FIFTH EDITION

THE HANDBOOK OF EMPLOYEE BENEFITS

Design, Funding and Administration

Edited by Jerry S. Rosenbloom

McGraw-Hill

New York   Chicago   San Francisco
Lisbon   London   Madrid   Mexico City   Milan
New Delhi   San Juan   Seoul   Singapore
Sydney   Toronto

Library of Congress Cataloging-in-Publication Data

The handbook of employee benefits / [edited] by Jerry S. Rosenbloom. — 5th ed.
    p. cm
    Includes bibliographical references and index.
    ISBN 0-07-137183-4
    1. Employee fringe benefits—United States. 2. Employee fringe benefits—
Law and legislation—United States. 3. Employee fringe benefits—
Taxation—Law and legislation—United States.
I. Rosenbloom, Jerry S.
HD4928.N62 U6353   2001
658.3'25'0973—dc21   00–051533
                                                CIP

McGraw-Hill

A Division of The McGraw·Hill Companies

1 2 3 4 5 6 7 8 9 0 AGM/AGM 0 9 8 7 6 5 4 3 2 1

ISBN 0-07-137183-4

This book was set in Times by Hendrickson Creative Communications.

Printed and bound by Quebecor World/Martinsburg.

McGraw-Hill books are available at special quantity discounts to use as premiums and sales promotions, or for use in corporate training programs. For more information, please write to the Director of Special Sales, Professional Publishing, McGraw-Hill, Two Penn Plaza, New York, NY 10121-2298. Or contact your local bookstore.

This publication is designed to provide accurate and authoritative information in regard to the subject matter covered. It is sold with the understanding that neither the author nor the publisher is engaged in rendering legal, accounting, or other professional service. If legal advice or other expert assistance is required, the services of a competent professional person should be sought.

—From a Declaration of Principles jointly adopted by a Committee
of the American Bar Association and a Committee of Publishers.

PREFACE

Much has taken place in the employee benefits field since the publication of the fourth edition of *The Handbook of Employee Benefits* in 1996. The fifth edition has been modified and updated to reflect major new pieces of legislation, dramatic changes in health care delivery and retirement planning, and the development and implementation of many new employee benefit concepts. This edition of the *Handbook* recognizes these changes, with revisions of many of the chapters in the previous edition and the addition of chapters covering new and emerging areas in employee benefits. These changes reemphasize the basic premise that employee benefits can no longer be considered "fringe benefits" but must be regarded as an integral and extremely important component of an individual's financial security. The most recent U.S. Chamber of Commerce study on employee benefits indicates that, on average, employee benefits account for about 40 percent of a worker's total compensation. In light of the ever-increasing importance of benefit plans, those dealing with them must be well versed in the objectives, design, costing, funding, implementation and administration of such plans.

While *The Handbook of Employee Benefits* is intended for students in the benefits field and for professionals as a handy reference, it can serve as a valuable tool for anyone with an interest in the field in general or in a specific employee benefit topic. The *Handbook* can be used as a reference work for benefit professionals or as a textbook for college courses, and for professional education and company training programs. Each chapter of the *Handbook* stands alone and is complete in itself. While this produces some overlap in certain areas, in many cases it eliminates the need to refer to other chapters while providing important reinforcement of difficult concepts.

The chapters of the *Handbook* are structured into 9 parts, each covering a major component of the employee benefit planning process. These are: Part One, The Environment of Employee Benefit Plans; Part Two, Medical and Other Health Benefits; Part Three, Life Insurance Benefits; Part Four, Work/Life Benefits; Part Five, Social Insurance Programs; Part Six, Retirement Planning; Part Seven, Employee Benefit Plan Administration; Part Eight, Employee Benefit Plan Financial Management; and Part Nine, Employee Benefit Plan Issues.

The *Handbook* consists of 52 chapters written by distinguished experts—academics, actuaries, attorneys, consultants, human resources professionals and other benefit experts—covering all areas of the employee benefits field. Their practical experience and breadth of knowledge provide insightful coverage of the employee benefits mechanism, and the examples and case studies presented throughout the *Handbook* illustrate the concepts presented.

The chapters that remain from the fourth edition have been updated to incorporate legislative and other changes in the field, and several of the chapters from the fourth edition have been expanded to include new topic areas. The coverage of certain subjects has been amplified with additional chapters on disability income, flexible benefits and communication. New chapters have been added on: Time-Off and Medical Leave Programs, Stock Options Plans, Executive Compensation Plans, Investment of Defined Contribution Plan Assets, and Voluntary Compliance Resolution Programs.

In such a massive project, many people provided invaluable assistance, and it would be impossible to mention them all here. Special thanks must be extended, however, to the authors of the individual chapters for the outstanding coverage of their subject areas in a comprehensive and readable manner. I would like to thank, too, the late Dr. Davis W. Gregg, former president of The American College, for his encouragement over the years to undertake such a project. Appreciation also must go to my most able assistant who recently retired after working with me for 22 years, Diana Krigelman. She spent many hours on all aspects of the manuscript. I would also like to extend a grateful thanks to Fina Maniaci and Dennis F. Mahoney who work with me on the Certified Employee Benefit Specialist (CEBS) Program for their dedicated work in reviewing the entire manuscript.

In a work of this magnitude, it is almost inevitable that some mistakes may have escaped the eyes of the many reviewers of the manuscript. For these oversights I accept full responsibility and ask the reader's indulgence.

Jerry S. Rosenbloom

Mark S. Allen, William M. Mercer, Inc.

Everett T. Allen, Jr., Vice President and Principal, Towers Perrin (deceased)

Vincent Amoroso, FSA, Deloitte & Touche

Bruce L. Ashton, J.D. , Reish & Luftman. E-mail: bruceashton@reish.com

Burton T. Beam, Jr., CLU, ChFC, CPCU, Associate Professor of Insurance, The American College

Melvin W. Borleis, CEBS, Retired Managing Director, William M. Mercer, Incorporated

Tony R. Broomhead, FIA, ASA, Senior International Consultant, Watson Wyatt Worldwide. E-mail: Tony.Broomhead@WatsonWyatt.com

Gregory K. Brown, Esq., Partner, Seyfarth, Shaw, Fairweather & Geraldson. E-mail: gkbrown@gcd.com (www.gcdlawchgo@gcd.com)

Eugene B. Burroughs, CFA, Investment Consultant

Alan P. Cleveland, Esq., Sheenan, Phinney, Bass & Green

Dennis R. Coleman, Esq., PricewaterhouseCoopers LLP

Paula J. Conroy, National Director of Employee Benefit Plan Services, Ernst & Young, LLP

Ann Costello, Ph.D., Associate Professor of Insurance, Barney School of Business, University of Hartford

Kenneth E. Dakdduk, Partner, PricewaterhouseCoopers LLP

Craig J. Davidson, CEBS, e-Business Leader, Willis National Benefits Practice, and Lecturer, Graduate School of Business, University of Wisconsin, Milwaukee

Michele F. Davis, Associate Director of Education, TIAA-CREF Institute. E-mail: mfdavis@tiaa-cref.org

William E. Decker, Partner-in-Charge, PricewaterhouseCoopers LLP

Donald A. Doran, Partner, PricewaterhouseCoopers LLP

Cynthia J. Drinkwater, M.P.P.A, J.D., CEBS, Senior Director of Research, International Foundation of Employee Benefit Plans

David L. Durbin, Ph.D., Head of Group Product Management, Swiss Reinsurance

Anthony J. Gajda, Principal, William M. Mercer, Inc.

Charles P. Hall, Jr., Ph.D., CLU, CPCU, FACHE, Professor of Risk, Insurance, and Healthcare Management, and Director, International MBA, Temple University

G. Victor Hallman III, Ph.D., J.D., CPCU, CLU, Lecturer in Financial and Estate Planning, Department of Insurance and Risk Management, The Wharton School, University of Pennsylvania

Sarah Holden, Ph.D., Senior Economist, Research Department, Investment Company Institute

Charles E. Hughes, D.B.A., CLU, CPCU, Professor Emeritus, The American College

Ronald L. Huling, Senior Consultant, Watson Wyatt Worldwide. E-mail: Ronald.Huling@WatsonWyatt.com

Robert T. LeClair, Ph.D., Associate Professor, Finance Department, College of Commerce and Finance, Villanova University. E-mail: robert.leclair@villanova.edu

Serafina Maniaci, CEBS, MS, Certified Employee Benefit Specialist (CEBS) Program, The Wharton School, University of Pennsylvania

Dennis F. Mahoney, MS, CEBS, CFP, Associate Academic Director, Certified Employee Benefit Specialist (CEBS) Program, The Wharton School, University of Pennsylvania

Ernest L. Martin, Ph.D., FLMI, Assistant Vice President Emeritus, Examinations Department, Education & Training Division, LOMA (Life Office Management Association)

William J. Mayer, MD, M.P.H, President and Chief Executive Officer, QualityMetric, Inc.

David McCarthy, Ph.D. candidate in Insurance and Risk Management at the Wharton School, University of Pennsylvania

Olivia S. Mitchell, Ph.D, International Foundation of Employee Benefit Plans Professor of Insurance and Risk Management, The Wharton School, University of Pennsylvania

Linda Mondzelewski, SPHR, CBP, Director of Benefits and Work/Life Programs, ECS, Inc. E-mail: mondzell@ecsinc.com

Robert J. Myers, L.L.D., FSA, Professor Emeritus, Temple University, Chief Actuary, Social Security Administration, 1947-70; Deputy Commissioner, Social Security Administration, 1981-1982; and Executive Director, National Commission on Social Security Reform, 1982-83

Michael Norton, Principal of Norton Communications, Inc., Portland, Maine

Michael P. O' Donnell, Ph.D., MBA, MPH, Editor-in-chief and President, American Journal of Health Promotion

Kelly A. Olsen, Social Science Research Analyst, Office of Retirement Policy, Social Security Administration

Richard Ostuw, FSA, Global Health Care Practice Director, Watson Wyatt Worldwide

Bruce A. Palmer, Ph.D., CLU, Chairman, Department of Risk Management and Insurance, J. Mack Robinson College of Business, Georgia State University. E-mail: bpalmer@gsu.edu

Phillip D. Pierce, General Manager, Aetna U.S. Healthcare

Carol Quick, MPP

William H. Rabel, Ph.D., FMLI, CLU, Senior Vice President, Education & Training Division, LOMA (Life Office Management Association)

Thomas W. Ramagnano, Hewitt Associates LLC

George E. Rejda, Ph.D., CLU,V.J. Skutt Distinguished Professor of Insurance, Finance Department, College of Business, University of Nebraska-Lincoln

C. Frederick Reish, J.D., Reish & Luftman. E-mail: fredreish@reish.com

John S. Roberts, CLU, Senior Vice President Underwriting, UNUMProvident

Jerry S. Rosenbloom, Ph.D., CLU, CPCU, Frederick H. Ecker Professor of Life Insurance, Department of Insurance and Risk Management, and Academic Director, Certified Employee Benefit Specialist (CEBS) Program, The Wharton School, University of Pennsylvania

Daniel J. Ryterband, CEBS, Managing Director, Frederic W. Cook & Co., Inc.

Dallas L. Salisbury, President and CEO, Employee Benefit Research Institute

Lawrence J. Sher, FSA, PricewaterhouseCoopers LLP

Robert W. Smiley, Jr., L.L.B., Chairman and Chief Executive Officer, The Benefit Capital Companies, Inc. E-mail: rsmiley@benefitcapital.com (www.benefitcapital@gcd.com)

Morris Snow, Ph.D., FSA, MAAA, Principal, William M. Mercer, Inc.

Gary K. Stone, Ph.D., CLU, Executive Vice President, The American College

David M. Sugar, Hewitt Associates LLC

Richard L. Tewksbury, Jr., CLU, Senior Consultant, Towers Perrin

Jack L. VanDerhei, Ph.D., CEBS, Professor, Department of Risk, Insurance, and Healthcare Management, Temple University

JulieAnn C. Verrekia, Senior Manager, PricewaterhouseCoopers LLP

Nicholas J. White, J.D., Reish & Luftman. E-mail: nickwhite@reish.com

John D. Worrall, Ph.D., Professor of Economics, Rutgers University

Eugene J. Ziurys, Jr.

BRIEF CONTENTS

PART FOUR

WORK/LIFE BENEFITS   397

PART FIVE

SOCIAL INSURANCE PROGRAMS   497

PART SIX

RETIREMENT PLANNING   573

PART SEVEN

EMPLOYEE BENEFIT PLAN ADMINISTRATION   859

PART EIGHT

EMPLOYEE BENEFIT PLAN FINANCIAL MANAGEMENT   983

PART NINE

EMPLOYEE BENEFIT PLAN ISSUES   1173

CONTENTS

Chapter 8

Understanding Managed Care Health Plans: Understanding Costs and Evaluating Plans   171

Chapter 9

Health Care Quality: Are We Getting Our Money's Worth?   209

Chapter 10

Dental Plan Design   237

Chapter 11

Prescription Drug, Vision, and Hearing Care Plans   255

Chapter 16

Other Life Insurance Programs   375

PART FOUR

WORK/LIFE BENEFITS   397

Chapter 17

Work/Life Benefits: An Overview   399

Chapter 27

Section 401(k) Plans (Cash or Deferred Arrangements) and Thrift Plans   633

Chapter 28

Cash Balance Pension Plans and Other Evolving Hybrid Pension Plans   661

Chapter 29

Employer Stock Ownership Plans (ESOPs)   681

Chapter 34

Section 457 Deferred Compensation Plans   821

Chapter 35

Investment of Defined Contribution Plan Assets   837

Chapter 50

State and Local Pension Plan Developments   1241

Chapter 51

The Globalization of Employee Benefits   1259

Chapter 52

The Future of Employee Benefit Plans   1285

PART ONE

The Environment of Employee Benefit Plans

Employee benefits constitute a major part of almost every individual's financial and economic security. Such benefits have gone from being considered "fringe" benefits to the point where they may constitute about 40 percent of an employee's compensation, and the plans under which they are provided are a major concern of employers.

Individuals responsible for the design, pricing, selling and administration of employee benefits carry a broad range of responsibilities, and the role of the benefits professional has changed rapidly and radically in the past twenty-five years. During that period the number of employee benefits has virtually exploded with expansion occurring in many of the more traditional benefits and the addition of totally new forms of benefits.

Part One of the *Handbook* is concerned with the environment in which employee benefit plans are designed and operated, and Chapter 1 considers many important design issues. Chapter 2 extends the discussion of employee benefit plan design concepts by looking at the functional approach to designing and evaluating employee benefits, which provides a framework for various strategies for considering benefits on a risk-by-risk basis and as a part of total compensation. The third chapter in this part considers some of the risk and insurance concepts inherent in many approaches to employee benefit planning, and lays the foundation for many of the concepts throughout the *Handbook*.

The fourth and final chapter in Part One is a brief overview of the regulatory environment surrounding employee benefit plans. Later chapters cover in greater detail the extremely important regulatory issues that are so much a part of employee benefit planning.

CHAPTER 1

The Environment of Employee Benefit Plans

Jerry S. Rosenbloom

Employee benefits are an extremely important part of almost everyone's financial security. Once considered to be "fringe" benefits because of their relatively small magnitude, employee benefits cannot be considered as fringe anything today. Employee benefits account for approximately 37 percent of an individual's total compensation. In many firms, that percentage is even higher. Furthermore, many new types of employee benefits have emerged in recent years as employers compete for talented employees. Employee benefits also have become much more of a strategic matter for many firms. To ensure that both employers and employees utilize employee benefit plans in the most effective manner requires a thorough knowledge of all aspects of employee benefit plan design, funding, and administration, including benefit communications. This chapter gives the necessary background for the rest of the volume by outlining what employee benefits are, the reasons for their growth, what they are intended to achieve from both the employer and employee perspective, and what makes such plans work.

EMPLOYEE BENEFITS DEFINED

Broad View of Employee Benefits

Many definitions of employee benefits exist, ranging from broad to narrow interpretations. In the broad view, employee benefits are virtually any form of compensation other than direct wages paid to employees.[1] For example, in the annual U.S. Chamber of Commerce survey of employee benefits, such benefits are defined broadly to include the following:[2]

1. Employer's share of legally required payments.
2. Employer's share of retirement and savings plan payments.
3. Employer's share of life insurance and death benefit payments.
4. Employer's share of medical and medically related benefit payments.
5. Payments for time not worked (e.g., paid rest periods, paid sick leave, paid vacations, holidays, parental leave, et al.).
6. Miscellaneous benefit payments (including employee discounts, severance pay, educational expenditures, child care, et al.).

Table 1–1 illustrates the costs for benefits as a percentage of payroll for all companies as well as a breakdown by manufacturing and nonmanufacturing companies. As the table indicates, employee benefits are intertwined with almost every facet of an individual's economic and financial security.

A More Limited View of Employee Benefits

The broad view of employee benefits encompasses both legally mandated benefits such as Social Security and other governmental programs and private plans, while the narrow view can be summarized as "any type of plan sponsored or initiated unilaterally or jointly by employers and employees in providing benefits that stem from the employment relationship that are not underwritten or paid directly by government."[3]

This narrow definition of employee benefits will be the one primarily used in the *Handbook*. That does not mean in any way, however, that legally required benefits are unimportant. Quite the contrary, these benefits are extremely important and must be considered in employee benefit plan design and in integrating private employee benefit plans with the benefits provided by governmental bodies. This interrelationship is stressed throughout the book. In addition to benefits provided through

---

1 Jerry S. Rosenbloom and G. Victor Hallman, *Employee Benefit Planning,* 3rd ed. (Englewood Cliffs, NJ: Prentice Hall, 1991), pp. 2–3.
2 U.S. Chamber of Commerce, *Employee Benefits 1999* (Washington, D.C., 1999).
3 Martha Remey Yohalem, "Employee Benefit Plans—1975," *Social Security Bulletin* 40, no.11 (November 1977), p. 19.

government bodies and those provided through the employment relation-ship, benefits provided by an individual for his or her own welfare also are described when appropriate. This so-called tripod or three-legged stool of economic security underlies the foundation of individual and family financial security.

REASONS FOR THE GROWTH OF EMPLOYEE BENEFIT PLANS

There are numerous reasons why employee benefit plans have evolved from a fringe benefit to a major component of financial security today. They arise from external forces as well as the desire of employers and employees to achieve certain goals and objectives.

Business Reasons

A multitude of business reasons explain why employee benefit plans were established and why they have expanded greatly. Employers want to attract and hold capable employees. Having employee benefit plans in place helps to serve this objective. Also, in many cases an employer's competition has certain benefit plans and, therefore, it is necessary to have equal or better plans to retain current employees. Moreover, employers hope that corporate efficiency, productivity, and improved employee morale will be fostered by good benefit plans. Concern for employees' welfare and social objectives also encouraged employers to provide benefits.

Collective Bargaining

Labor unions, through the collective bargaining process, have had a major impact on the growth of employee benefit plans. The Labor Management Relations Act (LMRA), which is administered by the National Labor Relations Board (NLRB), requires good-faith collective bargaining over wages, hours, and other terms and conditions of employment. A notable event occurred in 1948 when the NLRB ruled that the meaning of the term wages includes a pension plan, and this position was upheld in the landmark case of *Inland Steel Co.* v. *National Labor Relations Board* in the same year. Shortly thereafter, in 1949, the good-faith bargaining requirements were held to include a group health and accident plan (*W. W. Cross & Co.* v. *National Labor Relations Board*). As a result of these two

TABLE 1-1

Employee Benefits, by Type of Benefit: All Employees, 1999

Type of Benefit	Total, All Companies	Total, All Manufacturing	Total, All Nonmanufacturing
Total employee benefits as percent of payroll	37.2%	33.1%	38.2%
1. Legally required payments (employer's share only):	8.4	8.5	8.4
a. Old-Age, Survivors, Disability, and Health Insurance (FICA taxes) and Railroad Retirement Tax	6.9	6.8	6.9
b. Unemployment Compensation	0.5	0.6	0.5
c. Workers' Compensation (including estimated cost of self-insured)	0.9	1.0	0.9
d. State sickness benefit insurance	0.0	0.0	0.0
e. Other	0.1	0.0	0.1
2. Retirement and Savings Plan Payments (employer's share only):	8.7	6.5	9.3
a. Defined benefit pension plan contributions	3.3	1.2	3.9
b. Defined contribution plan payments (401(k) and similar)	1.9	1.4	2.1
c. Profit sharing	1.4	2.3	1.2
d. Stock bonus and employee stock ownership plans (ESOP)	0.1	0.6	0.0
e. Pension plan premiums (net) under insurance and annuity contracts (insured and trusteed)	0.1	0.1	0.1
f. Administrative and other costs	1.9	1.0	2.1
3. Life Insurance and Death Benefit Payments (employer's share only)	0.3	0.4	0.3
4. Medical and Medically Related Benefit Payments (employer's share only):	8.5	8.3	8.6
a. Hospital, surgical, medical, and major medical insurance premiums (net)	5.5	5.7	5.4
b. Short-term disability, sickness, or accident insurance (company plan or insured plan)	0.2	0.2	0.2

(continued)

Employee Benefits, by Type of Benefit: All Employees, 1999 *(concluded)*

c. Long-term disability or wage continuation (insured, self-administered, or trust)	0.2	0.2	0.2
d. Retiree (payments for retired employees) hospital, surgical, medical, and			
major medical (net)	0.9	1.0	0.9
e. Dental insurance premiums	0.5	0.5	0.5
f. Vision care and prescription drugs	0.3	0.3	0.4
g. Other	0.9	0.4	1.0
5. Payments for Time Not Worked:	10.6	8.8	11.0
a. Paid rest periods, coffee breaks, etc.	1.7	1.9	1.6
b. Payments for vacations	4.6	3.6	4.8
c. Payments for holidays	2.9	2.5	3.0
d. Sick leave pay	1.1	0.5	1.3
e. Maternity and paternity leave payments	0.0	0.0	0.0
f. Other	0.3	0.3	0.3
6. Miscellaneous Benefit Payments (employer's share):	0.6	0.7	0.6
a. Discounts on goods and services purchased from company by employees	0.0	0.1	0.1
b. Severance pay	0.3	0.3	0.3
c. Child care, on-site	0.0	0.0	0.0
d. Child care, third-party provided	0.0	0.0	0.0
e. Employee education expenditures (tuition refunds, etc.)	0.2	0.2	0.2
Total employee benefits as cents per payroll hour, per employee	710.9¢	681.2¢	719.2¢
Total employee benefits as dollars per year per employee	$14,655	$14,414	$15,034

Source: U.S. Chamber of Commerce, *Employee Benefits 1999* (Washington, D.C., 1999), p. 10.

decisions, it was clearly established that the LMRA provisions applied to both retirement and welfare benefit plans, and their subsequent growth has been substantial.

The LMRA, or Taft-Hartley Act, as it commonly is known, also has played other significant roles in the development of employee benefit plans. It, along with the Internal Revenue Code (IRC), established the distinction between retirement benefits and welfare benefits. Additionally, the statute sets forth the basic regulatory framework under which both of these major categories of benefits are to be jointly administered within the collective bargaining process. As such, it is the legislative basis on which jointly trusteed benefit plans are founded.

Favorable Tax Legislation

Over the years the tax laws have favored employee benefit plans. Such preferential tax legislation has greatly encouraged the development of employee benefit plans as well as helped to shape their design, because many plans seek to maximize the tax treatment or tax consequences of various employee benefit plans. The main tax benefits of employee benefit plans are as follows: (1) most contributions to employee benefit plans by employers are deductible as long as they are reasonable business expenses; (2) contributions from employers within certain limits on behalf of employees are generally not considered income to employees; and, (3) on certain types of retirement and capital accumulation plans, assets set aside to fund such plans accumulate tax-free until distributed. Some additional tax benefits may be available when such distributions are made. All in all, favorable tax legislation has had great impact on the development and expansion of employee benefit plans.

Efficiency of the Employee Benefits Approach

The bringing together after the industrial revolution of employees and employers in cities and in business firms made it possible for the employee benefits concept to flourish by covering many employees under one contract or plan instead of each employee having to go out and purchase an individual contract. The simplicity and convenience of providing coverage to people through their place of employment made sense from many standpoints. Employee benefit providers and suppliers, such as insurance companies, banks, and various types of health organizations, all found the marketing of such benefits through the employer to be a cost-effective and administratively efficient channel of distribution.

Other Factors

Many other factors have contributed to the growth of employee benefit plans. One such factor was the imposition of limitations on the size of wage increases granted during World War II and the Korean War. While wages were frozen, employee benefits were not. As a result, compensation of employees could effectively be increased by provision of larger benefits. The result was a major expansion of employee benefits during these two periods.

Some have argued that various legislative action over the years has encouraged employee benefit plans not only through providing favorable tax treatment but also by the government's "moral suasion" that, if such benefit plans were not established voluntarily by employers and employees, additional governmental programs might result. Allowing employee benefits to be integrated with governmental benefits also has enhanced the private employee benefit approach by taking into consideration benefits provided by governmental plans in benefit plan design.

Development of the group approach to certain employee benefits also has helped expand the employee benefit mechanism. The techniques inherent in the group selection process made it possible for employers to provide benefits that previously could only be provided on an individual basis, with coverage often determined by medical selection.

GROUP TECHNIQUE

In many types of insurance programs, such as group life insurance and group health insurance, the group technique enables these coverages to be written as employee benefit plans.[4] Unlike individual insurance, group insurance is based on a view of the group as a unit, rather than on the individual. Usually, individual insurance eligibility requirements are not required for group insurance written under an employee benefit plan.[5] The concepts that make the group technique work are all designed to prevent "adverse selection"—that is, to reduce the possibility that less-

---

4 See Chapter 15 for additional discussion of the "group mechanism" to providing employee
   benefits.
5 A discussion of the insurance technique and how and why it works is presented in Chapter 3.

healthy individuals may join a group or be a larger percentage of a group than anticipated because of the availability of insurance or other benefits.

Characteristics of the group technique of providing employee benefits include some or all of the following:[6]

1. *Only certain groups eligible.* While most groups qualify, this requirement is intended to make sure that the obtaining of insurance is incidental to the group seeking coverage. Thus, a group should not be formed solely for the purpose of obtaining insurance.

2. *Steady flow of lives through the group.* The theory behind this concept is that younger individuals should come into the group while older individuals leave the group, thus maintaining a fairly constant mortality or morbidity ratio in the group. If the group doesn't maintain this "flow through the group" and the average age of the group increases substantially, costs could increase dramatically.

3. *Minimum number of persons in the group.* A minimum number of persons, typically 10, must be in the group to be eligible for group benefits. However, this requirement has been liberalized to the point where two or three individuals in a group may obtain coverage. This minimum-number provision is designed to prevent unhealthy lives from being a major part of the group and to spread the expenses of the benefits plan over a larger number of individuals.[7]

4. *A minimum portion of the group must participate.* Typically in group life and health insurance plans if the plan is noncontributory (i.e., solely paid for by the employer), 100 percent of eligible employees must be covered. If the plan is contributory (both employer and employee share the cost), 75 percent of the employees must participate. The rationale for this provision is also to reduce adverse selection and spread the expense of administration.[8]

5. *Eligibility requirements.* Frequently, eligibility requirements are imposed under group plans for the purpose, once again, of preventing adverse selection. Such provisions can include only full-time employees who are actively at work on the date[9] the benefits become effective. A waiting or eligibility period may be used for certain benefits. Also, if employees don't join when eligible and want to enroll at a later date, some form of medical information may be required.

---

6 See Rosenbloom and Hallman, *Employee Benefit Planning*, pp. 15–20.

7 Ibid., p. 17.

8 Ibid., p. 17.

9 At print time, clarification of the Health Insurance Portability and Accountability Act (HIPAA) of 1996 regulations (that were being temporarily postponed by the new Bush administration) made "the actively at work" provision illegal.

6. *Maximum limits for any one person.* In certain cases, maximum limits on the amount of life or health benefits may be imposed to prevent the possibility of excessive amounts of coverage for any particular unhealthy individual.

7. *Automatic determination of benefits.* To prevent unhealthy lives in a group from obtaining an extremely large amount of a particular benefit or benefits, coverage is determined for all individuals in the group on an automatic basis. This basis may be determined by an employee's salary, service, or position, may be a flat amount for all employees, or may be a combination of these factors.

8. *A central and efficient administrative agency.* To keep expenses to a minimum and to handle the mechanics of the benefit plan, a central and efficient administrative agency is necessary for the successful operation of an employee benefit plan. An employer is an almost ideal unit because he or she maintains the payroll and other employee information needed in meeting appropriate tax and recordkeeping requirements.[10]

Over the years many of the requirements just described have been liberalized as providers of employee benefits have gained experience in handling group employee benefits, and because of the competitive environment. Nevertheless, the basic group selection technique is important in understanding why employee benefits can work on a group basis and how any problems that exist might be corrected.

OVERALL EMPLOYEE BENEFIT CONCERNS

Because employee benefits, as noted previously, provide such an important dimension of financial security in our society, some overall questions need to be asked to evaluate any existing or newly created employee benefit plan. While future chapters in the *Handbook* analyze benefit design, cost, funding, administration, and communication issues, some principles permeate all these areas and need brief mention early in this text.[11]

Employer and Employee Objectives

The design of any employee benefit plan must start with the objectives of the benefit plan from the standpoint of both employer and employee.

---

10 Ibid.
11 Some of the ideas presented here are based on Rosenbloom and Hallman, *Employee Benefit Planning,* 3rd ed., Chapter 23. For a more detailed analysis, consult this publication.

What Benefits Should Be Provided?

There should be clearly stated reasons or objectives for the type of benefits to be provided. Benefits provided both under governmental programs and by the individual employees also should be considered.

Who Should Be Covered by the Benefit Plans?

Should only full-time employees be covered? What about retirees or dependents? What about survivors of deceased employees? These and a host of similar questions must be carefully evaluated. Of course, some of these issues depend on regulatory and legislative rules and regulations.

Should Employees Have Benefit Options?

This is becoming more and more of a crucial question under employee benefit plans. With the growth of flexible or cafeteria benefit plans, employee choice is on the increase. Even in nonflexible benefit plan situations, should some choices be given?

How Should Benefit Plans Be Financed?

Several important questions need to be answered in determining the approach to funding employee benefit plans. Should financing be entirely provided by the employer (a noncontributory approach) or on some shared basis by the employer and employee (a contributory approach)? If on a contributory basis, what percentage should each bear?

What funding method should be used? A wide range of possibilities exists, from a total insurance program to total self-funding with many options in between. Even when one of these options is selected, still further questions remain concerning the specific funding instrument to be used.

How Should the Benefit Plan Be Administered?

Should the firm itself administer the plan? Should an insurance carrier or other benefit plan provider do the administration? Should some outside organization such as a third-party administrator (TPA) do this work? Once the decision is made, the specific entity must be selected.

How Should the Benefit Plan Be Communicated?

The best employee benefit plan in existence may not achieve any of its desired objectives if it is improperly communicated to all affected parties. The communication of employee benefit plans has become increasingly important in recent years with increased reporting and disclosure requirements. Effective communication of what benefit plans will and won't do is essential if employees are to rely on such plans to provide part of their financial security at all stages of their lives. Technology has provided many new options in this area.

Future of Employee Benefits

With the spate of legislation affecting certain aspects of employee benefit plans, and the varying needs of today's changing workforce and the outsourcing of many benefit functions, some benefit experts believe there may be more changes than ever before. While certain new approaches and techniques may be utilized, employee benefit plans are woven into the fabric of our society in such a way that the basic character or importance of such plans will not be changed. With pressures to contain costs ever increasing, greater efficiencies in the benefits approach, more tailoring to individual needs in the growth of flexible benefits or cafeteria compensation plans, and other refinements will drive the employee benefits mechanism. While it seems certain that employee benefits will not grow as rapidly as they have in the past, their place is secure and there will continue to be a demand for people who are knowledgeable about all aspects of the design, funding, administration, and communication of employee benefits in order to make such plans more effective while helping to provide for the economic security of society at large.

CHAPTER 2

Functional Approach to Designing and Evaluating Employee Benefits

G. Victor Hallman III

This chapter deals with the functional approach toward analyzing an existing employee benefit program and evaluating the need for new employee benefits. The functional approach can be defined as an organized system for classifying and analyzing the risks and needs of active employees, their dependents, and various other categories of persons into logical categories of exposures to loss and employee needs. These exposures and needs may include medical expenses, losses resulting from death, losses caused by short- and long-term disabilities, retirement income needs, capital accumulation needs, needs arising out of short- and long-term unemployment, custodial care (long-term care) needs, and other employee needs.

THE FUNCTIONAL APPROACH IN CONCEPT

As indicated above, the functional approach essentially is the application of a systematic method of analysis to an employer's total employee benefits program. It analyzes the employer's program as a coordinated whole in terms of its ability to meet employees' (and others') needs and to manage loss exposures within the employer's overall compensation goals and cost parameters. This approach can be useful in overall employee benefit plan design, in evaluating proposals for new or revised benefits, for evaluation of cost-saving proposals, and in effective communication of an employer's total benefits program to its employees. It can be seen that the functional approach, which is essentially a planning approach, fits logically with the total compensation philosophy, as explained later in the chapter.

The functional approach to employee benefits is not really a new concept. In 1967, George C. Foust outlined the approach in the American Management Association book, *The Total Approach to Employee Benefits*.[1] Similarly, Robert M. McCaffery in his pioneering 1972 work, *Managing the Employee Benefits Program*, stated:

> The "package" or total approach to employee benefits is simply the purposeful management of an integrated program. Rather than continually reacting to current fads, outside pressures, and salesmen's pitches, the contemporary businessman relies on fundamental principles of management in developing, organizing, directing, and evaluating systems of employee benefits for his organization.[2]

The functional approach represents such systematic management of the employee benefits function.

NEED FOR THE FUNCTIONAL APPROACH

The functional approach is needed in planning, designing, and administering employee benefits for several reasons.

First, in most instances, employee benefits are a very significant element of the total compensation of employees. Benefits have become an important part of the work rewards provided by employers to their employees. Therefore, it is important to employees, and hence to their employers, that this increasingly important element of compensation be planned and organized to be as effective as possible in meeting employee needs.

Second, employee benefits currently represent a large item of labor cost for employers. Depending on the industry, the particular employer, and how employee benefits are defined, benefits may range from less than 18 percent to more than 65 percent of an employer's payroll.[3] Therefore, effective planning and hence avoidance of waste in providing benefits can be an important cost-control measure for employers.

---

1 George C. Foust, Jr., "The Total Approach Concept," in *The Total Approach to Employee Benefits*, ed., Arthur J. Deric (New York: American Management Association, 1967), chapter 1.

2 Robert M. McCaffery, *Managing the Employee Benefits Program* (New York: American Management Association, 1972), p. 17. There also is a revised (1983) edition of this book. These farsighted concepts are developed further by McCaffery in Chapter 2, "Planning a Total Program," of Robert M. McCaffery, *Employee Benefit Programs: A Total Compensation Perspective* (Boston: PWS–KENT Publishing Company, 2nd ed., 1992).

3 U.S. Chamber of Commerce, *Employee Benefits 1999* (Washington, D.C.: 1999), p. 18.

Third, in the past, employee benefits often were adopted by employers on a piecemeal basis without being coordinated with existing benefit programs. Thus, some benefit plans just sprouted in every direction. For this reason, it usually is fruitful to apply the functional approach in reviewing existing employee benefit plans to determine where overlapping benefits may exist and costs may be saved, and where gaps in benefits may exist and new benefits or revised benefits may be in order.

Fourth, because of new benefits and coverages, changes in the tax laws, changes in the regulatory environment, and other developments in employee benefit planning have come about so rapidly in recent years, it is important to have a systematic approach to planning benefits to keep them current, competitive, and in compliance with regulatory requirements.

Finally, a given employee benefit or program, such as a pension plan, often provides benefits relating to several separate employee needs or loss exposures. Therefore, an employer's benefit plan needs to be analyzed according to the functional approach so its various benefit programs can be integrated properly with each other.

CONSISTENCY WITH AN EMPLOYER'S TOTAL COMPENSATION PHILOSOPHY

In designing the total compensation package, an employer should seek to balance the various elements of its compensation system, including basic cash wages and salary, current incentive compensation (current cash bonuses and company stock bonuses), longer-term incentive plans (including stock-based and performance-based plans), and so-called employee benefits, to help meet the needs and desires of the employees on the one hand and the employer's basic compensation philosophy and objectives on the other. Thus, it is clear that the functional approach to planning and designing an employee benefit plan must remain consistent with the employer's total compensation philosophy. A particular employer, therefore, may not cover a certain employee desire for benefits, or may cover it in a rather spartan manner, not because the desire is not recognized but because the employer's total compensation philosophy calls for a relatively low level of employee benefits or, perhaps, benefits oriented in a different direction.

Employers may adopt different business policies regarding the general compensation of their employees. For example, many employers want to compensate their employees at a level in line with that generally prevailing in their industry or community, or both. They do not wish to be much above or below average compensation levels. The employee bene-

fit programs of such employers also frequently follow this general philosophy. Other employers may follow a high-compensation philosophy
(including employee benefits) with the goal of attracting higher levels of
management, technical, and general employee talent. This may be particularly true in industries where the need for a highly skilled work force is
great. On the other hand, there may be employers that follow a low-com-
pensation policy, feeling that, for them, the resultant lower payroll costs
more than outweigh the resulting higher employee turnover and lower
skill level of their workforce. An employer with this kind of philosophy
may want to adopt more modest employee benefit programs.

Type of industry and employer characteristics also will have an
impact on an employer's total compensation philosophy and on the
design of its employee benefit plan. Figure 2–1 is a grid presented by one
employee benefit consulting firm showing the relationship between type
of organization, working climate, and compensation mix.

Thus, a larger well-established employer in a mature industry, a financial institution, or a nonprofit organization may take a relatively liberal

FIGURE 2–1

Organizational Style and Compensation Mix

| Type of Organization | Working Climate | Reward Management Components | | | |
| | | Cash | | Noncash | |
		Base Salary	Short-Term Incentives	Level	Characteristics
Mature industrial	Balanced	Medium	Medium	Medium	Balanced
Developing industrial	Growth, creativity	Medium	High	Low	Short-term oriented
Conservative financial	Security	Low	Low	High	Long-term, security-oriented
Nonprofit	Societal impact, personal fulfillment	Low	None	Low to medium	Long-term, security-oriented
Sales	Growth, freedom to act	Low	High	Low	Short-term oriented

Source: Hay-Huggins, member of the Hay Group.

approach toward meeting the benefits needs and desires of its employees. But developing industrial firms, high-tech companies, and other growth companies, which may have considerable current needs for capital and seek a highly-skilled and motivated workforce, may seek to rely more heavily on short-term oriented incentive types of compensation. Further, industries that are highly competitive, subject to cyclical fluctuations, or perhaps in a currently depressed state, may not be willing to add to their relatively fixed labor costs by adopting or liberalizing employee benefits, even if there may be a functional need for them. In fact, such firms may seek to cut back on their employee benefit commitments when possible. However, even in these situations firms should attempt to allocate their available compensation dollars in as consistent and logical a manner as possible to meet the needs and goals of their employees as well as their own corporate compensation objectives. In fact, the functional approach may be even more appropriate in such cases, because their resources for compensating employees are relatively scarce.

Another area of employer philosophy that affects the functional approach and how it is actually applied is whether the employer tends to follow a compensation/service-oriented benefit philosophy or a benefit- or needs-oriented philosophy. Employers having a compensation/service-oriented philosophy tend to relate employee benefits primarily to compensation or service, or both, in designing their employee benefit plans. Thus, the level of benefits would tend to be tied in with compensation level, and eligibility for benefits may be conditioned directly or indirectly on salary level. For example, separate benefit plans may be provided for salaried and for hourly-rated employees, with more generous benefits being made available to the former group. Further, some types of benefits may be available only to certain higher-paid employees or executives. In addition, such employers tend to emphasize service with the employer in determining benefit levels and eligibility for benefits. The theory of this approach is that employee benefits generally should be aimed to reward the longer-service employees who have shown a commitment to the employer. The benefit- or needs-oriented philosophy, on the other hand, tends to focus primarily on the needs of employees and their dependents, rather than on compensation and service.

In practice, the design of employee benefit plans tends to be a compromise between these two philosophies. On one side, certain kinds of employee benefits, such as medical expense benefits, tend to be primarily benefit- or needs-oriented. On the other side, benefits like group life insurance and pensions customarily are compensation-oriented, at least for nonunion employees. Thus, this distinction in philosophy really is one of degree. However, the extent to which eligibility for benefits, participation requirements, and levels of employee benefits reflect compensation or service, or both, may affect the extent to which the needs of employees or certain categories of employees will be met by an employee benefit plan.

APPLICATION OF THE FUNCTIONAL APPROACH

While the functional approach to planning employee benefits has been actively discussed since the early 1960s, no clearly developed procedure or technique exists for the application of this approach to individual benefit plans. However, based on the underlying concept and the way it is applied in practice, here are the logical steps in applying the functional approach to employee benefit plan design, revision, or review. For convenience of presentation, these steps can be listed as follows:

1. Classify employee (and dependent) needs or objectives in logical functional categories.
2. Classify the categories of persons (e.g., employees, some former employees, and dependents) the employer may want to protect, at least to some extent, through its employee benefit plan.
3. Analyze the benefits presently available under the plan in terms of the functional categories of needs or objectives and in terms of the categories of persons the employer may want to benefit.
4. Determine any gaps in benefits or overlapping benefits, or both, provided from all sources under the employer's employee benefit plan and from other benefit plans in terms of the functional categories of needs and the persons to be protected.
5. Consider recommendations for changes in the employer's present employee benefit plan to meet any gaps in benefits and to correct any overlapping benefits, including possible use of the flexible benefits (cafeteria plan) approach.
6. Estimate the costs or savings from each of the recommendations made in step 5.
7. Evaluate alternative methods of financing or securing the benefits recommended above, as well as the employee benefit plan's existing benefits.

8. Consider other cost-saving techniques in connection with the recommended benefits or existing benefits (i.e., plan cost-containment strategies).

9. Decide upon the appropriate benefits, methods of financing, and sources of benefits as a result of the preceding analysis.

10. Implement the changes.

11. Communicate benefit changes to employees.

12. Periodically reevaluate the employee benefit plan.

Each of these steps is considered in greater detail below. Naturally, it must be recognized in applying this process to a particular employee benefit plan that some of these steps may be combined with others and some will be taken implicitly. However, each step represents a logical decision point or consideration in the design or revision of an employee benefit plan.

Classify Employee and Dependent Needs in Functional Categories

The needs and exposures to loss of employees and their dependents can be classified in a variety of ways, some being more complete than others. The following classification appears to cover most of the commonly accepted needs and exposures to loss that may be covered under an employee benefit plan:

1. Medical expenses incurred by active employees, by their dependents, by retired (or certain otherwise terminated, suspended, or temporarily not in service) employees or former employees, and by their dependents.

2. Losses due to employees' disability (short-term and long-term).

3. Losses resulting from active employees' deaths, from their dependents' deaths, and from the deaths of retired (or certain otherwise terminated, suspended, or temporarily not in service) employees or former employees.

4. Retirement needs of employees and their dependents.

5. Capital accumulation needs or goals (short-term and long-term).

6. Needs arising from unemployment or from temporary termination or suspension of employment.

7. Needs for financial counseling, retirement counseling, and other counseling services.

8. Losses resulting from property and liability exposures and the like.

9. Needs for dependent care assistance (e.g., child-care services or elder-care services).

10. Needs for educational assistance for employees themselves or for employees' dependents, or for both.

11. Needs for custodial-care expenses (long-term care) for employees or their dependents or for retired employees or their dependents.

12. Other employee benefit needs or goals (such as a desire to participate in corporate stock plans or other longer-term incentive programs).

Naturally, a given functional analysis often does not encompass all these needs, goals, or loss exposures. The above classification is intended to be more exhaustive than frequently is included in a functional analysis. However, the history of employee benefit planning, particularly since the end of World War II, generally has been one of expanding the areas of employees' (and others') needs for which the employer is providing benefits of various kinds. It seems likely, therefore, that additional categories of needs, goals, and loss exposures will be added to the above list from time to time. Also, some of those needs and exposures mentioned only incidentally in the above list may become more important in the future.

Figure 2–2 provides an illustration of the functional approach to employee benefit planning, using the employee benefit plan of a large corporation and the functional categories used by that corporation. Note that the employee needs, goals, and exposures to loss are shown on the left-hand margin of the grid, while the components of this corporation's employee benefit plan are shown across the top of the grid. This arrangement shows how each benefit plan applies to each of these employee needs, goals, or loss exposures. Any gaps or duplications in coverage (or need for further information) can be seen more easily through this systematic process of analysis.

Classify by Categories the Persons the Employer May Want to Protect

This step basically involves the issues of who should be protected by an employee benefit plan, for what benefits, for what time period, and under

F I G U R E   2–2

Illustration of Functional Approach to Employee Benefit Planning

Employee Needs, Goals, or Exposures to Loss	Health Care Plan	Basic Salary Continuation Plan	Extended Salary Continuation Plan	Long-Term Disability Plan	Basic Life Insurance Plan
Medical expenses	Choice among 3 types of plans (HMO options, preferred provider option, or indemnity plan) with different levels of employee contributions and cost-sharing. Dental, hearing, and vision care also covered.				
Disability losses	Coverage continues while employee receives disability benefits under company plans.	Full salary for up to 30 days of absence each year for illness or injury.	After the basic allowance is exhausted, employee's full salary less offsetting benefits is maintained up to a maximum of 25 months depending on length of service.	After extended plan ends, 75% of base monthly pay less offsetting benefits for up to 25 months; then, a voluntary payroll deduction LTD benefit of 50% of salary.	Coverage continues while employee receives disability benefits under company plans.
In case of death	Dependent coverage continues for 4 months plus an additional period depending upon employee service, at the employer's expense. Thereafter, the plan meets COBRA requirements.	Coverage terminates.	Coverage terminates.	Coverage terminates.	Provides beneficiary with a benefit of $3,000.
Retirement	Modified plans may be continued for life during retirement on a contributory basis.	Coverage terminates.	Coverage terminates.	Coverage terminates.	$3,000 coverage continues after retirement for as long as employee lives.
Capital accumulation					
Dependent care assistance					

(continued)

F I G U R E   2–2 (continued)

Employee Needs, Goals, or Exposures to Loss	Primary Life Insurance Plan	Travel Accident Plan	Savings Plan	Employees' Stock Purchase Plan
Medical expenses				
Disability losses	Coverage continues while employee receives disability benefits under company plans.	Pays a benefit of up to 3 times employee's annual base pay if disability involves an accidental dismemberment while traveling on company business.	Contributions are discontinued when long-term disability benefits begin. Participation may continue unless employee becomes permanently and totally disabled or until formal retirement. Withdrawals are permitted.	Employee receiving disability benefits may suspend any payments being made to the plan for a period not to exceed 6 months or a specified date in the offering.
In case of death	Provides beneficiary with a benefit of 3 times employee's current annual base pay (offset by pension plan's preretirement survivor benefit). Employee also has the option to purchase additional life insurance at favorable group rates, up to 3 times current base pay.	Pays beneficiary a lump-sum benefit of 3 times employee's annual base pay if death is the result of an accident while traveling on company business.	Beneficiary receives the amount credited to employee's account.	Payment is made of any amount being accumulated during a "purchase period" with interest.
Retirement	Continues after retirement with the amount and duration of coverage depending on the option employee chooses.	Coverage terminates.	Employee may receive the balance in the plan account upon retirement under various payout options.	Stock purchased under plan available at and before retirement; retirees not eligible for future offerings.
Capital accumulation			Employees may contribute up to 16% of pay or $7,000 (indexed) before-tax per year. Employer matches 50% of contributions, up to 6% of pay. Six investment options available. Withdrawals permitted on termination of employment or in service in special cases. Plan loans available subject to tax law requirements.	Employees can purchase company stock in amounts based on salary up to tax law maximum at 85% of stock price at either the beginning or the end of any purchase period; payment in installments by payroll deduction.
Dependent care assistance				

F I G U R E   2–2 (concluded)

Pension Plan	Social Security	Workers' Compen-sation	Supplemental Workers' Compensation	Flexible Spending Accounts (FSAs)
		Pays if illness or injury is job-related under the workers' compensation laws.		Allows employees to set aside before-tax up to $3,000 per year for tax-eligible health care expenses.
Participation continues while employee receives company disability benefits; service credits accumulate until end of extended disability period or up to 3 months.	Pays after 5 months of continuous total disability when approved by Social Security.	Pays if disability is job-related under the workers' compensation laws.	Increases disability income if employee receives workers' compensation benefits.	
Active employees: preretirement survivors benefit for vested employees' spouses if employees die before retirement; no cost to employee; coordinated with primary life insurance plan. Retired employees: retiree may elect pension option to provide benefits to beneficiary upon retiree's death, subject to QJSA rules.	Pays a lump-sum death benefit and monthly survivor income to spouse and children.	Pays if death is job-related under the workers' compensation laws.	Coverage terminates.	
Defined benefit plan integrated with Social Security pays regular benefit at 65, with alternatives for early retirement before age 65.	Pays unreduced retirement benefits at full-benefit retirement age (currently age 65) or reduced benefits as early as age 62. In addition, health care expenses may be covered under Medicare.	Coverage terminates in accordance with the workers' compensation laws.	Coverage terminates.	
				Allows employees to set aside before-tax up to $5,000 per year for tax-eligible child or other dependent care.

what conditions. These issues have become increasingly important in employee benefit planning as the scope of employee benefit plans has increased not only in terms of the benefits provided but also in terms of continuing to protect employees or former employees once the formal employment relationship has ended and of protecting dependents of employees in a variety of circumstances. It is a logical part of the functional approach because the needs, goals, and loss exposures of employees imply consideration not only of the kinds of benefits to be provided but also of the persons to be protected and when they will be protected. Thus, in designing its employee benefit plan, the employer should consider how the various functional categories of needs and goals will be met for different categories of persons under a variety of circumstances.

In this type of analysis, the following are among the categories of persons whom the employer may want to consider protecting under its employee benefit plan—under at least some circumstances and for at least some benefits:

1. Active full-time employees.
2. Dependents of active full-time employees.
3. Retired former employees.
4. Dependents of retired former employees.
5. Disabled employees and their dependents.
6. Surviving dependents of deceased employees.
7. Terminated employees and their dependents.
8. Employees (and their dependents) who are temporarily separated from the employer's service, such as during layoffs, leaves of absence, military duty, strikes, and so forth.
9. Other than full-time active employees (e.g., part-time employees, directors, and so forth).

The employer basically must decide how far to (or in some cases it may be required to) extend its employee benefit program, and for what kinds of benefits, to persons who may not be active full-time employees. This represents a significant issue in employee benefit planning both in terms of adequacy of employee protection and the cost for the employer. Some extensions of benefits, such as provision of medical expense benefits to retirees and perhaps their dependents (retiree medical benefits), and continuation of group term life insurance (normally in reduced amounts) on retirees' lives, can be quite expensive. The importance of this issue has been heightened for employers by the adoption by the *Financial Accounting*

Standards Board (FASB) of Financial Accounting Standard (FAS) 106—Employers' Accounting for Postretirement Benefits Other Than Pensions. *FAS 106* generally requires employers to recognize during covered employees' periods of service the accrued benefit cost of these post-retirement benefits (the net periodic post-retirement benefit cost) as a current business expense, and to recognize the liabilities for and any plan assets funding these benefits for balance-sheet purposes.

The extent to which employers may want to extend coverage of their benefit plans to one or more of these categories of persons varies with employer philosophy, cost constraints, funding and accounting considerations, union negotiations, and employee benefit practices in the particular industry and geographic area involved. Such extensions also vary considerably among the different kinds of benefits. Regulatory requirements also must be observed.

For example, medical expense benefits may be extended to active employees, various categories of dependents of active employees, retired former employees, dependents of retired former employees, surviving spouses and other dependents of deceased retired former employees, disabled employees, dependents of disabled employees, and surviving dependents of deceased active employees. Further, medical expense coverage must be made available for specified periods under the terms of the *Consolidated Omnibus Budget Reconciliation Act of 1985* (COBRA), as amended, for terminated employees, certain dependents of terminated employees, certain dependents of active employees who no longer meet the definition of an eligible dependent under the regular employee benefit plan, certain dependents of deceased employees, and in certain other situations. In addition, under the *Family and Medical Leave Act of 1993*, employers are required to maintain an employee's group health (medical expense and health flexible spending account) coverage during an allowed period of family or medical leave (generally for a total of 12 weeks during any 12-month period) as if the employee had been continuously employed during the period of permitted leave. Also, the *Uniformed Services Employment and Reemployment Rights Act of 1993* requires employers to offer up to 18 months of health coverage to employees who are on military leave and to their dependents.

Group term life insurance, however, may be provided to active full-time employees, disabled employees who meet the definition of disability under the plan, and retired employees in reduced amounts. Also, some plans provide dependents group life insurance to eligible dependents of active employees.

Another factor to consider in this analysis is to what extent, and on what contribution basis, certain employee benefits will be provided to or continued for various categories of persons. Benefits may be provided or continued without contribution by the employee or covered person in full or in reduced amounts. Or, the benefits could be provided or continued with contribution to the cost by the employee or covered person in full or on a reduced basis. Finally, benefits may be provided or continued to covered persons on an elective basis at the covered person's own cost.

Analyze Benefits Presently Available

The next step in the functional approach is to analyze the benefits, terms of coverage, and plan participation by employees in terms of how well the existing or proposed employee benefit plan meets employee needs and goals in the various functional categories for those classes of persons the employer wants to protect or benefit. This step involves measuring the employee benefit plan against the objectives and coverage criteria set up for it under the functional approach just outlined.

Types of Benefits

A common application of the functional approach to employee benefit planning is to outline the different types of benefits under an employee benefit plan that apply to each of the categories of employee needs and goals. This may be done in the form of a grid as shown in Figure 2–2. In that figure, for example, employee needs, goals, and exposures to loss are shown on the left-hand margin of the grid, while the components of the corporation's employee benefit plan are shown across the top of the grid.

Levels of Benefits

In a similar fashion, the levels of benefits under the various components of the employee benefit plan can be determined or shown, or both, for each of the categories of needs or goals.

To supplement this analysis, it may be helpful to use benefit illustrations to determine or illustrate the levels of benefits that would be provided under the various components of the employee benefit plan or proposed plan in the event of certain contingencies and using certain assumptions. For example, it might be assumed an employee with certain earnings and using certain salary projections will retire at age 65 with 30 years of service with the employer. This employee's total retirement income then may be estimated from various components of the employer's employee benefit plan as well as from Social Security as of the assumed retirement date. This can be expressed as a percentage of the employee's estimated final pay, which often is referred to as the employee's retirement income "replacement ratio." The employee benefits used in such an analysis may include only the employer's pension plan and Social Security, but it would be more logical to include all potential sources of retirement income available through the employee benefit plan, such as a pension plan, profit-sharing plan, thrift or savings plan, supplemental executive retirement plans, and perhaps other kinds of plans or benefits intended primarily to provide capital accumulation or stock-purchase benefits. Naturally, assumptions must be made for a variety of factors if all these sources of retirement income are considered. Also, different assumptions as to employee earnings, year of retirement, final pay, years of service, and so forth may be used to test the adequacy of retirement income for employees.

The same kind of analysis can be made for disability benefits from all sources under the employee benefit plan. When the analysis of disability benefits is made, it may be found that excessive benefits will be paid under certain conditions and for certain durations of disability, while inadequate benefits will be paid under other conditions. Thus, better coordination of disability benefits may be called for in making recommendations for changes in the plan.

This approach also may prove fruitful for other employee loss exposures, such as death, medical expenses at various levels and under various conditions, long-term care (custodial care), and so forth. Finally, the adequacy of benefit levels can be tested for different categories of persons the employer may want to protect.

Another interesting kind of analysis in terms of benefit levels is to estimate the potential for capital accumulation available to employees under the components of an employee benefit plan designed primarily for this purpose. These may include, for example, profit-sharing plans, thrift or savings plans, stock-purchase plans, stock options, restricted stock, employee stock ownership plans (ESOPs), other stock-based performance plans, and so forth. Employees often are pleasantly surprised to learn how much capital can be accumulated under such plans over a period, even using relatively conservative investment assumptions.

In evaluating levels of benefits and benefit adequacy, consideration also may be given to optional benefits that may be available to employees under the employee benefit plan. Such options may involve the opportunity for employees to purchase coverage or additional levels of coverage beyond a basic level of benefits. Through such optional benefits, the employer in effect is giving employees the opportunity at a given cost to themselves to make their total benefits more adequate in certain specific areas. As an example, the life insurance plan shown in Figure 2–2 allows eligible employees to purchase additional life insurance at favorable group rates up to three times their base pay over and above the employer-provided benefit of three times annual base pay (subject to certain individual underwriting requirements). Another such area of optional benefits exists when employers allow employees to purchase long-term care (LTC) insurance for themselves or specified dependents on an employee-pay-all group basis. At present, this generally is the way employers make LTC coverage available to their employees, if they do so at all.

Of course, an employer may extend the idea of optional benefits or employee choice-making even further by adopting a flexible benefits (cafeteria compensation) program as part of its employee benefit plan. This idea is discussed again in this chapter with regard to "Flexibility Available to Employees."

Probationary Periods

In assessing how well an existing employee benefit plan meets the needs and loss exposures of employees and certain other individuals, it also is helpful to analyze the probationary periods required for the various types of benefits contained in the plan. Such probationary periods, or the length of service otherwise eligible employees must have with the employer before they become eligible to participate in the various types of benefits, will have an effect on the plan's protection for employees, their dependents, and possibly others. The longer the probationary period required, the greater the exposure of employees and others to a loss not covered by the plan. But, many employers believe only employees with certain minimum periods of service, and hence demonstrable connection with the employer, should be eligible for at least certain types of benefits.

Probationary periods by their nature create gaps in coverage for newly hired or newly eligible employees and their dependents. Thus, probationary periods should be analyzed as part of the functional approach to determine whether the resulting gaps in coverage are appropriate and consistent with the employer's objectives and the employees' needs.

It seems desirable that the use of probationary periods in an employee benefit plan should be based on a reasonably consistent employer philosophy. One possible philosophy in this regard is to divide employee benefits into "protection-oriented" benefits and "accumulation-oriented" benefits. *Protection-oriented* benefits would consist of medical expense benefits, life insurance benefits, short- and long-term disability benefits, and so forth. These benefits protect employees and their dependents against serious loss exposures which, if they were to occur, could spell immediate financial disaster for the employees or their dependents, or both. For such benefits, where the need/protection orientation is great, there might be no probationary period, or a relatively short one. The rationale for this would be that the need for immediate coverage would override the traditional reasons for using probationary periods or longer probationary periods.

Accumulation-oriented benefits, such as pension plans, profit-sharing plans, thrift plans, stock-bonus plans, stock-purchase plans, and so forth, could involve relatively long probationary periods if desired by the employer and could be subject to legal requirements. The theory might be that these kinds of benefits should be a reward for relatively long service with the employer. Also, an employee who stays with the employer would have a relatively long time in which to accumulate such benefits, and thus longer probationary periods would not really place the employee at any serious disadvantage or risk.

Eligibility Requirements

Requirements for eligibility for benefits, including definitions of covered persons, obviously affect those who may benefit from or be protected by various employee benefits. In this area, for example, the employer, or the employer and the union or unions with whom the employer negotiates, should consider such issues as:

1. Which dependents of active employees (and perhaps dependents of retired former employees, disabled employees, and deceased employees—see 2, 3, 4, and 5 below) should (or must) be covered for medical expense benefits?

2. Should retirees (and perhaps their spouses and other dependents) continue to be covered, and if so, for what benefits?

3. Should survivors of deceased active employees continue to be covered, and if so, for what benefits and for how long?

4. Should survivors of retired former employees continue to be covered, and if so, for what benefits?

5. Should employees or former employees on disability (and perhaps their dependents) continue to be covered, and if so, for what benefits, how long, and under what conditions?

6. Should (or must) coverage be extended to employees during layoffs, leaves of absence, strikes, and other temporary interruptions of employment, and if so, for what benefits, how long, and under what conditions?

7. Should coverage be limited only to full-time employees (or employees meeting ERISA requirements) or should coverage, or some coverage, be extended to part-time employees as well?

8. What coverage should (or must) be continued or made available to persons (or for the dependents of such persons) after termination of employment with the employer and on what basis?

The resolution of some of these issues depends in part on statutory or other legal requirements, insurance company underwriting rules, collective bargaining agreements, and similar factors. However, the philosophy or rationale of the employer, or the employer and union, concerning the employee benefit program will have a substantial impact on how some of these coverage and eligibility issues are resolved. At the heart of many of these issues is the basic question of how far an employer (or union) should feel obligated to go, either legally or morally—or possibly can afford to go—in meeting the various needs and loss exposures of its employees, their dependents, and persons who once were employees or dependents of employees but who now have various other relationships or no relationship with the employer.

Employee Contribution Requirements

If certain employee benefits under an employer's employee benefit plan are contributory (i.e., the employees or possibly their surviving dependents must contribute to the cost of the benefit), this will have an impact on employee participation and hence on how well the plan meets the needs of the employee group as a whole. This really represents a trade-off: between the financing and other advantages of a contributory plan— and the loss of employee participation in the plan, which results from requiring employee contributions, assuming employee participation in the contributory plan is voluntary. Thus, an employer, and union if the plan is negotiated, may have to decide whether a particular employee benefit will be noncontributory or contributory, and, if it is to be contributory, how much the employees will have to contribute toward the cost of the plan. Further, if the plan is contributory, the employer (or employer and union) will have to decide whether participation will be voluntary or mandatory as a condition of employment. Making a contributory plan mandatory solves the employee participation problem, but it may create serious employee relations and morale problems. Therefore, most employers do not have mandatory contributory plans. Still another possibility is for employers simply to make the coverage available to employees (usually on a more favorable basis than they could purchase it individually) on an employee-pay-all basis.

In the context of this cost/employee participation trade-off, one approach that can help planners strike an agreeable balance is to rank employee benefits in terms of the relative degree to which the employer feels that all employees and their dependents should be protected, and hence what benefits should the plan aim for 100 percent participation, compared with benefits for which such a high level of participation is not deemed essential. This same kind of analysis also might be helpful in determining the level of employee contribution if it is decided to have the plan be contributory. Another factor bearing on this decision is whether other benefits in the employer's overall plan also may be available to meet the same functional need. For example, employee benefit plans frequently contain a number of kinds of benefits intended to help provide retirement income for employees. Still another factor to consider is the extent to which employees or their dependents, or both, may have similar benefits available to them elsewhere. Those employees or dependents who have an alternative source of similar benefits may opt not to participate if the plan is made contributory, thereby helping to avoid duplication of benefits. An example of this is the availability of multiple plans of medical expense benefits when both a husband and wife are employed outside the home.

There is a tendency toward providing employees with alternative benefits or levels of benefits, with varying degrees of employee contributions (if any) required. In any event, as part of its benefit planning system, it will be helpful for an employer to make a benefit-by-benefit analysis, within the context of its total benefit and compensation philosophy, to evaluate the desirability of any employee (and possibly dependent) contributions to the cost of the various employee benefits or levels of benefits.

Of course, to the extent that voluntary salary reduction (normally before-tax) is part of a flexible benefits (cafeteria compensation) plan, the covered employees themselves really are making the decision as to the level of their contributions (through salary reduction) to pay for the benefits they select within the scope of the plan. To this degree, the decision-making regarding contributions into these plans is at least partly shifted to the covered employees, depending on the benefit options they select.

Flexibility Available to Employees

The degree to which employees have flexibility in making such choices as to whether they will participate in a given employee benefit; the amounts of additional coverage they may wish to purchase; the opportunity to select from among two or more alternative plans of benefits; and even the opportunity to structure their own benefit program, as under a flexible benefits (cafeteria compensation) approach, clearly has an impact on the extent to which employees may tailor an employee benefit plan to meet their own needs and goals within the functional categories described previously. In fact, it may be argued that the more flexibility employees have, the more likely it is that the benefit program they select will meet their individual needs and goals. It thus can be argued, on the one hand, that flexibility in employee benefit plan design should facilitate the goals of the functional approach to employee benefit planning. On the other hand, it also can be argued that allowing too much employee flexibility in choosing types and amounts of employee benefits may work against the functional approach, because employees may misperceive or not understand their and their families' needs and hence leave some important needs uncovered. This concern often is addressed by limiting the choices of employees or by specifying a core of benefits that are not subject to employee choice.

A distinct trend exists toward giving employees more flexibility in the structuring of their own benefits. As just discussed, this trend probably buttresses the functional approach, in that it may be presumed that rational employees will opt for those benefits and benefit amounts that will best meet their individual needs and goals.

Actual Employee Participation in Benefit Plans

It was noted previously that, under the functional approach, an employer may analyze the types of benefits provided to employees and their dependents according to the various functional categories. The employer also may estimate or project benefit levels for the benefits in the different categories under certain assumptions and given certain contingencies or events. However, these analyses and estimates of benefits and benefit levels may not completely show how well certain employee benefits actually reach a given employee group. Therefore, an employer also may want to calculate the actual participation ratios for its employees and their dependents for given employee benefits. These ratios can be calculated in terms of the employees (and their dependents) actually participating in the plan as a ratio of total full-time employees, as a ratio of total eligible employees, or both.

A given employee benefit plan may have many good features, and may even be quite liberal in some respects; but if the ratio of employee participation is low, the particular benefit may not be meeting the employer's objectives in terms of its total compensation system.

Of course, if a given employee benefit is noncontributory, and if its eligibility requirements are reasonably liberal, all the eligible employees will be covered and, probably, a reasonably high percentage of total employees also will be covered. However, when employee benefit plans are contributory, or are optional benefits under a flexible benefits plan, and/or eligibility requirements are tighter, participation ratios may drop significantly. When this is the case, an employer may wish to evaluate the reason(s) for the low participation and what steps, if any, it might take to increase participation in the particular plan or plans.

Determine Gaps in Benefits and Any Overlapping Benefits

From the preceding steps, it is possible to more effectively analyze any gaps in the employer's present employee benefit plan. These gaps may exist in terms of the benefits available from all sources to meet the various categories of employee needs, and goals, in terms of the projected levels of benefits for those needs, in terms of coverage of the various categories of persons the employer may want to protect, and finally in terms of the actual participation of employees in the various components of the employee benefit plan. In a similar fashion, the employer will want to determine any overlapping benefits that presently may be provided from all sources in its employee benefit plan to meet certain categories of needs.

Consider Recommendations for Changes in Present Plan

As a result of the functional approach described here, the employer may consider various recommendations or alternative recommendations for changes in its present employee benefit plan to not only eliminate gaps in benefits or persons covered but also to avoid any overlap in benefits. Part of this step also may involve consideration of adopting or modifying an existing flexible benefits (cafeteria compensation) plan to meet employee needs. Essentially, this step involves the consideration of alternatives, which is implicit in any decision-making system.

Estimate Costs (or Savings) for Each Recommendation

The cost or savings estimate is an important step before any recommendation for improvements, reductions, or changes in an employee benefit plan can be adopted. These estimates are based upon certain assumptions and may be expressed in terms of ranges of possible cost (or savings) results. An employer normally will have certain overall cost constraints on its employee benefit planning. Therefore, recommended improvements or changes in the plan may have to be assigned certain priorities in terms of which benefits the employer can afford to adopt.

Evaluate Alternative Methods of Financing Benefits

This step involves the evaluation of how recommended changes in benefits or existing benefits, or both, should be financed or secured. While this may not strictly involve the functional analysis of benefits in relation to needs, it is an essential step in analyzing any employee benefit plan.

Consider Cost-Saving or Cost-Containment Techniques

At this point, the employer also should consider cost-saving techniques concerning its employee benefits. These may involve changes in benefit plan design, elimination or reduction of certain benefits, adoption or modification of a flexible benefits (cafeteria compensation) approach, use of alternative methods of financing certain benefits, use of managed care approaches for medical benefits, use of utilization review for medical expense benefits, use of disability management and rehabilitation, adoption of wellness and similar programs, changes in insurers or servicing organizations, changes in investment policies or advisors, the decision to self-fund or retain certain benefits, and other similar techniques. Again, while consideration of such techniques may not be directly involved in the functional analysis of an employee benefit plan, it is a logical step in the planning process once such a functional analysis is begun.

Decide on Appropriate Benefits and Financing Methods

Once the preceding analysis is complete, the employer, or employer and union, is in a position to decide on the particular benefit recommendations it wants to adopt or bargain for. The employer also may decide on appropriate financing methods. This is essentially the selection of the best alternative or alternatives in the decision-making process.

Implement Any Changes

This step involves the implementation of the changes or recommendations decided on above. It is the implementation phase of the decision-making process.

Communicate Benefit Changes to Employees

The effective communication of employee benefits and changes in such benefits is a vital element in the overall success of any employee benefit plan. It often is a neglected element. An employer may go to a great deal of time, trouble, and expense in making improvements in its employee benefit plan, but all this effort and cost may not be as effective as it could be in terms of good employee relations and meeting the employer's total compensation policies if the improvements are not effectively communicated to employees.

Many employers periodically communicate to employees the current overall status and value of their employee benefits. Frequently this is done annually. Such a communication concerning the status and total value of an employee's benefits may be accomplished, at least in part, by using categories of benefits similar to those classified in the functional approach described above. See Chapter 40 of the *Handbook* for a more detailed discussion of communications.

Periodically Reevaluate the Plan

Employee benefit planning is a task that is never complete. Concepts of employee needs, the benefits available to meet those needs, how those benefits should be made available to employees, and regulatory requirements are constantly changing. Therefore, the employee benefit plan must be constantly reevaluated and updated to change with them.

CHAPTER 3

Risk Concepts and Employee Benefit Planning

Gary K. Stone

RISK AND EMPLOYEE BENEFITS

Definition of Risk

The concept of risk is fundamental in any discussion of employee benefit planning. For our purposes, risk will mean *uncertainty* with respect to possible *loss*. In other words, it is the inability to determine a future loss and to figure out how expensive it will be should the loss take place. For example, individuals have very little ability to know when they will die, become ill, disabled, or unemployed. All the typical potential losses associated with employee benefits are "risks" from the standpoint of the individual. *Loss* is meant to convey any decrease in value suffered. A hospital bill associated with an illness could result in a loss, because it would cause a decrease in the value of assets held by a person.

Peril and Hazard Distinguished from Risk

The concept of risk is different from the concepts of peril and hazard, but the three have an interrelationship. Peril and hazard are insurance terms, used primarily in property and liability insurance but also in life and health insurance. They also have considerable application in employee benefit planning.

A peril is defined as the cause of personal or property loss, destruction, or damage. Common perils involving property are fires, floods, earthquakes, thefts, and burglaries. These same perils also can cause personal harm. Other perils that cause personal losses are illnesses, bodily injuries, and death. A number of insurance policies are identified by the perils covered. Life insurance and health policies normally do not name the perils but usually cover all perils associated with those policies. Actually they originally were called *death insurance policies* and *accident and sickness policies*, but their names were changed for euphemistic and marketing reasons.

A hazard is a condition that either increases the probability that a peril will occur or that tends to increase the loss when a peril has struck. The three basic types of hazards are designated as physical hazards, moral hazards, and morale hazards.

Physical hazards are physical conditions that fit within the definition of hazard. In the workplace, there can be numerous physical hazards—for example, the presence of flammable materials and the absence of fire extinguishing equipment, machines without appropriate safety devices, and faulty heating and air conditioning units.

Dishonest, unethical, and immoral people are moral hazards. Unfortunately, some employees qualify as moral hazards. The category includes those who steal from the employer, purposely damage employer property, file fraudulent medical claims, abuse sick leave and personal time off, or file false overtime and expense statements.

Morale hazards exist when people act with carelessness or indifference. Some individuals appear to be accident- or disaster-prone and, as such, are morale hazards. On the other hand, specific morale hazards include the failure to lock rooms, vaults, or areas from which valuable items are stolen; forgetting to notify the employer of faulty materials that ultimately cause personal injuries to a handler; or ignoring the fact that a number of employees all experience the same symptoms of physical discomfort, which ultimately can be traced to a job-related cause.

Types of Risk

Risk can be classified into many categories depending upon the use of the term. For the purposes of this chapter, a simple classification is used. Risk is divided into two types or classes, (1) pure risk and (2) speculative risk.

Pure risk is risk in which only two alternatives are possible: (1) either the risk will *not* happen (no financial loss) or (2) it *will* happen, and a financial loss takes place. Nothing positive can result from a pure risk. An example is illness. The best thing that can happen is that a person does not become ill. If a person does become ill, a negative result takes place. Many examples of pure risk are available. The risks of loss from fire, auto accidents, illness, unemployment, disability, theft of property, and earthquake all would be pure risks. Many of the risks covered by employee benefits fall into this classification. Pure risks for the most part can be insured.

Speculative risk inserts another possibility not existing in pure risk. The additional alternative is the possibility of a gain. Speculative risks then would have three potential outcomes: (1) a loss, (2) no loss, and (3) a gain. Examples of speculative risk would be the purchase of a share of common stock, acquiring a new business venture, or gambling. The emphasis of this chapter is on pure risk, rather than on speculative risk.

Pure Risk

Pure risk can be subclassified depending upon the type of financial loss. The three classifications of pure risk are:

1. Personal risk.
2. Property risk.
3. Legal liability risk.

The most important classification of pure risk from an employee benefit standpoint is personal risk. Personal risks are losses that have a direct impact on an individual's life or health. Many risks involving employee benefit plans fall into the category of personal risk. Death, illness, accidents, unemployment, and old age would all be considered to be personal losses. This type of risk can be measured with some degree of accuracy. It is difficult to be precise, but by estimating potential lost income from a particular risk and the medical and other costs associated with it, one can approximate the potential loss. With that information, one can estimate needed protection and seek insurance or whatever other risk-handling measure is appropriate.

Property risks are the uncertainty (possible loss) that decreases the value of one's real or personal property. Fire, flood, earthquake, wind, theft, and automobile collisions all are examples of types of property risks. The home, furniture, cars, and jewelry would be the types of property subject to possible loss. Legal liability risk is a loss resulting from negligent actions of a person that result in injury to another person. It stems from lawsuits by the injured party seeking damages from the negligent party. Common sources of legal liability would be negligent behavior associated with automobiles, one's home or business, the sale of products, or professional misconduct (malpractice). A serious difficulty connected with liability risk is that it has an unlimited potential loss. The dollar impact of this risk is a function of the seriousness of the negligence and the status of the parties involved. Malpractice awards against physicians or awards resulting from automobile accidents are examples in which potential losses can extend into the millions of dollars.

As previously noted, employee benefit plans deal substantially with personal risks. The magnitude of life insurance, medical expense, disability income, retirement, and other personal risk-oriented benefit plans reflect this. However, property and liability risk coverage also can be found in a number of benefit plans. For example, homeowner's insurance, automobile insurance, group legal services, and financial planning services all are examples of property and liability risk coverages available through employee benefit plans. Nevertheless, there is a considerably greater emphasis on personal risk coverages, and there are important factors that explain why benefit plans are less likely to include various property and liability coverages.

Methods of Handling Risk

There are several methods of handling risk. Although the main focus of this chapter is on the use of some type of insurance method to handle the risks associated with benefit plans, it should be recognized that other alternatives are available and are used. The primary risk-handling alternatives are:

1. Avoidance.
2. Control.
3. Retention.
4. Transfer.
5. Insurance.

Avoidance

Avoidance is a perfect device for handling risk. It means one does not acquire the risk to begin with and hence would not be subject to the risk. For example, if a person does not want the risk associated with driving automobiles, he or she won't drive a car. The problem with avoidance is that many times one cannot help but have the risk (the nondriver as a pedestrian or passenger still is exposed to the risk of other persons' driving), or one does not want to avoid it. For risks covered by employee benefits, it is almost impossible to use the avoidance technique. How does one avoid the risk of death or illness? The point is that one is unable to avoid some risks. Attention, then, must be focused on the other alternatives.

Control

Control is a mechanism by which one attempts either to prevent or reduce the probability of a loss taking place, or to reduce the severity of the loss after it has taken place. Many examples of control devices exist. Smoke detectors, fire-resistant building materials, seat belts, air bags, crash-resistant bumpers on autos, nonsmoking office buildings, physical examinations, and proper diets would be considered control devices.

Employee benefit plans can use control in conjunction with other risk-handling techniques, such as insurance. Any procedure used to reduce or prevent accidents, illnesses, or premature death would help in lowering the cost of most benefit plans. It is not unusual for employers to adopt accident-prevention programs, wellness programs, a smoke-free environment at work, and other programs with the intent of lowering workers' compensation and other employee benefit costs as well as improving employees' health and welfare.

Retention

Retention means that the risk is assumed and paid for by the person suffering the loss. Assumption or retention can be used with losses that are small in terms of their financial impact on a person or company. The cost of insurance or some other risk-handling device could be higher than paying for such a loss when it happens, and some losses can be handled more efficiently simply by paying for them as they occur. For example, assume you have an old automobile worth $600. Collision insurance with a typical deductible of $250 would give you only a $350 recovery upon a total loss. In other words, the cost of the insurance plus the deductible could be higher than the value of the loss. In such cases, it may be more economical to retain the risk than to insure it. One has to be careful with retention in that it should be used only with the types of loss that will not cause a financial disaster. Retaining or assuming risks with high severity potential can result in financial catastrophe. It should not be assumed that because a loss is unlikely to happen (low probability), it could or should be retained. The crucial factor is the financial result (severity), if it does take place. A fire that destroys one's home is unlikely, but it is devastating if it happens.

Retention can be a useful tool in handling employee benefit plans. An employer (insured) might decide to retain the first $1,000 of employee medical costs, by purchasing an insurance plan with a $1,000 deductible. Another use of retention can be found in the administration of benefit plans. Employers can take over many of the administrative duties of the insurance company. Payroll deduction, claims administration, answering questions from plan members, and filing of forms sometimes can be done more efficiently by the insured than the insurance company, and by carrying out these functions itself, an employer may be able to lower its direct dollar outlay. However, this form of retention should be examined carefully before being adopted, because the administrative burden and other negative factors may outweigh any potential savings.

Transfer

Transfer is a concept in which one switches or shifts the financial burden of risk to another party. Two forms of transfer usually are recognized. They are (1) insurance, which is covered in the next section of this chapter, and (2) noninsurance transfers, which can take place in many different forms. For example, a landlord may require new tenants to pay extra money up front as a security deposit for potential damage to the premises. This would be a form of transfer. The landlord would be transferring his or her possible loss to the tenant. Another example involves travel agents. A client may want to travel to the Middle East during a time of potential military conflict. The travel agent suggests avoiding the area. The client insists upon taking the trip, but the travel agent has the client sign a form waiving legal claims against the travel agent for dissatisfaction with a trip that the travel agent has not recommended. The hope is that, if a lawsuit develops, the travel agent can assert that the traveler took the responsibility for the burden of any loss upon himself or herself.

Employee benefit plans use transfer extensively, but it usually is in the form of insurance contracts. Noninsurance transfers typically do not serve as risk-handling mechanisms in benefit plans.

Insurance

Insurance is a common method of financing employee benefits. The definition of insurance varies depending upon whether one is looking at insurance from an economic, legal, social, or mathematical viewpoint.

However, for purposes of this chapter, the following definition of insurance will be used.

> Insurance is the pooling of fortuitous losses by transfer of such risks to insurers who agree to indemnify insureds for such losses or to render services connected with the risk.[1]

From the standpoint of an employee benefit plan, insurance would be a mechanism in which the insured (employer/employee) would pay money (premiums) into a fund (insurance company). Upon the occurrence of a loss, reimbursement would be provided to the person suffering the loss. Thus, the risk has been reduced or eliminated for the insured, and all the individuals who paid into the fund share the resulting loss.

Insurance is but one method by which an employee benefit plan may be financed. Large benefit plans may rely on insurance, self-funding, and various combinations of the two. However, many small- to medium-size firms rely almost exclusively on the insurance mechanism.

Before continuing with the discussion of insurance, it is important to clarify the difference between insurance and gambling. Since both insurance and gambling have a relationship to risk, they sometimes are viewed erroneously as essentially the same. However, there are several important features of insurance that distinguish it from gambling. First, insurance is a mechanism for *handling an existing risk*; whereas gambling *creates* a risk where one did not previously exist. Second, the risk created by gambling is a speculative risk; whereas insurance deals with pure risks. Third, gambling involves a gain for one party, the winner, at the expense of another, the loser; whereas insurance is based on a mutual sharing of any losses that occur. Fourth, the loser in a gambling transaction remains in that negative situation; whereas an insured who suffers a loss is financially restored in whole or in part to his or her original situation. Obviously, the insurance-gambling discussion is more appropriate to individual, rather than to group insurance, but the comparison also has some applicability to the group mechanism.

Additionally, the use of insurance to make the victims of losses whole reflects the principle of indemnification on which insurance is structured. An insured is indemnified if a covered loss occurs. That is, he or she is placed somewhat in the same situation that existed prior to the loss (e.g., by reimbursement for damaged property or medical bills, disability income, and the like).

---

1. George E. Rejda. *Principles of Risk Management and Insurance*, 6th ed. (Reading, MA: Addison-Wesley Education Publishers Inc., 1998), p.19.

Summary of Risk-Handling Alternatives

It is possible to use a number of alternatives in the design of employee benefit plans. One or more of the alternatives in some combination is common. The one alternative that is mutually exclusive of the others is avoidance. If you avoid the risk, you are not subjected to potential losses, so that no need exists for insurance, loss control, or any other risk-handling technique. The remaining alternatives, however, could be used in combination.

Assume a typical medical benefit plan for a firm's employees. The firm might purchase a medical insurance plan with a deductible of $1,000 per year per covered member. The plan is insured, and so transfer has been used. In addition, someone must pay the $1,000 deductible, so there is retention or assumption of part of the risk. Further, assume that the firm is interested in keeping the cost of medical benefits down. It may initiate a number of control devices, such as a smoke-free work environment and an accident-prevention program to aid the effort. Thus, a number of the risk-handling alternatives are used together.

What factors should be considered in deciding upon the "best" method of handling the risk of a particular benefit plan? In general, consider the most economical from a financial standpoint, but with proper consideration given to employee welfare. What is being suggested is that there is nothing wrong with opting for the lowest-cost alternative as long as proper consideration is given to the nonfinancial aspects of the employees' welfare. Failing to put a guard on a machine to prevent injury is generally unacceptable, even if it might cost less to let the accident take place. Firms must consider employee welfare and mandatory requirements set forth by the state and federal government in evaluating the alternatives for handling risk.

INSURANCE AND INSURABLE RISK

Insurance is one of the most popular methods of funding employee benefit plans, but, as explained in later chapters of the *Handbook*, many other options exist. The advantages and disadvantages of using insurance in the design of a benefit plan are discussed in the next section.

Advantages of Insurance

A number of reasons account for why insurance can be used effectively in an employee benefit plan. One advantage is the known premium (cost); it is set in advance by the insurance company. The employer may have better control over its budget with a known premium, because any high shock losses would be the problem of the insurance company and not the insured. Having an outside administrator also can be an advantage to the employer. The employer does not have to get involved in disputes involving employees over coverage of the plan, because these would be handled by the insurance company. Employees may prefer insurance to some other form of funding in order to obtain the financial backing of an outside financial institution. This, of course, depends upon the financial strength of the insurance company selected, and care should go into this choice. Insurance companies often are leaders in the area of loss control and may help in the design and implementation of systems designed to control costs for the employer. A final advantage is that it may be more economical for an employer to use insurance rather than other alternatives. The insurance company may be more efficient and able to do the job at a lower total cost.

Disadvantages of Insurance

Insurance is not always the preferred method of funding employee benefit plans. A number of costs are involved that must be considered. Insurance companies charge administrative expenses that are added to the premium (or loaded) to compensate for their overhead expenses. Home office costs, licensing costs, commissions, taxes, loss-adjustment expenses, and the like all must go into the loading. One must realize that the premium covers not only direct losses but also the insurance company's overhead as well. The amount may vary from a small percent of the premium (e.g., 2 percent to 5 percent) to potentially a very high amount (25 percent or more) depending on the type of contract involved. Another potential disadvantage is that employer satisfaction is directly affected by the insurer's ability to handle claims and solve problems. Slow payment or restrictive claim practices can have an adverse effect on employees.

Whether something is an advantage or disadvantage often depends upon the specific insurance company involved. It is important to use care in the selection of an insurer. Checking out the insurer with other clients and carefully analyzing the carrier's financial stability are critical elements in the selection process.

Characteristics of an Insurable Risk

It often is said that anything can be insured if one is willing to pay the premium required. Insurance companies, however, normally will insure a risk only if it meets certain minimum standards. These standards or prerequisites are needed for an insurer to manage the company in a sound financial manner. Without suitable risks, an insurance company can find itself in serious financial trouble. An insurance company is subject to the same problems as any other business—inadequate capitalization, a weak investment portfolio, or poor management. Insurance companies have the additional problem of insuring risks that could result in catastrophic losses.

The following is a list of the characteristics of a risk that are desired in order for it to be considered an "insurable risk":

1. There should be a large number of homogeneous risks (exposure units).
2. The loss should be verifiable and measurable.
3. The loss should not be catastrophic in nature.
4. The chance of loss should be subject to calculation.
5. The premium should be reasonable or economically feasible.
6. The loss should be accidental from the standpoint of the insured.

It should be noted that this list is what is considered ideal from the standpoint of the insurance company. Most risks are not perfect in all aspects, and insurance companies have to weigh all aspects of a risk to determine if, overall, it meets the criteria of an insurable risk.

Large Number of Homogeneous Risks

The insurance company must be able to calculate the number of losses it will incur from the total number of risks it insures. Assume that a life insurance company has just been formed and it is to insure its first two people. Each wants $100,000 of life insurance. The company needs to know what the chance of dying for each of the two people is in order to calculate a premium. Without this information, the company will have no idea of whether these people will live or die during the policy period. Should both die during this period, $200,000 would be needed for the claims. If neither dies, the company would need nothing for the claims. The conclusion one reaches is that the premium should be somewhere between $0 and $200,000. This information is not very helpful, and the insurance company could not insure the risk. What is needed is a large number of similar risks so statistics can be developed to determine an accurate probability of loss for each risk being evaluated. Insurance is based on the *law of large numbers*, which means that, the greater the number of exposures, the more closely the actual results will approach the probable results that are expected from an infinite number of exposures. For example, life insurance companies have accumulated information over the years that enables them to develop mortality tables that reflect the expected mortality for a given type of risk. They are able to do this because of the large number of lives that have been insured over the years. Medical, dental, disability, and life risks all require large numbers of cases to determine proper premium rates.

Employee benefit plans may or may not have the numbers needed to determine loss expectations accurately. This would depend upon the specific plan. Those plans with large numbers of homogeneous risks can be experience rated. This means the premiums will be calculated with the data from the plan experience itself. Smaller plans would not have an adequate number of risks, and other alternatives would be needed. For example, small plans can be combined with other small plans to get creditable statistics, or insurance companies might ignore small-plan statistics and rely on loss statistics developed independently of the plan.

Loss Should Be Verifiable and Measurable

It is important that an insurance company be able to verify a loss and to determine the financial loss involved. Certain risks pose no problem in determining if a loss has taken place. Examples would be fire and windstorm losses with a home or a collision loss with one's auto. Furthermore, the financial value of these losses can be determined accurately by the use of appraisals and other forms of valuation. Other risks are harder to evaluate. An example is a claim for theft of money from a home. Did the theft take place? Did the person have any money at home to be stolen? With risks that are difficult to evaluate, the insurance company has to take other precautions to protect itself from false and inflated claims.

Employee benefits are subject to the same types of problems. Death claims and retirement benefit claims probably would be the easiest in which to determine whether a loss has taken place or not. Once a death claim is verified, the amount of loss is normally the face value of the insurance contract. Few problems result from death claims. The same is true of retirement benefits. Assuming the age of the retiree can be verified, then the benefit promised by the plan will be paid. The other extreme might be disability income claims. In some situations, an insurer might be uncertain whether a valid claim exists or not. Some disability losses, such as back injuries, are very difficult to determine. Is the insured actually disabled or not? Still other employee benefit losses may fall between these two extremes. Medical and dental losses might fall into this category. When an employee benefit loss is difficult to verify or measure, the insurer may attempt to overcome the problem through several methods. Policy provisions are helpful in such situations. Benefit maximums, waiting periods, preexisting conditions clauses, alternate medical verification, required second opinion on certain surgical procedures, and hospital-stay monitoring are a few of the provisions that help in these situations.

Loss Should Not Be Catastrophic in Nature

A serious problem occurs when a large percentage of the risks insured can be lost from the same event. Assume a fire insurance company insured all of its risks in one geographical location. A serious fire could result in catastrophic losses to the company. This did happen in the early history of fire insurance. Fires in London, Chicago, Baltimore, and San Francisco resulted in insurance company bankruptcies and loss of confidence in the industry. It became obvious that a geographic spread of the risks insured was essential, because a concentration of losses from one event could seriously impair or even bankrupt a company. Cases exist in which it is almost impossible to obtain a spread of the risks. In such cases, insurance becomes difficult or impossible to obtain. Flood and unemployment losses would be examples. Unemployment can cover wide geographic areas, and a geographic spread would not help prevent a catastrophic loss. The same could be true for flood losses. The federal or state government might insure this type of risk, but it would be necessary for it to subsidize the premium rates to make them affordable.

Employee benefits are seldom subject to problems relating to inability to get a geographic spread of the risk. Benefit plans often insure life risks, hospital and dental risks, and disability income losses. For the most part, these types of risks are not subject to catastrophic loss due to geographic location, but examples can be imagined in which catastrophic losses might exist. The possibility of a plant explosion or a poison gas leak causing a large number of deaths or medical losses, or a concentration of certain diseases because of the exposure to certain elements that are indigenous to a specific employee group theoretically exist. Usually, however, this is not an important consideration in underwriting typical benefit plans. Policy limitations, reinsurance, and restrictions on groups insured all can be used to minimize the problem to the extent it exists.

Chance of Loss Should Be Subject to Calculation

For an insurance company to be able to calculate a premium that is reasonable to the insured and that represents the losses of a particular risk, certain information is essential. Data on both the frequency of losses and the severity of the losses must be available to determine the loss portion of the premium. This often is referred to as the pure premium portion of the premium. Essential to the pure premium calculation would be a large number of homogeneous exposure units as previously discussed. If an employer is large enough, the plan losses alone could be used to determine the *pure premium* portion. The meaning of "large" depends upon the type of risk involved. At least several hundred employees probably would be needed for full reliance upon the data.

Premium Should Be Reasonable or Economically Feasible

For an employee benefit plan to be acceptable to an employer and to employees, the plan must have a premium that is considered reasonable relative to the risk being insured; that is, the insured must be able to pay the premium. An insurance company's expenses not related to the losses covered by the pure premium must be added to that premium to obtain the total premium. The expense portion may be referred to as the *loading* associated with the risk. The "pure premium" plus the "loading" would make up the total premium to be paid by the plan. Employees who pay a part or all of the premium (participating plan) will not participate if they can obtain a lower premium in an individual insurance plan or if they can be insured through a spouse's plan at a lower cost, and the employer will be unable or unwilling to pay the premium if the rate is not reasonable.

Why would a premium be noncompetitive? This could happen for any number of reasons. For example, a plan could be populated by a high number of older employees. The resulting rate may mean that the younger employees can find lower-cost insurance outside of the plan. The younger employees are unwilling to subsidize the rates for the older employees. Also, the employer may not want to pay the needed premiums. Other reasons for noncompetitive plans could be poor loss experience from a high number of sick and disabled in a plan, or a plan having specific benefits that have resulted in high loss payout. For example, a plan may provide unlimited benefits for drug- or alcohol-related sickness, and the plan member makeup may have resulted in heavy payout for these problems. The bottom line is that the resulting loss experience has made the plan noncompetitive. It is not unusual for an employee group initially to pay a rate that is considered reasonable only to have the plan premiums become unreasonable over time. Failure to keep the average age of the members in the plan low or a higher incidence of illness could be the reason.

The employer must keep track of the factors contributing to premium increases. Inflation related to medical benefits has in recent years resulted in plan costs increasing beyond the regular cost-of-living index. This is particularly true with plans covering prescription drugs. The cost of this coverage has dramatically increased during the 1990s. Constant review of benefits, benefit levels, employees covered by the plan, and competitive rates for alternative plans must take place. It has become common for plans to move away from "first dollar" medical benefits and to incorporate deductibles, waiting periods, and other cost-saving features. An obvious factor to review is the cost of alternative plans. Would it be financially sound to use an alternative insurance plan or an alternative method of delivering the benefits, such as a health maintenance organization (HMO) or a preferred provider organization (PPO)?

Loss Should Be Accidental from the Standpoint of the Insured

This problem can be serious in some forms of insurance, such as property and liability coverage, but is of less importance in the life and health areas of employee benefits. The insurance company does not want to pay for a loss if it is intentionally caused by the insured. It is obvious that payment should not be made if one intentionally destroys his or her home by arson or purposely wrecks an automobile.

An employee could intentionally cause a personal loss, but it would mean causing harm to himself or herself. For example, suicide or attempted suicide could result in death or medical claims. This type of problem can be reduced or eliminated by policy provisions restricting benefits in some manner if it is necessary. Determining whether a loss is accidental normally is not a problem in life, medical, and disability claims.

Insurable Risk Summary

Insurance companies consider providing insurance to employee benefit plans if they meet the minimum standards of an insurable risk. Benefit plans in general fit the minimum standards as set forth above. Such plans would include life insurance, medical and dental insurance, disability income, and retirement programs. Policy provisions, benefit restrictions, and reinsurance can be used to help alleviate problems to the extent they exist. Life insurance probably is the best example of a plan that meets all the desirable standards of an insurable risk. Disability income, although normally insurable, creates more of a problem from an insurability stand-point. Although not a common employee benefit, excess unemployment insurance would be a benefit that borders on being uninsurable.

Handling Adverse Selection

Adverse selection is the phenomenon in the insurance mechanism where-by individuals who have higher-than-average potentially insurable risks "select against" the insurer. That is, those with the greater probabilities of loss, and who therefore need insurance more than the average insured, attempt to obtain the coverage. For example, people who need hospital-ization or surgical coverage seek to purchase medical insurance, those who own property subject to possible loss by fire or flood obtain insur-ance, and individuals who own valuable jewelry or objects of art purchase appropriate coverage. This tendency can result in a disproportionate num-ber of insureds who experience losses that are greater than those antici-pated. Thus, the actual losses can be greater than the expected losses. Because adverse selection is of concern to insurers for both individual and group contracts, certain safeguards are used in each case to prevent it from happening.

Under a block of individual insurance contracts, the desirable situa-tion for an insurance company is to have a spread of risks throughout a range of acceptable insureds. The so-called spread ideally will include some risks that are higher and some that are lower than the average risk within the range. Insurers attempt to control adverse selection by the use of sophisticated underwriting methods used to select and classify appli-cants for insurance and by supportive policy provisions, such as pre-existing-conditions clauses in medical expense policies, suicide clauses in life insurance policies, and the exclusion of certain types of losses under homeowners policies.

The management of adverse selection under group insurance con-tracts necessarily is different from the approach used in individual insur-ance. Group insurance is based on the group as a unit and, typically, indi-vidual insurance eligibility requirements are not used for the group insur-ance underwriting used in employee benefit plans. As an alternative, the group technique itself is used to control the problem of adverse selection. The characteristics of the group technique are covered in Chapter 1 of the *Handbook* in the discussion of the factors that have contributed to the development of employee benefits, and again in Chapter 15 in the context of its application to group life insurance contracts.

Self-Funding/Self-Insurance

Self-funding, or self-insurance, is a common method of providing financing for employee benefit plans. Essentially this means that the organization is retaining the risk. It is important to realize, however, that many of the activities performed by the insurance company under an insured plan still have to be done. The identical problems associated with insurable risks for an insurance company exist for the firm that is self-funding or self-insuring. Therefore, the characteristics of an ideally insurable risk would be just as important for those firms that use self-funding as they are for an insurance company. The mechanism used for funding is not directly related to the question of whether a risk is a good one to include in the benefit plan. One should realize that only large firms with many employees would be able to meet all the characteristics of the ideally insurable risk. It is not uncommon to find that firms that say they self-fund or self-insure have, in fact, some arrangement with an insurance company or companies to insure part or all of a particular benefit. Many firms use insurance to provide backup coverage for catastrophic losses or coverage for losses the firm feels cannot be self-funded. The self-funded or self-insured plan has most of the characteristics found in the definition of insurance and has many of the same problems.

SUMMARY

Risk may be defined as uncertainty with respect to future loss or decrease in financial value. Risk can be classified as either pure or speculative. The difference between the two types is that speculative risk has the possibility of gain associated with it as well as loss. Pure risk on the other hand involves only the possibility of loss. Insurance is designed to handle pure risk but not speculative risk. Most employee benefit plans involve pure risk, so it is not uncommon to find these plans funded with insurance.

Pure risk can be classified as property, liability, or personal risk. Personal risk was the focus of this chapter and would include any loss suffered directly to a person, such as death, disability, illness, unemployment, or old age. Many risk-handling methods are used to solve the problems connected with the uncertainty of risk. Avoidance, retention, control, noninsurance transfer, and insurance are typical methods. Employee benefit plans often use a combination of methods, such as control, retention, and insurance.

Insurance is a mechanism by which one's risk (uncertainty) can be handled by transferring the risk to a third party called the insurance company. Although insurance is a popular risk-handling device, it is not appropriate for all risks. Insurance companies prefer that the risk have certain characteristics. The risk must have a large number of similar exposure units, the loss should be able to be verified and measured, the risk should not be subject to catastrophic loss, the chance of loss should be subject to calculation, the premium should be reasonable, and the loss should be accidental from the standpoint of the insured. Fortunately, most employee benefit plans cover insurable risks, thus insurance is a feasible solution. Life risks are very good from a desirable-risk standpoint, with unemployment being poor as an insurable risk for private insurance companies.

The functional approach to planning employee benefits (Chapter 2) considers the factors discussed in this chapter. Risk alternatives, characteristics of insurable risks, and types of risk all are important concepts in developing an employee benefit plan, and failure to consider these factors could result in eventual failure of the plan itself.

Regulatory Environment of Employee Benefit Plans

Dallas L. Salisbury

The regulatory environment of employee benefit plans has changed dramatically over the past 50 years. Major legislation was passed in 1942, 1958, and 1974, with a continuous flow of legislation, regulations, and rulings since. The combined effect of these laws and rules has been to make the administration of employee benefit plans increasingly complex.

This chapter briefly reviews the regulatory environment for private pension and welfare plans; insurance programs; federal, state, and local government pension plans; and disability programs. It is intended to heighten awareness of the complexity of the regulatory environment. It is not intended to provide legal guidance or to be a guide to compliance. Many of the issues touched upon here are explained more fully in subsequent chapters of the *Handbook*, and there are several "loose-leaf" services available that should be consulted to keep abreast of the constant changes taking place.

PRIVATE PENSION AND WELFARE PLANS

Pre-ERISA

Before the enactment of the Employee Retirement Income Security Act (ERISA) on Labor Day 1974, only three principal statutes governed private pension plans: the Internal Revenue Code (IRC), the Federal Welfare and Pension Plans Disclosure Act of 1958 (WPPDA), and the Taft-Hartley Act, more formally known as the Labor Management Relations Act of 1947. The latter regulated collectively bargained multiemployer pension plans.

Amendments to the Internal Revenue Code enacted in 1942 established standards for the design and operation of pension plans. The principal purposes were to prevent plans from discriminating or disproportionately benefiting one group of employees over another and to prevent plans from taking excessive or unjustified tax deductions. Until 1974, the Internal Revenue Service was not concerned with the actuarial soundness of plans.

The Federal Welfare and Pension Plans Disclosure Act was enacted to protect plan assets against fraudulent behavior by the plan administrator. The act mandated that, upon request, participants concerned with plan malpractice would be provided with information concerning the plan. If misuse or fraud were suspected, it was up to the participant to bring charges against the administrator. A significant amendment to the WPPDA was enacted in 1962. That amendment authorized the Department of Justice to bring appropriate legal action to protect plan participants' interests and authorized the Department of Labor to interpret and enforce the act. For the first time, the burden of plan asset protection was placed upon the government, rather than on the individual participants.

Employee Retirement Income Security Act of 1974 (ERISA)

The shift to government protection of participants' rights enacted in 1962 would carry through to ERISA. It reflected a concern for workers, which was confirmed by President John Kennedy in 1962 with appointment of the Committee on Corporate Pension Funds and Other Retirement and Welfare Programs. That committee issued its report in 1965, concluding that private pension plans should continue as a major element in the nation's total retirement security program. The report advocated many changes in the breadth of private plan regulation.

The report received widespread attention and led to the introduction of a number of legislative proposals. Congress concluded that most plans were operated for the benefit of participants on a sound basis, but some were not. To solve this problem, Congress enacted ERISA to govern every aspect of private pension and welfare plans and require employers that sponsor plans to operate them in compliance with ERISA standards.

TITLE I: PROTECTION OF EMPLOYEE BENEFIT RIGHTS

Title I of ERISA placed primary jurisdiction over reporting, disclosure, and fiduciary matters in the Department of Labor. The Department of the

Treasury is given primary jurisdiction over participation, vesting, and funding. During the first years of ERISA, this "dual jurisdiction" led to a number of problems, which were addressed in 1979 by Reorganization Plan Number 4, discussed later in this chapter. As a result of reorganizations and administrative experience under ERISA, many requirements have been adjusted, resulting in a reduction of the regulatory burden.

Reporting and Disclosure

Plan sponsors are required to provide plan participants with summary plan descriptions and benefit statements for the plan. Participants also are provided access to the plan's financial information. These documents are to be written in "plain English" so they can be easily understood.

Plan sponsors file an annual financial report (Form 5500 series) with the IRS, which is made available to other agencies. In addition, sponsors must file amendments when modifications to the plan are made. Taken together, these provisions seek to ensure that the government has accurate information on employer-sponsored plans.

Fiduciary Requirements

Plan sponsors are subject to an ERISA fiduciary standard mandating the plan be operated solely for the benefit of plan participants. The fiduciary standard, or "prudent man standard," requires the plan fiduciary perform duties solely in the interest of plan participants with the care a prudent person acting under like circumstances would use. This means any person who exercises discretion in the management and maintenance of the plan or in the investment of the plan assets must do so in the interest of the plan participants and beneficiaries, in accordance with the plan documents, and in a manner that minimizes the risk of loss to the participant. The standard applies to plan sponsors, trustees, and co-fiduciaries, as well as to investment advisers with discretionary authority over the purchase and sale of plan securities. Underlying the standard are prohibitions against business or investment transactions between the plan and fiduciaries or interested parties. Upon violation of the prohibitions, the fiduciary may be held personally liable to the plan for any misuse, fraud, or mismanagement. Exemptions can be applied for when parties feel that actions are not to the detriment of the plan and its participants and should be allowed. Both the IRS and the Department of Labor are responsible for enforcing the fiduciary standards. The Department of Labor may file charges on behalf of the participants if the fiduciary has breached or violated the standards imposed by ERISA. The IRS may fine the employer and revoke the plan's favorable tax treatment. Both civil and criminal actions may arise from violations.

TITLE II: MINIMUM STANDARDS

Title II of ERISA contains minimum standards for participation, vesting, and funding of benefits, which must be satisfied for qualification of a plan. It also contains amendments to the IRC that increase the scope of federal regulation over certain pension plans, whether tax qualified or not.

Participation

Although ERISA (as amended) does not require every employer to set up an employer pension or welfare benefit plan, it does impose requirements on those who do. For those employers sponsoring plans, the age of employee eligibility cannot be higher than 21. A maximum of one year of service and 1,000 hours of work also may be required for eligibility.

Vesting

Upon satisfying the participation requirements, further conditions must be met for the participant to become entitled to receive a benefit—that is, to have a vested right to the benefits. There are two alternative vesting requirements contained in ERISA (as amended):

- Full vesting after five years of service, with no vesting before the five-year requirement is met.
- Graduated vesting from the time the participant completes three years of service (full vesting after seven years).

Benefits

Under ERISA, benefits generally must be earned in a uniform manner while the participant is employed. This does not affect the levels of benefits provided by the plan, only the rate at which the benefits are earned.

Funding

The minimum funding standards attempt to ensure that plans will have sufficient assets to pay benefits. Those employers with plans subject to the standards must establish and maintain a funding standard account. The sponsor must annually contribute the normal cost—the annual cost of future pension benefits and administrative expenses—plus amounts necessary to amortize in equal installments unfunded past service liabilities and any experience losses less experience gains. The presence of these standards has changed the environment for pension plans, creating greater need for long-range planning.

Tax-Qualified Plans

Requirements for tax qualification of plans has not materially changed since 1942. Meeting these requirements allows the employer to deduct contributions from income and makes investment earnings on plan assets exempt from current taxation.

The structure of tax-qualified plans is determined by ERISA requirements. The terms of the plan must be set forth in a written document. Copies of the plan and related documents must be made available to participants. In addition, a summary of the plan must be made available. The plan sponsor must have created the plan with the intent of permanency.

The provisions of the pension plans also are dictated by the requirements of the IRC.

- As referred to above, the plan must meet minimum participation, vesting, and funding standards, and plan assets must be legally segregated from other assets of the sponsor.
- The plan must not benefit only a limited number of favored employees but must benefit employees in general in such a way as to be deemed nondiscriminatory by the IRS. This status must extend to contributions and benefits such that officers, shareholders, or highly compensated employees are not favored when the plan is viewed in its entirety.
- The pension plan must provide definitely determinable benefits.

Overall, implementing the IRC regulations and rulings has had the goal of fostering accrual and preservation of benefits for present and potential plan participants and beneficiaries.

The requirements for a tax-qualified profit-sharing plan are somewhat different in that the plan must cover all employees and the benefit is not determinable.

Fulfillment of all tax qualification requirements entitles the employer to a current deduction from gross income for contributions to the plan.

The participating employee recognizes no taxable income until the funds are distributed in the form of benefits or are distributed as a lump-sum distribution. When the distribution is made upon termination of service, taxes become due unless, in the case of a lump-sum distribution, the funds are rolled over into another plan.

Employees may voluntarily be allowed, or in some cases required, to make contributions to qualified plans. The employee's required contributions are limited to the maximum amount provided in the plan, and no tax deduction is allowed.

Nonqualified Plans

Nonqualified employee benefit plans have different requirements and may either be funded or nonfunded. Under the funded plan, the employer agrees to make contributions to the plan for the benefit of the employee. Under an unfunded plan, the employer promises to provide a benefit to the participant at some future time. Most funded plans must satisfy ERISA, while unfunded plans must only meet ERISA's reporting and disclosure provisions. Tax treatment varies, as does the security of any assets in the event of bankruptcy. Each time Congress restricts qualified plan funding, the universe of nonqualified plans grows.

TITLE IV: PLAN TERMINATION INSURANCE

Title IV of ERISA established the Pension Benefit Guaranty Corporation (PBGC), a governmental body that insures payment of plan benefits under certain circumstances.

Most defined benefit pension plans (those that provide a fixed monthly benefit at retirement) are required to participate in the program and pay premiums to the PBGC.

There are certain restrictions and limitations on the amount of benefits insured, and the amount is adjusted annually to reflect the increasing average wages of the U.S. workforce. The limit applies to all plans under which a participant is covered so it is not possible to spread coverage under several plans to increase the guaranteed benefit. To be fully insured, the benefit must have been vested before the plan terminated, and the benefit level must have been in effect for 60 months, or benefits are proportionately reduced. Further, the guarantee applies only to benefits earned while the plan is eligible for favorable tax treatment.

In an effort to protect against employers establishing plans without intending to continue them, ERISA introduced the concept of contingent employer liability in the event of plan termination for single-employer plans and for multi-employer plans in the event of employer withdrawal or insolvency. Additional complex requirements that apply to multi-employer plans also were established by Congress in 1980.

The PBGC has served to substantially change the environment in which plans operate. The PBGC now has substantial ability to involve itself in mergers, acquisitions, and sales when the sponsor of an under-funded plan is involved. For present sponsors, and for those thinking of establishing new defined benefit plans, Title IV should be carefully reviewed so that its implications are fully understood.

LEGISLATION 1980–2000

During the years since ERISA, there have been a series of legislative measures with common themes enacted into law. The laws include the Economic Recovery Tax Act of 1981 (ERTA), the Tax Equity and Fiscal Responsibility Act of 1982 (TEFRA), the Retirement Equity Act of 1984 (REA), the Deficit Reduction Act of 1984 (DEFRA), the Consolidated Omnibus Budget and Reconciliation Act of 1985 (COBRA), the Tax Reform Act of 1986 (TRA '86), the Omnibus Reconciliation Act of 1987 (OBRA '87), the Omnibus Budget Reconciliation Act of 1989 (OBRA '89), the Budget Act of 1990, the Omnibus Budget Reconciliation Act of 1993 (OBRA '93), the Family and Medical Leave Act of 1993, the Uniformed Services Employment and Reemployment Rights Act of 1993, the Pension Annuitants Protection Act of 1993, the Uruguay Round Agreements Act (Retirement Protection Act) of 1994, the Bankruptcy Reform Act of 1994, the Deduction for Health Insurance Costs of Self-Employed Individuals (1995), the Small Business Job Protection Act of 1996, the Health Insurance Portability and Accountability Act of 1996 (HIPAA), the Taxpayer Relief Act of 1997 (TRA '97), the Savings Are Vital to Everyone's Retirement Act of 1997, the Transportation Equity Act for the 21st Century of 1998, the Omnibus Consolidated and Emergency Supplemental Appropriations Act of 1998, the Ticket to Work and Work Incentives Improvement Act of 1999, and the Medicare, Medicaid, and SCHIP Balanced Budget Refinement Act of 1999.

COBRA established rules to ensure that individuals and their dependents would have access to continued group health insurance upon job termination and certain other qualifying events, and Congress can be expected to expand this concept to one of assured access for all Americans.

OBRA '87 significantly tightened funding standards for defined benefit plans, further restricted plan terminations, and moved the PBGC to a much higher and variable premium. Legislation consistent with the themes just noted will continue to be considered and enacted, with emphasis on the larger theme that employers should be responsible for keeping promises once made *regardless of the financial implications for the business*.

In 1989, Congress again consolidated employee benefits changes into the budget, restricting tax incentives for employee stock ownership plans (ESOPs), reforming the method of physician payment in the Medicare program, expanding COBRA protections, and repealing the 1988 Medicare Catastrophic Coverage Act and Section 89 (nondiscrimination tests for welfare plans) of TRA '86.

The year 1990 saw the enactment of child-care legislation, expansion of Medicaid, further restrictions on asset reversions, allowance for some pension asset transfers for retiree medical expenses, Age Discrimination in Employment Act (ADEA) amendments to expand protections in early retirement programs, and passage of the Americans with Disabilities Act.

In 1991, Congress limited the employee deduction of employer-provided parking benefits, increased the tax-exempt employer-provided transit benefit, passed the Civil Rights Act of 1991, eliminated pass-through coverage for benefit responsive bank investment contracts (BICs), and limited federal deposit insurance.

In 1992, Congress imposed a 20 percent withholding tax on lump-sum distributions that are not rolled over into qualified retirement accounts and required pension plan sponsors to transfer eligible distributions directly to an eligible plan at the participant's request.

Congress modified ERISA in 1993 as it relates to group health plan coverage of pediatric vaccines, compliance with medical child-support orders, and coverage of adoptive children as dependents. In addition, Congress reduced the compensation limit for qualified pension plans and placed a cap on the deduction of executive compensation not tied to performance. The legislation also included a veterans' rights bill guaranteeing veterans' rights to pension benefits that would have accrued during military service and clarifying the right for military personnel to continue receiving employer-sponsored health insurance for up to 18 months if they are absent due to military service. Finally, it provided, through the Family and Medical Leave Act, that firms with more than 50 workers provide up to 12 weeks of unpaid leave with continued health coverage to employees for the birth or adoption of a child or for serious illness of the employee or the employee's child, parent, or spouse.

In 1994, Congress passed a trade bill that included pension provisions that required greater contributions to underfunded plans, limited the range of interest rate and mortality assumptions used to establish funding targets, phased out the variable rate premium cap, modified certain rules relating to participant protection, and required private companies with underfunded pension plans to notify the PBGC before engaging in large corporate transactions. The law also slowed pension cost-of-living adjustments and extended a provision to allow excess pension assets in certain pension plans to be transferred into a retiree health benefits account. Congress also passed legislation to give the PBGC and state and local government pension plans seats on creditors' committees in corporate bankruptcies. The Social Security Administration also became an independent federal agency in 1995, with the passage of Social Security Administration Reform legislation in 1994.

In 1995, Congress made no permanent legislative changes for benefits.

In 1996, Congress made changes to COBRA, established a tax exclusion for adoption assistance, and repealed the $5,000 death benefit exclusion. Congress also simplified many pension rules, restricted the ability of states to tax nonresidents' pension incomes earned while working in another state, added length-of-stay requirements for health plans, added mental health parity provisions, established new requirements for health plans and insurers and HMOs (including limiting preexisting-condition exclusions), established limited medical savings accounts, and provided favorable tax treatment for long-term care insurance.

In 1997, Congress was very active. TRA '97 included numerous simplification provisions while increasing the full funding limit, repealing the 15 percent tax on excess distributions, expanded deductible IRAs, created non-deductible "Roth" IRAs, enacted the SAVER Act which led to the 1998 National Summit on Retirement Savings, and enacted a budget that included many Medicare and health coverage expansion provisions.

In 1998, Congress added new tax incentives for transportation benefits, restructured the IRS, and enacted a number of mandatory coverage provisions for health plans.

In 1999 and 2000, Congress enacted changes for Medicare and Medicaid, but passed no ERISA benefits provisions that were signed into law.

ADDITIONAL REGULATORY AGENCIES

Labor Laws

A number of laws, from both statutory and case law, give the Department of Labor authority to monitor and regulate employee benefit plans.

Among them is the National Labor Relations Act, which promotes collective bargaining between employers and employees' representatives. The Taft-Hartley Act contains specific provisions similar to ERISA and the IRC relating to plan structure and content. The landmark case of *Inland Steel Company* v. *the National Labor Relations Board* prohibits an employer from refusing to bargain with employees upon a properly presented demand to bargain regarding employee benefit plans.

Equal Employment Opportunity Commission (EEOC)

The EEOC's interest in employee benefit plans stems from various acts that prohibit discriminatory plan practices. The Civil Rights Act of 1964, Title VII, is interpreted by the EEOC as defining discrimination between men and women with regard to fringe benefits as an unlawful employment practice. The Equal Pay Act of 1963 makes employer discrimination between the sexes in the payment of wages for equal work unlawful. Benefits under employee benefit plans are a form of wages and must be free from discrimination, held one EEOC decision. The Age Discrimination in Employment Act of 1967 and its 1975 and 1979 amendments clearly prohibit discrimination on the basis of age. The so-called Betts changes enacted in 1990 and relating to early retirement programs make clear the significant role of the EEOC in regulating retirement plans. In 1999 and 2000, new attention was paid to the EEOC as discussion turned to the application of age discrimination regulations to cash balance defined benefit retirement plans.

Securities and Exchange Commission (SEC)

Under the Securities Act of 1933, information concerning securities publicly offered and sold in interstate commerce or through the mail is required to be disclosed to the SEC. At first blush, the act does not seem to apply to employee benefit plans. However, a security is defined by the act as including participation in any profit-sharing agreement. The Securities Act of 1934 affects the administration of plans by imposing disclosure and registration requirements as well as antifraud provisions. The SEC has not actively enforced requirements, but the scope of legal SEC jurisdiction has been debated and litigated.

The Investment Company Act of 1940 regulates reporting and disclosure, structure, content, and administration of investment companies. A pension benefit plan could be subject to this act if it fits the definition of an investment company. An investment company, as defined by the act, is one engaged in the business of holding, trading, investing, or owning securities.

The SEC has expanded its interest in pension plan proxy voting and corporate governance on an ongoing basis. And, the agency has become active in savings and investing education for the general public.

Other Acts and Agencies

The Small Business Administration (SBA) receives complaints from small businesses regarding the relationship of small business to agencies of the federal government.

Banking laws also apply. The National Bank Act permits national banks to act as trustees in a fiduciary capacity in which state banks or trust companies are permitted to act under the laws of the state where the national bank is located. This affects private employee benefit plans because banks act as fiduciaries. The Federal Reserve Act and the Federal Reserve System can affect pension and welfare plans, because plans may either be borrowers or lenders. Because there is regulation of interest payable on deposits in banks that are members of the Federal Reserve System, IRA and Keogh plans are affected in terms of possible rates of return. The Federal Deposit Insurance Act also affects these plans if they are not covered by the PBGC since funds held by an insured bank, in its capacity as fiduciary, will be insured up to $100,000 per participant.

The Commerce Department is concerned with ERISA's impact on the health of the economy. The Department of Health and Human Services (HHS) tries to keep track of individuals with deferred vested benefit plans and administers Social Security and other public programs that have a substantial impact on private plan design. HHS is also involved with implementation of the health care continuation provisions of HIPAA. In addition, HHS is charged with issuance of health care data confidentiality regulations that affect employee benefit plans.

THE REGULATION OF INSURANCE

Both individual state governments and the federal government regulate insurance. The states regulate rates, financial examination, formation of the company, qualification of officers, licensing, and taxing. The federal government provides for regulation as noted above, in addition to the activity of the Federal Insurance Administrator, the Interstate Commerce Commission, and the Federal Trade Commission.

A growing concern exists over which level of government is the most appropriate for the regulation of insurance. Many contend that there should be greater federal involvement. Advocates of federal regulation argue that state regulation lacks uniformity and that multiple state regulation is more costly than federal regulation, that the state insurance commissioners are unqualified, and that the states cannot effectively regulate interstate companies. Those who favor state regulation argue that the states are more responsive to local conditions and needs, that state regulation encourages innovation and experimentation, and that the decentralization of power is advantageous.

At present there exists an ongoing disagreement between the states and the federal government over the extent to which state laws are preempted by ERISA. The federal government believes it could move toward greater regulation without legal difficulty. This is based upon the federal ability to regulate interstate commerce, to provide for the general welfare, and to tax. Section 514(a) of ERISA states that it shall supersede any and all state laws insofar as they may now or later relate to any employee benefit plan. The preemption does not apply to any state law that regulates insurance. But a question remains: To what extent does ERISA preempt laws enacted under the insurance codes of the states, when such laws are designed specifically to apply to the insurance-type functions of employee benefit plans?

The Department of Labor advocated a broad interpretation of Section 514, which would preempt most state statutes even if the laws deal with areas not explicitly covered by ERISA, such as the content of health benefit plans. The federal courts have not been so consistent in their interpretation of the statute. In one case, *Fleck* v. *Spannaus*, the court decided ERISA does not preempt causes of action occurring before January 1, 1975. But in another case, *Azzaro* v. *Harnett*, the court held that Congress intended absolute preemption in the field of employee benefits. Even the insurance exception found in Section 514 is subject to limitations: "No employee benefit plan shall be deemed to be an insurance company or engaged in the business of insurance for the purpose of any law of any state purporting to regulate an insurance company."

In general, the courts, including the Supreme Court, have tended to preempt state regulation that relates to employee pension and retirement plans. This stems from the broad-based protections incorporated in ERISA for pension plan participants. The courts are less inclined to preempt state laws that apply to employee health and insurance plans. ERISA has had a more limited application to welfare plans and a more narrow view of the preemptive effect in the health and welfare plan area. When health insurance benefits are mandated in traditional insurance contracts, rather than through comprehensive health care legislation, claims of federal preemption will not hold. However, when an employer's prepaid health care plan satisfies the ERISA definition, state regulation is preempted.

Where the line eventually will be drawn between state and federal regulation of health and welfare plans continues to be uncertain. The debate centers on the degree to which arrangements have insurance versus noninsurance characteristics, with states arguing that even stop-loss coverage makes the underlying plan "insured," thus subject to state regulation. The courts continue to be heavily involved, but are increasingly reaching decisions that reinforce the strength and breadth of ERISA preemption.

The ongoing debate over national health policy will ensure legislative consideration of where the state-federal regulatory line should be drawn. The more limited the future federal role, the more likely ERISA will be modified. The debate surrounding Patient's Protection initiatives has continued to highlight differences between insured and ERISA plans.

The U.S. Department of Labor issued significant health benefits claim regulations in late 2000, and the U.S. Department of Health and Human Services issued significant regulations on health data privacy and confidentiality. These actions are expanding the federal role in health regulation.

FEDERAL, STATE, AND LOCAL GOVERNMENT PENSION PLANS

Public plans represent a substantial level of retirement income promises for federal, state, and local employees. Benefit levels promised in public plans exceed those of the private sector. Public plans exist free of federal regulatory controls like those imposed by ERISA. For practical purposes, there is only a limited "regulatory environment."

Public employee pension programs are receiving a considerable amount of attention today because of the sharp increases in current appropriations necessary to support retirement programs, the increased activism of public plans in the realm of corporate governance, and the greater frequency of public pension purchases of public debt to "bail out" deficits. Federal regulation of private plans has given rise to a congressional commitment to the study of public plans and to an assessment of whether a public plan version of ERISA should be enacted.

Research has revealed that large cities with their own pension plans are likely to provide some of the most generous benefits available in the public sector. Public employees generally have more liberal early retirement provisions in their pension plans than private employees, and public plans usually include a provision for automatic increases in retirees' benefits when the cost of living increases.

State and local plans are viewed by many as being underfunded as a group. Actuarial, financial, auditing, and disclosure requirements are viewed as deficient. Many charge that fiduciary standards are seriously breached. Other characteristics of public plans have led to criticisms, including the following:

- Their retirement benefits replace a substantial percentage of final pay after only 20 to 25 years of service.
- Their normal retirement ages are set well ahead of the end of productive working lifetimes.
- They are generous in granting a high proportion of early disability retirements in "high risk" professions (police, firefighters, and the like), rather than retaining the workforce in less hazardous positions.

There is also substantial concern because some federal, state, and local employees currently are not covered by the Social Security program. Because of noninclusion, or lack of integration when both programs are involved, there is a belief that public employees obtain "windfall" benefits or unnecessarily large benefits, or both. For example, a recent government study indicated that income replacement ratios for public employees serving 30 years at average wages received more than 100 percent of salary in 53 percent of all cases, and 125 percent of salary in more than 10 percent of all cases.

These and other issues have led to the development of state commissions to advise state legislators on pension issues. The threat of an impending federal intervention in the form of the Public Employee Retirement Income Security Act (PERISA) has stimulated efforts in many states to monitor state and local pension funds more closely and to improve reporting and disclosure practices.

DISABILITY PROGRAMS

In 1975, cash disability payments equaled 25 percent of all cash payments to retirees, survivors, and the disabled. Disability programs resemble pension programs in that their purposes are similar (generally, both are intended to maintain the income of workers and their dependents or survivors when they are unable to work), program finances are intertwined, and disability programs are sometimes used to substitute for retirement programs.

Disability program trends indicate that cash disability programs have grown rapidly and that the federal role in disability programs has increased. Analyses indicate workers of all ages are being awarded disability benefits more frequently than in previous years. Per capita benefits generally have grown more rapidly than earnings and the difference in growth rates has been larger since 1970. Social factors also add to the increase in disability payouts. Society is doing more to support the disabled. More and more people identify themselves as disabled. There are indications that disability programs may be repeating the welfare crisis of the 1960s, the dramatic increase in beneficiaries largely representing a growing percentage of eligible persons claiming benefits.

Social Security Disability Benefits

To qualify for Social Security disability benefits, the wage earner must be unable to engage in any substantial activity by reason of a medically determined physical or mental impairment that can be expected to result in death or to last for a continuous period. Total disability exists if the claimant's disability equals or exceeds the standards as established and is documented by a medical report using the language required by the regulations. The Social Security Act considers age, education, and previous work experience when applying the disability standard. The wage earner also must meet special earnings requirements to be covered. The wage earner must have performed 20 quarters of employment in the 40 quarters immediately prior to the alleged onset of disability. The benefit payout begins on the sixth month of disability. For a detailed discussion of Social Security disability benefits, see Chapter 22 of the *Handbook*.

CONCLUSION

The regulatory environment of employee benefit programs is far-reaching and complex. It involves all levels of government in at least some areas, and numerous different agencies at each level, all with the purpose of protecting the potential recipient and adding security to the benefit promise.

The degree to which the environment is refined is constantly changing. There has been no rest from discussion of new legislative proposals or new regulatory initiatives. Some proposals aim at reducing regulation, others at increasing it. Frequently the short-term effect is the same: creation of uncertainty, which inhibits the growth and development of employee benefit programs. The year 2000 saw continuation of a focus by the Congress on expansion of individual prerogatives, reinforced by proposals of the Clinton administration. The trend began in 1994 when the Republican Congress moved towards more libertarian and individual approaches, as compared to more socialist and paternalistic policies. A return to Democratic control in both the House and the Senate in the 2002 election, or an extended economic downturn, could be the next turning point in these trends. Should that not occur, the present trend line is likely to continue.

The challenge for the practitioner is to understand the environment, how it affects particular situations, and to affect it when the opportunity arises.

Medical and Other Health Benefits

In this part the critically important topic of medical benefits and issues is explored. Of prime importance in any discussion of medical benefits is the subject of cost containment—a topic so important today it is referred to, either explicitly or implicitly, in all the chapters in this part.

Part Two opens with a discussion of the environment of health benefit plans in Chapter 5. Following this stage-setting chapter, the basic designs and strategic consideration of health plans are covered in Chapter 6. Chapters 7 and 8 present a detailed discussion of managed care health plans while Chapter 9 examines how to evaluate the quality of health care provided by plans. Chapters 10 and 11 expand health benefits coverage to dental, prescription drugs, vision, and hearing care plans. Employers can mitigate the costs of health care benefits through preventive health care programs, a topic covered in Chapter 12. The topics of long-term care and disability income benefits are discussed in Chapters 13 and 14, which complete this series of chapters.

CHAPTER 5

The Environment of Health Plans in the New Millennium

Charles P. Hall, Jr.

INTRODUCTION

It takes very little modification of the opening statement in the previous edition of the *Handbook* to "set the stage" for a discussion of health plans in the new millennium. The "severe and continuing escalation of medical care costs" which were referred to at that time have returned with a vengeance in the past year after a relatively brief period during which it actually seemed that some control had been achieved. There were a couple of years where medical care costs and the costs of benefit plans were held nearly constant—even one year where they were reduced just slightly. But those days have now passed. Indeed, Scott Serota, acting CEO of the Blue Cross & Blue Shield Association was quoted as early as February 2000 as predicting that employers renewing health insurance plans could expect rate increases of 10 percent to 15 percent in 2000, a prediction that appeared to be coming true by midyear.[1]

Then, with the truly remarkable announcement in late June of 2000 that scientists had completed mapping the human genetic code, the stage was set for speculation as to the long-term implications of that accomplishment for health in general and health plans in particular. One speculates that, in the short run, it may lead to even more costs, both because of the new tests and treatments that certainly will evolve and because of the inevitable law-

---

1 Jerry Geisel, "Health Plan Rates Hikes Up To 15% Seen," *Business Insurance*, February 28, 2000, p. 3.

suits that probably are equally inevitable. These may stem from claims that some of the new tests either should or should not have been performed, or from those who will sue over the ethical issues that are already being raised about how this new knowledge can or should be used. In the longer run, however, there is certainly great potential for eliminating or curing a wide range of diseases, and that spawns the hope for ultimate cost reductions.

Once again, the cost of health care has assumed center stage as a topic of concern to both public and private providers of coverage as well as to state and federal legislators and—perhaps most important—to the public in general. This fulfills the predictions of those many pundits who, after the defeat of the Health Security Act (a.k.a. the "Clinton Health Plan") in 1993, said that health-related issues would become a major factor in Washington again in the year 2000.

True, there were some incremental actions taken in the interim, perhaps the most important being the Health Insurance Portability and Accountability Act (HIPAA) in 1996. But, clearly, the 2000 presidential campaign brought a range of health-related matters back to center stage. Much of the discussion focused on concern about the long-term financial viability of the Medicare and Medicaid programs funded and operated by the federal and state governments. President Clinton's push for full prescription drug coverage for Medicare recipients was backed by Vice President Gore, who made the issue one of the centerpieces of his campaign. As the election neared, the Republican standard bearer, George W. Bush, had clearly committed to a prescription drug plan of his own. Thus, while the rhetoric from both sides attempted to claim the high ground as proposing the better plan, there appeared to be little doubt that some kind of prescription drug program would get early legislative attention in the coming year. Special attention also was directed to the growing number of children who lack meaningful health insurance benefits, with both candidates expressing concern about the matter. More inclusive coverage for mental health problems also received considerable attention. More to the point of employer health plans, the growing number of uninsured and underinsured citizens was also a matter of great concern. According to a Kaiser Family Foundation report issued May 26, 2000, ". . . almost three-quarters (74 percent) of the uninsured are in families where at least one person is working full-time. . . " And while the decrease in job-based coverage has slowed since the early 1990s, the number of workers covered by employee benefit plans continues to decline as a percentage of the total workforce. This disclosure that most of the uninsured are fully employed workers or their dependents constitutes a wake-up call to many who incorrectly believe that most fully employed individuals had at least *some* coverage.[2]

There are, of course, several factors that can explain, at least in part, why this is true. Among them is the change in the composition of American business. As the economy shifted rapidly toward a more dominant service sector, the impact of labor unions, whose traditional strength was found in the manufacturing sector, declined in recent years. Traditionally, big unions such as the United Automobile Workers (UAW) and others had been "pattern setters" for employee benefits, from life and health insurance plans to pension plans. As the influence of unions waned, benefit plans clearly have been affected. One study reported that there was a decline of more than 6 percent in the number of civilians under age 65 with employer-based health insurance between 1977 and 1996.[3] Dramatic growth in the "high-tech" business sector, where union activity has been limited, accounts for some of the problem. Labor Department predictions that most growth in the U.S. economy in the next decade will be in the service sector indicate that the decline in those covered by employer-sponsored health plans may continue. The decline has been further exacerbated because the majority of workers in this field tend to be quite young and they often fail to see the need for costly health insurance programs. This is especially true in the case of the thousands of young workers who have never experienced anything but economic growth during their working lifetimes. Some undoubtedly feel that a combination of salary and stock options will be more than adequate to protect them against any medical expenses that they are likely to encounter in the next few years.

Another factor in the decline of covered workers is the fact that many employers—particularly those in relatively small businesses, including the thousands of high-tech start-ups that have been spurring our economic growth—simply feel that they cannot afford to provide health benefits at current premium levels. Again, workers in many of these firms also have shown a preference for greater take-home pay when given the choice between a substantial reduction in salary and health insurance. The "give backs" of health benefits that characterized labor negotiations during the economic slowdown in the early 1980s, have been a matter of passionate

2 www.kaiser.org, "The Uninsured and Their Access to Health Care," May 2000, reported by the Kaiser Commission on Medicaid and the Uninsured.
3 Jon R. Gabel, "Job-based Health Insurance, 1977–1998: The Accidental System Under Scrutiny," *Health Affairs*, Chevy Chase; Nov/Dec 1999; Vol. 18:6, p. 65.

concern to older workers with families who have tried vigorously to regain those lost benefits. However, to a new generation of young workers in booming "dot.com companies" who have never seen a recession, and many of whom still have no family obligations, these benefits apparently have less appeal.

Switching to the actual cost of health care, there appear to be many causes for both the escalating costs and the growing concern. First, much of the "fat" that clearly existed in the system under the cost-based reimbursement structure of Medicare in its early years has already been eliminated through reimbursement reform and the efforts of managed care over the past quarter century. There has been a dramatic reduction in unnecessary hospitalization. Many surgical procedures that formerly required extended hospitalization have now been moved to outpatient or short-procedure units. However, much of the savings came from the one-time elimination of inefficiencies, while at the same time, new technology and new expectations have added costs to the system. Coverage now exists and is routinely expected for activities that were never covered in the past. Add to this the aging of the population, which carries with it the increasing cost of dealing with chronic conditions and other debilities of age, and it is no wonder that total expenditures on health care have continued to grow.

The continued explosion of new medical technology, much of it costly, has been matched—if not exceeded—by the public's demand for broader and deeper protection against the potentially disastrous costs of treatment. There continue to be periodic reports of egregious examples of abuse by some insurers and medical delivery systems that arouse both fear and anger among the public. However, there is no convincing evidence that these situations are widespread or that the health of Americans has declined. Indeed, the opposite is true. Most traditional indicators of health status have shown improvement.

It seems strange that the same government that spent so much energy and money for a quarter century after the passage of the Health Maintenance Organization (HMO) Act of 1973 encouraging their development should now be attacking managed care organizations for doing exactly what they were asked to do—save money! These organizations have been under increasing legal and legislative attack in the past few years. Indeed, we have witnessed laws designating the minimum length of stay for infant deliveries enacted by Congress (The Newborns' and Mothers' Health Protection Act of 1996) and several state legislatures, even going so far as to stipulate the differences between normal and Cesarean deliveries. A case can be made for a wide range of regulatory legislation, perhaps even that which requires certain *types* of coverage to be provided—though there are those who object even to that. But in a field where technology is changing so rapidly, it may be difficult to justify the micro management, via legislation, of the *duration* of any specific treatment.

Someone has attacked virtually every technique that managed care plans have explored in their attempts to control costs as being inappropriate. Indeed, legislative proposals have been introduced that would virtually strip providers of any meaningful ability to control costs. Attacks have been directed against everything from "gatekeepers" to financial incentives to avoid overuse of specialty physicians. Proposals to give virtually unlimited ability to patients to sue their health plans generally wrapped in the politically attractive name of "patient bill of rights" legislation, have already been passed or are pending in several venues. Another proposal, to provide physicians exemption from antitrust laws when banding together to negotiate managed care contracts would, if enacted, clearly eliminate another hitherto effective tool of controlling costs and would undoubtedly lead to a new round of escalating costs.

The U.S. Supreme Court on June 12, 2000 handed down its long-awaited decision in the *Lori Pegram et. al.* v. *Cynthia Herdrich* case and upheld the right of HMOs to use financial incentive clauses in their contracts with physicians as a tool to contain costs. This reversed a 1998 decision by the 7th U.S. Circuit Court of Appeals that would have made HMOs liable to actions for breach of a fiduciary duty under the Employee Retirement Income Security Act (ERISA) for such provisions. Though this unanimous decision was immediately hailed as a victory for both managed care plans and employers, some fear that it may have only opened the door for later enactment of more onerous legislation by Congress or state legislatures. Speaking for the court, Justice Souter said, "Although it is true that the relationship between sparing medical treatment and physician reward is not a subtle one under (this) scheme, no HMO could survive without some incentive connecting physician reward with treatment rationing."

Shortly before this Supreme Court decision was handed down, yet another challenge had been mounted in federal court against managed care contracting procedures. The California Medical Association (CMA) filed a civil action against the three largest managed care organizations in the state under the Racketeer Influenced and Corrupt Organizations Act (RICO). RICO was designed for and generally has been used only in organized-crime cases. In its suit, the CMA alleges "coercive, unfair and fraudulent means to dominate and control physician-patient relationships for their own financial gains."[4] Though few expect this action to be successful, it is just one more example of the kind of attacks managed care is facing, both on the judicial and legislative fronts. Another example was the action taken by the U.S. House of Representatives on June 30, 2000, when it voted to allow physicians to bargain collectively with insurers and HMOs over fees, treatments, and other contract items while enjoying an exemption from antitrust rules. Stiff resistance was anticipated in the Senate to this bill, whose chief sponsor was Congressman Tom Campbell of California. If it becomes law, there is little question that it will lead to higher prices, while its impact on quality of care is questionable.

Thus, the start of the new millennium finds little evidence of lasting solutions having been developed for the ongoing problems of providing adequate health benefits to the American public. Significant changes have continued to take place in the delivery, financing, and organization of medical care since the *Handbook* was first published, and many proposals for further change continue to surface. However, the "light at the end of the tunnel" in the seemingly endless battle against soaring costs that was flickering in 1996 seems to have dimmed again, as health care cost increases once more have begun to outstrip increases in the overall consumer price index (CPI). The safest prediction for the first decade of the new millennium remains the same as before—continued turmoil and change!

Health Expenditures

Total health expenditures have continued to rise since the previous edition of the *Handbook*, though at a somewhat slower pace than had been expected. Nevertheless, as a nation our annual health care expenditures now exceed $1 trillion, and the U.S. still spends a larger percentage of its gross domestic product (GDP) on health than any other nation in the world. According to one study,[5] the U.S. spent 14 percent of its GDP on health care in 1998. Our per capita expenditures were also the highest in the world, at $4,270. However, the gap between the U.S. and some other major countries had clearly narrowed, with both Germany and Switzerland now also spending over 10 percent of GDP on health, and per capita spending also gaining ground in those countries. Furthermore, at

---

4 Cited in *The Wall Street Journal Interactive Edition*, May 26, 2000.
5 Gerard F. Anderson, et al, "Health Spending and Outcomes: Trends in OECD Countries, 1960–1998," *Health Affairs*, Chevy Chase; May/June 2000; vol. 19:3.

least part of the gap in expenditures reflects what many feel is a difficult-to-measure quality-of-life issue. Americans spend more on such items as cosmetic surgery and various high-tech procedures for prolonging life than most other countries. We have more technology available at more sites, thus providing more choices. Despite complaints about the costs, then, we find very few Americans suggesting that these kinds of choices should be limited. Indeed, quite the opposite seems to be true. One of the major challenges to managed care has consistently been the charge that it has limited consumer choice. It appears that we can't have it both ways. Note, too, that virtually every election year policy proposal for "protecting" or "expanding" health care benefits involves a further increase in health spending. As the comic strip character Pogo used to say, "We have met the enemy, and he is us!"

Benefit Plan Costs

As noted above, though there was a short period during which employers appeared to have gained some control over increases in their health benefit costs, recent trends once again show those costs to be increasing at a more rapid pace than the CPI. Current proposals for even more expanded benefits provide little room for optimism in the short run. It is now obvious that the glimmer of hope for control over rising costs that was reported in the previous edition of the *Handbook* was not sustainable over the long run. Much of the early gains were accomplished by implementing one-time corrections and efficiencies. Once made, however, it has been difficult to find similar savings in subsequent years. There has, of course, also been an even greater emphasis placed on quality of care in recent years, but many employers continue to rank cost over quality as the most important factor in their health plan decisions. That point continues to be made by many consumer and provider groups. Physicians have become even more united than before in their attacks on what they perceive as interference in medical decisions by "administrators," and politicians have picked up on the theme of "giving your health care decisions back to the medical profession." These allegations, which further claim that by putting profit above good care, managed care plans are a threat to overall patient health, are not supported by any convincing evidence, but they have a very strong appeal to a public that increasingly fears the specter of runaway cost for care. Sometimes overlooked, too, is the fact that a substantial percentage of managed care organizations around the country are not only not making outrageous profits, some are even losing money or going bankrupt!

Meanwhile, widespread publicity given to the growing number of uninsured Americans gives credibility to the fears of runaway health care costs. Some estimates now place the number of uninsured at about 44 million, and it has been growing at nearly a million per year.[6] Consumer fears have been further exacerbated by the volatile business climate. The growing number of corporate mergers and acquisitions in recent years has cost many workers both their jobs and their health care coverage. Yet most medical care organizations and employers fully realize that poor treatment or under treatment of patients is, in the long run, the most costly care of all, so they have very little incentive to behave in ways that would undermine their members' (or employees') health. Controversy over how best to deal with benefit plan costs continues, with an increasing number of firms, especially the new, smaller ones in the service sector, deciding not to offer any company plan. Others have taken advantage of the opportunity to provide medical savings accounts (MSAs) as provided for in HIPAA, rather than bear the problems of a traditional health insurance plan with its inevitable cost increases and controversies. There have even been those who have begun to challenge the entire system of employer-based health insurance, which has been the backbone of health protection in this country since World War II. In turn, articles defending the system also have appeared.[7] Any kind of momentous change, however, seems still a distant hope. So we probably will see continued tinkering with the various reforms that have apparently worked best in terms of cost containment, despite the continuing challenges they face on grounds of limiting consumer choice, threatening quality, and taking control of medical decisions out of the hands of doctors and their patients. Well-known health economist Uwe Reinhardt of Princeton, speaking at a session sponsored by the Alliance for Health Reform in June 1999, perhaps stated the situation best when he said, "No group of health policy analysts, if they started from scratch, would ever put together this system . . . [but] . . . at the moment, the employer-based system is the best there is." How long this will be true in a changing economy that relies more and more on part-time, temporary and contract workers is not known.

Managed Care, Cost Containment and Control

It remains true that the term "managed care" still can refer to a wide range of health care financing and delivery systems. In its most generic use, it

---

6 See previous reference to the Kaiser Family Foundation web page.
7 William S. Custer, "Why We Should Keep The Employment-Based Health Insurance System," *Health Affairs*, Chevy Chase; Nov/Dec 1999; 18:6, pp 115-123.

still means any arrangement that incorporates features that distinguish it from the "traditional" indemnity insurance or service benefit (e.g., Blue Cross/Blue Shield) plans by utilizing specific controls designed to limit the cost of or access to unrestricted care. These controls include the use of "gatekeeper" physicians, active utilization review (UR) procedures, contracting for negotiated service prices with selected hospitals or for capitation rates with physicians, or both, and promotion of preventive care services. While not all of these controls exist in every managed care plan, most plans contain at least several of them. Other control techniques, such as mandatory second opinions on all elective surgery, clearly have lost favor. It is used far more sparingly now than in the early days of managed care.[8]

To review, the hallmark of an HMO remains that it consists of a panel of doctors and hospitals that have contracted to provide a defined, usually very comprehensive, set of benefits to a group of subscribers or enrollees on a prepaid basis. Although similar organizations existed earlier, the term "HMO" emerged around 1970. The intent of a prepaid arrangement such as an HMO was to change the incentives found in the traditional fee-for-service (FFS) system. Under FFS, prescribing additional services clearly added to the providers' income, whether or not it was needed by, or improved the health status of, the patient. Many considered this to be a clear conflict of interest. By promising services on the basis of a prepaid and fixed fee, it was reasoned, the conflict would be removed and providers would have a strong incentive to keep subscribers well (i.e., to "maintain their health"), so the demand for services would not get out of control. Furthermore, it was felt that the peer pressure of other participating providers would be a guarantor of quality since the entire group's reputation could be undermined by one "bad apple."

Although managed care has continued to capture a larger share of the overall market, its rate of growth has slowed. Most observers still give HMOs and the "alphabet soup" of related medical care organizations (MCOs) credit for cutting substantial costs from the system. However, there are an increasing number of critics who claim that the concern for costs has been carried too far. They argue that the "fat" is gone and that further cuts are a threat to all that use the system. The most frequent complaints are that the quality of care and patient choice has been undermined and that "bureaucrats" have replaced the doctor in making key medical decisions.

While there is little evidence that overall patient care quality has suffered, there are just enough anecdotal incidents to provide continuing fuel

---

8 See Chapter 7 for definitions of these terms.

for that statement. There is little doubt that some patient choice has been limited, especially in the selection of particular physicians or treatment centers. That, after all, was one of the major points of contention in the *Pegram* case. It also is true that physician decisions are being questioned in many cases. But what is often omitted from the discussion is that the questions are frequently related to quality issues, not simply costs. In fact, many MCOs have been among the leaders in the growing effort to measure and guarantee quality treatment, often following so-called "best-practice" guidelines as soon as they are developed.

Most HMOs continue to utilize a "gatekeeper." That is, they require patients to see a primary care physician (PCP) first, and the PCP controls referrals to specialists. Indeed, it was (and still is) not unusual to find HMOs using financial incentives to discourage PCPs from making "unnecessary" referrals (the basis for the charge under the *Pegram* case). Not surprisingly, complaints soon arose that the new incentive was to under-prescribe services or, even worse, for the PCP to overreach his or her expertise, thus endangering the patient's well being. Many people fail to realize that over-treatment often may involve more risk than no treatment at all, and in a culture that had not experienced much oversight of physicians in the past, any attempt to question a recommendation was viewed suspiciously by patients and with outrage by physicians. Patients and providers have often found common cause in the complaint that patients are denied a free choice of physician. This usually occurs when a particular provider is not included on an MCO's approved panel of providers, and also when a PCP refuses a request to recommend a specialist. Clearly, some individual choice has been limited, but is this all bad? Without some control over physicians, we might return to the days of runaway health costs that so many people have apparently forgotten was one of the major reasons for encouraging managed care in the first place. Of course, there are also many who are too young to remember the nature of the problems that gave rise to the HMO Act of 1973. A major concern at that time was the alleged over-treatment by "greedy" physicians who often prescribed "unneeded" hospitalization (as a matter of convenience so they could see more patients per day) and performed "unnecessary" surgery (because of the desire to increase their personal incomes). In the absence of that institutional memory, one can almost imagine some current proposals as heading us "back to the future." While all still is not well with managed care, there is no doubt that the evidence of unneeded surgeries and hospitalizations in pre-HMO days was far better documented than recent claims of under-treatment and poor quality.

One example of an innovation that has been widely adopted is that the gatekeeper or PCP has been redefined by many plans. As the patient population has aged, there is an increasing tendency to designate physicians previously identified as "specialists" as the PCP for enrollees with certain chronic conditions. For example, a patient with diabetes may now have an endocrinologist designated as the PCP, thus removing the need for a referral in order to see this physician. Similarly, older patients may be assigned to geriatricians as their PCPs.

Another major tool of cost containment has been the use of capitation rates to pay physicians and, sometimes, hospitals whereby providers are paid a set amount for each plan participant regardless of the number of visits or services provided. This, too, seems to be changing. It has been clear for some time that capitation has been a major point of controversy, because it shifts the ultimate burden of risk from the MCO (or insurer) to the provider. As managed care groups have continued to ratchet down their capitation rates, an increasing number of physicians and hospitals have been faced with bankruptcy. There have been several reasons for this. First, the MCOs often have been in a superior bargaining position and have forced providers to accept their rates "or else." Equally important, in many cases, is the fact that the providers, lacking detailed knowledge or training in economic and business matters, simply agreed to bad deals. However, observers believe that the trend of squeezing capitation rates cannot continue. A recent article states that, "The peak may have passed for capitation." It further notes that this issue has become a major concern for many providers, especially those who have been "burned" by the arrangement. The author goes on to state that, while capitation is not likely to disappear any time soon, some HMOs have decided that "the negative response to capitation now outweighs its benefits in controlling costs."[9] Indeed, the squeeze on capitation rates has possibly been the underlying cause of some class-action suits against HMOs for allegedly improperly denying or delaying access to certain kinds of treatment. It should also be pointed out that some of the draconian cuts imposed on Medicare and Medicaid by Congress and the states have made both providers and MCOs unwilling victims and forced them into adopting either higher prices or more restrictive practices in order to survive.

There are still some physicians who remember all the charges of "unjust enrichment" in the old FFS days, when suggesting an additional office visit was viewed as an attempt to fatten the physician's wallet.

---

9 Michael Prince, "Capitation in Decline," *Business Insurance*; April 10, 2000; pp. 1, 23.

Some of those doctors still prefer capitation as a means to avoid such charges. Another interesting view has recently been expressed that capitation may, in conjunction with the traditionally low or no deductible provisions that exist in most HMOs, have contributed to overuse by patients who never are faced with the "pain in their own pocketbook" from seeking additional care. To the extent that this was not anticipated, some providers agreed to very bad bargains, and patient expectations may have been unrealistically raised.

Employers, too, were among those most reluctant to accept HMOs when they first appeared, preferring to continue negotiations over employee health plans with "traditional" insurance carriers. In part, this reflected the same reluctance to change that patients and providers felt, but it also arose, undoubtedly, from the traditional suspicion of anything that government advocated, especially after passage of the federal HMO Act in 1973. Later, as real cost-savings were observed, many employers became firm advocates of managed care.

Over time, different types of HMOs developed (group, staff, independent practice associations, and so on), with varying degrees of control over providers, slightly different organizational structures, and more or less flexibility over where care was delivered. But they all retained the same basic characteristics. In the early 1980s, a new "player" appeared—the preferred provider organization (PPO)—and it quickly became a favorite of employers and workers. The PPO offered more flexibility than the HMO, allowing free choice to seek out-of-system services in exchange for a higher participation cost, generally a larger coinsurance payment or deductible, or both. A virtual "alphabet soup" of hybrid managed care organizations emerged over the next decade, and often the distinctions became blurred. The so-called point-of-service (POS) plan permits the patient to defer a decision until the final moment about whether to use a physician or hospital that is in the employer's "network" of contracted providers. It is the most flexible managed care option. POS plans typically incorporate some traditional indemnity principles with PPO and HMO components. While PPO and POS plans remain most popular with most patients and providers, HMOs have grown rapidly both in enrollment and in favor with employers in recent years. HMO enrollment growth, in the face of consumer preference for less-restrictive models, reflects more aggressive action by employers to get employees into more cost-effective plans.

Cost containment remains a central issue for employers and others. Benefit innovations continue to be limited only by the imaginations of plan designers. Some innovations are soon discarded, having proved to be either ineffective or so offensive as to be impractical. Others work and become part of a new "tradition." In any case, there still are only a few basic approaches to effective control of the cost of medical expense benefit plans. One can either control the factors that affect costs, invent ways to minimize the impact of changes that can't be controlled, or reduce the magnitude and scope of the benefits offered. State and federal mandates have made it increasingly difficult to achieve these controls.

A primary goal of this chapter is to set the stage for what will follow. To accomplish this, it is necessary to have some understanding of the history of health insurance as an employee benefit. The following discussion outlines the changing roles of the various players in the health care arena, the continuing market changes, and the major public policy issues that face the country and employers and other sponsors of health plans.

HISTORY OF HEALTH INSURANCE AS AN EMPLOYEE BENEFIT

The Pattern Is Set

Employee benefits as we know them today are essentially a product of the last half of the 20th century. That is a relatively recent development in historical terms. While some examples of health insurance, life insurance, and private pensions existed early in the 20th century, they were by no means widespread. Particularly with respect to health insurance, there were several "defining moments" that were decisive in shaping the way Americans are covered today.

The first of these moments came in the 1930s, when President Franklin D. Roosevelt directed those who were developing his Social Security program to exclude health insurance from the package. Rightly or wrongly, the president felt that opposition of the medical profession to such a plan was so strong that to try to incorporate health insurance would threaten passage of the entire program. Thereafter, with the government on the sidelines, the private sector had to take the lead in sponsoring health insurance coverage. At the time, most commercial insurance companies were also on the sidelines because they believed that health insurance was not a viable product for a variety of reasons. At the same time, nonprofit Blue Cross and Blue Shield plans began to develop to fill the void. As they grew and prospered, commercial insurers took note and slowly began to follow suit.

The next major development came in the early stages of World War II when the federal government froze wages and salaries to prevent runaway inflation. This opened the door to a wide range of non-cash arrangements and gave rise to the first major step in employer-sponsored employee benefits including health insurance, life insurance, and pensions. Employers used these plans to reward loyal service, boost employee morale, and attract the best available employees. When the wage freeze ended after the war, many employers were no longer interested in funding these plans, most of which had no vested benefits and had been unilaterally introduced by the firm. Employees, however, had come to feel that these benefit packages were their right, and they took industry to court to preserve them. Their victory came when the U.S. Supreme Court decreed that these benefits were, in fact, subject to collective bargaining under the Taft-Hartley labor law. At this point, in the late 1940s, another dramatic surge in growth of benefit plans took place. On the health insurance side, the basic benefit was hospital insurance, with a lesser, but significant, growth in surgical benefits.

Most plans had very modest benefits by today's standards, with the Blues generally offering so-called first-dollar service benefits, which were defined in terms of days of hospitalization or specific surgical procedures. This was made possible by the special relationship that the Blues had with the major provider organizations—the American Hospital Association and the American Medical Association—which were sponsors of Blue Cross and Blue Shield, respectively. Through a dual contract arrangement (i.e., Blue/provider and Blue/subscriber), the insureds, or subscribers, as the Blues called their members, never received any cash. Rather, cash benefits were paid directly to the provider organization or professional on the basis of a contractually determined fee for service, while the patients simply got the defined service. Limiting the number of days of service that were promised held down premiums.

The commercial insurers, by contrast, offered indemnity (cash) benefits to the subscriber after the fact, and they did not have any contractual guarantee of service cost with providers because it was felt that it would violate antitrust laws. The cash limits, typically stated in terms of both maximums per unit of service and total outlay, were quite low, as an underwriting protection, but so were charges in those days!

In the early years, commercial insurers often provided the same first-dollar coverage that the Blue plans offered. In a sense, they were coerced into this by the fact that insureds had come to expect it from the way the pioneer Blues did business.

Another feature that distinguished the Blues was the use of "community rating," or charging all subscribers in the same geographical area the same premium. This arose from the strong sense of social commitment that motivated the founders of the Blue plans. Indeed, many perceived the Blues to be quasi-social institutions, because of their nonprofit status and the special enabling legislation under which many of them were started, which also provided tax advantages in many states. The commercial insurers, by contrast, used rating distinctions based on perceived risk factors, just as they did in the rest of their business. The majority of the plans were also limited to coverage of the employee in the early days, though family coverage developed rather rapidly.

When President Harry Truman's attempt to pass a national health insurance program failed, the pattern of employment-based health insurance for the vast majority of Americans seemed to be firmly entrenched, a fact that set the United States clearly at odds with most of the rest of the industrial world. That distinction has persisted, with some exceptions—notably the elderly—until the present and seems destined to continue at least through the end of this decade.

Innovation, Growth, and Challenges

The introduction of the first major medical policies in 1949 was another milestone, and one that had a major impact. The policies were characterized by high benefit limits, usually combined with a deductible and coinsurance. This design not only broke ranks with the first-dollar coverage concept but also introduced more comprehensive benefits, extending far beyond the traditional hospital and surgical services. Major medical policies were often used as a supplement to basic hospital, surgical, and medical policies after benefits had been exhausted; they also were used in some cases as stand-alone coverage by those who felt they could bear modest medical costs without any serious hardship. It did not take long for insurers to develop policies that combined both basic and major medical coverage in a single contract, variously referred to as either "comprehensive" or "comprehensive major medical" policies. These policies used a number of internal limits, consisting of varying deductibles and/or coinsurance provisions for selected services, (e.g., mental health benefits). This had the dual effect of containing costs and affecting choices of service.

Another surge in the growth of group insurance benefits occurred as a result of the wage and price freeze during the Korean War. Around that time, the Blues lost some of their market dominance, as commercial underwriters used rate differentials to attract the healthiest groups. Ultimately, the Blues also used experience rating for their group contracts. For most of the 1950s, however, both the number and percentage of non-elderly Americans with group health insurance coverage sponsored by an employer continued to grow, and the benefits continued to develop greater breadth and depth. Other developments during the 1950s included escalating health care costs and the recognition, for the first time, of a serious problem in providing health insurance for the elderly.

During the decade, a combination of factors came together that forced attention on retiree health care. The first wave of retirements under the federal Social Security law began to appear. During the war, because of the need to keep up with defense production, many of those eligible to retire had not done so, but the impact of the law, which effectively "institutionalized" 65 as "old age," did not take long to become clear. Many firms had designed their retirement programs around age 65. Workers, who had by then become accustomed to health insurance coverage through their place of work, suddenly found themselves without health insurance by virtue of their retirement (often forced) and without many companies willing to offer them affordable coverage as individuals. As pressure grew to address the problem, some private insurers, fearing the entry of the government, joined so-called state-65 plans, under which several states permitted insurers to pool their efforts on a nonprofit basis in order to establish a viable market for senior-citizen health insurance at an affordable price. Despite good intentions, however, this approach was destined to be too little and too late. Ultimately, of course, the federal government stepped in with the Medicare program in the mid-1960s.

Throughout the 1960s and 1970s, health insurance benefits continued to expand. One of the major changes during the 1960s was a dramatic expansion of psychiatric benefits, which had been either nonexistent or extremely limited in previous years. But despite the spread of more and more generous benefits, there were many troubling developments, too, the most important of which was the rapidly increasing cost of plan benefits.

The single biggest event of the decade was the enactment of the Medicare and Medicaid programs (Titles XVIII and XIX of the Social Security Act) in 1965 and their implementation in 1966. Health care costs, which already had been escalating more rapidly than the overall consumer price index, began to soar. The combination of an explosion of new scientific breakthroughs in medicine, a rapidly aging population, and a growing sense of entitlement—health care as a right, not a privilege—fed the inflationary pressures. Furthermore, both the Medicare and Medicaid programs clearly emphasized access to care, not cost containment as their primary objective. The initial policy of full-cost retrospective reimbursement for hospitals added fuel to the inflationary fires, because it provided absolutely no incentive for economy. Rather, it encouraged what, in retrospect, seems like an overly ambitious investment in physical plant and equipment, while also following the historic trend established in the early days of private health insurance of encouraging inpatient hospital care, the most expensive place of treatment. By giving what economists call "effective demand" to millions of elderly Americans, the Medicare program contributed significantly to the rampant inflation of the medical care sector, which has had a profound and long-lasting impact on the cost of benefit plans.

Cost Concerns Grow

By the early 1970s, cost had become a major concern for both government and private programs, but benefits continued to be expanded in both sectors even as the explosion of new medical knowledge and equipment added to the inflationary pressure. With the extension of Medicare benefits to those suffering with end-stage renal disease in 1972, a veritable Pandora's box of added costs was opened. Now, nearly 30 years later, the parade of new diagnostic and treatment techniques and equipment, each seemingly more expensive than the last, still shows no sign of abatement. New developments in the past decade have, if anything, been even more rapid.

There were many who believed that, with the enactment of Medicare and Medicaid in 1965, some form of national health insurance would inevitably follow quite soon. By the early 1970s, pressure was mounting for such a program, but there was very little agreement on what form it should take, and there was no solid public outcry to support it, despite the fact that two dozen or more proposals were introduced in each session of Congress. Many experts felt that the combination of the civil rights movement, the women's movement, the Vietnam War, and the Watergate scandal distracted attention from the health insurance issue and, in the case of the latter two, seriously undermined public confidence in government. Thus, no national health insurance program emerged at the time.

As noted earlier, HMOs appeared on the scene in about 1970, and supporters felt they offered real opportunities for cost containment. Unfortunately, health care professionals, consumers, and employers resisted them because of reservations about the dramatic changes they would bring about. HMOs were given a boost, with the passage of the federal HMO Act in 1973, but they were still very slow to develop.

During the decade, the federal government undertook several initiatives to try to contain health care costs and to ensure the viability of private benefit plans. The Employee Retirement Income Security Act of 1974 (ERISA) introduced vesting requirements for pensions and provided protection (the ERISA "preemption") of qualified employee benefit plans against state efforts to regulate certain aspects of those programs.

During the 1970s, many states began to enact mandated benefit laws for health insurance plans. Despite the constant expansion of benefits, there were always special-interest groups demanding more. Provider groups, in particular, have always been powerful at the state level. These laws took several forms, ranging from requirements that specific benefits be offered to requirements that the benefits be included in any group plan issued and, in some cases, specifying which providers' services had to be included. By the mid 1990s, there were hundreds of these laws, and the specific mandates were wide-ranging. Just a few examples include the mandating of maternity benefits; in vitro fertilization services for sterile couples; and services from Christian Science readers, chiropractors, and various medical or social workers other than traditional physicians. At least one state even mandated payment for hairpieces when hair loss resulted from a specific disease or treatment! These laws motivated many firms to drop commercial health insurance plans and self-insure their workers' benefits because the ERISA preemption protected self-insured firms from state-mandated requirements. The law also protected them from having to pay insurance premium taxes.

A series of federal laws relating to health planning also were enacted during the 1960s and 1970s. Most of them had, as at least one of their goals, the mission of containing or slowing cost increases. None succeeded.

In 1976, President Carter took office as the first president since Truman with a formal commitment to national health insurance. Within six months of taking office, however, he decided that no such program could be undertaken until control was gained over escalating costs. There followed a series of initiatives by the federal government to gain that control. Some of President Carter's more aggressive proposals were never enacted, especially when the so-called "voluntary effort" by the private sector, which the proposals spawned, appeared, however briefly, to be working.

In the early 1980s, changes to Medicare served to marginally slow the increases in the program's costs, although they did little to control the overall rise in health care costs. The first of such changes included stricter limits on what costs were reimbursable under Medicare, but the major change was the shift to a prospective payment system based on diagnostic related groups (DRGs) of services in 1983. The resulting cost-shifting of millions of dollars in medical expenses to private benefit plans had a profound impact on the attitude of employers toward their benefit programs and their willingness to consider a governmental solution. It also began to have an impact on the willingness and ability of firms, especially small ones, to provide any coverage at all to their workers.

The Tide Turns

At this point, two watershed events occurred. For the first time since the introduction of private group health insurance plans 50 years earlier, both the number and percentage of the civilian population covered by such plans began to fall. And for the first time since organized labor won the right to collectively bargain health benefits, they were forced (however reluctantly) to accept givebacks of previously won gains in order to save jobs because of employers' unwillingness and/or inability to bear the high costs involved. In the climate of the early 1980s, when the economy had slowed, there seemed to be no other choice. However, as the economy rebounded, attempts to recover the lost benefits and to expand them even further became a primary goal. In the pursuit of this goal, however, success was elusive. The vast majority of labor stoppages during both the 1980s and the early 1990s were primarily, if not exclusively, tied to disputes over health benefits.

A dramatic side effect of this development was the persistent and growing problem of the uninsured. As some firms dropped their group plans, it was found that very few insurers offered affordable health insurance plans to individuals. As the numbers of uninsured grew, so did the pressure to reconsider a national health care solution. Another important factor in the growth of the uninsured has been the dramatic restructuring of the American economy since the 1970s. As the number of jobs in the manufacturing sector, traditionally the bastion of strong labor unions and often the source of benefit innovations and broad "pattern benefit" plans, dwindled because of strong foreign competition (e.g., in the auto and steel industries), union membership dropped. Despite strong job growth in the United States during the Reagan years in the 1980s, most of the new jobs were in smaller, non-unionized service industry companies, which often did not have formal health insurance plans.

Also during the 1980s, private insurers began adopting some of government's techniques to control plan costs. This was facilitated initially when the California legislature, while debating ways to control costs of the state Medicaid plan, MediCal, decided to let private health plans use the same technique that the state was adopting, that is, to seek bids for fixed-price service delivery contracts with selected health care providers. Thus protected from charges of antitrust or price fixing, private insurers and self-insured firms gave birth to the preferred provider organization (PPO). PPOs grew exponentially over the next few years. They were far more popular with workers than HMOs, as noted earlier, because PPOs provided greater flexibility and freedom. Some employers also preferred them initially. However, PPOs have been less effective than HMOs in controlling costs, and by the-mid 1990s, HMOs had become more favored by plan sponsors.

At the same time that health insurance coverage and benefits were changing in the late '70s and '80s, the hospital industry was undergoing its own transformation. At this time, there was dramatic growth in for-profit hospital corporations, some growing to several hundred hospitals in multiple states. Indeed, at one time there were predictions, which later proved to be well off the mark, that by the end of the century the hospital industry would be dominated nationally by just a handful of these mega-organizations. This was a dramatic departure from the American tradition of community-based not-for-profit hospitals that had dominated the industry for most of the century. Some hospital groups tried to regain control of their destinies by creating wholly owned health insurance companies to avoid, or so they hoped, destructive pressure from various managed care organizations that were constantly pushing for lower costs of service. Most of these ventures were less than successful, and the entire for-profit hospital movement slowed dramatically.

Nevertheless, hospital mergers and acquisitions continued to take place at a rapid rate, and newly emerging efforts to maintain control of their destinies led hospitals to enter into a variety of new ventures, including some of the previously mentioned "alphabet soup" varieties of managed care. One such venture was the physician–hospital organization, or PHO, which was an attempt to "capture" a specific segment of a market area by offering prepaid services in much the same way that an HMO would, while doing away with any intermediary. This never became a major factor, however, for a variety of reasons, one of which may have been that their geographical limitations were crippling in a mobile society. In addition, it was difficult to balance the needs of physicians and hospitals in the face of continuing change.

The most significant event of the early 1990s, from a health insurance point of view, was undoubtedly the failure, after much fanfare, of the Clinton health plan. Despite the fact that it failed, however, the initial expectation of passage motivated many insurers and providers to dramatically reposition themselves in hopes of surviving after the federal government acted. Furthermore, a few states went ahead with plans that incorporated some aspects of the Clinton plan, and this experimentation continues today, with many state initiatives already enacted that will, sooner or later, probably also appear in federal legislation.

Another major initiative by some hospital groups after the defeat of the Clinton Health Plan was the purchase of private physician practices. Originally entered into as a defensive technique to preserve referral relationships and market share, most of these ventures turned out to be disastrous. Institutional managers, some of whom had been "stars" in their own organizations, found that they were totally unprepared for the challenge of managing physicians who had sold them their practices in exchange for salaried positions within a corporate structure. Not only did they discover that they had paid far too much for these practices, because they did not know how to value them, but they also discovered that doctors on salary had very different motivations from those in purely private fee-for-service practice. In one of the more spectacular failures of this approach, the Allegheny Health System of Philadelphia declared bankruptcy late in the decade, and other area health systems which had followed a similar strategy also found themselves in serious fiscal trouble. Needless to say, this strategy is now being seriously re-evaluated by others who had adopted it.

THE PUBLIC POLICY ISSUES AROUND HEALTH CARE SPENDING

As health care costs have escalated, so too has the attention devoted to this sector of the economy. Indeed, it would have been difficult to identify more than a handful of "health economists" a half century ago. Today they are everywhere! Unfortunately, despite their growth in numbers and sophistication, they have been unable to solve the health care cost problems. Because of the extremely high cost of much of medical care today, health insurance has taken on a more important role in society.

Indeed, many people equate the absence of health insurance with the inability to obtain medical care. Recently, a judge held an insurer liable for not covering a treatment on the grounds that failure to insure the service was tantamount to denial of service in today's expensive medical care environment—even though the policy in question clearly did not cover the treatment. In reality, this equation of coverage and treatment overstates the problem to a considerable degree because existing laws require hospitals and physicians to treat patients in need regardless of their insurance status. Several public programs, notably Medicaid, also provide a significant amount of care to persons who have either inadequate or no health insurance. Some charitable organizations also make services available.

Nevertheless, there is a widespread perception that people without insurance are not able to obtain needed care, and perception is reality for most. In the current era of corporate mergers and industrial downsizing, many people are extremely worried about the "what if" situation if they should lose their job. It is clear that most would not be able to either locate or afford individual or family coverage comparable to whatever group benefits they currently have. Even those protected under the provisions of the Consolidated Omnibus Budget Reconciliation Act (COBRA), who would have the right to stay under their former employer's group plan for up to 18 months, would have to come up with 102 percent of the full premium. This is an option that is not only unattractive, but also probably unaffordable when one is unemployed.

Health care benefits have been a major factor in labor contract negotiations since shortly after the end of World War II. These negotiations have taken on a sharper edge in recent years because of the very high cost of care and the perception, just mentioned, that no insurance might mean no treatment. Negotiations over health benefits have, thus, increasingly become make-or-break contract issues and the cause of most strikes for nearly two decades.

Articles in the popular press as well as several television specials have done a great deal of hand wringing over the fact that Americans "spend too much on health care." Undoubtedly some, perhaps many, health care expenditures are "excessive" or "unnecessary." Services that do little or nothing to improve health status or charges that are out of proportion to the service rendered fall into this category. But realistically, how much is "too much" in terms of a percentage of GDP, and who should decide? Clearly, a substantial proportion of health care spending is elective, and in many cases the major benefit may come only from the recipients' sense of well being for having had the treatment or discussion with the health care professional. For elective service, it seems that the only basis for a case against it being rendered would be if someone other than the recipient is held responsible for payment. Thus, the pertinent public policy question is not whether or not the service should be available or utilized but which services, and how much of them, should be a public responsibility?

In looking at the pattern of spending on health care in the United States, several observations seem pertinent. First, Americans have always been fiercely independent and protective of their freedom—including, as some would put it, the right to make bad choices or even to be downright stupid! Thus, if an individual decides to spend money on services of little or no value, it could be argued that it is his or her right, so long as it does not prevent someone else from obtaining needed treatment.

One explanation for "excessive" health spending in this country may be that, as a nation, we have enjoyed a higher standard of living than most, resulting in more money available for discretionary spending. When combined with the so-called baby boom generation's much-publicized concern with remaining youthful, this has produced significant expenditures on things such as cosmetic surgery, for example. Another factor involved in our high level of spending is our love affair with the latest technologies. Most of us also want our local community hospital to have all the same equipment and services that every other hospital has, even if it would be more rational to share the equipment and consolidate services at a single site. Economic pressure may some day force providers to take this step, some "centers of excellence" address this to some extent, but it is doubtful that government will mandate it any time soon.

Finally, we have, in the eyes of many, a less mature view of death than did our forebears. There appears, at times, to be a need, both in individuals and in the health care professions, to prolong life at any cost, often without regard for the quality of life that results. This may be changing slowly, as measured by the increasing number of people who have prepared living wills, advanced directives and durable powers of attorney to indicate their desire to be spared extreme measures. However, a November 1995 editorial in the *Journal of the American Medical Association* reported on the results of a study showing that entrenched patterns of care still view death as the enemy rather than the natural end of life. This view often results in enormous expenditures made against the wishes of the patient and the family. At the same time, these costly procedures may cause the patient great pain and deny him or her the right to die with dignity.[10] The public policy debate on these economic issues has barely begun, but the implications for health insurance, both public and private, could be significant. And with the completion of the mapping of the human genetic code, more people than ever may want to hang on to life in the belief that additional cures will soon be forthcoming.

---

10 "Improving Care Near the End of Life: Why Is It So Hard?," Editorial commenting on "A Controlled Trial to Improve Care for Seriously Ill Hospitalized Patients: The Study to Understand Prognoses and Preferences for Outcomes and Risks of Treatment (SUPPORT)," *Journal of the American Medical Association*, 274, No. 20, November 22/29, 1995, pp. 1634–1636 (editorial); 1591–1598 (study).

PLAYERS AND THEIR ROLES IN HEALTH CARE

In earlier and simpler times, the players and their roles were quite clear and almost universally understood. Doctors were the caregivers whose services were covered under health insurance policies, and coverage pertained primarily to hospital and surgical services. Over time, coverage expanded to include a broader range of physician's services, and eventually benefits were extended to a whole range of both inpatient and outpatient services provided by medical paraprofessionals and technicians needed to operate much of the new technology. As the population aged because of longer life expectancy, and as acute care services became more expensive, new benefits emerged to cover services provided in a variety of outpatient settings and in nursing homes, rehabilitation centers, and even in home care settings. Often the caregivers came from outside the usual orbit of the medical community and could more appropriately be identified as social workers.

Employers became the primary purchasers of health benefit plans early on in the development of health insurance. At the outset, the insurers basically defined the coverage, set the price, and offered the benefits on a take-it-or-leave-it basis. They operated largely as a "fiscal funnel," in that they adjusted premiums to the costs of a group's utilization and passed the cost back to the employer, usually through some form of "experience rating" formula. Over time, employers demanded more services from insurers, including things like utilization review. They also wanted some evidence that the insurer was providing the maximum bang for the buck in terms of coverage and service. Indeed, employers began to demand a greater say in the definition of coverages and no longer accepted whatever the insurer offered. They moved from accepting the premium charge as a necessary cost of doing business to demanding insurer accountability and the institution of cost controls, and they began to shop for better coverage, service, and prices.

By the 1970s and 1980s, employers began to self-insure in large numbers so that they would have almost complete control over their benefit plans. Many continued to use insurers or other third parties not as risk bearers but as administrative service only (ASO) providers. Finally, as HMOs and other managed care plans evolved, combining the care giving and financing responsibilities in one organization, the health insurance industry recreated itself to the point where it is now a major sponsor of managed care programs. Indeed, the largest number of both HMO and PPO plans today are sponsored by Blue Cross and Blue Shield plans and insurance companies, some of whom have almost completely phased out their "traditional" indemnity benefit plans.

Labor unions, which had originally opposed group insurance plans as a form of "paternalism," became active advocates of these plans and exerted considerable clout in the broadening and deepening of benefits through their collective bargaining agreements. Indeed, they were probably the driving forces for the inclusion of many, if not most, of the added benefits that evolved over several decades. Though their power has waned since the rapid decline in union membership as the result of changing industry patterns, they continue to be a major voice in the development and maintenance of coverage for their members. They also have been a strong lobbying presence for government programs, and that continues to be the case today.

Clearly, the role of the federal government, despite the absence of a comprehensive and universal health plan in this country, has grown significantly over the years. As regulator, financier, and sometimes as a direct provider of services, the government's role has constantly expanded since the end of World War II. It regulates drugs through the Food and Drug Administration. It has played a significant role in funding medical research and the construction of facilities through the National Institutes of Health and the Hill–Burton Act. It directly provides care through the Veterans' Administration, the military, and the Indian Health Service, for example. And its role in funding coverage for the elderly, poor, and other specific groups through Medicare, Medicaid, and other programs now runs to billions of dollars annually. State and local governments also play an important role. Though they have historically taken a back seat to the federal government, this has changed dramatically in the past few years as national policy has been stalled. States, which have always had primary responsibility for insurance regulation, have been passing health-related legislation at a dizzying pace in the past decade.

Indeed, a major concern of employers and insurers is the problems that they will face from dual regulation. While some dual regulation has existed for years, an article in *Business Insurance* states that it is feared that the passage of a federal "patients' bill of rights" could cause "confusion and chaos if adopted nationally." The article goes on to say: "States have focused on consumer protection and access to health insurance for well over a decade, and the legislation that is pending before Congress threatens to undermine and undo access to affordable health insurance as well as to pre-empt the effective and user-friendly consumer complaint and appeals networks in place around the country."[11] In addition, the article contained a

---

11 Meg Fletcher, "Employers Fear Dual Regulation," *Business Insurance*; April 10, 2000, pp. 1, 26.

report from the National Association of Insurance Commissioners (NAIC) which listed over 590 existing state mandates directed at managed care alone as of March 2, 2000.

After years of hesitating to enact significant new national health legislation at least in part because of huge budget deficits, lawmakers in Washington suddenly find themselves awash in a massive and growing surplus. They are currently struggling to find a compromise or common ground for spending these anticipated surpluses. Among the goals that have been reported are the following: to guarantee the solvency of Medicare; reduce the number of uninsured; provide much needed support for education; reduce the federal deficit; and also provide the American public with some sort of tax relief.

CHANGES IN THE MARKET ENVIRONMENT

The complications and challenges of the health insurance market in recent years have caused many of the old, traditional commercial health insurers to phase out of the business or at least to completely change their approach to the market. There has also been a significant shift among the Blues, many of which have converted to for-profit status in recent years. Also, the Blues no longer strictly adhere to their traditional "exclusive territory" pattern, which was once a requirement for membership in the National Association of Blue Cross and Blue Shield Plans. Many now compete against each other for subscribers. Most Blues abandoned any across-the-board effort to maintain community rating many years ago in order to compete effectively with insurers that experience-rated their customers. Recently, however, community rating concepts—though with some modifications—have come back into favor as the government imposed them on federally qualified HMOs. Even many commercial insurance company plans generally utilize modified community rates today.

The often desperate search for ways to control health care plan costs over the years has forced many significant market changes. Between the constant flood of new technology and the desire for cost containment, pressure on providers to accept lower reimbursement for services became so great that many providers—both institutional and individual—are now struggling to survive. Some have failed. Newer technologies have made it possible for many procedures that once required lengthy inpatient stays to be handled on a lower-cost outpatient basis. Even at tertiary care teaching hospitals, it is now common to find more than 60 percent of the surgical procedures performed in outpatient or short-procedure units that do not involve an overnight stay. For years hospitals were the undisputed nerve center or "hub" of health care activity and the dominant institutional provider. But some now see them becoming more of a last-resort facility where research and highly technical and sophisticated "cutting edge" services will be provided to the diminishing number of patients who will require acute inpatient services. They may well become subsidiaries of comprehensive clinics or outpatient facilities. Nursing homes or life care communities may well replace hospitals as the dominant inpatient facility as the population continues to age over the next several decades.

Facing mounting pressure from managed care organizations to accept lower fees, eliminate unnecessary services, and conform to defined practice guidelines and "best practice" measures of quality, both hospitals and physicians have been forced to contemplate a very different future than they would have faced just a few short years ago. All parties seem to realize that the provision of the most appropriate service delivered in the most appropriate setting by the most appropriate provider at the most appropriate time holds the best long-term promise of cost control and consumer satisfaction along with improved health. Clearly, patterns of service delivery will continue to face change.

While solo medical practitioners are not likely to totally disappear, it has become increasingly difficult for them to survive. As enrollments in managed care organizations continued to grow, these groups were increasingly able to direct patients to their own networks of providers. Thus, it became important for providers to make themselves attractive to the HMO, PPO, or other organization because the managed care plans exercise considerable control over where patients go for treatment. Market share has become the dominant concern of most hospitals and physicians. With lower reimbursements per unit of service, they need to capture more patients in order to maintain their level of income. If they fall out of favor with their managed care group because of substandard performance, failure to meet the economic targets of the organization, or any other reason, it can be difficult, if not impossible, to survive.

It has already been noted that attempts to develop viable physician–hospital organizations (PHOs) did not meet with great success, and the widely adopted hospital strategy of buying up physician practices in an effort to ensure their referral base and, ultimately, their survival also has largely been a failure. While we have seen some return to prominence of primary care physicians, who form the heart of most managed care networks, the American love affair with medical specialization that has dominated the bulk of the 20th century is likely to remain a major factor in the new millennium. While many managed care plans offer a variety of incentives to minimize referrals to specialists except where deemed absolutely medically necessary, continuing concerns about the potential impact on quality and the inexorable development of new technology is likely to ensure a continued prominent role for many specialists. The debate will continue as to who should call the medical shots, the doctor or the accountant. But there has been sufficient evidence of a backlash against managed care tactics to ensure that, while cost control will remain a major concern, the role of the physician is likely to be bolstered in coming years. However, the common assumption that more costly is better is no longer supportable in all cases, as more and better measures of quality are developed.

Finally, despite the current market supremacy of managed care organizations, there is certainly no assurance that they themselves will ultimately survive the 21st century. Even if they do, it will undoubtedly be in modified form, but who knows what future organizational structure might emerge to supplant current MCOs? One clue may be found in recent reports of a variety of new initiatives which are, not surprisingly, related to the emergence of the internet and e-commerce. Two articles that were featured on the front page of *Business Insurance* on March 20, 2000 tell of how a Hewitt Associates initiative may "revolutionize the way that employers purchase and deliver health care benefits to employees and retirees" and how employers and HMOs "trying to shield themselves from expanded liability under proposed federal patient protection legislation are reversing earlier positions and now voluntarily funding research into experimental medical treatments."[12] In the latter case, the article notes an increasing tendency for health plans to *voluntarily* pay for selected experimental treatment regimens even before they have been proven effective, provided that the treatments are delivered in high quality clinical trials. Such trials are typically conducted under guidelines provided by the National Institutes of Health, and though they may still be experimental, nevertheless, there have been several instances where patients have successfully sued for damages after being denied payment for the services. The more enlightened position now being taken by many plans is that it is in their best interest to pay under certain circumstances, not only to avoid litigation, but also to help speed the development of potentially more effective treatment protocols. Indeed, some other insurers are expected to follow the lead of the Blue Cross and Blue Shield Association

---

12 Jerry Geisel, "Hewitt Starts Health Care E-Business," and Joanne Wojik Kochaniec, "More
   Insurers Funding Research—New Coverage Stance," *Business Insurance*, March 20, 2000,
   p. 1, 35.

of Chicago and establish their own technology assessment committees to determine just what the latest medical research indicates would be appropriate with respect to coverage decisions.

The Hewitt initiative described in the front page articles, was scheduled to begin operation in the fall of 2000 under the name Sageo. It will use the technological expertise and long-standing relationships of Hewitt with health plans "to provide complete administration of health programs while enabling employers to eliminate the time and expense of enrolling participants, collecting premiums, transferring premiums to insurers and communicating benefits to participants." The plan enables participants to compare and select health care plans on-line, to access health care information provided by the Mayo Clinic, and communicate with other participants. Sageo is said to have completed arrangements that will enable it at the outset to provide standard benefit designs in nearly 100 markets. Initial offerings will be to retirees, but active employees will have the same options available shortly. Selection and enrollment will be done over the Internet, with participants having the ability to make personal choices among a variety of standardized plans on the basis of cost, quality, access and member satisfaction, with all of the variables displayed on-line. This "full administrative solution" is seen as being both cost-effective and user-friendly. It will allow a wider choice for participants at reduced cost. Sageo claimed to have pre-launch commitments from plans representing more than 50 percent of all participants in group plans. The article provides additional details on the finer points of the proposal.

Two more articles in the same publication on May 22, 2000 introduce an even more revolutionary concept—letting employees "set up their own customized network of providers and let providers set their own fees, while limiting employers' financial obligation to pay for health care to a fixed amount."[13] In a companion article dealing with the same phenomenon, which is described as borrowing elements from both managed care and traditional indemnity insurance, it is stated that the program "is based on the idea of giving employees control over how their health care dollars are spent—the so-called consumer driven model . . . The program's approach all but abandons the traditional components of health maintenance organization style managed care—such as gatekeepers and utilization review—relying instead on discounted-provider arrangements and consumer education to control health care costs."[14]

---

13 Jerry Geisel, "Cutting Complexity," *Business Insurance*; May 22, 2000, p. 1.
14 Joanne Wojik Kochaniec, "Employees Call Shots," *Business Insurance*; May 22, 2000, p. 1.

These and other developments yet to be articulated and tested will undoubtedly get a good deal of attention as we move into the new millennium. Each will present new challenges and opportunities.

PUBLIC POLICY ISSUES

Anyone involved with the design or operation of employee medical plans ignores public policy issues relating to health care at his or her peril. Health care has been a politically charged arena for decades, never more so than at present. That in the near future there will be some legislation dealing with the long-term solvency of Medicare is pretty much assured no matter which party dominates Congress or is in the White House. There is also likely to be some action dealing with prescription drug coverage at least for the elderly. The emergence of a huge federal budget surplus makes these and possibly other expansions of health programs probable. One can immediately recognize the enormous change in circumstance since the last edition of the *Handbook*, when deficits were still looming. Yet, while some added benefits for Medicare beneficiaries and others are likely to be forthcoming, there is no reason to believe that the emphasis on cost containment will diminish, though if surpluses continue to grow this could reduce the pressure.

Employers have learned the hard way that "cost containment" under government programs such as Medicare and Medicaid often leads to "cost shifting" to the private sector, so they will need to pay close attention to what goes on. Congressional changes in Medicare ground rules in the past have usually added costs to the private sector, and even with projected budget surpluses, that could still be true. Past examples include: shifting reimbursement from a retrospective cost-related basis to a prospective system based on diagnostic related groups (DRGs); making Medicare secondary coverage to employer-sponsored benefits for workers over age 65; and, requiring that employers retain benefits for such workers at the same level as for younger workers. Where employers formerly utilized "carve-out" provisions to make their group plans responsible only for items not covered by Medicare for over-65 workers, Congress made the employee benefit plan primary for all active workers regardless of age. Other actions including COBRA and its subsequent amendments also had serious implications for employee plans. These and other actions have had a profound and lasting impact, not only on the financing of care, but also on the access to insurance and on the organization and delivery of medical services. There is no question that they gave rise to redoubled efforts on the part of employers to search for ways to protect themselves against federal cost shifts and to discover meaningful cost-control measures of their own.

Both state and federal legislators have often been more willing to grant "entitlements" than to fund them. In the past, the federal government has often mandated that state governments or employers provide those benefits it deems desirable but is unable or unwilling to fund. States, too, have enacted countless mandates related to health insurance and health care. There are now nearly 600 state mandates dealing with managed care alone, but they constitute only a fraction of the total of mandates that relate to employee health benefits. They have probably done as much to exacerbate the problems as they have to solve them.

In trying to avoid the higher premiums that state legislation has produced, as well as the payment of premium taxes that typically range from 2 percent to 3 percent in every state, more and more large employers have shifted to self-insurance. Then, by taking advantage of the preemption provision of ERISA, they are able to cover their workers with plans that are exempt from both state mandates and taxes. Savings for large employers can be substantial, but in reducing the pool of privately insured plans, to which providers traditionally shifted costs resulting from deficits under government programs or other bad debt, premium increases that forced many small employers to drop coverage were accelerated. Thus, mandates often produce both fewer regulated health insurance plans and fewer insureds. While the impact of mandates varies from state to state, there is little doubt that it has been significant in many cases. Ironically, some mandates designed to extend medical insurance benefits have unintentionally resulted in decreased access to coverage. This, in turn, has accelerated the growth in the number of uninsured Americans.

In the 1990s seniors were given the option of electing to have their Medicare coverage provided through private HMOs rather than via the traditional fee-for-service structure that had characterized Medicare benefits since their origin. Under the plan, the government agreed to pay HMOs directly on a capitation basis in exchange for the HMOs agreeing to provide benefits at least as generous as those provided for under the law. Among the enhanced benefits were such popular items as prescription drugs, reduced or eliminated deductibles, and lower co-payments. Most HMOs literally jumped at this opportunity and launched massive marketing campaigns to attract this growing market. Millions of Medicare participants were happy to accept the bonus coverage at no extra cost. But after continual government tightening of the payments to providers, managed care plans soon discovered that this business, which was originally welcomed and heralded as a boon to both providers and recipients, is no longer attractive. Recently, many managed care plans have been bailing out and announcing that they will no longer participate in the plan. As this is being written, one of the largest national players in this field, Aetna U.S Healthcare, announced that it, too, will join the growing parade of MCOs that have decided that they can no longer afford to provide this kind of coverage. Naturally, this creates tremendous angst among those who are losing their coverage, and it immediately leads to more charges of irresponsibility on the part of the HMOs that withdraw from the field. In defending their position, the retort is that "the government forced us out by cutting its payments so far that it has become impossible for us to survive." At this stage, one can only speculate as to the political fallout that will result.

We do know that federal legislation to provide prescription drug coverage under Medicare is currently under debate. While some action on this is likely soon, the differences between the Republican and Democratic positions are significant, and the final form of the legislation is still very much in doubt. However, with drug prices now rising more rapidly than any other health-related services or products, some action seems inevitable, and soon.

The previous edition of the *Handbook* predicted that after "the debacle of the Clinton Health Plan" only more modest proposals were likely to succeed in the short run, and several of the specifically identified proposals that were under discussion at the time did in fact become laws. In most cases, this happened with a flurry of legislation in 1996. We have already alluded to the Newborns' and Mothers' Health Protection Act of 1996, with its seemingly ill-advised legislation mandating duration of care.

HIPAA, in addition to providing for portability of benefits and special tax credits for qualified long term care insurance, also amended portions of COBRA and ERISA to provide more generous rules on pre-existing-condition exclusions as well as modifications in notification requirements when plan benefits change. But perhaps its most controversial section provided for a four-year pilot project to test the viability of the concept of medical savings accounts (MSAs). It was thought by some that allowing individuals to accept more responsibility for their own health care would lead to wiser behavior in the use of the health care system and in personal health habits. Individuals were allowed to set up tax-free savings accounts from which unexpected medical bills could be paid. This was supposed to encourage them to rely on lower-cost, higher-deductible health insurance policies and make less "unnecessary" use of professional services. Nearing the end of the pilot period, the concept remains controversial and there is some question as to whether or not it will endure. Some still project potential savings of billions of dollars annually, while others continue to condemn the plans, claiming that they serve only the rich and healthy.

Even with passage of the Mental Health Parity Act of 1996, there is still pressure for additional action to further broaden mental health benefits, but it is difficult to predict whether any new developments will occur in the near future.

No widespread movement calling for a total overhaul of the health care system has emerged since the Clinton debacle, but there is no shortage of ideas for reform. Hardly a day goes by without some article appearing that either defends the current system or suggests a radical reform. Critics of the current employment-based health insurance system are many, but there are also defenders. No one believes that the current system is anywhere near perfect, but even the strongest critics admit that it is so well entrenched that it would be very difficult to replace.[15] There are, however, those who envision a radically different future, even if they fail to explain just how we will get to their envisioned nirvana.[16]

CONCLUSIONS

This discussion has necessarily been limited in scope. It has only touched a few of the most current and controversial issues. Yet it should be sufficient to convince any prudent benefits planner or manager to keep a close watch on emerging issues, with a view to anticipating changes and designing plans that will minimize any undesirable impact on the employer or the employees. It also may be possible to lobby successfully either for or against proposals that are of direct concern.

Usually it is quite natural to think largely in terms of legislation when discussing policy, but at this point in history it would be foolish not to consider the enormous role of the courts. Recent Supreme Court decisions dealing with a wide range of controversial health related issues, ranging from abortion rights, to causes of action against managed care providers, have certainly provided fuel for continued debate over these issues. They will undoubtedly lead to even more legislative activity as lawmakers attempt to react according to their own and their constituents' biases on these issues.

---

15 See Jon R. Gabel, "Job-Based Health Insurance, 1977–1998: The Accidental System Under Scrutiny," *Health Affairs*, Chevy Chase, Nov/Dec 1999; 18:6, pp. 62-74, and William S. Custer, "Why We Should Keep The Employment-Based Health Insurance System," *Health Affairs*, Chevy Chase; Nov/Dec 1999; 18:6, pp. 115-123.

16 See David Levy, MD, "Health Care in the New Millennium: It's About the Patient," *Compensation & Benefits Management*, Greenvale; Summer 1999; 15:3, pp. 50-59.

Perhaps more so than any time in history, technology also may play a major role in shaping health policies in the near term. We are only beginning to tap the awesome resources of the Internet, and the legal and ethical issues related to this technology as it will be used in health care will take years to sort out. The same can be said about the "human instruction book" of the genome map. Questions of privacy, the potential for various kinds of discrimination, and the potential for other misuses of these new tools come immediately to mind as major concerns. Some have observed that science is moving too fast for policy makers today. Discoveries happen so fast and unexpectedly in some areas that we don't have time to anticipate and plan our responses to them. In the litigious society in which we live, this results in major threats to all concerned, including corporate benefits managers and their firms.

In all probability, there will be many changes in health care and health insurance in the new millennium, though no one knows just what those changes will be or exactly when they will occur. Will managed care, which was the "darling" of government and private policymakers for so long, be able to reshape itself in the face of current criticisms in time to survive? Will we see a return to fee-for-service medicine and private practice as it once existed? Or will something that has not even been dreamed of today become the new pattern for the U.S.? How much of medical care and health insurance will remain in the private sector? Will a totally government sponsored national health insurance system develop in the U.S. in the next decade? How will the emergence of the Internet impact the world of medicine and health insurance? What about the mind-boggling potential of the newly discovered genome map? How will the answers to these vexing questions affect corporate benefit plans? Stay tuned!

In a world of volatile and unpredictable science and politics, benefit professionals must be alert observers of both judicial and legislative activities at the federal and state levels. But that may not be enough. They also need to become astute observers of related technologies. All of these factors can and will have an impact on the cost and operation of benefit plans. Working together, benefit professionals may be able to help guide the ongoing search for a viable national health policy that achieves the needed delicate balance of rights and responsibilities and that will guarantee an acceptable level of care to all citizens without bankrupting the government or unduly burdening the private sector. The most crucial question that must be resolved before any real progress can be made is to determine the minimum acceptable standard of care.

Health Plan Design Evolution

Dennis F. Mahoney

INTRODUCTION

Medical plans have changed considerably since first introduced as an employee benefit. The early medical plans were either prepaid service plans providing a set allowance for hospitalization/medical services or traditional indemnity-type plans providing cash reimbursement for specific covered services. These approaches to medical insurance have become far less popular among employers because of the inability to manage costs and the inability to place a value on the health care received. Although traditional prepayment and indemnity designs are still offered in employee benefit plans and as choices in flexible benefit programs, medical care increasingly moved to managed care programs in the 1980s and 1990s. However, even managed care plans have faced significant rate increases and employers continue to review their plan designs in search of better values. A study by Hewitt Associates in October 2000 projected average increases in 2001 of 10 percent to 13 percent in employer health plans. The study's authors indicated this would mark the third year in a row for major health care cost hikes. Furthermore, the authors did not foresee any imminent slowdown in health care cost escalation.[1]

This chapter describes the traditional fee-for-service prepayment and indemnity plan structures and chronicles the evolving plan configurations that have led to today's managed care programs. Actual benefits

---

1 Hewitt Associates, *Employers to Face Double Digit Health Care Cost Increases for Third Consecutive Year*, October 23, 2000.

and coverage levels vary widely among plans. It is useful to have a full understanding of the benefits commonly provided and, in the case of traditional indemnity plans, to understand which benefits were provided under the various component parts of the plan. The exact level of benefits is defined by the insurer or plan sponsor, and the benefits described throughout this chapter are representative of benefits commonly provided. The chapter also discusses issues in developing a health care strategy. Other chapters in the *Handbook* cover in greater detail various types of managed care delivery systems, how to assess quality in health care, and specific approaches to controlling health care costs.

HOSPITAL/MEDICAL PLAN DESIGNS–THEN AND NOW

Prepayment Service and Indemnity Plans

Because the primary distinction between original prepayment and insured indemnity products was whether the benefit coverages were stipulated as a set level of benefits or an indemnified dollar amount to cover a certain amount of benefit, these two types of plans are described together.

Hospitalization Coverage–Background

Insurance that covered hospital stays was traditionally obtainable as a stand-alone product separate from insurance for medical services. Although medical benefit insurance has evolved into a more comprehensive product that covers hospital stays, physician services, and other medical expenses, it is still useful to examine the separate components.

The Blue Cross/Blue Shield organizations played a dominant role in the emergence of these early plans, setting up separate entities to handle hospital insurance and medical care insurance. Their hospital insurance products were configured as prepayment plans in which benefits were set in terms of allowable days of hospitalization. These plans emerged in the early 1930s. They contracted with hospitals and reimbursed them directly for patient lengths of stay. The Blue Cross organizations provided insurance to all policy seekers under their own charter. Insurance companies entered the marketplace soon thereafter but provided a hospital-day benefit that was based on a fixed dollar figure, which was the amount for which the insurance company indemnified the subscriber. This dollar figure was calculated based on the expected cost of the hospitalization. While the Blue Cross organizations were nonprofit entities, the insurance companies were for-profit organizations, were not community rated, and were not open to all those seeking coverage.

The early hospitalization plans were configured as first-dollar plans, in which benefits were paid from the first dollar of expense incurred, and the subscriber did not incur any expense with the hospitalization. This first-dollar coverage was in keeping with the model of a prepayment plan and was doable because the cost and utilization patterns for medical care were quite different from what they are today. Many of these plans, particularly the Blue Cross plans, were underwritten by community rating, an insurance approach whereby a uniform rate is used for all subscribers or insureds within a given geographical area.

Hospitalization Benefits Today

The hospitalization portion of today's plans generally covers all services, supplies, and procedures provided and billed through a hospital. These include the following:

- Inpatient room and board. This benefit usually covers hospital charges for a semiprivate room and board and other necessary services and supplies. If confinement in an intensive care unit is necessary, it is usually paid at two or three times the semiprivate room rate or at a set charge.
- Emergency care for services obtained at a hospital emergency room.
- Intensive and specialty care.
- Maternity and required associated newborn care for a set number of days or a stipulated dollar amount.
- X-ray, diagnostic testing, and laboratory expenses when the insured is hospital confined or when these services are performed by a hospital on either an inpatient or outpatient basis.
- Skilled nursing facility care. A plan will pay for confinement in a skilled nursing facility if it meets prescribed requirements. Usually there is a daily limitation either on a yearly basis or per confinement. Historically, a hospital stay of at least three consecutive days immediately prior to confinement was required to trigger allowance for skilled nursing facility care. Many plans have eliminated this prior hospitalization requirement.
- Radiation and chemotherapy. This benefit typically covers materials and their preparation as well as use of hospital facilities.
- Inpatient mental and nervous care.
- Inpatient drug and alcohol substance abuse care.
- Physical, inhalation, and cardiac therapy.

- Home health care. This benefit is provided for a specific number of visits per year by physicians, nurses, and home health aides. Care usually must be under a treatment plan supervised by a home health agency.
- Hospice care. This benefit is provided when the subscriber's attending physician certifies that the subscriber has a terminal illness with a limited medical prognosis, in many plans six months or less. This type of care allows the subscriber to receive care primarily at home, to help relieve pain and provide comfort rather than curing the patient. Hospice care will typically allow for admission into a hospice facility, and benefits will usually be provided until the earlier of either a patient's death or discharge from a hospice.
- Respite care. Coupled with hospice care, this benefit allows the terminal patient short-term inpatient care in a skilled nursing facility or member hospice when it is necessary to relieve primary caregivers in the patient's home. An example of this benefit might be an allowance of seven days every six months.

Under a major medical plan (described below) when allowances for hospitalization services are exceeded by a plan participant, the excess charges typically flow to the major medical component of the plan where the plan reimburses the participant after he or she pays the applicable deductible and coinsurance amounts.

Medical/Service Coverage—Background

Just as Blue Cross provided *hospital* insurance coverage, Blue Shield provided for insured *medical* care, including physician and other health care provider expenses. Similar to Blue Cross, the Blue Shield plans were service type plans, which provided a limit on the services covered rather than a strict dollar indemnification. Blue Shield plans followed the creation of the Blue Cross hospitalization plans. The insurance companies that followed Blue Shield into the marketplace provided indemnification to the subscriber up to certain dollar amounts for covered medical services.

Medical/Service Benefits Today

Today's medical/service benefits parallel the benefits provided under the earlier medical/service plans. The medical/surgical portion of today's plans covers most services of health care practitioners. Their fees are reimbursed either on a scheduled fee basis or on a "reasonable and customary (R&C) basis." A scheduled fee basis provides a maximum allowance for itemized procedures in terms of either a flat dollar amount or a unit value per procedure, which is then multiplied by a conversion dollar amount. The reasonable and customary basis is reimbursement based on the individual practitioner's customary charge for the procedure and the charges made by peer physicians in the given geographic area. Typically, "reasonable and customary" covers the equivalent of the full charge of 85 percent to 90 percent of all physicians within a geographic region. The plan then reimburses the lesser of the individual practitioner's charge or the reasonable and customary fee. The advantage to a medical/surgical plan that pays on an R & C basis is that, unlike a scheduled fee plan, it is not necessary to amend the medical plan to account for medical inflation. However, in times of dramatic medical inflation, an insurer might not update the reasonable and customary database as frequently to exercise some restraint on price escalation.

The following services typically are covered in the medical/surgical insurance component:

- Surgeons.
- Anesthesiologists.
- Nurses and other surgical assistants.
- Service fees associated with inpatient medical care.
- Second surgical opinions.
- X-ray, diagnostic, and laboratory expense benefits made in a doctor's office or by an independent laboratory.
- Skilled nursing care.
- Obstetricians and pediatricians associated with prenatal, delivery, and postnatal care.
- Inpatient intensive care and concurrent care in a hospital.
- Allergy testing.
- Transplant services.
- The administration of radiation and chemotherapy.
- Inpatient physical therapy.
- Immunizations for children.

Today, an insurer may contract with physicians and other health care practitioners to establish fees for services. This agreement with physicians was common practice in the past with Blue Shield plans. With these plans, in agreeing to be a "participating doctor," the physician would agree to accept as payment in full, Blue Shield's usual, customary, and reasonable (UCR) fee. Thus the doctor agreed that he or she would not balance bill the plan participant an additional amount if the doctor's fee was higher than the fee assigned by Blue Shield. The benefit that the doctor received for being a participating provider with Blue Shield was that she or he would be paid directly and would not have to seek collection from the individual patient. Most physicians were participating providers with Blue Shield.

If, on the other hand, the plan participant were to receive medical services from a "nonparticipating" doctor, the basic component of the plan might reimburse the participant a dollar amount that was less than the doctor's charge. In this case, the participant could often submit the excess billed amount to the supplemental major medical portion of the plan and receive a second level of reimbursement after paying the required deductible and coinsurance amounts required on the major medical insurance component of the plan.

As managed care organizations have become more prominent, they have been able to exert greater influence over physician fee arrangements.

Major Medical Coverage—Background

The third component that was joined with hospitalization and medical service to comprise traditional plans was supplemental major medical insurance. Major medical insurance is characterized by high limits of coverage; it is not typically written as first-dollar coverage, but involves reasonable up-front deductibles and coinsurance. Two of the earliest attempts at health care cost containment, deductibles and coinsurance amounts, are two distinct methods of cost sharing with plan participants. The deductible is an amount of eligible covered medical expense that the insured subscriber must incur before the plan pays benefits. The rationale for a deductible is to lower plan costs. Coinsurance is another means by which plan participants share in the cost of their medical care. After an insured participant exceeds his or her deductible, the plan reimburses at less than 100 percent. This cost-sharing device ensures that the insured participant has a financial stake in the cost of medical care. The major medical insurance policy is written as "all-except" coverage rather than as "named peril" coverage, which specifically identifies the services that are covered. Major medical coverage includes a widely defined array of medical expenses, and names those services or medical items that are either limited in or precluded from coverage. A major medical policy also can be issued as a stand-alone policy, which was prevalent when this type of coverage was first introduced.

Major Medical Benefits Today

The supplemental portion of today's plans covers eligible expenses that may not be covered in full or that are specifically excluded from either the basic hospitalization or the basic medical/surgical portions of the plan. Typically, these charges include the following:

- Excess hospitalization charges if the limit for services or a dollar amount on the hospitalization portion of the hospitalization component of the plan is exceeded.
- Excess medical/surgical expenses experienced in receiving medical services from a "nonparticipating" doctor (if the plan is a Blue Cross/Blue Shield Plan).
- Diagnostic home and office visits.
- Ambulance service.
- Durable medical and surgical equipment.
- Blood transfusions.
- Oxygen and its administration.
- Prescription drugs not used in a hospital or outpatient facility.
- Prosthetics and orthotics.
- Skilled nursing facility care in excess of the basic benefit allowance.
- Outpatient mental and nervous care.
- Outpatient drug and alcohol substance abuse care.

These expenses are generally reimbursed after the participant pays an annual deductible in a major medical plan. He or she is then responsible for the relevant coinsurance amount. A plan may require a deductible of $200 worth of eligible major medical type expenses per person before the plan begins to reimburse. A typical level of coinsurance required by the participant is 20 percent. Therefore, under this type of arrangement, the plan would begin to reimburse at 80 percent after the deductible is satisfied. Typically, the plan reimburses at 100 percent after an individual incurs a certain amount of coinsurance. For instance, the plan may reimburse at 80 percent for the first $10,000 of expenses and then pick up at 100 percent above the $10,000 threshold after the individual has paid $2,000 worth of co-payments out of pocket. The rationale for eliminating the coinsurance after a certain level and establishing an out-of-pocket maximum payment by the subscriber is the recognition that even requiring a coinsurance amount of 20 percent can cause extreme financial hardship in the event of a catastrophic illness.

Major medical plans have some lifetime maximum cap on eligible benefit charges, after which the plan ceases reimbursing the participant. For instance, an individual might be subject to a $1 million lifetime plan maximum, meaning that the plan will no longer cover expenses if the individual incurs eligible major medical expenses in excess of this limit.

Comprehensive Plans—Background

It is not hard to imagine the change in design of medical plans that occurred as the economics of medical care, utilization patterns, and technological enhancements increased the cost of the prepayment and traditional indemnity plans. Comprehensive medical plans were an adaptation of the major medical approach. Essentially, the structural approach of up-front deductibles and coinsurance was applied not only to supplemental medical services but to hospitalization and basic medical services. What was a supplemental insurance approach to items not covered in the base medical plan became the mode of providing all medical insurance. The cost of medical insurance has decreased for two primary reasons. First, plan participants are cost sharing each time medical expenses are incurred through the up-front deductible and coinsurance. Second, because plan participants are required to pay a portion of medical costs when incurring services, they are given a financial incentive to be better health care consumers, unlike with first-dollar coverage where there is no incentive to curb unnecessary utilization or choose less costly care. Comprehensive plans tend to be easier to communicate to plan participants because there is no need to explain different component parts of a plan, which benefits are in each component, and which benefits are subject to deductibles and coinsurance.

Cost-Control Features of Comprehensive Plans

Because many comprehensive plans were designed with cost savings as a primary objective, they had other cost-controlling features. Some of these features were applied later to other plan designs when organizations wanted to restrain the cost escalation in these programs. Some of the cost-controlling features included requiring second surgical opinions, full coverage for certain diagnostic tests, pre-admission certification requirements for hospitalizations, utilization reviews by the insurer or a third-party administrator, and enhanced reimbursements if procedures were performed at an outpatient facility.

These plan features were intended to control costs and reduce unnecessary care. A plan sometimes exempted certain items such as second surgical opinions and diagnostic testing from the deductible and coinsurance provisions, and either required or encouraged their use. The belief was that second surgical opinions could decrease unnecessary surgical procedures and diagnostic tests could result in early detection of certain medical conditions that were more cost effectively treatable if identified early. Pre-admission certification required either plan participants or the admitting hospital to check with a specialist at the insurer or the plan before admitting an individual for treatment. The intent was to allow insurers to review provider decisions as to the cost-effectiveness and necessity of the treatment before hospitalization and to intervene if necessary. Utilization review involved an examination of medical patterns to determine whether plan participants or certain health care providers seemed to be outside average utilization patterns or expected practice patterns. Utilization review was concurrent, prospective, or retrospective. Enhanced reimbursements or waiving of deductibles and co-payments would occur if certain procedures were performed on an outpatient basis. The belief here was that a financial incentive would encourage plan participants to opt for a less costly outpatient treatment rather than a more costly treatment involving hospital inpatient care.

Comprehensive Plan Benefits Today

The cost-control features just described have carried over into today's comprehensive plans, which subject virtually all expenses to a deductible and then reimburse an amount that excludes the coinsurance the participant must pay. However, certain benefits might be paid at 100 percent if they are viewed as contributing to a more economical means of accessing care, primarily as an alternative to inpatient hospital care. Also, as with major medical programs, most comprehensive plans have a maximum out-of-pocket payment, after which the plan would reimburse 100 percent of the UCR fee. Special daily limitations and annual maximum and lifetime caps also apply. A typical plan with a 20 percent coinsurance amount might have benefits configured in the following way:

Benefits Paid at 80 Percent of the Insurer's Established UCR Fee (Subject to Deductible)

- Inpatient days room and board (pre-admission certification required for admission).
- Maternity and newborn care.
- Administration of radiation and chemotherapy.
- Inpatient surgical services.
- Physician office visits.

- Chiropractic care.
- Anesthesia.
- Outpatient hospitalization services.
- Emergency accident and medical emergency expenses.
- Prescription drugs.
- Private duty nursing.
- Pre-admission hospital testing.
- Skilled nursing facility care.
- Hospice care.
- Respite care.
- Physical and respiratory therapy.

Benefits Paid at 100 Percent of the Insurer's Established UCR Fee (Not Subject to Deductible):

- Outpatient diagnostic tests, X-rays, and lab examinations.
- Outpatient surgery or procedures performed at an ambulatory care facility, doctor's office, or surgi-center.
- Home health care.
- Second surgical opinions for specific medical procedures.

In obtaining medical services from a Blue Cross/Blue Shield Comprehensive Plan, it could still be beneficial to seek services from the "participating" doctors because a "nonparticipating" provider could charge an amount in excess of the insurer's UCR fee schedule. This could result in a plan participant having to pay more than 20 percent coinsurance because the plan will reimburse based upon the UCR fee.

MANAGED CARE PLAN DESIGNS

Managed care delivery systems go beyond the cost-control features detailed above and attempt to control costs through active ongoing health care management. Health care management can entail many different aspects. Some of the more common managed care delivery systems are detailed below.

Health Maintenance Organizations (HMOs)

The introduction of the health maintenance organization was seen by many as the first real attempt at managed health care. An HMO differs from traditional approaches to health care in that it stresses wellness and preventive care. The HMO's intent is to maintain the participant's health, and therefore its orientation is toward health maintenance rather than toward treatment of illness only. Accordingly, HMOs provide richer preventive benefits, such as wellness programs, health screenings, and immunizations. Also, the financial incentives and cost controls are structured differently. Whereas comprehensive and major medical programs have up-front cost sharing to discourage "excess" medical utilization, HMOs usually have no up-front costs or charge only modest copayments for routine physician visits. Theoretically, HMOs control plan costs by maintaining health, managing care more cost-effectively, and controlling specialist referral. Most HMOs assign a primary care physician (PCP) to the plan participant. This PCP is charged with providing routine medical care to the subscriber and serves as a "gatekeeper," steering the subscriber to appropriate and cost-effective care should referral to specialists be required.

HMOs can take a variety of forms. The *individual practice association model* (IPA) is one in which an HMO contracts with individual physicians or associations of individual physicians to provide services to the health plan's subscribers. A *group model* is one where the HMO purchases services from an independent multispecialty group of physicians. A *network model* HMO is similar to the group model, but more than one multispecialty group practice provides services to members. Yet another variation in organizational design and service delivery is the *staff model* HMO. Here, rather than the HMO contracting with independent physicians or multispecialty groups, the physicians are full-time, bona fide employees of the HMO that pays their salaries. As many HMOs have grown, the clear distinction between individual practice model, group model, network model, and staff model has been somewhat blurred. The dramatic and ongoing growth of various health systems has meant the aggregation and merging of these disparate models.

Health Maintenance Organization Benefits

As mentioned earlier, most managed care providers offer broader health care coverage especially in the areas of wellness and preventive care. Often a fundamental difference is the manner in which one accesses the delivery of care. At the time of initial enrollment in the plan, the subscriber and his or her dependents select a PCP who is responsible as the primary caregiver for most routine medical care. This PCP is the person to make referrals and provide authorization for specialty care when needed. Different managed care organizations have different approaches to the process by which specialty care referrals can occur. For instance, some managed care companies publish a listing of specialists in the network and leave a referral to the discretion of the PCP. Other companies have this function centralized and require the assignment of specialty authorizations to a centralized unit that ensures steerage to the most cost-effective specialty providers. This centralized approach to specialty care can be beneficial in ensuring that serious illnesses are directed to a "center of excellence," a provider known to have unique procedures or competence in treating certain types of injury or illnesses.

Wellness and preventive care benefits are key coverages that HMOs (and other managed care plans) provide that traditional plans have not provided. Expenses for these services have not been historically covered in the traditional fee-for-service type of plan:

- Routine physical exams.
- Preventive screenings and diagnostic tests for early detection of certain diseases.
- Prenatal and well-baby care.
- Immunizations for prevention of diseases (particularly for children).
- Vision and dental checkups.
- Allowances for health club memberships.

See Chapter 12 for a complete discussion of preventive care benefits and strategies.

Because of the growing understanding of the benefits of preventive care, some states have enacted legislation requiring all health plans to offer certain benefits such as childhood immunizations and screenings for diseases that clearly would benefit from early detection. Hence, some of the distinctions between plan models in terms of benefits offered have been blurred as preventive measures have been added to the traditional insurance plans.

Preferred Provider Organizations (PPOs)

A preferred provider organization is formed when a group of medical providers such as hospitals and doctors contract with employers, insurance companies, or other plan sponsors to provide various medical services. The medical providers usually offer discounted pricing because of the volume of business received from the contracting organizations. The medical providers are reimbursed on a fee-for-service basis, but the fees are lower than in a traditional plan because of the negotiated discounts.

Preferred Provider Organization Benefits

Benefits provided through a preferred provider organization vary depending on the capabilities of the providers in the organization and the overall size of the PPO. A PPO could be the only source of medical care for an employee group, or the PPO may be one choice among several medical plans the employer offers. Alternatively, a PPO may provide the in-network benefit for a point of service plan, described below.

Point of Service (POS) Programs

Another type of managed care program is the point of service program. This managed care product is somewhat of a cross between an HMO and the comprehensive major medical plan. Essentially, the plan sponsor either contracts with a number of health care providers or a managed care company to provide cost-effective medical care through a preferred provider organization of health care providers. Plan participants are free to use the network of preferred providers when they need health care. Alternatively, the plan participants can decide to utilize other medical providers who are not included in the network. However, if the participant uses out-of-network providers, he or she incurs additional expense in the form of greater deductibles and copayments. It is at the point of service that the plan participant is making the decision whether to remain in-network and receive a higher level of coverage or, alternatively, to select a medical provider who is out-of-network and be personally responsible for a larger share of the cost for this care. The POS program can be an attractive delivery system for participants who do not want to be restricted to receiving medical care only from network providers yet still would like to receive the same coverage and wellness benefits provided through a managed care system. This system of health care delivery suits some medical providers who are willing to join the PPO and provide medical services for discounted fees but are unwilling to assume the financial risks of HMO participation where a monthly fee is often paid to the doctor for each member regardless of the frequency of visits and the care provided. However, the particular financial arrangement and whether service providers bear any financial risk can be determined in various ways. These points are discussed later in the chapter.

Point of Service Plan Benefits

The point of service plan is a hybrid of sorts, offering managed care case-management features and health maintenance approaches to medical care within the network but allowing plan participants the added flexibility of going outside the network if they are willing to bear a larger share of the cost for such flexibility. The extent to which subscribers are either penalized for going outside the network or rewarded for staying within the network can be determined by the deductible and coinsurance levels that are set. An organization could have varying reasons for setting the deductible and coinsurance levels either low or high. Also, these coinsurance levels can vary by various types of medical services. For instance, if the network of medical providers is not particularly well-developed in certain specialty areas, such as pediatrics, a company would find it difficult to penalize employees for not utilizing an in-network benefit. Another example could be that on certain types of medical services, for instance, psychiatric benefits, a company may perceive it as intrusive to require use of an in-network benefit. This may be particularly true if the POS plan is newly installed and would result in disruption of ongoing treatment. Some organizations have used POS plans as a means to transition from an indemnity plan to an HMO. In this situation, deductibles and coinsurance might initially be set slightly higher than in the traditional indemnity plan for employee relations reasons and later be increased as utilization grows in the managed care environment and employees become more comfortable with using in-network providers.

Integrated Health Systems

As the managed care delivery structures continue to grow, what started out as HMOs or PPOs are evolving into larger health systems that may include a managed care company, various physician and multispecialty practices, as well as entire hospitals and ancillary service providers. The preceding discussion of health care delivery structures is not meant to provide strict classifications into which each health plan must be distinctly assigned. Rather, it is hoped this characterization will be helpful in understanding basic differences between existing health care delivery systems and a starting point for understanding the relative merits of alternative designs. An employer's health plan should be configured matching the plan sponsor's objectives and assisting in meeting total compensation and human resource objectives.

Special Provisions

Mental Health/Substance Abuse Benefits

Special provisions and limitations historically have applied to mental illness and substance abuse (drug/alcohol treatment) benefits. These limitations were a very common plan design feature. In 1993 for example, 97 percent of participants in medium and large private establishment health plans were eligible for some level of outpatient mental health services, while only 3 percent had the same benefits as those for other illnesses.[2] Similarly, while 98 percent of full-time participants in medium and large private establishment medical plans in 1993 were covered for inpatient detoxification for alcohol and drug abuse treatment, 28 percent and 29 percent, respectively, had the same level of coverage for these illnesses as they had for other illnesses.[3] However, on September 26, 1996, the Mental Health Parity Act (MHPA) was signed into law. The MHPA requires that annual or lifetime limits on mental health benefits be no lower than that of the dollar limits for medical and surgical benefits offered by the group health plan. The MHPA applied to group health plans for plan years beginning on or after January 1, 1998 and contained a "sunset" provision providing that the parity requirements do not apply to benefits received on or after September 30, 2001. Many believe these parity requirements will be extended or made permanent. The MHPA does not apply to benefits for substance abuse or chemical dependency.

In the past, substance abuse benefits were not separately delineated in many plans but covered under mental and nervous benefits. However, because new treatment approaches have been developed and because the federal government and some states have enacted legislation mandating minimum levels of treatment for mental and nervous benefits, more plans separate these benefits today into distinct categories. Most plans in the past had limitations on both mental/nervous and drug/alcohol benefits that resulted in greater cost sharing by the participant. There were two common forms of limitations on these benefits. The first was to set the coinsurance at a higher level, say 50 percent in a 20 percent reimbursement plan, and establish an annual maximum for this benefit, such as $1,500. Additionally, a different lifetime maximum applied to this benefit, say $10,000. A

---

2 Carolyn Pemberton and Deborah Holmes, eds. Cecelia Silverman, Michael Anzick, Sarah Boyce, Sharyn Campbell, Ken McDonnell, Annmarie Reilly, and Sarah Snider, *EBRI Databook on Employee Benefits*, 3rd ed. (Washington, DC: Education and Research Fund, 1995), p. 328.
3 Ibid., p. 328.

second form of limitation was to set a maximum number of outpatient visits per year, such as 20 visits, with a maximum covered charge, such as $50. Similarly with inpatient coverage on the basic hospitalization portion of the plan, it was common to have a lifetime cap on this specific type of care and a maximum number of days allowable per plan year or calendar year. Since the MHPA prohibited specific dollar limitations for mental and nervous benefits different from other medical and surgical benefits offered by the plan, many plans eliminated such provisions but kept limitations in terms of days of treatment and outpatient visits. Some plans have used this same approach for substance abuse benefits although dollar limitations are still permissible.

"Carve Out" and Separate Management of Costly Expense Items

Many organizations have "carved out" prescription drug benefits from their plans and are managing those benefits on a separate basis. This is because prescription drugs have been among the fastest growing cost components in many medical plans. The emergence of drug management firms provides opportunities for cost savings through pharmacy networks, mail-order discount programs, inclusion of generic drug substitutes, drug formulary management, prescription utilization review, and disease management programs. Mental health and substance abuse benefits also have been carved out and are separately managed by many medical plans.

VARIATIONS IN PLAN DESIGN

The preceding descriptions of benefit provisions are intended to acquaint the reader with standard types of medical plans. The reader should be aware that there is wide latitude in design alternatives within the frameworks described. For instance, with the traditional prepayment and indemnity products, which benefits are included in the medical/surgical component and which benefits are covered by supplemental major medical can dramatically alter the nature of a plan. Through the use of its fee schedule, an insurer might exert greater control over provider price escalation, including procedures in the medical/surgical component. An alternate design could include more items from the medical/surgical component in the supplemental major medical portion, subjecting these to deductibles and coinsurance, or the plan could characterize hospitalization benefits as the only form of basic benefits. Some supplemental major medical plans, called wraparounds, only supplement basic hospitalization benefits.

With a comprehensive plan, variation as to which benefits are subject to deductibles and coinsurance can lead to very different plan designs. Some comprehensive plans, the so-called "full-pay hospital" plans, waive deductibles and coinsurance on hospitalizations, making the comprehensive plan resemble a first-dollar plan. Even payments to providers can combine different reimbursement systems, with payment on a fee schedule up to a certain level and then above that on a reasonable and customary basis, with subscribers paying a deductible and coinsurance at the reasonable and customary level. Some flexible benefit programs offer plan participants various alternative comprehensive plans with different levels of deductibles and coinsurance.

Accordingly, a plan sponsor can use this flexibility in designing plans that best suit the organization's objectives. The sponsor should consider designs that balance human resource and organization goals with administrative, communication, and funding realities.

UNDERWRITING AND FUNDING APPROACHES

Health care cost control has become of paramount importance as the cost of medical care has increased. Medical costs are a significant expense and a risk exposure that can have a substantial impact on an organization's overall compensation costs and operating results. In light of this, it is not surprising that many organizations have looked to innovative financial arrangements at the same time they restructure benefit design and health care delivery.

Community Rating

The early prepayment plans offered by the Blue Cross and Blue Shield organizations were offered as community-rated products. Under this financing approach, all insureds in a given geographic area paid a uniform rate. Because the Blue Cross and Blue Shield organizations were chartered with the intention of providing insurance to all those seeking coverage and because they negotiated contractual reimbursement arrangements with providers, this method of underwriting was possible in the early years when costs were lower and the Blue Cross/Blue Shield plans were the principal underwriter of medical care. HMOs at their inception also used community rating and, in order to be qualified under the Health Maintenance Organization Act of 1973, were required to adhere to specific rules regarding it. These requirements were relaxed with the 1988 amendments to the Health Maintenance Organization Act. Community rating is still used for individual subscribers and for smaller group contracts. However, community rating is much less popular in the group insurance market where larger organizations prefer to experience rate rather than be rated with other organizations, which potentially have less-favorable risks.

Adjusted Community Rating

At times, an insurer will offer a plan sponsor insurance rates that have been calculated using adjusted community rates. The baseline claims data used to establish these rates are the claims and utilization patterns in the community at large. However, based on certain favorable characteristics of the plan sponsor's own past claims data, the insurer is willing to offer more favorable rates, which have been approved by the state's insurance department and the insurer's underwriting department, for a client that exhibits favorable claims characteristics.

Experience Rating

An organization that is willing to proactively manage its health care costs through benefit plan redesign and innovative delivery of care will seek to capture the cost savings generated by these actions. An experience-rated plan uses recent claims and utilization data of a particular organization to establish the appropriate insurance rates for a future time period. If an organization has had a history of favorable claims experience, the experience-rated insurance product may offer substantial cost advantages over an underwriting approach that uses aggregate community claims experience to establish insurance rates.

Cost-Plus and Self-Insured Approaches

An organization of sufficient size may finance its health care benefits using a cost-plus or self-insured approach. Under such a scenario, the organization will pay for the actual claims of its group, along with an administrative charge to an insurer or third-party administrator who handles claims processing. Such an agreement is often called an administrative services only (ASO) agreement. Under this type of arrangement, it is important to understand provider reimbursement methods. For instance, are hospital daily room costs based on actual charges or a discounted amount below charges? Will the hospital be paid for each day a patient is hospitalized, or will the hospital be paid for a fixed number of days commensurate with the expected length of stay usually associated with the medical condition and its course of treatment? This latter approach would give the hospital an incentive to ensure that patient lengths of stay are in line with practice norms.

Stop-Loss Insurance

If an organization utilizes a cost-plus or self-insured method of financing, it may choose to limit its potential aggregate medical claims exposure by purchasing insurance that would make payment if claims exceeded a certain predetermined amount for the entire group. This insurance coverage for capping the total claims experience of the group is known as *aggregate stop loss*. A firm also might limit its liability using *specific stop loss*. Specific stop loss sets a limit on the amount that a plan sponsor will pay for an individual case. If a catastrophic medical case occurs, the employer will only be responsible for paying covered medical costs on that individual case up to the stop-loss amount.

Because the insurer is assuming risk for excess claims, the contractual document will clearly define when the insurer assumes the risk. It is extremely important when contracting for stop-loss protection to carefully analyze terms and conditions to ensure that the intentions for protecting against loss are matched by the insurer's policy. For instance, the period for claims coverage could be specified either on the basis of when a claim is incurred or when a claim is paid. It is also important to ensure that definitions for coverable expenses in the employer's health plan match coverages in the stop-loss agreement. Medical plans and stop-loss coverage typically exclude medical care that is deemed experimental in nature. Do both documents have the same definition of experimental medical care? Other issues to examine would be whether specific subscribers undergoing treatment are excluded from the stop-loss coverage and how the run-out of claims payments going beyond the stop-loss coverage period are handled.

PROVIDER REIMBURSEMENT APPROACHES

Fee-for-Service

Under this payment method, health care providers charge separately each time services for care are rendered. This is a common reimbursement method under traditional indemnity plans. Providers commonly set their own charge and are paid accordingly. Sometimes, insurers negotiate a fee schedule that establishes the maximum amount the plan will pay for any given medical procedure or service. Fee-for-service has been the most common provider reimbursement approach for the traditional prepayment, indemnity, and comprehensive plan designs.

Capitation

Under capitation, providers are paid a set amount (generally monthly for PCPs) for each plan participant, regardless of the number of visits or services provided.

Capitation payment methods are used extensively by HMOs. This form of payment shifts some risk to the medical provider, who accepts the capitation amount, assuming the increased enrollment will level out the risks. Some plans reimburse PCPs and certain specialists using capitation, and have a fee schedule for other medical specialists.

Other Provider Reimbursement Approaches

Health Care Purchasing Cooperatives/Coalitions

Some employers have banded together into purchasing cooperatives to have greater health care buying power in the marketplace. Such an arrangement is used to gain favorable pricing from medical providers because of the large volume of business that can be supplied. This means of purchasing health care can be particularly attractive to a small employer who would not be able to procure the same discount on services that a large employer could. In some ways, the insurance company or managed care provider plays this role for smaller groups. However, the emergence of health care purchasing cooperatives provides another alternative for employers to negotiate pricing with medical providers.

DEVELOPING A HEALTH CARE STRATEGY

Developing a health care strategy for providing employee health and medical care benefits can be viewed as a program for managing risk exposures on a variety of levels. In its most elementary form, managing this risk involves a three-pronged strategy. First, the organization sponsoring the plan must decide what mode of health care delivery system will be used. Second, the organization must decide on the benefits that will be provided through the selected system. Third, the plan sponsor must decide what contractual, financial, or payment arrangement will be negotiated with insurers or providers of medical care. Negotiation of the financial arrangement also includes what level of risk is assumed by the plan sponsor and whether certain types or levels of risk will be shifted to a third party such as an insurer or the providers of the medical care itself. Increasingly, plan sponsors shift some of this risk to ensure that medical providers have a stake in providing cost-effective and quality care. All three of these macro decisions involve many other tiers of decisions at the micro level, which can have a profound impact on the levels of risk assumed and the financial costs assumed by the plan sponsor.

Designing the Plan and Delivery System

Multitiered Decisions

Not only is the plan sponsor selecting one of the delivery systems discussed previously, but the plan sponsor has latitude to select various plan designs offered by alternate delivery systems or to include plan-specific provisions or procedures particular to the employer group. Unless state law requires certain benefits, an employer quite often has flexibility to design its own schedule of benefits, assuming it is of sufficient size to gain this degree of customization by an insurer or managed care company. At times, even state insurance law is not an immovable constraint because certain administrative service financing arrangements exempt plans from state insurance mandates. Limitations on specific coverages, uses of deductibles/co-payments, and the systems for case management and precertification can profoundly impact both risk exposure and cost. The delivery system and plan design, its oversight, and financial incentives also can have behavioral impacts on plan participants influencing the utilization of health care services.

Self-Administration, Third-Party Administrators, and Unbundled Services

The decision to purchase an assembled delivery system from an insurer or managed care company, or to directly contract with providers is generally dependent on employer size and the geographical concentrations of an organization's employees. When an employer is of sufficient size, it might want to deal directly with medical providers and eliminate the costs associated with the intermediary insurer. Even if an employer does not want to assume the burden of self-administration, it is not necessary to purchase all medical care management services through a single provider. An employer can decide to unbundle specific services that might be more effectively performed by separate entities or purchase an integrated set of services or programs through one provider. Moving specific, specialized functions to third-party vendors with specific expertise in one area can sometimes address specific goals. At the very least, an employer should understand the costs of these services if they are left bundled with the insurer and review claims and other reports to evaluate the services' effectiveness and contributions to cost control.

Use of Multiple Plan Offerings and Single or Multiple Administrators

Medical care delivery systems and benefit design are not an "all-or-nothing" decision for many large employers. Though some employers place their entire block of business with a single insurer or managed care company, many other employers have configured a variety of health plan alternatives and give employees the choice of selecting the health plan that best meets their individual needs. This can be accomplished through a simple choice of medical plan options or through a flexible benefit plan. In large part because of limited dollars available to expand benefit programs and a recognition that a diverse workforce may have varying benefit needs, flexible benefit programs proliferated in the 1980s. In a flex plan, employees are allocated a set amount generally in the form of credits or dollars from the employer, which they can "spend" to select the benefits and plan options of their choice or receive those credits in the form of cash if not spent on benefits. Nevertheless, many managed care companies and insurers offer employers an array of multiple plan designs. Price concessions are often offered if an employer agrees to place the entire block of business with a single administrative entity. An employer must balance the price concessions it will receive and assess the effectiveness of the administrative entity at managing health care costs against the loss of competition that occurs when multiple plan offerings through various administrators are eliminated.

Pricing Plan Options and Designing Employer Subsidies

Regardless of whether multiple administrators or a single administrator is used for separate plan offerings, the plan sponsor must look at the pricing of plan options and make decisions regarding the form and amount of employer subsidy provided to employees. An employer offering a flexible benefit program may price various plan options at prevailing market rates, assign all employees an equal credit amount, and allow them to spend the credits as they prefer. Other employers provide a direct subsidy to their medical plans and only show employees the remaining employee costs they will be required to pay. Some employers subsidize family contracts to a greater extent than single coverage. The employer also must decide how to relate the subsidy to each medical plan option. Plan pricing will affect employee selection patterns. Premiums are impacted by the level of deductibles and co-payments that have been included in the front-end plan design. Accordingly, an employer can determine whether plan costs and certain benefits are being borne by those utilizing those particular benefits or are being spread over the employee group at large.

The Effects of Multiple Plan Offerings on Employee Selection Patterns and Pricing

The offering of multiple benefit offerings can create an exodus of favorable risks from existing offerings and result in price escalations for those who choose to stay with a previously offered plan. In some cases, the offering of a new plan at favorable pricing can cause such dramatic migration out of a plan that the remaining plan will experience a price spiral that causes termination of the plan. This was particularly true in the mid-1980s for many employers who offered traditional indemnity plans. The offering of either a less expensive comprehensive plan or an HMO can result in those employees with low utilization for major services migrating to the less costly plans, seeking to reduce their expenditures on monthly health care premiums. With this loss of favorable risks, the indemnity plan retains less favorable risks with higher utilization patterns. Because there is a smaller pool of favorable risks in the plan over which to spread plan costs, the premiums charged to those who remain increase. This increase in plan costs results in another group of more favorable risks choosing to leave the plan rather than bear the increased costs of the plan. Again costs increase, giving further incentive for favorable risks to migrate from the plan. Ultimately, a cost spiral like this will cause a plan to become prohibitively expensive and result in its demise.

Designing the Underwriting and Financial Arrangements

As indicated in the discussion of alternative financing techniques, an employer can dramatically alter the financial arrangement of its medical benefits program by determining the amount of risk it will accept. The strategic issue is to select a financial arrangement that controls costs and allows management to assume the level of risk that it believes appropriate for its employee group. The financial arrangement selected can have a behavioral impact on both the providers managing care and the insurer or administrator responsible for management of the plan. Increasingly, employers have explored arrangements that shift more risk to health care providers and that promote incentives to provide quality care. Much research is being done on measuring quality of care and developing information systems that can be used to evaluate cost and quality of care (see Chapter 9 on Quality of Care).

The financial strategy for a medical benefits program will have multiple tiers. This is particularly true if multiple plan options are available and employees choose between plan offerings. Plan pricing and plan offerings can alter enrollment patterns and affect the effectiveness of a given financial arrangement or risk-management strategy.

Determining cost-effective medical providers and health plans is not an easy exercise. Certain plans will attract employees from certain demographic and geographical constituencies because of plan benefits or the convenience of provider locations. Health care costs are directly correlated with age, in that older individuals tend to need more care and need to access more extensive and thus more expensive care. Likewise, there can be regional differences in the cost of medical care. Sometimes base premium costs or allocated costs per participant are not the best indicator of cost-effective medical care. Analyzing plan costs by adjusting for demographic, geographic, and other variables in the plan population is the best way to evaluate the cost efficiency.

Measuring Performance and Managing the Plan

A final attribute of health care strategy is to create a system of monitoring and measuring the attainment of plan objectives. It is also important to have a system of controls that ensures that the plan is being effectively managed. A well-developed plan design is of little use if a third-party administrator is unable to administer the design as it was intended. A system for auditing plan results, ensuring quality outcomes and reporting utilization is necessary. For this reason, any delegation of responsibilities for health plan management should involve negotiation on the management reporting responsibilities of the administrator and the performance standards it is expected to achieve. Assigning financial penalties or providing rewards associated with these performance standards can be very effective. For instance, with a traditional insured product, a plan sponsor can require claims payment within a certain number of days for a percent of the claims. With a managed care provider operating a staff model HMO, reporting could be required on the telephone systems for contacting PCPs. There could be performance criteria on the amount of time it takes to reach a physician by phone, and scheduling standards for the amount of time between the initial call and an available appointment.

SUMMARY AND CONCLUSIONS

There are many different approaches to providing medical benefits to plan participants. Some of these approaches are less popular today because of various trends in medical care, particularly the need to provide a delivery system that controls costs and provides appropriate care. Nevertheless, it is important to understand the different models for providing medical benefits and the historical context out of which these plan designs have emerged. The plan structure, delivery system, and employer subsidy chosen can have important implications on the plan selection decisions of employees and the choices they make in procuring individual medical care for themselves and their families. These choices will affect the effectiveness of the plan in meeting human resource and budget objectives. The financial arrangements to insure the plan or pay for care are also critical. The plan sponsor must decide how to insure the plan and how to pay providers, and then must negotiate price. Any financial arrangement involves a decision on what amount of risk will be retained by the employer and what amount of risk will be transferred to another party—whether an insurer, third-party administrator (TPA), managed care company, or medical provider. Structuring the financial arrangement properly can drive the incentives that promote effective cost and quality management of medical care. Development of a health care strategy involves not only strategic decisions at the macro level, but a series of micro decisions that together should ensure the plan meets its goals and objectives. Any plan design, delivery system, and financial arrangement that is configured to manage this risk and meet organizational objectives is of little consequence unless the program is effectively executed and managed at all levels and from multiple vantage points. It is precisely the challenge to create and effectively manage a plan from the multitude of possible configurations in the realms of plan design, health care delivery systems, and financial arrangements that makes medical care benefits management an exciting area in which to work.

B I B L I O G R A P H Y

Association of Private Pension and Welfare Plans (APPWP). *Health Notes*, September 15, 2000.

Department of Labor, *General Facts on Women & Job Based Health Benefits*. April 2000.

Geisel, Jerry. "Health Plan Inflation Held to 8% in 1993," *Business Insurance*, February 14, 1994.

Goldsmith, Jeff C., PhD; Michael J. Goran, MD; and John G. Nackel. "Managed Care Comes of Age." *Healthcare Forum Journal*, September–October 1995.

Herzfeld, Jeff. "Optimizing the Value of a Pharmacy Benefit Management Plan." *Managing Employee Health Benefits* 3, No. 10 (Fall 1995).

Hewitt Associates. *Employers to Face Double Digit Health Care Cost Increases for Third Consecutive Year*, October 23, 2000.

KPMG Peat Marwick. "Health Benefits in 1995." *Benefits Spectrum*, October 1995.

O'Leary, James S. "The Evolving Role of Pharmacy Benefits Management Firms in a Managed Care Environment." *Benefits Quarterly* 11, No. 3, (Third Quarter 1995).

Pemberton, Carolyn and Deborah Holmes, eds. Cecelia Silverman, Michael Anzick, Sarah Boyce, Sharyn Campbell, Ken McDonnell, Annmarie Reilly, and Sarah Snider. *EBRI Databook on Employee Benefits*. 3rd ed. Washington, DC: Education and Research Fund, 1995.

Reiff, Michael and L. Kenneth Sperling, CEBS. "Measuring the Savings from Managed Care: Experience at Citibank." *Benefits Quarterly* 11, No. 2 (Second Quarter 1995).

CHAPTER 7

Understanding Managed Care Health Plans: The Managed Care Spectrum

Phillip D. Pierce

INTRODUCTION

At the start of the new millennium, the burden of health care benefit costs, which had abated slightly in the early 1990s, had begun to increase at double-digit levels more common during the last quarter of the 20th century. Despite historic efforts at cost containment and despite the considerable attention focused on health care reform in recent years, health care expenses are now the largest single nonwage labor cost for many organizations. Both private- and public-sector employers have been forced to evaluate the growing variety of "managed care" plans that have evolved over the past two decades.

Since 1973, with the passage of the Health Maintenance Organization (HMO) Act, which provided federal initiatives for the establishment of HMOs, many alternatives to traditional health insurance have evolved. Under the various names of preferred provider organizations (PPOs), exclusive provider organizations (EPOs), point-of-service (POS) programs, and swing-out (or open-ended) HMOs, managed care programs now dominate as the standard form of health care benefit plan offered by plan sponsors to their participants, covering almost 90 percent of total non-governmental health benefit enrollees.

In 1999, an estimated 38 percent of covered workers were enrolled in PPOs, 28 percent in HMOs, 25 percent in POS plans, with barely 10 percent still enrolled in traditional indemnity plans. By contrast, enrollment shares in PPO, POS and HMO plans were 28 percent 31 percent and only 14 percent, respectively, in 1996.[1] While HMO enrollments were flattening by 2000, the rapid nationwide growth of HMOs during the late 1980s and 1990s reflects the increased importance that plan sponsors have placed on managed care in controlling costs and improving quality of health benefit plans. Total enrollment in HMOs grew from approximately 33.3 million members in 1990 to more than 81.3 million by the end of the decade.[2]

Yet, the widespread dominance of managed care has not altered the disagreement among employers, consultants, health care providers, managed care companies, insurers, and governmental regulators about how to define managed care and how to identify its fundamental characteristics. The purpose of Chapter 7 is to provide a history of the development of managed care plans, as well as to introduce a framework within which to analyze their fundamental characteristics, particularly as compared to traditional indemnity health plans. Chapter 8 examines how managed care plans are designed to save money and how managed care plans are increasingly focusing on quality and value.

These chapters are not an exhaustive study of all managed care strategies available today. Managed care has become an industry of its own, and hundreds of managed care companies, insurers, third-party administrators (TPAs), HMOs, PPOs, and even medical provider groups have developed their own sets of products.[3] This chapter focuses on the most commonly recognized forms of managed care and provides a basis from which the reader can identify and evaluate the many products and services.

ECONOMIC TRENDS FACING THE EMPLOYER

During the 1990s, both public and private employers in the United States faced multiple economic and financial challenges, in spite of broad-based economic prosperity within the country. Powerful economic trends are forcing corporations to reduce operating costs and improve productivity in

---

1 Kaiser Family Foundation and Health Research and Education Trust, as quoted in *Managed Care Week*, Vol. 9, No. 38, November 1, 1999; Atlantic Information Service, Inc., Washington DC; www.aispub.com.

2 Interstudy's *Competitive Edge HMO Directory*, 9, as quoted in *Managed Care Week*, Vol. 9, No. 34, September 27, 1999; Atlantic Information Service, Inc., Washington DC; www.aispub.com.

3 For example, see Mary Jaklevic, "Docs Try To Own Managed Care," *Modern Health Care*, Vol. 25, April 24, 1995, and Bruce Goldfarb, "Corporate Health Care Mergers," *Medical World News*, Vol. 34, February 1993.

order to survive in an increasingly competitive global environment. Simultaneously, employers face labor shortages entering the 21st century, with unemployment levels near record lows in many key positions that require specialized expertise critical to businesses' new growth and development. Plan sponsors are caught in the paradox of needing to maintain a trained, productive workforce while limiting health care benefit expenses. Creative and cost-effective approaches are needed to attract, retain, and motivate talented people who are vital to corporations' and public-sector employers' success in today's economy. Some of the economic pressures facing employers are discussed below.

Federal Government Cost Shifting

Government-funded health care programs continue to experience escalating cost increases, particularly the Medicare and Medicaid programs. Attempts to contain federal health care expenditures have shifted costs indirectly and directly to the state and local governments and to the private sector. There is no doubt that private health care plans have borne the burden of federal cutbacks to Medicare providers. Squeezed by Medicare reimbursements that often are below their costs of operation, hospitals and physicians are forced to shift costs to other payers to make up for lost revenues.

Beginning with the Consolidated Omnibus Budget Reconciliation Act of 1985 (COBRA), federal legislation has shifted portions of Medicare costs directly to private employer plans. Federal law requires that active employees over age 65 select either Medicare or their employer's health plan as the primary source of medical coverage. Employers are prohibited from providing secondary or supplemental coverage to employees who select Medicare as their primary coverage. Because employer plans typically provide richer benefits and easier access to medical providers than Medicare, it is not surprising that many employees continue their primary coverage through their employer's plan. As a result, employers have been forced to accept greater responsibility for financing the medical care costs of an aging population.

Competitive Global Environment

U.S. companies also face increased economic pressure from new global competitors. In addition to dominant economic players in Western Europe and Japan, entrants from developing nations and former European communist bloc nations are playing a greater role in international production. Alliances among foreign capital markets, such as the European Economic

Community pact of 1992, test the ability of U.S. companies to compete with the collective strength of nations linked by free-trade agreements.

Furthermore, much of employees' medical care in competing foreign companies is provided through governmental programs (for example, Canada, Japan, Germany). Because medical care is often funded by federal or provincial taxes, the costs are less directly identifiable as part of a company's costs of production. Other top industrialized nations spend considerably less on a per capita basis for healthcare. In 1997, the United States per capita healthcare spending of $4,090 was 82 percent higher than Germany ($2,239), 95 percent higher than Canada ($2,095), 134 percent higher than Japan ($1,741), and more than 200 percent higher than the United Kingdom's ($1,347) per capita expenditures.[4]

In contrast, the United States is the only major industrial country in which employers bear most of the cost of their employees' health insurance—a clear competitive disadvantage. Thus, U.S. employers have a real incentive to investigate alternatives that can lower these costs while maintaining an attractive level of benefits for employees.

Shrinking Workforce

Both private- and public-sector employers are operating today with a tightening supply of trained labor for critical new positions. Since the 1970s, most industrialized nations—including the United States—have faced negative net population growth. In addition, the baby boom generation is now well into midlife and will start retiring in the next 5 to 10 years. Confronting a shrinking workforce, employers have been forced to offer more competitive wages and benefits in order to attract qualified employees. Acute labor shortages are projected in the areas of science and technology, health care, and hospitality services. Thus, employers must maintain competitive compensation packages to attract and maintain a stable and highly qualified workforce. Doing so will require employers to offer an enticing and well-developed package of employee benefits.

National Resources Spent on Health Care

As shown in Figure 7–1, national health care expenditures exceeded $1 trillion in 1996, an increase of 50 percent over the $699 billion spent in

---

4 *Multinational Comparisons of Health Care: Expenditures, Coverage and Outcomes*, The Commonwealth Fund, New York, New York; www.cmwf.com., as published in *Modern Healthcare*, Crain Communications, Chicago: July 19, 1999.

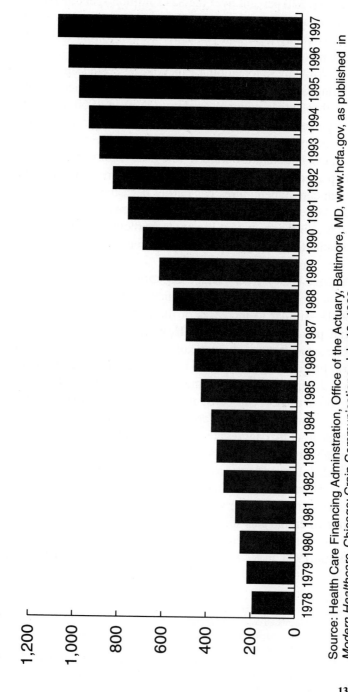

FIGURE 7-1

Growth in National Healthcare Expenditures over 20 years (U.S. 1978 through 1997)

Billions $

1978 1979 1980 1981 1982 1983 1984 1985 1986 1987 1988 1989 1990 1991 1992 1993 1994 1995 1996 1997

Source: Health Care Financing Adminstration, Office of the Actuary, Baltimore, MD, www.hcfa.gov, as published in *Modern Healthcare*, Chicago: Crain Communications, July 19, 1999.

1990 and 320 percent over the $247 million spent in 1980. While growth in national health care expenditures had dropped in the late 1990s, to approximately 5 percent per annum, the rate was still more than double the general consumer price index (CPI).

While these total dollar expenditures seem staggering, perhaps more startling is the fact that health care costs, which accounted for about 5.2 percent of gross national product (GNP) in 1960, consumed more than 13.5 percent of GNP by 1997, according to Department of Labor statistics.

Put simply, health care expenditures are taking a greater share of available national resources. While little argument exists about the importance of delivering high-quality health care, this dramatic increase in health care expenditures has hardly been the result of national deliberation. More resources devoted to health care means less spent on education and training, investment in new technology and research, which are also essential to keeping American companies competitive and growing.

Impact on the Plan Sponsor

Employee health benefit costs increased an average of 21.6 percent in 1990[5]—similar to increases of the last 20 years, except for a couple of brief periods of lower rates. However, by mid-1993, most health care trend rates dropped dramatically, and a national study by the consulting firm Foster-Higgins reported that average health costs actually decreased by 1.1 percent in 1994. Some observers suggested that this swing was a temporary effect caused by industry efforts to slow cost increases during the federal health care reform debate. However, the Foster-Higgins study pointed out that aggregate costs were flattened more by the shift in membership from traditional indemnity health plans to managed care plans, which exhibited lower average per capita costs.

However, by the late 1990s, health care cost trend rates were rising again, particularly for those employers with significant portions of their covered employees still in indemnity benefit programs. A William Mercer national study showed average total health benefit costs increasing 6.1 percent in 1998 and 7.3 percent in 1999.[6] A Towers Perrin survey estimated

---

5 The 1994 study conducted by Foster-Higgins also showed that all types of health plans actually had increased costs, but the rate of increase for managed care plans was significantly below that for standard indemnity benefits. As reported in *Managed Care Week*, February 27, 1995, Atlantic Information Services, Inc., Washington, DC.

6 William M. Mercer, Inc.'s *14th Annual National Survey of Employer-Sponsored Health Plans*, as published in *Managed Care Week*, Vol. 9, No. 45, December 20, 1999; Atlantic Information Service, Inc., Washington DC; www.aispub.com.

that health cost increases for 2000 would average 9 percent for most managed care plans and 11 percent for traditional indemnity plans.[7]

Even if aggregate health benefit cost trend rates stay below the levels of the 1970s and 1980s, the compounded results are clearly seen on the "bottom line." Health care benefit costs represented about 5 percent of corporate profits in the 1960s; that figure increased to between 25 percent and 50 percent of earnings in the 1990s.[8] For many smaller, growing companies, this financial burden can threaten the very survival of the firm, and even the country's largest corporations feel the need to actively pursue new and dramatic means of delivering their employees' health care in more cost-effective ways.

So employers continue to face a challenging and delicate balance in the new millennium: effectively managing health care costs while maintaining value and quality.

THE DEVELOPMENT AND GROWTH OF MANAGED CARE

History of Managed Care

In the strictest sense, the very earliest forms of group health insurance were managed care. Such insurance was started as a prepaid health plan, under a contract with Baylor University Hospitals, in the late 1920s. This led to the eventual development of today's Blue Cross/Blue Shield plans, most of which were started as prepaid plans.[9] However, these early prepaid plans differed greatly from today's managed care programs, in that they had no provider restrictions or utilization management programs. See Chapter 6 for a discussion of the early medical plans.

Insurance companies introduced major medical and comprehensive medical plans in the 1950s and 1960s, and group health coverage grew tremendously. However, as medical plan costs began to spiral upward, the health insurance industry was compelled to start addressing employer concerns. During the 1970s, most traditional health insurers developed few products to compete directly with the newly emerging HMOs, preferring instead to encourage clients to use plan design techniques alone to

---

7 Towers Perrin *2000 Health Care Cost Survey*, as published in *Managed Care Week*, Vol. 10, No. 3, January 17, 2000; Atlantic Information Service, Inc., Washington DC; www.aispub.com.

8 "Corporate Chiefs See Need for U.S. Health-Care Action," *The New York Times*, April 8, 1991, p. D4.

9 Today, most Blue Cross and Blue Shield plans offer a full range of managed care programs in addition to their traditional group health plans.

control cost increases. During this time, insurance companies, third-party administrators (TPAs), and the benefits consulting community recommended a variety of refinements—from greater employee contributions to expanded coverage for "cost-effective" forms of treatment, such as home health care or generic drugs.

However, for the most part, these efforts provided only short-term relief, and there is little evidence today to prove that plan design changes by themselves lead to long-term cost control of indemnity insurance plans. This lack of significant positive results from incremental efforts, coupled with growing competition from HMOs in the late 1970s and 1980s, forced insurers and many Blues plans to develop new managed care products and to add utilization management to their traditional programs. In many cases, they also pursued the purchase or development of wholly owned HMO plans.

In fact, the origins of today's managed care plans are founded in health maintenance organizations. The HMO concept is not new, and its earliest roots parallel those of the prepaid plans before World War II. While some of the earlier prepaid plans evolved into Blues plans, others evolved into HMOs. Several group practice-based HMOs were established in the Pacific Northwest and California, but the most well-known plan—Kaiser Permanente—was started in the early 1930s by Sidney Garfield, MD, to serve workers building an aqueduct to bring fresh water from the Colorado River to the city of Los Angeles. Kaiser opened to the general public following World War II and has continued on a steady growth that has brought it to a premier position nationally, serving almost 9 million members, in 11 states and the District of Columbia, by 1997.[10]

Other HMOs started in Washington, D.C., New York City, and Minneapolis, although their initial development was slow due to heavy opposition from the proponents of fee-for-service medicine. Major HMO growth began after the passage and enactment of the HMO Act of 1973 (P.L. 93-222). The act, named and promoted as the "health maintenance strategy" by Dr. Paul Ellwood, consisted of federal grants and loans to organizations wishing to investigate the feasibility of what would be called "federally qualified HMOs."

The federal government continued to nurture the growth of the HMO industry through the 1970s and early 1980s, and the Department of Health and Human Services issued hundreds of millions of dollars to start-up HMOs. However, as part of its overall reduction in federal government regulation, the Reagan Administration encouraged HMOs to

---

10 Kaiser Permanente Web site, www.kaiserpermanente.org., January 20, 2001.

look to private capital sources for future funding and expansion. Many smaller plans, especially those in early development, did not survive the 1980s, while others consolidated or were purchased by large national insurance companies that were expanding their managed care capabilities. In fact, by the end of 1998, corporate HMO chains and national insurance companies owned almost 75 percent of the total 902 licensed HMOs operating in the United States, and they accounted for nearly 85 percent of HMO enrollment nationwide.[11] Managed care had not only become mainstream health care, it had become big business.

In the late 1970s and 1980s, PPOs also grew rapidly, sponsored heavily by national insurance companies, third-party administrators, Blue Cross/Blue Shield plans, hospital organizations, and benefit consulting firms that needed to offer their customers alternatives to compete against emerging HMOs. PPOs gained quick popularity with employers that wanted cost savings but were unwilling to reduce provider choice as much as required in HMOs.

In 1983, there were about 115 PPOs.[12] By 1999, that number had increased to more than 1,125 plans, covering an estimated 98.3 million members nationwide, including those in specialty-only PPOs (e.g. mental health benefit treatment). Similar to the direction of HMO ownership, corporate chains and national insurance companies operated more than 70 percent of the PPO plans by 1999.[13]

Early PPO plans were primarily discounted fee arrangements with little focus on utilization control, and, as a result, many employers never achieved long-term cost savings. PPO companies responded by increasing the monitoring of utilization, implementing quality control, and surveying member satisfaction. In some structural aspects, PPOs resemble individual practice association (IPA) model HMOs, since both organizations contract with private practice physicians. However, opponents argue that PPOs are a weak form of managed care, coupled with rich benefits, which make them more expensive than HMOs. Nonetheless, PPOs are a significant part of the group health market today and will likely continue to be a factor for some time.

11 SMG Marketing Group, Inc., as reported in HMO-PPO Digest, *Managed Care Digest Series 1999*, published by Hoechst Marion Roussel, Kansas City, MO; www.managedcaredigest.com.

12 Dorothy L. Cobbs, *Preferred Provider Organizations: Strategies for Sponsors and Networks*, Chicago: American Hospital Publishing, Inc., 1989, p. 9.

13 SMG Marketing Group, Inc., as reported in *HMO-PPO Digest, Managed Care Digest Series 1999*, published by Hoechst Marion Roussel, Kansas City, MO; www.managedcaredigest.com.

Newest and fastest growing among managed care programs are point-of-service (POS) plans. In 1988, the first national POS plan was established for the employees of Allied Signal Corporation by CIGNA Health Plans. Since then, virtually all national managed care companies have developed POS products, and many local and regional HMO companies rely heavily on their POS products for new membership growth.

POS plans are a "hybrid" between the PPO and HMO approach. They offer members the choice of network or non-network providers, but members are required to select a primary care physician (PCP), who then handles basic medical services for the plan member and oversees access to more specialized levels of care, including hospitalization. POS plan designs are discussed in detail later in this chapter.

Over the last decade, there has been a dramatic shift from traditional indemnity plans to managed care programs, as shown in Figure 7–2. Virtually all forms of managed care show growth, with HMOs estimated at about 30 percent of total enrollment in 2000, up from 18 percent in 1998. POS plans, which only started in the late 1980s, garnered about 16 percent of total enrollment by the end of the decade, but it was PPO plans that experienced dramatic growth, rising from an estimated 11 percent of total enrollment in 1998 to 43 percent by 2000. Traditional indemnity plans, as stated earlier, have flattened out, to barely double-digit market share.[14,15]

Definition of Managed Care

For purposes of this chapter, *managed care* includes those programs intended to influence and direct the delivery of health care through one or more of the following techniques:

1. Plan-design features, including incentives and disincentives in the level of coverage, intended to redirect delivery of medical care;
2. Access restricted to a specified group of preselected providers; or,

---

14 A report by Group Health Association of America states that, at the end of 1994, more than 52 percent of HMOs offered a PPO option and 50 percent offered POS, both of which helped fuel a 13 percent membership growth from 1993. *Managed Care Week*, June 19, 1995, Atlantic Information Services, Inc., Washington, DC.

15 According to a KPMG report on market share, "Premium Growth Moderates: POS Plans Have Lowest Increase," *Managed Care Week*, January 3, 1994, Atlantic Information Services, Inc., Washington, D.C., and a Foster-Higgins study on 1994 market share, "Firms Use More Managed Care for Workers: PPOs Cheapest," *Managed Care Week*, February 27, 1995, Atlantic Information Services, Inc., Washington, DC. Year 2000 estimates from internal reports of Aetna Health Plans, Hartford, CT.

F I G U R E   7–2

Managed Care Market Share

Year	FFS	PPO	POS	HMO
1988	71%	11%	0%	18%
1991	53%	21%	3%	23%
1994	37%	24%	15%	26%
2000	11%	43%	16%	30%

Source: *Managed Care Week (1988–1994 data).* William Mercer 2000 *Employer-Sponsored Survey* (2000 data), www.wmmercer,com.

3. Utilization management (UM) programs, also called utilization review (UR), intended to preauthorize certain forms of medical care use and/or concurrently monitor the use of more expensive forms of care such as inpatient treatment.

This definition includes the broad range of "managed" indemnity plans, HMOs, PPOs, and the newer POS plans. There is disagreement within the industry about whether managed indemnity plans are managed care, particularly since there are no formal contractual obligations between providers and payers. Some experts like to classify managed indemnity plans and PPOs as "soft-form" managed care, and HMOs and POS plans as "stronger-form" managed care since they commonly include a "gatekeeper" to manage utilization.

While there is validity to this perspective, this chapter includes managed indemnity in the overall definition in order to provide a complete picture of all common forms of group health coverage today. Strong-form managed care arranges for selected providers to furnish comprehensive health care services to members under a set of formal programs of ongoing quality assurance and UM review, coupled with significant financial incentives for members to use contracted providers. In managed care programs, medical care is delivered by health care professionals who are committed to providing effective and efficient health care services, and who are willing to evaluate their own treatment patterns using medical outcomes data.

The medical provider—whether hospital or physician or ancillary provider—is an integral player in managed care plans. The provider's definition of managed care also differs from that noted above, referring to a patient's treatment program rather than to a specific benefit design or provider reimbursement method. The ultimate definition of managed care may need to be one that embraces some financial risk and responsibility, a particular set of benefits, quality of care mechanisms, and payment initiatives. Unfortunately, employers, payers, consumers, providers, and plan managers all see the puzzle based on their own perspective and experience, often without seeing the other pieces. In short, they often define managed care through the lenses of their own self-interest.[16]

The specific definition used for managed care is not as important as having an understanding of the context in which it is applied. Managed care is best understood as a *change in the process* of health care delivery, rather than as distinct products. The definition of managed care as a process helps the reader understand how a specific product operates and how it can best address a plan sponsor's objectives. This chapter provides the reader with effective tools to analyze the process of competing products and hopefully understand those characteristics that distinguish managed care products.

Health care delivery is a complex business, shaped in the local community and influenced by social environment, clinical culture, and economic realities. Most managed care companies, whether HMO or insurers, recognize the importance of developing an infrastructure in the local markets in which they operate, even if they are headquartered outside of the market. This local perspective means doing the following:

1. Understanding the local health care delivery systems.
2. Developing an appropriate panel of providers.
3. Incorporating the necessary managed care mechanisms in the network.

TYPES OF MANAGED CARE PLANS

Plan sponsors and participants often define managed care in terms of plan design characteristics, such as benefit levels. This is understandable since plan design is the simplest, and most visible, means of distinguishing various health plans.

Plan Design Considerations

Most managed care plans pay different benefits when members use non-contracted (out-of-network) providers instead of contracted (in-network) providers. This concept is called *steerage*. When members use in-network

---

16 Maria R. Traska, "Defining Managed Care," *Medical Benefits*, Vol. 8, No. 4, January/February 1991.

providers, the members pay less, the plan sponsor benefits from preferential prices, and providers theoretically gain more patients—but they are also typically obligated to follow utilization management procedures. Use of steerage is critical to maximize financial results of managed care. The managed care company's ability to negotiate favorable provider reimbursement rates is directly related to its ability to steer large numbers of members to contracted providers.

The degree of benefit differential depends on type of plan, but it generally ranges from 10 percent to 30 percent. Obviously, the greater the degree of benefit differential, the greater the degree of cost savings associated with the managed care program. Standard plan designs are frequently used by managed care companies since it makes the plans easier to administer for the plan sponsor as well as to communicate to members and providers. A plan sponsor must be careful about implementing nonstandard plan features since these require considerably greater advance preparation and ongoing support to minimize employee complaints and provider confusion.

Managed Indemnity

Managed indemnity is a very broad form of group health benefits and includes most standard fee-for-service plans. It is characterized by combining various stand-alone utilization management programs with traditional indemnity benefits often including:

1. Precertification of inpatient medical, surgical, and some other admissions; concurrent review of ongoing confinements for medical necessity; and discharge planning to encourage alternative treatment.
2. Precertification for selected outpatient surgical and diagnostic testing procedures, whether performed in a physician's office, hospital outpatient center, or ambulatory facility.
3. Second surgical opinion.
4. Case management for high-dollar cases.

Plan design features in a managed indemnity plan, as shown in Figure 7–3, need to consider the following points:

1. Deductibles should be increased to keep pace with inflation, or their cost-effectiveness deteriorates and the plan sponsor pays greater percentages of total health costs. Low deductibles do not encourage prudent use of the health care system.

F I G U R E   7–3

How Managed Indemnity Works

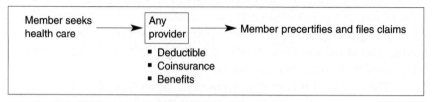

Sample Managed Indemnity Plan Design	
Plan Feature	**Benefits**
Annual Deductible	
Individual	$500 (applies to all services)
Family limit	2× or 3× individual level
Inpatient Deductible	$250 per confinement (no annual limit)
Coinsurance Rate	
Hospital inpatient	80%, after deductible
Emergency care	80%, after deductible
Physician office visit	80%, after deductible
Other physician	80%, after deductible
Mental/nervous/substance	
Inpatient	80%, after deductible
Outpatient	50%, after deductible
Prescription drugs	80%, after deductible
Skilled nursing facilities	80%, up to 120 days per confinement
Home health care	80%, up to 120 visits per calendar year
All other covered expenses	80%, after deductible
Coinsurance limit	$2,000 (due to member's 20% coinsurance)
Lifetime maximum benefit	Unlimited

2. Coinsurance percentages typically cover expenses at 80 percent after the deductible but at lower rates (e.g., 50 percent) for certain services, such as outpatient mental/nervous and substance abuse, subject to state requirements. (Managed indemnity plans generally include consumer advisory services as a supplement to their standard member services, which allow members to discuss health questions with a registered nurse or other clinically trained professional.)

3. Coinsurance limits, like deductibles, should be adjusted to keep pace with inflation. Once limits are met, all expenses are payable at 100 percent for the remainder of the calendar year.

Preferred Provider Organizations (PPOs)

PPOs provide comprehensive benefits through networks of contracted providers who have negotiated preferred prices with the managed care company. Network providers agree to preferred pricing with the expectation of increased member flow or maintenance of their existing member base. A PPO plan can either totally replace an existing health plan or be an option alongside other health plans. PPO members decide, at the time of services, whether to use a preferred provider within the established network or to use a nonpreferred provider.

PPO plans offer members some flexibility in choosing providers since they can see any provider within the network without a prior referral through a primary care physician; this "gatekeeper" procedure, which is required under most other forms of managed care, is discussed later in this chapter.

An additional advantage to a PPO member is that providers are typically required to handle all utilization management, claim submissions, and other paperwork when the member selects a network provider. The member must assume these responsibilities if he or she visits a nonpreferred provider.

A neutral level of benefits (e.g., 80 percent) typically applies for those services when a network provider is unavailable or if the network does not offer a specific type of medical service, so as not to penalize or reward the member for something that is outside the member's control.

Plan design under a PPO creates an incentive for use of a preferred provider:

1. Deductibles in the PPO typically feature two applications: an individual calendar-year deductible and an inpatient per-confinement deductible. The deductible for nonpreferred benefits should be significantly higher (e.g., twice as large) than the preferred deductible, to influence appropriate steerage.

2. The coinsurance differential is typically 20 percent between preferred and nonpreferred benefits, although some plan sponsors may opt for a 10 percent differential when introducing managed care for the first time to their employee population.

3. Coinsurance limits for nonpreferred benefits should be higher than for preferred benefits, to complement the steerage elements in deductibles and coinsurance rates.

In designing a PPO, employers or plan sponsors should determine which of the following approaches matches their own objectives:

1. An *incentive approach* is used when the plan sponsor's primary objective is to introduce managed care with the least employee disruption. It offers members richer preferred benefits while maintaining existing benefit levels for nonpreferred benefits. Compared to a standard comprehensive medical plan, which may pay 80 percent for covered services, an incentive approach would pay, for example, 100 percent for preferred expenses, while nonpreferred expenses would be maintained at the prior 80 percent benefit level. Note that premiums will likely increase, because of higher benefit payments, unless negotiated provider arrangements and the impact of utilization controls are sufficient to offset the benefit increase and additional administrative expenses.

2. A *disincentive approach* is used when the primary objective is cost savings, with preferred benefits equal to the prior plan and nonpreferred benefits being significantly reduced. Compared to the standard indemnity plan, preferred benefits remain at 80 percent after deductible, and nonpreferred benefits are paid at 60 percent, with a higher calendar-year deductible. Savings are maximized, since plan design differentials, negotiated prices, and utilization management controls more than offset the administrative expense of operating the managed care plan.

3. A *combination approach* is for the plan sponsor who wants to introduce managed care with some improvement in benefits but also wants to save money. Using the presumed current 80 percent standard indemnity plan, the preferred benefits are set at a slightly higher level, for example 90 percent, and the nonpreferred benefits at a lower level, for example 70 percent. Deductibles also would be adjusted accordingly to match the higher and lower coinsurance benefit levels. Adequate steerage would be built into the plan design while balancing employee acceptance against the plan sponsor's need for savings. Figure 7–4 shows how PPOs work.

Point-of-Service (POS)

This newest form of managed care was developed to respond to plan sponsors who wanted more cost control than in PPO plans but wanted to

F I G U R E   7–4

How PPOs Work

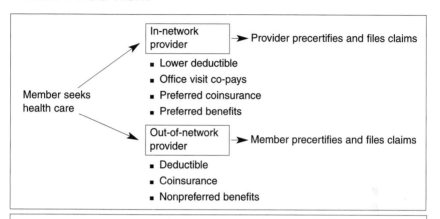

	Sample Preferred Provider Plan Design	
Plan Feature	**Preferred Benefits**	**Nonpreferred Benefits**
Annual Deductible*		
Individual	$200 (waived for certain services below)	$400 (applied to all services)
Family limit	2× or 3× individual level	2× or 3× individual level
Inpatient Deductible	None	$250 per confinement
Coinsurance Rate		
Hospital inpatient	100%, no deductible	70%, after deductible
Emergency care	90%, after deductible	90%, after deductible
Physician office visit	100%, after $10 co-pay	70%, after deductible
Other physician	80%, after deductible	70%, after deductible
Mental/nervous/substance		
Inpatient	100%, no deductible	70%, after deductible
Outpatient	50%, after deductible	50%, after deductible
Prescription drugs**	100%, after $5 co-pay	70%, after deductible
Skilled nursing facilities	100%, up to 120 days	70%, after deductible
Home health care	100%, up to 120 visits	70%, after deductible
All other covered expenses	90%, after deductible	70%, after deductible
Coinsurance limit	$1,000	$3,000***
Lifetime maximum benefit	Unlimited	Unlimited

*   In-network annual deductible is typically waived for hospitalization, emergency room, outpatient surgery, and
   physician office visits.

**   Outpatient prescription drugs are often covered under a separate drug card program in combination with a PPO plan.

*** Higher coinsurance limit needed to maintain benefit differential for large claims.

allow members greater provider choice than in HMO plans. POS plans were initially intended as full replacement products to all other health plans offered, but they are now commonly offered as one option among several. This design is becoming a more common method of introducing "stronger-form" managed care.

The primary care physician (PCP) is the key component of the POS concept, and preferred benefits are only available for care rendered by or coordinated through the member's PCP. Care rendered by non-network providers, as well as any other self-referred care, even if rendered by a network provider, is payable at the nonpreferred benefit level. In other words, preferred benefits are only received for care that is accessed, or referred, through the member's assigned PCP. The primary care physician generally is a family practitioner (FP), general practitioner (GP), internist (IN), or pediatrician (for children). Some networks include obstetricians and gynecologists (OB/GYNs) as primary care physicians, in response to demand from female members, although most plans handle OB/GYNs as specialists.[17]

Plan features (see Figure 7–5) are designed to encourage care within the network, through the PCP, often including the following:

1. No deductible and 100 percent coverage after small office visit co-pay, for care rendered through selected PCP.

2. Preventive services (e.g., physical exams, immunizations, eye and ear exams) when obtained through the member's PCP.

3. One routine gynecological exam per year.

4. No member claim submission when the PCP treats or refers the member within the network; member claims submission required when member self-refers or when the PCP refers member to a provider outside the network.

5. PCP directs medical care and obtains necessary precertification for hospital confinements and referral care. For self-referred, nonpreferred services, the member is responsible for obtaining any required precertification and handling any other utilization management (UM) requirements.

---

17 A 1994 study by Towers Perrin indicated that only 15 percent of the nation's 593 HMO plans included OB/GYNs as primary care physicians. The study also pointed out that a recent Gallup poll conducted for the College of Obstetricians and Gynecologists found that 75 percent of female HMO members object to having to go through a primary care physician in order to be referred to an OB/GYN. Only a few states (California, Maryland, and New York) either require inclusion of OB/GYN as a primary care physician, or allow female members to make a self-referral without penalty. *Managed Care Week*, March 20, 1995, Atlantic Information Services, Inc., Washington, DC.

FIGURE   7–5

How POS Plans Work

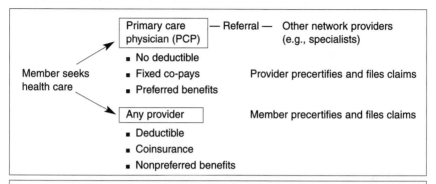

	Sample Point-of-Service Plan Design	
Plan Feature	**Preferred Benefits***	**Nonpreferred Benefits****
	(In-Network)	(Out-of-Network)
Annual Deductible		
Individual	None	$250 (applied to all services)
Family limit	None	2× or 3× individual level
Inpatient Deductible	None	$250 per confinement
Coinsurance Rate		
Hospital inpatient	90%, no deductible	60%, after deductible
Emergency care	$25 co-pay	90%, after deductible
Physician office visit	100%, after $10 co-pay	60%, after deductible
Routine exams	100%, after $10 co-pay	Not covered
Other physician	90%, after deductible	60%, after deductible
Mental/nervous/substance		
Inpatient	90%, no deductible	60%, after deductible
Outpatient	100%, after $20 co-pay max. 20 visits/year	50%, after deductible max. 20 visits/year
Prescription drugs***	100%, after $5 co-pay	60%, after deductible
Skilled nursing facilities	90%, up to 120 days	60%, after deductible
Home health care	90%, up to 120 visits	60%, after deductible
All other covered expenses	90%, after deductible	60%, after deductible
Coinsurance limit	$1,000	$3,000****
Lifetime maximum benefit	Unlimited	Unlimited

*   "Preferred" benefits applies to services provided by or referred by member's PCP.

**   "Nonpreferred" benefits applies to any and all services when not provided by, or referred by, PCP, except for emergency services, which are payable as preferred.

***   Outpatient prescription drugs are often covered under a separate drug card program in combination with a POS plan.

**** Higher coinsurance limit needed to maintain benefit differential for large claims.

Like PPOs, POS plans can use incentive, disincentive, or combination approaches to plan design, but there must be a greater differential (e.g., minimum 30 percent) between preferred and nonpreferred benefits than in a standard PPO. Inadequate steerage works against the objectives of controlling health care delivery and costs through the PCP, where quality of care is best coordinated and monitored.

Health Maintenance Organizations (HMOs)

As prepaid health plans, HMOs provide members with comprehensive benefits through an established provider network. Members receive rich benefits (virtually 100 percent coverage) in exchange for exclusive use of the HMO network and for compliance with its requirements. No coverage is provided for any health care received outside of the HMO, except for emergency treatment or when traveling out of the network's coverage area.

Plan highlights, as shown in Figure 7–6, include the following:

1. No annual deductibles and small office visit co-payments.
2. Comprehensive coverage with minimal co-payments.
3. No claims forms or other paper work to file.
4. Preventive care, including well baby care, immunizations, and routine exams.

HMOs have evolved into three basic types, the distinguishing feature being the relationship between the HMO and the participating physicians.

1. *Group Model HMOs* contract with medical groups of physicians and usually link the financial well-being of the HMO company to the medical group through various forms of financial risk sharing. While the physicians are not employed by the HMO company, they typically have large numbers of patients who are HMO members, which forms a strong financial tie with the company. Members receive primary care at the medical group's clinic or health center, with specialty referral care and hospital confinements handled through other contracted arrangements.

2. *Staff Model HMOs* are nearly identical to the group model, but the critical difference is that physicians are employed by the HMO company, which pays them a salary rather than payments per service to covered members. Typically, staff model HMOs deliver all levels of care, although the HMO may contract with certain specialists or facilities to provide services it cannot handle. Kaiser Permanente is the most well-known example of a staff model HMO, although there are others in many metropolitan areas.

F I G U R E   7–6

How HMOs Work

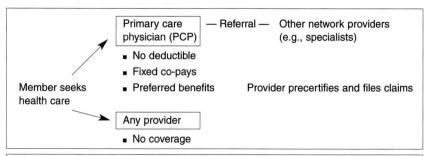

Sample HMO Plan Design		
Plan Feature	**Preferred Benefits***	**Nonpreferred Benefits****
Annual Deductible		
Individual	None	No coverage
Family limit	None	No coverage
Inpatient Deductible	None	No coverage
Coinsurance Rate		
Hospital inpatient	100%	No coverage
Emergency care	100%	100%
Physician office visit	100%, after $10 co-pay	No coverage
Routine exams	100%, after $10 co-pay	No coverage
Other physician	100%	No coverage
Mental/nervous/substance		
Inpatient	100%, 30-day limit	No coverage
Outpatient	50%, after $20 co-pay max. 20 visits/year	No coverage
Prescription drugs***	100%, after $5 co-pay	No coverage
Skilled nursing facilities	100%	No coverage
Home health care	100%	No coverage
All other covered expenses	100%	No coverage
Coinsurance limit	No limit	No coverage
Lifetime maximum benefit	Unlimited	No coverage

*   Benefits only payable for services provided by or referred by member's PCP.

**   "Nonpreferred" benefits applies to any and all services when not provided by or referred by PCP, except for emergency services, which are payable as preferred.

***   Outpatient prescription drugs are often covered under a separate drug card program in combination with a HMO plan.

3. *IPA Model HMOs*, also called "open-panel" plans, contract with individual practice associations (IPAs) or directly with private-practice physicians. This is the most common form of HMO structure today since it requires less capital to establish and operate. It is also often the most popular form of HMO among members, whose current physician may already be on the panel (members usually have to switch physicians to join a staff model or group model HMO).

By 1998, IPA model HMOs accounted for more than 67 percent of the 902 licensed HMO plans in the United States. Group models constituted about 30 percent and staff models only about 3 percent of licensed plans nationwide. Percentages of the total 105.3 million covered HMO members for IPA, group and staff HMOs models were 59 percent, 38 percent and 3 percent, respectively.[18]

Comparing Managed Care Plans: The Managed Care Spectrum

To put the various managed care plans into perspective, it is helpful to view their key features along a continuum. Figure 7–7 depicts the managed care alternatives along a spectrum allowing the user to compare managed indemnity, PPO, POS, and HMO plans. With this spectrum, the reader can evaluate virtually any product to determine precisely where it falls along the continuum. This helps differentiate among competing managed care plans in the request for proposal (RFP) process and helps to understand differences among options in flexible benefit plans.

The horizontal scale of the spectrum shows the major types of managed care alternatives, as well as a traditional fee-for-service medical plan, for comparison. The vertical scale lists fundamental components that distinguish the alternatives, including these:

1. Degree of freedom in the members' *choice of providers*, either among primary care practitioners or specialists.

2. *Degree of steerage* to encourage members to use selected providers.

3. Responsibility for *claims handling* (i.e., the member or the provider).

---

18 SMG Marketing Group, Inc., as reported in HMO-PPO Digest, *Managed Care Digest Series 1999*, published by Hoechst Marion Roussel, Kansas City, MO; www.managedcaredigest.com.

FIGURE 7-7

The Managed Care Spectrum

Key Features	Standard Indemnity	Managed Indemnity	Managed Care Alternatives		
			Preferred Provider Plan	Point-of-Service Plan	Health Maintenance Organization
Choice of Provider	Unrestricted	Unrestricted	Choice of network or non-network	PCP directed or self-referral	Network only; no coverage outside
Degree of "Steerage"	None	None	Moderate (10%–20%)	Considerable (30%)	Maximum
Claims Handling	Patient files	Patient	Provider in-network Patient non-network	Provider in-network Patient non-network	Provider only
Utilization Management	None	Limited and patient initiated	Moderate with provider handling	Considerable with provider handling	Maximum with provider handling
Referral Management	None	None	None	PCP must refer all care in network	PCP must refer all care in network
Provider Reimbursement	Fee for service at "R&C" levels	Fee for service at "R&C" levels	Discounted for in-network care; "R&C" non-network	Discounted for in-network care; "R&C" non-network	Discounted for all care delivered; no non-network
Balance Billing	Patient billed for unpaid balance	Patient billed for unpaid balance	Network provider accepts fee	Network provider accepts fee	No balance billing
Rating/Financial Methods	Experience rated	Experience rated	Experience rated	Prospectively and experience rated	Community rated; some experience rated
Expected Net Savings* (versus standard indemnity)	None	4%–6%	10%–12%	14%–16%	20%–24% (IPA model)

* Expected net savings based on 1994 survey commissioned by the Healthcare Leadership Council and conducted by Lewin-VHI.

4. Degree of external *utilization management* (UM) controls within the plan and who is responsible for initiating UM review.

5. Whether prior *referral management* is required for the member to receive approved specialists' care (if applicable, then typically handled by the PCP).

6. Method of *provider reimbursement* for services, for example, straight fee-for-service basis, discount, or capitation. (Risk-sharing models are discussed in detail in Chapter 8.)

7. Whether the patient is responsible for any *balance billing* if actual charges exceed the amount of provider reimbursement.

8. *Rating and financial methods* indicate whether the plan is available on an experience-rated basis (where future costs are based on actual plan experience) or on a community-rated basis (where future costs are based on claims experience of all plans).

9. *Expected net savings* reflect the average expected "value" of the combined and utilization management controls and network discounts incorporated in the managed care alternative plans.[19]

Standard Indemnity

For comparative purposes, a standard indemnity (fee-for-service) plan is listed on the spectrum. Although not discussed in detail above, indemnity plans dominated the group health benefit industry for decades. Today, standard indemnity plans are probably the least common form of group health insurance,[20] since most plans have introduced some form of utilization management.

Some plan designs use a combination of basic medical benefits superimposed with major medical benefits, although most have evolved to comprehensive medical plan design, which combines the use of deductible and coinsurance features. Both of these approaches are described further in Chapter 6 of the *Handbook*.

As Figure 7–7 shows, indemnity plans make no restriction on the member's choice of providers. As long as the physician or health care facility is duly licensed and operating within the scope of that license, the indemnity plan typically covers the expense. While most claims payers apply a

19 Expected net savings based on 1994 survey commissioned by the Healthcare Leadership Council and conducted by Lewin-VHI.
20 While little industrywide data are available, internal studies at Aetna Health Plans indicates that fewer than 5 percent of its customers have standard indemnity benefits.

variety of controls and edits to eliminate unnecessary or excessive charges, there is no plan steerage to move members to precontracted providers.

Claims handling is the responsibility of the member, although some providers may handle it as a courtesy. Claims handling has been refined over the past 30 years, and most operations today are automated. Most major insurance carriers participate in the National Electronic Information Corporation (NEIC), which serves as an electronic clearinghouse with providers. Most Blue Cross and Blue Shield organizations have automated claims and reimbursement systems established with their participating providers. Nonetheless, it is still ultimately the employee's responsibility to make sure the employer receives all necessary claim information.

There is no structured utilization management or referral management. Although claims payers typically apply retrospective analysis of submitted expenses to identify unnecessary or unreasonable services, these steps rarely include any prospective or concurrent intervention. Providers are under no negotiated-pricing arrangements, and most payers cover prevailing fees based on type of service and geographic area in which the service is performed. Any excessive charges, or those charges not covered above plan limitations, are the responsibility of the plan participant, and the provider may balance bill for any nonreimbursed expenses.

For the most part, standard indemnity plans have a complete array of experience rating and other financial alternatives available. Although smaller plans often are pooled, the premiums for medium- and large-employer plans usually are based on the prior plan experience. In addition, such plans can take advantage of various funding arrangements such as retrospective premium, deferred premium, or minimum premium, as discussed in Chapter 43, which can improve the cash flow associated with funding benefits. As mentioned earlier, a large number of plan sponsors self-fund their indemnity plans, sometimes using individual and aggregate stop-loss insurance to limit their financial exposure.

Managed Indemnity Medical Plans

Managed indemnity plans are virtually identical to standard indemnity, but with the introduction of basic utilization management programs, such as precertification, second surgical opinion (SSO), concurrent review, and case management.

These UM programs are relatively limited in scope as compared to the enhanced UM programs of stronger managed care programs. The member is responsible for initiating the UM review procedures. Failure to adhere to the UM requirements typically reduces the benefit payable, by either a flat-dollar deductible penalty or a higher coinsurance.

Although some providers may assist the member in handling the UM procedures, managed indemnity does not bind the provider to accept any specific level of reimbursement, nor does it establish any other contract obligation between medical provider and claims payer.

Preferred Provider Organizations (PPOs)

With PPOs, we start to see more distinguishing features of managed care. Choice of provider is introduced with the PPO, since members must select care between network or non-network providers. Plan designs use steerage to encourage use of the provider network. Providers are responsible for all claims handling in network, although the member must handle claim submission for non-network expenses.

Utilization management is similar to managed indemnity plans, although in-network providers typically initiate and handle the ongoing UM procedures as part of their agreement with the managed care company. Failure to comply with UM requirements can be a basis, by some network managers, to penalize the provider for noncompliance. However, there is no mandatory referral management process between preferred providers. PPO providers are usually required to refer care within the PPO network, but they do not have to get preauthorization to make the referral.

Benefits to network providers are paid at established rates (i.e., discounted fees), which the provider has agreed to accept as payment in full for the service. Thus, there should be no balance billing to plan members when they use network providers, although they may still get "balance-billed" for services by out-of-network providers. Since PPO provider reimbursement is typically on a discounted fee basis, there can be a full array of experience rating and financial alternatives available to the plan sponsor, similar to those available for standard indemnity programs.

Point-of-Service (POS)

As discussed earlier, point-of-service plans are a new and fast growing form of managed care. In large part, the popularity of POS plans is due to the blending of key features of the PPO and HMO approach.

Like PPOs, POS plans use an established network of contracted providers, to which enrolled members are steered through the use of benefit plan design differentials. However, an important distinction is that POS plans, like HMOs, require the member to select a primary care physician, who acts as the "gatekeeper" for all levels of care accessed within the network. Thus, the choice of provider is more limited than with a PPO since the member selects the primary provider but is removed from selecting specialists or other providers. Furthermore, any visits to specialists require a preauthorization or visit to the PCP.

Benefit differentials in POS plans must be much more significant than in PPOs to create greater incentives to access care through the PCP. Effective communication to the member and coordination between the PCP and the managed care company is critical to ensure members receive prompt care in the most cost-effective setting. Members are penalized for failing to go through their PCP, so nonpreferred benefits apply to services rendered by non-network providers and also to network care that was not referred through the PCP. Self-referral, without a prior visit to the PCP, often requires the specialist to take a full personal health history and perform other basic tests before they can render treatment—steps that cost more money and reduce the effectiveness of delivering coordinated quality care through the POS plan.

Provider reimbursement in POS plans varies, from a discounted fee to full capitation, although more health plans are moving their PCP reimbursements to reflect the methods used by their HMO product lines. As such, PCPs often participate in some form of structured risk-sharing arrangement even under POS arrangements.

Experience rating and funding alternatives are typically available to a plan sponsor, although this depends largely on the provider reimbursement method used by the health plan. Capitated models, which are often built from an HMO network platform, usually provide less ability to experience-rate claims or to finance benefits outside of conventional funding. Many insurance carriers and managed care organizations (MCOs), especially those that build their POS products on their PPO network platform, can offer a full array of experience rating and funding options.

Health Maintenance Organizations (HMOs)

At this point, the reader can appreciate how the features in managed care plans interrelate. The *degree of choice* is linked to the *level of steerage*. The greater the intensity of *utilization management programs*, the more important is proper *referral management*. The *provider reimbursement* contract outlines its responsibilities with respect to *claims handling* and *balance billing*; and the greater the degree of *expected net savings*, the lower the long-term level of expected annual trend.

Health maintenance organizations lie at the far end of the spectrum since they represent the greatest restriction of provider choice. All care must be delivered in network to be covered, except for certain emergency services rendered out of the service area of the HMO. Like POS plans, the member must select a PCP and have care coordinated through him or her. Choice of the PCP is made once each year at the time of annual enrollment.

Claims processing is done entirely within the HMO, and there is rarely any paperwork for the plan member, a real attraction to HMO members—which PPOs and POS plans try to mimic as much as possible. Utilization management, including referral management, is internal to the HMO, with the medical staff handling all procedures among network specialists. Procedures may vary slightly among different HMOs, but these features are generally common whether the HMO is group model, staff model, or IPA-based.

Fully pooled rating, or community-rating pricing, is common among HMOs, where premium rates are determined based on the broader experience of the HMO's insured population, rather than of the specific plan sponsor. There are practical reasons why HMOs tend to use the pooled/community-rate approach: Most HMO coverage is sold as an option to members, along with traditional health benefits, and thus the HMO may cover only a percentage of the employer's group. Furthermore, community rating is required by state HMO regulations.

However, as other group health companies have developed competing products, there has been a need to expand rating and funding flexibility. This has led to the development of the exclusive provider organization (EPO), which essentially is a self-funded HMO plan and thus can offer greater financial options to plan sponsors. The HMO may directly sponsor the EPO or may sell its managed care network and UM services to a stand-alone TPA or smaller insurance company. These types of "rental" arrangements are increasingly common in today's managed care marketplace, even to the point of plan sponsors directly contracting with health care providers for selective services.

Emerging Managed Care Applications

Using Managed Care with Medicare/Medicaid [21]

With the burgeoning over-age-65 population and growing entitlement costs, cost control is as much a priority for those state and federal agencies responsible for health care delivery as it is for employer-sponsored plans. Not sur-

---

21 Medicare is the federally sponsored health care program for eligible persons who are over age 65. Medicaid is the federally funded, but state administered, health care program for poor and indigent persons. See Chapter 22 for further information.

prisingly, both Medicare and Medicaid programs are actively introducing managed care options to those populations covered by these programs.

By 1998 more than 6.5 million Medicare beneficiaries received care through health maintenance organizations. Similar to members of private managed care plans, Medicare and Medicaid recipients in HMOs are restricted to using network providers and must comply with all applicable utilization management requirements. However, in return, participating members receive full HMO benefits, which are better than standard Medicare benefits, saving members hundreds of dollars per year. Many HMOs offer supplemental benefits, including prescription drug, vision, and dental benefits—sometimes free, but typically with a small additional premium.

Medicare payment levels to HMOs equal 95 percent of the prevailing expected Medicare fee-for-service level. In mid-1995, the U.S. Congress introduced proposed revisions to the Medicare program, which include expanding managed care options to help control skyrocketing government costs.

Of the nation's 30 million Medicaid recipients in 1998, 15.8 million (52 percent) were enrolled in some form of managed care, with licensed HMOs accounting for 9.2 million of these Medicaid members. In 1982, Arizona became the first state to implement managed care for its Medicaid population, under a demonstration waiver from the federal government.[22] By mid-1995, 10 more states had received waivers from the Health Care Financing Administration (HCFA) to convert their Medicaid populations to managed care, and some also had been permitted to expand Medicaid eligibility to the uninsured. By 1998, 48 states and the District of Columbia were permitting licensed HMOs to enroll Medicaid membership.[23]

Some observers have suggested that quality of health care provided by Medicare and Medicaid HMOs is inferior to fee-for-service plans. Available studies indicate that quality of health care in Medicaid HMOs is no less than the care received under the comparable fee-for-service plans. For example, a 1990 study found that Medicaid HMO patients received more immunization, Pap smears, and breast examinations than non-HMO patients. Another study done by the Centers for Disease Control (CDC) and the National Center for Health Statistics found that HMOs improve access to preventive services among women with lower

---

22 Based on listing of HCFA-Approved, Section 1115 State Medicaid Demonstration in Managed Care Perspectives. *Managed Care Week*, July 31, 1995, Atlantic Information Services, Inc., Washington, DC.

23 Op. Cit. SMG Marketing Group, Inc.

levels of education. Among women with 12 years of education or less, HMO members had higher levels of screening for breast and cervical cancer than members of fee-for-service plans and uninsured women.[24]

Similarly, Medicare HMO members with cancer are more likely to be diagnosed at an earlier stage than in fee-for-service plans, according to an HCFA study that compared Medicare records for HMO and fee-for-service patients to find the stage of diagnosis for 12 types of cancer, including breast, cervical, and colon cancers, as well as melanomas. Authors of the study attributed the difference to Medicare HMOs' coverage of cancer screenings—such as mammograms, Pap smears, fecal blood tests, and annual physicals—which are not covered by standard fee-for-service Medicare.

Mental Health/Substance Abuse Benefits

Among the fastest growing medical costs are those associated with mental health and substance abuse (MH/SA). Combined inpatient and outpatient expenses average about 10 percent of total health benefit expenses for many plan sponsors and sometimes the figure reaches as high as 35 percent. Moreover, the growth rate is more than twice that of medical/surgical costs. These expenses don't include costs associated with increased absenteeism and lost time for employees with ill dependents.

One reason for the higher trend rate is less uniformity associated with accepted patterns of treatment for mental health and substance abuse than for other physiological causes. Clinical opinions regarding what constitutes effective, quality mental health care widely differ, so payers have difficulty determining effective care alternatives. These gaps often provide opportunity for fraud and abuse.

A 1992 Congressional hearing investigated fraud in mental health care.[25] According to testimony, perpetrators subjected mental health patients to unnecessary, costly, and potentially harmful treatments and routinely overbilled insurers. Fraud can flourish when employer-sponsored plans pay claims without monitoring care, which perhaps is the most compelling reason for the plan sponsor to consider using managed care techniques for mental health and substance abuse expenses.

---

24 CDS/NCHS, Advance Data No. 254, August 3, 1994.

25 *The Profits of Misery: How Inpatient Psychiatric Treatment Bilks the System and Betrays Our Trust.* Transcript of the Hearing before the Select Committee on Children, Youth, and Families, House of Representatives, 102nd Congress, April 28, 1992 (Washington, DC: US Government Printing Office, 1992).

Most standard indemnity plans deal with excessive MH/SA costs by limiting benefits. For example, outpatient benefits may be payable at a 50 percent coinsurance rate. The Mental Health Parity Act of 1996 (scheduled to expire on September 30, 2001) prohibits lifetime or annual limits on mental health care, unless comparable limits apply to medical or surgical treatments. Unfortunately, limiting benefits in many ways fails to address the underlying problem and may lead to longer-term cost for the employer.

Many employers, recognizing the need to care for the tangible impact of such problems, have established employee assistance programs (EAPs) to identify potential problems and steer potential cases into a managed environment.

Figure 7–8 is an adaptation of the Managed Care Spectrum (Figure 7-7) on page 157, showing various managed care methods for MH/SA benefits. Indemnity benefits are shown on the left-hand side of the chart as a baseline. There is no incentive for effective utilization; the plan participant selects treatment as desired, and there are no negotiated prices and no expected savings other than those stemming from plan features.

Standard EAP programs provide access to professional resources by providing early and controlled intervention to personal problems to help decrease unnecessary admissions and promote appropriate use of outpatient services. Most EAP programs are prepaid capitated arrangements and therefore are not experience-rated through claims, but the pricing can vary according to program utilization. Most EAPs do not include negotiated pricing at inpatient or outpatient facilities.

An *EAP gate plan* operates the same as the standard EAP, except that the EAP is encouraged by health plan design, thus directing more clients to managed care. For example, maximum MH/SA benefits may only be available when members certify through the EAP in all but emergency situations. Through better utilization control, EAP gate plans are expected to produce greater savings than standard EAP programs.

An MH/SA network introduces a preferred network of providers who are selected on the basis of their clinical expertise, cooperation with utilization management procedures, and agreement to preferential prices. This approach is similar to the PPO approach for medical/surgical programs. Such networks typically consist of special inpatient facilities (hospitals and clinics), outpatient providers (MDs, PhDs, and master-level therapists), and alternative care resources (nonacute residential centers, structured day/evening programs, and halfway houses). The plan relies on plan-design incentives to encourage employees to use network providers. This approach has the added advantage of being experience rated.

FIGURE 7-8

Mental Health/Substance Abuse Access and
Treatment Options

Options / Services Provided	Indemnity	EAP	EAP Gate	MH/SA Network	MH/SA Network with EAP Gate
Employee incentives for use	No	Free short-term counseling	EAP and plan	Plan design	EAP and plan
Treatment approach consistent with managed care philosophy	Maybe	Yes	Yes	Yes	Yes
Experience rating	Yes	No	No	Yes	Yes
Negotiated pricing at facilities	No	No	No	Yes	Yes
Expected savings	None	$	$$	$$	$$$

An *MH/SA network with EAP gate* combines the benefits of simple
and early mental health access with experience rating and preferred pricing arrangements. Such arrangements can be purchased either with the
established medical/surgical plan or as stand-alone managed mental
health/EAP services from specialized vendors. In this case, the MH/SA
benefit is "carved out" of the rest of the health care benefit. Either way,
the best long-term costs savings are expected from this combination of
EAP and network since there is consistent utilization control from initial
identification of the problem through treatment and outcome.

Managed care has been shown to reduce the cost of mental health
care services. Between 1993 and 1995, mental health care costs increased
9.5 percent per year under indemnity plans but just 1 percent per year in

network plans.[26] And by assuring that care is clinically effective, managed care also reduces the indirect cost to employers of mental illness, such as medical care and absenteeism.[27]

Managed Disability

Short- and long-term disability income plans are invaluable methods of providing employees with security surrounding the sudden loss of income due to accident or illness.[28] However, disability benefits are a significant expense to plan sponsors. Disability costs can approach 8 percent of covered payroll when replacement labor, lost productivity, and benefit payments are taken into account.

For many years, long-term disability programs have used formal rehabilitation and other return-to-work programs to reduce costs and bring disabled employees back to productive status. However, most control efforts usually start three to six months after the employee becomes disabled, long after many employers are forced to hire and train replacement workers. Most short-term disabilities are unmanaged, other than cursory independent examinations.

In the early 1990s, insurers started applying utilization management techniques, learned through the development of managed health care benefit programs, to their disability insurance products. Several also offer their managed disability expertise to those employers who self-fund their short-term disability benefit plans. Managing short-term disabilities provides an improved integration with long-term disability programs and deals more effectively with the total disability period of the employee.

The most successful approaches employ a team approach, coordinated by a nurse consultant, starting from the onset of disability. The teams commonly include the plan sponsor, physician consultants, and vocational and rehabilitation specialists, if necessary. Either the plan sponsor or the disabled employee contacts the managed care company

---

26 *Managed Behavioral Health Care Quality and Access Survey Report*, Foster-Higgins, for the American Managed Behavior Healthcare Association (AMBHA). The survey covered 48 million enrollees in various types of managed mental health programs.

27 Employees with untreated mental health problems are absent 15 percent to 30 percent more frequently than healthy employees (Mental Health Policy Resource Center, as reported in Lind). In a mid-1985 study, medical costs dropped sharply after emotionally distressed patients received mental health treatment. See Harold D. Holder, Ph.D., and James O. Blose, M.P.P., "Changes in Health Care Costs and Utilization Associated with Mental Health Treatment," *Hospital and Community Psychiatry 38*, No. 10, October 1987.

28 Chapter 14 provides a detailed discussion of these plans.

upon onset of the disability (typically after the third day, to ignore common short-term illnesses), or the managed disability company may collect the information automatically if it also administers UM certification programs under the managed health care program.

The nurse consultant will then use automated protocol-based systems, combined with input from other team members to determine the expected length of disability (LOD). Concurrent review enables the nurse consultant to continue to check on an employee's disability and to initiate rehabilitation services if appropriate.

In one study, employees covered under a managed disability program returned to work an average of 10 days sooner than under traditional programs, with savings between 10 percent and 25 percent of short-term disability benefit costs.[29]

Managed Workers' Compensation

The origins and development of workers' compensation programs, which provide disability income and medical expense coverage for occupational accidents and illnesses, are covered in Chapter 23 of the *Handbook*. It is a no-fault, social insurance, state-regulated system that provides injured workers with predetermined and prompt compensation in exchange for the worker's inability to sue the employer. Essentially, workers' compensation laws involve an economic and legal principle of liability without fault. However, it is not without cost to the employer, and some employers have begun applying managed care techniques to workers' compensation programs.

Between 1985 and 1992, while the consumer price index (CPI) grew at an average annual rate of 4.4 percent, workers' compensation medical costs increased at an annual rate of 10.9 percent.[30] Medical expenses now account for about half of workers' compensation costs and run as high as 60 percent in some states. Many states have passed reforms to focus on cost containment and tightening of compensability rules; and formal managed care programs, pilot projects, or comprehensive health plans have been authorized in at least 14 states. In addition, the National Association of Insurance Commissioners (NAIC) has drafted the "24 Hour Coverage Pilot Project Model Act" to determine if "24 hour coverage" plans should contain managed health care.

---

29 Aetna Health Plans internal studies of customers with managed disability programs.
30 Stephen M. Mulready, "Cutting-Edge Concepts for Trimming Workers' Comp Medical Costs," *Perspective*, (Hartford, CT: Aetna Casualty and Surety, February 1995).

Ensuring that an injured person visits the right provider as soon as possible greatly improves the individual's chance to fully recover. The proper type of care—physical therapy to regain use of a limb or corrective surgery to relieve pain—is important for full recovery. Two distinct general managed care models can be applied to work-related illnesses and injuries.[31]

1. The *passive discount PPO model* is the most prevalent managed care delivery model but the least effective. It involves contracting with a broad-based PPO to increase the chance of a worker selecting a discounted provider. Since many states do not allow employers to require claimants to use a PPO or particular physicians, cost savings can be sporadic. Furthermore, few clinical standards are used to assess appropriateness of treatment.

2. The *proactive model*, which is newer and still evolving, applies the cost-control attributes of an HMO to the workers' compensation environment. However, the model is limited to those states that permit employers to direct worker care to selected providers. A network of primary care "entry points" is created to ensure prompt initial treatment and appropriate referral management. These providers include occupational clinics, urgent care centers, or other primary care physicians. There is approval of treatment and frequent contact between an assigned case manager and the injured worker. The role of the employer is crucial under the proactive role, particularly in educating supervisors about prompt injury reporting, directing workers to a primary treatment site, and immediate notification of the HMO/PPO.

The latter model is also being integrated with group managed care products into what are called "24 hour" packages by some managed care companies, and many industry experts expect managed workers' compensation (also called occupational managed care) to be among the fastest growing areas of managed care.

---

31 James Sullivan, "Healthcare Networks and Their Roles in Workers' Compensation Cost Reduction, *Perspective*, (Hartford, CT: Aetna Casualty and Surety, February 1995).

CHAPTER 8

Understanding Managed Care Health Plans: Understanding Costs and Evaluating Plans*

Phillip D. Pierce

As stated numerous times in the *Handbook*, the growth of health care costs has been the driving force behind the development of new forms of managed health care plans. However, to understand how managed care plans seek to control costs, it is important to understand why costs have increased historically and why traditional, fee-for-service health insurance plans have not provided an adequate solution to this problem.[1] Although there is some disagreement over the reasons for rising health care costs, some of the more commonly cited ones include these:

1. *Increased input prices* in health care, including both supply and labor costs, such as wages paid to medical personnel. However, other nonwage expenses have added to overall higher prices, such as the rapid acceleration of malpractice insurance premiums, and the cost shifting among providers to make up for

---

* Many of the acronyms used in this chapter are defined in Chapter 7 of the *Handbook* where they are first used.

1 Health insurance premiums are further affected by other factors that do not directly affect costs: (1) antiselection—younger, healthier people often buy less insurance; therefore, insurance premiums are often more reflective of the risk associated with an older, less healthy population; (2) leveraging effect of co-payments and deductibles—when co-pays and deductibles do not keep pace with overall medical cost increases, health insurance premiums must make up the difference.

unpaid bills (indigent care) and governmental underpayments mentioned earlier (i.e., Medicare and Medicaid).[2]

2. *Increased service intensity* associated with new medical technologies and new medical protocols (e.g., prescribed procedures).

3. *Increased demand for services* caused by more intensive societal problems, such as the growth of AIDs, substance abuse, and violence. In our third-party payment system of health insurance, by paying most of the bill, third-party payers (e.g., employer-sponsored and governmental coverage) distort the economic supply/demand equilibrium between buyer (member/patient) and supplier (provider) and also remove any financial incentive consumers might otherwise have to help contain costs.

4. *Changing demographics* in the 1990s characterized by a rising average age (as baby boomers entered their 40s and 50s), which increases health care costs; and rising life expectancy, which means people are receiving health care for longer periods.

HEALTH CARE COST EQUATION

Since the last edition of the *Handbook* the questions of "Should we move our plan into managed care?" and "Does managed care save money?" have evolved into "What *type* of managed care is best for our health care benefit plan?" and "*How* does managed care save us money?" Few questions in the vast industry of employee benefits are getting more attention today, and this text would not be complete without trying to answer them. However, it is important to note that these are distinctly different questions.

The first question requires a response more complex than just how much savings are produced by the various forms of managed care. While cost control has been the primary driver behind the establishment of managed care products, there are many other fundamental considerations for the plan sponsor offering the various forms of managed care, such as the impact on employee satisfaction, the degree of plan design flexibility, and whether managed care networks are available to enough plan participants.

Also, the plan sponsor must consider the types of managed care in the broader context of its employee benefit philosophy. If senior management does not understand, nor fully support, the offering of managed

---

2 Cost shifting adds 20 percent to 25 percent to the cost of private health insurance, according to a Lewin/ICF study for the National Association of Manufacturers, *Employer and Cost Shifting Expenditures*, September 1991.

care, the plan sponsor may not devote adequate internal resources to ensure proper employee education and acceptance of the plan. Since managed care plans rely heavily on proper understanding of and acceptance by the member population, the plan sponsor may not realize the expected savings. So, the first step to achieving expected savings from any managed care plan requires the plan sponsor to establish clear expectations and to make the necessary commitment to its success.

The second question is the primary subject of this chapter: *How* does managed care save money? To answer that question, it is first important to understand the elements that drive health care costs. As noted in Chapter 7, a plan sponsor can generally expect greater savings with stronger forms of managed care. Savings will reflect the initial cost reductions from transitioning membership from a traditional indemnity plan to some form of managed care, as well as the level of provider discounts, the change in benefits, and the degree of utilization control included in the new managed care plan.

To understand the potential impact of managed care alternatives on the costs of medical care, it is important to understand the basic health care cost equation: Cost = Price × Use, where *Price* is the average cost per unit of health services delivered, and *Use* (or utilization) represents the average number of units of health services.

Effective managed care strategies must address both portions of the cost equation: *price* management, which is a function of network development and provider reimbursement strategy; and *utilization* management, which is a function of medical management capabilities and quality controls employed by the managed care company.

Elements of Price Management

Provider Reimbursement Methods

Provider reimbursement methodology is the cornerstone of price management. It must cover broad provider service categories, and it must be actively managed, with regular review and renegotiation. Those group health plans that fail to take advantage of negotiated pricing will bear greater and greater cost shifting from governmental and other managed care plans.

Hospital reimbursement strategies are most important, since facility expenses account for, on average, more than 40 percent of total health care expenditures. Common strategies include the following:

1. *Straight discount (percentage off)* is simply a negotiated percentage (e.g., 15 percent) off billed charges with no risk sharing by the provider. Managed care companies disfavor straight discounts because they do not protect expenses against general medical inflation; hospitals can still increase their prices, while the managed care company can only take the same discount off higher and higher costs. Furthermore, this method does little to control increased utilization of hospital services.

2. *Diagnostic (diagnosis) related group (DRG)* pays a prenegotiated amount to the hospital for the total cost of treatment, for each of about 475 specific "diagnoses." (Medicare reimburses hospitals in this manner.) With DRGs, the hospital is given an incentive, by being put at some financial risk to effectively manage length of stay and intensity of services per admission. However, since the number of admissions is not limited, hospitals could discharge patients early and readmit them. Stop-loss arrangements are often set up to protect the hospital from catastrophic cases. Additional problems with DRGs include setting the price, which can require significant claims data; artificially high charges if the base is determined before utilization has been aggressively managed; and the additional administrative burden of assigning a DRG number which requires grouping software to avoid DRG creep whereby a hospital raises the classification of an illness in order to receive the higher amount. Even with a grouper, the payer should have an audit program to verify DRGs.

3. *Case rates* are flat negotiated reimbursements for a specific type of service (e.g., outpatient surgery rates or OB case rates), rather than for all services related to a specific diagnosis. With this arrangement, the hospital is at risk for managing cost as well as increases in cost for services but not for managing the number of services.

4. *Per diem* entails a prenegotiated fixed daily rate, usually set up by broad major categories, such as medical/surgical, delivery, intensive care, and so on. Per diem allows the managed care company to share some risk with the hospitals and gives the hospital an incentive to effectively manage cost per day. However, in contrast to DRG reimbursement, the hospital is paid for each day of care and thus has no incentive to control admission rates or length of stay per admission.

5. *Global rates* pay a specific fee for an episode of care (e.g., all costs related to cardiovascular surgery or organ transplant). It is broader than DRG reimbursement because the negotiated fee includes all professional, ancillary, anesthesia, and facility fees associated with the episode of care, so one payment is made for all services rendered (usually to the facility). Under global rates, the hospital is at risk for effectively managing all health costs related to the negotiated episodes as well as increases in the cost of these services.

It is not uncommon for HMOs to engage in multiple reimbursement arrangements with various hospitals and other inpatient facilities. Based upon the *HMO Industry Report 9.1*, in July, 1998, 72 percent of hospital contracts used discounted charges, 86 percent used per diems, 50 percent used DRGs, and 33 percent used a combination of case or global rates.[3]

Physician reimbursement strategies depend largely on the type of managed care plan. Physicians costs are influenced two ways in a managed care environment:

1. Through specific utilization management procedures that employ medical protocols, coupled with advanced information measurement systems to intervene, monitor, and regulate physician practice.
2. Through risk-sharing reimbursement arrangements that give providers financial incentives to control patient utilization.

Most managed care programs rely on both of these strategies, depending on the readiness and sophistication of the local provider community. But it is the physician reimbursement strategy that is key in controlling costs.

FEE-FOR-SERVICE

In nonmanaged plans and even in managed indemnity and many PPO plans, fee-for-service is the standard reimbursement method. While discounts are sometimes applied to fees, fee-for-service has no real way to control utilization.

1. *Fee-for-service—Reasonable and Customary (R&C) or Usual, Customary and Reasonable (UCR)* utilizes a schedule of maximum allowable fees for covered services, based on prior payment practices within a particular geographic area. The prevailing R&C fee is set at the most frequently occurring charge within a particular range. Physicians are paid the lesser of billed charges or the R&C maximum fees. This is the way traditional plans have operated for years, and most patients don't even realize an allowance (or fee schedule) is being used unless the provider "balance-bills" the patient. Since this arrangement reimburses the provider for each service, there is no incentive for providers to effectively manage utilization. R&C reimbursement is common with indemnity and managed indemnity plans since it requires no established contract with providers.

---

3 *HMO Industry Report 9.1*, Interstudy Publications, as published in *Managed Care Week*, Atlantic Information Services, Inc., Washington, DC; www.aispub.com.

2. *Fee-for-service—Fee Schedule* reimburses physicians based on negotiated rates (e.g., relative value scale). The physician is reimbursed the lesser of billed charges or the negotiated maximum which is based on the current procedural terminology (CPT) code and set below the average charge sometimes using a relative value scale (RVS) to factor in specialty and location. Like the R&C method, this arrangement reimburses the physician for each service, resulting in little incentive to manage utilization. These fee schedules are common in PPOs, in which a negotiated contract sets the fee schedule in advance with contracted physicians. It is crucial that the managed care company provide monitoring and review of physician utilization patterns in order to avoid unnecessary expenses.

3. *Resource-based relative value scale (RBRVS)* is a variation of RVS under which the relative value assigned to a procedural code is derived from the components of physician work units (including time and skill), practice expense units, and malpractice expense units with the intent of reimbursing according to comparable costs of doing business, not according to specialty. Medicare adopted this approach in 1992.

RISK-SHARING STRATEGIES

A reimbursement strategy that lacks risk sharing often sees little provider interest in controlling overall costs since providers are only concerned with the "price management" side of the managed care cost equation.

Risk sharing is best suited for stronger-form managed care plans, such as HMO and POS plans, since these models rely on the primary care physician (PCP) as the central control point for member health care delivery. The PCP is best positioned to monitor a member's care and to control benefit utilization. Furthermore, integrated delivery systems (e.g., group practices, IPAs, physicians hospital organizations [PHOs]) have shown interest in risk-sharing models because they have the administrative systems to monitor broad levels of member care and can better assume the risks associated with shared financial incentives.

The risk-sharing model has to be flexible enough to adapt to local market conditions and to grow and change over time. An effective risk-sharing model should generally include the following conditions.

1. A PCP in place for each member to serve as the entry point for referral and hospital care.
2. Risk pools that include about 10 to 12 PCPs per pool, in order to aggregate experience.

3. A given PCP that has a minimum concentration of membership (e.g., 150 to 200 members) in order to make the revenue flow significant enough to be "at risk."

4. Risk sharing within group and IPA HMO models that takes a variety of forms depending on the following conditions:

   a. Receptivity of the provider community.

   b. Membership leverage by the managed care company among its participating providers.

   c. Sophistication of the provider group and the managed care company.

Types of risk-sharing models include:

1. *Case management fee* where the managed care company pays the PCP a set fee per member for overall case management services. This fee is paid in addition to charges for medical services rendered. It is intended to compensate physicians for the added work of acting as case manager for their membership, but this approach is typically not favored by managed care companies. Many companies feel PCPs already serve as overall case manager for their membership and should not receive additional compensation. Furthermore, case management fees alone do not provide an effective vehicle to influence specific physician behavior.

2. *Physician incentive/bonus* rewards positive performance in specific measurable categories, such as financial results (e.g., average monthly costs per member), quality assurance compliance, and member satisfaction surveys results. Results are shared with providers on a regular basis to improve effectiveness of performance-based incentives. Some advantages of using bonus plans are that they are relatively easy to develop and establish, and can be administered in conjunction with other risk arrangements. Concerns include whether bonus payments are large enough to outweigh gains from potential plan overutilization and whether comparative systems need to be developed to measure performance among PCPs.

3. *Fee-for-service with a "withhold"* reduces provider reimbursement by a withheld amount (e.g., 15 percent) at the time the claim is adjudicated, and this withhold is placed in specially assigned risk pools. Cumulative withholds are either returned or retained each year based on the results of the risk pool compared to expected results. Typically, catastrophic claim costs are not charged against the selected risk pool so that they do not unfairly influence the results of the risk pool. Some advantages of the withhold arrangement are that it is relatively easy to develop and administer, and it encourages PCPs to deliver services within its practices rather than refer to other specialists, which helps control utilization. Concerns include the following: There is the possibility of overutilization of physician services to increase revenue in order to offset the withhold; the plan can be "nickeled and dimed" on PCP services; and providers often perceive withholds as part of their discounts and do not put serious effort into adjusting performance to regain the withholds. Effective use of withhold arrangements requires critical information system tools, physician profiling data systems to monitor performance criteria, a limit on the number of specific fees for office visits, and regular communication with PCPs, so they can properly manage their practices.

4. *Capitation for defined services* provides a fixed regular payment for each member selecting a PCP, as compared to payment for each service delivered by that physician. It is critical to define exactly what services are to be covered in that capitation payment so that a physician knows what level of care is being covered through the reimbursement. PCP services typically include the following:

- Office visits, including routine exams and well-baby care.
- Immunizations and therapeutic injections.
- Inpatient visits while member is confined in a hospital or other facility.
- Specific list of routine lab and diagnostic services (e.g., EKGs).
- Specific list of routine office procedures (e.g., minor surgical procedures).

To supplement the capitation for defined services, the managed care company also may pay the PCP additional fee-for-service reimbursement for after-hour and emergency treatment to avoid the higher cost of sending the member to the emergency room.

Capitation rates are usually age/sex specific (e.g., different rates for adult versus child, male versus female) to recognize differences in the member population. It is possible to capitate most types of providers or groupings of providers (e.g., hospitals, IPAs, PHOs, labs, drug vendors), provided there are clear definitions as to the services to be provided and the expectations of the provider. Advantages of capitation for defined services are that it rewards prudent utilization of services (PCPs "keep" excess capitation payments above their actual costs of delivering care), and it eliminates claims processing for low-cost, routine, high-volume services.

Concerns about capitation models include the following: It can be more difficult to recruit physicians if they are not willing to accept capitated services; and it can be difficult to collect accurate and relevant encounter (claims) data because physicians have no incentive to complete paperwork. Effective audit systems must be established to ensure that services contracted under the capitation agreement are not also submitted and reimbursed as under fee-for-service; physicians must have sufficient financial strength to assume the risk inherent in capitation; and the managed care organization (MCO) must closely monitor the practice to make sure PCPs are delivering appropriate care, rather than simply referring care to other providers (for which the MCO pays additional fees). Thus, critical tools for implementing a capitation for defined services include a clear and workable definition of capitated services, monitoring reports to identify inappropriate referrals, systems support to give PCPs information necessary to manage their budgets, and quality screens to protect against underutilization.

5. *Capitation with a withhold* is the same as capitation for defined services, except that a portion of the capitation payment is withheld as a tool to reduce PCP "triaging" (i.e., making too many referrals) to other providers. The withhold is returned at the end of the fiscal year, depending on PCP performance. The key advantage is that the PCP has a financial stake in properly managing referral care. The same concerns about capitation exist, and recruiting primary care physicians who will accept this model is tricky.

6. *Capitation for complete services* capitates the PCP for all services rendered to a member, including referrals to specialists and hospital services. The capitation payments are used to establish a PCP budget, against which the costs for all services are charged. The PCP has a stake in managing the total care for assigned members. However, unless PCPs are careful, a string of catastrophic cases can be financially devastating (usually protected against by some type of stop-loss coverage).

7. *Budgeted capitation* sets up a pool, which is funded directly from premiums, for a group of PCPs. Claims are charged directly against the budgeted pool during the fiscal year; if the pool runs dry, no further monies are paid out for services, but excess monies in the pool at the end of the fiscal period can be available as surplus and shared with providers. Advantages of budgeted capitation include those noted above for other methods of capitation, plus the added feature that medical expenses cannot exceed premiums collected. However, an added concern is that the PCP's average member costs vary by plan group and the PCP has no control over them.

8. *Salaried physicians* are employed by staff model HMOs. Like capitation models, a key advantage is that the supposed financial incentives for overutilization are removed, and more importantly this "vertically integrated" approach to health care delivery allows for efficiencies not possible in other types of arrangements. However, it is crucial that the appropriate "corporate" goals/policies are developed and broadly communicated to give staff providers direction on utilization and quality.

Elements of Utilization Management

While price management is the first step in managing the health care cost equation, some regard it as a "one-time" savings once the plan sponsor gains discounts. This is not entirely correct since ongoing price management is crucial to controlling ongoing costs. However, the long-term cost advantage of managed care rests in its ability to *reduce the rate of increase*. The rate declines, with stronger and stronger forms of managed care by reducing the *number of units* of health care services delivered. Reducing that number is the principal function of medical utilization management (UM).

Primary Utilization Management

Primary utilization management programs are found in most managed indemnity and PPO plans. They have generally focused on controlling hospital confinements, either through reducing the number of admissions and/or reducing the average length of stay (LOS). The following programs are typically included:

1. *Precertification* reviews the medical necessity of inpatient admissions and identifies potential case management opportunities.

2. *Concurrent review* monitors patient care during hospital stays with the intent of identifying alternate settings that can provide less-costly care.

3. *Discharge planning* assesses whether additional services are needed and prepares the patient's transfer to less-costly alternate settings for treatment (e.g., skilled nursing facility or home health care).

4. *Large case management* provides a continuous process of identifying members with high risk for problems associated with complex, high-cost health care needs and of assessing opportunities to improve the coordination of care.

Primary UM programs are typically handled by telephone (e.g., a toll-free help line) to the managed care company's central member services offices, although selected cases may be supplemented with local on-site review, either through clinical representatives of the managed care company or through contracted medical professionals.

Expanded Utilization Management

Expanded utilization management programs are more commonly included with stronger forms of managed care, such as POS and HMO plans (although they are increasingly available with PPO plans on a stand-alone basis). Some programs are fairly sophisticated, combining protocol-based telephonic intervention services with more intensive clinical analysis of specific treatments of care. Because of the nature of HMO and POS plans, many of these advanced UM programs are initiated by the primary care physician and are supposed to be transparent to the member. Provider compliance with the requirements of these programs is essential to managing care. Elements of these programs often include the following:

1. *Referral management* is the primary technique differentiating HMO and POS plans from PPO plans. It requires members to access care through their PCPs, who then manage referrals to specialists within the provider network. Properly handled, referral management, also known as the gatekeeper approach, ensures that high-quality care is delivered in the most cost-effective setting possible by coordinating care through one source (the PCP) and eliminating unnecessary or inappropriate care.

2. *Outpatient precertification* requires prior authorization from the managed care company for certain outpatient surgical and medical procedures, with the intent being to reduce unnecessary, inappropriate, and potentially harmful procedures.

3. *Managed second surgical opinion* replaces voluntary second surgical opinion programs (used in the 1980s) and requires the member to contact the managed care company, which evaluates the necessity of surgery and recommends less invasive medical treatment if appropriate.

4. *On-site concurrent review* complements telephone-based concurrent review in basic UM services by placing clinically trained nurses at hospitals and other inpatient facilities to review the necessity of continued confinements, proposed tests, and procedures.

5. *Centers of excellence* include a network of designated, nationally recognized medical facilities that perform selected, highly sophisticated, and high-cost procedures (e.g., organ transplants, open-heart surgery, advanced forms of cancer treatment). The managed care organization typically negotiates preferred rates with the centers.

6. *Prenatal advisory services* (also called prenatal planning and maternity management services) help identify women who may be at risk for delivering low-birth-weight, preterm, or unhealthy babies and provides education and counseling on proper prenatal care.

Most managed care companies use sophisticated protocols and medical guidelines to develop and administer their UM programs. Whether their operations are centrally based or located in local member service centers, today's UM programs are highly automated and integrated with the claims payment systems, so that there are minimal delays in the handling of member claims after UM procedures are approved. Similarly, the managed care company will usually provide toll-free numbers for both members and providers and extended customer service hours to decrease the "hassle factor" often associated with having to preauthorize confinements, referrals, or outpatient procedures.

Patient Care Models

Even with the growth of advanced clinically based UM programs, managed care companies are continually developing new models of patient care treatment to better manage the total health care delivered to their membership. This is an example of evolution of standard utilization management into a more proactive form of health management.

Figure 8–1 depicts a framework for evaluating how three patient care models apply to members and their providers at various levels of illness. The general population has a wide variety of health needs, and different people respond to different types of patient care at different times of their lives. It is essential that a managed care company approach its membership with a high level of sensitivity to these differences so that each member's needs are handled in the most appropriate manner, as opposed to being forced through a common set of UM protocols and methods that are designed to apply on a generalized basis.

FIGURE 8–1

Patient Care Model

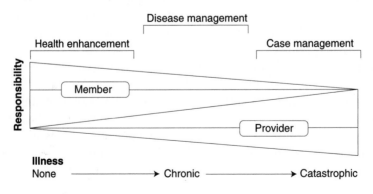

Many industry experts believe that a patient care treatment continuum will continue to be a critical area of focus in the 21st century. There will be a shifting emphasis from micromanaging specific episodes of care to macromanaging the member's continuous health status, using the patient care model that most effectively addresses the member's specific needs. The models include the following:

- *Health enhancement* programs, which help assess the broad lifestyle of the individual member, provide broad-based education on proper self-care techniques, and provide more tailored, individualized counseling on preventive care, such as stress management, nutrition and weight control, smoking cessation, and safety instruction. Working with case managers, members can improve their personal health awareness, identify specific risk factors that may affect their future health care needs, and tailor specific behavioral change programs to help avoid potential health problems.

- *Disease management* is more appropriate for those members with identified chronic conditions (e.g., asthma, diabetes, heart disease, some types of mental illnesses) that require continuous monitoring and occasional, or regular, treatment. Broader in scope than traditional UM programs, which primarily focus on managing specific episodes of care, disease management is a more systematic approach to health management, coordinating all levels of care, including prevention, control, and self-care to maximize cost savings and improve the quality of care delivered. It involves physicians as well as patients, and sometimes workplace medical personnel, in following clinical treatment guidelines, in educating patients on self-care, and in proactive intervention of chronic situations. Case managers monitor prior treatment history and current treatment regimes as well as ensure that information is provided to physicians and patients.

- *Case management* programs deal with specific, severe illnesses, in order to avoid unnecessary, inappropriate, or excessive care. Ideally, the member progresses through the prior stages of the patient care continuum to minimize the need for large case management, or at least start case management before the health problem has already reached the severe phase.

Increasingly, managed care companies are employing clinical specialists with expertise in areas of more common case management activity, such as AIDS, cancer, high-risk pregnancy and neonatology, head and spine injury, pediatrics, cardiovascular disease, and organ transplants. At this point, patient care shifts from primary care to highly specialized disciplines.

Carve-out arrangements, for benefits such as prescription drugs, mental health and substance abuse treatment, and certain medical/surgical expenses (e.g., lab, maternity) are becoming increasingly popular among larger plan sponsors who wish to apply case management on specific services. Some companies have developed very specialized expertise in such areas. On the other hand, many diseases cannot be easily isolated into specific types of treatment and therefore must be treated more holistically. Cancer treatment, for example, often stretches across the spectrum of medical services—surgery, inpatient medicine, drugs, lab, and X-ray therapy—and treatments must be coordinated to ensure the best quality care of the patient in the most cost-effective manner possible.

Sample Pricing Model

Now that we have examined the *Price* and *Use* elements of the cost equation, let us bring them together in a pricing model.

Figure 8–2 is a sample pricing model showing the net savings an employer can expect when transferring from a fee-for-service indemnity plan to a PPO. (HMO and POS plans also can be used in this model. They are discussed later under certain assumptions). The model helps illustrate some of the basic pricing components used to evaluate the net cost advantage of establishing a managed care plan.

The model uses a hypothetical plan sponsor with 1,000 employees incurring $4 million in recorded medical benefit costs in 2000, estimated to increase 20 percent in 2001 in a completely unmanaged environment,[4] to an estimated $4.8 million, as shown in steps 1 through 6.

With implementation of a PPO plan, the net expected plan costs would be a combination of in-network and non-network expenses. Steps 7 through 13 illustrate how the PPO in-network costs are projected. Using the starting point of historical indemnity claims, line 8 shows a lower expected trend of 14 percent, as compared with the 20 percent for non-managed plans, which produces a lower claims-per-employee cost, before PPO adjustments.

---

4 Trend increase figures used are based on historic averages for indemnity and PPO plans.

F I G U R E   8–2

Sample Managed Care Pricing Model for 1,000-Employee Plan

Steps	Amounts
1. 2000 recorded medical claims indemnity	$4,000,000
2. Covered employees	1,000
3. Average 2000 claims per employee (lines 1/2)	$ 4,000
4. Projected indemnity trend increase	× 20%
5. Expected 2001 claims per employee (lines 3 x 4)	$4,800
6. Expected 2001 indemnity costs (lines 2 x 5)	$4,800,000
Projected PPO In-Network Claim Costs	
7. Average 2000 claims per employee (line 3)	$ 4,000
8. Projected PPO trend increase	× 14%
9. PPO claims per employee before adjustments	$ 4,560
10. PPO claim cost adjustments	
a. Increased value of benefits (90% in-network)	× 107%
b. Network discounts	× 88%
c. Effect of utilization management	× 95%
11. Projected 2001 PPO claims per employee	$ 4,080
12. Expected average PPO participants (75 percent in-network usage)	× 750
13. Projected 2001 PPO claims costs	$3,060,000
Projected Non-network Claims Costs	
14. Average 2000 claims per employee (line 3)	$ 4,000
15. Projected indemnity trend increase (non-network)	× 20%
16. Expected 2001 claims per employee (lines 3 × 4)	$ 4,800
17. Non-network claim cost adjustments	
a. Decreased value of benefits (70 percent non-network)	× 92%
b. Network discounts	N/A
c. Effect of utilization management	x 97%
18. Projected 2001 PPO claims per employee	$ 4,284
19. Expected average PPO participants (75 percent in-network usage)	× 250
20. Projected 2001 PPO claims costs	$1,071,000
Summary Comparison	
21. Expected 2001 PPO total costs (lines 13 + 20)	$4,131,000
22. Expected 2001 indemnity costs (line 6)	$4,800,000
23. Net savings (line 22–21)	$ 669,000
% Savings (line 23/22)	14%

Note: Excludes additional costs of PPO network operation and UM administration.

Assumptions: Plan sponsor with 1,000 covered employees is covering a standard indemnity plan (80 percent after $200 deductible) to a full-service PPO plan (90 percent in-network/70 percent non-network). There are no provider networks or utilization management programs under the current group health plan. All employees are located in one location, with access to the new PPO network. Expected 75 percent average PPO network usage.

The PPO adjustments on line 10 include (a) an adjustment for higher in-network benefit level (90 percent versus standard 80 percent);[5] (b) an adjustment for the estimated value of PPO network discounts;[6] and (c) an adjustment to reflect the expected value of reduced utilization brought about by the precertification and concurrent review programs associated with the PPO.

These adjustments total an 11.5 percent reduction, which when multiplied by line 9, yields a net 2 percent increase in 2001 claims costs per employee in the PPO network. The expected average usage of the PPO network is 75 percent, so the claims of an average of 750 employees (and their covered dependents) will flow through the network side of the equation. (Note: The actual degree of network utilization will depend largely on the success of employee education about the PPO plan and the accessibility of network providers to employee locations.) While the illustration assumes 100 percent availability of PPO network providers, this assumption is generous, and in the majority of instances there will be some employees who live outside the available service area and therefore continue to receive indemnity benefits (80 percent after deductible).

However, that is only half of the story. The plan sponsor needs to understand that non-network benefits also are impacted, as shown in lines 14 through 20. Starting again with unadjusted 2000 claims per employee of $4,000, we apply the nonmanaged trend level (20 percent), to get a projected claims cost of $4,800 per employee before adjustments. The PPO non-network adjustments, on line 17, include (a) net benefit because of lower reimbursement levels and penalties for noncompliance (70 percent versus indemnity of 80 percent); (b) no adjustment for network discounts; and (c) a smaller adjustment for UM features, since the stand-alone programs generally are not as comprehensive as those integrated into the PPO plan operations. Assuming 25 percent non-network usage among eligible participants (line 19), the combined plan costs are increased about 7.1 percent between 2000 and 2001 versus 20 percent in the indemnity plan.

---

5 The actual benefit adjustment will vary, depending on other specific plan features, although it typically is not worth a full 10 percent since both plans eventually cover expenses above the coinsurance limits at 100 percent for catastrophic benefits.

6 Again, the exact value of discounts will vary among networks, although this adjustment reflects the full value of various discounts over the entire array of covered expenses. Therefore, even if the PPO network has an average hospital discount of 20 percent, this will only cover about half of total benefits, the balance going to physician, prescription drugs, and ancillary services. For our illustration, we show an overall 12 percent discount adjustment; again, this is a one-time adjustment in the level of expected paid claims, and future years' costs are influenced only by the continued impact of utilization management procedures, except for minor adjustments in average discount levels negotiated by the PPO manager.

On a composite basis, total 2001 PPO claims costs (network and non-network) are shown at $4,131,000 (line 21) as contrasted with the original projected indemnity claim costs of $4,800,000 (line 22), resulting in an estimated savings of $669,000 or 14 percent less than nonmanaged care. Instead of a 20 percent cost increase for 2001, the plan sponsor would see about 6 percent. As mentioned above, this pricing model is used here for illustrative purposes only. Actual network discounts and UM adjustments will vary among networks and vendors. The point here is to understand some of the components that impact the value of PPO plan pricing.

The results are even more dramatic over longer periods. Unmanaged costs in 2002 would increase another 20 percent, to $5,760 per employee, for a total of $5,760,000. For the PPO plan, trend levels are expected to be at 14 percent per annum, for a resulting expected cost of $4,709 per employee, for total annual costs of $4,709,000, or 19 percent lower than the nonmanaged plan. The spread in cost differences continues to grow in additional years because trend levels are expected to be higher among nonmanaged plans, as compared to managed care plans.

Point-of-service plans also can be evaluated using the same model with essentially the same methodology. There would be higher UM savings, brought about by referral management. The net difference can be significant, since referral management more directly controls utilization of medical services.

Health maintenance organizations' net savings are not as easily evaluated using the above pricing model, especially when capitation is the method of reimbursement with provider revenues capped; the frequency of services (utilization) is a more direct concern for the provider. When capitation reimbursement is used, the traditional methods of evaluation shown in the pricing model become obscure. The fixed revenue of capitation translates into a fixed level of paid claims. In fact, if all providers within an HMO are capitated, the premium becomes one fixed prospective payment to providers.

Studies show HMOs produce better control over trend levels than other forms of managed care alternatives. Indeed, several national insurers that operate both PPO and HMO plans expect lower premium increases among their HMOs.[7] Furthermore, a 1994 Congressional Budget Office study indicated that HMOs, in general, reduced utilization 7.8 percent over comparable fee-for-service plans and also found that the result-

---

7 *Medical Benefits 8*, No. 2, (January 20, 1991), quoting Michael Schachner in *Business Insurance*, December 17, 1990.

ing cost savings would have been even greater if the benefit differentials were the same between HMO and fee-for-service plans.[8]

The premise under which managed care was conceived was that virtually any form of managed health care would be less expensive than nonmanaged health care.[9] This often intuitive assumption on the part of plan sponsors is now supported by growing amounts of statistical data showing that managed care plans offer greater potential for lower cost increases.

EVALUATING MANAGED CARE

As with any facet of employee benefit planning, it is important for the plan sponsor to consider the value of managed care within the context of its broader employee benefits/human resources objectives and company culture.

Picking a managed care product "off the shelf," without prior analysis of the plan sponsor's goals and benefits philosophy is generally an ill-advised step, regardless of the proposed cost savings of the program. Health benefits are perhaps the most visible part of employee benefits since they are the most frequently used by plan participants and often the most expensive. Thus, implementing a managed care plan can have a profound impact on the way employees view their total benefits. The plan sponsor must carefully consider and balance the impact of any managed care plan on member satisfaction against the potential for cost savings, remembering that the realities of the local health care environment play a critical part in this evaluation.

Functional Approach to Evaluating Health Care Plans

A thorough evaluation of employee needs, company compensation philosophy, and other considerations, in a functional approach model as dis-

---

8 The Congressional Budget Office study indicated that group and staff model HMOs reduced plan utilization by 19.6 percent versus fee-for-service, but that IPA-based HMOs were only marginally effective. However, IPA models were judged to be equivalent to group and staff model HMOs in terms of cost effectiveness if they actively employed best practices, risk sharing, and improved information management systems. *Managed Care Week*, March 20, 1995, Atlantic Information Services, Inc., Washington, DC.

9 For example, in a speech at the 1990 Certified Employee Benefit Specialist Conference, Patricia M. Nazemetz, director of benefits for the Xerox Corporation, expressed a strong feeling that managed care, over the long term, can produce savings over the fee-for-service indemnity business, although "that side of the business (fee-for-service) is in such a very bad state of repair that almost anything should be able to improve that process."

cussed in Chapter 2, are critical steps before adopting any managed care plan. Figure 8–3 may prove helpful in this evaluation. Like the managed care spectrum analysis, using a functional approach to evaluating health plans provides a way to compare plan sponsor needs and objectives across the spectrum of health plan alternatives.

1. *Planning orientation* addresses the plan sponsor's readiness to implement a health care program that requires a long-term commitment. Indemnity and PPO plans are better in a shorter-term orientation because changes in plan design can be adopted fairly easily without a large disruption to the membership population. HMO and POS plans are typically less flexible in plan design, and because members are required to select a PCP, they may be more reluctant to switch physicians if the plan sponsor later decides to change managed care plans. Thus, the plan sponsor must be fairly comfortable with the HMO or POS plan at the outset and be willing to avoid frequent intervention.

2. *Member satisfaction* is often difficult to obtain because there are many aspects to satisfaction: provider access, quality of care, claims processing, member service responsiveness, and adequate and appropriate communications. Managed care plans require greater member understanding of process and procedure than do traditional plans and often limit choice; initial member satisfaction is commonly not high. However, as participation grows, members usually reach a comfort level with how managed care operates. HMO membership survey results show improving satisfaction rates. This seems to be particularly true among longer-term members.[10] It is important for the plan sponsor to understand and address member concerns with managed care. This often requires additional communications and regular surveys.

3. *Provider choice* becomes more restricted as managed care becomes stronger. Most employees are concerned with being able to select their physicians without outside interference and to choose when, where, and how to receive health care services. Managed care products are deliberately designed to steer members to more cost-effective providers and treatment settings, which limits freedom of selection. HMOs and POS plans, which require the use of a PCP to access services, are the most restrictive. However, members who are pleased with their PCPs may not express dissatisfaction with this aspect of the plan.

4. *Cost savings*, as discussed in the managed care pricing analysis above, is best achieved with stronger-form managed care plans, which

---

10 As reported in *Managed Care Week*, March 21, 1995, Atlantic Information Services, Inc., Washington, DC.

FIGURE 8-3

Functional Approach to Evaluating Health Plans

Plan Sponsor Needs and Objectives	Standard Indemnity	Managed Indemnity	Managed Care Alternatives		
			Preferred Provider Plan	Point-of-Service Plan	Health Maintenance Organization
Planning orientation	Short term	Short term	Moderate term	Long term	Long term
Member satisfaction	High degree	High degree	High to moderate	Moderate	Moderate
Provider choice	High degree	High degree	Moderate	Moderate to low	Low degree
Cost savings	Low degree	Low to moderate	Moderate	Moderate to high	High degree
Cost-control features	Low degree	Low to moderate	Moderate	Moderate to high	High degree
Financial reporting/ funding features	High degree	High degree	High degree	High to moderate	Low degree

have proven abilities to control both the price and use components of the cost equation.

5. *Cost containment features* are more prevalent and stronger with stronger forms of managed care programs.

6. *A broader range of financial reporting/funding alternatives* is generally more available with fee-for-service and PPO plans because these plans typically reimburse providers on a "reasonable and customary" or fee schedule basis. Some POS and HMO plans can offer funding alternatives; however, commercial HMOs are typically restricted, by statutory regulation, to offering only prospective funding. Furthermore, the extent to which HMOs reimburse providers on a capitated basis affects the value of experience rating to the plan sponsor; that is, claims payments are more or less equal to the sum of prospective cap payments made to providers. HMOs commonly have had difficulty in providing detailed utilization and cost reports because of the nature of paying on a capitated basis.

Evaluating Managed Care Proposals: Network Adequacy

To evaluate health plan alternatives and potentially select an appropriate managed care option, a plan sponsor may hire an agent, broker, or consulting firm that specializes in group/health and managed care plans. This analysis typically results in the development of a request for proposal (RFP), a detailed document that provides information to managed care companies about the plan sponsor and invites those companies to offer proposals in response to the request. Evaluating RFP responses can be exhausting, and this is where the assistance of a qualified professional can be most valuable. Managed care consultants each have their own method of evaluating proposals depending on the plan sponsor's objectives and their own experience. Commonly, different weights are assigned to portions of the RFP, with competing companies compared on the weighted results of their proposal.

Typically, the first step is to conduct a review of network adequacy or access to providers. While the request for information (RFI, a shorter, less formal document than the RFP) "site match" process provides some preliminary information, conducting a more detailed "disruption analysis," which compares members' most commonly used physicians to those in competing networks, is a good idea. The results will show the number of members who would need to switch providers in the new managed care plan. Minimizing member disruption is important for two reasons: to improve member acceptance of the managed care program since fewer members will need to switch providers in order to receive favorable network benefits, and to increase the probability of increased network utilization. On the other hand, a close provider match should not be the sole basis for network selection, especially if the managed care company otherwise fails to demonstrate proper price management and utilization controls. A broad network does not necessarily mean effective cost control or provision of quality health care. Network configuration and provider adequacy are also important criteria in examining the adequacy of a network. Networks must be well-dispersed geographically and include the necessary medical disciplines to be able to deliver services at all levels of care. That is a difficult challenge in many parts of the country since managed care network development varies significantly across the United States. Differences in population demographics, availability of medical care and hospital facilities, the influence of local provider associations, and the statutory regulations of medical providers have influenced the ability of managed care vendors to build viable, cost-effective networks and products.

For example, managed care is well developed in California and other western states. A 1999 study of HMO penetration within the largest metropolitan statistical areas (MSAs) showed that the West accounted for 6 of the top 10 cities, with 59.5 percent HMO penetration in California, 55.4 percent in Utah, 52 percent in Colorado, and 47.8 percent in Arizona.[11]

In contrast, HMO penetration in New York City and the northern New Jersey area was 39.2 percent and 35.8 percent, respectively. Pockets of significant HMO market presence also exist in such diverse areas as Minneapolis/St. Paul, Boston, and Washington, D.C., all of which are in the top 10 MSAs. To the extent HMO market penetration is indicative of the availability and acceptance of managed care alternatives, these data show that managed care plans are evolving at different paces across the country. This presents a very real challenge for the plan sponsor that has multiple locations across the country and yet wishes to maintain a uniform approach to its health plan offerings.

Although most national managed care organizations are able to provide uniform administrative systems for managed care plans, the underlying delivery platform may vary from area to area in order to conform to accepted practices within those areas. Plan sponsors need to be aware of these possible differences in advance of committing to a given managed care product so they can be prepared to accept modifications in plan

---

11 SMG Marketing Group, Inc., as reported in HMO-PPO Digest, *Managed Care Digest Series 1999*, published by Hoechst Marion Roussel, Kansas City, MO; www.managedcaredigest.com

design or product offerings and can take advantage of the best offerings available in each geographical area. Frequently, this may result in selecting several different organizations, depending on which is strongest in a given geographic area of the country.

The plan sponsor also may consider whether to seek bundled versus unbundled managed care services. The bundled approach provides as many services as possible—access to a network, contract negotiations, UM, QA, claims and reporting—from a single vendor, such as a national managed care company or regional HMO. A bundled approach simplifies administration by reducing the number of organizations and contracts to be managed.

Conversely, the unbundled approach allows the plan sponsor to contract directly with a variety of organizations for different services or to develop its own network through direct negotiations with providers. In an unbundled approach, one company may be used for utilization management and quality assurance, another for claims payment. Sometimes, the plan sponsor handles some functions internally, hiring staff to assume the new responsibilities. Some plan sponsors feel that the unbundled approach is the best way to obtain the best quality services because the different vendors theoretically have specialized expertise in the area chosen. Unbundling is particularly concerned with prescription drug and mental health services. An obvious disadvantage to this approach is the resulting administrative complexity occurring with multiple vendors.

Many employers find themselves somewhere in the middle between the purely bundled and the purely unbundled approach. For example, an employer may contract with one vendor to insure the indemnity plan and one or more HMOs and/or PPOs to serve the employer's different geographic locations.

Evaluating Managed Care Proposals: Quality Assurance

Traditional indemnity health plans do not actively monitor the quality of care being delivered. Members select the providers, and the providers' patients are responsible for the quality of care. The growth of managed care has spawned increased interest in quality assurance. Because much of the cost savings from managed care comes from managing and sometimes restricting utilization, MCOs must ensure that decreased utilization still results in appropriate health care delivery. Thus, insurers and HMOs are investing in methods to measure quality and ensure that quality health care is being provided. In evaluating MCO proposals, quality assurance programs are a critical component. While Chapter 9 provides an in-depth look at quality issues in health care, including evaluating quality in networks, the following discussion presents a high-level profile of key quality considerations for a proposal.

Assuming that the general network configuration matches well with employee locations, the plan sponsor must next understand how the managed care company selects its network providers and what types of quality assurance mechanisms are incorporated into plan management. The network provider is "front line" with plan members, and members' overall plan satisfaction level is often determined by their interaction with providers. This point cannot be overstated since the principal element in managed care plans is the deliberate alignment of contracted providers with membership. Not surprisingly, therefore, many quality assurance programs place considerable emphasis on the selection and credentialing process for providers.

Selection is primarily focused on ensuring that there are sufficient numbers of providers within a geographic area to ensure adequate availability of providers to patients. The plan also must ensure that there is a sufficient mix of PCPs and specialists to meet membership needs.

Credentialing helps ensure that providers meet acceptable levels of expertise and professionalism. While each managed care company has its own set of credentialing requirements, the following are representative of some of the standard areas considered:

Sample Physician Guidelines

1. Graduation from an accredited medical school.
2. Valid state license/Drug Enforcement Administration (DEA) registration.
3. Clinical privileges at a licensed participating hospital.
4. Current malpractice coverage/history.
5. Federation check of state licensure.
6. No mental/physical restriction on performing necessary services.
7. No prior disciplinary action/criminal conviction or indictment.
8. No prior involuntary termination of employment or contract.
9. No evidence of inappropriate utilization patterns.
10. Agreement to follow utilization programs, including periodic on-site review of procedures and adherence to contractual obligations.

Sample Hospital Credentialing Guidelines

1. Joint Commission on Accreditation of Hospitals (JCAHO) accreditation.
2. Contractual warranty of state license.
3. Agreement to participate in the various utilization control programs.

While credentialing does not guarantee the provision of quality medical care, it is an important indicator of the managed care company's commitment to provide high-quality levels of care for plan members. In fact, adherence to established credentialing standards is among the most important evaluation areas for the National Committee on Quality Assurance (NCQA).

NCQA standards for accreditation cover the following areas:

1. Quality management and improvement including:
   a. How effectively the plan works to continuously improve the quality of care.
   b. How the plan makes sure that members have access to the care needed.
   c. What demonstrable improvement in quality the plan can show.
2. Physician credentials including:
   a. How thoroughly the plan reviews physician qualifications.
   b. How the plan monitors physicians on a continuous basis.
3. Utilization management including:
   a. How fairly, consistently, and promptly the plan makes UM decisions.
   b. The basis of medical judgment used in making such decisions.
   c. How the plan reduces administrative hassles in authorizing services.
4. Member's rights and responsibilities including:
   a. How the plan communicates to members about how to get care and services.
   b. How member complaints are handled.
   c. How membership satisfaction is measured.
5. Preventive health including:
   a. How the plan promotes health and encourages members to use preventive services, such as immunization and mammograms.

    b. How the plan measures what percentage of membership receive such care.

6. Medical records including;
    a. The completeness of medical records.
    b. How those records show communication between PCPs and specialists.

NCQA is largely recognized as the leading accrediting body for managed care plans, primarily HMOs, in the United States.[12] While NCQA accreditation is not required by either federal or state government, a growing number of HMOs and other managed care plans are voluntarily seeking accreditation. As of mid-1995, over one-third of the country's licensed HMOs had sought NCQA accreditation, with 149 receiving some form of approval and 23 plans denied accreditation.[13]

An increasing number of large employers are requiring managed care plans to either have received NCQA accreditation or have an established plan towards accreditation in order to be offered to plan members. NCQA accreditation has become a way for plan sponsors to measure the performance of a health plan and assess the value of their health care purchase.

Evaluating Managed Care Proposals: Site Visits

Once the plan sponsor has narrowed down potential vendors based on an evaluation of the proposal responses to the RFP, visits to the sites of the finalists' operations are recommended to further verify the written materials and to meet the staff responsible for operating the health plan. Agendas for such meetings vary, although it is common for the plan sponsor to list specific areas they wish to discuss during the visit. Most site visits will seek to at least interview and question those health plan personnel who will service the business. It is also common for the bidding company to demonstrate the computer systems that are used to support its business, including claims administration, member services, UM protocol programs, and other medical management information systems.

Because there are often expert staff from different areas of the bidding company present at the site, it is advisable for the plan sponsor to

---

12 For a full description of NCQA requirements, contact the National Committee on Quality Assurance, 1350 New York Avenue, N.W., Suite 700, Washington, DC 20005; (202) 628-5788.

13 As reported in *Managed Care Week*, June 19, 1995, Atlantic Information Services, Inc., Washington, DC.

consider bringing individuals who have the appropriate expertise to ask the necessary questions and understand the operation. Preparation is important in this phase, and the consultant should help the plan sponsor establish objectives for the site visit and conduct a post-visit debriefing to make sure all outstanding issues and questions have been addressed. For plan sponsors with multiple locations, it may be appropriate to conduct site visits in each of the principle locations because health plan management and operation may vary from site to site.

In addition to the site visit, the plan sponsor may wish to consider contacting current customers of the bidding companies to assess references. Employer and employee satisfaction of managed care will be largely affected by the ability of the managed care company to follow through on commitments and meet the objectives of the plan sponsor. The Health Plan Employer Data and Information Set (HEDIS) reports provide one means of plan comparisons for plan sponsors. While surveys show members are generally satisfied with managed care, satisfaction rates will vary among different managed care plans.[14]

MANAGED CARE OUTLOOK AND EVALUATION

At the start of the 21st century, the health care insurance system in the United States is at a brink. Managed care plans have grown to dominate the system, as noted above. While managed care has saved plan sponsors significant costs over the past 20 years, as compared to traditional fee-for-service plans, the system is now facing increased criticism from virtually all constituents for its complex processes, administrative burden, and perceived access restrictions to desired providers. Some believe that managed care plans have effectively run their course and, as a result, many provider organizations and legislatures, at both the state and federal level, are pressing for fundamental changes to dramatically revise or eliminate much of what the managed care industry has built.

However, proponents of managed care generally see beyond the immediate system problems and point to an ongoing evolution of the health care delivery and financing system. Managed care, in this context, is not an end point, but a continually improving process to control costs and demonstrably improve the quality of care delivered. At the center of the evolution is a huge paradigm shift in health care accountability, with

---

14 A survey of 132,000 members under age 65 and 14,000 aged 65 and over by the Group Health Association of America (GHAA) found that HMO plans rated same or better levels of member satisfaction as FFS plans. "Managed Care Stats & Facts," *Managed Care Week*, July 31, 1995, Atlantic Information Services, Inc., Washington, DC.

members in much greater control of information and selecting those health plans and providers who demonstrate results.[15]

This shift towards increased consumerism in health care challenges the long-held premise that important health care decisions were primarily delegated to physicians and that health plan costs were primarily hidden from members through the third-party insurance coverage system. Health plans are investing heavily in new technology and data management systems to help members get access to information that can support a much broader role for them in making health decisions.

They also are using these new tools to help physicians practice evidence-based medicine. Improved performance will be increasingly expected as providers gain greater exposure to the best practices and outcomes measurement.[16] Transforming health care delivery into a systematic, evidence-based approach based on best practice also will require proper realignment of financial incentives with clinical practices. Provider compensation models, which historically have relied on discounted fees in a managed care environment, also will continue to evolve to reward demonstrated quality.[17]

A more detailed exploration of the impact of e-commerce and Internet technology upon the health care delivery and insurance system is covered later in this chapter.

Development of Defined Contribution Health Plans

An increasing number of plan sponsors are considering a new strategy for their health benefits, to maintain control of employer costs while giving plan members an increasing degree of choice and decision-making. While managed care continues to be the main component of most employers' health benefits, employees are demanding a greater ability to select those plans which best suit their individual needs – another aspect of increased consumerism.

15 Managed Care, "What's Next?," Vol. 8, No. 11, November, 1999; MediMedia USA, Trenton, NJ, Peter Lee, Executive Director of the Center for Health Care Rights reports that increased consumerism and patient empowerment are powered by several elements: (a) greatly informed consumers who approach their physicians with considerably more information than historically available; (b) much closer scrutiny of costs of alternative procedures, especially as members have increased benefit options that give them increased incentives to reduce costs; and a growing demand for action to address the health care needs of an exploding uninsured population.

16 Ibid. Karen Ignagni, CEO of American Association of Health Plans also points to greater demands upon health plans to coordinate care and expand disease management programs.

17 Ibid. Peter Kuhn, MD, VP, Kaiser Permanente further points out that the speed of health system transformation will demand on how quickly embattled providers feel relief from excessive administrative processes and external demands of payors and regulators.

Some analysts see the defined contribution concept as being driven by the convergence of several factors, including:

- General backlash against existing managed care plans;
- Broad popularity and acceptance of 401(k)-style retirement plans;
- Rapid rise of Internet access to help members gain information about medical care choices; and
- A sense that accountability demanded by end-consumers will have more real impact on health plans and providers than can be demanded by the plan sponsor (e.g. members ultimately vote by their enrollment).[18]

The concept is similar to 401(k) retirement plans in that the plan sponsor would contribute a fixed amount for each employee's health benefits, often tied to either the lowest cost plan available or some composite index of available plans. Then, plan participants typically would be able to select from several types of health plans often including several managed care plans and perhaps traditional fee-for-service.

Any difference between actual plan premiums and the plan sponsor's contribution would be paid by those participants who select that particular health plan. In this manner, the fixed contribution serves to cap current and future plan sponsor costs, with any future premium cost increases being borne in whole or in part by plan participants.

Several impediments still remain before defined contribution health plans gain broader acceptance, including:

- Certain federal tax code changes to permit full deductibility of unused employer contributions;
- Lack of consistent performance data among competing managed care health plans, or no data in the case of traditional fee-for-service plans;
- Plan sponsor concerns about employees making poor selections relative to their health needs or high-risk employees being able to qualify for affordable coverage;
- Rising health care costs, and employee contributions, forcing some participants to drop coverage altogether further increasing the number of working uninsured.[19]

---

18 Ron Winslow and Carol Gentry, "Companies Consider Letting Employee Handle Health Benefits Decision," *The Wall Street Journal*, February 8, 2000.

19 Ibid.

Nonetheless, there is significant plan sponsor interest in the development of the defined contribution health plan strategy. A 1999 study by management consultant firm Booz-Allen & Hamilton showed that 23 percent of plan sponsors surveyed were willing to actively advocate for changes and ready to implement them when they become available. Further, another 67 percent were watching developments with plans ready to consider when changes become available.[20]

The Overshadowing of the Uninsured

Despite the increased emphasis on health care issues in the last decade, and although there are millions more people working as a result of a prolonged period of economic prosperity, the number of uninsured Americans rose in the 1990s. While economic growth generally increased family income levels, the costs of health coverage rose faster, which dampened the expansion of health coverage for many working families. Wherein 34.7 million people, about 13.9 percent of the U.S. population, were uninsured in 1990, an estimated 44.3 million Americans, or 16.3 percent of the population, were without health insurance by 1998.[21]

The Health Insurance Association of America (HIAA) commissioned a study in 1998, and a follow-up one in 1999, with the Center for Risk Management and Insurance Research of Georgia State University. A summary of the sources of health insurance coverage among the 1998 U.S. population is shown in Figure 8–4.[22]

Among the key findings was that despite the rise in employment levels and a relative increase in average family income levels, the percentage of those without health insurance actually rose in the 1990s. Furthermore, while males constitute a larger share of the uninsured in virtually every age group, the fastest growing share of uninsured were females. The study ominously points to a dramatic worsening of the problem in the event of an economic downturn. With a recession, uninsured ranks could grow to an estimated 60 million people, more than 25 percent of the total U.S. population, by 2008.[23]

---

20 "Employers Mixed in Attitudes Toward Defined-Contribution Health Programs," *Managed Care Week,* Vol. 10, No. 9, March 6, 2000; Atlantic Information Services, Washington, D.C.; www.ManagedCareNewsWeb.com

21 Charles Ornstein and Laura Beil, "Medically Insured Up in 90s," *The Dallas Morning News.* September 26, 2000.

22 "Health Insurance Coverage and the Uninsured: 1990-1998", Health Insurance Association of America, www.hiaa.org

23 Ibid.

FIGURE 8—4

Sources of Health Insurance

	U.S. Population	
Employer—direct	87,587,483	32%
Employer—indirect	80,620,406	30%
Individual coverage	24,546,744	9%
Total Private Coverage	190,488,214	71%
Medicare	35,886,608	13%
Medicaid	27,851,854	10%
Total Public Coverage	65,355,267	24%
Uninsured	44,278,762	16%
TOTAL POPULATION	271,004,107	100%

Note: The total for insurance categories may exceed 100 percent because individuals may have multiple sources of coverage.

Source: Health Insurance Association of America

The primary predicator of lack of insurance is income level. According to the HIAA study, 41 percent of uninsured are below 150 percent of the poverty level, 55 percent are below 200 percent of the poverty level, and almost 85 percent of the uninsured make less than 400 percent of the poverty level.[24]

Aggravating the problem is higher costs of health insurance for smaller businesses, which do not have the same ability to spread risks or to self-insure as larger companies. Other concerns deal with employers who feel pressured to pass along additional costs to their employees if health care costs continue to increase faster than general inflation, or if employers face additional costs due to legislation permitting plan members to sue plan sponsors.

A 1999 survey of 400 plan sponsors commissioned by the American Association of Health Plans indicates that more than 70 percent would pass along costs to members if health care premiums increase by $125 per month. More than 75 percent indicated they would either raise contributions or reduce benefits if they incur additional costs associated with legislation allowing employees to sue employers over health care coverage decisions.[25]

---

24 Ibid.

25 "Firms Would Reduce Health Coverage If Liability of Costs are Increased," *Managed Care Week*, Vol. 10, No. 6, February 7, 2000; Atlantic Information Services, Washington, D.C.; www.ManagedCareNewsWeb.com.

According to HIAA, the states with the highest rates of uninsured include: Texas and Arizona (27 percent); California, New Mexico, and Nevada (24 percent); Mississippi (23 percent); Montana (22 percent); and Florida, Louisiana, and West Virginia (21 percent). Those with the lowest rates include Minnesota and Nebraska (10 percent); Iowa and Vermont (11 percent); and Hawaii, Kansas, Massachusetts, Missouri, Ohio, Pennsylvania, and Rhode Island (12 percent).[26]

The growth in public and private initiatives on ways to extend coverage to the uninsured, especially children, underscores the societal importance being placed on tackling this issue. Without consistent health care coverage, medical treatment is often deferred until conditions reach acute stages. General health also can be further jeopardized without regular preventive care and recommended screening tests.

The apparent correlation between increases in health care costs and the growth in the number of uninsured persons underscores the importance of continuing to evolve managed care in a manner that can continue to control costs and make benefits more affordable. As public policy is shaped to further extend coverage, managed care programs will continue to be an important vehicle used to deliver health coverage.

THE E-MERGENCE OF E-HEALTH

Perhaps no single non-clinical factor holds greater promise in fostering the continued evolution of health care delivery and financing in the United States than the explosive growth of "e-health," which uses the Internet and Web-based technology to dramatically enhance communication and information transfer among various health care constituents.

Information technology has been vitally important to the health insurance industry for decades. In fact, the insurance industry was one of the earliest, broad-scale users of mainframe data systems for record keeping and claims processing. Today, few health plans could operate effectively without fully automated eligibility, billing, claims and medical management systems.

However, the advent of the Internet has dramatically changed business operations throughout the country, in virtually every industry. The impact in health care is monumental, with the ability to greatly expand the flow of information among providers, health plans, plan sponsors, and consumers unlike any venue to date.

---

26 Op. Cit. HIAA Study.

Realities of Managed Care Today

As mentioned earlier in this chapter and in Chapter 7, some form of managed care is the prevalent means of health care coverage for most Americans. As a result, the vast majority of medical claim payments today are already discounted or reimbursed in some negotiated manner. With the continued consolidation of MCOs and health care systems, coupled with the tremendous financial pressures placed on hospitals and health care systems because of Medicare/ Medicaid payment reductions in the late 1990s, discounts in many metropolitan areas have reached practical limits. While there will continue to be active management of unit costs, the days of purely discounted managed care are past.

Similarly, the days of micro-inspection forms of utilization management are waning. Many of the largest MCOs have significantly loosened or eliminated their prospective methods of utilization approvals for many medical services. Some HMOs have even eliminated the referral management systems between primary care physicians and specialists. In lieu of a prior PCP referral, these plans often have higher co-payments for direct, self-referred specialist treatment. Such "open access" plans provide greater flexibility for plan members in seeking care as well as eliminating the time-consuming processes previously required for referrals.

In addition, the rapid increase in state and federal mandates (e.g., 48-hour maternity confinements), coupled with the potential passage of federal legislation allowing plan participants to sue their health benefits plan has forced the moderation or elimination of many standard UM procedures.

As managed care continues to evolve, it is evermore apparent that the key to effective health care is getting the right patient the right medical service at the right time. Central to facilitating this process is the need to significantly change communication and knowledge-sharing within the patient/provider relationship, including:

- Immediately accessible and correct data on plan benefits, member eligibility, and claims status;
- Increased patient knowledge of illness and treatment options;
- Continuous communication among the patient, the provider, and the health plan to aid in the timely and appropriate level of medical service.

Increasing consumer demand in health care delivery is aiding this evolution. As information becomes more timely, more accurate and more usable, consumers will be more willing to accept responsibility for their health care, and to be more involved in specific decisions regarding the quantity, quality, and cost of health care selected. This degree of increased "consumerism" is leading a paradigm shift in an industry which traditionally placed the patient largely outside of the decision-making circle.

Realities of E-Commerce Today

Virtually all sectors of American business have incorporated some degree of e-commerce strategies into their business operations, whether through sales distribution on external Web sites or e-mail communications with other business partners through the Internet. The growth of business-to-business ("B2B") relationships has improved communication and information management among suppliers and business vendors. Likewise, the growth of business-to-consumer ("B2C") applications on the Internet has generated new sales and marketing opportunities as well as a wider variety of direct customer services.

Furthermore, the Internet has created a time compression in information exchange previously unseen in corporate business, especially within service-based industries. Web-based service models, which rely much more on the use of automated assistance, can be created, changed to meet consumer preferences, or completely eliminated in much shorter time periods than traditional service models, which were largely dependent on human assistance.

Through Internet-based technology, many service-based companies and consumer product manufacturers, can make changes in product/service type and distribution and can even respond to market pricing changes in a fraction of the time previously required. As consumers grow increasingly able to access this quicker form of information, those companies who do not take full advantage of Internet technology will find themselves at a great competitive disadvantage.

The Internet also facilitates the ability of different companies to blend their specialized expertise in various new combinations. With the formation of unique partnerships, "virtual" companies can create end-to-end product/service development and management. This permits the quick formulation of new types of products, often faster than a single company could devote internal resources to accomplish the same objective.

More than 100 e-health care companies were launched in 1999.[27] In the managed health care industry, examples of emerging partnerships

---

27 Ellen Licking, "E-Health May Be Just What Managed Care Ordered," *Business Week*, January 10, 2000.

include: InteliHealth, which is owned by Aetna, Inc. and receives medical content information from the Harvard Medical School; and, Humana, Inc., whose Internet Web site holds content agreements with Healtheon/ WebMD.[28]

E-Health Development Stages

Managed health care is an excellent industry for capitalizing on the benefits of e-commerce, the collective aspects of which are referred to as e-health. The development of e-health capabilities for managed health care companies falls broadly into the following stages:

1. Quality web page awareness is the simplest stage in development, with web page development now readily available through business and consumer software applications. Virtually all health plans have at least a basic web page, with company information and product portfolio information. While the basic web page may allow hyper links to other Web sites, most information is static and there is no transactional capabilities or data inquiry allowed.

2. Building basic interaction capabilities with constituents, which includes members, providers, and plan sponsors. Virtually all national and many regional/local health plans and carriers have varying abilities to provide e-mail communication and to access detailed databases for information retrieval. However, these interactions tend to be limited to specific functions, such as accessing on-line provider directories or pulling down health plan information.

3. Building self-service capabilities for constituents marks a critical leap in the use of Internet technology since it requires real-time transactional competence combined with the ability to coordinate data from various information systems. This stage is the biggest growth area for health care plans in the 2000-2002 time period, as they increase their ability to offer on-line enrollment, referrals, and claim submission. While this stage will greatly improve the administrative quality of plan operations, most transactions are still "stove-pipe," with the constituent interacting in a specific function.

---

28 "Internet Strategies of Major Managed Care Organizations," *Managed Care Week*, Vol. 10, No. 8, February 21, 2000; Atlantic Information Services, Washington, D.C.; www.ManagedCareNewsWeb.com.

4. Transformation into seamless integrated operations is the ultimate stage in e-health development for health plans, wherein all transactions are real-time and span end-to-end across different operations, without interruption. Cross-functional electronic capabilities will enable specific business areas and systems (e.g., claims, plan eligibility) to interact simultaneously to serve the customer. In addition to further improving administrative capabilities, this stage holds significant potential for accelerating a patient's access to proper treatment, such as in the integration of information needed for effective disease management programs.

The Benefits of E-Health Development

At the center of the e-health evolution is the health plan member, who is the ultimate consumer of medical services as a patient. Eligibility data, enrollment data, claims data, treatment data, payment data all converge on the member/patient. Members are becoming more self-sufficient as they become more empowered with usable information, which in turn helps them maximize the value of their health plans. For members, the benefits of e-health include:

1. Maintaining personal health and family eligibility information;
2. Selection of a primary care physician as well as being able to inquire about other types of providers;
3. Checking on claim status, family eligibility, and flexible-spending account reimbursements;
4. Accessing health plan information such as the summary plan description; and
5. Searching general health care information about specific illnesses or general health topics.

Empowered and satisfied members reduce the administrative burden on plan sponsors. With e-health tools to speed up and improve operational duties, the plan sponsor can concentrate more on tailoring its benefit programs to best fit the needs of its employees. For plan sponsors, the benefits of e-health transactions include:

1. Plan set-up and maintenance, which can review for state benefit requirements and proper underwriting of benefit plans;
2. On-line member enrollment, which can provide immediate notification of enrollment errors and provide for direct production of member ID cards; and

3. On-line summary plan description, booklet, and certificate of coverage editing and production.

Similarly, with reduced manual intervention and paperwork, medical providers can return to practicing medicine and focusing on the best medical solutions for their patients. For providers, e-health benefits include:

1. Ability to submit claims electronically;
2. Checking patient plan benefits and eligibility;
3. Maintaining patient rosters for each type of health plan; and,
4. Receiving reimbursements electronically.

CHAPTER 9

Health Care Quality: Are We Getting Our Money's Worth?

William J. Mayer

INTRODUCTION

Employers have a number of reasons for offering medical benefits to their employees. Principal among them, perhaps, are the desire to be competitive in the recruitment and retention of employees, and the advantages of maintaining a productive workforce. As employers increasingly turn to managed care organizations (MCOs)—preferred provider organizations (PPOs), health maintenance organizations (HMOs) and point-of-service (POS) plans—to help control the cost of these benefits, many have recognized the need to address issues of quality of care to ensure that their medical benefit plan serves the purposes for which is was designed.[1] The risk is that employers will continue spending vast resources to provide a health care plan that is not valued by current and/or prospective employees and that fails to maintain the health and productivity of the workforce.

Despite the obvious importance of this value equation in health care purchasing, as in all other purchasing, many employers, employees, and families do not explicitly factor quality of care into their health care purchasing decisions. There may be many reasons for this apparent paradox. Some individuals may be skeptical of their own or their employer's ability to define and measure quality of care. Some may be intimidated in their dealings with health professionals because of a lack of technical knowledge of health care. Some may view managed care organizations as

---

1 I. Fraser, et al. "The Pursuit of Quality By Business Coalitions: A National Survey," *Health Affairs* 18 (1999), pp. 158–165.

contract and claims administrators, assuming that MCOs have little or no impact on quality of care.

This chapter describes further why it is important for employers to focus on quality of care in purchasing health care. It offers a definition of quality and discusses what we know about how to improve it. The chapter also presents suggestions for improving quality through changes in consumer and employer purchasing behavior, including practical approaches to evaluating the quality of MCOs, with options based on resources available for evaluation. Recommendations will be offered for setting quality performance standards and performance guarantees for managed care contracting. And, finally, additional resources will be suggested for those who wish to pursue efforts to improve the quality of their health care purchases. The chapter is intended to help the reader better appreciate the importance of quality of care in health care purchasing, gain a higher level of confidence in his or her ability to evaluate and improve quality of care, and become aware of resources available to further pursue the subject.

IS QUALITY OF CARE IMPORTANT?

Quality of health care is an important issue for employer and employee purchasers for a number of reasons. First, there are widespread documented errors in the delivery of health care services. Second, there is substantial evidence for extensive overuse and underuse of various health care services. Third, poor quality of care erodes the value of health care purchases. Fourth, failure to exercise due diligence in evaluating quality of care may increase an employer's liability for a bad outcome of care. And, finally, lack of attention to quality of care can have negative consequences for an employer in employee relations and relationships with providers and others in the local business community. Each of these reasons is discussed below.

Errors in the Delivery of Health Care Services

Almost 10 years ago, the Harvard Medical Practice Study found that injuries caused by medical management occurred in 3.7 percent of hospital admissions in New York State. Among these injuries were drug complications, wound infections, and technical complications. Fully 27.6 percent of these injuries were the result of negligence, and 13.6 percent of the injuries led to death.[2] Extrapolating these results to all U.S. hospital admissions in 1997, as many as 98,000 Americans may have died because of errors during their hospitalization in a single year.[3] Other studies have confirmed the order of magnitude of this estimate for injuries during hospital admissions. Yet, we must assume this is a gross understatement of the impact of medical errors, given that it does not include injuries because of outpatient care.

Recently, the Institute of Medicine focused attention on the impact of errors in medicine through the work of its Quality of Health Care in America Project. Its first published report—*To Err is Human: Building a Safer Health System*—notes: "More people die in a given year as a result of medical errors than from motor vehicle accidents (43,458), breast cancer (42,297), or AIDS (16,516)."[4] The group estimates that preventable adverse events result in total national costs of between $17 billion and $29 billion, over one-half of which are direct health care costs. Clearly, medical errors have a significant negative impact on employer health care costs, as well as employee health outcomes and productivity. These findings beg the question of what employers and individuals can do to help minimize the likelihood and the impact of medical errors in the health care services they purchase and receive – a question to be taken up later in this chapter.

Overuse of Health Care Services

Investigators have long noted dramatic geographic variations in the use of health care services, without apparent differences in the health of the populations being served. For example, Medicare hospitalization rates are 60 percent higher in Boston than in New Haven, yet Medicare mortality rates do not differ between the two cities.[5]

There is a large and growing body of research on the extent of medical care that is inappropriate or unnecessary. Studies of appropriateness of care have found that as much as 32 percent of selected procedures are

---

2 T. Brennan, et al., "Incidence of Adverse Events and Negligence in Hospitalized Patients: Results of the Harvard Medical Practice Study I." *New England Journal of Medicine* 324 (1991), pp. 370–376.

3 American Hospital Association, Hospital Statistics. Chicago, 1999.

4 Institute of Medicine, Committee on Quality of Health Care in America, L. Kohn, J. Corrigan, and M. Donaldson, editors. *To Err is Human: Building a Safer Health System*, National Academy Press, Washington, DC. 2000.

5 E. Fisher, et al., "Hospital Readmission Rates for Cohorts of Medicare Beneficiaries in Boston and New Haven," *New England Journal of Medicine* 331 (1994), pp. 989–995.

inappropriate.[6] An excellent example of current research supporting this estimate is the series of studies commissioned by the State of New York Cardiac Advisory Committee on the appropriateness of various cardiac procedures in New York State. Evaluation of coronary angiographies (inserting a catheter into coronary arteries and injecting contrast material) found that 20 percent were of uncertain appropriateness and 4 percent were clearly inappropriate.[7] When percutaneous transluminal coronary angioplasty (PTCA) (using a balloon catheter to open blood flow through a coronary artery) was evaluated, 38 percent were of uncertain appropriateness and 4 percent were clearly inappropriate. At some hospitals, as many as 57 percent of PTCAs were either inappropriate or of uncertain appropriateness.[8] In a companion study, inappropriate and uncertain use of coronary artery bypass graft surgery was found to be 2.4 percent and 7 percent, respectively. Though these rates may appear relatively low, they have significant health implications, given that the average mortality rate for patients undergoing surgery in the study was 2 percent, and the complication rate was 17 percent.[9]

These are but a few recent examples of research suggesting that inappropriate and unnecessary medical care has substantial negative consequences both for employee health and the cost of health care.

Underuse of Health Care Services

Another deficiency identified in health care quality is the failure to apply services known to be beneficial in improving health. In a study of patients hospitalized for acute myocardial infarction ("heart attack"), Marciniak and colleagues found that between 11 percent and 68 percent of patients nationwide did not receive particular standard treatments for this condition, despite being "ideal candidates" for therapies.[10] An earlier study found that internists and family physicians were less knowledgeable

---

6 R. H. Brook and M.E. Vaiana, "Appropriateness of Care: A Chart Book," (Washington, DC: National Health Policy Forum, 1989).

7 S.J. Bernstein et al., "The Appropriateness of Use of Coronary Angiography in New York State," *Journal of the American Medical Association,* 269 (1993), pp. 766–769.

8 L.H. Hilborne et al., "The Appropriateness of Percutaneous Transluminal Coronary Angioplasty in New York State," *Journal of the American Medical Association,* 269 (1993), pp. 761–765.

9 L.L. Leape et al., "The Appropriateness of Use of Coronary Artery Bypass Graft Surgery in New York State," *Journal of the American Medical Association,* 269 (1993), pp. 753–760.

10 T. Marciniak, et al., "Improving the Quality of Care for Medicare Patients With Acute Myocardial Infarction: Results From the Cooperative Cardiovascular Project," *Journal of the American Medical Association,* 279 (1998), pp. 1351–1357.

about, and less inclined to practice, state-of-the-art advances in treatment of acute myocardial infarction than were cardiologists.[11]

Similarly, a study of patients with diabetes treated in primary care offices found that between 55 percent and 84 percent of these patients did not receive optimal services recommended for their condition according to national guidelines in use. Optimal use of services varied by location of practice by as much as 238 percent.[12]

Some studies suggest that physicians are more likely to underuse health care services when treating women, particularly black women. Recently published research by Roger, et al. found that women with unstable angina (chest pain from blockages in arteries supplying blood to heart muscle) were 27 percent less likely to undergo non-invasive cardiac tests, and a startling 72 percent less likely to receive invasive cardiac procedures.[13]

There is also evidence to suggest that underuse varies by type of health plan. For example, Wells and colleagues found that patients in health plans financed by prepayment were less likely than fee-for-service plan patients to have depression detected or treated during an office visit.[14] A more recent study found that Medicare patients with joint pain who were enrolled in HMOs reported less improvement in symptoms than similar fee-for-service Medicare beneficiaries.[15] Yet, other research suggests no significant difference between quality of care in HMO and fee-for-service environments in such areas as hypertension and diabetes.[16]

Failure to apply services known to be beneficial in improving health is a substantial and widespread problem. Clearly, this type of quality problem has negative implications for employee health and productivity. The

11 J.Z. Ayanian et al., "Knowledge and Practices of Generalist and Specialist Physicians Regarding Drug Therapy for Acute Myocardial Infarction," *New England Journal of Medicine,* 331 (1994), pp. 1136–1142.

12 J.P. Weiner et al., "Variation in Office-Based Quality: A Claims-Based Profile of Care Provided to Medicare Patients with Diabetes," *Journal of the American Medical Association,* 273 (1995), pp. 1503–1508.

13 V. Roger, et al., "Sex Differences in Evaluation and Outcome of Unstable Angina." *Journal of the American Medical Association,* 283 (2000), pp. 646–652. See also D. Mark, "Sex Bias in Cardiovascular Care: Should Women Be Treated More Like Men?," *Journal of the American Medical Association,* 283 (2000), pp. 659–661.

14 K.B. Wells et al., "Detection of Depressive Disorder for Patients Receiving Prepaid or Fee-for-Service Care," *Journal of the American Medical Association,* 262 (1989), pp. 3298–3302.

15 D.G. Clement et al., "Access and Outcomes of Elderly Patients Enrolled in Managed Care," *Journal of the American Medical Association,* 271 (1994), pp. 1487–1492.

16 S. Greenfield et al., "Outcomes of Patients with Hypertension and Non Insulin Dependent Diabetes Mellitus Treated by Different Symptoms and Specialties," Results from the Medical Outcomes Study, *Journal of the American Medical Association,* 274 (1995), pp. 1436–1444.

implications for cost of care are more variable, because some of the under-used services may result in a net increase in direct medical care costs, despite being effective in preventing negative and costly health outcomes. Nevertheless, in purchasing health care for ourselves or for employees, these are services we would want to receive as part of state-of-the-art quality in health care delivery. Whether one looks at quality from the perspective of individual providers, practices, or health plans, these recent landmark studies shed new light on deficiencies in quality of care, and suggest how appropriate to health care is the maxim: "Let the buyer beware."

Employer Liability

One reason employers should be concerned about health care quality is their potential liability for managed care programs they may purchase. In one 1995 survey, employers with more than 200 employers reported that an average of only 4 percent of employees were enrolled in conventional medical plans with no precertification of medical services.[17] Thus, in this survey, which covered 1,000 employees, an average of 96 percent of respondents' employees were enrolled in some type of managed care programs with their attendant potential liability. The evidence for payer liability for managed care stems from two legal cases: *Wickline* v. *State of California* and *Wilson* v. *Blue Cross of Southern California*. In *Wickline*, the court concluded that a third-party payer can be legally liable for negligence in utilization review decisions.[18] In *Wilson* the court determined that a third-party payer cannot escape liability for negligent utilization review based on the argument that the treating physician bears all legal responsibility for a hospital discharge decision.[19]

In *Fox* v. *Health Net*, the estate of Nelene Fox was awarded damages from a managed care organization for its refusal to cover bone marrow transplantation and high-dose chemotherapy for advanced breast cancer. The total jury award was $89 million, $77 million of which was punitive damages.[20] Some observers believed that the impact of this case on the

---

17 *KPMG Surveys of Employer Sponsored Health Benefits*, KPMG Peat Marwick, Montvale, NJ, 1995.

18 *Wickline* v. *State of California*, Court of Appeals of California, Second Appellate District, Division Five, 192 Cal. App. 3d 1630; 239 Cal. Rptr. 810.

19 *Wilson* v. *Blue Cross of Southern California* No. B040597, Court of Appeals of California, Second Appellate District, Division Five, 222 Cal. App. 3d 660; 1990 Cal. App. LEXIS 1006; 271 Cal. Rptr. 876.

20 E. Eckholm. "$89 Million Awarded to Family Who Sued H.M.O.," *The New York Times*. December 30, 1993, p. Al.

liability of employers and MCOs was limited by the Employee Retirement Income Security Act (ERISA).

More recently, in the case of *Goodrich* v. *Aetna U.S. Healthcare*, a jury awarded the widow of David Goodrich $120 million for delays in approving coverage of high-dose chemotherapy and bone marrow transplantation for a form of stomach cancer. Although ERISA did not apply to this case because Goodrich was covered under a state-sponsored health plan, the size of the award and recent legislative action to limit ERISA protection have raised new concerns about the exposure of MCOs and employer-sponsored health plans to litigation and resulting damage awards.[21] At the time of this writing, the U. S. House of Representatives has passed legislation that would support suits by plaintiffs. The bill is now in conference committee, being reconciled with a Senate version that does not contain such provisions. Bills permitting consumers to sue MCOs have been introduced in many state legislatures, and such laws have been enacted in Texas, Missouri, and Georgia.[22]

These developments suggest a future in which the courts broadly interpret the potential liability of third-party payers for poor quality, negligent managed care processes. Given this legal environment, it seems prudent for employers to address the issue of quality of care in their medical benefits plans.

Employee, Provider, and Community Relations

When medical benefits decisions are made without substantive consideration of quality of care, employees can take away the message that their health and well-being are not valued by their employer. This message can undermine one of the key objectives of offering medical benefits: to promote the recruitment and retention of employees. When quality of care is measured as patient satisfaction, health plans also have been found to differ in performance. Rubin and colleagues found considerable variation in patient ratings, with solo or single specialty fee-for-service care rated best and HMO care rated worst among different practice types.[23] A *Consumer Reports* survey of more than 70,000 subscribers found that one-half of respondents were dissatisfied with at least one aspect of their medical

---

21 D. Studdert and T. Brennan, "The Problems With Punitive Damages in Lawsuits Against Managed-Care Organizations," *New England Journal of Medicine,* 342 (2000), pp. 280–284.
22 Ibid.
23 H.R. Rubin et al., "Patients' Ratings of Outpatient Visits in Different Practice Settings," *Journal of the American Medical Association,* 270 (1993), pp. 835–840.

care.[24] Incorporating quality assurance and continuous quality improvement (CQI) processes into medical benefits decisions, and effectively communicating these processes to employees, can help avoid this employee relations pitfall.

Disillusioned providers also can undermine the extent to which employees value their medical benefits. Employee opinion may be influenced by negative assessments from physicians about the quality of an employer's health plan. In addition, physician performance may be adversely affected by a poor quality health plan, with consequences for employee health and productivity.

Failing to demonstrate a commitment to quality assurance and CQI in health care decisions can leave employers vulnerable to the charge of neglecting corporate social responsibility as well. This can have obvious negative implications for community relations.

Value of Medical Care Expenditures

The value of health care services can be defined as the health benefit per dollar spent.[25] Chassin and the National Roundtable on Health Care Quality have observed that errors in the delivery of health care services, as well as overuse of services, can reduce the value of health care services by both decreasing the numerator and increasing the denominator of this equation. Conversely, by reducing errors and overuse, the value of health care services can be increased. (The impact of underuse on value is more variable, as it tends to move the numerator and denominator in the same direction.) Most businesses would not view as prudent the practice of purchasing from suppliers based upon price alone. When viewing health plans and providers as you would view other suppliers to your business, considerations of quality and service, as well as cost, become essential components of the value equation.

DEFINING QUALITY

Brook has defined health care quality as consisting of three components: appropriateness, excellence, and satisfaction.[26] Quality care is care that is

24 "How Is Your Doctor Treating You?," *Consumer Reports*, February 1995, pp. 81–88.
25 M. Chassin, et al., "The Urgent Need to Improve Health Care Quality," *Journal of the American Medical Association*, 280 (1998), pp. 1000–1005.
26 R.H. Brook, "Define and Review the Purpose of Guidelines," Presentation at Measuring Performance and Implementing Improvement Conference, April 27, 1995, Chicago.

appropriate given the current state of the art in medicine. It is also care that is excellent in its execution and that produces a high degree of patient satisfaction.

One of the positive, and in this author's view essential, attributes of this definition is the fact that it is measurable. The literature cited above on cardiac services in New York State provides examples of how appropriateness can be quantified. Excellence in execution can be measured in terms of both the processes and outcomes of care. Examples of process measures of excellence might include transfusion rates in coronary artery bypass surgery. Outcome measures might include operative mortality or complication rates for this type of surgery.

In the area of patient satisfaction, there is well over a decade of research demonstrating that this component of quality of care also can be measured in ways that are reliable and valid.[27] Resources to assist in evaluating these elements of quality will be provided later in this chapter.

EVALUATING QUALITY

Let us assume that an employer is convinced of the importance and feasibility of considering quality in health care purchasing. How should it go about assessing quality or promoting employee evaluation of quality, whether at the level of the physician, hospital, ancillary services provider, or health plan?

Physician Quality

Most assessments of physician quality begin with the physician's training, experience, and professional certifications. The literature on the link between these factors and quality is limited. Nevertheless, these characteristics can serve as a starting point for evaluating a physician's level of knowledge and skills, which we might postulate would be related to the appropriateness and excellence of his or her practices. In addition, a review of physician credentials might reveal that small proportion of physicians for whom glaring quality-of-care problems have been identified. Characteristics to consider in this assessment include the following:

■ Current unrestricted license to practice in your state.

---

27 U.S. Congress, Office of Technology Assessment, Ware, J.E. Jr., Davies, A.R., and Rubin, H.R., "Patients' Assessments of Their Care," *The Quality of Medical Care: Information for Consumers*, Washington, DC: U.S. Government Printing Office, 1988.

- Current unrestricted license to dispense prescription drugs from the Drug Enforcement Agency.
- Certification by a specialty board recognized by the American Board of Medical Specialties.
- Current active, unrestricted hospital staff privileges.

The latter of these criteria may not apply to physicians who choose not to see patients in a hospital setting. It may be difficult, however, to determine if a physician's privileges were dropped as a result of his or her own choice or because of a quality-driven decision by the hospital. The advantages of using a physician with hospital privileges include having continuity of both inpatient and outpatient care and having the benefit of the hospital's QA and/or CQI program apply to your physician. This latter benefit includes hospital access to the National Practitioner Data Bank, a national database on physician quality problems that is not accessible to the public.[28]

Conspicuously absent from the above list is malpractice experience. There are questions about the extent to which malpractice experience is a reflection of physician quality.[29] On the other hand, research indicates that any history of malpractice claims, paid or unpaid, is associated with an increased likelihood of future claims.[30] Therefore, it may be worth evaluating a physician's malpractice claim history, if only to reduce your risk of being involved in a future malpractice claim.

A physician's credentials can be evaluated directly by employees, by benefit managers, or by health plans. The following are some of the resources for employees and benefit managers to consider in conducting such an evaluation:

- American Board of Medical Specialties. *Directory of Medical Specialists*. Evanston, IL: American Board of Medical Specialties Research and Education Foundation, 1999.
- Public Citizen Health Research Group. *16,638 Questionable Doctors*. Washington, DC: Public Citizen Health Research Group, 1998.

28 S.L. Horner, "The Health Care Quality Improvement Act of 1986: Its History, Provisions, Applications and Implications," *American Journal of Law and Medicine,* 16 (1990), pp. 455–498.

29 U.S. Congress, Office of Technology Assessment, *The Quality of Medical Care: Information for Consumers*, OTA-H-386 (Washington, DC: U.S. Government Printing Office, 1988).

30 R.R. Bovbjerg and K.R. Petronis, "The Relationship Between Physicians' Malpractice Claims History and Later Claims: Does the Past Predict the Future?," *Journal of the American Medical Association,* 272 (1994), pp. 1421–1426.

- E.L. Bradley, *A Patient's Guide to Surgery*. Philadelphia, PA: University of Pennsylvania Press, 1994.
- M.S. Miller, ed., *Health Care Choices for Today's Consumer*. Washington, DC: Families USA Foundation, 1995.

The state physician licensing board is a good place to call for questions about the state licensing status of individual physicians. Some malpractice claim information on individual physicians may be available from the court clerk in the jurisdiction(s) where the physician has practiced.

If your physician participates in any managed care programs, he or she may receive periodic performance report cards from the MCO and may be willing to share the results with you. Some of these results may be published. For example, the Pacific Business Group on Health has published performance data on medical groups that make up California health plans (though the data are not broken out by individual physician). The Pennsylvania Health Care Cost Containment Council has published heart attack mortality data for physician groups.[31] While "report cards" on physicians promise to be increasingly available, they should be interpreted with caution. A number of potential pitfalls with such reports have been identified. For example, multiple physicians may participate in a patient's care, making it difficult to assign primary responsibility for the patient's outcome to any one physician or medical group.[32] In a study of physician report cards for diabetes care, Hofer and colleagues found that they were unable to reliably detect true practice differences among physicians at three practice sites. They also found that physicians could easily "game" the reporting system by avoiding or deselecting patients with high prior cost or with poor adherence or poor response to treatment.[33]

The quality-related issues described above pertain to all physicians, regardless of their specialty. When assessing physician quality as it relates to specific diagnoses or conditions, additional factors should be considered. For example, physicians being evaluated for their quality in performing a particular surgical procedure should be asked such questions as these:

- What kind of advanced training and/or certification has the physician had in performing the procedure?

31 *Focus on Heart Attack in Pennsylvania in Western Pennsylvania*, Harrisburg, PA: Pennsylvania Health Care Cost Containment Council, June 1996.
32 J. Jollis and P. Romano. "Pennsylvania's Focus on Heart Attack—Grading the Scorecard," *New England Journal of Medicine,* 338 (1998), pp. 983–987.
33 T. Hofer, et al., "The Unreliability of Individual Physician 'Report Cards' for Assessing the Costs and Quality of Care of a Chronic Disease," *Journal of the American Medical Association,* 281 (1999), pp. 2098–2105.

- What is the annual volume of the procedure performed by the physician?
- What is the complication/mortality rate for the procedure as performed by the physician?
- What is the success rate for the procedure as performed by the physician?
- What is the average length of hospital stay for the procedure?
- What is the average length of disability following the procedure?

The applicability of these and other questions will vary by specialty, condition, and procedure. Generally speaking, however, the quality of a physician's performance, as in the example of percutaneous transluminal coronary angioplasty described above, is related to the frequency with which he or she performs the procedure. For some conditions and procedures, there may be regional or national research centers or centers of excellence. Helpful resources in learning about such centers, and obtaining consumer information about various health issues include the following:

- National Cancer Institute, Cancer Information Service.
  Tel: 800-4-CANCER
- American Cancer Society local affiliates
  (see local phone book)
- American Heart Association local affiliates
  (see local phone book)
- American Lung Association local affiliates
  (see local phone book)
- National Institute of Mental Health. Tel: 800-421-4211

Finally, there is a large body of research suggesting that physician–patient communication is related to the quality and outcome of care. Perhaps the best way to evaluate a physician's communication skills is to do so firsthand, scheduling an office visit to get to know a physician you may not already be familiar with. If you make such a visit, it may be helpful to prepare both general questions and questions particular to your circumstances in advance of your appointment. Some of the publications noted in this chapter's bibliography may be of assistance in this regard.[34]

Investigating even this minimum set of criteria for physician quality care requires a significant investment of time and resources. And such

---

34 "How Is Your Doctor Treating You?," *Consumer Reports*, February 1995, pp. 81–88. D. Roter and J. Hall, *Doctors Talking with Patients/Patients Talking with Doctors* (Westport, CN: Auburn House, 1992).

assessments should be repeated periodically to ensure that there has been no change in physician status. The extensive nature of this undertaking points to one advantage of purchasing medical care from a health plan that includes a network of providers. The various aspects of physician quality described above and others can be consistently and rigorously assessed by the plan on an ongoing basis, with associated economies of scale.

Hospital Quality

Some of the same approaches to quality assessment described for physicians can be applied to hospitals. A useful starting place for assessing a hospital's quality is its accreditation. Accreditations to look for include these:

- Current, unrestricted license from the state.
- Current, unrestricted, nonprobationary accreditation from the Health Care Financing Administration for participation in Medicare and Medicaid.
- Current, unrestricted, nonprobationary accreditation from the Joint Commission on Accreditation of Healthcare Organizations.

The Joint Commission on Accreditation of Healthcare Organizations has an extensive process for assessing hospital quality with an on-site survey[35] Beginning January 1, 1995, the Joint Commission made available summaries of the results of its new surveys.[36] These summaries, however, are brief and offer only general information. In addition, the Joint Commission's surveys have been criticized by the Inspector General of the U.S. Department of Health and Human Services as "unlikely to detect patterns, systems, or incidents of substandard care."[37] Among the improvements being pursued by the Joint Commission are the inclusion of outcomes measures in its review process, such as acute myocardial infarction, congestive heart failure, and complications of surgery. This data collection effort is scheduled to begin in 2002.[38]

---

35 Joint Commission on Accreditation of Healthcare Organizations, 1995 Accreditation Manual for Hospitals (Oakbrook Terrace, IL, 1994).
36 For information on whether a survey summary is available for a particular hospital, contact the Joint Commission at 708-916-5600. If your hospital has not undergone a survey since January 1, 1995, you can contact the hospital administration and request a summary of its most recent survey.
37 HHS Inspector General Reports on The External Review of Hospital Quality, OEI-01-97-00050; -00051; -00052 and -00053.
38 Information from www.jcaho.org, January 2000.

General information on hospital facilities, personnel, and services are published annually by the American Hospital Association.[39] This information can sometimes be helpful in making inferences about quality for particular conditions or procedures. For example, if you are having a high-risk delivery, you may wish to choose a hospital that has an advanced level nursery, including a dedicated neonatal intensive care unit. Or if you are planning a percutaneous transluminal coronary angioplasty, you might be well-advised to choose a hospital that offers high-quality emergency coronary artery bypass graft surgery, in the event it may be required.

The Health Care Financing Administration makes data publicly available on hospital performance through its Medicare Provider Analysis and Review (MEDPAR) files. Commercial services can provide extracts of the MEDPAR files for selected hospitals in a more easily readable form.[40] In some states (e.g., Pennsylvania and New York), data are publicly available on hospital performance for specific conditions and procedures.[41] These data can include the volume of cases, outcomes (mortality and complication rates), average length of stay, and average cost per case. Whether or not such data are publicly available for the condition or procedure of interest to you, you may wish to consider approaching the hospital administration directly with the following questions:

- What is the hospital's volume of admissions for the condition/procedure of interest?
- What is the complication/mortality rate for the condition/ procedure as performed at the hospital?
- What is the success rate for the treatment/procedure at the hospital?
- What is the average length of stay for the condition/procedure?
- What are the results of your patient satisfaction survey for the most recent period (including response rate)?
- Does the hospital participate in any managed care networks (e.g., HMO, PPO, or POS plans)?

39 American Hospital Association, *Guide to the Health Care Field* (Chicago: American Hospital Association, 1995).

40 (e.g., The Center for Healthcare Industry Performance Studies, *Clinical Assessment Profile.* Columbus, OH. Tel: 800-859-2447, www.chipsonline.com)

41 Pennsylvania Health Care Cost Containment Council, *A Consumer Guide to Coronary Artery Bypass Graft Surgery* (Harrisburg, PA: Pennsylvania Health Care Cost Containment Council, 1991). Pennsylvania Health Care Cost Containment Council, *Hospital Effectiveness Report* (Harrisburg, PA: Pennsylvania Health Care Cost Containment Council, 1994).

■ Has the hospital been designated as a center of excellence for the condition/procedure by a health plan?

The final question will apply to only a small number of conditions/ procedures and hospitals. Nevertheless, one can find designated regional and national centers of excellence for high-risk, high-cost conditions/procedures, such as organ transplantation, open-heart surgery, and burns. The National Institutes of Health also designates research centers for selected conditions. One might postulate that these centers are more likely to provide quality care for these conditions due to their successful research programs.

One variable to consider in assessing hospital quality is whether it is a major teaching hospital (defined as more than 0.097 teaching residents per hospital bed set up and staffed for patient care). Such hospitals have been found to have a lower risk of death than other hospitals, when evaluated for mortality due to hip fracture, stroke, coronary heart disease, and congestive heart failure.[42]

The question pertaining to volume of patients treated with a particular condition or procedure can be extremely useful as a surrogate measure of quality. More than twenty years of research and dozens of published studies have linked better outcomes to hospitals and doctors delivering higher volumes of particular health care services.[43] Recently, research has confirmed the link of high volume to better outcomes in acute myocardial infarction (hospitals with more than 6.3 Medicare patients with acute myocardial infarction per week on average), major cancer surgery (hospitals with more than one Medicare patient per year on average for a given procedure), and carotid endarterectomy, surgery removing blockages from the carotid arteries to prevent stroke, (hospitals with more than 62 Medicare patients undergoing the procedure per year).[44]

In interpreting hospital satisfaction survey results, it is important to consider the validity of the survey instrument and response rates. Ask whether the survey is based on a standard instrument that has been evaluated for its reliability and validity. If the survey has a response rate of less than 50 percent, the results should be considered suspect. Research

42 D. Taylor, D. Whellan, and F. Sloan. "Effects of Admission to a Teaching Hospital on the Cost and Quality of Care for Medicare Beneficiaries," *New England Journal of Medicine,* 340 (1999), pp. 293–299.

43 E. Hannan, "The Relation Between Volume and Outcome in Health Care," *New England Journal of Medicine,* 340 (1999), pp. 1677–1679.

44 Op. cit., D.Thieman, et al., 1999. C. Begg, et al., "Impact of Hospital Volume on Operative Mortality for Major Cancer Surgery," *Journal of the American Medical Association,* 280 (1998), pp. 1747–1751. R. Cebul, et al., "Indications, Outcomes, and Provider Volumes for Carotid Endarterectomy," *Journal of the American Medical Association* (1998), pp. 1282–1287.

suggests that nonrespondents to such surveys have lower levels of satisfaction than respondents.[45]

Resources to consider when evaluating hospital quality include the following:

- American Hospital Association, Chicago. Tel: 312-422-3000, www.aha.org
- Health Care Financing Administration, Baltimore, MD. Tel: 410-786-3000, www.hcfa.org
- The Center for Healthcare Industry Performance Studies, Columbus, OH. Tel: 800-859-2447, www.chipsonline.com
- Joint Commission on Accreditation of Healthcare Organizations, Oakbrook Terrace, IL. Tel: 630-792-5000, www.jcaho.org

Assessing hospital quality, both initially and on an ongoing basis, can be a labor-intensive process. As in the case of physician quality assessment, this kind of assessment and more should be obtainable with economies of scale through a quality health plan offering a provider network (see below).

Managed Care Organization Quality

One of the great potential advantages of purchasing health care through a managed care organization is the cost-effective ongoing quality assurance and continuous quality improvement that these plans can provide. The question for the employer/purchaser of an MCO is how to evaluate the quality of its supplier's QA/CQI programs. One approach to this question is to look for accreditation by an independent organization that has evaluated the quality of the MCO. Today, there are two major accrediting organizations for MCOs: the Joint Commission on Accreditation of Healthcare Organizations (JCAHO) and the National Committee for Quality Assurance (NCQA).

The NCQA is probably the most experienced of the MCO accrediting organizations. It has reviewed more than one-half of all MCOs in the United States at the time of this writing.[46] The NCQA accreditation process involves a review of MCO quality-related systems, including quality management, utilization management, credentialing, members' rights and responsibilities, preventive health services, and medical

---

45 William Mayer, telephone conversation with J.E. Ware, Jr., 1995.
46 www.ncqa.com, February 2000.

records.[47] Documentation of these processes provided by the MCO are analyzed, and a site survey is conducted involving both physician and administrative reviewers. The MCO is then assigned to one of the following accreditation categories based upon its level of compliance with NCQA standards:[48]

- *Full accreditation:* Full or substantial compliance with standards in each of the quality-related areas reviewed.

- *Accreditation with recommendations:* Full or substantial compliance with standards in each of the quality areas reviewed but with one or more significant areas of noncompliance. If NCQA recommendations to address the area(s) of noncompliance are implemented within 90 days, the MCO receives full accreditation. If not, the MCO receives one-year accreditation.

- *One-year accreditation:* Significant compliance with standards in each of the quality areas reviewed but with additional action required for full accreditation.

- *Provisional accreditation:* Partial compliance with standards in each of the quality areas reviewed but no deficiencies with significant risk to quality of care. The term of such accreditation is not to exceed a total of 27 months.

- *Denial/revocation of accreditation status:* Failure to meet the standards for accreditation described above, violation of NCQA policies and procedures, or failure to comply with NCQA recommendations or agreed-upon improvement plans.

In addition to its accreditation processes, the NCQA has developed the Health Plan Employer Data and Information Set (HEDIS) to help standardize the measurement and reporting of health plan performance. HEDIS includes measures of health care quality, access to care, satisfaction with care, membership, health services utilization, financial performance, and plan management. HEDIS measures have become the basis of performance measures produced by many health plans and purchasing coalitions.[49]

The latest version of HEDIS at the time of this writing is HEDIS 2000. This version has a total of 56 measures applicable to commercial plans, Medicaid, and/or Medicare. In the area of effectiveness of care, the

---

47 National Committee for Quality Assurance, *Standards for Accreditation* (Washington, DC: National Committee for Quality Assurance, 1995).
48 Ibid.
49 National Committee on Quality Assurance, *HEDIS 2000* (Washington, DC: NCQA, 1999).

measures include such items as breast cancer screening, controlling high blood pressure, and follow-up after hospitalization for mental illness. In the area of access/availability of care, measures include adults' access to preventive/ambulatory services and availability of language interpretation services. Measures of health plan stability include practitioner turnover and indicators of financial stability. For use of services, such measures as well-child visits and cesarean section rates are included. HEDIS 2000 also covers measures of satisfaction, cost of care, informed health care choices, and health plan descriptive information. In the area of satisfaction, HEDIS 2000 incorporates the Consumer Assessment of Health Plans (CAPS) instrument—a reliable and valid survey and reporting kit developed by a consortium of Harvard Medical School, the RAND Corporation, and the Research Triangle Institute under the sponsorship of the Agency for Health Care Policy and Research.[50]

Theoretically, the performance of health plans could be compared using HEDIS 2000 measures. Not all health plans collect and publish these data, however, and NCQA does not require HEDIS data for its accreditation process. In addition, although NCQA audits HEDIS data, the data are collected and analyzed by the health plans themselves, with potential for bias that is inherent in this approach.

The approach of the Joint Commission on Accreditation of Healthcare Organizations to accrediting MCOs is comparable to that of the NCQA and results in assignment of an MCO to one of the following categories of accreditation: provisional accreditation, accreditation with commendation, accreditation with or without recommendations, conditional accreditation, or nonaccreditation.[51]

In assessing health plan quality of care, it would be worthwhile to ask the following questions:

- Has your MCO applied for accreditation from either NCQA or the Joint Commission on Accreditation of Healthcare Organizations?
- If so, when was your most recent review, and what category of accreditation did your MCO receive?
- Will the MCO provide a summary of the findings of the accreditation process?

---

50 www.ncqa.org, January 2000.

51 Joint Commission on Accreditation of Healthcare Organizations, *1999 Accreditation Manual for Health Care Networks* (Oakbrook Terrace, IL: JCAHO, 1999).

A list of health plans reviewed by NCQA for accreditation is available on-line at http://www.ncqa.org. While reviewing the results of these accreditation processes can be informative, the accreditation organizations explicitly warn that they do not warranty any third parties (e.g., employers) regarding the quality of care of an MCO. In addition, many MCOs have not yet undergone accreditation. Therefore, whenever an employer or employee is purchasing MCO services, it would be advisable to do some additional evaluation, including contacting your state departments of insurance and/or public health, reviewing some minimal documentation related to MCO quality, and making a site visit.

State governments generally have some regulatory authority over MCOs operating within their borders. This regulatory authority may reside with the department of public health, the department of insurance, or some combination of these. A call to one or both of these agencies in your state, asking for information about the status of a particular MCO, can be informative. If the MCO of interest is an HMO, you may want to ask for a copy of the HMO's annual report, which must be filed with the state department of insurance. This report includes information on consumer grievances, utilization, payments of provider incentives, and financial stability.[52]

Additional information about the quality of a health plan may be commercially available. At least one commercial enterprise has gathered data on health plan satisfaction nationwide and made them available for purchase.[53]

Requesting and reviewing the following information from the MCO also can be helpful:

■ *Credentialing criteria/processes for network physicians, hospitals, and ancillary providers* (e.g., laboratory, X-ray, home health agencies): Do these criteria and processes include those mentioned above under physician and hospital quality? Are provider credentials verified by the MCO, or do they accept a provider's self-report? How frequently are providers recredentialed? Does the recredentialing process include routine, systematic consideration of member complaints, member satisfaction, and other quality indicators?

■ *A copy of the most recent quality assurance, quality management, or CQI plan and annual report* (individual provider and patient identifiers

52 Public Citizen Health Research Group "How You Can Make HMOs More Accountable," *Public Citizen Health Research Group Health Letter* 7, No 11 (1991), pp. 1–4.

53 William Mayer, Telephone conversation with National Research Corporation. Personal Communication, 1995.

can be removed to protect confidentiality): Does the plan include reliable and valid measures and standards of appropriateness of care, excellence in care, and satisfaction with care as described above? Are providers educated about these measures and standards? Are performance measures documented and routinely fed back to providers? Is meaningful reinforcement and support provided for performance improvement? Are there credible, specific documented examples of performance improvement over the preceding year?

■ *Routine provider quality profiles* (i.e., sample reports on provider performance routinely analyzed by the MCO): How reliable, valid, and useful to quality improvement are the data contained in the reports? To what extent has the quality performance monitoring described in the QA plan been incorporated into MCO reporting systems?

■ *Reimbursement formula for physicians in the MCO:* Are there substantial financial incentives for physicians to withhold necessary care? Conversely, are there substantial financial incentives for physicians to provide quality care? (It has been this author's observation that MCOs providing such financial incentives are more likely to have reliable and valid measures of physician quality and systems for monitoring and feedback of these measures.)

■ *Preventive care programs offered and participation rates:* What preventive care programs does the MCO offer, at what location, and with what frequency? What member cost sharing, if any, is required? What are the participation and success rates for these programs?

■ *Plan-wide measures of quality:* Will the MCO provide the most recent report of performance using HEDIS measures? Did it use survey instruments recommended in HEDIS for assessing member satisfaction and health status? If not, how did it ensure the reliability and validity of the instruments? What were the response rates to these surveys?

An additional step that can be immensely helpful in assessing the quality of an MCO is to conduct a brief site visit to "kick the tires." In this author's experience, it is not uncommon to come away from such a visit with an entirely different assessment of MCO quality than is conveyed in written material from the organization. Consultants with some knowledge of managed care can be helpful but are not necessary. For a site visit to be most helpful, the following guidelines are recommended:

■ Allow four to eight hours for the visit.

■ Try to limit the time devoted to marketing and formal presentations.

- Arrange to meet key staff, including the medical director and the heads of member services, quality assurance, utilization management, and finance: What is their relevant training and experience? Are they credible and involved? What is their level of commitment?

- Devote the most time on site to direct observation and questioning of MCO operations staff, and listening to staff on the telephone in member services, claims administration, and utilization management: What is their relevant training and experience? What is their level of commitment? What is the quality of their customer service? Do they document members' complaints, concerns, and questions, and follow up? Do you see signs of a pervasive CQI program with posted performance standards and measures?

- Discuss quality-related information provided prior to the site visit (see above). What are the processes for collection and quality control of data? What were the most successful improvement initiatives in the preceding year? Review minutes of the most recent quality assurance committee meetings.

- Assess the philosophy of the MCO: Is it a good fit with your own and that of your organization? Is the MCO interested in you as a customer, your quality concerns, and your business needs?

Patient, member, and/or physician confidentiality should not be a barrier to conducting a site visit as long as reviewers are willing to sign confidentiality agreements.

Resources to consider when evaluating MCO quality include the following:

- National Committee for Quality Assurance (NCQA), Washington, DC. Tel: 888-275-7585, www.ncqa.org
- American Association of Health Plans (AAHP), Washington, DC. Tel: 202-778-3200, www.aahp.org
- National Coalition on Health Care, Washington, DC. Tel: 202-638-7151, www.nchc.org
- Institute for Health Care Improvement (IHI), Roxbury, MA. Tel: 617-754-4800, www.ihi.org
- Health Care Financing Administration, Baltimore, MD. Tel: 410-786-3000, www.hcfa.gov

- Agency for Health Care Research and Quality, Rockville, MD.
  Tel: 301-594-6662, www.ahcpr.gov
- Foundation for Accountability, Portland, OR. www.facct.org

Evaluating MCO quality, like physician and hospital quality assessment, can be a time-consuming process. Yet, this may be a relatively small investment of time when weighed against the resources spent by employer and employee on health care and the risks posed by the purchase of poor-quality health care.

Improving Quality

Conceptually, approaches to improving quality of health care fall into two major categories: provider or supply-side approaches and patient/consumer or demand-side approaches.

Supply-Side Approaches

The resources required to significantly change provider behavior, whether at the level of the physician, hospital, or MCO, make it unlikely that relatively small purchasers of health care (e.g., individuals and small businesses) acting alone will be successful in driving this approach to quality improvement. However, by banding together in purchasing or policy making, a supply-side quality improvement agenda can be advanced. Business coalitions on health care have proliferated throughout the United States, most with a focus on controlling costs.[54] Many, however, also have addressed issues of quality of care, with some effect. In Michigan, for example, the Southwest Michigan Healthcare Coalition championed the adoption of a uniform hospital database for analyzing severity of illness, health care outcomes, and cost. The information derived and published from the database has been used to identify deficiencies in quality and to inform and monitor quality improvements in area hospitals. The coalition is also active in promoting the concept of a statewide uniform provider database.

Providing feedback on hospital and medical staff performance, with encouragement to initiate quality improvement activities, can produce significant results. This approach was applied by Medicare in its Cooperative Cardiovascular Project, yielding improvements in the use of

---

[54] *National Business Coalition on Health, Health Care Data and Quality: The Role of the Business Coalition* (Washington, DC: National Business Coalition on Health, 1995).

state-of-the-art care for acute myocardial infarction and reducing mortality for this condition.[55]

Large employers and purchasing coalitions can use quality data to selectively contract with providers. A recent survey of business coalitions found that 35 percent directly contract with providers, and 20 percent contract with "centers of excellence" for high-cost and/or high-risk conditions or procedures.[56]

In another effort to improve quality, the Managed Health Care Association, a group of large employers, has collaborated with the Health Outcomes Institute to create a program to develop, implement, and evaluate guidelines for care for selected medical conditions and procedures.[57] While guidelines can be a useful tool in quality improvement, a number of concerns have been raised about the ways in which guidelines are currently developed and implemented. A study of clinical practice guidelines found that fully half of those recently published did not adhere to established methodological standards.[58]

For information on business coalition activity in your area, contact the National Business Coalition on Health, Washington, DC 20036, Tel: 202-775-9300.

Larger businesses and health care purchasing cooperatives may have the ability to influence quality of care more directly through their managed care purchasing decisions. By increasing the numbers of covered lives at stake in a managed care bid process, large employers and purchasing cooperatives can generally enhance the responsiveness of MCOs to the quality evaluation described above. This can help ensure the selection of an MCO with superior quality. Ensuring that the MCO will maintain or improve quality of care, however, may require the purchaser to take additional steps.

When contracting with an MCO, the following approaches to promoting CQI are recommended:

■ Identify key deficiencies in the MCO's QA/CQI and stipulate that they be remedied in a specified reasonable period. Failure to remedy deficiencies in the agreed-upon period should result in financial penalties

---

55 Op. cit., T. Marciniak, et al., 1998.

56 I. Fraser, et al., "The Pursuit of Quality By Business Coalitions: A National Survey," *Health Affairs,* 18 (1999), pp. 158–165.

57 M.R. Huber, "MHCA OMS Consortium Focuses on Results of Care," *Update: The Newsletter of the Health Outcomes Institute,* 2, No. 2 (Spring 1995), pp. 1, 3.

58 T. Shaneyfelt, M. Mayo-Smith, and J. Rothwangl, "Are Guidelines Following Guidelines? The Methodological Quality of Clinical Practice Guidelines in the Peer-Reviewed Medical Literature," *Journal of the American Medical Association,* 281 (1999), pp. 1900–1905.

to the MCO. In a self-insured, administrative-services-only arrangement, this penalty may be a significant portion of the MCO's administrative fee (e.g., 10 percent). In a fully insured arrangement, the penalty may be cost sharing by the MCO in noninsured, employer health-related costs (e.g., worksite health promotion/disease prevention).

■ Specify reliable and valid measures to be used to track MCO quality over the life of the contract. Ideally, these will be measures already tracked by the MCO and will include appropriateness of care, excellence of care, and satisfaction. It may be necessary to stipulate that the MCO adopt new measures, or to hire an independent organization to do the MCO quality measurement.

■ Require periodic reporting of the above quality measures and track the MCO's performance. Arrange to meet with key MCO staff to review the reports. Financial penalties and rewards should be specified in the contract for failing to meet or exceeding agreed-upon targets for improved performance, respectively.

By monitoring MCO performance in routine reports, providing feedback in periodic meetings, and reinforcing CQI with financial rewards and penalties, employers can continue to enhance the value of their health care expenditures over the life of an MCO contract. This approach has been taken by the Pacific Business Group on Health in negotiating more than two dozen performance guarantees with 13 California HMOs. Of more than $8 million at risk for meeting performance targets, nearly $2 million was refunded for sub-par performance. Eight of 13 plans missed their targets in the area of childhood immunization. Most plans met or exceeded their targets in such areas as satisfaction, cesarean section rates, mammography, Pap smear, and prenatal care.[59]

Demand-Side Approaches

Demand-side approaches to improving quality of care can be considered under the broad heading of "demand management." Demand management is a relatively new term and has been defined as "the support of individuals so that they may make rational health and medical decisions based on a consideration of benefits and risks."[60] Viewed in this way, traditional health

---

59 H. Schauffler, C. Brown, and A. Milstein, "Raising the Bar: The Use of Performance Guarantees By the Pacific Business Group on Health," *Health Affairs,* 18 (1999), pp. 134–142.

60 D.M. Vickery and W.D. Lynch, "Demand Management: Enabling Patients to Use Medical Care Appropriately," *Journal of Occupational & Environmental Medicine,* 37, No. 5 (May 1995), pp. 551–557.

promotion and disease prevention can be regarded as quality of care-related demand management. Much of the more recent attention received by demand management has been directed at controlling utilization and cost of health care.[61] Yet, there is intuitive appeal to the concept of modifying consumer behavior to improve quality of care. There is also some research evidence to suggest such an approach can be effective.

It has long been apparent that providing preventive services is an important element of quality health care. The U.S. Preventive Services Task Force, a panel of medical and health experts appointed in 1994 by HHS, has published guidelines that have set the standard for quality in preventive care since 1989.[62] Since that time, the NCQA has incorporated measures of delivery of selected preventive services into its HEDIS measures of MCO performance. Clearly, employers can improve the quality of care received by their employees by increasing employee demand for these preventive services, see Chapter 12 on health promotion for more information.

Recent research also suggests that consumer-directed decision support, in the form of interactive video, can be effective in improving the appropriateness of medical treatment. This approach, referred to as shared decision-making programs, has produced dramatic changes in patient preferences for treatment of benign prostatic hypertrophy (BPH) or benign enlargement of the prostate gland. Patients with BPH participating in early shared decision-making programs showed a 44 percent to 60 percent reduction in surgery rates, opting more frequently for "watchful waiting" as an alternative.[63] These results suggest the tremendous potential for targeted and well-designed demand management programs to improve quality. For more information on shared decision-making programs contact the Foundation for Informed Medical Decision-Making, Hanover, NH, Tel: 603-646-6180.

Another approach attempting to modify consumer care-seeking behavior has been the dissemination of information about provider quality. This approach has been used by the Minnesota Health Data Institute, the Cleveland Health Quality Choice program, the Foundation for Accountability (FAACT), the Pennsylvania Health Care Cost Containment

---

61 J.F. Fries et al., "Reducing Health Care Costs by Reducing the Need and Demand for Medical Services," *New England Journal of Medicine,* 329, No. 5 (July 29, 1993), pp. 321–325.

62 U.S. Preventive Services Task Force, *Guide to Clinical Preventive Services* (Washington, DC: U.S. Government Printing Office, 1989).

63 J.F. Kasper et al., "Developing Shared Decision-Making Programs to Improve the Quality of Health Care," *QRB,* 18, No. 6 (June 1992), pp. 183–190.

Council, and others. Schneider and Epstein studied the impact of this approach, as implemented by the Pennsylvania Health Care Cost Containment Council in its Consumer Guide to Coronary Artery Bypass Graft (CABG) surgery. The Guide provided CABG mortality ratings of all cardiac surgeons and hospitals in the state. A telephone survey of patients who had undergone CABG in one of four hospitals included in the Guide revealed that only 12 percent of patients were aware of the Guide, and fewer than 1 percent knew the correct rating of their surgeon or hospital and reported that it had a moderate or major impact on their selection of provider.[64] The authors conclude: "Efforts to aid patient decision-making with performance reports are unlikely to succeed without a tailored and intensive program for dissemination and patient education."

More general approaches to demand management have produced suggestive, though less well-documented results. One such approach undergoing tremendous growth is telephonic nurse counseling. These services offer telephone access to nurses to discuss health issues in general and answer clinical questions in particular. Vendors of these services purport to be effective in reducing costs and improving appropriateness of health care, and they appear to have convinced a growing number of employers and health plans. Enrollment in these services has grown to an estimated 13 million covered lives.[65] Some of the larger providers of these services are:

- Access Health, Rancho Cordova, CA, Tel: 916-851-4000
- Health Decisions International, Golden, CO, Tel: 800-403-0099

Telephonic nurse case management is also being targeted to patients with specific medical conditions, such as congestive heart failure, diabetes, and asthma. A variety of organizations offer this type of service, including pharmacy benefit management firms, MCOs, hospitals, and others. This approach appears to hold promise for improving compliance with state-of-the-art treatment through improved self-care and patient-provider communication.

The explosive growth of the Internet and its widespread use in the arena of health, suggests that it may be a medium that can contribute to

---

64 E. Schneider and A. Epstein, "Use of Public Performance Reports: A Survey of Patients Undergoing Cardiac Surgery," *Journal of the American Medical Association,* 279 (1998), pp. 1638–1642.

65 G. Borzo, "1-800-Get-Advice: Phone Counseling Services Are Booming, as Physicians and Health Plans Seek New Ways to Manage Patient Use of Medical Care," *American Medical News* 38, No. 39 (Oct. 16, 1995), p. 3.

health care quality improvement. Yet, its growth and use have raised a number of new quality-related issues. One study of Internet-derived information on clinical questions found that:

- 89 percent of retrieved pages were not applicable to the question that prompted the search.
- Fewer than 1 percent of pages consisted of original research or systematic reviews.
- 69 percent of pages did not indicate an author.
- Only 1 percent of pages provided information on financial or other conflicts of interest.
- Fewer than 18 percent of pages gave the date they were posted or most recently updated.[66]

While the Internet represents a tool with great promise for health care quality improvement, consumers, purchasers and providers should employ the same rigor in evaluating its application as we do for other quality improvement interventions.

Demand management represents a wide variety of concepts and products with potential application to quality improvement. The most cost-effective of these are likely to be focused on well-defined, measurable target behaviors, and to include education and skill-building, monitoring, and reinforcement of target behaviors. Effective integration of such demand-management programs with supply-management programs will likely bring about the greatest impact on quality improvement.

CONCLUSION

Quality is an essential component of the value equation in health care purchasing. There are a number of reasons employers and/or employees should make efforts to evaluate and improve health care quality, including errors in the delivery of health care services; overuse and underuse of health care services; employer liability; employee, provider, and community relations; and the potential to improve the value of health care expenditures. Quality of care can be defined and measured. Furthermore, these measures can be used to evaluate the quality of physicians, hospitals, other providers, and managed care organizations. Through both supply

---

66 W. Hersh, P. Gorman, and L. Sacherek, "Applicability and Quality of Information for Answering Clinical Questions on the Web," (letter) *Journal of the American Medical Association,* 280 (1998), pp. 1307–1308.

and demand management, employers, in particular, have the potential to improve quality of care. Supply management opportunities include the use of employer coalitions, purchasing cooperatives, and/or contractual provider/MCO performance guarantees. Opportunities for quality improvement through demand management include health promotion/disease prevention, shared decision-making programs, dissemination of quality information, telephonic nurse counseling, and telephonic disease management. The most effective strategy to improve quality will likely involve a combination of these approaches.

Dental Plan Design

Ronald L. Huling

INTRODUCTION

Dental plans are one of the nation's most popular employee benefits. In 2000, it is estimated that more than 175 million individuals were covered by workplace-based dental benefit plans. These individuals represent a significant portion of the U.S. full-time workforce.

It is not surprising that dental plans are so popular. Most of the U.S. population visits a dentist at least once each year.

DIFFERENCES BETWEEN MEDICINE AND DENTISTRY DRIVE PLAN DESIGN

Medicine and dentistry have many differences, and sound dental plan design recognizes these. These differences include practice location, the nature of care, cost, and emphasis on prevention.

Location

The practice of the typical physician is hospital-based, while dentists practice almost exclusively in an office setting. Partly because of these practice differences, physicians tend to associate with other physicians with greater frequency than dentists associate with other dentists. This isolation, along with the inherent differences in the nature of medical and dental care, tends to produce a greater variety of dental practice patterns than is the case in medicine. In addition, practicing in isolation does not afford the same opportunities for peer review and general quality control.

Nature of Care, Cost, and Prevention

Perhaps contributing more significantly to the differences in medicine and dentistry are the important differences between the nature of medical and dental care.

First and perhaps foremost, because of the importance of preventive dentistry, the need for dental care is almost universal to ensure sound oral hygiene. Many individuals sometimes require only preventive or no medical care for years. Individuals routinely visit their dentists for preventive dental care, but in medicine the patient typically visits a physician with certain symptoms—often pain or discomfort—and seeks relief.

Dental treatment, because of its emphasis on prevention, often is considered elective. Unless there is pain or trauma, dental care is sometimes postponed. The patient recognizes that life is not at risk and as a result has few reservations about postponing treatment. In fact, postponement may be preferable to some patients—perhaps because of an aversion to visiting the dentist, rooted many years in the past when dental technology was less developed.

Because major dental care is not life-threatening and time-critical, dentists' charges for major courses of treatment often are discussed in advance of the treatment when there is no pain or trauma. As with any number of other consumer decisions, the patient may opt to defer the treatment to a later time or spend the money elsewhere.

A second difference in the nature of care is that, while medical care is rarely cosmetic, dental care often is. A crown, for example, may be necessary to save a tooth, but it also may be used to improve the patient's appearance. Many people place orthodontics into the same category, although evidence exists that failure to obtain needed orthodontic care may result in problems ranging from major gum disease to temporomandibular joint (TMJ) disorders in later life.

A third major difference between the nature of medical and dental care is that dentistry often offers alternative procedures for treating disease and restoring teeth, many of which are equally effective. For example, a molar cavity might be treated by a two-surface gold onlay, which may cost 10 times as much as a simple amalgam filling. In these instances, the choice of the appropriate procedure is influenced by a number of factors, including the cost of the alternatives, the condition of the affected tooth and the teeth surrounding it, and the likelihood that a particular approach will be successful.

There are other significant differences in medical care and dentistry that will have an effect on plan design. These include the cost of the typical treatment and the emphasis on prevention.

Dental expenses generally are lower, more predictable, and budgetable. The average dental claim check is only about $130. Medical claims, on average, are much higher.

The last significant difference is the emphasis on prevention. The advantages of preventive dentistry are clearly documented. While certain medical diseases and injuries are self-healing, dental disease, once started, almost always gets progressively worse. Therefore, preventive care may be more productive in dentistry than in medicine. Certainly the value of preventive dentistry relative to its cost is acknowledged.

PROVIDERS OF DENTAL BENEFITS

Providers of dental benefits generally can be separated into three categories: insurance companies, Blue Cross and Blue Shield organizations, and others, including state dental association plans (e.g., Delta plans); self-insured, self-administered plans; and group practice or HMO-type plans. Insurance companies and Blue Cross/Blue Shield plans cover the largest share of the population. However, enrollment in self-administered, self-insured plans; plans employing third-party administrators; dental association plans; and HMOs is in an upsurge.

The types of dental benefit plans resemble today's medical plans. There are three basic design structures: the fee-for-service indemnity or reimbursement approach, the preferred provider (PPO) approach, and the dental health maintenance organization. The point-of-service design, which is still relatively rare, is a combination of the three.

Insurance company-administered dental benefits and most self-insured, self-administered plan benefits are provided on either an indemnity or preferred provider basis. Under the indemnity approach, expenses incurred by eligible individuals are submitted to the administrator, typically an insurer, for payment. If the expense is covered, the appropriate payment is calculated according to the provisions of the plan. The indemnity plan payment generally is made directly to the covered employee, unless assigned by the employee to the treating dentist.

Preferred provider benefits are payable directly to the treating dentist, generally according to a contract, which fixes the reimbursement level between the dentist and the plan. In most instances, this payment actually may be lower than what would be charged to a direct-pay or indemnity patient.

The dental benefits of both dental service corporations and Blue Cross/Blue Shield plans are generally provided on a preferred provider basis. The major differences between indemnity and preferred provider benefits relate to the roles of the provider and the covered individual. Under either approach, the plan sponsor normally has substantial latitude in determining who and what is to be covered and at what level.

Under the group practice or HMO-type arrangement, a prescribed range of dental services is provided to eligible participants, generally in return for a prepaid, fixed, and uniform payment. Services are provided by dentists practicing in group practice clinics or by those in individual practice but affiliated for purposes of providing plan benefits to eligible participants. Some individuals eligible under these arrangements are covered through collectively bargained self-insurance benefit trusts. In these instances, trust fund payments are used either to reimburse dentists operating in group practice clinics or to pay the prescribed fixed per capita fee. Group practice HMO-type arrangements, which often have cost, quality assurance, and administrative advantages but more limited provider selection, generally offer little latitude in plan design. As a result, the balance of this chapter, since it is largely devoted to the issue of plan design, may have limited application to these types of arrangements.

COVERED DENTAL EXPENSES

Virtually all dental problems fall into 10 professional treatment categories:

1. *Diagnostic.* Examination to determine the existence of oral disease or to evaluate the condition of the mouth. Included in this category would be such procedures as X-rays and routine oral examinations.
2. *Preventive.* Procedures to preserve and maintain dental health. Included in this category are topical fluoride applications, cleaning, space maintainers, and the like.
3. *Restorative.* Procedures for the repair and reconstruction of natural teeth, including the removal of dental decay and installation of fillings.

4. *Endodontics.* Treatment of dental-pulp disease and therapy within existing teeth. Root canal therapy is an example of this type of procedure.

5. *Periodontics.* Treatment of the gums and other supporting structures of the teeth, primarily for maintenance or improvement of the gums. Periodontal curettage and root planing are examples of periodontic procedures.

6. *Oral Surgery.* Tooth extraction and other surgery of the mouth and jaw.

7. *Prosthodontics.* Construction, replacement, and repair of missing teeth. Examples include onlays, crowns and bridges, which are fixed prostheses, and dentures and partials, which are removable prostheses.

8. *Orthodontics.* Correction of malocclusion and abnormal tooth position through repositioning of natural teeth.

9. *Pedodontics.* Treatment for children who do not have all their permanent teeth.

10. *Implantology.* Use of implants and related services (e.g., overdentures, fixed prostheses attached to implants, etc.), to replace one or all missing teeth on an arch.

In addition to the recognition of treatment or services in most of these 10 areas, the typical dental plan also includes provision for palliative treatment (i.e., procedures to minimize pain, including anesthesia), emergency care, and consultation.

These 10 types of procedures usually are categorized into three, four, and sometime five general groupings for purposes of plan design. The first classification often includes both preventive and diagnostic expenses. The second general grouping includes all minor restorative procedures. The third broad grouping, often combined with the second, includes major restorative work (e.g., prosthodontics), endodontic and periodontic services, and oral surgery. A fourth separate classification covers orthodontic expenses. Although excluded under most plans, implantology services are usually covered under a separate fifth classification.

Pedodontic care generally falls into the first two groupings. Later in this chapter, plan design is examined in greater detail, with specific differences evaluated in traditional plan design applicable to each of these general groupings.

TYPES OF PLANS

Dental plans covering the vast majority of all employees can be divided broadly into two types: scheduled and nonscheduled. Other approaches discussed below are essentially variations of these two basic plan types.

Scheduled Plans

Scheduled plans are categorized by a listing of fixed allowances by procedure. For example, the plan might pay $50 for a cleaning and $400 for root canal therapy. In addition, the scheduled plan may include deductibles and coinsurance (i.e., percentage cost-sharing provisions). Where deductibles are included in scheduled plans, amounts usually are small or, in some cases, required on a lifetime basis only.

Coinsurance provisions are extremely rare in scheduled plans since the benefits of coinsurance can be achieved through the construction of the schedule (i.e., the level of reimbursement for each procedure in the schedule can be set for specific reimbursement objectives). For example, if it is preferable to reimburse a higher percentage of the cost of preventive procedures than of other procedures, the schedule can be constructed to accomplish this goal.

There are three major advantages to scheduled plans:

1. *Cost control.* Benefit levels are fixed and therefore less susceptible to inflationary increases.
2. *Uniform payments.* In certain instances, it may be important to provide the same benefit regardless of regional cost differences. Collectively bargained plans occasionally may take this approach to ensure the "equal treatment" of all members.
3. *Ease of understanding.* It is clear to both the plan participant and the dentist how much is to be paid for each procedure.

In addition, scheduled plans sometimes are favored for employee-relations reasons. As the schedule is updated, improvements can be communicated to employees. If the updating occurs on a regular basis, this will be a periodic reminder to employees of the plan and its merits.

There also are disadvantages to scheduled plans. First, benefit levels, as well as internal relationships, must be examined periodically and changed when necessary to maintain reimbursement objectives. Second, where participants are dispersed geographically, plan reimbursement levels will vary according to the cost of dental care in a particular area unless multiple schedules are utilized. Third, if scheduled benefits are established at levels that are near the maximum of the reasonable and customary range, dentists who normally charge at below prevailing levels may be influenced to adjust their charges.

Services under the typical dental HMO are also provided on a scheduled basis—in a fashion. Since the contract between the participating dentist and the HMO generally specifies the basis on which the provider will be paid by the HMO and also fixes the amount that can be charged to the participant, the schedule furnished to participants typically identifies the amount the participant is required to pay rather than the amount the plan pays.

Nonscheduled Plans

Sometimes referred to as comprehensive plans, nonscheduled plans are written to cover some percentage of the "reasonable and customary" charges, or the charges most commonly made by dentists in the community. For any single procedure, the usual and customary charge typically is set at between the 75th and 90th percentiles depending on the administrator. (The trend is toward the lower number.) This means that the usual and customary charge level will cover the full cost of the procedure for 75 percent to 90 percent of the claims submitted in that geographical area.

Nonscheduled plans generally include a deductible, typically a calendar-year deductible of $50 or $75, and reimburse at different levels for different classes of procedures. Preventive and diagnostic expenses typically are covered in full or at very high reimbursement levels. Reimbursement levels for other procedures usually are then scaled down from the preventive and diagnostic level, based on the design objectives of the employer.

There are two major advantages to nonscheduled plans:

1. *Uniform reimbursement level.* While the dollar payment may vary by area and dentist, the percent of the total cost reimbursed by the plan is uniform.

2. *Adjusts automatically for change.* The nonscheduled plan adjusts automatically, not only for inflation, but also for variations in the relative value of specific procedures.

This approach also has disadvantages. First, because benefit levels adjust automatically for increases in the cost of care, in periods of rapidly escalating prices cost control can be a problem. Second, once a plan is installed on this basis, the opportunities for modest benefit improvements, made primarily for employee-relations purposes are limited, at least relative to the scheduled approach. Third, except for claims for which predetermination of benefits is appropriate, it rarely is clear in advance what the specific payment for a particular service will be, either to the patient or the dentist.

Preferred provider benefits are usually provided on an unscheduled basis. Reimbursement for services provided, however, is based on an agreed-upon discounted charge level, rather than the reasonable and customary charge. Deductible, coinsurance, percentage co-payment, and other benefit provisions are generally applied to the discounted charge level, not the reasonable and customary amount.

Other approaches are, for the most part, merely variations of the two basic plans. Included in this list are combination plans, incentive plans, and dental combined with major medical plans.

Combination Plans

This simply is a plan in which certain procedures are reimbursed on a scheduled basis, while others are reimbursed on a nonscheduled basis. In other words, it is a hybrid. While many variations exist, a common design in combination plans is to provide preventive and diagnostic coverage on a nonscheduled basis (i.e., a percentage of usual and customary, normally without a deductible). Procedures other than preventive and diagnostic are provided on a scheduled basis.

The principal advantage of a combination plan is that it provides a balance between (1) the need to emphasize preventive care and (2) cost control. Procedures that traditionally are the most expensive are covered on a scheduled basis, and except where benefit levels are established by a collective bargaining agreement, the timing of schedule improvements is at the employer's discretion. Preventive and diagnostic expenses, however, adjust automatically, so the incentive for preventive care does not lose its effectiveness as dental care costs increase.

The combination approach shares many of the same disadvantages as the scheduled and unscheduled plans, at least for certain types of expenses. Benefit levels—for other than preventive and diagnostic expenses— must be evaluated periodically. Scheduled payments do not reimburse at uniform levels for geographically dispersed participants. And dentists may be influenced by the schedule allowances to adjust their charges. Also, actual plan payments for preventive and diagnostic expenses rarely are identified in advance. Finally, it can be said that the combination approach is more complex than either the scheduled or unscheduled alternatives.

Incentive Plans

This type, a second variation, promotes sound dental hygiene through increasing reimbursement levels. Incentive coinsurance provisions generally apply only to preventive and maintenance (i.e., minor restorative) procedures, with other procedures covered on either a scheduled or non-scheduled basis. Incentive plans are designed to encourage individuals to visit the dentist regularly, without the plan sponsor having to absorb the cost of any accumulated neglect. Such plans generally reimburse at one level during the first year, with coinsurance levels typically increasing from year to year only for those who obtained needed treatment in prior years. For example, the initial coinsurance level (i.e., the benefit paid by the plan) for preventive and maintenance expenses might be 60 percent, increasing to 70 percent, 80 percent and, finally, 90 percent on an annual basis as long as the individual visits the dentist regularly. If, in any one year, there is a failure to obtain the required level of care, the coinsurance percentage reverts back to its original level.

The incentive portion of an incentive plan may or may not be characterized by deductibles. When deductibles are included in these plans, it is not unusual for them to apply on a lifetime basis.

The incentive concept, on the one hand, has two major advantages. In theory, the design of the plan encourages regular dental care and reduces the incidence of more serious dental problems in the future. Also, these plans generally have lower first-year costs than most nonscheduled plans.

On the other hand, there are major disadvantages. First, an incentive plan can be complicated to explain and even more complicated to administer. Second, little evidence exists to suggest that the incentive approach is effective in promoting sound dental hygiene. Finally, this particular plan is vulnerable to misunderstanding. For example, what happens if the participant's dentist postpones the required treatment until the beginning of the next plan year?

Plans Providing Both Medical and Dental Coverage

The last of the variations is the plan that provides both medical and dental coverage. During the infancy of dental benefits, such plans were quite popular.

These plans generally are characterized by a common deductible amount that applies to the sum of both medical and dental expenses.

Coinsurance levels may be identical, and sometimes the maximum applies to the combination of medical and dental expenses. However, recent design of these plans has made a distinction between dental and medical expenses so that each may have its own coinsurance provisions and maximums.

The advantages of this approach are the same as for the nonscheduled plan (i.e., uniform reimbursement levels, adjusts automatically to change, and relatively easy to understand). But this approach fails to recognize the difference between medicine and dentistry unless special provisions are made for dental benefits. It must be written with a medical carrier, whether or not this carrier is competent to handle both medical and dental protection; it makes it extremely difficult to separate and evaluate dental experience; and it shares the same disadvantages as the nonscheduled approach.

ORTHODONTIC EXPENSES

With possibly a few exceptions, orthodontic benefits never are written without other dental coverage. Nonetheless, orthodontic benefits present a number of design peculiarities that suggest this subject should be treated separately.

Orthodontic services, unlike nonorthodontic procedures, generally are rendered only once in an individual's lifetime; orthodontic problems are unlikely to recur. Orthodontic maximums, therefore, typically are expressed on a lifetime basis. Deductibles, which are applicable only to orthodontic services, also are often expressed on a lifetime basis. However, it is quite common for orthodontic benefits to be provided without deductibles, since a major purpose of the deductible—to eliminate small, nuisance-type claims—is of little consequence.

Because adult orthodontics generally are cosmetic and also because the best time for orthodontic work is during adolescence, many plans limit orthodontic coverage to persons under age 19. However, an increasing number of plans are including adult orthodontics as well, and many participants are taking advantage of this feature.

The coinsurance level for orthodontic expenses typically is 50 percent, but it varies widely depending on the reimbursement levels under other parts of the plan. It is common for the orthodontic reimbursement level to be the same as that for major restorative procedures.

Reflecting the nature of orthodontic work, and unlike virtually any other benefit, orthodontic benefits often are paid in installments instead of at the conclusion of the course of treatment. Because the program of treatment frequently extends over several years, it would be unreasonable to reimburse for the entire course of treatment at the end of the extended time. It would be equally unreasonable to pay for the entire course of treatment at its beginning.

IMPLANTOLOGY AND ITS SERVICES

Today's typical dental plan excludes implantology, partly because it is expensive to cover these services but, more importantly, because it was considered experimental for many years. Still, as these services move into the mainstream of dentistry, more plans are electing to cover them.

Implants, like orthodontic services, are generally rendered only once in an individual's lifetime. As a result, implant benefits design typically includes the following features:

1. The maximum benefit is expressed on a lifetime basis, typically at the same level that applies to orthodontic services.
2. Deductibles, where they apply, are also on a lifetime basis.
3. Coinsurance levels are the same as that for orthodontic services.

Because implants are not usually appropriate until an individual has reached adulthood, benefits are usually not extended to children.

FACTORS AFFECTING THE COST OF THE DENTAL PLAN

A number of factors, including design of the plan, characteristics of the covered group, the employer's approach to plan implementation, and plan administration affect the cost of the dental plan.

Plan Design

Many issues must be addressed before a particular design that is sound and reflects the needs of the plan sponsor can be established. Included in this list are the type of plan, deductibles, coinsurance, plan maximums, treatment of preexisting conditions, whether covered services should be limited, and orthodontic coverage.

An employer's choice between scheduled and nonscheduled benefits requires a look at the employer's objectives. The advantages and disadvantages of scheduled versus nonscheduled plans, combination plans, and others have been described earlier in this chapter.

Deductibles may or may not be included as an integral part of the design of the plan. Deductibles usually are written on a lifetime or calendar-year basis, with the calendar-year approach by far the more common.

Numerous dental procedures involve very little expense. Therefore, the deductible eliminates frequent payments for small claims that can be readily budgeted. For example, a $50 deductible can eliminate as much as 15 percent of the number of claims. A deductible can effectively control the cost of claim administration.

However, evidence exists that early detection and treatment of dental problems will produce a lower level of claims over the long term. Many insurers feel the best way to promote early detection is to pay virtually all the cost of preventive and diagnostic services. Therefore, these services often are not subject to a deductible.

A few insurance companies are advocates of a lifetime deductible, designed to lessen the impact of accumulated dental neglect. It is particularly effective when the employer is confronted with a choice of (1) not covering preexisting conditions at all, (2) covering these conditions but being forced otherwise to cut back on the design of the plan, or (3) offering a lifetime deductible, the theory being, "If you'll spend X dollars to get your mouth into shape once and for all, we'll take care of a large part of your future dental needs."

Opponents of the lifetime deductible concept claim the following disadvantages:

■ A lifetime deductible promotes early overutilization by those anxious to take advantage of the benefits of the plan.
■ Once satisfied, lifetime deductibles are of no further value for the presently covered group.
■ The lifetime deductible introduces employee turnover as an important cost consideration of the plan.
■ If established at a level that will have a significant impact on claim costs and premium rates, a lifetime deductible may result in adverse employee reaction to the plan.

Most dental plans are being designed, either through construction of the schedule or the use of coinsurance, so that the patient pays a portion of the costs for all but preventive and diagnostic services. The intent is to reduce spending on optional dental care and to provide cost-effective dental practice. In addition, many believe that employees that participate financially in the plan make better use of it. Preventive and diagnostic expenses generally are reimbursed at 80 percent to 100 percent of the usual and customary charges. Full reimbursement is quite common.

The reimbursement level for restorative and replacement procedures generally is lower than that for preventive and diagnostic procedures. Restorations, and in some cases replacements, may be reimbursed at 70 percent to 85 percent. In other cases, the reimbursement level for replacements is lower than for restorative treatment.

Orthodontics, implantology (where covered), and occasionally major replacements, have the lowest reimbursement levels of all. In most instances, the plans reimburse no more than 50 percent to 60 percent of the usual and customary charges for these procedures.

Most dental plans include a plan maximum, written on a calendar-year basis, which is applicable to nonorthodontic expenses. Orthodontic and implantology expenses generally are subject to separate lifetime maximums. Also, in some instances, a separate lifetime maximum may apply to nonorthodontic expenses.

Unless established at a fairly low level, a lifetime maximum will have little or no impact on claim liability and serves only to further complicate design of the plan. Calendar-year maximums, though, encourage participants to seek less costly care and may help to spread out the impact of accumulated dental neglect over the early years of the plan. The typical calendar-year maximum is somewhere between $1,000 and $1,500. To put things in perspective: In 1999, only about 20 percent of people visiting a dentist spent from $300 to $999 annually, including insurance company payments, and just 17 percent spent $1,000 or more, including insurance company payments. Most claims are small (40 percent spent $100 or less), and therefore the maximum's impact on plan costs is minor.

Another major consideration is the treatment of preexisting conditions. The major concern is the expense associated with the replacement of teeth extracted prior to the date of coverage. Preexisting conditions are treated in a number of ways:

■ They may be excluded.

■ They may be treated as any other condition.

■ They may be covered on a limited basis (perhaps one-half of the normal reimbursement level) or subject to a lifetime maximum.

If treated as any other condition, the cost of the plan in the early years (nonorthodontic only) will be increased by about 5 percent to 7 percent.

Another plan design consideration is the range of procedures to be covered. In addition to orthodontics and implantology, other procedures occasionally excluded are surgical periodontics and temporomandibular joint (TMJ) dysfunction therapy. It is difficult to diagnose TMJ disorders, and many consider them a medical and not a dental condition. Claims are large, and the potential for abuse is significant.

Although rare, some plans cover only preventive and maintenance expenses. These plans are becoming more common in flexible benefit plans where employees often may pick either a preventive plan or one that is more comprehensive.

Orthodontic expenses, as noted, may be excluded. However, where these are covered, the plan design may include a separate deductible to discourage "shoppers." The cost of orthodontic diagnosis and models is about $300, whether or not treatment is undertaken. The inclusion of a separate orthodontic deductible eliminates reimbursement for these expenses. Also, orthodontic plan design typically includes both heavy coinsurance and limited maximums to guarantee patient involvement.

An indication of the sensitivity of dental plan costs to some of the plan design features discussed can be seen in the following illustration. Assume a nonscheduled base model plan with a $50 calendar-year deductible applicable to all expenses other than orthodontics. The reimbursement, or employer coinsurance, levels are as follows:

- Diagnostic and preventive services (Type I): 100 percent.
- Basic services, including anesthesia and basic restoration (Type II): 75 percent.
- Major restoration, including oral surgery, endodontics, periodontics, and prosthodontics (Type III): 50 percent.
- Orthodontics (Type IV): 50 percent.

There also is an annual benefit maximum of $1,500 for Types I, II, and III services and a lifetime maximum of $1,500 for orthodontics. Based on this base model plan, Table 10–1 shows the approximate premium sensitivity to changes in plan design. If two or more of the design changes shown in this table are considered together, an approximation of the resulting value may be obtained by multiplying the relative values of the respective changes.

The change in deductibles has a significant impact on cost, as much as a 14 percent reduction in cost to increase the deductible from $50 to $100. The change in benefit maximums has some impact, but it is minor. Coinsurance has a definite effect, especially changes in restoration, replace-

TABLE 10–1

Model Dental Plan

	Relative Value (in percent)
Base model plan	100%
Design changes	
Deductible	
Remove $50 deductible	122
Lower to $25	112
Raise to $100	86
Benefit maximum (annual)	
Lower from $1,500 to $1,000	92
Raise to $2,000	101
Coinsurance	
Liberalize percent to: 100—80—60—60*	110
Tighten percent to: 80—70—50—50*	92
Orthodontics	
Exclude	84

* For Types I, II, III, and IV services, respectively.

ment, and orthodontic portions of the plan, all of which represent about 80 percent to 85 percent of the typical claim costs. Finally, the inclusion of orthodontics in the base plan is another item of fairly high cost.

Characteristics of the Covered Group

A second factor affecting the cost of the dental plan is the characteristics of the covered group. Important considerations include, but are not limited to, the following:

■ Age.
■ Gender.
■ Location.
■ Income level of the participants.
■ Occupation.

The increased incidence of high-cost dental procedures at older ages generally makes coverage of older groups more expensive. Average charges usually increase from about age 30. As one ages, the need for more expensive restorative services increases for those who need dental care.

Gender is another consideration. Women tend to have higher utilization rates than men. For a given age, costs among females are approximately 15 percent higher than the costs among males. One study showed that women average 1.9 visits to dentists per year, compared with 1.7 for men. These differences may be attributable to a heightened sensitivity to personal appearance by women rather than to a higher need.

Charge levels, practice patterns, and the availability of dentists vary considerably by locale. Charge levels within the United States range anywhere from 75 percent to 135 percent of the national average, except for Alaska, California, and certain metropolitan areas. Differences exist in the frequency of use for certain procedures as well. There is evidence, for example, that more expensive procedures are performed relatively more often in Los Angeles than, say, in Philadelphia.

Another consideration is income. One study shows that dental care expenditures per participant were 5 percent to 30 percent higher for members of families with higher incomes. Generally, the higher the income, the greater the difference.

Essentially four reasons may account for income being a key factor. First, the higher the income level, the greater the likelihood the individual already has an established program of dental hygiene. Second, in many areas there is greater accessibility to dental care in high-income neighborhoods. Third, a greater tendency exists on the part of higher-income individuals to elect higher-cost procedures. Last, high-income people tend to use more expensive dentists.

Another important consideration is the occupation of the covered group. While difficult to explain, evidence suggests considerable variation between plans covering blue-collar workers and plans covering salaried or mixed groups. One possible explanation is differences in awareness and income levels. One insurer estimates that blue-collar employees are 15 percent to 25 percent less expensive to insure than white-collar employees.

Sponsor's Approach to Implementation

The last of the factors affecting plan costs is the sponsor's approach to implementation. Dental work, unlike medical care, lends itself to "sandbagging" (i.e., deferral of needed treatment until after the plan's effective date). Everything else being equal, plans announced well in advance of the effective date tend to have poorer first-year experience than plans announced only shortly before the effective date. Advance knowledge of the deferred effective date easily can increase first-year costs from 10 percent to 20 percent or even more.

Employee contributions are another consideration. Dental plans, if offered on a contributory basis, may be prone to adverse selection. While there is evidence that the adverse selection is not as great as was once anticipated, many insurers continue to discourage contributory plans. Most insurance companies will underwrite dental benefits on a contributory basis, but some require certain adverse selection safeguards. Typical safeguards include the following:

- Combining dental plan participation and contributions with medical plan participation.
- Limiting enrollment to a single offering, thus preventing subsequent sign-ups or dropouts.
- Requiring dental examinations before joining the plan and limiting or excluding treatment for conditions identified in the exam. The Health Insurance Portability and Accountability Act (HIPAA) limitations do not apply as long as the dental benefits are "limited in scope" and are available under a separate policy or rider.
- Requiring participants to remain in the plan for a specified minimum time period before being eligible to drop coverage.

Plan Administration

The last item to be addressed is claims administration. The nature of dentistry and dental plan design suggests that claims administration is very important. While several years may lapse before an insured has occasion to file a medical claim, rarely does the year pass during which a family will not visit the dentist at least once. Therefore, claims administration capability is an extremely important consideration in selecting a plan carrier—and might very well be the most important consideration.

One key element of claims administration is "predetermination of benefits." This common plan feature requires the dentist to prepare a treatment plan that shows the work and cost before any services begin. This treatment plan generally is required only for nonemergency services and only if the cost is expected to exceed some specified level, such as

$300. The carrier processes this information to determine exactly how much the dental plan will pay. Also, selected claims are referred to the carrier's dental consultants to assess the appropriateness of the recommended treatment. If there are any questions, the dental consultant discusses the treatment plan with the dentist prior to performing the services.

Predetermination is very important both in promoting better quality care and in reducing costs. These benefits are accomplished by spotting unnecessary expenses, treatments that cannot be expected to last, instances of coverage duplication, and charges higher than usual and customary before extensive and expensive work begins. Predetermination of benefits can be effective in reducing claim costs by as much as 5 percent. Predetermination also advises the covered individual of the exact amount of reimbursement under the plan prior to commencement of treatment.

Also important are alternate treatment provisions. These provisions enable the plan administrator either to approve the least costly, equally effective treatment option or to cover more expensive procedures only at the level of the less expensive alternative. Alternate treatment provisions, adopted by most plan sponsors, can reduce plan costs up to 5 percent.

Prescription Drug, Vision, and Hearing Care Plans

Eugene J. Ziurys, Jr.[*]

Despite greater employee cost sharing in both premiums and claims, ancillary benefits such as prescription drugs, vision care, and hearing care maintain their presence in many benefit packages. The presidential election of 2000 focused attention once again on the issue of providing a prescription drug plan for seniors as well as bringing the high cost of pharmaceuticals for just about everyone into the national spotlight.

PRESCRIPTION DRUGS

"Twenty years ago prescription drug benefits represented an average of 4 percent of total health plan costs; today they represent four times that amount and are increasing geometrically."[1] The emphasis on outpatient care, lifestyle, and biotech drugs has further exacerbated the cost increases in prescription drug costs.

Inpatient prescriptions are covered by basic hospital, major medical, or comprehensive medical plan benefits. This chapter concentrates on prescription drugs strictly in an outpatient environment, and the discussion essentially is limited to federal legend drugs or state-restricted drugs, which cannot be dispensed without a prescribing physician or dentist.

As new and increasing expensive "wonder" drugs continue to be introduced, new generics are entering the marketplace. The use of generics

---

[*] Revised by Jerry S. Rosenbloom

[1] "Prescription Drug Costs: Confronting the Issues," *Employee Benefit Practices*, International Foundation of Employee Benefits Plans, 2nd Quarter 2000, p. 1.

is increasing continuously as a percentage of the total prescription drug market. Antisubstitution laws have been repealed in all states and the District of Columbia, and the passage of the 1984 Drug Price Competition and Patent Restoration Act (Hatch/Waxman) accelerated the introduction of generic products. It is estimated that close to half of prescriptions dispensed are generics. Several states mandate that some of the substitution savings be passed on to the consumer. Generic substitutes have a wide price variation, often from close to that of the innovator to substantially lower. In a mail-order benefit plan, the average brand-name drug can be up to five times the cost of the average generic drug.

The matter of generic drug quality surfaces from time to time. However, the Food and Drug Administration (FDA), charged with monitoring the quality and safety of all prescription drugs, has reassured the American public periodically of generic integrity. Leading research shows that drug manufacturers produce more than 50 percent generic drugs, and some research companies purchase generic drugs and sell them under their own labels.

Prescription drug benefit programs can be designed in various ways to encourage the use of generic drugs. The simplest is patient incentive, offering a lower co-payment (two-tier) when a generic is dispensed. A pharmacy can be paid a surcharge for dispensing a generic, and some health maintenance organizations (HMOs) mandate their use. Often plans require the patient to pay the differential when a brand product is requested.

There are several modes of reimbursing outpatient prescriptions. One is a traditional indemnity product as part of a major medical or comprehensive medical benefits package. Others stand as a distinct benefit from these basic plans. They are service-type card plans with per-prescription cost sharing, mail-order programs, and managed care arrangements through HMOs in which a patient's pharmacy selection is often limited.

Traditional Indemnity Approach

In the indemnity environment, drugs are covered under major medical or comprehensive medical policies. The majority of outpatient drug benefits are no longer provided in this manner, as most plans are now under some form of managed care. Nevertheless, it is useful to understand the indemnity approach.

To obtain prescription drug benefits under these plans, the employee must fulfill an annual deductible and thereafter is subject to coinsurance, usually at 20 percent. The total charge is paid at the pharmacy, and the patient files a claim. Though the convenience of having the prescription filled by any retail provider (pharmacy) is an advantage, the total charge almost always is the usual and customary one. The beneficiary participates in prescription drug price inflation by contributing a percentage of the total cost through the 20/80 percent coinsurance provision. For a variety of reasons including inertia on the part of the employee, many claims are never submitted to the payor. This is commonly known as the "shoebox effect." While the extent of this is impossible to quantify, it is guessed that between 15 percent and 20 percent of prescription drug charges are never claimed under these traditional plans. Even when submitted these plans yield limited statistical information.

Prescription drug claims submitted separately from other medical charges are expensive to process when compared with the total cost of the drug. For example, because the cost of issuing a check ranges between $6 to $9, a prescription-only reimbursement can cost more to process than the drug itself. In addition, claims for some noncovered drugs may slip through the system with relative ease.

Service Plans

The impetus for service-type card plans was a result of collective bargaining between the Big Three automakers and the United Auto Workers in the late 1960s. Prior to that time, few health plans had separate prescription drug benefits. In such a plan, an insurance company, Blue Cross organization, or administrator (also called a clearinghouse, fiscal intermediary or more recently a pharmacy benefit manager [PBM]) solicits pharmacies nationwide or on a regional, as-needed basis to join the plan. Several insurance companies and Blue Cross plans manage their own prescription benefits rather than outsourcing it to a PBM. While under a master contract, the pharmacy usually has the latitude to accept or reject a particular offering.

The covered employee is issued an identification card, has a selection of participating pharmacies, and can obtain a prescription drug by paying a per-prescription co-payment. Today, this generally ranges from $5 to $15. The card is similar to a credit card and gives the pharmacy ample information to process the claim transaction.

Employees electing to patronize a non-network pharmacy must pay for the prescription out of pocket. A claim form must be completed (a portion by the employee and the balance by the pharmacy) and mailed to the insurance company or PBM. Provided that the employee and the drug are eligible, reimbursement less any per-prescription co-payment will be sent to the employee's residence. In many cases, these prescriptions are tested for reasonableness, and a charge beyond the co-payment may be made. Some plans have an additional penalty if a nonmember provider is used within a designated service area. Claims processed through a non-network pharmacy are called direct or nonparticipating reimbursements.

Reimbursement Levels

A reimbursement level is decided by insurers or employers when contracting directly with a PBM. A common reimbursement formula has these components:

Ingredient cost + Professional (dispensing) fee + State sales tax
(where applicable) – Cost sharing (coinsurance or co-payment)

The ingredient cost usually is based on the published average wholesale price (AWP). Many plans have been able to take substantial discounts off the AWP as pharmacies often are able to purchase drugs below these published "sticker" prices. The professional fee paid to the pharmacy is a flat amount. This fee usually is set by region or state based partly on the cost of doing business in that particular part of the country. More recently, there has been a trend toward capitation where the risk is shared based on the number of people covered.

Covered Costs and Exclusions

Benefits under a managed care plan most often cover the following:

- Federal legend drugs.
- State-restricted drugs. In several states, some drugs that are non-legend under federal law must have a physician's prescription to be dispensed.
- Compound items containing a federal legend drug or state-restricted drug.
- Injectable insulin. Needles and syringes often are covered when purchased with injectable insulin.

Quantity limitations often are based on whichever is greater: a 30- to 34-day supply or 100 units.

Common exclusions are contraceptives, experimental drugs, drugs covered under federal and state workers' compensation programs, fertility drugs, immunizing agents, cosmetic drugs, and the administration of drugs. However, plans do differ. In certain states, contraceptives must be covered, while in others coverage can be offered voluntarily by the employer. Also, a recent Equal Employment Opportunity Commission (EEOC) decision found that a health plan that covers prescription drugs and preventive care, but does not cover birth control prescriptions violates equal employment rights under the Pregnancy Discrimination Act (PDA).

On-Line Adjudication of Claims

Today, the pharmacist processes the prescription claim by keying in certain information from the identification card on-line directly to the PBM. The claim is adjudicated while the patient is in the store. Factors such as patient eligibility, drug coverage, potential drug interaction, and amount of cost sharing are all considered and answered in a matter of seconds. The employee signs a log acknowledging receipt of the prescription, assigning benefits (beyond the cost-sharing amount) to the pharmacy, and authorizing release of information to the payor if requested.

Nonautomated pharmacies make an imprint from the employee identification card onto a universal claim form (UCF), completing the drug information and requiring the employee to sign the claim form, in lieu of the log. The card imprint shows employer/employee information; the pharmacist then completes the balance of the needed data elements, e.g., drug information, cost, etc.

Most managed care claims are processed by PBMs. The PBM receives most claims on-line, processes them, and sends checks or wires funds to the banks of its network of pharmacies. Funds are transferred from the insurer (payor) to the PBM for these prescriptions. Modern computerized technology lends itself well to handling the high volume of claims combined with the still relatively low charge per prescription. Economies of scale apply, and the administration usually costs substantially less than $1 per claim.

Advantages and Disadvantages

Certain features make managed care plans desirable. An important consideration is the ability to place a reimbursement ceiling on each drug. Useful statistics are available from the highly automated procedures and include pharmacy and employee profiles, particular therapeutic classes of drugs being dispensed, and average costs by therapeutic class, per prescription and per employee. These statistics benefit the employer and can be the basis of pharmacy audits.

On the negative side, in the absence of an annual deductible, all prescriptions are covered (less the per-prescription co-payment), and many claims are paid. However, with proper compliance, savings are possible. If the benefit package is not designed with ample exclusions and realistic co-payments, the net payout could exceed traditional indemnity plans. Also, there is speculation in some circles that card plans result in increased drug utilization.

Limited Networks

When service programs started, the large PBMs rushed to sign up most retail pharmacies. While this produced economies of scale in processing and limited ingredient cost allowances, the share of market in a given community did not change appreciably except for the few pharmacies not joining available networks.

With torrid prescription drug price inflation and the demand of payors to limit the acceleration of health care, pressures to tighten the reimbursement to the pharmacy mounted, hence the emergence of the preferred provider organization (PPO). In this setting, a select number of pharmacies in a community, region, or nation (with limitations) are given a measure of exclusivity in which, for a substantial reduction of AWP, dispensing fees, or both, they would receive a more substantial share of the market. The employee was steered into these stores with a substantially lower cost-sharing amount.

While selected pharmacies, specifically large drugstore chains and payors have benefited, it has caused a major uproar in the balance of the pharmacy community, especially in the independent pharmacy sector. As a result, there are many state legislative proposals requiring that "any willing pharmacy provider" meeting certain (usually financial) criteria be admitted to a network. Some states have passed such measures into law.

A provision used in some plans is the limitation of benefit differentials the employee must pay when patronizing an out-of-network pharmacy. Some states are moving to legislate statutory limits on the differential.

Mail-Order Prescription Programs

Prescriptions by mail began after World War II with the U.S. Veterans Administration and the American Association of Retired Persons (AARP) Pharmacy Service Programs. The private sector got off to a slower start, and mail-order programs did not become an employee benefit to an appreciable segment of the population until the 1980s. The mail-order market is most practical for maintenance drugs in the treatment of chronic conditions. It is estimated that up to 70 percent of prescriptions and prescription expenditures are for chronic conditions. Mail order has a special relevance for the senior citizen population, as more than half of those 65 and older have at least one such chronic condition, and the convenience of ordering by mail is appealing to the aged, disabled, and those residing in rural areas. Complete self-addressed packets are provided, simplifying the mail-order process. With the first order, detailed information is requested to create a patient profile. The mail-order company fills prescriptions generally within 10 to 14 days (from residence, to pharmacy, back to residence). Home delivery is a convenience rarely offered today by retail pharmacies. Toll-free phone numbers for both patients and physicians are also common.

Plan Design

A mail-order benefit program can be an add-on to a major medical or comprehensive medical plan. Such a plan usually waives the annual deductible and imposes a modest per-prescription co-payment or coinsurance amount as an incentive to use the mail-order arrangement. An additional incentive is a more liberal quantity allowance, typically up to a 90-day supply, compared with the usual 30- to 34-day arrangement at the retail level. For example, the employee can receive up to a 90-day supply for $12 per prescription. In a traditional indemnity plan, the same employee would have to fulfill the annual deductible and pay a 20 percent coinsurance charge thereafter for a lesser quantity. Another method of designing a mail-order plan is to integrate it with a card arrangement with a lower co-payment coupled with larger quantity as an incentive to use the mail-order option. While some plans mandate use of the mail-order segment after one refill, most still only offer an incentive to use it.

Advantages and Disadvantages

Because of mail-order company volume buying, substantial discounts off the AWP are commonplace. The employer and insurer can add to these savings by negotiating a discounted reimbursement formula with the mail-order (central fill) pharmacy. In addition, the professional (dispensing) fee is lower than in a retail setting or even waived at times, and most mail-order pharmacies are committed to fill prescriptions generically whenever legally permissible, further managing benefit dollars.

Although the unit price is virtually always lower at a mail-order pharmacy, opinions differ on the extent of savings for the employer. The matter of "wastage" often is debated. Ability to obtain up to a 90-day supply of a needed medication is beneficial. However, should the employee's drug regimen change after a week, for whatever reason, there is substantial extra cost. An employee also might terminate employment after "stocking up" on several prescriptions, thereby receiving an extended benefit. Regardless of the plan's design, instituting realistic cost-sharing amounts while simultaneously providing incentives to use the mail-order plan increases the savings potential.

The Future

With the aging population and pressures to manage health care costs in general, mail-order arrangements are becoming a larger segment of the prescription drug market. The retail pharmacy community is being hurt by the mail-order prescription industry. To counter this, it has introduced, and some states have have passed, laws requiring licensure in the state the prescription is being sent. Several large pharmaceutical chains have opened mail-order facilities as a defensive measure.

Cost-Management Techniques

Maximum Allowable Cost (MAC)

MAC programs reimburse only up to a certain threshold on selected, often-dispensed generics. This maintains a substantial price differential between the innovator drug and generic ceiling. MAC programs were initiated by the U.S. Health and Human Services Department, are used in many state Medicaid programs, and have become more common in the private sector.

Formularies

Basically a formulary is a listing of drugs approved for dispensing. A formulary mandates specific innovators and generics within therapeutic classes to limit inappropriate utilization and to aggressively price frequently prescribed drugs. Formularies are in general use in hospitals and managed care health plans that utilize a primary care physician (PCP) or "gatekeeper." Some formularies have drugs tied to manufacturers' rebates once certain volume thresholds are reached. The formulary considerations are both medical and economic and are set mainly by pharmacy and therapeutics (P&T) panels of physicians and pharmacists. Step-care protocols utilizing a sequence of drug therapy lend themselves well to such medical management techniques. Formulary compliance is becoming a key factor in assessing pharmacy panels.

Drug Utilization Review (DUR)

With the growth of managed care and more attention to cost and quality control, DUR systems are widespread. They connect drug utilization to a medical condition on a per-case basis. This is especially prominent with the increased use of a primary care physician. Computerized on-line prescription profiles link both the retail pharmacy(ies) and the mail-order house with a patient's record. Vital interventions can be made on drug interactions, unnecessary prescribing, and patient compliance. DUR can be utilized on a prospective, concurrent, or retroactive basis.

In-House Pharmacy

Most staff-model HMOs have in-house drug dispensing units. Here the ideal cost-management situation can occur when drugs are prescribed by a primary care physician and dispensed using strict formularies, thus minimizing "dispense as written" (DAW) situations that often result in the use of more expensive drugs.

Individual practice association HMOs (IPAs) commonly give a pharmacy chain or chains with major presence in a service area a measure of exclusivity at a discounted reimbursement in exchange for channeling a large segment of eligible participants to the provider.

Some employers with large facilities have on-site pharmacies as a convenience to employees and tie-in incentives to utilize the "company pharmacy."

Point of Sale (POS)

State-of-the-art telecommunication has enabled PBMs to have on-line prescription drug claim adjudication performed while the beneficiary is present at the pharmacy. This has created the capability to administer a separate annual prescription drug deductible and/or annual maximum per patient.

Today, the vast majority of pharmacies are connected with one or more data centers. In a matter of seconds, the pharmacist can tell if the employee has prescription drug coverage, whether the drug prescribed is covered and appropriately priced, and the exact amount of cost sharing to collect. In addition, most plans add on DUR and alert the pharmacist to a possible drug interaction, early refill, and formulary compliance.

VISION CARE

Most of us would rank vision as a very important, if not the most important, of our senses. Yet vision care is often neglected. Eye disease, treatment, and surgery traditionally are covered under hospital, surgical, major medical, and comprehensive medical policies. However, most of these plans exclude routine vision examination and eyewear from coverage. Separate (freestanding) vision plans cover services such as routine examinations and materials (products) such as lenses, frames, and contact lenses. In a purist sense, some do not consider this coverage insurance because of the absence of illness or disease. Nevertheless, the need for appropriate vision care is real, as over 60 percent of the adult population wears corrective eyewear. A routine vision exam not only confirms whether prescription eyewear is necessary but may detect unrelated problems such as diabetes and high blood pressure. Aside from the obvious medical benefits to employees, vision care plans have the potential of reducing accidents and increasing production, factors that are of major importance to the employer. Vision care often is compared to dental care because of its frequently elective and predictable nature. However, despite holding patterns for certain new benefits, some employers are adding vision care to their benefit portfolio.

Providers

There are three types of vision care professionals.

Ophthalmologists are medical doctors (MDs) specializing in the total care of the eye, including diagnosis, treatment of eye diseases, and surgery. Many perform eye examinations and prescribe corrective lenses. Some also dispense corrective eyewear. An ophthalmologist typically completes four years of premedical training, another four years of medical school, and subsequent internship/residency.

Optometrists are doctors of optometry (ODs) who are licensed to examine, diagnose, treat, and manage diseases and disorders of the visual system, the eye, and associated structures as well as diagnose related systemic conditions. They are trained to detect eye disease and/or symptoms requiring the attention of ophthalmologists. In addition to performing vision examinations and prescribing lenses, most optometrists dispense glasses and contact lenses. An optometrist typically completes undergraduate work and is graduated from a college of optometry.

Opticians fit, adjust, and dispense eyewear (lenses, frames, and contact lenses) prescribed by ophthalmologists and optometrists. They are eyewear retailers and provide advice on which lenses and frames are most appropriate. Many grind and fabricate eyewear, verify the finished products, and repair and replace various ophthalmic devices. Optician certification, licensure, and registration vary by state, as do training and apprenticeship.

Covered Benefits

Vision Examination

A thorough examination includes a history of general health, vision complaints, and an external and internal eye exam. Other services may include various ocular tests, usually including but not limited to coordination of eye movements, tonometry, depth perception (for children), and refraction testing for distance and near vision. In addition to the possible need for corrective eyewear, the exam could detect cataracts, glaucoma, diabetes, and brain tumors. Some plans allow an examination at 12- or 24-month intervals, and it is up to the employee to arrange for eyewear if needed. HMOs often feature "exam-only" plans.

Lenses

The lens is the heart of sight-corrective material. Single-vision lenses are the most widely used, with multivision lenses (bifocal, trifocal) also being dispensed in large quantities. Plastic has replaced glass as the predominant lens material, and a wide array of lenses, such as oversized, photochrometric, and tinted, are available. Most plans consider these "cosmetic extras" and outside normal plan limits. As contact lenses have gained popularity, some plans are providing benefits for them even though they are likely to be worn for cosmetic rather than for medical reasons.

Many dispensers have an in-house laboratory for grinding and fabrication of the more routinely prescribed eyewear, while others use full-service labs.

Frames

The cosmetic element is much more obvious in the area of frames than in lenses. Frames are increasingly being selected for cosmetic purposes and at times are part of a fashion wardrobe. The cost can run into hundreds of dollars for plastic or metal frames of almost limitless sizes, shapes, and colors. Herein lies a dilemma for the payor. The frame is a must, but how does one avoid paying for fashion while giving a fair reimbursement for utility? Certain plans make allowances up to a specified dollar figure, while others approve a limited selection; for example, 50 frames each for men, women, and children.

Plan Design

Frequency Limits

To control unnecessary use and keep administrative costs down, plans use a time limit (frequency) with which a participant may utilize a benefit plan for covered expenses. Examples of frequencies allowed by four plans are noted in the following table.

		Month Intervals		
	Plan 1	Plan 2	Plan 3	Plan 4
Exams	24	12	12	12
Lenses	24	24	12	12
Frames	24	24	24	12

Schedule-of-Benefits Approach

This type of plan has maximum allowances for each service and material and a limit on the frequency of use. A typical schedule pays the lesser of the claimed or schedule maximum.

Service/Material	Maximum Allowed
Examination	$ 50
Lenses (pair)	
Single vision	60
Bifocal	90
Trifocal	110
Lenticular	140
Contacts (elective)	100
Frames	60

Schedules can be national or regional, based on a geographical percentage of UCR charges.

Advantages of a schedule-of-benefits plan are that it is easy to understand, it has no restriction on the choice of provider, and it encourages the thrifty employee to shop around. The employer is cognizant of premium outlay, as the schedule ceiling does not change with inflation, and administration is simplified for the insurer or administrator because the frequencies and caps are determined in advance.

Preferred Provider Networks

Preferred provider plans steer employees to a network of participating providers that have agreed to provide certain services for a negotiated fee. Employees who use a provider in the network may have many of the plan benefits covered 100 percent or pay only a minimum co-payment, usually from $5 to $20. There is no claim form for the employee. An employee simply shows an identification card, which can be subject to confirmation at the provider's place of business, or the employee can mail a request for vision services and materials to the administrator and receive a benefit form stating which benefits are available, for what length of time, and the extent of the copayment.

Providers are solicited by the insurer or administrator with the expectation of increased patient volume. In return, the provider agrees to reimbursement of discounted material costs plus dispensing fees. Some plans also mandate the use of specific laboratories. Various quality-control measures are inserted into these plans, and peer review is common. In some plans, participating providers can charge the regular retail price for oversized or tinted lenses, and designer frames, while others call for reduced charges for these extras.

Most plans allow reimbursement even when a participating provider is not utilized. In these instances, the employee must pay the provider's charge and file a claim. Reimbursement is based on a schedule or UCR determination. When a non-network provider is used, the employee's out-of-pocket expense is almost always greater than it would be with a participating provider. Figure 11-1 illustrates a sample plan.

These plans usually follow a medical plan pattern, with a percentile of the charges in a given area prevailing. A higher figure is allowed for examination and lenses, and less for lenses of a cosmetic nature. Inflation is shared with the employee, with a percentage of coinsurance applied with the medical reimbursement. A separate means of administration is unnecessary.

Vision Benefits in Flexible Benefit Plans

Flex plans increasingly include ancillary benefits, including vision care. They enable an employee to choose among various coverages, taking into account factors such as overall health, spouse coverage, and specific family needs. Although the design of these plans varies, employers commonly allocate a certain number of "flex credits" to each employee, who then uses these to "purchase" benefits. Each employee chooses the benefits that best fit his or her needs. Once the employer allocation has been used, the employee may purchase additional benefits at his or her own cost. They place vision care in competition with other coverages.

Flexible Spending Accounts (FSAs)

If not covered under a medical plan or a freestanding plan, vision benefits are usually covered by a flexible spending account if the employer maintains one. Under an FSA arrangement, the employee may reduce

F I G U R E   11–1

Preferred Provider Network Sample Plan

	In-Network	Out-of-Network (Program Allowance)
Exam (every 12 months)	100%	$32
Frames (every 12 months)	100% (up to $60 retail value)	$24
Lenses (every 12 months)	100%	$24 single vision $36 bifocal $46 trifocal $72 aphakic/lenticular
Contact lenses (every 12 months in lieu of glasses)		
Prescription and fitting	100%	$20 daily wear $30 extended wear
Standard	100%	$48
Specialty	100% (up to $75 retail value)	$48
Vision Care Options* (such as tints, contact lens solution)	10% discount off charge	Not covered

*These allowances and discounts are only available at the point of purchase.

income and Social Security taxes by funding benefits such as vision care with pretax dollars.

At the beginning of the plan year, employees can designate a certain amount of money (up to a maximum) to be deducted from salary, thereby reducing the base upon which taxes are paid. The employer holds the money and "reimburses" the employee upon verification of covered expenses. (See Chapters 37 and 38 for a complete discussion of flex plans and FSAs.)

Occupational Safety and Health Administration (OSHA)

OSHA requires employers to provide protective eyewear to employees in positions exposing them to the danger of eye injury. These "safety glass" programs are usually outside the normal health benefit package.

HEARING CARE

A majority of benefit packages still do not contain this coverage. The aging population, coupled with a noisy contemporary society, contribute to hearing loss/impairment, and it is estimated that more than 10 percent of the population is affected. Despite the generally acknowledged increase in the number of hearing-impaired persons and the substantially improved technology of hearing-aid instruments available, many would rather continue with this impairment than bear the stigma of wearing a hearing aid in public.

Coverage

Surgical procedures affecting the ear are normally covered in standard medical policies. Beyond this, some HMOs, major medical, and comprehensive policies include hearing aids. However, more complete coverage is afforded by plans designed specifically to cover hearing care.

Hearing Care Benefits

A common benefit package includes an 80 percent reimbursement of services and materials up to a ceiling of $300 to $600. The frequency of benefit availability is usually every 36 months. The following items are often covered:

- Otologic examination (by a physician or surgeon).
- Audiometric examination (by an audiologist).
- Hearing instrument (including evaluation, ear mold fitting, and follow-up visits).

Preferred provider plans in which access to a panel would result in discounts for audiologist fees as well as hearing-aid instruments are also available. Several administrators have developed service plans in which co-payments apply when participating providers are utilized. Material costs can be reimbursed on a cost-plus dispensing-fee basis. However, identical procedures vary in different geographic areas and even within specific metropolitan areas.

As with vision care expenses, an FSA is a convenient vehicle through which to budget for hearing care expenses in the absence of employee benefit coverage.

CONCLUSION

Because of continuing prescription drug inflation, drugs are no longer an inconsequential portion of an employer's benefit cost. New technology combined with managed care is quickly tracking the use of drugs for more effective use. The increased percentage of the health care dollar spent on prescription drugs is a common target for managed care, and insurer intervention is increasing.

The advent of accessible up-to-date personal profiles because of on-line drug adjudication is now forcing the prescription drug benefit from a carve-out mode to integration with the medical record.

This will result in a shift from management of the prescription drug benefit from a "vacuum" toward concentration from wellness (lifestyle) to early detection and on to programs of outcomes such as disease management. This will enable outcomes research resulting in a more informed patient, resulting in better coverage decisions, greater drug regimen discipline, and a reduction of physician visits, medical procedures, and hospitalization.

Vision care in traditional benefit plans or as an elective part of a flexible benefit plan is growing. It is a frequently used benefit with a relatively low cost. A barrier to the growth of coverage is the lack of awareness by many employees of their possible need for vision care and its still relatively affordable cost.

Hearing care benefits are still absent from the majority of benefit packages, but this coverage, too, is growing.

With an aging population, the public and private sectors will continue to pay more attention to these ancillary benefits. The costs for prescription drug, vision care, and hearing care benefits represent a large financial commitment in the absence of coverage by former employers or Medicare.

CHAPTER 12

Preventive Health Care Strategies: An Overview for Employers

Michael P. O'Donnell

INTRODUCTION

Evidence continues to mount that well-designed preventive health care strategies contribute to reductions in absenteeism; increases in productivity; health care cost containment; and improved recruitment, retention, and employee morale.[1] The remarkable growth and evolution in employee preventive health care strategies are documented in both academic and business literature. Fueled in large part by the increased science base supporting the role of prevention, interest in and commitment to preventive initiatives have accelerated in the past decade. Research indicates that disease prevention and health promotion can postpone up to 70 percent of all premature deaths; in contrast, traditional high-tech curative medicine can postpone no more than 10 percent to 15 percent of such deaths and disabilities. The Employee Benefit Research Institute's special report, *Health Promotion: Its Role in Health Care*, and the special report from *Business and Health Magazine* called *Preventive Medicine: Strategies for Quality Care and Lower Costs,* illustrate the growing recognition that the leading causes of illness and disability relate to factors that individuals can control.

Former Surgeon General C. Everett Koop comments that, "The plain fact is that we Americans do a better job of preventive maintenance on our cars than on ourselves." Dr. Koop states: "We incorrectly assume

---

1 Office of Disease Prevention and Health Promotion, Public Health Service, U.S. Department of Health and Human Services, *Health Promotion Goes to Work: Programs with an Impact*, (Washington, D.C.: U.S. Government Printing Office, 1993).

that high-tech medicine means high-quality, when actually timely, low-tech, low-cost preventive measures can often do more to improve health and cut costs."[2] He points out that preventable illness makes up approximately 70 percent of the burden of illness, which should have major implications for our debate on health care reform and for the use of our health dollars. Unfortunately, this message has been slow to reach the majority of providers and purchasers of medical care services.

The current U.S. health care system is based on the traditional medical model. The focus of this medical model is to "diagnose and treat," with no incentives in place for consumers and providers to pursue prevention strategies. Employers have structured the design and delivery of "health care" benefits on a medical model that provides incentives for patients, providers, and facilities to maximize the most expensive tertiary care services. However, the escalating costs of providing "medical" care has generated a shift to a new model that aims to "prevent and empower"—a public health model.

The emerging public health model seeks to promote health and control the development and presence of disease or disorders. The concepts of primary, secondary, and tertiary prevention are used in public health. Primary prevention seeks to promote health and prevent illness. Secondary prevention is related to early diagnosis and treatment of illnesses in order to prevent, control, or minimize their serious impact on the community. Examples of tertiary prevention are rehabilitation to restore or maintain functioning and other programs to limit the morbidity of illness.

The purpose of this chapter is to provide human resources professionals with the information necessary to decide if a health promotion program is appropriate for their organization and briefly describe a process that can be followed to design a program. References are provided for more detailed protocols. A review of the empirical evidence linking lifestyle factors and financial outcomes such as medical care costs and productivity is provided to give human resource professionals a sense of the quality of this evidence.

Definition of Health Promotion

Before an organization develops a health promotion program, it needs to have a clear sense of the concept of health promotion. The design princi-

---

2 C. Everett Koop, "A Personal Role in Health Care Reform," *American Journal of Public Health*, 85, No. 6 (June 1995), pp. 759–760.

ples in this chapter are consistent with the definition of health promotion offered by the *American Journal of Health Promotion*: "Health promotion is the science and art of helping people change their lifestyles to move toward a state of optimal health. Optimal health is defined as a balance of physical, emotional, social, spiritual, and intellectual health. Lifestyle change can be facilitated through a combination of efforts to enhance awareness, change behavior, and create environments that support good health practices. Of the three, supportive environments will probably have the greatest impact in producing lasting changes."[3] The multiple dimensions of optimal health are represented graphically in Figure 12–1. Complementing this definition of health promotion are the concepts of a health continuum (Figure 12–2), the health matrix (Figure 12–3), and multiple levels of programs, which are discussed below.

Health Continuum

The health continuum shown in Figure 12–2 is adapted from the work of John Travis, MD.[4] The left end of the continuum represents a state of extreme illness or premature death. The right end represents a state of optimal health. The midpoint is a neutral point of no discernible illness or wellness.

Medicine has traditionally focused attention on the left side of the continuum, working with people who have disabilities, symptoms, and signs of disease, because the goal of medicine is to help people who have such disabilities, symptoms, and signs of disease. However, once a patient has reached the midpoint of the continuum, a point of no discernible disease but also no discernible wellness, medicine does not have much to offer in helping people move further along the continuum toward optimal health. While that neutral point represents a very desirable goal for someone who is seriously ill, it is not enough for the individual who wants to excel in his or her personal and professional life. Those people want to move toward optimal health and that is where health promotion has begun to make its greatest impact. Working with people who are overtly healthy, but often at risk of becoming ill, health promotion helps people move toward optimal health by improving health-related knowledge, attitudes, and, most importantly, health behaviors.

3 M.P. O'Donnell, "Definition of Health Promotion: Part III; Stressing the Impact of Culture," *American Journal of Health Promotion*, 1989, 3,3,5.
4 D. Ardell, "Meet John Travis, Doctor of WellBeing," *Prevention*, 1975, 4:62–69.

FIGURE 12-1

Dimensions of Optimal Health

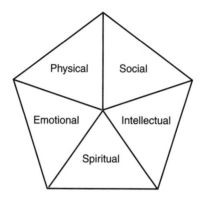

Source: M.P. O'Donnell, Design of Workplace Health Promotion Programs, 2000.

FIGURE 12-2

Health Continuum

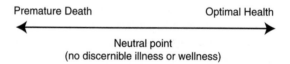

Premature Death   Optimal Health

Neutral point
(no discernible illness or wellness)

Source: M.P. O'Donnell, Design of Workplace Health Promotion Programs, 2000.

Health Matrix

The health continuum has guided much of our work in health promotion during the past two decades, but we are now realizing it may be conceptually flawed. Illness and wellness really are not part of the same continuum. For example, a person could be highly evolved in his or her emotional, spiritual, intellectual, and social health and have a high level of physical fitness but also have an unknown terminal illness. A health matrix, with illness on one axis and wellness on the other axis, may be a more accurate conceptualization than a continuum. As shown in Figure 12–3, optimal health would be in the top right corner, representing ab-

F I G U R E   12–3

Optimal Health Matrix

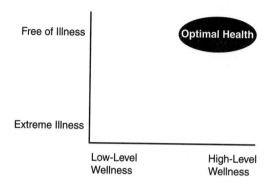

Source: M.P. O'Donnell, Design of Workplace Health Promotion Programs, 2000.

sence of illness and a high-level wellness. Using this matrix also allows us to better apply health promotion principles in clinical care settings and with people who have physical disabilities. For example, despite the physical deterioration that might be experienced by people living with cancer, there is no reason they cannot develop the other aspects of optimal health. In fact, developing their social, spiritual, and emotional health probably will help them deal with their physical disability and may even help them recover physically. These principles also apply to people recovering from heart attacks and other physical injuries. As employers continue to develop programs to help employees return to work after injuries or heart attacks, this refined model will become even more useful. The use of lifestyle change programs to facilitate recovery of ill patients also will increase as leaders in traditional medicine are trained in the disciplines of health promotion, and as more health promotion professionals work in clinical settings. Regardless of the condition of the patient or client, the goal of health promotion is to help people move toward a state of optimal health.

CURRENT STATE OF HEALTH PROMOTION PROGRAMS IN THE UNITED STATES

Approximately 90 percent of all workplaces with 50 or more employees and virtually all employers with more than 750 employees offer some form of health promotion program at their workplaces.[5] Comparison to previous years[6] shows continual growth in the total number of programs (Table 12–1), and in specific types of programs (Table 12–2). Note: Direct comparisons between 1999 and earlier years on the prevalence of some of the specific types of programs is not possible because the 1999 survey measured presence of "programs" while the earlier surveys measured presence of "activities or information."

It is clear from these data that most large employers recognize that there are some benefits to be derived from employee health promotion programs. The reasons cited by employers for offering programs are shown in Figure 12–4. "Keeping workers healthy" is the most frequently cited reason, but it is important to recognize that employee health is usually not a top priority for most employers. As Figure 12–5 shows, health is the number one priority for only 4 percent of employers, and near the top of the priority list for only 35 percent. Therefore, most employers will need to see tangible financial returns, usually in the form of medical care cost reduction, productivity enhancement, or image enhancement, to sustain a health promotion program through good and bad financial cycles. Recognition of these motivations must be incorporated into program design efforts.

T a b l e   12–1

Prevalence of Any Health Promotion Programs at the Worksite

Employer size	1999	1992	1985
50–99	86	75	N/A
100–249	92	86	N/A
250–749	96	90	N/A
750+	98	99	N/A
All employees	90	81	66

Source: Association for Worksite Health Promotion, U.S. Department of Health and Human Services, William M. Mercer, Inc., 2000, *1999 National Worksite Health Promotion Survey*, and William M. Mercer, Inc., Northbrook, Illinois.

5 Association for Worksite Health Promotion, U.S. Department of Health and Human Services, William M. Mercer, Inc., 2000, *1999 National Worksite Health Promotion Survey*, Association for Worksite Health Promotion and William M. Mercer, Inc., Northbrook, Illinois.

6 U.S. Department of Health and Human Services, Public Health Service, 1992 National Survey of Worksite Health Promotion Activities: Summary, *American Journal of Health Promotion*, 1993, 7,6, pp. 452-464.

T a b l e   1 2 – 2

Prevalence of Specific Types of Health Promotion Programs at the Worksite

Type of Program	1999	1992	1985
Blood pressure screenings	29	32	N/A
Cholesterol screenings	22	20	N/A
Cancer screenings	9	12	N/A
Health risk assessment	18	14	N/A
Fitness programs	25	N/A	N/A
Nutrition or cholesterol education	23	N/A	N/A
Weight control classes or counseling	14	N/A	N/A
Smoking cessation classes or counseling	13	N/A	N/A
Stress management classes or counseling	26	N/A	N/A
Alcohol or drug abuse programs	28	N/A	N/A
Back injury prevention	53	N/A	N/A
Maternal or prenatal programs	12	N/A	N/A
Balancing work and family education	18	N/A	N/A
HIV/AIDS education	25	N/A	N/A
Workplace violence prevention programs	36	N/A	N/A
Smoking policy	79	59	27

Information or Activities	1992	1985	
Job hazard/injury prevention	64	22	
Exercise physical fitness	41	36	
Smoking control	40	27	
Alcohol/other drugs	36	29	
Back care	32	17	
Nutrition	31	16	
High blood pressure	29	N/A	
AIDS education	28	N/A	
Cholesterol	27	N/A	
Mental health	25	15	
Weight control	24	N/A	
Cancer	23	N/A	
Medical self-care	18	22	
Off-the-job accidents	18	N/A	
Sexually transmitted diseases	10	N/A	
Prenatal education	9	N/A	

Source: U.S Department of Health and Human Services, Association for Worksite Health Promotion, 2000, and U.S. Department of Health and Human Services, 1993.

F I G U R E   12-4

Business Reasons for Offering Health Promotion Programs

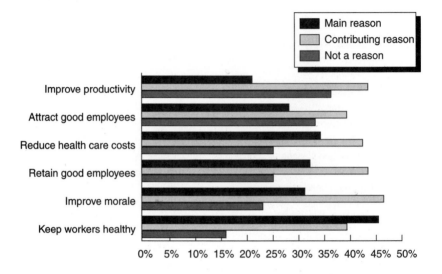

Source: Association for Worksite Health Promotion, 2000.

F I G U R E   12-5

Where on the List of Senior-Management Priorities Does Employee Health Fall?

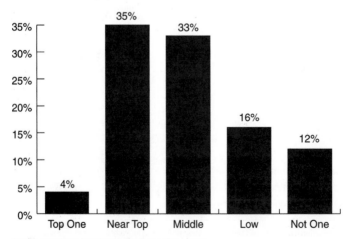

Source: Association for Worksite Health Promotion, 2000.

The prevalence of actual health screening, health risk appraisal, awareness or behavior change programs provided by employers based on number of employees is shown in Figure 12–6. Programs are clearly more prevalent among larger employers, but more than one-third of the smallest category of employers (50 to 99 employees) offer programs.

Spouses, dependents, and retirees are not eligible for programs among most employers (Figure 12–7). This is unfortunate for a number of reasons. First, from a behavioral perspective, employees will be most successful in changing and maintaining health habits if those habits are supported by their spouses and dependents. Therefore, involving spouses and dependents in programs can increase the likelihood of success. Second, one-half to two-thirds of an employer's medical care costs are typically incurred by spouses and dependents. If one of the goals of a program is to reduce medical care costs, all those who incur those costs should be eligible for the program.

Figure 12–8 shows the types of programs provided to employees at the worksites, through their health plans, or in either location. The most common programs offered at the worksite are back injury prevention, violence prevention, blood pressure screening, alcohol or drug abuse support, and stress management programs. Programs offered for employees by their health plan are typically more medically focused; the most common programs are maternal or prenatal programs, alcohol or drug abuse support, blood pressure screening, cholesterol screening, and cancer screening.

Face-to-face and print programs are the most common communications media, but electronic media are used by a significant portion of employers, especially those with more than 750 employees (Figure 12–9). Attracting employees to participate in programs remains a challenge. More than half of the employees participate in awareness and health risk appraisal programs, but only a quarter participate in actual lifestyle change efforts (see Table 12–3).

DEVELOPING A HEALTH PROMOTION PROGRAM

The process recommended in this section on how to design a health promotion program is significantly influenced by the results of a benchmark study by the American Productivity and Quality Center[7] on the best workplace health promotion programs. The goal of that study was to identify the best workplace health promotion programs in the United States and determine what made them different from the hundreds of other programs

---

7 M.P. O'Donnell, C. Bishop, K. Kaplan, "Benchmarking Best Practices in Workplace Health Promotion," *The Art of Health Promotion*, 1,1, March/April, 1997.

F I G U R E   12–6

Worksites Where Employees are Eligible for at Least One Type of Program* (by workplace size)

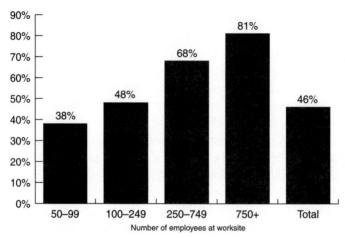

* Health risk appraisal, awareness, or behavior change program.

Source: Association for Worksite Health Promotion, 2000.

F I G U R E   12–7

Eligibility of Spouses, Dependents, and Retirees to Participate in Programs (by workplace size)

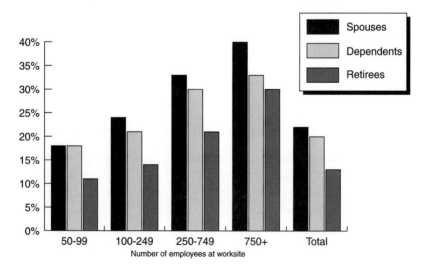

Source: Association for Worksite Health Promotion, 2000.

F I G U R E   12–8

Percent of Employers Offering Types of Programs

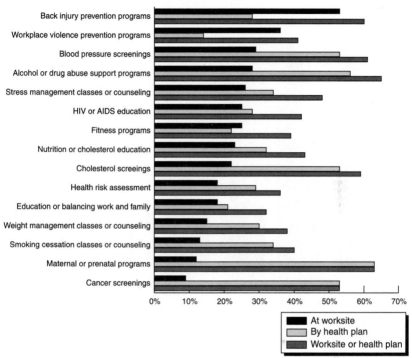

Source: Association for Worksite Health Promotion, 2000.

T a b l e   12–3

Health Promotion Program Participation Rates

Health awareness	59%
Health screenings	46%
Health risk appraisals	54%
Lifestyle behavior change	27%

Source: Association for Worksite Health Promotion, 2000.

F I G U R E   12–9

Communication Channels (by workforce size)

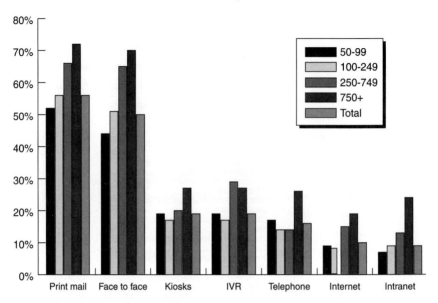

Source: Association for Worksite Health Promotion, 2000.

in other worksites. The eight elements unique to these programs are shown in Table 12–4. These elements are organized in a matrix based on the impact of the element on program outcome and the level of control a typical program manager would have over building that element into his or her program. For example, linking the program goals to the business goals of the organization has a major impact on the effectiveness of the program and is also something the typical program manager can control. The manager can learn the goals of the organization and align the program goals to support these organization goals. Predictably, another factor that was very important in determining the success of the program was strong top management support. Unfortunately, in the short term, the typical program manager has little control over how much support is received from top management. Interestingly, having a strong program budget was only moderately important in determining the success of a program. Most of the programs studied—even those not deemed among the "best"—did have generous budgets. Yet while a strong program budget is important, it is not sufficient to make a program successful. Not surprisingly, these excellent programs did not have program features which have low impact, therefore that column is empty.

T a b l e   12–4

Characteristics of the Best Health Promotion Programs

	Low Impact	Medium Impact	High Impact
High Control	None	• Effective communication • Communicate evaluation results	• Link programs to business goals
Medium Control	None	• Evaluation component	• Incentive program
Low Control	None	• Strong budget	• Supportive culture • Top management support

Source: O'Donnell, Bishop, Kaplan, 1997.

The striking finding of this study was that management-related factors were more important than programming factors in determining the success of the program. The typical health promotion program manager who is trained as a health expert tends to focus on the health dimensions of a program and often neglects how the program ties into the organization.

A team putting together a new health promotion program should build each of these eight qualities into a new program. The process of preparation, research, and design described here draws from a process described in other literature.[8]

Preparation

The first step in the program design process is to determine the extent to which employees will be involved. In general, employees should have a significant role in the design process, or they will not participate in the program. An employee committee should be organized to help design the program. Committee members should include representatives from top management, middle management, unions, and two employees at large. Other members should include a health promotion expert and representatives from human resources departments that might be affected by the program

---

[8] M.P. O'Donnell, *Design of Workplace Health Promotion Programs*, 6th edition, American Journal of Health Promotion Programs, Inc., 2000, Keego Harbor, Michigan.

such as medical, training, and benefits. The authority of the committee in the design process needs to be clearly articulated and should be consistent with the organization's norm for program development.

Research

The second step in designing a health promotion program is to conduct research to determine if a health promotion program would be advantageous and feasible for an organization and, if so, to understand the needs and capabilities of the organization. The research should focus on the following issues:

- Organization motives and goals.
- Cost/benefit analysis.
- Management and employee support.
- Organization capabilities.

Organization Motives and Goals The first step in the research process is to determine the organization's reasons for being interested in developing a health promotion program and the resultant goals for the program. The results of this step will dictate the type of program most appropriate for the organization. For example, if interest in a program was stimulated by the heart attack of a top executive, and the goal of the program is to prevent heart attacks among other employees, the program should focus on cardiovascular health programs such as smoking cessation, nutrition, exercise, and possibly stress management. Alternatively, if interest was stimulated by the elaborate program launched by a critical competitor, and the goal is to recruit the best employees and maintain an image superior to the competitor, the program might focus on highly visible and even flashy programs such as a fitness center, community fun runs, health fairs, and similar programs. If interest was stimulated by continually increasing medical care costs, and the goal of the program is to control those costs, the program should focus on programs with a clear relationship to medical care costs such as back injury prevention, hypertension control, prenatal care, and smoking cessation. In most cases, organizations will have a combination of motivations and goals for the program. In these cases, the priority of the various goals needs to be determined.

Despite the obvious importance of clarifying motives and goals, doing so is often difficult. Many organizations fail to articulate their goals and motives before they develop a program. This failure occurs for many reasons. In some cases, the person charged with developing the program is a low-level manager far removed from the top manager who authorized the program. In other cases, the top managers who authorized the program do not understand the range of program possibilities and how these will vary depending on program goals. In other cases, the program developer has a clinical health background and is not familiar with organization politics or goal clarification processes. Whatever the cause, when the motives and goals are not clarified, the program developed has little chance of being successful in achieving those goals or of surviving on a long-term basis.

Finally, to give the program the greatest chance of success, it is important to identify all parties whose support is critical to the success of the program and to determine what outcomes are necessary to satisfy each of them.

Cost/Benefit Analysis   For a program to survive on a long-term basis, the benefits of the program must be greater than the costs. Conducting a prospective cost-benefit analysis of a health promotion program is difficult because some of the benefits are difficult to quantify, and those that can be quantified are difficult to specify. For example, it is hard to quantify the value of enhanced morale or community image. And while benefits such as reduced medical care costs or enhanced productivity can be quantified, it is very hard to project the extent to which benefits will be realized in these areas. This process is complicated by the time value of money and the fact that some benefits will occur by the mere presence of a program, while others will be in direct proportion to the number of participants.

Because of these difficulties, it usually makes sense to use a cost/benefit analysis process that does not overstate the precision of the data available. One such process involves the seven steps detailed below.

1. *Identify and quantify the areas affected by the health promotion program.*

In this first step, all of the areas that might be affected by the health promotion program need to be identified. Next, data must be collected to estimate the magnitude or importance of each area to the employer. Finally, the data must be quantified to the extent possible. Areas identified might include medical care costs, workers' compensation claims, productivity, morale, turnover, absenteeism, recruiting, health crises suffered by employees, and image problems and goals. As a beginning point in quantifying productivity, the cost of the total payroll could be estimated. Other areas, such as company image, might be more difficult to quantify but can be estimated. In this case, it might be wise to determine how much is spent for advertising and other programs designed to enhance image.

2. *Estimate the cost ranges of the health promotion program.*

The general cost of the health promotion program should be determined by interviewing local program vendors. In general, basic awareness programs cost about $10 to $50 per employee, programs that help employees change behavior cost about $40 to $120 per employee, and programs that create a health-enhancing environment, possibly including fitness facilities, cost about $100 to $500 per employee.

3. *Determine the percentage savings required, by area, in order to pay for the program.*

The savings required in a particular area affected by the program should pay for the program. To determine savings required, divide the projected cost of the program by the cost of each area affected. For example, if the program was projected to cost $100 per employee annually and medical care costs $4,000 annually, the program would need to reduce medical care costs 2.5 percent ($100 ÷ $4,000 = .025) to pay for itself solely through savings in medical care costs. If the average employee salary is $25,000 and the program costs $100 per employee per year, the program would need to increase productivity by 0.4 percent ($100 ÷ $25,000 = .004) to pay for itself through enhanced productivity alone. This process should be repeated for all of the areas expected to be affected by the health promotion program. Considering multiple benefit areas, of course, reduces the amount of saving required in each area to pay for the program.

4. *Ask if it is reasonable to achieve the savings needed to pay for the program.*

Program developers and top managers need to decide if it is reasonable to expect the program to produce the level of savings required in each of the areas discussed above to pay for the program. Reviewing the published research on the financial impact of programs will help program developers get a sense of the level of savings that can be expected; but because of the limitations of this research, the final decision needs to be gut-level judgment rather than highly scientific deduction. The quality of the evidence supporting the cost impact of health promotion programs is discussed later in this chapter.

5. *Add other nonquantifiable benefits.*

Because some of the areas that might be impacted by the program may not be quantifiable, it may be impossible to determine the amount of savings required to cover the cost of the program. For example, the organization may not have adequate estimates of the cost of employee health crises, improved image in the community, or other areas, and therefore would be unable to calculate the percentage savings required in these areas to pay for the program. Nevertheless, expected benefits in these areas may be sufficient to help justify a program.

6. *Compare costs to other current expenditures.*

Examining other expenditures made by the organization can help put the costs of the health promotion program in perspective by comparing the benefits expected of the program to the benefits experienced as a result of other expenditures. Expenses that could be considered might include the cost of equipment maintenance and other employee benefits such as tuition reimbursement, vacation time, travel to conferences, and so on. In most cases, the cost of a health promotion program will be modest compared to costs in these other areas. For example, a basic health promotion program will usually cost about the same as a large annual holiday party, installing new carpeting, or maintaining landscaping.

7. *Decide if the program is a good investment.*

After considering all the issues in the first six steps, most managers will have sufficient information to determine if the health promotion program is a good investment for their organizations.

Management and Employee Support A critical next step is measuring management and employee support in the organization. A health promotion program will be most successful if it has broad-based and strong support. Levels of support among top managers, middle managers, and employees in general should be determined.

Support among senior managers is best measured through personal interviews. Senior managers should be asked if they will support funding for the program, personally participate, encourage their subordinates to participate, promote the program in the organization, and be available as a troubleshooter if the program has a problem. They also should be asked what kinds of programs they would like to see as part of the program, the most important benefits they would hope to obtain, what they consider reasonable budget levels, and the best strategies for successful implementation.

Support among middle managers and employees in general should be measured by a combination of interviews or focus groups and written survey questionnaires. Middle managers should be asked if they will participate and encourage their employees to participate. Middle managers also should be invited to be part of the development effort to determine the best strategies for successful implementation.

Employees should be asked about their current health practices, their interest in improving those practices, and their interest in participating in specific programs. Employees also should be invited to participate in the design of the program. Questionnaires to be used with managers and employees are available from a number of sources, including local program vendors.

If these analyses show strong support for the program at all levels, it is likely the program can be implemented effectively. If there is resistance at any of these levels, additional work may be necessary to build support before the program is implemented.

Organization Capabilities In addition to having clear goals, a positive cost/benefit situation, and strong management and employee support, a health promotion program needs specific resources to be successfully implemented. These include technical expertise, space for offices and programs, and funding. Each needs to be secured before the program is implemented. After the research phase is complete, the program content can be determined and the administrative structure developed.

The Wellness Councils of America (WELCOA) is a nonprofit organization created to encourage employers to launch, maintain, and upgrade their health promotion programs. WELCOA has developed a set of guidelines that describe the administrative structures necessary to support an effective program at three levels: bronze, silver, and gold. The criteria for each level of program are shown in Table 12–5. For details, see the WELCOA Web site (www.welcoa.org).

Program Design

In developing program content, decisions need to be made about the desired level of program impact, the level of intensity, and the program topics. The most important decision is the level of desired impact. Most programs fall into one of three basic levels:

- Programs that enhance awareness.
- Programs that produce health behavior changes.
- Programs that create a supportive environment that sustains long-term change.

The organization's goals for the program will dictate the level of impact most appropriate. In general, the higher the level pursued, the greater the impact on organization goals.

The level of intensity is determined by how intensively the health change goal is promoted. For example, offering a "quit smoking" pro-

T A B L E   12–5

The Well Workplace Application (Bronze, Silver, and Gold)

Bronze	Silver	Gold
Basic information	Basic information	Basic information
CEO sign-off	CEO sign-off	CEO sign-off
Organizational overview	Organizational overview	Organizational overview
Management support	Management support and participation	Management support and participation
		Health promotion as part of the strategic plan
	Integration into the organizational structure (3 questions)	Integration into the organizational structure (4 questions)
Organizational/employee assessments—health risk survey or HRA, facility survey, demographic data, culture audit, and 1 additional.	Organizational/employee assessments—health risk survey or HRA, facility survey, demographic data, culture audit, and 2 additional.	Organizational/employee assessments—health risk survey or HRA, facility survey, demographic data, culture audit, and 3 additional.
Operating plan	Operating plan	Operating plan
Employee feedback and ownership	Employee feedback and ownership	Employee feedback and ownership. Additionally, document actions taken on suggestions.
	Diverse employee groups—2 examples.	Diverse employee groups— explain how needs were identified, strategies used to reach them, and programs implemented.
Policy and benefit options— need at least 4	Policy and benefit options— Need at least 6	Policy and benefit options— Need at least 8
Required policies and procedures—*tobacco and emergency.*	Required policies and procedures—*tobacco, emergency, alcohol/drug, safe driving practices, and healthful food options.*	Required policies and procedures—*tobacco, emergency, alcohol/drug, safe driving practices and healthful food options.*
	Community resources— what's available through the community.	Community resources— what's available through the community.
		Work and family—organization recognizes importance of work/life issues and has responded.

Continued

T A B L E 12–5

The Well Workplace Application (Bronze, Silver, and Gold) (concluded)

Bronze	Silver	Gold
	Community involvement—activities and organizations supported.	Community involvement—activities and organizations supported
Self-care—need at least 2 awareness programs.	Self-Care—need at least 2 educational programs.	Self-Care—programs must be ongoing.
		Employees' families and retirees—at least 5 programs offered to them.
Other programs—5 total programs offered—only 2 awareness.	Other programs—7 total programs offered—only 2 awareness and a minimum of 2 behavior change.	Other programs—9 total programs offered—only 2 awareness and a minimum of 4 behavior change.

Source: The Wellness Councils of America.

gram only once will have little impact on the smoking habits of people in an organization, while offering a wide range of programs repeatedly will have more impact. Program topics can be selected fairly easily once the health and organization goals are specified. Program topics appropriate for various health goals are shown in Table 12–6 and for various organization goals in Table 12–7.

Another option to consider in developing topics is to model the programs after those found to be the best programs in the benchmark study.[7] "Best practice" programs include incentive efforts, effective communication efforts, and supportive cultures.

The effective communication programs should include awareness programs to reach the employees in precontemplation and contemplation. They also should include effective marketing programs to communicate program offerings to all employees. The key here is not just to have a communication effort, but to have a communication effort that is professional in appearance and effective in reaching all employees.

The primary impact of incentive programs is to enhance participation. This is critically important, because, as discussed previously, only the employees in preparation will be ready to join actual programs, and this typically represents only 20 percent of the employees. Incentives may be an effective way to attract the attention of the other 80 percent.

T A B L E   12–6

Programs Most Appropriate for Health Goals
Best Programs for Specific Health Conditions

Problem Area	Program/Initiative
Hypertension	**Obesity**
Medical evaluation and prescription	Fitness
Fitness	Nutrition
Nutrition	Self-esteem training
Weight control	Stress management
Smoking cessation	Weight control
Stress management	
Stress	**Smoking**
Fitness	Smoking policy
Child care	Smoking cessation
EAP	Fitness
Policy review	Weight control
Stress management	Stress management

Source: M.P. O'Donnell, 2000.

Incentives can be simple small prize giveaways to people who complete a health screening or class, or rebate programs for those successful in making behavior changes. They also can be more elaborate ongoing systems. To date, most incentive programs do not seem to have much impact in actually changing health behaviors.[9]

Management Options

Important management decisions include the following:

- What will be the program's implementation schedule?
- Where will the program be placed in the organization structure, and what support will be provided by top management?
- Will it be managed internally or through an external vendor?
- What staffing levels will the program require?

9 D. Matson, Jerry Lee, J. Hopp, "The Impact of Incentives and Competitions on Participation and Quit Rates in Worksite Smoking Cessation Programs," *American Journal of Health Promotion*, 1993, 7-4, pp. 270-280.

T A B L E   12–7

Best Programs for Specific Organizational Problems

High Medical Care Costs	Low Morale	Low Productivity
Medical self-care	Dependent-care facilities & programs	Policy review
Risk rating	Visible fitness facilities	Fitness programs
Hypertension control	EAP programs	Dependent-care facilities & programs
Injury control	Policy review	Stress management
Smoking policy	Incentive programs	Comprehensive programs
Smoking cessation	Recreation programs	
Medical coverage	Other visible programs	

Source: M.P. O'Donnell, 2000.

- What will be the program's budget and how will it be financed?
- Who will be eligible to participate?
- How will it be evaluated?

Having strong top-management support is one of the characteristics of the best health promotion programs. Which came first? In most cases, strong support preceded good programs. Many programs become excellent programs because they have strong top-management support. Despite this fact, program developers should focus on this point as they organize their program. First, they should tell top management that strong support is one of the eight ingredients for a successful program. This may motivate some top managers to become more involved. Second, developers should ask top managers what the program must do to ensure strong support from top management, make sure those things are done, and make sure top management knows these things are being done. Probably the most important factor in developing top-management support is linking the program to the organization's goals, and making top management aware of how the program is supporting those goals.

Staffing Levels   The benchmark study by the American Productivity and Quality Center cited earlier determined that the best programs have approximately one full-time professional staff person for every 1,800 employees. This figure is also consistent with the staffing ratio recommended by a number of major program management companies and with the author's personal experience.

Budget   This study also found that the average annual budget among the best programs was approximately $200 per eligible employee (not per participant), in 1996 dollars. This is consistent with the author's experience that an internally managed comprehensive program that includes awareness, behavior change, and supportive environment programs costs approximately $135 per eligible employee (not per participant) in an organization with at least 4,000 employees. These figures include staff salaries, but do not include office space, employee benefits, overhead benefits, staff recruitment or initial training costs, or the cost of top management's supervision of the program. If fitness facilities are included, this will add an additional $100 to $200 per eligible employee (not per participant), including amortization of construction costs over 15 years, but not including land acquisition or space costs. Fitness facility costs often can be reduced by charging employees a modest membership fee.

Program eligibility   This will be determined by organization goals and available resources. For example, if the goal of the program is to contain medical care costs, the program should be offered to all those who are receiving medical care coverage: all employees, spouses, dependents, and perhaps retirees. However, in a large organization or an organization that has limited resources to implement a program, the program offered to spouses, dependents, and retirees may need to be phased in over time. Alternatively, if the program is limited to a specific health area such as back care, it would be offered only to those experiencing back problems or at high risk for developing back problems.

Financing   Options include the employer paying for the entire program, employees paying for the entire program, and cost sharing.

Program Evaluation   This chapter precludes a detailed analysis of program evaluation, but it is important to stress a few points. An evaluation effort is an important part of every health promotion program. The benchmark study showed that the best programs have evaluation efforts in place and, equally important, that they communicate their evaluation results. In addition to measuring the impact of the program on health outcomes, the evaluation effort should measure the extent to which the program addresses the organization's long-term goals and current priorities. These findings should, of course, be communicated to top management.

The evaluation plan—including what will be evaluated, when it will be evaluated, how, by whom and for what purpose—should be specified as the program plan is developed. If the evaluation plan is not developed and approved as part of the basic program plan, it will be very difficult to start the evaluation once the program is up and running. Also, some baseline measures will need to be recorded before programs are launched, so progress against these values can be assessed. If the evaluation plan is not developed, it will be difficult to know which baseline measures need to be taken.

Program evaluation budgets should range from 1 percent to 10 percent of the total budget. One percent will be sufficient to measure implementation progress, participation rates, and satisfaction levels. Approximately 5 percent will be required to measure changes in health risks and health behavior. Approximately 10 percent will be required to measure changes in organizational outcomes such as medical care costs and productivity.

WHAT IS THE QUALITY OF THE EVIDENCE DEMONSTRATING THE IMPACT OF HEALTH PROMOTION PROGRAMS ON FINANCIAL OUTCOMES?

The quality of the evidence demonstrating the impact of health promotion programs on financial outcomes has evolved significantly since 1984 when the first scholarly text on workplace health promotion was published.[10] At that time, one could only speculate about the financial impact of health promotion programs. Only a handful of studies had been published, and all of them had serious methodological flaws. By the mid-1990s, hundreds of studies had been published on the impact of workplace health promotion programs and a large number of them addressed financial outcomes.[11] The general conclusion by that time was that most of the studies did have flaws in methodology, which prevented making conclusive statements that programs do save money. Despite these flaws, it was already clear that the amount and quality of research supporting the financial returns from health promotion programs was, even then, far superior to the research supporting business investments for decisions with costs similar to those of a health promotion program. After all, these programs cost only $50 (or less) per employee for a basic program and

10 M.P. O'Donnell, Y. Ainsworth, *Health Promotion in the Workplace*, 1984, Albany, NY: Delmar Publishers.
11 M.P. O'Donnell, "Employer's Financial Perspective on Health Promotion," in O'Donnell, M., Harris, J., (eds.) *Health Promotion in the Workplace*, 1994, 2e Delmar, pp 54–57.

$200 for an excellent comprehensive program. This cost is about as much as a year-end party, new carpeting, landscaping, and the like. The quality of the evidence by that date was more than sufficient for an employer to make a decision to invest in a health promotion program. Indeed, by 1990, 81 percent of employers had decided to develop some form of health promotion program.[12]

Between the mid-1990s and 2000, numerous additional studies were published and the quality of studies continues to improve. A review by Aldana[13] is probably the best available source of information on the financial impact of workplace health promotion programs from the perspective of having a systematic search process, and summarizes results of the literature as a whole. In addition, this article also critiqued the methodology of each study.

The most important methodological problems in the research on the financial impact of workplace health promotion programs are the lack of enough randomized controlled designs, small sample sizes, short duration of the studies, inadequate measurement tools, and inappropriate analysis of data that is not normally distributed. Despite these limitations, it is difficult to find many higher quality research studies in health care, business, or any of the social sciences, for investments of a similar order of magnitude. From a practical perspective, the quality of evidence is certainly good enough for a business executive trying to determine if health promotion is a good investment. From a scientific perspective, we still must strive to produce better research. Despite these programs, we can draw a number of conclusions on the financial impact of health promotion programs.

Medical Care Cost Containment

The first significant study on the link between modifiable health risks and medical care costs was conducted by Control Data Corporation.[14] After following 10,000 employees for four years, the auditors concluded that medical care claims were lowest for employees who did not smoke cigarettes,

---

12 Association for Worksite Health Promotion, U.S. Department of Health and Human Services, William M. Mercer, Inc. 2000, *1999 National Worksite Health Promotion Survey*, Association for Worksite Health Promotion and William M. Mercer, Inc., Northbrook, IL.

13 S. Aldana, Financial Impact of Worksite Health Promotion and Methodological Quality of the Evidence, *The Art of Health Promotion*, 1998, March/April, 2,1.

14 S. Brink, *Health Risks and Behavior: The Impact on Medical Care Costs*. Brookfield, WI, Millman and Robertson, Inc., 1987.

exercised regularly, ate nutritious foods, fastened their seat belts, and were not hypertensive. Consistent results were found at Steelcase.[15,16] Between 1985 and 1990, employees with zero risk factors had average annual medical care costs of only $250, while employees with six risk factors had costs of $1,600.

One of the most impressive studies to date[17] on the link between medical care costs and risk factors was produced through a collaboration of six employers (Chevron, Health Trust, Hoffman-LaRoche, Marriott, the State of Michigan, and the State of Tennessee), which was organized by the Health Enhancement Research Organization (HERO). StayWell, a health promotion vendor, and MEDSTAT, a medical care cost data management organization, had medical care cost data on these six employers. With the assistance of HERO and the permission of the employers, these two databases were merged to determine the relationship between 10 modifiable risk factors and medical care costs. The strengths of this study include the large sample size, measurement of a wide range of risk factors, and the multivariate nature of the analysis. Eight of the risk factors (depression, stress, blood glucose, body weight, current or previous tobacco use, hypertension, and sedentary lifestyle) are associated with higher costs even after controlling for the other risk factors. Depression and stress were the most expensive risk factors; employees with those risk factors had costs 70 percent and 46 percent higher than those who did not have those risk factors (Table 12–8). One of the strengths of this study was the multivariate control for multiple risk factors. This is illustrated in the third and fourth columns of numbers in Table 12–8. For example, the third column shows that people who were depressed had medical care costs that were 90 percent higher than those who were not depressed. As the fourth column shows, medical care costs remained 70 percent higher even after controlling all of the other risk factors (stress, blood glucose, etc).

Costs were higher for those with elevated cholesterol, but not after adjusting for the other nine risk factors. The finding that higher levels of alcohol consumption are not related to higher costs is initially surprising, but has been found in other studies. People who drink excessively often neglect their health and do not seek medical care when they need it. The

15 L. Yen, D. Edington, P. Witting, "Associations Between Health Risk Appraisal Scores and Employee Medical Claims Costs," *American Journal of Health Promotion*, 1991, 6,1, pp. 46–54.

16 L. Yen, D. Edington, P. Witting, "Prediction of Prospective Medical Claims and Absenteeism Costs for 1,284 Hourly Workers from a Manufacturing Company," *Journal of Occupational Medicine*, 1992, 34, 4, pp. 428–435.

17 R. Goetzel, "Relationship Between Modifiable Health Risks and Health Care Expenditures," *Journal of Occupational and Environmental Medicine*, 1998, 40,10.

T A B L E   12–8

Medical Care Costs Associated with Risk Factors

Risk Factor	Mean Cost with Risk Factor	Mean Cost without Risk Factor	Percentage Difference (unadjusted)	Percentage Difference (adjusted)*
Depression	$3,189	$1,679	90%	70%
Stress	$2,287	$1,579	45%	46%
Blood glucose	$2,598	$1,691	54%	35%
Body weight	$2,318	$1,571	48%	21%
Tobacco (former)	$1,950	$1,503	25%	20%
Tobacco (current)	$1,873	$1,503	30%	14%
Hypertension	$2,123	$1,716	24%	12%
Sedentary lifestyle	$2,011	$1,567	28%	10%
Cholesterol	$1,962	$1,678	17%	–1%
Alcohol use	$1,431	$1,726	–17%	–3%
Nutrition	$1,498	$1,772	–15%	–9%

* The adjusted difference is the difference that persisted after adjusting for all of the other risk factors for those with the risk factor and those without it.

Source: Goetzel, "Relationship Between Modifiable Health Risks and Health Care Expenditures," *Journal of Occupational and Environmental Medicine*, 1998, 40,10.

finding related to nutrition was surprising. This study showed the medical costs for those with good nutrition habits were actually higher, before and after adjustment. Our suspicion is that the tool used to measure nutrition habits within the health risk appraisal (HRA) was too short to fully capture the full scope of nutrition habits that would impact health and medical care utilization.

This study also showed that employees who had a cluster of risk factors had strikingly higher costs. Employees with a cluster of seven heart disease risk factors had average annual costs of $3,804, those with a cluster of risk factors for stroke had average annual costs of $2,349, and those with a cluster of psychological (depression and stress) risk factors had average annual costs of $3,368. Employees with no risk factors had average costs of $1,166 (Table 12–9).

A follow-up study coordinated by HERO[18] used the data in the earlier study to estimate the percent of total costs attributable to these risk

---

18 D. Anderson, et. al., "Relationship Between Modifiable Health Risks and Health Care Expenditures: A Group Level Analysis of the HERO Research Data Base," *American Journal of Health Promotion*, 2000, 15, 1, pp. 45–52.

T A B L E   12–9

Medical Care Costs Associated with Clusters of Risk
Factors (United States)

Risk Factor Cluster	With Risk Factors	Without Risk Factors	Percentage Difference
Heart disease risks	$3,804	$1,158	228%
Stroke risks	$2,349	$1,272	85%
Psychological risks	$3,368	$1,368	147%
No risk factors		$1,166	

Source: Goetzel, "Relationship Between Modifiable Health Risks and Health Care Expenditures," *Journal of Occupational and Environmental Medicine*, 1998, 40,10, pp. 843–857.

factors. The first study identified the most expensive risk factors among those who had these risk factors. The second study identified the total cost of the risk factors, factoring in the number of employees who had each of those risk factors. This changed the order of the most costly risk factors. For example, in the first study, depression was the most costly risk factor per person, but because less than 3 percent of employees suffered from depression, it did not have a significant impact on total costs. Stress was the most costly risk factor because almost 20 percent of employees experienced high levels of stress. Almost 8 percent of total medical care costs were attributable to stress. Furthermore, this study showed that 24.9 percent of total costs were attributable to these 11 risk factors, all of which we feel are manageable through health promotion programs. This study is very important because it indicates that 25 percent of annual medical care costs, or about $1,000 per employee, are attributable to risk factors that health promotion programs have been shown capable of managing. This information will better help an employer make a decision to invest the $50, $100, or $200 needed to pay for a program, or at least give the employer the objective data required to justify an emotional or gut-level decision to invest in a program (Table 12–10).

The work of The Health Management Research Center (formerly the Fitness Research Center) at the University of Michigan provides additional support for the connection between health risks and medical care costs. This center has collected health care utilization and lifestyle behavior data during the past 20 years on almost 2 million individuals working in more than 1,000 worksites. They have established long-term data man-

T A B L E   12–10

Cost of Risk Factors as a Percentage of Total Medical Care Costs

Risk Category	Cost/ High Risk	Number at High Risk	Total Cost Due to Risk	Percentage of Total Costs	Cost/ Capita
Stress	$732	8,518	$6,236,880	7.9%	$136
Former tobacco smoker	$311	14,329	$4,455,029	5.6%	$97
Body weight	$352	9,197	$3,239,919	4.1%	$70
Exercise habits	$173	14,908	$2,574,760	3.3%	$56
Current tobacco user	$228	8,797	$2,004,045	2.5%	$44
Blood glucose	$587	2,271	$1,332,646	1.7%	$29
Depression	$1,187	997	$1,183,439	1.5%	$26
Blood pressure	$199	1,827	$363,317	.5%	$8
Excess alcohol use	-$52	1,723	–$89,027	–1.1%	$2
High cholesterol	-$14	8,641	–$117,431	–1.5%	–$3
Nutrition habits	-$162	9,278	–$1,500,623	–1.9%	–$33
Total Expenditures Attributable to High Risk Per Capita			$19,682,953	24.9%	$428
Total Medical Care Expenditures			$78,959,286		

Source: D. Anderson, et. al: "Relationship Between Modifiable Health Risks and Health Care Expenditures: A Group Level Analysis of the HERO Research Data Base," *American Journal of Health Promotion*, 2000, 15, 1, pp. 45–52.

agement relationships with nine large employers. This data allowed them to formulate and test a wide range of relationships between health risks and medical care costs.

One of the center's most interesting findings reports changes in cost related to changes in risk. The center found that medical care costs decrease an average (median) of $153 with every decrease in number of risk factors, and increase an average (median) of $350 with every increase in number of risk factors. The finding that reduced risk factors are associated with reduced costs provides further support for risk reduction. The finding that increases in risk factors are associated with increases in costs is a breakthrough discovery if it holds up to further scrutiny, because it demonstrates how important it is to keep healthy employees healthy. This is a critical finding because health promotion programs have often been criticized for attracting the people who already practice healthy lifestyles and not attracting people who do not. Programs do need to do a better job of attracting those with unhealthy lifestyle practices, but this finding underscores the importance of helping those with healthy practices continue those healthy practices.[19]

The link between medical costs and risk factors that can be modified by health promotion programs is fairly clear from the studies cited above. However, a separate question is whether health promotion programs can reduce medical care costs. At least two dozen studies have addressed this question and a number of reviews have attempted to summarize these.[20, 21, 22, 23] The most systematic of these reviews was written by Aldana[24] who conducted a thorough review of the literature to identify all the research on the impact of workplace health promotion programs on medical care costs. He then examined the methodology of each study and determined which ones had experimental, quasi-experimental, and pre-experimental designs.

Aldana found 24 studies on the impact of workplace health promotion programs on medical care costs. Twenty-one of these studies (88 percent) showed that programs reduced medical care costs and three (12 percent) showed no impact on medical care costs. Eight of the studies reported the cost of the program and the amount of savings achieved thus allowing a calculation of the cost/benefit ratio. Savings ranged from $2.30 to $5.90 for every dollar invested and averaged $3.35 (Table 12–11). Also, the studies with experimental designs reported the highest levels of savings. How should these findings be interpreted? The total number of studies published (24) is rather small, and it is likely that studies that found negative or neutral results were not submitted for publication or were more likely to be rejected if they were submitted. Nevertheless, the trend is very persuasive. It can conservatively be concluded that some health promotion

19 Edington, *Worksite Wellness; 20th Century Year Cost Benefit Analysis and Report: 1979 to 2000,* 2000.

20 K. Pelletier, "A Review and Analysis of the Heath and Cost Effectiveness Outcome Studies of Comprehensive Health Promotion and Disease Prevention Programs at the Worksite," *American Journal of Health Promotion,* 1991; 5,4, pp. 311–315.

21 K. Pelletier, "A Review and Analysis of the Heath and Cost Effectiveness Outcome Studies of Comprehensive Health Promotion and Disease Prevention Programs at the Worksite," *American Journal of Health Promotion,* 1991–1993 Update; 1993; 8, pp. 43–49:

22 K. Pelletier, "A Review and Analysis of the Heath and Cost Effectiveness Outcome Studies of Comprehensive Health Promotion and Disease Prevention Programs at the Worksite," *American Journal of Health Promotion,* 1993–1995 Update, 1996; 10, pp. 380–388.

23 K. Pelletier, "A Review and Analysis of the Heath and Cost Effectiveness Outcome Studies of Comprehensive Health Promotion and Disease Prevention Programs at the Worksite," *American Journal of Health Promotion,* 1995–1998 Update 1999; 13,5: pp. 66–78

24 S. Aldana, 1998, "Financial Impact of Worksite Health Promotion and Methodological Quality of the Evidence," *The Art of Health Promotion,* March/April, 2,1, pp. 1–8.

T A B L E   12-11

Impact of Health Promotion Programs on Medical Care Costs

	Studies	
	Numbers	**Percentage**
Reduced medical care costs	21	88%
No change	3	12%
Increased medical care costs	0	0%
Total	24	100%

Cost/benefit analysis: 8 studies

Range of savings: $2.30–$5.90 per $1 invested

Average savings: $3.35 per $1 invested

Source: S. Aldana, Financial Impact of Worksite Health Promotion and Methodological Quality of the Evidence, *The Art of Health Promotion*, 1998, March/April, 2,1, pp. 1–8.

programs are clearly able to reduce medical care costs. The number of studies (8) reporting cost/benefit ratios is far too small to be conclusive, but again the findings are very impressive. It also can be concluded that some programs are apparently able to produce medical care cost savings that far exceed their cost. These cost benefit values need to be put into perspective. An employer never expects to *make money* on an employee benefit (like a health promotion program), and rarely expects the program to pay for itself in direct measurable savings. Almost any employer would be more than satisfied with an employee benefit that produces a cost/benefit ratio of 1.00, $1.00 in savings for every $1.00 invested; returns of $3.35 for every dollar invested are clearly outstanding.

In conclusion, the relationship between risk factors that can be modified by health promotion programs and medical care costs is quiet clear. Also, research on the impact of programs on medical care costs does support the claim that programs can reduce medical care costs. The quality of the research methodology is also adequate. This body of research should be sufficient to persuade an employer that health promotion programs can reduce medical costs. This statement could not be made in previous editions of the *Handbook*. Furthermore, we can probably increase the savings potential of health promotion programs if we design programs with the explicit goal of reducing medical care costs. To do this, we need to focus more attention on the health risks that are most costly, such as injury and musculoskelatal problems, instead of the health risks with the strongest links to death and chronic disease, such as cardiovascular disease and cancer. We also need to incorporate programs on wise use of medical services in our programs. A large percentage of services provided are medically unnecessary, and it is possible to train employees to avoid using these. Finally, we need to focus on improving the health of the small number of employees who are at greatest risk for high cost *and* focus more attention on keeping the healthy employees healthy. Many programs have already adopted the strategy of focusing on high-risk employees, but few have recognized the importance of keeping healthy employees healthy as a strategic focus.

Productivity

We have long argued that health promotion programs enhance productivity, yet little research has attempted to measure this impact, primarily because productivity is often difficult to measure and the impact of a specific factor such as a health promotion program, which may or may not contribute to it, is even more difficult to measure.

In general terms, employee productivity is defined as output per unit of labor. Among blue-collar workers, this might be measured in terms of automobiles, toys, tables, or any other product produced per hour. For white-collar workers, it might be pages typed, insurance claims processed, or airplane reservations taken per hour. For a salesperson, it might be sales closed per month, and for a film producer, it might be films produced per year. In addition to the quantity of units produced, the quality of each unit produced is an important element of productivity; the automobiles, toys and tables must meet all production standards. To be of value to the organization, the pages typed, claims processed and reservations taken must be free of errors. The sales closed must not be canceled and the films made must be well made.

Within the health promotion community, most of our focus to date on productivity has been on absenteeism, primarily because absenteeism is easy to measure. Absenteeism is an important part of productivity. When a worker is absent, he or she normally continues to get paid, but produces no work. In some cases, he or she is replaced by someone else. This raises the cost of producing the same level of output. In other cases, he or she is not replaced and coworkers are required to disrupt their work to fill in for the absent employee. This reduces total output. In either case, output per unit of labor (productivity) drops. Health promotion programs are expected to reduce absenteeism by helping people stay healthy, and thus reduce the need to be absent. This is reasonable as long as illness is the cause of the absence. Sometimes people take a "mental health" day when they need a break. Other times they "call in sick" when in fact they are staying home with a sick child. However, absenteeism is only a small part of the productivity equation. The impact of a heath promotion program on these cases is more complex and is better explained within a broader conceptual approach illustrated in Figure 12–10.

The basic concept is that human performance is higher when people are physically and emotionally able to work and have the desire to work. Higher levels of human performance lead to higher levels of productivity which in turn can lead to higher profit levels. Health promotion programs play a central role in this model because they can improve health by reducing health risks, helping to manage controllable diseases, and reducing use of avoidable substances. These health improvements lead to the improved physical and emotional ability to work. Health promotion programs also improve the organizational climate, which enhances the employee's desire to work and directly enhances human performance. This model also asserts that the improved organizational climate and higher profit levels also directly reduce health risks. This is a preliminary model that must be tested and refined. We fully expect that the elements within each of the boxes will change and that new mechanisms will be discovered.

F I G U R E   12–10

Mechanisms Linking Health, Productivity, and Profit

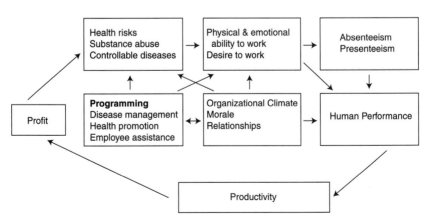

Source: M.P. O'Donnell, et al., 2000.

How much more productive are employees who are physically and emotionally able to work and motivated to work because they feel their employer is concerned about their well-being? This remains an open question that we expect will receive considerable attention in the next decade. The author has posed this question in formal discussions with dozens of executives and dozens of scientists during the past few years. The most common response from scientists is that employees will be 5 percent to 10 percent more productive. The most common response from executives is that employees will be 100 percent more productive! As we would expect and hope, scientists are more conservative in their estimates. However, executives think of themselves when they answer this question. They know how much more productive they are when then are full of energy, not distracted by emotional problems, and really want to work. They know they are far more likely to be effective in their creative thinking, negotiating, motivating people, strategic planning, and any other challenging activities when they feel good and are motivated.

In reality, factory workers and clerks who have little control over their work environment might be able to increase productivity by 5 percent, 10 percent, or even 30 percent. A non-factory worker such as a lawyer, scientist, writer, salesperson, or senior manager might be able to increase productivity by 50 percent, 100 percent, or even more.

To make this relevant to business, we need to quantify the value of productivity increases. The data supporting a financial payoff from health promotion is probably strongest in the area of medical cost savings, but the greatest potential payoff for health promotion is probably in productivity enhancement. The reason for this is simple. The maximum benefit we can achieve in medical cost savings is to eliminate the cost, or more realistically, to eliminate the costs related to lifestyle risk factors. If we eliminate the total medical care cost, this will save approximately $4,000 per year per employee. If we eliminate the 25 percent of costs that are related to lifestyle risk factors,[25] we will save approximately $1,000 per year per employee. More realistically, if we eliminate one quarter of the 25 percent of costs which are related to lifestyle risk factors, we will save approximately $250 per year per employee. Savings at any of these levels would be significant, and more than enough to pay for the health promotion program, but they are minor compared to the additional revenue and profit we could earn by increasing productivity.

---

25 L. Yen, D. Edington, P. Witting, "Prediction of Prospective Medical Claims and Absenteeism Costs for 1284 Hourly Workers from a Manufacturing Company," *Journal of Occupational Medicine*, 1992, 34, 4, pp. 428–435.

If productivity increases by 1 percent in a company with a 10 percent profit margin, and that increased productivity can be translated into increased revenues, this will increase profits by 10 percent. If the profit margin is 5 percent, profits will increase 20 percent. If productivity increases by 10 percent, profits will increase 100 percent with a 10 percent profit margin and 200 percent with a 5 percent profit margin. A 1 percent increase in profits in the United States would be worth $100 billion per year, a 10 percent increase worth $1 trillion, and a 20 percent increase worth $2 trillion. Potential returns of this magnitude will grab the attention of even the most skeptical executives and policy makers.

As already mentioned, measuring productivity is very difficult and measuring the impact of programs on productivity is even more difficult. As we acknowledged previously, most efforts to measure the impact of health promotion on productivity have focused on absenteeism as an outcome measure. Aldana[26] reviewed the research on the impact of absenteeism on productivity in the study cited previously. He found 16 studies on this topic; fourteen (87 percent) of the studies reported reductions in absenteeism after the introduction of the health promotion programs, one (6 percent) study reported no change, and one (6 percent) study reported an increase in absenteeism as a result of the program. Five of the studies reported cost/benefit analysis values, with a range of $2.50 to $10.10 saved for every $1 invested, and an average savings of $4.90. The studies with experimental designs had the highest level savings values (Table 12–12).

These results are very encouraging, and we should be comfortable in concluding that some health promotion programs can reduce absenteeism, and in some cases, those savings may more than pay for the cost of the program. However, given the small number of studies, we should view these results as preliminary.

Productivity enhancement has become an important focus for American business, and efforts are underway to measure the impact of health promotion on productivity. In the next decade, we should be able to say a lot more about the topic.

Image

We have very little data to support the positive impact of health promotion on image, but it remains a very important motivation for many

---

26 S. Aldana, Financial Impact of Worksite Health Promotion and Methodological Quality of the Evidence, *The Art of Health Promotion*, 1998, March/April, 2,1, pp.1–8.

T A B L E   12–12

Impact of Health Promotion Programs on Absenteeism

	Studies	
	Numbers	**Percentage**
Reduced absenteeism	14	87%
No change	1	6%
Increased absenteeism	1	6%
Total	16	100%

Cost/benefit analysis: 5 studies

Range of savings: $2.50 – $10.10 per $1.00 invested

Average savings: $4.90 per $1 invested

Source: S. Aldana, Financial Impact of Worksite Health Promotion and Methodological Quality of the Evidence, *The Art of Health Promotion*, 1998, March/April, 2,1, pp. 1–8.

employers who develop health promotion programs. The recent survey of workplace health promotion programs did show that attracting new employees was identified as an important reason for developing a health promotion program by 67 percent of employers and retaining existing employees was cited by 76 percent.[27]

CONCLUSION

Workplace health promotion programs are beginning to become the norm for large and medium size employers. There are hundreds of successful programs in place and a growing body of literature that describes how to develop and manage successful programs as well as the financial returns many of these employers are receiving. However, there is a large gap between the best programs and the typical ones. The best programs are described in the literature; the best programs are the ones that have enhanced their employees' health; and, the best programs are the ones that have produced savings through medical care cost containment, absenteeism reduction, and productivity enhancement. For other pro-

---

27 Association for Worksite Health Promotion, U.S. Department of Health and Human Services, William M. Mercer, Inc., 2000, *1999 National Worksite Health Promotion Survey*, Association for Worksite Health Promotion and William M. Mercer, Inc., Northbrook, IL.

grams to produce these results, they need to follow the protocols recommended for developing an excellent program. The time for dabbling in workplace health promotion has passed. Employers should use a rational process to determine if a health promotion program will produce the returns they need to justify it, if they have the organizational resources required to develop and support it, and if so, to do it right.

CHAPTER 13

Long-Term Care

Anthony J. Gajda

Morris Snow

WHAT IS LONG-TERM CARE?

Long-term care (LTC) usually is thought of in the context of old people in nursing homes, but actually it is a much broader concept. A little-known fact is that a considerable portion of LTC expenses is incurred by the non-elderly: 29 percent of institutional care and 42 percent of non-institutional care is provided to working-age adults. Frequently, it is needed because of a medical problem, but often it encompasses services beyond those covered by most medical plans because they are not "medically necessary." It often is not oriented toward rehabilitation. It may be needed by people of all ages and can be provided through a wide range of delivery systems and in a variety of settings.

Long-term care can be defined as a system of health and custodial services to support people who have chronic, or long-term, nonremediable physical or mental conditions. Under this umbrella definition, there are many kinds and classifications of long-term care. One classification is by *level of service*—skilled, intermediate, or custodial—differentiated by the degree of medical care involved. Another basic distinction is between *informal services*—provided by family and friends—and *formal services* purchased from individuals or institutions. Somewhere between 60 percent and 80 percent of the long-term care provided in the United States still falls into the category of informal services.

Within the category of formal services, the market is diverse and fragmented. The list of providers includes nursing homes; long-term care units in hospitals; continuing care retirement communities; home health agencies; assisted living facilities; adult day-care centers; and social health maintenance organizations, an experimental system that includes some prepaid long-term care services along with traditional medical services. Even such unusual players as the hotel and real-estate industries are exploring business opportunities in long-term care, through residential facilities that offer some health and support services.

Why Is Long-Term Care a Big Issue?

Long-term care is an important public concern for several reasons:

1. *Medical advances*, ironically, have helped to convert many critical short-term health problems into long-term health problems. New techniques and technology permit us to "save" the lives of heart attack and stroke victims, premature babies, and many other people whose diseases or injuries would have been fatal in the past. Yet while modern medicine prevents death, in many cases it cannot restore health. Particularly for older people, life-saving medical treatment often is the threshold to months or years of custodial care.

2. *The demographics* of the baby boom mean that we are on the verge of a population explosion in the higher age groups. In 1995, more than 35 million people, 13 percent of all Americans, were older than 65. By 2030, that age group will have grown to 70 million, more than 20 percent of the population.

People who think the need for long-term care "won't happen to me" stand on increasingly shaky ground; for example, at age 65, there is a 40 percent probability of being in a nursing home before death.

3. *Changes in the way we live* have made it less likely that long-term care can be provided at home by the patient's family. Now that many women are employed (59.8 percent of women age 16 and over are in the workforce), they are not available to care for their ailing parents or husbands. Children frequently live far from their parents, and few people enjoy the built-in support system of a large extended family in the same city, let alone the same house. This distance also means that parents cannot as easily get help from their children for nonmedical affairs, such as financial paperwork, meal preparation, or transportation.

4. *Public awareness* about the risks and costs of long-term care has traditionally been low. Unless one's own family has seen the financial effects of a long nursing home stay, one is likely to believe that Medicare or Medigap insurance policies will cover long-term care. Typically, surveys find that about half the population has this misunderstanding.

As the public becomes more aware of the problems of long-term care, many people look to government programs as a possible solution. Because the cost would be enormous, passage of any publicly funded comprehensive long-term care program seems unlikely in the near future. For many reasons, it is much more difficult to try to cover long-term care through social insurance than it is to provide basic medical services. If there is a public solution, which is not likely, it will be expensive, complex, and, no doubt, imperfect.

That leaves the bulk of the long-term care problem firmly in the lap of the private sector—the responsibility of individuals and families. While more than 120 insurance companies and Blue Cross plans—as well as associations such as the American Association of Retired Persons (AARP)—offer individual LTC coverage, many policies provide low levels of coverage or have restrictive underwriting rules, and the product is still new enough that pricing and marketing can be confusing to consumers who try to purchase coverage.

5. *Existing medical coverage* is inadequate to pay for long-term care. Neither government nor private insurance health programs cover much long-term care, and it can be staggeringly expensive.

A 1997 survey of LTC costs (Table 13–1) showed that those costs vary considerably around the country.

LTC can be very expensive. Current private health insurance plans—as well as Medicare—provide little or no coverage of LTC expenses, while traditional sources of LTC caregiving are contractual. This means that

T A B L E   13-1

LTC Costs in Selected Cities

	Annual Cost of:	
	Nursing Home Confinement	5 four-hour home care visits/week
Atlanta	$39,420	$16,411
Chicago	37,352	15,465
Dallas	31,755	13,905
New York	100,375	15,340
Philadelphia	50,735	15,558
Phoenix	35,770	14,913
San Francisco	46,355	19,115
Seattle	47,085	16,723

Source: *Long-Term Care Insurance: New Reasons to Consider Offering This Group Benefit*, Metropolitan Life Insurance Company, New York, 10010, 1997.

employees are exposed to a potentially huge financial risk with little or no protection.

LONG-TERM CARE AS AN EMPLOYEE BENEFIT

Employers' interest in long-term care has increased dramatically for many reasons:

1. *Preventing productivity losses* may be a significant benefit of an LTC program from the employer's standpoint, although this may not be apparent at first glance. Many employees are responsible for providing care to older or disabled people, a responsibility that often cuts into work time and creates stress, fatigue, and even illness.

Surveys have revealed that many employees in the workforce have responsibility for caring for an elderly person—either for managing the care or actually providing it.

- 23 percent to 46 percent of employees manage or provide some care to an elderly person
- 2 percent to 12 percent of employees provide personal care to an elderly person

The conclusion reached in each survey is that employees involved in providing care to an elderly person:

- quit their jobs;
- are absent from work to manage or provide care; and,
- are interrupted in their workday because of care responsibilities.

The further conclusion reached is that the availability of LTC insurance would reduce time and productivity lost by employees who have caregiving responsibility.

2. *Protecting employees' financial security* has been a traditional employer concern since destitute employees and retirees are bad for morale, productivity, and public image. Long-term care insurance can protect against financial devastation, just as pensions and life insurance do.

3. *Increasing employee satisfaction* with benefits is an important concern as employers try to make benefit dollars stretch farther. As people become aware of the need for long-term care, they will appreciate LTC coverage, and as more employers offer LTC benefits, employers may want to match their competitors.

4. *Companies can use their purchasing power* to negotiate more attractive premium rates, terms, and conditions than employees can obtain in the many individual LTC products that are available in the marketplace.

Some employers have added LTC coverage to the benefits offered to their employees. According to the Health Insurance Association of America, by the middle of 1998, more than 2,100 employers had adopted group LTC insurance programs covering nearly 800,000 employees and retirees. At present, most of the plans are paid for entirely by contributions from employees or retirees, with the employer's involvement limited to selecting an insurance carrier and handling communication and administration. Beyond that, there is little uniformity in how the programs operate, since few standard policies exist, and the pioneering employers have, in effect, required carriers to tailor the coverage to the employer's specifications. Although they want to proceed with LTC plans, some employers feel that the insurance market for such plans is still too immature. But the market is changing so rapidly that employers determined to wait and see won't have to wait long.

A Decade of Legislation and Regulation

In the beginning, when long-term care insurance was a new and radical idea, government was content to stimulate its growth and development by allowing the coverage to grow and develop unfettered by legislation and regulation. As the coverage became more mainstream and as abuses, real or perceived, became more commonplace, ever stricter laws and regulation became the norm. These laws seek to eliminate some of the abusive products and sales tactics in the marketplace. But as with other insurance products, compliance with both state and federal law has become a major headache for insurance companies as well as for employers.

The National Association of Insurance Commissioners (NAIC), an association of insurance commissioners of all of the states, meets regularly to adopt model laws and regulations (L&R) with respect to virtually all insurance products sold throughout the United States. The NAIC, however, lacks the power to make law so that its model L&R are only models and have no legal standing until adopted by the various states. While one of the purposes of the model L&R is to provide uniform rules across the various jurisdictions, with respect to long-term care the model L&R is only partially successful. First, not all of the states adopt the model L&R. Second, the laws are adopted by states at different times and oftentimes with material modifications. Currently:

- Somewhat more than 40 states base their laws primarily on one of the model L&R.
- However, none of the state laws are based upon the most recent model law passed in mid-2000.

- Approximately five of the states have laws that while based on the model L&R, they deviate from the model L&R in a number of significant ways.
- Several of the states have L&R that are not based upon the model laws.

These L&R passed by the states require filing and state approval of all policy forms, rates, and marketing materials before they may be used. Policy forms, rates, and marketing materials are strictly reviewed by the states for compliance with a host of detailed requirements.

A key feature of the L&R of many states is their extra-territoriality. Even if a group long-term care insurance contract complies fully with the laws and regulations of the state to which, for purposes of legal jurisdiction it is deemed to belong, the LTC contract must nevertheless be filed and comply with the L&R of any other state in which the contract is marketed and sold. This extra-territoriality, makes the filing process very lengthy and the administration process very complex. It also may force different versions of the employer plan to be marketed in different states.

On the federal level, the Health Insurance Portability and Accountability Act of 1996 (HIPAA) had a major effect on LTC. It created *qualified* LTC policies that have some distinct advantages over *nonqualified* policies. These advantages include favorable tax treatment for insurance company reserves as well as for individual purchasers of qualified plans. Premiums paid by individuals for qualified LTC insurance are potentially deductible as medical expenses and benefits paid are excluded from income. In order to be qualified, an LTC insurance plan must pay benefits only to "chronically ill" individuals, meet certain other definitional requirements, and include certain design and consumer protection features. Contracts issued prior to 1997 may automatically be accorded qualified status under a grandfather rule. HIPAA specifically prohibits the offering of LTC under a Section 125 cafeteria plan.

State Plans

State plans sold by insurance companies, are long-term care policies, that meet special state-defined minimum provisions. A handful of states have developed such plans, which carry special state endorsement to encourage the purchase by the general public of significant LTC insurance.

States are interested in LTC plans because states pay for a portion of Medicaid costs. And, in many states, one of the largest Medicaid expenses is long-term care—nursing homes and home health care. States have developed policies that protect the purchasers' assets or income. If a purchaser of a state plan requires long-term care, then the purchaser will receive some type of protection of his or her assets or income while still qualifying for Medicaid coverage of LTC services.

States win because the long-term care policies pay some of the expenses that their Medicaid programs would otherwise pay. Consumers win because they don't have to spend down all of their assets or income in order to qualify for Medicaid.

However, there is a downside to state plans: They are not extra-territorial in their protection of assets and income. In other words, while the policies will pay benefits for LTC services in any state, the asset/income protection is effective only in the state in which the policy was sold. Because many persons retire to other states, the value of a state plan may be diminished, at least in terms of asset/income protection.

State plans have been developed in only a handful of states. Sales to date have been disappointing, especially in the group market where few policies have been offered and sales results have been negligible.

Principles of Long-Term Care Plan Design

In designing a long-term care plan, the benefit manager should keep several principles in mind:

1. Most importantly, the employer must retain enough control over the LTC product to protect employees. An important premise of LTC as an employee benefit is that the employer can design a plan and negotiate terms and provisions with insurance carriers that produce more attractive protection than an employee can find in the individual LTC insurance market.

2. Levels of coverage should be both adequate and appropriate. As in any emerging insurance market where no rules of thumb have yet been developed, it is difficult to determine how much insurance is enough.

3. To the extent possible, an employer should offer a choice of LTC coverage levels. As shown earlier, LTC costs differ considerably around the country. Offering a single coverage level may force employees to pay for more coverage than they need and/or preclude employees from buying as much coverage as they need or would like.

4. A quick-fix solution to the problem does not exist. Off-the-shelf insurance programs are not likely to satisfy either the employer or employees. Employees should recognize that the LTC plan installed this year will likely need future revisions, perhaps major ones, as the laws and the marketplace change. Employees also should recognize that premiums may rise in the future as health care costs and utilization increase and that coverage levels may have to be increased to provide adequate coverage.

5. A single approach to employer-sponsored LTC coverage does not exist either. Employee needs and preferences differ from one workplace to another; health care supply varies by geography; corporate culture also is a great variable. The plan that works well for one employer may work less well at another organization.

6. Policy termination provisions need to be negotiated in advance. Employers need to be able to transfer adequate reserves to a successor carrier should the need develop.

7. Policies should be simple and easy to communicate. For most groups, it is wise to keep benefits modest, lest they get too expensive. Otherwise enrollment will likely be quite poor.

Despite all the uncertainties, employers should try to get everything right the first time. It is harder to make changes in an LTC insurance plan than in the typical medical group plan because in LTC plans employees generally begin building reserves with their first premium payments. These reserves greatly complicate the process of changing carriers or benefits.

What Should a Long-Term Care Insurance Plan Include?

The employer beginning to design an LTC program has many choices to make. From the benefit side, the choices include the following:

1. How will benefits be paid? Will the plan reimburse for a given service at a fixed rate or pay a certain percentage of care costs?
2. What level of coverage is appropriate? Should it be defined as a daily maximum, a lifetime maximum, or in some other way?
3. Will the plan include an inflation escalator?
4. What kinds of services are covered? Will the plan cover just nursing home stays and, if so, what kind? Will it cover services such as home health visits, assisted living facilities, adult day care, or respite care? Will inpatient and outpatient services vary?
5. Certain diseases and conditions should not be excluded from coverage. Are they being excluded?
6. Does the insurance carrier have a network of facilities and providers that have been screened for quality or that have agreed to attractive reimbursement levels that will control costs? How is the network accessed?

7. The plan should have a waiting period – sometimes called an elimination period—before benefits are paid. How long should the waiting period be?

8. How will eligibility for benefits be defined? Activities of daily living (ADLs), e.g., bathing, shopping, preparing meals, etc. are the typical method. How are ADLs defined? How many ADLs must be absent to trigger benefit eligibility? Note that for qualified plans under HIPAA, the number and type of ADLs are regulated.

9. Will the plan's maximum benefit be expressed in dollars of benefit payments, years of benefit payments? What will the maximum benefit be?

10. How will the plan provide inflation protection? Will the plan include automatic increases? Will employees be able to buy additional layers of coverage in the future? What will be the premium rates for future layers of coverage?

11. What, if any, benefits will be paid upon the death of the employee or lapse of the coverage?

12. What are the insurance carrier's underwriting rules? Will coverage be guaranteed for current employees? current retirees? new hires? dependents?

13. Who will be eligible for coverage? Will the plan be offered to employees and retirees or just to retirees? To increase the size of the group and thus spread risk, will employees be allowed to enroll their parents or children as well as themselves and their spouses?

14. Employees who leave the employer should be able to keep their policy or convert their coverage to an individual policy. Will their premium rates be the same as for the remaining group?

15. What utilization controls will be in effect? Will the plan include practices typical in medical plans, such as preadmission screening or advance certification of treatment? Will it include case management? Will the employer or a third-party attempt to monitor quality of care?

There are important decisions to be made on the financing side of LTC plan design as well as on the benefit side. Among them are these:

1. How will the reserves built up from the policy be valued? The plan may want to move them from one carrier to another in the future, and it may want to offer certain portability options to participants.

2. Premium rates should vary by age. The plan should charge lower premiums if employees enroll at early ages, to minimize adverse selection. But there are many variations in how steeply the premium rates increase with age of entry and, in turn, how quickly reserves will build up.

3. Will coverage be paid up at retirement, or will retirees continue to pay premiums? Will premiums be waived while the participant is collecting benefits?

4. What underwriting guidelines should be used in deciding which applicants will be permitted to enroll? Will the plan cover preexisting conditions or establish a waiting period? Will medical examinations or tests be required? State insurance laws will affect the options and decisions on these issues.

5. What actuarial assumptions will be used? How will the costs of future care and utilization be projected, especially since availability of coverage may increase utilization?

Employer Financing of Long-Term Care Programs

Group LTC plans are almost always employee-pay-all plans; only a handful of employers contribute to the cost of their plans. This practice may continue for several reasons. Even if long-term care doesn't come up as a bargaining issue for labor unions, employers may want to introduce it themselves as a preemptive move. Another impetus toward employer contributions may be the growing concern over skyrocketing liabilities for retiree medical coverage. With the issuance of Financial *Accounting Standards Board Statement 106* putting retiree medical liabilities on corporate balance sheets, employers are looking for ways to cap these commitments. It is difficult, and sometimes impossible, to cut back on a promise to provide medical care to retirees—but retirees can voluntarily agree to a new arrangement. In such a situation, long-term care could be an incentive for retirees to reopen the discussion and, in return for LTC coverage, accept a less-expensive medical plan.

HIPAA has made it more cost-effective for employers to contribute to long-term care plans for their employees. Under HIPAA, if the plan is qualified, the employer contributions are tax deductible to the employer and excluded from the taxable income of the employee. Benefits also are excluded from taxation. However, while it was hoped that these HIPAA provisions would stimulate employer contributions to LTC plans, there is little evidence that this is happening.

Whatever their reasons for contributing to LTC plans, employers, if they do contribute, will learn from their recent experience with medical plans, and probably will prefer a "defined contribution" approach to plan funding rather than a "defined benefit" approach. In other words, they will express their financial commitment as a fixed dollar amount, rather than promising to cover a share of all costs.

THE INSURANCE COMPANIES' VIEW

Long-term care coverage is a relatively new market for the insurance industry, and carriers are testing the waters cautiously. LTC coverage is a curious hybrid, which in some ways resembles several different kinds of traditional insurance products.

1. LTC resembles medical insurance because it involves health services and health facilities.
2. LTC resembles disability insurance, because in many cases, the insurance benefit is simply a daily or monthly amount, paid to a nursing home rather than directly to the beneficiary when disabilities or inabilities to function reach a certain level.
3. LTC resembles life insurance because the risk curves have the same shape, and many years pass before the carrier has good information on experience and pricing.
4. LTC resembles deferred annuities because reserves build up over many years before payout, making long-term investment decisions an essential factor in pricing and profitability.

As a result, carriers wanting to enter the LTC market have many different models to look at for guidance—but based on past experience, LTC is unlike any single one of them.

Insurance companies have been issuing individual LTC policies for about 20 years, but only a few companies have been in the market long enough to have credible experience available to analyze. Even those companies that have been in the business long enough for credible experience, have difficulties projecting that experience because:

- The early policies were very different from those sold now. They were underwritten differently and most of the older policies had prior hospital stay requirements for benefits and had little if any home health benefits.
- People are now living longer, but it is uncertain if they are living longer and healthier or longer and sicker.

■ Health care delivery systems have been changing rapidly, making it more difficult to predict costs and utilization with any degree of confidence.

Although some inter-company experience is available, it is usually scanty; of short duration; and, because within the industry there is no standard set of benefits, difficult to interpret. Nevertheless, there is ample evidence that many companies have significantly underpriced their products. Specifically:

■ Companies have been filing for rate increases in increasing numbers. The NAIC is very concerned that the elderly will be hit with increases they can ill afford just when they need the benefits most.

■ Some companies have sold their business and exited the market.

■ A few companies have declared bankruptcy.

■ A number of reinsurers are complaining about being badly burned.

As more experience emerges, it is reasonable to expect some market corrections. For this reason, employers would be wise to use a thoughtful process in choosing a LTC insurer and to resist the temptation to simply select the low-cost carrier. A lower rate today may result in much higher rates tomorrow.

What We've Learned

In a survey of employers that sponsor group LTC benefit plans, 70 percent give the programs positive ratings.

Rating	% of Respondents
Positive	70%
Too early to tell	17%
Negative	13%

Nearly all respondents reported that administering the group LTC benefit plan was easy or extremely easy.

Ease of Administration	% of Respondents
Extremely easy	42%
Fairly easy	55%
Somewhat difficult	3%

Roughly one-fourth (26 percent) of respondents said they would change nothing about their LTC programs. Other respondents would have changed some aspects of their LTC programs in the following ways:

- Communicate better during rollout and enrollment (38 percent).
- Coordinate LTC more closely with employees' retirement planning (29 percent).
- Find out more about employee wants and needs beforehand (27 percent).
- Negotiate a better rate structure with carrier (14 percent).

Three of the four most-cited changes are communication-related.

Communicating an LTC Benefit Plan

The evidence is already strong that the success of a group LTC plan—defined by the level of employee participation—depends on how well it is communicated to employees. As mentioned earlier, the American public generally is not informed of the facts about long-term care—either about the probability that they will need such care or the adequacy of existing insurance to pay for it. Unless people understand these facts, they are not likely to want LTC coverage. In turn, low participation tends to create adverse selection and drives up costs, thus making the program less attractive. The first step in successfully introducing LTC coverage, therefore, must be education. As with life insurance, people's reluctance to contemplate their own declines or demises presents an obstacle, but the subject can be made more palatable by broadening the focus from nursing home care to other services, such as adult day care or home health assistance.

Employers can further diffuse the clinical response by positioning LTC in the context of financial planning and retirement planning.

Employees see the financial threat that LTC expenses pose. A survey of employees revealed that their top three concerns about LTC were as follows:

Concerns About LTC	% of Respondents
It is irresponsible not to plan for my own LTC needs.	82%
The cost of LTC will significantly reduce my retirement income and assets.	76%
LTC is the greatest threat to my standard of living during retirement.	67%

LTC coverage can be an important element of financial and retirement planning that can alleviate some of the concern that employees have about the threat of LTC expenses. In this regard, three points are important.

First, LTC premium rates are age-based. They are lower at younger ages and higher at older ages. These rates reflect the fact that LTC expenses and claims are usually incurred at older ages and reserves must be built up to pay the claims. Consequently, lower premium rates can be charged to younger persons because those lower rates will be paid for longer periods of time.

The point is that premium rates will be lower if employees elect coverage at younger ages. An LTC benefit plan is not a plan for only older employees and retirees. It can be important for employees in their 40s as well. Further, younger employees are better able to afford LTC coverage. Their incomes are higher relative to older employees and retirees, and their premium rates are lower. In fact, 70 percent or more of employees age 35 to 54 can afford LTC coverage if premium rates are 2 percent or less of their incomes, but only 31 percent of older employees and retirees can afford LTC coverage if premium rates are 2 percent or less of their incomes.

Second, even at younger ages, LTC premium rates may be unaffordable. Table 13-2 shows the composite premium rates of five large LTC insurance carriers for typical LTC coverage. Even a $507 annual premium—or about $42 per month—may be more than some employees can afford.

Third, the simple fact is that some employees do not need LTC coverage. The employee with a net worth of $5 million or more is likely to be better off by self-insuring against LTC expenses. That employee can afford the

T A B L E   13-2

Composite Premium Rates by Age Groups

Ages	Annual Premiums
35–39	$507
40–44	605
45–49	734
50–54	905
55–59	1,204
60–64	1,709
65–69	2,432
70–74	3,610
75 and older	5,274

Source: *Who Will Pay for the Baby Boomers' Long-Term Care Needs?*, American Council of Life Insurance, Washington, D.C., 2004, 1998.

exposure and will not have to incur the administrative expenses and charges that are built into LTC premium rates. Similarly, LTC insurance is probably inappropriate for an employee with a net worth of less than $20,000 who probably cannot afford to pay for LTC coverage. More importantly, that employee would likely qualify for Medicaid LTC coverage.

So there is some upper level of net worth above which self-insuring is preferable to insuring against LTC expenses, and there is some lower level of net worth below which self-insuring is likely preferable to insuring against LTC expenses. While some commentators have said with some certainty what those upper and lower levels are, we believe that they can be very different for different employees because of family responsibilities, geographic location, degree of risk aversion, etc. The point is that employees should be apprised of the possibility that self-insuring may be preferable in some circumstances.

Communication of a LTC benefit plan is more complex than communication of most other benefits. A LTC communication program must educate employees about their exposure to risk and the consequences of those risks. It must educate employees on how to evaluate risk and how to use LTC coverage to protect against risk.

And communication cannot stop after the initial enrollment nor focus solely on plan details. If people have unrealistic expectations about the risk of LTC expenses and the ability of the plan to protect against it, they may be disappointed, and this can jeopardize the continued appeal of the plan for new participants. Continuing communication with both active employees and retirees is critical to getting the most out of an LTC program.

What to Expect

Many employers that decide to offer an LTC benefit plan to their employees seek to get as high an employee enrollment as possible. As already stated, there are circumstances in which employees will not be able to afford LTC benefits and in which employees may be better off by self-insuring against LTC expenses.

There are other explanations for low LTC participation rates:

■ Employees in their 20s probably give very little serious thought to a risk that is most likely 50 or 60 years into the future. They may view the accumulation of wealth in a 401(k) plan—which can be used for LTC expenses as well as any other expenses in retirement—as more important.

- There were 5 million individual LTC insurance policies in force in 1996 indicating that some employees may already have individual LTC coverage.
- Though declining, there still are cultural groups and communities in which caring for the elderly is taken for granted, making LTC unnecessary.
- Employees over the age of 45, the target market for this product, generally are under the financial stress of family expenses such as mortgage payments and college tuitions. Oftentimes they feel that they have no available funds to pay for another benefit.
- Some employees may still believe that Medicare will cover their LTC expenses.

The fact is that participation in employer-sponsored group LTC benefit plans is usually less than 10 percent of the eligible workforce. An International Foundation of Employee Benefit Plans survey found that 78 percent of group LTC benefit plans had a participation rate of less than 10 percent. A research study by the Health Insurance Association of America estimated that only 5.3 percent to 8.8 percent of eligible employees would purchase employer-sponsored LTC coverage. Consequently, an employer that decides to offer a group LTC benefit plan should:

- Design a plan that is especially attractive to its employees.
- Communicate effectively to maximize participation.
- Have realistic expectations about employee participation in the plan.

CAREGIVERS–ALSO IN NEED OF ASSISTANCE

The recipients of LTC benefits generally are thought of as the people who must receive custodial care. But another type of benefit program has as its recipients the people who provide care to family members or friends. Across the country, the best research indicates that 20 percent to 25 percent of employees are responsible for taking care of aged or disabled parents or spouses. Employers are coming to realize that it is in their best interests to help caregivers with these responsibilities that can erode productivity.

Various studies have attempted to quantify the burdens of caregiving upon people and their employers. Among the statistics are the following:

- Caregivers to brain-damaged older people lost an average of 9.3 hours every month from their jobs.

- Caregivers tend to get sick themselves as a result of the physical and emotional strain of their responsibilities; they were 25 percent more likely to be under physicians' care, almost twice as likely to have frequent headaches, and almost three times as likely to have frequent anxiety or depression.

- Thirty-five percent of employed caregivers said their work is affected, 13 percent had to decline overtime work, and 18 percent had to pass up training opportunities.

The cost to employers of their employees' caregiving responsibilities, therefore, is significant. Employees simply cannot operate at top quality if they are exhausted from nursing an invalid at night or visiting the hospital or nursing home every day. They cannot put in a full day's work if they are on the phone arranging a parent's doctor appointments, handling his or her legal affairs, getting him or her into a nursing home, or checking whether he or she ate a decent lunch. The situation can be even more difficult if the parent lives 1,000 miles away.

In their own interest, employers are beginning to look for ways to ease these burdens, through a wide variety of programs that have come to be described by the term *elder care*. Elder-care activities fall into two categories: indirect and direct. Indirect programs are those that may help many employees, not just those with caregiving responsibilities. Such programs can provide emotional support and reduce conflicts between work and caregiving. They include flextime, liberal personal-leave policies, job sharing, employee assistance programs, and dependent-care spending accounts. Use of spending accounts for pretax payment of dependent-care expenses, unfortunately, is quite restricted. Under IRS regulations, the employee must claim the older person as a dependent for income tax purposes and provide at least 50 percent of support. The dependent must spend at least eight hours a day in the caregiver's home, and the care purchased through the spending account must be necessary to allow the employee to work.

Direct programs are designed specifically to help caregivers, and include several types:

- *Information* programs can include printed materials, seminars and meetings, or fairs to which many local agencies send representatives.

- *Direct service* programs might include support groups or individual counseling services for caregivers, an adult daycare center affiliated with the employer, or subsidized slots in a community center.

- *Referral and linkage* programs put caregivers in touch with community agencies, geriatric case managers, nursing homes, daycare programs, or other resources that can help the caregivers or the patient.
- *Reimbursement* programs subsidize various services for caregivers, such as respite care to allow the caregiver time away from the patient.

Eldercare programs often are perceived by employees as being far more valuable than their costs might indicate. Employed caregivers, above all, lack time in which to gather information or investigate alternative arrangements or even to take care of their own emotional or physical health.

In addition, there are no tax problems involved in most eldercare benefits, because many of these programs are similar to employee-assistance programs and do not provide any tangible, thus taxable, benefits.

CHANGING LTC CARRIERS

As was noted earlier, once a group LTC insurance plan has been implemented with an insurance carrier, it is difficult to transfer the plan to a different carrier. Thus, caution should be exercised in judging whether to transfer coverage from one carrier to another. If an employer decides to make a change, then efforts should be concentrated in the following areas:

Reserve Transfer. Unless the existing long-term care insurance contract was very specific about:

- How the transfer amount is to be calculated,
- The timing of the transfer of funds, and
- Any termination penalties or market value adjustment, there will almost certainly be a serious disagreement between the incumbent carrier and the employer about the magnitude and timing of the reserve transfer. The transfer of funds needs to be artfully negotiated.

Benefits Under New Contract. The new contract should offer substantially the same benefits as the existing contract. Unless the benefits are substantially the same, there may be some unpleasant legal implications with regard to the existing contract's guaranteed renewable provisions.

Premiums. Every effort should be made to keep the premiums stable during the transition period. Usually this requires securing an adequate reserve transfer from the existing carrier *and* negotiating effectively with the new carrier.

HIPAA Effects. For contracts that are qualified under HIPAA's grandfathering provisions, care must be taken not to unravel the grandfathering. Significant changes to the plan may result in loss in the grandfathering and the disqualification of the plan under HIPAA.

Fiduciary Responsibilities under ERISA. In changing carriers, care should be taken not to violate any fiduciary responsibilities under ERISA. These responsibilities can be significant because the coverage is for a lifetime, substantial reserves are built up, and some of the covered population could be impaired.

Carrier transfers are not simple, but with care and attention they can be accomplished when necessary.

CONCLUSION

While long-term care is a hot issue and likely to get even hotter, employers need to be careful in making decisions. Special care must be taken by the employer in the following areas:

- Plan design.
- Plan termination provisions.
- Premium rates.
- Vendor selection.
- Communication efforts.

When a group LTC program is well designed, it will be a valuable financial and retirement planning tool for employees and a productivity-enhancing tool for the employer as progressive, work-family sensitive, etc. Further, a group LTC program will differentiate the employer, as progressive, work-family sensitive, etc., and likely will enhance its recruitment and retention efforts at a very modest or no cost.

S o u r c e s

Who Will Pay for the Baby Boomers' Long-Term Care Needs?, American Council of Life Insurance, 1998

Preliminary Data from a Survey of Employers Offering Group Long-Term Care Insurance to Their Employees—Interim Report, The Lewin Group, 1999.

Long-Term Care Insurance in 1996, Health Insurance Association of America, 1999.

State-of-the-Art in Long-Term Care Insurance, William M. Mercer, Inc., 1997.

Can Private Insurance Solve the Long-Term Care Problems of the Baby Boomer Generation?, The Urban Institute Testimony before the Senate Special Committee on Aging, 1998.

Stanger, Janice, "Long-Term Care Insurance: A Unique and Versatile Benefit," *Compensation & Benefits Management,* Winter, 1998.

Hotze, Christopher, "Selecting Long-Term Care Insurance," *HR Magazine,* 1999.

New Reasons To Consider Long-Term Care Insurance, MetLife, 1997.

The MetLife Study of Employer Costs for Working Caregivers, Washington Business Group on Health, 1995.

1999 Long-Term Care Survey, John Hancock/The National Council on the Aging, 1999.

CHAPTER 14

Disability Income Benefits

John S. Roberts

Michael Norton

Loss of income because of disability is among the most devastating losses a person can face. This chapter focuses on disability income benefits, both short-term and long-term. It begins with an overview of disability risk and an explanation of how disability income protection, both public-sector and employment-based programs, evolved in the United States. Plan design issues associated with sick leave, short-term disability, long-term disability, self-insurance options, integration of plans, and integration with public programs are discussed.

DISABILITY RISK

About 17.1 million Americans are out of work at any given time because of a health problem or disability.[1] Most of these are short-term conditions, but millions of workers have severe conditions that can keep them from work. In 1998, 4.7 million workers qualified for disability benefits under Social Security OASDI (Old Age, Survivors, and Disability Insurance).[2] By definition under Social Security these were severe disabilities that prevented the person from doing any kind of work for which he or she is suited and that can be "expected to last for at least a year or to result in death."[3]

---

1 U.S. Department of Commerce, Bureau of the Census, *Statistical Abstract of the United States,* 1999, Oct. 1999, p. 396.

2 Ibid.

3 Social Security Administration, *Social Security Disability Benefits,* (SSA Publication No. 05-10029), May 1996, p. 3.

Estimates of the number of people with disabilities vary depending upon how disability is defined. The most recent U.S. Census Bureau figures estimate that roughly one in four people age 15 and older in the U.S. have some type of disability, with disability defined generally as a reduced ability to perform tasks one would normally do at a given stage in life. By this definition, the Census Bureau reported that about 48.5 million of the 202.4 million people over age 15 had a disability.[4]

The risks of both short-term and long-term disability increase with age. The average incidence of a disability lasting three months or longer is 3.5 per 1,000, according to Society of Actuaries estimates.[5] The figure grows to 20 per 1,000 near age 65 and can be as low as .5 per 1,000 in younger age groups. Disability is a low-incidence event in comparison to some other insurable events. However, if one makes the same comparison in terms of impact, disability is a dramatically more serious financial threat. A 40-year-old earning a gross salary of $50,000 will forgo almost $2.4 million in pay if he or she is disabled and is not able to return to work before age 65. (See Table 14–1.)

EARLY HISTORY

The first disability-type insurance policies were created as the United States made the transition from an agricultural to an industrial economy.

T A B L E   14–1

Potential Lost Salary (000s) Due to Disability at
Various Ages to Age 65

Gross Pay at Disability	Age at Disability			Estimated Composite FIT & FICA Rates (%)
	25	40	50	
$ 7,500	$ 906	$ 358	$ 162	12
18,000	2,174	859	388	17
50,000	6,040	2,386	1,079	21

Note: Assumes a 5 percent salary increase per year if disability had not occurred. For example, if disabled at age 40 with a salary of $18,000, then future earnings lost would be $859,000 to age 65.

---

4 U.S. Department of Commerce, Bureau of the Census, *Current Population Reports*, pp. 70-61.
5 *Commissioner's Disability Table*, Society of Actuaries, Vol. 39, 1987.

These forerunners of disability income insurance—called "establishment funds"—were seen in the industrial regions of the Northeast in the early 1800s. Employers created the funds and paid employees a small cash payment if they became sick or were injured on the job.

Insurance companies followed with other measures to protect against accident or illness. The first disability policies were sold to individuals in the late 1840s, and related-travel-accident type coverages followed in the 1850s.

Few people were covered by these early policies, but their existence signaled that society was beginning to think about disability risk and how to protect against it. The industrial revolution had created new industries, new machinery, and faster production. In turn, this progress created new hazards for employees and business. By 1900, businesses were seeking insurance to protect against accident-related lawsuits. At the same time, government was responding to the new economic and social conditions. In 1911, state governments enacted the first workers' compensation laws, requiring employers to provide employees with insurance protection for job-related injury and sickness.

The workers' compensation laws created more awareness of disability risk and marked a new stage of development for disability insurance. The first group disability insurance came on the market in 1915, modeled after group life insurance.

These early chapters of the nascent disability income insurance market were virtually closed by the Great Depression. By 1932, 14 million Americans were unemployed. Sales of disability and accident-related insurance to both individuals and groups fell, and claims under existing policies climbed.

Looking back, it seems clear that even without the vast economic disruption of the 1930s, the disability income insurance contracts of that day were destined for poor results. These early contracts used a flat rate structure, applying the same rate to all ages. In addition, contracts did not include a number of underwriting safeguards that are common today, such as a maximum age beyond which benefits cannot be received.

THE MODERN ERA OF DISABILITY INCOME BENEFITS

The modern era of disability income benefits took shape in the 1950s and 1960s. Two demand factors are worth noting. First, organized labor became more active in seeking noncash compensation. Second, government addressed the problem of disability. In 1960, an amendment to the Social Security program extended disability income protection to all workers. This initiative had a strict definition of disability and a six-month waiting period, so it hardly met the full need for disability income protection. However, it did propel awareness of the need for protection, encouraging bargaining units and individual workers to seek disability income benefits through the workplace.

In the 1960s, the quality of disability income insurance products caught up with the emerging demand of a modern economy and workforce. Before this time, group long-term disability (LTD) contracts provided a low level of benefits. Insurance carriers did not understand how to manage LTD risk and, in the wake of their 1930s experience, they took a highly conservative approach. In the 1960s, innovative insurers developed the methods for insuring the unique risks of disability. One of the most important changes was insuring the loss of income specifically. By contrast, contracts of the past triggered payment when a person was disabled, without attention to loss of income. The focus on income protection allowed insurers to manage risk more effectively and offer more appropriate and meaningful benefits.

The recent decades also have been characterized by a new level of awareness about disability issues and the capabilities of people with disabilities. This culminated in 1990 with passage of the Americans with Disabilities Act (ADA). The law prohibits discrimination on the basis of disability. In relation to employment, the ADA states that employers cannot discriminate against qualified individuals with disabilities. Qualified individuals with disabilities are those who can perform the essential functions of the job they hold or desire, with or without reasonable accommodation.

Other ADA sections cover the issues of discrimination in public services, public accommodations and services operated by private entities, and telecommunications.

In addition, public policy has begun to focus more on aiding people with disabilities in returning to work. In 1999, the Work Incentives Improvement Act broadened access to the major federal health insurance programs—Medicare and Medicaid—in supporting a return to work among those who receive Social Security disability benefits (both under OASDI and Supplemental Security Income). Under prior policy, those on Social Security disability risked loss of their access to federal health insurance programs if they attempted to return to work. Advocates for people with disabilities consider the new Work Incentives law as the most important policy step in supporting return to work since ADA.[6]

---

6 "Clinton Signs Law to Help Workers With Disabilities," *The New York Times*, Dec. 18, 1999.

TYPES OF DISABILITY INCOME IN THE PUBLIC AND PRIVATE SECTORS

This section describes the various public and private income replacement programs. Four major areas are covered within each program:

- Eligibility.
- Benefit levels/approximate replacement ratios.
- Duration of benefits.
- Definition of disability.

Specified limitations and exclusions also are pointed out where appropriate. A description of the public programs is followed by a discussion on private-sector benefit programs, including sick pay, short-term disability (STD), and long-term disability (LTD). Plan design and funding issues also are addressed.

Public Programs

Public-sector disability programs include the following:

- Social Security (OASDI/SSI).
- Workers' compensation.
- Veterans' benefits.
- State retirement systems (disability rider).
- State-mandated (short-term) plans.

These various public-sector programs provide a modest yet important foundation of disability income protection to the working population.

The most comprehensive level of coverage is provided by the state workers' compensation programs covered in Chapter 23. However, those apply only to work-related disabilities and, work-related disabilities represent less than 10 percent of total disabilities that last more than 90 days.

Social Security disability income provides protection for both occupational and nonoccupational disabilities, but its strict definition of disability and general benefit levels are not intended to support disability protection needs at all income levels. Similarly, state retirement systems often apply in lieu of participation in the Social Security disability income system, with equivalent replacement ratios and claim approval rates.

The state-mandated (short-term) programs also are modest and, by definition, apply only to short durations.

Veterans' benefits can provide significant income protection, depending on the degree of disability. These benefit levels normally are provided regardless of benefits received from other programs.

Private group disability plans generally integrate with public programs. The income replacement remitted under private plans usually reflects income replacement that was not available from public programs or is an addition to payments received under public programs. The most significant exception to this rule are payments under veterans' disability income, which do not normally offset with private group disability plans.

Social Security: SSDI and SSI

Chapter 22 discusses eligibility and insured status of individuals participating in Social Security OASDI (Old Age, Survivors, and Disability Income). This section addresses Social Security disability income (SSDI) and supplemental security income (SSI). Both are administered by the Social Security Administration. Employers and employees share the funding of SSDI through regular withholding. SSI is funded through general revenue of the federal government.

SSDI A worker is generally eligible for Social Security disability income (OASDI) if the following five conditions are met:

1. The person is insured. In most circumstances, the standard that will apply here is that the person has worked under Social Security for at least five of the last 10 years before becoming disabled.
2. The person is under age 65.
3. The person has been disabled for 12 months, is expected to be disabled for at least 12 months, or has a disability that is expected to result in death.
4. The person has filed an application for disability benefits.
5. The person has completed a five-month waiting period or is exempted from this requirement.

Benefits

The benefit generally equals the worker's Primary Insurance Amount (PIA) as defined by Social Security. This amount is determined as if the worker were 65 (normal retirement age under Social Security) and eligible for benefits in the first month of his or her waiting period.

Disability benefits are normally lowered by any workers' compensation benefits. Auxiliary beneficiaries receive a portion of the PIA (see Table 14–2).

Duration

Benefits are payable to age 65.

Definition of Disability

It is vital to keep in mind that the definition of disability under Social Security is narrow. Disability is defined as the inability to engage in any substantial gainful activity by reason of any medically determinable physical or mental impairment that can be expected to result in death or that has lasted or can be expected to last for a continuous period of not less than 12 months.

In 1998, 52 percent of applications for disability benefits under OASDI were approved. Applicants usually receive initial approval or denial within 60 days.[7] The benefit process, viewed as a whole, is a difficult course of applications, denials, and appeals. Nearly all workers are eligible for disability income under OASDI, but this narrow definition of disability excludes many who apply for benefits. The average benefit

T A B L E   14–2

Benefits as a Percentage of PIA

Disability benefit = 100% of PIA
Spouse's benefit (husband or wife of retired or disabled worker) = 50% of PIA*

Child's benefit
Child of retired or disabled worker = 50% of PIA*

Mother's or father's benefit
Caring for child under 16 or disabled = 75% of PIA*

Disabled widow(er)'s benefit
Starting age 50–59 = 71.5 % of PIA

*Subject to a Maximum Family Benefit.

7 *Social Security Bulletin Annual Statistical Supplement*, 1999, p. 269.

under OASDI (or Social Security disability income) was $746.[8] (See Table 14–3).

Supplemental security income (SSI) is a need-based program that makes cash payments to individuals who fall under designated income thresholds and are disabled. In 1998, more than 5 million people with disabilities received SSI payments. The average monthly payment was $380.[9]

Workers' Compensation

Workers' compensation provides reasonable income and medical benefits to work-accident victims, or income benefits to their dependents, regardless of fault. Most employees have a solid replacement level of income for a good-to-excellent duration of benefit payments for disabilities that result from work-related injuries and diseases. However, as stated previously, these work-related disabilities represent less than 10 percent of all disabilities that occur to the employee population.

The following provides a brief description of the benefits under the workers' compensation program. Chapter 23 explains the program in detail. All 50 states have workers' compensation laws. Although there is broad agreement that coverage under these laws should be universal, in

T A B L E 14–3

OASDI Disability Benefits Awarded–Number and Average Monthly Benefit, 1998

Age	Number	Avg. Monthly Benefit
Under 30	35,000	$468.20
30–39	87,000	$639.30
40–49	150,500	$737.60
50–54	112,400	$789.00
55–59	127,000	$808.50
60 or older	89,900	$834.50
Total	603,000	$746.30

Source: Social Security Bulletin, Annual Statistical Supplement, 1999, p. 256.

---

8 Social Security Bulletin, Annual Statistical Supplement, Social Security Administration, 1999, p. 256.
9 SSI Annual Statistical Report, Social Security Administration, June 1999, p. 6.

fact no state law covers all forms of employment. In 1995, 113 million wage and salary employees were covered by job injury laws.[10] In 14 states, smaller employers are exempt from the law. Generally these are firms with fewer than three to five employees. Interpretations of the law in different states also can affect uniformity of coverage among all workers, but the intent of the laws is to cover all work-related injuries and diseases. These compensation laws are theoretically compulsory or elective. Under an elective law, the employer may reject the act, but if it does so, it loses the three common-law defenses: assumption of risk, negligence of fellow employees, and contributory negligence. As a practical matter, this means that workers' compensation laws are generally "compulsory." Coverage is still elective in Texas, although Texas law provides for mandatory workers' compensation for occupations engaged in transportation as defined in state law. In Wyoming, the law is compulsory for all employees engaged in extra-hazardous occupations and elective for all other occupations. Most states require employers to obtain insurance or prove financial ability to carry their own risk. Self-insurance is permitted in all but a few states. Employers may set up a reserve fund for self-insurance to pay compensation and other benefits.

Benefits Provided   Because workers' compensation imposes an absolute liability upon the employer for employee disabilities caused by employment, the benefits payable to the injured employee attempt to cover most of the worker's economic loss. Specifically, the benefits provided are the following three:

1. *Cash benefits*, which include both impairment benefits and disability benefits. The former are paid for certain specific physical impairments, while the latter are available whenever there is an impairment and a wage loss. Four classes of disability are used to determine cash benefits: (1) temporary total, (2) permanent total, (3) temporary partial, and (4) permanent partial. Most cases involve temporary total disability: The employee, although totally disabled during the period when benefits are payable, is expected to recover and return to employment. Permanent total disability generally indicates that the employee is regarded as totally and permanently unable to perform gainful employment.

10 U.S. Department of Commerce, Bureau of the Census, *Statistical Abstract of the United States, 1999*, Oct. 1999, p. 397.

In general, most states provide payments extending through the employee's lifetime on permanent total disability. Replacement ratios vary somewhat by various states but are always reasonable and are a percentage of "current" predisability income.

2. *Medical benefits*, which usually are provided without dollar or time limits. In the case of most workplace injuries, only medical benefits are provided since substantial impairment or wage loss is not involved.

3. *Rehabilitation benefits*, which include both medical rehabilitation and vocational rehabilitation for those cases involving severe disabilities.

Veterans' Benefits (Disability Income)

Members of the military are provided with a noncontributory pension plan. Retirement is provided for after 20 years of service. If a member is disabled before retirement, he or she becomes eligible for veterans' compensation, provided the disability is service-connected. Compensation varies by degree of disability, ranging in 1999 from $98 per month for a 10 percent disability to $2,036 for a 100 percent disability.

Additional amounts above those base disability-compensation rates are paid when an individual has a severe disability as defined in law. In addition, those with at least a 30 percent disability can receive additional allowances for dependents. These additional allowances are tied to the level of disability. For example those with a 30 percent disability received an additional $18 per month in 1999 for each child or an additional $55 per month for each school-age child. Those with 100 percent disability received an additional $61 per month for each child and an additional $186 for each school-age child.

State Retirement Systems (Disability Features)

Pension programs, especially public employee retirement systems (PERS), frequently have a disability component to protect the income of disabled members. The PERS programs are usually a substitute for the OASDI program of Social Security. State and local governments can opt out of the Social Security system if their employees are covered by their own retirement system.

Eligibility

The PERS programs are established by each state to provide for the retirement and disability income needs of their employees. The eligibility point for disability benefits varies from immediate to up to five years of service; in some states, 10 years of service is required to qualify for benefits.

Benefits

The benefit levels frequently are based on a service-type formula, such as 2 percent of salary for each year of service times a final average salary (FAS), to a maximum percentage of salary. Other states provide straight formulas, such as 50 percent of FAS or 62.5 percent of average monthly salary (AMS). The number of years required in these averages varies by state, but the most frequent requirements are "latest x years," or all years since a certain date, excluding the five years of lowest earnings. In general, replacement ratios are not applied to current incomes prior to disability, and benefit levels generally are in the range of the Social Security disability income programs, with some exceptions.

Duration

Benefits usually are paid to normal retirement (age 65).

Definition of Disability

The definition of *disability* usually is permanent and total disability. The approval rates on PERS programs (i.e., of the claims submitted, how many are approved for payment by the PERS) generally are not available. However, because the definition of disability is permanent and total, similar to that of the Social Security disability income system, there probably is a sizable declination rate that may be more severe than that of Social Security. The Social Security Administration declines about 50 percent of applications for disability benefits under OASDI.

State Mandated Plans (STD)

California, Hawaii, New Jersey, New York, Rhode Island, and the territory of Puerto Rico have modest programs that provide or require employers to provide disability benefits for all workers. These programs all provide benefits for short-term disabilities.

Public-Sector Benefits Changes on the Horizon

Public-sector benefits may face changes in the coming years as the U.S. government deals with the problem of an aging population and the potential impact on budget deficits. The Social Security Board of Trustees 1999 annual report noted that trust fund expenditures will begin to exceed tax revenues in 2015. Beginning in 2025, the report said, trust fund assets will be drawn down to pay benefits until the funds are exhausted in 2037.

The strong economy and resulting payroll tax revenue helped extend the solvency date to 2037, but the trustees have urged bipartisan legislative action to restore the long-term balance to Social Security. Other major programs, most notably Medicare and Medicaid, also are expected to feel the financial strain of an older population requiring more benefits.

In 1950, there were 16.5 covered workers for every Social Security beneficiary; in 1994, there were 3.2 workers per beneficiary, according to Social Security Administration figures. By 2040, this figure is projected to fall to about two workers per beneficiary. Potential reforms for coping with this situation include raising the eligibility age and/or changing eligibility criteria for Social Security benefits.

Workers' compensation has undergone significant reform at the state level. Between 1992 and 1994, 30 states enacted substantial workers' compensation reforms aimed at lowering costs and stabilizing the market for corporations and insurers. These reforms have included use of managed care practices to contain costs. Some states and businesses also have turned to 24-hour coverage plans, which integrate disability management, workers' compensation, and group health insurance in a single program. This approach is designed to reduce the complexity and cost of managing workplace disabilities and to increase productivity.

Public-sector programs provide a critical foundation for disability coverage, yet they do not cover all disabilities or income protection needs sufficiently. That makes additional disability income protection a fundamental need to be met through private-sector insurance or self-insurance plans.

Private-Sector Benefits

Three major benefits in the private sector address group disability concerns: sick leave, short-term disability (STD), and long-term disability (LTD). An employer can elect to provide these benefits through a self-insured, partially insured, or fully insured plan. What follows is an overview of each benefit and related plan design issues.

Sick Leave

Employers often will continue full salary for the time missed when an employee is ill. These sick leave or medical leave plans generally cover a period of up to 10 days. Most often, the plan is self-funded by the employer.

Salaried personnel are more likely to have a sick-leave plan that is combined with a long-term disability plan. A short-term disability plan that follows a brief period of sick pay also may be part of this package. These benefits should be explained to employees in writing as part of the total benefits package.

The design of the sick-leave plans can allow employees to accumulate unused "sick days" over several years. This permits employees to apply their accumulated time to an extended illness or disability. Some employers also increase the number of sick days per year based on time of service. Such a design will have a maximum for accumulated sick-leave days; most often, 180 days is the limit.

Short-Term Disability (STD)

Employees generally must be off the job for five days because of illness or one day because of a non-job-related accident to qualify for benefits under a group STD plan. Such a plan, unlike sick pay, is more likely to be insured. The waiting periods before STD benefits begin will vary among workplaces. The goal is to structure a waiting period so that the plan does not encourage staying off the job. The level of income replaced also is a key part of this design goal. Most STD plans replace 50 percent to 66.6 percent of income for up to 26 weeks. Some plans may base benefits on a percentage of take-home pay or spendable income.

Whether an STD plan is insured or self-insured, payments during this 26-week period are considered wages and are subject to income, Social Security, and unemployment taxes.

Long-Term Disability (LTD)

LTD plans usually provide income replacement after 13 or 26 weeks under a two-part definition of disability. The first part usually applies to the initial two years that LTD benefits can be paid and concerns the employee's own occupation. It states that employees must be disabled to an extent that they cannot perform the duties of their own occupation. Employers also have the option of plan structures that will extend the "own occupation" definition of disability beyond the initial 24 months.

The second part of the definition usually applies to the time frame after the initial 24 months of LTD benefits. It states that benefits will continue to be paid if the person is unable to engage in any work or occupation for which he or she is reasonably fitted by education, training, or experience.

The benefits continue until normal retirement age. While that is often age 65, many contracts now extend to age 67 in order to cover younger workers who may have a Social Security retirement age of 67. Some workers also may be eligible for benefits after age 67. The Age

Discrimination in Employment Act (ADEA) requires that the benefit period provide cost-equivalent benefits for older workers when compared to younger workers. (This is covered in more detail in the section on age under "Elements in Plan Design.")

Benefits cease if the person is able to return to work or dies before normal retirement age. The percentage of income replaced is normally a percentage of gross salary and can vary significantly from one plan to another. Some plans replace as much as 75 percent to 80 percent of gross income; others replace 50 percent to 66.6 percent of gross income. In addition, some higher-income professionals will supplement these group benefits with an individually purchased disability income protection plan.

In comparison to medical and life insurance, LTD is relatively under-penetrated in the marketplace. The coverage is most commonly found among professional and technical employees (see Table 14–4).

Unlike STD benefits, Social Security and unemployment taxes do not apply to LTD benefits. However, LTD benefits are subject to income tax because the premiums are employer-paid. In circumstances where the employees paid for a disability plan with their own post-tax dollars, benefits are tax-free. This is most likely to be the case with an individual disability plan, which executive and professional employees often access and buy through the workplace. When a portion of the plan was paid by the employer and a portion by the employee with post-tax dollars, the proportion of plan benefits funded by the employer are taxable as income.

Integrated Disability

Disability insurance is moving toward designs that integrate traditional occupational coverage such as workers' compensation and the coverage

TABLE 14–4

Percentage of Employers Providing LTD Programs in Businesses With Over 100 Employees

	All Employees	Professional/ Technical	Clerical/ Sales	Blue Collar/ Service
Medical	76%	79%	78%	74%
Life	87%	94%	91%	81%
LTD	43%	62%	52%	28%

Source: U.S. Department of Labor, Bureau of Labor Statistics, *News*, USDL 99-02, Jan. 7, 1999.

more oriented to non-occupational risk (e.g., STD, LTD, individual disability, and certain voluntary employee benefits). These designs offer a single point of entry to the benefits process for employees, making coverage more seamless. Employers have a more seamless picture of the coverage as well through integrated information reporting. Information that follows trends across the full spectrum of coverage is a valuable tool in assessing effectiveness of the benefits program design and disability management initiatives.

Elements in Plan Design

Group Size

Many LTD carriers require at least 10 participants in a group plan. Individual underwriting applies to smaller groups. In general, individuals and extremely large groups tend to produce the highest incidence. In the case of groups with 5,000 or more participants, higher incidence is attributable to a lower level of employer contact and control. By contrast, on the individual and small groups end of the spectrum, small numbers and antiselection play the larger role in the incidence picture.

Age

Age of a group is the key factor in determining rate. However, it is discriminatory under the Age Discrimination in Employment Act (ADEA) to use age to determine eligibility for the group. Some employers prefer offering disability benefits based on years of service. This is not a discriminatory practice because all employees have access to the plan once they have been employed for the predetermined amount of time.

Table 14–5 illustrates the relationship between age and disability incidence. Younger workers, in addition to experiencing fewer disability events, have higher motivation for both rehabilitation and retraining.

The rule on discrimination issues generally is that all employees within an eligible class must be included in the plan. In voluntary or contributory plans, all employees in the eligible class must be asked to participate in the plan.

Under ADEA, benefit programs can define benefit periods without discriminating against the older employee. The contract can specify the maximum number of months of income replacement for other older employees. The key issue is that this benefit period must provide cost-equivalent benefits when compared to benefits of younger workers. The

T A B L E   14–5

Group Long-Term Disability Insurance Rate of
Disablement in Men and Women per 1,000 Lives
Exposed (Calendar Years of Experience 1976–1980)

Six-Month Elimination Period	Male Experience	Female Experience
Under 40	1.02	1.39
40—44	2.02	3.04
45—49	3.56	4.52
50—54	6.33	7.41
55—59	12.20	10.88
60—64	16.63	12.98
All ages	3.78	3.40
Three-Month Elimination Period	**Male Experience**	**Female Experience**
Under 40	1.70	2.83
40—44	3.41	4.84
45—49	5.75	7.67
50—54	8.35	9.50
55—59	15.41	13.30
60—64	21.26	17.63
All ages	4.85	5.24

Source: *Transactions of the Society of Actuaries,* 1982 Reports on Mortality and Morbidity Experiences, 1985, p. 279.

ADEA also specifies that employees age 70 or older must receive a minimum of 12 months of disability benefits.

Preexisting Conditions

Preexisting-condition exclusion clauses are used in LTD contracts to minimize the risk of antiselection. For example, one common clause in LTD
contracts allows for an examination of the three months prior to policy
purchase to determine if an insured filed a claim within 12 months of the
policy purchase. If the policyholder received care, treatment, or took prescribed medication during that three-month period for a condition that is
now claimed as a disability, the insurer will not pay benefits.

Preexisting conditions are normally not used as part of STD plans but are almost always a standard for LTD plans, given the increased exposure. As a result, an employee could be eligible for benefits under the STD plan and later be denied benefits because his or her condition existed prior to the effective LTD contract date. When STD benefits are offered on a voluntary basis, preexisting condition language may apply to the short term as well.

Gender

As Table 14–5 indicates, women have a higher incidence of disability than men at younger ages but a lower incidence at older ages. This can increase disability incidence in some groups with a high percentage of young female employees.

Occupation

Claim frequency will vary from one occupation to the next. Some of these differences are obvious. Blue-collar workers, for example, face more physical hazards on the job. Other occupational connections with incidence are more complex. An economic downturn in a particular type of business or major changes in the job environment of professional groups will increase disability incidence.

The existence of workers' compensation insurance also does not eliminate the impact of occupational hazards on disability plans. Medical leave or STD are needed in some states before workers' compensation is available. LTD benefits are paid when workers' compensation is not adequate.

Hourly workers and lower-paid workers historically have been declined or heavily rated in LTD plans. This is related to the likelihood of overinsurance. The percentage of hourly paid or lower-paid jobs and the type of work done often will determine whether a group is insurable. Seasonal work, such as agriculture and construction, generally are more tightly underwritten as well.

Duration

Plans may exclude new employees from both short-term and long-term disability coverage for a set period of time. Benefits will continue under the LTD plan until the age of retirement if the person cannot work in any occupation. Pension plans should include some provision for accrual of pension benefits during the time of disablement. When disability plans are not in place, some employer plans allow early retirement benefits because of disability.

Funding

Risk is the primary concern in designing a disability-income benefits plan. Long-term disability is a catastrophic coverage. Employers must take great care in fully self-insuring this kind of risk. A fully insured or partially insured plan is often the best course. The following are among the considerations for employers:

- *Size of the employee group.* The high predictability of experience in a large group is important in evaluating the risk of any self-insured or partially self-insured plan.
- *Structure of the plan.* Employers should look to structure a plan that makes their exposure predictable, for example, in LTD, self-insuring only the first two years of a claim.
- *Stop-loss insurance.* Stop-loss insurance is a sound option for employers that need special design components. For example, stop-loss insurance can be applied to one or a small number of highly paid employees with very high maximum benefits.

Limiting Exposure

No employer should self-insure any part of its LTD risk without carefully evaluating and limiting its maximum benefit exposure on any given individual. The impact of accounting standards on self-funded plans also must be assessed. In 1993, new accounting standards (*Financial Accounting Standard No. 112*) required employers to switch from a pay-as-you-go accounting to an accrual method for liabilities associated with self-funded disability benefits, COBRA plans, life insurance, severance pay, salary continuation plans, and workers' compensation.

Other changes also have given employer's more incentive to seek out greater claims-management expertise. Disability is becoming more complex. New causes of disability, social trends, and the evolution of health care delivery are affecting the success of claims management. LTD insurance carriers have the most developed expertise in claims management and are more aware of changes in the medical, social, and economic environment.

Employers face less risk in self-insuring STD, and most employers do self-insure sick leave. However, these also are areas of potential savings for employers that partner with insurance carriers. STD and sickness benefits have become recognized as high payback targets for disability management programs and can produce cost savings.

The claims-management expertise of insurers should be allocated to those disability risks where recovery or rehabilitation have a direct impact on the insurer's profit levels. It is distinctly in the insurer's best interest to fully manage any front-end self-insured portion of these risks. Recoveries within this window create the insurer's desired experience results for the catastrophic insured portion of the claim duration; that is, claim payments in excess of that two-year limit are the liability of the insurer. The insurer's full expertise and resources, including rehabilitation resources, should come to bear as early as feasible and within any self-funded period.

Related plan design issues also are important to weigh in the insure-versus-self-insure evaluation. Insurance carriers with a specialty in disability understand issues of eligibility and nondiscrimination, among other considerations. This expertise often is not available from other sources or is costly to create within the employer's organization.

Disability Management

Disability management is an important consideration in disability benefits plan design. Disability management encompasses the range of activities that prevent disabilities from occurring or minimize the impact of disabilities on employers and employees. These initiatives can include wellness programs, employee assistance plans, medical clinics focused on minimizing disability, employee safety programs, claims management activities, and return-to-work programs.

The direct costs of disability were 6.3 percent of payroll in 1999.[11] These included payments or premiums for workers' compensation, sick pay, STD, and LTD. According to Watson Wyatt Worldwide's annual survey of employers, the highest direct cost item was workers' compensation at 2.5 percent of payroll; the lowest was LTD at 0.6 percent of payroll. The disability cost area where employers see some of the greatest impact and opportunities for better management is indirect costs. These include items such as overtime costs and replacement workers needed when an employee is out on disability, or workstation accommodations. The Watson Wyatt Worldwide survey found that these items totaled 8 percent of payroll in 1999 and were growing more rapidly than direct costs.

Employers are finding that effective disability management programs reduce total cost. Among the most effective interventions, accord-

---

11 "Stay at Work, Fourth Annual Survey Report," *Watson Wyatt Worldwide*, 1999, p.3.

ing to employers, are return-to-work programs, prevention and behavioral health programs, and case management.[12]

The best disability management programs begin before a disability occurs. The foundation is a comprehensive, well-integrated disability plan design. In addition, a cost analysis specific to each business is useful to reveal the areas with the most potential savings. The ability of the insurance carrier to help the employer analyze and understand cost impact across the full range of benefits and programs that touch on disability has become increasingly important. The best plan designs integrate information across this spectrum to help improve outcomes. Once a claim does occur, early intervention, rehabilitation, case management resources and long-term follow-through are critical. Specialized knowledge of the impairment from both a medical and vocational perspective is highly valuable in managing complex claims.

Given the high cost and complexity of disability today, quality disability management efforts have taken on greater importance. Employers with well-coordinated disability management programs can save up to 1 percent or more of payroll.

SUMMARY

A significant likelihood of disability exists for the working population, and the loss of income has a devastating impact. A number of public income sources are provided for the disabled, but these programs do not cover all employees or all types of disabilities. As a result, private-sector insurance coverage is needed on both a short-term and long-term basis to provide adequate and reliable protection. Such private programs usually integrate with the public programs before remitting the additional income support to the covered individual.

Self-insurance of the long-term disability exposure is not a normal solution for employers because of the catastrophic and volatile nature of the coverage. The lowest costs are achieved through appropriate plan design that includes disability management programs.

---

12 "Stay at Work, Fourth Annual Survey Report," Watson Wyatt Worldwide, 1999, p. 3.

Life Insurance Benefits

Most employers, large and small, provide some form of life insurance benefit for their employees. Life insurance benefit plans must be designed in terms of employer and employee objectives.

Part Three begins with a discussion in Chapter 15 of some of the most important considerations involved in the design of a life insurance benefit plan and an overview of the most popular method of providing life insurance benefits—group term life insurance. Included in Chapter 15 are permanent forms of group life insurance and their uses in employee benefit planning. This is followed with a discussion in Chapter 16 of other life insurance programs, including group universal life programs and corporate owned life insurance, which are forms of life insurance benefit plans that provide substantial flexibility for meeting certain employer and employee objectives.

Group Life Insurance: Term and Permanent

William H. Rabel

Jerry S. Rosenbloom

INTRODUCTION

Death benefits are a nearly universal employee benefit in the United States. Almost all employers, regardless of size, provide death benefits for their employees as an integral part of their employee benefit programs, and they also are made available through public-sector programs such as Social Security and workers' compensation. Some of the forms of death benefits provided through the employee benefit mechanism include the following:[1]

Group term life insurance.

Group paid-up life insurance.

Group permanent life insurance.

Group universal life insurance.

Group survivor income benefit insurance.

Group dependent life insurance.

Group accidental death and dismemberment (AD&D) insurance.

Group travel accident insurance.

Joint and survivor annuity benefits under retirement plans.

Preretirement annuity benefits.

Supplemental/optional life insurance.

---

1 See Jerry S. Rosenbloom and G. Victor Hallman, *Employee Benefit Planning*, 3rd ed. (Englewood Cliffs, N.J.: Prentice Hall, 1991), pp. 32–33.

The emphasis in this chapter is on group term life insurance—the most common means of providing death benefits as an employee benefit. This chapter and Chapter 16 review some of the permanent forms of group life insurance. Other chapters in the *Handbook* cover the forms of death benefits specific to their topic areas.

Traditionally, group life insurance has covered employees against death during their working years. The protection usually provided is one-year renewable group term life insurance with no cash surrender value or paid-up insurance benefits. However, a relatively small amount of permanent group life insurance is in force. Furthermore, with the growth of retirement plans, other forms of death benefits, such as arrangements for the payment of a lifetime pension to the spouse of a career employee who dies before retirement, have developed.

In some cases, life insurance also is provided for dependents of employees, typically in such small amounts as $1,000 or $2,000, and some employee benefit plans may continue a reduced amount of death benefits on retired employees.

Survivor income benefit insurance (SIBI) plans also have become a part of employee benefit programs in recent years. These plans differ from traditional employer-sponsored death benefit plans in that a benefit is payable only to certain specified surviving dependents of the employee and only in installments. Additionally, mandated survivor benefits to spouses are available under certain conditions under the Employee Retirement Income Security Act of 1974 (ERISA). The Retirement Equity Act of 1984 (REA) also provides for a preretirement survivor annuity under pension plans for surviving spouses of vested employees who die in active service and who were not yet eligible for early retirement.

GROUP MECHANISM

While it is beyond the scope of this chapter to discuss fully the intricacies of the group mechanism, it is helpful to develop some basics to understand when the mechanism can be used. Five essential features of group insurance should be understood.

First, unlike individual insurance in which the risk associated with each life is appraised, group insurance makes use of group selection. In other words, an entire group is insured without medical examination or other evidence of individual insurability. For many years, state regulation and prudent practice have mandated stringent underwriting rules concerning such things as the minimum number of individuals in a group and the minimum proportion to be insured. However, in recent years, these rules have been relaxed somewhat as a result of competitive pressure and decades of experience with the group underwriting process.

A second feature of group insurance is that premiums on a plan usually are subject to experience rating. The larger the group, the greater the degree to which its cost of insurance reflects its own loss experience. Experience rating can either be on a prospective or retrospective basis. Normally, if experience has been favorable, an experience credit (sometimes called a *dividend*) may be paid at the end of the year to adjust the renewal premium for the next year (prospective basis), or credits may be applied to the current year's original premium (retrospective basis).

A third feature of the group mechanism calls for economies of administration. The plan is administered by an employer, a union, or some other agency positioned to obtain administrative efficiencies through payroll deductions or other centralized functions, or both.

Group insurance makes use of a fourth feature—a master contract—containing all conditions concerning the coverage. Insured individuals receive a group certificate as proof that they are covered, which shows the coverages provided and the amounts of those coverages. Often insureds receive a booklet (a summary plan description [SPD]) describing the plan in easy-to-read language.

The existence of a master contract indicates a fifth feature: that the plan may last long beyond the lifetime (or participation in the group) of any one individual.

GROUP TERM LIFE INSURANCE

The importance of group term life insurance in employee benefit plans is shown by data in Table 15–1. This table reveals that, at the end of 1998, group life insurance in force in the United States totaled $5,735.3 billion. While the amount of group life insurance in force continued to increase during the 1990s, the number of group certificates has not increased significantly since 1989 (not shown). Group coverage has remained fairly constant as a percentage of life insurance sold during this decade. Taken together, these figures suggest that the market has reached maturity. However, recent growth in sales suggest that a comeback may be in the offing.

Table 15–2 shows that while only 56.8 percent of group life insurance certificates in force at year-end 1993 covered members of employer-employee groups, they accounted for 88.7 percent of the total amount of group life insurance in force. More recent data are not available, but anecdotal evidence suggests that employer-employee groups remain the dominant type, as they have been since the inception of group coverage.

TABLE 15-1

Group Life Insurance in Force and Purchased in the United States (selected years: 1940–1998)

Years	In Force					Purchased		
	Number of Master Policies	Number of Certificates	Average Amount per Certificate	Group in Force (millions)	Percent of Total Insurance in Force	Number of Certificates	Amount (millions)	Percent of Total Insurance Purchases
1940	23,000	8,800,000	1,700	$ 14,938	12.9%	285,000	691	6.4%
1950	56,000	19,288,000	2,480	47,793	20.4	2,631,000	6,068	21.1
1960	169,000	43,602,000	4,030	175,903	30.0	3,731,000	14,615	19.7
1965	234,000	60,930,000	5,060	308,078	34.2	7,007,000	23,585	20.6
1970	304,000	79,844,000	6,910	551,357	39.3	5,219,000	46,590	26.5
1975	378,000	96,693,000	9,360	904,695	42.3	8,146,000	93,490	32.4
1980	586,000	117,762,000	13,410	1,579,355	44.6	11,373,000	183,432	31.2
1985	642,000	129,904,000	19,720	2,561,595	42.3	16,243,000	319,503	26.0
1990	707,000	140,966,000	26,627	3,753,506	40.0	14,592,000	459,271	30.0
1995	N/A	147,000,000	31,326	4,604,856	39.4	19,404,000	537,828	34.1
1996	N/A	139,000,000	36,459	5,067,804	39.9	18,761,000	614,565	36.1
1997	N/A	142,000,000	37,176	5,279,042	39.5	19,973,000	688,589	36.4
1998	N/A	152,000,000	37,732	5,735,273	39.8	20,332,000	739,508	35.8

Note: Data includes group credit life insurance on loans of more than 10 years' duration; totals include all life insurance (net of reinsurance) on residents of the United States, whether issued by U.S. or foreign companies.

Source: American Council of Life Insurance.

T A B L E   15–2

Group Life Insurance in Force by Type and by Size of Insured Group in the United States 1993

	Insurance in Force		
	Percent of Master Units	**Percent of Total Members**	**Percent of Amount in Force**
Type of Group			
Related to employment or occupation:			
Employer-employee	66.1%	56.8%	88.7%
Union and joint employer-union	0.1	0.4	0.2
Multiple employer trusts	26.9	1.8	1.9
Professional society	0.4	1.1	3.2
Employee association	0.2	0.9	2.1
Other—related to employee benefit program		0.1	0.1
Other—not related to employee benefit program			
Total	93.7	61.1	96.2
Not related to employment or occupation:			
Fraternal society		0.1%	0.1%
Savings or investment group	3.5%	35.4	0.9
Credit card holders	0.1	0.8	0.3
Mortgage insurance	1.8	1.5	1.7
Other	0.9	1.1	0.8
Total	6.3	38.9	3.8
Total all groups	100.0%	100.0%	100.0
Size of Group			
Fewer than 10 members	N/A	2.5%	1.4%
10–24 members	N/A	2.8	1.8
25–99 members	N/A	8.9	6.9
100–499 members	N/A	11.1	10.1
500 or more members	N/A	74.7	79.8
Total all groups		100.0%	100.0%

Note: Data exclude dependent coverage, Federal Employees Group Life Insurance, and Servicemen's Group Life Insurance. Group credit life insurance on loans of over 10 years' duration is included.
* Less than 0.05%. N.A. means not available.

Source: American Council of Life Insurance.

Benefits

Group term life insurance benefit amounts should be based on a plan designed to avoid or minimize possible adverse selection either by the employees or the employer. Factors to consider in the selection of a benefit schedule include (1) the employees' needs, (2) the overall cost of the plan, (3) the nondiscrimination requirements of the law, and (4) the employees' ability to pay if the plan is contributory. The interrelationship of these factors has resulted in the development of group term life insurance benefit schedules related to earnings, occupation or position, or a flat benefit amount for everyone covered. Benefit schedules that are a combination of these types of benefits schedules also have been used in the past, but today the practice is somewhat rare.[2]

The most common benefit schedule bases the amount of insurance on the employee's earnings. An illustration of such a schedule is seen in Table 15–3. It is worth noting that schedules often provide up to $100,000 or more, depending on the salary structure of the firm.

Such a schedule would not discriminate in favor of key employees (including executives), thus making the plan eligible for favorable tax treatment if other conditions are met. The tax treatment and nondiscrimination requirements for group life insurance are discussed later in this chapter.

Financing

Any employee benefit program, including group term life insurance, may be financed on either a *noncontributory basis* (where the *employer pays the total amount for the insurance*) or a *contributory basis* (where *the employees share the cost with the employer*). A number of advantages are claimed for each approach. The following advantages are claimed for noncontributory plans.[3]

All Employees Insured   All eligible employees who have completed the probationary period and are actively at work have coverage. Thus, the plan has maximum participation and minimizes adverse selection.

Tax Advantages   Under conditions described later in this chapter, employer premium costs are deductible as an ordinary business

---

2 See Davis W. Gregg, "Fundamental Characteristics of Group Insurance," in *Life and Health Insurance Handbook*, 3rd ed., eds. Davis W. Gregg and Vane B. Lucas (Burr Ridge, Ill.: Richard D. Irwin, 1973), pp. 357–58.

3 Gregg, pp. 358–60.

T A B L E   15–3

Sample Schedule Basing Benefits on Amount of Employee Earnings

Monthly Earnings	Group Term Life Insurance
Less than $1,500	$25,000
More than $1,500 but less than $2,000	30,000
More than $2,000 but less than $2,500	35,000
More than $2,500 but less than $3,000	40,000
More than $4,500 but less than $5,000	65,000
More than $5,000	70,000

expense for federal income tax purposes, whereas employee contributions under a contributory plan are not unless under an Internal Revenue Code (IRC) Section 125 flexible benefit plan up to a maximum of $50,000 of life insurance.

Simplicity of Administration Records for individual employees are easier to maintain than under contributory plans primarily because no payroll-deduction procedures are involved.

Economy of Installation Because all employees are covered, it is not necessary to solicit plan membership among individual employees.

Greater Control of Plan The employer may have more control over changes in benefits under noncontributory plans because, in the absence of collective bargaining, unilateral action may be more feasible when employees are not sharing in the cost of the plan.

The following advantages are claimed for the *contributory plans*:[4]

Larger Benefits Possibly more liberal benefits are possible if employees also contribute.

Better Use of Employer's Contributions A contributory plan, provided enough individuals participate to meet the nondiscrimination requirements, may permit the employer to direct group term life insurance funds to the employees with the greatest needs. Employees who elect not to contribute, and hence who are not covered, tend to be

---

4 Gregg, pp. 358–60.

young single individuals who may have few life insurance needs and among whom employee turnover also may be high. In such a case, a contributory plan allows employer funds to be used most effectively by sharing the cost of benefits for the employees who have greater needs for life insurance and who also are most likely to be long-service employees.

Employees May Have More Control The contributory plan may afford employees a greater voice in the benefits, because they are paying part of the cost.

Greater Employee Interest Employees may have a greater interest in plans in which they are making a contribution.

Important Group Term Life Insurance Provisions[5]

Beneficiary Designation

Under group term life insurance, an employee may name and change his or her beneficiary as desired. The only restriction is that the insurance must benefit someone other than the employer. If, at the death of the employee, no beneficiary is named, or if a beneficiary is named but does not survive the employee, the proceeds may be payable at the insurer's option to any one or more of the following surviving relatives of the employee: wife, husband, mother, father, child or children, or the executor or administrator of the estate of the deceased employee. If any beneficiary is a minor or otherwise incapable of giving a valid release, the insurer is able to pay the proceeds under a "facility of payment" clause, subject to certain limits.

Settlement Options

The covered employee or the beneficiary may elect to receive the face amount of the group term life insurance on an installment basis, rather than in a lump sum. The installments are paid according to tables listed in the group master policy. An insurer generally offers optional modes of settlement based on life contingencies. But the basis is seldom mentioned or guaranteed in the contract and is governed by insurance company practices at the time of death.[6]

---

5 See William G. Williams, "Group Life Insurance," in *Life and Health Insurance Handbook*, 3rd
    ed., eds. Davis W. Gregg and Vane B. Lucas (Burr Ridge, Ill.: Richard D. Irwin, 1973), pp.
    373–77.
6 Ibid., p. 376.

Assignment

Group term life insurance generally may be assigned if the master policy and state law both permit. Assignment of group term life insurance is important as a means for an employee to remove the group life insurance proceeds from his or her gross estate for federal estate-tax purposes by absolutely assigning all incidents of ownership in the group term life insurance to another person or to an irrevocable trust. In the past, this was an important estate-planning technique for some employees whose estates potentially were subject to federal estate taxation. However, because the Economic Recovery Tax Act of 1981 (ERTA) allows an unlimited estate-tax marital deduction, the attractiveness of assigning proceeds has decreased.

Conversion Privilege

If an employee's life insurance ceases because of termination of employment, termination of membership in a classification(s) eligible for coverage, or retirement, he or she may convert the group term insurance to an individual permanent life insurance policy. The employee must apply to the insurer in writing within 30 days of termination and pay the premium for his or her attained age, the type of insurance, and the class or risk involved; however, medical evidence of insurability is not necessary. Under the law, employers must notify employees of their conversion rights within 15 days after they take effect.

A more restricted conversion privilege may be provided for an employee if the group master policy is terminated or amended so as to terminate the insurance in force on the employee's particular classification. The employee may not convert more than $2,000 worth of coverage. The reason for such a limitation is to avoid the situation where an employer purchases group life insurance and quickly terminates the plan to allow individually uninsurable individuals to obtain, by conversion, large amounts of individual life coverage.

Thirty-One-Day Continuation of Protection

This provision gives a terminated employee an additional 31 days of protection while evaluating the conversion privilege or awaiting coverage under the group life insurance plan of a new employer.

Continuation of Insurance

The employer can elect to continue the employee's group term life insurance in force for a limited period, such as three months, on a basis that precludes adverse selection during temporary interruptions of continuous, active, full-time employment. Upon expiration of the continuation period, premium payments are discontinued, and the employee's insurance is terminated. However, in this event, the insurance, as well as the right to exercise the conversion privilege, is still extended for 31 days after termination of the insurance.

Waiver of Premium Provision

Because employees may become disabled, group life insurance policies generally contain a waiver-of-premium provision. Under a typical waiver-of-premium provision, the life insurance remains in force if (1) the employee is under a specified age, such as 60 or 65, at the date of commencement of total disability; (2) total disability commences while the person is covered; (3) total disability is continuous until the date of death; and (4) proof of total and continuous disability is presented at least once every 12 months.[7]

The waiver-of-premium provision is one of three types of disability benefit provisions used for group life plans. The second, the maturity value benefit, pays the face amount of the group term life insurance in a lump sum or monthly installments when an employee becomes totally and permanently disabled. A third type of disability provision, the extended death benefit, pays group life insurance death claims incurred within one year after termination of employment. It requires that the employee be continuously and totally disabled from the date of termination of employment until death occurs.

Accelerated Benefits

Some plans provide for the payment of all or part of the death benefit if a patient can prove that he or she has a terminal illness. These so-called accelerated benefits have become increasingly popular where permitted by law, and barriers to the practice have evaporated as third-party organizations have emerged to purchase the rights to life insurance benefits covering the terminally ill. Insurance regulators have reasoned that it is better to allow insureds, who may need funds to cover medical expenses or for other emergency purposes, to exercise a contractual right, rather than to be held hostage to the highest bidder in a limited market where the scientific assessment of risk is difficult and may be impossible.

Dependent Coverage

Dependent group life insurance may be offered either as part of the basic group term life insurance plan or as optional additional coverage. The

7 Williams, pp. 374–75.

growth of dependent group life insurance has been relatively slow, partly because of the taxation of amounts greater than $2,000. When provided, a typical schedule of benefits might give the dependent spouse life insurance equal to 50 percent of the employee's coverage but not more than $2,000. Typical benefits for dependent children often are graded from $100 between the child's age of 14 days to six months up to, for example, $1,000 or $1,500 between ages 5 and 19 years. Much larger amounts of coverage sometimes are offered under supplementary plans fully paid for by the employee.

The death benefit normally is payable automatically in one lump sum to the insured employee or, in the event of the prior death of the employee, either to the employee's estate or, at the option of the insurer, to one of certain specified classes of "order-of-preference" beneficiaries.

Coverage of Employees After Retirement[8]

Retired Employees

Upon retirement, a former employee's group term life insurance normally would be discontinued, and the high cost of conversion at the retiree's advanced age usually makes use of the conversion privilege impractical. Therefore, many employers continue to provide reduced amounts of group term life insurance on retired employees under various types of reduction formulas. One formula reduces the insurance by 50 percent at retirement. Another uses a graded percentage system decreasing the amount of coverage each year after retirement age until a certain minimum benefit is reached; for example, 10 percent per year until 50 percent of the amount in force immediately prior to retirement is attained. Still other employers provide a flat dollar amount, such as $15,000 or $20,000, at retirement. Taxation of the post-retirement benefits is the same as for active employees. Because continuing group life insurance on retired lives is costly, employers may consider funding coverage for retired employees through some other means such as group paid-up, group ordinary, or a separate "side fund" to pay the premiums at retirement.

Active Employees

Coverage requirements for active employees after age 40 are strongly influenced by the Age Discrimination in Employment Act of 1967 (ADEA), as amended in 1978 and then by HR–4154, which became effective on January 1, 1987. This latest amendment to ADEA eliminated

---

8 See Rosenbloom and Hallman, *Employee Benefit Planning*, pp. 48–49.

the age-70 ceiling on active employment. Essentially, employees aged 40 and above are considered the protected group. Plans may be "cut back," but individual plans must be actuarially analyzed to determine cost-justified reductions.

The U.S. Supreme Court in *Public Employees Retirement System of Ohio* v. *Betts* created some ambiguity when it ruled that age-based distinctions in employee benefits are not prohibited by ADEA if they are not intended to discriminate. However, the Older Workers Benefit Protection Act amended ADEA in 1990 and restored the "equal benefit of equal cost" requirements for age-based differences in employee benefits.[9]

The guidelines allow cost-justified reductions that permit an employer to (1) reduce an employee's life insurance coverage each year starting at age 65 by 8 percent to 9 percent of the declining balance of the life insurance benefit, or (2) make a one-time reduction in life insurance benefits at age 65 of from 35 percent to 40 percent and maintain that reduced amount in force until retirement. The 8 percent to 9 percent annual reduction is justified by mortality statistics showing that, for example, the probability of death increases by that amount each year for the age-60-to-70 group. The one-time 35 percent to 40 percent reduction is justified by the difference in mortality expected, for example, by employees in the age-65 through age-69 bracket, compared with the mortality expected in the age-60 through age-64 bracket. An employer also may be able to cost justify greater reductions in group term life insurance benefits on the basis of its *own* demonstrably higher cost experience in providing group term life insurance to its employees over a representative period of years.

ADEA also permits use of a "benefit package" approach for making cost comparisons for certain benefits. This benefit package approach offers greater flexibility than a benefit-by-benefit analysis as long as the overall result is of no lesser cost to the employer and is no less favorable in terms of the overall benefits provided to employees.

Advantages and Disadvantages of Group Term Life Insurance

In summary, employers and employees are interested in evaluating the relative advantages and limitations of group term life insurance as an employee benefit.[10]

---

9 "A Special Report to Clients," Hewitt Associates, October 16, 1990.
10 See William G. Williams, *Group Life Insurance*, pp. 377–78.

Advantages to the Employer

From the employer's perspective the following might be considered advantages of including a well-designed group term life insurance program as one of its employee benefits:

- Employee morale and productivity may be enhanced by offering this element of financial security.
- The coverage is necessary for competitive reasons, since most employers offer this form of protection.
- The life insurance protection is an aid to attaining good public and employer-employee relations.

Advantages to Employees

Group term life insurance dovetails into an employee's financial security planning in the following ways:

- It adds a layer of low-cost protection to personal savings, individual life insurance, and Social Security benefits.
- It helps reduce anxieties about the consequences of the employee's possible premature death.
- If the plan does not favor key employees, the employer's contributions are not reportable as taxable income to the insured employee for federal income-tax purposes unless the total amount of group insurance from all sources exceeds $50,000; then the employee is only taxed on the value of amounts in excess of $50,000, as determined by a table in the Internal Revenue Code, less any contributions the employee made to the plan. However, if the plan discriminates in favor of key employees, the actual cost of all coverage (or the amount of its value as determined in the code, whichever is greater) will be taxable to the employee. In other words, the employee loses the $50,000 worth of tax-free life insurance, and may end up paying a higher rate on amounts in excess of $50,000. However, even if the plan is discriminatory, "rank-and-file" employees will not suffer adverse tax consequences. A group term life insurance plan may be considered to discriminate in favor of key employees unless (1) the plan benefits at least 70 percent of all employees; (2) at least 85 percent of the participants are not key employees; (3) the plan is part of a cafeteria type plan; or (4) the plan complies with a reasonable classification system found by the Internal Revenue Service (IRS) to be nondiscriminatory. In applying

these IRS rules, part-time and seasonal workers as well as those with fewer than three years of service do not have to be considered. Employees covered by a collective bargaining agreement by which group term life insurance has been bargained for also may be excluded. Special rules apply to groups of fewer than 10 employees.

- If employees are contributing toward the cost, their contributions are automatically withheld from their paychecks, making payment convenient and also reducing the possibility of lapse of insurance.
- The conversion privilege enables terminated employees to convert their group term life insurance to individual permanent policies without having to provide individual evidence of insurability.
- Liberal underwriting standards provide coverage for those who might be uninsurable or only able to get insurance at substandard rates.

Disadvantages

Despite its many advantages, group term life insurance has some disadvantages. First, the employee usually has no assurance the employer will continue the group policy in force from one year to the next. Group life insurance plans seldom are discontinued, but business failures can and do occur, and the conversion privilege upon termination of a group life policy may be of limited value to the employees because of the high cost of conversion on an attained-age basis.

Another limitation exists when employees change employers, because group term life insurance is not "portable." Only about one out of every 100 departing employees uses the conversion privilege. However, most employees changing jobs expect to be insured for the same or a higher amount of group life insurance with their new employers. Group term life insurance provides "protection only," while employee needs, at least partially, may dictate some other form of life insurance that has a savings or cash-value feature. Also, with salary-related plans, coverage may be lowest when it is most needed (e.g., for a young employee with dependents). The next section looks at some permanent forms of group life insurance.

PERMANENT FORMS OF GROUP LIFE INSURANCE

Given the expense of providing retired employees with group term life insurance, it is not surprising that permanent forms of group life have engendered some degree of interest over the years. After all, even though most retired workers do not have dependent children, many of them have dependents, most often spouses, and some have problems of estate liquidity. Furthermore, a lifetime of work may not be sufficient to provide the legacy hoped for by many retirees, and their financial goals are made particularly elusive by the high level of inflation that has plagued most countries since World War II. Therefore, the thought of obtaining permanent insurance through the relatively low-cost group mechanism has a certain amount of appeal.

Several forms of group permanent life insurance have been developed over the years, mostly in response to government policies that have provided favorable tax treatment to group term life insurance. Among those to be examined here are group paid-up insurance and various forms of continuous premium coverage, including level-premium group, supplemental group, and group ordinary life insurance. However, it is important to note that only a relatively insignificant amount of group permanent remains in effect, because of (1) potential adverse tax consequences, and (2) the advent of employee-pay-all supplemental policies that have many advantages of the group mechanism, such as payroll deduction.

GROUP PAID-UP LIFE INSURANCE

Group paid-up life insurance was first written in 1941. Although today it is largely superseded by other types of plans, it is nevertheless useful to understand how it works in order to understand the development and current status of tax laws on group insurance, which are a driving force in plan design.

Group paid-up life insurance allows all or part of an employee's scheduled group coverage to be so written that it will be fully paid up when the employee retires. During his or her working life, the employee makes a regular contribution that is used to purchase paid-up increments of whole life insurance. Each purchase increases the total amount of paid-up insurance owned. Figure 15–1 illustrates how units of paid-up insurance accumulate.

For tax reasons, discussed in the next section, employers do not purchase permanent insurance for their employees under this plan. Rather, they supplement the employees' purchases of permanent insurance with decreasing amounts of term insurance. After each contribution, the amount of term insurance decreases by exactly the amount by which the paid-up insurance increases. Thus, the combined amount of both types of insurance remains constant at the amount set by the benefits schedule. Figure 15–1 illustrates the combination of coverages in this product.

F I G U R E   15–1

Interrelationship between Increasing Increments of Paid-Up Group Life Insurance and Decreasing Increments of Group Term Life Insurance

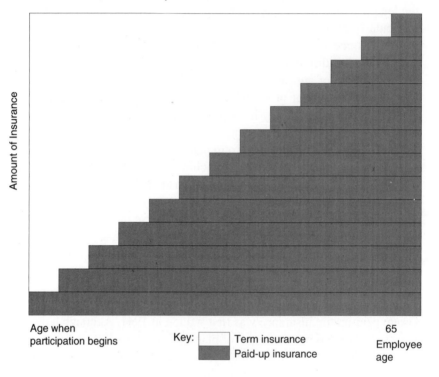

Contributions

Employee contributions generally are designed to be level throughout the employee's working life. Naturally, because of actuarial considerations, the amount purchased with each contribution decreases as the employee gets older. Furthermore, costs are higher for individuals who enter the plan at older ages, because they have fewer years in which to accumulate paid-up coverage. Therefore, in theory, a schedule of contributions should be graded for age of entry into the plan and anticipated length of service, and this is a common practice.

To provide certain minimum benefits for all employees and to encourage a high level of participation (particularly among older employees), some employers have set a single contribution rate for all employees. Table 15–4 illustrates the amounts of paid-up insurance that can be accumulated by workers at various ages with a monthly contribution of

T A B L E   15–4

Accumulated Amounts of Paid-Up Insurance Based on $1 Monthly Contribution

Entry Age	Number of Years in Plan				
	5	15	25	35	45
20	$229	$609	$905	$1,139	$1,329
30	178	474	708	899	—
40	139	373	563	—	—
50	110	301	—	—	—
60	91	—	—	—	—

Source: Robert W. Batten et al., *Group Life Insurance* (Atlanta, Ga.: Life Office Management Association, 1979), p. 111.

$1. When the flat contribution results in inadequate coverage for older employees, the employer may supplement the paid-up insurance by continuing the necessary amount of term insurance after the employee retires. Sometimes a flat contribution schedule is limited to those who have been with a firm for a minimum time when the coverage starts, while new employees pay according to an age-graded schedule. All such arrangements should be reviewed carefully to ensure that they do not run afoul of the nondiscrimination prohibitions in the tax laws.

Plan Provisions

As is normal for group insurance, benefits are determined by a schedule. In general, the provisions found in group term contracts apply to the term portion of the paid-up plan as well. These include conversion and disability (such as waiver-of-premium) benefits.

Coverage is not automatically surrendered if the master contract terminates. Paid-up coverage remains intact as long as employment is not terminated and for life unless it is surrendered. Term coverage is convertible under the same rules as under a group term plan.

Premium Rates and Experience Rating

Group term policy owners (usually an employer) normally receive a dividend or "experience credit" each year if plan experience has been favorable. As a result of revenue rulings beginning in 1971, the term account may not subsidize the permanent account, or vice versa. In other words, each account must stand on its own feet. Thus, favorable experience credits must be allocated to the account from which they originate, whether it is the term or the paid-up account. Favorable experience may be passed on to the paid-up account in the form of a dividend to insureds or as reduced rates for future purchases.

All normal or customary practices in experience rating are subject to change under the pressure of competition. When competition is intense, insurers may expand their tendency to pool the underwriting experience of different coverages or even different lines (e.g., group term and group permanent, or group life and group health). Pooling may lead to changes in the experience-rating practices.

Uses of Group Paid-Up Insurance

Group paid-up tends to appeal to firms with fewer than 500 employees. Furthermore, it generally is underwritten only for groups that display certain characteristics. As a first requirement, only those employers that provide stable employment can purchase group paid-up. Because strikes and layoffs interrupt employee contributions and therefore interfere with the accumulation of paid-up coverage, such events must be most unusual for the industry in which the policy owner operates. Furthermore, some carriers will not underwrite a case until the firm has been in business for a minimum period (e.g., three years).

Insurers also require that turnover be very low for the employer. To a degree, the turnover problem can be controlled by a long probationary period. However, the underwriting rules of some carriers exclude employers that have an annual turnover rate in excess of 5 percent. In addition, some establish minimum-age requirements for participation (e.g., age 30 to 35).

Advantages of Group Paid-Up
Life Insurance

Adherents of group paid-up life insurance claim it provides several advantages to employers or employees, or both. First and foremost, as contrasted with group term, it does provide permanent protection. Related to this is the advantage of cash-value accumulations by the insured that can be made available when employment terminates. Both these features are related to a third, which is that group paid-up provides a scientific way to fund post-retirement coverage over the working life of the employee.

Group paid-up plans facilitate the conversion by long-service employees of any term coverage remaining at age 65, because it usually is a relatively small proportion of the scheduled amount and because converted coverage is purchased at net rates. For these two reasons, retirees may end up being able to afford even more permanent coverage than they had anticipated.

A sixth advantage to group paid-up is that employers electing to continue all or part of the coverage on retirees find the scheduled amount of term reduced well below the amount needed in the absence of paid-up insurance. This smaller financial burden may be easier for a business to justify.

A seventh advantage, when group paid-up is compared with other forms of permanent group coverage (discussed later), is that the status of these plans is well established with the Internal Revenue Service. They are a known commodity, and no serious modification of existing plans has been required by tax rulings to date. Therefore, it is highly unlikely that they will be subject to unfavorable rulings in the future. Another important tax factor is that the employer-purchased term coverage receives the favorable tax treatment accorded to all group term coverage.[11]

The group paid-up system provides still other advantages. Being contributory, the plan encourages participation only by those who need insurance. At the same time, in contrast to group term plans, employees may be more willing to contribute to the cost of group paid-up because they can see a permanent benefit growing out of their premiums.[12]

It is worth noting that insurers may be willing to offer higher limits on group plans containing permanent coverage than on term alone. The amount at risk for each individual continually diminishes throughout his or her working life. Furthermore, margins in interest earnings on reserves may support a more liberal benefit schedule.

Disadvantages of Group Paid-Up Life Insurance

Among the greatest disadvantages of group paid-up insurance is that the type of employer that can use it is limited, as explained previously. Another drawback is the relatively high cost of administering the plan, when compared with term insurance, because more professional advice is

---

11 See William H. Rabel and Charles E. Hughes, "Taxation of Group Life Insurance," *Journal of Accounting, Auditing, and Finance* 1, No. 2, p. 177, for a thorough discussion of this topic.

12 For a discussion of the advantages of contributory group life plans, see Robert Batten et al., *Group Life and Health Insurance* (Atlanta, Ga.: Life Office Management Association, 1979), p. 42.

needed in designing, installing, and operating it. Furthermore, changes in benefits, eligibility status, and the like often require more record changes than would be required for term. A third disadvantage is that employer costs are higher in the early years of the plan than they would be for group term. Thus, the employer may delay the plan until it can be afforded. The high cost in the early years is caused by start-up costs. In some cases, the employer may decide not to purchase a term plan to provide temporary protection, with the result that there is no protection at all.

Finally, the principal advantage of group paid-up is also its principal weakness. Employee contributions purchase permanent coverage, and, therefore, afford less current protection for each premium dollar.

LEVEL-PREMIUM GROUP PERMANENT LIFE INSURANCE

In exploring various approaches to providing post-retirement coverage through the group mechanism, it was only a matter of time before someone suggested taking standard, level-premium, whole life insurance and writing it on a group basis. The idea was to have the employer pay all or part of the premium and to have the employee pay any amount not paid by the employer. However, before this approach could develop much of a following, the Treasury Department quashed it for all practical purposes in a 1950 tax ruling (Mimeograph 6477). The ruling required employees to include as current taxable income any employer contribution toward the cost of permanent insurance, unless the insurance is nonvested and forfeitable in the case employment is terminated. As a result of this ruling, the use of traditional level-premium group life insurance has been limited principally to supplemental group life plans. A prominent form of supplement life, group universal (sometimes called GULP) is discussed in Chapter 16.

GROUP ORDINARY LIFE INSURANCE

In the mid-1960s, a new type of permanent coverage was introduced; it purported to allow employers to contribute to permanent policies because of some newly introduced standards in the tax law. Over the years these products have varied widely in design, but are known collectively as "group ordinary" or "Section 79" plans.

In concept, group ordinary allows employees to elect to take all or a part of their term insurance as permanent coverage. In effect, the contract is divided into protection and savings elements. Employer contributions are used to pay only for the term insurance component of the permanent contract, while employee contributions are credited to cash values. The plan can be limited-payment (e.g., life paid up at 65) or ordinary whole life. Had plans been limited to this simple design, the taxation of group life insurance would be less complex than it is today.

However, inherent in the group ordinary concept is the fact that premium contributions will vary from year to year, as the amount at risk under the policy and the insured group's death rate vary. This variability of premium limited the attractiveness of the product, and companies began to seek ways of smoothing or leveling the premium. Of course, such designs fly in the face of the tax rules providing that payments can be used to purchase term insurance only; premium leveling by its very nature creates a reserve. Furthermore, the IRS suspected that some products were so designed that employers were paying more than their fair share of expenses under the contract. (This practice had been common under group paid-up, and was never brought into question until the IRS began to scrutinize group ordinary.) As a result, during the 1960s and 1970s a tug of war developed in which the IRS would write regulations and carriers would try to design plans that would comply while still being attractive in the marketplace. The final result is that today all group permanent insurance issued must meet stringent, complex rules that ensure that (1) employer contributions are not used to purchase permanent insurance and (2) employee-owned benefits are self-supporting. A few group ordinary plans remain in force under these circumstances, but the coverage is not widely marketed.

FUTURE OF PERMANENT GROUP LIFE INSURANCE

In 1974, permanent forms of group insurance constituted eight-tenths of one percent of the total amount of group insurance outstanding, and they constituted a similar percentage as late as 1993. Subsequent to that time, statisticians have ceased to differentiate between "true" group permanent, carve-out plans, and employee-pay-all supplemental plans, that offer permanent life insurance. Now, for statistical purposes, group permanent also includes any form of "noncontributory" coverage under which individual insurance is issued through the efficiencies of the group mechanism (sometimes including some form of group underwriting). Table 15–5 illustrates the importance of "group permanent," when the more liberal definition is applied. Whereas group term constituted more than 99

T A B L E   15–5

Group Life Insurance In Force in the United States, 1998

	Certificates (thousands)	Percent (%)	Face Amount (millions)	Percent (%)
Permanent insurance				
Traditional whole life*	7,962	5.2	$258,417	4.5
Universal life	9,859	6.5	454,851	7.9
Variable-universal life	83	0.1	98,174	1.7
Total permanent insurance	17,904	11.8	811,443	14.1
Term insurance	134,190	88.2	4,923,830	85.9
Total group	152,094	100.0	5,735,273	100.0

* Includes paid-up and level premium and other whole life.

Source: American Council of Life Insurance *Fact Book 1999*, Washington, D.C., p. 8.

percent of the group in force under the old set of definitions, it now constitutes only about 88 percent of the policies in force and 86 percent of the face value.

Briefly described, the other forms of life insurance mentioned in the table are as follows. Group whole life has a fixed premium with fixed death benefit and cash values. Group variable-universal life combines the flexible premium features of group universal life (see below) with a variable death benefit and cash values.

The group insurance business is a dynamic, ever-changing arena. Large purchasers are highly sophisticated and are constantly seeking better products and services for their money. By the same token, carriers compete fiercely for the business and are always innovative in their products and administrative procedures. As time passes, the distinctions among various product lines will continue to blur, and already scholars and practitioners have begun to develop an entirely new taxonomy for describing the group life insurance business.

RETIRED-LIVES RESERVE

Another approach used to fund life insurance benefits for retired employees is a retired-lives reserve plan. A retired-lives reserve arrangement can be set up as a separate account through a life insurance company or through a trust arrangement for providing group term life insurance for retired employees. Such an approach provides for the funding of retiree life insurance over the employees' active employment period.

Retired-lives reserve plans were once a popular mechanism for providing life insurance for retired employees, because of very favorable tax implications for the employer. Restrictions imposed by the Deficit Reduction Act of 1984 (DEFRA) have limited the previous favorable tax aspects of retired-lives reserve plans for both employers and employees, and such plans have decreased in importance.

ACCIDENTAL DEATH AND DISMEMBERMENT (AD&D) INSURANCE

In addition to providing group term life insurance or some form of group insurance with cash values, employers typically also provide accidental death and dismemberment insurance. The AD&D benefit usually is some multiple of the amount of group term life insurance provided the employee under the plan's benefit formula. AD&D insurance is payable only if the employee's death is a result of accident. Percentages of the AD&D coverage amount are payable in the event of certain dismemberments enumerated in the contract or employee booklet.

SUPPLEMENTAL GROUP LIFE INSURANCE

In the past few years, interest has been kindled in an employee-pay-all approach to providing permanent insurance, which has some features of both group and individual insurance. Sometimes called supplemental insurance, it may be provided under a master policy with a certificate being issued to each employee. Alternatively, sometimes individual policies are issued when the coverage is written. Premiums are paid through payroll deduction and do not receive favored tax treatment. Depending on competitive factors and amounts available, coverage may be purchased with minimal individual underwriting. Since the employee owns the coverage, it goes with him or her if employment is terminated.

Supplemental group life insurance appears to be giving way to "mass-marketed" or "wholesale" life insurance. This approach involves the issue of individual insurance through the endorsement (and sometimes the administrative support) of a third party. Over $45 billion of mass-marketed insurance is now in force, including almost $9 billion that has been issued through employers. It seems likely that much of this coverage would have been sold as supplemental group if the mass-marketed coverage were not available.

GROUP CARVE-OUT PLANS

While supplemental coverage may be purchased above and beyond group term benefits, another approach provides that all or part of a group term benefit may be "carved out" and permanent insurance substituted. Typically, amounts in excess of $50,000 are carved out. While premiums are paid with dollars that are taxable to the employee, the actual cost for the employee typically may be favorable when contrasted with imputed income (based on government tables) for term insurance of an amount equal to the carve out. Thus, an overall advantage is created for the employee. Various forms of permanent coverage are used, depending on employee objectives.

GROUP UNIVERSAL

Interest in supplemental protection was substantially increased through the addition of *group universal life* (GULP) in the mid-1980s. GULP is a permanent form of insurance that (like individual universal life) has two separate parts: (1) pure term protection, and (2) an accumulation fund. The employee contributes periodically to the fund, which is credited with interest at a competitive rate. Each month the carrier deducts the cost of pure term protection for the amount at risk under the policy and the cost of administering the policy. The insured may elect to increase the face amount of the policy, provided that certain requirements are met. Like other insurance products, reserves accumulate on a tax-deferred basis and are tax-free if paid as a death benefit. Since GULP is becoming such an important form of benefit for many employees, Chapter 16 covers this subject in detail.

Other Life Insurance Programs*

GROUP UNIVERSAL LIFE INSURANCE PROGRAMS

To understand group universal life insurance programs (GULP), it is helpful to begin with a look at its direct forebear—individual policy universal life (UL). This form of permanent life insurance is a major product line for almost all life insurers.

The hallmark of UL is flexibility. Among its distinguishing characteristics are the following:

- Policyholders decide on the amount and timing of premium payments. They can, for example, fund the policy up front with a single premium and make additional payments at irregular intervals and in irregular amounts. They also can arrange premium "holidays" for any payments scheduled at a specific time.

- Premiums—minus mortality charges and expenses—create policy cash values that are credited with interest, typically at current

---

* This chapter is based on Chapters 16 and 17 of the fourth edition of the *Handbook of Employee Benefits*, both written by the late Everett T. Allen, Jr. Chapter 16, Group Universal Life Programs, had been reprinted with the permission of Towers Perrin. Chapter 17, Corporate-Owned Life insurance, had appeared originally in *The Handbook of Executive Benefits*, Towers Perrin (Burr Ridge, IL: Irwin Professional Publishing, 1995).

The Group Universal Life Insurance Programs (GULP) section has been reviewed for the fifth edition by Burton T. Beam, Jr. and Ed Graves.

The editor acknowledges the significant contribution of G. Victor Hallman III in updating for the fifth edition, the Corporate-Owned Life Insurance (COLI) and the Split-Dollar Insurance sections of this chapter.

rates for new investments with some applicable guaranteed floor amount (e.g., 3 percent). This interest accumulates tax-free (as it does with most forms of permanent life insurance) and can totally escape income taxes if ultimately paid out as a death benefit.

■ Policyholders can usually choose between a *level death benefit* (i.e., the policy's cash value plus whatever amount of term insurance is required to provide the level benefit selected) and an *increasing death benefit* (i.e., a level amount of term insurance plus the policy's cash value). They also may be able to increase their amount of term insurance—subject to some controls to prevent adverse selection.

■ Policyholders can withdraw or borrow against cash values or use the money to purchase paid-up life insurance. If they do not pay future term premiums, both mortality charges and administrative expenses (including premium taxes) are withdrawn from the cash values. If cash values are used up for any reason, leaving nothing to cover term premiums due, the policy is terminated.

In essence, UL offers individuals the chance to "buy term and invest the difference." GULP provides the same opportunity, but with a key difference: Coverage is available on a group basis in a form similar to the coverage available under an employee benefit plan. Thus, GULP can be written as a supplement to, or replacement for, an existing group term life insurance plan. In addition, GULP may well have other important applications for employers. These include:

■ Funding ERISA-excess and top-hat plans (both defined benefit and defined contribution).

■ Replacing coverage lost under discriminatory post-retirement life insurance plans.

GULP CHARACTERISTICS

Although GULP works much the same way that individual UL does, there are some differences:

■ Because GULP is underwritten on a group basis, mortality charges may or may not be based on the underlying experience of the group. In addition, coverage amounts are guaranteed up to some limit without evidence of insurability. These limits vary from plan to plan, depending on plan provisions, the size of the participating group, and the insurer's underwriting standards.

■ Rates are set on a prospective basis (although the experience of the group may be used for this purpose) and the contracts are generally *nonparticipating* (i.e., dividends or experience-rating credits are not generated by favorable experience).

■ Group underwriting requirements are used to avoid adverse selection and may limit GULP's flexibility to some extent. Actively-at-work requirements, for example, generally apply, and some formula is used to determine amounts of coverage available (e.g., one or two times pay). Health statements or other proof of insurability also may be required in some situations— for example, if participation falls below some predetermined level. In addition, while an individual UL policyholder may be able to choose between a level or increasing death benefit, a GULP purchaser may be limited to one of these choices. But despite such constraints, overall plan design remains significantly more flexible than that available through a traditional supplemental group insurance contract.

■ GULP is not typically sold by insurance agents and is, therefore, available on a no-commission basis. (Individual UL policies, by contrast, are usually sold by agents who receive commissions for their sales and service efforts, even in cases where an employer permits "mass marketing" of such policies to employees.)

■ Charges for any administrative services provided by the carrier should be lower for GULP than for individual coverage.

Finally, note that GULP is written on an employee-pay-all basis. Introducing employer contributions could eliminate most of its advantages, particularly its exemption from compliance under Section 79 of the Internal Revenue Code (IRC or code) as an employee-pay-all plan.

SPECIFIC GULP FEATURES

Coverage Options

Under GULP, the purchase of term insurance can be separated from the savings or cash-value element. Thus, employees can buy only term insurance or whatever combination of term insurance and savings best meets both their death benefit and capital-accumulation objectives.

Employees select an amount of term insurance from the choices available—either a flat amount or a multiple of pay. In the latter case, the plan could provide for coverage to increase automatically in relation to pay. Although some plans limit coverage to employee life insurance, it is possible to include accidental death and dismemberment insurance, and dependent coverage for spouses and children. Typically, children are covered only for term insurance, but spouses may be able to accumulate cash values. It is also possible to add waiver-of-premium coverage (payable in the event of an employee's disability) to the term insurance.

Payment Arrangements

Employee contributions for both the cost of the term insurance and administrative expenses are automatically withheld from after-tax pay (pretax contributions are not available). Employees who wish to add a savings element authorize an additional amount to be deducted from pay as well. In theory, these latter contributions can be variable; but in practice, design and administrative considerations may limit employee choices. Even so, employees might be able to change their rate of savings, suspend savings contributions from time to time, or contribute lump-sum amounts (called "drop-ins"). In many respects, given these features, GULP more closely resembles a defined contribution plan than it does a traditional life insurance "product."

Insurance Rates

Premium rates for term insurance are negotiated and are usually based on the experience and characteristics of the participating group and can be quite attractive. (Table 16–1 illustrates the rates used for one existing plan.) Generally, the rates are guaranteed from one year, up to three or five years, with higher rates presumably applicable for coverage with extended guarantees.

While rates (even though guaranteed) can be designed to increase each year by age, linking rates to five-year age brackets is a common practice. Premiums are usually lower for nonsmokers than for smokers. Or nonsmokers might be given additional term insurance (e.g., 20 percent more) for the standard premium.

Cash Values

The interest credited to cash values varies, depending on current rates for new investments and insurer practices. Once a rate is declared, however, it may apply for a limited period, such as one year. A permanent guaran-

TABLE 16-1

Illustrative Term Insurance Rates (per $1,000)

Age	Monthly Rate
Under 30	$0.069
30–34	0.089
35–39	0.099
40–44	0.152
45–49	0.259
50–54	0.428
55–59	0.669
60–64	1.040

teed floor rate of interest is also set for purposes of state insurance and federal tax laws.

As noted earlier, participating employees may withdraw cash values at any time and for any reason, and may replace them later with supplemental contributions. Employees also may be able to borrow from the insurer, using their cash values as collateral security. The interest charged for such loans exceeds the rate being credited to cash values—possibly by 1.5 percent or 2.0 percent. In addition, a withdrawal or loan transaction may trigger a transaction charge (e.g., $10 or $20) against the cash value.

Benefit Portability

An attractive feature of GULP is that individual coverage may be portable when insured employees terminate employment or retire. Specifically, some insurers permit employees to continue coverage on a premium-paying basis—making payments directly to the insurance company—for the full duration of the mortality table (e.g., to age 100). In such a case, different mortality costs and expense charges may apply to continued coverage. Some insurers pool all nonactive insureds for this purpose, using a different rate basis that reflects the experience of the pool. It is also possible to distinguish between retirees and other terminations, allowing retirees to pay premiums based on the employer's plan, while assigning other terminations to the pool. In any event, if coverage is continued, it is important to clarify whether the subsequent experience of former employees will be charged back to the employer group and reflected in future premium levels.

As the above discussion illustrates, GULP is not a product. Rather, it is a highly flexible type of coverage that involves many of the design and financial issues applicable to other employee benefit plans. Some of these issues are:

- Selecting eligibility requirements.
- Establishing insurance schedules.
- Fixing contribution schedules.
- Obtaining competitive bids and negotiating contract provisions.

Clearly, given these considerations, the insurance "product" ultimately used is not "off the shelf," but rather is the result of a careful design and negotiation process. Moreover, an insurer's underwriting and administrative requirements can influence design or become a factor in carrier selection.

ADVANTAGES AND DISADVANTAGES OF GULP

GULP offers a number of advantages to employers. Specifically:

- A successfully implemented plan may relieve pressure on the employer to provide post-retirement life insurance coverage.
- GULP is a low-cost "benefit improvement," much like an unmatched 401(k) plan.
- GULP offers a way to move away from an existing subsidized flat-rate plan.
- Significant benefits are available for key employees.
- Because GULP is generally sold on a group basis, there is no need for individual insurance agents to solicit employees.
- If an employee continues coverage after termination of employment, the employer will not face conversion charges. (If subsequent experience is charged back to the employer as indicated above, a similar effect results albeit at a later date. If it isn't charged back, presumably the initial premium will be higher.)

GULP also offers many advantages to employees. Among them are the following:

- Employees can consolidate all coverages for themselves and their dependents under one contract.
- Upon termination of employment, the coverage may be portable.
- Premiums are flexible in amount and timing.

- Investment income is on a tax-deferred or tax-free basis.
- GULP appears to be a very low-cost way to purchase term or permanent life insurance.
- GULP is a convenient way to purchase insurance; premium payments are made on a payroll-deduction basis.
- Guaranteed issue amounts are available at levels sufficiently high to cover most employee needs.
- Cash values offer a source of funds for emergencies. This may be very attractive, because withdrawals from qualified defined-contribution plans are often limited and may be subject to excise taxes.
- Employees receive periodic reports and are kept up to date on the status of their life insurance program.
- Upon retirement, employees can use their cash value to purchase paid-up insurance.

The appeal and versatility of GULP notwithstanding, employers should be aware of certain potential disadvantages before adopting such a program for any reason. Among the major issues to consider are the following:

- Employees may view GULP as a more attractive savings vehicle than an employer-sponsored 401(k) plan. If that occurs and precipitates a drop in 401(k) participation, the 401(k) plan could have trouble meeting actual deferral percentage (ADP) tests for nondiscriminatory participation by higher-paid employees.
- GULP cannot be funded with before-tax employee contributions if it is to remain outside the scope of Section 79. Thus, it cannot be a direct part of a flexible benefit program.
- Although employers are not technically involved in operating GULP, they may well bear the brunt of employee dissatisfaction if servicing problems arise.
- To preclude financial selection, insurers may move toward short-term interest guarantees. In such a case, the interest credited to individual accounts will probably depend on when the moneys are invested. Although the yields on current investment vehicles are likely to be as good as or better than those available from other investment vehicles, there is no guarantee that the total cash value will enjoy similar results, especially in a period of rising inflation.

- Changes in laws, regulations, and rulings could bring GULP within the purview of Section 79 or make taxable the buildup of cash values.

- As with any form of permanent life insurance, participants could face adverse financial results if coverage is surrendered early.

- Low GULP participation may saddle employers with administrative burdens and no offsetting advantages.

Communicating GULP to Employees

GULP's very flexibility necessitates careful employee communication. After all, employees are being offered an opportunity to participate in a program with many choices—generally, without the benefit of face-to-face explanations and enrollment by insurance agents or insurance company personnel. Although insurance carriers will undoubtedly provide communication assistance (at no additional specified cost), bear in mind that they want to sell the product. Generally, therefore, it will be up to employers to ensure their employees receive a balanced presentation and understand both the advantages and disadvantages of participation.

Pretesting the concept with employees in focus groups can help employers determine the magnitude of the communication challenge. Based on this information, employers can then prepare appropriate communication materials to explain how the program works and the various options available to employees. Trained employer personnel also should be available to answer questions and help employees make appropriate choices. Although strategies and techniques will be much the same as those used for other employee benefit plans (particularly savings or 401(k) plans), employers may have to place extra emphasis on communicating initial and ongoing choices and their implications. Employers that wish to encourage participation for a specific area (e.g., to replace post-retirement life insurance) also may have to use specific "selling" techniques.

Design

What follows is a list of the issues involved in designing GULP. Many have to be negotiated with the insurer and must be included in the competitive bidding process. Key considerations include the following:

Eligibility requirements:
- Age.
- Service.
- Minimum pay level.
- Employment classification.

Coverage to be included:
- Term only.
- Term plus savings.
- Accidental death and dismemberment.
- Declared interest rate.
- Policy loan interest rate.
- Regular administrative charges.
- Transaction fees.
- Reserve basis for paid-up insurance.

Underwriting:
- Guaranteed issue amount.
- Evidence of insurability requirements.
- Open enrollment availability.
- Dependent coverage.
- Waiver of premium.

Term coverage amounts to be included:
- Number of choices.
- Flat amounts.
- Multiples of pay.
- Initially frozen.
- Automatically increased with pay.

Savings provisions:
- Number of choices.
- Maximum contribution level.
- Regular contributions.
- Variable contributions.
- Floor rate of interest.
- Declared rate of interest.

Other provisions:
- Withdrawals.
- Policy loans.
- Paid-up insurance options.
- Portability.

Premiums and other financial considerations:
- Level.
- Guarantees.
- Renewal rating process.
- Floor interest rate.

SUMMARY

Many employers are utilizing GULP—either in addition to or as a replacement for conventional group life insurance. They are doing so to achieve a number of the advantages previously described but, in particular, to avoid the tax implications of Section 79. GULP also has proven to be an effective way of providing additional benefits for highly compensated employees. Its value in allowing employees to continue meaningful amounts of coverage after retirement is also a significant factor. And, of course, the savings opportunities presented are important to employees at all pay levels.

Employers still must consider the potential disadvantages of using GULP. Also, they need to recognize the additional and somewhat complicated administrative issues that GULP entails. However, it does not appear that these disadvantages outweigh the positive results, both for employers and employees, that this coverage creates.

GROUP VARIABLE UNIVERSAL LIFE INSURANCE

In the mid-1990s, many insurers that wrote group universal life insurance introduced a variable product. This product differs from group universal life insurance in one important aspect—employees have a series of investment accounts to which they may allocate their net premiums. There are no investment guarantees (except in the one instance described later), and the full investment risk rests solely with the employee.

An insurer may have 20 or more available investment options, including money market funds, growth funds, bond funds, international funds, and index funds. The options available to employees are selected by the employer, and for administrative reasons are usually from four to six in number.

Many group variable universal products also have an account that has a minimum interest rate guarantee. An employee who elects to put 100 percent of his or her net premium into this account in effect has the equivalent of coverage under a group universal contract rather than a variable contract.

CORPORATE-OWNED LIFE INSURANCE

Employers often receive proposals to use permanent life insurance to "fund" benefits for their executives on an informal basis. Coverage may be written as corporate-owned life insurance (COLI), where the corporation is owner and beneficiary of the insurance; it also can be written on a split-dollar basis, with ownership and beneficial interest split between the corporation and the executive. In either situation, leveraging through loans has been involved, but this is limited by the interest deductibility rules noted later

The purchase of COLI is separate and distinct from the employer's plan or agreement to provide benefits for the executive. While the plan or agreement might, for example, provide for ERISA-excess benefits, the restoration of other benefits lost because of the tax law, deferred compensation, or other supplemental retirement or death benefits, or both, there is generally no legal link between the policy value and the employer's benefit promise.

With COLI, the employer is both owner and beneficiary of permanent life insurance purchased on the lives of participating executives. The amount of insurance is usually related to the benefits expected to be paid on the basis of current pay, although it is not unusual for initial amounts of insurance to anticipate some future pay increases. Because the employer owns the policy, the arrangement does not provide benefit security for the executive.

Upon death, the employer collects the proceeds of the policy and, depending on the nature of the arrangement, may pay a death benefit to the executive's beneficiary. Any benefit payable to a living executive is paid from employer assets, with the employer recovering the funds through policy loans or from insurance proceeds payable when executives die. Because funding largely flows from the payment of generally tax-free life insurance proceeds, it is important that insurance be kept in force until the executives die. Thus, most COLI programs continue insurance on the lives of executives who have retired or otherwise terminated employment.

Federal tax treatment of COLI and certain executive benefits is as follows:

For the employer:

- Premiums paid by the employer are not tax-deductible.
- The employer generally receives life insurance death proceeds free of income tax, though proceeds may be considered in determining whether a company must pay the corporate alternative minimum tax.[1]
- The inside buildup of cash values is not currently taxable to the employer-company, but may be considered in determining whether a company must pay the corporate alternative minimum tax.[1]
- If the employer surrenders the policy before it matures as a death claim, any excess of the gross cash surrender value (without regard to any outstanding policy loans that might reduce the cash surrender value actually available) over the premiums paid will be considered a taxable gain. Hence, as noted previously, it normally is desirable to continue the policy in force until the insured's death when the entire proceeds will be income-tax-free.
- The tax situation regarding the deductibility of interest paid or accrued on loans with respect to COLI is complicated.[2] The general rule is that no income tax deduction is allowed for any interest paid or accrued on any indebtedness with respect to one or more life insurance policies owned by a taxpayer covering the life of any individual. However, there is an exception to this general nondeductibility rule for interest paid or accrued on indebtedness with respect to policies on the lives of "key persons" (officers or 20-percent-or-more owners of the employer), but only to the extent that aggregate indebtedness on each such "key person" does not exceed $50,000.[3] Interest within this exception is deductible. Further, there is another provision that

---

1 It may be noted, however, that pursuant to the Tax Reform Act of 1997 the corporate alternative minimum tax (AMT) no longer applies to "small business corporations" for tax years beginning after 1997. "Small business corporations" generally are those whose initial average gross receipts do not exceed $5 million and thereafter do not exceed $7.5 million. Thus, for these smaller corporations the corporate AMT is not a factor.

2 See, in general, IRC Section 264.

3 The number of such "key persons" for any taxpayer may not exceed the larger of: 1) 5 individuals, or 2) the lesser of 5 percent of all officers and employees of the taxpayer, or 20 individuals.

denies a tax deduction for that portion of a taxpayer's total interest expense (from whatever source) that is allocable to unborrowed policy cash values.[4] However, for entities engaged in a trade or business, there is an exception to this rule for policies covering one individual who is a 20 percent or more owner, an officer, a director, or an employee of the trade or business. There also are rules applying to the nondeductibility of interest on indebtedness to purchase or carry life insurance policies and other rules for interest on indebtedness to purchase or carry other policies. Finally, there are transition rules for certain previously purchased policies.[5]

For the insured executive and his or her beneficiary:

- The value of the death benefit protection provided under the COLI each year does not create imputed income for the insured executive.
- Payments made by the employer to the executive or beneficiary under the separate benefit plan are generally tax-deductible by the employer.
- Payments received by the executive under the separate benefit plan are taxable income to him or her.
- Payments received by the beneficiary under the separate benefit plan are taxable income to him or her as income in respect of a decedent (IRD) and generally are includable in the employee's gross estate for estate tax purposes.
- The death benefit may qualify for the marital deduction if paid to a spouse. In large estates, this may serve only to defer estate taxation because the benefit may remain in the spouse's estate and be taxed on his or her subsequent death.
- An income tax deduction by the beneficiary for any estate tax attributable to the distribution can mitigate, but not eliminate, the combined effect of federal income and estate taxes.

State income and estate or inheritance taxes vary. In most situations, however, it is reasonable to assume that state tax treatment will be consistent with that of federal tax law.

---

4 This portion is the same ratio as the taxpayer's average unborrowed policy cash values bears to the sum of 1) the average unborrowed cash values, and 2) the average adjusted income tax bases of the taxpayer's other assets.

5 For example, different rules apply under the general rule and the pro rata rule, noted above, for policies issued prior to June 9, 1997.

SPLIT-DOLLAR LIFE INSURANCE

Split-dollar is a generic term that covers a variety of funding procedures using permanent life insurance. The employer usually purchases permanent life insurance on the life of an executive, and ownership of the policy (death proceeds and cash value) is split between the employer and the executive. Premiums may be paid entirely by the employer or they can be split between the employer and executive. The split of ownership generally can be handled in one of two ways: (1) the employer can own the policy and create the executive's interest by endorsement, or (2) the employee can own the policy and collaterally assign a portion of the proceeds to the employer.[6]

In one possible split-dollar arrangement, the employer pays all premiums and ownership is split by assignment. The employer's interest in the cash value or the death proceeds, as the assignee, might be the larger (or the smaller if it is so-called "equity split-dollar") of the amount of its premium payments (with or without an additional credit to reflect the time value of money) or the cash value. When the executive retires, the employer withdraws its interest from the cash value of the policy. If the executive dies, the employer receives its interest through the payment of part of the insurance proceeds, with the executive's beneficiary receiving the balance. As with COLI, the transaction can be leveraged through the use of loans but subject to the interest deductibility rules noted previously. Early in 2001, the IRS stated (in Notice 2001-10, 2001-5 IRB_) that it was reviewing the tax treatment of split-dollar plans. The Service provided some new rules and guidelines for use until it publishes further guidance. These guidelines allow split-dollar plans to be characterized under the traditional rules that have governed these plans as well as in other ways. The following are the major federal tax aspects of split-dollar insurance plans under these traditional rules:

- The employer's premium payments are not tax-deductible.
- The executive will have imputed income each year equal to the value of the term insurance provided—that is, the difference between the face amount of the policy and the employer's interest—less any payments by the executive.[7]

---

6 Another arrangement, often called sole-owner split dollar, may be used in some cases. Here all ownership rights are held by a third-party owner and there is a separate agreement between the owner and the employer.

7 The amount taxable to the executive is determined under rates published by the Internal Revenue Service. For taxable years ending on or before December 31, 2001 taxpayers may continue to use the PS 58 rates, but these rates are not allowed to be used after 2001. Instead, taxpayers may use the new, and lower, "Table 2001" rates for taxable years ending after December 31, 2001. Alternatively, taxpayers may continue to use the insurer's published and available one-year term insurance rates, if they are lower than the IRS published rates.

- If, prior to the executive's death, the employer receives payment of any part of the cash value that exceeds the premiums it paid, this excess will be taxable as income.
- Death proceeds paid to either the employer or the insured executive's beneficiary (including that part of the proceeds that consists of cash values) will generally not be subject to federal and state income taxes.
- Federal estate taxes (and state inheritance or estate taxes) will apply to any death proceeds payable to the executive's beneficiary, but the marital deduction will be available if the beneficiary is the insured's spouse. However, proceeds can be entirely excluded from the insured executive's gross estate if the executive's ownership rights are assigned at least three years prior to death to a third party (such as an irrevocable life insurance trust).
- The inside buildup of life insurance cash values is generally not taxable unless withdrawn from the policy, and it has been assumed by most practitioners that this rule applies to the cash value buildup under split-dollar coverage. However, if the executive is entitled to cash values created by employer contributions (referred to as "equity-split dollar"), there is risk that the buildup will become currently taxable to the executive. This is the position taken by the Internal Revenue Service in a Technical Advice Memorandum.[8] As of this writing, the tax status of equity split-dollar is unclear.

Split-dollar coverage offers potential security for executive retirement benefits over the long term. Also, use of the pension values of a split-dollar arrangement to offset benefits under an employer's Supplemental Executive Retirement Plan (SERP) could reduce the accounting cost of the SERP program.

ANALYZING PROPOSALS: GENERAL ISSUES

COLI and split-dollar arrangements are complicated, and they warrant careful scrutiny and analysis. General considerations are summarized below, followed by an analysis of financial issues.

Tax Treatment

Insurance proposals typically quite properly project financial results that reflect current tax law. However, changes in tax treatment are always a

---

8 Internal Revenue Service, TAM 960 4001.

possible (and even likely in the case of split-dollar), and any such changes, whether by statute or by administrative or judicial rulings, could have an adverse impact on projected results. While no one can predict what changes might come about, prior legislation and administrative activity suggest that COLI and split-dollar insurance may not be viewed with complete favor when used as discussed in this chapter.

Time Period

It is important to recognize that COLI and split-dollar arrangements are long-term programs that produce maximum financial advantages only when policies mature as death claims. Projected results of COLI and split-dollar programs typically reflect several long-term assumptions (in addition to the assumption that the tax law will not change), including the following:

- Interest will be credited for the entire period at the rate specified in the proposal.
- There will be no loss or deferral of projected tax benefits due to changed circumstances of the employer.
- Mortality will occur in accordance with the table used in the proposal—typically, the insurer's mortality table for that class of business.

Each of these assumptions deserves additional comment.

Interest Rates. The interest credited under a participating traditional whole life insurance policy has two components: the guaranteed interest rate and the excess or nonguaranteed dividend interest rate. The interest rate typically used in a COLI or split-dollar proposal is based on a total rate of return that includes projected dividends. Prior experience tells us that interest rates will vary over time. Thus, projected results under a COLI or split-dollar proposal should be analyzed with several different assumptions as to future interest rates. In this regard, it would be helpful to look at the insurer's investment performance for prior years as well as the history of interest rates it has credited for dividend purposes.

Loss or Deferral of Tax Benefits. Employers cannot be certain that they will receive expected tax benefits from a COLI or split-dollar arrangement in any given year or years. Proposals typically assume that the employer will always pay taxes at regular corporate rates. This may not always be the case. If the employer becomes an alternative minimum taxpayer, for example, it will have to include a part of the life insurance proceeds and the inside buildup of cash values in determining its alternative minimum tax exposure. An employer also may suffer tax losses. Thus, it is important to assess the implications of losing or deferring tax benefits at various times.

Mortality Rates. Projections of the tax-free life insurance proceeds that will be payable to the employer are usually based on the insurer's mortality table. An employer whose actual mortality rate is lower will collect death proceeds more slowly. On the other hand, their mortality experience may be less favorable than assumed in the insurer's mortality table, which would be favorable for COLI projections.

Employer Objectives

Insurance proposals often focus on program funding, rather than on program design and objectives. Thus, it is important for an employer contemplating the purchase of insurance to determine exactly what it wants to accomplish. Once the employer has set its objectives, it can evaluate an insurance proposal against them and consider alternatives that may be available.

Assume, for example, that the employer's primary objective is to prefund an executive's supplemental retirement benefits—amounts that cannot be provided under the employer's qualified plan because of tax law restrictions. These benefits could be quite substantial for a highly paid employee. As a result, the amount of life insurance required to generate sufficient cash values might far exceed the employer's objectives in terms of providing death benefits. Other alternatives, including a rabbi or secular trust or a stock-based SERP, might prove to be more efficient for this objective.

ERISA Compliance

Executive retirement plans fall within the purview of Title I of ERISA. While pure excess benefit plans (limited to benefits lost by reason of IRC Section 415) are generally exempt, other plans must comply with all of Title I's requirements unless they are limited to a select group of management or highly compensated employees and are unfunded.

FINANCIAL CONSIDERATIONS

One of the difficulties in analyzing proposals for COLI or split-dollar coverage is that they often are combined and thus may confuse issues of plan design and funding. The cost of the plan itself should be separated from the financial aspects of funding.

Plan Costs

From a cost standpoint, an executive benefit plan is the same as any other employee benefit plan: In general, the cost of the plan will ultimately equal the sum of the benefits actually paid plus the expense of the plan operation. If the plan is funded, this outlay of principal will be reduced by any investment income on plan assets. If the investment income is less than the company could earn investing the funds elsewhere, however, funding could create additional costs. If a company can earn a 10 percent after-tax return on retained assets, but plan assets (an insurance policy, a pension fund, and the like) earn only 8 percent, the company should acknowledge a cost of 2 percent for the opportunity loss associated with the choice of investment vehicle.

If an employer buys permanent life insurance for a group of executives and maintains this insurance in force, actual mortality experience over the long run may or may not parallel that used in the insurer's table. The larger the insured group and the longer the plan is in effect, the more likely it is that actual experience will track the table. If so, the cost of the program should reflect the cost formula referred to above—the cost will equal the sum of benefits paid and expenses of operation, adjusted for investment considerations. Put another way, amounts paid to the insurer, together with investment income (and less the insurer's expenses and profit), may be returned to be paid as benefits. This principle has long been recognized in group life insurance, where experience-rating formulas develop costs in this fashion.[9]

If this formula correctly expresses the long-term cost of an executive benefit plan, it follows that the benefits paid to the executives or their beneficiaries will be a function of the actual mortality experience of the covered group and the effect of plan provisions on amounts payable.

---

9 Not surprisingly, the cost and pricing of insurance works the same way from the insurer's viewpoint. The insurer must collect enough money from premiums and investment income to cover its expenses, profit, and the amount of benefits it pays; in other words, the price of insurance is equal to the sum of the claims paid plus expenses (and profit), less income received on investments.

Many proposals claim that there is no cost for executive benefits funded with permanent life insurance, because "money advanced by the company to fund the program will be returned to the company together with a factor for the use of the money"—a statement that often finds its way into proxy statements. This claim warrants close examination, because it may arise from a confusion of basic accounting concepts.

Suppose, for example, that an employer agrees to pay Executive A the sum of $1,000 in exactly one year. In order to have funds on hand to meet this obligation, the employer invests $909 in a 12-month certificate of deposit yielding a 10 percent annual rate of return. At the end of one year, the certificate matures for $1,000 and the employer uses this amount to pay Executive A.

Most people would agree that the employer in this simple example incurred a cost of $1,000 to provide Executive A with a benefit in that amount even though it invested only $909 for the certificate and did not have to expend any current income to meet the obligation when it came due. The interest earned during the year that became part of the total payment made to Executive A was the employer's property. The fact that the employer used an existing asset to make the payment (rather than current income) does not mean that it did not incur an expense.

This is basically what happens when an employer purchases life insurance. The employer assumes an obligation to pay benefits to the executive (or his or her estate); this obligation will produce a cost. The fact that insurance proceeds may become available to provide liquid funds that can be used to pay benefits does not mean that the benefits cost nothing. The insurance proceeds, over the long term, represent employer assets, partly a return of the principal amounts advanced and partly the investment return that could have been realized if the employer had otherwise invested the principal. In other words, setting aside an asset to meet a future cost does not eliminate that cost; it is a separate and distinct transaction.

Financial Analysis

Employers should view the purchase of permanent life insurance primarily as an investment. Thus, the effective rate of return that will be credited to the funds invested—a rate that is highly sensitive to the amount of tax leverage generated—is a critical consideration.

A discounted cash-flow analysis, incorporating the time value of money, can be used to compute the employer's after-tax yield on an insurance product. Employer cash flow would include the following elements:

- *Income to the employer:* any annual policy loans and any net death benefits received from the insurer (i.e., gross policy death benefits less any policy loans outstanding at date of death).

- *Outgo from the employer:* annual premiums and (after-tax) interest on any policy loans. (But note the severe limitations on the deductibility of policy loan interest indicated earlier. In general, only interest paid or accrued on indebtedness with respect to policies on the lives of "key persons" (officers, or 20 percent or more owners of the taxpayer) up to $50,000 per key person is deductible.)

Annual dividends typically are not considered as cash flow, because they are usually used to purchase additional death benefits, which are included in the total proceeds received at death.

The discounted cash-flow analysis includes these steps:

1. First, each year's income and outgo are adjusted to reflect the probability of occurrence (i.e., either survival or death).
2. Second, the adjusted annual amounts are discounted to determine the highest interest rate for which the current value of the income equals the current value of the outgo.

The interest rate determined in this manner is called the *internal rate of return*. This rate is often used to compare investment alternatives. If an employer can realize a higher rate of return elsewhere, the policies have a cost—the loss of the excess earnings otherwise available. Several factors should be kept in mind when making this analysis.

Tax Implications.   Permanent life insurance can be a very effective tax-sheltered investment. As noted, the payment of policy proceeds at death will not be subject to income tax, and investment income that accumulates to the employer (through cash value buildup or dividends, or both) over and above premiums paid will be tax-deferred—taxable only when and if the policy is surrendered. Further, investment income will not be subject to income tax at all if paid as part of the policy's death proceeds. An exception is that both the inside buildup and the death proceeds will be considered in determining the corporate alternative minimum tax, if applicable. However, while the basic statement that life insurance death proceeds are income-tax-free is true, this tax advantage in essence only applies to part of the proceeds. To the extent the employer receives back an amount equal to the premiums it paid, there is no advantage. These amounts were already after-tax or tax-free when paid to the insurer (i.e., they were not tax-deducible).

Further tax advantages may accrue to the extent that policy loans are made (within the strict permissible limits just noted). This occurs when the after-tax cost of borrowing is less than the rate of interest credited by the insurer. If a corporation borrows money from the insurer at an 8 percent interest rate, for example, its after-tax cost of borrowing (assuming a 35 percent tax bracket) is 5.2 percent. If the insurer is crediting interest to the policy with the equivalent of a 7 percent return, there is a difference of 2.8 percent. The effect of this can be illustrated by the following analysis of a $1,000 loan using the assumptions in this example:

Cost of Borrowing	Guaranteed Plus Dividend Interest	Tax Saving	Net Gain
–$80	+$70	+$28	+$28

But again it must be emphasized that any such tax advantage depends on the deductibility of the interest. As noted previously, this deductibility has been sharply curtailed by recent tax legislation.

Early Termination. As noted earlier, the financial analysis should measure the potential after-tax financial results of early termination of an insurance program—at the end of the 1st, 5th, 10th, 15th, and 20th years, for example.

A program terminated after only a few years will often produce minimal returns and even losses. If the policies are surrendered, any investment gain will be taxable as income. Further, early year cash values will not reflect significant investment gains, because traditional insurance policies are front-loaded to recover acquisition expenses. Also, most universal life-type policies will impose a surrender charge if the policy is terminated within a certain number of years after it has been issued. Long-term investment projections also rely on the payment of significant tax-free life insurance proceeds; these anticipated death claims may not have materialized in the early years of the program's operation.

Assumed Interest. Insurance proposals project financial results that are premised on assumptions about dividend payments by the insurer; these projections about financial results are not guaranteed but are based on best estimates as to the insurer's future financial performance. Thus, proposals should be analyzed under several different future dividend or interest scenarios. In selecting these scenarios, it is helpful to look at the historical investment performance of the insurer's total asset portfolio, the insurer's dividend history with respect to the specific type of policy being contemplated, and how well it performed in the past compared with the dividend projections it made.

Other Factors. The following points are also important in analyzing insurance proposals:

- All costs and cost summaries should be shown on an after-tax basis—both for the employer and the executive.
- Costs to the executive, including direct contributions, taxes, or the time value of any money he or she has advanced, should be taken into account in looking at the total cost implications.
- Possible changes in anticipated financial results that could occur if the employer has tax losses or becomes an alternative minimum taxpayer should be determined.
- Financial results should be projected over the life expectancies of insured individuals.
- Any additional costs for executives who are not insurable at standard rates should be established.
- Because the purchase of permanent insurance is a long-term investment, the creditworthiness of the insurer should be carefully investigated.

Other matters may warrant scrutiny in specific proposals. And every analysis of permanent life insurance should include consideration of alternative ways of achieving employer objectives

Work/Life Benefits

Part Four consists of five chapters dealing with work/life programs and several service type plans. Chapter 17 begins by discussing the environmental factors that have motivated and continue to motivate employers to design work/life programs for the diverse workforce of the Information Age. The balance of the chapter provides an overview of the various forms of work/life programs, highlighting the characteristics of successful ones.

Chapter 18 reviews traditional time-off benefits and family leave programs that are the basis of all work/life programs. Chapter 19 focuses its attention on two major forces behind most work/life programs—child care and elder care needs. This chapter explores the several approaches that have been developed as employee benefits to help meet the financial needs of employees for these special concerns.

Educational assistance programs, and the nature and uses of legal service plans provided through the employer are covered in Chapter 20.

Part Four concludes with Chapter 21, which discusses financial planning as an employee benefit.

Chapter 17

Work/Life Benefits:
An Overview

Linda Mondzelewski, SPHR, CBP

Why should organizations today have work/life programs? Haven't employees always had children and elderly parents to care for, routine housework to do, and outside activities to pursue? They have, yes, but times have changed and so have the workplace and workforce.

FACTORS LEADING TO WORK/LIFE PROGRAMS

Baby Boomers

In 1944, the nation's builders sold 100,000 houses. Just two years later they sold a million, and in 1950, they built 1.7 million houses, a record that lasted well into the 1980s. This postwar building boom provided housing for all the baby boomers and gave birth to the suburb—putting greater distances between homeowners and their places of work.

More Women Working

According to one mid-1950s survey, people "liked" being at work. That appeal carried across the family, as increasing numbers of women started reporting to work. Female employment increased 400 percent between 1940 and 1960, and during the 1950s rose four times faster than male employment. Once at work, men and women trusted that helping to nourish the company's bottom line meant growing their own personal bottom line.

Family Income Doubled

Company bottom lines grew. Between 1937 and 1958, Dow Chemical grew by 750 percent. IBM's net earnings rose from $11 million in 1945 to $250 million in 1960 and on to $3.4 billion in 1980. Between 1959 and 1977, ITT bought and acquired its way from $765 million in annual sales to $28 billion. This steady growth in production and profits returned Americans to their basic belief that work was worth it. Companies flourished, and the rewards they offered their hardworking employees followed. By 1960, family income had doubled from the already high level of 1945 and the American economy prospered.[1]

Credit Offered-Debt Increases

When television and advertising grew in the marketplace, consumer wants exceeded their financial capabilities; and when the acquisition of goods and services implied a rising standard of living, conflicts developed. Extended credit eased those conflicts. Short-term credit leaped from $8.4 billion in 1946 to $45.6 billion in 1958; and by 1975, consumers held $167 billion in personal debt (excluding mortgages). Within another 10 years, the number rose to $517 billion. Overall, between 1965 and 1985, consumer debt as a percentage of disposable income averaged 15 percent—moving to a record high of 19 percent in 1988.

Employees Work More Hours

Leisure hours shrank throughout the 1980s as work demands increased. In 1984, Americans managed only 18.1 hours of weekly leisure time, down from 24.3 hours in 1975. Meanwhile, the average workweek edged upward from 40.6 hours in 1973 to 47.3 in 1984. As the number of work hours increased, most managers believed that what employees did at work was the company's business and what employees did outside work was their own business. But, during the 1970s and 1980s, most managers assumed that employees would put the company's interests first.[2]

Major Recession Hits

When the recession of 1990 hit, large numbers of employees began questioning the viability and attractiveness of their work lives. In 1994, the

---

1 Kenneth Hey, & Peter Moore, "The Caterpillar Doesn't Know," *How Personal Change is Creating Organizational Change* (New York, NY: Simon & Schuster) 1998.
2 Ibid.

fourth year of an economic recovery, corporations reported profit increases of 11 percent (after 13 percent in 1993). In the midst of this growth, however, corporations let go more than 516,000 employees. By 1995, workweeks for the survivors of downsizing expanded to 50.6 hours[3] This recession was different from any previous ones. Even when the recovery started, laid-off employees did not find old jobs waiting for them. Fifty-four percent of the job cutbacks made during the recession became permanent. Overall, from 1989 through 1997, American companies cut 4 million jobs. From the late 1970s through the middle 1990s, the lowest earning 10 percent of workers lost 10 percent of their earning power. For blue-collar males in general, hourly wages measured in constant dollars shrank 14.6 percent from 1978 to 1994. By 1996, the minimum wage had reached a 40-year low in real terms. More people than ever were working full-time, yet 20 percent were still living below the poverty line ($15,141 for a family of four). Census Bureau figures for 1993 revealed earnings declined for 60 percent of U.S. households. Of the 120 million people working in 1995, 8 million held two jobs, a 38 percent increase in one decade. Of the 22 million part-time workers, 4.5 million wanted full-time work but could not find it. The number of temporary workers tripled in the same decade to 2.1 million.

Change in Employee Mindset

As the surviving employees' work schedules increased with more work, personal lives suffered. The mindset of employees changed along with what they valued:

Old Employee Mindset	New Employee Mindset
Career	Learning
Profit	Growth
Success	Inner contentment
Loyalty to employer	Loyalty to self
Financial rewards	Personal rewards
Promotion	Development
Standard of living	Quality of life

Increased demands on employees, both men and woman, meant there was less time in their day to tend to life's routine tasks, such as shopping, child care, elder care, hobbies, spouses, and friends. The quality of the relationship between an employee's work and personal life was

---

3 Joanne Cuilla, *The Working Life* (New York, NY: Time Books) 2000.

drastically out of balance. If an employee did not speak up regarding his or her out-of-balance work/life, it became apparent through increased absenteeism, decreased work performance, or both. Work/life issues were delegated to the human resources department and problems were dealt one at a time. When enough problems arose, corporations responded by creating programs such as flextime and on-site child daycare.

Birth of Work/Life Programs

Over the years, employee benefit programs have evolved along with the workplace and workforce. The first kinds of benefits—life, disability, health insurance, and retirement—known as traditional benefits, established uniform financial security. In the 1970s, flexible benefits were introduced. These benefits were designed to meet the baby boomers' more diverse needs. Flexible benefits entailed more plan options in the area of supplemental and dependent life insurance, medical plans, and 401(k) contributions, as well as full "cafeteria" plans and flexible spending accounts. In the 1980s, family-friendly benefits arose. Then, a backlash arose from employees who did not have families. In 1984, a social group with 46 chapters worldwide was formed. Called "No Kidding," the basic purpose of the organization is to ensure childless workers are not subsidizing parenthood in the workplace. Childfree workers said they were getting trapped more often to work holidays and overtime because they didn't have "families." In 1997, a study conducted by the Families and Work Institute found that 60 percent of workers said they would not resent their employer's providing work/family benefits that did not benefit them personally. Nevertheless, work/family benefits became known as work/life benefits to send the message of inclusion.

In the early 1990s, work/life issues and programs to help employees balance their lives, such as flexible work arrangements and paid time off, were viewed by management as "soft issues" and not taken seriously. In the early developmental stages of work/life programs, managers believed that every time an employee's personal interests "won," the organization "lost." Even though human resources departments created work/life programs, they did not help a large segment of the employee population because they did not permeate into a company's culture or change managers' beliefs. By the late 1990s, work/life programs made giant leaps, moving from a focus on work/family issues primarily involving child daycare to a variety of issues impacting employees' lives. Work/life programs no longer target only employees with children—they are for everyone. As the workforce has become increasingly diverse, work/life issues have become broader and more complex. Organizations have started asking: "How can we link the diverse work/life issues our employees face to broad organizational issues?" In the late 1990s, a growing number of managers began to approach work/life issues differently. Slowly, the mindset of managers transformed from viewing work and personal life as competing priorities to seeing work and personal life as complementary ones.

DIVERSITY A MAJOR PART OF WORK/LIFE BENEFITS

According to Workforce 2000, only a minority of employers' new hires will be Anglo-American males by the year 2010. The remaining 85 percent will be females, Hispanics, Asians, and Native Americans. To remain competitive, it will be necessary for employers to embrace diversity and seek out all available strategies that will attract the talent they need in the future. One such strategy is work/life benefits. To make work/life benefits effective in an organization requires an understanding of diversity in the workplace.

Working Mothers

"To work or not to work?" is a question many mothers ask themselves. There are no simple answers and there are as many ways of solving the work versus stay-at-home dilemma as there are women experiencing the conflicting tugs of children, home, and gainful employment. This question haunts women whether their children are infants or teenagers. Work/life programs alleviate many working mothers' concerns and enable many mothers to work who might not have chosen to if the programs were not in place. Many mothers choose to stay at home until their young children enter full-day school. But a recent U.S Bureau of Labor Statistics study shows that only 7 percent of American families conform to the wage-earning dad, stay-at-home mom, and at least one child. In 1969, that figure was 20 percent. In 1995, 83 percent of new mothers who worked before having a child returned full-time to the labor force within six months of giving birth. A 1999 *Monthly Labor Review* study shows that female work patterns are influenced by the ages of children. Mothers with children under the age of 6 are less likely to work full-time than mothers with older children; 36.8 percent are employed full-time, compared to 52.6 percent of mothers with children over the age of 6. For many mothers, staying at home is not an option. Almost 50 percent of mothers contribute more than half of their household's income, according to the Families and Work Institute. Mothers are also more likely to work part-time than other categories of women. Among all mothers, 37.1 percent work part-time, compared to 13.6 percent of childless women and 8.4 percent of men. Working mothers spend 32 hours a week doing household chores and 28 hours a week caring for their children, including helping with homework and carpooling—seven hours a week less than what a stay-at-home mother would spend on household chores and caring for children.

NEW PRIORITIES, NEW BENEFIT DEFINITIONS

To help employees achieve the work/life balance they need, employers are rethinking employee benefits and asking: "What do employees consider to be benefits?" As already mentioned, traditional benefit programs, such as health, survivor, disability, and retirement benefits, were motivators for the prior generation. Today's employees view these benefits as a given. Flexible benefits or cafeteria benefits have been around since the 1970s. Work/family benefits produced a backlash that evolved into what we call work/life benefits today.

Employers not offering these benefits are eliminated from job consideration by many employees. The present generation of employees wants to know what an employer is going to do to enhance their work experience and help balance their work and personal life. The same is true of the "downsized" generation of older workers who originally came into a workforce that promised continuing employment for loyal service. They found that midway through their careers, the employer/employee social contract was rewritten to their disadvantage. Whether or not these employees were actually downsized, they felt "burned" because the rules changed without their input, and those who were not downsized were working more hours to do the work of those who were let go. Feeling mistreated and wary, they invested in themselves and their personal skills. Instead of individuals asking one another where they worked as they did in the 1970s and 1980s, now individuals asked each other: "What do you do?" "What do you know?" Employees began concentrating on building and acquiring the tools for their own toolboxes that could be used anywhere, anytime. Much wiser now, employees learned how to negotiate, and they, too, adopted new ideas of what constitutes benefits.

Further fueling this drive toward a reconsideration of benefits is the shortage of qualified people in today's labor market. While pay remains a significant motivator, it is not as dominant as it once was. More and more, people are considering their total life needs. When evaluating employment options, they want to know how employers are meeting those needs. Given the labor shortage, employers with innovative ideas for addressing their employees' life needs have the advantage.

CURRENT WORK/LIFE BENEFITS

In the late 1990s, many employers began offering a new array of benefits to their employees. The focus was primarily on helping employees:

1. Manage their physical and mental health.
2. Care for dependents (spouses, children, elders).
3. Save time.
4. Work in a flexible environment.

Currently, employers realize how fast society is changing. Rising divorce rates, the trend toward dual-income families and increased life expectancy are having profound effects on the way employees manage their lives. Recent statistics show that approximately one-half of all children under the age of 16 will spend some time as part of a single-parent household. Three-fifths of two-parent families boast dual-wage earners, one-half of working mothers have a child under one year of age, and two-thirds have children under the age of 18.[4] By the year 2005, women are expected to comprise one-half of the workforce. More of today's parents are also spending time caring for elderly relatives who are expected in the near future to outnumber children under age 18 for the first time ever.

In our workplaces, we continue to be challenged by change as companies downsize, reengineer, and globalize; while they flatten, implement total quality management, and improve cycle time. Businesses are operating 24 hours a day, seven days per week. Managers and employees alike are asked to do more with less and are pulled in many directions at once.

Despite technological advances, Americans continue to work longer and longer hours. All these demands add up to stress as we try to balance the many pieces of our lives. Adopting work/life programs sends the message to employees that they work for forward-looking organizations. A discussion of the types of programs currently offered along with some case examples follows.

Child-Care Assistance

Eighty-six percent of employers offer some kind of child-care assistance to their employees (up from 66 percent in 1991). Dependent care spending accounts and resource and referral services are the two most prevalent programs used. Ninety-seven percent of employers providing child care

---

4 Ann Vincola, "Work/Life Balance: Not Just a Women' Issue," *Benefits and Compensation Solutions*, Publication of Intermedia Solutions, July 2000, pp. 22-23.

assistance offer dependent-care spending accounts, and 40 percent offer resource and referral services. It is estimated that employer-based centers (including those sponsored by companies, government agencies, hospitals, and large nonprofits) have grown at a rate of about 25 percent per year over the past five years. Less than 10 percent of Fortune 500 companies currently provide on-site child care. Still, the number of employer-sponsored sites is estimated at 8,000 nationwide (an increase from 204 in 1982). That number is predicted to grow by 10 percent a year. Once the exclusive domain of larger companies, the typical center-sponsoring employer has about 2,100 employees and a center serving 105 children. Sick/emergency child-care programs are an emerging trend, offered by 13 percent of employers with child-care assistance. Many smaller employers who cannot afford emergency care services on their own join with each other to find a solution.

> **Child Care.** The human resources director of San Jose National Bank recalls the day her boss, the bank's president and CEO, asked her: "How would you like to bring your baby to work?" The HR director, who at the time was pregnant with her first child, gave her boss what seemed to be a good HR answer: "The bank can't afford on-site daycare." The CEO explained that he wasn't talking about a formal daycare program. He was talking about the HR director literally bringing her baby with her to the job. To the CEO, the benefits of such an arrangement—perhaps impractical for most employers—outweighed the risks. He wanted employees to return eight weeks after giving birth instead of taking the extended vacation and sick time they may have accrued. Not only did the bank save hundreds of thousands of dollars in leave costs, it minimized the use of consultants and temporary workers. At the time, the bank had four women who were pregnant and two of them managed departments. Faced with the idea of using consultants or temporary employees, the bank came up with a plan to curb leave costs and get employees back to work sooner. In place for three years, the program allows new parents to bring their babies to work until the children are six months old or start to crawl. The program has three basic ground rules:
>
> - Feeding and diaper changes take place in private.
> - The parent is primarily responsible for the baby.
> - Other employees can request a baby-free workspace. Management decides which employee moves, based on space and equipment considerations. Since the program started, no employee has requested a baby-free workspace.

Emergency Care of Children and Elders. ConAgra, Union Pacific Railroad, Mutual of Omaha, Commercial Federal Bank, and

First Bank joined together to create an emergency child-care and elder-care program. ConAgra figures it cost them about $10,000 per year. All participating companies confirm the costs are covered by increased productivity. The services are provided by the local Visiting Nurses Association and cost $10.50 to $14.00 per hour. The visiting nurses care for mildly ill children and adults with temperatures and each company limits the hours the program can be used.

Elder-Care Programs

Elder-care programs are now offered by nearly one-third of employers, an increase of 17 percent over the number of employers offering elder-care assistance in 1991.[5] The most common approach to elder-care assistance is a resource and referral program, offered by 79 percent of the employers with elder-care programs. Long-term care insurance is now offered by 25 percent of employers with elder-care programs (up from 5 percent in 1991).

Flexible Work Options

Flexible work options represent a critically important trend in today's workplace. This trend will continue and increase in impact as employers are forced to adapt to a changing environment that includes both working across time zones and locations, and competition for skilled employees with a wide range of personal concerns and responsibilities. A flexible work schedule is any work arrangement that is not standard for all or most of the other jobs in the company or industry. Flexible work schedules range from coming or going home an hour later than the norm to working part-time hours during nontraditional business hours from a home office. Full-time or part-time, home office or company office, regular business hours or nontraditional hours, jobs filled by one person or two partners, flexible work schedules live up to their name. They are *flexible*. They allow employees to creatively manage the need to balance the many facets of their work and personal lives. They also allow business managers to manage the workforce by lifting the traditional restriction of standard days, hours, and office locations. Flexible work options are offered by 68 percent of companies, up from 53 percent in 1991. The most common arrangements offered by these employers are flextime (provided by 72 percent of employers) and part-time employment (provided by 64 percent of employers). More than a third

5 Hewitt Associates, *Work and Family Benefits Provided by Major US Employers in 1996.* Based on practices of 1,050 employers.

of employers have job sharing, 22 percent offer compressed workweeks, and 20 percent allow work at home. Fifteen percent of employers offering flexible scheduling have summer hours.

Telecommuting. By various estimates, there are somewhere between 9 million and 15 million salaried corporate telecommuters in the United States, who spend at least one day per week working at home during normal work hours. We have seen, and continue to see, overwhelming changes in what people do, who those people are, and where they do their work. It is this last change in work location itself that seems to be the most profound. It's one thing to change from a paper spreadsheet to a software spreadsheet, or to change from a full-time predominantly male workforce to a much more diverse one. But, it is significantly different to consider changes in the "office" part of office work that we have taken for granted. The deconstruction of the term "office work" is at the heart of many changes we are seeing. This results from the explosion of hardware, software, and telecommunications technologies that are shaking up the workplace of the past 300 years. This is the first time in the history of the workplace that we can separate activity from location. In the agricultural age, we had no choice but to bring all the workers to the workplace; that's where the fields were. In the industrial age, we had no choice but to bring all the workers to the workplace; that's where the machinery and assembly lines were. But, in this information age, we have the option of separating what people do from where they do it.

Implications of Telecommuting. When an employee starts telecommuting (which in most cases means working at home one to three days a week), the only thing that changes is the work location. Pay, benefits, employment status, and all other company and regulatory protections and entitlements are unchanged. Some employers have tried to use the shift to telecommuting to justify a shift from employee to independent contractor status for telecommuters, which, in most cases, is done to avoid benefits costs and coverage. The IRS, however, has taken a dim view of this. Another concern expressed by some employers is non-exempt employees telecommuting. As long as all existing requirements for work hours, time recording, and the like are met, as they would be if the person were in the office full-time, there is no reason a non-exempt employee cannot telecommute. Some employers argue that the work hours and schedule for a telecommuter at home can't be monitored and verified as they are in the office. That's true, but it's also true for the thousands of installers, service representatives, health care aides, etc., who worked away from the workplace before telecommuting became an official work/life benefit. Bell Atlantic began a telecommuting pilot in 1991 that has grown and allowed 20,000 telephone operators to work at home, supervising themselves, and seeking a coach when necessary. United Airlines agents used to drive several hours each day to central reservation centers in Los Angelos, San Francisco, and Chicago. Many said they were exhausted when they arrived at work. Now they work at neighborhood satellite offices, using a new call distribution system developed by AT&T. Each of the three neighborhood satellite offices has 125 employees. One woman who used to commute 75 miles each way now uses that extra two hours to be with her child; another who put more than 100,000 miles on her car in six years now has time to volunteer.

Flextime Employment. Coach, the Manhattan-based maker of classic leather goods, is considered one of the nation's friendliest places to work. Their human resource director believes "the workplace should be a healthy environment where careers are nurtured through support, not prodded by intimidation." That wasn't how it was for her in the '70s. "I never took a day off. I worried I'd be viewed as less professional if family needs crept into my work life, so I left my kids home sick. We used to believe in face time. Now we look for the contribution employees make." Some employees at Coach work three days a week. One with an ailing parent has totally flexible hours. It fits with Coach's vision of itself: a company that serves the needs of women. And a company with steadily increasing sales.

Education and Training

John Hazen White, owner of privately held Taco, Inc. in Rhode Island, is proud of the fact that educating his employees has contributed to doubling his sales in the past four years and keeping turnover at less than 1 percent. With 450 employees and $90 million in revenues, Taco is a small manufacturer with a huge commitment to learning. *Fortune* magazine reports that just a few of the six dozen courses Taco offers are work-related—blueprint reading, ISO auditing, and employment law. Employees have taken Spanish, algebra, computing, speech, art, gardening, and business ethics courses. Employees' children have gone whale watching with oceanographers, learned to play stringed instruments, and put on musicals. Cost to employees: nothing. Cost to Taco: $250,000 for the Learning Center and about $700 per employee per year—$200,000 to run the center and $100,000 in extra wages and lost production. White believes he receives a great return on his education investment. RJR Nabisco declared a commitment to education and made available the means for employees and their children to receive education and skills training beyond high school. Time off is allowed to accompany children on the first day of school or to attend school conferences. A workshop series is offered to help parents learn how to be leaders in the school, and grants of $2,000 are made to help those who help the schools. As part of a Scholastic Savings Plan, Nabisco matches employee contributions up to $1,000 per year for four years for each child's post-secondary education, including options such as computers. Employees can pay their share from pre-tax dollars. With interest, the two contributions grow to nearly $10,000 by the time each student graduates from high school.

Family and Medical Leave Act

Employers are now required by the Family and Medical Leave Act of 1993 to provide 12 weeks of unpaid family and medical leave for the birth/adoption of a child or for the serious illness of a family member. Sixty-four percent of employers provide the required 12 weeks of leave; 67 percent of employers require unpaid leave to be offset with some or all paid leave provided.

Adoption Benefits

Adoption benefits are now offered by 23 percent of employers (up 12 percent from 1991). Reimbursement levels vary, but $2,000 per adoption is the most common benefit provided.

Employee Assistance Programs (EAPs)

EAPs are offered by 84 percent of employers (up 9 percent from 1991) and are most commonly provided through a contract with an outside provider. EAPs give employees an accessible source of counseling about problems relating to relationship issues, family issues, alcohol, gambling, and other compulsive and addictive problems. Personal debt and family illness problems also are addressed.

Emerging Benefits

Emerging benefits that employers are beginning to offer more often include:

- Supplemental life and/or disability insurance for employees, their spouses, and/or dependents.
- On-site health club facilities, health club discounts, exercise classes, walking clubs, on-site yoga, softball, baseball, volleyball, golf teams, and on-site massage.

■ Wellness and/or health promotion programs for improving employees' health and reducing health insurance costs. Many companies provide programs that may include health assessments or lunch-time seminars on topics such as cancer prevention, cardiac health, diabetes, nutrition, stress, first aid, CPR, smoking cessation, or managing weight. Some organizations also provide on-site medical facilities for physicals, work-related injuries, minor first aid, and/or routine check-ups and tests.

■ Dry cleaning and shoe repair services.

■ Corporate discount buying programs where company products or services that save employees time and money are available at work.

■ Credit unions to save employees time with various banking transactions, as well as providing them with more favorable financial terms.

■ Pre-paid legal services.

■ Computers.

■ Cell phones.

■ Travel services.

■ Mailing services and ATM machines.

■ Floral services.

■ Lactating rooms for nursing mothers.

■ Home mortgage and loan services.

■ Auto insurance, renter's insurance, and homeowner's insurance through payroll deduction.

■ Financial planning.

■ Pick-up/drop-off programs for car repairs, oil changes, and inspections.

■ On-site cafeterias to save employees time at mealtime and provide them with meals at a discount. Grocery shopping and delivery service also may be available by phone or fax.

■ Pet care referral and pet insurance.

■ Twenty-two percent of employers provide some type of commuting assistance. Of these companies, the most common form of assistance (49 percent) is to pre-pay or partially reimburse transportation system expenses. Many of these companies make free or discounted "transit passes" available at work. Forty percent of those with a commuting assistance program provide company vans, buses, or cars, while 32 percent coordinate employee carpools. A recent change to the Transportation Equity Act for the 21st Century (HR2400, June 9, 1998) allows employee expenses for parking and mass transit expenses to be tax-free under an employer plan.

- Providing casual dress days is considered a work/life benefit with 73 percent of employers participating.
- Personal use of the company PC and personal use of the Internet or Intranet also are common benefits.

DELIVERY SYSTEM FOR WORK/LIFE BENEFITS

Growing simultaneously with work/life benefits is the use of on-line technology for delivery and administration of benefits. This is a result of more and more technology being deployed in the workplace. As workplace Internet access grows, employers are increasingly allowing employees to take advantage of this access for personal, benefit-related reasons—within certain parameters. For example, as 401(k) and other defined contribution plans grow in number and asset value, employers are not only allowing, but encouraging employees to use corporate Internet access to view their accounts and make transactions on-line. Investment fund sponsors have grown their Web sites not only to allow on-line transactions, but also to provide financial planning tools for a variety of purposes: saving for a house, vacation, college education, retirement, estate planning, and budgeting, etc. Additionally, health care sponsors provide access to information regarding providers of health care, participating physicians, hospitals, labs, pharmacies, and others—all available on-line. On-line technology gives employees the benefit of easy access to integrated benefits information and transaction capabilities—whenever and wherever they need it—7 days a week/24 hours a day. This kind of employee self-service takes human resources out of the middle of transactions and gives employees three things: control, responsibility, and choice.

On-line benefits access provides advantages for both employees and employers. In December 1999, Aon Consulting surveyed employers about Web-based benefits delivery and financial planning. While work/life benefits such as workplace Internet access enhance employee commitment, the survey results revealed that employers strongly believe Internet access to both benefits and financial information reduces the cost and time spent by human resources staff in administering the organization's benefits. In addition, most employees said a Web-based system would help them communicate this information to spouses and families.

Self-service is always less expensive than assisted service and self-service through the Internet or other on-line resources is the least expensive service alternative. Specifically, the cost of Internet transactions is measured in pennies per transaction; interactive voice response is measured in dollars per transaction; and, human interaction is measured in tens of dollars per transaction.

Employers are now looking to expand their on-line delivery of benefits with particular interest in the work/life benefits that are low- or no-cost to employers. Paramount in their decision-making will be delivery mechanisms that are relatively easy for them to establish and inexpensive to maintain. This has led many employers to internally develop enhanced Intranets, coordinating their Web-based work/life benefits themselves.

ADVANTAGES OF WORK/LIFE BENEFITS

Some employers are finding work/life benefits effective in 1) reducing absenteeism, 2) reducing turnover, 3) increasing productivity, and 4) retaining customers.

Reduced Absenteeism

According to the 1996 Unscheduled Absence Survey by Commerce Clearing House, Inc., the rate of absenteeism has increased more than 14 percent since 1992. On average, annual absenteeism costs $603 per employee, and more absences are now attributed to family responsibilities and personal stress. To curb costs associated with unplanned absences, the Arnold and Porter law firm in Washington, D.C. made it easier for employees to come to work even when a child is ill. By offering backup child care, including sick care, for employees' children, the partners concluded that in 1993 alone, the firm saved $800,000. A Xerox customer operations site reduced absenteeism by 30 percent by allowing work schedules other than 8:30 a.m. to 5 p.m., five days a week. Some employees chose to work four long days a week, leaving the fifth day off for errands and more time with their children.

Reduced Turnover

Alternative work arrangements, such as part-time or reduced hours, have proven to curtail turnover costs. At Aetna in the late 1980s, the turnover rate was 23 percent among high-potential, professional women who took leave for childbirth. By modifying policies to allow employees to return part-time after family leave, attrition was cut by more than 50 percent.

The result: about a 90 percent retention rate for leave-takers after five years, and an annual savings of more than $1 million in recruiting and hiring costs. Aetna's director of work/life strategies said the costs really totaled $2 million, but Aetna wanted to be conservative in quantifying the success. Many employers believe that managers do not appreciate the total costs associated with turnover. Aetna uses 93 percent of a person's outgoing salary to figure the costs of hiring and training a new person. This formula also accounts for lost productivity and the supervisor's time. The cost of replacing a person making $25,000, for example, is $48,250. Ninety-three percent of salary is $23,250, which is added to the current salary of $25,000 to get the total in turnover costs. In 1997, ECS, an XL Capital Company, built the first employer-sponsored on-site daycare center in Chester County, Pennsylvania, adjacent to the firm's corporate headquarters. Prior to 1997, less than 65 percent of new mothers returned to work. Since 1998, at least 88 percent have returned.

Increased Productivity

Because employers can track productivity in various ways, the effect of work/life benefits on productivity is one of the best-documented benefits. In 1998, employees of Hewlett-Packard's Financial Services Center in Colorado approached management about working compressed workweeks of four 10-hour days. The employees, who handled financial transactions for the company, argued that the schedule would have two advantages: Customer service would improve because longer shifts would better span time zones for customer calls, and a weekday off would relieve stress and boost morale. Thirty-eight of 60 employees chose to work compressed workweeks, and overlapped their schedules to cover all their responsibilities on their weekday off. The immediate result was productivity almost doubled. Each employee in the group that worked compressed workweeks completed 63 transactions per day, while employees working traditional eight-hour schedules completed 37 transactions daily. What employees discovered is that when you work 10-hour days, you get into a set pace. There are gains in productivity because there is more quiet time available in the early morning hours when fewer people are in the office. According to Hewlett Packard's work options program manager, overtime hours were cut in half. Previously, overtime accounted for 7 percent of the hours worked by employees. Compressed workweeks reduced the figure to 2.7 percent of hours worked per employee.

Customer Retention

The newest discovery about the business benefits of work/life programs is their direct correlation with increased customer retention and satisfaction. First Tennessee Bank surveyed employees and customers at its branches and analyzed the financial performance of each branch. Results showed that the bank, by meeting employee's needs, encouraged employees, in turn, to provide more value to customers. The bank's first step was training managers on how to focus on employee's performance instead of their time in the office. Employees at all levels are allowed to work schedules other than the traditional ones. By overhauling work processes and time schedules, First Tennessee Bank actually increased profits. The account processing department instituted longer shifts at the beginning of the month because this was considered a "crunch" period. The change reduced the time required to reconcile customer accounts from 10 days to four, increasing customer satisfaction with no added cost. Business units run by managers who ranked highest—as measured by employee surveys—in the work/life arena have a 7 percent higher customer retention rate than other units. "This may not seem like a lot, but it amounts to multimillion dollars," says First Tennessee's vice president of work/life strategies. Employees with more supportive managers stay employed at the bank 50 percent longer than others. As a result, the bank saved more than $1 million in turnover costs in the past three years. First Tennessee has the highest customer retention rates of any bank in the country. Once reduced hours and full benefits were instituted, 85 percent of the employees who switched over from full-time hours said they would have quit otherwise. The bank estimates that total replacement costs saved $5,000 to $10,000 per nonmanagerial employee, and $30,000 to $50,000 per managerial employee.

STAGES OF WORK/LIFE BENEFITS

Human resources departments are most often asked to develop work/life initiatives or benefits for their companies. Typically, most companies move from one stage to the next—some more quickly than others.

STAGE 1–PROGRAMMATIC APPROACH[6]

Companies typically move from this narrow view of work/life by first overcoming resistance from managers. Convincing managers that the per-

---

6 The National Study of the Changing Workforce, *Family and Work Institute*, 1998. Published by Work and Family Connection, Inc., 5197 Beachside Drive, Minnetonka, MN 55343.

sonal lives of their employees have a significant impact on employees' work environment and work productivity is paramount. After this hurdle is cleared, there are four parts to the programmatic approach:

1. **Determine the needs of employees.** The first stage of the programmatic approach usually entails defining the problems that employees within the culture are experiencing. This is accomplished through interviews, surveys, and/or focus groups. Ask questions such as: How many times in the past year did you miss work because of an ill child? How many times did you miss work because your child-care arrangements fell through? Are you caring for an aging parent? How long does it take for you to commute to work? How do you use your lunch hour? Have you needed a lawyer in the past year?

   Typically, child-care concerns rank as the most prevalent work/life concern. Many employees develop their own proposals for work/life options as follows and their managers respond. Some managers block the new approach to balancing work and life because they are bound by tradition and continue to value face time for its own sake. Some managers fear that taking an employee's personal priorities into account will create either a sense of entitlement or feelings of resentment. These beliefs and feelings are understandable, but the new breed of manager deals with his or her people individually. Every employee of the new breed manager receives "special" treatment in terms of a workplace that takes personal priorities into account. Typically, in this Stage 1 programmatic approach, there are a few "new breed" managers in the organization.

   From Employee's Point of View

   - Employee outlines reasons for electing work/life option.
   - Ideal schedule is outlined, with acceptable schedule as backup.
   - Employee thoroughly describes how job responsibilities will be accomplished with business concerns addressed in detail.
   - Type and cost of equipment and supplies needed are noted.
   - Employee outlines mechanism for accounting for performance.

   From Manager's Point of View

   - Managers first consider business requirements to assess whether employees requesting flexible work options can be accommodated. Typically, managers will seek out other managers who have successfully implemented flexible work options and ask about the pros and cons. Managers are forced to rely much less on "face time" and more on managing to achieve goals and results.

- Managers need to evaluate such issues as process changes, task completion, and project scheduling. During the change process, communication is critical. All those involved need information and answers to their questions about how flexible schedules will impact everyone. Employees who continue to work a standard schedule may resent someone else's flexible hours. However, if employees contribute to the success of flexible work options and understand how they may apply to them at a future date, even employees with traditional hours may become supporters/contributors of work/life programs.

- It is highly unlikely that all or even a majority of employees will want to work less than a full-time schedule because most people want and/or need to earn their full salaries, but it is possible. If this occurs, managers should challenge their teams to develop a plan or work schedule that accommodates flexible schedules. Managers who view this as a challenge help grow their own management skills and create an opportunity for redesigning how work gets done.

2. **Develop a model.** The model will help determine the specific needs of employees at different stages of life.

3. **Match your company's current work/life offerings with the model.** Place your existing programs into a larger framework and identify potential gaps in benefits. Perhaps your company already has an effective EAP but lacks flexible work options.

4. **Use company data.** Use your organization's demographic data—age, gender, marital status, ethnicity, educational background, tenure with the company, etc. Keep statistics on the number of sick days that employees use and why, other absenteeism trends, turnover statistics, pregnancy leaves, other leaves of absence, exit interview data, and employee assistance program data.

STAGE 2–INTEGRATIVE APPROACH

At Stage 2, management has a more broadened view about work/life benefits. They consider it a business issue and assume centralized responsibility for making the benefits work effectively. The human resources department and/or a work/life advisory committee represented by various employees throughout the organization make recommendations for improvement that would not necessarily be equal to all employees—but they would be equitable. Policies and programs are packaged together and solutions are offered to employees that ask. In Stage 2, employees usually reveal concerns that different managers treat employees differently. For instance, while one manager encourages employees to use flextime or work four days a week, another manager may make employees feel guilty or deny the request.

STAGE 3–CULTURE CHANGE

This view of work/life benefits is mainstream and integral to the business achieving its strategic objectives. Usually, mandatory leadership training is conducted and the changing role of the manager is integrated within the company culture. Whether or not formal training is provided for work/life benefits depends upon the organization and the nature of the policies and/or guidelines. Informal sessions, such as panel presentations with discussion, may be just as effective. However, detailed policies often require more formal training. Managers are given case studies reflective of work/life initiatives and/or policies and asked to come up with win-win solutions. Managers become proactive advocates of work/life benefits, and are given tools to communicate their new beliefs and attitudes based on the following three principles:

1. **Clarify What Is Important.** Managers clearly inform their employees about business priorities *and* encourage their employees to be just as clear about personal interests and concerns—to identify where work falls in the spectrum of their overall priorities in life. The objective is to hold an honest dialogue about both the business's and the individual's goals and then to construct a plan for fulfilling all of them. The key to integrating work/life benefits with business operations is to understand the business and how it makes profits.

2. **Managers Recognize and Support Their Employees as Whole People.** This means managers openly acknowledge and even celebrate the fact that employees have roles outside of work. These managers understand that skills and knowledge can be transferred from one role to another and also that bound-

aries where these roles overlap and where they must be kept separate need to be established. Even in an open and flexible work environment where employees have a lot of leeway in making decisions and are provided flexible work opportunities, managers don't accede to every employee request.

3. **Managers Continually Experiment With The Way Work Is Done.** Xerox and the Ford Foundation proved what work/life proponents have believed for some time. If organizations take the time to question the way work is done, taking into account employees' personal needs, solutions that substantially improve both work and life would evolve.[7] The research team studied the corporate environments of Xerox, Corning, and Tandem Computers to see how work and business goals were accomplished. Through interviews with managers and employees, researchers discovered what bottlenecks existed and defined the clashes between work and employees' personal lives. One of the project's prime researchers, a professor of management at the Massachusetts Institute of Technology's Sloan School of Management, discovered that the very things hindering people's ability to lead fuller personal lives were the same factors hindering work flow and outcomes. "The project began with the belief that changes in work practices that were designed to make the workplace more friendly could be accomplished with no loss to business productivity," said Xerox CEO Paul Allaire. But this view underestimated the benefits of a work/life approach. The research showed that this approach offered companies a strategic opportunity to achieve a more equitable and productive workplace. By altering work processes, managers and employees at Xerox exceeded sales goals and improved customer satisfaction. Because the new methods of working took into account some of their personal needs, employees felt more supported by their managers, less stressed, and more in control of their lives.

Managers sometimes resist the three principles because they think that taking an employee's personal priorities into account will create either a sense of entitlement or feelings of resentment. It is understand-

---

7 Stewart Friedman, Perry Chistensen, Jessica DeGroot, "Work and Life: The End of the Zero-Sum Game." *Harvard Business Review*, Nov.–Dec., 1998.

able that managers worry about setting off waves of entitlement and/or resentment. But, *Harvard Business Review* (December, 1998) reports that managers who use the three principles rarely run into that. Because these managers deal with all of their people individually, every one of their employees does receive "special" treatment in terms of a work plan that takes personal priorities into account. Therefore, there is less chance for resentment to fester. As for entitlement, it is usually outweighed by the enormous loyalty these employees feel toward their managers.

CONCLUSION

No two companies—indeed, no two managers—approach the relationship between work and life exactly the same way. But it is fair to say that all organizational practices fall along a continuum. On one end is the tradeoff approach, whereby either the business wins or personal life wins, but not both. Further along is the integrated approach, in which employee and manager work together to find ways to meet both the company's and the employee's needs. That approach is becoming more common, as an increasing number of companies use work/life benefits to attract and retain talented people. Taken together, the three principles fall at the far end of the continuum—the leveraged approach, in which the practices used to strike a work/life balance actually add value to the business. Not only do the three principles seem to help people live more satisfying personal lives, but they also help identify inefficiencies in work processes and illuminate better ways to get work done.

Businesses and organizations continue to be under tremendous pressure to attract and retain talent. Employers want to be on a list, whether it's "Employer of Choice" or "Fortune's 100 Best Companies to Work For." Business is more competitive than ever and a productive, committed, and knowledgeable workforce is critical to the bottom line in this global economy. The competition for such a workforce is fierce. Companies are now in a position where they must engage their employees "where they are," meaning what's happening in their lives. No longer can employers expect employees to keep their working lives and personal lives separate. Even with more and better technology (cellular phones, electronic mail, facsimile machines, laptop computers, palm pilots, etc.) business and personal demands have made employees' lives more complicated. While the evidence in favor of flexibility is compelling, it is still not well integrated or widely accepted at many companies. Businesses and organizations still face a steep climb on the learning curve. In most companies, this will require changing the culture and implementing these important concepts:

1. Technology is here today and can substantively redefine how work is done.
2. Self-management is an essential skill that must be developed for tomorrow's workplace and workforce.
3. Management philosophy must embrace innovative and creative forms of scheduling and staffing.
4. Flexibility is the key to any long-term business strategy.

In the author's experience, programs that use quantitative measures to promote work/life benefits are in danger of becoming too formalized. After all, work/life benefits are rooted in deep subliminal values like work ethics, responsibility, morality, sensitivity, unselfishness, and generosity. It is difficult to quantify these through conventional research and opinion surveys. Yet, human resources needs to get its arms around these somewhat "soft issues" if a company or organization is to build and maintain a good relationship with employees. The challenge is to combine a strategic perspective with conceptual thinking. In the real world, this means thinking creatively, but staying within a pragmatic framework.

Time-Off Benefits and Family and Medical Leave Programs

Serafina Maniaci

INTRODUCTION

Today's technological revolution is enabling companies to reengineer work processes and transform many job duties. Business literature is replete with stories describing the latest innovations in production, distribution, and marketing. Many of these technological advancements are creating unprecedented flexibility in work schedules and permit work to be done at irregular times and off-site, many times from the employee's home. Work-life programs attempt to allow employees to balance employment and personal commitments by providing more flexible work arrangements. The emergence of work/life programs and their characteristics are discussed in Chapter 17 of the *Handbook*. This chapter discusses more traditional time-off benefits. These are the benefits that employees in many industries, including the manufacturing sector and the financial sector, have depended on and continue to depend on to balance work life and personal life. Companies have relied on these types of traditional time-off benefits to manage employee burnout and unscheduled absences and to reward longer-service employees when that is a desired objective. The U.S. Chamber of Commerce in its *1999 Employee Benefits Study* reported that of the 37.2 percent of payroll spent on benefits, 10.6 percent was for paid time off. The chamber defines paid time off as: (1) paid rest periods, coffee breaks, lunch periods, wash-up time, etc., (2) payments for vacations, (3) payments for holidays, (4) sick leave pay, (5) maternity and paternity leave payments, and (6) payments for miscellaneous reasons.

Not included in the Chamber of Commerce category of "paid time off" are payments for short-term disability, sickness or accident insurance, or severance.

This chapter's focus is on:

1. Paid Leave Time.
   a. Nonproduction time.
   b. Holidays.
   c. Sick days.
   d. Personal days.
   e. Vacation days.
2. Paid Time-Off (PTO) Plans.
   a. Miscellaneous Paid Leave Time.
   b. Bereavement leave.
   c. Jury duty pay and leave required by law.
   d. Military pay and leave required by law.
3. Extended Leaves of Absences.
   a. Time included as eligible leave under the Family and Medical Leave Act.
   b. Sabbatical leave.

PAID LEAVE TIME

Nonproduction Time

The payment of nonproduction time such as rest periods and clothes-change time is considered an intrinsic part of labor costs. The federal Fair Labor Standards Act (FLSA) mandates such payments.[1] Specifically FLSA requires payments for:

- Break periods shorter than 20 minutes. (Rest periods and lunch periods are not required under FLSA.)
- Preparation and cleanup before and after shifts.
- Travel between job sites.

---

1 The Fair Labor Standards Act (FLSA) was passed in 1938 and since then amended many times. Its basic requirements are: payment of the minimum wages, overtime pay for time worked over 40 hours in a work week, restrictions on the employment of children, and record keeping. The act covers employees who are engaged in the production of goods for interstate and foreign commerce, including those whose work is closely related to or essential to such production.

■ Downtime or call-in time, where the employee must be readily available for work.

There also are state labor laws that regulate whether paid or unpaid rest periods must be provided. State laws also require meal breaks to be provided but in general they do not require that the meal breaks be paid. Employees who are likely to be paid for meals are blue-collar workers in large private establishments and workers who cannot leave their worksite or are on constant call, such as coal miners, police officers and firefighters.[2]

Holidays

Although payments for holidays are not mandated by law, they are perceived by employers as an unavoidable component of labor costs especially for full-time permanent employees. After completing a probationary or introductory period, most employees are eligible to receive paid time off for holidays. Part-time employees and seasonal workers may receive full or prorated pay for holidays. If employers pay for holidays, the six holidays that virtually every company provides paid time for are:

1. New Year's Day.
2. Memorial Day.
3. Independence Day.
4. Labor Day.
5. Thanksgiving Day.
6. Christmas Day.

Many employers also pay employees for the day after Thanksgiving. Other paid holidays are provided by some employers. The next most popular days are President's Day and Christmas Eve Day. Because it is of rather recent origin, Martin Luther King, Jr. Day is not universally provided. However, this holiday is gaining as an observed paid holiday. Another popular holiday in the public sector is Election Day. In the private sector, Election Day is not a paid holiday unless negotiated in a collective bargaining agreement. There are, however, state laws that mandate time off for voting. Companies also may provide one or two floating holidays (the time may be prorated during the first year of employment) for employees to use at their discretion for personal holidays such as Good Friday and Martin Luther King, Jr. Day.

2 "Time-Off Benefits in Small Establishments," *Monthly Labor Review*, March 1992, 115(3): pp. 3–8.

A general requirement particularly for FLSA nonexempt (hourly paid) employees of holiday pay is that the employee must work the day before and after a holiday. (See Appendix 18–1 for information on the FLSA designation of exempt and nonexempt workers.)

Employees who take an unscheduled day off either before or after a holiday often are denied payment for the holiday if they are unable to provide medical documentation for the absence. Also, nonexempt employees who are required to work on a company designated holiday are likely to receive a pay differential for that day or compensatory time. Compensatory time is an option only if the nonexempt employee has worked less than 40 hours in the workweek; otherwise, according to FLSA rules the employee must receive overtime pay. According to the Bureau of Labor Statistics (BLS), the average number of holidays provided each year to full-time employees by private and public sectors ranges from 7.6 to 11.5 days with the public sector at the high end of this range.[3]

Sick Days

Eligibility for sick days is determined by length of service and, in some cases, employment category. A common variable used for employee differentiation regarding sick time is the FLSA exempt or nonexempt status. For example, a nonexempt employee may accrue one sick day or a stated number of hours of sick time per one completed month of service, while an exempt (salaried) employee may accrue one and-one-half days during the same period. In general, the total number of sick days are available immediately for use upon the completion of the accrual period. Some plans may allow employees to use a limited number of sick days to care for immediate family members.

To promote the conservation of sick days companies may permit employees to accumulate sick-days from one year to another up to a maximum amount. A sick-leave program allows employees to transfer unused, carried-over sick days at a one-to-one or two-to-one exchange rate to a short-term disability (STD) bank for an employee to use in the event of an extended illness or when applicable during the waiting period before long-term disability benefits begin. BLS data show that about 90 percent of full-time employees at medium and large private establishments (100 or more employees) with one year of service receive between five and nine days of sick paid leave.[4]

---

3 "Employee Benefits Survey Technical Note," *Compensation and Working Conditions*, Fall 1999,
    Vol. 4, No. 3, p. 76.
4 Ibid., p. 89.

Personal days

Paid time for personal days grants employees a few extra days off a year without requiring employees to identify the reason for the absence. The availability of personal days is believed to reduce unscheduled absences. With less restrictive advance-notice requirements than those for vacation days, personal days are likely to reduce the incidence of employees calling in sick to attend to a personal matter. For part-time employees and employees in their first year of service, personal leave days typically are prorated. Paid time-off plans which are discussed later in the chapter extend this concept of employee discretion in using an alloted number of days as the employee wishes, rather than necessitating that specific types of leave time be used for specific purposes. BLS data show that for full-time employees the average amount of personal leave granted by private and public sectors is 3.2 days.[5]

Vacation Days

Paid vacation time also is not mandated by law although there are state labor laws that protect vacation time once it has been accrued. A typical vacation policy grants two weeks of vacation after one year of employment with days being prorated during the first year of employment. Some companies may have varying accumulation rates with lower rates for nonexempt employees or non-executive staff. The amount of vacation time generally increases with the length of service often capping at four or five weeks after 15 or 20 years of service. BLS data show that full-time participants in the combined private and public sectors receive 9.3 days after one year of service, 15.7 days after 10 years, and 17.3 days after 15 years.[6]

A number of employers (15 percent according to Hewitt Associates[7]) supplement vacation plans by offering in their flexile benefit programs the option to buy additional vacation days. Under the Internal Revenue Code (IRC) Section 125, employers may allow on a tax-favored basis the option of purchasing (or selling) vacation days. These plans appeal not only to current employees, but also to prospective employees who may be reluctant to switch jobs if it means a reduction of one or two weeks of vacation time. In a typical flex vacation plan, an employee can

---

5 Ibid., p. 75.

6 Ibid., p. 75.

7 "Workers Around the World Gear Up for Summer Vacation," *Hewitt Press Release*, June 6, 2000.

purchase up to five additional vacation days with the cost usually being based on the employee's base salary.[8] When vacation days are purchased under a Section 125 arrangement, the IRC places restrictive conditions on the operation of the plan. The employee must use all of his or her non-elective (core) days before accessing the vacation days purchased and the law prohibits carryovers of these elective days to a succeeding tax year. However, companies are permitted to reimburse employees for unused days as long as they do it by the end of the employer's tax year or the plan year, whichever is earlier. Some companies that offer the option to buy vacation time also offer their employees the option of selling back the vacation time to the employer. In these plans, the number of days that an employee is eligible to sell, regardless of whether he or she sells them, is subject to Section 125 forfeiture rules. If a week of vacation that could have been sold is not used in the plan year, the week must be cashed out by the end of the plan year—or employee tax year, if earlier—in which the election is made; otherwise, it will be forfeited. Offering the option to buy and sell vacation time in a flexible benefit program enables employees to buy vacation days with flex credits or sell vacation days back for flex credits or cash. Offering a similar program outside of Section 125 on an after-tax basis allows plan participants to avoid the forfeiture penalties required by Section 125.

PAID TIME-OFF PLANS

Paid time-off (PTO) plans have gained in popularity for two reasons. First, these plans are appealing given the diversity in the workforce because they allow employees to use their block of time as they choose. Secondly, such plans typically reduce administrative record keeping because time need not be tracked for separate purposes. Under a PTO plan, employers bundle most of their paid time-off benefits into one package. A PTO plan consolidates the benefits of floating and personal days, vacation, sick days, and, in some cases, salary continuation programs and holidays into one single plan that provides benefits for scheduled and unscheduled short-term absences. The absences require no specific designation from the employee. The objective of a PTO is to give employees

---

8 Depending on employer objectives, the price for buying vacation days can be discounted from the base salary price, and for selling vacation days it can be set higher than the base salary price. Also, employers can establish a salary cap and exclude highly paid employees from participating in a flex vacation plan.

more control over their work schedule by eliminating the restrictions found in traditional paid time-off policies. Under a PTO plan, in non-emergency cases, employees have the freedom to take a day off to attend to personal matters without worrying about whether their managers will approve the leave. For example, an employee can schedule a day off for the delivery of an appliance without having to designate the day as a vacation day, a personal day, or a floating day. PTO advocates believe that this kind of freedom dissuades employees from calling in sick on the day of the delivery. By freely notifying the employer of absences in advance, unscheduled absences, which are more disruptive and costly to work processes, are reduced. Unscheduled absences are estimated to cost employers $600 per employee per year—a loss of $10,000 for a very small business, or $3 million annually for a large organization.[9]

Other savings may be derived from the implementation of a PTO plan. Employers often reduce the total amount of paid time that they provide[10] although in some cases the reduction affects only new hires. The combined amount of time off under these converted PTO plans is less than the sum of what was available under the separate policies. The justification for the reduction is that by combining the various categories of time off—especially sick time with vacation time—many employees have access to more paid time under the new PTO plan. Also, under some PTO plans, those employees who have not used all the time available at the end of the plan years may be allowed to carry over or cash-out unused time.

MISCELLANEOUS PAID LEAVE TIME

Bereavement Leave

Bereavement leave is specifically designated for use when a member of the employee's immediate family dies. Employers today are granting bereavement leave in other situations. Companies recognizing the diversity of today's family arrangements have expanded the definition of a family and are granting the leave not just for mothers, fathers, spouses and children, but also for stepparents, domestic partners, in-laws, and ex-spouses. BLS

---

9 Based on the 10th annual survey of human-resource executives conducted for CCH Inc. by market researcher Harris Interactive. "Missed work costs $600," *CNN America, Inc.*, October 23, 2000.

10 An employer implementing a PTO plan should consider state laws governing accrued vacation time.

data show that for full-time employees the average bereavement leave is 3.5 days.[11]

Jury Duty Pay and Leave Required by Law

Jury duty pay is provided by many employers with some paying up to a designated number of days and others paying for the entire leave regardless of the number of days the employee serves on a jury. Some companies that do provide some paid jury duty benefits reduce the employee's pay by any fees the employee receives for jury duty service. No BLS datum is available on the average number of days employers pay for jury duty leave, but BLS data do show that 76 percent of full-time employees in the public and private sectors receive paid jury duty leave.[12]

As for legislation regulating jury duty leave, the Federal Jury System Improvement Act of 1978 makes it unlawful for an employer to discharge, intimidate, and coerce employees because of their service on jury duty. However, the law does not require employers to pay salaries during jury duty. The law only requires that jury duty be considered an excused leave of absence with no loss of seniority and with benefits continuing to accrue. There are also state laws that govern jury duty leave, but only a few states stipulate that the time off must be with pay.

Military Pay and Leave Required by Law

Military leave is paid time off granted to employees who are members of the National Guard or a reserve component of the United States Armed Forces. Typically the leave grants time off with pay for annual military duty provided it is obligatory to maintain military status. Any period of time spent on military duty in excess of the maximum time allowed by the leave may be taken as vacation or personal days. BLS data show that the average paid military leave is 14.4 days annually.[13]

This type of leave obviously is not meant to address non-peacetime situations. In the event of war (e.g., the Persian Gulf War in 1991) or a conflict (e.g., the conflict in Kosovo in 1999), the time off needed by employees who are called to or volunteer for active military duty cannot be accommodated by paid military leave policies. Employees can look to federal law in such situations. Under the provisions of the Uniform Services Employment and

---

11 "Employee Benefits Survey Technical Note," *Compensation and Working Conditions*, Fall 1999, Vol. 4, No. 3, p. 75.

12 Ibid., p.75.

13 Ibid., p. 75.

Reemployment Act (USERRA) of 1994, veterans, reservists, and National Guard members participating on *active duty* or *required training* must be allowed up to five years of excused absences for military service. This is required as long as, when possible, advance notice is provided to the employer and the employee returns to work in a "timely manner" after completion of his or her tour of duty. The USERRA defines what is considered a timely manner. The applicable time limits are as follow.[14]

- Less than 31 days of service: By the beginning of the first regularly scheduled work period after the end of the calendar day of duty plus time required to return home safely. If this is impossible or unreasonable, then as soon as possible.

- 31 to 180 days: Application for reemployment must be submitted no later than 14 days after completion of a person's service. If this is impossible or unreasonable through no fault of the person, then as soon as possible.

- 181 days or more: Application for reemployment must be submitted no later than 90 days after completion of a person's military service.

- Service-connected injury or illness: Reporting or application deadlines are extended for up to two years for persons who are hospitalized or convalescing.

In addition to granting reemployment rights after a military leave, USERRA also provides other rights that include continuation of medical benefits up to 18 months and the accrual of retirement benefits during a military leave.

EXTENDED LEAVES OF ABSENCES

Family and Medical Leave Act (FMLA)

Signed into law in 1993 the Family and Medical Leave Act[15] allows 12 weeks of unpaid leave within a 12-month period with job protection and continued health care. Eligible employees are entitled to FMLA for the following reasons:

---

14 U.S. Department of Labor. *Small Business Handbook: Wage, Hour and Other Workplace Standards, Uniformed Services Employment and Reemployment Rights.* Updated December 1999. See www:dol.gov.

15 FMLA applies to employers that have had 50 or more employees for at least 20 weeks in the current or preceding calendar year. Only employees who have worked for at least 12 months and for at least 1,250 hours during the preceding 12-month period are entitled to take a leave.

a. The employee's serious health condition. (See Appendix 18–2.)

b. The birth and care of the employee's child.

c. Placement with the employee of a child for adoption or foster care.

d. Care of the employee's spouse, child, or parent with a serious health condition.

FMLA leave for the birth and care, or placement and care of a child must be completed within a one-year period, beginning on the date of the birth or placement of the child.[16] The act also provides that the leave can be taken intermittently or on a reduced work schedule. Most employers have integrated FMLA into their existing paid and unpaid time-off programs. Provided employees are immediately notified of the designation,[17] companies are permitted to designate any leave request because of a reason that qualifies for FMLA event as an FMLA leave. The effect of the designation is to draw down time from the FMLA's 12-week bank. In such cases, the employee does not have the choice of selecting FMLA's unpaid leave and not accessing paid leave, such as vacation or sick days if the leave is because of the employee's medical condition. For those employees who already had access to generous paid time-off benefits and liberal unpaid leave programs before the passage of the FMLA, the benefits of FMLA are statutory protection of employment and insurance, but not an extra 12 weeks of unpaid leave. However, FMLA does compel recalcitrant employers to acknowledge and accommodate the needs of employees when attributable to FMLA covered events. An example is paternity leave. Before the passage of FMLA, in companies where such a leave was unheard of, a father who wanted to take time off to care for his newborn child could only do so if he had vacation available and the duration of the leave could not exceed the vacation time available. FMLA mandates that he be granted up to 12 weeks of leave with no threat of retaliation. Successful lawsuits brought against employers attempting to deny or circumvent the law are ensuring the accessibility of FMLA benefits across all sectors of the labor market.

---

16 Also, if the father and mother work for the same employer, the leave they are entitled to take for the birth or placement of a child is limited to a combined total of 12 weeks if they are both eligible for FMLA leave.

17 FMLA imposes notification requirements also on employees. Employees must give their employers at least 30 days prior written notice of the proposed leave. Where advance notice is not possible, such as in the event of a medical emergency, notice should be given as soon as practicable.

Sabbatical Leave

In the past, sabbatical leave has been available only to employees of a select group of organizations such as educational and religious institutions. But sabbatical leave plans have been surfacing in more traditional corporate settings. A sabbatical program allows an employee to take an extended unpaid leave (or paid leave, in a few cases) with a guarantee of a job upon returning to work with no risk of being demoted. The program may restrict the types of projects or endeavors for which a leave will be granted, perhaps allowing a leave for community service or job-related education, but not for an extended vacation; and the program is likely to limit eligibility to employees with more than five years of service. The actual leave time allotted can vary from several weeks or months to a year. Sabbatical leaves are being considered for and, in some cases, incorporated in work/life programs with the view that they enhance employee morale and foster employee loyalty, creativity, and productivity. But there also are reports of companies that sponsor sabbatical leave plans scaling back on the plans or discontinuing them entirely. The sponsors cite problems of poor administration, of disruptions in the workplace, and, ironically, of retention efforts being undermined by participants job-hunting during the sabbatical leave periods.[18]

SUMMARY

Paid time-off benefits have a tremendous effect on recruitment efforts, employee relations, productivity, and, ultimately, on profitability. Companies face many challenges in maintaining paid time-off benefits that meet the needs of their workforce and their business strategies. In administering the benefits, companies must contend with a myriad of federal and state laws that can precipitate employee litigation if human-resource managers and line supervisors overtly or inadvertently fail to adhere to the legislation. Also, a company's time-off policies contribute to the attitudes and perceptions employees possess about a company. Paid time off from work is just as important to employees as medical and retirement benefits. Therefore, as companies look to establish the latest innovative work/life initiatives, they should begin by examining their traditional paid time-off benefits.

---

18 "It's About Time," *Industry Week*, February 7, 2000, Vol. 249, No. 3, pp. 47, 49–50.

FLSA EXEMPT AND NONEXEMPT WORKERS

In the broadest terms, the Fair Labor Standards Act (FLSA) exempts from its basic rules employees who require minimal supervision and exercise much discretion in performing their duties. According to the Department of Labor (DOL), the exact terms and conditions of an exemption must be made in light of the employee's actual duties and not just the designation of the position as a nonexempt position. The ultimate burden of supporting the actual application of an exemption rests on the employer. The act also exempts specific categories and businesses. Examples of exemptions include:[19]

1. White-collar employees employed in executive, administrative, professional (physicians, CPAs, engineers) or outside sales positions (as defined in DOL regulations) and who are paid on a salary basis are exempt from both the minimum wage and overtime provisions of the FLSA.

2. Employees employed by certain seasonal and recreational establishments are exempt from both the minimum wage and overtime pay provisions of the FLSA.

3. Commissioned sales employees of retail or service establishments are exempt from overtime if more than half of the employee's earnings come from commissions *and* the employee averages at least one and one-half times the minimum wage for each hour worked.

4. Certain computer professionals under Section 13(a)(17) of the FLSA who are paid at least $27.63 per hour are exempt from the overtime provisions of the FLSA.

5. Farmworkers employed on small farms are exempt from both the minimum wage and overtime pay provisions of the FLSA. Other exemptions and regulations apply to farmworkers.

6. Salespeople, partsmen, and mechanics employed by automobile dealerships are exempt from the overtime pay provisions of the FLSA.

---

19 See www.elaws.dol.gov/flsa/screen75.asp.

A P P E N D I X   18–2

GUIDELINES FOR THE TERM SERIOUS HEALTH CONDITION UNDER THE FAMILY AND MEDICAL LEAVE ACT[20]

Serious health condition means an illness, injury, impairment, or physical or mental condition that involves either:

1. Inpatient care in a hospital, hospice or residential medical care facility, or
2. Continuing treatment by a health care provider.

Continuing treatment means, in broad terms:

1. A period of incapacity (i.e., inability to work, attend school, or perform other regular daily activities due to the serious health condition, treatment thereof, or recovery therefrom) of more than three consecutive calendar days (and any subsequent treatment or period of incapacity involving the same condition) involving treatment two or more times by a health care provider or treatment by a health care provider on at least one occasion that results in a regimen of continuing treatment under the health care provider's supervision.
2. Any period of incapacity due to pregnancy or for prenatal care.
3. Any period of incapacity or treatment for such incapacity due to a chronic serious health condition that requires periodic visits for treatment by a health care provider; continues over an extended period of time; and may cause episodic rather than a continuing period of incapacity (e.g., asthma, diabetes, epilepsy, etc.).
4. A period of incapacity that is permanent or long-term due to a condition for which treatment may not be effective (e.g., Alzheimer's, severe stroke, terminal stages of a disease).
5. Any period of absence to receive multiple treatments by a health care provider either for restorative surgery after an accident or injury or for a condition that would likely result in a period of

---

20 See www.dol.gov/dol/allcfr/ESA/Title_29/Part_825/29CFR825.114.htm.

incapacity of more than three consecutive calendar days in the absence of medical intervention or treatment (e.g., chemotherapy for cancer, physical therapy for severe arthritis, or dialysis for kidney disease).

Health care provider means a physician, dentist, podiatrist, clinical psychologist, or optometrist who is authorized to practice medicine or surgery in the state in which the individual practices his/her profession. A chiropractor is limited to treatment consisting of manual manipulation of the spine to correct a subluxation, as demonstrated by X-ray to exist.

Examples of conditions that do not, by themselves, qualify for FMLA are:

1. A regimen of continuing treatment that includes the taking of over-the-counter medications such as aspirin, antihistamines, or salves; or bed rest, drinking fluids, exercise, and other similar activities that can be initiated without a visit to a health care provider.

2. Conditions for which cosmetic treatments are administered (such as most treatments for acne or plastic surgery) without inpatient hospital care or medical complications.

3. Without any other complications, the common cold, the flu, ear aches, upset stomach, minor ulcers, headaches other than migraine, routine dental or orthodontia problems, periodontal disease, etc.

4. A substance abuse absence because of the employee's use of the substance, rather than for treatment.

CHAPTER 19

Dependent Care Programs

Ann Costello

Increasingly, employers recognize the conflict that employees face between work and family stemming from dependent care responsibilities. As a result, the offer of dependent care as an employee benefit has grown dramatically. Dependent care benefits, originally thought of as child-care assistance, actually encompass employer support for the care of other dependents including elderly parents; elderly, ill, or disabled spouses; and dependent adult children. An employer that offers dependent care benefits usually considers them an important element of its human resources policy directed at maintaining or improving its competitive position.

In the last 20 years, the benefit portion of employee compensation began to change in a number of ways in response to social and demographic changes in the American family. The family stereotype composed of working father, housewife, and two or three children was rapidly being replaced by a family unit that reflected workplace and demographic realities. By 1998, both husband and wife worked in more than 70 percent of families, as compared to 15 percent in 1980. More than half the mothers of children under six and more than 75 percent of mothers with school-age children were employed.[1] The number of single-parent families with children under age 18 had increased dramatically to 28 percent, and more than 83 percent were headed by women. At the same time, life expectancy had increased; a 65-year-old male could expect to live until age 80.8 and a female to age 84. The U.S. Census Bureau estimated that there were 35.3 million persons age

---

1 U.S. Bureau of the Census, *Statistical Abstract of the United States: 1999* (119th edition), Washington D.C. 1999, Table 659, p. 417.

65 and over in 2000, and that number will double to 70.2 million by the year 2030. This will be approximately 20 percent of the population. A 1996 survey by the National Alliance for Caregiving and the American Association of Retired People found that more than 64 percent of elder caregiving was done by employed individuals. A national opinion poll reported that 54 percent of Americans believed that they would have elder-care responsibilities in the next 10 years.[2] Thus, family responsibilities were not only extended to children but also to the older generation. With far more of the adult population participating in the labor force, the need for some accommodation on the part of employers for employees' dependent care needs came forcefully to both the public's and employers' attention.

EMPLOYEE PROBLEM

For the past 20 years, the more troubling aspects of working parents and child care have received increasing attention. First, child care represents a considerable expense for employed parents; second, the desired quality of child care may be difficult to obtain and too costly to be a realistic alternative; and, third, employers of working parents have had to face the issue of either providing or subsidizing child care.

The Children's Defense Fund has estimated the cost of child day-care as being between $4,000 and $10,000 per child a year. The National Child Care Information Center estimates that a family spends as much as 10 percent of its income and as much as $15,000 depending on the number of children and services.[3] Further, consultant Sandra Burud has stated that employees spend as much as $700 a month for pre-school care and up to $1,400 a month for infant care.[4] There is tremendous variation depending on the age of the child, location of care, geographic region, and services desired. Elder care, depending upon the degree of skill needed for the caregiver or for special treatments, can be inexpensive for occasional at-home services or very expensive for a special daycare center with a nursing staff. A further example of a low cost program that would cost only $1 to $2 per employee is one that includes a dependent care fair, a resource library, and resource kit.[5]

---

2 U.S. Department of Labor, *Facts on Working Women Report*, "Work and Elder Care: Facts for Caregivers and Their Employers," No. 98–1, May 1998, gatekeeper.dol.gov.

3 U.S. Department of Health and Human Services, Child Care Bureau, Children Partnership Project, *Employer Toolkit Template: Child Care Options for Employers*, Washington, D.C. 2000, p.4, www.nccic.org/ccpartnerships/toolkit/section4.htm.

4 "Family Benefits Help Workers Keep Their Balance," *Business and Health*, March 1998, p. 15.

5 Charlene Solomon," Elder-Care Issues Shake the *Workplace*," *Workforce*, 78, October 1999, p. 61.

Both child care and elder care can best be seen as part of the human resource challenge facing employers in the United States. Employers are challenged to provide the type of employee benefits that make the greatest contribution to overall productivity and employee morale and to do so in a cost-effective manner. Well-designed dependent child-care and elder-care benefits offer an important means to meet this challenge.

CHALLENGE FOR EMPLOYER

Thus, employers who recognized they had human resource management problems—such as recruiting and retention of certain categories of workers, high turnover rates, high rates of absenteeism, and requests for time off the job—turned to employer-supported child care as a problem-solving technique.[6] Several factors have stimulated the growth of the dependent care benefit. These include information given to employees by labor organizations, media attention to child care as a significant issue, and a gradual understanding that dependents other than children required similar care and that employers could increase management efficiency by assisting their employees in solving these problems.[7] Also, the granting of tax-preferred status to employee benefit dependent care and the use of flexible spending accounts have encouraged the growth of these plans.

In 1997, 10 percent of full-time employees in medium and large private establishments (100 or more employees) were eligible for child-care assistance.[8] Employers with fewer than 100 employees had 2 percent of employees eligible for child care in 1996. Elder-care statistics are not available in these studies, but a major private study of 4,091 employers showed that 31 percent offer some type of elder-care assistance (mainly leaves of absence with 10 percent offering resource and referral).[9]

TYPES OF EMPLOYER DEPENDENT CARE BENEFITS

The mass media often present child care and elder care as synonymous. While there are similarities, human resource and benefit consultants should be aware of the differences. Families often seek elder-care assistance in a

---

6 See Joan P. Fernandez, *Child Care and Corporate Productivity* (Lexington, Mass.: D.C. Heath, 1986).

7 Allan Halcrow, "IBM Answers the Elder Care Need," *Personnel Journal*, 67 1989; William H. Wagel, "Elder Care Assistance for Employees at the Travelers," *Personnel* 4, 1987.

8 U.S Department of Labor, Bureau of Labor Statistics, *Employee Benefits in Medium and Large Firms*, 1997 (Washington, D.C.: U.S. Government Printing Office, 1998).

9 Business And Legal Reports, *2000 Survey of Employee Benefits*, 2000, p. 26, www.bir.com.

time of emotional crisis. The types of care needed can change quickly, and the strain of dealing with physical and mental deterioration of the dependent is extremely stressful on the caregiver. They often do not know where to seek help. Many times there may be need for care in a geographical location different than the employee's.

In contrast, the types of child care that are needed are typically routine (except for a child with special needs). The major stress factor is trying to do the two full-time jobs of parent and employee at once. Table 19–1 shows a comparison of two forms of dependent care—child and elder care—as an employee benefit. A discussion of the different programs follows. Categorizing the programs by costs is made difficult by the different degrees of possible actions. In designing the program, the cost should be viewed in relation to the cost of the problem it is attempting to address.

The different types of benefits can be classified according to the function or purpose of the program and according to ease of administration. The purposes of dependent care programs include:

1. Information or resource assistance.
2. Referral services.
3. Emotional support or counseling services.
4. Emergency or short-term services.
5. Direct or contractual provision of services.
6. Financial approaches.

Employers should consider the ease of administration, the cost/benefits, and the risk of implementation of the particular form of the benefit. They should examine questions of employee equity that may arise, so employees do not feel that only limited numbers of their coworkers will benefit from dependent care. The six categories of employer-provided dependent care assistance serve different purposes, take different forms, and vary in relation to the nature of the dependent because children and the elderly differ in caregiving and service needs. In any event, employers should understand the nature of the forms of dependent care benefits that have been implemented by a variety of private- and public-sector employers in the United States.

Recent surveys demonstrate companies' choices. The Families And Work Institute did a survey of 1,057 companies for its 1998 Business Work-Life Study (BWLS).[10] The sample was composed of 84 percent for-profit

---

10 Ellen Galinsky and James T. Bond, *The 1998 Business Work-Life Study: A Sourcebook* (New York's Families And Work Institute 1998) pp.V and VI.

T A B L E   19–1

Dependent Care as an Employee Benefit

	Child Care	Elder Care
Eligibility of dependent	Child under 13— worker claims as tax exemption.	Mentally or physically incapacitated dependent or spouse of the taxpayer—lives in employee's home for 8 hours a day.
Annual limit	Lesser of $5,000 total; $2,500 if separate tax return of married individual or earned income of either spouse.	Lesser of $5,000 total; $2,500 if separate tax return of married individual or earned income of either spouse.
Tax code	IRC Section 129 subject to definition and requirements of Section 21.	IRC Section 129 subject to definition and requirements of Section 21.
Care	Very routine—generally same type for almost all children of same age.	Individualized with rapid change in needs—must be closely monitored.
Decision-making on care and type	Parent-employee for child.	Employee in conjunction with dependents or spouse—level of resistance or resentment possible.
Benefit options	Straight benefit, flexible spending account (FSA), flexible benefits, vouchers, resource and referral, employee assistance program (EAP), family daycare, worksite daycare.	Straight benefit, FSA, flexible benefit, vouchers, resource and referral, EAP, family daycare, adult day-care.

and 16 percent non-profit companies. For child-care assistance, 36 percent offered resource and referral services, 9 percent offered child care at or near the workplace, and 5 percent paid for vouchers for subsidized care. The overwhelming form of assistance was flexible spending accounts (50 percent), but 5 percent did provide sick care for children and 4 percent back-up or emergency care. As far as elder care, 23 percent offered resource and referral services and 5 percent provided direct financial help for the use of local programs. Larger companies were more likely to offer elder care. A 1998 Survey of Work/Life Initiatives by Mercer and Bright Horizons found that more than 25 percent of employers with more than 500 employees offered some type of resource and referral elder-care benefit.

In the International Foundation of Employee Benefit Plans' study of 219 companies, dependent care was offered by 68 percent; three-quarters of them offered elder care as well as child care.[11] The most common benefit provided was flexible spending accounts, offered by 97 percent of the respondents. Negotiated employee discounts were provided by 9 percent, vouchers to provide services were offered by 5 percent, and 5 percent provided near or on-site dependent care centers. Only 1 percent made payments to dependent care providers.

One of the growing techniques to offer dependent care is by the use of partnerships or consortium, which is "defined as a joint venture of two or more businesses, community or government agencies, dependent care providers, and educational or religious institutions that provide money and/or resources to help workers meet the needs of these children, parents, or dependents."[12] The Conference Board in its survey found that 62 percent of 121 companies provide this and the previously cited BWLS study cited 5 percent of 1,057 companies with such arrangements. The American Business Collaboration for Quality Dependent Care with more than 100 major corporate members is seen to be a major influence on this movement.[13]

Dependent Care Resource and Referral Services

Employers may choose to limit their dependent care assistance programs to the provision of information pertinent to their employees' needs or to combine this with an actual referral service. The use of employer resource and referral services for child-care services has been well established, and, while employer experience in using these services for employee elder care is more limited, the results appear to be positive. The great contrast in the nature of the two different kinds of information and referral services means that very different types of community resources are involved in service provision.

For child care, the employer's objective in establishing an information service is to provide employees in need of child care services with a

---

11 "74% of Dependent Plans Cover Elder Care," *Business Insurance*, January 9, 1995, p. 6.
12 "Firms Share Duties in Work/Family Assistance," *Employee Benefit Plan Review*, August 1994, p. 39.
13 "It Pays To Share," *Employee Benefit News*, October 1, 1998, pp. 33–36.

listing of available providers; these providers control the quality of care. Employers can exercise quality control only insofar as they limit information and referrals to state-licensed, registered, or certified providers. Employers generally have to make a financial contribution to support the information system. Frequently, employers may contract with a nonprofit agency, such as the United Way, to provide the information service and to make referrals if that service is included. The nonprofit agency then has the responsibility to compile the listing of providers and, frequently, to attempt to ensure quality control through an on-site inspection process. The quality of service, however, is not guaranteed. The addition of referral services usually entails additional costs for the employer. If the information service is contracted out, it may mean an additional charge for the actual referral, since this involves the attempt to match the employees' need with the availability and type of service provided in the listings. If the employer is providing the referral system in-house, the additional time involved in finding an appropriate provider adds to the employer's costs for the service. This additional cost, however, needs to be weighed against the possible work time lost by requiring the employee to find a service provider, particularly on short notice.

This type of assistance may be used by any size company and would provide an employer with documentation on how many employees need some form of child-care assistance. Also, an employer with more than one location could easily use such a system. However, this option depends on a high supply of quality daycare assistance and does not provide any direct financial support. The service for elder care is similar to that for child care. However, the range of community resources and the types of service provided may be much greater. Some of the types of services are adult daycare, home health care, nursing homes, elder law assistance, home-delivered meals, respite care, senior centers, companion visits, emergency response, continuing care communities, and special transportation. Whether the service is provided in-house or is contracted out, it is of great importance that the information provider is knowledgeable about the various types of services and the special needs of the elderly. Unless the employer is of sufficient size to have specialists with gerontological knowledge and precise knowledge of community programs, the employer should look to contract with an external source for the provision of the service. In most U.S. communities of any size, a wide range of services exist to meet the needs of elderly persons, and, since the enactment of the Older Americans Act in 1965, a network of community services has developed. Most communities in the United States have developed local agencies, called Area Agencies on Aging, to follow the mandate of the federal act as amended to plan, coordinate, monitor, and evaluate local services available to the elderly. Community services funded through the Older Americans Act are provided without charge, as they are an entitlement based on age. Other community-based services charge fees, usually based on a sliding scale to match the income of the elderly person.

Elder-care services, nevertheless, are quite different from child-care services. The structure of the dependent care benefit for each of the two groups of dependents may be similar, but the specific services and programs differ greatly. The elderly dependent, unless mentally incapacitated, likely will want to be involved in the choice of service. Care arrangements may change more frequently in instances where the elderly dependent insists upon service changes or criticizes the care provider. This may add to the emotional stress of the employee.

As a result of these problems, resource and referral service may be linked to the employer's employee assistance program (EAP).[14] The employer may structure the information service so that it is linked to a counseling service. This may facilitate the employee's ability to express the tension and frustration that often are found in a dependent care situation for an elderly parent. Some employers have made use of employee support groups for those employees who serve as care providers for elderly parents or other relatives.

Resource services for either child care or elder care are intended to provide information on the range of available services, their nature, their costs, their schedule of availability, and often the qualifications of the caregivers. The addition of a referral system provides assistance in matching the specific employee need with the available service. A hotline service may be included for either child care or elder care to provide immediate information in the case of a crisis, such as a sudden illness or the disruption of the existing dependent care services.

Emotional Support or Counseling Services

As employers began exploring the need for elder-care assistance with their employees, they came to realize that the emotional problems and tensions surrounding dependent care for parents, spouses, or elderly relatives were often destructive to an employee's well-being and ability to function on the job. It became apparent that extending EAP services to

---

14 An example of this type of company is Child and Elder Care Insights, a national dependent care consulting firm based in Cleveland, Ohio. This company provides work and family support services and has national databases for both child care and elder care.

cover these problems might serve as a source of support to the employees and reduce associated productivity problems. Because the nature of the problems involved in elder care are different, employers who wish to extend EAP services to assist their employees in coping with elder-care problems will need to add specialists trained to handle gerontological problems or contract out for such services.

Emergency or Short-Term Services

Even if parents have made satisfactory arrangements with a child-care center to care for their child or children, a sudden illness can leave the working parents with the need to make alternative arrangements on short notice. In many cases, the demands of a job make it extremely difficult for a parent to stay at home to care for the sick child. In a few cases, employers have joined together to create an at-home emergency child-care service that covers a wide variety of situations. For children who are ill or whose usual care arrangements are not available, some companies offer emergency child care in centers established for the care of sick children. The children are cared for in a safe environment with professional help, so the parents are able to continue working. For some employers, it is less expensive to pay for this service than to pay for temporary help or to bear the cost of absenteeism. In some communities, the Visiting Nurse Association attempts to coordinate the startup of sick child programs to service a number of cooperating employers in private or public organizations.

Emergency child care encompasses not only sick-child care, but also the failure of the regular child-care options. This may be due to something as common as a snowstorm and the parent has to stay home. Some have estimated that a working parent misses up to eight days a year due to the lack of emergency care.[15] The benefit provides last-minute child care; it may be on-site slots in an existing center or home or a center only for back-up care. At one center the average usage is six times a year per eligible employee and if not available it would cost participating employers an estimated $2,000 to $4,000 per employee.[16] This benefit has shown growth among firms that offer child-care assistance in general. The cost will vary tremendously depending on the services offered and geographic location of the employer, but must be compared to productivity losses of absent workers. Emergency care for elderly dependents has not been a benefit given great consideration, other than through the resource and referral service that

15 Nancy Hatch Woodward, "Child Care To The Rescue," *HR Magazine*, 44 No. 8, August 1999, p. 84.

16 Charlotte Adamis, "Emergency Breaks," *Human Resource Executive*, 13 No. 6, May 4, 1999, p. 60.

links the employee with existing resources in the community. Area Agencies on Aging provide information on service availability and also coordinate many services. Local units of the Visiting Nurse Association can be contacted for the provision of nursing services in the home.

Contractual or Direct Provision of Services

There are obvious limitations to the financial-assistance programs employers may provide to employees for dependent care, because these programs depend on existing child-care facilities which may or may not meet employee needs, and employers have no control over the quality of the care provided. If employees are not satisfied with the available services, the employer can attempt to find new providers, terminate the benefit program, or consider providing various dependent care services itself. Employers may directly provide, or provide through a contractual arrangement, an array of services ranging from resource and referral or employee counseling programs to the provision of emergency care and even on-site daycare services. While only a limited number of employers offer on-site elder-care services, there is a possibility that use of them may expand in the future for those employers who have exceptional need for that type of service among their employees.[17]

Family Daycare Home Support

In some communities, daycare services for children and the elderly are available in family homes as well as in daycare centers, and some employers have made arrangements to make use of these facilities as an alternative to on-site care. Family daycare homes offer care by an individual for up to six children in a home. This form of care often is cited as being preferred for children from one to three years old, and many homes accept infants and toddlers. The family daycare home often is more convenient and less expensive than daycare centers and provides a homelike atmosphere. This benefit is cited as being the best for companies that have employees living in a broad geographical area who must commute distances to work. The individual employees have a broader choice in the selection of provider and can leave their children close to home. The cost of this care is less expensive due to lower overhead. However, while these advantages make this an attractive option, the quality of care may vary

---

17 Refer to Wagner, *Employees and Elder Care: Designing Effective Responses for the Workplace* (Bridgeport, Conn.: University of Bridgeport Center for the Study of Aging, 1989) for a thorough discussion of elder-care programs.

greatly. Employers in some localities have provided financial support to cover start-up costs and assisted in the hiring of workers and the development of daycare homes. The homes usually agree to carry the necessary insurance and to act as independent contractors[18] and, in some cases, may agree to price ceilings. The employer does not have management or financial control over the homes and is, therefore, not legally liable. The employer may or may not use some form of financial assistance to help employees with the cost of using the homes. (Vouchers, discounts, flexible benefit plans, and reimbursement accounts also can be used, subject to Internal Revenue Code [IRC or Code] requirements.)

Daycare Centers

Analysis of the information gathered in a feasibility study may lead employers to establish a daycare center to meet their objectives. Child-care centers provide institutional care for more than six children, from infants through school age (but normally over the age of three), and as many as 100 children may be cared for at one center. Centers usually are licensed, and extensive safety, health, and sanitation requirements are imposed on centers by local and state laws. If there are any educational services, such as preschool or kindergarten, the programs must meet the appropriate educational standards of the community and state.

Employers may offer child care in one of the several ways identified by Adolf and Rose. Centers may be:

1. Owned and managed by the employer.
2. Owned by the employer and operated by an outside group.
3. Contracted out to a nonprofit agency.
4. Contracted with a profit-making service.[19]

An employer may act alone or join a consortium of other firms. The consortium concept has been used by some employers in locating care in downtown urban areas, but difficulty in meeting varying employer objectives has limited its use. Another option is the building and operating of centers by developers for their office tenants. The centers are used as a marketing technique to attract employers to lease space.

Employer-supported daycare centers may be at the worksite (on-site) or located elsewhere (off-site), and the financial arrangements of the

---

18 Sandra Burud, Pamela R. Aschbacher, and Jacquelyn McCroskey, *Employer Supported Child Care: Investing in Human Resources* (Boston: Auburn House, 1984), p. 189.

19 Barbara Adolf and Karol Rose, *The Employer's Guide to Child Care* (New York: Praeger Publishers, 1985), p. 37.

employers may vary. Some firms have supplied the startup costs and expect the program to be self-sustaining; others have supplied full financial support and subsidized yearly center losses. Major employer concerns are cost, usage, and quality. These programs have high startup costs, and attendance may fluctuate. In exchange for financial support, employers may want preferential treatment for their employees, reduced rates, or reserved spaces.

The positive aspect of this option is that the center may be more flexible in providing the types of service required by the company's employees. The center may be open for different shifts of workers[20] and be easily accessible during breaks and lunch, parents may be able to visit their children, and the available resources may permit children to have broader experiences than available with a babysitter or daycare home. The employer has the greatest amount of control with this arrangement, and the center may enable the employer to recruit new employees from a broader range of the community population and foster a positive image for the firm in the community.

However, there are negative considerations for the firm. The employer must be concerned with pricing. The benefit may be provided free to the employee; or, more commonly, the employee will pay part of the cost. The existence of other child-care services in the community that offer lower prices and more desirable locations may offer competition for the center. If the center is in an urban location, employees may not want to transport their children long distances daily or on public transportation. Also, the employer may incur extensive administrative and legal problems imposed by providing a center. Liability for the center may become a major issue and liability insurance may be expensive or unavailable. Some companies set up a 501(c)(3) nonprofit corporation to avoid financial loss, but a firm's reputation can be severely damaged by claims of injury to children.

Financial Approaches

Dependent care assistance plans may be financed totally by the employer and treated as a separate benefit following IRC Section 129 and Section 21 guidelines. However, if employee contribution is involved, Section 125 of the Code allows this to be done on a pretax basis subject to the dependent care assistance plan (DCAP) requirements. Flexible spending accounts and flexible benefit (Section 125) plans provide attractive options for dependent care.

---

20 The General Accounting Office (1999) stated that 12 percent to 35 percent of the centers are open during nontraditional work hours.

Flexible Spending Accounts (FSAs)

FSAs, commonly referred to as reimbursement accounts, can be used to provide employees with dependent care benefits. Such an account may be established at a very low or negligible cost to the employer, and employees can pay for dependent care expenses with pretax dollars by using a salary reduction program. Table 19–2 illustrates the tax savings available through the use of an FSA for dependent care expenses. Money going into the dependent care account must be kept separate from the other possible form of reimbursement account—accident and health. Employers may contribute to the account but often do not. The total amount of the dependent care account is restricted by the requirement of Section 129 of the Code—the total maximum amount that may be in the account is $5,000 for a single person or married couple filing jointly, or $2,500 for a married person filing separately. This also is subject to the earned-income limitation. The employer pays no Social Security taxes or unemployment taxes on the amount of the employee's salary reduction.

As discussed later, *eligible employment-related expenses* provided for *qualifying individuals* by *approved caretakers* are governed by IRC Sections 129 and 21. While the plan may be funded by employee and employer contributions, if any form of salary reduction is used, the plan is subject to the Section 125 flexible benefit plan regulations. The amount of funds to be committed to the account must be decided in advance by the employee and must cover the whole period of the plan. Thus, an individual may not choose to participate for only three months, rather than 12 months, in order to protect the tax exclusion. A change in contribution amount is allowed only when there is a change in family status, such as a change in marital status, addition or loss of a dependent, or addition or loss of spousal employment. The plan also requires that any money left in an account at the end of the year is forfeited by the employee—"Use it or lose it"—and the employer must use the remaining funds for the exclusive benefit of the employees. This forfeiture requirement can strongly affect the desirability of such a benefit, and the employee should be conservative in estimating expenses. Also, it is essential that the employee do the comparison between the benefit of a salary reduction versus the tax credit of Section 21 discussed later. A Section 125 plan document is required for all salary-reduction plans, and the nondiscrimination rules and reporting requirements must be strictly adhered to.

The reimbursement account satisfies the equity issue so often raised about dependent care. Those not needing the benefit are not deprived of employer funds that could be used for some more desired benefit. Also,

T A B L E   19–2

Usage of Flexible Spending Account Tax Savings on Elder-Care or Child-Care Expenses

Information: $9,000 eligible expenses—Head of household tax status (1999 rates)	With Dependent Care Assistance Plan	Without Dependent Care Assistance Plan
Taxable income	$40,000	$40,000
Contributions to FSA (elder or child)	5,000	0
Net taxable income	$35,000	$40,000
Taxes—Federal	$ 5,316	$ 6,716
State*#	1,400	1,600
Social Security	2,678	3,060
	$9,394	$11,376
Disposable income	$25,606	$28,624
Elder or child expense	4,000	9,000
Spendable income after dependent care expenses	$21,606	$19,624
Increase in spendable income with FSA	$ 1,982	

* Assume 4% rate.
\# Assume state is following federal laws for withholding.

because the employer does not pay Social Security or unemployment taxes on the amount of the employee's salary reduction, these savings often are used to offset the administrative costs of setting up an individual account and reimbursing the employee—usually biweekly, monthly, or quarterly— for eligible expenses. Thus, in effect, the employee is paying for the cost of the benefit by trading Social Security and unemployment earnings credits for it, and the cost is borne only by those participating in the plan.

DCAP as Part of a Flexible Benefit Plan

While a dependent care assistance plan (DCAP) may be offered as a separate benefit, it also may be one of a choice of benefits under a Section 125 flexible benefit or "cafeteria" plan. A cafeteria plan is a written plan under which participants may choose among two or more benefits consisting of taxable benefits and certain other permissible nontaxable benefits. Whether or not the flexible benefit plan offers the DCAP choice to employees, it must meet numerous requirements under Section 125 of the IRC that are beyond the scope of this chapter and are covered in detail in Chapters 37 and 38 of the *Handbook*.

The flexible benefit plan must follow the dependent care assistance plan rules of Section 129 for the DCAP to be a qualified benefit. The plan may allow for care of children, handicapped dependents, and elderly parents. Reimbursement accounts using salary reduction are governed by Section 125. Requirements for dependent care administration exist for salary-reduction plans as well as the flexible benefit program, both being governed by Section 129. Flexible benefit feasibility studies are used to decide which qualified benefits and options should be included. The incorporation of a dependent care option often results after examination of the whole benefit package, rather than from a consideration of the need for dependent care benefits.

A flexible benefit plan provides an ideal situation for dependent care coverage. Recognizing that only a portion of employees need the benefit, the plan allows them to have it without depriving other employees of some portion of compensation. The employee who chooses dependent care elects it instead of some other benefit, thereby eliminating the equity issue. Also, the needs of employees change over time; some may want dependent care now but not in the future, and for others the reverse will be true.

Other Financial Approaches

Instead of or in addition to the methods just described, there are methods of more direct financial assistance for employees' dependent care expenses. These, by providing assistance through reduction of taxes, are employer-negotiated discounts at local daycare centers, subsidies, and child-care or elder-care vouchers.

Employer Discounts and Subsidies

Certain national child-care provider chains offer employers a discount on employee child-care services if the employer meets the provider's requirements for use. The Department of Labor found that a number of employers match the discount with an equivalent subsidy. The employer subsidy can be either a flat amount or a percentage of child-care/elder-care expenses and can be available for all employees or for only those employees in the lower-income brackets.

Vouchers

Vouchers for elder-care services are relatively new and vouchers are used more widely for dependent child care payments. Most voucher programs operate as Section 125 flexible spending accounts for dependent care, but they can be attractive to firms that cannot afford or choose not to adopt flexible benefits plans. The programs are limited to licensed care and are more common in the retail field.

Employers usually contract with a voucher vendor to administer the voucher program. Employees enroll in the program during an enrollment period and select a specific amount of pretax dollars to be deducted from each paycheck to cover all or part of the dependent care expenses. The employer advances monthly payments to the voucher vendor, who issues four vouchers per month to individual program participants. The voucher represents a fixed amount of available funds. The employee receives the voucher from the vendor and either endorses it over to the dependent care service provider or directly pays the provider and then turns the voucher in for reimbursement. To be reimbursed, the employee must submit identification information on the provider, as required by the IRC.

To implement a dependent care voucher program, an employer enters an agreement with the vendor firm and pays both a startup fee (based on the employer's total number of employees) and a small monthly administrative fee. Major voucher vendors can provide a complete program that provides employer/employee summaries, communication kits, administrative forms, utilization statistics, and annual IRS reports. The fees paid to the vendor are structured so that the employer incurs little or no cost, because of the savings on Social Security and unemployment taxes.

Vendor Plan

An employer may join other employers and buy "slots" or spaces from a local daycare provider. Their employees have priority for these openings; this is especially common for emergency daycare.

TAX POLICY

As already mentioned, the tax treatment of dependent care costs is governed by IRC Sections 21 and 129. Section 21 was passed by Congress in 1976 in response to rising dependent care costs and provides a tax credit on the individual's federal income tax liability. Also, important definitions such as "dependent" and "employment related expenses," required for Section 129 plans are stated in this part of the Code. The tax-preferred treatment of employer-provided dependent care assistance programs

(DCAPs) was added in 1981 by Section 129 and amended several times in the 1980s. Under the provision, payments made in accordance with the tax law are deductible for the employer and excluded from the employee's gross income. The maximum exclusion for a tax year is the lesser of $5,000 or the earned income of the worker or spouse. Eligible expenses and the method for determining the earned income of a spouse who is disabled or is a student are set forth in Section 21 of the Code. The employee must provide over one-half of the financial support of the dependent.

A dependent care program organized to meet Section 129 requirements can assist employees in securing services required for the supervision and care of children and of elderly or disabled dependents of the employee so long as the employee is employed full-time. The term *dependent care assistance* must meet the Code definition.[21] The Code requires that dependent care assistance be in connection with "employment-related expenses" incurred to enable the employee to be gainfully employed.[22] The expenses must be incurred for household services and the care for a "qualifying individual,"[23] defined as (1) a dependent of the taxpayer under the age of 13; (2) a dependent who is physically or mentally incapable of caring for himself or herself; or (3) the spouse of the employee if the spouse is physically or mentally incapable of caring for himself or herself.[24] For services provided outside the home, dependents in the last two categories also must live at the taxpayer's residence each day for eight hours.

If the dependent care services are provided by a dependent care center, to meet the Code requirements the center must comply with all applicable laws and regulations of a state or local government and receive a fee for the provisions of care for more than six individuals.[25] In addition, the DCAP must pass a special nondiscrimination test. The average employer-provided benefit for those not defined by the Code as highly compensated must be at least 55 percent of the employer-provided benefits given to those who are so defined.[26] Employees who are covered by collective bargaining agreements, who are under 21 years old, or who have less than one year of service may be excluded from the calculation. For plans that involve the use of salary reduction, employees with compensation below $25,000 may be disregarded, also. The reasoning for this provision is that

---

21 IRC Sec. 129 (e) (1) and as defined under Section 21 (b) (2).
22 IRC Sec. 21 (b) (2).
23 IRC Sec. 21 (b) (1).
24 IRC Sec. 21 (b) (1) (A,B,C).
25 IRC Sec. 21 (b) (2) (c).
26 IRC Sec. 129 (d) (2) and Section 129 (d) (8).

the existence of the tax credit for dependent care would benefit this group of employees more than would a salary reduction.

In order to meet the requirements for the federal income tax exclusion, a DCAP must meet the following eligibility requirements:

1. The plan must be in writing.
2. The employee's rights under the plan must be enforceable.
3. Employees must be given reasonable notification of the benefits available under the plan.[27]
4. The plan must be maintained for the exclusive benefit of employees.

Employees must be informed that they have to make a choice between use of the DCAP and use of the dependent care tax credit (DCC) in a given tax year, and employees are responsible for determining whether the tax credit offers them more tax savings than the use of the DCAP. Employers can assist employees in understanding which option provides the employee with the greater tax savings. For an example, see Table 19–3.

Currently, Section 21 of the IRC provides a credit against tax liability for individual income tax equal to 20 percent to 30 percent (depending on the taxpayer's adjusted gross income) for employment-related child-care expenses.[28] The amount of the employment-related expenses incurred on behalf of the qualifying dependent during any taxable year is limited to $2,400 for one dependent or $4,800 for two or more dependents of the taxpayer.[29] The dollar amount determined under Section 21 is reduced dollar for dollar by the amount of expenses excludable from the taxpayer's income under the Section 129 dependent care exclusion. Consequently, the employee who has the opportunity to make use of the DCAP benefit needs to assess carefully, based on his or her income or the

---

27 The notification must include a description of the dependent care credit (IRC Sec. 21) and the circumstances under which the credit is more advantageous than the exclusion. Also, on or before January 31, the employee must be given a written statement showing the employer's expenses or amount paid for the dependent care during the previous year. This may be done on Form W–2.

28 IRC of 1986 Sec. 21. "Employment-related expenses" is defined by Sec. 21 (b) (2) to mean expenses incurred (a) to enable the taxpayer to be gainfully employed and (b) for household service or for the care of a qualifying individual. Thus, expenses can qualify for the credit even though incurred for domestic services, such as cleaning and meal preparation, rather than actual care of a child or incapacitated person. Any amount paid for services outside the taxpayer's household at a camp where the qualifying individual stays overnight is excluded. This is provided the household includes a "qualifying" individual as defined by Sec. 21 (b) (1).

29 IRC Sec. 21 (c) (1) and (2).

T A B L E   19–3

FSA (Dependent Care) vs. Tax Credit

Karen	—Head of household tax status.
	—One child; $2,400 eligible expense.
	—$18,000 adjusted gross income.
Ann and Dan	—Married; both (filing jointly) work.
	—Two children; $4,800 eligible expenses.
	—$70,000 adjusted gross income.

Assumptions:
1. 1999 income tax rate and Social Security (OASDI and Medicare).
2. Standard deduction used.
3. Children are qualified dependents.

	Karen	**Ann and Dan**
1. Dependent care—FSA:		
A. Taxes gross income:		
Adjusted gross income	$18,000	$70,000
Taxable income	6,150	51,800
Federal income tax	926	8,915
Social Security tax	1,377	5,355
Total tax	2,303	14,270
B. Taxes with FSA:		
Adjusted gross income	$18,000	$70,000
FSA contribution	2,400	4,800
Adjusted gross income	15,600	65,200
Taxable income	3,750	47,00
Federal income tax	566	7,571
Social Security tax	1,193	4,988
Total tax	1,749	12,559
C. Tax saving with FSA	$ 544	$ 1,711
2. Child-care credit		
Karen 0.25 ($2,400)	$ 600	
Ann and Dan 0.20 ($4,800)		$ 960
3. Comparison		
A. Tax savings with FSA	$ 544	$ 1,711
B. Tax saving with child-care credit	600	960
4. Choice	Credit	FSA

Note: State and local taxes should also be considered—may increase tax saving differential for FSA.

Source: Compiled from information provided by The Segal Company, July 1995.

combined income of a married couple, which exclusion provides the greater tax advantage.[30] If the employee's marginal tax rate is less than the percentage used in the tax credit formula, then the tax credit generally is more favorable than the dependent care spending account. For employees in the lowest income brackets, it is important to understand the additional tax benefits received through the earned income tax credit.

The dependent care credit under Section 21 and the exclusion for employer-provided dependent care assistance benefits under Section 129 both require the taxpayer to report on his or her tax return the correct name, address, and taxpayer identification number of the dependent care provider.[31] If the caregiver refuses to provide the correct information, he or she may be penalized. If the taxpayer cannot report the required information, he or she must be able to prove to the Internal Revenue Service that the taxpayer exercised due diligence in attempting to provide the information on the service provider; otherwise, the taxpayer may forfeit the Section 21 or the Section 129 exclusion.[32] The reporting requirement often restricts the use of either benefit because some care providers do not report the income to the IRS and may not be providing "legal" services. Thus, they are unwilling to provide the required information and the taxpayer must choose between the needed services or the benefit. There are also employer reporting requirements for plan years starting December 31, 1988, and after.[33]

EMPLOYER OBJECTIVES

In the context of its overall benefit philosophy, an employer may decide to offer dependent care benefits when it finds it advantageous to meet its objectives. These objectives fall into three major categories:

1. Employee needs.
2. Employer productivity goals.
3. Improved external relations.

---

30 For example, if a taxpayer with one child incurred $6,500 of child-care expenses during a taxable year, of which $3,000 is excluded under the DCAP, the amount excluded under the DCAP ($3,000) exceeds the expenses eligible for the DCC ($2,400) and no dependent care credit could be claimed for the taxable year. If the amount excluded under the DCAP was only $1,000, then the employee could claim $1,400 ($2,400 − $1,000) under the DCC.

31 Taxpayers report this information on Form 2441, the form on which the credit for child and dependent care expenses is computed. If the dependent care provider is exempt from federal income taxation under Sec. 501 (c) (3) of the Code, the taxpayer is only required to report the correct name and address of the exempt organization.

32 IRC Sec. 21 (e) (9).

33 IRC Sec. 6039 (D).

Employee Needs

If the absence of available dependent care alternatives or the high costs of available care are creating hardships for employees, the employer may find it advantageous to offer dependent care benefits in recognition of employee needs. Personal considerations often dictate whether an individual accepts a particular employer's job offer or another's. Willingness to relocate is not as common as it was in the past, and family considerations are much more important. Individuals examine what the employer is willing to provide in total compensation, of which benefits are a major component. Employees see the employer's commitment to a benefit, such as dependent care, as recognition that employees are more than just workers, and assistance in finding high-quality dependent care or in reducing its cost bonds the employee to the company. The design of the actual benefit affects the level of freedom from concern, but almost any form of assistance provides some form of relief. An employee with dependent care concerns may see the need for and importance of such a benefit as greater than such benefits as a pension: The dependent care problem exists now; the other benefits are something for the future.

Employee Productivity

With increasing health care costs and the passage of more restrictive and demanding employee benefit legislation, employers are hesitant to add benefits or to increase existing benefits. An employer considering the addition of a benefit wants to know how the additional benefit will promote its goals. If the addition of dependent care benefits will contribute to productivity goals by reducing absenteeism and employee turnover and the attendant costs of hiring and training new employees, then the employer may decide that potential improvements in productivity outweigh the additional costs of the benefit.

Three separate national surveys done in the 1980s asked employers who offered child-care services how the company had been affected by the addition of the benefit.[34] The respondents in two of the studies were predominantly employers who sponsored their own daycare centers. The data were of a subjective nature but did present a positive relationship between

---

34 The three studies that provided the surveys are: Sandra Burud, Pamela R. Aschbacher, and Jacquelyn McCroskey, *Employer Supported Child Care: Investing in Human Resources* (Boston: Auburn House, 1984); Renee Y. Magid, *Child Care Initiatives for Working Parents: Why Employers Get Involved* (New York: American Management Association, 1983); and Kathryn S. Perry, *Employers and Child Care: Establishing Services through the Workplace* (Washington, D.C.: Women's Bureau, U.S. Department of Labor, 1982).

corporate child care and productivity, and improvements were seen in recruitment, employee morale, absenteeism, turnover, and employee work satisfaction. Recently, a Wayne State University study cited individual surveyed companies' costs ranging from $66,000 to $3.5 million for child-care related absences.[35] ChildrenFirst calculates the cost for such absences as $4,000 per employee annually.[36] The Hartford Area Child Care Collaborative reported in a survey of 930 employees from 18 organizations that more than one-quarter had suffered some employment problem at least once a month from family responsibilities.[37] Major studies have shown that offering child-care services dramatically lowers absences and turnover and increases productivity.[38]

Studies on elder care and productivity have centered on employment problems, caregiver characteristics, and diversity of required caregiving. Similar work problems such as absenteeism, excessive phone calls, tardiness, high stress, and emotionalism have been cited. A MetLife study projected a productivity loss of $11.4 billion to $29 billion to businesses annually due to elder-care responsibilities.[39]

In 1997, Transitions, Inc. reported that 50 percent of those in its survey worried about elder-care problems and 37 percent suffered tardiness, absenteeism, and lack of concentration due to caring for an older relative.[40] Employers have started to realize that if an employee is late, absent, or disturbed because of a child-care or elder-care problem, productivity will be affected. Someone else will have to perform the individual's duties, and this creates not only stress for other workers but also scheduling problems. Unforeseen problems, such as a late babysitter or a sick child, may mean that a project is not completed on time. At certain periods of the day, an employee's attention may not be on his or her work but on whether the child has arrived at home after school or whether a parent is receiving medication.

The studies cited here and other recent studies suggest a positive relationship between employer-supported dependent care and productivity. Articles about firms that have adopted dependent care plans are appearing constantly in the press, and individual firms are noting improved

---

35 Ann Vincola, "Back-Up Child Care: An Effective Solution to A Growing Need," *Benefits & Compensation Solutions,* 22, No. 2 (February 1999), p. 52.

36 Ibid.

37 Mary Carsky, "Balancing Work And Family Responsibilities," Unpublished, August 1999, p. 11.

38 U.S. Department of Health And Human Services, *op.cit.* p.3.

39 MetLife Mature Market Group, *MetLife Study of Employer Costs For Working Caregivers,* (Westport, CT: 1999).

40 Beth S. Offenbacker and Stacy A. Puskar, "Eldercare And Childcare Needs Challenge Workers," *Employee Services Management,* 42, No. 9, October 1999, p. 17.

morale, increased employee retention, reduced recruiting costs, and reduced absenteeism as results. All of these appear to have led to increased individual employee productivity. The *1997 National Study of the Changing Workforce* done by the Families And Work Institute found that employees were more committed, loyal, and satisfied working for companies that offered a supportive workplace.

Improvements in External Relations

Besides productivity gains, an employer may gain additional advantages external to the organization. The installation of new benefits often is announced in the local press and industry publications. The image of a "caring" employer is reinforced; a message is transmitted that the company is progressive and a leader in human resource management.[41] Other firms may use the plan as a prototype for their benefit packages, and the company's name is often repeated as a trendsetter. Positive public relations may be furthered by actual involvement of the company in increasing the quantity and quality of dependent care in the community; this depends, however, on the actual design of the benefit.

ISSUES

While dependent care may offer many advantages to a company, there are major issues that affect its acceptance and are probably causing many firms to hesitate.

Equity

In a conventional employee benefit plan option, such as health care coverage, an employee may or may not use the benefit during a given year; but all employees are eligible to use it any time, and over time all employees may have occasion to rely on it. However, dependent care may be used only by those who have "qualifying individuals" as dependents. While employees who do use and do not use it will change over time, resentment could arise among employees who have no need for such a benefit; compensation funds are being spent for something that does not help them at all. Equity is a fundamental issue in employee benefits, as can be seen from the nondiscrimination rules applicable to many benefits

---

41 An example of this is being named as one of the "100 Best Companies for Working Mothers" by *Working Mother*. The magazine is inundated by companies trying to be named. Also, it is very common for the media to report the findings.

that exist to protect against a disproportionate amount of funds for a benefit being spent on top management, owners, and stockholders. The equity issue in dependent care benefits could lead to individual personnel issues, and the actual composition of the employee group is important in determining the size of the potential problem.

Dependent-Child Care Industry

One of the major obstacles to providing dependent-child care is the nature of the industry itself. High-quality child care requires dedicated and informed care providers who have an understanding of child development and the patience to provide the appropriate personal care in stressful situations. The ability to attract and retain qualified workers is difficult, for the best paid child-care teachers received an average annual pay of only $19,000 in 1997 and have one of the highest turnover rates of any occupation (31 percent). Quality of care is hard to maintain with such a high turnover. Two major studies have found the quality of care provided in many family daycare homes and daycare centers to be low. The child-care center study presented a connection between child-care cost and the quality of care and the overall effect on the children.[42] Centers that have employers' subsidies tend to have lower teacher turnover rates, higher staff/child ratios, and higher pay; thus they tend to provide higher quality of care.

There also is a major shortage of available care. Connecticut, often cited among the states as having a highly progressive dependent care environment, still needs care for thousands more children. The market for child care is one of high demand and low supply—the seller exercises control, because the parent needs the service. Parents who have to work are forced to look for acceptable alternatives, and an "underground" industry exists in which payments made to providers are not reported for income tax or Social Security tax purposes, thus making it impossible even for parents to use, legally, the federal tax credit.

Upper Management

Decision-making about dependent care benefits is done by upper management. Some have argued that senior managers may be older and not really

---

42 Ellen Galinsky et. al., *The Study of Children in Family Child Care and Relative Child Care: Highlights of Findings* (New York: Families & Work Institute, 1994): and *Cost, Quality, and Child Outcomes Study Team, Cost, Quality, and Child Outcomes in Child Care Centers—Public Report*, 2nd ed. (Denver, CO: Economics Department, University of Colorado at Denver, 1995).

aware of the sociological changes that have affected the demographics of the labor force. Their sensitivity to the issue of dependent care may not be as acute as is necessary, and they may not be aware of the different options available for plan design. However, this may be changing. The Conference Board found in a 1999 study that 94 percent of corporate executives polled believed that elder care will be an increasing concern in the next five years and 58 percent believed child care would. Also the 1998 BWLS found that companies with women in one-half or more of the top executive positions are more likely to offer dependent care assistance plans.

Firm's Reputation

While there are positive outcomes for the reputation of a company offering dependent care, a risk manager would advise caution when considering the benefit from an external relations perspective. Firms do not want to be involved with a program that may be substandard, as the expected gain from such a plan would be more than offset by the problems presented. Personnel complaints and, ultimately, liability suits could severely damage the company's reputation. A firm must be very careful about the qualifications of any daycare provider with which it associates and may decide to deal only with state-licensed or registered providers. Attempts to limit liability by having a nonprofit foundation or a professional daycare chain control and manage the on-site or off-site facility have been utilized. In plans that simply make referrals, the choices given have often been limited to licensed care; here the purpose is to inform, not to be the provider. Flexible benefit plans and reimbursement accounts merely provide financial aid; choosing the provider, within the requirements of the IRC, is left to the employee, and the employer would not be liable for the actions of the dependent care provider.

Usage

Studies have explored nonusage by some caregivers of workplace dependent care plans, specifically elder care. While the results are not conclusive, they do raise interesting points. One is that social norms about caregiving for the elderly have not really been established.[43] In the past, people did not live as long nor need the types of care now necessary; thus

43 Lee Velker, "Elder Care Referral Services Gaining Employees' Interest," *Business Insurance*, July 31, 1995, p. 10; and Joan S. McGill and Larry S. Kelley, "Elder Care—The Employee Caregiver," *AAOHN Journal 38*, No. 6, June 1990, p. 281.

behavior models for those responsible for the care of an elder are not well known. Also, many workers are uncomfortable seeking workplace counseling and discussing caregiving with supervisors and coworkers.[44] The discussion often involves financial issues and the use or possible use of Medicaid. Workplace dependent care programs must stress confidentiality and provide extensive communication processes to achieve the employer's objectives. Recently, experts have cited the great variation in the types of care needed and the geographical location of employees' parents as detriments to the growth in elder care.[45]

DESIGN OF BENEFITS

The Feasibility Study

In the process of designing or redesigning a benefit package, feasibility studies often are conducted to explore the possibilities of a particular benefit. Employers considering adopting or modifying dependent care benefit policies need to research the specific needs and opportunities of their labor force. The analysis may be undertaken by management, but outside consultants often are used for their specific expertise. Expert assistance may be needed not only in the employee benefit field but also in the child-care and elder-care fields as well and may require the use of more than one consultant.

Set Objectives

The employer's overall employee benefit philosophy is the first consideration, after which the employer's objectives in adding dependent care should be established. With the objectives clearly defined and the need of the employees and their dependent care problems identified, those responsible for designing the new benefit may proceed.

The personnel problems that appear to diminish productivity should be reinforced by the benefit design. For example, to meet employer productivity objectives of reducing training costs, the level of acceptable turnover and the demographic characteristics of employees are important considerations. Some firms may accept a high turnover of employees, while others may spend large sums for recruiting and training and will

---

44 Donna L. Wagner and Gail G. Hunt, "The Use of Workplace Elder Care Programs by
     Employed Caregivers," *Research on Aging 16*, No. 1, March 1994, p. 78.
45 Amanda Milligan, "Elder Care Programs Fail to Generate Interest," Business Insurance, June
     1999, p.15.

want a very low turnover rate. Some industries, such as health care, have predominantly female employees in their child-bearing years. The feasibility study should identify and further examine those relevant employee characteristics that suggest child care would meet the company's objectives, keeping in mind that, while dependent care may not be useful for all employees, the productivity impact of dependent care problems on the entire organization may make alleviating those problems a priority.

Assess Employee Needs

Economic projections about future requirements for employees will help management to understand not only the immediate situation but also long-term implications as well. Data from personnel records are an important source of information. Examination of demographics of the employee group will show how many present employees are members of two-income families or are single parents; these data will assist in making projections on future child-care requirements. Comparative data about tardiness, absenteeism, and turnover can be collected for groups of employees with and without children. From this, the company can cost out the possible personnel problems as well as advantages associated with child-care programs. Since the collected data are very limited, other techniques may be implemented. Adolf and Rose, in *The Employer's Guide to Child Care*, recommended that a company use informal means and target groups for the feasibility study.[46] Information as to whether child care has been mentioned as a problem by employers is gathered from individuals by the personnel department and supervisors. Focus groups involve discussions among a small number of specifically selected individuals led by an expert whose purpose is to elicit individual viewpoints concerning dependent care needs and propose alternative responses to the identified needs. The leader tries to keep the discussion focused on plan design options that would be acceptable to the company.

Analysis of personnel records will not disclose the need for elder care, so the use of employee surveys is the most recommended tool.[47] There may be a wide variation between the need and the types of care

---

46 Adolf and Rose, *The Employer's Guide to Child Care*, p. 88.

47 Proper analysis of elder-care survey responses is important to measure the prevalence of employee caregiving. See K.M Gorey, R.W Rice, and G.C Brice, "The Prevalence of Elder Care Responsibilities Among the Work Force Population," *Research on Aging* 14, (1992), pp. 399–418. Past estimates often have been overstated due to different definitions and statistical techniques. However, future numbers will be larger due to an increasing aged population.

involved from one employee group to another. Also, the type of care needed may change drastically with the normal process of aging, and the "dependent" most likely will be involved in the selection and acceptability of the care. The survey may provide important information totally unknown to management, and the data will demonstrate which elder care benefit options are viable.

Evaluate Local Market

Management or its consultant, or both, should have the most current cost and tax implications of the different options available. To assist in choosing those possible for the firm, information must be collected on dependent care in the local community. The employer must try to establish the existing availability of daycare homes and dependent care facilities. The ages of children and appropriate facilities for each age group are important considerations; children may be infants, toddlers, preschoolers, school age, or those with special needs. Care for infants is the most expensive and often is in the shortest supply. Special children may be handicapped or temporarily sick; care of this type may not be available at all. Data are gathered about licensed or registered caretakers' costs, hours of operation, and services provided. If any other local businesses offer dependent care assistance, their programs should be examined.

As with child care, the availability of elder-care services is an important factor in the employer's decision-making process, and a similar study should be done for elder care by an employer considering that benefit. The employer-supported benefit plan should not duplicate but complement any programs the community provides and to which the dependent may be entitled.

Select Option

At this point in the feasibility study, company executives should be equipped to decide which design options are viable. Besides the obvious factor of cost, the firm must decide what level of involvement should exist in actually providing the dependent care. Low involvement would be a referral system; very high involvement would involve an on-site facility. A firm's ability to spend additional dollars on a new benefit will place constraints on acceptable alternatives. A flexible benefit plan that includes dependent care but also allows the employer more financial control may be attractive. For the child-care benefit, after analyzing the possible acceptable options, the firm does a formal needs assessment. The firm should be seriously committed before doing this, as the employees' expectations may be raised, and negative feelings toward the employer could result if the process is not handled properly. Adolf and Rose state that the questionnaire should cover (1) demographics, (2) attitudes, (3) the connection between child-care needs and work problems, and (4) special needs.[48] Besides the normal demographics, the first section also would cover the types and operating features of dependent care currently available. This assessment data, similar to the elder-care survey data, will assist the firm in deciding which of the acceptable options would most satisfy employees' needs now and in the future. On completion of the feasibility study, the employer should have identified the dependent care needs and associated problems that inclusion of dependent care as an employee benefit may alleviate, thus meeting the employer's objectives.

CONCLUSION

Employers concerned with their responsibility to design benefits that both meet employee needs and contribute to productivity will continue to search for ways to integrate dependent care into their existing benefit plans. Employers have gained an increased understanding that parents in the labor force who have young children currently comprise, and in the foreseeable future will continue to comprise, a substantial portion of the labor force. An even greater number of employees have and will have elder-care needs. The high cost of good-quality elder care and child care and problems with their continuing availability can contribute to the economic insecurity of those employees, particularly single parents and those with low incomes. Current evidence indicates that concerns over dependent care affect employee performance detrimentally. Responsible employers will seek to improve their ability to analyze the dependent care needs of their employees and to design benefits that meet employee needs as well as employer objectives and that are administratively feasible.

---

48 Adolf and Rose, *The Employer's Guide to Child Care*, p. 91.

Educational Assistance Programs & Group Legal Services Plans

Craig J. Davidson, CEBS

EDUCATIONAL ASSISTANCE PROGRAMS (SECTION 127 PLANS)

INTRODUCTION

The relationship between education and work is well known. Education has a positive effect on incomes, job potential, and workplace performance. The importance of education in today's workplace is particularly acute given the shortage of qualified workers. Employee benefits that offer workers educational assistance are a win-win proposition. Employers gain through a more highly educated and skilled workforce, increased employee morale, possible tax deductions, and a strategic hiring and retention advantage over employers who do not offer educational assistance benefits. Similarly, employees gain from employer-sponsored educational assistance through increased knowledge and skills that can lead to higher pay and better career opportunities.

Research suggests that this message resonates strongly with a growing number of employers. According to a survey of 460 U.S. companies, one-third of employers have increased their educational reimbursement offerings since 1993 as part of an effort to attract and retain employees. The survey also found that education programs are offered to more employees, with 38 percent of companies offering educational reimbursement to at least some of their part-time employees.[1]

JOB-RELATED VS. NONJOB-RELATED EDUCATIONAL ASSISTANCE

Employer-sponsored educational assistance represents a variety of arrangements. Those arrangements, and the accompanying tax issues, can be separated into two categories—job-related and nonjob-related. The most common form of job-related educational assistance is an educational reimbursement program (ERP). Employers that offer ERPs can reimburse an employee for job-related educational expenses as a *working condition fringe* and exclude the expense from the employee's gross income.[2] Educational assistance is job-related if it helps to maintain or improve skills required for a job, trade, or business, or meets the requirements imposed by an employer (or by law) as a condition to retaining an employee's job, status, or salary. Exclusions or deductions are not permitted for: (1) education required for the employee to meet the minimum educational requirements for qualification in his or her employment or other trade or business, or (2) expenditures made by an individual for education that is part of a program of study that will qualify him or her in a new trade or business.[3] Employers are not limited on the amount of excludable assistance if the education is job related. An example could include software training for an employee who needs to use that software on the job.

The remainder of this chapter will deal with programs that can offer both nonjob-related educational assistance and job-related educational reimbursement. These arrangements, known as *educational assistance programs*, are sanctioned under Section 127 of the Internal Revenue Code (IRC).

OVERVIEW AND HISTORY OF EDUCATIONAL ASSISTANCE PROGRAMS

Congress created educational assistance programs with passage of the Revenue Act of 1978. Under these programs, employees can exclude up to $5,250 of employer-provided educational assistance from gross income.[4] Amounts of educational assistance provided above the $5,250

---

1 See *Design and Administration of Educational Reimbursement Plans*, (Lincolnshire, IL: Hewitt Associates 2000).
2 See IRC Sec. 132.
3 Treas. Reg. Sec. 1.162-5.
4 See IRC Sec. 127(a).

limit for educational assistance programs may be excludable under other sections of the Internal Revenue Code if the conditions of those sections are met. Actual amounts excludable from an employee's gross income are reported on the employee's W-2. Where an employee works for more than one employer, the $5,250 limitation applies to the aggregate amount of educational assistance benefits received from all employers.[5]

Congress designed Section 127 with sunset provisions that have allowed these programs to expire and lose their tax-qualified benefits over the years. Most recently, the Tax Relief Extension Act of 1999, enacted as part of the Ticket to Work and Work Incentives Improvement Act of 1999, extended Section 127 through December 31, 2001. Employers can exclude from employees' gross incomes the cost of undergraduate courses that begin before January 1, 2002.[6] Graduate-level courses are not eligible for tax-preferred payment or reimbursement.[7]

DEFINITION AND ADMINISTRATION OF AN EDUCATIONAL ASSISTANCE PROGRAM

Educational assistance programs are qualified plans under the Internal Revenue Code and must meet strict requirements set forth in the Code. Unlike the process for qualified retirement plans, employers who sponsor educational assistance programs do not have to request a determination letter from the Internal Revenue Service (IRS) for the plan to be qualified.[8]

An educational assistance program is an arrangement under which an employer provides education to an employee or pays the employee's educational expenses. The term *education* includes any form of instruction or training that improves or develops the capabilities of an individual.[9] Eligible educational assistance provided under these arrangements may include tuition, fees, books, supplies, and equipment. Expenses for tools and supplies (other than textbooks) that an employee may retain after the course ends, and/or meals, lodging, and transportation are not

---

5 See H.R. Rep. 1049, 98th Congress, 2nd Session, 6, 1984.

6 See IRC Sec. 127(d). According to IRS Notice 96-98, the start day of a class is the first day on which regular classes generally begin for courses offered during a regular academic term. A regular term is, for example, a semester or session during which the course is offered. Registration and enrollment dates do not determine when a course begins.

7 See IRC Sec. 127(c)(1)(B). Congress repealed the gross income exclusion for graduate-level courses in the Small Business Job Protection Act of 1996.

8 Treas. Reg. Sec. 1.127-2(a).

9 Treas. Reg. Sec. 1.127-2(c)(4).

considered eligible expenses. Other ineligible expenses include any payment or benefits for any course involving sports, games, or hobbies.[10]

Separate Written Plan

Section 127 requires that these plans be written exclusively for educational assistance benefits and solely for the exclusive benefit of employees.[11] Plans must be administered in a nondiscriminatory manner. Employers can, and typically do, offer educational assistance programs as part of a more comprehensive employee benefit arrangement. These arrangements may include cafeteria plans. Benefits under Section 127 cannot, however, be offered through a cafeteria plan that provides employees choice between taxable cash and educational assistance.[12] The written plan must set forth the details of the program and the employer must provide reasonable notice to eligible employees of the plan's terms and conditions.[13]

Exclusive Benefit of Employees

Educational assistance programs must be established exclusively for employees. Spouses and other dependents are ineligible to participate in the plan, unless they are also employees. The term *employee* includes certain self-employed individuals; retired, disabled, or laid-off employees; and employees on leave.[14] For purposes of an educational assistance program, any individual who owns an entire interest in an unincorporated business is considered both the employer and the employee. A partnership includes the employer and of each of the equity partners, if any. The partners are considered employees of the partnership.[15]

Nondiscrimination Rules

Employers that offer educational assistance plans to their employees must comply with nondiscrimination rules or risk plan disqualification and the loss of Section 127 tax benefits. An explanation of the nondiscrimination rules for educational assistance plans is as follows:

---

10 See IRC Sec. 127(c)(1).
11 IRC Sec. 127(b)(1).
12 IRC Sec. 127(b)(4); Treas. Reg. Sec. 1.127-2(b); and Treas. Reg. Sec. 1.127-2(c)(2).
13 IRC Sec. 127(b)(6) and Treas. Reg. Sec. 1.127-2(g).
14 IRC Sec. 127(c)(2) and Treas. Reg. Sec. 1.127-2(h)(1).
15 Treas. Reg. Sec. 1.127-2(h)(2).

1. **Highly Compensated Employees**—An employer's educational assistance plan cannot discriminate in favor of highly compensated employees (HCEs) with respect to eligibility for benefits under the plan. An HCE includes owners, officers, or self-employed individuals, or their spouses or dependents who are employees.[16]

2. **Five-Percent Owners**—The plan cannot provide more than 5 percent of the benefits paid under the program during the year to shareholders or owners (or their spouses or dependents) who on any day of the year owned more than 5 percent of the stock, capital, or profits of the employer.[17]

The IRS will not treat a plan as discriminatory merely because different types of educational assistance available under the plan are used to a greater degree by employees for whom discrimination is prohibited. Similarly, a plan may base benefits on the successful completion of a course, attainment of a particular grade, or satisfaction of a reasonable condition (such as remaining with an employer for a period of time after completion of a course).[18] Finally, employees participating in a collective bargaining agreement unit are excluded from nondiscrimination testing if the educational assistance benefits were established through good-faith bargaining.[19]

Reporting and Record-keeping Requirements

Section 127 plans are required to comply with certain reporting and record-keeping requirements under the Employee Retirement Income Security Act of 1974 and the Internal Revenue Code. An employer's reporting requirements include filing information annually with the IRS, on behalf of the plan, that includes the following:

- Number of employees.
- Number of employees eligible to participate in the plan.
- Number of employees actually participating in the plan.
- Plan's total cost for the year.

---

16 IRC Sec. 127(b)(2) and Treas. Reg. Sec. 1.127-2(e).
17 IRC Sec. 127(b)(3) and Treas. Reg. Sec. 1.127-2(f). The term *shareholder* includes an individual who is a shareholder as determined by the attribution rules under IRC Sec. 1563(d) and IRC Sec. 1563(e) without regard to IRC Sec. 1563(e)(3)(C).
18 IRC Sec. 127(c)(5) and Treas. Reg. Sec. 1.127-2(e)(2).
19 IRC Sec. 127(b)(2) and Treas. Reg. Sec. 1.127-2(e)(1).

- Name, address, and taxpayer identification number of the employer and the type of business in which the employer is engaged.
- Number of highly compensated employees.

The vehicle for providing this information to the IRS is Form 5500 and Schedule F.[20] Educational assistance program sponsors must also retain records of information sent to the IRS and other information relative to the financial transactions on behalf of the plan.[21]

SUMMARY

Support for educational programs can play a vital role in an employer's overall mix of employee benefits. Reimbursement for job-related educational expenses is the most common approach. Increasingly though, employers recognize the need for formal employee assistance programs under IRC Section 127 that help employees expand their knowledge and skills beyond their current job responsibilities.

That strategy squares nicely with a new, unwritten contract that has emerged among forward-thinking organizations and their employees during the late 1990s. That contract places less emphasis on job security and more emphasis on investment in worker education and skill training to attract and retain qualified employees. Educational assistance programs represent a powerful tool for organizations that adopt this philosophy.

---

20 IRC Sec. 6039D.
21 Ibid.

GROUP LEGAL SERVICES PLANS

INTRODUCTION

Contemporary employee benefit systems are a reflection of societal needs, economic constraints, laws, and demographic trends. Group legal services plans are one such reflection of our current times. The American Bar Foundation estimates that 37 percent of all employees will face a legal problem every year that a lawyer can help with, but fewer than one in 10 will seek legal help.[1] While a relative minority of individuals seek professional legal help with their legal problems, the need for such assistance is certain and growing. Population demographics also play a role in the advent of group legal services plans. According to one researcher, "a high correlation exists between age and the use of lawyers because most people wait until they are older to consider estate planning issues"—a highly utilized service in group legal assistance plans.[2]

LEGISLATIVE BASIS FOR GROUP LEGAL SERVICES PLANS

Congress provided the early incentive behind group legal services plans with the passage of key laws in the 1970s and subsequent provisions in the IRC. For example, the Labor Management Relations Act (LMRA) gave organized labor the right to collectively bargain for legal plans. In 1974, President Ford signed into law the Employee Retirement Income Security Act (ERISA) which preempted state insurance regulations. ERISA effectively provided a federal framework for group legal services plans.

The Tax Reform Act of 1976 added a new section to the tax code—Section 120. Under Section 120, employees, spouses, and dependents could exclude from gross income:

- Amounts contributed by an employer under a qualified group legal services plan, or
- The value of legal services received under a qualified group legal services plan.

---

1 See Sandra H. Dement, "Advice for Employers: How to Select a Prepaid Legal Benefit," *Employee Benefits Journal*, June 1999, p. 22, citing American Bar Foundation study.
2 Ibid., p. 22.

IRC Section 120 also permitted the creation of tax-exempt trusts to fund qualified group legal services plans.

Congress capped the amount that could be contributed to a group legal services plan at $70 per person.[3] This exclusion cap applied to the plan's "premium value" for insured and self-insured plans. The exclusion did not apply to the value of legal services provided under the plan. Under an insured plan, the premium value was equal to the premium paid by an employer for the plan. For self-insured plans, the premium value was the total amount paid by the employer under the plan during the year divided by the total number of individuals entitled, in their own right, to benefits under the plan.[4]

Qualification under Section 120 required the plan to:

- Be in writing and for the exclusive benefit of employees, their spouses, and dependents.
- Provide only personal legal services.
- Not discriminate in favor of highly compensated employees with respect to contributions or benefits and eligibility.
- Provide that no more than 25 percent of amounts contributed be provided to shareholders or owners (or their spouses or dependents) owning more than 5 percent of the stock, capital, or profits.
- Notify the IRS of application for qualified status.
- Be financed through payments to insurance companies, or persons or organizations providing legal services or indemnification against the cost of such services; trusts or organizations described in IRC Section 501(c) (20); other 501(c) organizations permitted to receive employer contributions for qualified group legal services plans; providers of legal services; or a combination of the above.[5]

Passage of the Revenue Act of 1978 established cafeteria plans under IRC Section 125. This section of the Code permitted employers to set up plans that gave employee participants a choice between taxable cash and non-taxable employee benefits. This tax provision proved to be popular and many employers established cafeteria plans as a result. The tax advantages under Section 120 made group legal services benefits ideal for cafeteria plans. As a result, group legal services plans grew in popularity during the 1980s.

---

3 IRC Sec. 120(a).
4 See *Benefits Coordinator* (New York: Research Institute of America, 1992), pp. 20, 102A, citing *Congressional Record,* October 11, 1988, p. S 15458.
5 See IRC Sec. 120(b); IRC Sec 120(c); Prop. Treas. Reg. Sec. 1-120-2; Treas. Reg. 1.120-3.

In 1992, Congress voted to sunset Section 120, effectively removing any tax advantage for employers to set up or maintain group legal services plans. Employers may still establish group legal services plans. Most common today, those services are offered as voluntary, employee-pay-all benefits. Despite the loss of tax advantages, employees still benefit through group purchasing of legal services and the advantages of group administration.

DEFINITION OF A GROUP LEGAL SERVICES PLAN

The term *group legal services* describes a variety of plan arrangements that offer legal services as the core benefit. In general, plans take on one of two basic forms—access plans and comprehensive plans.

Access plans are the more basic of the two forms. These arrangements provide participants with easy access, usually over the telephone, to legal advice and consultation for simple legal issues. Access plans can typically cost employees between $5 and $10 per month.[6]

Comprehensive plans typically offer the same benefits as access plans, but are usually established based on a traditional group benefits design. These plans can offer services for more complex legal problems such as financial guidance, consumer protection, property protection, family matters, and standard wills. Comprehensive plans typically also cover in-office consultation, research, negotiation, and trial presentation. The cost of comprehensive plans can run between $15 and $20 per employee, per month.[7]

Legal services plans are also referred to as "prepaid" plans. A "prepaid" legal services plan is an individual or group arrangement that is funded in advance of services being rendered through employer or employee contributions to a trust, group of legal service providers, or through insurance premiums.[8] These programs can be designed as either access plans or comprehensive plans.

GROUP LEGAL SERVICES PLANS AS AN EMPLOYEE BENEFIT

Many employers today offer these plans as a response to the tight labor market that has gripped the United States for the past few years. The

---

6 See Todd Ruopp, "The Growing Popularity of Group Legal Plans as an Employee Benefit," *Network*, Vol. 9, No. 9, May 1999, p.4.

7 Ibid.

8 Some researchers maintain that a plan funded with insurance premiums is not a prepaid plan. Research suggests that an insured plan is merely a prepaid plan where the insurance company holds the risk of loss.

maxim that employee benefits are offered to attract and retain qualified employees holds true with group legal service benefits. According to a recent study, respondents indicated an 80 percent likelihood that they would use legal and financial services if they were available. The same study found that more than 69 percent of men surveyed and 54 percent of women surveyed felt a legal insurance benefit would influence their choice of employer.[9]

DESIGN, FUNDING, AND ADMINISTRATION

The decision to add group legal services as an employee benefit launches a series of questions and processes. What type of plan best suits my organization and its employees? How should the plan be funded? What administrative burden does my organization assume in adopting a group legal services benefit plan? These are all valid questions.

Type of Plan

Selection of a plan design should start with an examination of the characteristics of the workforce. Is the employee population older or younger? A low-cost telephone access plan may be ideal for an older workforce. Where are employees located? Try to match your organization's choice of a legal provider network with the geographic distribution of employees. Telephone access plans may be ideally suited for rural workforces, while urban workforces may be better matched with legal provider office locations. What is the compensation level of employees? A population with more highly compensated employees may require a plan that offers financial counseling as a benefit.[10] Finally, and perhaps most importantly, these plans are designed so an employer or family member cannot use the program to sue the employer.

Administration

An organization's funding method will determine, in large part, the type of administrative procedures required to be compliant with federal and state laws. Employee-pay-all plans, for example, may be exempt from ERISA and therefore do not have to comply with the reporting and disclosure requirements found in Title I of the Act. To receive this exemption, the

9 See Ruopp, p. 6., citing study by Mercer Consulting, Inc.
10 See Sandra H. Demet, p. 23.

plan must comply with each of the following four conditions set by the Department of Labor:

1. No contributions are made by the employer or employee organization.

2. Participation in the program is completely voluntary for employees or members.

3. The sole functions of the employer or employee organization with respect to the program are, without endorsing the program, to permit the insurer to publicize the program to employees or members, to collect premiums through payroll deductions or dues checkoffs, and remit them to the insurer.

4. The employer or employee organization receives no consideration in the form of cash or otherwise in connection with the program, other than reasonable compensation, excluding any profit, for administrative services actually rendered in connection with payroll deductions or dues checkoffs.[11]

Plans that do not meet these criteria are subject to ERISA and required to comply with the following reporting and disclosure requirements identified in Table 20–1.[12]

Record-keeping

Administrators of group legal services plans (if the program is subject to ERISA) also are required to keep records that support and verify information required in Form 5500 or disclosed under ERISA in summary plan descriptions or summary annual reports. Records must be retained for six years after the Form 5500 filing date.

Enrollment

Enrollment in a group legal services plan can be voluntary or automatic. Voluntary enrollment plans require employees to make an election to participate in the plan and pay the enrollment fee or premium. Fees or premiums are generally paid through payroll deduction. Voluntary enrollment periods are generally held once a year. An automatic enrollment plan requires that all employees participate in the plan as a condition of employment. These automatic enrollment plans will be subject to ERISA.

---

11 See DOL Regs. 2510.3-1(j).
12 See ERISA Sec. 101.

T A B L E   20–1

Reporting and Disclosure Requirements for
Organizations (100 or more participants)

Item	File With	Disclose to Participants	When Due
Form 5500 (Annual Report) and Schedules	ERISA Filing Acceptance Systems (EFAST)	On written request; available for viewing	Last day of 7th month after the end of the plan year (unless extension is obtained)
Summary Annual Report	None	Yes, if plan is insured or otherwise funded	9 months after the end of the plan year (unless extension is obtained)
Summary Plan Description	Department of Labor (DOL) on written request	Yes	120 days after the plan becomes effective; for new participants, 90 days after becoming a participant
Summary of Material Modification	Department of Labor (DOL) on written request	Yes	210 days after the end of the plan year in which the change occurs

Source: *Willis Regulatory Compliance Manual for Health and Welfare Benefit Plans, 1999.*

SELECTING AN ATTORNEY PANEL

Providers in group legal services plans fall into one of two broad categories—open and closed panels. Employers must decide how much choice plan participants will have in selecting an attorney. If freedom of choice is important, the plan can be designed using an open panel of attorneys. Participants can use any licensed attorney on a fee-for-service basis. Under this design, plan participants utilize the services of an attorney of their choice and are billed directly by the attorney. When services are complete, the participant submits a claim form and the attorney's billing statement for reimbursement according to plan limits.[13]

---

13 See Jim Brennan, "Group Legal Insurance: An Effective Recruiting and Retaining Tool," *Compensation & Benefits Review*, May/June 1999, p. 88.

The closed panel approach allows a plan to contract with a group of attorneys to form a network. Using a network of attorneys affords the plan an opportunity to negotiate rates and services with a single entity. Generally, the plan design will provide financial incentives for participants to use attorneys in the network, or may restrict participants to using in-network attorneys.

Administrators of plans that use a network of providers have a responsibility to perform due diligence on the qualifications of the attorneys in the network. This due diligence can be performed by establishing and enforcing written guidelines of performance. Following is a sample list of reliable indicators of an attorney's level of expertise that can be incorporated into a plan's guidelines for attorney participation:

- Licensed to practice in a particular state.
- Member in good standing with the state bar association.
- Maintains an office for regularly engaging in the practice of law.
- Agrees to the methods and rates of payments for covered services.
- Agrees to provide services to plan members.
- Committed to client service.
- Adequate number of years in practice and breadth of practice (knowledgeable in areas frequently generating questions from plan members).
- Adequate level of support (associate attorneys, staff, etc.) and technology (phone lines, computer equipment, etc.).
- Accessibility during regular business hours and for emergencies.
- Good telephone demeanor.
- Acceptable levels of professional liability coverage ($100,000 is standard).
- Foreign languages spoken.
- Percentage of time spent offering advice and counsel.
- Reasons the attorney wishes to provide services to plan members.
- No record of fraud or felony convictions.
- Disclosure of any complaints or disciplinary actions filed and the outcomes.
- Community involvement.[14]

---

14 Ibid, p. 89.

SUMMARY

Providing legal services through a group benefit plan offers an employer an opportunity to meet a need among its workforce and to offer an attractive recruitment tool if communicated properly. Employers today struggle to compete for skilled employees who will bring maximum productivity to the workplace. Group legal services plans offer those employees important peace of mind for when inevitable legal issues arise.

Financial Planning as an Employee Benefit

Charles E. Hughes

Robert T. LeClair

Today's modern business environment places many demands on individuals, couples, and families. Two-career couples, downsized corporations, home computers and laptops, telecommuting, globalization, and other factors have contributed to a hectic and fast-paced modern lifestyle. Few people today have the luxury of adequate personal time to plan and manage their own affairs, including their financial situations. They are rightly concerned that, despite all their hard work, they may not achieve the security and peace of mind they desire.[1]

Similarly, corporations, faced with tight labor markets and intense competition, are anxious to attract and retain capable employees. In addition to paying higher salaries, firms have greatly expanded the menu of benefits available to their employees. Included in this menu, especially for officers and other highly compensated individuals, is the availability of personal financial planning services. Hopefully, freed from at least this one burden of modern life, employees will feel more relaxed and secure personally, and be able to contribute even more effectively in their work.

To make an informed decision on whether to offer such services as an employee benefit, an employer must understand the elements of financial planning. The first part of this chapter provides background information on the need for financial planning and the role of the financial planner and then outlines the financial planning process. The chapter con-

---

1 For a discussion of these concerns see, "The Overworked American: The Unexpected Decline of Leisure," by Juliet B. Schor, *Basic Books*, 1992.

cludes with an examination of financial planning as an employee benefit, discusses the providers of the needed services, and looks at the cost factors involved in providing them.

FINANCIAL PLANNING

Personal financial planning is concerned with acquiring and employing funds in a manner consistent with established financial objectives. Because money is a limited resource that can be spent in an endless variety of ways with widely different results, financial planning plays a critical role in the satisfactory achievement of objectives.

Individuals or families may experience problems in managing debt, current income and expenditures, protection, savings, investments, conflicting objectives, and haphazard or impulsive financial decisions. Perhaps most important, the individual or family may fail to meet needs and objectives in an economical and satisfactory way. Therefore, advice or consultation on the management of financial matters becomes a valuable service.

At one time it was common to think that only the wealthy needed to be concerned with personal financial planning. This is no longer the case. Increased income levels and benefits, taxation, inheritances, sophisticated financial markets and instruments, increasing longevity, and a generally higher standard of living have all added to the complexity of managing personal finances. The growth and change of our economy and social structure have contributed to the widespread acceptance of the need for planning.

The need for and applicability of financial planning is much broader in our society today than most individuals realize. Many people look only at their bank accounts or investment portfolios in determining the extent of their wealth. They fail to consider other assets, including their equity in a home, personal property (such as automobiles, furniture, and paintings), the cash value of life insurance, pension benefits, divorce settlements, profit-sharing programs, Social Security benefits, and other hidden assets as part of their financial position. Finally, individuals or couples concentrating on the demands of careers simply do not have time to explore all the possibilities for putting money to work and may fail to consider the consequences that can occur if financial planning is neglected.

The Role of the Financial Planner

The management of financial affairs has been changing through the years. There was a time when setting a budget for household expenditures was considered to be adequate financial planning. If adhering to that budget was difficult, or if carrying out the plan seemed impossible, an individual might have sought the advice of a counselor. Such an adviser would have reviewed the client's income and expenditures and devised a spending plan that made efficient use of the available income.

As income levels increased, larger amounts of surplus disposable income became available. Individuals and families sought ways of making money work harder for them. Various investments may have looked interesting, but the complexities of the securities markets appeared to be overwhelming. At this point, the counselor also was asked to take on the role of an investment adviser. However, investment opportunities were much broader than just securities. The adviser also was expected to be knowledgeable concerning real estate, tax-advantaged investments, and even such "hard" assets as gold or diamonds.

Added to this were the client's needs for an accountant to prepare tax returns, a lawyer to draft wills and other documents, and an insurance agent to assist in the protection, preservation, and distribution of an estate. Today, the adviser has become someone who counsels clients in all of these areas and who serves as an intermediary in all these functions. From the growing needs of consumers has emerged a new professional, the financial planner.

The role of the financial planner is to provide total financial management for individuals or families to enable them to realize the maximum enjoyment of their finances in an efficient and economic manner. The best way to accomplish the financial objectives of a client is to develop specific plans to direct and control financial activity and progress. The financial planner must assess the client's current financial position, assist in establishing his or her objectives, consider all constraints and variables that bear on those objectives, and develop realistic projections and plans based on these factors. Financial planning is a process, an ongoing series of interrelated activities.

The Financial Planning Process

It is most important to understand the concept of financial planning not as a product or service, but as a process. Many persons who claim to provide planning services are really selling products and nothing more. For them, a "good plan" is simply one that requires extensive use of their products whatever they may be. Similarly, a view of financial planning as a service provided at one point in time is also inadequate. This concept does not provide for the continuing needs of an individual or family for information, analysis, and review of its program.

Financial planning should be thought of as a series of *interrelated activities* that a person participates in on a continuing basis. It is not something that is completed, even successfully, and then put away or forgotten. This is similar to the modern view of education that embraces learning not only through formal schooling but throughout one's lifetime. In the same way, financial planning must be done regularly and continuously to take account of changes in an individual's circumstances, the availability of new products, and varying financial market conditions.

New tax legislation, fluctuating market interest rates, and the introduction of new or modified investment vehicles are examples of changes that can alter the way people and businesses handle money as well as the rates of return earned on liquid funds. As new products appear and market conditions change, even the best-prepared financial plan will tend to become obsolete. Changes in an individual's personal situation also may require adjustments in the overall plan. Births, deaths, marriages, divorces, or a new business venture can have a great impact on financial as well as personal planning.

The following activities in the process of financial planning must be carried out regularly and, when necessary, should involve qualified, professional advisers:

1. Gathering background information.
2. Establishing objectives.
3. Developing financial plans.
4. Executing and controlling plans.
5. Measuring performance.

The flowchart shown in Figure 21–1 provides a summary of the individual activities involved in the process and shows the relationships among them.

Background Analysis

Financial planning requires comprehensive data on everyone participating in the program. Such information includes a record of income and expenditures as well as the current financial position of the individual or family. Prior to determining objectives, the financial planner needs information regarding the sex, health, age, lifestyle, tastes, and preferences of individual family members. Much of this information is subjective, and attitudes may shift considerably over the years. Such changes make it important that the financial planner maintain frequent contact with the client to be aware of important changes in these personal and family characteristics.

FIGURE 21–1

The Financial Planning Process

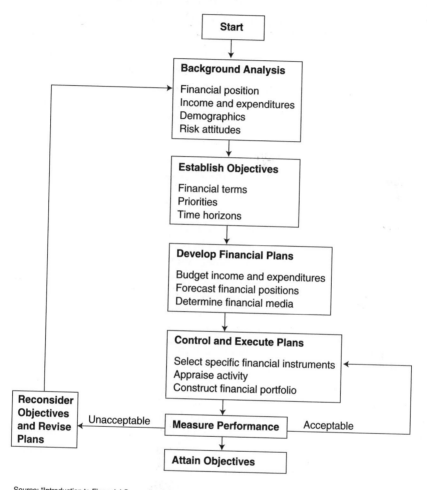

Source: "Introduction to Financial Counseling," *Financial Counseling* (Bryn Mawr, PA: The American College, 1982), p. 133.

Another important area of background analysis is the client's attitude toward the degree of risk in the overall financial plan. Feelings about investment risk, personal financial security, and independence are just as important as the client's income statement or net worth. An awareness of risk attitudes permits realistic, acceptable objectives to be established with the individual or family. By ignoring these feelings, the adviser runs the risk of developing a "good plan" that is simply out of touch with the client's personality. Such plans are not likely to be accepted or implemented, and a great deal of time and effort will have been wasted.

Unfortunately, for a number of reasons, attitudes toward risk are very difficult to measure or to judge. First, defining the nature of "risk" is highly subjective and varies considerably from one person to another. Second, attitudes about risk are likely to change dramatically over an individual's or family's life cycle. What seemed perfectly reasonable to a 25-year-old individual may be totally unacceptable to a 40-year-old mother or father of several children. Finally, risk attitudes are a function of many personal, psychological factors that may be difficult for the financial planner to deal with. Yet, the counselor should try through discussions and interviews with clients to determine their feelings about risk and to be alert to significant changes that may occur in this area.

Setting Financial Objectives

Stating worthwhile financial objectives in a meaningful way is a difficult but necessary part of the planning process. One reason why many plans fail is that financial goals are not described in operational terms. Objectives often are presented in vague language that is difficult to translate into action.

Each objective statement should have the following characteristics. First, it should be *well-defined* and clearly understood by all participants, including members of the financial planning team. Unless individuals really know and understand what they are trying to accomplish, it is not likely they will succeed. Writing down objectives is one way of working toward a set of clear and useful statements. Such comments as, "I want a safe and secure retirement income," do not provide much guidance for financial planners. They merely express an emotion that may be very real to the speaker but one that is hard to translate into effective terms and plans.

Second, good financial objectives generally are stated in *quantitative terms*. Only by attaching numbers to our plans can we know when the objective has been accomplished. For example, the objective could be stated as: "I want to have an inflation-adjusted monthly income of $10,000 in retirement." This is a particularly important factor for long-term objectives, such as those concerning educational funding or retirement. It is desirable to measure progress toward these goals at various points along the way.

The goal of having a particular sum for retirement in 20 years can be reviewed annually to see if the necessary progress has been made. If earnings have been lower than anticipated, larger contributions may have to be made in succeeding years. If a higher rate of return has been realized, future contributions can be reduced. Such fine-tuning is impossible unless numbers are associated with plan objectives. Adding numbers to objectives also helps to make them more understandable to all members of the planning team as well as to participants in the plan.

Finally, each goal or objective should have a *time dimension* attached to it. When will a particular goal be accomplished? How much progress has been made since the last review? How much time remains until the goal is to be accomplished? These questions and similar ones can be answered only if a schedule has been established with objectives listed at particular points in time.

Some aspects of the plan, such as retirement objectives, will have very long timelines associated with them. Others, such as an adjustment to savings, may be accomplished in a few months or a year. Whether long-term or short-term in nature, the timing feature of objective statements is very important. Even long-term goals can be broken down into subperiods that can coincide with an annual review of the plan.

After the objectives have been stated, they must be put in *priority order*. This ranking process is necessary since different objectives normally compete for limited resources. It is unlikely that a planner will be able to satisfy all the client's objectives at the same time. Some goals are more important, more urgent, than others. Critical short-term needs may have to be satisfied ahead of longer-range plans.

Once certain goals have been reached, funds may be channeled to other areas. An example would be the funding of children's education. After this goal has been met, resources previously spent on education costs may be allocated to building a retirement fund or some other long-range objective. Unless these and other goals have been assigned specific priorities, it is impossible to organize and carry out an effective plan. Conversely, a set of well-integrated financial objectives can make the actual planning process a relatively easy task.

Individuals and families should have workable objectives in each of the following areas:

1. Standard of Living. Maintaining a particular "lifestyle" normally takes the majority of an individual's financial resources. Setting an objective in this area calls for an analysis of required expenditures, such as food and shelter, as well as discretionary spending on such items as travel, vacations, and entertainment. If almost all income is being spent in this area, it is virtually impossible to accomplish any other objectives.

One widely used rule of thumb states that no more than 80 percent of income should be spent on maintaining a given standard of living. The remaining 20 percent of disposable income should be allocated among the other financial objectives. Obviously, this guideline varies from one person or family to another. But, *unless a significant portion of income can be channeled toward the remaining objectives*, those goals are not likely to be reached.

2. Savings. Almost everyone recognizes the need for funds that can be used to meet an emergency or other special needs. However, determining the ideal level of savings can be a complex problem. It is influenced by the nature of income received, individual risk attitudes, stability of employment, and other factors, such as the type of health and dental insurance coverage.

It is recommended that savings balances be equal to at least three months' disposable income. These funds should be maintained in a safe and highly liquid form where rate of return is a secondary consideration. Today, the typical bank money market account or money market mutual fund offers an excellent vehicle for maintaining savings balances. These funds offer a high degree of safety, ready access through the use of checks, telephone, or on-line redemption of shares, and an acceptable rate of return for this type of highly liquid asset.

3. Protection. This objective incorporates property, liability, disability, life, and medical insurance coverage. It should be designed to provide protection against insurable risks and related losses. Objectives in this area should take account of coverage provided through public programs, such as Social Security, as well as group insurance offered as an employee benefit.

4. Accumulation (investment). This is possibly the most complex objective in a number of ways. It relates to the buildup of capital for significant financial needs. These needs can be as diverse as a child's college education, a daughter's wedding, or the purchase of a vacation home. The sheer number and variety of such goals makes it difficult to define this objective and to set priorities.

Adding to the difficult nature of planning in this area is the generally long time horizon that may encompass 20 years or more. Finally, the wide variety of possible investment vehicles that can be used in the planning process adds to the overall complexity. Regardless of the reason for building capital, the critical ingredients in this objective are the ability to quantify the needed amount and to state a target date for its accumulation.

5. Financial independence. This objective may be thought of as a particularly important subset of the accumulation objective. It concerns the buildup of assets over a relatively long time in most cases. Such independence may be desired at a particular age and may or may not actually correspond with retirement from employment. Many persons may wish to have complete financial security and independence while continuing to work in a favored occupation or profession.

Since the planning horizon is such a lengthy one, this objective should be broken down into subgoals that can be evaluated, analyzed, and reworked over the years. More than most others, this area is affected by changes in government programs, such as Social Security, and in benefits paid by employers. For example, the recent removal of the Social Security earnings test will increase the retirement income of many working "retirees."

6. Estate planning. Objectives in this area typically are concerned with the preservation and distribution of wealth after the estate owner's death. However, accomplishing such goals may call for a number of actions to be taken well before that time. Writing a will probably is the most fundamental estate-planning objective, and yet thousands of persons die each year without having done so. These people die "intestate" and the distribution of their assets is determined by state laws and the courts.

For larger estates, avoidance or minimization of estate taxes is an important consideration. These objectives can be accomplished but call for careful planning and implementation prior to the owner's death. The use of various trust instruments, distribution of assets through gifts, and proper titling of property all can result in a smaller taxable estate. Carrying out such a program, however, takes time and should be considered as various assets are being acquired. This also is an area where professional guidance generally is necessary. If the financial planner is not an attorney, one should be consulted in drafting a will or in preparing a trust document.

Developing Financial Plans

Once a realistic, well-defined set of objectives has been established, the financial planner can begin to develop actual plans. This planning stage includes the budgeting of income and expenditures for the near term, along with a forecast of future activity. A projection of the client's financial position for the next several years also should be made.

These plans should identify the financial instruments to be included in programs to meet specific objectives. For example, specific savings media should be recommended for those who need more in the way of emergency funds. Should a family increase its regular savings accounts, purchase money market certificates, or buy shares in a money market fund? If an investment program is called for in the plan, recommendations should be made on the appropriate types of investments, such as securities, real estate, or tax shelters.

Executing and Controlling Plans

The next stage of the model calls for the financial planner to assist in setting the plan in motion. This may involve the purchase or sale of various assets, changes in life insurance protection, additional liability coverage, and other changes. All these activities should be monitored closely and appraised to see that they are effective in accomplishing the stated objectives. The outcome of some actions will be quickly apparent, while others may take a long time to produce results that can be evaluated.

Measuring Performance

The financial planner is responsible for gathering data on the plan's operations that are used to evaluate his or her performance and the actions of other professionals who may be involved. Such persons may include a banker, an attorney, a life insurance consultant, and an accountant.

This important step determines progress made toward the attainment of objectives. If performance to date is acceptable, no particular corrective action need be taken until the next scheduled review. However, if it is discovered that progress to date is unacceptable, several actions may need to be taken. These would include a review of the plans to see if they are still valid and an analysis of the market environment to take note of unanticipated changes.

It also may be necessary to review and alter the original objectives if they are no longer realistic and desirable. When this occurs, the entire plan may have to be recycled through each of the stages described previously. This model of financial planning is a dynamic one that is repeated continually as personal, financial, and environmental factors change.

FINANCIAL PLANNING AS AN EMPLOYEE BENEFIT

The array of programs, plans, and services that have been added to an employee's benefit package has expanded greatly over the past several years. Most benefits, by design, are selected or offered as part of a package for all employees; some are offered only to specific employees or groups of employees.

Financial planning is one benefit that has been limited primarily to key executives or other highly compensated employees. This came about partly from the belief that aspects of the program dealing with estate planning apply only to those individuals who will accumulate sufficient wealth to be subject to significant estate taxes.[2] Also, because programs recommended by financial planners may include forms of tax shelters that contain considerable risk, employees other than top executives might not have sufficient assets or income to justify the amount of risk involved. Finally, from the point of view of the employer, the full financial planning process generally is expensive, and this inhibits extending the benefit to large numbers of lower-income employees.

Despite these logical reasons for limiting the financial planning benefit to employees in top management, financial planning is gradually growing in importance as a benefit for those employees in the middle-management category. The increasing cost and complexity of pension, health, and other non-cash benefits, increases in the use of flexible benefit plans, the need for counsel regarding the expanding investment options in defined contribution plans, and the growing importance of retirement planning are all reasons why financial planning as an employee benefit is receiving increasing interest.

Services Provided

Because of the relatively high cost, many firms have opted for a partial financial planning service rather than the full process. These separate services include:

1. Estate planning—disposition at death, insurance arrangements, minimization of taxes, and estate liquidity.
2. Tax preparation—federal, state, and local returns; estate and gift tax returns.
3. Investment management—short- and long-term investment programs, tax shelters.
4. Compensation planning—analysis of options available, explanation of benefits.
5. Preparation of wills.

Some of these services may be provided by employees of the firm, while others are contracted for and performed by outside specialists

---

2 The Taxpayer Relief Act of 1997 made major changes in the law relating to federal estate taxes. The schedule of future excluded amounts is: 2000 and 2001—$675,000; 2002 and 2003—$700,000; 2004—$850,000; 2005—$950,000; and 2006 or thereafter—$1,000,000.

knowledgeable in a particular area. As the number of individual services available expands, the need for full financial planning becomes more apparent. Many companies now are providing financial planning benefits to their top executives, and some have expanded it to middle managers as well.

Advantages

The major advantages of financial planning as an employee benefit are:

1. Because of such factors as downsizing or corporate reengineering, many executives do not have sufficient time to devote to their own financial affairs. Financial planning as a benefit relieves them of having to spend time on financial planning and permits them to concentrate on business matters.

2. By reducing the likelihood a poor decision will be made on his or her own finances, the executive has greater personal peace of mind.

3. The employer probably is better able to screen and select financial planners. Thus, the executive is less likely to receive poor advice from unqualified planners.

4. Salaries offered may appear more attractive and competitive when such compensation is being used more efficiently to reach each executive's goals.

Disadvantages

Although financial planning as an employee benefit would appear to be attractive to both employer and employee, there are several reasons for not providing such services:

1. Financial planning might be construed as meddling in an employee's personal affairs.

2. There is a risk that the company could be held accountable for inaccurate or poor advice, since it has endorsed the services or employed the counselor.

3. Although the planning service is considered helpful to highly compensated employees, many companies are reluctant to provide benefits that are restricted to select groups of employees.

4. The cost can be substantial.

Who Provides Financial Planning?

Financial planning services are provided by numerous individuals and firms, including banks, insurance companies and agents, investment brokers, benefit consultants, lawyers, accountants, and others. The major firms specializing in financial planning services generally have staffs of professionals who are experts in investments, insurance, tax shelters, and so on, and who work as a team to provide the financial planning service. Smaller organizations may concentrate on one area and hire consultants to complete the planning team.

The selection of a financial planning firm requires care. It is important that the objectives of the employer are satisfied, and, from the employees' standpoint, that their individual confidences be protected and the advice be in their best interests. Some employers have attempted to provide financial planning services through in-house personnel. This is most effective when the benefit is limited to a single service, such as tax advice. However, problems occur because many executives are hesitant to discuss details of their personal financial affairs with fellow employees.

The selection decision sometimes is simply one of identifying the best financial planning firm available. Generally, a firm that operates on a fee-only basis is the preferred type. However, the objectives of the employer may warrant consideration of product-oriented financial planners. For example, if the objective of the benefit is limited to advice on life insurance planning, a competent life insurance agent may be able to satisfy the need. Further, banks, brokerage firms, and life insurance companies have formed financial planning divisions that provide support services for their personnel. Therefore, although an adviser may be product oriented, he or she has substantial breadth of assistance available to analyze and design broad-based financial plans. In these cases, a fee may be charged even though commissions exist.

Individual professionals call themselves financial counselors, financial planners, or financial advisers. Many of these persons still depend solely on commissions for their income. However, since it is difficult for any single individual to give professional advice in all areas included in a comprehensive plan, the trend is to join together to form firms that are rich in experience and professionally qualified in all aspects of financial planning and that are compensated through fees or a combination of commissions and fees. There exist today many quality individuals and firms that provide financial counseling. The most important ingredient, therefore, is to seek the individual or firm that understands financial planning as a process, one that can have important beneficial results for employers and employees alike.

Fiduciary Responsibility

As financial planners take on a wider range of responsibilities for their clients, a special fiduciary relationship develops between them. This arrangement arises whenever one person places confidence and trust in the integrity and fidelity of another. A fiduciary relationship is character-ized by faith and reliance on the part of the client and by a condition of superior knowledge of financial matters and influence on the part of the financial planner.

The existence of a fiduciary responsibility does not depend upon the establishment of any particular legal relationship. Nonlegal relationships can be fiduciary in nature, especially where one person entrusts his or her business affairs to another.

When a fiduciary relationship exists, the fiduciary (adviser) has a duty to act in good faith and in the interests of the other person. A fiduciary is not permitted to use the relationship to benefit his or her own personal inter-est. Transactions between the client and counselor are subject to close scrutiny by the courts. Especially sensitive are transactions in which the fiduciary profits at the expense of the client. Fiduciaries must subordinate their individual interests to their duty of care, trust, and loyalty to the client.

The Investment Advisers Act of 1940 is particularly important in defining the nature of a fiduciary relationship. One objective of the act is to expose and eliminate all conflicts of interest that could influence an adviser to be other than disinterested. Congress thus empowered the courts to require full and fair disclosure of all material facts surrounding the fiduciary relationship. The adviser must disclose in a meaningful way all material facts that give rise to potential or actual conflicts of interest. For example, an adviser who receives commissions on products, such as securities or life insurance, sold to clients should disclose the amount of sales compensation received on recommended transactions.[3]

Cost

The cost of financial planning varies, based on the range of services to be provided and the type of individuals employed to provide them. A finan-

---

3 Robert W. Cooper and Dale S. Johnson, "The Impact of the Investment Advisers Act of 1940 on CLUs and Other Financial Services Professionals," *CLU Journal*, April 1982, p. 35.

cial counselor or counseling firm may operate on a fee-only basis, a commission-only basis, or some combination of commissions and fees. The existence of commissions, which may eliminate or greatly reduce costs to the employer, can be a strong incentive for companies to seek product-oriented purveyors of financial planning services. It should be understood, however, that insurance or investment advice given to employees could be heavily weighted in favor of products available from the counseling firm. For this reason, employers usually prefer financial counseling on a fee-only basis, since the belief is that this provides the most objective analyses and unbiased recommendations.

Because the financial planning process often is extremely detailed and complicated, costs of $3,000 to $10,000 or even higher per executive are common for a complete counseling program. Another approach used by some counseling firms involves seminars where the counseling process and available services are explained to groups of eligible employees. Some firms charge a separate fee of $1,000 to $3,500 for the initial data-gathering or fact-finding visit with the employee. In addition, if legal documents or certified financial statements are required, there may be additional legal and accounting fees. Finally, after the initial year of the program, the annual fees for maintaining and updating the program are based on required time and effort, generally averaging $1,000 to $2,000 per employee.

The relatively high cost of financial planning as an employee benefit has undoubtedly contributed to its limited availability to only highly compensated executives or perhaps to its adoption at all. The cost of financial planning to the firm can be reduced by offering the benefit to employees on a contributory basis.

The fees paid for financial planning generally are deductible by the corporation for tax purposes if the total compensation to the employee, including the counseling fee, is not considered unreasonable compensation by the IRS.[4] When this benefit is offered to highly compensated executives, the fee generally would be small, compared with the executive's total compensation, and it is unlikely that total compensation would be considered unreasonable.

The amount the employer pays to the planning firm for services performed for an employee is considered taxable income to the employee and is subject to withholding tax.[5] However, an offsetting tax benefit may be available to the employee because deductions are allowed for services

---

4 IRC Sec. 106.
5 IRC Sec. 61.

related to tax matters or allocable to investment advice.[6] Therefore, it could be possible for the employee to contribute the cost associated with those services allowed as deductions. The financial planning firm should indicate clearly the charge for these services as a separate item on its billing.

In addition to the tax aspects, when supplemental legal or accounting fees are necessary, these expenses should be borne by the employee. Overall, contributions by employees could reduce the cost to the employer and make it possible for the firm to offer financial planning as an employee benefit.

CONCLUSION

Financial planning will become an increasingly important employee benefit as more employers offer such services and as more employees qualify for eligibility. Other factors contributing to this growth will be the maturity of the financial planning industry itself, and an increased need for financial counseling by employees who need to make investment decisions because of their pension plans being changed from the defined benefit to the defined contribution variety. While the costs associated with offering financial planning services as a benefit are not insignificant, clear advantages exist for both the employer and the employee. There also are areas of concern, however, and employers should carefully analyze the nature of their employees and the qualifications of those offering to provide financial planning services for them.

---

6 Fees paid for investment counsel are deductible only to the extent that *all second-tier* miscellaneous itemized deductions cumulatively exceed 2 percent of adjusted gross income.

Social Insurance Programs

Part Five covers the fundamentals of several social insurance programs that provide a basic layer of protection against various exposures. Chapter 22 discusses Social Security and Medicare, Chapter 23 explores workers' compensation programs, and Chapter 24 examines unemployment compensation systems. It is essential to understand these social insurance programs because their coordination with private benefit programs is vital to sound employee benefit planning.

CHAPTER 22

Social Security and Medicare

Robert J. Myers

Economic security for retired workers, disabled workers, and survivors of deceased workers in the United States is, in the vast majority of cases, provided through the multiple means of Social Security, private pensions, and individual savings. This is sometimes referred to as a *three-legged stool* or the *three pillars of economic-security protection*. It also can be seen as a layered arrangement, with Social Security providing the floor of protection, private-sector activities building on top of it, and public assistance programs, such as Supplemental Security Income (SSI), providing a net of protection for those whose total retirement income does not attain certain levels or meet minimum subsistence needs.

Although some people may view the Social Security program as one that should provide complete protection, over the years it generally has been agreed that it should only be the foundation of protection.

As described elsewhere in the *Handbook*, private pension plans have, to a significant extent, been developed to supplement Social Security. This is done in a number of ways, both directly and indirectly. The net result, however, is a broad network of retirement protection.

This chapter discusses in detail the retirement, disability, and survivor provisions of the Social Security program, not only their historical development and present structure but also a summary of the financial crises of the late 1970s and early 1980s (and what was done to solve them) and possible future changes. Following this, the Medicare program is described. Also, descriptions of the two public assistance programs

(Supplemental Security Income and Medicaid) that supplement Old-Age, Survivors, and Disability Insurance (OASDI), and Medicare are given.

The term Social Security is used here with the meaning generally accepted in the United States, namely, the cash benefits provisions of the OASDI program. International usage of the term social security is much broader than this and includes all other types of governmental programs protecting individuals against the economic risks of a modern industrial system, such as unemployment, short-term sickness, work-connected accidents and diseases, and medical care costs.

OLD-AGE, SURVIVORS, AND DISABILITY INSURANCE PROGRAM

Persons Covered under OASDI

OASDI coverage—for both taxes and earnings credits toward benefit rights—currently applies to somewhat more than 90 percent of the total workforce of the United States. About half of those not covered have protection through a special government employee retirement system, while the remaining half are either very low-paid intermittent workers or unpaid family workers.

The vast majority of persons covered under OASDI are so affected on a mandatory or compulsory basis. Several categories, however, have optional or semi-optional coverage. It is important to note that OASDI coverage applies not only to employees, both salaried and wage earner, but also to self-employed persons. Some individuals who are essentially employees are nonetheless classified as self-employed for the sake of convenience in applying coverage.

Compulsory coverage is applicable to all employees in commerce and industry (interpreting these classifications very broadly) except railroad workers, who are covered under a separate program, the Railroad Retirement system. However, financial and other coordinating provisions exist between these two programs, so that, in reality, railroad workers are covered under OASDI. Members of the armed forces are covered compulsorily, as are federal civilian employees hired after 1983. Compulsory coverage also applies to lay employees of churches (with certain minor exceptions), to employees of nonprofit charitable and educational institutions, to employees of state and local governments that do not have retirement systems (first effective after July 1, 1991; before then, coverage was elective, on a group basis, by the employing entity), and to American residents who work abroad for American corporations. Self-employed persons of all types (except ministers) also are covered compulsorily unless their earnings are minimal (i.e., less than $400 a year); beginning in 1990, covered self-employment is taken as 92.35 percent of the self-employment net income (such figure being 100 percent minus the OASDI–Hospital Insurance tax rate applicable to employees).

From a geographical standpoint, OASDI applies not only in the 50 states and the District of Columbia but also in all outlying areas (American Samoa, Guam, the Northern Mariana Islands, Puerto Rico, and the Virgin Islands).

Elective coverage applies to a number of categories. Employees of state and local governments who are under a retirement system can have coverage at the option of the employing entity and only when the current employees vote in favor of coverage. Similar provisions are available for American employees of foreign subsidiaries of American corporations, the latter having the right to opt for coverage. Once that coverage has been elected by a state or local government, it cannot be terminated. Approximately 70 percent of state and local government employees are now covered as a result of this election basis and the compulsory coverage applicable when the entity does not have a retirement plan.

Because of the principle of separation of church and state, ministers are covered on the self-employed basis, regardless of their actual status. Furthermore, they have the right to opt out of the system within a limited time after ordination on grounds of religious principles or conscience. Americans employed in the United States by a foreign government or by an international organization are covered compulsorily on the self-employed basis.

Historical Development of Retirement Provisions

When what is now the OASDI program was developed in 1934–35, it was confined entirely to retirement benefits plus lump-sum refund payments to represent the difference, if any, between employee taxes paid, plus an allowance for interest, and retirement benefits received. It was not until the 1939 act that auxiliary (or dependents) and survivors benefits were added, and not until the 1956 act that disability benefits were made available. The likely reason that only retirement benefits were instituted initially is that such type of protection was the most familiar to the general public, especially in light of the relatively few private pension plans then in existence.

The "normal retirement age" (NRA), also called the "full retirement age," was originally established at 65. This figure was selected in a purely empirical manner; it was a middle figure between two perceived extremes. Age 70 seemed too high, because of the common belief that relatively so few people reached that age, while 60 seemed too low, because of the large costs that would be involved if that age had been selected. Many of the existing private pension plans at that time had a retirement age of 65, although some in the railroad industry used age 70. Furthermore, labor force participation data showed that a relatively high proportion of workers continued employment after age 60. A widely cited, but erroneous, explanation of why age 65 was selected is that Bismarck chose this age when he established the German national pension program in the 1880s; the age used originally in Germany actually was 70 (actually, the plan was primarily a disability benefits one). The 1983 act provided for the NRA to increase from age 65 to age 67 in a deferred, gradual manner. Specifically, the NRA is 65 for those attaining this age before 2003 and first becomes 67 for those attaining this age in 2027.

The original program applied only to workers in commerce and industry. It was not until the 1950s that coverage was extended to additional categories of workers. Now, almost all are covered, including the self-employed.

The initial legislation passed by the House of Representatives did not require eligible persons to retire at age 65 or over in order to receive benefits, although it was recognized that inclusion of a retirement requirement would be essential in the final legislation. The Senate inserted a requirement of a general nature that benefits would be payable only upon retirement, and this was included in the final legislation. Over the years, this retirement earnings test, or work clause, has been the subject of much controversy, and it has been considerably liberalized and made more flexible over the years.

Beginning in the 1950s, pressure developed to provide early-retirement benefits, first for spouses and then for insured workers. The minimum early-retirement age was set at 62, again a pragmatic political compromise, rather than a number based on any completely logical reason. The three-year differential, however, did represent the approximate average difference in age between men and their wives; but, of course, as with any averages, the difference actually is larger in many cases. The benefit amounts are reduced when claimed before the NRA is reached, and are increased, although currently to not as great an extent, when the claim for benefits is delayed beyond the NRA. As the NRA increases beyond age 65, the reduction for claiming benefits at age 62 becomes larger.

Eligibility Conditions for Retirement Benefits

To be eligible for OASDI retirement benefits, individuals must have a certain amount of covered employment. In general, these conditions were designed to be relatively easy to meet in the early years of operation, thus bringing the program into effectiveness quickly. Eligibility for retirement benefits—termed *fully insured status*—depends on having a certain number of "quarters of coverage" (QCs), sometimes referred to as "credits," varying with the year of birth or, expressed in another manner, depending on the year of an individual's attainment of age 62.

Before 1978, a QC was defined simply as a calendar quarter during which the individual was paid $50 or more in wages from covered employment; the self-employed ordinarily received four QCs for each year of coverage at $400 or more of earnings. Beginning in 1978, the number of QCs acquired for each year depends on the total earnings in the year. For 1978, each full unit of $250 of earnings produced a QC, up to a maximum of four QCs for the year. In subsequent years the requirement has increased, and it will continue to increase in the future, in accordance with changes in the general wage level; for 2001, it is $830.

The number of QCs required for fully insured status is determined from the number of years in the period beginning in 1951, or with the year of attainment of age 22, if later, and the year before the year of attainment of age 62, with a minimum requirement of six QCs. As a result, an individual who attained age 62 before 1958 needed only six QCs to be fully insured. A person attaining age 62 in 1990 has a requirement of 39 QCs, while a person attaining age 65 in 1990 needs 36 QCs. The maximum number of QCs that will ever be required for fully insured status is 40, applicable to persons attaining age 62 after 1990. It is important to note that, although the requirement for the number of QCs is determined from 1951, or from year of attainment of age 22, and before attainment of age 62, the QCs to meet the requirement can be obtained at any time (e.g., before 1951, before age 22, and after age 61).

Beneficiary Categories for Retirement Benefits

Insured workers can receive unreduced retirement benefits in the amount of the Primary Insurance Amount (PIA), the derivation of which will be discussed next, beginning at the NRA, or actuarially reduced benefits beginning at earlier ages, down to age 62. For retirement at age 62 before 2000, the benefit was 80 percent of the PIA, while for retirement at age

62 in 2000, it is 79⅙ percent. As the NRA increases beyond 65, the reduction will become larger (eventually being 30 percent).

Retired workers also can receive supplementary payments for spouses and eligible children. The spouse receives a benefit at the rate of 50 percent of the PIA if claim is first made at the NRA or over, and at a reduced rate if claimed at ages down to 62 (before 2000, a 25 percent reduction at age 62—i.e., to 37.5 percent of the PIA); as the NRA increases beyond 65, the reduction for age 62 will be larger, eventually being 35 percent, 25⅚ percent in 2000). However, if a child under age 16 (or a child aged 16 or over who was disabled before age 22) is present, the spouse receives benefits regardless of age, in an unreduced amount. Divorced spouses, when the marriage had lasted at least 10 years, are eligible for benefits under the same conditions as undivorced spouses.

Children under age 18 (and children aged 18 or over and disabled before age 22, plus children attending elementary or high school full-time at age 18) also are eligible for benefits, at a rate of 50 percent of the PIA; prior to legislation in 1981, post-secondary-school students aged 18–21 were eligible for benefits, and spouses with children in their care could receive benefits as long as a child under age 18 was present. Grandchildren and great-grandchildren can qualify as "children" if they are dependent on the grandparent and if both parents of the child are disabled or deceased.

An overall maximum on total family benefits is applicable, as is discussed later. If a person is eligible for more than one type of benefit (e.g., both as a worker and as a spouse), in essence only the largest benefit is payable.

Computation Procedures for Retirement Benefits

As indicated in the previous section, OASDI benefits are based on the PIA. The method of computing the PIA is quite complicated, especially because several different methods are available. The only method dealt with here in any detail is the one generally applicable to people who reach age 65 after 1981.

Persons who attained age 65 before 1982 use a method based on the average monthly wage (AMW). This is based essentially on a career average, involving the consideration of all earnings back through 1951. To take into account the general inflation in earnings that occurred in the past, automatic-adjustment procedures were involved in the benefit computations. However, these turned out to be faulty, because they did not—and would not in the future—produce stable benefit results (as to the relationships of initial benefits to final earnings). Accordingly, in the 1977 amendments, a new procedure applicable to those attaining age 62 after 1978 was adopted, but the old procedure was retained for earlier attainments of age 62. The result has been to give unusually and inequitably large benefits to those who attained age 62 before 1979 and who worked well beyond age 62, as against similar people who attained age 62 after 1978, thus creating a "notch" situation.

Persons who attained age 62 in 1979–83 can use an alternative method somewhat similar to the AMW method (but with certain restrictions) if this produces a larger PIA than the new, permanent method. In actual practice, however, this modified-AMW method generally produces more favorable results only for persons attaining age 62 in 1979–81 and not continuing in employment after that age.

Still another method is available for all individuals who have earnings before 1951. In the vast majority of such cases, however, the new-start methods based on earnings after 1950 produce more favorable results.

The first step in the ongoing permanent method of computing the PIA applicable to persons attaining age 65 in 1982 or after is to calculate the Average Indexed Monthly Earnings (AIME). The AIME is on a career-average earnings basis. For persons who attain age 62 in 1991 or after, the AIME is based on the highest 35 years of indexed earnings after 1950. Actual earnings are indexed (i.e., increased) to reflect nationwide wage inflation from the particular year up to the year of attaining age 60. Details on the computation of the AIME are given in Appendix A.

Now, having obtained the AIME, the PIA is computed from a benefit formula. A different formula applies for each annual cohort of persons attaining age 62. For example, for those who reached age 62 in 1979, the formula was 90 percent of the first $180 of AIME, plus 32 percent of the next $905 of AIME, plus 15 percent of the AIME in excess of $1,085. For the 2001 cohort, the corresponding dollar bands are $561, $2,820, and $3,381. These bands are adjusted automatically annually, according to changes in nationwide average wages.

A different (and less favorable) method of computing the PIA for retirement benefits (and also for disability benefits, but not for survivor benefits) is applicable for certain persons who receive pensions based in whole or in part on earnings from employment not covered by OASDI or Railroad Retirement (in the past or in the future, and in other countries as well as in the United States). This is done to eliminate the windfall benefits (due to the weighted nature of the benefit formula) that would otherwise arise. Appendix A gives details on the application of the Windfall Elimination provision.

Prior to legislation in 1981, if the PIA benefit formula produced an amount smaller than $122 in the initial benefit computation, then this amount was nonetheless payable. However, for persons first becoming eligible after 1981, no such minimum is applicable.

A special minimum applies to the PIA for individuals who have a long period of covered work, but with low earnings. As of December 2000, this minimum is approximately $30 times the "years of coverage" (see Appendix A for definition) in excess of 10, but not in excess of 30; thus, for 30 or more years of coverage, the minimum benefit is $600.90. In practice, this procedure rarely applies for current retirees.

The resulting PIAs then are increased for any automatic adjustments applicable, because of annual increases in the consumer price index (CPI-W) that occur in or after the year of attaining age 62, even though actual retirement is much later. These automatic adjustments are made for benefits for each December. Such CPI increases were as high as 14.3 percent for 1980 and 11.2 percent for 1981, but have been much lower in recent years (3.5 percent in 2000).

The resulting PIA then is reduced, in the manner described previously, for those who first claim benefits before the NRA. Conversely, retired workers who do not receive benefits for any months after they attain the NRA, essentially because they elect not to receive them (usually because they have high earnings and do not need them currently), receive increases that are termed delayed-retirement credits (DRCs). Such credits for those who attained age 65 in 1982–89 are at the rate of 3 percent per year of delay (actually 0.25 percent per month) for the period between ages 65 and 70. For those who attained age 65 before 1982, the DRC is at a rate of only 1 percent per year. For those who attain the NRA after 1989, such credit is gradually increased from 3.5 percent for the 1990–91 cases to 4 percent for the 1992–93 cases, 4.5 percent for the 1994–95 cases, 5.0 percent for the 1996–97 cases, 5.5 percent for the 1998-99 cases, and 6 percent for the 2000-01 cases, until it is 8 percent for those attaining the NRA (then 66) in 2009. The DRC applies only to the worker's benefit and not to that for spouses or children (but it does apply to any subsequent widow(er)'s benefits).

A Maximum Family Benefit (MFB) is applicable when there are more than two beneficiaries receiving benefits on the same earnings record (i.e., the retired worker and two or more auxiliary beneficiaries). Not considered within the limit established by the MFB are the additional benefits arising from delayed-retirement credits and the benefits payable to divorced spouses. The MFB is determined prior to any reductions made because of claiming benefits before the NRA, but after the effect of the earnings test as it applies to any auxiliary beneficiary (e.g., if the spouse has high earnings, any potential benefit payable to her or him would not be considered for purposes of the MFB of the other spouse).

The MFB is determined from the PIA by a complex formula. This formula varies for each annual cohort of persons attaining age 62. The resulting MFB is adjusted for increases in the CPI in the future (in the same manner as is the PIA). For the 2001 cohort, the MFB formula is 150 percent of the first $717 of PIA, plus 272 percent of the next $317 of PIA, plus 134 percent of the next $315 of PIA, plus 175 percent of PIA in excess of $1,349. For future cohorts, the dollar figures are changed according to changes in nationwide average wages. The result of this formula is to produce MFBs that are 150 percent of the PIA for the lowest PIAs, with this proportion rising to a peak of 188 percent for middle-range PIAs, and then falling off to 175 percent—and leveling there—for higher PIAs.

Earnings Test and Other Restrictions on Retirement Benefits

From the inception of the OASDI program, there has been some form of restriction on the payment of benefits to persons who have substantial earnings from employment. This provision is referred to as the retirement earnings test. It does not apply to nonearned income, such as from investments or pensions. The general underlying principle of this test is that retirement benefits should be paid only to persons who are substantially retired.

The basic feature of the earnings test is that an annual exempt amount applies, so full benefits are paid if earnings, including those from both covered and noncovered employment, are not in excess thereof. Then, for persons under the NRA (which is age 65 until 2003), for each $2 of excess earnings, $1 in benefits is withheld; the reduction was on a "$1 for $3" basis for those at and above the NRA in 1990-99. Legislation in 2000 eliminated the test for the month of attaining the NRA and later months; the test still applies for earlier months in the year of attaining the NRA, but applicable only to earnings in such months. For persons aged 65–69 (at any time in the year), the annual exempt amount is $17,000 for 2000, $25,000 for 2001, and $30,000 for 2002, with the amounts for subsequent years being automatically determined by the increases in nationwide wages. Beginning with the month of attainment of age 65, the test no longer applies (this limiting age was 70 before 2000). For persons under age 65, the exempt amount is $10,680 in 2001, with automatic adjustment thereafter.

An alternative test applies for the initial year of retirement, or claim, if it results in more benefits being payable. Under this, full benefits are payable for all months in which the individual did not have substantial services in self-employment and had wages of $\frac{1}{12}$ of the annual exempt amount or less. This provision properly takes care of the situation where an individual fully retires during a year, but had sizable earnings in the first part of the year, and thus would have most or all of the benefits withheld if only the annual test had been applicable.

Earnings of the "retired" worker affect, under the earnings test, the total family benefits payable. However, if an auxiliary beneficiary (spouse or child) has earnings, and these are sizable enough to affect the earnings test, any reduction in benefits is applicable only to such individual's benefits.

If an individual receives a pension from service under a government-employee pension plan under which the members were not covered under OASDI on the last day of her or his employment, the OASDI spouse benefit is reduced by two-thirds of the amount of such pension. This provision, however, is not applicable to women—or to men who are dependent on their wives—who become eligible for such a pension before December 1982, while for December 1982 thorough June 1983 the provision applies only to those (both men and women) who cannot prove dependency on their spouse. This general provision results in roughly the same treatment as occurs when both spouses have OASDI benefits based on their own earnings records; and then each receives such benefit, plus the excess, if any, of the spouse's benefit arising from the other spouse's earnings over the benefit based on their own earnings, rather than the full amount of the spouse's benefit

Benefits are not payable to prisoners convicted of crimes involving confinement that lasts for at least 30 days, except for prisoners who are in an approved rehabilitation program (although payable to auxiliary beneficiaries of such prisoners)—also applies to disability and survivor benefits.

Historical Development of Disability Provisions

It was not until the 1956 act that monthly disability benefits were added to the OASDI program, although the "disability freeze" provision (in essence, a waiver-of-premium provision), described later, was added in the 1952 act.[1] It may well be said that long-term disability is merely premature old-age retirement.

The monthly disability benefits initially were available only at age 50 and over—that is, deferred to that age for those disabled earlier, with no auxiliary benefits for the spouse and dependent children. These limitations were quickly removed, by the 1958 and 1960 acts.

Eligibility Conditions for Disability Benefits

To be eligible for disability benefits, individuals must be both fully insured and disability insured.[2] Disability insured status requires 20 QCs earned in the 40-quarter period ending with the quarter of disability, except that persons disabled before age 31 also can qualify if they have QCs in half of the quarters after age 21.[3] The definition of disability is relatively strict. The disability must be so severe that the individual is unable to engage in any substantial gainful activity, and the impairment must be a medically determinable physical or mental condition that is expected to continue for at least 12 months or to result in prior death. Benefits are first payable after completion of six full calendar months of disability. For persons with alcoholism or drug abuse, disability benefits are not payable unless they have another severe disabling condition which, by itself, would be qualifying.

Beneficiary Categories for Disability Benefits

In addition to the disabled worker, dependents in the same categories that apply to old-age retirement benefits can receive monthly benefits.

Benefit Computation Procedures for Disability Benefits

In all cases, the benefits are based on the PIA, computed in the same manner as for retirement benefits, except that fewer dropout years than five are allowed in the computation of the AIME for persons disabled before age 47.[4] The disabled worker receives a benefit equal to 100 percent of

---

1 Actually, it was so written in the 1952 legislation as to be inoperative, but then was reenacted in 1954 to be on a permanent, ongoing basis.
2 Blind persons need be only fully insured.
3 For those disabled before age 24, the requirement is six QCs in the last 12 quarters.
4 Specifically four such quarters for ages 42–46, grading down to none for ages 26 and under.

the PIA, and the auxiliary beneficiaries each receive 50 percent of the PIA, subject to the Maximum Family Benefit.

An overall maximum on total family benefits is applicable, which is lower than that for survivor and retirement benefits—namely, no more than the smaller of 150 percent of the PIA, or 85 percent of AIME (but not less than the PIA).

Eligibility Test for Disability Benefits and Other Restrictions on Benefits

The earnings or retirement test applies to the auxiliary beneficiaries of disabled workers, but not to the disabled worker beneficiary. However, the earnings of one beneficiary (e.g., the spouse of the disabled worker) do not affect the benefits of the other beneficiaries in the family (e.g., the disabled worker or the children). The test does not apply to disabled worker beneficiaries, because any earnings are considered in connection with whether recovery has occurred, except those during trial work periods (which earnings may possibly lead to removal from the benefit roll later).

OASDI disability benefits are coordinated with disability benefits payable under other governmental programs (including programs of state and local governments), except for needs-tested ones, benefits payable by the Department of Veterans Affairs, and government employee plans coordinated with OASDI. The most important of such coordinations is with Workers' Compensation (WC) programs, whose benefits are taken into account in determining the amount of the OASDI disability benefit (except in a few states that provide for their WC benefits to be reduced when OASDI disability benefits are payable—possible only for states that did this before February 19, 1981). The total of the OASDI disability benefit (including any auxiliary benefits payable) and the other disability benefit recognized cannot exceed 80 percent of "average current earnings" (generally based on the highest year of earnings in covered employment in the last six years, but indexed for changes in wage levels following the worker's disablement).

Disability Freeze

In the event that a disability beneficiary recovers, the so-called disability-freeze provision applies. Under this, the period of disability is "blanked out" in the computation of insured status and benefit amounts for subsequent retirement, disability, and survivor benefits.

Historical Development of
Survivor Provisions

When what is now the OASDI program was developed in 1934–35, it was confined entirely to retirement benefits (plus lump-sum refund payments to represent the difference, if any, between employee taxes paid, plus an allowance for interest, and retirement benefits received). It was not until the 1939 act that monthly survivor benefits were added with respect to deaths of both active workers and retirees, in lieu of the refund benefit.

The term *widow* is used here to include also widowers. Until 1983, the latter did not receive OASDI benefits on the same basis as widows, either being required to prove dependence on the deceased female worker or not being eligible at all. Now, because of legislative changes and court decisions, complete equality of treatment by sex prevails for OASDI survivor benefits.

The minimum eligibility age for aged widows was initially established at age 65. This figure was selected in a purely empirical manner, because it was a round figure (see the earlier discussion about retirement benefits on why this was selected as the minimum retirement age).

Beginning in the 1950s, pressure developed to provide early-retirement benefits, first for widows and spouses and then for insured workers themselves. The minimum early-retirement age was set at 62, again a pragmatic political compromise, rather than a completely logical choice and was later lowered to 60 for widows. The three-year differential, however, did represent about the average difference in age between men and their wives (but, of course, as with any averages, in many cases the actual difference is larger). The benefit amounts were not reduced for widows when they claimed before age 65 under the original amendatory legislation, but this is no longer the case.

Eligibility Conditions for Survivor Benefits

To be eligible for OASDI survivor benefits, individuals must have either fully insured status or currently insured status. The latter requires only six QCs earned in the 13-quarter period ending with the quarter of death.

Survivor Beneficiary Categories

Two general categories of survivors of insured workers can receive monthly benefits. Aged survivors are widows aged 60 or over (or at ages 50–59 if disabled) and dependent parents aged 62 or over. Young survivors are children under age 18 (or at any age if disabled before age 22), children aged 18 who are full-time students in elementary or high school (i.e., defined just the same as in the case of retirement and disability beneficiaries), and the widowed parent of such children who are under age 16 or disabled before age 22. In addition, a death benefit of $255 is payable to widows or, in the absence of a widow, to children eligible for immediate monthly benefits.

The disabled widow receives a benefit at the rate of 71.5 percent of the deceased worker's PIA if claim is first made at ages 50–59. The benefit rate for other widows grades up from 71.5 percent of the PIA if claimed at age 60 to 100 percent if claimed at the NRA, which is age 65 for those attaining age 60 before 2000, grading up to 67 for those attaining age 60 in 2022 and after. Any DRCs that the deceased worker had earned also are applicable to the widow's benefit. Widows, regardless of age, caring for an eligible child (under age 16 or disabled before age 22) have a benefit of 75 percent of the PIA. Divorced spouses, when the marriage lasted at least 10 years, are eligible for benefits under the same conditions as undivorced spouses.

The benefit rate for eligible children is 75 percent of the PIA. The benefit rate for dependent parents is 82.5 percent of the PIA, unless two parents are eligible, in which case it is 75 percent for each one.

The same overall maximum on total family benefits is applicable as is the case for retirement benefits. If a person is eligible for more than one type of benefit (e.g., both as a worker and as a surviving spouse), in essence, only the largest benefit is payable.

Benefit Computation Procedures for Survivor Benefits

In all cases, the monthly survivor benefits are based on the PIA, and then are adjusted to reflect the Maximum Family Benefit, both of which are computed in essentially the same manner as is the case for retirement benefits.[5]

---

5 For individuals who die before age 62, the computation is made as though the individual had attained age 62 in the year of death. In addition, for deferred widow's benefits, an alternative computation based on indexing the deceased's earnings record up to the earlier of age 60 of the worker or age 60 of the widow is used if this produces a more favorable result.

Eligibility Test for Survivor Benefits and Other Restrictions

Marriage (or remarriage) of the survivor beneficiary generally terminates benefit rights. The only exceptions are remarriage of widows after age 60 (or after age 50 for disabled widows) and marriage to another OASDI beneficiary (other than one who is under age 18).

From the inception of the OASDI program, there has been some form of restriction on the payment of benefits to persons who have substantial earnings from employment, the earnings or retirement test. The same test applies to survivor beneficiaries as to retirement benefits for retirees who are under NRA. However, the earnings of one beneficiary (e.g., the widowed mother) do not affect the benefits of the other beneficiaries in the family (e.g., the orphaned children).

If a widow receives a pension from service under a government-employee pension plan under which the members were not covered under OASDI on the last day of her employment, the OASDI widow's benefit is reduced by two-thirds of the amount of such pension. This provision, however, is not applicable to women (or to men who were dependent on their wives) who became eligible for such a pension before December 1982 or to individuals who became first so eligible from December 1982 through June 1983 and who were dependent on their spouses.

Financing Provisions of OASDI Program

From its inception until the 1983 act, the OASDI program has been financed entirely by payroll taxes (and interest earnings on the assets of the trust funds), with only minor exceptions, such as the special benefits at a subminimum level for certain persons without insured status who attained age 72 before 1972. Thus, on a permanent ongoing basis, no payments from general revenues were available to the OASDI system; the contributions for covered federal civilian employees and members of the armed forces are properly considered as "employer" taxes.

The 1983 act introduced two instances of general-revenues financing of the OASDI program. As a one-time matter, the tax rate in 1984 was increased to what had been previously scheduled for 1985 (i.e., for both the employer and employee, from 5.4 percent to 5.7 percent), but the increase for employees was, in essence, rescinded, and the General Fund of the Treasury made up the difference to the OASDI Trust Funds. On an ongoing basis, the General Fund passes on to the trust funds the proceeds of the income taxation of 50 percent of OASDI benefits for upper-middle-income and high-income persons (first effective for 1984), and, in fact, does so somewhat in advance of actual receipt of such moneys.[6]

The payroll taxes for the retirement and survivors benefits go into the OASI Trust Fund, while those for the disability benefits go into the DI Trust Fund, and all benefit payments and administrative expenses for these provisions are paid therefrom. The balances in the trust fund are invested in federal government obligations of various types, with interest rates at the current market values for long-term securities. The federal government does not guarantee the payments of benefits. If the trust fund were to be depleted, it could not obtain grants, or even loans, from the General Fund of the Treasury. However, a temporary provision (effective only in 1982) permitted the OASI Trust Fund to borrow, repayable with interest, from the DI and HI Trust Funds. A total of $17.5 billion was borrowed ($12.4 billion from HI). The last of such loans was repaid in 1986.

Payroll taxes are levied on earnings up to only a certain annual limit, which is termed the earnings base. This base is applicable to the earnings of an individual from each employer in the year, but the person can obtain a refund (on the income tax form) for all employee taxes paid in excess of those on the earnings base. The self-employed pay OASDI taxes on their self-employment income on no more than the excess of the earnings base over any wages they may have had.

Since 1975, the earnings base for OASDI has been determined by the automatic-adjustment procedure, on the basis of increases in the nationwide average wage. However, for 1979–81, ad hoc increases of a higher amount were legislated; the 1981 base was established at $29,700. The 1982 and subsequent bases were determined under the automatic-adjustment provision. The 2000 base was $76,200, while that for 2001 is $80,400.

The payroll tax rate is a combined one for OASI, DI, and HI, but it is allocated among the three trust funds. The employer and employee rates are equal. The self-employed pay the combined employer-employee rate. In 1984–89, they had an allowance for the reduction in income taxes as if half of the OASDI-HI tax were to be considered as a business expense (as it is for incorporated employers); such allowance was a uniform reduction in the tax rate—2.7 percentage points in 1984, 2.2 per-

---

6 The income taxes on the next 35 percent of benefits (first effective in 1994) anomalously go to the Hospital Insurance Trust Fund.

centage points in 1985, and 2.0 percentage points in 1986–89. After 1989, the direct procedure of considering half of the OASDI-HI taxes as a deduction from income is done for the self-employed. Also, until 1991, the earnings base was the same for OASDI and HI, but in 1991, the base for HI was raised to $125,000, and it was $130,200 in 1992 and was eliminated for 1994 and after.

The employer and employee rates were 1 percent each in 1937–49, but have gradually increased over the years, until being 7.15 percent in 1986–87 (the latter subdivided 5.2 percent for OASI, 0.5 percent for DI, and 1.45 percent for HI). These rates increased to 7.51 percent in 1988, and then to 7.65 percent in 1990 (and after), the latter being subdivided 5.3 percent for OASI, 0.9 percent for DI, and 1.45 percent for HI for 2000 and after.

Past Financing Crises of OASDI Program

In the mid-1970s, the OASI and DI trust funds were projected to have serious financing problems over both the long range and the short range. The short-range problem was thought to be remedied by the 1977 act, which raised taxes (both the rates and the earnings bases). At the same time, the long-range problem was partially solved by phased-in significant benefit reductions, by lowering the general benefit level, by freezing the minimum benefit, and by the "spouse government pension" offset, although an estimated deficit situation was still present for the period beginning after about 30 years.

The short-range problem was not really solved. The actuarial cost estimates assumed that earnings would rise at a somewhat more rapid rate than prices in the short range; but the reverse occurred—and to a significant extent—in 1979–81. Because increases in tax income depend on earnings and because increases in benefit outgo depend on prices, the financial result for the OASI Trust Fund was catastrophic. It would have been exhausted in late 1982 if not for legislation enacted in 1981. The DI Trust Fund did not have this problem, because the disability experience, which had worsened significantly in 1970–76, turned around and became relatively favorable—more than offsetting the unfavorable economic experience.

The 1981 act significantly reduced benefit outgo in the short range by a number of relatively small changes, shown in detail in Appendix B.

Further action beyond the 1981 amendments was essential to restore both the short-range and long-range solvency of the OASDI program. Because of the difficult political situation, President Reagan established the National Commission on Social Security Reform—a bipartisan group whose members were appointed both by President Reagan and the congressional leadership—to study the problem and make recommendations for its solution. Such recommendations were adopted almost in their entirety in the 1983 act. The most significant changes made by this legislation are described in Appendix B.

The changes made by the 1983 act were eminently successful over the short run. In the following years, the assets of the OASDI Trust Funds grew steadily from their very low level then and were about $1 trillion at the end of September 2000. Further, they are estimated to increase rapidly for the next two decades and reach a height of $6 trillion in 2024. However, thereafter a decline is estimated, and the balance will be exhausted in 2037 unless changes are made before then (which will most certainly occur). Ideally, the fund balance should be at least equal to one year's outgo at all times during the 75-year valuation period.

Possible Future OASDI Developments

Advisory groups have, over the years, advocated so-called universal coverage. Following the 1983 amendments, relatively little remains to be done in this area, except perhaps to cover compulsorily all new hires in state and local government employment (as was done in the federal area).

The NRA was increased from the present 65 to age 67, phased in over a period of years, by the 1983 act. This was done in recognition of the significant increase in life expectancy that has occurred in the last 40 years, as well as likely future increases. If life expectancy increases even more rapidly than currently projected, a further increase in such age would reduce the higher long-range future cost of the program resulting from such increase.

The earnings test has always been subject to criticism by many persons, who argue that it is a disincentive to continued employment and that "the benefits have been bought and paid for, and therefore should be available at age 65." The 1983 act, by increasing ultimately (beginning with those who attain age 66 in 2009) the size of the delayed retirement credits (to 8 percent per year) to approximately the actuarial-equivalent level, virtually eliminated the earnings test after the NRA insofar as the cost aspects thereof are concerned. In other words, when the DRC is at an 8 percent level, the individual receives benefits for delayed retirement having approximately the same value as if benefits were paid without regard to the earnings test, beginning at the NRA. Some persons have advocated that the DRC should be at the 8 percent rate as soon as possible. As mentioned earlier, the earnings test was eliminated in 2000 for the month of attaining NRA, although insured workers can waive receipt of benefits and receive DRCs.

As to disability benefits, the definition might be tightened, such as by using "medical only" factors (and not vocational ones). Conversely, the definition could be liberalized so as to be on an occupational basis at age 50 and over. Also, the five-month waiting period could be shortened.

The general benefit level was significantly increased in 1969–72 (by about 23 percent in real terms), but financial problems caused this increase to be partially reversed in subsequent legislation (1974 and 1977). Nonetheless, there will be efforts by many persons to reverse the situation and expand the benefit level.

Over the years, the composition of the OASDI benefit structure—between individual-equity aspects and social-adequacy ones—tended to shift more toward social adequacy. The 1981 amendments, however, moved in the other direction (e.g., by phasing out student benefits and the minimum-benefit provision). There may well be efforts in the future to inject more social adequacy into the program—or, conversely, more individual equity.

It frequently has been advocated that people should be allowed to opt out of the OASDI system and provide their own economic security through private-sector mechanisms, using both their own taxes and those of their employer. Although this approach has certain appealing aspects, it has some significant drawbacks. First, it is not possible to duplicate to any close extent the various features of OASDI, most notably the automatic adjustment of benefits for increases in the CPI.

Second, because the low-cost individuals (young, high-earnings ones) would be the most likely to opt out, there is the question of how the resulting financing shortfalls of the OASDI program would be covered. Those who make such proposals (or even the more extreme ones, which involve terminating OASDI for all except those currently covered who are near retirement age) do not answer this question. The only source of financing would be from general revenues, and this means more general taxes, which would be paid to a considerable extent by those who have opted out.

Proposals have been made to means-test (actually, income-test) OASDI benefits. Then, high-income persons would have their benefits sharply reduced (or even eliminated). Although this may seem appealing to solve budget deficits or OASDI financing problems, it has serious faults. Middle-income persons would tend to save less, because they would fear that saving would only mean a reduction in their OASDI benefits. Further, fraud and abuse would occur as people hid their assets and income therefrom or else transferred them to their children and had the income given back secretly.

Many have argued that part of the cost of OASDI should be met from general revenues. At times, an indirect manner of implementing such a funding method has been advocated, such as by moving part of the HI tax rate to OASDI and then partially financing HI from general revenues. The difficulty with this procedure is that no large amounts of general-revenues moneys are available for all future years to come; the General Fund of the Treasury is now estimated to have relatively small surpluses for the next 10 to 15 years or so, but not thereafter. In turn, this would mean either that additional taxes of other types would have to be raised or that any budget deficit would become larger, and inflation would be fueled. Those opposed to general-revenues financing of OASDI, and of HI as well, believe that the financing, instead, should be entirely from direct, visible payroll taxes. Nonetheless, it is likely that pressure for general-revenues financing of OASDI will continue.

According to the latest intermediate-cost estimate for present law, the OASDI Trust Funds will have large annual excesses of income over outgo for the next two decades. As a result, mammoth fund balances will accumulate—amounting to about $6.0 trillion in 2024. Under current budgetary procedures, such annual excesses are often considered as meeting the budget-deficit targets, and thus they hide the extent of titanic general-budget deficits. Further, the presence of such large fund balances could well encourage over-liberalization of the OASDI program now— for example, by raising benefit levels or by postponing the scheduled increases in the NRA beginning in about a decade.

To prevent these undesirable results from occurring, former Senator Daniel Patrick Moynihan proposed that the financing basis of the OASDI program be returned to a pay-as-you-go basis. This would be done by an immediate reduction in the contribution rates and the introduction of a graded schedule of increases in the contribution rates, beginning in about 20 years. This proposal produced a vast amount of discussion (and also education of the public). Such a proposal will undoubtedly continue to be raised, although it has strong opposition from those who are concerned with the general-budget deficits and seek to hide them through "counting Social Security surpluses."

SUPPLEMENTAL SECURITY INCOME PROGRAM (SSI)

The SSI program replaced the federal/state public assistance programs of aid to the aged, blind, and disabled, except in Guam, Puerto Rico, and the Virgin Islands. Persons must be at least age 65 or be blind or disabled to qualify for SSI payments.

The basic payment amount, before reduction for other income, for 2001 is $530 per month for one recipient and 50 percent more for an eligible couple. An automatic-adjustment provision closely paralleling that used under OASDI is applicable.

A number of "income disregards" are present. The most important is the disregard of $20 of income per month per family from such sources as OASDI, other pensions, earnings, and investments. The first $65 per month of earned income is disregarded, plus 50 percent of the remainder.

SSI has certain resource exemptions. In order to receive SSI, for 2001, resources cannot exceed $2,000 for an individual and $3,000 for a couple. However, in the calculation of resources, certain items are excluded—the home, household goods, and personal effects (depending on value), an automobile with value of $4,500 or less, burial plots, and property needed for self-support—if these are found to be reasonable. Also, if life insurance policies have a face amount of $1,500 or less for an individual, their cash values are not counted as assets.

Some states pay supplements to SSI.

In addition to SSI, a public assistance program provides payments for widowed mothers (and fathers) with children. This is on a state-by-state basis, with part of the cost borne by the federal government.

MEDICARE PROGRAM

Health (or medical care) benefits for active and retired workers and their dependents in the United States is, in the vast majority of cases, provided through the multiple means of the Medicare portion of Social Security for persons age 65 and over and for long-term disabled persons, private employer-sponsored plans, and individual savings. As mentioned earlier, this is sometimes referred to as a "three-legged stool" or the three pillars of economic security protection. Another view of the situation for persons age 65 and over and for long-term disabled persons is of Medicare providing the floor of protection for certain categories, or, in other cases, providing the basic protection. Supplementing this, private insurance is present, with public assistance programs such as Medicaid, providing a safety net of protection for those whose income is not sufficient to purchase the needed medical care not provided through some form of prepaid insurance.

Private health benefit plans supplement Medicare to some extent. In other instances—essentially for active workers and their families—health benefit protection is provided by the private sector. The net result, however, is a broad network of health benefit protection.

Historical Development of Provisions

Beginning in the early 1950s, efforts were made to provide medical care benefits (primarily for hospitalization) for beneficiaries under the OASDI program. In 1965, such efforts succeeded, and the resulting program is called Medicare.

Initially, Medicare applied only to persons age 65 and over. In 1972, disabled Social Security beneficiaries who had been on the benefit rolls for at least two years were made eligible, as were virtually all persons in the country who have end-stage renal disease (i.e., chronic kidney disease). Since 1972, relatively few changes in coverage or benefit provisions have been made. In 1988, legislation that provided catastrophic-coverage benefits—to be financed largely through a surtax on the income tax of eligible beneficiaries—was enacted. However, as a result of massive protests from those who would be required to pay the surtax, these provisions were repealed in 1989.

Medicare is really two separate programs. One part, Hospital Insurance (HI),[7] is financed primarily from payroll taxes on workers covered under OASDI, including those under the Railroad Retirement system. Beginning in 1983, all civilian employees of the federal government were covered under HI, even though, in general, not covered by OASDI. Also, beginning in April 1986, all newly hired state and local government employees are covered compulsorily (and, at the election of the governmental entity, all employees in service on March 31, 1986, who were not covered under OASDI can be covered for HI). The other part, Supplementary Medical Insurance (SMI), is on an individual voluntary basis and is financed partially by enrollee premiums, with the remainder, currently about 75 percent, coming from general revenues.

As an alternative to "traditional" Medicare, persons eligible under both HI and SMI (except those previously diagnosed with end-stage renal disease) can elect to participate in a Medicare + Choice plan. There are

---

7 Sometimes referred to as Part A. Supplementary Medical Insurance is Part B.

several types of such plans, but generally they must provide at least the same benefits as Medicare (usually, they provide more, such as some drug benefits and lower cost-sharing payments). These plans receive per capita payments from Medicare (the participant continues paying the SMI premium to Medicare), which hopefully are equitable reimbursement. In theory, these plans are supposed to provide better health care at a lower cost (through managed-care principles), but some critics believe that they do not always provide adequate care, especially because they usually do not allow free choice of physicians to provide the services (and generally little or no choice at all).

Persons Protected by HI

All individuals age 65 and over who are eligible for monthly benefits under OASDI or the Railroad Retirement program also are eligible for HI benefits (as are federal employees and state and local employees who have sufficient earnings credit from their special HI coverage). Persons are "eligible" for OASDI benefits if they could receive them when the person on whose earnings record they are eligible is deceased or receiving disability or retirement benefits, or could be receiving retirement benefits except for having substantial earnings. Thus, the HI eligibles include not only insured workers, but also spouses, disabled children (in the rare cases where they are at least age 65), and survivors, such as widowed spouses and dependent parents. As a specific illustration, HI protection is available for an insured worker and spouse, both at least age 65, even though the worker has such high earnings that OASDI cash benefits are not currently payable because of election to defer receipt of benefits.

In addition, HI eligibility is available for disabled beneficiaries who have been on the benefit roll for at least two years (beyond a five-month waiting period). Such disabled eligibles include not only insured workers but also disabled child beneficiaries aged 18 and over who were disabled before age 22, and disabled widowed spouses aged 50–64.

Further, persons under age 65 with end-stage renal disease (ESRD) who require dialysis or renal transplant are eligible for HI benefits if they meet one of a number of requirements. Such requirements for ESRD benefits include being fully or currently insured, being a spouse or a dependent child of an insured worker or of a monthly beneficiary, or being a monthly beneficiary.

Individuals aged 65 and over who are not eligible for HI as a result of their own or some other person's earnings can elect coverage, and then must make premium payments, whereas OASDI eligibles do not. The standard monthly premium rate is $300 for 2001 (but only $165 if they have at least 30 quarters of coverage).

Benefits Provided Under HI

The principal benefit provided by the HI program is for hospital services. The full cost for all such services, other than luxury items, is paid by HI during a so-called spell of illness, after an initial deductible has been paid and with daily coinsurance for all hospital days after the 60th one, but with an upper limit on the number of days covered. A spell of illness is a period beginning with the first day of hospitalization and ending when the individual has been out of both hospitals and skilled nursing facilities for 60 consecutive days. The initial deductible is $792 for 2001. The daily coinsurance is $198 for the 61st to 90th days of hospitalization. A nonrenewable lifetime reserve of 60 days is available after the regular 90 days have been used; these lifetime reserve days are subject to daily coinsurance of $396 for 2001. The deductible and coinsurance amounts are adjusted automatically each year after 2001 to reflect past changes in hospital costs.

Benefits also are available for care provided in skilled nursing facilities, following at least three days of hospitalization. Such care is provided only when it is for convalescent or recuperative care and not for custodial care. The first 20 days of such care in a spell of illness are provided without cost to the individual. The next 80 days, however, are subject to a daily coinsurance payment, which is $99 in 2001, and it will be adjusted automatically in the future in the same manner as the hospital cost-sharing amounts. No benefits are available after 100 days of care in a skilled nursing facility for a particular spell of illness.

In addition, an unlimited number of home health service benefits are provided by HI and/or SMI without any payment being required from the beneficiary. Also, hospice care for terminally ill persons is covered if all Medicare benefits, other than physician services, are waived; certain cost restrictions and coinsurance requirements apply with respect to prescription drugs.

HI benefit protection is provided only within the United States, with the exception of certain emergency services available when in or near Canada. Not covered by HI are those cases where services are performed in a Department of Veterans Affairs hospital or where the person is eligible for medical services under a workers' compensation program. Furthermore, Medicare is the secondary payor in cases when (a) medical care is payable under any liability policy, especially automobile ones; (b) during the first 30 months of treatment for ESRD cases when private group health insurance provides coverage; (c) for persons aged 65 and over (employees and spouses) who are under employer-sponsored group health insurance plans (which is required for all plans of employers with at least 20 employees) unless the employee opts out of it; and (d) for disability beneficiaries under the plan of an employer with at least 100 employees when the beneficiary is either an "active individual" or a family member of an employee.

Financing of HI

With the exception of the small group of persons who voluntarily elect coverage, the HI program is financed by payroll taxes on workers in employment covered by OASDI. This payroll tax rate is combined with that for OASDI. The HI tax rate is the same for employers and employees; self-employed persons pay the combined employer-employee tax rate, but have an offset to allow for the effect of business expenses on income taxes (as described earlier in connection with OASDI taxes). Such HI tax rate for employees was 1.45 percent in 1990 (and in all future years). The maximum taxable earnings base for HI was the same as that for OASDI for all years before 1991, but thereafter was a higher amount, and, beginning in 1994, no limit is applicable. Also, beginning in 1994, part of the income taxes on OASDI benefits is diverted to finance HI. It should be noted that long-range actuarial cost estimates indicate that this rate will not provide adequate financing after about 2025 (or perhaps even sooner).

The vast majority of persons who attained age 65 before 1968, and who were not eligible for HI benefit protection on the basis of an earnings record, were nonetheless given full eligibility for benefits without any charge. The cost for this closed blanketed-in group is met from general revenues, rather than from HI payroll taxes.

The HI Trust Fund receives the income of the program from the various sources and makes the required disbursements for benefits and administrative expenses. The assets are invested and earn interest in the same manner as the OASDI Trust Funds.

Although the federal government is responsible for the administration of the HI program, the actual dealing with the various medical facilities is through fiscal intermediaries, such as Blue Cross and insurance companies, which are reimbursed for their expenses on a cost basis. Beginning in 1988, reimbursement for inpatient hospital services is based on uniform sums for each type of case for about 490 diagnosis-related groups.

Persons Protected under Supplementary Medical Insurance

Individuals aged 65 or over can elect SMI coverage on an individual basis regardless of whether they have OASDI insured status. In addition, disabled OASDI and Railroad Retirement beneficiaries eligible for HI and persons with ESRD eligibility under HI can elect SMI coverage. In general, coverage election must be made at about the time of initial eligibility; that is, attainment of age 65 or at the end of the disability-benefit waiting period. Subsequent election during general enrollment periods is possible but with higher premium rates being applicable. Similarly, individuals can terminate coverage and cease premium payment of their own volition.

Benefits Provided under SMI

The principal SMI benefit is partial reimbursement for the cost of physician services, although other medical services, such as diagnostic tests, ambulance services, prosthetic devices, physical therapy, medical equipment, home health services, and drugs not self-administerable are covered. Not covered are out-of-hospital drugs, most dental services, most chiropractic services, routine physical and eye examinations, eyeglasses and hearing aids, and services outside of the United States, except those in connection with HI services that are covered in Canada. Just as for HI, there are limits on SMI coverage in workers' compensation cases, medical care under liability policies, private group health insurance applicable to ESRD, and employer-sponsored group health insurance for employees and their spouses.

SMI pays 80 percent of "recognized" charges, under a complicated determination basis that usually produces a lower charge than the reasonable and prevailing one, after the individual has paid a calendar-year deductible of $100 for 1991 and after. Special limits apply on out-of-hospital mental health care costs and on the services of independent physical and occupational therapists. The cost-sharing payments ($100 deductible and 20 percent coinsurance) are waived for certain services (e.g., home health services, pneumococcal vaccine, and influenza shots, and certain clinical diagnostic laboratory tests). Beginning in 1993, physicians cannot charge Medicare patients more than 115 percent of Medicare "recognized" charges.

Financing of SMI

The standard monthly premium rate is $50 for 2001. The premium is higher for those who fail to enroll as early as they possibly can, with an increase of 10 percent for each full 12 months of delay. The premium is deducted from the OASDI or Railroad Retirement benefits of persons currently receiving them, or is paid by direct submittal in other cases.

The remainder of the cost of the program is met by general revenues. In the aggregate, persons aged 65 and over pay only about 25 percent of the cost, while for disabled persons such proportion is only about 20 percent. As a result, enrollment in SMI is very attractive, and about 95 percent of those eligible to do so actually enroll.

The enrollee premium rate will be changed every year after 2001, effective for January. According to "permanent" law, the rate of increase in the premium rate is determined by the percentage rise in the level of OASDI cash benefits in the previous year under the automatic adjustment provisions, and in part by the percentage rises in the per capita cost of the program. However, for the premium years 1996–98, the premium rate was set at 25 percent of the cost for persons aged 65 or over. (The premium rates for 1992–95 were established by legislation.)

The SMI Trust Fund was established to receive the enrollee premiums and the payments from general revenues. From this fund are paid the benefits and the accompanying administrative expenses. Although the program is under the general supervision of the federal government, most of the administration is accomplished through "carriers," such as Blue Shield or insurance companies, on an actual cost basis for their administrative expenses.

Possible Future Development of Medicare

Over the years, numerous proposals have been made to modify the Medicare program. Some of these would expand it significantly, while others would curtail it to some extent.

Among the proposals that would expand the program are those to establish some type of national health insurance program, having very comprehensive coverage of medical services applicable to the entire population. Somewhat less broadly, other proposals would extend Medicare coverage to additional categories of OASDI beneficiaries beyond old-age beneficiaries aged 65 and over and disabled beneficiaries on the roll for at least two years—such as to early-retirement cases at ages 62–64 and to all disability beneficiaries.

In another direction, liberalizing proposals have been made to add further services, such as out-of-hospital drugs, physical examinations, and dental services. Still other proposals have been made in the direction of reducing the extent of cost-sharing on the part of the beneficiary by lowering or eliminating the deductible and coinsurance provisions and by eliminating the duration-of-stay limits on HI benefit eligibility.

Proposals have been made to reduce the cost of the Medicare program by increasing the cost-sharing payments made by the beneficiary. For example, the cost-sharing in the first 60 days of hospitalization could be changed from a one-time payment of the initial deductible to some type of daily coinsurance that would foster the incentive to shorten hospital stays. Another proposal is to adjust automatically, from year to year, the SMI annual deductible, which, unlike the HI cost-sharing payments, is a fixed amount, although it has been increased by ad hoc changes from the initial $50 in 1966 to $75 in 1982 and to $100 in 1991. Also, it has been proposed that the minimum age for non-disabled persons should rise above 65 when the NRA for OASDI does so.

A major risk for persons aged 65 and over that is not covered by Medicare is the cost of long-term custodial nursing-home care and homemaker services for disabled or frail persons. Although many persons recognize the serious nature of this problem, it is currently being met only on a means-test basis by the Medicaid program. Some people believe that the problem should be met on an "insurance" basis under a new part of Medicare, but others think that it is not an "insurable" risk and must be handled on a means-test basis (possibly liberalized somewhat).

Proposals have been enacted to lower the cost of the HI programs as far as reimbursement of hospitals and skilled nursing facilities is concerned, although this would have no effect on the Medicare beneficiary directly.

MEDICAID

Over the years, the cost of medical care for recipients of public assistance and for other low-income persons has been met in a variety of ways. Some years ago, these provisions were rather haphazard, and the medical care costs were met by inclusion with the public assistance payments. In 1960, a separate public assistance program in this area was enacted— namely, Medical Assistance for the Aged (MAA), which applied to persons aged 65 and over, both those receiving Old-Age Assistance and other persons not having sufficient resources to meet large medical expenses.

Then in 1965, the MAA program and the federal matching for medical vendor payments for other public assistance categories than MAA were combined into the Medicaid program. This new program covered not only public assistance recipients but also persons of similar demo-graphic characteristics who were medically indigent.

The Medicaid program is operated by the states, with significant federal financing available. Some states cover only public assistance recipients.

Medicaid programs are required to furnish certain services, to receive federal financial participation. These services include those for physicians, hospitals (both inpatient and outpatient), laboratory and X-ray tests, home health visits, and nursing home care. Most other medical services, such as drugs, dental care, and eyeglasses, can be included at the option of the state, and then federal matching will be made available. Also, as a result of legislation enacted in 1988, states must pay the SMI premiums and the HI and SMI cost-sharing payments for persons who are eligible for Medicare and who have incomes below the poverty level and have resources of no more than twice the standard under the Supplemental Security Income program. Thus, the states have the advantage of the relatively large general-revenues financing in the Medicaid program.

The federal government pays a proportion of the total cost of the Medicaid expenditures for medical care that varies inversely with the average per capita income of the state. This proportion is 55 percent for a state with the same average per capita income as the nation as a whole. States with above-average income have a lower matching proportion, but never less than 50 percent. Conversely, states with below-average income have a higher federal matching percentage, which can be as much as 83 percent. The federal government also pays part of the administrative costs of the Medicaid programs; generally, this is 50 percent, although for certain types of expenses that are expected to control costs the federal percentage is higher.

A P P E N D I X   22-1

Detailed Descriptions of Several Social Security Benefit Elements

This appendix describes the features of three complex elements involved in the computation of OASDI benefits.

COMPUTATION OF AVERAGE INDEXED MONTHLY EARNINGS

The AIME is a career-average earnings basis, but it is determined in such a manner as to closely approximate a final-average basis. In a national social insurance plan, it would be inadvisable to use solely an average of the last few years of employment, because that could involve serious manipulation through the cooperation of both the employee and the employer; whereas in a private pension plan, the employer has a close financial interest not to do so. Furthermore, OASDI benefit computation is not proportionate to years of coverage or proportion of worklife in covered employment, as is the case for private pension plans generally.

The first step in computing the AIME is to determine the number of years over which it must be computed. On the whole, the number depends solely on the year in which the individual attains age 62. The general rule is that the computation period equals the number of years beginning with 1951, or with the year of attaining age 22, if later, up through the year before attainment of age 62, minus the so-called five dropout years. The latter is provided so the very lowest five years of earnings can be eliminated. Also, years of high earnings in or after the year of attaining age 62 can be substituted for earlier, lower years.

As an example, persons attaining age 62 in 1990 have a computation period of 34 years (the 39 years in 1951–89, minus 5). The maximum period is 35 years for those attaining age 62 after 1990. For the infrequent case of an individual who had qualified for OASDI disability benefits and who recovered from the disability, the number of computation years for the AIME for retirement benefits is reduced by the number of full years after age 21 and before age 62 during any part of which the person was under a disability.

The AIME is not computed from the actual covered earnings, but rather after indexing them, to make them more current as compared with the wage level at the time of retirement. Specifically, covered earnings for each year before attainment of age 60 are indexed to that age, while all subsequent covered earnings are used in their actual amount. No earnings before 1951 can be utilized, but all earnings subsequently, even before age 22 or after age 61, are considered.

The indexing of the earnings record is accomplished by multiplying the actual earnings of each year before the year that age 60 was attained by the increase in earnings from the particular year to the age-60 year. For example, for persons attaining age 62 in 1990 (i.e., age 60 in 1988), any earnings in 1951 would be converted to indexed earnings by multiplying them by 6.90709, which is the ratio of the nationwide average wage in 1988 to that in 1951. Similarly, the multiplying factor for 1952 earnings is 6.50251, and so on. Once the earnings record for each year in the past has been indexed, the earnings for the number of years required to be averaged are selected to include the highest ones possible; if there are not sufficient years with earnings, then zeroes must be used. Then, the AIME is obtained by dividing the total indexed earnings for such years by 12 times such number of years.

APPLICATION OF WINDFALL ELIMINATION PROVISION

Excluded from the operation of this provision are the following categories: (1) persons who attain age 62 before 1986; (2) persons who were *eligible* for a pension from non-covered employment before 1986; (3) disabled-worker beneficiaries who became disabled before 1986 (and were entitled to such benefits in at least one month in the year before attaining age 62); (4) persons who have at least 30 "years of coverage" (as defined hereafter); (5) persons who were employed by the federal government on January 1, 1984, and were then brought into coverage by the 1983 amendments; and (6) persons who were employed on January 1, 1984, by a nonprofit organization that was not covered on December 31, 1983, and had not been so covered at any time in the past.

Under this method of computation of the PIA, beginning with the 1990 cohort of eligibles, the percentage factor applicable to the lowest band of earnings is 40 percent, instead of 90 percent. As a transitional measure, those who became first eligible for OASDI benefits in 1986 have an 80 percent factor, while it is 70 percent for the 1987 cohort, 60 percent for the 1988 cohort, and 50 percent for the 1989 cohort.

For persons who have 21–29 "years of coverage," an alternative phase-in procedure is used (if it produces a larger PIA). The percentage factor applicable to the lowest band of earnings in the PIA formula is 85 percent for 29 years of coverage, 80 percent for 28 years, down to 45 percent for 21 years.

In any event, under any of the foregoing procedures, the PIA as computed in the regular manner will never be reduced by more than 50 percent of the pension based on noncovered employment (or the pro rata portion thereof based on noncovered employment after 1956 if it is based on both covered and noncovered employment).

DETERMINATION OF "YEARS OF COVERAGE" FOR SPECIAL MINIMUM BENEFIT AND FOR WINDFALL ELIMINATION PROVISION

For purposes of the special minimum benefit, for periods before 1991, a "year of coverage" is defined as a year in which earnings are at least 25 percent of the maximum taxable earnings base; while after 1990, a factor of 15 percent is used. However, for 1979 and after, the maximum taxable earnings base is taken to be what would have prevailed if the ad hoc increases in the base provided by the 1977 act had not been applicable, but, instead, the automatic annual increases had occurred.

For the purposes of the Windfall Elimination Provision, a "year of coverage" is defined in the same way, except that the 25 percent factor continues after 1990.

In 2001, a "year of coverage" is $8,955 for purposes of the special minimum benefit and $14,925 for the Windfall Elimination Provision.

A P P E N D I X   22–2

Changes in Social Security Program Made by Amendments in 1981 and 1983

This appendix describes the most important changes that were made in the OASDI program in 1981 and 1983, when it experienced a significant financial problem, of both a short-range and a long-range nature. The 1981 amendments were of a "stop-gap" nature, while the 1983 amendments were intended to provide a complete solution to the problem.

The 1981 act significantly reduced benefit outgo in the short range by the following actions:

1. The regular minimum benefit (an initial PIA of $122) was eliminated for all new eligibles after 1981, except for certain covered members of religious orders under a vow of poverty.

2. Child school attendance benefits at ages 18–21 were eliminated by a gradual phase out, except for high school students aged 18.

3. Mother's and father's benefits with respect to nondisabled children terminate when the youngest child is aged 16 (formerly 18).

4. Lump-sum death payments were eliminated, except when a surviving spouse who was living with the deceased worker is present, or when a spouse or child is eligible for immediate monthly benefits.

5. Sick pay in the first six months of illness is considered to be covered wages.

6. Lowering of the exempt age under the earnings test to age 70 in 1982 was delayed until 1983.

7. The Workers' Compensation offset against disability benefits was extended to several other types of governmental disability benefits.

8. Interfund borrowing among the OASI, DI, and HI Trust Funds was permitted, but only until December 31, 1982, and then no more than sufficient to allow payments of OASI benefits through June 1983.

Further action beyond the 1981 amendments was essential to restore both the short-range and long-range solvency of the OASDI program. President Reagan established the National Commission on Social Security Reform—a bipartisan group whose members were appointed both by him and the Congressional leadership—to make recommendations for its solution. Such recommendations were adopted almost in their entirety in the 1983 act.

This legislation made the following significant changes in the OASDI program (as well as some in the HI program):

1. OASDI and HI Coverage Provisions
  a. OASDI-HI coverage of new federal employees and current political appointees, elected officials, and judges. (HI coverage of all federal civilian employees was effective in 1983 under previous law.)
  b. Coverage of all employees of nonprofit charitable, educational, and religious organizations.
  c. State and local employees once covered are prohibited from withdrawing.
  d. Employee contributions to cash-or-deferred arrangements (Sec. 401[k]) and employer contributions under nonqualified deferred-compensation plans when no substantial risk of forfeiture is present are covered.

2. OASDI Benefit Provisions
  a. Cost-of-living adjustments are deferred for six months (i.e., will always be in checks for December payable in early January).
  b. The indexing of benefits in payment status is changed from being based only on the CPI to the lower of CPI or wage increases when the trust funds are relatively low.
  c. Gradual increases will be made in the normal retirement age from the present 65, beginning with those attaining age 62 in 2000—so it will be 66 for those attaining such age in 2009–20, then rising to 67 for those attaining such age in 2027 and after. Age 62 is retained as the early-retirement age, but with appropriate, larger actuarial reductions.
  d. Gradual increases will be made in the credit for postponing claiming (or not receiving) benefits beyond the normal retirement age from 3 percent per year for persons attaining age 65 in 1982–89 to 8 percent for persons attaining normal retirement age in 2009 and after.

    e. The retirement earnings test for persons at the normal retirement age up to age 70 is liberalized, beginning in 1990, by changing the "$1 for $2" reduction in benefits for earnings above the annual exempt amount to a "$1 for $3" basis.

    f. Several minor changes are made to liberalize benefits that primarily affect women (e.g., indexing deferred widow(er)'s benefits by whichever is more favorable, prices or wages, and increasing the benefit rate for disabled widow(er)s aged 50 to 59 from 50 percent to 71.5 percent, depending on age at entitlement, to a uniform 71.5 percent.)

    g. The situation about windfall benefits for retired and disabled workers, with pensions from noncovered employment and OASDI benefits based on a short period of covered employment is alleviated.

    h. The offset of government employee pensions based on employment not covered by OASDI against OASDI spouse and widow(er) benefits is reduced from a full offset to a two-thirds offset.

    i. Restrictions are placed on the payment of benefits to prisoners receiving retirement and survivor benefits (previous law related essentially to disability beneficiaries).

    j. Restrictions are placed on the payment of benefits to aliens residing abroad who have, in general, not had at least five years of residence in the United States.

3. Revenue Provisions, OASDI and HI

    a. OASDI tax rate scheduled for 1985 was moved to 1984 for employers, but not employees. Trust funds receive, from general revenues, additional amount of taxes as if employee rate had been increased.

    b. Self-employed pay the combined OASDI-HI employer-employee rate, minus (for 1984–89) a credit (in lieu of a business expense deduction for such taxes). The trust funds receive, from general revenues, the additional amount of taxes as if the full employer-employee rate had been paid.

    c. About 72 percent of the OASDI tax rate increase scheduled for 1990 was moved forward to 1988.

    d. Part of OASDI benefits (but not more than 50 percent) will be subject to income tax for persons with high incomes, with the proceeds going into the OASDI Trust Funds.

    e. A lump-sum transfer of general revenues will be made to meet the cost of certain gratuitous military-service wage credits (which, under previous law, would have been paid for in future years).

    f. Interfund borrowing (which, under previous law, was permitted only in 1982) was allowed in 1983–87, with specific repayment provisions (before 1990 at the latest) and with prohibitions against borrowing from a fund that is relatively low.

    g. Operations of OASDI and HI trust funds will be removed from Unified Budget after FY 1992 (subsequent legislation moved this up to 1986 for OASDI).

    h. Two public members will be added to the boards of trustees.

4. HI Reimbursement Provisions

    a. A new method of reimbursement of hospitals will be gradually phased in. This will be done on the basis of uniform amounts (but varying among nine geographical areas and between rural and urban facilities) for each of 467 Diagnosis-Related Groups.

    b. No change is made in the minimum eligibility age for HI benefits for the aged (i.e., it remains at 65).

5. SMI Provisions

    a. The enrollee premium rate is changed to a calendar-year basis (to correspond with the OASDI Cost-of-Living Adjustments (COLAs). The rate for July 1982 through June 1983 was to continue through December 1983.

    b. No change is made in the minimum eligibility age for SMI benefits for the aged (i.e., it remains at 65).

These changes in OASDI were about equally divided, over the long run, between increases in income and reductions in outgo. They were supposed to solve both the short-range problem (in the 1980s), which they did, and the long-range problem (of the following 75 years), which, as it turned out, they did not completely do.

CHAPTER 23

Workers' Compensation Insurance

John D. Worrall

David L. Durbin

The United States has several social "insurance" programs: the massive Social Security Program (discussed in Chapter 22 of the *Handbook*) that includes Old-Age, Survivors, and Disability Insurance (OASDI); the Temporary Disability Insurance Program (TDI), which is available in five jurisdictions and provides benefits for up to six months for nonwork-related illnesses or injuries; the unemployment insurance (UI) program; and workers' compensation insurance (WC). Workers' compensation, a no-fault insurance program that provides both wage replacement (indemnity) and medical benefits to workers for injuries arising "out of and in the course of employment," is the oldest and one of the largest of these programs. The workers' compensation program was paying cash benefits 25 years before the advent of unemployment insurance and 40 years before the Social Security Disability Insurance (SSDI) program. As of 1998, employers pay approximately $50 billion annually for workers' compensation insurance.

Workers' compensation issues and cost problems attracted significant media attention in the late 1980s and early 1990s. At that time, costs and the insurance premiums paid by employers were experiencing double-digit annual increases. Many employers could not afford these increases; business decisions on hiring employees and where to locate were affected. Fraud was thought to be rampant and trust in the workers' compensation system was very low. However, as a result of a number of legislative initiatives, favorable economic conditions, and lower medical inflation, the workers' compensation system enjoyed a revival in the mid-to-late 1990s. Indeed, insurance premiums have declined 20 percent to 30 percent since their peak earlier in the decade.

Yet there are even now signs that problems might once again be on the horizon and that costs and premiums may be on the verge of increasing. To understand the cyclical nature of the workers' compensation system it is instructive to consider the nature of the program, its design, the structure of benefits, and how insurance prices are determined and established.

The first state workers' compensation laws to pass constitutional muster were enacted by nine states in 1911. Most of the remaining states passed workers' compensation acts by 1920. Prior to the enactment of workers' compensation statutes, injured workers had to bring legal actions against their employers and rely on common law remedies. However, to succeed with these legal actions, workers had to prove their injuries resulted from employer negligence. Employers also had other legal defenses, including contributory negligence, assumption of risk, and negligent acts of other workers, which made winning a legal action highly uncertain. With the increase in industrialization of the late 19th and early 20th centuries, the number of workplace accidents rose and so did the number of personal injury lawsuits.

The cumbersome legal process at that time was highly uncertain and variable. Workers could become destitute as a result of a workplace injury; employers could potentially lose large lawsuits. Issues of fairness and equity were behind the *quid pro quo* concept that is the heart of today's workers' compensation system. In exchange for relinquishing legal rights to bring suit, workers would be guaranteed indemnity (lost wage) and medical benefits. Workers' compensation insurance became the sole remedy for workplace accidents. In effect, the statutory changes of the early 20th century internalized the costs of industrial accidents to employers, employees, and consumers.

With the enactment of specific workers' compensation statutes, a number of issues needed to be addressed. On the benefits side, issues of how they should be determined (especially for indemnity benefits), their adequacy and equity, how they should be delivered and administered, and government oversight were addressed either through additional legislation or by regulation. The determination of workers' compensation insurance premiums was also an issue similarly addressed.

In general, the oversight and regulation of workers' compensation insurance has been left to the states, and there has been much controversy over state, rather than federal, administration of the program. This controversy emerges from time to time, with some parties pushing for more federal involvement in all aspects of the program. Indeed, the failed national health legislation in 1994 contemplated folding workers' compensation into a national health system. The cost pressures of the early 1990s also caused some to argue for federal oversight. With the decrease in costs later in the decade there has been a revival of support for the state-based system and the issue of federal oversight has quieted.

Although the individual state workers' compensation laws have some features in common, the benefit levels, program structure, offset provisions, and self-insurance requirements (where permitted) differ greatly from state to state. Although intended to be a no-fault system, in practice the state workers' compensation laws and their administration are so complex that legal, actuarial, and underwriting advice is often sought from attorneys, Fellows of the Casualty Actuarial Society, and licensed agents and brokers, respectively.

Of course, the issues of workplace injuries and their costs involve more than just workers' compensation insurance. Loss prevention and safety programs are strategies used by employers to avoid or reduce workplace accidents. If an injury occurs, there are various strategies employers can use to hasten the injured worker's return to work and to manage the duration of disability and costs of the injury. As the costs of workplace accidents and workers' compensation insurance rose dramatically in the 1980s and early 1990s, there was a growing interest in ways to contain costs. Even with the apparent success of some of these programs, the interest in containing workers' compensation costs and improving return-to-work outcomes continues. Recent legislation and some specific cost containment programs will be discussed later in this chapter.

This chapter is an introduction to the topic of workers' compensation insurance and should not be construed as professional advice. The differences in benefit levels and utilization, method of administration, propensity to litigate, industrial structure, and injury frequency and severity are among the major factors resulting in the differences in workers' compensation insurance costs among states. Workers with the same injury in two different states can receive very different cash benefits. In fact, because of the effect of litigation and negotiations over actual cash benefits, workers with the same injury within the same state can receive very different cash benefits. However, in virtually every state, they would receive nearly unlimited medical coverage.

Workers' compensation is part of a larger disability income system designed to provide income maintenance or income support. Some of the programs in the disability income system are based on labor-force attachment. For example, a person who suffers an injury "in and out of the course of employment" may be eligible for cash benefits designed to maintain his or her income (workers' compensation). Benefits provided through other programs in the disability income system, such as veterans' benefits, are based on other statuses and affiliations, and some of the programs designed to provide income support, such as public assistance, are entitlement programs.

Each of the programs in the disability income system give rise to questions of program efficiency and the adequacy and equity of benefits. There is also a considerable body of research that explores the work disincentives of income maintenance or support systems. This research finds that as benefits become more attractive, the use of these programs increases. In times of significantly rising costs, such as the 1980s and early 1990s, questions about the appropriate level of benefits have increased.

Since workers' compensation laws vary dramatically by state, a careful reading of each state's statute is essential. Similarly, there is a large body of case law on workers' compensation. A cottage industry has arisen to follow changes in legislative and case law. The National Council on Compensation Insurance (NCCI), the largest workers' compensation data collection, research, and insurance rating organization in the United States, maintains a staff that does in-depth analyses of the laws of each state in which it is licensed. The U.S. Chamber of Commerce publishes an annual *Analysis of Workers' Compensation Laws* that provides valuable information on each state's program. The state legislatures set the coverage conditions and benefit provisions, but the workers' compensation program is typically financed through the private sector.

Workers' compensation insurance prices are regulated by the insurance department of each state; the prices will vary by state and by the nature of the business being insured. Yet, the workers' compensation insurance business is competitive, with approximately 700 insurers offering coverage. Over the past several years, there has been a significant growth in alternative financing schemes, whereby employers fund their workers' compensation benefit obligations through other risk-sharing arrangements (discussed below), rather than through the direct purchase of insurance.

Workers' compensation insurance is a mandatory, "no fault" program in 48 of the 50 states. In exchange for giving up their right to sue, under the workers' compensation laws employees are expected to get swift and certain payment of medical and cash benefits for injuries or occupational diseases regardless of fault. In exchange for giving up their right to contest claims, employers are protected against the risk of negligence suits for occupational injury or disease brought by their employees.

The state workers' compensation laws were intended to eliminate or minimize the litigation that characterized workplace injury before their adoption. Unfortunately, litigation rates remain high in a number of states.

Workers' compensation insurance is technically elective in New Jersey and Texas; although, most employers are required to carry coverage in New Jersey. In Texas, a growing number of firms are opting out of the workers' compensation system and using other forms of insurance, such as extended disability policies or self-insurance. Employers who fail to elect coverage and provide benefits expose themselves to tort actions and a much greater likelihood of losing in court because they forgo the right to the three common-law defenses: contributory negligence, assumption of risk, and negligence of other workers.

Some workers are covered by federal legislation. Under the Jones Act and the Federal Employers Liability Act, maritime and railroad workers are exempt from state workers' compensation laws. Such workers retain their right to sue their employers. Maritime workers are covered under the Longshoremen's and Harbor Workers' Compensation Act. Federal employees also have a workers' compensation program. They are covered under the Federal Employees Compensation Act, which is administered by the U.S. Department of Labor.

FINANCING WORKERS' COMPENSATION

Employers can meet their requirements to provide workers' compensation insurance by purchasing insurance from private insurance companies or state-run insurance funds, or by self-insuring. Workers' compensation is unique among other forms of social or health insurance. It is a "prefunded" system in that employers or their insurers are required to set aside funds (called reserves) for all future benefit payments once an injury occurs, even if those payments (especially for very serious injuries) may not occur for many years. This is to ensure that injured workers will indeed collect their benefits, which is a fundamental part of the social compact or *quid pro quo* agreement underlying workers' compensation.

Five states do not permit employers to buy primary workers' compensation insurance from private insurance carriers. In the states that allow private property-casualty insurance companies to write policies, employers may insure with stock or mutual insurers, or, in some states, with reciprocal insurers. A growing trend in the private workers' compensation insurance market is for employers to purchase insurance policies with deductibles. This was not allowed until the early 1990s. In this fashion, employers essentially self-insure their workers' compensation obligations up to some threshold and purchase insurance for costs above that amount.

North Dakota, Ohio, Washington, West Virginia, and Wyoming have monopoly state insurance funds. Employers in North Dakota and Wyoming are required to purchase their insurance through the state monopoly. In the other three states, they can either self-insure or buy insurance from the state fund. In 21 states—Arizona, California, Colorado, Hawaii, Idaho, Kentucky, Louisiana, Maine, Maryland, Michigan, Minnesota, Montana, Nevada, New York, Oklahoma, Oregon, Pennsylvania, Rhode Island, Tennessee, Texas, and Utah—the state has a "competitive state fund" that competes with private insurers for workers' compensation insurance business. Each of these states also permits employers to self-insure.

Forty-eight states permit some form of self-insurance. Thirty-four states permit individual firms to self-insure. Firms that self-insure generally are required to meet minimum financial standards set by the state, and most employers are too small to qualify for self-insurance. Those firms that do self-insure generally are required to post a bond or deposit securities with a government regulatory agency (such as the Industrial Commission or the Workers' Compensation Board). Thirty-two states permit employers, typically in the same industry and general line of business, to form groups for the purpose of self-insuring. Firms electing to self-insure, individually or in groups, may purchase excess insurance or self-insure for fixed amounts for individual or aggregate claims. This helps protect them against the cash drain that would accompany a large claim. Firms that self-insure are subject to different tax treatment than firms that buy primary coverage from a private insurance carrier. Private insurance carriers can deduct paid losses and the discounted present value of the change in loss reserves when calculating their tax liability under the Tax Reform Act of 1986. Firms that self-insure can deduct paid losses and expenses but not loss reserves. Hence, firms that self-insure lose the tax deduction for premiums paid that they would get if they purchased a policy from a private insurance carrier. They are subject to less-favorable tax treatment on incurred losses, and subject themselves to unlimited liability (unless they insure excess amounts of coverage with private carriers). Firms that self-insure may have some cash-flow advantages and may reap the benefits of good claim frequency and severity experience. Over the past several years, as costs have accelerated dramatically, there has been a tremendous growth in the use of self-insurance in workers' compensation. Although estimates are imprecise, perhaps as much as 40 percent or more of the market now self-insures.

During certain periods, when the workers' compensation market is unprofitable for insurers (as was the case in the early 1990s), employers may have trouble securing insurance coverage from the private market. In such times, some employers, especially small or riskier businesses, are forced to buy their insurance from an assigned risk pool (sometime also called the residual market). These pools serve as a market of last resort, generally charging higher prices and providing fewer services. During the early 1990s, the assigned risk pools were actually the largest writers of workers' compensation insurance. Since then, the workers' compensation market revival has significantly reduced the size of these pools.

WORKERS' COMPENSATION PRICES

Workers' compensation insurance is regulated in every state. The state regulates the solvency of insurers, the insurance contract and policy forms, and the various pricing programs including experience rating, dividend plans, and a host of other items. Most states also regulate workers' compensation rates. Employers are charged workers' compensation insurance rates per hundreds of dollars of payroll. As the rate for certain types of employers may exceed $30 per $100 of payroll, workers' compensation insurance can be a major cost of doing business. Workers' compensation cash benefits increase every year in virtually every state. This is caused not only by changes in the state laws, but also by the fact that most current state laws tie workers' compensation benefits to the nominal statewide average weekly wage. As the statewide average weekly wage increases with changes in labor market conditions or inflation, new claimants are paid a fixed percentage of the higher nominal wage. Medical costs for treating injured workers also tend to be higher than medical costs for the general population. Workers' compensation rate-making is quite complicated, and the requirements differ by state. The scope of this chapter does not allow an exhaustive treatment of workers' compensation rate-making, and the following is a brief overview.

The regulation of workers' compensation prices takes several forms. In many states, rating bureaus file proposed rates on behalf of members and subscribers. The state insurance department either approves the rates for use or it orders a rate hearing, at which a hearing officer attempts to determine if the proposed rates are adequate and not unfairly discriminatory. Although the issues to be resolved in such hearings are diverse, common themes include the accuracy of projected medical and cash claims, frequency and severity costs, the cost of capital and the allowed rate of return, and current and projected expenses. In a growing number of states, the regulation takes the form of "competitive rating" based on "loss costs." This means the regulators set a benchmark rate that only considers the projected losses or costs from insurance claims. Individual insurers then file their own expense and profit margins, with the theory being this will not only ensure enough funds are available in the system to pay claims but also encourage competition in the market. States that require insurance department formal review before insurance companies issue new policies at the proposed rates are called "prior approval" states. In other states ("file and use" states), insurers can file proposed rates and use them after a suitable period for insurance department review. Several states do not permit rating bureaus or rate making in concert.

Historically, rating bureaus filed proposed rates using losses, expenses, and a markup (a profit and contingency factor) that can be positive or negative. More recently, most states require rating bureaus to file "pure premiums" or "loss costs" only (no expense or profit provisions). Individual insurance companies now use their own expense experience and profit needs, together with bureau loss projections to file individual proposed workers' compensation rates with state insurance departments.

As a result of the McCarran-Ferguson Act, property-casualty insurance companies have been granted a partial exemption from the antitrust laws, and this exemption has enabled the companies to make rates in concert. From time to time, the U.S. Congress considers amendments that would repeal the exemption. If such amendments pass, the rating bureaus may be able to file the "pure premiums" discussed previously. After a transition period, they would not be able to promulgate the "trend factors" discussed in the following section. As of 2000, the antitrust exemption seems unlikely to be repealed in the near future.

Manual Rates

Manual rates (price per $100 of payroll) are the starting point for an understanding of workers' compensation prices. Premium and loss data is collected for each employer insured by a private insurance carrier or competitive state fund. Firms are separated into five areas of economic activity: manufacturing, contract construction, producers/dealers, office/clerical, and "all other," and then are classified further by the type of business in which they are engaged and assigned to one of more than 600 workers' compensation class codes. (The number of classes varies by state.) The idea is to group the firms into homogeneous classifications based on the type of business activity and, thus, risk of injury. For example, it would not make sense for an office staff/clerical operation to have the same manual rate as a contractor. The risk and type of injury and hence costs would be very different for these two types of employers. These codes are analogous to but not quite the same as a standard industrial classification (SIC) or a census code. To determine what manual rates they will propose for a future time period, rating bureau actuaries examine all relevant available data on historical and projected costs and revenues. The projected ratio of losses (costs) and loss-adjustment expenses (to premium) is compared with a permissible or target loss and loss-adjustment ratio established by the state regulators.

Complicating this calculation is the fact that prices are set for a future period and are supposed to generate enough revenue to cover the medical and cash benefits for injured workers, which may be paid out over many years. By law, employers or their insurers are required to set aside funds to pay for all the future costs once a workplace injury occurs. Actuaries must then make a number of estimates not only about the number of accidents but they also must estimate the amount of benefits that need to be paid out over time.

Historical data must be adjusted to reflect "development" (how the payment of benefits changes over time), subsequent changes in rates, and changes expected in payrolls during the future period in which proposed rates will be in effect. A ratio of these adjusted losses to premiums is compared with a permitted (the permissible) ratio to arrive at an indicated change in rates. The indicated change in rates is further adjusted to reflect both legislatively mandated changes in benefits that will take effect during the period that the proposed rates will be in force and recent trends (called "trend factors," which are the difference in the rate of growth in expected costs and premiums) in adjusted loss ratios. An overall change in rate level is determined for each of the five major subdivisions: manufacturing, contract construction, producer/dealer, office/clerical, and all others. The rate change is then distributed to each of the workers' compensation class codes, depending on the relative contribution or weight (class relativity) of the class within the major subdivision.

Small firms are charged these manual rates, which represent the average experience for their workers' compensation class code. Small firms also may be charged minimum premiums, loss constants, and expense constants. Loss constants are applied to small firms to attempt to stabilize loss ratios across all firm sizes. Expense constants are the fixed costs of issuing the insurance policy and reflect the fact that insurers must devote a higher percentage of each premium dollar from small policies to the cost of writing and processing that policy than they do for larger policies. Minimum premiums are charged, because insurers do not want to subject themselves to unlimited liability unless they receive some minimum premium in return. Additionally, there are many programs, some mandatory and others voluntary, that affect workers' compensation insurance prices.

Adjustments to Manual Rates

Employers with premiums greater than $5,000 per year are given mandatory premium discounts that increase with the size of their manual premiums. These discounts can be close to 15 percent for premiums greater than $1 million. Where allowed, stock insurers and mutual insurers use different discount tables to reflect their different operating and policyholder dividend policies, but not all states permit the use of different discount tables. Stock company discounts are greater than mutual company discounts, and, as can be seen from the example above, premium discounts can reduce workers' compensation prices substantially.

Firms with workers' compensation manual premiums in excess of a specific threshold, which vary by state (typically either $5,000 or $7,500 per year), are subject to mandatory experience rating. Experience-rated firms have their manual rates adjusted up or down by a modifier (their "mod"), which is a weighted average of the firm's own prior loss experience and that of all other firms in its own class based on the information from the three latest years. If a firm's experience is better or worse than the average or expected experience for its class, its manual rate will be reduced or increased accordingly. The weight given to the firm's own experience varies directly with the size of the firm (called "credibility").

Because of the paucity of claims and the inability to predict the nature of all work injuries, the experience of small (manually rated) firms receives little or no weight (zero credibility). Large firms, whose experience is more stable and, thus, easy to predict, receive higher weight; that is, their modifier, and, hence, the price they are charged, is determined more by their own experience. Experience-rating plans provide safety incentives for employers. Employers can directly reduce their experience-rating modification factor and price they pay for workers' compensation insurance by maintaining a safe workplace.

Firms that generate $25,000 of standard premium for a one-year policy, or $50,000 for three years, can elect to purchase a retrospective rating plan (retro). This option, which usually is selected by larger firms, is similar to cost-plus insurance. The employer pays the loss costs, subject to negotiated minimums and maximums, and an insurance charge. Insureds have several different plans from which to select, but each provides the opportunity to capitalize on above-average safety standards and good loss experience.

Most mutual insurance companies and many stock (participating) companies pay dividends to policyholders. Some of these dividend plans pay a flat percentage rate to all policyholders (flat-rate plans), while others pay sliding scale dividends based on the loss performance of the individual insured (sliding scale plans). Countrywide dividends to workers' compensation insureds have been in the 4 percent to 5 percent range recently, although they are higher in some states and vary considerably by insurance carrier. Some stock companies pay smaller dividends but offer higher premium discounts.

Many states permit private insurance carriers to deviate from filed bureau rates, and such deviations can play an important role in the competition for workers' compensation business. Deviations can be up or down, and usually are in terms of flat percentages. Insurers may choose to deviate downward, because they believe their expenses are much lower than average, or that their underwriting is superior. They may choose to deviate upward, because they believe that the rating bureau has filed inadequate rates (or the regulatory authority has mandated them). Some insurers may own multiple insurance companies that write workers' compensation insurance in a state; one member of the group or fleet may deviate from bureau rates, while another does not.

"Scheduled rating" also is allowed in many states, and this can be a powerful underwriting tool. Insurers are allowed to reduce the rate charged to insureds to reflect characteristics of the insured (e.g., strong management or outstanding safety programs) that are likely to result in lower-than-average loss costs. The state insurance department typically establishes the maximum scheduled rating credit that can be applied. Over the past few years, there has been a substantial growth in scheduled rating programs especially for small firms that may not qualify for experience rating. Discounts may be given for establishing safety committees, having no accidents in a year, or having a drug-testing and drug-free workplace policy.

In some states, employers can negotiate the amount and timing of deposits they pay insurers. These "deposit premiums" can be waived in some cases. As the timing of cash flows can be negotiated, the real (discounted present) value of an employer's workers' compensation premium is not necessarily fixed.

CLAIMS AND BENEFITS

There are five basic workers' compensation insurance claims. The five types include:

1. Noncompensatory medical or medical-only claims.
2. Temporary total disability claims.
3. Permanent partial disability claims.
4. Permanent total disability claims.
5. Death claims.

Explanations of each type follow.

Noncompensatory Medical or Medical-Only Claims

"Medical only" claims result from injuries or occupational disease "arising out of and in the course of employment" that do not result in lost work time sufficient to generate lost wage (cash benefit) claims. These claims are by far the most common type, accounting for approximately 75 percent to 80 percent of all workers' compensation claims. Although the state workers' compensation laws provide for virtually unlimited medical coverage, most medical-only claims do not exceed a few hundred dollars and account for less than 10 percent of the cost of workers' compensation. The medical cost component of the lost-time claims described below is far more expensive. As the medical cost component of all workers' compensation claims, including the lost-time claims to be discussed shortly, now accounts for more than 45 percent to 50 percent of system costs, states have adopted cost-containment strategies to rein in escalating medical expenses. Cost-containment issues and statutory reforms to the workers' compensation systems will be discussed later.

Temporary Total Disability Claims

Temporary total disability claims are those claims for injuries or occupational diseases serious enough to prevent someone from working but from which full recovery is expected. Most state laws have both *waiting periods* and *retroactive periods*. The waiting period in most states is between three to seven days. Injured workers begin to draw cash benefits if they have lost work time that exceeds the state waiting period. Should their temporary total disability result in lost work time that exceeds the state-mandated retroactive period—two to three weeks in most states—

they receive retroactive cash benefits for the waiting period. Temporary total disability benefits are the most common form of cash claim, accounting for roughly three of every four cash claims and 25 percent of workers' compensation costs. Although more than one-half of temporary total disability claims close within one month, some are long-duration claims, and others become permanent claims. States limit the amount of time that a temporary total disability claimant can collect benefits and, in some instances, the amount of cumulative cash benefits.

A typical state's workers' compensation law provides that workers who suffer temporary total disability receive cash benefits equal to two-thirds of their pre-injury wage subject to maximum and minimum payments. The maximum generally is based on a percentage of the statewide average weekly wage, 100 percent being the most common. Consequently, workers who earned a wage greater than the statewide average may have wage *replacement rates* that actually are less than two-thirds of their wages. Similarly, virtually all states provide minimum cash benefits for temporary total disability. The most common method of determining the minimum payment is to use a percentage of the statewide average weekly wage or to specify the injured worker's wage as the minimum. In some states, the minimum is as high as 50 percent of the statewide average weekly wage. Consequently, the replacement rate for low-wage workers can be greater than 100 percent. Because workers' compensation benefits are not taxable, it is not unusual for workers to receive larger amounts in cash benefits than their normal take-home pay. The higher the *real* (after-tax) replacement rate, the stronger the incentive both to file a workers' compensation insurance claim and to lengthen the duration of a nonwork spell. There is strong research evidence that a 10 percent increase in real workers' compensation cash benefits results in a 4 percent increase in claims filed with no underlying change in the mix of jobs or risks of injury.

Less than one-quarter of the states adjust temporary total disability benefits for inflation, and several of these only after two or three years from the injury date. As most temporary disability claims close fairly rapidly, inflation does not have a chance to erode the value of cash benefits for the majority of temporary total disability beneficiaries. However, for long-duration cases and permanent claims, to be discussed later, the real replacement rate falls with the passage of time as inflation erodes the value of cash benefits.

Workers' compensation programs also provide for vocational rehabilitation benefits for injured workers. More than one-third of the states have special funds to finance the provision of vocational rehabilitation services. More than half the states have their own workers' compensation vocational rehabilitation sections, although many states refer injured workers to public or private providers for vocational rehabilitation services. Vocational rehabilitation services are used almost exclusively by long-duration temporary total disability claimants and permanent disability claimants. These services involve evaluation of potential return-to-work possibilities and retraining as appropriate. Temporary total claimants whose injuries are serious and will eventually make the transition to permanent disability claimants can have the amount of their cash benefit determined by a disability rating (see below), they may have an incentive to forestall or forgo rehabilitation services that could restore them to the world of work.

Permanent Partial Disability Claims

Permanent partial disability claims account for most of the costs of the workers' compensation program. Although these claims represent only 5 percent to 7 percent of all workers' compensation claims and 25 percent to 30 percent of cash claims, they constitute 70 percent of program costs. They also are responsible for a good deal of the litigation in workers' compensation. Permanent partial claims usually begin with a period of temporary total disability, but the claimants eventually are evaluated as having a permanent but partial disability. These partial disabilities can be quite severe, and some permanent partial disability claimants show up on the Social Security disability insurance rolls.

The method of evaluating the extent of permanent partial disability, as well as the rationale for awarding benefits, varies among (and sometimes within) states. Most permanent partial benefits fall into two broad categories: "scheduled" and "nonscheduled" benefits. States with scheduled benefits award a specific dollar amount, depending on the specific type and nature of the injury. States that have schedules tend to list awards for amputations and loss of hearing. For example, the state of Illinois pays almost a quarter of a million dollars to a worker who loses his or her arm at the shoulder. A few states have no schedule but pay disability benefits on the basis of the "impairment," "whole man," or "loss of earnings capacity" principles. As the amount of cash benefits to be paid varies directly with the impairment rating assigned to injured workers by the treating physician under these three schemes, and for nonscheduled injuries in general, there is little uniformity and much contention over impairment ratings.

Permanent partial disability benefits can be substantial, essentially making up (in part) for the loss in lifetime earning capacity. As lifetime awards can run well into the hundreds of thousands of dollars, there are incentives for both employers, as represented by their insurers, and employees to litigate these claims. Attorneys have incentives to litigate them on a contingency-fee basis because many states permit injured workers to receive lump-sum settlements called "redemptions," "washouts," or "compromise and release" in some states, of which attorneys receive a fixed share. Employers and insurers also prefer in many instances to provide a lump-sum settlement to satisfy their statutory obligations and, thus, no longer have to carry a liability on their books (i.e., they can release the dollar reserves they otherwise must hold).

Permanent Total Disability Claims

Permanent total disability claims are rare. Less than one-half of 1 percent of all cash claims are permanent total claims. These claims tend to have the highest *average* claim cost, more than $400,000 per claim, and account for about 7 percent of workers' compensation costs. Workers who receive permanent total awards are expected to remain totally disabled even after reaching the point of maximum medical improvement for the remainder of their lives. States tend to award benefits for life, or for the duration of the disability. The replacement rates and inflation adjustments tend to be the same as those for temporary total disability, although some states provide inflation protection for permanent total cases.

Death Claims

Death claims have become quite rare over the past few decades and constitute less than one-half of 1 percent of cash claims. The average cost of a death claim is lower than that of the average permanent total disability claim. Fatalities account for about 2 percent to 3 percent of workers' compensation insurance costs. Cash benefits are paid to surviving spouses and children. The replacement rates are similar to those paid for total disability claims, with two-thirds of the pre-injury wage being a common benefit rate, although some states reduce the replacement rate substantially if a surviving spouse has no minor children.

Death benefits are subject to maximum and minimum weekly amounts, as well as to maximum lifetime amounts. The lifetime amount may be specified in the law or may be implied as the duration of benefit receipt is restricted in most states. Remarriage of a surviving spouse can result in the cessation of benefit payments, frequently with an accompanying lump-sum settlement. Actuaries use remarriage tables to reserve or price these claims. All states provide burial allowances for fatal injuries covered under the workers' compensation law.

Recent research suggests that the safety incentives embedded within workers' compensation insurance premiums and the various pricing programs have been responsible for the significant decline in the observed workplace fatality rates over the past 40 to 50 years. Other government mandated programs such as those regulated and administered by the Occupational Safety and Health Administration (OSHA) also have played a role.

Coordination of Benefits

Since workers' compensation is one of a host of programs designed to assist people with work disabilities, it is not unusual to find workers' compensation cash beneficiaries receiving payments from one or more additional programs. The various Social Security benefits are those most commonly received with workers' compensation, but veterans' benefits, public assistance, private insurance, and other programs provide joint benefits as well. As mentioned previously, the workers' compensation laws were in force long before Social Security or unemployment insurance. When workers' compensation was introduced, there was no need to consider offsets or coordination of benefits. When Social Security was introduced, there was no offset provision in the law; one was initiated in 1965, which limits the combined workers' compensation and Social Security payment to 80 percent of pre-injury current earnings. Twenty-one states have Social Security offset provisions in their state workers' compensation laws. The federal government has prohibited any further state offset provisions. Only 10 states have offset provisions for unemployment benefits. Although there are exceptions, a good rule of thumb is that workers' compensation benefits take precedence over other programs.

WORKERS' COMPENSATION IN THE 1990s AND 2000s

As alluded to previously, workers' compensation costs escalated dramatically in the 1980s into the early 1990s. In the 1980s, the costs of workplace accidents more than doubled, increasing at the rate of more than 10 percent per year. Medical costs rose even faster. By some estimates, the medical cost portion of workers' compensation rose 1.5 times faster than medical costs in the general economy and were the major workers' compensation cost-driver. At the same time, premiums in the private insurance market also rose almost 10 percent per year. As a result, workers' compensation costs became a significant public policy issue. Workers' compensation issues took on even more importance as employers struggled to keep production costs down to remain competitive. In many states, workers' compensation costs became an economic growth and jobs issue.

Beginning in the late 1980s and continuing through the mid 1990s, a number of states attempted to address workers' compensation cost growth through statutory reforms to the system. The reforms have focused on three main areas: the structure of permanent partial disability benefits, safety initiatives, and, most importantly, medical issues.

More than 30 states have now adopted medical fee schedules that list the maximum amounts that will be paid for certain procedures. More than half of the states limit the choice of medical care providers and the ability to switch providers after the initial choice has been made. A growing number of states have adopted billing and utilization review procedures as well. In the last few years, several states have embraced so-called managed care strategies for controlling workers' compensation costs. Use of health maintenance and preferred provider organizations has grown dramatically. By some estimates, maybe as many as two-thirds of injured workers are treated by such arrangements. By 1995, 29 states had passed legislation promoting or allowing the use of managed care arrangements for delivering care to injured workers.

MANAGED CARE IN WORKERS' COMPENSATION

Significant managed care initiatives have been adopted by California, Florida, Minnesota, New Jersey, New York, New Hampshire, North Carolina, and South Dakota, among others. We should point out that "managed care" schemes vary tremendously across state programs. Some are part of a plan that may include other delivery systems such as traditional fee-for-service. However, in 1997, Florida made the provision of service through approved workers' compensation managed care arrangements mandatory. South Dakota has required insurance carriers (since 1995) and self-insurers (since 1996) to provide managed care as part of their workers' compensation policies. As the legislative environment is quite dynamic and subject to change in many states, interested readers should consult their State Insurance Department or the National Association of Insurance Commissioners for the latest provisions of law in a specific state.

The nature of workers' compensation especially its *quid pro quo* (swift and sure treatment in exchange for the lack of recourse to recovery by lawsuit) means that managed care in workers' compensation will differ in some important aspects from general managed care plans. The state is interested not only in the provision of appropriate medical care of a high quality, but also in the return, where possible, of injured workers to employment, preferably with their pre-injury employer. Indeed, because lost-wage benefits account for roughly half of overall workers' compensation costs, traditional preventive medicine and gatekeeper models employed by more general managed care programs may not be suitable. This can result in a different service delivery mix, and in different economic incentives to the key agents in the workers' compensation system.

For example, some have argued that a more active and aggressive form of medicine may be more appropriate for treating injured workers. Some so-called "sports medicine" models promote immediate medical interventions, which in the short run may actually cost more money in terms of medical expense. The payback is thought to be in the long run if workers are healthy and can return to work more quickly. However, some fear that quality of care will actually suffer and that workers will be pressured to return to work too quickly. It is too soon to tell yet the merits of these arguments.

Although the provider arrangement (HMO, PPO, or other network) varies across states, all must typically be certified by a state authority. The Agency for Health Care Administration in Florida is an example of a mandatory state managed care scheme. Certification by a regulatory authority holds regardless of the nature of the financing scheme or the size of the program. For example, California and New York have both a State Fund and private carriers; and, South Dakota and New Jersey, which are largely financed through private carriers or self-insurance, all require that managed care service providers be certified by the state before they deliver health care services to injured workers. South Dakota is an interesting example because it will also certify the managed care plans of employers that self-insure. Some states require employers to notify workers if their insurance arrangement includes a managed care provider, Minnesota is a good example.

Another important consideration for workers' compensation managed care is that roughly half of the states permit injured workers to select their treating physician. This limits the ability of employers to direct workers to their preferred managed care network, and quite likely diminishes the potential cost-effectiveness of such programs. On the other hand, injured workers may be more comfortable with their own physicians and less likely to litigate their workers' compensation claims.

The convergence of state regulation and employer desire for cost-containment, together with the widespread adoption of managed care in the general provision of health services have been proximate causes of the rapid rise of managed care arrangements in workers' compensation programs during the last decade of the century. Whether such arrangements will ultimately reduce total social costs associated with the workers' compensation program appears promising but ultimately remains to be seen. There have been claims of large cost reductions associated with the adoption of managed care. (Estimates for pilot projects in California, Florida, and New Hampshire range from 20 percent to 45 percent.) However, for several reasons, it is best to be cautious about these estimates.

First, legislation that introduced managed care in some states also enacted other changes to the system, and cost savings attributed to the delivery system may be because of other aspects of reform, including benefit reductions. Second, there are tradeoffs between costs and quality of care and their concomitant outcomes. Third, cost savings may be calculated primarily on the medical component of cases which entail little or no lost work time, and, perhaps on closed claims only. Clearly, the most important claims, in terms of cost, are permanent partial disability claims. Such claims take a long time to develop. Eliminating open claims may bias estimates of cost savings. Fourth, the 1990s were largely characterized by an expanding economy, when workers were less likely to file and go out on a workers' compensation claim. Fifth, we do not, as yet, know the impact of changes in the delivery system on the duration of non-work spells. Given the huge expenditures on medical care in workers' compensation, both academic and industry researchers are devoting attention to data collection, reporting, and evaluation

Even in those states that have adopted managed care, some of the traditional issues that affect medical costs remain. Perhaps, the most telling is the continuing debate about choice of physician. Organized labor has fought to enable employees to retain physician choice, while management, in an attempt to contain cost and manage return to work, has, through its legislative efforts, fought to control physician assignment. Some managed care arrangements present injured workers with lists or panels of physicians they may use, but employees may not have a choice of health plans. Injured workers may be assigned to a physician within a single plan. Employees may be able to switch physicians in some states if they are not satisfied with the service that their original choice provides, but such switching is limited. For example, Florida limits employees to one change within the same provider network. The issue of employer-employee control is unlikely to recede in the near future. Its footprints are on the California, Florida, and other legislative changes. Employee satisfaction with managed care is currently under study, but it is safe to say that it is unclear if organized labor is satisfied with the ability to appeal in cases where they believe medical care has been inadequate.

The tension over physician choice is one manifestation of competing interests in the system. Another issue concerns return to work. If the delivery system offers financial incentives to physicians based on a fixed cost contract, injured workers may feel that they are being pushed to return to work too soon, or that they have not received the service intensity their injuries deserve. This perception on the part of labor may exist in a traditional fee-for-service scheme, but it may be exacerbated in some managed care contractual arrangements.

We should close this brief discussion of managed care in workers' compensation by pointing out that the introduction of a national health scheme, as was contemplated by one of the political parties during the 1990s, would have made the rate of adoption of managed care moot if workers' compensation health care delivery was absorbed into the system. Again, it is wise to remember that workers' compensation is a social insurance disability program, and it is too early to tell whether such schemes would reduce total social costs in workers' compensation.

OTHER LEGISLATIVE INITIATIVES

Besides managed care initiatives, two other areas have received considerable legislative, employer, and media attention. These relate to the benefit provisions for permanent partial disability claims (PPD) and to fraud. A growing number of states have tried to address the inequities in PPD awards where workers with the same or similar injuries receive very different dollar awards, or where very seriously injured workers do not receive as much as less seriously injured workers. Instead of a fixed award for a specific injury, some states are linking PPD awards more directly to lost wages. They also are splitting PPD awards into two (or more) categories with one set of benefits for less seriously injured workers (often with explicit benefit caps or maximums) and one set for the more seriously injured. Injury severity as measured by impairment or disability ratings is still quite subjective and may be influenced by the treating physician. Litigation also plays a role. Many states have moved to a more objective system of impairment ratings based on recommendations from the American Medical Association. While costs seem to have been mitigated, similar to the issue of the effectiveness of managed care programs, it is too soon to tell definitively how successful these efforts will be. The issue of the adequacy and equity of PPD awards has historically been the most vexing for policymakers in designing workers' compensation systems. It is quite likely that social and economic cycles will continue to affect this issue.

A number of states also have enacted specific fraud legislation making certain actions by employers and employees crimes with stiff penalties. Stories of supposedly injured workers collecting workers' compensation benefits and then working at other jobs, collecting unemployment benefits, or otherwise malingering were common earlier in the decade. At the same time, some employers tried to bypass the classification and experience-rating systems to avoid paying insurance premiums. Dedicated fraud bureaus with prosecutorial authority have been established in some states to pursue these activities. Advances in information technology also allow linking computer files among the workers' compensation, unemployment, Social Security, and other systems to identify potential repeat offenders. Again the preliminary evidence suggests these efforts have reduced fraud and thus lowered costs for other system participants.

SUMMARY

Workers' compensation is a mandatory, no-fault social insurance program that provides medical and cash benefits and rehabilitation services to workers who suffer injuries or occupational diseases arising "out of and in the course of employment." The program is strictly regulated by the states. Employers pay for this program as an employee benefit; but there is research evidence that, as workers' compensation costs increase for employers, employees bear much of the cost burden through a wage tradeoff. Most small employers pay manual rates, or close to manual rates. However, about 85 percent of covered payrolls are experience-rated. There are many competitive pricing devices that have a major impact on the price of workers' compensation insurance.

Most workers' compensation claims are simple medical-only claims, and the most frequent cash claims, temporary total disability claims, usually close within a month. Unfortunately, permanent claims that result from serious injuries are expensive and prone to litigation. Medical benefits are virtually unlimited in all states, but cash benefits usually are capped. Federal law limits the combined workers' compensation and Social Security benefit to 80 percent of pre-injury earnings. Less than half of the states offset Social Security, and even fewer offset unemployment insurance. In most other cases, workers' compensation is primary.

During the 1980s and early 1990s, workers' compensation costs rose dramatically and captured employer and policymaker attention. A number of new initiatives and reforms have come on line in the mid-1990s to deal with the cost issues. There are now many opportunities for employers to handle their workplace safety and workers' compensation insurance issues; the challenge will be to find the right fit of insurance programs and medical providers, given the statutory and regulatory environment in each state.

As of 2000, many state workers' compensation programs have enjoyed a resurgence to health. Employer costs are down, fewer workers are being injured, and insurers have regained some profitability. Yet, the history of workers' compensation is one of cycles. In the past, costs and injuries have risen after periods of reform and profitability. Indeed, in certain states there is already evidence of the cycle turning with double-digit premium increases on the horizon. This will undoubtedly once again give rise to introspection regarding the design of the system and then legislative attempts to address perceived problems. Perhaps that is one of the most important messages about the workers' compensation system: Namely, in its 80- to 90-year history, the program, its costs, and benefit structures have not stood still for long. Employers need to keep abreast of changes in order to design and implement effective programs.

CHAPTER 24

State Unemployment Compensation Programs

George E. Rejda

Unemployment compensation is an important employee benefit. Weekly cash benefits are paid to workers who are involuntarily unemployed and who meet certain eligibility requirements. The weekly cash benefits enable unemployed workers to maintain their consumption and reduce the economic insecurity that results from extended unemployment.

The primary purpose of this chapter is to discuss the fundamentals of state unemployment compensation programs. Unemployment compensation in the United States consists of several distinct programs. First, regular state unemployment compensation programs exist in all states, the District of Columbia, Puerto Rico, and the Virgin Islands. The regular state programs came into existence as a result of the Social Security Act of 1935. Second, a permanent extended-benefits program that pays additional unemployment benefits in states with high unemployment also is available. In addition, separate government-provided programs exist for civilian employees of the federal government, for ex-service members, and for railroad employees. Private employers also may provide unemployment-related benefits, such as severance pay, and, in conjunction with unions through collective bargaining, supplemental unemployment benefits (SUBs).

The treatment in this chapter is limited to the regular state programs and the permanent program of extended benefits. More specifically, the following areas are discussed: (1) objectives of unemployment compensation; (2) state unemployment compensation provisions; (3) extended benefits program; (4) financing unemployment compensation; (5) administration of unemployment compensation; and (6) unemployment compensation problems and issues.[1]

OBJECTIVES OF UNEMPLOYMENT COMPENSATION

Unemployment compensation programs have several objectives. The most important include the following:

- Provide weekly cash benefits during periods of involuntary unemployment.
- Help stabilize the economy during recessions.
- Encourage employers to stabilize their employment.
- Help unemployed workers find jobs.

Unemployment can cause great economic insecurity. Thus, the primary purpose of unemployment compensation is *to pay weekly cash benefits to workers who are involuntarily unemployed.* The benefits paid provide for the partial replacement of earnings to workers who are involuntarily unemployed for temporary periods and, thus, help the unemployed workers to maintain their previous standard of living. As a result, economic insecurity from involuntary unemployment is reduced.

Unemployment compensation programs *help stabilize the economy during business recessions.* Unemployment compensation is an automatic stabilizer. During business recessions, when unemployment increases, unemployment benefits also increase in a desirable counter-cyclical manner. Thus, personal income and consumption spending can be maintained, which reduces the severity of the business recession and helps stabilize the economy.

Another important objective is to *encourage employers to stabilize their employment.* This is done by experience rating, in which employers with favorable employment records pay reduced unemployment compensation tax rates. Experience rating is an important financing issue that will be discussed later in the chapter.

---

1 The material in this chapter is based largely on George E. Rejda, *Social Insurance and Economic Security,* 6th ed. (Upper Saddle River, NJ: Prentice Hall, 1999), Chaps. 14 and 15; Committee on Ways and Means, U.S. House of Representatives, *1998 Green Book, Background Material and Data on Programs within the Jurisdiction of the Committee on Ways and Means* (Washington, D.C.: U.S. Government Printing Office, 1998), pp. 327-359; and *Highlights of State Unemployment Compensation Laws,* January 2000. (Washington, D.C.: National Foundation for Unemployment Compensation and Workers' Compensation, 2000).

Another important objective is to *help unemployed workers find jobs*. Applicants for unemployment benefits are required to register for work at local employment offices, and officials assist unemployed workers in finding suitable employment. The unemployment benefits give the unemployed workers time to find jobs that are consistent with their education, skills, and experience. Computer job banks are especially helpful in matching the available jobs in the community with the skills and experience of unemployed workers.

STATE UNEMPLOYMENT COMPENSATION PROVISIONS

The characteristics of regular state unemployment compensation programs vary widely among the states. Each state is free to determine coverage, eligibility requirements, and benefit amounts, subject to certain minimum federal standards. However, certain common provisions are present in all programs.[2]

Covered Occupations

Most occupations today are covered for unemployment compensation benefits. About 97 percent of all wage and salary workers or 89 percent of the civilian labor force are covered by unemployment compensation programs.[3]

The Federal Unemployment Tax Act (FUTA) requires coverage of certain occupations under state unemployment compensation programs if the state wants to qualify for the 5.4 percent federal tax credit (discussed later). *Private firms* are covered if they pay wages of at least $1,500 during any calendar quarter or employ at least one worker on at least one day of each of 20 weeks in the current or prior year.

Agricultural firms are covered if they pay cash wages of at least $20,000 for agricultural labor during any calendar quarter or employ 10 or more workers on at least one day in each of 20 different weeks in the current or prior year. *Domestic service employers* also are covered if they pay cash wages of $1,000 or more for domestic service during any calendar quarter in the current or prior year.

Most occupations in *state and local government* also are covered for unemployment compensation benefits. However, state and local govern-

---

2 G. Rejda, *Social Insurance and Economic Security*, pp. 304-319.
3 *1998 Green Book*, p. 328.

ment employers are not required to pay the federal unemployment tax and have the option of reimbursing the state for any unemployment benefits paid to laid-off employees, rather than paying regular state unemployment compensation contributions.

Nonprofit organizations of a charitable, religious, or educational nature are covered if the nonprofit organization employs at least four workers for at least one day in each of 20 different weeks in the current or prior year. Like state and local governments, a nonprofit organization is exempt from FUTA taxes and has the option either to pay the state unemployment tax or to reimburse the state for the benefits paid. Many jurisdictions have expanded coverage of nonprofit employers beyond that required by federal law. A number of jurisdictions now cover nonprofit organizations that employ one or more workers, rather than four or more.

Finally, the states can elect to cover certain occupations not covered by FUTA, but most states have not expanded FUTA coverage significantly. Occupations generally not covered include (1) self-employment, (2) certain agricultural labor and domestic service, (3) certain student interns, (4) service of patients in hospitals, (5) certain alien farm workers, (6) certain seasonal camp workers, and (7) service for relatives.[4] Railroad workers are not covered under state programs but have their own program under the Railroad Unemployment Insurance Act.

Eligibility Requirements

Unemployed workers must meet certain eligibility requirements to qualify for unemployment benefits. Eligibility requirements vary among the states. However, the most common eligibility requirements include the following:

- Earn qualifying wages.
- Be able to work and be available for work.
- Actively seek work.
- Satisfy a waiting period.
- Be free of any disqualifying act.

Unemployed workers must earn a certain amount of qualifying wages during their base period to receive unemployment benefits. Most states define a base period or base year as the first four of the last five completed calendar quarters before the unemployed worker receives benefits. Most states also require employment in at least two calendar quarters in

---

4 *1998 Green Book*, p. 331.

the base period. The purpose of the qualifying wages requirement is to limit benefits to workers who have a current attachment to the labor force.

The amount of wages earned during the base period determines the benefits that are paid during the benefit year. The *benefit year* usually is a 52-week period during which the claimant can receive benefits. In 1997, qualifying wages for minimum weekly benefits ranged from $130 in Hawaii to $3,400 in Florida. Qualifying wages for maximum weekly benefits ranged from $5,450 in Nebraska to $29,432 in Colorado.[5]

Unemployed workers also must be able to work and be available for work. *Able to work* means the unemployed worker is capable of working. *Available for work* typically means being ready, willing, and able to work. Registration for work at a public employment office provides some evidence that the unemployed worker is available for work.

In addition to registration for work, unemployed workers must actively seek work or make a reasonable effort to obtain suitable work. Suitable work generally is work in a worker's customary occupation that meets certain safety, moral, and labor standards. An unemployed worker is not required to take any job. However, if the claimant refuses suitable work without good cause, he or she may be disqualified. In general, as the length of unemployment increases, the claimant is required to accept a wider range of jobs.

In most states, unemployed workers also must satisfy a one-week waiting period. Some states have no waiting period. The purposes of the waiting period are to hold down claim costs, reduce administrative expenses by eliminating short-term claims, and give claims personnel time to process claims.

Finally, the worker must not have committed a disqualifying act. Examples of disqualifying acts include quitting a job voluntarily without good cause; discharge for misconduct; refusal of suitable work; or being an active participant in a labor dispute. In addition, benefits cannot be paid to professional athletes between sport seasons, to illegal aliens, or to professional and administrative employees of educational institutions during summer and other vacation periods if they have reasonable assurance of reemployment after the vacation period.

Weekly Benefit Amounts

A weekly cash benefit is paid for each week of total unemployment after the worker meets the waiting period. The benefit amount depends on the

---

5 *1998 Green Book*, p. 334.

amount of wages earned during the base period, subject to certain minimum and maximum amounts.

Several methods are used to determine the weekly benefit amount. Some states compute benefits based on a fraction of the worker's high-quarter wages. For example, some states use the fraction 1/26, which results in a weekly benefit of 50 percent of the full-time wage for a worker who is employed 13 weeks on a full-time basis. Thus, if a worker earns $400 weekly or $5,200 during his or her high quarter, 1/26 of this amount produces a weekly benefit of $200. Many states use a lower fraction to provide relatively higher benefits to low-wage workers.

In January 2000, the minimum weekly benefit amount ranged from $5 in Hawaii to $94 in Washington. The maximum weekly benefit amount ranged from $133 in Puerto Rico to $646 in Massachusetts.[6]

The vast majority of states pay regular weekly benefits for a maximum of 26 weeks; Massachusetts and Washington pay benefits for up to 30 weeks. However, not all claimants qualify for 26 weeks of benefits. The majority of states have a variable duration of benefits that depends on the amount of the claimant's wages during the base year.

Finally, under the extended-benefits program (discussed later), up to 13 additional weeks of benefits can be paid to claimants who have exhausted their regular benefits in states with relatively high unemployment rates.

Reduced benefits can be paid for part-time work. The partial unemployment benefit usually is the weekly unemployment benefit less wages earned, but with a certain amount of earnings disregarded in computing the benefit.[7]

Disqualifications

Unemployed workers can be disqualified for unemployment compensation benefits for a variety of reasons. The most important are the following:

- Not able or available for work.
- Voluntarily quit without good cause.
- Refusal of suitable work without good cause.
- Unemployment as a result of direct participation in a labor dispute.

---

6 *Highlights of State Unemployment Compensation Laws January 2000.* (Washington, D.C.: National Foundation for Unemployment Compensation and Workers' Compensation, 2000), Table 18, pp. 50-51.

7 G. Rejda, *Social Insurance and Economic Security*, p. 309.

Disqualification for one of the above reasons can result in (1) post-ponement of benefits for a certain period or until certain conditions are met, (2) cancellation of benefit rights, or (3) a reduction in benefits that otherwise are payable.

Disqualification rates are relatively high. Of the 17.3 million work-ers who were monetarily eligible for initial unemployment compensation benefits in 1996, 23.8 percent were disqualified. Reasons for disqualifi-cation included not being able to or available for work, voluntarily quit-ting without good cause, being fired for misconduct on the job, and refus-ing suitable work.[8]

In addition, unemployed workers can be disqualified for benefits if they receive certain types of *disqualifying income*. This includes severance pay, wages in lieu of notice, and workers' compensation. Also, unemploy-ment benefits must be reduced by the amount of any public or private pen-sion based on the worker's own work, which includes a primary Old-Age, Survivors, and Disability Insurance (OASDI) or Railroad Retirement ben-efit. However, only the pension benefit paid for a "base period" or "chargeable employer" is considered. A chargeable employer is an em-ployer whose account is charged for the unemployment compensation benefits received by the individual. However, the unemployment compen-sation offset must be applied to OASDI benefits without regard to whether the worker's base period employment contributed to that entitlement.

States can reduce the amount of the unemployment compensation offset by any amount consistent with the contributions made by the em-ployee toward the pension. This policy allows states to limit the unem-ployment compensation offset to one-half of the amount of OASDI retire-ment benefits received by an individual who also qualifies for unemploy-ment benefits.[9]

Finally, certain groups are disqualified from receiving benefits. As noted earlier, these groups include professional and administrative em-ployees of educational institutions during summer months and other vacation periods if they have a reasonable assurance of reemployment; professional athletes between seasons; or aliens not legally admitted to work in the United States. Many states also have disqualification provi-sions that apply to students while attending school or to individuals who quit work to attend school.

---

8 *1998 Green Book*, p. 337.
9 Ibid., p. 338.

Taxation of Benefits

As a result of the Tax Reform Act of 1986, all unemployment compensation benefits are now subject to the federal income tax. From 1979 through 1986, only part of the unemployment benefits was subject to taxation.

EXTENDED-BENEFITS PROGRAM

Many unemployed workers exhaust their regular benefits and are still unemployed. In 1970, Congress enacted a permanent state-federal extended-benefits program that pays additional benefits to workers who exhaust their regular benefits in states with high unemployment. The weekly extended benefit amount is identical to the regular state benefit. *Claimants can receive up to 13 additional weeks of extended benefits or one-half of the regular benefits that have been received, whichever is less.* However, the duration of both regular and combined benefits is limited to a maximum of 39 weeks.

Extended benefits can be paid only if the state's insured unemployment rate exceeds a certain level. The *insured unemployment rate* is the ratio of unemployment insurance claims to total employment covered by unemployment compensation programs. The insured unemployment rate is substantially below the total unemployment rate, because some unemployed workers have not met the eligibility requirements, have not satisfied the waiting period, have exhausted their benefits, or are not covered for unemployment compensation benefits.

Extended benefits can be paid in a state only under certain conditions: (1) the state's 13-week average insured unemployment rate (IUR) in the most recent 13-week period is at least 120 percent of the average of its 13-week IURs in the last two years for the same period, and its current 13-week average IUR is at least 5 percent; or (2) at the state's option, the current 13-week average IUR is at least 6 percent. Most states have adopted this second option.

In addition, as a result of the Unemployment Compensation Amendments of 1992, states have the option of electing an alternative trigger that will pay extended benefits for up to 20 weeks under certain conditions. During the 1990–91 recession, large numbers of recipients exhausted both regular and extended benefits. The alternative trigger provides an additional seven weeks of extended benefits in those states with unusually high unemployment rates.

The alternative trigger is based on a three-month average of the total unemployment rate (TUR) using seasonally adjusted data, rather than the insured unemployment rate. If the average TUR exceeds 6.5 percent and is at least 110 percent of the same measure in either of the prior two years, an additional 13 weeks of extended benefits can be paid. However, if the average TUR exceeds 8 percent and meets the same 110-percent test, *a total of 20 weeks of extended benefits can be paid.* At the time of this writing, however, only eight states have adopted the optional TUR trigger.

FINANCING UNEMPLOYMENT COMPENSATION

State unemployment compensation programs are financed by employer payroll taxes on the covered wages of employees. A few states also require employees to contribute to the program. All unemployment tax contributions are deposited in the Federal Unemployment Trust Fund. Each state has a separate account, and the state's unemployment benefits are paid out of that account.

In 2000, each covered employer paid a federal unemployment tax of 6.2 percent on the first $7,000 of wages paid to each covered employee. However, if the state program meets certain federal requirements, employers are eligible for a maximum tax credit of 5.4 percent, which reduces the federal tax rate to 0.8 percent. The 0.8 percent that is paid to the federal government is used for administrative expenses, for loans to states that have depleted their unemployment reserve accounts, and for the federal government's share of the cost of the extended benefits program.

Because of a desire to strengthen their unemployment reserve accounts, the majority of states have a taxable wage base in excess of $7,000. In these states, the taxable wage base in 2000 ranged from $8,000 to $27,500.[10]

All states use experience-rating to determine individual employer tax rates. There is considerable variation among the states with respect to experience rates. In January 2000, only 22 jurisdictions used the standard 5.4 percent rate as the maximum tax rate subject to experience-rating. In the remaining jurisdictions, maximum tax rates were much higher, ranging from 5.7 percent to 10 percent. Minimum tax rates for some employers with low unemployment were as low as 0 percent in 19 jurisdictions.[11]

Various experience-rating formulas are used to determine employer tax rates. The most common is the reserve ratio method. Under the reserve ratio method, each employer has a separate account. The total benefits paid since the program became effective are subtracted from the total

---

10 *Highlights of State Unemployment Compensation Laws January 2000*, p. 33.
11 Ibid., Table 11, pp. 30-31.

employer contributions over that period. The balance is then divided by the employer's taxable payroll (usually an average of the last three years). The higher the reserve ratio, the lower the contribution rate. The reserve ratio formula can be summarized as follows:[12]

$$\frac{\text{Total employer contributions} - \text{Total benefits paid}}{\text{Taxable payroll (usually an average of last three years)}} = \text{Reserve ratio}$$

Experience-rating is a controversial subject. The major arguments for experience-rating are (1) experience-rating encourages firms to stabilize their employment, (2) the costs of unemployment are allocated to the firms responsible for the unemployment, and (3) employers have a greater interest in unemployment compensation programs.

The major arguments against experience-rating are (1) some cyclical and seasonal firms have little control over unemployment and should not be penalized by higher tax rates; (2) employers may oppose an increase in unemployment benefits because of higher tax rates; and (3) experience-rating may result in inadequate income to finance the system.[13]

ADMINISTRATION OF UNEMPLOYMENT COMPENSATION PROGRAMS

Each state administers its own unemployment compensation program. The majority of states administer their programs through employment security offices in the Department of Labor or some other state agency. Other states have independent boards or commissions to administer their programs.

State agencies operate through local unemployment insurance and employment offices. The local offices process unemployment compensation claims and provide a variety of job placement and job development services. Federal law provides that personnel who administer the programs must be appointed on a merit basis, except for personnel in policy-making positions.

The federal functions of unemployment compensation programs are the responsibility of the Employment and Training Administration, Unemployment Insurance Service, in the U.S. Department of Labor. The Internal Revenue Service collects the FUTA taxes, and the Treasury Department maintains the unemployment insurance trust fund.

---

12 G. Rejda, *Social Insurance and Economic Security*, pp. 316-317.
13 Ibid., pp. 314-316.

In general, claims must be filed within seven days after the week for which the claim is made unless there is a good cause for a late filing. The unemployed worker files a weekly claim form at the same office. In most cases, claims may be filed by mail and in some cases by telephone. The benefits are paid weekly or biweekly after the waiting period is met.

In addition, all states have interstate agreements for the payment of benefits to workers who move to another state. All states also have special wage-combining agreements that apply to workers who earn wages in two or more states.

Finally, federal law requires that workers who are denied benefits must be given the opportunity of a fair hearing. The claimant can appeal first to a referee or tribunal and then to a board of review or a board of appeals. The board of review decision may be appealed to the state courts.

UNEMPLOYMENT COMPENSATION PROBLEMS AND ISSUES

Regular state unemployment compensation programs have numerous problems and issues that limit their effectiveness in reducing economic insecurity from involuntary unemployment. The following section discusses several important issues.[14]

Declining Proportion of Unemployed Who Receive Benefits

One important issue is the declining proportion of unemployed workers who receive benefits. On average, only 36 percent of the unemployed received benefits in an average month in 1996, a period of relatively low unemployment. This figure compares with a peak of 81 percent of the unemployed who received benefits in April 1975 and a low point of 26 percent in June 1968 and October 1987.[15]

Researchers have attempted to determine the reasons why the proportion of unemployed workers receiving benefits has declined over time. An earlier study by Mathematica Policy Research showed that the decline in the proportion of workers who received benefits during the 1980s included the following: (1) a decrease in the ratio of unemployed workers in the manufacturing sector where historically unemployment compensation claims have been high; (2) geographic shifts in the composition of the

---

14 This section is based on G. Rejda, *Social Insurance and Economic Security*, pp. 322-335.
15 *1998 Green Book*, pp. 331-332.

unemployed in different geographical regions in the country; (3) more stringent state eligibility requirements; (4) changes in federal policy, such as the taxation of unemployment compensation benefits; and (5) changes in unemployment as measured by the Current Population Survey.[16]

The fact that only a relatively small proportion of unemployed workers receive unemployment compensation benefits during an average month violates a well-established and fundamental social insurance principle—*that of providing broad coverage of workers against well-defined social risks, including the risk of unemployment.* Because only a small proportion of the unemployed receive benefits during a typical month, the effectiveness of unemployment compensation programs in reducing economic insecurity from unemployment can be seriously questioned.[17]

Inadequate Reserves

Another serious problem is that many states have inadequate trust-fund reserves. As a result, such states would be unable to pay unemployment benefits during a severe recession without borrowing from the federal government.

One common measure of the adequacy of a state unemployment reserve account is a complex measure known as the "high-cost multiple."[18] A value of 1 means that the state's current balance in its reserve account could support 12 months of payments at the highest unemployment rate historically experienced in the past. The U.S. Department of Labor has recommended a high-cost multiple of 1.5, which would enable a state to pay benefits for at least 18 months without a tax increase or borrowing from the federal government. However, in 1996, 38 jurisdictions had high-cost multiples below 1. Only five jurisdictions had a high-cost multiple of 1.5 or higher.[19]

Several worthwhile recommendations have been made to improve the financing of unemployment compensation benefits. Such recommendations include (1) an increase in the taxable wage base, (2) higher max-

---

16 Ibid., p. 331.

17 G. Rejda, *Social Insurance and Economic Security*, p. 326.

18 The high-cost multiple is determined by the following formula:

$$\text{High-cost multiple} = \frac{\text{Ratio of current net trust-fund reserves to total wages in insured employment in the current year}}{\text{Ratio of highest state benefits during 12 consecutive months to total wages in insured employment during those 12 months}}$$

19 *1998 Green Book*, pp. 347–349.

imum tax rates subject to experience-rating, (3) greater refinement of experience-rating formulas to charge more of the cost of unemployment to those firms responsible for the unemployment, and (4) requiring employees to contribute to the program.

Inadequate Benefits

Another serious problem is that unemployment compensation benefits generally are inadequate for many unemployed workers, with the possible exception of low-wage earners. One common measure of benefit adequacy is that the weekly benefit should restore at least 50 percent of the unemployed worker's average weekly wage. This standard when applied nationally is not being met at the present time. The ratio of average weekly benefits to average weekly wages nationally has remained roughly constant over the years at about 35 percent to 36 percent. The average replacement rate was only 35 percent for the quarter ending December 31, 1996.[20] Thus, many claimants are not receiving benefits equal to half of their average weekly wages at the present time. The result is that many unemployed workers are exposed to serious economic insecurity during extended periods of unemployment and must deplete their savings or go into debt despite receiving unemployment benefits.

Misclassification of Employees

Some workers are misclassified as independent contractors rather than as employees, which can be either unintentional or deliberately done. State and federal laws are complex. Some employers make honest mistakes and classify workers as independent contractors. However, some employers hire workers and intentionally classify them as independent contractors. By classifying the workers as such, employers avoid paying payroll taxes, including Social Security and unemployment compensation taxes, and employee benefits as well. Thus, employers can reduce labor costs and gain a competitive advantage over other employers that obey the law.

Misclassification of employees results in a loss of tax revenues to the state's regular unemployment compensation program. Also, misclassified employees may be initially denied benefits because unemployment taxes have not been paid on their behalf. After an investigation, benefits

---

20 *1998 Green Book*, p. 339.

can be paid if the state determines that the workers are employees rather than independent contractors. The state then attempts to collect the unpaid taxes from the employer.

Paying Unemployment Benefits During Family Leave

Another timely issue is a proposal to pay unemployment benefits to employees during a family leave of absence. Under the federal Family and Medical Leave Act, parents can take an unpaid leave of absence for up to 12 weeks to care for newly born or adopted children or sick relatives. Regulations introduced by the federal government in 2000 would allow the states to pay unemployment benefits to parents of newly born or adopted children while on leave from their jobs.

The issue is controversial. At the time of this writing, at least 15 states are considering partial use of their unemployment funds for paid family leaves. Proponents argue that many workers are financially unable to take a leave of absence after the birth or adoption of a child without regular income. However, business groups representing employers generally are opposed to paid family leaves by using unemployment compensation taxes to pay benefits. Critics argue that many state unemployment programs are inadequately financed and could run out of money if the economy slows and a recession ensues. As a result, payroll taxes would have to be increased, and labor costs to employers would be substantially increased.

SUMMARY

All states have regular state unemployment compensation programs that pay weekly cash benefits to eligible workers who become involuntarily unemployed. The programs have several basic objectives: (1) pay weekly cash benefits to unemployed workers during periods of involuntary unemployment, thereby enabling them to maintain their consumption and economic security; (2) help stabilize the economy during periods of business recessions; (3) encourage employers to stabilize their employment; and (4) help unemployed workers find jobs.

Unemployed workers must meet certain eligibility requirements to qualify for unemployment benefits. Workers must earn certain qualifying wages during their base period, be able and available for work, actively seek work, satisfy a short waiting period, and be free of any disqualifying act.

Weekly cash benefits are paid after the worker meets a short waiting period. The weekly benefit amount depends on the worker's wages earned during his or her base period, subject to certain minimum and maximum amounts. Most states pay benefits up to a maximum of 26 weeks. However, not all claimants qualify for 26 weeks of benefits. The majority of states have a variable duration of benefits that depends on the amount of the claimant's wages during the base year.

Under the state-federal extended-benefits program, up to 13 additional weeks of benefits can be paid to claimants who have exhausted their benefits in states with relatively high unemployment rates. Complex provisions trigger the payment of additional benefits in states with high unemployment.

Regular state unemployment compensation programs are financed by employer payroll taxes paid on the covered wages of employees. A small number of states also require employees to contribute. Covered employers typically are experience-rated and pay unemployment taxes based on the amount of unemployment in the firm.

Unemployment compensation programs face a number of problems and issues. These issues include a declining proportion of unemployed workers who receive benefits; inadequate unemployment reserves in many states; inadequate benefits in many states, especially for middle- and upper-income workers; misclassification of employees as independent contractors; and proposals to pay unemployment benefits to workers who take a leave of absence to care for newly born or adopted children or sick relatives.

SELECTED REFERENCES

1. Committee on Ways and Means, U.S. House of Representatives. *1998 Green Book, Background Material and Data on Programs Within the Jurisdiction of the Committee on Ways and Means.* Washington, D.C.: U.S. Government Printing Office, 1998, pp. 327-359.

2. National Foundation of Unemployment Compensation & Workers' Compensation. *Highlights of State Unemployment Compensation Law, January 2000.* Washington, DC: National Foundation for Unemployment Compensation and Workers' Compensation, 2000.

3. National Foundation of Unemployment Compensation & Workers' Compensation. *Highlights of State Unemployment Compensation Law, January 1999.* Washington, DC: National Foundation for Unemployment Compensation and Workers' Compensation, 1999.

4. Rejda, George E. *Social Insurance and Economic Security.* 6th ed. Upper Saddle River, NJ: Prentice Hall, 1999, Chapters 14 and 15.

PART SIX

Retirement Planning

This part begins in Chapter 25 with an overview of the important issues involved in the design of retirement plans in general—both defined benefit and defined contribution plans.

Chapter 26 deals with profit-sharing plans, and this is followed by a discussion of 401(k) plans and thrift plans in Chapter 27.

Chapter 28 reviews cash balance and other evolving hybrid pension plans, and Chapter 29 provides an in-depth look at the various types of employee stock ownership plans (ESOPs). Chapter 30 covers stock option plans.

Chapter 31 deals with retirement plans for the self-employed, concentrating on individual retirement accounts (IRAs), simplified employee pension plans (SEPs), and Keogh (HR-10) plans.

Executive compensation plans that provide nonqualified (supplemental retirement) benefits are examined in Chapter 32.

Chapters 33 and 34 cover retirement arrangements for employees in certain nonprofit organizations and government sectors of the economy, Section 403(b) and Section 457 plans.

This section on retirement planning concludes with Chapter 35, which examines the investment choices made by defined contribution plan participants under various plan option scenarios.

Retirement Plan Design*

Everett T. Allen, Jr. *

Although pension plans vary in terms of specific provisions, they generally fall into one of two categories—they are either *defined benefit* or *defined contribution* in nature. Large employers and unions historically have favored the defined benefit approach. Since the mid-1970s, however, a significant percentage of all new plans established have utilized the defined contribution approach.

A defined benefit plan provides a fixed amount of pension benefit. The amount of each employee's benefit usually depends on length of service and pay level; for example, a pension of 1 percent of pay for each year of service. In collectively bargained plans, however, pay often is not taken into account; the monthly pension might be a fixed dollar amount (such as $15) for each year of service. In any event, a defined benefit plan promises a fixed level of benefit, and the employer contributes whatever is necessary to provide this amount.

By contrast, the defined contribution approach focuses on contribution levels. The employer's contribution may be fixed as a percent of pay or as a flat dollar amount, or it may be based on a variable, such as a percentage of profits. In some cases, the employer contribution is totally variable and is established each year on a discretionary basis. However it is determined, the contribution (along with any amount contributed by the

---

* This chapter originally appeared in *Employee Benefits Today*; Concepts and Methods
     (Brookfield, WI: International Foundation of Employee Benefit Plans, 1987).
** Revised by Dennis F. Mahoney.

employee) is accumulated and invested on the employee's behalf. The amount of pension an employee receives, thus, will vary depending on such factors as length of plan participation, the level and frequency of contributions, and investment gains and losses.

There are several different types of defined contribution plans. The two most commonly used for pension purposes are the *deferred profit-sharing plan* and the *money purchase pension plan*. In a profit-sharing plan, the employer contribution is related to profits or made on a discretionary basis. The money purchase pension plan requires a fixed employer contribution, regardless of profits. Other defined contribution plans (such as Section 401(k) or savings plans) can be used as primary pension vehicles but often are adopted to supplement basic defined benefit pension plans. Because the focus in this chapter is on pension arrangements, only deferred profit-sharing and money purchase plans are discussed; other defined contribution programs are covered in subsequent chapters.

It also should be noted there is growing interest in hybrid arrangements—plans that involve features of both defined benefit and defined contribution plans. Target benefit, cash balance, and floor offset plans are examples of these hybrid approaches and are discussed later in this chapter as well as in detail in Chapter 28 of the *Handbook*.

Regardless of the approach chosen, a pension plan should be designed so it supports overall employer objectives. This chapter begins with a discussion of these objectives and how they are influenced by the employer's environment and attitudes. Specific design features are then described, with differences between the defined benefit and defined contribution approaches noted, as appropriate. Finally, these two approaches are evaluated from the viewpoint of both employers and employees.

EMPLOYER OBJECTIVES

Business organizations do not exist in a vacuum. They possess individual characteristics and operate in environments that influence what they can and want to accomplish in providing employee benefits. Factors that can affect employee benefit planning and, in particular, the choice between defined benefit and defined contribution programs, include the following:

■ *Employer characteristics.* Is the organization incorporated or unincorporated, or is it tax-exempt? Is it mature, or young and growing? Are profits stable or volatile? What growth patterns are anticipated? What are the firm's short- and long-term capital needs? What are its personnel needs, now and in the future?

■ *Industry characteristics.* Is the employer part of a clearly defined industry group? Is this industry highly competitive? Does it have a distinct employee benefit pattern? Is it important, from the standpoint of attracting and retaining employees or for cost considerations, to provide benefits or maintain cost levels that are consistent with those of other companies in the same industry?

■ *Employee characteristics.* What is the composition of the employee group? How are employees distributed in terms of age, gender, service, and pay? Is this distribution likely to change in the future? How many employees are in the highly compensated group?

■ *Diversity of operations.* Does the employer operate its business on a diversified basis? If so, should the same or different benefits be provided for employees at each location or in each line of business? How will such factors as profit margins, competitive needs, costs, employee transfer policies, and administrative capabilities affect this decision?

■ *Collective bargaining.* Are any employees represented by a collective bargaining unit? Are benefits bargained for on a local basis or is a national pattern followed? Is a multiemployer plan available for some employees and is it an acceptable alternative? How will benefits gained through collective bargaining affect benefits for nonrepresented employees?

■ *Community.* Is the employer (or any of its major operating units) located in a large urban area or is it a dominant employer in a discrete geographic location? What is the role of the employer in the community? What social and civic responsibilities does the employer want to assume? How important is its image in the community? What other employers compete for labor in the local marketplace?

Answers to these questions (and the list is only illustrative) need to be taken into account in setting specific employee benefit plan objectives. The employer's basic compensation philosophy is also important in the objective-setting process, as is its attitude on:

■ The role of employee benefits in protecting income in the event of economic insecurity.

■ The extent to which employee benefits are considered a form of indirect or deferred compensation.

■ Whether employee cost sharing is necessary or desirable.

■ Whether employees can or should bear the risks of inflation and investment performance.

■ The use of employee benefits in meeting personnel planning needs.

- The amount of choice to be given employees in structuring their own benefits.
- The importance of cost levels, cost controls, and funding flexibility.
- The desirability of integrating plan and statutory benefits.
- The treatment of highly compensated employees.

Each employer will have specific and sometimes unique objectives in establishing or modifying an employee benefit plan. And, as noted, these objectives will be influenced by the employer's environment and its attitudes on such matters as those listed above.

Most employers want to attract and retain desirable employees. An adequate benefit program will certainly be of value in achieving this objective. It also seems reasonably clear that the absence of an adequate benefit program will have a negative effect on recruiting and retention efforts. What is not clear, however, is whether a generous benefit program will have an increasingly positive effect in this regard. In the opinion of many employers, money otherwise spent on extra benefits would be more useful in meeting recruitment and retention objectives if it were directed to other elements of compensation.

A competitive benefit program is another common employer objective. This objective must be clarified before it can be implemented. For example, will competitiveness be measured by industry or local standards, or by both? Industry standards might be more relevant for highly skilled employees and executives. For employees whose skills are readily transferable to other industries, however, local practice could be much more important. Once the competitive standard is established, the employer must decide where it wants to rank—as average, above or below average, or among the leaders. It is also important to establish the means by which competitiveness will be measured. The most common technique compares benefits payable at certain times (e.g., at normal retirement) for employees with different pay and service combinations. This approach must be used with caution, because it tends to focus on single events and does not consider the value of other plan provisions. More sophisticated techniques, which measure the relative value of plans by provision, in total, and with reference to both employer- and employee-provided benefits, can be used for this purpose.

Cost objectives can have a major impact on plan design. Employers should set specific objectives for liabilities that will be assumed as well as for annual cost accruals. They also must consider the need for contribution flexibility and the control of future costs that are sensitive to inflation and investment risk.

Employer objectives for income-replacement levels are critical to the design of pension plans. Most employers seek to provide a pension benefit that, together with primary Social Security benefits, replaces a percentage of the employee's preretirement gross income. In establishing income-replacement levels, these factors should be taken into account:

- Employers rarely contemplate full replacement of gross income, primarily because of tax considerations. Most employers also feel that employees should meet some of their own retirement needs through personal savings (many maintain supplemental plans to help employees in this regard). Further, they expect that most employees will have lower living expenses after they retire.

- Income-replacement objectives are often set with reference to the employee's pay level during the final year of employment or average pay during the three- or five-year period just prior to retirement.

- The percentage of income replaced is generally higher for lower-paid employees than for higher-paid employees.

- Income-replacement objectives are usually set so that they can be achieved in full only by employees who have completed what the employer considers to be a "career" of employment (usually 25 or 30 years); objectives are proportionately reduced for individuals who have shorter service.

Obviously, income-replacement objectives that are set with reference to an employee's final pay and length of service can best be met through a defined benefit plan that bases benefits on final average pay. Achieving such objectives with a career pay defined benefit plan is more difficult, but not impossible. Accrued benefits under a career pay plan can be updated periodically to keep benefits reasonably close to final pay objectives. Although it is almost impossible to establish and meet final pay income-replacement objectives with a defined contribution plan, contribution levels can be set so that, under reasonable expectations for pay growth and investment return, final pay objectives might be approximated. As a practical matter, though, actual experience is not likely to coincide with the assumptions used. Thus, actual benefits will probably be larger or smaller than anticipated, depending on experience. Table 25–1 sets forth a typical set of income-replacement objectives.

T A B L E   25–1

Illustrative Income-Replacement Objectives
(Employee with 30 Years of Service)

Final Pay	Retirement Income as a Percentage of Final Pay*
Under $25,000	80–70%
$25,000 to $50,000	75–65%
$50,000 to $100,000	70–60%
$100,000 to $200,000	65–55%
Over $200,000	60–50%

*Including primary Social Security benefits.

Many other objectives—for example, the desire to provide employee incentives or to foster employee identification with overall corporate goals through stock ownership—can affect plan design. In any event, once objectives have been established, they should be ranked in order of priority. In some situations, certain objectives can be achieved only at the expense of others. If this is the case, the relative importance of all objectives should be clearly understood.

PLAN PROVISIONS

A pension plan must contain provisions governing which employees are covered, what benefits they will receive, and how and under what conditions these benefits will be paid. Federal tax law plays an important role in this regard, because a plan, to be tax-qualified, must meet the requirements of the Internal Revenue Code (IRC) and supporting regulations and interpretations issued by the Internal Revenue Service (IRS) through various public and private rulings.[1]

Employers have no choice with respect to certain mandatory plan provisions (e.g., if an employer wants to change the plan's vesting schedule, employees with at least three years of service must be given the right to elect vesting under the prior provision). Other mandatory provisions give the employer some latitude (e.g., a plan must provide for vesting, but

---

1 A detailed discussion of the IRC requirements for qualified retirement plans is beyond the scope of this chapter. They are referred to here only in general terms and are described in the following 10 chapters of the *Handbook* in the context of the individual plans to which they apply.

the employer can choose between two permissible schedules). Some provisions are not mandatory but must meet certain requirements if they are included in a plan (e.g., a plan need not require employee contributions, but if it does, contributions made by highly compensated employees cannot exceed those made by lower-paid employees by more than a percentage established under the tax law). By and large, the requirements of federal tax law revolve around the central concept that a plan cannot discriminate as to coverage, contributions, and benefits—as well as in operation—in favor of highly compensated employees.

The discussion that follows covers the major plan features an employer must consider and the approaches most commonly used in establishing actual plan provisions. The emphasis is on the practical aspects of design, rather than on legal requirements.

Service Counting

With rare exceptions, an employee's service will be relevant to his or her benefits under the plan. Specifically, service can be used to determine eligibility for (1) participation in the plan, (2) vested benefits, (3) benefit accruals, (4) early retirement, and (5) ancillary benefits (e.g., spouse or disability benefits). In most plans, service also will be a factor in determining the amount of an employee's benefit.

The law imposes explicit requirements on how service is to be determined for the first three purposes listed above. Generally, service must be measured over a 12-month period (a computation period) that may be a plan, calendar, or employment year. Any such period in which an employee is credited with 1,000 hours of service will be considered a full year of service. The employee's hours of service can be established by counting actual hours worked or by using one of several "equivalency" methods permitted by regulations. Alternatively, an "elapsed time" method can be used to measure service. The law also requires the inclusion of provisions dealing with breaks-in-service and the conditions under which service before and after such breaks must be aggregated.

For purposes of early retirement and ancillary benefits, service can be determined on any reasonable basis the employer establishes, provided the method does not discriminate in favor of highly compensated employees. As a practical matter, however, most employers adopt a uniform method of calculating service for all plan purposes.

Administrative considerations are important in choosing a service-counting method. Actual hours-counting, for example, may prove impractical for a plan covering exempt employees who do not maintain detailed records of hours worked. One of the most popular of the available equivalency methods is "monthly" equivalency, which credits an employee with 190 hours for any month in which at least one hour of service is credited. The elapsed time method, which—with the exception of break-in-service aspects—measures service from date of employment to date of termination, is also popular. However, these methods give part-time employees the equivalent of full-time service. In situations where this could be a problem, different methods of counting service can be used; for example, service for part-time employees could be determined by actual hours-counting, and the elapsed time method could be used for full-time employees. The use of different methods is permissible only if it does not result in discrimination.

Eligibility for Participation

A plan may require that an employee complete a minimum period of service and attain a minimum age to be eligible to participate. In general, the maximum permissible service requirement is one year, although up to two years may be used in plans (without cash or deferred arrangements [CODAs]) that provide for full and immediate vesting. The highest minimum age that can be used is 21.

These minimum age and service requirements can be useful in plans that necessitate maintenance of individual records for participants—defined contribution plans, contributory plans, or plans funded with individual life insurance or annuity contracts. Some administrative cost and effort is avoided by excluding young or short-service employees from such plans until they are beyond what is considered the high-turnover stage of their employment. By contrast, there is very little (if any) administrative work associated with early terminations under a noncontributory defined benefit plan funded with an arrangement that does not require individual employee allocations—for example, a trusteed plan—and plans of this type often provide for eligibility immediately upon employment. However, if the plan bases benefits on years of participation (rather than years of service), the use of minimum age and service requirements will reduce the period of participation and, as a result, will reduce benefit costs to some extent. Also, Pension Benefit Guaranty Corporation (PBGC) premiums can be avoided (in plans insured by the PBGC) for those employees who have not met the plan's eligibility requirements. Thus, these requirements are sometimes used in noncontributory defined benefit plans.

In the past, maximum-age provisions—typically excluding employees hired after age 60—were common in defined benefit plans. However, the law now prohibits the use of a maximum-age provision in any type of qualified plan. Instead, plans may provide that the normal retirement age for individuals hired after age 60 will coincide with the completion of five years of participation.

Another type of eligibility requirement relates to employment classifications. A plan may be limited to hourly or to salaried employees, to represented or nonrepresented employees, or to individuals employed at certain locations or in specific lines of business. An employee will have to fall within the designated classification to be eligible to participate. Employers must take care that such plans meet the coverage requirements of the IRC.

Plans are not permitted to limit eligibility to employees who earn more than a stipulated amount.

Employee Contributions

Some employers prefer that employees contribute toward the cost of their pension benefits. This preference may be philosophical or it may be founded on more pragmatic considerations of cost and benefit levels. Arguments in favor of noncontributory plans seem to have been more persuasive, however. Employee contributions involve additional administrative effort and cost. Further, if a plan is contributory, an employer may face problems with nonparticipating employees who reach retirement age and cannot afford to retire. Another practical consideration is that almost all collectively bargained plans are noncontributory. An employer that has such a plan will find it difficult to require contributions under plans for nonrepresented employees.

The most compelling factor favoring noncontributory plans is federal tax law. Employer contributions to a pension plan are tax deductible; employee contributions are not.[2] Thus, on an after-tax basis, it is more cost-efficient to fund benefits with employer contributions.

Most defined benefit plans do not, in fact, require employee contributions, nor do deferred profit-sharing plans. Both types of plans may permit voluntary employee contributions—that is, contributions that are not required as a condition of participation. Although many pension plans

---

2 Employee contributions can, of course, be made on a before-tax basis under a deferred profit-sharing plan or employee stock ownership plan that has a cash or deferred option meeting the requirements of Section 401(k).

have such an option, very few employees have taken advantage of the opportunity to make these additional contributions.

Employee contributions are more often required as a condition of participation in money purchase pension plans. In theory, the arguments for and against employee contributions are the same for these plans as they are for other arrangements. However, employers often choose the money purchase approach because of cost constraints; where this is the case, employee contributions may be necessary to bring total contributions to a level that will produce adequate benefits. Further, these plans are often viewed—and communicated to employees—as being similar to savings plans where employee contributions are matched by employer contributions.[3]

If employee contributions are required, they are usually set as a percentage of compensation—typically, from 2 percent to 6 percent. If the plan benefit formula is integrated with Social Security by providing a higher accrual rate for pay over a stipulated level, the same pattern is followed with the contribution rate. If the benefit formula is 1 percent of pay up to $10,000 and 1.5 percent on pay over this amount, for example, the contribution rate might be 2 percent of pay up to $10,000 and 3 percent over this amount.

Retirement Ages

Normal Retirement Age

Almost all pension plans specify 65 as normal retirement age. Those plans that have permitted employees to enter after age 60 have usually set the normal retirement age as 65 or, if later, after the completion of five years of participation. Because the law now prohibits the use of a maximum age for participation, this latter definition of normal retirement age is used in many plans.

It is possible—but relatively uncommon—to specify an age under 65 as the plan's normal retirement age. For one thing, providing full benefits before age 65 can be expensive. For another, provisions of this type can result in a violation of age discrimination laws unless they are carefully designed and operated.

At one time, the concept of a normal retirement age was very significant for defined benefit plans. It was the age at which employees

---

3 Matching employer contributions under a defined contribution plan as well as after-tax employee
   contributions have to satisfy an "actual contribution percentage" (ACP) test. This test is
   similar to the "actual deferral percentage" (ADP) test used for elective contributions under a
   Section 401(k) plan.

could retire with full, unreduced benefits and without employer consent. Moreover, it was the age at which most employees were expected to retire and the age at which full, unreduced Social Security benefits became available. In most plans, it also marked the point at which pension accruals stopped; continued employment beyond normal retirement usually did not result in increased benefits.

This concept has become diffuse in recent years. Many employers now provide for the payment of full accrued benefits, without reduction, on early retirement after the completion of certain age and service requirements. And, in fact, many employees do retire before age 65. Because of changes in age discrimination laws, benefits must accrue for service beyond normal retirement; also, for individuals born after 1937, the Social Security normal retirement age has been raised. For all practical purposes, a plan's normal retirement age remains significant primarily for determining the value of accrued benefits at any point in time and for determining the amount of any reduction for benefits payable in the event of early retirement. The normal retirement age concept has even less significance in defined contribution plans: Once an employee is vested, the value of plan benefits is the same regardless of the reason for the employee's termination (although a retiring employee might have more options as to how the benefit is to be paid).

The distinction between retirement and termination of employment can be important for other employee benefit programs. Some employers, for example, continue employer-supported life insurance and medical expense benefits for retired employees, but not for those who terminate employment before qualifying for early retirement. Further, distributions on account of termination of employment after age 55 will not be subject to the 10 percent additional tax levied on early distributions from a qualified plan.

Early Retirement

Most pension plans permit an employee to retire and receive benefits prior to the plan's normal retirement age. It is customary to require that the employee have attained some minimum age and completed some minimum period of service to qualify for this privilege. The minimum age most frequently used is 55. Minimum service is often set at 10 years, although both shorter and longer periods are used.

The benefit amount payable at early retirement is less than that payable at normal retirement, because, in most plans, the employee will not have accrued his or her full benefit. This will not be the case if a defined benefit plan limits service that can be counted in calculating benefits and the employee has already completed the full service period. Even in this situation, however, the benefit could be smaller if it is based on final average pay and the employee loses the advantage of the higher pay base he or she would have achieved if employed until normal retirement age.

Early retirement benefits can be reduced for another reason as well. When benefit payments start before the employee's normal retirement age, they will be paid over a longer time; a reduction factor may be applied to recognize these additional payments. This could be a true actuarial factor or, as is more often the case, a simple factor such as one-half of 1 percent for each month by which early retirement precedes normal retirement. This type of reduction takes place automatically in a defined contribution plan, because the annuity value (in the marketplace) of the employee's account balance will reflect the employee's age and life expectancy.

Many defined benefit plans do not fully reduce the retirement benefit to reflect the early commencement of benefit payments. For example, some plans use a factor of one-quarter of 1 percent instead of the one-half of 1 percent factor mentioned above. Another common approach is to apply no reduction factor at all if the employee has attained some minimum age (e.g., 60 or 62) and has completed some minimum period of service (e.g., 25 or 30 years) or if the sum of the employee's age and service equals or exceeds a specified number, such as 85 or 90.

It is important to understand that there will be additional plan costs when less than a full actuarial reduction (or its equivalent) is used. It is also important to recognize that this type of provision will encourage early retirement and must be considered in the context of the employer's personnel planning needs and objectives.

Deferred Retirement

Prior to the advent of age discrimination laws, it was uncommon for plans to permit deferred retirement solely at the employee's option. If deferred retirement was permitted, it was customary to provide that the benefit payable at actual retirement would be the same as that available at normal retirement—that is, there would be no increase in benefits due to continued employment.

Age discrimination laws, particularly the amendments enacted in 1986, have changed all this. An employee can no longer be discharged for reasons of age; this protection also has been extended to all employees at advanced ages.[4] Further, benefits must continue to accrue under the plan

4 A limited exception allows the use of a mandatory retirement age of 65 for "bona fide" executives whose annual employer-provided retirement benefit (from all sources) is at least $44,000.

formula for pay and service after the plan's normal retirement age. Thus, as a practical matter, deferred retirement will be permitted under all plans, and it will be common for benefits to accrue until the time of actual retirement. However, many plans have a provision that limits the total period of service that can be taken into account for calculating plan benefits; service after this maximum has been reached, whether before or after normal retirement age, will not be taken into account, but pay will be considered up until actual retirement.

Retirement Benefits

Because the defined contribution and defined benefit approaches are totally different in terms of plan provisions for determining retirement benefits, they will be discussed separately in this section. A description of the basic concepts of each of these approaches is followed by brief discussions on hybrid plans, Social Security integration, federal tax law limits on contributions and benefits, and the restrictions applicable to "top-heavy" plans.

Defined Contribution Plans

An employee's retirement benefit under a defined contribution plan—at normal, early, or deferred retirement—is his or her account balance at the time of retirement. This account balance depends on the amounts credited to the employee's account by way of (1) direct contributions, (2) reallocated forfeitures, and (3) investment gains or losses. The annuity value of this account balance—that is, the amount of pension it will generate—depends on then-current interest rates and the employee's age at the time the balance is applied to provide a benefit. If the employee purchases an annuity from an insurance company, the annuity value also may reflect the employee's gender. (Even though laws prevent an employer from discriminating on the basis of gender, insurers are not yet required to use unisex factors in pricing their annuity products.)

The contributions made on an employee's behalf under a money purchase pension plan can be made by the employer or by the employee from after-tax income. These contribution rates are fixed and are stipulated in the plan. Although they can be stated in dollar amounts, they are usually expressed as a percentage of pay. For example, the employer contribution to a noncontributory plan might be set as 6 percent of pay. A contributory plan might require an employee contribution of perhaps 3 percent of pay with a matching employer contribution.[5] Contribution rates are usually established on the basis of projections, using reasonable assumptions for growth in pay and investment results, as to the level of replacement income the contributions will generate for employees retiring after completing a career of employment with the employer. Actual experience is likely to differ from the assumptions employed, with the result that actual benefits will be more or less than those projected.

Contributions under a profit-sharing plan typically are made by the employer only—that is, employee contributions are not mandatory. These contributions are allocated to employees in proportion to pay. Allocations also can be weighted for service; most plans, however, allocate on the basis of pay only. If the plan has a cash or deferred arrangement, an employee electing to defer is, in a sense, making a contribution; however, the deferred amount is considered to be an employer contribution for most purposes under the tax law. In any event, the employer contribution may be determined by formula or, as is often the case, on a discretionary basis from year to year. The contribution amount may be established with a view toward ultimate benefit levels. However, unlike the money purchase pension plan, the profit-sharing plan does not require an employer commitment as to contribution levels and thus provides flexibility as to cost levels and funding.[6]

Both money purchase pension plans and profit-sharing plans may permit employees to augment their account balances by making voluntary or supplemental contributions. These can be made on an after-tax basis or, in the case of a profit-sharing plan (and within permissible limits), through a reduction in pay.

Forfeitures, the second source of credits for an employee's account, arise when employees terminate employment without being fully vested in their account balances. These nonvested amounts can be used to reduce employer contributions or they can be reallocated to employees in the same manner that employer contributions are allocated. Profit-sharing plans often reallocate forfeited amounts. In the past, money purchase plans were required to use forfeitures to reduce employer contributions. This practice may change in the future since these plans can now reallocate forfeitures also.

---

5 As noted earlier, matching employer and after-tax employee contributions under a money purchase plan must satisfy an actual contribution percentage test.
6 Although this contribution flexibility exists, the tax law does require that there be "substantial and recurring" contributions. To date, this requirement has not been clearly defined by the IRS.

A third and very important source of credits to an employee's account consists of investment results. Contributions and forfeitures allocated to an employee are invested and the employee's account balance is credited with any investment gains or losses. A few plans invest only in a single fund and all employees share in the aggregate gains and losses. It is more common, however, for employers to offer two or more investment funds and allow employees to choose how their account balances are invested. Available choices might include a fixed-income fund (or a guaranteed interest contract with an insurance company) and several types of equity or balanced funds. In the case of a profit-sharing plan, the employee also might be given the choice of investing in an employer stock fund. (In some profit-sharing plans—and many savings plans—a minimum amount must be invested in employer stock.)

Defined Benefit Plans

A defined benefit plan is structured to provide a fixed amount of pension benefit at the employee's normal retirement age. The benefit can be a flat dollar amount or flat percentage of pay. It is more common, however, for employees to accrue a unit of benefit for each year of service or participation in the plan. This unit can be a percentage of pay (e.g., 1 percent) or, in the case of some negotiated or hourly employee plans, a dollar amount (e.g., $15).

If a plan provides for a pay-related benefit, the benefit can be determined with reference to the employee's pay each year (a career pay plan) or it can be determined with reference to the employee's pay averaged over a period (such as three or five years) just prior to retirement (a final pay plan). The final pay plan has the advantage of establishing an employee's pension amount on a basis that reflects preretirement inflation, but the employer assumes the cost associated with such inflation. The career pay plan does not protect employees to the same extent, but employers who adopt such plans generally update accrued benefits from time to time to bring actual benefits in line with current compensation. An employer who does this retains some control over the cost of inflation. (A defined contribution plan is, in effect, a career pay plan, but there is no equivalent practice of updating accrued benefits; however, employees might have some degree of inflation protection if the investment return credited to their account balances is higher because of such inflation.) The value of benefits under a nonpay-related plan also can be eroded by inflation. Most of these plans are negotiated, however, and benefits are periodically updated through the collective bargaining process.

The actual formula used in a plan may provide for a full unit of benefit for each year of service or participation, or there may be a maximum period (e.g., 30 years) for which benefits are credited. Some plans provide for a full credit for a specified number of years and a partial credit for years in excess of this number. In any event, the actual design of the formula (including the choice of a career or final pay approach) should reflect the employer's objectives as to income replacement levels.

Hybrid Plans

Some employers have adopted hybrid pension arrangements—plans that incorporate some of the features of both the defined contribution and defined benefit approaches.

One such arrangement is the "target benefit" plan. In this type of plan, a defined benefit formula is used to determine each employee's targeted retirement benefit. An acceptable actuarial cost method, along with acceptable assumptions, is used (although not necessarily by an actuary) to determine a contribution for each employee assumed to be sufficient to provide the targeted benefit. At this point, the plan becomes defined contribution in operation. Individual accounts are established for employees, and all investment gains and losses are credited to their accounts; ultimate retirement benefits will be determined by actual account balances. For most tax law purposes, including Section 415 limits, a target benefit plan is treated as a defined contribution plan. Also, it is not subject to the plan termination insurance provisions of the Employment Retirement Income Security Act (ERISA).

Another hybrid arrangement is the "floor-offset" plan. Here, a defined contribution plan (typically a deferred profit-sharing plan) is used as the primary vehicle for providing retirement benefits. Recognizing that many factors (e.g., investment performance and inflation) might result in the defined contribution plan providing less than adequate benefits in some situations, the employer also maintains a defined benefit floor plan. This floor plan uses a defined benefit formula to establish a minimum benefit. If the defined contribution plan provides a benefit that equals or exceeds this minimum, no benefit is payable from the floor plan; if the defined contribution benefit is less than this minimum, the floor plan makes up the difference. Thus, the total benefit from both plans is equal to the minimum described in the floor plan.

A third hybrid arrangement that has attracted much interest is the "cash balance" plan. This type of plan is, in fact, a defined benefit plan that provides a definitely determinable benefit, requires an annual actuarial valuation, and is subject to all of the tax law requirements that apply to defined benefit plans. Thus, for example, the defined benefit Section 415 limits apply to cash balance plans. Further, these plans are subject to the plan termination insurance provisions of ERISA. In operation, however, the cash balance plan appears to have defined contribution characteristics. Typically, an employee's retirement benefit is based on career average pay, and each year's benefit accrual is indexed to increase at some stipulated rate. This same rate is used to discount the present value of the employee's accrued benefit. The overall actuarial structure of the plan is such that the employee's accrued benefit may be expressed as an "account balance," and the annual "addition" to this account may be expressed as a percent of the employee's current pay. The effect of this is that the plan may be communicated to employees as though it were a defined contribution plan. It should be noted, however, that actual employer contributions and actual investment return on plan assets may not be the same as the annual additions and rate of increase credited to employee accounts. Hybrid plans are discussed in more detail in Chapter 28.

Integrated Formulas

Most pay-related plans are integrated in some fashion with Social Security benefits. The concept of integration recognizes that Social Security benefits are of relatively greater value to lower-paid employees than they are to the highly compensated—particularly on an after-tax basis. Thus, integrated formulas are weighted to compensate for this difference. This approach is sanctioned by federal tax law, but stringent rules must be followed to prevent the plan from discriminating in favor of highly compensated employees.

There are, in general, two ways for integrating plan and Social Security benefits. The first approach—the "excess" method—provides a contribution or benefit for pay over a stipulated level (the integration level) that is higher than that provided for pay below this level. The second approach—the "offset" method—is used only in defined benefit plans and provides that the employee's gross plan benefit is reduced by some amount representing the employer-provided portion of the employee's Social Security benefit.

For defined contribution plans, the contribution rate for pay above the plan's integration level is limited to two times the rate for pay below the integration level. (The integration level for a defined contribution plan may be any amount up to the Social Security taxable wage base at the beginning of the plan year.) Also, the spread between the two contribution rates cannot exceed the greater of (1) 5.7 percent, or (2) the Social Security tax for old-age benefits. This percentage gap is further reduced if the plan's integration level is set at a level which is more than 20 percent but less than 100 percent of the current Social Security taxable wage base. If set between 20 percent and 80 percent of this base, the gap becomes 4.3 percent; if set between 80 percent and 100 percent, it becomes 5.4 percent.

For defined benefit excess plans, the accrual rate for pay above the plan's integration level cannot be more than two times the accrual rate for pay below this level. In addition, the spread between these accrual rates cannot exceed a "permitted disparity"—three-quarters of 1 percent for each year of participation up to a maximum of 35 years, or a maximum spread of 26¼ percent. The integration level for these plans may be any amount up to the Social Security taxable wage base at the beginning of the plan year. The permitted disparity will be reduced, however, if the plan's integration level exceeds the Social Security covered compensation level—the average of Social Security taxable wage bases for the preceding 35 years. The permitted disparity also will be reduced for early retirement benefits.

For defined benefit offset plans, the benefit otherwise accrued cannot be reduced, by the offset, by more than 50 percent. Also, the offset cannot exceed three-quarters of 1 percent of final average pay up to the Social Security covered compensation level, multiplied by years of service up to a maximum of 35 years. The three-quarters of 1 percent factor will be reduced if the offset is based on pay in excess of the Social Security covered compensation level, and for early retirement benefits.

A plan that does not meet these integration requirements may still be able to achieve a tax-qualified status by demonstrating that contributions or benefits, or both, do not discriminate in favor of highly compensated employees under the provisions of Section 401(a)(4) of the IRC.

Limitations

The IRC imposes several limitations on contributions and benefits for highly compensated employees. One, which was added by the Tax Reform Act of 1986, limits the amount of pay that can be taken into account for most qualified plan purposes. This limit was initially set at $200,000 but, beginning with 1994, was rolled back to $150,000. This dollar limit will increase with changes in the consumer price index (CPI), but only when the cumulative changes will increase the limit by at least $10,000. For 2001, the limit was $170,000.

Another change affects profit-sharing plans with a cash or deferred arrangement; the maximum amount that can be deferred each year by an employee on an optional basis is limited to a dollar amount that was initially set at $7,000. This limit, too, will increase with changes in the CPI and, by 1994, had reached $9,240. General Agreement on Tariffs and Trade (GATT) legislation in 1994 provided that, beginning with 1995, this dollar limit will be rounded to the next lower multiple of $500. For 2001, the limit is $10,500.

Under Section 415 of the IRC, a defined benefit plan cannot provide an annual benefit that exceeds the lesser of $140,000 (indexed) or 100 percent of pay for the participants high three-year average compensation. This $140,000 (indexed) limit is adjusted for various factors and, in particular, is actuarially reduced for retirements before the Social Security retirement age. The annual addition limit under a defined contribution plan for any employee cannot exceed the lesser of $35,000 (indexed) or 25 percent of pay. Both of these dollar limits are indexed to increase with changes in the CPI and, under GATT, are rounded to the next lower multiple of $5,000. For 2001, the defined benefit dollar limit was $140,000 and the annual addition limit was $35,000.

Most employers maintain nonqualified restoration plans to restore benefits lost by reason of one or more of the above limits.

Top-Heavy Plans

Special rules apply to any plan that is considered top-heavy. In general, this occurs when the value of accrued benefits for key employees is more than 60 percent of the value of all accrued benefits. If this happens:

- The benefit accrual for non-key employees under a defined benefit plan must be at least 2 percent of pay for up to 10 years.
- The contributions made for non-key employees under a defined contribution plan must be at least 3 percent of pay.
- Special and more rapid vesting requirements will apply.

Vesting

A tax-qualified pension or profit-sharing plan must provide that the value of any employee contribution is vested at all times. In addition, an employee must be vested in the accrued benefit attributable to employer contributions at normal retirement and, in any event, after a reasonable length of service. An employer may satisfy this requirement with either of two vesting schedules. The first, and simplest, is five-year "cliff" vesting—all accrued benefits fully vest after five years of service. The second schedule permits graded vesting; 20 percent of accrued benefits vest after three years of service and that percentage increases in 20 percent multiples each year until 100 percent vesting is achieved after seven years. Top-heavy plans must provide for 100 percent vesting after three years of service or provide for graded vesting with a 100 percent interest achieved in six years.

It should be noted that vesting refers to the right to receive accrued benefits in the form of a retirement benefit. The law does not require an employer-provided death benefit if an employee dies after meeting the plan's vesting requirements; however, the law does require automatic joint and survivor protection if a vested employee dies.

Defined benefit plans usually provide that, if an employee terminates employment, his or her vested benefit will be payable at retirement. Defined contribution plans usually pay the employee's vested account balance at termination, although the employee must be given the opportunity to leave the balance in the plan to be paid at a later time. Most plans, including defined benefit plans, have a provision permitting the payment of small benefit amounts (worth less than $5,000) at termination.

Death Benefits

Qualified plans must comply with the joint and survivor requirements of the IRC—whether the vested employee dies before or after retirement. These benefits, however, need not be provided at any cost to the employer.

Even though the inclusion of employer-provided death benefits is fully optional, if they are included the IRS requires that they be incidental to the primary purpose of the plan, which is to provide retirement benefits. This requirement limits the amount of preretirement lump-sum death benefits to 100 times the employee's expected monthly pension or the reserve for this amount, if greater. (An employee's full account balance, of course, can be paid under a defined contribution plan.) Post-retirement death benefits provided under an optional form of payment are generally so limited that no more than 50 percent of the value of the employee's pension can be used to continue death benefits to individuals other than the employee's spouse.

Although death benefits are optional, most defined contribution plans provide for a death benefit of the employee's remaining account balance at time of death—whether before or after retirement.

The practice for defined benefit plans varies. If plan benefits are funded with individual life insurance policies, there is likely to be a pre-retirement death benefit up to 100 times the employee's expected monthly pension. Except for this type of insurance, however, it is unusual for defined benefit plans to pay lump-sum benefits from employer contributions. (If employees have made contributions, these are almost always payable as a death benefit, usually with interest but less any pension payments made to the employee prior to death.) The most common form of employer-provided death benefit under defined benefit plans is a spouse or survivor benefit, under which some part of the employee's accrued benefit is payable, in periodic installments, to the employee's spouse or some other survivor. This benefit is usually payable for life in the case of a spouse or another adult such as a dependent parent; in the case of surviving children, the benefit is usually payable until the child reaches a stipulated age. Although such a benefit could be paid for deaths occurring both before and after retirement, post-retirement survivor benefits are provided less frequently by employers, because of their higher cost. For the most part, survivor benefits are limited to surviving spouses. As noted, however, some plans will pay benefits to dependent parents or children if there is no surviving spouse.

An employer can provide a survivor benefit indirectly by subsidizing the rates used for joint and survivor protection—that is, by not charging the employee the full actuarial cost of the protection. The customary practice of employers who want to pay for this benefit, however, is simply to do so on a basis that involves no cost to employees.

Disability Benefits

A pension or profit-sharing plan need not provide a disability benefit as such. Of course, if an employee is otherwise vested and terminates employment, because of disability, then regular benefits payable on termination of employment must be available.

Most employers provide disability income benefits under separate plans. When this is the case, the employer's pension arrangement usually operates to complement the disability income plan by providing for continued benefit accruals or contributions during the period of disability.

Some employers, however, make their pension arrangement the major source of benefits for employees who incur a long-term disability (usually one that lasts for more than six months). Under a defined contribution plan, for example, the employee might be fully vested in his or her account balance, regardless of service, and this amount could be made available in the case of disability—either in a lump sum or in the form of installment payments. A defined benefit plan could treat the disability as an early retirement, even though the employee had not satisfied the regular requirements, and might even waive the reduction in benefit that would otherwise occur at early retirement. A defined benefit plan might also provide for a separately stated benefit in the case of disability, possibly with more liberal age and service requirements than those that apply for early retirement. Disability income benefits from defined benefit plans are found more often in negotiated plans than they are in plans covering nonrepresented employees.

From the standpoint of benefit adequacy, employees are usually better off with separate, pay-related disability benefits. Those benefits payable from qualified plans (whether defined contribution or defined benefit) reach reasonable levels only for those employees who have long periods of service or participation.

Other Plan Provisions

Provisions dealing with the following matters also must be included in any pension arrangement:

- The employer's right to amend and terminate the plan.
- Protection of employee rights in the event of plan mergers or the transfer or acquisition of plan assets.
- Treatment of employees on leave of absence (including military leave).
- Rehiring of retirees who are receiving benefits.
- The ability to make benefit payments to a payee who is a minor or otherwise incompetent.
- A prohibition against employees making assignments (except for qualified domestic relations orders [QDROs]).
- The rights and obligations of plan fiduciaries, including the right to delegate or allocate responsibilities.

DEFINED CONTRIBUTION VERSUS DEFINED BENEFIT PLANS

A critical decision for any employer who is about to adopt a pension plan is whether to use the defined contribution or defined benefit approach, or a combination of the two. As noted at the outset of this chapter, the defined contribution approach has grown in popularity since the passage of the Employee Retirement Income Security Act (ERISA). Some of this popularity is attributable to the positive treatment afforded these plans by legislation over the past 20 years; for example, the laws dealing with individual retirement accounts (IRAs), simplified employee pensions (SEPs), savings incentive match plans for employees (SIMPLE plans), 401(k) plans, employee stock ownership plans (ESOPs), and flexible compensation arrangements. Some is also due to legislation that has made it increasingly difficult to design and administer defined benefit plans— changes in the Social Security normal retirement age, joint and survivor requirements, age and gender discrimination laws, provisions relating to qualified domestic relations orders, and the like.

Whatever the reason, more and more employers, including those who maintain defined benefit plans, are examining the defined contribution approach to providing retirement benefits. Thus, it is important to understand and evaluate the basic characteristics of both approaches. The following lists some of the factors that should be considered in deciding which approach is appropriate in a given situation:

1. Most employers have specific income-replacement objectives in mind when they establish a retirement plan. A defined benefit plan can be structured to achieve these objectives. The defined contribution approach will probably produce benefits that either fall short of or exceed these objectives for individual employees.

2. By the same token, most employers want to take Social Security benefits into account so the combined level of benefits from both sources will produce the desired results. Defined contribution plans can be integrated with Social Security benefits to some extent by adjusting contribution levels, but integration can be accomplished more efficiently under defined benefit plans.

3. The defined benefit plan requires an employer commitment to pay the cost of the promised benefits. Thus, the employer must assume any additional costs associated with inflation and adverse investment results. The defined contribution plan transfers these risks to employees and allows the employer to fix its cost.

4. A deferred profit-sharing plan offers an employer the ultimate in contribution and funding flexibility. The money purchase pension plan, however, offers little flexibility, because contributions are fixed and must be made each year. Although the defined benefit plan involves an employer commitment as to ultimate cost, there can be significant funding flexibility on a year-to-year basis through the use of various actuarial methods and assumptions, the amortization of liabilities, and the operation of the minimum-funding standard account. (There is less flexibility with respect to establishing the annual charge to earnings for defined benefit plans, however, as a result of accounting standards.)

5. The other side of the cost issue concerns benefits for employees. A defined benefit plan can protect the employee against the risk of preretirement inflation. In a defined contribution plan, this risk is assumed by the employee, who must rely primarily on investment results to increase the value of benefits during inflationary periods.

6. Employees also assume the risk of investment loss under a defined contribution plan. Some observers feel it is inappropriate for the average employee to assume such a risk with respect to a major component of his or her retirement security.

7. The typical defined contribution plan provides that the employee's account balance is payable in the event of death and, frequently, in case of disability. This, of course, produces additional plan costs or, alternatively, lower retirement benefits if overall costs are held constant. An employer who is interested primarily in providing retirement benefits can use available funds more efficiently for this purpose under a defined benefit plan.

8. Many observers believe that a more equitable allocation of employer contributions occurs under a defined benefit plan, because the employee's age, past service, and pay can all be taken into account; the typical defined contribution plan allocates contributions only on the basis of pay. On the other hand, the very nature of a final pay defined benefit plan is that the value of total benefits accrued becomes progressively greater each year as the employee approaches retirement; under a defined contribution plan, a greater value will accrue during the early years of participation. As a result of the greater values accrued in earlier years, defined contribution plans, unless they use age-weighted allocation formulas, produce higher benefits and costs for terminating employees than do defined benefit plans.

9. Profit-sharing and savings plans offer two potential advantages that are not available under defined benefit and money purchase pension plans. Profit sharing can create employee incentives. These plans also can invest in employer securities, giving employees, as shareholders, the opportunity to identify with overall corporate interests.

10. Younger employees are apt to perceive a defined contribution plan, with its accumulating account values, to be of more value than a defined benefit plan. The reverse is probably true for older employees. Thus, the average age of the group to be covered can be critical.

11. Defined benefit plans are subject to the plan-termination provisions of ERISA, thus requiring the employer to pay annual Pension Benefit Guaranty Corporation (PBGC) premiums and exposing the employer's net worth to liability if the plan is terminated with insured but unfunded benefit promises. Defined contribution plans do not have this exposure.

These factors will have different significance for different employers, and a choice that is appropriate for one organization may be inappropriate for another. Many employers will find that a combination of the two approaches is the right answer—a defined benefit plan that provides a basic layer of benefits, along with a defined contribution arrangement that is a source of supplemental benefits.

CHAPTER 26

Profit-Sharing Plans

Bruce A. Palmer

Programs providing retirement income have received great attention in recent years. The reasons for this attention are many and varied but most relate fundamentally to inflation, other economic problems, and the inability of individuals to provide for their own retirement security without assistance from some formal group savings or social program. With the growth in concern over the future viability of the Social Security program and its ability to provide meaningful benefits to most retirees, substantial additional attention has been focused on employer-sponsored retirement programs.

This chapter continues the discussion of retirement plans that began in Chapter 25 and extends throughout Part Six. Specifically, this chapter focuses on profit-sharing plans as defined in Section 401(a) of the Internal Revenue Code (IRC). Collectively, these plans constitute a major component of the overall retirement benefit structure existing in the private sector.

DEFINITION OF PROFIT SHARING

A profit-sharing plan is a plan or program for sharing company profits with the firm's employees. The contributions to a qualified, deferred profit-sharing plan are accumulated in a tax-sheltered account to provide income to employees during their retirement years. Historically, deferred profit-sharing plans also have provided for the distribution of moneys on other prescribed occasions to employees or their beneficiaries.

According to federal income tax regulations:

A profit-sharing plan is a plan established and maintained by an employer to provide for the participation in its profits by its employees or their beneficiaries. The plan must provide a definite predetermined formula for allocating the contributions made to the plan among the participants and for distributing the funds accumulated under the plan after a fixed number of years, the attainment of a stated age, or upon the prior occurrence of some event such as layoff, illness, disability, retirement, death, or severance of employment.[1]

Under the Employee Retirement Income Security Act of 1974 (ERISA) and the IRC, profit-sharing plans are treated as defined contribution or individual account plans. As such, an employer is under no financial obligation to provide a specific dollar amount of benefit at retirement in these plans.

Periodic (e.g., annual) employer contributions to profit-sharing plans are allocated to individual accounts set up for each plan participant.[2] These contributions are augmented by each employee's share of investment earnings and possibly further by forfeitures of account balances created when nonvested (or partially vested) participants terminate their employment with the sponsoring firm. The amount of benefit available to the participant will be solely a function of the amount in the individual account at the time of retirement and the level of monthly income that the accumulated amount will purchase.

The concept of profit sharing, in its broadest sense, encompasses any program under which the firm's profits are shared with its employees. Thus, it includes both cash plans and deferred-distribution plans. Under cash plans, profit-sharing amounts are distributed to employees currently as a bonus or a wage/salary supplement. Consequently, these distributions are includable in the employees' income in the year of distribution and taxed on top of their wages, salaries, and other income.[3] Deferred-distribution profit-sharing plans are programs in which the profit-sharing amounts are credited to employee accounts (held under trust) and accumulated for later distribution (for example, upon retirement or some other specified event, such as death, disability, or severance of employment, or according to the terms of any plan-withdrawal provisions).

---

1 Reg. 1.401–1(b)(1)(ii).

2 Federal regulations require that an individual account be maintained for each plan participant in defined contribution plans.

3 Payments under cash profit-sharing plans may be made as soon as the respective participants' allocations are determined. Thus, the structure of these plans is simplified because there is no trust fund, no assets to be invested, and so on. Of course, the major disadvantage of these plans is that the payments are currently taxed to the participants.

In actuality, there is a third approach to profit sharing since it is possible for a firm to have a combination cash and deferred profit-sharing plan covering essentially the same group(s) of employees. Under this arrangement, a portion of the profit-sharing allocation is distributed currently to the participant, with the remainder deferred. A combination plan can be designed in one of two ways: (1) two separate plans may be established—one cash and the other deferred—or (2) only one plan is created, and it possesses both current and deferred features.

In this chapter, the term *profit-sharing plan* shall refer to the deferred-distribution form and will not include cash profit-sharing or 401(k) (cash or deferred) arrangements within profit-sharing plans unless otherwise noted. Cash profit-sharing plans are not qualified plans within the meaning of IRC Section 401(a), and 401(k) plans are discussed in detail in Chapter 27.

On rare occasions, profit-sharing plans provide for the payment of supplementary contributions (usually voluntary) by the covered employees. However, this chapter does not address any distinctive features that might be attributed to contributory profit-sharing plans nor does it cover thrift or savings plans,[4] which are described in Chapter 27 along with the coverage of 401(k) plans under which a substantial majority of them operate today.

IMPORTANCE OF PROFIT-SHARING PLANS

While several notable profit-sharing plans had been in existence prior to 1939, that year seems to signal the beginning of the major growth experienced in profit-sharing plans. In 1939, the U.S. Senate's endorsement of the profit-sharing concept, together with subsequent favorable tax legislation, provided the stimulus for the establishment of profit-sharing plans. In the 25 years preceding the enactment of ERISA, the number of deferred profit-sharing plans doubled approximately every five years. However, the

---

4 The IRS does not have a separation or division of requirements addressing only thrift plans. Thus, many thrift and savings plans qualify with the IRS under the profit-sharing rules and hence would be deemed to be profit-sharing plans. However, the purist would argue that there still exists a fundamental difference between a contributory profit-sharing plan and a thrift or savings plan. In the latter case, employer contributions to the plan are usually fixed at some predetermined percentage "match" (e.g., 25, 50, or 100 percent) of the employee contributions for the purpose of encouraging thrift on the part of the employee. Thus, employer contributions to a thrift plan are dependent primarily on the "level of employee thrift." In contrast, employer contributions to a contributory profit-sharing plan are primarily a function of the "level of profits." Further, in contributory profit-sharing plans where the employee contributions are voluntary, employer contributions to a participant's account usually are not made contingent on the payment of contributions by the participant.

reforms and uncertainties created by ERISA's enactment had a major deterrent effect on the establishment of all types of qualified plans, initially even including profit-sharing plans. Today, profit-sharing plans are extremely important in terms of the number of annual new plan approvals. This prominence is largely due to the strong interest in 401(k) plans.

The importance of profit-sharing plans is further underscored by the dual purpose that they serve in the overall structure of retirement-income planning. Profit-sharing plans often exist as the sole retirement-income plan in many firms, particularly in firms of small to medium size in which employers may feel unable to assume the financial commitment associated with a money purchase or defined benefit pension plan. In larger firms, profit-sharing plans often are established as a supplement to a defined benefit pension plan. There are several advantages to this combination approach. In addition to enhancing the possibility of greater total benefits, the pension plan can provide employees with protection against the downside risk that corporate profits will be low, leading to minimal contributions to the profit-sharing plan and ultimately to the payment of inadequate profit-sharing plan benefits.

EMPLOYER OBJECTIVES IN ESTABLISHING A DEFERRED PROFIT-SHARING PLAN

An employer normally has a number of specific objectives in electing to establish a qualified deferred profit-sharing plan. A major objective, of course, is to provide a vehicle, on behalf of covered employees, for the accumulation of tax-favored assets that, in turn, will constitute a primary source of income at retirement. As part of the overall objectives in establishing a qualified plan of any type, employers seek the various tax advantages associated with such a plan. These include the deductibility (within limits) of employer contributions, the tax-free accumulation of moneys held in trust under the plan, and the current nontaxability to employees of employer contributions and investment earnings on plan assets. In addition, employers typically have one or more other important objectives in establishing a qualified profit-sharing plan.

As part of a firm's overall compensation scheme, profit-sharing plans play a significant role in compensating employees and achieving various employee benefit objectives. In addition, many firms establish profit-sharing plans in the hope of improving their productivity and efficiency. Establishment of a profit-sharing plan may lead to improved employee morale and provide a source of motivation to employees to perform in a more productive and efficient manner. Since employer contributions to the plan are tied to the firm's profits, a profit-sharing plan provides employees with a direct incentive to become more efficient and more productive, resulting in lower costs and higher profits to the firm.[5] To the extent that these anticipated results are realized, employees, management, and stockholders alike should all benefit from the establishment of a profit-sharing plan.

Although both profit-sharing and pension plans create asset accumulation and financial security for covered employees and their dependents, these two approaches provide the employer with substantially different levels of funding flexibility. Under a money purchase or a defined benefit pension plan, the employer has a fixed commitment (not contingent on profit levels) to contribute amounts that meet certain ERISA-prescribed minimum requirements.[6] In most instances, these requirements will result in the employer having to make contributions to the plan during each and every year. In contrast, it is possible to design a profit-sharing plan such that the firm is not required to make a contribution each and every year, even when there are profits. This so-called "discretionary" approach provides employers with great contribution flexibility. The lack of a fixed yearly contribution obligation under profit-sharing plans is especially advantageous for small businesses and for new firms that may be unable to assume the fixed costs required of pension plans. In years of no profits, or when profits fall below a predetermined level, employer contributions do not have to be made. In contrast, in years of high profits, larger-than-average contributions can be made to the profit-sharing plan. For these reasons, profit-sharing plans may possess maximum flexibility with regard to employer contributions.

In establishing any new retirement-income plan, most employers will want to take employee desires into account. Younger and middle-aged employees may prefer the individual account approach inherent in a profit-sharing arrangement. The individual account approach often provides an opportunity to accumulate large sums on behalf of younger employees. Conversely, older employees generally tend to prefer a defined benefit plan (with its predetermined level of promised benefits) to either

---

5 Arguments also can be presented against this line of reasoning. For example, it is argued that profit-sharing plans reward poor performance equally as well as good performance, thereby questioning whether profit-sharing plans are truly motivational. Further, there is an issue as to how many employees in a firm can really influence profitability. In summary, the relationships among motivation, increased productivity, and the establishment of deferred profit-sharing plans are still strongly debated issues.

6 For money purchase plans, this entails the payment of a fixed rate of contribution; for defined benefit plans, it requires the payment of contributions at a level necessary to fund the promised benefits. In both cases, it means a specific contribution commitment without regard to the firm's profitability.

a profit-sharing or a money purchase pension plan. A profit-sharing or money purchase plan generally will not provide an accumulation of moneys sufficient to provide adequate retirement benefits for those employees near retirement at the time the plan is established. In choosing between the two approaches, profit-sharing (or money purchase) and defined benefit, the employer should consider the age distribution of the employee group to be covered by the plan. In the decision-making process, the employer should also take into consideration the firm's hiring objectives. A defined contribution plan may be preferred if the firm is interested primarily in hiring younger employees. In contrast, a defined benefit plan is likely to be more attractive to older executives and managers hired from other firms. The employer may decide to have a combination profit-sharing and defined benefit plan to appeal to both young and older workers.

An employer may be influenced by other objectives in deciding to adopt a profit-sharing plan. For example, the individual account feature provides employees with the opportunity to share in favorable investment results, which potentially could lead to much higher levels of monthly benefits at retirement.[7] In contrast, favorable investment earnings reduce employer costs under defined benefit plans. In addition, profit-sharing plans can permit the reallocation of forfeitures of nonvested (and partially vested) terminated participants to the accounts of the remaining participants, thus providing the possibility of even greater benefits to those employees who remain with the firm for long periods.[8] To the extent an employer wants the firm's long-service employees to share in both forfeitures and favorable investment earnings, the profit-sharing approach may be preferred.

An employer also may prefer certain other features that can be incorporated into the design of a profit-sharing plan whose inclusion in pension plans is either prohibited or substantially restricted. Specifically, the employer may want to provide covered employees with the option to make withdrawals from their individual accounts while still actively employed, or the employer may desire that the funds held in the profit-sharing trust be invested in employer stock or other employer securities to a greater

---

[7] However, the employee also is exposed to the downside risk of low or otherwise unfavorable investment results. This may be a potential source of employee (and possibly employer) dissatisfaction with the plan and, in addition, requires a greater sensitivity on the part of the employer to fiduciary obligations associated with the investment of plan assets.

[8] The issue of forfeitures and their reallocation has become somewhat less important today because of the faster vesting requirements imposed by the Tax Reform Act of 1986.

extent than permitted under a pension plan. When profit-sharing plan assets are invested in employer securities, employees have the opportunity to participate to an even greater extent in the success of the company.

Finally, the employer may want to avoid certain regulatory requirements imposed on defined benefit pension plans. These include satisfying minimum funding standards, payment of plan termination insurance premiums to the Pension Benefit Guaranty Corporation (PBGC), and the exposure to contingent employer liability and the attendant impact on the firm's accounting and financial reports.

In addition to their many advantages, profit-sharing plans possess several important disadvantages. One relative disadvantage of profit-sharing plans centers on the difficulty of providing employees with adequate credit for any period of past service (i.e., service prior to plan inception). Past service credits can be incorporated with relative ease in most defined benefit pension plans. Second, the ultimate benefit payable at retirement under a profit-sharing plan (or any other defined contribution plan) may be inadequate for those employees near retirement at the time the plan is established. Third, profit-sharing amounts contributed to the plan in any year usually are allocated among the individual employee accounts on the basis of each employee's annual compensation, ignoring both age and service factors. Although, historically, age and years of service generally have been ignored in profit-sharing allocation formulas, there is increasing interest today in incorporating employee age into the allocation formula. Fourth, the allocation patterns under profit-sharing plans are such that relatively larger amounts are provided to short-service employees who terminate with vested rights compared to what occurs under defined benefit plans. Additional disadvantages of profit-sharing plans relate to the employee's assumption of the inflation and investment risks (see footnote 7) and the risk of little or no profits to the firm, which, collectively, could result in inadequate benefits at retirement.

QUALIFICATION REQUIREMENTS APPLICABLE TO DEFERRED PROFIT-SHARING PLANS

For the most part, the same or similar qualification requirements apply equally to both pension plans (defined benefit and money purchase) and deferred profit-sharing plans. These requirements relate to (1) the plan provisions being contained in a written document (ensuring a formal, enforceable plan), (2) plan permanency, (3) communication of plan provisions to the employees, (4) the plan being established and operated for the exclusive benefit of plan participants and their beneficiaries, (5) minimum age and service provisions, (6) nondiscrimination in coverage and contributions/benefits, (7) minimum vesting standards, and so forth. Because of the similarity of regulatory treatment between pension plans and profit-sharing plans, the discussion of the general legal requirements for plan qualification are minimized here.

A few differences exist in the qualification requirements pertaining to profit-sharing plans and pension plans, however. Additionally, although pension and profit-sharing plans alike are subject to the same eligibility and vesting rules, the actual eligibility and vesting provisions included in profit-sharing plans are frequently more liberal in nature.

A significant regulatory difference between pension and profit-sharing plans relates to the investment of plan assets in employer securities. Pension plans (including both defined benefit and money purchase plans) are restricted in terms of their ability to invest plan assets in employer stock. These plans are subject to the ERISA Section 404 requirement that no more than 10 percent of the fair market value of plan assets can be invested in qualifying employer securities and employer real property.[9] This limitation does not apply to profit-sharing plans. As a result, profit-sharing plans may invest their assets in qualifying employer securities and employer real property without restriction as to percentage limitation.[10]

Many employers believe that the investment of a portion of profit-sharing plan assets in employer stock provides employees with an additional incentive to be more productive. The extent to which profit-sharing plans invest a portion of the plan assets in employer stock is likely to be related to several factors, including company size, overall profitability of the firm (including future prospects as regards profitability), marketability of the stock, and others. Historically, the investment of profit-sharing plan assets in employer stock has been widespread among very large companies and also among companies whose ownership is closely held. Because of important advantages and disadvantages, great care should be exercised in making decisions concerning the investment of plan assets in employer stock.

As indicated earlier, profit-sharing plans are not subject to certain ERISA provisions affecting qualified defined benefit pension plans. These primarily relate to minimum funding standards and the various

---

9 From the covered employee's standpoint, this limitation is not likely as important under a defined benefit plan as it is under a money purchase plan. Any appreciation in the employer's stock under a defined benefit plan serves to reduce future employer contributions, resulting in no direct benefit to the employee.

10 Of course, investment of profit-sharing plan assets in employer stock (along with other investment media) must meet the prudent expert standard of ERISA.

plan-termination insurance requirements. Further, in defined benefit plans, forfeitures must be used to reduce future employer contributions to the plan. In contrast, under profit-sharing plans, forfeitures may either be used to reduce future employer contributions or be reallocated among the remaining participants (the usual case), thereby increasing the amounts in the participants' individual accounts.[11]

In addition to those qualification requirements that are distinctive of profit-sharing plans, as described above, other requirements imposed on all qualified plans are often satisfied differently under profit-sharing plans. The following discussion focuses on two areas: (1) eligibility requirements and (2) vesting requirements.

Permissible eligibility requirements include (a) a minimum age requirement of 21 and (b) a minimum period of service of one year. (A two-year service requirement is permitted, together with age 21, if the plan provides for full and immediate vesting upon satisfying the plan's eligibility requirements and if there is no 401(k) feature in the plan.) These eligibility requirements apply to profit-sharing and pension plans alike. Qualified plans also must satisfy a complex set of coverage and benefit nondiscrimination rules. For many deferred profit-sharing plans in existence today, the eligibility and coverage provisions tend to be more liberal than what are required as minimum standards for qualification purposes, and they also tend to be more liberal than those commonly employed in pension plans.

Most profit-sharing plans provide broad coverage of employees, although they often exclude seasonal and part-time employees (e.g., those who work fewer than 1,000 hours per year). (Note: Once employees meet the "one-year-at-1,000-hours requirement," the plan cannot thereafter exclude them due to their seasonal or part-time status, although they still may be excluded as a part of a broad classification of employees excluded from the plan, subject to the minimum coverage requirements under IRC Section 410(b).) Some plans make employees eligible on the date of hire, and many others use a minimum service requirement of less than one year. In addition, most profit-sharing plans do not use a minimum age requirement, and historically, these plans rarely have been integrated with benefits payable under Social Security.

Regarding vesting, the Tax Reform Act of 1986 specifies that profit-sharing plans must meet one of two alternative minimum vesting standards:

---

11 From the standpoint of remaining plan participants, the advantage inherent in profit-sharing plans that accrues from forfeiture reallocation is somewhat mitigated by the presence of more rapid vesting typically found in profit-sharing plans. See *infra*.

(1) five-year cliff vesting or (2) seven-year graded vesting. Under the five-year rule, plan participants are not required to have any vested rights in employer-provided benefits until after the completion of five years of service, at which point the participants must be 100 percent vested. Under the seven-year graded vesting rule, participants must be at least 20 percent vested after the completion of three years of service, with the required vesting percentage increasing by 20 percent each year, until 100 percent vesting is reached at the end of seven years.[12]

A substantial majority of profit-sharing plans provide more liberal vesting than prescribed under the IRC Section 411(a) alternative minimum vesting standards. In fact, a significant percentage of profit-sharing plans provide full and immediate vesting upon plan participation. Other plans provide full vesting if a participant's employment is terminated "through no fault of the employee." This might occur, for example, at the closing of a plant, department, or smaller organizational unit. Finally, while the law requires that full vesting occur at the normal retirement date specified in the plan and also upon plan termination, nearly all deferred profit-sharing plans also provide full vesting in the event of the participant's death or total and permanent disability.

The liberal coverage and eligibility and vesting provisions typically found in most profit-sharing plans are consistent with an overall employer objective of providing employees with an incentive to work more efficiently, which, it is hoped, will lead to increased profits for the firm.[13] This objective can be maximized in a deferred profit-sharing plan only

---

12 These rules became effective for plan years beginning after December 31, 1988. They replaced the original "10-Year Rule," the "5-to-15 Year Rule," and the "Rule of 45" created by ERISA. Plans that are classified as "top-heavy" must comply with additional vesting requirements imposed under the Tax Equity and Fiscal Responsibility Act of 1982 (TEFRA). Specifically, if a plan is "top-heavy," its vesting schedule must comply with one of two rules: (a) "three-year cliff vesting" or (b) "six-year graded vesting."

13 It also should be noted that the employer's contributions (costs) to a profit-sharing plan are not increased or otherwise affected either by a larger number of participants (through more liberal eligibility requirements) or through more rapid vesting; assuming, of course, that non-vested forfeitures are reallocated among the remaining participants (the typical case) rather than used to reduce future employer contributions. (While this statement is generally true, it is not applicable to those profit-sharing plans that base their contribution on a percentage of compensation subject to a maximum contribution based on profit.) This is in direct contrast to the situation that occurs in either a money purchase or a defined benefit pension plan. Pension plans that are designed with more liberal eligibility and vesting rules result in higher costs to the employer. Thus, to reduce total plan costs, pension plans generally impose more restrictive eligibility rules and less liberal vesting requirements than those used in deferred profit-sharing plans. It is important to note, however, that under profit-sharing plans, the *allocation* of both contributions (profits) and forfeitures among plan participants would be affected by a plan's eligibility and vesting requirements.

through broad participation, through the imposition of few eligibility restrictions, and through the providing of liberal vesting.

In conclusion, the employer's reason(s) for establishing a deferred profit-sharing plan should have a direct bearing on the specific eligibility and vesting requirements adopted by the plan. That is, an objective of creating employee incentives would indicate short periods for vesting and minimum or no eligibility requirements. Other objectives, such as maximizing the retirement income that may be provided to long-service employees from a specified amount of employer contribution, might indicate longer vesting periods and more stringent eligibility requirements subject to the minimum qualification standards.

CONTRIBUTIONS TO DEFERRED PROFIT-SHARING PLANS

The issue of profit-sharing contributions constitutes a most important topic in regard to the overall design of deferred profit-sharing plans. It is these amounts, together with investment earnings and forfeiture reallocations, that ultimately determine the funds available to plan participants at retirement or upon other prescribed occasions.

The discussion of profit-sharing contributions is divided into three major subsections. These subsections describe, respectively, the various methods of ascertaining contribution amounts to deferred profit-sharing plans, alternative formulas for allocating the profit-sharing contributions among plan participants, and the maximum limits imposed under federal tax law on contributions and allocations.

Methods of Determining Profit-Sharing Contributions

A most important concern in profit-sharing plans centers on the question, "How much of the profits should be shared with the employees?" For a specific employer, the portion or percentage of profits that should be contributed is likely to depend on several factors, including the (1) amount and stability of the firm's annual profits; (2) capital requirements of the firm (e.g., needs for working capital, reserves, and expansion); (3) level of return to be provided to stockholders on their investment in the firm; (4) presence (or absence) of other capital accumulation or retirement income programs sponsored by the firm; (5) portion of profits that is to be used in upgrading the (cash) payroll levels of the employees; (6) federal tax law, which places limitations on annual contributions, deductions, and allocations to participants' accounts; and, of course, (7) objectives of the plan, particularly the extent to which management believes that the profit-sharing plan serves as a motivator to covered employees and the extent to which employee behavior can affect, in a significant way, the profit levels of the particular firm in question.[14]

A second area of interest relating to profit-sharing contributions concerns how profits are to be defined in the plan. Employers have considerable flexibility in making this determination since "profits" are not defined in great detail under federal tax law. Traditionally, "profits" have related to current-year profits, although it is legally permissible for deferred profit-sharing plans to base their profit-sharing contributions on both current profits and profits accumulated from prior years. With the passage of the Tax Reform Act of 1986, profits are no longer required for contributions, and employers are permitted to make contributions even when there are no current or accumulated profits. Further, profits can be defined either in terms of "before-tax profits" or "after-tax profits," with the majority of companies basing their profit-sharing contributions on before-tax profits.[15] Additionally, a significant number of plans provide that only profits in excess of some stipulated minimum dollar amount (e.g., $100,000) or in excess of a minimum return to stockholders (e.g., 30 cents per share) are available for profit sharing.[16] Conditions such as these are commonly referred to as "prior reservations for capital," or simply, "prior reservations." Their purpose is to protect the financial interests of the company's shareholders. Employers who incorporate a prior reservation in determining their profit-sharing contributions commonly share a greater percentage of profits, once the reservation has been satisfied, than plans that do not include a prior reservation.

---

14 One fairly basic concept in this regard is to split profits equally into three shares: (a) one-third to employees in the form of profit-sharing contributions, (b) one-third to stockholders in the form of dividends, and (c) one-third to customers, either through price reductions or expenditures for product improvement. In some instances, element (c) is eliminated, with that share going into company surplus and being available for reinvestment in the company's operations. It is important to note that when companies provide as much as a one-third share of profits to employees, it may be that not all of these moneys will flow into a deferred profit-sharing arrangement because of limitations on tax deductions and allocations (and possibly for other reasons). Rather, a substantial portion of these profit-sharing moneys might be distributed immediately to the employees.

15 It should be noted that employers are permitted to determine "profits" in accordance with generally accepted accounting principles, even when this may differ from the calculation of profits under federal income tax law.

16 Even when a minimum return on capital is not expressly provided in the profit-sharing formula, the concept generally is taken into consideration in the profit-sharing deliberations in an indirect way.

Most importantly, profit-sharing contribution methods differ according to whether profits are shared on the basis of a fixed formula, with its terms and conditions communicated in advance to plan participants, or whether the company's board of directors in a discretionary manner determines the annual percentage of profits to be shared. Although the use of a predetermined, fixed-contribution formula is not required by law (and, consequently, no specific minimum level or rate of contribution is required),[17] profit-sharing contributions must meet two other legal requirements. Specifically, the contributions must be "substantial and recurring,"[18] to lend support to the qualification requirement pertaining to plan permanency, and these contributions cannot be applied in any manner (either in amount or time) that would result in discrimination in favor of highly compensated employees. So long as these general restrictions are complied with, an employer may establish any method or formula for determining the profit-sharing amounts that are to be contributed to the plan.

The major advantage of the discretionary approach is its tremendous flexibility in the annual determination of contributions. Under this approach, the board of directors has the opportunity of viewing past experience along with the firm's current financial position and capital requirements before making the decision as to the portion of profits to be shared in the current year. Contribution rates may be adjusted upward or downward from previous years' rates based on any number of factors, including the current financial picture of the firm. Under the predetermined formula approach, the plan itself would have to be amended to accommodate an employer's desire to adjust the profit-sharing contribution rate. Use of the discretionary method also ensures that the firm will not have to make contributions to the deferred profit-sharing plan in amounts that exceed the maximums that may be deducted currently for federal income tax purposes.[19]

When the discretionary approach is used, the plan often stipulates minimum and maximum percentages of profits to be distributed (e.g., 10 percent to 30 percent of profits). These limitations restrict the range within which the board of directors may exercise discretionary authority in regard to contributions to the profit-sharing plan. Other illustrations of

---

17 Reg. 1.401–1(b)(2).

18 Reg. 1.401–1(b)(2).

19 While this is a legitimate concern when fixed-contribution formulas are used, satisfactory results may be obtained through the inclusion of a condition in the plan specifying that contributions not be in excess of the maximum deductible amount. Thus, this concern should not be viewed as a deterrent to the use of predetermined, or fixed-contribution formulas.

discretionary arrangements include "discretionary, but not to be less than 10 percent of before-tax profits," and "discretionary, but approximately 20 percent of before-tax profits." The purpose of such arrangements is to provide some guidelines or constraints to the board of directors as it exercises its discretionary authority. Any of these guidelines could include some form of a prior reservation for capital.

At one time, the Internal Revenue Service (IRS) required that deferred profit-sharing plans include a fixed-contribution formula. However, as a result of several court decisions to the contrary, IRS rules were liberalized to permit employers to determine profit-sharing amounts without a predetermined formula. Although approved by the Internal Revenue Service, the discretionary method is not without its disadvantages. For example, a discretionary approach may lead to lower employee morale and a weakened sense of financial security. Without a fixed formula, employees may feel uncertain about whether they can count on sharing in the profits they have helped produce. In this context, the argument for using a fixed formula is that the "ground rules" are established in advance. At the beginning of each year, employees have the knowledge that their share of the profits will be determined in accordance with the terms contained in the formula.

Second, some type of formula method takes many of the burdens and pressures off the board of directors in making decisions on profit-sharing amounts during periods of economic instability (for example, when the firm has experienced high profits during the current year, but a severe economic downturn is forecast for next year; or, conversely, there are low profits in the current year with much brighter prospects for next year). Previously established guidelines are helpful to the board of directors when these circumstances arise.

Finally, the discretionary method exposes the contributions to the potential risk that they will come under any wage (and price) guidelines in effect at the time the contributions are made to the plan. For example, in 1979 the President's Council on Wage and Price Stability released its decision on the treatment of profit-sharing plans. Profit-sharing contributions determined under a discretionary approach were treated as incentive pay and therefore fell within the wage guidelines. In contrast, qualified deferred profit-sharing plans that used a fixed formula did not come under the wage guideline calculations to the extent that the formula was not changed.

Despite the tremendous flexibility of the discretionary approach, its disadvantages are major reasons why many large employers use a fixed formula method. Smaller companies (up to 1,000 plan participants) have a greater tendency to determine profit-sharing contributions on a discretionary basis, since these terms appear to be more concerned with contribution and financing flexibility.

An unlimited variety of fixed profit-sharing formulas exist from which an employer may choose. These formulas can specify a fixed percentage or sliding scale of percentages (either ascending or descending) based on before-tax or after-tax profits, with or without a prior reservation. Examples using a fixed percentage are "10 percent of before-tax profits" and "25 percent of before-tax profits but no more than the amount that is available as a current tax deduction." An illustration of a formula involving a sliding scale (ascending) used by one large company is "3.5 percent on the first $100 million of before-tax profits, 5 percent on the next $50 million, and 6 percent on before-tax profits in excess of $150 million." (Because of obvious concerns about employee motivation, a formula providing for a scale of decreasing percentages rarely is used.) An example of a fixed formula with a prior reservation is "20 percent of before-tax profits in excess of 5 percent of net worth." Certainly, many other examples of predetermined formulas exist.

In addition to its relative inflexibility, a predetermined formula poses difficulties, from an employee relations perspective, in changing the formula when the amended formula clearly produces a lesser share of profits for the employees. Thus, careful consideration must be given to the initial decision as to the profit-sharing percentage(s) that will be included in the formula. To take advantage of the desirable features of both discretionary and fixed formulas, some employers (especially smaller firms) choose a combination method that provides a minimum fixed-contribution rate with additional profit-sharing amounts determined by the board of directors on a discretionary basis. The specific approach adopted, whether discretionary, predetermined formula, or some combination, and the precise details of the method chosen should be reflective of the employer's goals and objectives for the plan and the perceived impact of the plan and its profit-sharing method on the covered employee group.

Methods of Allocating Employer Contributions Among Plan Participants

Once the amount of profit-sharing contributions has been determined for the year, these moneys must then be allocated to the individual participants' accounts. Although not requiring a fixed (or predetermined) formula for calculating the level of contributions, the law does require that a predetermined formula for allocating profit-sharing contributions among employee accounts be specified in the plan. This is to ensure that the contribution allocation does not discriminate in favor of the firm's highly compensated employees. In judging whether a plan meets the qualification requirements, the IRS must be able to examine the allocation formula to determine that allocations will be made in a nondiscriminatory manner.

A wide range of alternative methods exists for allocating profit-sharing contributions among individual employee accounts, depending on the nature of the plan and employer objectives. The most commonly used approach is based on compensation (with age and years of service ignored), whereby amounts are allocated according to the ratio of each individual employee's compensation to the total compensation of all covered participants for the year. To illustrate, assume employee A has compensation of $20,000 during the year. If total covered compensation for all plan participants is $400,000 for the year, employee A would be entitled to 5 percent ($20,000 divided by $400,000) of the total profit-sharing allocation. If aggregate profit-sharing contributions are $50,000 for the year, employee A's share would be $2,500 (5 percent of $50,000). In using this allocation formula, the plan sponsor must specify the amounts to be included in determining compensation. For example, compensation for an individual participant may include all compensation paid during the plan year, even though this individual was a plan participant for only part of the year, or it may be defined to include only amounts earned during the portion of the year that the employee was a participant. Compensation also must be defined in terms of whether it consists of base (or regular) pay only, or if it includes bonuses, overtime, commissions, or other forms of cash compensation as well. An allocation method based on compensation usually presents no discrimination problems so long as compensation is determined in a nondiscriminatory manner.

Another type of contribution allocation formula bases the allocation on both compensation and length (years) of service. Formulas incorporating both compensation and service typically allocate profit-sharing contributions on the basis of each participant's number of "points" awarded for the current year in proportion to total credited points of all plan participants for the year. Commonly, one point might be awarded for each $100 of compensation. An additional point, for example, might be given for each year of service.[20] To illustrate, an employee earning $25,000 with 15 years of

---

20 It is possible to credit more than one point to each year of service. Further, units other than $100 might be used in determining the number of points to be awarded for a specific amount of compensation.

service would be credited with 265 points [($25,000/$100 = 250) + 15]. The contribution allocation to this employee's account is determined first by dividing 265 by the total number of points credited to all plan participants during the year. This ratio is then applied to the total profit-sharing contribution to derive the employee's share.

Relatively few deferred profit-sharing plans allocate contributions according to length of service only. However, there is growing interest and utilization of so-called "age-weighted" profit-sharing plans. These plans, often established by small employers, incorporate employee age into the profit-sharing allocation formula. Through this process, older employees receive relatively larger contribution allocations due to their higher ages. Like all qualified plans, "age-weighted" profit-sharing plans must meet the nondiscrimination requirements contained in IRC Section 401(a)(4), which are designed to prevent discrimination favoring highly compensated employees. Since it is often the case that highly compensated employees are also older than most of the firm's other employees (and this may be particularly true in smaller firms), careful attention should be given to the design of contribution allocation formulas that are weighted by age or service to ensure compliance with the nondiscrimination requirements.

In summary, a contribution allocation formula determines participant shares for accounting and record-keeping purposes. These moneys are allocated to individual employee accounts. However, contribution dollars are not necessarily segregated for investment purposes. While the profit-sharing trust may permit each participant's account to be invested in "earmarked" assets (e.g., an insurance contract), profit-sharing contributions also may be received, administered, and invested by the trustee as commingled assets. In the latter case, the balance in each participant's account at a specific time simply represents his or her current share of the total trust assets.

Maximum Limits

A number of maximum dollar limits apply to deferred profit-sharing plans. Several relate to maximums placed on the amount of profit-sharing contributions that may be deducted, for federal income tax purposes, by an employer in any one tax year. In addition, the IRC Section 415 "annual additions limit" places maximums on certain allocations to individual employee accounts in defined contribution plans, including profit-sharing plans. Collectively, these limits place important constraints on what employers can do for their covered employees through deferred profit-sharing arrangements.

An overriding consideration here is that profit-sharing contributions, when added to all other compensation paid to an employee for the year, must be "reasonable" for the services performed by the employee and, in addition, be shown to be an "ordinary and necessary expense" of doing business.[21] If this is not the case, the IRS may deny the employer a tax deduction for any part or all of the profit-sharing contributions (and possibly other compensation amounts as well) made on behalf of the employee.[22]

As regards specific maximums, probably the single most important constraint is the IRS limit on deductible contributions. This limit is set forth in IRC Section 404. For deferred profit-sharing plans, the basic limit is that annual deductible contributions may not exceed "15 percent of compensation otherwise paid or accrued during the taxable year to all employees under the plan."[23] The 15 percent limitation applies regardless of the manner in which employer contributions are determined (i.e., discretionary versus fixed formula, or type of formula). However, this limit applies only to employer contributions to a deferred profit-sharing arrangement. Employers who provide for both cash and deferred profit sharing are subject to the 15 percent deduction limit only on contributions to the deferred portion of the profit-sharing arrangement. Thus, if an employer's profit-sharing arrangement calls for sharing 30 percent of before-tax profits, and if 40 percent of this amount is to be distributed in cash (with the balance deferred), then the limit of IRC Section 404(a)(3) applies only to the 18 percent [30% − (30%) × (40%)] of before-tax profits that is contributed to the deferred plan. Furthermore, the 18 percent of before-tax profits (or a portion thereof) will be deductible as a contribution to the deferred profit-sharing plan only to the extent that this amount does not exceed 15 percent of the total compensation of plan participants.

Prior to the passage of the Tax Reform Act of 1986, employers were permitted to create "credit carryovers" and "contribution carryovers." A "credit carryover" occurred whenever the employer's contribution for the year was less than the maximum allowable deduction of 15 percent of covered compensation. This credit was carried forward to be available for employer use in any subsequent tax year in which contributions exceeded the 15 percent limit, up to a 30 percent cap. This enabled employers to take larger tax deductions in later years of higher profits (and larger prof-

---

21 This statement is not restricted to profit-sharing contributions but is equally true for all forms of compensation.

22 In most large publicly held firms, the issue of "unreasonable compensation" arises infrequently. When this question is raised, it tends to be in those businesses whose ownership is closely held by a small number of individuals.

23 IRC Section 404(a)(3).

it-sharing contributions). A "contribution carryover" was created whenever the employer's contributions for a given year exceeded the maximum allowable deduction for that year. This amount could be carried forward and deducted in a subsequent year in which the employer's contribution that year was less than the otherwise allowable deduction (e.g., 15 percent of covered compensation). This permitted employers to make large contributions in earlier, high-profit years that exceeded the deductible amount, with the excess carried forward and available for deduction in later years of lower profit-sharing contributions.

Unfortunately, the 1986 tax law repealed the "credit carryover" provisions and applies a 10 percent excise tax penalty to employer contributions exceeding the current allowable deduction. ("Credit carryovers" created and accumulated prior to 1987 can still be used to increase the otherwise available deduction limitations for tax years beginning after December 31, 1986.) Since these carryover provisions enhanced employer contribution flexibility, their restriction may lead to an eventual decrease in the popularity of profit-sharing plans.

Additional deduction limits apply when an employer sponsors both a pension plan and a profit-sharing plan that cover a common group of employees. A 25 percent (of covered compensation) aggregate limit applies when both a profit-sharing plan and a money purchase pension plan exist. Further, in the case of a combination profit-sharing plan and defined benefit pension plan, the maximum annual deductible contribution to the combined plans is limited to 25 percent of covered compensation or, if larger, the amount necessary to meet the minimum funding requirements of the defined benefit plan alone.[24] If circumstances are such that the minimum funding rules require the employer to contribute amounts to the defined benefit plan during a year that are in excess of 25 percent of covered compensation, the employer, in effect, is precluded from making a deductible contribution to the profit-sharing plan that year. The separate 15 percent deduction limit on employer contributions to the profit-sharing plan still applies in combination pension and profit-sharing plans.

Contributions, together with forfeiture reallocations, in deferred profit-sharing plans are subject to the "annual additions limit" of IRC Section 415(c). This section of the code prescribes limitations on the amounts of moneys that can be added, on an annual basis, to individual participants' accounts under defined contribution plans. Specifically, a qualified defined contribution plan may not provide an annual addition,

---

24 See IRC Section 404(a)(7).

in any year, to any participant's account that exceeds the lesser of: (a) 25 percent of compensation (for that year) or (b) a stipulated dollar amount ($35,000 in 2001). A separate qualification requirement that applies for all purposes (e.g., basic contribution, nondiscrimination testing, etc.) and not just for IRC Section 415, specifies that in determining (a), only the first $150,000 indexed ($170,000 in 2001) of compensation can be considered.[25] Contributions in excess of the IRC Section 415 limits will result in disqualification of the plan. Thus, employers must be certain that these limits are satisfied. Conceivably, the annual additions limit could reduce the contribution that an employer might otherwise make to the account of an individual participant in a given year.

The term *annual additions* includes: (a) employer contributions, (b) forfeiture reallocations, and (c) employee contributions. For purposes of the annual additions limit, investment earnings allocated to employee's account balances, rollover contributions, and loan repayments are not part of annual additions. Since this chapter is concerned primarily with deferred profit-sharing plans funded exclusively with employer contributions, component (c) of the annual additions limit is of little importance here and therefore will be ignored.

Many employers have combination pension and profit-sharing arrangements designed to provide significant amounts of retirement income from the pension plan and to provide for asset accumulation through the establishment of the required individual accounts under the profit-sharing plan. In essence, there are two basic ways of having a combination plan that includes a deferred profit-sharing arrangement: (1) a money purchase pension plan together with a profit-sharing plan; and (2) a defined benefit pension plan plus a profit-sharing plan. In the first arrangement, because both plans are defined contribution plans (and assuming the plans cover the same group of employees), the combined plans must comply with the annual additions limit of the lesser of 25 percent of pay or a stated dollar maximum ($35,000 in 2001). In addition, the 15 percent annual maximum on *deductible* employer contributions would act as an "internal" limit, in the aggregate for all employees, with regard to the portion of the 25 percent that is accounted for by employer contributions to the deferred profit-sharing program. Further, any forfeiture reallocations under the profit-sharing plan may cause a reduction in the amounts that otherwise could be contributed to either the profit-sharing plan or the money purchase plan to comply with the annual additions limit.

---

25 The compensation limit is indexed to changes in the consumer price index (CPI). The limit is increased only when cumulative CPI changes require an adjustment of at least $10,000.

Prior to 1996, a combined limit under IRC Section 415(e) restricted the amount of aggregate contributions and benefits to individual participants in those situations where an employer sponsored both a defined benefit plan and a defined contribution plan (including profit sharing) covering the same group of employees. The Small Business Job Protection Act of 1996 (SBJPA) eliminated the combined plan limit effective for limitation years beginning after December 31, 1999. Thus, employers can establish separate defined benefit and profit-sharing plans covering the same employees, and, if desired, provide maximum benefits and contributions up to the individual plan limits contained in IRC Section 415 (e.g., the year 2001 limit of $140,000 for defined benefit plans and $35,000 for defined contribution plans.)

ALLOCATION OF INVESTMENT EARNINGS AND FORFEITURES

In addition to specifying a contribution allocation formula, deferred profit-sharing plans also must prescribe methods for allocating investment earnings and forfeitures among the participants' accounts. These allocation methods, depending on the specific circumstances, may differ from the method applied in allocating employer contributions.

Allocation of Investment Earnings

Unless profit-sharing allocations are "earmarked" for specific investments (when life insurance contracts are purchased), these moneys will be pooled and invested on an aggregated basis. The investment earnings generated from these commingled funds, in turn, must then be allocated to each participant's account. The most equitable approach is to base the allocation on the respective sizes of the individual account balances. Presumably, the funds assigned to each participant's account contribute in a pro rata fashion to the total investment earnings of the plan. As such, each account should share on a pro rata basis in these earnings. Thus, if a participant's account balance comprises 10 percent of the total of all account balances, that participant's account should be credited with 10 percent of the total investment earnings. Because investment earnings invariably are allocated on the basis of individual account balances, the method allocating investment earnings will differ from the approach used in allocating employer contributions.

Investment earnings accruing to a profit-sharing trust are typically measured on a "total return" basis. That is, investment earnings for a given year are defined to include interest and dividends, as well as adjustments in the market value of the underlying assets during the year of measurement. The net result is that the assets of the profit-sharing plan should be valued periodically to determine their market value. In fact, the IRS requires that the accounts of all plan participants be valued in a uniform and consistent manner at least once each year.[26] It is common for large plans to conduct valuations as often as daily. Frequent asset valuations accommodate more rapid benefit payouts after employment separation and, in addition, enhance the plan's ability to permit participants to change their investment selections periodically. Frequent market valuation of plan assets also leads to more equitable treatment of plan participants. This is particularly important in the general overall treatment of plan transactions (primarily withdrawals) that occur between valuation dates. On the occasion of withdrawals (whether partial or total), an issue arises as to the appropriate values to be placed on the account balances and consequently the dollar amounts available for distribution. More frequent asset valuations will assist in achieving equitable results (a) between individuals making withdrawals and those who do not, and (b) among individuals making withdrawals at different times. There is also the policy question of whether investment earnings are to be credited to individual account balances for the period between the last valuation date and the date the funds are withdrawn. If interest is not credited for this period, the amounts (interest) lost to the participants making withdrawals could be substantial unless relatively frequent valuations (e.g., monthly or every two months) are made.

Allocation of Forfeitures

Forfeitures arise when participants terminate employment and the funds credited to their accounts are less than fully vested. As described earlier, the qualification requirements applicable to deferred profit-sharing plans permit the periodic reallocation of forfeitures among the remaining plan participants. While profit-sharing plans are also permitted to use forfeitures to reduce future employer contributions, this is seldom the case. The

---

26 Certain exceptions exist. For example, an annual valuation is not required when all of the plan assets are invested, immediately, in individual annuity or retirement contracts meeting certain requirements. See Revenue Ruling 73-435, 1973-2 C.B. 126.

advantage of being able to reallocate forfeitures is somewhat lessened by the rapid vesting typically provided in profit-sharing plans which, in turn, reduces the amount of forfeitures available for reallocation. Further, forfeiture reallocations, together with employer contributions, must comply with the "annual additions limit" contained in IRC Section 415.[27]

All methods of forfeiture reallocation are subject to the principal requirement that they not discriminate in favor of the firm's highly compensated employees. Potential discrimination is of particular concern when forfeitures are reallocated on the basis of account balances. This concern centers on the premise that highly compensated employees are more likely to have longer periods of service and, therefore, will have much larger account balances than other plan participants. Thus, if account balances constitute the basis for reallocating forfeitures, highly compensated employees may be entitled to substantially larger shares of forfeitures than other employees. The IRS will not permit forfeitures to be reallocated on the basis of account balances to the extent that discrimination in favor of highly compensated employees occurs. Because of concern about possible discrimination (and subsequent loss of the plan's qualified status), "account balances" is a seldom-used method in reallocating forfeitures. Instead, forfeitures generally are reallocated on the basis of each participant's compensation—the same method typically used in allocating employer contributions. Under normal circumstances, a compensation-based method will create an equitable reallocation of forfeitures among plan participants and will not be viewed as discriminatory.

LOAN AND WITHDRAWAL PROVISIONS

A large number of deferred profit-sharing plans provide participants with access to funds on prescribed occasions earlier than actual retirement. This is accomplished through inclusion of loan or withdrawal provisions in the plan.

Loan Provisions

Many profit-sharing plans contain loan provisions. These allow participants to borrow up to a specified percentage (e.g., 50 percent) of the vested amounts in their individual accounts. While profit-sharing plans are not legally obligated to contain a loan provision, certain regulatory require-

---

27 See *supra*.

ments will apply when such a provision is included. One requirement is that loans must be made available to all plan participants on a reasonably equivalent basis. Specifically, loans cannot be made available to highly compensated employees on a basis that is more favorable than that available to other employees. In addition, loans must be repaid in level payments (made at least quarterly) and must bear a reasonable rate of interest. The IRS may view any loans not repaid as withdrawals, in which case they must meet the conditions described below. So long as the specified terms are properly drawn and prudent, the loans will be exempted from the prohibited transaction provisions and also should comply with the fiduciary standards under ERISA.

It is possible that certain loans will be treated as plan distributions and, therefore, subject to current income taxation. Generally, loans will be treated as plan distributions unless two conditions are met:

1. The participant's total outstanding loan amount does not exceed the *lesser* of (a) one-half of the present value of the participant's nonforfeitable benefit, or (b) $50,000. Further, the $50,000 limit is reduced by any principal repayments during the preceding 12-month period.
2. The loan (according to its terms and conditions) must be repaid within five years; however, the five-year repayment rule is waived for loans whose proceeds are applied to purchase a dwelling used as a principal residence of the participant.

Withdrawal Provisions

In the past, some deferred profit-sharing plans have provided for the automatic distribution of plan assets to employees (during active employment) after the completion of a stated period of participation or after the lapse of a fixed period of years.[28] Other plans provided employees with the option to withdraw portions of the moneys in their individual accounts on "the attainment of a stated age or upon the prior occurrence of some event such as layoff, illness, disability, retirement, death, or severance of employment." Distributions to participants on these prescribed occasions are permitted under Reg. 1.401–1(b)(1)(ii). Distributions of

---

28 The inclusion of such provisions is prohibited in IRC Section 401(k) cash or deferred profit-sharing plans. In general, withdrawal provisions applicable to 401(k) plans are much more restrictive than the rules that apply to traditional deferred profit-sharing plans as described here. The reader is referred to Chapter 27 for a discussion of these more restrictive provisions.

profit-sharing funds made sooner than the occurrence of any one of the aforementioned events may lead to the disqualification of the plan.

An employee's right to withdraw funds from a deferred profit-sharing plan is dependent on the actual plan provisions because the plan is under no legal obligation to permit such distributions. In fact, some plans do not permit withdrawals prior to a participant's termination of employment. In any event, only vested amounts are available to be withdrawn.

When a profit-sharing plan provides for automatic distributions (or permits voluntary withdrawals) after a fixed number of years, IRS regulations require that only funds that have been deposited for at least two years be distributed. Thus, if employer contributions have been credited to a participant's account for three years, only contributions made in the first year plus investment income credited that year, are eligible to be withdrawn.[29] Of course, distributions of funds held less than two years may be made in the event of ". . . disability, retirement, death, or the occurrence of an event (such as completion of five years of participation) . . ." without affecting qualification. Further, distributions of moneys held less than two years may be made upon the showing of "hardship" if this term is sufficiently defined and consistently applied under the plan. In any event, the actual amounts withdrawn are taxable to the participant in the year in which the distribution is received and will be subject to an additional 10 percent tax if the amounts are deemed to constitute "premature" distributions (see *infra*). Thus, the automatic and other early distributions from profit-sharing plans are not particularly attractive from a tax standpoint.

Relative Advantages and Disadvantages of Loans and Withdrawals

Plan provisions permitting loans or withdrawals prior to termination of employment provide participants with much added flexibility. Employees may use these funds for down payments on homes, children's college education expenses, or other financial needs. A potential disadvantage is that these provisions (particularly withdrawal provisions) may prevent the plan from accumulating sufficient funds at retirement.

Loan provisions have certain inherent advantages over withdrawal provisions. Specifically, funds made available through a loan do not create

---

29 After completion of five years of participation in the plan, an employee is legally permitted to withdraw all employer contributions credited to his or her account, including moneys contributed during the two years preceding the date of withdrawal. The completion of five years of participation is an "event" within the meaning of Reg. 1.401–1(b)(1)(ii), making the two-year rule inapplicable.

taxable income to the borrowing employee. In addition, since loans are likely to be repaid, the retirement income objective of the profit-sharing plan is protected. Some potential disadvantages of loan provisions are as follows:

1. The administrative expense associated with processing loans.
2. An employee objection to being charged interest on his or her "own money."
3. A reduction in overall investment earnings to the trust when the loan interest rate is below the earnings rate at which the trustee could otherwise invest the borrowed funds.[30]

Previously, profit-sharing plans containing withdrawal provisions had to be concerned with the "constructive receipt doctrine." The question arose whether the right to withdraw any moneys from a participant's individual account, whether or not exercised, constituted constructive receipt of all (withdrawable) moneys allocated to the account. If the constructive receipt doctrine applied, all such amounts available to be withdrawn would be taxable currently to the participant, even though the moneys are not actually withdrawn. To avoid application of the constructive receipt doctrine to amounts not withdrawn, plans usually assessed a substantial penalty (e.g., denying participation rights for six months) on employees who made withdrawals. Today, however, the constructive receipt doctrine no longer presents a problem in deferred profit-sharing plans. The Economic Recovery Tax Act of 1981 (ERTA) amended IRC Section 402(a)(1), which deals with the taxation of benefits from qualified retirement plans. Under the amended provision, distributions from qualified plans are taxed only when actually received by the participant; they are not taxed simply because they are made available to the participant. Thus, the basis for the constructive receipt doctrine has been removed from IRC Section 402(a)(1). This affects the tax treatment of all qualified plans, including profit-sharing plans, and it applies both to distributions at termination of employment and to withdrawals made by active employees. The amended provision became effective for taxable years beginning after December 31, 1981. Today, profit-sharing plans need not contain withdrawal penalties or restrictions simply to avoid constructive receipt issues. However, plan sponsors should determine whether, and to what extent, these penalties and restrictions are desirable in order to meet plan objectives and to control administrative costs.

---

30 This last disadvantage exists only to the extent that the plan treats participant loans as loans from the entire assets of the trust, rather than treating them as loans from the participants' own individual accounts.

Since the passage of the Tax Reform Act of 1986, the biggest drawback to including withdrawal provisions is the additional, nondeductible 10 percent tax on premature distributions. This additional tax is applied to early distributions from all qualified retirement plans, including profit sharing. An early distribution is one made prior to age 59½, death, or disability. Exemptions are permitted for (1) periodic annuity benefits, after separation from service, paid over the life (or life expectancy) of the employee or the joint lives (or joint life expectancies) of the employee and beneficiary; (2) distributions to an employee that are used to pay medical expenses that are deductible under IRC Section 213; (3) distributions to a participant who separated from service after age 55; (4) payments to a former spouse or dependent under a qualified domestic relations order (QDRO); and, (5) distributions made on account of plan termination, or termination of employment, that are rolled over into an individual retirement account (IRA) or into another qualified plan.

ADDITIONAL FEATURES OF DEFERRED PROFIT-SHARING PLANS

Two additional features pertaining to deferred profit-sharing plans are worthy of mention. These features relate to the inclusion of life insurance benefits and the integration of the plan with Social Security benefits.

Life Insurance Benefits

Life insurance benefits may be incorporated into the design of qualified deferred profit-sharing plans.[31] First, life insurance coverage on key personnel may be purchased by the trust as an investment. It can be argued that the profit-sharing trust has an insurable interest in the lives of certain employees who are "key" to the successful operation of the firm. These key employees may include officers, stockholder-employees, and certain other employees of the company. Contributions to the profit-sharing trust are dependent on the continued success and profitability of the firm. If future profitability is contingent on the performance of these key employees, the profit-sharing trust is likely to suffer a substantial reduction in

---

31 Only a limited treatment of life insurance in qualified profit-sharing plans is provided here. For more information, see Allen, Melone, Rosenbloom, and VanDerhei, *Pension Planning*, 8th ed. (New York, NY: McGraw-Hill, 1997), p. 150; and McGill, Brown, Haley, Schieber, *Fundamentals of Private Pensions*, 6th ed. (Philadelphia, PA: University of Pennsylvania Press, 1996) pp. 272-275.

future contribution levels upon the death of one or more of these individuals. Under these circumstances, if permitted by the trust agreement, the trustee may protect the profit-sharing trust against potential adverse consequences by purchasing insurance on the lives of the key employees. In such cases, the life insurance contracts are purchased and owned by the trust, with the necessary premiums paid out of trust assets. The trust is designated as the beneficiary under such contracts, and at the key employee's death the insurance proceeds are allocated among the individual participant accounts, generally according to the size of the respective account balances.[32]

Second, most deferred profit-sharing plans provide a benefit payable at the death of a participant. At a minimum, a death benefit equal to the participant's individual account balance is generally paid. Reg. 1.401–1(b)(1)(ii), however, permits amounts allocated to participants' accounts to be used to purchase incidental amounts of life insurance coverage. There are several reasons why a participant might want explicit life insurance benefits provided under the profit-sharing plan including (1) the relatively small accumulation (and, consequently, available death benefits) in the participant's account during the early years of participation; and (2) inadequate amounts of coverage provided under the employer's group life insurance program.

Profit-sharing contributions used to purchase life insurance on plan participants are subject to certain limitations. However, the limitations are sufficiently liberal that, in many cases, it is possible for plan participants to acquire substantial amounts of life insurance coverage. Specifically, if the funds used to pay life insurance premiums have been accumulated in the participant's account for at least two years, or if the funds are used to purchase either an endowment or a retirement-income contract, there are no IRS limits on the amount of life insurance that can be purchased (or the portion of the account balance that may be used to pay premiums). If neither of these requirements is met, the aggregate amount of funds used to pay life insurance premiums must be less than one-half of the total

---

32 In contrast to the purchase of life insurance on plan participants (see *infra*), the purchase of life insurance on key employees, for the collective benefit of the trust, does not create any current income tax liability for the participants. Furthermore, the tests requiring that life insurance be incidental in amount do not apply to the types of life insurance purchases described above. However, as a practical matter, the trust is not likely to invest a substantial portion of its assets in such life insurance coverage. Also, under ERISA's fiduciary provisions, the trustee is under the obligation to show that the purchase of life insurance on key personnel is a prudent investment and in the best interests, collectively, of the plan participants.

contributions and forfeitures allocated to the participant's account. Additional restrictions pertaining to the inclusion of life insurance (on plan participants) in profit-sharing plans are that (1) the plan must require the trustee to convert the entire value of the life insurance contract at or prior to retirement either to cash or to provide periodic income (in order that no portion of such value is available to continue life insurance protection into the retirement years), or to distribute the insurance contract to the participant; and (2) the participant must treat the value of the pure life insurance protection as taxable income each year.

To maintain its qualified status, a plan must meet the requirements of Reg. 1.401–1(b)(1)(ii). However, life insurance need not be purchased on all plan participants to achieve qualification. Rather, the purchase of life insurance can be the decision of individual participants (with some electing coverage and others not) so long as all participants are offered the same opportunity. To accomplish this, the trust agreement should expressly allow each participant, individually, to direct the trustee to purchase specific investments (e.g., insurance contracts) and "earmark" them for the participant's account. Normally, the trustee is the applicant and owner of any life insurance contracts purchased on the lives of the plan participants. In addition, the trustee pays the premiums on the policies, although these amounts are then charged directly to the individual accounts of those participants electing insurance coverage. Typically, the insured participants designate their own personal beneficiaries. In this case, death proceeds are paid by the insurer directly to the named personal beneficiary. If the trustee is designated as beneficiary, the death proceeds are paid to the trustee, who, in turn, credits the proceeds to the deceased participant's account.

Integration with Social Security

Deferred profit-sharing plans are seldom integrated with the benefits payable under Social Security (OASDI). A major reason is that any "employee incentive" objective sought by the employer would tend to be diminished by a plan design that calls for contributions at a lower rate on behalf of employees earning less than a specified minimum.

If a profit-sharing plan is to be integrated, it must be done on a step-rate excess-earnings basis. This requires that an integration level be established. The integration level is a chosen dollar amount such that the employer contribution rate differs between earnings above and below this amount. Specifically, the employer contribution rate is greater on compensation in excess of the integration level. While lesser dollar amounts are permitted, the integration level often is defined as the current Social Security maximum taxable wage base (e.g., $80,400 in 2001).

Current law requires that the *difference* between the employer contribution rate applied to compensation in excess of the integration level and the contribution rate applied to compensation below the integration level not exceed the *lesser* of: (1) 5.7 percent (or the tax rate for the old-age insurance portion of OASDI, if greater), or (2) the contribution rate applied to compensation below the integration level.[33] To illustrate, if a 3 percent contribution rate is applied to earnings below the integration level, a maximum of 6 percent can be contributed on excess compensation above the integration level. Similarly, if the employer contributes 7 percent on earnings below the integration level, no more than 12.7 percent can be applied to excess compensation.[34]

Frequently, an employer sponsors both a pension plan and a deferred profit-sharing plan covering the same overlapping group of employees. If both plans are integrated, the regulations prohibit the combined integration under both plans from exceeding 100 percent of the integration capability of a single plan. If maximum integration is desired, the simplest approach is to integrate one plan fully and not integrate the other plan at all. Other combinations are permissible, however.

DISTRIBUTIONS

Earlier sections described specific events leading to distributions under profit-sharing plans. The discussion here is limited to the form and taxation of distributions from qualified deferred profit-sharing plans.

Form

Distributions from profit-sharing plans may take several forms, including lump-sum installment payments, or a paid-up annuity. Withdrawals during active employment or distributions to employees who have terminated employment (for reasons other than death, disability, or retirement)

---

33 The 5.7 percent must be reduced if the integration level utilized is less than the Social Security taxable wage base. In addition, IRC Section 401(a)(4) can permit a plan to qualify even if it violates (1) and (2) above.

34 For a general rule, let x denote the employer contribution rate applied to compensation below the integration level. Then the maximum contribution rate that can be applied to compensation in excess of the integration level is (a) $2x$, when $x < 5.7$ percent or (b) $x + 5.7$, when $x > 5.7$ percent.

generally are made in the form of a lump-sum payment.[35] At death or disability of the plan participant, distributions usually consist of lump-sum or installment payments. Distributions at retirement typically are payable either as a lump sum, in installments, or as a life annuity provided through an insurance company. To the extent that the plan permits an annuity payout form, it must satisfy ERISA's rules relating to qualified joint-and-survivor annuities.

Taxation

In general, the tax treatment of distributions from qualified profit-sharing plans is identical to the tax treatment accorded distributions from qualified pension plans. However, the tax treatment accorded distributions consisting of employer securities holds particular importance to profit-sharing plans. Profit-sharing plans are not subject to ERISA's 10 percent limitation on the investment of plan assets in employer securities and tend to invest more heavily in employer securities as a result. When employer securities are distributed as part of a lump-sum distribution under such conditions that otherwise qualify the distribution for favorable tax treatment, IRC Section 402(e)(4)(J) permits the entire net unrealized appreciation on the securities (excess of fair market value over cost basis of the securities to the trust) to escape taxation at the time of the distribution. In effect, the participant can elect, at the time of distribution, to be taxed only on the amount of the original employer contributions (i.e., the trust's cost basis) and defer the tax on any unrealized appreciation until the securities are sold at a later date. Alternatively, the participant can choose to be taxed on the entire value of the employer securities at the date of distribution.

---

35 As indicated earlier, the applicability of an additional 10 percent tax on premature distributions may cause employers to limit the availability of in-service withdrawals from profit-sharing plans. Further, when terminating employment prior to age 59½, participants may choose to roll the funds into an individual retirement account (IRA) to avoid imposition of the penalty tax.

CHAPTER 27

Section 401(k) Plans (Cash or Deferred Arrangements) and Thrift Plans*

Jack L. VanDerhei

Kelly A. Olsen

This chapter deals with Section 401(k) cash or deferred arrangements (CODAs) and thrift plans. Under a CODA, an employee can receive automatic employer contributions to a qualified retirement plan. This is no different from the way conventional deferred plans operate. With a CODA, however, the employee may also have the option of receiving the amount of the employer's contribution in cash as currently taxable income. Additionally, under a CODA, an employee is entitled to make elective contributions of amounts that could otherwise be received in cash to an employer's qualified plan on a before-tax basis, thereby reducing the employee's current taxable income and avoiding any federal (and possibly state) income tax on the amount and its investment income until it is received as a plan distribution.

A thrift plan is the name given to an employee benefit plan that promotes savings and thrift among employees by requiring participants to make periodic contributions to the plan in order to be credited with an employer contribution on his or her behalf. The amount of the employer contribution usually relates, in whole or in part, to the amount the participant contributes. These plans also are referred to as savings plans, thrift incentive plans, savings and investment plans, and by a variety of other

---

* Parts of this chapter are based on material that appears in Everett T. Allen, Jr., Joseph J. Melone, Jerry S. Rosenbloom, and Jack L. VanDerhei, *Pension Planning*, 8th ed. (Homewood, IL: Richard D. Irwin, 1997). Other portions are based on material from Chapter 31 of *The Handbook of Employee Benefits*, 4th ed.

names that generally denote an employee savings feature. Many, but not all, thrift plans have a 401(k) CODA feature.

This chapter reviews the legislative history of 401(k) CODAs and thrift plans, the technical requirements they must meet, some special considerations that must be taken into account, and their relative advantages and disadvantages to employers and employees.

401(k) CASH AND DEFERRED ARRANGEMENTS

HISTORY OF CODAS

CODAs are not a new concept; they have existed since the 1950s. Before 1972, the Internal Revenue Service (IRS) provided guidelines for qualifying "cash-option" CODAs in a series of revenue rulings.[1] In essence, more than half the total participation in the plan had to be from the lowest-paid two-thirds of all eligible employees. If this requirement was met, employees who elected to defer compensation were not considered to be in constructive receipt of the amounts involved even though they had the option to take such amounts in cash. Salary-reduction plans satisfying these requirements also were eligible for the same favorable tax treatment.

In December 1972, the IRS issued proposed regulations that stated that any compensation an employee could receive as cash would be subject to current taxation even if deferred as a contribution to the employer's qualified plan. Although directed primarily at salary-reduction plans, the proposed regulations also applied to cash-option profit-sharing plans.

As the gestation period for the Employee Retirement Income Security Act (ERISA) was coming to an end, Congress became increasingly aware of the need to devote additional time to studying the CODA concept. As a result, ERISA included a section that provided that the existing tax status for CODAs was to be frozen until the end of 1976. Plans in existence on June 27, 1974, were permitted to retain their tax-favored status; however, contributions to CODAs established after that date were to be treated as employee contributions and, as a result, were currently taxable. Unable to meet its self-imposed deadline, Congress extended the moratorium on CODAs twice, the second time until the end of 1979.

The Revenue Act of 1978 enacted permanent provisions governing CODAs by adding Section 401(k) to the Internal Revenue Code (IRC or

---

1 U.S. Department of Labor, Pension and Welfare Benefit Administration, *Abstract of 1995 Form 5500 Annual Reports* (Washington, DC: U.S. Government Printing Office, 1999).

Code), effective for plan years beginning after December 31, 1979. In essence, CODAs are now permitted, as long as certain requirements are met.

This legislation, in itself, did not result in any significant activity in the adoption of new CODAs, and it was not until 1982, after the IRS issued proposed regulations in late 1981, that employers began to respond to the benefit-planning opportunities created by this new legislation. By providing some interpretive guidelines for Section 401(k), and by specifically sanctioning salary-reduction plans, the IRS opened the way for the adoption of new plans and for the conversion of existing, conventional plans. For example, many employers converted existing after-tax thrift plans to CODAs to take advantage of the Section 401(k) tax shelter on employee contributions. CODA growth since then has been significant. By 1995 (the most recent data available), 401(k)-type plan contributions accounted for more than half of all new defined benefit and defined contribution retirement plan contributions.[2]

The Tax Reform Act of 1984 provided some subtle modifications to Section 401(k). The original specification of the nondiscrimination standards for cash or deferred plans appeared to permit integration with Social Security. This ambiguity was resolved by applying both the general coverage tests and a special actual-deferral-percentage (ADP) test to all CODAs (both are described later in this chapter). The 1984 legislation also extended cash or deferred treatment to pre-ERISA money purchase plans, although contributions were limited to the levels existing on June 27, 1974.

The changes imposed by the Tax Reform Act of 1986 (TRA '86) were much more substantive. In addition to reducing the limit on elective deferrals, this legislation provided a new definition of highly compensated employees (HCEs), restricted the ADP test, modified the list of contingencies on which distributions from CODAs are permitted, and reduced the employer's flexibility in designing eligibility requirements for these arrangements.

In 1988, the IRS released final regulations reflecting changes made by the Revenue Act of 1978 and simultaneously issued newly proposed regulations for CODAs as affected by the Tax Reform Act of 1986. The

---

2 Cash-option CODAs differ from salary-reduction CODAs. An example of a cash-option CODA is when an employer offers an employee a bonus at the end of the year and allows that employee to decide whether to take it in cash or defer it by allowing the employer to place it in a tax-exempt trust for the benefit of the employee. A salary-reduction CODA is a plan in which the employee and employer enter into a contract where the employee agrees to take a reduction in salary (either as a percent of compensation or a dollar amount), and the employer places that amount in a tax-exempt trust for the benefit of the employee.

proposed regulations were modified in May 1990, and additional guidance was contained in proposed regulations under Section 401(a)(4) in September 1990. The IRS later released final regulations replacing all the 1988 proposed and final regulations on these subjects and the amendments to regulations under Section 401(k) issued in May 1990.

The Small Business Job Protection Act of 1996 (SBJPA) applied many changes that were intended to improve 401(k) retirement benefits and coverage as well as simplify 401(k) plan sponsors' administrative requirements. Most notably for purposes of this chapter, the SBJPA created savings incentive match plans for employees (SIMPLE plans) that may be established as 401(k) plans. The legislative intent of SIMPLE plans was to create a retirement savings vehicle for small employers that was not subject to the complex rules associated with qualified plans, such as the nondiscrimination requirements. The SBJPA also created a safe-harbor contribution formula; relaxed compensation-based limitations; and simplified the definition of highly compensated employees (HCEs),[3] which, in turn, simplified nondiscrimination testing.

The Taxpayer Relief Act of 1997 (TRA '97) made less sweeping changes to 401(k) plans than did the SBJPA. Yet, like the SBJPA, the intent of the majority of the TRA '97's 401(k)-related provisions was to simplify plan administration and to increase 401(k) benefits and coverage. In this chapter, changes made by the TRA '97 are noted where they are applicable.

Recent Developments

Negative Elections

In summer 1998, the IRS issued Rev. Rul. 98-30, which gave a stamp of approval to negative elections for 401(k) plans. In a negative election 401(k) plan, a certain percentage or dollar amount (e.g., 3 percent) of each eligible employee's compensation is automatically contributed to the 401(k) plan unless the employee designates a different amount or affirmatively elects not to contribute. The negative election takes effect only after the employee has had a reasonable period following receipt of the notice to make a contrary election; either to have no withholding or to withhold salary reduction contributions at a different rate. In Rev. Rul. 98-30, the

---

3 Highly compensated employees for purposes of a given year are those who (1) were a 5 percent owner of the employer at any time during the year or the preceding year; or (2) had compensation in excess of $85,000 (in year 2001, indexed) for the preceding year and, if the employer elects, were in the top-paid 20 percent group for such year.

IRS' original guidance on negative elections, the IRS dealt only with a situation where a newly eligible employee was subject to the negative election provision. More recently, the IRS issued Rev. Rul. 2000-8, which added a situation where an existing 401(k) plan makes the automatic enrollment provision applicable to already-eligible employees who are deferring at a rate which is less than the automatic enrollment rate. Whether or not to use negative elections in a 401(k) plan is a plan fiduciary decision.

Use of Electronic Technology

Both the IRS and the Department of Labor (DOL) have issued guidance regarding the use of electronic technologies in retirement plans. In IRS Notice 99-1, the IRS proposed regulations that would permit participant consent to the receipt of benefits given electronically. They would also allow electronic delivery of the notice. In Notice 99-1, the IRS confirmed that there are no specific Code requirements regarding the use of electronic media for participant enrollments, contribution elections, investment elections, beneficiary designations (other than designations requiring spousal consent), electing direct rollovers, or plan and account information inquiries.

In January 1999, the DOL published guidance on the use of electronic technologies for satisfying ERISA's disclosure requirements. These proposed rules establish a safe-harbor method for furnishing summary plan descriptions, summary of material modifications, and summary annual reports using electronic media if certain conditions are satisfied.

TECHNICAL REQUIREMENTS FOR CODAS

Section 401(k) states that a qualified CODA is any arrangement that:[4]

1. Is part of a profit-sharing or stock-bonus plan, a pre-ERISA money purchase plan, or a rural electric cooperative plan[5] that meets the requirements of Section 401(a) of the Code.

2. Allows covered employees to elect to have the employer make salary reduction contributions to a trust under the plan on behalf

---

4 The regulations generally provide that a partnership arrangement that permits partners to vary the amount of contributions made to a plan on their behalf on a year-to-year basis will be deemed to constitute a CODA.

5 For purposes of IRS Sec. 401(k), the term *rural electric cooperative plan* means any pension plan that is a defined contribution plan and is established and maintained by a rural electric cooperative or a national association of such cooperatives. For further details see IRC Sec. 457(d)(9)(B).

of the employees rather than receiving that portion of their salary in cash.

3. Subjects amounts held by the trust that are attributable to employer contributions made pursuant to an employee's election to certain specified withdrawal limitations.

4. Provides that an employee's right to his or her accrued benefits derived from employer contributions made to the trust pursuant to his or her election is nonforfeitable.

5. Does not require, as a condition of participation in the arrangement, that an employee complete a period of service with the employer maintaining the plan in excess of one year.

As a tax-qualified plan, a CODA must meet all the general nondiscrimination requirements applicable to such plans. The special requirements for CODAs are covered in the following material. Before discussing these requirements, however, it is important to know the different types of employee and employer contributions that can be made to a CODA:

1. *Elective contributions* are amounts an employee authorizes the employer to contribute to a CODA on a pretax basis—either by way of salary reduction, in the case of a typical thrift plan, or through an election to defer, in the case of a cash-option profit-sharing plan. Elective contributions are sometimes called pretax contributions or elective deferrals.

2. *After-tax employee contributions* consist of contributions an employee is deemed to have received and taken as income.

3. *Matching contributions* are employer contributions made when an employee authorizes an elective deferral or, less typically, an employee's after-tax employee contribution.

4. *Nonelective contributions* are employer contributions made on behalf of eligible employees regardless of whether they have made elective deferrals.

5. *Qualified nonelective contributions (QNECs)* are nonelective contributions to which two special rules apply: (1) the contribution must be fully vested at all times, and (2) it generally may not be distributed to the employee on an in-service basis for any reason before the employee reaches age 59½.

6. *Qualified matching contributions (QMACs)* are matching contributions that meet the same rules a nonelective contribution must meet to become a QNEC.

7. *Safe-harbor contributions* are employer contributions made to allow a plan to meet safe-harbor requirements and avoid the need for actual deferral percentage (ADP) testing. Like QNECs, they must be fully vested and are subject to distribution restrictions.

8. *SIMPLE contributions* take the form of employer 100 percent matching contributions equal to 3 percent of the employee's compensation or nonelective contributions equal to 2 percent of compensation for each eligible employee who earns at least $5,000 during the year. Like safe-harbor contributions and QNECs, all contributions to a SIMPLE account must be fully vested.

Type of Plan

As noted, a CODA may be part of a profit-sharing or stock-bonus plan. This, of course, includes thrift and savings plans. In addition, CODAs may take the form of profit-sharing plans that meet the safe-harbor contribution requirements, which were established by the SBJPA. These plans are called "safe-harbor" plans. Finally, SIMPLE plans may be established as 401(k) plans. The only qualified defined contribution plan that cannot be established as a CODA is a post-ERISA money purchase plan.[6]

In practice, the greatest number of CODAs fall into one of two categories—either cash or deferred profit-sharing plans, or thrift and savings plans. CODAs also can be subdivided into plans that involve employer contributions only, both employer and employee contributions, and employee contributions only. Plans involving only employee contributions are not used to a great extent, largely because of the difficulty these plans experience in satisfying the special tests that are described later in this chapter.

Individual Limitations

Three individual limitations apply to CODAs: a limit on elective deferrals, a limit on the amount of compensation that can be taken into account for determining contributions and benefits, and the IRC Section 415 contribution limit.

---

6 CODAs are not available to state or local governments unless adopted before May 6, 1986. Because of the SBJPA, they are now available to many other nonprofit organizations.

Elective Deferral Limits

TRA '86 imposed a $7,000 annual limitation on the exclusion of elective deferrals. This limit is indexed annually for changes in the cost of living and reached $10,500 in 2001.[7] Any excess amounts (and investment earnings thereon) are included in the employee's gross income. This limitation applies to the aggregate elective deferral made in a taxable year to all CODAs and simplified employee pensions (SEPs, which are described in Chapter 31). The limit is reduced by any employer contributions to a tax-deferred annuity under a salary-reduction agreement; however, the limitation is increased (but not to an amount in excess of $10,500 in 2001) by the amount of these employer contributions.

For SIMPLE plans, the SBJPA established an elective deferral limit of $6,000. This amount became subject to annual adjustments for changes in the cost of living (in $500 increments) under the TRA '97. As of 2001, the limitation remains unchanged at $6,500.

Elective deferrals in excess of the annual limit (plus the earnings on such amounts[8]) may be allocated among the plans under which the deferrals were made. This means that an employee may have deferred more than $10,500 (in 2001) for one year by March following the close of the taxable year, and the plan may distribute the allocated amount back to the employee by April 15. Although such a distribution will be includable in the employee's taxable income for the year to which the excess deferral relates, it will not be subject to the 10 percent excise tax that may otherwise apply to distributions prior to age 59½. Any income on the excess deferral will be treated as earned and received in the taxable year in which the excess deferral is distributable.

Any excess deferral not distributed by this date will remain in the plan, subject to all regular withdrawal restrictions and penalties. Plus, the amount will again be treated as taxable income when it is later distributed. Finally, the amount will be taken into account in applying the special nondiscrimination tests.

Compensation Base Limit

This limit caps the amount of compensation that can be taken into account for most qualified plan purposes, including the determination of contri-

---

7 Pursuant to the TRA '97, matching contributions made to a 401(k) plan on behalf of partners and sole proprietors are not subject to this limit. The only exception is if the employer uses matching contributions on behalf of non-highly compensated employees (NHCEs) to satisfy the ADP test, then the matching contributions of the partners or sole proprietor will be subject to the limit on elective deferrals.

8 Plans do not need to include income for the period between the end of a plan year and the date excess amounts are distributed.

butions and benefits, at $170,000 in the year 2001 (indexed to changes in the cost of living). The exception is SIMPLE plans, under which non-elective contributions are subject to the compensation cap, but matching contributions are not subject to this limitation. Pursuant to the SBJPA, private employers may define compensation to include pretax elective deferrals to a 401(k) plan and deferrals under a cafeteria plan.

Section 415 Contribution Limit

IRC Section 415 imposes limits on the contributions and benefits that might be provided for an employee under qualified plans. The Section 415 contribution limit restricts the amount that can be added to an employee's account each year by the employee and/or the employer to the smaller of: (1) 25 percent of the employee's compensation, or (2) $35,000 (indexed to changes in the cost of living).

These limitations should affect only a few, if any, employees in most situations. Nevertheless, it is important that they be observed. A plan will be disqualified if it violates these limitations and does not remedy the problem within the manner and time period prescribed by the IRS.

Nondiscrimination in Coverage

To be qualified, a CODA (with certain exceptions for SIMPLE and safe-harbor plans) must satisfy the general coverage provisions for all quali-fied plans. A plan must satisfy any one of the minimum coverage tests under Code 410(b).

In applying these requirements, it is permissible to exclude from consideration any employees covered by a collective bargaining agree-ment if there is evidence that retirement benefits were the subject of good-faith bargaining. It also is possible to exclude nonresident aliens who receive no income from the employer from sources within the United States, certain airline pilots, and employees not meeting minimum age and service requirements.

Nondiscrimination in Contributions

ADP and ACP Tests for Non-SIMPLE and Non-Safe-Harbor Plans

For a CODA to be qualified, the contributions under the plan must be nondiscriminatory. To satisfy this requirement, the plan must meet an ADP test by the close of each plan year.

The first step in applying this test is to determine the ADP for each eligible employee; that is, the percentage of each eligible employee's salary that is deferred into the plan. Plans may use prior-year data for non-highly compensated employees (NHCEs).[9] The percentage of each eligible employee's salary that is deferred into the plan is computed by dividing the amount of an employee's elective deferrals (contributions) by the amount of the employee's compensation. In addition, the employer may include in the numerator any matching or nonelective contributions that satisfy the CODA nonforfeitability and distribution requirements (described later in this chapter). Excess deferrals must be taken into account in this testing even if they later are distributed to comply with the annual cap on elective deferrals (as discussed previously).

For purposes of a 401(k) plan, compensation refers to compensation as defined by IRC Section 414(s). An employer may limit the period taken into account to that portion of the plan year or calendar year in which the employee was an eligible employee, provided that this limit is applied uniformly to all eligible employees under the plan.

It should be noted that this percentage is determined individually for all eligible employees, whether or not they actually participate. Thus, the ADP for an eligible but nonparticipating employee is zero. For this reason, employers often provide incentives to encourage eligible employees—particularly those who are lower-paid—to participate, as discussed below.

The next step is to divide the eligible employees into two groups—the HCEs and all other eligible employees (the NHCEs). For each of these groups, the individual ADP for each employee is computed, and the group average is found. If the average ADP for the HCEs does not exceed the average ADP for the NHCEs by more than the allowable percentage, the test is satisfied for the year. Formulas for the allowable percentages are set forth in Table 27-1.

Note that the ADP test determines a maximum average ADP for the HCEs and does not indicate the maximum deferral percentage for any individual in this group. As long as the average deferral percentage for the HCEs as a group is less than or equal to the maximum allowed, it is permissible for an individual in this group to defer an amount in excess of that limitation.

If any HCE is a participant under two or more CODAs of the employer, all such CODAs will be treated as one CODA for purposes of determining the employee's ADP.

---

9 However, once this election is made, it cannot be reversed for future years without approval from the IRS.

T A B L E   27-1

Maximum Allowable Average ADPs for Highly Compensated Employees

If Average ADP for Non-highly Compensated Employees (ADP$_{NHC}$) Is:	Then Average ADP for Highly Compensated Employees (ADP$_{HC}$) May Not Exceed:
Less than 2 percent	2 times ADP$_{NHC}$
At least 2 percent but less than 8 percent	ADP$_{NHC}$ plus 2 percent
8 percent or more	1.25 times ADP$_{NHC}$

Examples

1. If the ADP for the non-highly compensated employees is determined to be 1 percent, then the ADP for the highly compensated employees can be as much as 2 percent (2 × 1%).

2. If the ADP for the non-highly compensated employees is determined to be 4 percent, then the ADP for the highly compensated employees can be as much as 6 percent (4% + 2%).

3. If the ADP for the non-highly compensated employees is 10 percent, the ADP for the highly compensated employees can be as much as 12.5 percent (1.25 × 10%).

Where a plan combines salary deferral with employer contributions and/or employee after-tax contributions, it is necessary to satisfy a multiple-use test based on both the ADP and the actual contributions percentage (ACP) tests.[10] The average contribution percentage for each group of employees is the average of the contribution percentages of all employees in that group. The contribution percentage of each individual is determined by dividing the sum of the employee's own contributions (both basic and voluntary) and the employer's matching contributions made on the employee's behalf during the year by the amount of compensation that he or she received during the year.

If a plan must meet both the ADP and ACP tests, there is a restriction on the multiple-use of the alternative limitation—in other words, one of these tests must be met using the basic, or 125 percent, test. An aggregate limit test is available for plans that can pass each test only by using

---

10 It is important to note that the regulations do not allow the full flexibility inherent in Table 27-1 for both ADP and ACP tests simultaneously. Specifically, the mathematical formula represented by the first two rows in the right-hand column of the table may only be used for one of the two tests.

the alternative limitation. The first step in this test is to add up the ADP and ACP for HCEs to arrive at the "aggregate HCE percentage." Then, the *larger* of the ADP or ACP for the NHCEs is multiplied by 1.25. Next, the *smaller* of the ADP or the ACP for NHCEs is multiplied by two. The resulting product is compared with the sum of two plus the *smaller* of the NHCE ADP or ACP. Whichever of the two results is smaller is added to the result produced from the 125 percent test. If the resulting sum equals or exceeds the aggregate HCE percentage, the aggregate limit test is passed. This test also can be run in a different way by reversing the items just described. Thus, the *smaller* of the NHCE ADP or ACP is multiplied by 1.25, and it is the *larger* of the NHCE ADP or ACP that is multiplied by or added to two. The employer may choose whichever way produces the most favorable result.

Safe-Harbor 401(k) Plans

As a result of the SBJPA, a CODA plan sponsor will no longer have to worry about nondiscrimination tests for elective contributions starting in 1999 if the employer satisfies one of two safe harbors by either: (1) providing certain matching contributions to NHCEs, or (2) making a contribution of 3 percent of compensation for all employees, regardless of whether these employees contribute to the plan. Also, ACP testing is not required for matching contributions if: (1) the plan provides for a safe-harbor matching contribution, and (2) no match is provided on contributions in excess of 6 percent of compensation. (The ACP test is still required, however, for after-tax employee contributions.)

The safe-harbor matching contribution must be at least 100 percent of the first 3 percent of pay contributed and 50 percent of the next 2 percent of pay contributed. Other formulas for matching contributions will qualify for this safe-harbor treatment if the formula provides an amount of matching contribution at least as large as the safe-harbor formula and the percent matched does not increase as the employee's contribution increases. In addition, the rate of match for HCEs cannot be greater than the rate of match for NHCEs.

To meet the safe-harbor requirements, eligible employees must be informed of their opportunity to participate in the CODA prior to the beginning of the year, and the matching contributions used to satisfy the safe-harbor must be fully vested and subject to the same restrictions on distributions as QNECs or QMACs—that is, they can be distributed only on account of separation from service, death, disability, or attainment of age 59½.

While these safe harbors eliminate the need and expense of annual testing, as well as the necessity of recharacterizing (described below) or refunding excess contributions, they can result in additional plan costs caused by the full-vesting and annual-notice requirements.

The IRS issued IRS Notice 2000-3, which modified Notice 98-52, which made the following changes to the 401(k) safe-harbor rules:

- Providing an extended period of time—until May 1, 2000—for 401(k) plan sponsors adopting the 401(k) safe-harbor methods for the first time in 2000 to provide the required safe-harbor notice to employees, assuming the employer contribution and other safe-harbor requirements are met for the entire plan year.

- Permitting 401(k) safe-harbor plans to match pretax or after-tax employee contributions on the basis of compensation for a payroll period, month or quarter, if the plan so provides and if the matching contributions are actually contributed to the plan by the last day of the following plan year quarter.

- Encouraging adoption of 401(k) safe-harbor plans by allowing sponsors of existing 401(k) plans to wait as late as December 1 of a calendar plan year to decide to adopt the 3-percent employer nonelective contribution method for that calendar plan year, if the employer has given employees prior notice of this possibility.

- Permitting plan sponsors using the 401(k) safe-harbor matching contribution method to exit the safe-harbor prospectively during a plan year (and adopt ADP and ACP nondiscrimination testing) if employees are notified beforehand and given a chance to change their contribution levels.

- Permitting 401(k) safe-harbor plans to provide matching contributions on an employee's aggregate pretax and after-tax contributions.

- Permitting plan sponsors to provide the 401(k) safe-harbor notice to employees electronically if employees are also able to request a paper version, and otherwise simplifying the notice requirement by allowing the notice to cross-reference the plan's summary plan description for certain required information.

SIMPLE Plans

As indicated previously, the legislative intent of SIMPLE plans was to create a retirement savings vehicle for small employers that was not subject to the complex rules associated with qualified plans, such as the nondiscrimination requirements. In exchange, SIMPLE 401(k) plans must meet very specific contribution rules. Employers must either match 100 percent of employee plan contributions equal to 3 percent of the employee's compensation or make nonelective contributions equal to 2 percent of compensation for each eligible employee who earns at least $5,000 during the year. See Chapter 31 for a complete description of SIMPLE-IRA plans.

Nondiscrimination Rules for Combined Plans

Except for safe-harbor and SIMPLE plans, if a CODA consists of both elective contributions and nonelective contributions, the nonelective portion of the plan must satisfy the general coverage tests for all qualified plans and the general nondiscrimination requirements with regard to contributions. Elective deferrals under a CODA may not be taken into account for purposes of determining whether a plan has met these requirements.

Combined plans can satisfy the nondiscrimination requirements by one of two methods. In both cases, the nonelective portion must satisfy the general coverage rules; however, the special CODA qualification rules may be met either by the elective portion of the plan alone or the combined elective and nonelective portions of the plan.

The following example, adapted from Proposed Regulation Section 1.401(k)-1, illustrates the application of these rules. An employer with nine employees maintains and contributes to a profit-sharing plan the following amounts:

- 6 percent of each employee's compensation, where such amounts do not satisfy the Section 401(k) nonforfeitability and distribution requirements;
- 2 percent of each employee's compensation, where such amounts do satisfy the Section 401(k) nonforfeitability and distribution requirements; and
- Up to 3 percent of each employee's compensation, which the employee may elect to receive as a direct cash payment or to contribute to the plan.

In 2000, employees M through S received compensation and deferred contributions as indicated:

Employee	Compensation	Elective contributions	Actual deferral ratio (percent)
M	$100,000	$3,000	3
N	85,000	1,600	2
O	60,000	1,800	3
P	40,000	0	0
Q	30,000	0	0
R	20,000	0	0
S	20,000	0	0

Assuming that none of the employees is a 5 percent owner, only employees M and N are HCEs. The ADP test will not be satisfied if only the elective contributions are measured, because the average ADP for the NHCEs is 0.6 percent, and as can be seen from Table 27–1, the maximum allowable average ADP for the HCEs also would be 1.2 percent (2 × 0.6 percent). As a result of the fact that the HCEs generated an average ADP of 2.5 percent in this example, the combined plan would not satisfy the nondiscrimination tests.

However, the nondiscrimination test may be satisfied if the elective contributions meet the Section 401(k) nonforfeitability and distribution requirements. In that case, the average ADP for the NHCEs will be 2.6 percent (0.6 percent elective + 2 percent nonelective) and, as can be seen from the table, this would allow a maximum average ADP for the HCEs of 4.6 percent (2.6 percent + 2 percent). The actual average ADP for the HCEs is 4.5 percent (2.5 percent elective + 2 percent nonelective). Therefore, the ADP test is not violated.

Note that the plan also must satisfy the coverage requirements described earlier. However, there will be no difficulty satisfying such a test in this example, because all employees were eligible to benefit under the arrangement.

Increasing the Probability that the ADP Test Is Met

There are several ways in which an employer can minimize or eliminate the possibility that a plan will not meet the ADP test. Some of the techniques that might be used for this purpose are listed here.

1. The plan can be designed so that it is automatically in compliance. That is, the plan can be designed so that even under the worst case scenario in which HCEs' accounts receive maximum contributions and

NHCEs' accounts receive none at all, the plan will always satisfy the ADP test. For example, the employer can make an across-the-board nonelective 5 percent contribution for all employees that satisfies the CODA nonforfeitability and distribution requirements. Employees can then be given the option of contributing up to 1.5 percent of pay by way of salary reduction, and the plan will always satisfy the ADP test since the maximum allowable average ADP for the HCEs could be as much as 7 percent (5 percent + 2 percent) but, in fact, does not exceed 6.5 percent (5 percent nonelective + 1.5 percent elective).

2. The plan can be designed to encourage maximum participation from the NHCEs. This can be done under a savings plan, for example, by providing for higher levels of employer contributions with respect to lower pay levels.

3. Limits can be placed on the maximum amounts allowed to be deferred.

4. The plan can include a provision allowing the employer to adjust deferrals (either upward or downward) if the plan is in danger of failing to meet the ADP test (as opposed to recharacterizing the deferrals as after-tax contributions or refunding them, as described below).

5. The employer can make additional nonelective contributions at the end of the plan year to the extent necessary to satisfy the test. (Such contributions, of course, would have to satisfy the CODA nonforfeitability and distribution requirements.)

6. Contributions for a plan year can be determined in advance of the plan year and, once established on a basis that satisfies the ADP test, fixed on an irrevocable basis (except, possibly, that NHCEs could be given the option of increasing their contributions).

Eliminating Excess Contributions

An excess attributable to a failure of the ADP test is called an excess contribution. Excess contributions are defined as the difference between: (1) the aggregate amount of employer contributions actually paid over to the trust on behalf of HCEs for such a plan year, and (2) the maximum allowable contributions for HCEs, based on the average ADP for NHCEs as shown in Table 27–1. If the ADP tests are not satisfied, the plan must eliminate excess contributions to keep the plan qualified.

A CODA will not be treated as failing to meet the ADP requirements for any plan year if one of two conditions is met before the close of the following plan year:

1. The amount of the excess contributions for such plan year (and any income allocable to such contributions[11]) is distributed.

2. To the extent provided in regulations, the employee elects to treat the amount of the excess contributions as an amount distributed to the employee and then contributed by the employee on an after-tax basis to the plan. (This procedure is known as *recharacterization.*)

Excess contributions were once distributed by returning contributions made on behalf of HCEs in order of the actual deferral percentages beginning with the highest of such percentages. The SBJPA changed the method for correcting excess contributions by requiring employers to return the excess starting with the HCEs who have the highest dollar amounts rather than those who have the highest deferral or aggregate contribution percentages. Returns must be made under this procedure until one of the following occurs:

1. The ADP test is satisfied (that is, the relationship between ADP_{nhc} and the adjusted ADP_{hc} satisfies the requirements expressed in Table 27–1).

2. The ADP for the HCE with the largest ADP is reduced to the level of the HCE with the second-largest ADP.

Successive iterations of this procedure are continued until the ADP test is satisfied.

Distributions of excess contributions (and income) may be made without regard to any other provision of law (e.g., qualified domestic relations orders (QDROs) will not be violated). Moreover, although the returned amounts are treated as taxable income to the employee, the 10 percent penalty tax on early distributions from qualified retirement plans does not apply to any amount required to be distributed under this provision.

Although the plan has until the close of the following plan year to distribute or recharacterize excess contributions to avoid disqualification, an excess contribution may result in a 10 percent penalty for the employer unless it is distributed (together with any income allocable thereto) before the close of the first two and one-half months of the following plan year. Any amount distributed or recharacterized will be treated as received and earned by the recipient in his or her taxable year for which the contribution was made.

---

11 Plans do not need to include income for the period between the end of a plan year and the date excess amounts are distributed to participants.

For nondiscrimination purposes, recharacterized amounts are treated as employee contributions for the year in which the elective contribution would have been received (but for the deferral election). Thus they must be tested under the ACP tests. In addition, recharacterized amounts are subject to the CODA withdrawal restrictions, they must be nonforfeitable, and they will count against the employer's maximum deductible limit.

Nonforfeitability Requirements

The value of all elective contributions to a CODA must be fully vested at all times. The value of nonelective contributions must vest in accordance with one of ERISA's prescribed vesting standards.[12] It should be noted, however, that the vested amount of elective contributions cannot be considered for this purpose. Thus, the vesting of nonelective contributions must be accomplished independently.

Distribution Requirements

Limitations on Withdrawals

A common provision in many profit-sharing and savings plans permits an actively employed participant to make a withdrawal of some part of his or her vested account balance. Sometimes this withdrawal right is limited to hardship situations, but more often a withdrawal can be made for any reason subject to some period of suspension from plan participation.

In the case of a CODA, in-service withdrawals are severely limited. The value of elective contributions (and nonelective contributions that are aggregated with elective contributions to meet the special CODA nondiscrimination rules) are distributable only on one of the following conditions:

1. Death.
2. Disability.
3. Separation from service.
4. The termination of the plan, provided no successor defined-contribution plan (other than an ESOP or SEP) is established.[13]

---

12 Two vesting standards are available (unless the plan is top-heavy). The first standard requires that all accrued benefits must be 100 percent vested after five years of service. The second standard permits graded vesting, with 20 percent of accrued benefits vesting after three years of service and that percentage increasing in 20 percent multiples each year until 100 percent vesting is achieved after seven years.

13 A successor plan does not include a plan that does not overlap the 401(k) plan (that is, a plan under which fewer than 2 percent of employees eligible for the 401(k) plan are eligible).

5. The sale of substantially all of the assets used by the corporation in a trade or business if the employee continues employment with the corporation acquiring the assets.

6. The sale of a corporation's interest in a subsidiary if the employee continues employment with the subsidiary.

Distributions on account of a plan termination or because of a sale of a subsidiary or assets must be a distribution of the participant's entire interest in the plan. The Technical and Miscellaneous Revenue Act of 1988 (TAMRA) expanded these exceptions to cover other transactions that have the effect of sales of assets or subsidiaries.[14]

Hardship Withdrawals

In the case of profit-sharing or stock-bonus plans, distributions of elective contributions are permitted at age 59½, or before 59½ for hardships. However, hardship withdrawals are limited to the amount of an employee's elective deferrals, without investment income. Although not specified in the regulations, the IRS has allowed a plan provision permitting withdrawal of employer contributions on account of hardship, as long as it does not exceed the participant's vested account.

Limiting the withdrawal of elective contributions to hardship cases can be of significance to many employers, because it can have a negative effect on the participation of lower-paid employees, thus creating problems in meeting the ADP test. The regulations define hardship in a very narrow way. The hardship must be caused by immediate and heavy financial needs of the employee for which other resources are not reasonably available.[15] Plans may use a "safe harbor" under which certain expenses are deemed to be heavy and immediate needs. These expenses include: medical expenses (and amounts needed in advance to obtain medical care) for the employee, spouse, and dependents; the purchase (excluding mortgage payments) of a principal residence for the employee; the payment of tuition (and related medical fees) for the next 12 months of post-

---

14 To qualify for the exception, the Technical and Miscellaneous Revenue Act of 1988 (TAMRA) reconfirms that distributions upon termination of a plan without the establishment or maintenance of another defined-contribution plan (other than an ESOP), or upon disposition of assets or disposition of a subsidiary, must be lump-sum distributions without regard to the age 59½ requirement, as well as other required events for income-averaging eligibility, the election of the lump-sum-distribution treatment requirement, and the five-year minimum plan participation requirement.

15 Plans may ignore the fact that the expense was foreseeable or voluntarily incurred by the employee. Employers are permitted to make changes in the hardship distribution rules (even for existing account balances) without causing a prohibited cutback in accrued benefits.

secondary education for the employee, spouse, children, and dependents; and a payment to prevent eviction from or foreclosure on the employee's principal residence.

The plan may reasonably rely on the employee's representation that a heavy and immediate financial need cannot be met by insurance; reasonable liquidation of assets of the employee, spouse, or children (unless protected by the Uniform Rights to Minors Act); cessation of the employee's 401(k) or after-tax contributions to the plan; other distributions or loans from any plans maintained by the participant's current employer or any previous employer; or by a loan from any commercial source on reasonable terms.

A plan may provide that a distribution will be deemed necessary to satisfy a financial need if all of the following requirements are met:

- The distribution is not in excess of the amount necessary to meet the need.
- The employee has taken all distributions available and all loans permissible under all plans maintained by the employer.
- The employee is precluded from making any 401(k) or after-tax contributions to any plan maintained by the employer for a period of 12 months.
- The employee's 401(k) contributions of the following taxable year are limited to the $7,000 (adjusted) annual limit reduced by the amount of 401(k) contributions made in the taxable year when the hardship withdrawal was made.

Hardship distributions may be grossed up for federal, state, and local taxes and penalties, including the 10 percent additional income tax on early distributions.

Nonhardship In-Service Withdrawals

It should be noted that some amounts might still be available for non-hardship, in-service withdrawals. As already noted, nonelective contributions may be withdrawn (unless they are designated to be part of the ADP test). In addition, even elective contributions may be withdrawn from a profit-sharing or stock-bonus plan on a nonhardship basis after the employee attains age 59½.

OTHER CONSIDERATIONS FOR CODAS

The preceding discussion dealt with the requirements of federal tax law for the qualification of CODAs. There are, however, other issues that must be addressed. The following section discusses the federal income taxation of

CODA distributions and the status of elective contributions for purposes of Social Security, other employer-sponsored plans, and state and local taxes. It also discusses the express limits on 401(k) contributions, the treatment of excess deferrals, the effect of such contributions on deduction limits, and the Section 415 limitations on contributions and benefits.

Federal Income Taxation of CODA Distributions

CODA distributions arising out of employer contributions, before-tax employee contributions, and investment income (on all contributions) are subject to the same federal income tax treatment as any other qualified plan distribution when the employee has no cost basis.[16] If after-tax employee contributions were made to the CODA, a portion of the withdrawal will be excluded from federal income tax; otherwise, the entire withdrawal will be taxable. Moreover, with certain limited exceptions, a 10 percent penalty tax will apply to distributions (other than those that are not subject to the regular federal income tax because they are returns of employee contributions) made before the participant's death, disability, or attainment of age 59½.[17]

---

16 Briefly, IRC Section 72 provides that an employee's cost basis includes the following:
- The aggregate of any amounts the employee contributed on an after-tax basis while employed.
- The aggregate of the prior insurance costs the employee has reported as taxable income, but only for distributions made under that policy. (If the employee has made contributions and the plan provides that employee contributions will first be used to pay any cost of insurance, the employee's reportable income for any year is the excess, if any, of the insurance cost of protection over the amount of the employee's contribution for the year, and not the full cost of insurance protection.)
- Other contributions made by the employer that already have been taxed to the employee. An example could be where the employer has maintained a nonqualified plan that later was qualified.
- Loans from the qualified retirement plan to the participant that were treated as taxable distributions.
- There also is provision for the inclusion of other items in an employee's cost basis, such as contributions made by the employer after 1950 but before 1963 while the employee was a resident of a foreign country. For the most part, however, the items listed above will constitute an employee's cost basis in the typical situation.

17 Specifically, exceptions are granted if the distributions are:
1. Part of a series of substantially equal periodic payments made for the life (or life expectancy) of the employee or the joint lives (or joint life expectancies) of the employee and his or her beneficiary.
2. Used to pay medical expenses to the extent the expenses exceed 7 percent of adjusted gross income.
3. Payments to alternate payees pursuant to a qualified domestic relations order (QDRO).

Social Security

Originally, elective contributions to a CODA were not considered to be wages for purposes of Social Security. Thus, they were not subject to Social Security (FICA) tax, nor were they taken into account when calculating Social Security benefits.

This was changed by the 1983 Social Security amendments. As of 1984, elective contributions are considered as wages for Social Security (and federal unemployment insurance) purposes. Thus, FICA taxes are paid on such amounts (if they are under the taxable wage base) and are taken into account when calculating an employee's Social Security benefits.

Other Employer-Sponsored Plans

A matter of some concern to employers was the question of whether an employee's elective contributions could be considered as part of the compensation base for purposes of other tax-qualified plans. This uncertainty was resolved in 1983 when the IRS ruled that the inclusion (or exclusion) of elective contributions under a CODA as compensation in a defined benefit pension plan does not cause the pension plan to be discriminatory. The IRS also noted that the inclusion of nonelective contributions will still be subject to the discrimination standards.

Employers also maintain other pay-related employee benefit plans. These include short- and long-term disability income plans, group term life insurance, survivor income benefits, and, in some cases, medical expense benefit plans. There appear to be no legal reasons why pay, for the purpose of these plans, cannot be defined to include elective contributions made under a CODA. If such contributions are to be included, care should be taken to make sure that necessary plan and/or insurance contract amendments are made so that compensation is properly defined.

To be qualified, a CODA must not condition any other benefit provided by the employer, either directly or indirectly, on the employee electing to have the employer make or not make contributions under the arrangement. This does not apply to matching contributions.

Prior to the SBJPA, employers that sponsored both defined benefit and defined contribution plans were subject to combined limitations on benefit accruals under the defined benefit plans and on allocations to the defined contribution plan in regard to employees who participated in both plans. Pursuant to the SBJPA, the combined limitation no longer applies.

State and Local Taxes

The treatment of elective contributions under state and local tax laws is not uniform. For years, many states followed principles of federal tax law in the treatment of employee benefits. This practice was also followed by many local governments that impose some form of income tax.

With the increased use of individual retirement accounts (IRAs) in the 1980s, and with the publicity that CODAs have received, concern has grown among state and local tax authorities over the potential loss of tax revenue. As a result, the question of state and local taxation of elective contributions has become an important issue.

At this time, the tax treatment of these amounts is uncertain in many jurisdictions. Some state and local authorities have indicated that they will follow federal tax law. However, a few have announced that elective contributions will be taxable and subject to employer withholding. It seems reasonable to expect that many more state and local authorities will adopt this latter position.

Deduction Limits

IRC Section 404 imposes limits on the amount an employer can deduct for contributions made to qualified plans. For profit-sharing plans, this limit is expressed as 15 percent of the payroll of the employees covered. The only exception is SIMPLE 401(k) contributions, which TRA '97 established as deductible even if they exceed the 15 percent of compensation limit that applies to profit-sharing 401(k) plans. If the employer has both a defined benefit plan and a defined contribution plan, the combined limit is 25 percent of the covered payroll.

Elective contributions affect the maximum deduction in two ways. First, they reduce the amount of the covered payroll to which the percentage limitations apply, thus reducing the dollar amount available as a maximum deduction. Second, even though participants actually make elective contributions, they are considered to be employer contributions for purposes of plan deduction limits. As a result, elective contributions count against the amount that the employer can contribute from its own money and deduct for tax purposes.

As a practical matter, the effect of CODAs on these tax deduction limits should not be of great concern to most employers. In the past, employers who maintained liberal plans may have needed to limit the level of elective contributions permitted in order to preserve deductions for regular employer contributions. However, TRA '97 relaxed the 10 percent excise tax on nondeductible contributions by excluding elective deferrals and matching contributions from that limit.

ADVANTAGES AND DISADVANTAGES OF CODAS

Advantages

The advantages of CODAs are significant, although most of them accrue to employees, rather than to employers. Nevertheless, the advantages to employers are important.

From an employer's viewpoint, CODAs have all the advantages normally associated with any employee benefit plan. Thus, they should be of material value in attracting and retaining employees, improving employee morale, achieving a better sense of corporate identification (when employer securities are involved), and so forth. In addition, they can serve specific corporate objectives, such as increasing the level of participation in an existing plan that has had conventional after-tax employee contributions. For some employers, converting a conventional savings plan to a CODA, and thus increasing take-home pay for participating employees,[18] could alleviate pressures for additional cash compensation.

Under a CODA, employees have the flexibility of determining on a year-to-year basis whether to take a portion of their salaries in cash or to defer a portion in the form of elective contributions to the plan. Since employee needs and goals change from time to time, this element of flexibility could be important.

If a conventional savings plan is converted to a CODA, the participating employees not only realize an immediate increase in take-home pay, but their contributions are also accumulating under a tax shelter. This means that an employee can receive investment income on amounts that otherwise would have been paid in taxes. Over a period of years, the cumulative effect of accumulating interest on contributions on a tax-free

---

18 Take-home pay is increased because, for example, a $5,000 annual contribution to a non-qualified plan will reduce take-home pay by $5,000. The same $5,000 contribution to a CODA will equal $5,000 *minus* that tax that would otherwise be paid on the amount if it were included in the participant's federal (and possibly state) income tax.

basis can result in a substantially larger account balance at distribution than would otherwise be the case.

Finally, when amounts are distributed and subject to tax, the actual amount of tax paid might be considerably less than would otherwise have been the case. Installment distributions could be taxed at a lower effective tax rate (because of lower levels of taxable income and indexed tax brackets).

Disadvantages

The disadvantages of CODAs also should be recognized. From the employer's viewpoint, these plans involve complex and costly administration. Also, the employer must be prepared to deal with employee relations and other problems that can occur in any year that the plan fails to satisfy the ADP test. These plans also involve more communications efforts than are associated with conventional employee benefit plans.

From the viewpoint of employees, the disadvantages of CODAs are not as great. In fact, the only significant disadvantage is that elective contributions are subject to the previously mentioned withdrawal limitations and the possible application of the early distribution tax. This could be of major importance to some employees, particularly those at lower pay levels, and could be a barrier to their participation in the plan.

THRIFT PLANS

HISTORY OF THRIFT PLANS

With a few exceptions, all thrift plans have been established since the late 1950s. Their prevalence among employers of all sizes has grown continuously. However, their growth in the 1980s was phenomenal. This, no doubt, is due in large part to the fact that thrift plans are ideally suited to accommodate CODAs. In fact, in recent years, thrift plans are often referred to as 401(k) plans. Still, note that not all 401(k) plans are thrift plans, and not all thrift plans are 401(k) plans.

TECHNICAL REQUIREMENTS AND OTHER CONSIDERATIONS FOR THRIFT PLANS

The IRC does not generally recognize thrift plans as a separate category of deferred compensation plans. Thrift plans generally have been considered in the category of profit-sharing plans[19] and are distinguished by their employee and employer contribution patterns, which are described below.

Thrift plans generally are designed to meet the qualification requirements applicable to profit-sharing plans and therefore possess most of the general characteristics of deferred profit sharing plans (see Chapter 26). Because many thrift plans have a 401(k) feature, they also must meet the technical and other considerations discussed earlier for CODAs.

Employee and employer contribution patterns for thrift plans are discussed in greater detail following this list of these plans' significant characteristics:

1. Employee participation in the plan is voluntary and, to participate, an employee must agree to make contributions.

2. An employee usually has the option of determining the level of his or her contributions—that is, the employee may choose to make contributions at the minimum or maximum level set by the plan or at permitted intermediate levels.

3. Employer matching contributions usually match or are equal to some fraction of the contributions made by employees up to a specified level. In most thrift plans, the employer contributes a fixed percentage of employee contributions, although employer contributions sometimes are made in full or in part by means of a profit-sharing formula or on a discretionary basis.

4. Both employer and employee contributions generally are made to a trust fund.

5. Assets of the trust usually are invested in one or more investment funds, with the employee frequently having the option of choosing how his or her own contributions (and sometimes the employer contributions on the employee's behalf) are invested. In some plans, employer contributions are invested automatically in employer securities, with the employee having an investment option only for his or her own contributions.

6. An employee's account is generally paid to or on behalf of the employee in the event of retirement, death, disability, or termination of employment. Benefits on termination of employment are limited to the employee's vested interest, but thrift plans usually have relatively liberal vesting provisions.

---

19 Thrift plans also may take the form of money purchase plans that require after-tax employee contributions in order to receive an employer contribution. Unlike profit-sharing thrift plans, money-purchase thrift plans cannot provide that the employer, at its discretion, may make contributions in excess of the defined amount of contribution. (In such an instance, the requirement that money-purchase plan benefits must be definitely determinable would be violated.)

7. Most thrift plans permit an employee, during active employment, to withdraw the value of employee contributions as well as all or part of the employee's vested interest in employer contributions. Such withdrawals, however, are often subject to some form of penalty (such as a period of suspended participation). Some plans limit withdrawals to those made for specific financial needs, such as those associated with illness, the purchase of a home, college education, and the like.

Employee Contributions

As mentioned above, the requirement for employee contributions is a distinguishing characteristic of all thrift plans. This is because the amount of the employer's contributions and the predetermined formula for allocating those contributions among the participants are almost always based on the amount that each participant contributes.

Many thrift plans permit the employee contributions to be made on a tax-deferred basis. Under these arrangements, the employee contributions are deducted from the employee's pay and no federal income taxes are due on them until they are paid to the employee or his or her beneficiary. Plans that use this type of arrangement are referred to as 401(k) thrift plans and are subject to special nondiscrimination, withdrawal, and other provisions that do not apply to other thrift plans.

All thrift plans require one type of employee contribution, and some thrift plans permit a second type. The first type is that which determines the employee's share of the employer's contribution. The second type is an employee contribution in excess of the maximum employee contribution of the first type. Employee contributions of the second type have no effect whatsoever on the amount of the employer's contribution or on the employee's allocated share of the employer's contribution. For convenience, these types of employee contributions are referred to in this chapter as basic employee contributions and supplemental employee contributions, respectively.

Basic Employee Contributions

It is not necessary for a thrift plan to require or permit all participants to contribute at the same rate. Most plans permit employees to choose the amount to be contributed, up to the maximum permissible, and some plans have different maximums for different classifications of employees. For example, a plan may permit employees with fewer than a certain number of years of service or participation to contribute within a specified range, while this range may be greater for employees with more years of service or participation. In addition, many plans specify that a minimum contribution, expressed either as a dollar amount or as a percentage of pay, is required.

Supplemental Employee Contributions

A provision for supplemental employee contributions is an optional feature included in some thrift plans. This provision enables participants to take advantage of the favorable tax treatment afforded plan contributions and investment earnings. Supplemental employee contributions normally are accounted for separately.

Employer Contributions

The employer's contribution to a thrift plan generally is defined as a fixed percentage of basic employee contributions. That percentage may vary for different classifications of employees as long as the classifications are nondiscriminatory. Some thrift plans qualified as profit-sharing plans provide that the employer, at its discretion, may make contributions in excess of the defined amount of contribution.

The employer's contribution is most often allocated among the participants in direct proportion to the basic employee contribution of each participant. However, other methods of allocation (such as a varying percentage based on years of service or participation) may be used, provided they are not discriminatory.

ADVANTAGES AND DISADVANTAGES OF THRIFT PLANS

Unlike other employee benefit plans, which usually are designed with a specific purpose or objective in mind, savings plans generally meet a number of objectives and provide for the payment of benefits under several different contingencies. From an employer's viewpoint, they offer most of the advantages of profit-sharing plans at a considerably lower cost. As a result, many employers have instituted savings plans to provide relatively low-cost supplemental benefits in the event of the retirement, death, or disability of an employee, as well as to provide meaningful benefits during active employment. Further, they may be used to provide employees with some protection against the erosive effects of post-retirement inflation. It generally is recognized, however, that because of relatively lower contribution levels, savings plans do not have the same incentive value for employees as do profit-sharing plans.

CHAPTER 28

Cash Balance Pension Plans and Other Evolving Hybrid Pension Plans

Dennis R. Coleman

Lawrence J. Sher, FSA

ONE EMPLOYER'S STORY

The origins of the cash balance pension plan lend credence to the maxim: "Necessity is the mother of invention." The cash balance plan concept was "invented" in the mid-1980s in response to a perceived need that could not be adequately met by more traditional retirement vehicles. The seeds were sown when Bank of America attempted to redress some of the shortcomings of its traditional retirement plan.

A RETIREMENT PLAN DILEMMA

The bank's final-average-pay, Social Security offset, defined benefit pension plan was like those of many other U.S. companies. It provided ample and secure benefits for its long-service employees and retirees but very little in the way of benefits to its younger, shorter-service workers, many of whom were unaware that the plan even existed. Those who were aware of it were indifferent to its promise of a future income equal to some percentage of future pay, starting at some time in the distant future. In fact, in one attitude survey, 30 percent of the bank's employees responded that they had so little understanding of the plan's complicated formula that they were incapable of expressing an opinion as to whether or not they were satisfied with the plan. That statistic alone spoke volumes for the plan's ineffectiveness as a people motivator, and clearly it did little to facilitate the bank's efforts to attract and retain its mostly young, mobile work-force.

Equally troubling were certain other aspects of the bank's traditional plan that had not kept pace with the bank's changing objectives:

- The "blank check" design inherent in the plan's final-average-pay benefit formula resulted in fluctuating costs and liabilities that were escalating unpredictably.

- Generous incentives for early retirement and retiree cost-of-living increases were becoming too costly.

- The Social Security offset—subtracted directly from the gross benefit amount—was seen as a double-edged sword. Participants perceived it as a direct "takeaway," whereas the bank recognized that a portion of any future reductions in Social Security benefits (or slowdown in their rate of growth) would have to be picked up by the plan.

- Employee misunderstanding and confusion were exacerbated by the fact that two key elements of the plan's benefit formula—the determination of final average pay and the amount of the Social Security offset—are unknown until actual retirement and are very difficult to predict.

Anticipated Improvements

After an exhaustive study, the bank tentatively concluded that a defined contribution approach might, in principle, better address its needs because:

- The "age neutral" benefit-accrual pattern of traditional defined contribution plans, under which the amount of company contributions allocated to accounts each year is unrelated to age, would fit with the bank's philosophical compensation objective of providing "equal pay for equal work, regardless of age." Such an accrual pattern would be far more appealing to younger employees, since plan benefits accrue at a more rapid pace in the earlier years of plan participation as compared to the more "backloaded" accrual patterns typically found in defined benefit plans.

- In contrast to the complex benefit formula contained in its traditional plan, a defined contribution formula would be straightforward and easy for employees to comprehend. Employees' appreciation of a defined contribution plan would be reinforced at regular intervals through periodic statements reflecting contributions and earnings credited to their individual accounts since the last valuation date and their new balances at the end of the current valuation period.

- Defined contribution plans provide distributions upon termination of employment in the form of lump-sum cash distributions—a feature not usually seen in traditional defined benefit plans and one that holds great appeal to employees.

Reservations About the Change

In spite of these considerations, the bank was nevertheless reluctant to abandon the defined benefit approach and switch to a defined contribution approach for the following reasons:

■ Switching would result in older employees accruing less benefits as they approached retirement than if they had continued participating in the defined benefit plan.

■ No effective mechanism exists within a defined contribution framework to provide past service benefits, updated accrued benefits, or directly provide lifetime annuities—features of its existing plan the bank considered vital.

■ A defined contribution format transfers the investment risk to the employee. If the employee makes unwise investment elections, retires, or terminates in a down market, or if the fund's managers achieve unsatisfactory results, the adequacy of the employee's retirement income could be jeopardized. The bank was concerned that employees, having limited resources and a shorter "time horizon" than the bank, might be ill-equipped to accept or handle this level of risk. (A 401(k) savings plan was already in place, which earmarked the bank's match for investment in bank stock.)

■ Retirement benefit adequacy also can be undermined by preretirement withdrawals and, in contributory plans, by inadequate employee participation.

■ Defined contribution plans have only limited funding flexibility. The bank's existing defined benefit plan, on the other hand, allowed it to anticipate turnover, amortize gains and losses, and provide a range of contribution levels, thereby facilitating its ability to manage the incidence of cash costs.

A Decision Is Made

The bank concluded that the ideal vehicle to satisfy its disparate needs would be an entirely new kind of plan that melded the best features of both a defined benefit plan and a defined contribution plan into a single vehicle. Thus the cash balance concept was born—the invention necessitated by the call for a more comprehensible retirement plan that would not sacrifice essential employee benefit security.

WHAT IS A CASH BALANCE PLAN?

How does a cash balance plan blend, within a single vehicle, the seemingly inconsistent characteristics of defined benefit and defined contribution plans? A cash balance plan is a defined benefit plan that, like all defined benefit plans, embodies a firm promise to pay a formula-determined benefit at retirement. However, it is designed to operate—and to be perceived by employees—like a defined contribution plan. So, instead of expressing the retirement benefit promise as a monthly pension that is a function of final or career-average pay or a flat dollar amount per year of service, it is expressed in terms of an ever-increasing individual account to which benefit dollars and interest are credited at predetermined rates. At any point in time, in effect, the account represents the present value of the underlying earned pension benefit. The plan typically works this way:

1. A "cash balance" account is established for each employee when he or she becomes a member of the plan. These accounts are not directly related to plan assets; they are merely a record-keeping device to keep track of and communicate the current lump-sum value of each participant's accrued pension benefit. If the plan is replacing an existing pension plan, usually an initial account is established—the "opening" balance — typically equal to the actuarial present value of the employee's accrued benefit under the prior plan formula.

2. The employee's account balance is updated periodically (e.g., monthly) to reflect additional employer-provided benefit credits. These often are computed as a flat percentage, such as 4 percent or 5 percent, of the employee's pay; alternatively, such pay-based credits may be weighted to take into account age or years of service in order to skew the benefit in favor of older or longer-service employees. (Some hourly plans provide benefits that are independent of pay, such as $50 or $100 per month.) In addition, Social Security integration can be achieved by crediting a benefit rate on a portion of the employee's pay above a specified level. (Note that although such cash balance benefit credits are perceived as "employer contributions," they are unrelated to the amount the employer actually contributes to the plan.)

3. Employees' account balances are also credited with interest based on a rate specified in the plan. However, the rate is not tied to the actual investment performance of the plan's assets and, in most cases, is related to some recognized outside index, such as the yield on a designated U.S.

Treasury security (e.g., one-year bills or 30-year bonds). Because this rate usually is intended to vary from year to year, its value generally is communicated to employees before the start of each year.

4. Because it is a qualified pension plan, withdrawals may not be made during employment before the employee's normal retirement age.

5. Employees who terminate usually may choose to receive an immediate distribution of their vested accounts in a lump sum, perhaps to be rolled over into an individual retirement account (IRA), or in the form of an annuity commencing immediately. Alternatively, terminating employees may elect to leave their balances in the plan, accruing interest credits, until retirement age.

6. Most cash balance plans provide a pre-retirement death benefit equal to the full account balance. Where the beneficiary is the spouse, the spouse typically has the choice between a lump-sum distribution equal in value to the account and a benefit in the form of an annuity that is the actuarial equivalent of the account.

7. At retirement, the accumulated balance is available as a lump sum or is convertible into any of a number of optional forms of annuity the plan makes available. Of course, because the plan is a qualified pension plan, the normal form of benefit for a married employee must be a "qualified joint and survivor annuity" unless spousal consent to an alternate benefit form is obtained.

An Example

Let's look at an example of how an employee's cash balance account grows over time. Table 28–1 illustrates a typical pattern for a new employee earning $30,000 in each of the first five years of service. The plan provides 5 percent pay-based credits and 7 percent interest credits. Note that after one year this employee has a $1,552 account balance. Further, after five years the account represents about 30 percent of pay, and the employee is probably fully vested at that point.

COMPARISON WITH TRADITIONAL PLANS

Let's examine a little more how cash balance plans combine within a single vehicle significant aspects of both defined contribution and defined benefit plans. From the defined contribution side, they incorporate a number of features with broad employee appeal:

■ An easy-to-understand benefit formula.

T A B L E   28–1

Cash Balance Example

Year	Account Value (Beginning of Year)	Pay-Based Credit	Interest Credits*	Account Value (End of Year)
1	$ 0.00	$1,500.00	$ 52.50	$1,552.50
2	1,552.50	1,500.00	161.17	3,213.67
3	3,213.67	1,500.00	277.46	4,991.13
4	4,991.13	1,500.00	401.87	6,893.00
5	6,893.00	1,500.00	535.01	8,928.01

* Assuming credit based on midyear value of account.

- Individual accounts, the current value of which is communicated through periodic statements as a lump-sum cash amount.
- Payouts available in the form of lump-sum cash distributions.
- The ability to provide benefit accruals that are "age neutral."

However, unlike defined contribution plans, cash balance plans retain certain inherent defined benefit advantages that are beneficial to both employers and employees:

- The ability to eliminate "takeaways" by continuing, as a grandfathered minimum, a preexisting plan's final-average-pay formula for employees near retirement.
- The ability to provide past service benefits and benefit updates if necessary and affordable.
- Funding flexibility. The plan is funded on an actuarial basis, which allows the employer to contribute any cash amount within the usual Internal Revenue Service (IRS) minimum and maximum deductible contribution limits.
- Benefit guarantees—implicitly by the minimum funding requirements of the Employee Retirement Income Security Act (ERISA) and explicitly by the Pension Benefit Guaranty Corporation (PBGC).
- Attractive annuity options, such that if an employee wants a life annuity there is no need to take the account outside the plan to an insurer, where selling expenses and profit margins would make the same annuity benefit more costly.
- The shielding of participants from investment risk.
- The ability of the employer to invest for the long term and thereby provide more benefits for the same costs (or the same benefits for lower costs) as compared to a defined contribution plan.

Since its inception in the mid-1980s, the cash balance concept has grown by leaps and bounds. Many design variations have evolved to fit each employer's objectives, including the introduction of some elements of employee "choice," for example, in the interest credit rates. Today, the concept is embraced by hundreds of plan sponsors, many of them Fortune 500 companies. Several million employees already participate in such plans. This rapid growth in only 15 years is probably due to the fact that cash balance plans offer tangible "rewards" to both employers and employees.

The Employee's Perspective

From the employee's perspective, a typical cash balance plan looks like a money purchase pension plan under which the employer contributes a fixed percentage of payroll and the interest rate appears roughly comparable to what might be obtained in a fixed-income investment such as a guaranteed investment contract (GIC). (A key difference is that unlike a GIC, the plan's specified interest rate is a guarantee that extends, not just for one, three, or five years, but for as long as the employee remains a plan participant.) Thus, the employee perceives his or her benefit to be an individual account, the current value of which is expressed as a lump-sum cash amount that grows systematically from year to year. And if the annual credits to the employee's account are stated in terms of a fixed percentage of compensation, growth of account values mimics the age-neutral accrual pattern characteristic of defined contribution plans.

Contrast this pattern with traditional final-average-pay pension plans, which target relatively more financial firepower on older employees who stay until retirement. Under such plans, employees of different ages with equal pay typically *appear* to accrue the same benefit; that is, the same amount of normal retirement annuity income for a given year of service. Actually, however, because the money required to provide the same dollar amount of normal retirement annuity on behalf of a younger employee is lower than for an older employee (i.e., due to the longer time period available to earn interest), the current "value" of the same dollar amount of annuity is lower for the younger employee. The prior service benefits already earned under a final-average-pay plan automatically increase each year in line with increases in the average salary upon which pension benefits are based (in addition to the growth for interest), but such salary-related growth occurs only while the employee continues to work and get pay increases from the employer. For these reasons, younger employees have less dollar value "put away" for them under traditional plans than do their older coworkers, and are at significant risk for inflation due to termination of employment with the employer before retirement. For example, in a typical final-average-pay plan, the value of the identical incremental pension benefit earned by an employee aged 60 could be expected to be more than 10 times that of an employee aged 35!

Thus, compared to the traditional pension plan, the cash balance approach tends to be relatively more generous to younger employees and employees who terminate earlier in their careers and work for more than one employer. (This is a fairness issue with which employers must be comfortable, and many have concluded that the advantages of a cash balance approach are well worth this investment. In truth, most have already crossed this bridge philosophically by providing level accruals under their savings plans.) The graph in Figure 28–1 illustrates these differences by comparing the annual cost at various ages, as a percentage of current pay, of providing an equivalent pension benefit commencing at age 65 under a typical cash balance plan versus a typical final-average-pay plan.

Like a money purchase plan, a cash balance plan typically would offer a choice of distribution in the form of a lump sum or an annuity. (The latter choice is, of course, a legal requirement.) If the employee is 100 percent vested upon termination, the lump-sum amount is equal to the current value of his or her cash balance account, whereas if the participant chooses an annuity form of distribution, the annuity amount would typically be the actuarial equivalent of the account balance.

The Employer's Perspective

As noted, from the employee's perspective, the cash balance plan looks more like a defined contribution plan than it does like a traditional defined benefit pension plan. From the employer's perspective, on the other hand, things look quite different. Since the plan is in actuality a defined benefit plan that is actuarially funded on an aggregate basis, participant "accounts" are merely a record-keeping device and not directly related to the underlying assets of the plan. Similarly, the investment earnings of the trust are unrelated to the predetermined rate of interest credited to the accounts as specified in the plan. Thus, the employer bears the investment risk (and reward) and may experience fluctuating costs as a result.

Over the long run, however, because most cash balance plans credit an interest rate roughly equivalent to a 30-year Treasury bond rate, actual earnings of the trust can be expected to exceed the predetermined rate specified in the plan to be credited to participant accounts, thereby resulting in employer costs somewhat below the plan's pay-based credit rate. In the event that poor investment experience by the employer would

F I G U R E   28–1

Annual Cost of Benefit Earned as a Percentage
of Current Pay

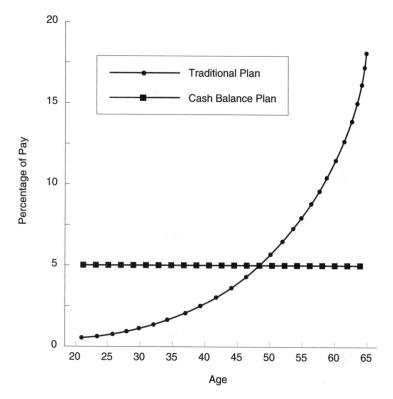

result in the actual earnings of the trust failing to keep up with the predetermined interest rate specified in the plan, employees' accounts would
nevertheless grow by the predetermined interest rate. The employer will
gradually absorb such loss, typically on an amortized basis.

In practice, the fact that there is no direct connection between the
interest rate credited to employee accounts and the actual return on the
plan's underlying assets can prove beneficial. It can enable the employer
to invest for the long run, thereby increasing the plan's potential to earn a
rate of return on plan assets in excess of the plan's predetermined interest
rate. In actuality, this interest rate "differential" (sometimes cynically
referred to as "arbitrage") is present in the financing of any defined benefit plan. It is just more obvious in a cash balance plan because benefits are
expressed as current values rather than deferred annuities that also grow in
value with "fixed income" interest as the employee approaches retirement.

Employees as well as their employers can benefit from this arrangement—employees by receiving the guaranteed return specified in the plan document; the employer by retaining the investment potential to earn a greater actual return. This arrangement usually is considered as an appropriate tradeoff, given employees' natural aversion to risk where their retirement income is concerned and the plan's relatively long-term horizon.

In the typical situation where the employee also is covered in a 401(k) plan with a wide array of investment choices, a cash balance plan can be viewed as the employee's "fixed income" investment, thereby enabling the employee to invest somewhat more aggressively in the 401(k) plan. Finally, to the extent that investment returns are favorable in the cash balance plan trust and employer costs decrease, employers can opt to share the savings with employees in the form of account adjustments or other plan enhancements.

PLAN FUNDING

Because cash balance plans are qualified as defined benefit plans, they are subject to the generally applicable defined benefit plan funding rules. Accordingly, contributions are actuarially determined, thereby providing flexibility as to both the timing and amount of contributions. For example:

- A range of funding methods is available. Turnover and other expected experience under the plan can be anticipated and discounted for in advance, and gains or losses that arise can be amortized.
- Subject to legal limitations as to minimum and maximum contributions, employers can vary the amount of funding from year to year.
- If a plan is overfunded, no cash outlay may be required (or even allowed without a tax penalty) until the overfunding is eliminated.
- Employers in temporary difficulty can use a "funding waiver" to defer a contribution without immediate consequences to employees who can continue to accrue benefits under the plan.

CONVERSION OF AN EXISTING PLAN

Conversion of a traditional pension plan to a cash balance plan is accomplished by amendment; no plan termination is required. Like any amendment to a defined benefit plan, the law prohibits any decrease in the employee's previously accrued benefit. Therefore, the first step in the transition process typically involves the determination of employees' accrued benefits under the prior benefit formula as of the conversion date. In many, but not all cases, the accrued benefit is converted into a lump-sum equivalent amount, which becomes the initial "opening" account balance. (In some cases, no opening balance is determined and the prior accrued benefit is paid in addition to the employee's cash balance account at retirement. In other cases, the opening balance may be determined in some other way, for example, by determining or estimating what the employee's account balance would have been had the plan always been a cash balance plan.)

One concern that invariably is addressed in the conversion process is the desire to keep "whole" certain employees who might otherwise be adversely affected by the changeover. In other words, unless special provision is made for such employees, a cash balance conversion might mean lower benefits at retirement than would have been provided by the preexisting plan had it remained in effect. One group that often is granted such protection is older employees who will be retiring in the next several years.

Potential benefit shortfalls incident to the transition may also arise for long-service mid-career employees (ages 40 to 54). However, whether and the extent to which the protection of the expectations of those employees is appropriate is a subjective question that each employer has to address. Many employers have not considered it to be appropriate to fully protect the benefit expectations under the prior plan for employees in this age range, especially those younger employees who have many years of future employment in the workforce remaining.

Probably the most common means of dealing with these issues, particularly in the case of older employees, is through the mechanism of "grandfathering"; that is, providing that their benefits will in no event be less than if the preexisting plan had remained unchanged. This involves the administrative burden of running two plans—the old and the new—for several years; but, many employers have concluded that such an iron-clad guarantee is worth the added administrative work involved.

Other common approaches to dealing with potential benefit shortfalls include:

■ Subsidizing the opening balance. This might involve computing the initial balance using a somewhat lower interest discount rate; a mortality table that reflects a longer life expectancy; or in plans that subsidized early retirement, an average retirement age (such as age 62) rather than normal retirement age (age 65). Alternative approaches along the same lines would be to provide a minimum opening balance equal to (1) what the balance would have been had the cash balance plan been in effect in the past (that is, an enhanced "retrospective" transition opening balance) or (2) an enhanced "prospective" opening balance equal to the present value of any difference between old-plan and new-plan benefits projected to retirement date. In either case, appropriate measures should be taken to prevent windfalls for employees who terminate before reaching retirement. One approach used to address this concern is to attach an "earn out" provision to these enhanced benefits.

■ Use of so-called transitional credits. That is, supplementary service credits, in addition to the regular pay-based credits, for older, longer-service employees. For example, if the regular annual cash balance credits are 5 percent of pay, eligible employees might receive an extra 5 percent (or 10 percent in total) until termination of employment or for a specified number of years. Along the same lines, the amount of the supplementary credits could vary based on a "point criterion" (age plus service) at date of conversion, or some other sliding scale, so as to more accurately target anticipated benefit shortfalls. In such a case the formula for determining the varying amount of the supplementation typically would be calculated by reference to a comparison of the old- and new-plan benefits projected to a specified retirement age and designing a supplemental credit stream such that it will bridge any undesirable shortfalls at that age. Employers utilizing this approach have run the gamut from a simple, "smoothed" table of supplemental credits applicable to all, to individually computed supplemental credits (different for each employee).

■ Offering a one-time choice to remain in the prior plan. An approach that has gained attention recently is to offer some or all employees a one-time choice to either remain under the prior plan benefit formula or to become covered under the new cash balance formula. As discussed later, the recent cash balance controversy has made this approach appealing to employers who otherwise may not have considered it.

Many employers consider adopting a cash balance plan in the broader context of a study of their entire retirement program—including 401(k) and retiree medical—and some bring in other benefits and compensation programs (e.g., stock compensation). Therefore, in any analysis of the potential impact on employees of a cash balance conversion, it also is appropriate to consider what effect changes to the other programs will have. Thus, for example, an enhancement to the match in the company's 401(k) plan offers all employees, including those who might otherwise experience a retirement shortfall, the opportunity to add to their retirement income.

LEGAL CONSIDERATIONS

Since cash balance plans are qualified under the Internal Revenue Code (IRC) as defined benefit pension plans, they are subject to the generally applicable qualification requirements that apply to defined benefit plans, including:

- Minimum participation rules that limit the age and service requirements an employer can impose as a condition of participation in the plan.
- Coverage and nondiscrimination rules designed to prevent the plan from discriminating in favor of highly compensated employees.
- Vesting rules, which limit the period of required service before an employee earns or becomes entitled to a nonforfeitable benefit under the plan.
- Accrual rules, which limit the extent to which a plan may "backload" benefit accruals and prohibit accrual rates from reducing on account of attaining any age.
- Surviving spouse and minimum lump-sum distribution requirements.
- Rules limiting the amount of contributions and benefits that may be provided through qualified plans on behalf of plan participants.
- Minimum funding rules designed to ensure the solvency of defined benefit pension plans.
- Minimum distribution rules that govern the timing, duration, and form of benefit payments.

In addition, like other defined benefit plans, cash balance plans are subject to Employee Retirement Income Security Act (ERISA), including the reporting and disclosure requirements of Part 1 of Title I of ERISA, the fiduciary-responsibility provisions of Part 4 of Title I of ERISA, and the plan termination insurance provisions of Title IV of ERISA.

Note, however, that applicable law has evolved over the years with traditional defined benefit plans, not cash balance plans, in mind. The IRS has issued only limited guidance directly related to cash balance issues, including a "safe-harbor" to satisfy nondiscrimination requirements (1991) and preliminary guidance on minimum lump-sum distributions (1996). Despite this, many employers have received favorable determination letters from the IRS on cash balance conversions. However, the lack of comprehensive guidance has been the source of certain technical issues over the years which have yet to be definitively resolved. This technical vacuum has contributed to the recent cash balance controversy discussed later.

THE RECENT CASH BALANCE CONTROVERSY

Until late 1998, employer conversions to cash balance plans occurred with little fanfare and employees seemed to accept and like the new plans. Press coverage had been rather sparse, primarily appearing in trade publications from time to time. The IRS had issued limited guidance (as discussed above) but had continually put off issuing more comprehensive guidance.

That rather benign picture changed almost overnight with a series of provocative articles that began appearing in *The Wall Street Journal* in December 1998. The articles painted a cynical picture of cash balance plans, the sponsors that adopted them, and their advisers. Since then, many others joined what became an attack on cash balance plans.

What are the major criticisms? The first *Wall Street Journal* article suggested that companies are switching to cash balance plans to save money. There appears to be no credible data or other evidence to support that contention. In fact, the evidence is to the contrary. Studies by Watson Wyatt Worldwide and PricewaterhouseCoopers LLP (PwC) reveal that in less than half of the conversions studied were retiree costs expected to reduce after a cash balance conversion. The PwC survey of 100 conversions indicates that in 70 percent of the cases overall retiree costs were expected to remain about the same or increase.

Another criticism seems to be that employers are slashing the benefits of middle-aged and older employees overnight and in the range of 20 percent to 50 percent. This criticism seems to lack foundation for a number of reasons:

■ Any reductions would occur gradually, not immediately, because of the anti-cutback provisions of the law.

■ We have found that these claims are often overstated because they focus on the worst-case scenario while ignoring other situations where reductions are much more modest or where there actually may be improvements. In most cases, the potentially large reductions can occur at the earliest retirement ages where the prior plan subsidies are highest. The gloomy outcomes presume that: (1) the employees will (or would have) remained with the employer until such age (sometimes 15 or more years in the future), (2) if it weren't for the cash balance conversions no other changes would have occurred to the plan in the interim, and (3) the employee would have retired at that very early age.

■ To suggest that employers do not take the conversion process seriously is not the case. In our experience, every employer that converts to a cash balance plan is very sensitive to the possible adverse impact the change could have on certain employees. For example, more than 97 percent of the plans in the PwC survey included transition provisions that go beyond the legal minimum to eliminate or mitigate the possible negative impact on some or all employees. Employers that do not go beyond the legal minimum should be viewed no less favorably than employers that elect to suspend or terminate their defined benefit plans.

The so-called "wear-away" effect—employees not receiving any increases in pensions for a period of time following the conversion—has received quite a bit of attention in the media and in Congress. Employers have been accused of intentionally understating opening balances by using interest rates much higher than prevailing rates to discount the value of future annuity payments to current lump-sum amounts. Based on the PwC survey, such alleged practice is not widespread. More than 70 percent of the plans with opening balances in the survey used an interest rate for determining opening balances that was equal to or lower than prevailing rates on 30-year Treasury bonds. Most of the wear-away effect has actually been caused by a decline in interest rates following cash balance conversions and the phasing-out of early retirement subsidies.

There is no question that one of the objectives that many employers have in converting to a cash balance plan is to move away from the rich early retirement subsidies provided under their traditional defined benefit plans. Given the changes that already have been occurring in the workforce and the anticipated heightening of labor shortages as more baby boomers retire, employers increasingly are looking to provide retirement benefits that are more "work neutral." According to the 1999 Statement on "New Opportunities for Older Workers" issued by the Committee for Economic Development: "Businesses have heretofore demonstrated a preference for early retirement to make room for younger workers. But this preference is a relic from an era of labor surpluses; it will not be sustainable when labor becomes scarce." Thus, whether through a conversion to a cash balance plan or otherwise, scaling-back or eliminating both early retirement subsidies and the loss of pension value because of continued employment after early or normal retirement age seems inevitable.

Another area of the cash balance debate is the claim that cash balance plans are age discriminatory, particularly in the conversion from a traditional plan. It seems apparent that, aside from the legislative relief that Congress granted in the late 1980s, traditional plans with their rich early retirement subsidies followed by anti-subsidies discourage continued employment of older employees and thus are a classic example of age bias in the workplace. Cash balance plans level the playing field by eliminating those subsidies and anti-subsidies. It is therefore surprising that these plans have been attacked by those interested in promoting opportunities for older workers.

Another aspect of cash balance plans that has been getting attention, especially in the courts, relates to minimum lump sum requirements. Although the promise in a cash balance plan is expressed as a lump-sum current value, in 2000 federal appeals courts in two cases—*Lyons* v. *Georgia Pacific* (11th Circuit) and *Esden* v. *Bank of Boston* (2nd Circuit) ruled that employees might be entitled to more than their account balances. In both cases, the district courts had sided with the employers by taking a pragmatic view of the relevant statutory provisions. The appeals courts embraced IRS preliminary guidance on cash balance lump sums that seemed to endorse the whipsaw approach despite its consequence— to force employers to provide lower interest credits to all employees to avoid paying more than account balances to those who take lump sums at the young ages. At the same time as giving deference to IRS preliminary guidance, the appeals courts gave no deference or respect to the IRS favorable determination letters on plan language that provided for lump sums equal to account balances. In fact, in the Georgia Pacific case, the IRS urged the appeals court to give no deference to its determination letter and to adopt the whipsaw approach. The IRS argued that determination letters should apply only to the tax provisions of the law and that the IRS agents might have granted the letters in error.

What is this controversy leading to? Cash balance critics, including certain members of Congress, succeeded in getting the IRS to suspend issuing determination letters on virtually all cash balance plans beginning in late 1999. Thus, rather than issuing more guidance on cash balance plans, the IRS entered a holding pattern apparently waiting either for Congress or the courts or both to deal with whipsaw and other legal issues. Given the highly politicized nature of this debate, it seems likely that some legislation may be enacted in the near future. The most likely area is an expansion of the ERISA 204(h) disclosure rules. Anti-wear-away legislation was proposed in 1999 and 2000 and some variation has a chance of becoming law in 2001. It seems much less likely that legislation to mandate providing choice for employees to remain in the prior plan will become law, although one should not totally discount that possibility.

Meanwhile, the question of age-discrimination looms and there is considerable pressure on the IRS to more clearly state its position. The Equal Employment Opportunity Commission (EEOC) is pursuing this question both on a coordinated basis with the IRS and Treasury Department and on its own by joining and initiating actions against employers. The IRS and Congress seem disinclined to deal with this issue so it seems likely that the courts will decide whether the basic cash balance design is age discriminatory and whether or under what circumstances a conversion results in age discrimination. In fact, in 2000 a federal district court in *Eaton et. al.,* v *Onan Corporation* (Southern District of Indiana) decided that the basic cash balance plan design does not violate age discrimination laws.

We think that the criticisms launched at cash balance plans are largely unfair and have the potential to do much more harm than good. The private defined benefit system has been in a decline for quite some time and the introduction of new mandates and restrictions on cash balance plans surely will encourage a further exodus from defined benefit plans.

OTHER NONTRADITIONAL QUALIFIED PLAN DESIGNS

The proliferation of cash balance plans since Bank of America pioneered the concept indicates that cash balance is more than just a passing fad. Despite the recent attack on cash balance plans, for the most part they continue to be received with enthusiasm both by plan sponsors who have embraced the concept and by their employees, and more employers are looking closely at the concept.

But cash balance is by no means the only hybrid qualified plan format that has caught the attention of plan sponsors in recent years. Other formats that are now in vogue include other defined benefit account balance hybrid variants such as "pension equity plans," age-weighted profit-sharing plans, and target benefit plans.

Other Account Balance Hybrid Variants

Recently, a number of variations of the account balance defined benefit plan have been developed. These plans, rather than expressing the current value in terms of an account, define a lump sum based on the participant's final average compensation.

For example, under a so-called "pension equity plan," each employee is annually credited with a percentage that will be applied to his or her final average earnings. The percentage that employees earn increases with age. (The rationale for the larger lump-sum credits at an older age is to maintain retirement income adequacy late in the career, while lower lump-sum credits earlier in the career avoid giving too large of lump sums to early-leavers.) A measure of integration can be achieved by crediting additional percentages to earnings above a threshold amount.

When employees retire or otherwise terminate employment, they can receive a lump-sum benefit equal to the sum of the percentages they have earned during their careers multiplied by their final average earnings. At the employee's option, the plan benefits typically are payable as a lump sum, as an annuity, or may be rolled over into an IRA or another employer's plan.

For example, assume a participant retires at age 65 with 20 years of service and a final average salary of $50,000. Assume further that, over his or her career, the employee earned (i) credits of 220 percent, which are applied toward the full $50,000 of final average pay, plus (ii) an additional 55 percent in excess credits that are applied to final average pay in excess of $20,000. The total of the credits comes to $126,500. The lump sum could be converted into an annuity approximating 25 percent to 30 percent of final average pay, depending on the annuity factors used.

Age-Weighted Profit-Sharing Plans

Traditional profit-sharing plans typically allocate each year's employer contribution in accordance with a formula that results in each participant's share being proportional to such participant's recognizable compensation. The cross-testing rules of IRC Sections' 410(b) and 401(a)(4) regulatory scheme specifically sanction an allocation formula for profit-sharing plans that permits age to be taken into account without violating the applicable nondiscrimination requirements, thereby opening the door to age-weighted profit-sharing plans.

Prior to the Tax Reform Act of 1986, target benefit plans were generally the only defined contribution format that specifically permitted age to be reflected in the allocation formula. However as discussed later, target benefit plans, which are a type of money purchase pension plan, have had limited popularity, due to the fact that they require a long-term commitment and permit little funding flexibility.

Age-weighted profit-sharing plans demonstrate that they are nondiscriminatory under IRC §401(a)(4) by means of the cross-testing rules of Reg §1.401(a)(4)-(8). These rules permit a plan to comply by demonstrating that the *benefits* attributable to the contributions are nondiscriminatory in amount. This is accomplished by expressing the contributions in terms of benefits provided at each employee's testing age (e.g., age 65).

The general idea is to target the share of employer contributions and for-feitures allocated during a year to each participant's account as the amount needed to provide an annual benefit payable for life, at age 65, of the same percentage of each participant's pay. Therefore, when each participant's annual allocated share is accumulated to age 65 at a permissible interest rate and converted to a benefit expressed as a percentage of pay, the resulting percentage is the same for all employees.

The allocations for a year are converted to "equivalent accrual rates" by projecting them to age 65 and converting them into hypothetical benefits using a "standard interest rate" (i.e., a rate between 7½ percent and 8½ percent), one of several specified mortality tables, and a straight life annuity factor. The "equivalent accrual rates" of all participants are then tested for compliance under the so-called "general" nondiscrimination test for defined benefit plans. (Practically speaking, because the age-weighted formula results in a uniform benefit accrual rate at normal retirement age, all participants in the plan typically will have the same uniform accrual rate.)

In other respects, an age-weighted profit-sharing plan is similar to conventional profit-sharing plans:

- No actuarial valuation is required.
- The plan is not subject to PBGC insurance coverage.
- There are no unfunded liabilities.
- Contributions can be at the employer's discretion, and generally may range from 0 to 15 percent of covered payroll.

The effect of age-weighting the allocation is that significantly more can be put away for older participants than under a conventional allocation formula. For example, assume three employees, one age 55, one age 45, and one age 35, each with the same compensation; the age-weighted formula results in an allocation for the 55-year-old that is more than twice as large as for the 45-year-old, and more than four times as large as for the 35-year-old.

Target Benefit Plans

A target benefit plan is a money purchase pension plan under which the amount of required contributions is determined by reference to an assumed predetermined retirement benefit for each participant, but under which the amount of retirement benefit actually payable is dependent on the market value of the assets in the participant's account from which such benefit is payable. The contributions—which are determined on the basis of the employee's age and certain actuarial assumptions—are the amount that would be required to fund the target benefit over the employee's career on a level annual basis. But note that the level of contributions does not vary by reason of the actual investment experience of the plan assets. The theory is that if the actual return on plan assets equals the assumed return, the participant will receive the "targeted benefit." The employee, rather than the employer, bears the risk of favorable or unfavorable investment experience, however. If the fund fails to meet expectations, the employees' retirement accumulations will be less than the targeted benefit. By the same token, if the fund performs better than anticipated, the employees' benefits will be larger than the targeted amount.

The contributions and any forfeitures are allocated and separately accounted for with respect to each participant. The benefits provided under the plan are provided solely from employer contributions, forfeitures, employee contributions, and any investment experience.

The employer contribution on each employee's behalf constitutes the "definitely determinable benefit" as required by applicable law. The target benefit formula may not allow any discretion on the part of the employer with respect to the amount of its contribution to the plan. The investment risk and reward under a target benefit plan reside with the participant, not the plan sponsor.

Whether a target benefit plan satisfies IRC §401(a)(4) is generally determined on a benefits basis by means of the cross-testing rules as provided in Reg. §1.401(a)(4)-8. Note that there is a target-benefit plan safe harbor, using the cross-testing rules, set forth in Reg. §1.401(a)(4)-8(b)(3), which might prove useful in certain circumstances.

CHAPTER 29

Employee Stock Ownership Plans (ESOPs)

Robert W. Smiley, Jr.

Gregory K. Brown

INTRODUCTION AND OVERVIEW

Employee Stock Ownership Plans (ESOPs)

Employee stock ownership plans (ESOPs) have evolved from a novel academic concept into a sophisticated tool of corporate succession and finance that is well integrated into the mainstream of the American business community. During the period of this evolution, a fairly well-developed body of law has emerged at a legislative and regulatory level as well as through judicial interpretation. ESOPs have been used not only for business succession and capital formation by owners of closely held companies but as an employee benefits tool and defensive measure by many publicly held corporations, or as a means of taking a publicly held company private. This chapter provides the reader with a road map to the development of ESOPs as well as the legal, financial, and accounting considerations that must be dealt with to implement an ESOP. As this chapter will evidence, great care in planning is necessary for a corporation (and its shareholders) to decide whether an ESOP is feasible and will serve its (and their) goals and objectives and, if so, to implement the ESOP to serve those ends.

Kelsoism, Two-Factor Economics, and the Results

Louis Kelso started a movement almost 30 years ago that has, through his own efforts and the efforts of many other capable people, resulted in millions of Americans owning part or all of the companies they work for—"a piece of the action." His concept is "universal capitalism," and its thrust is to spread the benefits of capital ownership to all Americans, not just to a few. There are now well in excess of 11,000 such plans across the country, and more are being adopted every day.

Background and Description

The first stock bonus plans were granted tax-exempt status under the Revenue Act of 1921. In 1953, the Internal Revenue Service (IRS) first recognized the use of a qualified employees' plan for debt financing the purchase of employer stock when it published Revenue Ruling 46. In recent years, Congress has encouraged the use of the ESOP financing technique in at least 21 different pieces of legislation.

ESOPs generally can be described as defined contribution, individual account plans similar to stock bonus plans and profit-sharing plans. By relating ESOPs to these familiar employee benefit plans, a base can be established from which these plans can be analyzed and reviewed. As a form of stock bonus plan, ESOPs differ from profit-sharing plans in that an ESOP must make distributions in employer stock—although cash can be distributed—provided the employee is given the option to demand his or her distribution in employer securities or if the other special requirements discussed later in this chapter are met. It is the ESOP's ability to borrow based on the credit of the company that allows the ESOP to be used as a technique of corporate finance. An ESOP is essentially a stock bonus plan that uses borrowed funds to finance the purchase of a company's stock for the firm's employees. The ESOP is a tax-sheltered employee benefit plan on the one hand, and a bona fide technique of corporate finance on the other.

The statutory definition of an ESOP is a defined contribution plan:

1. Which is a stock bonus plan that is qualified, or a stock bonus and a money purchase plan both of which are qualified under IRC Section 401(a), and that are designed to invest in qualifying employer securities; and
2. Which is otherwise defined in IRS regulations.

An ESOP also must meet special distribution, put option, nonallocation, and voting requirements (discussed later in this chapter).

The following example illustrates the simplest and most basic use of a nonleveraged ESOP:

> Assume that a company in a 40 percent combined federal and state income tax bracket has pretax earnings of $150,000, a covered payroll of $600,000, and makes a $90,000 (15 percent of $600,000) contribution to the plan, which then buys stock from the company.
>
> Compare this situation with a profit-sharing plan to which the company contributes the same amount. Table 29–1 shows the effect of different plans and Table 29–2 shows the effect of the ESOP tax shield.

Leveraged ESOPs

An ESOP also may leverage its investments to acquire employer stock, something that a normal pension or profit-sharing plan (except under very limited circumstances) is not permitted to do. This feature makes an ESOP very useful in debt financing. For example, assume the ESOP borrows $500,000 for seven years at a below-market annual interest rate of 6.14 percent. (The lender relies on the solvency of the company.) The ESOP then buys $500,000 worth of stock from the company (which will result in some dilution of existing shareholders' equity), and the company can use this money as additional working capital in any way it wishes. The company then contributes to the ESOP approximately $90,000 each year, which is used to pay the principal and interest on the $500,000 loan. The

T A B L E   29–1

Comparing Plans

	Qualified Plan	Profit-Sharing Plan	ESOP
Pretax income	$150,000	$150,000	$150,000
Less contribution	0	90,000	90,000
Net taxable income	150,000	60,000	60,000
Income tax (federal and state)	60,000	24,000	24,000
Net after-tax income	$ 90,000	$ 36,000	$ 36,000
Company cash flow	$ 90,000	$ 36,000	$126,000

The $90,000 contribution goes to work inside the corporation as additional equity capital.

T A B L E   29–2

ESOP Tax Shield

	Without ESOP	With ESOP
Operating pretax income	$1,000	$1,000
Less: ESOP contribution	0	500
Pretax income	1,000	500
Less: Income taxes	400	200
Net income	600	300
Equity		
Start of year	$5,000	$5,000
Add: Retained earnings	600	300
Add: ESOP stock purchase	0	500
	$5,600	$5,800

Source: Benefit Capital, Inc., Logandale, Nevada.

company gets a tax deduction for the entire $90,000, even though part of it is used to pay the principal. Assuming a 40 percent corporate tax rate, the company has reduced its ultimate tax bill by $200,000, and the cash flow of the company has been increased by $200,000, the amount of the tax reduction. At the same time, the employees have become beneficial stockholders of the company and, presumably, now have a greater interest in making the company more profitable and in generating the profits necessary to repay the loan. Of course, if the ESOP purchases the stock from existing shareholders (rather than the company), this will not create additional working capital, but the tax results will be the same.

The Economic Recovery Tax Act of 1981 (ERTA) altered the funding limits applicable to leveraged ESOPs. Whereas prior to ERTA the combination of limits on deductible contributions and maximum allowable annual additions created a practical limit to the amount of an ESOP loan, ERTA greatly expanded that limit. After ERTA, a plan sponsor may contribute on a deductible basis an amount up to 25 percent of covered payroll to be used solely for principal reduction on an ESOP loan. In addition, the sponsor may contribute on a deductible basis an unlimited amount to service interest on the loan. Relevant adjustments were made to Internal Revenue Code (IRC or code) Section 415 to allow for the allocation of all released shares (i.e., forfeited and reallocated loan shares need not be considered "annual additions" for purposes of the limitations). Obviously, this allows a much larger block of stock to be purchased than could have been under pre-ERTA law.

For purposes of this chapter, an ESOP is defined as a qualified stock bonus plan, or a combination stock bonus and money purchase pension plan, that meets certain requirements under the Employee Retirement Income Security Act of 1974 (ERISA), as amended, and under the Internal Revenue Code of 1986, as amended, that allows the plan to borrow from, or on the credit of, the company or its shareholders, for the purpose of investing in the company's securities. The trust gives the lender its note for the money borrowed, which may or may not be secured by a pledge of the stock. Alternatively, the company borrows the money and makes a back-to-back loan to the ESOP on similar terms. The company or the shareholders, or both, guarantee the loan. Usually there is an agreement with the lender that the company will make contributions to the trust in sufficient amounts to repay the loan, including interest. As the plan contributions are used to repay the loan, a number of shares are released to be allocated to the employees' individual accounts. As with other qualified plans, benefits usually are paid after employees die, retire, or otherwise leave the corporation.

Alternatives to an ESOP

Plans other than an ESOP can aid employers in their financing and also provide employees with the benefits of stock ownership. Compliance with the requirements of the definition of an ESOP is necessary only if the trust forming part of the plan is to be a borrower for the purpose of acquiring stock. If stock is to be acquired without this debt financing, any plan of the eligible individual account variety can be used to accomplish essentially the same purpose. Such plans include profit-sharing plans, stock bonus plans, savings plans, and thrift plans as well as ESOPs. However, certain benefits, including the tax-free rollover and the dividend deduction explained later in this chapter, are available only through an ESOP.

The most common alternative is a profit-sharing plan (including a 401(k) profit-sharing plan). While trust borrowing with corporate or shareholder guarantees is prohibited, most if not all of the benefits of an ESOP are available to the company and to the employees through a well-designed profit-sharing plan. Distributions may be made to participants in either cash or stock. Contributions may be made in cash or stock; and cash, once contributed, may be used to purchase company stock from the company or the shareholders, as long as certain rules are followed.

The next-most common alternative is a stock bonus plan, which is similar to a profit-sharing plan except that benefits normally are distributable in stock of the employer. IRC Section 401(a)(23) now permits a stock bonus plan to distribute cash in lieu of stock, provided the employee has the right to have his or her distribution in employer securities, unless the special cash-only distribution provisions of IRC Section 409(h)(2) apply. The primary purpose of a stock bonus plan is "to give employee-participants an interest in the ownership and growth of the employer's business."[1] This distinction in purpose from pension plans and profit-sharing plans is important in interpreting the fiduciary responsibility provisions of ERISA.

Thrift plans and savings plans[2] were not previously defined in federal income tax law but would encompass the whole gamut of very successful plans that match employee contributions on some basis. Under many thrift and savings plans, especially the larger ones, a very high percentage of the investments is in company stock.

As for these non-ESOP plans being able to repay company debt, the same amount that an ESOP would have borrowed can usually be borrowed by the company directly, and then contributions to the non-ESOP plan can be made in company stock having a value equal to the amount of the amortization payments on the debt. If the stock goes up in value, from the point of view of company costs, it will be less costly for the company than for the trust to incur the debt. The reason is that less stock will be contributed by the company if the shares increase in value as the future contributions are made, thereby reducing the repurchase liability for closely held companies because fewer shares of stock have to be redeemed.[3] Additional stock will not have to be contributed to the ESOP to pay the interest, because the interest already is deductible as an expense by the company.

A money purchase pension plan may be structured as part of an ESOP. As discussed earlier, after ERTA a leveraged ESOP can be structured to provide contributions in excess of 15 percent of covered payroll. If a contribution of more than 15 percent of payroll is desired without using a leveraged ESOP, a money purchase pension plan, combined with a stock bonus plan, may be in order. The pension plan could be a savings

---

1 Rev. Rul. 69-65, 1969-1 C.B. 114.

2 ERISA Sec. 407(d)(3).

3 Robert W. Smiley, Jr., "How to Plan for an ESOP's Repurchase Liability," Prentice Hall's *Pension and Profit-Sharing Service* (Englewood Cliffs, NJ: Prentice Hall, April 3, 1980), pp. 1, 431–440; and "How to Plan for an ESOP's Repurchase Liability," Prentice Hall's *Pension and Profit-Sharing Service* (Englewood Cliffs, NJ: Prentice Hall, February 27, 1987), pp. 1, 215–229.

plan, and because savings plans generally require the employee to contribute, some assurance of employee contributions can be made by establishing an attractive matching rate. The two plans combined then would permit a deductible contribution of up to 25 percent of covered payroll.

A money purchase pension plan alone is not an ESOP, and only 10 percent of assets may be invested in employer securities, but can be if combined with a stock bonus plan as part of an ESOP. The money purchase plan that forms a part of an ESOP will generally be subject to some of the requirements applicable to money purchase plans [except, for example, the 10 percent limit on investments in employer stock under ERISA Section 407(a) and the joint and survivor annuity requirements of IRC Sections 401(a)(11) and 417 and ERISA Section 205], as well as the special requirements (described below in "Plan Design Considerations") that apply to an ESOP under IRC Section 4975(e)(7) and the regulations thereunder.

The primary purpose for including a money purchase plan as part of an ESOP is to increase the tax-deductible limits on employer contributions from the normal 15 percent of compensation limit applicable to stock bonus plans to 25 percent of compensation. After the enactment of ERTA, however, such use of a money purchase pension plan will generally no longer be necessary if leveraging is used, because ERTA increased the deduction limits applicable under IRC Section 404(a)(9) with respect to employer contributions used to repay an ESOP loan. In the case of a nonleveraged ESOP, the use of a money purchase plan may still be attractive to increase tax-deductible contributions, provided the employer is willing to make the definite contributions required each year under the money purchase plan.

CORPORATE OBJECTIVES IN ESTABLISHING ESOPS

ESOP as a Financing Vehicle

Generally, ESOPs serve a variety of corporate objectives above and beyond the primary objective of providing an employee benefit. ESOPs also serve as a technique of corporate finance. In this hybrid role, ESOPs also can be used for:

■ Capital formation.
■ Low-cost borrowing.
■ Solving succession-of-ownership issues.

- Refinancing existing debt.
- Estate planning.
- Financing an acquisition or divestiture.

Considerable care is required in structuring the ESOP for these various uses.

ESOP as an Employee/Employer Benefit Plan

Advantages to the Employer

The principal reasons for the continuing rise in interest in ESOPs are the number of potential advantages of their use by the employer [and shareholder(s)]. From an employer's standpoint, their primary objectives are to:

1. Increase employee motivation and productivity through ownership participation.
2. Increase cash flow by creating tax deductions with stock contributions.
3. Transfer business to key employees on a tax-favored basis.
4. Refinance existing debt at more favorable rates with pretax dollars.
5. Create a market for shares of stock held by current shareholders.
6. Aid in estate planning for one or more shareholders.
7. Create an alternative to sale of the company to outsiders or to a public offering.
8. Divest a subsidiary, acquire an existing subsidiary or division, or finance the acquisition of a company or business.
9. Convert existing pension/profit-sharing plan(s) from pure cash expense items to tax-saving or corporate finance vehicles.
10. Serve as a means of charitable giving.

ESOPs are recognized as being able to solve corporate financial needs in the following ways:

1. Financing future growth with pretax dollars.
2. Refinancing existing debt, repaying both principal and interest with pretax dollars, while simultaneously providing an employee retirement benefit.
3. Increasing cash flow without increasing sales or revenue.

4. Motivating employees to regard the company through the eyes of an owner by letting them share in a "piece of the action" and possibly receive tax-deductible dividends.

5. Creating a friendly base of stockholders (employees) as opposed to disinterested speculators in the public marketplace.

6. Creating a tool to help attract and retain high-quality management and supervisory personnel while cutting down on employee turnover.

7. Encouraging employee ownership of closely held company stock (without relinquishing voting control).

8. Improving employee relations.

9. Ensuring the future growth of the company through increased employee productivity and increased company profitability.

10. Converting present employee benefit plans from pure expense items and liabilities to vehicles that increase working capital and net worth.

11. Providing an in-house, liquid market for stock while remaining private.

12. Enabling private shareholder(s) to sell all or part of their holdings at fair-market value without the expense and uncertainty of a public securities offering.

13. Enabling private shareholder(s) to defer paying federal capital-gains taxes, perhaps indefinitely.

14. Divesting an incompatible subsidiary without the publicity, expense, and uncertainty of finding an outside buyer.

15. Acquiring a company with pretax dollars, and amortizing acquisition financing with pretax dollars.

16. Using in conjunction with takeover defense strategy, retiring stock, or "going private."

17. Increasing the yields to stockholders.

Disadvantages to the Employer.

As with almost all things, ESOPs have some disadvantages. The value of the company's stock may be independent of company performance. If the company's stock experiences a market decline or a decline based on appraised values, a substantial risk of employee dissatisfaction may occur. This dissatisfaction may be accentuated if there is leveraging in the ESOP. In most cases, however, the direct link between company performance and trust fund performance will be a disadvantage only if the company stock performs poorly.

Further, because an ESOP may have to make distributions in stock, and because the employee may owe taxes, the company must be certain that the employee has sufficient cash to pay taxes. Otherwise, the stock must be sold to pay taxes, possibly creating a morale problem. The put option provision (described later in this chapter) usually alleviates this problem.

Dilution is a key disadvantage. When new stock is contributed to the trust, or purchased from the company, the earnings per share on each remaining share may be reduced. A careful analysis must be made to determine whether this potential disadvantage is offset by the increase in working capital and the increased cash flow from the tax savings.

The emerging repurchase liability is another problem that must be dealt with. Again, a careful analysis and the series of solutions available here must be worked through, scheduled, and acted on.[4]

Voting control may become an issue, unless the ESOP is monitored with considerable forethought. Sometimes, this change of voting control is what is desired; if it is not, the safeguards that are available should be established to avoid a loss of control.

The degree of risk is another factor. The ESOP invests primarily in employer securities and may subject the trust funds to capital risks. The value of the benefit to both the employer and the employee depends on the performance of company stock and the timing of the financing. Finally, an ESOP may not use the permitted disparity rules of section 401(l) in allocating contributions to participants' accounts.

Advantages to Employees

The advantages of an ESOP to employees are obvious: they receive stock in the company that employs them, usually without any cash outlay or financial liability, and without any income tax liability until they receive the stock.

If employees receive company stock in a lump-sum distribution, they can escape current taxation of the unrealized appreciation in the company stock until they sell the stock. They are required to pay tax only on the trust's basis (or fair-market value, whichever is lower) in the year a lump-sum distribution is made; however, an election to be taxed on the unrealized appreciation may be made. This can be quite a benefit if the stock has done well and the employees hold the stock until the tax year in which a

---

4 Robert W. Smiley, Jr., "How to Plan for an ESOP's Repurchase Liability," pp. 1, 215-29.

sale appears most advantageous to them. In smaller companies, the stock usually is sold immediately, either to the trust or to the company.

Other advantages to employees include:

1. The participant may effect a direct rollover of such distribution on a tax-deferred basis under code Section 402(c).

2. Dividends paid on ESOP stock are taxable to the recipient and deductible by the employer when paid or distributed to participants (or their beneficiaries). If the dividends are used to repay ESOP loans, the dividends are not taxable to the recipients, but allocations may be accelerated to participants. Nondeductible dividends may also be paid to the ESOP and allocated as trust earnings.

Disadvantages to Employees

The major potential drawback is the "all eggs in one basket" problem, the lack of diversification. If the employer company has financial difficulties, the employee can suffer a double loss; he or she can lose both the ESOP benefits and the job.

Having to sell a block of stock in a closely held corporation can be very difficult. With the put option requirements the problem is easier, but an employee could let his or her put option expire and be faced with this problem well into retirement.

Because most distributions are in company stock, ESOPs will place the employees in the position of having to sell the stock they receive, because they usually will not have the cash to pay the taxes due on the amount of the distribution. An individual retirement account rollover, or a rollover to another qualified plan, may eliminate this need for cash to pay taxes at the time of the distribution.

Employees also must face the problem of a liquidity crisis if the employer (or ESOP) does not have sufficient cash on hand to purchase distributed shares. Proper planning by the employer can generally eliminate this problem; however, it must be considered.

Leverage to purchase employer securities is rarely a disadvantage to the employees if the employer is assuming the risk of the loan.

More Effective Capital Formation

The primary advantage resulting from the use of ESOP financing techniques is greater cash flow. The basic ESOP model provides for financing new capital formation and corporate growth, with pretax dollars being used to repay debt. While conventional loans require repayment of principal with after-tax dollars, ESOP financing enhances the ability of the employer company to meet debt-service requirements with pretax dollars.

Transfers of Ownership

Code Section 1042 provides that, if stock of a closely held corporation is sold to an ESOP under circumstances where the sale would otherwise qualify as a long-term capital gain, no tax must be paid at the time of the sale, on all or part of the realized gain, provided the following requirements are satisfied. The seller must have held such stock for at least three years before the time of the sale. The ESOP must own either (1) at least 30 percent of the value of the outstanding equity of the company after the sale, on a fully diluted basis (other than certain nonvoting, nonconvertible preferred stock), or (2) at least 30 percent of each class of outstanding stock of the company on a fully diluted basis (other than certain nonvoting, nonconvertible preferred stock), after the sale, and the sales proceeds must be reinvested in replacement securities ("qualified replacement property") within a 15-month period that begins three months before and ends 12 months after the sale. The replacement securities must be securities of a domestic (i.e., United States) operating company and may be public or private securities, giving the seller a virtually unlimited choice. In practice there are very few restrictions, although care must be taken to avoid certain passive-income company pitfalls for the unwary. Tax is then deferred until the qualified replacement property is sold; or, if the replacement securities become a part of the seller's estate, the capital gains tax is never paid, because the replacement securities enjoy the advantage of a step-up in basis at the holder's death.

An excise tax is imposed on the employer for certain dispositions of the stock acquired by the ESOP in the transaction within three years after sale. The stock that is purchased by the ESOP may not be allocated to the seller, members of his or her family (brothers, sisters, spouse, ancestors, and lineal descendants), and to anyone related to the seller within the meaning of code Section 267(b) during the period beginning on the date of sale and ending on the later of 10 years after the date of sale or the date of the plan allocation attributable to the final payment of acquisition indebtedness in connection with the sale. Similarly, that stock may not be allocated at any time to any shareholder who owns more than 25 percent of the value, or number of outstanding shares, of any class of outstanding employer stock (or a controlled group member). In determining whether a person owns more than such 25 percent in value or number, the constructive ownership rules of code Section 318(a) apply, taking into account stock held by a qualified plan (including the ESOP).

However, individuals who would be ineligible to receive an allocation of qualified securities just because they are lineal descendants of other ineligible individuals may receive an allocation of code Section 1042 securities (i.e., the employer securities acquired in a tax-deferred sale) as long as the total amount of the securities allocated to the lineal descendants is not more than 5 percent of all code Section 1042 securities. In computing this percent amount, all employer securities sold to the ESOP by the seller that are eligible for nonrecognition treatment (including outstanding stock options) are taken into account, according to the Tax Reform Act of 1986 (TRA '86) Conference Report.[5] Existing shareholders may dispose of all or a portion of their shares without the potential dividend treatment that may apply to a corporate redemption under code Section 302. ESOP financing permits the acquisition of stock from existing shareholders using pretax dollars, and the existing shareholders are selling capital assets that can be taxed as long-term capital gains. Normally, for closely held companies, corporate stock redemptions are fraught with potential dividend treatment problems and require the use of after-tax dollars.

Refinancing Existing Debt

An ESOP may be used to refinance existing corporate debt and to repay it with pretax dollars, thereby lowering the borrowing costs. Besides cash contributions, the company could issue new shares of stock to the ESOP equal in value to the amount of debt assumed by the ESOP, thus helping cash flow. This will effectively make the repayment of debt tax-deductible (within the limits of code Section 404(a)(9)). Sophisticated lenders generally understand that they have greater security with an ESOP, because their payment is made out of pretax earnings. Dividends are now deductible by the employer if used to repay ESOP debt. In addition, ESOP loans may be refinanced.

---

5 At p. II-852. IRC Sec, 409(n) appears to exclude lineal descendants of a 25 percent owner; in other words, the lineal descendants' exception would not apply to a 25 percent owner, including shares deemed owned by such owner through attribution. If so, this would severely limit application of this exception. However, this interpretation seems contrary to the use of the words "any other person" in IRC Sec. 409(n)(1)(B).

Alternative to Going Public

The costs of a public stock offering, a Securities and Exchange Commission (SEC) registration, and the high expense of operating as a publicly owned company can be avoided through ESOP financing. The shares may be acquired by the ESOP from the company or existing shareholders, or both. Because employee shareholders are usually more loyal as shareholders than outsiders, and because an in-house market is usually more stable, the value of the stock may not be subject to the sometimes wild fluctuations found in the public market. In some situations, the ESOP shares will have a higher value than a comparable public company, because the ESOP shares may not be subject to a "minority-interest discount." A minority interest is usually worth somewhat less than a proportionate share of the total value of the company when the company is valued on an "enterprise (or control) basis." This is because minority shareholders cannot control company policy in many important areas that affect them, such as compensation, dividends, selection of officers, sale or purchase of assets, and other crucial corporate decisions.

Financing an Acquisition or Divestiture

ESOP financing provides a way for a company to spin off a division or subsidiary to a new company owned by the employees in whole or in part through an ESOP. The new company earnings then would be available to pay off the purchase price, which may have been financed by an installment purchase from the divesting company—or through loans and equity provided from outside lenders, venture capitalists, or investor/operators expert in leveraged buyouts (LBO) or a specialized ESOP leveraged buyout fund. The success of any LBO turns on the capacity of the ongoing business to amortize the acquisition debt. The increased after-tax cash flow available through ESOP financing can enhance materially the probability of a successful transaction, because repayment of the acquisition indebtedness may be accelerated. In an ESOP leveraged buyout transaction, the employer may effectively amortize both principal and interest payments from pretax income. In contrast, only interest is deductible in a conventional LBO. As a result, ESOP LBOs are able to support acquisition debt more easily, and the viability of the transaction may not be affected as adversely by fluctuations in interest rates or economic cycles.

The same technique in reverse may be used to finance the acquisition of other companies. The often increased pretax earnings of the acquired company and the generally increased employee payroll (because of the added payroll of the acquired company), are variables that may permit accelerated repayment of the debt incurred for financing an acquisition.

Estate Planning

An ESOP may provide a ready market for the shares of a deceased shareholder. Acquisitions of employer stock from the estate can be debt-financed and then repaid with pretax dollars. Note, however, that the ESOP purchase of those shares, which cannot be at a price in excess of appraised fair-market value, will then set a price for estate tax valuation purposes and for the shares held by any remaining shareholders.

Problem Areas in ESOP Financing

Acquisition of Stock

ESOPs may acquire stock from parties-in-interest if no more than "adequate consideration" is paid. If the purchase price exceeds fair-market value, the acquisition from a "party-in-interest" or "disqualified person" would constitute a prohibited transaction subject to penalty taxes and corrective action under code Section 4975 and ERISA Section 406, would probably violate the fiduciary duty of prudence, and the fiduciaries would have liability for any resulting losses.

Care must be taken, if the stock is not publicly traded, to determine the value of the company stock. Use of an independent appraisal is now mandatory with the addition of the independent-appraiser requirement of IRC Section 401(a)(28) and the issuance of proposed regulations under ERISA Section 3(18). The IRS and the Department of Labor (DOL) are currently closely scrutinizing ESOP acquisitions of employer stock, especially with respect to fair-market value and equity allocation issues.

Section 502(1) of ERISA requires that the DOL assess a penalty equal to 20 percent of the "applicable recovery amount" involved in any judgment or settlement involving a breach or violation of fiduciary liability, or against a nonfiduciary who knowingly participates in such breach or violation. The penalty is also reduced by the amount of any excise tax on prohibited transactions paid to the IRS.

Debt Financing

ERISA Section 408(b)(3) and IRC Section 4975(d)(3) provide for a prohibited-transaction exemption for an ESOP loan primarily for the benefit of participants. The collateral given for a party-in-interest loan by the ESOP must be limited to employer stock, and the loan must bear no more than a reasonable rate of interest. However, if these conditions are not met, the entire loan may be subject to prohibited transaction penalty taxes, corrective action, and, of course, fiduciary liability.

Usually a loan will be primarily for the benefit of participants if the proceeds are used to acquire company stock on fair terms for the benefit of employees in connection with the financing of corporate capital requirements. Primary security for the loan should be corporate credit, and the company will generally be required to either guarantee the loan, or make a commitment to pay sufficient dividends on the company stock or make sufficient contributions to pay off the debt, or both. Liability of the ESOP for repayment of the loan must be limited to payments received from the company, including dividends, and to any stock remaining in the ESOP that is still used as collateral. The loan, by its nature, must be *non-recourse* on other ESOP assets. In other words, no person entitled to payment from the ESOP will have any right to any other asset of the ESOP than the payments received from the company, including dividends, and the pledged stock not yet received from the suspense account.

The employer contributions required to service debt principal must not exceed the allocation limitations under IRC Section 415. However, because forfeitures of loan shares and dividends used to repay ESOP debt on such shares are effectively allocated at cost (not current fair-market value), and forfeitures of leveraged shares and dividends are not considered annual additions, the value of actual allocations may exceed 25 percent of pay or the then-in-effect dollar limit. However, when more than one-third of the contribution for the plan year is allocated to highly compensated employees, forfeitures of leveraged shares are considered as annual additions, as are ESOP interest payments, for the plan year.

Determination Letter

The usual IRS determination letter issued under code Section 401(a) offers little protection for the more difficult compliance issues in ESOP financing. While the letter applies to the formal requirements for the tax exemption of the ESOP, it does not apply to issues of operational compliance with the prohibited transaction exemptions under ERISA Section 408(b)(3) and (e) and under code Section 4975(d)(3) and (13). It is possible to request and to receive a determination letter that the ESOP is qualified under IRC Section 4975(e)(7) by completing and filing IRS Form 5309 in addition to the regular application materials. The ERISA

Conference Report and the leveraged ESOP regulations direct the IRS and DOL to give all aspects of ESOP financing special scrutiny—ostensibly to protect the interests of participants and to prevent abuses of the ESOP technique. Where operational defects are discovered by a plan administrator prior to a governmental audit, it may be advisable, to retain the plan's tax-qualified status, to apply for relief under the Voluntary Compliance Resolution Program or the Closing Agreement Program sponsored by the IRS.[6]

Existing Plan Conversions

If the prudence requirement (discussed later in this chapter) of ERISA is satisfied, the assets of an existing plan may be used to acquire company stock either directly from the company or from existing shareholders by converting the existing plan into an ESOP. The conversion of an existing plan into an ESOP is accomplished by means of an amendment to the plan. (This subject is covered in more detail later in the chapter.)

Which Type of ESOP Provides What Benefits?

Even though ESOPs are a technique of corporate finance, they are also compensation programs. The company contributions to these plans involve real economic costs incurred in exchange for employee services. As a form of compensation, they have the advantage of making the employees owners of a company. This may, in fact, be their main advantage.

Not all ESOPs, however, are the same. Selecting the proper form depends on the characteristics and goals of the sponsoring company and how the plan is to be used. Careful consideration must be given on how the plans differ. Often, the use of an ESOP and its many tax and other benefits is not desired, and another type of plan may be in order. It should be remembered that there is a wide range of options available, which allows employers great flexibility in tailoring a plan to their needs.

Simplicity is a virtue in the benefits field. Stock bonus plans have this major attribute. They are not subject to code Section 4975(e)(7) regulations. They can use any equity security, including nonvoting or nonconvertible stock, or both, which may be an important consideration when voting control is a key issue. Stock bonus plans, which do not meet

---

6 Rev. Proc. 2000-16, *Internal Revenue Bulletin* 2000-6, February 7, 2000.

the ESOP requirements, cannot be leveraged if the loan is guaranteed by the company, nor can the stock bonus plan acquire company stock from a shareholder using the popular tax-deferred rollover provisions of code Section 1042. (Nor may the stock bonus plan facilitate the use of the many other tax benefits discussed in this chapter that are available only to ESOPs.) Stock bonus plans may distribute cash in lieu of employer securities, but the employee still has the option to require that his or her distribution be made in employer securities. A profit-sharing plan that invests primarily in company stock is not subject to this demand from employees to distribute company stock.

Leveraged ESOPs enhance immediate transfers of the ownership of companies, subsidiaries, and divisions from the existing owners to the employees. They are, however, subject to the ESOP regulations, including the put option requirements and the "special scrutiny" mandates. The leveraged ESOP is required to invest primarily in common stock or non-callable, convertible preferred stock of the employer.

ESOPs and Corporate Performance

Increased employee productivity often is cited as one advantage of ESOPs. *Productivity* is a term with a decidedly nonspecific meaning. It can be expressed in terms of dollar output per hour of labor, but little, if any, agreement exists among experts on how to increase it—and how to break down the relative contributions of capital and labor. It is almost impossible to prove that giving millions of workers a piece of the action will motivate them to increase productivity. Each company has a group of diverse employees with diverse temperaments, interests, goals, and objectives, and each group may react differently. Some employees are "long-term oriented"; they think and talk years ahead. Other employees are much more "short-term oriented." Obviously, there are millions of employees in between. Each company has to analyze its own employee base, make careful and well thought-out value judgments, and decide what kind of employees it has and wishes to attract.

It is the most fundamental tenet of capitalist theory that economic efficiency is based on individual incentive. The idea that employee-ownership companies would be more efficient than conventionally owned companies follows this commonsense conclusion. If an employee's reward is fixed, what reason is there to work harder, smarter, faster, or more creatively? When the rewards are tied directly to productive effort, as they can be in an ESOP company, most employees *should* be more motivated and productive. Employee attitudes should be consistent with their work ethic. Since the late 1970s, researchers have put this reasoning to measurement in numerous studies that can be found by contacting the National Center for Employee Ownership or The ESOP Association.

The authors' own experience, consisting of observations of several hundred ESOP companies, would tend to confirm these results, as does the Rosen, Klein, and Young book, *Employee Ownership in America: The Equity Solution*, (Lexington, MA: Lexington Books, 1986). Several other studies have been done and are explained and referenced in *Employee Stock Ownership Plans: Business Planning, Implementation, Law, and Taxation* by Robert W. Smiley, Jr., Ronald J. Gilbert, and David Binns, (Warren Gorham & Lamont). (See Footnote 11, see Chapter 3 and the *1998 Yearbook*.) Most recently a study done by Hewitt Associates and Hamid Mehran confirms these results and provides that the power of engaged ownership is derived from the number and strength of the connections between people, information, and action.

SPECIAL FIDUCIARY LIABILITY RULES UNDER ERISA FOR ESOPS

There are special fiduciary liability rules under ERISA for ESOPs. The primary purpose of a stock bonus plan (the ancestor and major building block of an employee stock ownership plan) is "to give employee-participants an interest in the ownership and growth of the employer's business" (Revenue Ruling 69-65). This distinction is critical to interpreting the fiduciary responsibility provisions of ERISA. ERISA Section 404(a)(1) requires that fiduciaries act for the "exclusive purpose of providing benefits to participants," and serving as a "prudent man acting in a like capacity . . . would . . . in the conduct of an enterprise of a *like character* and with *like aims*."

The purpose of ESOP financing is two-fold:

1. To use corporate credit to acquire ownership of employer stock for participants.
2. To finance the capital requirements of the employer corporation.

No other qualified plans may incur debt to be used to finance corporate capital requirements or may be used as vehicles for debt financing transactions involving parties-in-interest. Revenue Ruling 79-122 properly recognizes the ESOP "as a technique of corporate finance." The *prudent man, exclusive purpose,* and *document rule* requirements of ERISA Section 404(a)(1) and the *exclusive benefit* rule of IRC Section 401(a) must be analyzed and interpreted with the understanding that the ESOP is a technique of corporate finance. The *diversification rule* is generally not applicable to ESOPs.

As long as an ESOP prudently acquires and holds company stock as the benefit to be provided to employees, ERISA's Sections 404(a)(2) and 407(b)(1) (which specifically permit an ESOP to be wholly invested in employer stock) are satisfied. Also under Revenue Ruling 69-494, the exclusive benefit rule generally is satisfied if:

1. The purchase price does not exceed fair-market value.

2. The prudent man standard also is complied with.

Section 803(h) of the Tax Reform Act of 1976 makes it clear that Congress intended for ESOPs to be used under ERISA as a technique of corporate finance. IRC Section 4975(d)(3) and ERISA Section 408(b)(3) provide for prohibited-transaction exemptions, which are available only to an ESOP and are not applicable to conventional stock bonus or profit-sharing plans.

The legislative history of the Tax Reform Act of 1986, including statements by a number of Senators on the floor of the Senate, indicate Congress's clear intention that ESOPs be a technique of corporate finance.[7]

Prohibited Transactions and Special Exemptions and Exceptions

Fortunately for employers and shareholders, ERISA contains statutory exemptions from many of the restrictions that would otherwise prohibit ESOP transactions. ERISA's Sections 406 through 408 contain the prohibited-transaction restrictions and the related exemptions. These restrictions apply independently of the fiduciary standards. Violation of any of the fiduciary standards or of the prohibited transaction restrictions by a fiduciary may result in civil penalties and personal liability. ERISA Section 409 provides that a fiduciary in breach will be personally responsible for any losses to the ESOP as a result of his or her breach, and that profits must be restored.

Several exemptions from ERISA's general fiduciary provisions apply to ESOPs. An ESOP is not subject to the prohibition on acquiring and retaining an investment in qualifying employer securities that ex-

---

7 *Congressional Record*, June 19, 1986, pp. S7901-S7912, and S. Rep. No. 313, 99th Cong., 2nd Sess. p. 677 (1986).

ceeds 10 percent of the fair-market value of its assets. ESOPs also are exempt from the diversification requirement, but not from the prudence requirement.

An ESOP also may purchase stock from (or sell stock to) the employer, a major shareholder, or any other party-in-interest without violating the prohibited transaction rules, provided the transaction is for adequate consideration and no commission is charged to the plan. See, for example, Prop. Labor Reg. Section 2510.3-18.

An ESOP may leverage its stock purchases, if the interest rate is reasonable, if the loan is primarily for the benefit of plan participants and their beneficiaries, and if certain other stringent requirements are met.[8] For example, the only collateral acceptable for certain exempt loans is the stock purchased with the loan proceeds. The employer, however, may give any collateral it may have available.

The ESOP loan documents for an exempt loan must specifically provide that all the foregoing relating conditions be met, and that:

1. The loan will be repaid only from employer contributions made to enable the trustee to repay debt, earnings attributable to contributions, earnings on unallocated shares, and dividends on stock acquired with the loan proceeds or the proceeds of another exempt loan.

2. The lender's recourse on the note against the trust must be limited to the stock used as collateral and to the contributions and other amounts described in condition Number 1 above.

3. Each year, as the loan is repaid, the stock is allocated to the accounts of active participants as payments are made under the loan, according to the prescribed formulas.

4. The loan must be for a fixed term and satisfy certain requirements in the event of default, including that a party-in-interest lender may not accelerate payments in the event of default and that the loan must not be payable on demand of the lender, except in the case of default.[9]

Special ESOP Problems

Securities Exchange Act of 1934

The 1934 Securities Exchange Act relates to the rules regarding transactions in securities normally conducted on national securities exchanges and in the over-the-counter markets. It contains both registration and

---

8 Sec. 408(b)(3) of ERISA and Sec. 4975(d)(3) of the IRC.
9 Labor Regs. Sec. 2550.408 b-3(m); Treas. Reg. Sec. 54.4975-7(b)(13).

antifraud provisions, both of which are beyond the scope of this chapter. Because the rules in regard to all qualified plans (including ESOPs) are in a state of change, the current securities aspects should be carefully checked prior to engaging in transactions with the ESOP. For example, on February 19, 1981, the SEC eliminated Rule 10b-6 for all employee benefit plans. Previously this rule on trading by persons interested in a distribution of securities required that ESOPs (and other employee benefit plans) stick to a strict set of criteria. In another example, the SEC exempted a qualified plan from the SEC requirement of the 5 percent beneficial-owner disclosure rule in company proxy statements. The SEC reasoned that the true beneficial owners of the stock are the plan participants when there is full voting pass-through, and when the plan documents and participants control the disposition of the stock.

Blue-Sky Laws

Various states have laws and rules relating to transactions of employer securities. These laws generally require disclosure of the transactions and can be extremely complicated. Normally, there are exemptions for transactions with an ESOP, but there are exceptions, and care should be exercised that the applicable state laws are complied with.

Tender Offers

In recent years corporations subject to tender offers have established an ESOP after the tender offer is made, or used a previously established ESOP to secure loans to purchase additional employer securities in an effort to defeat the tender offer. This allows for more employer securities to be in "friendly" hands. The tender offer area is complicated and fraught with potential problems for an ESOP that borrows or purchases stock, or both, in an effort to defeat the tender offer, particularly if the trustees purchase employer securities at a premium price. If the tender offer is successful, the ESOP will generally be a minority shareholder in a debt-ridden corporation, and, if the tender offer is unsuccessful, the ESOP will own stock for which the trustees paid too much. If these transactions violate the exclusive-benefit rule:

- The trust could lose its tax-exempt status.
- Any contributions to the ESOP could be nondeductible.
- The earnings of the trust could become taxable.

Any borrowing by the ESOP that is not primarily for the benefit of the participants is a prohibited transaction that subjects disqualified persons to excise taxes.

Even the decision on how shares are to be tendered became subject to special consideration. For a more detailed analysis, see the most recent "BNA Tax Management Portfolio on ESOPs" (354-6th) 1999 by Jared Kaplan, John E. Curtis, Jr., Helen H. Morrison, and Gregory K. Brown.

Procedural Prudence and Leveraged Buyouts

Procedural prudence requires that independent ESOP fiduciaries be represented by one or more independent fiduciaries, or that the ESOP fiduciaries be represented by independent financial and legal counsel, and that the interests of the ESOP and the participants and beneficiaries be fairly represented in meaningful negotiations. The ultimate responsibility for the decisions made by an ESOP fiduciary rests with the fiduciary. Procedural prudence must be strictly observed. The DOL advisory letters in the Blue Bell, Inc. ESOP transaction provide meaningful guidance.[10]

PLAN DESIGN CONSIDERATIONS

Application of Issues Inherent in All Qualified Plans to ESOPs[11]

Coverage

The requirements of IRC Section 410, which impose the age and service conditions for eligibility to participate, are applicable to ESOPs. In practice, however, most ESOPs are more liberal. This is partially because employers adopting ESOPs have expressed a desire to permit employees

---

10 See letter dated September 12, 1983, from Mr. Charles M. Williamson, Assistant Administrator for Enforcement, Pension and Welfare Benefit Programs, to Gareth W. Cook, Esq., Vinson & Elkins, Houston, Texas, regarding Raymond International, Inc., and letter dated November 23, 1984, from Mr. Norman P. Goldberg, counsel for Fiduciary Litigation, Plan Benefits Security Division, to Charles R. Smith, Esq., Kirkpatrick, Lockhart, Johnson & Hutchison, Pittsburgh, Pennsylvania, regarding Blue Bell, Inc.

11 See, Kaplan, Brown, Morrison and Curtis, "BNA Tax Management Portfolio on ESOPs" (354-6th), 1999; and Smiley, Gilbert, and Binns, *Employee Stock Ownership Plans: Business Planning, Implementation, Law, and Taxation* (New York: Maxwell MacMillan/Rosenfeld Launer, 1991, especially the *1998 Yearbook* thereto, New York, NY: Warren Gorham & Lamont). The book was formerly published by Warren, Gorham & Lamont. Annual updates now are published by the Employee Ownership Institute Foundation, Inc. and the American Institute for Advanced Studies, Inc. (Cost: $95 plus shipping and handling. To order, contact ESOP Book Services, P.O. Box 400, Scottsville, VA, 24590; Phone: 888-443-4485; Fax: 804-286-3815; e-mail: esopserv@cfw.com).

to participate in a "piece of the action," and also to provide the maximum compensation base for purposes of ensuring that contributions to the ESOP are sufficiently large to make the loan payments and are deductible under Section 404 of the code. Many ESOPs do not have minimum age requirements. They may provide for a single, retroactive entry date. However, certain individual limitations on these generally liberal plan provisions may be important.

The rules that apply to all qualified plans for the inclusion or exclusion of particular groups or classes of employees are applicable to ESOPs and are covered elsewhere in the *Handbook*. Two different ESOPs may be established for purposes of satisfying the nondiscrimination and coverage tests if the proportion of employer securities to the total plan assets is substantially the same in each ESOP, and if either the securities held by each ESOP are the same class or the *ratio* of each class of employer securities to all classes of employer securities in each ESOP is substantially the same.[12]

The regulations on ESOPs[13] specifically prohibit a plan designated as an ESOP after November 1, 1977, from being integrated, directly or indirectly, with contributions or benefits under Social Security. These regulations are excise tax regulations, and a prohibited transaction would exist if the plan engaged in a loan or another extension of credit to a disqualified person, and therefore, an excise tax would be due.

The proposed regulations issued under both IRC Sections 401(a)(26) and 410(b)(1) require that the ESOP features of a 401(k) plan and the non-ESOP features thereof are to be considered separately in determining compliance with the minimum coverage and minimum participation rules. Moreover, the final regulations issued under the nondiscrimination rules of IRC Sections 401(k) and 401(m), concerning elective deferrals and matching contributions, provide that these ESOP and non-ESOP features are to be treated separately in determining compliance with those nondiscrimination rules.

Break-in-Service Rules

The two groups of break-in-service rules that are important for solving ESOP design and drafting problems are the eligibility break-in-service rules and the vesting break-in-service rules. Under these rules, an employee may have a one-year break in service if he or she fails to complete more than 500 hours of service in the relevant computation period. These

---

12 Treasury Reg. Sec. 54-4975-11(e)(2).
13 Treasury Reg. Sec. 54.4975-11(a)(7)(ii).

rules are identical for ESOPs and other qualified plans. These rules are covered in detail in other chapters of this book and apply to ESOPs the same as to other qualified plans.

Under the regulations, if any portion of a participant's account is forfeited at the time the vested portion is paid to him or her, or commences to be paid, employer securities that have been acquired with the proceeds of an exempt loan may be forfeited only after other assets have been forfeited. For example, if a participant's account reflects both company stock acquired with the proceeds of an exempt loan and other investments, the participant's forfeiture(s) first must come from the other investments—if the amount forfeited is greater than the other investments available, then some of the company stock may be forfeited. If the distribution is to be deferred, say, until some specified age or actual retirement, or both, the ESOP must generally provide for separate accounts for pre-break and postbreak service.

Most ESOPs do not have a "repayment" provision under the cash-out and buy-back rules of ERISA, and instead, provide automatic restoration of forfeited amounts for partially vested reemployed participants. Any such repayment could present an issue under the Securities Act of 1933 and relevant state securities laws. The amount is repaid voluntarily on the part of the employee, and, therefore, none of the exemptions discussed later would be available, because employee "contributions" are being used to acquire employer securities. If state securities laws permit, an alternative is to establish a separate account-vesting schedule or to provide that any repayments will not be used to purchase employer stock.[14]

Reemployment Problems

It is possible for a plan to require that a former participant who is reemployed after a one-year break in service meet the eligibility requirements of the plan again. However, once the eligibility requirements are again satisfied, participation is retroactive at least to the reemployment date; if overlapping plan years are involved, great care must be taken to defer final allocations, and distributions may need to be either deferred or reduced and reconciled.

Additionally, some care should be taken in utilizing the complex set of rules that relate to crediting and disregarding service for eligibility purposes.[15] When designing this section of the plan, and when designing the vesting computation period, several well thought-out and well-presented

---

14 Treasury Reg. See. 1.411 (a)-7(d)(5)(iii).
15 Labor Reg. Sec. 2530.202-2(b)(2).

examples can go a long way in educating the plan sponsor on just what the provisions mean. ESOPs traditionally have been used by larger companies, and larger companies generally rehire employees on a more regular basis than smaller companies.

Section 415 Considerations

As a condition of tax qualification, a defined contribution plan must provide that the annual addition to the account(s) of a participant for a limitation year may not exceed the lesser of a stated dollar amount or 25 percent of the participant's compensation. This annual addition includes contributions to all defined contribution plans of the sponsor in which the employee is a participant, forfeitures allocated to his or her account, and, if participant contributions are permitted (or required), the participant's own contributions. For employer contributions used to repay acquisition indebtedness, IRS Announcement 95-33 provides that the annual addition is the lesser of the cost or fair-market value of shares released and allocated to a participant's account that are attributable to such repayment. Dividends paid on employer securities that are used to repay ESOP debt are not counted as annual additions.[16]

Section 415(c)(6) of the IRC excludes employer contributions used to pay loan interest and also excludes forfeitures of leveraged employer securities from the annual-additions limitations in the case of ESOPs that are established under 4975(e)(7) of the code. However, these exclusions apply only if no more than one-third of the employer contributions to the ESOP for a limitation year are allocated to the accounts of participants who are highly compensated employees within the meaning of IRC Section 414(q) (the "one-third rule"). When securities are released from the suspense account provided for the holding of the "unpaid-for securities," the contributions (but not dividends) used by the ESOP to pay the loan are treated as annual additions to participants' accounts, not the value of the securities released from the suspense account, which could conceivably be much greater (or much less).

If the special one-third rule is violated, then the forfeitures of leveraged employer securities are included in the computation of the annual addition at fair-market value—that is, the share forfeitures are normally valued at fair-market value. Several potential problems arise because of

---

16 U.S. Senate, Committee on Finance, *Report to Accompany* H.R. 3838, 99th Cong., 2nd sess., May 29, 1986, Rept. 99-313, p. 682.

this treatment of the forfeitures. First, accurate and timely valuations are critical so as to permit a proper and timely allocation. Second, in the event of an audit, if the employer securities that were forfeited and reallocated to participants' accounts in a plan year were undervalued, the plan could be disqualified if the additional value, as determined by the IRS, increased any participant's annual addition beyond the permissible maximum amount. Third, because most loans require fixed payment dates, timely valuations are necessary to know whether the plan is qualified by the time the employer's contribution is due, because of forfeitures being revalued. The forfeiture suspense accounts, which are permitted by the final code Section 415 regulations, require limiting employer contributions first—so, with forfeitures high enough, an ESOP may end up in default on the loan, because large enough contributions cannot be made on a timely enough basis to amortize the loan repayment on schedule. To solve this problem, an employer may vary the plan year for which contributions (made after the end of the year but before the tax-year due date, including extensions) are attributed. The employer also may set up individual Section 415 suspense accounts, which defer annual additions to a later plan year, or alternatively (or concurrently), not permit forfeitures to arise until a terminated participant incurs five consecutive one-year breaks in service.

The resolution to this problem comes to a certain extent from amendments to both Section 415 (the allocation limits) and Section 404 (the deductibility limits). After ERTA, an employer contributing to a leveraged ESOP may contribute and deduct an amount up to 25 percent of covered participants' compensation for purposes of principal reduction. Additional contributions used to service interest due on the ESOP loan are deductible in any amount. TRA '86, as amended by the Technical and Miscellaneous Revenue Act (TAMRA) of 1988 and Omnibus Budget Reconciliation Act (OBRA) of 1989, also permits a corporate deduction for dividends on leveraged shares (whether or not allocated) if used to repay principal or interest, or both, on any loan used to acquire those shares, provided the dividends are reasonable (and do not make the participants' total compensation unreasonable). These dividends are not considered annual additions. Dividends on allocated shares, however, may be used to make loan payments only if the account to which dividend(s) would have been allocated is allocated shares having a fair-market value not less than the amount of such dividend(s). Furthermore, the allocation must be made in the year the dividend(s) otherwise would have been allocated.

The allocation limits in Section 415 eliminate from consideration as annual additions employer contributions used to make interest payments on an ESOP loan and reallocated forfeitures of ESOP stock originally purchased with an exempt loan.

These amendments partially resolved the obvious difficulty arising when three equally inflexible requirements (debt service, deduction limits, and allocation limits) are applied on different, sometimes unrelated, bases to the same transaction. For a particular company, therefore, the deductible and allocable contribution will set the practical limit for the amount of an ESOP loan after giving consideration to deductible dividends.

When designing the ESOP, the other plans of the employer have to be taken into account. The other plan(s) might be drafted to provide for a reduction in benefits under the other plans before reducing benefits under the ESOP. This would help to minimize the code Section 415 problems and, at the same time, maximize the allocations to the ESOP participants. The typical order of priority appears to be to first refund participants' contributions under all plans; second, if more of a reduction is required, then place the excess forfeitures in a forfeiture suspense account or reduce or reallocate them in the other defined contribution plans; and, third, defer the creation of forfeitures until a terminated participant has incurred five consecutive one-year breaks in service.

Reversion of Employer's Contributions

As a qualified plan, an ESOP must provide that no part of the plan's assets are to be used for or diverted to other purposes than the primary benefit of participants. In an ESOP, there are *unallocated* shares and *allocated* shares (disregarding the forfeiture suspense account). The nonreversion provision applies to both the allocated and unallocated securities.

Employer contributions may be returned if made under a good-faith mistake of fact (but not a mistake of law) or if deductions are disallowed and those contributions were conditioned on deductibility, if that condition is specifically stated in the plan document.

Employer contributions also may be conditioned on initial qualification, but not on continued plan qualification, according to Revenue Ruling 91-4 and the Revenue Act of 1987. That ruling also made clear that a permissible reversion will not be treated as a forfeiture in violation of Section 411(a) of the code, even if an adjustment is made to participants' accounts that are partially or wholly nonforfeitable. If this is done, participants' accounts should be adjusted by first withdrawing assets other than employer securities. Note, however, the nondeductible excise provisions of IRC Section 4972 for nondeductible contributions, which impose a penalty equal to 10 percent of a nondeductible contribution.

Compensation Used for Deductions

In Revenue Ruling 80-145, the IRS addressed the definition of *compensation* for computing the deduction limitation under code Sections 404(a)(3) and 404(a)(7). The IRS held that the deduction limits are based on total compensation, even in a situation where the plan defines compensation (for allocation purposes) as excluding certain items (such as limiting compensation to basic pay). Some ESOP companies may increase their deductible ESOP contributions by properly applying these guidelines, but must observe the restricted "safe harbor" definition of compensation reflected in code Section 414(s), the $150,000 ($170,000 for the year 2000 and subject to cost-of-living adjustments thereafter) limitation in code Section 401(a)(17), and the final nondiscrimination regulations issued under code Section 401(a)(4). However, no deductions are permitted for the amount of contributions that cause the Section 415 limits to be exceeded.

Leveraging Difficulties to Anticipate

While leveraging has its positive aspects, some potential negatives exist that should be considered. For example, there will be an immediate dilution of existing shareholders' interests if the company issues new shares, or shares not previously outstanding, to the ESOP; this may, however, be offset by the other benefits, and a careful analysis should be done.

The loan documents for leveraged ESOP transactions also may expressly require the employer to make contributions at least sufficient to amortize securities-acquisition debt. This "commitment" of cash flow is offset in many cases by increased employee morale and the use of many ESOP tax benefits.

Contributions and dividends used to pay for a large block of stock purchased all at once can be a substantial cash drain over a long time. Further, a contraction in business conditions resulting in fewer employees could be construed as a termination or a partial termination of the plan, triggering full vesting for affected participants. If the shares that are then distributed are subject to the put-option requirements (to be discussed in subsequent sections of this chapter), they may have to be purchased with nondeductible dollars, causing an additional and often untimely cash drain.

If the covered compensation for deduction (or allocation, or both) purposes drops below the threshold amount for making required payments on ESOP debt, or if the "one-third rule" is violated, then the ESOP may not be able to make its required payments on the ESOP note unless the employer makes an additional loan, the proceeds of which are used to repay the preexisting loan. If this could be a problem, careful negotiation with the lender is important at the outset.

Allocations to Employees' Accounts

Suspense Account

An ESOP is required to contain specific provisions governing annual accounting for employer securities purchased with the proceeds of an exempt loan. The ESOP must provide for a suspense account to which the securities acquired with the proceeds of an exempt loan must first be credited, even if the securities are not pledged as collateral for the loan. Also, all ESOPs must provide for the release of the securities and their allocation to participants' accounts as payments of principal or payments of principal and interest are made with respect to the loan. Further, if the income from the securities is to be used to repay the loan, both the ESOP and the loan agreement must provide for that. The provisions relating to the release of the shares from the suspense account for allocation to employees' accounts should be contained in the loan documents.[17] The regulations require that the securities be released from the suspense account of the ESOP in the same manner that the loan agreement provides. If there is no pledge of shares relating to the loan agreement, then the plan administrator, plan committee, or other relevant plan fiduciary must select a method of release.

Shares can be released from the suspense account in two ways. Under the first method permitted by the regulations, the number of securities released each year is equal to the number of securities held in the suspense account immediately before release—multiplied by a fraction, the *numerator* of which is the amount of principal and interest payments for the year, and the *denominator* of which is the sum of the numerator plus the amount of future principal and interest payments to be made during the remaining term of the loan, including the current year. The number of future years must be definite and cannot take into account any possible extensions or renewal periods. If the interest rate is variable, the interest is computed, for purposes of the fraction, by using the interest rate applicable at the end of the plan year in which the fraction is applied.

The second method entails releasing securities based on the payment of principal alone. When a loan is amortized over a period of years, the interest portion of the payment is higher in the early years than in the

---

17 Treas. Reg. Secs. 54.4975-11(c), 54.4975-7(b)(8); Labor Reg. Sec. 2550.408b-3(h).

later years. Many lenders would prefer that the shares be released based only on principal payments, so they stay secured. This second method permits more collateral coverage for lenders, because the shares are not usually released as quickly under this method. The only other restrictions on this second method provide that the release based solely on principal payments must be part of a term loan that provides for annual payments of principal and interest that are not cumulatively less rapid than level annual payments of principal and interest over 10 years. In computing amounts of principal under this method, interest is disregarded only to the extent it would be disregarded under standard loan amortization tables.[18] Apparently the agencies are concerned that the terms of the loan might provide greater interest payments during each year of the loan than would be permitted under standard loan amortization tables.

The unrealized appreciation or depreciation on the suspense-account securities is not allocated to the participants' accounts. Shares are allocated at cost, then the value is extended to show a dollar amount reflected at fair market value on the participant's periodic account statement. Employees who become participants in an ESOP after securities have been purchased and credited to the suspense account, but prior to these securities being released, will share in the unrealized appreciation or depreciation that occurred prior to their participation and will realize that appreciation or depreciation on distribution from the plan in the form of cash or, if the distribution is made in the form of stock, upon exercise of their put option or a subsequent sale. The reverse is also true, in that employees who were participants when the shares were credited to the suspense account will not share in the unrealized gains or losses if they are not participants when the securities are released.

The forfeiture provisions must be so drafted as to require that a participant forfeit other plan assets before a forfeiture of employer securities may occur. When more than one class of employer securities has been allocated to the participant's account, forfeitures must reduce each class of security proportionately.[19]

Dividends

Dividends paid on securities allocated to participants' ESOP accounts, to the extent not utilized to repay ESOP debt, may be allocated to participants' accounts with respect to which the dividends were paid and either reinvested in company stock or invested in other assets. Alternatively,

---

18 Treas. Reg. Sec. 54.4975-7(b)(1)(ii); Labor Reg. Sec. 2550.408b-3(h)(2).
19 Treas. Reg. Sec. 54.4975-11 (d)(4).

these dividends may be distributed to participants and their beneficiaries. If dividends on allocated shares are used to repay the loan, the shares allocated to each participant's account by reason of such use must have a fair market value at least equal to the amount of dividends used (as further discussed later in this chapter) for such dividends to be deductible.

Dividends from the securities purchased with the proceeds of an exempt loan but not yet allocated, to the extent not utilized to repay the loan, would be allocated entirely to participants' accounts either:

1. Based on prior account balances;
2. Based on current compensation; or
3. Per capita.

A conservative employer would use method 2 or 3 above to ensure that such allocation would be nondiscriminatory. Alternatively, the dividends paid on unallocated shares may be currently distributed to participants or be used to repay debt (both principal and interest) on the same basis as such dividends would be allocated to participants' accounts.

Allocation of Cost Basis of Shares

Most ESOP allocation sections specify two accounts for each participant. This practice occurs because of the suspense-account requirement, code Section 415, and the requirement that employer securities acquired with the proceeds of an exempt loan be allocated to participants' accounts in terms of share units, rather than in monetary terms.[20] The first account is the "company stock account," which contains employer securities. The other account is the "other investments account," which is maintained to account for the participant's share of plan assets other than employer securities.

Amounts contributed to an ESOP must be allocated as provided under Sections 1.401-1(b)(1)(ii) and 1.401-1(b)(1)(iii) of the regulations. These sections relate to the requirement for a definite, predetermined formula for allocating contributions among participants. Cost-basis accounting is used primarily to determine the net unrealized appreciation in employer securities upon distribution. Therefore, acquisition of employer stock must be accounted for, as provided under 1.402(a)-1(b)(2)(ii) of the regulations. The plan document need not specify which cost-basis rule is adopted, although the chosen rule should be reflected in the trustee's or plan administrator's permanent plan records.

---

20 Treas. Reg. Sec. 54.4975-11 (d)(2).

The reasons to track the cost basis of shares for the participants include some valuable options for participants' tax planning, such as enjoying a lower overall tax for participants' distributions, especially when long-term capital-gains tax rates are lower than ordinary income tax rates (which they have been historically). At the participant's election, a participant who receives stock in a single-sum distribution that qualifies for lump-sum distribution treatment may pay tax on his or her distribution based solely on the cost basis of the shares. The taxability of the gain is deferred until the participant sells the stock received in the distribution. This means if a participant holds onto the shares, no tax is due on the amount of the gain over the ESOP trust's basis in those shares until the shares are considered sold for tax purposes.

Voting Rights

Because the block of securities held in the ESOP may constitute a controlling interest, how voting rights are handled is very important, now and in the future. All ESOPs must satisfy the requirements of code Section 409(e) with respect to voting rights on employer securities acquired after 1979. A stock bonus plan that is not an ESOP is subject to these requirements for shares acquired after December 31, 1979, only if no class of the employer's securities is publicly traded. A stock bonus plan of a closely held company must provide that each participant is entitled to exercise any and all voting rights in the employer's securities allocated to his or her account with respect to corporate matters that involve the voting of shares for or against corporate mergers, consolidations, sales of all or substantially all of the corporation's assets, recapitalization, reclassifications, liquidations, and dissolutions, or such similar matters as the Secretary of the Treasury may prescribe by regulation, if (1) the plan is maintained by an employer whose stock is not publicly traded, and if (2) after acquiring securities of the employer, more than 10 percent of the plan's assets are invested in securities of the employer as required by code Section 401(a)(22). (Voting requirements for ESOPs other than stock bonus are treated elsewhere in this chapter.)

After December 31, 1986, code Section 401(a)(22) eliminated the pass-through voting requirement for ESOPs maintained by certain newspapers, and code Section 409(1)(4) also permitted such newspapers to acquire nonvoting common stock in certain instances after December 31, 1986. This passing-through of voting-rights requirements for closely held companies extends not only to ESOPs but to any eligible individual-account plan, other than a profit-sharing plan, that invests more than 10 percent of its assets in the plan sponsor's stock.

The voting requirements of code Section 409(e) apply only to shares of employer stock allocated to participants' accounts. To the extent that shares are not allocated or have been acquired with the proceeds of an exempt loan and not yet released from the suspense account, voting rights usually are exercised by designated fiduciaries at their own discretion. However, this is not the case when the little-used "one-person, one-vote" rule of code Section 409(e)(5) is used.

An ESOP of a publicly traded employer whose securities are of a type generally required to be registered under the Securities Exchange Act of 1934 must pass through voting rights on all matters for all allocated shares, even nonvested shares. Code Section 409(e)(2) requires that participants and beneficiaries be entitled to direct the manner in which securities of the employer [not just "employer securities" as described in code Section 409(l)] allocated to their accounts are to be voted on all matters. These provisions would appear to apply only to shares of employer securities acquired after December 31, 1979.

On or after October 22, 1986, an ESOP maintained by an employer that has no registration-type class of securities may permit each participant to have one vote with respect to each issue he or she is entitled to direct the trustee to vote, without regard to the actual number of shares allocated to his or her account.[21] The trustee may vote the shares held in the plan in the proportions so directed by the participants. An ESOP can be restructured with respect to its pass-through voting requirements whether or not the company has registration-type securities or where the ESOP document provides that unallocated shares will be voted in the same proportion as participants direct the voting of allocated shares, or where the ESOP plan document provides another voting method (i.e., where the shares are voted on a majority-rule basis). The ESOP also may provide each participant with one vote as long as the trustee votes the shares held by the ESOP in proportion to the votes of all participants. Therefore, the trustee must give up all voting discretion on unallocated shares in order to use this voting method. Under prior law, voting pass-through on a one-person, one-vote basis was only permitted with respect to issues for which the law did not require voting pass-through.

Recently, the IRS clarified in Revenue Ruling 95-57 that allocated shares for which no direction is received may be voted by the responsible fiduciary. The DOL agrees with the IRS on this point.

---

21 Code Sec. 409(e)(5).

When voting pass-through (the right of participants to direct the voting of their allocated shares) is required by law but not all of the shares held by the ESOP have been allocated to participants, the unallocated shares are voted in the manner prescribed by the ESOP document. The ESOP document may provide that the unallocated shares will be voted in the same proportion as participants vote allocated shares. In most cases, however, any unallocated shares are voted by the ESOP administrative committee or ESOP trustees and must be voted in the best interests of participants and beneficiaries. If the ESOP trustee is a bank or other institution, the trustee usually votes unallocated shares as directed by a committee appointed by the company. Only in extreme and unusual circumstances—when the trustee knows (or should know) that the voting instructions given to it are clearly improper (perhaps because of coercion or misinformation) and violate ERISA—may the trustee exercise its own judgment regarding the voting of such shares. Because there are no voting pass-through provisions contained in ERISA, the DOL takes the position that the trustees are ultimately responsible for the voting of all shares, both allocated and unallocated. This may be the case, according to the DOL, despite explicit plan provisions that, as required by IRC Section 409(e), vest voting direction authority in plan participants (and their beneficiaries) with respect to allocated shares and prescribe procedures for the voting of unallocated shares. No regulatory or legislative clarification of this point is in sight.

When voting pass-through is not required by law, the shares usually are voted by the fiduciary. However, voting rights may be provided to participants in excess of what is required by law, from full pass-through on all allocated shares on all issues requiring a shareholder vote, to limiting the vote to certain specific issues (such as the election of one or more corporate directors or limiting the vote to vested shares only). The procedures to be followed to solicit voting instructions should be established so as to permit participants to vote without any improper interference. Generally, participants will be sent the same shareholder meeting notice and any proxy solicitation materials that are sent to all other shareholders. The disclosure requirements for shareholder meetings are generally done in accordance with applicable state corporate laws and corporate bylaws (and SEC rules when a company is publicly traded). The proxy solicitation card or form instructs the ESOP trustee how to vote the shares and will generally be tabulated by the company on instructions given to or by the ESOP trustee. All participant voting must be kept confidential and free of duress or coercion.

Rights and Restrictions on Employer Securities

General Rule

Historically, employer securities held by a qualified plan must have "unrestricted" marketability.[22] This rule was further modified by Technical Information Release (T.I.R.) 1413's prohibition on a mandatory "call" option exercisable by the employer within a specified time. The regulations provide that employer securities acquired with the proceeds of an exempt loan may not be subject to a "put, call, or other option, or buyout, or similar arrangement," except that restrictions required under federal and state laws are permitted.[23] Since this applies only to securities purchased with the proceeds of an exempt loan, a violation of this provision will result in a prohibited transaction and the loss of tax benefits that depend upon the plan being an ESOP. However, since Revenue Ruling 57-372 continues to apply, a violation of this provision also would result in plan disqualification if the violation takes the form of a buy-sell, call option, or other market-restricting arrangement and could result in a loss of all of the tax benefits dependent upon qualified ESOP status.

Right of First Refusal

The regulations permit a customary right of first refusal to attach to certain securities. First, the securities must not be publicly traded at the time the right may be exercised. Second, the right of first refusal may be only in favor of the employer, the ESOP, or both, in any order. Third, the right must not be in favor of shareholders, other than the ESOP. Last, the right of first refusal must lapse no later than 14 days after written notice of the offer to purchase has been given to the party holding the right.

Further, the payment terms and purchase price must not be less favorable to the seller than the greater of (1) the purchase price and other terms offered by the buyer (other than the sponsor or the ESOP, which has in good faith made an offer to purchase), or (2) the value of the security determined on the most recent valuation date under the ESOP.[24]

If the seller of employer securities is a disqualified person and the ESOP is buying, a special valuation date applies. The purchase price is determined on the date of the proposed transaction. A disqualified person is a person described in 4975(e)(2) of the IRC and a party-in-interest is

---

22 Rev. Rul. 57-372,1957-2 C.B. 256, modified by Rev. Rul. 69-65 1969-1 C.B. 114.
23 Treas. Reg. Sec. 54.4975-7(b)(4); Labor Reg. Sec. 2550.408(b)-3(d).
24 Treas. Reg. Secs. 54.4975-7(b)(9), 54.4975-11 (d)(5); Labor Reg. Sec. 2550.408b-3(l).

described in ERISA Section 3(14)(A). The two definitions are identical with one key difference: ERISA says only that all employees are parties-in-interest; under the IRC only employees earning 10 percent or more of the yearly wages of an employer are disqualified persons. Thus, most employees receiving in-service distributions will not be disqualified persons, even though they are parties-in-interest.

Buy-Sell Agreements

An ESOP is not permitted to enter into agreements obligating it to acquire securities from a shareholder at an indefinite time in the future that is determined by the occurrence of an event—including certain events such as the death of a shareholder.[25]

An ESOP also is not permitted to be obligated to put-option arrangements.[26] Ostensibly the purpose of these prohibitions is to eliminate the possibility that plan fiduciaries may be required to act imprudently in the future, at the time of purchase.

Even agreements spelling out that the transaction will take place at fair-market value and for adequate consideration at the time the obligation becomes due will not be acceptable, because the purchase (for all of the reasons outlined in this chapter) may not be an acceptable transaction.

Option arrangements, however, are permissible. An ESOP may enter into an agreement that would provide the ESOP with an option to purchase employer securities from a shareholder at some definite or indefinite date in the future. This type of arrangement clearly is in the interest of both the ESOP and the participants, because it provides a place to purchase employer securities and gives the fiduciaries a chance to determine the prudence of the exercise of the option. Careful drafting would require that the ESOP trust provisions specifically permit such agreements but not require that they be entered into.

Put Options

One key question that has always troubled nearly everyone concerned with ESOPs is: "What good is stock without a market?" Part of the answer has been set forth in regulations[27] and modified by statute.[28]

Code Sections 401(a)(23) and 409(h) provide that participants or beneficiaries receiving a distribution of employer stock from an ESOP (or tax-

---

25 Treas. Reg. Sec. 54.4975-11 (a)(4)(ii).
26 Treas. Reg. Sec. 54.4975-7(b)(10); Labor Reg. Sec. 2550.408b-3(j).
27 Treas. Reg. Sec. 54.4975-7(b)(10); Labor Reg. Sec. 2550.408b-3(j).
28 Revenue Act of 1978, Sec. 17(n).

credit ESOP or stock bonus plan) generally must be given a put option for the stock if the employer securities are not readily tradable on an established market. This means that a participant who receives a distribution of stock from the plan has a right to require that the employer repurchase employer securities under a fair valuation formula.

As finally codified by the Revenue Act of 1978 and its legislative history and by TRA '86, the put option must give these benefits:

1. The trustee of the participant's IRA must be able to exercise the same option.

2. The participant must have at least 60 days after receipt of the stock to require that the employer repurchase the stock at its fair-market value[29] and make payment within 30 days if the shares were distributed as part of an installment distribution.

3. The ESOP *may* be permitted to take the employer's role and repurchase the stock in lieu of the employer.

4. The participant must have an additional 60-day period in which to exercise the put option in the following plan year.[30]

5. If the shares were distributed as part of a lump-sum distribution, payment for the shares must begin within 30 days after the exercise of the put option on a schedule at least as rapid as substantially equal annual payments over a period not exceeding five years, at the option of the party buying back the stock. Under code Section 409(h)(5), the seller must be given a promissory note that will accelerate (all become due at once) if the buyer defaults on any installment payment. The installment note must have adequate security and carry a reasonable interest rate. "Adequate security" means a tangible asset that can be sold, foreclosed upon, or otherwise be disposed of in the event of default; an unsecured note backed only by the employer's "full faith and credit" is insufficient.[31]

The legal obligation to grant a put option is applicable under a leveraged ESOP where the employer's securities are not readily tradable on an established market, if the shares were acquired by an ESOP in a leveraged transaction. This put-option requirement also applies to employer securities acquired after December 31, 1979, by unleveraged ESOPs qualified under code Section 4975(e)(7), whether leveraged or not. Under an ordinary stock-bonus plan sponsored by an employer without a readily tradable class of securities, the employer is legally obligated to grant a put option for its securities distributed to participants by the plan, but only if such securities

---

29 IRC Sec. 409(h)(4).

30 IRC See. 409(h)(5)(A).

31 IRC Sec. 409(h)(5)(B).

were acquired after December 31, 1986, and to any shares acquired after December 31, 1976, if the plan included a cash distribution option.

A put option is always required on distributed stock that was acquired with the proceeds of an exempt loan and that is not publicly traded, even if the plan is subsequently changed from an ESOP. After ERTA, this does not apply in the case of a bank that is prohibited from purchasing its own stock if participants are given the right to receive benefits in cash, thereby eliminating the need for the put option. Also, if it is known at the time the exempt loan is made that honoring the put option would cause the employer to violate federal or state law, the put option must permit the securities to be put to a third party having substantial net worth at the time the loan is made and whose net worth is reasonably expected to remain substantial. Very few individuals would, or could, accept the obligations of a perpetual putee. Also, the substituted putee rule was clearly not intended to cover situations in which the employer may be temporarily prevented from honoring the option, such as in the situation when the employer sponsor has no retained earnings from which to purchase securities (a requirement of many states). Not even companies whose shares are readily tradable on an established market can afford to ignore the put-option requirements. For example, if the shares held by the ESOP are not readily tradable on an established market, then the put-option rules apply. Sometimes public companies are acquired and are no longer public. Sometimes trading is suspended in certain securities, or perhaps the company goes "private" or fails to meet the continuing rules of the exchange(s) on which it is traded (i.e., no longer readily tradable on an established market). Sometimes a publicly traded company's ESOP distributes shares that are not freely tradable (e.g., subject to SEC Rule 144). In any case in which the employer securities are no longer readily tradable on an established market, the put-option rule becomes effective.

Payments under put options also may not be restricted by loan agreements, other arrangements, or the terms of the employer's bylaws or articles of incorporation, except to the extent necessary to comply with state laws.[32]

The ESOP will very likely lose its attractiveness as an employee benefit plan if terminating employees and their beneficiaries are liable for taxes on shares for which there is no immediate liquid market. Also, this lack of marketability is a factor in determining the value of the shares and, without a put option, there will likely be a lower valuation of the securities. The

---

32 Treas. Reg. Sec. 54.4975-7(b)(12)(v); Labor Reg. Sec. 2550.408b-3(l)(5).

company may offer to repurchase shares voluntarily, under even more favorable terms and conditions than the law requires, even when not required to do so by law and may do so under conditions that do not have to conform in any respect to the rules applicable to mandatory put options.[33] However gratuitous this desire may be, if these discretionary put options are granted in a manner that is not uniform and nondiscriminatory, prohibited plan discrimination may result. The problem can be eliminated if, for example, the discretionary put options are for a fixed number of securities for each and every party receiving a distribution.

Under the requirements of IRC Section 401(a)(28)(B), the ESOP must provide "qualified employees"—those who are at least 55 years old and who have at least 10 years of participation in the plan—an opportunity to diversify their plan holdings. This applies only to shares acquired after December 31, 1986. Section 401(a)(28)(B) imposes this as a qualification requirement that plans must permit qualified participants to diversify the investment of at least 25 percent of their ESOP account during the qualified election period. The qualified election period is the six-year period commencing with or after the plan year in which the participant attains age 55 (or, if later, starting with the plan year in which the participant has completed 10 years of participation). Further, in the final year of the qualified election period, the plan must afford the participant the opportunity to diversify the investment of at least 50 percent of the balance of his or her plan account (less any prior portion diversified). Participants are apparently entitled to one election each year during the election period. For companies whose ESOP shares are not readily tradable on an established market, this provision will have the practical effect of accelerating the repurchase liability created by the plan's distributions. However, under IRS Notice 88-56, IRB, 1988-19, no diversification need be provided if the fair-market value of the employer stock allocated to a participant's account is less than $500 and the plan document so provides. The 10 percent early-distribution tax is due under code Section 72(5) for a diversification distribution that is not rolled over.

An ESOP may satisfy this diversification requirement in two ways:

1. The plan may distribute, in stock or in cash, the portion of a participant's account subject to the diversification requirement to him or her within 90 days of the period in which the diversification election may be made. If the plan distributes stock (even though it is not required to do so), the put-option requirements apply and the stock may be rolled over into an IRA. The IRA retains the put right only if the stock is not readily

33 Treas. Reg. Sec. 54.4975-11 (a)(7)(i); Labor Reg. Sec. 2550.407d-6(a)(6).

tradable on an established market at the time of the distribution; if it distributes cash, the participant may roll the cash over into an IRA.

2. A plan may offer at least three investment options (other than employer stock) to qualified employees. Alternatively, an option to transfer assets to a qualified plan that permits at least three investment options (other than employer stock) can be provided to qualified employees. Because of the similarity to distribution options of cash or stock, the authors believe that the mere offering of the option to liquidate ESOP shares should not be considered as a "sale" and "purchase" under federal and state securities laws.

Valuation

For nonpublicly traded employer stock acquired after December 31, 1986, all determinations of fair-market value in connection with an ESOP must be based on an independent appraisal.[34] IRS regulations issued under code Section 170(a) may establish standards for determining what constitutes an independent appraiser; otherwise, the proposed DOL regulations on adequate consideration now deal with this issue. The final regulations under code Section 4975 and proposed DOL regulations require that a valuation be made in good faith on the basis of all relevant factors affecting the value of securities.[35]

Conversions and Mergers Involving ESOPs

Conversion to an ESOP

Under the proper circumstances, existing pension and profit-sharing plans may be converted (by amendment) into ESOPs. If the requirements of prudence and the exclusive-benefit rule under ERISA can be satisfied, existing assets of such converted plans may be used to acquire employer securities. However, *the conversion into an ESOP of an existing plan's investments in general assets that have been accumulated for the purpose of providing retirement benefits should be undertaken with extreme caution.* Fiduciaries should carefully document why the conversion was prudent and consistent with the exclusive-benefit requirement. Normally, it is only when the fortunes of the company and the value of the stock decline following a conversion that the fiduciaries are called upon to explain.

---

34 IRC Sec. 401(a)(28)(C).

35 Treas. Reg. Sec. 54.4975-11(d)(5). See also *Donovan* v. *Cunningham* 716 F.2d 1455 (5th Circuit, 1983), Cert. denied, June 18, 1984.

Almost all the rules discussed earlier in this chapter come into play with a conversion, and accelerated vesting may be required, depending upon the type of plan converted, along with the preservation of distribution options. The shares may be purchased from existing shareholders, the employer corporation, or the public market.

Conversion of a defined benefit plan into an ESOP involves both the amendment of the character of the plan from a defined benefit plan to a defined contribution plan, and the use of all or part of the plan assets to buy employer stock. Such a conversion is treated as a termination of the plan for purposes of Title IV of ERISA. Therefore, code Section 411(d) will require 100 percent vesting of participants' actuarially determined benefits. Annuity distributions must be offered to participants in addition to the plan's other distribution requirements. If the employees are given a choice between receiving their accrued benefits in the form of an annuity and having the present value of such benefits invested in employer stock, care must be taken to comply with all applicable federal and state securities law requirements. Other types of plans, such as thrift and savings plans, also may be converted.

Conversion of a money purchase pension plan into an ESOP may result in 100 percent vesting if the new ESOP does not constitute a comparable plan.

For taxable years beginning after December 31, 1986, the ability to deduct up to 25 percent of participants' compensation (instead of the normal 15 percent of compensation) for contributions to a stock bonus or profit-sharing plan is eliminated except to the extent that the increased deduction results from prior years' contributions is below 15 percent of compensation. The unused deduction carryforwards that accumulated for taxable years beginning prior to January 1, 1987, are preserved and may be used after 1986 to increase the deduction limit to 25 percent of participants' compensation. Finally, pre-1987 contribution credit carryovers attributable to the existing plan under IRC Section 404(a)(3)(A) are available for use under a converted ESOP, provided the preexisting plan was a stock bonus or a profit-sharing plan. No credit carryover is permissible if the converted ESOP is derived from a money purchase pension plan or a defined benefit plan.[36]

For any conversion, the provisions of such plans with respect to permissible investments are indeed critical. Because vested employee

---

[36] This is because pension plans had no pre-1987 contribution carryovers. See T.I.R. 1413, Q&A T-9 (1975).

accounts are being used to purchase qualifying employer securities, the plan provisions almost universally require substantial amendments.

Potential fiduciary liability for plan conversions may exist. Further information is available by reading the following decisions: (1) *Usery* v. *Penn*, 426 F. Supp. 830 (W.D. Okla. 1976), *aff'd sub nom. Eaves* v. *Penn*, 587 F.2d 453 (10th Cir. 1978); (2) *Marshall* v. *Whatley*, No. 77 Civ. 04-A (E.D. Va. Apr. 18, 1977); and (3) *Baker* v. *Smith*, No. 80 Civ. 3067 (E.D. Penn. Aug. 6, 1980).

A number of labor issues, including the existence of any collective bargaining agreements, may have to be considered.

Pension-Reversion Excise-Tax Exemption

Section 4980(d) imposes a 50 percent excise tax on a reversion from a qualified plan, unless the employer establishes or maintains a qualified replacement plan or provides for certain benefit increases. An ESOP may be a qualified replacement plan and, if 25 percent of the reversion amount is transferred to the ESOP and allocated to participants' accounts no less rapidly than ratably over seven plan years, then the excise tax is reduced to 20 percent of the reversion amount.

Mergers into an ESOP

Each qualified plan, as a condition of qualification, must provide that, in the case of merger or consolidation with or transfer of assets or liabilities to any other plan after September 2, 1974, each participant must receive a benefit immediately after the merger, consolidation, or transfer, determined as if the plan being transferred were then terminated. This means that any participant must receive no less than the benefit the participant would have been entitled to receive before the merger, consolidation, or transfer, determined as if the plan into which the transfer occurs had then terminated.[37] These conditions will be referred to as the *transfer rules*. The rules are extremely complicated and generally beyond the scope of this chapter. However, a few of the more essential rules are presented here.

If two or more defined contribution plans are merged or consolidated, the transfer rules will be met if all of the following conditions are met:

1. The sum of the account balances in the plans equals the fair-market value of the assets of the surviving plan on the date of the merger or consolidation.

---

37 IRC Secs. 401(a)(12), 414(l).

2. The assets of each plan are combined to form the assets of the plan as merged.

3. The participants' balances in the plans that survive right after the merger are equal to the sum of the participants' account balances (individually determined) in the plans just before the merger.

A defined benefit plan being merged into an existing ESOP is considered as being, first, converted to a defined contribution plan, and then, once converted, it is considered as merged.[38] The Pension Benefit Guaranty Corporation (PBGC) requires the plan administrator to allow each participant to elect in writing either to receive the value of the participant's accrued benefits in the form provided under the plan or to have plan assets equal in value payable as an annuity transferred to an individual account under the ESOP.[39] This election probably constitutes a sale within the meaning of Section 2(3) of the Securities Act of 1933 and would require compliance unless some exception from registration is available. In addition, care must be taken to preserve distribution options to the extent required under code Section 411(d)(6).

Conversion from an ESOP

If the conversion out of an ESOP is accomplished by plan merger, consolidation, or transfer of assets, the transfer rules would apply. There may be significant problems under the anticutback rules of code Section 411(d)(6), because the participant's right to demand stock may be considered a "protected right" for purposes of the anticutback rules. If the plan merger, consolidation, or transfer of assets out of an ESOP is into another type of defined contribution plan, it will not necessarily trigger a termination within the meaning of the vesting requirements of code Section 411(d)(3). The key issue is the fiduciary decision as to what extent employer stock will be sold in light of the conversion.

To the extent employer stock continues to be held under the plan, the conversion out of an ESOP also will not in itself relieve the employer from the put-option requirements. The put-option rule applies only when employer securities are distributed and enough securities of the employer could be converted to other assets to permit distributions in other assets or when future contributions may supply enough cash for

---

38 Treas. Reg. Sec. 1.414(l)-1(i).
39 PBGC Opinion 76-30 (March 8, 1976); PBGC Opinion 76-12 (January 27, 1976).

many years. Outstanding loans are a problem on the conversion out of an ESOP. To the extent unallocated shares held as collateral are sold, the proceeds should be used to retire ESOP debt, absent an extremely favorable ESOP interest rate. If indebtedness would still remain thereafter, however, the ESOP fiduciaries have three options: (1) defer the conversion until the loan is paid off, (2) seek a specific exemption from the prohibited transaction rules of ERISA Section 408(a) and IRC Section 4975(c)(2), or (3) proceed with the conversion risk and incur the penalties imposed with respect to prohibited transactions. There is a further risk that plan fiduciaries may be held liable for any losses incurred by the plan as a result of their violation of the prohibited transaction provisions of ERISA Section 409(a), and they may be removed by a court. The same fiduciary considerations applicable to converting *to* an ESOP are applicable in converting *from* one.

Last, converting to any other kind of plan but an eligible individual-account plan gives rise to an absolute 10 percent limitation of ERISA Section 407 on the holding of employer securities.

Types of Employer Securities

With the changes brought about by the Technical Corrections Act of 1979, the definition of *qualifying employer securities* in code Section 4975(e)(8) incorporates by reference the definition of *employer securities* set forth in code Section 409(1) (which was added by the Revenue Act of 1978). This definition includes stock of the employer and certain controlled group members, which meets one of the following requirements:

1. Common stock readily tradable on an established securities market.
2. If there is no readily tradable common stock, common stock having a combination of voting power and dividend rights at least equal to the classes of common stock having the greatest voting power and the greatest dividend rights.
3. Preferred stock convertible (at any time at a reasonable conversion price determined at the date of acquisition) into common stock meeting one of the above definitions.

This definition of employer securities is applicable to stock acquired by a statutory ESOP after December 31, 1979. Note that any kind of capital stock may be contributed or purchased on a nonleveraged basis, if the plan is a stock-bonus plan that is not an ESOP or an ESOP that is otherwise primarily invested in qualifying employer securities. However, to the extent that an ESOP acquires stock that is not a qualifying employer security, the special ESOP tax benefits (tax-free rollover, partial interest exclusion, special deduction limitations, and so on) do not apply.

Cash Versus Stock Distributions

Until the changes brought about by the Revenue Act of 1978, the Technical Corrections Act of 1979, and the Miscellaneous Revenue Act of 1980, the regulations for ESOPs required that the portion of an ESOP consisting of a stock bonus plan must provide for benefits to be distributable only in stock of the employer.[40] This provision restated the requirements applicable to stock-bonus plans set forth in Treasury Regulation Sections 1.401-1(a)(2)(iii) and 1.401-1(b)(1)(iii).

The Revenue Act of 1978 provided that a leveraged ESOP could distribute cash in lieu of employer securities so long as the participant could demand that his or her distribution be made in employer securities.

The Technical Corrections Act of 1979 provided that the cash-distribution option available to an ESOP under code Section 4975(e)(7) and 409A(h), which is now 409(h), be made effective with respect to distributions of benefits after December 31, 1978.

The Miscellaneous Revenue Act of 1980 added code Section 401(a)(23), which permits any qualified stock-bonus plan, not just an ESOP or Tax Reduction Act stock ownership plan (TRASOP), to make distributions of benefits in either cash or stock after December 31, 1980, so long as the participant or beneficiary has the right to demand distributions in the form of employer stock. ERTA further modified this to provide that mandatory cash distributions could occur if the articles or bylaws of the corporation restrict ownership of substantially all the company's stock to current employees and an employees' trust.

Finally, TAMRA provides that a participant does not have the right to demand that benefits be paid in the form of stock with respect to the portion of the participant's stock that the participant elected to diversify.

Special Distribution Requirements

TRA '86 imposed new requirements on the timing of distributions from an ESOP. These requirements apply to distributions attributable to employer stock acquired by the ESOP after December 31, 1986.

---

40 Treas. Reg. Sec. 54.4975-11 (f)(1).

Unless a participant otherwise elects, or resumes employment following a resignation or dismissal but before the distribution date, IRC Section 409(o) requires the distribution of his or her ESOP benefits to begin no later than the last day of the plan year following the plan year of normal retirement age, disability, or death, or of the fifth plan year following the plan year in which his or her employment terminates for other reasons. An exception to this general rule exists under IRC Section 409(a)(1)(B) for leveraged shares until the corresponding ESOP debt is repaid; however, code Sections 401(a)(9) and 401(a)(14) require that distribution begin by the earlier to occur of (1) the April 1 next following the calendar year in which the participant who is a 5 percent or more owner attains age 70½, or (2) the 60th day following the plan year during which the participant has attained the plan's normal retirement age, reached the 10th anniversary of the date he or she commenced participation in the plan, and separated from service.

Generally, unless a participant otherwise elects, distribution of ESOP benefits must be made at least as rapidly as substantially equal, annual installments over a period not exceeding five years. However, for participants whose benefits exceed $500,000 in value, the distribution period may be extended (up to an additional five years) by one year for each $100,000 ($150,000 in 2000), or fraction thereof, by which the value of benefits exceeds $500,000 ($755,000 in 2000).

Subject to these and other qualified plan nondiscrimination requirements, an ESOP may retain discretion in determining the timing and form of distributions without regard to the restrictions on discretionary distribution options generally applicable to qualified plans under the Retirement Equity Act of 1984 (REA).

Early Distribution Excise-Tax Exception

TRA '86 imposes a 10 percent excise tax on taxable distributions (after 1986) from a qualified plan to a participant prior to age 59, unless the distribution occurs as the result of the participant's death, disability, or terminated employment after age 55 under the plan; is made as a part of substantially equal periodic payments over the participant's life or the joint lives of the participant and a designated beneficiary; or is rolled over into an IRA. This excise tax generally did not apply to any ESOP distributions prior to 1990. In addition, cash dividends on employer stock that are passed through to ESOP participants are not subject to this excise tax even after 1990.

Which Distribution Is Best?

A nearly universal participant question is: "Which distribution type is best—cash or stock?" The answer depends on the tax picture of the employee, the interplay of the lump-sum distribution rules under the code, and the net unrealized-appreciation provisions of code Section 402(e)(4)(D) and (J) and regulations issued thereunder. Under those provisions, the employee has opted to exclude the net unrealized appreciation from taxable income. *Net unrealized appreciation* is the excess of the fair-market value of the employer securities at the time of distribution from a plan over the trust's adjusted basis in the securities. The net unrealized appreciation on the date of distribution is taxed as a long-term capital gain when the securities are subsequently disposed of. Any additional appreciation is either short- or long-term capital gain, depending on how long the stock is held by the distributee.[41] The participant may, however, not have a choice as to whether he or she receives a lump-sum distribution or installments; this decision may be reserved for the fiduciary, committee, or plan administrator that must consider plan and employer liquidity in making a choice as to the form of distribution.

To determine which distribution is most advantageous, calculate the total tax from lump-sum treatment with each of the various possibilities. Surprisingly, in many large distributions, taking stock may result in a lower tax, both currently and subsequently. However, it permits an ESOP distributee to elect to include any appreciation in value of employer stock while in the ESOP (net unrealized appreciation) as part of the taxable amount eligible for special income-tax averaging available for certain lump-sum distributions. Considerations also should be given to the excess-distribution tax provisions of code Section 4981 and the possible advantageous use of an IRA rollover. In a situation, for example, where the employee receives stock, excludes the net unrealized appreciation from income and dies before selling the stock, his or her survivors will get a stepped basis in the stock and avoid paying income tax on the net unrealized appreciation.

Rollovers

Rollovers are very flexible for lump-sum distributions (and certain "partial distributions") from ESOPs. The stock may be distributed, then sold, and the proceeds contributed to an IRA, provided the proceeds are contributed

---

41 Rev. Rul. 81-122 1981-1 C.B.

within the statutory 60-day period. Alternatively, partial rollovers are permitted, and of course, if the stock is acceptable to an IRA custodian or trustee, the stock can go right into the IRA. No tax is due by participants or beneficiaries if these special IRA rules are followed. The disadvantage of an IRA, however, is that the various options available by carefully calculating the tax effect of stock and cash in a lump-sum distribution are not available if the distribution stays in an IRA until distributions start. If a distribution is rolled over into an IRA, the benefit of the lump-sum and capital-gains provisions of the IRC are not available. The subsequent distributions from the IRA are taxed at ordinary earned-income tax rates, and the special averaging and capital-gains rates are lost forever. The only exception is when the amount rolled over is subsequently rolled over into another qualified plan.

Deduction of Employer Dividend Payments

Code Section 404(k) permits a deduction to a corporation for the amount of dividends paid in cash by such corporation with respect to employer securities if:

1. Such employer securities are held on the record date of the dividend by a tax-credit ESOP or an ESOP that meets the requirements of Section 4975(e)(7) of the code and regulations issued thereunder and is maintained by such corporation or a controlled group member thereof; and
2. In accordance with the ESOP provisions, one of the following occurs:
   a. The dividend is paid in cash directly to the participants and beneficiaries in the plan, or
   b. The dividend is paid in cash to the ESOP and is distributed to the participants and beneficiaries in the ESOP not later than 90 days after the close of the plan year in which paid.[42]

In addition, a deduction for dividends is permitted where the amount of cash dividends paid on employer stock held by an ESOP (both allocated and unallocated shares) are used by the ESOP to make payments (of principal and interest) on the ESOP loan used to acquire those shares. Code Section 404(k)(2) significantly enhances the ability to finance ESOP transactions on a pretax basis. Note that dividends on allocated shares may be used to make payments on such a loan only if the account to which the

---

42 IRC Sec. 404(k)(2)(A).

dividends would have been allocated is allocated shares with a fair-market value not less than the amount of the dividend that would have been allocated. Such allocation must be made in the plan year the dividend would otherwise have been allocated. The deduction, which applies for taxable years commencing after October 22, 1986, is allowed for the taxable year of the corporation in which the dividends are so applied.

The deductibility of dividends used to repay a securities acquisition loan is further limited to those dividends paid on the shares acquired with the loan proceeds, and not extended to dividends on other shares held by the plan. This restriction applies to employer securities acquired by an ESOP after August 4, 1989. While the legislative history and informal remarks by IRS representatives indicate that no inferences should be made with respect to the scope of the dividend deduction on employer securities acquired by an ESOP before August 5, 1989, Tax Advice Memorandum 9435001 and 9516003 rule that a corporation may deduct dividends it pays on stock that was acquired by its ESOP before August 5, 1989. No inferences should be made with respect to the permissible sources of payment on exempt loans under Title I of ERISA; it is theoretically possible under ERISA that dividends paid on allocated shares may not be used to repay ESOP debt.

Finally, reasonable dividends used to repay an ESOP loan will not be considered an annual addition for Section 415 purposes and such dividends will be disregarded for purposes of determining the maximum amount deductible under Section 404(a).

Stock Purchase by an ESOP

When a taxpayer sells shares of stock, he or she recognizes gain to the extent of the excess over the taxpayer's adjusted basis in the stock. When the stock is redeemed by the issuing corporation, the transaction is considered a distribution by the corporation, with respect to its stock, and will be taxable as a capital gain (or loss) only if the requirements of code Section 302(b) are satisfied. Otherwise, it is a dividend to the shareholder and taxed twice—once at the corporate level and then again at the shareholder level.

The ESOP is clearly a separate legal entity, and so under normal circumstances the sale by a shareholder to an ESOP would be taxed as a sale or exchange at capital-gains rates, too. Basis in the stock will not be taxed, only the proceeds in excess of the basis. However, the IRS may view certain transactions as a redemption by the sponsoring employer and, hence, subject to dividend treatment.

Revenue Procedure 87-22 sets forth operating rules with respect to the issuance of an advance ruling of the IRS: that the proposed sale of the employer's stock by a shareholder to a related employee plan is a sale or exchange, rather than a corporate distribution taxable under code Section 301.[43] The revenue procedure only provides a safe harbor, and failure to meet its tests will not be an automatic application of code Section 301 to the sale of stock to a qualified plan. These guidelines do not, as a matter of law, precisely define the only situations in which the sale of stock to a plan will avoid treatment as a corporate distribution of property under code Section 301. In the absence of such a ruling, the tax ramifications of such a sale will be subject to examination on audit.

Other ESOP Considerations

Characteristics of the Employer

An ESOP must be established by a corporate employer. Only two states, Minnesota and North Carolina, allow a professional corporation to establish an ESOP.

S Corporations

ESOPs may be S corporation shareholders beginning in 1998.[44] However, the following tax benefits applicable to ESOP sponsors do not apply to S corporations: (1) the special contribution deduction rules under Section 404(a)(9),[45] (2) the deduction of dividends paid on employer securities held in an ESOP,[46] and (3) the rules on the rollover of gain on the sale of stock to an ESOP under Section 1042.[47]

The Taxpayer Relief Act of 1997 corrected certain technical flaws in the corporation/ESOP legislation and made advantageous changes in the method of taxation of ESOPs that hold S corporation stock. The 1997 Tax Act enacted the following provisions:

The prohibited transaction provisions of code Section 4975 and ERISA Section 406 were amended to permit plans sponsored by S corporations to use the sale of employer securities prohibited-transaction exemption, previously available only to C corporations.

---

43 1987-1 C.B. 718.
44 IRC Sec. 1361 (b)(1)(B), as amended by the SBJPA, P.L. 104-188, Sec. 1316(a).
45 IRC Sec. 404(a)(9)(C).
46 IRC Sec. 404(k)(1).
47 IRS Sec. 1042(c)(1)(A).

Section 409(h)(2) was amended to provide that an S corporation ESOP may deny participants the right to demand their distributions in the form of stock in the same manner as a corporation whose charter or bylaws restrict ownership of its employer securities to current employees or a trust defined in Section 401(a).

Section 512(e) was amended to provide that the "unrelated business income tax" that the Small Business Job Protection Act (SBJPA) imposed on the ESOP's share of S corporation's earnings is repealed, effective January 1, 1998. This change achieves the single level of tax regime for ESOP participants that other S corporation shareholders enjoy.

An S corporation is a corporation for state law purposes that generally is not required to pay federal corporate income tax. (Many, but not all, states accord S corporations similar treatment.) Instead, the shareholders must pay tax on their proportionate share of the S corporation's income. This means that S corporation income is not subject to the two layers of tax applicable to other corporate income: a tax on corporate earnings payable once by the corporation, and a second tax payable by the shareholders when those earnings are distributed as dividends or liquidation proceeds.

The repeal of the unrelated business income tax may provide a strong incentive for some C corporations to convert to S corporation status.

Example: An S corporation is owned 50 percent by an ESOP and 50 percent by an individual and has $2 million of earnings for 2000. The individual will owe a tax on his or her $1 million share of the corporation's earnings on his or her 2000 tax return, but the ESOP will owe nothing because it is a tax-exempt entity. Presumably, either the value of the stock of the company will increase to reflect its share of the earnings, or those earnings will be distributed to the ESOP, so that when participants receive their ultimate taxable distributions, they will pay tax on their share of the 2000 earnings. The date of that tax payment could be many years off, however, because participants have the right to roll their ESOP distribution directly into an IRA.

In order for a C corporation to convert to an S corporation, the following requirements must be satisfied:

1. An S corporation cannot have more than 75 shareholders. An ESOP is considered as a single shareholder.[48]

2. An S corporation can have as shareholders only individuals, estates, certain trusts, and certain tax-exempt organizations,

---

48 IRC Sec. 1361(b)(1).

including qualified plan trusts. Nonresident aliens cannot be S corporation shareholders.[49]

3. An S corporation must have only one class of stock issued and outstanding. A corporation is treated as having only one class of stock if all of the outstanding shares confer identical rights to distribution and liquidation proceeds.[50]

As a result of the single class-of-stock requirement, in the case of a less than 100 percent ESOP-owned company, the ESOP must receive an S corporation dividend distribution in an amount equal to the distribution made to the other shareholders. Although the dividends paid to an S corporation ESOP are not tax-deductible under Section 404(k), dividends paid on the unallocated shares may still be used to make payments on an ESOP loan and will not count against the contribution (Section 404) or annual addition (Section 415) limitations. Depending on the amount of accumulated earnings and profits, dividends on allocated shares may not be used to repay ESOP indebtedness.[51]

Certain tax benefits may be lost upon conversion to S corporation status. For the 10-year period following its conversion to S corporation status, the corporation will be subject to a "built-in gains" tax on the disposition of any asset that it held on the day of its S corporation election. This tax, that is in addition to the tax payable by the shareholders, is imposed on the gain that had accrued in the asset before the corporation's conversion to S status. Corporations on the cash method of tax accounting may owe built-in gains tax on the amount of their receivables as of the date of their S corporation election.

In addition, "LIFO recapture tax" must be paid by a C corporation on the LIFO method when it converts to S corporation status, and certain fringe benefits for 2 percent or more shareholders are excludible from income if they are employed by C corporations, but not if they are employed by S corporations.

General Requirements

All employee benefit plans must be established pursuant to a written instrument. All assets of the plan must be held in a trust and be managed by a trustee named in the plan or appointed by a named fiduciary. The

---

49 Id.

50 Id.

51 IRC Sec. 404(k)(5)(B).

trustee has exclusive authority to manage and control the assets of the plan.[52] However, the plan may provide that the trustee is subject to the direction and authority of the named fiduciary.[53] The plan may provide that the named fiduciary may appoint an investment manager to manage the assets of the plan.[54]

Valuation of Employer Securities

Proper valuation of employer securities contributed or sold to the plan is an important and difficult aspect of plan administration. Improper valuation of employer securities contributed to the plan may result in the loss of some deductions if the valuation is overstated. If the value is understated, potential deductions also will have been forgone. If the ESOP purchases the securities for more than their fair-market value, an excise tax could be imposed (together with required corrections and liability to the responsible fiduciaries), and in egregious circumstances, disqualification of the ESOP might result.[55] For nonpublicly traded employer stock acquired after December 31, 1986, all determinations of fair-market value in connection with an ESOP must be based upon a valuation by an independent appraiser. Treasury regulations will establish standards for determining what constitutes an independent appraiser along the lines of regulations issued under the charitable-contribution provisions of IRC Section 170(a)(1).[56]

Accounting Considerations[57]

ESOPs must address some difficult accounting issues, both from the employer's point of view in preparing the financial statements, and in the trust accounting and participant accounting areas. Since 1976, the American Institute of Certified Public Accountants (AICPA) has published accounting guidelines and updates.

On November 22, 1993, the AICPA published *Statement of Position 93-6 (SOP 93-6)*. While the rules in regard to the accounting treatment are

---

52 ERISA Sec. 403(a).

53 ERISA Sec. 403(a)(1).

54 ERISA Sec. 402(c)(3).

55 IRC Sec. 4975, 401(a); ERISA Sec. 502(l).

56 IRC Sec 401(a)(28)(C).

57 This section has been intentionally prepared in brief. For further information, see the AICPA's *Statement of Position 93-6*; see also Smiley, Gilbert, and Binns, *Employee Stock Ownership Plans: Business Planning, Implementation, Law, and Taxation*, Chapter 12.

beyond the scope of this chapter, the basic rules are summarized below. Prior to *SOP 93-6*'s publication, *SOP 76-3* and several updates provided guidance. The revised SOP is effective for ESOP stock acquisitions after December 31, 1992. Sponsors of ESOPs that were formed prior to the effective date can elect the new standard. The reporting in the final standard is required for financial periods beginning after December 15, 1992.

Liabilities

All ESOP debt will be recorded on the balance sheet of the plan sponsor, with no exceptions. The issue of the "push down" of an obligation to a subsidiary is still present, but is not discussed.

Equity

The contra equity account will still be an offsetting entry. The contra equity account will change as compensation is recognized. Equity recorded may be adjusted for immediate post-transaction valuation changes.

Income

The compensation cost will be based upon the fair-market value of the shares released or deemed to be released for the relevant period.

Dividends

Any compensation cost obligation will not be reduced to the extent the obligation is satisfied with dividends on unallocated shares. Dividends on allocated shares retain the character of true dividends.

Earnings per Share

Unreleased shares will not be considered to be outstanding. All convertible preferred shares will be considered to be common stock equivalents.

Disclosures

The repurchase liability, as reflected by the current value of the allocated shares, must be disclosed. The use of an actuarial estimate of this future obligation is not authorized.

As evidenced by the new SOP, the AICPA has made an already difficult area more difficult, and with no discernible increase in any benefit to anyone. The underlying ESOP transactions governed by this new standard have not changed one iota. This change was not welcomed by anyone the authors know, except the AICPA and its constituents.

Repurchase Liability

The ESOP repurchase liability[58] has not been given much attention. Basically, it arises because the employer contributes cash or stock and the stock has to be bought back, usually at an increased price. And, the employer must buy it back—for cash. Since ESOPs are relatively new, the cash needed to repurchase company stock from departed employees and their beneficiaries has not yet created a problem for many companies. But there is a clear risk it will, unless companies properly plan for it. It is the authors' opinion that, potentially, this is the most serious difficulty the ESOP will experience. Since the repurchase liability affects the value of company stock, the balance sheet and income statement, the number of shareholders, and employee morale, it must be forecasted and planned for.

The first step in facing this potential problem is to develop a projection of future cash requirements. A computer model specifically suited for this purpose is particularly advantageous, because without one it is almost impossible to see how the plan operates under different assumptions, and how the company's income, cash flow, and balance sheet are affected. The final step is to analyze the various funding methods to determine what would work best in a particular situation. It is conceivable that the repurchase liability could consume more cash than the company could contribute in a given year, since the entire contribution may be used to make repurchases. All the more reason to plan!

The repurchase liability is partially alleviated by varying distributions over time, varying the size of the contribution, varying the stock and cash contributions mix, properly timing stock repurchases, and carefully planning for the proper use of dividends on employer securities and of income on other assets. Other solutions include going public, private placements, being acquired, or the creative use of corporate-owned life insurance.

The employee's diversification right is a concept added by TRA '86. It allows employees an elective diversification of their ESOP account balances as to securities acquired after December 31, 1986. This election is extended to any employee who is age 55 or older and has 10 years of plan participation in the ESOP. Elections for the first five years may cover up to 25 percent of an employee's account balance (less the portion diversified).

---

58 Robert W. Smiley, Jr., "How to Plan for an ESOP's Repurchase Liability," Prentice Hall's *Pension and Profit-Sharing Service*, (Englewood Cliffs, NJ: Prentice Hall, 1987), pp. 1, 215-29; and Robert R. Bunigamer and R. Alan Prosswimmer, "ESOP Repurchase Liability," *Journal of Employee Ownership, Law, and Finance*, National Center for Employee Ownership, vol. II, no. 4 (Fall).

The election in the final year may cover up to 50 percent of his or her account balance (less any prior portion diversified).

Companies should not be discouraged from adopting or continuing an ESOP because of the "unknown" repurchase liability, nor should a company adopt an ESOP without ample consideration of the potential repurchase liability. Instead, careful advance planning, ongoing review, good communications, increased productivity, and increased company profits, as well as continued flexibility and encouragement from Congress and the government agencies, should solve almost every problem created by the repurchase liability—but not without planning for it today. The repurchase liability plan must be implemented properly, carefully maintained, and revised as often as necessary to reflect the real world.

ESOPs and Plan Disqualification

If an ESOP is ruled not to meet the requirements of either code Section 401(a) or code Section 4975(e)(7), a variety of problems result. First, any sales to such a plan will not qualify for the tax-free rollover treatment provided under code Section 1042, since that section requires that the sales be made to a plan within the meaning of code Section 4975(e)(7).

Disqualification also will have a negative effect on both the employer and its employees. Plan contributions will no longer be deductible under code Section 404 (with its special limitations for ESOPs), but may be deductible under the ordinary and necessary provisions of code Section 162. For the employees, disqualification will mean that the value of their vested account balances will be immediately taxable to them as ordinary income, and all earnings of the ESOP will be subject to tax, thereby diminishing the account balances of the employees.

401(k) Plans and ESOPs

Most 401(k) plans maintained by employers are profit-sharing plans. However, a 401(k) plan also may be a stock bonus plan. Thus, the salary-reduction contributions made by participants and by employer matching contributions may be invested in employer stock. In that case, all of the requirements relating to stock-bonus plans would apply to the 401(k) stock-bonus plan. For example, final IRS regulations under code Sections 401(k) and 401(m) make it clear that plans or portions of plans that are required to be tested separately under the minimum coverage rules, such as combination 401(k)/ESOPs, must be tested separately under Sections 401(k) and 401(m). Particular care and attention also should be given to applicable federal and state securities law provisions because, if the participant's salary-reduction contributions are allowed to be invested in employer stock, plan registration and related disclosure may be required.

A further variation are 401(k)-leveraged ESOPs known as KSOPs (under which participant elective deferrals and stock dividends are used to purchase stock or repay stock acquisition debt, or both) and MSOPs (under which employer contributions and dividends on the stock are used to purchase stock or repay stock acquisition debt, or both). Both take careful planning and scrutiny of all ERISA and code issues; however, one KSOP, with its use of participant elective deferrals to repay ESOP debt, was recently approved by the IRS.[59]

Wage-Concession ESOPs

Several notable ESOPs—including those established by Eastern Airlines, Continental Airlines, Pan American World Airways, Inc., Republic Airlines, Inc., Western Airlines, Inc., Pacific Southwest Airlines, Inc., CF&I Steel Corporation, and PIE Nationwide, Inc.—have involved wage concessions in exchange for shared equity provided by an ESOP as a quid pro quo for stock ownership. These were companies in which productivity improvements and reduced labor costs were necessary to ensure corporate survival. In other ESOPs—such as those of United Airlines, Weirton Steel, Northwestern Steel & Wire Co., Rosauers Supermarkets, Inc., and Omak Wood Products, Inc.—employees accepted wage reductions to assist in the financing by which they acquired the company. Such ESOPs are the exception rather than the rule. In fact, according to surveys conducted by the National Center for Employee Ownership, less than 5 percent of the ESOPs established in the United States to date have involved wage concessions or contributions by employees.

COMPARISON OF ESOPS WITH OTHER EMPLOYEE STOCK OWNERSHIP ARRANGEMENTS

Stock ownership arrangements have been around for a long time. Sears Roebuck & Co. has had a profit-sharing plan invested primarily in employer securities since July 1916. The Proctor & Gamble Co. had a plan prior to 1900 where employees shared ownership. When the Revenue Act of 1921 was enacted, certain types of stock-bonus trusts and profit-sharing trusts were granted tax exemptions. Many of the qualified

---

59 Technical Advice Memorandum 9503002 (October 27, 1994).

deferred-compensation plans are currently permitted to invest and hold employer securities. The *Handbook* discusses many alternatives to an ESOP, as well as many compensation arrangements that can supplement an ESOP. (See Chapters 26, 27, 30, 32, and others.)

Other Defined Contribution Plans

Defined contribution plans generally can give the feeling of meaningful employee ownership. The account balances of the participants, like a mutual fund, reflect how much gain or loss there is for the year. The ESOP is unique among employee stock ownership arrangements. First, it generally involves a broad base of employees and is operated within the purview of qualified deferred-compensation plans, giving it considerable flexibility. Second, it permits financing acquisitions of employer securities through borrowing, by using the credit of the employer. Third, the initial purchase of stock on a leveraged basis generally means the employer is permanently committed to an ESOP-type plan, at least for the period of the loan repayment. From the employee's point of view, it's very hard for an employer to "back out" of a plan once the stock has been acquired by the trust. Other qualified plans cannot leverage to acquire the employer's stock by using the credit of the employer.

However, sometimes a non-ESOP eligible individual-account plan may serve many of the same purposes as an ESOP without some of the obvious disadvantages, such as put options, specific allocation of shares, required distributions in employer securities, and the like. The eligible individual-account plan, however, can help an employer add to its capital by means of contributions in employer securities or by cash contributions that purchase newly issued (or treasury) stock. Employees also share in the economic benefits of corporate success in a visible way. All of these plans must face the repurchase liability problem eventually, however.

Other Stock Plans

Stock ownership opportunities are granted to executives and other selected employees in many other ways. These include incentive stock plans under code Section 422A, nonqualified stock-option plans, stock-appreciation-rights plans, performance share plans, phantom stock plans, restricted stock plans, key-employee stock plans, employee stock-purchase plans under code Section 423, stock *gifts* by the employer, stock sales to employees by the employer or by shareholders, and so on. Most of these are aimed at a limited group of employees, and, because the context is so different, it is difficult to make comparisons. The qualified stock-purchase plan under code Section 423, while directed to a broad-based group, is substantially different from an ESOP, in that the contribution required of the employee is a major part of the acquisition cost. An ESOP's stock acquisition costs are, in most instances, borne solely by the employer! Compare this to the ESOP tax benefits shown in Tables 29–1 and 29–2.

Global Stock Plans

During the last decade many U.S. multinational corporations have extended their employee-ownership arrangement to employees of affiliates in other jurisdictions, oftentimes through trusts established in tax-haven jurisdictions such as Luxembourg, the Isle of Jersey, Bermuda, and the Cayman Islands. Because employees will be taxed according to the laws of their residence jurisdiction, as modified by applicable tax treaties, careful planning is involved to design a program that spreads employee ownership in a tax-efficient manner under the laws of multiple jurisdiction.

CONCLUSION

Several million Americans are covered by ESOPs, with millions more being included in ESOPs every year. Employee stock ownership plans involve a complex array of business, legal, tax, accounting, and investment-banking questions that are best handled by those with experience in employee ownership. These questions include the basic ones any employer asks, such as: "Do we want it?" "What will it do for us?" "How do we get out of it if something happens?" and "What do our employees get and when?" There are also many additional questions that require expertise in the ESOP area to answer fully. The legal questions include all the qualification questions under code Section 401; the distribution, eligibility, and vesting sections; the fiduciary and prohibited-transaction questions under ERISA; the accounting and financial questions; securities and corporate-law questions; alternative financing questions; and a myriad more. Congress has continually sought to encourage employers to share the fruits of capital and labor through profit participation and a "piece of the action." The ESOP is the latest, most popular, by far the most practical, and, in many ways, the least expensive approach to providing employees with a piece of the company in which they work on a tax-favored, creditor-proof basis. More than 11,000 companies are enjoying the many benefits of employee ownership.

Employee Stock Compensation Plans*

G. Victor Hallman III

Jerry S. Rosenbloom

Use of employer stock in compensating employees has grown tremendously in recent years. As a result, many employees have a substantial part of their investment portfolios in employer stock, stock options, and other stock-based compensation.

GENERAL CONSIDERATIONS

Employee stock options and other stock plans have been used for many years, and the tax law has had various provisions concerning them.[1] But for most of this time, stock options were granted only, or mainly, to senior executives. However, in recent years a significant percentage of corporations have begun adopting more broadly based plans covering more levels of management or even most of their full-time employees. Having said this, however, it must be recognized that employee stock options and many other stock plans still are often viewed as primarily for higher-paid, selected, managerial employees. Of course, many companies also have employee stock purchase plans that are designed to cover virtually all employees.

---

* Reprinted with permission from *Personal Financial Planning*, 6th edition, G. Victor Hallman III
and Jerry S. Rosenbloom, Copyright 2000 by McGraw-Hill, Inc. All rights reserved.
McGraw-Hill, Two Penn Plaza, New York, NY, 10121–2298.

1 At various times, tax-favored stock options were called *restricted stock options* and *qualified stock options*. These particular plans have been discontinued. The present tax-favored stock option is called an *incentive stock option* (ISO).

TYPES OF PLANS

In the classification that follows, we have divided employer stock plans into *statutory plans* and *nonstatutory plans*. Statutory plans are those to which the tax law accords special tax advantages but which also must meet certain requirements to be eligible for the advantages. On the other hand, nonstatutory plans are not based on any special tax provision but rather are governed by general tax principles.

STATUTORY PLANS

Incentive Stock Options (ISOs)

These options were created by the Economic Recovery Tax Act of 1981 (ERTA) in Section 422 of the Internal Revenue Code (IRC or Code). They can be made available at the employer's discretion to only some employees, normally certain highly compensated executives, and hence can be discriminatory in nature.

Requirements for ISOs

A number of requirements must be met before a plan can qualify as an ISO plan. For example, the term (duration) of an option cannot exceed 10 years; the option price must equal or exceed the value of the stock when the option was granted; no disposition can be made of the stock by the person within two years from granting the option or within one year of the transfer of the stock to him or her (i.e., after exercise of the option); the option must be nontransferable (except by will or inheritance at death); and the maximum value of stock for which an employee can exercise ISOs in any year generally cannot exceed $100,000.

Tax Treatment to Employees

The main tax advantage of ISOs is that there is no regular income tax levied at the *grant* or at the *exercise* of the option by the employee. However, the bargain element upon *exercise* of an ISO (i.e., the difference between the fair-market value of the stock at exercise and the option price) is an adjustment item for individual alternative minimum tax (AMT) purposes. Aside from this AMT issue, the employee is taxed only when he or she sells the stock purchased under the option plan, and then any gain realized is taxed as a capital gain. The capital gain would be the difference between the option price (the income tax basis of the stock) and the stock's fair-market value on the date of sale.

As an example, assume that in 1996 Laura Johnson was granted an ISO to purchase 1,000 shares of her employer's (Acme Corporation's) common stock at an option price (*strike price*) of $20 per share, which was its fair-market value at the time. The ISO's term was 10 years. Laura had no gross income for federal income tax purposes at the *grant* of this option. Assume further that in 1999 Laura *exercised* the option with cash and purchased 1,000 shares of Acme common from her employer for $20,000 (1,000 shares × $20 per share = $20,000). At that time (1999), the stock's fair-market value was $50 per share and the bargain element was $30,000 ($50 − $20 = $30 × 1,000 shares = $30,000). Laura had no regular gross income at exercise of the ISO, but she did have an AMT adjustment item of $30,000. Laura's regular income tax basis for the 1,000 shares is her cost (purchase price) of $20,000 or $20 per share.

Now assume that in 2001 Laura sells the 1,000 shares for $80 per share. At this point Laura realizes and recognizes long-term capital gain of $60 per share or $60,000 ($80 − $20 = $60 per share × 1,000 shares = $60,000).[2] Further, if Laura does not sell during her lifetime but holds the Acme stock until her death, it would get a stepped-up income tax basis and the gain to that point would never be taxed.

Tax Treatment for the Employer

The general principle is that an employer gets a corporate income tax deduction for compensation expense at the same time and in the same amount as the employee realizes gross compensation income from the stock plan. In case of an ISO, an employee never realizes compensation income and so the employer never gets a corporate tax deduction.

Employee Stock Purchase Plans

Basic Characteristics

These are option arrangements under which all full-time employees meeting certain eligibility requirements are allowed to buy stock in their employer corporation, usually at a discount. The option price cannot be less than the lower (1) 85 percent of the stock's fair-market value when the option was granted or (2) 85 percent of the stock's fair-market value

---

2 Note that in this example the holding requirements for an ISO have been met (i.e., two years from grant and one year from exercise). However if the requirements for an ISO had been violated, the option would be treated as a nonqualified stock option (NQSO) described later in this chapter.

when the option was exercised. Many employers use these maximum discounts as the option (strike) prices under their plans. Employees who participate agree to have an estimated amount withheld from their pay to provide the funds with which to exercise their options at the end of an option period. If an employee decides not to exercise an option, the plan will return the amounts withheld to the employee, usually with interest.

Employee stock purchase plans are nondiscriminatory in that they cannot favor the highly paid executives of a corporation. In fact, no employee who owns 5 percent or more of the stock of a corporation can be granted such an option, and the maximum annual value of stock subject to these plans (determined as of the grant of the option) is $25,000.

Tax Treatment to Employees

If the requirements of Section 423 of the IRC are met, there is no gross income for participating employees at the grant or exercise of options under employee stock purchase plans. However, to get this favorable tax treatment no disposition can be made of the stock by the employee within two years from grant of the option and within one year from its exercise. If such a disqualifying disposition were to occur, the employee would be taxed as ordinary compensation income in the year of disposition on the difference between the fair-market value of the stock and the option strike price when the option was exercised.

For dispositions (sales) of the stock after the two-year and one-year holding periods (or upon death whenever occurring), when the option price was between 85 percent and 100 percent of the stock's fair-market value at grant, the employee (or his or her estate) will be taxed as ordinary compensation income on the lesser of (1) the difference between the fair-market value of the stock and the option price at the time of disposition or death, or (2) the difference between the fair-market value of the stock and the option price as of the time the option was granted. The remainder of any gain at sale during the employee's lifetime would be capital gain. At the employee's death, his or her estate or heirs would get a stepped-up basis for the remainder of any gain and it would never be taxed.

Many corporations have adopted employee stock purchase plans. While a company's plan may not necessarily be as liberal as permitted by the tax law, a great many are. Therefore, it would seem that eligible employers normally would be well advised to participate in these plans if they are at all financially able to do so. If an employee really does not want to hold the stock, he or she can simply sell it at a profit (assuming the stock price was such that the employee should have exercised the option in the first place).

Tax Treatment for the Employer

The employer does not get a corporate income tax deduction at grant or exercise of options under employee stock purchase plans.

Qualified Retirement Plans Invested in Employer Securities

Stock-bonus plans permit investment in employer stock and allow distribution of that stock to participants. Employee stock ownership plans (ESOPs) must invest primarily in employer stock. Qualified savings plans with Section 401(k) options often allow significant portions of employee account balances to be invested in employer stock.

NONSTATUTORY PLANS

General Tax Law Principles Governing Stock Compensation Plans

General Provisions

Because there are no special provisions governing these plans, they are interpreted under provisions of the code related to income—Section 61 in general and Section 83 in particular. Section 61 is simply the all-inclusive definition of gross income for federal income tax purposes. The more significant provision is Section 83, which deals with taxation of property transferred in connection with the performance of services.

Section 83 in essence provides that the fair-market value of property (less any amount paid for the property) transferred to a person for the performance of services shall be included in that person's gross income in the first taxable year in which the person's rights in the property become transferable or are not subject to a substantial risk of forfeiture, whichever is applicable. A substantial risk of forfeiture might exist, for example, if an employee has to remain with the employer for a certain number of years to receive unfettered ownership or rights to the property. In effect, the property (less any amount paid for it) is taxable to the person rendering the services as soon as all substantial conditions on his or her having it are removed.

Section 83(b) Election

However, an important subsection, Section 83(b), provides that a person performing services (e.g., an employee) may elect within 30 days of a transfer to include the fair-market value of the transferred property (less any amount paid for the property) in his or her gross income, even though the property then was subject to a substantial risk of forfeiture or was not transferable and hence under Section 83 normally would not have been taxable at that point. This is called a *Section 83(b) election*. It can be an important planning tool.

However, if one makes a Section 83(b) election and the value of transferred property is included in the person's gross income, and the property subsequently is forfeited (because, say, the employee did not remain with the employer for the required period), no tax deduction is allowed for the forfeiture. The election also cannot be revoked without the consent of the secretary of the treasury. On the other hand, when the substantial risk of forfeiture expires, there is no tax then.

Normally, of course, one does not want to pay taxes any sooner than necessary. On the other hand, a person receiving property for the performance of services (e.g., an executive receiving restricted employer stock) might want to make a Section 83(b) election and be taxed on the current value of the stock; if the current value is relatively low and the person expects it to rise significantly in the future, and he or she expects to remain with the employer at least through the forfeiture period. These, of course, may be big "ifs." Much depends on the circumstances. But if the stock price currently is low and is expected to do well in the future (as in some start-up situations, for example), the only real risk the person would seem to be taking is the possible loss of his or her current tax payment.

If an employee makes a Section 83(b) election and is currently taxed, the employer gets a corporate income tax deduction for compensation paid in the amount taxable to the employee. The effects of a Section 83(b) election will be illustrated later in connection with the discussion of restricted stock.

Current Stock Bonus

Some employers pay part of employees' current compensation in unrestricted stock. In this case, the employees receive current compensation equal to the fair-market value of the stock. On the other hand, employers often pay part of a current bonus in cash and part in restricted stock (i.e., subject to the condition that the employee stay with the employer for a minimum period). In this case the rules for restricted stock apply.

Nonqualified Stock Options (NQSOs)

Basic Characteristics

These are stock options that do not meet the requirements for ISOs and so are taxed on the basis of the general principles just discussed. Correspondingly, NQSOs can have terms decided upon by the parties and are not limited in the amount of stock subject to such options exercisable by an employee in any one year (as are ISOs). Hence, NQSOs can be considerably more flexible for employers and employees. Like ISOs, they can be granted only to certain employees and hence may be discriminatory. NQSOs generally have become more popular than ISOs as a compensation technique. While there are no statutory requirements to do so, NQSOs are often granted with an option price equal to 100 percent of the fair-market value of the stock on the date of grant and for option terms of around 10 years.

Tax Treatment to Employees

There normally is no taxable event (gross income) at grant because the tax regulations view their value then as not being readily ascertainable.[3] On the other hand, upon exercise of an option (and transfer of the stock to the employee), the employee will receive ordinary compensation income for regular federal income tax purposes equal to the difference between the fair-market value of the stock at exercise and the option price (the bargain element). The employee's income tax basis in the stock is its fair-market value at exercise. This is because the employee paid the option price to the employer (a cost basis) and included the remainder of the stock's value (bargain element) in his or her gross income as compensation (basis under the tax benefit principle). Thus, an immediate sale of the stock by the employee (there are no two-year and one-year holding periods for NQSOs) will produce zero capital gain or loss because the amount realized would equal the adjusted basis for the stock.

Let us illustrate these principles by returning to our example involving Laura Johnson. If we assume the same facts except that Laura was granted a NQSO in 1996 instead of an ISO, the tax results would be as follows. Laura would have no gross income at grant of the option. However, when Laura exercised her NQSO in 1999, she would have had ordinary compensation income of $30,000 in that year.[4] Laura's income

---

3 Employee stock options, of course, are not traded on organized or over-the-counter markets, may not be be transferable, and normally are not vested at grant.

4 Note that the AMT is not involved here because the $30,000 bargain element is taxable for *regular* income tax purposes.

tax basis for the 1,000 shares is $50,000 or $50 per share ($20 per share of cost basis and $30 per share of basis due to the tax benefit rule).

Now when Laura sells her 1,000 shares of Acme common in 2001 at a price of $80 per share, she will realize and recognize long-term capital gain of $30 per share or $30,000 ($80 – $50 = $30 per share × 1000 shares = $30,000). Thus, for the NQSO the total gain on the option stock would still be $60,000, except that $30,000 would be ordinary compensation income and $30,000 long-term capital gain taxable at a maximum 20 percent rate.

Tax Treatment for the Employer

The employer gets a corporate income tax deduction for the amount of compensation income the employee realizes at exercise of the option.

Restricted Stock

Basic Characteristics

Restricted stock plans are arrangements whereby a corporation grants stock (or stock options) to an employee (or someone rendering services to the corporation), by where ownership of the stock is subject to a substantial risk of forfeiture (such as the employee's remaining with the employer for a certain number of years or the corporation's meeting certain profit goals). Such stock may be provided to employees in a variety of circumstances. It can be part of a general compensation package, perhaps to entice the person to join the employer. It can be part of a bonus plan as noted earlier. And in some cases, stock issued on exercise of an NQSO can be restricted stock in order to further postpone taxation.

Tax Treatment to Employees and the Section 83(b) Election

As explained earlier, an employee receives ordinary compensation income in the year the employee's rights to the stock are first not subject to the substantial risk of forfeiture or are transferable. The gross income is measured by the fair-market value of the stock at the time less any cost to the employee. However, depending on the circumstances, a Section 83(b) election (described earlier) may be considered. A person receiving restricted stock must make a planning decision regarding this election.

Again to illustrate these principles, let us assume that John Venturesome is a young information executive with a large corporation. Recently a former college classmate invited him to join a start-up company, XYZ.com, that has some exciting new products in information technology. The offer is for less salary than John is now earning, but XYZ.com, which recently went public, will give John a compensation package that includes NQSOs and 10,000 shares of restricted stock (which is conditioned on John's staying with the company for at least three years). John does not have to pay anything for the 10,000 shares. XYZ.com common stock currently is selling at $2 per share.

John accepts the offer in 2000 and makes no Section 83(b) election. First, John has no gross income from receipt of the 10,000 shares of restricted stock because it is subject to a substantial risk of forfeiture. Let us further assume that at the end of three years (2003) John is still with XYZ.com and that its stock has done very well. Its price in 2003 is $20 per share. When the substantial risk of forfeiture ends (in 2003), John will have ordinary compensation income of $200,000 (10,000 shares × $20 per share = $200,000). His income tax basis in the 10,000 shares also will be $200,000, or $20 per share.

Now let us change our facts and assume John made the Section 83(b) election in 2000 within 30 days of when the 10,000 shares were transferred to him. He then would be taxed on $20,000 in year 2000 ($2 per share × 10,000 shares = $20,000) as ordinary compensation income, and his basis in the 10,000 shares also would be $20,000, or $2 per share. If John is still with XYZ.com at the end of the three years (in 2003), the substantial risk of forfeiture would end and he would have unrestricted right to the stock. He would incur no further gross income then. On the other hand, if John should leave XYZ.com after, say, two years, he would forfeit the 10,000 shares and could take no tax deduction for that. In effect, he would lose the tax he paid in 2000 on the $20,000 of ordinary income.

Let us now assume that John stayed with XYZ.com until 2003 and that two years later (in 2005) John sells the 10,000 shares for $30 per share. If he had not made the Section 83(b) election in the year 2000, he would have $100,000 of long-term capital gain ($300,000 amount realized − $200,000 adjusted basis = $100,000 gain realized and recognized). In effect, he would have had $300,000 of total gain on the 10,000 shares of restricted stock ($200,000 of ordinary compensation income and $100,000 of long-term capital gain). On the other hand, if John had made the Section 83(b) election in the year 2000, he would have $280,000 of long-term capital gain ($300,000 amount realized − $20,00 adjusted basis = $280,000 gain realized and recognized). In this situation, he also would have had $300,000 of total gain on the 10,000 shares of restricted stock, but now it is divided as $20,000 of ordinary compensation income and $280,000 of long-term capital gain. Further, if John does not sell the 10,000 shares (or all of them) during his lifetime, he can still consider other techniques for possibly avoiding capital gains taxation. Finally, if he does not sell or otherwise dispose of his stock, it will get a stepped-up basis at death. On the other hand, if the market price of the stock falls or it becomes worthless, John would have been better off not making the Section 83(b) election.

Tax Treatment for the Employer

Again, the employer gets a corporate income tax deduction when the employee receives gross compensation income. This is either when the substantial risk of forfeiture ends or the Section 83(b) election is made.

Other Stock-Based Plans

This is a complex field and only a brief description of some of these plans will be given here.

Stock Appreciation Rights (SARs)

These are accounts, maintained for selected employees that reflect the appreciation in the employer's stock over a certain period. When an executive's rights to an SAR become final, it normally is paid out to him or her in cash and is taxable then.

Phantom Stock

These also are accounts maintained for selected employees, but they normally reflect the full value of a certain amount of employer stock. The account value varies with the stock's value and normally is paid to the executive in cash at some point. However, there is no actual stock in the account.

Performance Shares or Performance-Based Stock Options

In this case, selected employees are granted stock or stock options whose vesting is contingent on certain corporate or other performance measures being met.

PROVISIONS OF STOCK OPTION PLANS

Vesting of Options

This is the period of continuous employment that must elapse after an option is granted and before the employee can exercise the option. There generally are vesting requirements in a stock option plans. The periods required for vesting vary but often range from two to four years.

Transferability of Options

Traditionally, employee stock options have not been transferable by the employees receiving the options other than at death. They could not be sold or given away. One of the requirements to be an ISO is that the option by its terms must not be transferable (other than by will or intestate distribution) and must be exercisable during the employee's lifetime only by him or her.

There is no corresponding prohibition for NQSOs. But in the past, corporations in practice have not allowed their NQSOs to be transferable. Recently, however, this has changed. Some corporations have amended their stock option plans to allow NQSOs to be transferred by the holder to members of his or her family, trusts for such members, or possibly family limited partnerships with such members as partners, with the consent of the corporation. Thus, in these cases there might be gifts of NQSOs to family members or entities for them.

Effect of Certain Contingencies on Options

Stock option plans normally have certain forfeiture provisions in the event of termination of employment for various reasons. The option holder (or his or her estate or heirs) usually has a limited period of time to exercise the option after he or she retires (such as three to five years), becomes disabled on a long-term basis (such as three to five years), dies (such as one to two years), voluntarily terminates employment (such as three months), or leaves for other reasons. The option holder should be careful to observe any such time limits lest valuable option rights be lost. Some plans also provide that options will be automatically forfeited if the holder becomes employed by or associated with a competitor of his or her former employer. In such a case, if an option holder is planning to change jobs and join a competing firm, he or she should exercise favorable (i.e., "in the money") vested options before terminating employment.

Exercise of Options

Stock options generally can be exercised in several ways.

Cash Exercise

An option holder can make a *cash exercise* by paying the option price to the employer and having the stock transferred to him or her. In the case of an NQSO, the employer also will require withholding of federal, state, local, and FICA taxes on the taxable amount. The option holder must lay out the option price (and any withholding) in cash.

Stock-for-Stock Exercise

A plan may allow payment of the exercise price by delivering previously owned shares of stock of the employer that are equal in value to the option price to the employer and having the option stock transferred to the option holder. This may be referred to as a *stock-for-stock exercise.*

As an example, suppose that Ahmed Bastor exercises an NQSO to buy 1,000 share of ABC Corporation common stock at an option price of $20 per share at a time when the fair-market value of the stock is $50 per share. Ahmed already owns ABC common through previous stock option exercises. In a stock-for-stock exercise, Ahmed could deliver 400 shares of his previously owned ABC common to the corporation in payment of the $20,000 exercise price (1,000 shares × $20 per share = $20,000 exercise price ÷ $50 per share = 400 shares of stock to deliver). Assume the 400 shares of previously owned stock had an income tax basis to Ahmed of $10 per share. There is no gain recognized on the exchange of the 400 previously owned shares for 400 of the new option shares, and the new shares will have the same holding period for capital gain purposes as the previously owned shares. This is because this is a tax-free exchange of common stock in a corporation for common stock in the same corporation as provided in Section 1036 of the IRC.

The income tax basis for the exchanged shares ($10 per share) will be carried over to 400 of the new option shares. The remainder of the new option shares will be as if it were a cash exercise. The difference between the fair-market value of the stock received (600 shares × $50 per share = $30,000) less any cash paid for the stock (0 in this example) would be ordinary compensation income to Ahmed, and his income tax basis in these 600 shares would be $50 per share (or $30,000), which is the amount taken into his gross income for them. The corporation may require cash withholding or allow withholding in the form of stock otherwise issuable to the option holder. It can be seen that in this case the option holder is paying for some of the new option stock with existing stock in the same corporation. This reduces the option holder's overall stock position in the company as compared with a cash exercise and is the reason reload options (discussed later) may be granted in this situation.

Cashless Exercise

This type of exercise was first made possible by the Federal Reserve Board in 1988. It involves working through a stockbroker who can buy the option stock from the corporation at the exercise price, sell enough stock in the open market to cover the purchase price plus broker's commissions and a small amount of margin interest, and then deliver the remaining stock to the option holder. If the exercise is a taxable event, the broker also may sell enough stock to cover tax withholding, which the broker will remit to the employer. If the option holder wants to receive cash for the transaction rather than stock, the broker may sell all the option stock and credit the net cash to the option holder.

Reload Options

These are additional options that may be granted to employees when they pay the exercise price for stock with previously owned stock of the corporation (a stock-for-stock exercise). The reload option normally is for the same number of shares used to pay the exercise price (plus perhaps shares used for federal, state, local, and FICA withholding tax purposes) and is for the remainder of the option period of the underlying option that was exercised.

A stock-for-stock exercise of an underlying option when there is a reload option can be attractive for an option holder. Using our previous example of Ahmed Bastor, assume that ABC's plan provides for reload options. In this case, if the underlying option Ahmed exercised originally had a term of 10 years and Ahmed engaged in the stock-for-stock exercise described previously four years after the grant date, he might be granted a reload option for 400 shares (ignoring, for the sake of simplicity, any stock used for tax withholding purposes) at an option price of $50 per share (the current fair-market value of the stock) for a term of six years (the remaining term of the exercised underlying option).

Compared with a cash exercise and a stock-for-stock exercise with no reload option, Ahmed now is in a better position. Under a cash exercise, he would have an exposure to ABC Corporation stock of 1,400 directly owned shares (400 previously owned and 1,000 option shares), but he would have had to come up with the $20,000 needed to exercise the underlying option. Under a stock-for-stock exercise with no reload feature, Ahmed's exposure to ABC stock would be reduced to 1,000 directly owned shares (the option shares). However, under the stock-for-stock exercise with a reload feature, his exposure to ABC stock remains at 1,400 shares (1,000 directly owned option shares and 400 reload option shares), but he would not have needed to disturb his other assets or cash reserves to exercise the underlying option. This occurs because Ahmed has been given a new option (the reload option) which itself has value.

VALUATION OF STOCK OPTIONS

This is a very complex subject. It is made even more so by the fact that employee stock options are different in many ways from publicly traded stock and other options. In essence, however, employee stock options are really call options for the employees on employer stock.

People may be concerned about the valuation of employee stock options for many reasons. Employees want to know what they are really worth, because options have become an important part of many compensation arrangements. They also need to be valued for purposes of an employee's asset allocation planning. In some cases, employees may give up cash compensation in exchange for stock options and so they want to have an idea of what the options are worth to evaluate the exchange. Finally, employee stock options may need to be valued for estate-planning purposes.

Traded Options

The market prices of publicly traded options are readily available in the financial press and from other sources. Employee stock options, of course, are not publicly traded and have no readily ascertainable market value.

Most traded options are for relatively short durations, such as a few months. However, just to get an idea of how the market values longer-term options relative to the prices of the underlying stocks, it may be instructive to note the market premiums (prices) for leaps. *Leaps* are longer-term publicly traded options. For example, as of this writing, the price of a 30-month call option on one major company's stock with a strike price (i.e., exercise price) of $115 when the underlying stock's current market price was $94¹⁄₁₆ (i.e., this call option was out of the money) was $40 per share, or about 42.5 percent of the underlying stock's market price.

Naturally, the prices of such publicly traded long-term options will vary considerably with the characteristics of the underlying stocks and with market conditions. The only point we are making here is that the market itself sets a considerable value on longer-term options (30 months in this example), even when they have no intrinsic value (to be described next). Clearly then, the market value (as well as the economic or true value) of long-term options can be substantial.

Intrinsic Value

The intrinsic value of a stock option is the difference between the underlying stock's current market price and the option's strike price. For example, if an employee is granted a 10-year NQSO with an option price of $25 per share when the underlying stock's market price also is $25 per share, the intrinsic value of the option is $0 at grant. As we have just seen for traded options, the intrinsic value does not reflect the fair value or economic worth of an option. In fact, as will be shown in the next section, the economic worth of a long-term option such as that previously cited can be quite substantial.

Option Pricing Models

A number of models (mathematical systems of analysis) have been developed to compute the fair value or economic worth of options. Probably the best known is the Black-Scholes option pricing model. This model is based on the following six factors to determine the economic value of an option.[5] (Let us say for the following illustration of these factors that we are valuing an employee stock option.)

- Option exercise price (strike price).
- Current market price of the underlying stock.
- Risk-free interest rate during the expected term of the option.
- Expected dividend yield on the stock.
- Expected life of the option. The expected life is the time period the employee is actually expected to hold the option before exercising it. It may be shorter than the maximum option period in the plan.
- Expected volatility of the underlying stock's market price. This normally is the most important factor in the model. The greater the expected volatility, the more likely there will be time value gains (see note 5), and the greater the option value will be. Volatility can be estimated from the historical standard deviation of the stock's price changes over past time periods.

To illustrate the *fair value* of an option, let us continue our fact pattern for the NQSO noted earlier with respect to intrinsic value. Using the factors just listed, we assume that this NQSO has an option exercise price

---

5 The concept behind these option pricing models is that the fair value of an option (which, in general, is an instrument that allows, but does not require, a person to buy or sell an asset at a prearranged price during a set time period) consists of two elements: (1) the intrinsic value, and (2) a time value, arising because the option holder may benefit from favorable future price movements (volatility) in the asset without having the downside risk of actual ownership of the asset.

of $25 per share, a current market price of the underlying stock also of $25 per share, an expected dividend yield of zero, an assumed expected life of the option of 10 years, and an expected volatility of the underlying stock's price of 20 percent per month. Under these assumptions, the Black-Scholes model would produce a fair value of $19.75 per option. This equals 79 percent of the underlying stock's current price. Of course, if the assumed expected life of the option were reduced, the fair value would decline. For example, if the expected life were one year, the fair value would be $7.24 per option. Most employee stock options have an expected life of considerably more than one year. Software is available for calculating the fair value of options under option pricing models.

It is clear from this discussion that the *economic value (fair value)* of stock options granted to employees can be substantial. However, it also must be recognized that the *actual value* of such options may never reach the fair value at grant (from an option pricing model) and may even be zero if the actual market price of the underlying stock should decline (or fail to rise) from the option price.

Sometimes when a stock's price falls—and many executive stock options are "under water" (i.e., the stock's market price is below the option price and the option is out of money)—the employer will reprice the options to be equal to the stock's current market price (i.e., cancel the old out-of-the-money options and issue new ones at the stock's current market value). However, this is a controversial tactic.

SOME CAVEATS CONCERNING STOCK OPTIONS AND OTHER PLANS

While employee stock options and other stock compensation plans have been a boon for many employees and a bonanza for some, a few caveats concerning them are still in order.

What Goes Up Can Still Come Down!

It seems almost trite to say that while employee stock plans can be very attractive when the price of a company's stock is rising, the reverse will be true when the price is falling. However, some employees may not truly understand this. They can overcommit themselves financially on the basis of paper gains in their stock options and other plans.

Some Employees May Not Realize the True Economic Worth of Options

The other side of the coin is that some employees may not truly understand, or may have difficulty in analyzing, the economic value of options or other stock rights granted to them.

Risk of Excessive Concentration in Employer Stock

While employees usually are well advised to take advantage of these plans when they are attractive to them, they also should attempt to deal with any overconcentration issue, assuming they want a reasonably diversified investment portfolio.

PLANNING ISSUES REGARDING STOCK OPTIONS AND OTHER STOCK PLANS

Some of these issues may be summarized as follows:

- Whether to participate in employee stock purchase plan offerings. (This depends on the terms of the plan and the employer stock, but in general, these plans are advantageous for employees and are flexible as to whether participating employees will take the stock.)
- When to exercise stock options.
- Whether to change an ISO into a NQSO by breaking an ISO requirement.
- How to exercise options (including the possible availability of reload options).
- Whether to make a Section 83(b) election with regard to restricted stock or other plans.
- Whether to take option stock as restricted stock if available.
- Whether to take bonuses or other compensation in the form of stock options if available.
- How to maintain investment diversification in light of likely favorable terms for acquiring more and more employer stock.
- Any estate-planning actions with regard to stock plans if possible.

SUMMARY

Employee stock plans have become an important ingredient in many employee compensation systems. However, their use also depends on each employer's compensation philosophy. For example, some issues may be:

- Should stock options be granted only to top executives or to most employees?
- How soon should options vest/
- How can or should option stock be secured by the employer for the sale to employees?
- Should reload options be used?
- Should out-of-the-money options be repriced?

An equally important consideration is the motivational effect of stock compensation on employees. Such compensation can be highly motivational when the stock price is rising, but the impact can be equally strong (in the wrong direction) when the stock price "turns south."

Another consideration is the effect of employee stock plans, particularly stock options, on other (non-employee) investors and the investment community. Repricing of options (and other employer tactics to mitigate the effects on employees of declining stock prices) may upset other investors.

CHAPTER 31

Individual Retirement Arrangements (IRAs), Simplified Employee Pensions (SEPs), SIMPLE Plans, and HR-10 (Keogh) Plans

Ernest L. Martin

William H. Rabel

Millions of American taxpayers now enjoy the retirement savings benefits of individual retirement arrangements (IRAs), simplified employee pensions (SEPs), and HR-10 (Keogh) plans.[1] Though these plans are very different in features and requirements, they have in common the extension of tax-favored benefits to workers and others who wish to put aside funds to be used later to support the retirement years. This chapter will discuss the features of IRAs, SEPs, and Keogh plans. It will begin with a discussion of IRAs, including traditional IRAs and newer variations such as Roth IRAs and Education IRAs. After a discussion of SEPs and savings incentive match plans for employees (SIMPLE plans), it will conclude with a look at legislative and participation trends that indicate that these three major categories of retirement savings instruments are likely to have a permanent and an expanded existence well into the future.

INDIVIDUAL RETIREMENT ACCOUNTS

In 1974, Congress enacted the Employee Retirement Income Security Act (ERISA), which, as modified by subsequent legislation, provided in part that an individual could make an annual tax-deductible contribution of 100

---

1 The authors wish to express their gratitude to Glenn A. Reed, CPA, PFS, CFP, CLU, ChFC, REBC, CFS, Attorney at Law and Master of Law in Taxation, San Antonio, Texas for reviewing the manuscript of this chapter, although we retain any responsibility for errors of omission or commission.

percent of personal service compensation up to $2,000 to an individual retirement arrangement. The enabling legislation also permitted contributions for spouses to a spousal IRA. In addition, eligible individuals can make nondeductible contributions, even if they are not eligible to deduct contributions made to a traditional IRA. The funds in a traditional IRA accumulate on a tax-deferred basis, regardless of whether the contributions are deductible or nondeductible. During the authorized age period, an IRA owner could make withdrawals from the account and have them taxed at the owner's current tax rate. Later legislation greatly expanded the variety and features of IRAs. For example, in recent years Congress has created Education IRAs and Roth IRAs. In this section, we will discuss the features of the various IRA plans, beginning with traditional IRAs.

TRADITIONAL IRAS

There are two basic types of traditional IRAs. A traditional IRA may be set up as:

- An individual retirement account with a bank, a savings and loan association, a federally insured credit union, or with another qualified person as trustee or custodian. Technically, an individual retirement account is a trust or custodial account.

- An individual retirement annuity through the purchase of an annuity contract issued by an insurance company, in which case no trustee or custodian is required. An annuity contract purchased after November 6, 1978 must provide for flexible premiums.

While most owners of IRAs take a passive role in the investment activities associated with their accounts, an IRA owner may choose to establish a *self-directed* IRA and thus directly manage the investment activities. However, the owner of a self-directed IRA will still need to find a bank or other institution or trustee to handle the account.

Eligibility

Currently, any person age 70½ years or less may make a tax-deductible contribution to a traditional IRA, provided that person's income falls below certain amounts and the income is derived from personal services resulting in salary, wages, commissions, fees, net self-employment income, or bonuses. Taxable alimony and separate maintenance payments received under a decree of divorce also may be considered eligible personal services income. However, investment income and capital gains must be excluded from the income base used to determine eligibility to contribute to an IRA.

Deductible Contributions

The deductibility of contributions to a traditional IRA depends upon a number of factors aside from the upper age limit, including income from personal services, federal income tax filing status, and whether a worker is already an active participant in an employer retirement plan, including a self-employed retirement plan.

An individual who is not an active participant in an employer-sponsored or self-employed retirement plan may make an annual tax-deductible contribution of up to $2,000 or 100 percent of personal services income, whichever is less. A married couple filing a joint return when neither is covered by an employer-sponsored retirement plan may make an annual deductible contribution up to $2,000 each, provided the combined eligible compensation amounts to at least $4,000, even if one of the spouses does not have personal services income.

However, the rules governing deductibility of contributions are considerably more complex in a case in which an individual is an active participant in an employer retirement plan, including a self-employed plan. In that case, the amount of any deductible contributions is determined by the individual's *modified adjusted gross income* (MAGI). MAGI is generally equal to adjusted gross income shown on an individual's tax return with the following items added back:

- The amount of the IRA contribution;
- Excluded interest from savings bonds;
- One-half of Social Security (or railroad retirement) otherwise deducted by the self-employed;
- Foreign income excluded from the return;
- The foreign housing exclusion;
- U.S. possessions income;
- Puerto Rican income of a bona fide resident; and
- Tax-exempt interest.

For purposes of determining the deductibility of an IRA contribution made by a person who is an active participant in an employer retirement plan, the tax code establishes certain *phaseout thresholds* for MAGI. For example, for 2001 returns, the $2,000 annual deduction limit is subject to a reduction if MAGI exceeds:

- $32,000 if the person is single, head of household, or married filing separately and treated as single because he or she lived apart from a spouse for the entire year;

- $52,000 if the person is married, filing jointly, and both the person *and* the spouse were active plan participants during the tax year, or if the person is a qualifying widow or widower;
- $52,000 if the person is married, filing jointly, and the person is an active plan participant during the tax year, but the spouse was not. In this case, the married person uses the $52,000 threshold, but the spouse may use a $150,000 threshold;
- $150,000 if the person is married, filing jointly, and the person was not an active plan participant during the tax year, but the spouse was. In such a case, the person uses the $150,000 threshold, but the spouse uses the $52,000 threshold;
- $0 if the person is married, filing separately, and lived with a spouse at any time during the tax year.

The deduction phaseout occurs over a range of income beyond the threshold. The following chart illustrates the phaseout ranges:

If the phaseout threshold is	Deduction limit is phased out if MAGI is	No deduction if MAGI is
$32,000	$32,000–$42,000	$42,000 or more
$52,000	$52,000–$62,000	$62,000 or more
$150,000	$150,001–$159,999	$160,000 or more
$0	$0–$9,999	$10,000 or more

As an example of the application of the phaseout rules, suppose a single individual subject to the $32,000 phaseout threshold has MAGI of $33,000. The deductible limit would be calculated as follows:

Step 1. Excess of MAGI over phaseout threshold $1,000
Step 2. 20% of Step 1   200
Step 3. $2,000 – Step 2 = deductible limit $1,800

Congress developed the phaseout rules as a means of preventing abuse of tax-favored retirement vehicles as mere tax-avoidance schemes and for the purpose of targeting the benefits of deductibility to lower-income ranges. These phaseout rules will expand each year so that by 2005 the phaseout range will be $50,000 to $60,000 for single persons and $80,000 to $100,000 in 2007 for married persons filing jointly.

Nondeductible IRA Contributions

Even if a worker is barred by the phaseout rules from making a deductible IRA contribution, that worker can still make an annual nondeductible contribution to an IRA of 100 percent of personal services income or $2,000, whichever is less. If the worker is married and filing a joint return, then the nondeductible annual contribution may be as much as $4,000. Even if the contribution is nondeductible, earnings in the IRA account continue to accumulate on a tax-deferred basis. Of course, a person considering making a nondeductible IRA contribution should consult a tax adviser as to whether contributing to a Roth IRA (treated later in this chapter) would be more beneficial. A worker making a nondeductible contribution to a traditional IRA must report the contribution on IRS Form 8606 within the federal tax return for the year to which the contribution applies.

Making the Contribution to a Traditional IRA

Contributions to a traditional IRA must be made by the due date for filing the federal tax return, or by the date the return is actually filed, whichever is earlier, for the tax year to which the contribution applies. Even if an individual receives an extension to file a return, the contribution must be made no later than the due date for filing a return.

Withdrawals and Their Taxation

The traditional IRA was designed as a retirement savings vehicle, not as an account of banking convenience. Moreover, while both the earnings in and any deductible contributions to a traditional IRA are tax-deferred, they are not tax-exempt.

Provided an account owner is at least age 59½ at the time he or she makes a withdrawal from a traditional IRA account, that owner pays regular federal income taxes on the proportion of a withdrawal attributable to deductible contributions and the proportion attributable to tax-deferred earnings in the account. For example, if all the contributions to the IRA have been deductible, then the entire withdrawal from the account would be taxable. However, suppose that a traditional IRA account has a balance of $100,000, and that the owner has made $60,000 in deductible contributions and $24,000 in nondeductible contributions. The remainder, $16,000, represents earnings on the deposits made. Now suppose an owner, age 60, makes a $10,000 withdrawal. How much of the withdrawal is subject to federal income tax? In this case, an owner must make a calculation. The portion of the $10,000 withdrawal that is subject to tax is equal to the portion of the IRA account that is attributable to tax-deferred contributions and earnings. In this example, that portion would be a fraction equal to nondeductible contributions and earnings as the numerator, and the total account balance as the denominator:

$$\$60,000 + \frac{\$16,000}{\$100,000} = 76\% \times \$10,000 = \$7,600 \text{ taxable}$$

Because the owner has already paid federal income taxes on the amount of the nondeductible contributions, the entire withdrawal would not be taxed.

Taxation of Premature Distributions

As already stated, Congress intended that traditional IRAs be retirement savings instruments, not merely savings accounts. Accordingly, Congress established a tax penalty on any withdrawals made from a traditional IRA account before an account owner reaches age 59½, although there are certain exceptions that will not be discussed here. In general, an account owner who withdraws any amount from a traditional IRA before attaining age 59½ is subject to a tax penalty of 10 percent of the withdrawn amount plus regular federal income taxes. Suppose, for example, that a 40-year-old owner of a traditional IRA withdraws $10,000 from the account and that the entire amount is subject to regular federal taxation at a 28 percent marginal tax rate. In this case, the federal tax would be calculated as:

$$
\begin{array}{rcl}
\$10,000 \times .28 &=& \$2,800 \\
\$10,000 \times .10 &=& \underline{\$1,000} \\
&& \$3,800
\end{array}
$$

The penalty tax is designed to discourage early withdrawals from traditional IRA accounts.

An individual may avoid the 10 percent penalty (though not the regular tax) by choosing to take an IRA balance in the form of annuity payments under certain circumstances. The annuity payments must (1) continue for at least five years, and (2) be paid out according to the life expectancy method, the amortization method, or the annuity factor method of distribution.

Mandatory Distributions from a Traditional IRA

Although Congress intended to provide tax-favored treatment to encourage saving for retirement, it did not intend to defer taxes on IRA contributions and earnings forever. The owner of an IRA must start receiving IRA distributions in the year following the year in which the owner reaches age 70½.

Tax law and the IRS provide various methods for determining the minimum amount of required annual distributions, if an account owner chooses to take annual distributions. If an IRA owner fails to take the full amount of a required annual distribution under an approved schedule, the difference between the amount that should have been distributed and the amount actually distributed is subject to a 50 percent penalty tax. If, for example, an IRS-approved schedule calls for an annual distribution of $1,000 and an IRA owner takes only a $500 distribution, then the $500 distribution not taken will be subject to a penalty tax of $250. Of course, an account owner may also choose an accelerated distribution method as a means of avoiding a penalty. For example, the account owner may take the account balance in a lump sum or over fewer years that an annual schedule might require.

Rollovers

The law permits a tax-free transfer of assets from one IRA to another. Also, proceeds received as a distribution from a qualified plan because of the death of a spouse can be rolled over tax-free into an IRA. Rollovers provide an element of flexibility that fosters investment, administrative, and other benefits arising from consolidation.

Every IRA-to-individual-to-IRA rollover must meet two major requirements in addition to several other less important ones. First, an individual is limited to only one tax-free rollover per IRA in any one year. However, it is worth noting that it is possible to make a direct transfer of funds from one funding agency to another without being considered to have made a rollover subject to the one-year restriction. Second, the rollover must take place within 60 days after the distribution is made. Any funds withdrawn but not rolled over are treated as a premature distribution, as described later. However, the Tax Reform Act of 1986 (TRA '86) extended the period for deposits that are frozen in a financially distressed financial institution until 10 days after funds become available. Either whole or partial rollovers may be made, and the owner must notify the funding agency that a rollover is being effected. Funds from a regular IRA may not be rolled over into a qualified plan, although the reverse is not true.

Three tests must be met when an individual is rolling over money or other property from a plan qualified under Section 401(a) into an IRA. First, only employer contributions or deductible qualified voluntary employee contributions (discontinued under TRA '86) may be rolled over. If nondeductible employee contributions are rolled over, they shall be treated as excess contributions and subjected to the penalties discussed previously. Second, the rollover must be completed within 60 days. Third, the distribution must be made because the employee is separated from service, has reached age 59, has died or become disabled, or because the plan has been terminated. Unlike IRA-to-individual-to-IRA rollovers, there is no limit of one transfer per year.

However, the Unemployment Compensation Amendment of 1992 requires employers to withhold 20 percent of pension distributions received directly by a terminating employee, even if it is the intention of the employee receiving the distribution to roll the distribution over into an IRA. This withholding can be avoided through a direct transfer from the pension plan to the IRA, however.

Since 1993, a distribution that is less than the balance to the employee's credit may be eligible for tax-free rollover treatment. The amount of the partial distribution is not required to equal 50 percent of an employee's plan balance, as was the case for pre-1993 distributions.

Whether a partial or a total rollover of assets has been made from a qualified corporate or Keogh plan into an IRA, assets may then be rolled over again into the qualified plan of a subsequent employer; however, such a "re-rollover" is allowable only if it is permitted by the subsequent employer's plan and if the assets of the IRA consist solely of the assets from the first qualified plan and earnings on those assets. The individual should not contribute to an IRA that is set up as a conduit between two qualified plans. Rather, to keep from losing favorable tax treatment, he or she should set up a second IRA for his or her contributions.

Rollover amounts may not be deposited in a spouse's IRA except when resulting from the taxpayer's death.

Assets rolled over into an IRA from a tax-sheltered annuity can be re-rolled over into another tax-sheltered annuity.

ROTH IRAS

With the passage of the Taxpayer Relief Act of 1997, Congress created an alternative to the traditional IRA. The so-called Roth IRA permits a taxpayer to make an annual nondeductible contribution of up to $2,000 per account. Earnings on deposited contributions accrue on a tax-free basis. No income taxes apply to withdrawals if an account has been maintained for at least five years provided (1) the owner is age 59½, disabled or deceased, or (2) money from a withdrawal is used for purchase of a first home, regardless of an owner's age.

In addition, if a Roth IRA has been maintained for at least five years, an owner may withdraw from the account without incurring a tax penalty provided the withdrawal is used for educational purposes, although such withdrawals are subject to regular income taxes on IRA earnings if the account owner is otherwise not eligible for a tax-free withdrawal.

Other withdrawals are subject to a 10 percent penalty plus regular income taxes on the portion attributable to the earnings.

The maximum allowable annual contribution is subject to a phase-out, beginning with $95,000 in adjusted gross income (AGI) for single taxpayers and $150,000 in AGI for couples filing jointly.

A taxpayer's combined contributions to a traditional IRA and a Roth IRA may not exceed a total of $2,000 per year. A taxpayer may choose to convert a traditional IRA to a Roth IRA, provided the taxpayer's adjusted gross income is less than $100,000 in the year of the conversion and a married taxpayer does not file a separate return, as discussed later.

Aside from providing the opportunity for a taxpayer to accumulate tax-free earnings and withdrawals from contributions to a Roth IRA, these accounts offer other advantages. Unlike traditional IRAs, Roth IRAs permit an account owner to continue to make contributions after he or she attains age 70½. Moreover, the owner of a Roth IRA is not required to take minimum distributions from the account after age 70½.

Distributions from a Roth IRA

As discussed earlier, distributions from a Roth IRA are tax-free provided the distributions are made after the end of a five-year period beginning with the first day of the first taxable year for which any Roth IRA contribution was made and one of the following conditions is met:

- The account owner is age 59½ when the distribution is made;
- The account owner is disabled;
- The account owner uses the distribution to pay up to $10,000 of qualifying first-time home-buyer expenses; or
- The account owner is a beneficiary receiving distributions following the death of the account owner.

A surviving spouse who inherits a Roth IRA after the death of the account owner may choose to treat the Roth IRA as his or her own, just as though the account had been set up by the surviving spouse. In this case, the surviving spouse is not subject to minimum distribution rules. Alternatively, the surviving spouse who is the Roth IRA's only beneficiary may delay the start of distributions over his or her life expectancy until the owner would have reached age 70½, if that is later than December 31 of the year following the year of the owner's death.

However, the rules are more stringent for beneficiaries who inherit a Roth IRA account and are not surviving spouses. In these cases, if the Roth IRA plan gives a beneficiary the option of choosing to receive distributions over his/her life expectancy, that method must be selected and the first minimum distribution must be made by December 31 of the year following the year of the owner's death.

Converting a Traditional IRA to a Roth IRA

Federal tax law provides that a taxpayer with MAGI of $100,000 or less may make a taxable conversion of a traditional IRA to a Roth IRA, provided the taxpayer is not married and filing separately. Such a conversion may be made either by means of a trustee-to-trustee transfer or by a traditional IRA account owner's instructing the current trustee to change the registration of the account. Alternatively, a traditional IRA owner may receive a distribution from a traditional IRA and deposit it in a Roth IRA account. Other, more complex requirements apply under certain circumstances in determining the $100,000 MAGI limit for eligibility for a conversion. In the case of a conversion from a traditional IRA to a Roth IRA, a taxpayer must report the conversion on IRS Form 8606 as a taxable conversion in the year in which the conversion is made. Amounts converted from a traditional IRA to a Roth IRA are taxable according to the owner's current federal tax rate, but these amounts are not subject to a penalty tax.

Reconverting to a Roth IRA After a Recharacterization

A traditional IRA that has been converted to a Roth IRA may be transferred back to a traditional IRA in a recharacterization. Recharacterization of such an IRA requires an account owner to notify the trustee of the account being recharacterized and of the amount being transferred. Subsequently, that amount may be reconverted back to a Roth IRA. The IRS has established deadlines for such recharacterizations and reconversions.

The rules governing conversions, recharacterizations, and reconversions are complex. Moreover, these actions are accompanied by serious tax implications. An individual contemplating a conversion, recharacterization, or reconversion should always consult a qualified tax advisor before taking any of these actions.

EDUCATION IRAS

Effective starting with 1998 tax returns, taxpayers may establish IRAs as a means of accumulating tax-free savings for education expenses for children. Although bearing the title IRA, the so-called Education IRAs are not retirement accounts at all. Rather, they exist to encourage taxpayers to save for the education of children. According to the authorizing law, the child or children to benefit from the funded education need not be a relative of the account owner.

A taxpayer may make a nondeductible annual contribution of up to $500 per child to an education IRA, and there is no limit to the number of children for which education IRAs may be established. Any contribution must be made in cash, and no contribution may be made after the beneficiary reaches age 18. However, the tax-free earnings may continue to accumulate in an account until the beneficiary of the account reaches age 30, by which time the account must be used for education purposes. Withdrawals from an account for any purpose other than funding a beneficiary's education are taxed to the extent of earnings at the taxpayer's regular income tax rate and subjected to a 10 percent penalty.

If a student receives a tax-free distribution from an education IRA in a tax year, none of the student's expenses can be used as the basis for either the Hope Credit or the Lifetime Learning Credit.

There is an income phaseout for eligibility to contribute to an education IRA, beginning with $95,000–$110,000 of modified adjusted gross income for single taxpayers and with $150,000–$160,000 for taxpayers filing a joint return.

SIMPLIFIED EMPLOYEE PENSIONS

A simplified employee pension (SEP) plan is an arrangement under which an employer contributes to an IRA that is set up for each covered employee. First authorized in 1979, SEPs simplify the administration and reduce the paperwork associated with many other types of pension plans; for this reason, they have been especially attractive to smaller employers. In particular, SEPs have reduced the paperwork normally required for HR-10 or corporate plans covering common-law employees. New tax legislation and the creation of the SIMPLE IRA (discussed later) have effectively eliminated the salary-reduction SEP as a new pension plan option for employees after 1996. However, many salary-reduction SEPs created prior to 1997 continue to exist as vehicles by which employers can provide retirement coverage for employees.

Contributions on behalf of employees are excludable from their income as follows: 15 percent of total employee compensation up to $170,000, or $25,000, whichever is less.

Employer contributions to a SEP must be made for all eligible employees in a manner that does not discriminate in favor of any "highly compensated" employees—sometimes called "prohibited classes," as defined by IRC Section 414(q). Discrimination is automatically deemed to exist if contributions do not represent a uniform percentage of each eligible employee's total compensation and favor the prohibited group, although integration with Social Security is permissible. Unionized employees and aliens usually are excluded from the process of determining whether a plan is discriminatory.

The integration of pension plans with Social Security is an important benefit distribution technique for the employer. Rules generally applicable to qualified defined contribution plans permit a limited difference between the contribution percentage that is applied to salary below and above the Social Security wage base or some other integration level.

Some of the requirements typically associated with pension plans also apply to SEPs. For example, the plan must be in writing, it must set forth the eligibility requirements, and it must specify the ways in which contributions are computed. However, SEPs are somewhat unusual in that (1) all rights to contributions are 100 percent vested in the employee immediately, and (2) an employee may freely withdraw funds, subject to the penalties described above for withdrawing funds from an IRA. Most employers would consider these vesting provisions to be a disadvantage.

SIMPLE IRAS

A SIMPLE IRA is a salary-reduction plan that permits employers to make contributions of up to $6,000 per year on behalf of eligible employees. With their lower, flat annual $6,000 limit, SIMPLE IRAs replaced salary-reduction SEPs as an option for employers beginning in 1997.

A SIMPLE IRA may be maintained only by an employer that (1) in the previous calendar year had no more than 100 employees who earned compensation of $5,000 or more, and (2) does not maintain any other retirement plan (unless the other plan is for collective bargaining employees).

An employee must be permitted to contribute to a SIMPLE IRA for a year in which he or she is reasonably expected to earn $5,000 or more, provided that employee received at least $5,000 in compensation in any two prior years, whether or not these years were consecutive. However, an employer may lower the $5,000 compensation test in order to broaden participation in a SIMPLE plan. In establishing a SIMPLE IRA plan, an employer may not set other conditions of eligibility for participation, including age or hours of work.

The only contributions that may be made to a SIMPLE IRA are elective salary-reduction contributions by employees and matching or non-elective contributions by employers. All contributions are fully vested and nonforfeitable when they are made.

Under a SIMPLE IRA, an employer must make either a matching contribution or a fixed non-elective contribution to an employee's account. Under the matching option, the employer must match up to 3 percent of a participating employee's compensation for a year, although the matching percentage may be reduced to as low as 1 percent for up to two years within a five-year period. For tax year 2000, as an alternative to the matching option, an employer may make a "non-elective" contribution equal to 2 percent of each eligible employee's compensation up to $170,000. While the 3 percent matching is not subject to the $170,000 compensation limit, the "non-elective" contribution is. Thus, for 2000, the maximum 2 percent non-elective contribution was $3,400. These limits are subject to inflation adjustment each year.

Distributions from SIMPLE IRAs are generally subject to the same rules as apply to traditional IRAs.

Although SIMPLE IRA plans are often discussed in the context of employer and employees, it is important to note that SIMPLE plans are also very popular among many one-person businesses in which the only employee is also the employer. For sole proprietors with moderate incomes, the $6,000 contribution limit is often much higher than the 15 percent limit that applies to Keogh plans, discussed below.

HR-10 (KEOGH) PLANS

The Self-Employed Individuals Tax Retirement Act of 1962 established the framework by which unincorporated small business owners and partners could set up and participate in tax-qualified pension plans popularly referred to as HR-10 (for an early version of the bill) or Keogh plans (for U.S. Rep. Eugene Keogh, sponsor of the bill).

Prior to the passage of this act, owners and partners of unincorporated businesses were ineligible to participate in a tax-qualified pension plan. Whereas the owner and sole employee of an incorporated business could enjoy the tax benefits of participation in a qualified pension plan, his or her unincorporated counterpart could not. Moreover, while employees of an unincorporated owner or partner were eligible to participate in such a plan, their employer could not. The 1962 act eliminated much of the inequity. The 1962 act imposed considerably stricter limitations for Keogh plans than existed for corporate pension plans. Subsequent legislation, however, in the form of ERISA, the Economic Recovery Tax Act of 1981 (ERTA), the Tax Equity and Fiscal Responsibility Act of 1982 (TEFRA), and TRA '86 has so liberalized the provisions of Keogh plans that today there are few differences between them and corporate plans. Of all this legislation, TEFRA had the greatest impact on Keogh plans, rendering changes in eligibility rules, vesting, plan administration, discrimination rules, and many other aspects.

Eligibility

To be eligible to establish a Keogh plan, an unincorporated sole proprietorship or partnership must be engaged in a business with a profit motive. Both owners/partners and their common-law employees are eligible to participate. For Keogh plan purposes, a common-law employee is one for whom an employer has the right to control and direct the results of the work and how it is done. Ministers, members of religious orders, full-time insurance salespeople, and U.S. citizens employed in the United States by foreign governments are not generally considered self-employed common-law employees for Keogh plan purposes, although distinctions to determine whether income is from self-employment can be subtle. A lawyer, for example, who is employed by a corporation would not be considered a self-employed person; however, if that same lawyer established a sole proprietorship by practicing law during the evenings, the earnings from that practice would establish eligibility for that lawyer to participate in a Keogh plan. Similarly, a pastor of a church would not be regarded as self-employed with respect to income derived from those services; but, if the pastor also performed wedding ceremonies independent of his church duties, the income derived would qualify as self-employment income. In all cases, the law provides that earned income for Keogh plan purposes must be derived from self-employment in which the individual's services materially helped to produce the income.

Capital gains from disposal of property are not considered self-employment income, although net earnings (e.g., commissions) from the sale of property are.

Eligibility for participation in Keogh plans is the same as for corporate plans discussed elsewhere in the *Handbook*. Full-time employees who are below age 21 or have less than one year of service may be excluded from coverage.

Establishing a Keogh Plan

A Keogh plan must be in writing. It can be drafted in the form of an individualized trust instrument, or it can be described in either a master plan or a prototype plan, either of which uses a standardized plan form. In the case of a master plan, a sponsoring organization—a trade or professional association, a bank, an insurance company, or a mutual fund—both funds the benefits and acts as plan administrator. If a prototype plan is utilized, the sponsoring organization funds the benefits, but the employer administers the plan. Whether an employer chooses to draft an individualized trust instrument or to adopt a master plan or a prototype plan, the plan should be submitted for approval by the IRS. Since the passage of TEFRA, the owner-employee is no longer required to seek out an institutional trustee, and in fact can now serve as the plan trustee.

In addition to providing a written instrument describing the plan, the owner-employee must make a contribution to the plan to bring the plan into legal existence.

The plan must meet the minimum participation requirements generally applicable to all corporate qualified retirement plans.

Keogh plans are subject to the same nondiscrimination and vesting rules as apply to corporate pension plans.

An owner-employee setting up a Keogh plan may establish a defined contribution plan, including a profit-sharing plan, a money purchase pension plan, or a defined benefit plan.

A Keogh plan administrator must file annual reports to the IRS. IRS Publication 560 lists the forms and reports that must be filed.

Contributions

Contributions to Keogh plans are governed by the same limits applicable to corporate pension and profit-sharing plans. For purposes of these limits, "earned income" is compensation for self-employed individuals.

"Earned income" means, in general, net earnings from self-employment in a trade or business in which personal services of the individual are a material income-producing factor. For plan purposes, earned income must be derived from the trade or business with respect to which the plan is established.

Contributions to a Keogh plan generally are applied to the current tax year. However, they can be applied to a previous tax year if (1) they are made by the due date of the tax return for the previous year, including extensions; (2) the plan was established by the end of the previous year; (3) the plan treats the contributions as though it had received them on the last day of the previous year; and (4) the employer (a) specifies in writing to the plan administrator or trustee that the contributions apply to the previous year or (b) deducts the contributions on the tax return for the previous year.

A promissory note is not considered a contribution to a Keogh plan for tax-deductibility purposes.

For purposes of determining the maximum deductible contribution to a Keogh plan, all defined contribution plans must be treated as a single plan, and all defined benefit plans must be treated as a single plan.

Voluntary Nondeductible Contributions and Elective Deferrals

Participants, including the owner employee, may be permitted to make nondeductible voluntary contributions to a Keogh plan on the same bases as under a corporate plan.

While such voluntary contributions are currently taxable, the interest buildup on them is not taxed until such time as distributions begin, a major advantage in building the value of the account.

Employees who participate in a profit-sharing Keogh plan also can elect to defer a portion of compensation by making elective distributions to a 401(k) plan, a Section 501(c)(18) plan, a SEP, or a tax-sheltered annuity.

Rollovers

The amount in a participant's Keogh plan account can be rolled over into another qualified plan or an IRA. However, nondeductible contributions cannot be rolled over. The rollover must be completed within 60 days of receipt of the distribution from the Keogh plan. A plan participant cannot roll over distributions into a spousal IRA. A surviving spouse can roll over a Keogh plan distribution as though he or she were the plan participant, but only into an IRA. Rollovers for partial distributions must be made to an IRA only. The decision to roll over a distribution from a Keogh plan into an IRA must be in writing and is irrevocable.

Distributions

Penalty-free distributions from a Keogh plan may begin as early as attainment of age 59½ and must begin no later than the participant's attaining age 70½.

Distributions from plans covering self-employed individuals are taxed in the same manner as distributions from traditional IRAs and SIMPLE IRAs, with the following modifications for distributions from plans covering self-employed individuals:

1. A distribution to a self-employed individual because of separation from service does not qualify as a lump-sum distribution.

2. Self-employed individuals can qualify for lump-sum treatment on distributions before age 59½ only because of disability.

3. In determining the investment in the contract for purposes of the annuity rules, in the case of a self-employed individual "cost" does not include contributions paid for which deductions were allowed.

4. Plan loans to an owner-employee may be a prohibited transaction.

There is a penalty tax of 10 percent on premature distributions, subject to exceptions for death of the participant, total and permanent disability of the participant, early retirement, decreed divorce settlements, and other events. Keogh plans also are subject to the imposition of an excise tax on a participant who fails to take the minimum distribution, as discussed earlier in this chapter in the section on IRAs.

A Keogh plan must provide that, unless the participant otherwise chooses, the payment of benefits must begin within 60 days of the latest of (1) the plan year in which the participant reaches the earlier of age 65 or the normal retirement age, (2) the plan year in which occurs the 10th anniversary of the year in which the participant came under the plan, or (3) the plan year in which the participant separated from service. These requirements do not waive the minimum distribution rule that distributions must begin by age 70½.

LEGISLATIVE TRENDS

In recent years, various initiatives in Congress have sought to liberalize participation in IRA plans and extend the uses to which these plans can be put. Among the successful efforts in this regard are the creation of

Roth IRAs, Education IRAs, and SIMPLE IRAs. In addition, the creation of penalty-free withdrawal exceptions for medical expense and medical insurance expense, higher education expenses, and first-time home buyer expenses all reflect the modification of rules to accommodate recent political concerns. Because of budgetary constraints, Congress has rejected numerous proposals to expand the income limits for eligibility for IRA participation. These proposals, however, keep coming and the emergence of budgetary surpluses is making it more difficult for Congress to resist the temptation to liberalize eligibility rules.

Expressions of the national will to encourage saving for retirement and to reduce reliance on Social Security as a retirement income source are encouraging the trend toward liberalization. Given the present concern with encouraging taxpayers to save for retirement, it is reasonable to conclude that efforts to expand eligibility for tax-deductible contributions to IRAs will continue in the future.

Chapter 32

Executive Compensation Plans

Thomas W. Ramagnano

David M. Sugar

INTRODUCTION

The two primary objectives for executive compensation programs are to help an organization in its efforts to attract, retain, and motivate top-quality executives, and to align executives' interests with the interests of shareholders. To accomplish these objectives, most organizations provide several different forms of compensation including:

- Base salary.
- Annual bonus.
- Long-term incentives.
- Qualified and nonqualified (supplemental retirement) benefits.
- Perquisites.

This chapter provides an overview of two areas of executive compensation that often require significant attention: long-term incentives, and executive retirement (and capital accumulation) benefits.

LONG-TERM INCENTIVES

Long-term incentives can be described as variable compensation earned over a period of more than 12 months. Of all forms of compensation available, the executive long-term incentive compensation program is perceived to be the most influential in shaping individual efforts and decision-making in support of the organization's goals. This makes it especially important to carefully identify measures of performance that correlate well with organizational success and allow for appropriate levels of reward through the company's incentive compensation plans.

Recognizing that each component of compensation should have a well-defined purpose and role, the primary objective of a long-term incentive arrangement is to guide (or influence) executives to make decisions that are consistent with and reinforce the corporation's long-term goals. Corporate goals cover everything from shareholder wealth creation to finance (such as earnings per share or return on net assets) to corporate culture (encourage teamwork). Of these, much more weight is placed on shareholder wealth creation.

Therefore, long-term incentive arrangements must be designed to:

■ Match the strategic needs of the business;
■ Influence executive behavior in support of the organization's goals; and
■ Reinforce the corporate culture and management style of the organization.

To achieve these goals, many forms of long-term incentive compensation have been developed. Some of these devices lead to direct ownership of stock, while others do not. The more common approaches are described in the following sections along with general accounting, tax, and design considerations for each.

Stock Options

Stock option plans are the most prevalent form of long-term compensation, with approximately 80 percent of companies allowing for option grants.[1] Stock option plans provide executives with the opportunity to purchase the employer's stock at a set price for a fixed period of time. Typically, the option (purchase) price is the fair-market value (FMV) of the stock on the date the option is granted. However, the purchase price can be established above or below the grant date FMV, and the price may be fixed or may vary. Regardless of how the option price is determined, the expectation is that the option holder will purchase the shares at a point in time when the current FMV of the stock is above the (purchase) price.

---

1 Based on Hewitt Associates LLC 1999 private data survey results.

Once the shares have been purchased (i.e., the option is exercised), the executive is free to sell the shares at whatever the current market price is or hold the shares for the possibility of future appreciation. Because the option holder can purchase the shares at any time during the proscribed period (typically 10 years), the potential for financial reward is very high.

Stock options can be granted in one of two forms: incentive stock options (ISOs), or nonqualified stock options (NQSOs). ISOs must conform to special rules contained within the Internal Revenue Code (IRC). Options that fail to meet the requirements are classified as NQSOs. (The differences are described in more detail below.)

Accounting Considerations

Even though stock options are capable of providing a significant amount of value to executives, current accounting rules do not require a company to record compensation expense for the grant of options at the stock's current FMV. This makes stock options a very attractive form of compensation for companies that want to reward the executives, but do not want the reward to impact the company's income statement. (In contrast, most other equity-based long-term incentive vehicles create a charge against income for accounting purposes, resulting in a lower level of reportable earnings.) There are a number of situations, however, where stock options can create corporate expense. For example, the grant of discounted options (options with an exercise price less than FMV on the date of grant) would result in a charge to earnings equal to the difference between the exercise price and the grant-date stock price. The expense is recognized over the vesting period (i.e., generally the period of time during which the individual must remain employed before the option can be exercised). In addition, any stock option arrangement where either the purchase price or the number of shares that can be acquired is not fixed at the time of grant can result in an accounting expense.

In 1995, the Financial Accounting Standards Board (FASB) issued *Statement of Financial Accounting Standards No. 123, Accounting for Stock-Based Compensation (FAS 123)*, which uses the "fair value" method for determining the compensation cost of equity-based compensation. The fair value method seeks to establish the fair value on the date of grant of stock options or other equity instruments. The resulting fair value determination is the compensation expense to be recognized over the vesting period. Companies are not required to adopt this statement for expense recognition purposes. However, companies not adopting the statement will be required to disclose in a footnote in their annual reports the pro forma effect on net income and earnings per share, if presented, as if the statement had been adopted. Companies typically do not adopt FAS 123 due to the resulting accounting charge from use of the fair value method.

Tax Considerations of Incentive Stock Options (ISOs)

To be classified as an ISO under Internal Revenue Code (IRC) Section 422, certain requirements must be met. The more significant requirements include:

- No disposition (of the underlying stock) within two years of the grant date and within one year of the exercise date.
- The option plan must be approved by shareholders within 12 months of adoption.
- The option price (or "exercise price") cannot be less than the FMV of the employer's stock on the date of grant and the option term cannot exceed 10 years.
- The fair-market value of stock with respect to which ISOs are first exercisable cannot exceed $100,000 in each calendar year. The excess is treated as nonqualified stock options (NQSOs).
- The options may be granted only to employees.

If these and other minor requirements are met, the executive does not recognize ordinary income at the time of the grant or upon the exercise of an ISO. (However, the "spread" between the grant price and the stock's FMV at exercise is an adjustment subject to the alternative minimum tax.) Following the exercise of an ISO, income tax on the stock's appreciation is deferred until the stock is actually sold and, at that time, the entire "spread" is taxed at capital gains rates (provided the holding requirements are met). Therefore, unless an employee is in an alternative minimum tax position, ISOs can be advantageous to an employee from a tax perspective.

The employer receives no tax deduction under an ISO plan unless the holding period requirements are not fulfilled by the executive (i.e., a disqualifying disposition). The employer may be entitled to a tax benefit if the employer reports the disqualifying disposition to the IRS. Because of these requirements, employers generally track and report disqualifying dispositions to receive a tax deduction.

Prior to the enactment of the Omnibus Budget Reconciliation Act of 1993 (OBRA '93) the tax advantages of ISOs for executives were considered to be too small to outweigh the restrictions (and tax disadvantages to the employer) associated with them. This was largely due to the fact that capital gains rates had closely paralleled ordinary income tax rates. However, because the top marginal ordinary income tax rates increased under OBRA 1993 (and capital gains decreased under the Taxpayer Relief Act of 1997), ISOs now offer potentially more value to executives, and companies are once again considering granting ISOs.

Tax Considerations of NQSOs

As indicated earlier, stock options that fail to meet the requirements under IRC Section 422 are NQSOs. When NQSOs are used, the executive will recognize income upon the exercise of an NQSO, in an amount equal to the "spread" between the exercise price and the stock's current FMV. Following exercise, income tax on the stock's appreciation is deferred until the stock is sold (and, at that time, the appreciation occurring after exercise is taxed as a capital gain).

The employer will receive a tax deduction for compensation expense upon the exercise of the option in an amount equal to the income reported for the employee. Thus, an NQSO plan can be beneficial to the employer from a tax perspective.

Annual compensation in excess of $1 million may not be deductible by the employer unless certain conditions are met under IRC Section 162(m). This overall limitation can apply to stock option arrangements as well as the other long-term incentives discussed below.

Design Considerations

Although there are some technical differences in the plan designs of ISOs and NQSOs, there are common design considerations including award size, option price, vesting schedule, and effect of employment termination. Each of these areas can affect the ultimate value of the options and the strength of the link between pay and company performance.

Award Size. The size of the option award is generally dependent on competitive market practice and is most typically expressed as a percentage of base salary. However, due to the $100,000 limit for ISOs (discussed above), awards of ISOs are typically much smaller than awards of NQSOs. Awards should be capable of delivering value which (when combined with other forms of pay) are consistent with the pay philosophy of the company. However, the aggregate amount of options outstanding may also be considered when determining the size of annual awards. Under certain circumstances, (e.g., new hires, reorganizations, etc.) it may be necessary to make a nonrecurring grant of options, which may or may not be consistent with the size of annual grants.

Option Price. As discussed earlier, ISOs must be granted with an option price not less than the FMV of the stock on the date of grant. However, NQSOs may be granted without any such restrictions. The following are various option pricing alternatives, however, none is common market practice.

Premium Options. Establish an exercise price that is higher than the grant-date stock price, creating a minimum threshold level of stock price increase that must be attained in order to realize any gains. This might be used to create more of a "stretch" goal for the executive.

Discounted Options. Establish an exercise price that is lower than the grant-date stock price, building in immediate value to the holder (not available for ISOs). This might be used in lieu of cash to reward for past performance.

Indexed Options. The exercise price is tied to some external measure (e.g., stock prices of comparator companies). Thus, employees will only benefit if the company's stock price outperforms the chosen index (for ISOs, the company may want to set the minimum option price at the FMV at date of grant). This might be useful where the corporate goal is to improve performance relative to a peer group of companies.

- **Schedule.** Vesting of options may occur ratably over time, at the end of a prearranged vesting schedule, or less commonly, based on satisfaction of performance conditions. Generally, vesting is used as a retention tool.
- **Effect of Termination.** Based upon the reason for termination, options may immediately vest, remain subject to a vesting schedule, or lapse and be forfeited. Termination also can affect the remaining length of time during which the options may be exercised. Usually, termination shortens the exercise period.

Stock Appreciation Rights (SARs)

SARs are much less prevalent than stock options with approximately 10 percent of companies allowing for grants of SARs.[2] Similar to stock options, a SAR gives the employee the ability over an extended period of time to realize the appreciation in the value of the employer's stock from the grant date to the date of exercise. However, with an SAR, the executive

2   Based on Hewitt Associates LLC 1999 private data survey results.

does not actually purchase the stock. Rather, the company simply pays the executive the spread at the point of exercise. Although payment of the appreciation upon exercise is usually in cash, it may be in stock or a combination of cash and stock.

Accounting Considerations

Although SARs have economic characteristics that are virtually identical to stock options, they require a different accounting treatment. The employer must recognize as compensation expense any increase in stock price from the date of grant to the date of exercise. Once a SAR is fully vested, the periodic compensation cost is measured by the difference between the FMV of the stock at the end of the period over that at the end of the preceding period. If vesting takes place over several periods, the value of the newly vested SARs (as well as the change in value of the previously vested SARs) will be included in the computation of the current period compensation cost. This accounting treatment may result in erratic, unexpected fluctuations in earnings charges.

Tax Considerations

There are no tax consequences to the company or the employee upon the grant of a SAR. Upon exercise of the SAR, the employee must recognize ordinary income in the amount of the appreciation (or up to a specified amount if the SAR is capped). The employer receives a corresponding deduction in the same amount.

Design Considerations

As with stock options, the establishment of a SAR program requires evaluation of certain design characteristics.

■ **Award Size.** Similar to the case with stock options, the size of the SAR award is contingent on various circumstances (e.g., annual grants versus new hires, special situations, etc.). The ultimate size of the grant should take into consideration the pay level philosophy of the company.

■ **SAR Exercise Price.** Typically, the SAR exercise price is equal to the FMV of a share of stock on the date of grant. This sets the basis of measuring the appreciation in the stock price from the date of grant to the exercise date.

■ **Vesting Schedule.** As with stock options, vesting of SARs may occur ratably over time, at the end of a prearranged vesting schedule, or less commonly, based on satisfaction of performance conditions.

■ **Effect of Termination.** Again, similar to stock options, SARs may immediately vest, remain subject to a vesting schedule, or lapse and be forfeited based on the reason for termination.

In addition to the foregoing considerations, SARs can be granted in conjunction with stock options ("Tandem" SARs) or as stand-alone SARs ("freestanding" SARs).

Tandem SARs

In the case of Tandem SARs, the holder usually may choose to exercise either the option or the SAR, and the exercise of one extinguishes the right to exercise the other. If the holder chooses to exercise the SAR in lieu of the stock option, he or she may also choose whether the value of the SAR will be paid in cash or stock.

Tandem SARs are typically used where the employer wants to give the executive the means to realize the increase in market value of the underlying stock without having to expend cash or otherwise raise capital to pay the option exercise price. There are other methods of realizing value without raising capital (e.g., "cashless exercise" of a NQSO).

Alternatively, Tandem SARs may be granted in order to provide a source of cash with which to pay taxes on exercises associated with the option. In that case, the Tandem SAR is usually exercisable (or automatically exercised) in addition to, rather than in lieu of, the associated option, and the Tandem SAR is usually payable in cash.

Freestanding SARs

Freestanding SARs are used without options and essentially take the form of stock-based deferred compensation entitling the holder to a payment upon exercise of the SAR.

Restricted Stock

With approximately 50 percent of companies having restricted stock plans, restricted stock continues to play an important role in long-term incentive programs.[3] A restricted stock plan gives the employee actual shares of employer stock subject to restrictions on transferability, with clear ownership contingent upon the providing of substantial services in the future. If the employee does not fulfill the future service contingency,

---

3 Based on Hewitt Associates LLC 1999 private data survey results.

the shares are forfeited, and revert back to the employer. Though a risk of forfeiture exists, the executive usually has the same voting and dividend rights as other shareholders.

Accounting Considerations

For accounting purposes, the employer will amortize the initial FMV of the restricted stock, as of the grant date, over the restriction period, regardless of the actual performance of the stock over this period (the subsequent appreciation does not create an accounting expense).

Tax Considerations

From the employee's perspective, because the stock is subject to a substantial risk of forfeiture (loss of shares if employment terminates during the restriction period), the employee has no taxable income until the restrictions lapse (unless the employee makes a special election to be taxed on the date of grant). However, dividends paid to the employee during the restriction period are taxed as ordinary income when paid. When restrictions lapse, the employee has taxable (ordinary) income equal to the current FMV of the stock less the amount paid, if any. Subsequent appreciation is taxed at capital gains rates when the stock is eventually sold.

The employer will receive a deduction for compensation expense at the time the restrictions lapse. The deduction will be in the amount of the FMV of the stock upon vesting. Also, the employer may receive a deduction for any dividends paid to the employee during the restriction period.

If the stock price increases after the date of the grant, the employer's deduction for tax purposes will exceed its expense for accounting purposes.

Design Considerations

Grants of restricted stock can create an immediate ownership interest while delaying taxation. In addition, restricted stock subject to forfeiture can create a strong retention vehicle for executives. The ownership of the stock is subject to certain conditions or restrictions. The holder's right to ownership in some or all of the shares of the stock is generally contingent upon the holder's continued employment by the employer for a certain period. The nature of restricted stock leads to a number of design alternatives:

- ■ **Dividends.** Shares of restricted stock may not pay dividends, may pay dividends on a current basis, or may accrue dividends;
- ■ **Vesting.** Vesting of shares of restricted stock may occur ratably over time, at the end of a prearranged schedule, or less commonly, based on satisfaction of performance conditions; and

■ **Termination.** Based upon the reason for termination, restrictions on the shares of restricted stock may lapse or the shares may be subject to forfeiture.

Performance Unit/Performance Share Plans

Performance unit/performance share plans are offered by approximately 30 percent of companies surveyed.[4] Performance plans typically are designed to pay awards if the organization meets preset, long-term performance objectives. At the beginning of the performance period, the employer establishes goals designed to measure the degree of business success over the period. Typical performance periods range from three to five years. The company's compensation committee typically approves goals that are recommended by management and decides the manner in which payouts are to be calculated. Such goals may be financial or operational in nature. One or more measures may be used.

Generally, an employee receives a grant of units or "stock" at no cost. Usually, no stock is actually granted until the end of the performance period. The employee then earns the right to receive the monetary value of some or all of the units or stock at the end of a specified period. Usually, these plans provide for minimum, target, and maximum levels of performance and the payout levels associated with each.

At the end of the performance period, performance is assessed and awards are paid. The value to be received depends upon the company's long-term performance. For example, an employee may be granted 1,000 performance units that will pay $100 each if certain target goals are achieved. If performance is above the targeted amount, the employee may receive additional units (that pay out at $100 each) or a higher payout per unit ($150 each). The value to be received from a performance share is based on the market value of the employer's stock at the end of the performance period and the extent to which performance goals are achieved. Performance units are typically paid in cash, while performance shares are usually paid in stock. However, a combination of cash and stock may be used for either vehicle.

Accounting Considerations

Under current accounting practices, an estimated expense is accrued by amortizing the initial value of the awards, and subsequent appreciation, over

---

4 Based on Hewitt Associates LLC 1999 private data survey results.

the performance period. The compensation expense for each period is calculated by determining the cumulative compensation as of the current period and deducting the compensation expense recognized in prior periods.

Tax Considerations

The company will receive a tax deduction in the year in which the actual payouts are made (or in the year prior to payment if the payment was made within two and one-half months of year end). The employee must report taxable income in the year the award is received.

Design Considerations

Performance shares provide an extremely flexible incentive vehicle that may not require the use of actual shares. Furthermore, as the value of the payout provided under a performance share plan is affected by the attainment of performance objectives and ultimate share price, performance shares can provide an incentive for performance even with a falling share price (while helping to limit awards for minimal or nonperformance with an increasing share price).

Alternatively, the payout provided under a performance unit plan is based solely on the achievement of performance objectives. The inherent flexibility of performance shares/units allows for a number of design alternatives:

- **Awards.** Can be units or shares. With share awards, ultimate payout value also depends on the market value of stock.
- **Performance Objectives.** Performance objectives can be based on a wide range of financial and nonfinancial measures. Typical measures include earnings per share (EPS), return on net assets (RONA), total shareholder return (TSR), and customer satisfaction.
- **Dividend Equivalents.** Performance shares/unit awards can be designed to pay or accrue dividend equivalents.
- **Payment Options.** Performance shares/unit awards can be paid out in cash or shares or provide the holder with a choice.

Phantom Stock

This form of long-term incentive compensation typically uses the employer's stock as the basis for measurement, and it is used more frequently in private (or closely held) companies where share ownership cannot easily be given to employees. Designated executives receive units corresponding to shares of common stock, but not representing genuine ownership. The employer simply credits these units on its books to the account of the executive. Often, the value of a unit upon initial grant equals the market price of a share of stock. Alternatively, the employer may relate unit values to the book value of common stock. Executives' accounts also may be credited during employment with any dividends declared on a number of shares of stock equivalent to the number of units in the executive's account.

At a specified point in time, the employer computes the value of the units credited to the executive's account and either pays the full value of the shares or the appreciation in value. Payment usually occurs after a specified period of time has elapsed.

A phantom stock plan also may be used to defer compensation from a separate incentive plan by using the employee's incentive dollars to "purchase" a number of phantom shares at the then-current value of the employer's stock. Final payments may be made in cash, in stock, or in a combination of cash and stock.

Tax Considerations

The tax treatment of phantom stock plans closely resembles that of performance share plans. Participating executives incur no income tax liability upon the initial grant of phantom stock shares, but recognize ordinary income when the amounts are received. Dividend payments are treated as additional compensation and thus are subject to ordinary income tax when received by the employee. If final payments are made in stock, subsequent appreciation represents capital gain.

The employer receives a tax deduction in the amount of, and at the same time as, the employee's taxable income from the plan.

Accounting Considerations

If the phantom stock plan is structured like an SAR (i.e., only share appreciation is paid out), the employer does not recognize compensation expense when the phantom shares are granted. Instead, expense is recognized periodically based on the fluctuation in market price from the date of grant to the date of payout, less expense recognized in previous periods. In addition, expense recognition is further affected by vesting schedules or performance criteria related to the phantom shares.

If a phantom stock plan is structured like restricted stock (i.e., the full value is paid rather than the appreciation) and the award will be paid only in stock, the accounting treatment is similar to the accounting for restricted stock plans. The value of the phantom stock on the date of grant is amortized over the vesting period. Increases after the grant date in the stock's FMV are not recognized as compensation expense. If the award is payable in cash (or in cash and stock), increases in value are recognized as compensation expense.

Design Considerations

Phantom stock provides an alternative incentive vehicle for corporations that do not have publicly traded stock. In addition, phantom stock does not require the use of actual shares. The use of phantom stock allows for several design alternatives:

- **Award Determination.** A number of methods can be used to determine the size of phantom stock awards, including multiples of salary, predetermined amounts, or discretionary awards.
- **Dividend Equivalents.** Phantom stock awards can be designed to pay or accrue dividend equivalents.
- **Payment Options.** Phantom stock awards can be paid out in cash or shares, or provide the holder with an option. Certain plans allow for payments to be deferred.
- **Structure of the Awards.** Phantom stock awards can be designed to pay the full value of the stock at the payout date or the appreciation only from the date of grant.
- **Vesting.** Vesting of phantom stock may occur ratably over time, at the end of a fixed schedule, or according to other methods established by the company.

Omnibus Plans

Though employers may have more than one long-term incentive plan, it is becoming more and more common for companies to include multiple long-term incentive vehicles in one long-term plan. Plans of this type are frequently referred to as omnibus or umbrella plans. More than 40 percent of companies grant their long-term incentive awards under an omnibus plan. Generally, the language in such plans allows the administering committee considerable leeway in establishing the various terms of the plan (i.e., participants, grant size, type of incentive vehicle, timing of grants, etc.).

Omnibus plans have come into favor for two main reasons. First, they provide a great deal of flexibility. The administrators may switch among incentive vehicles in response to unanticipated events, such as new or revised accounting or tax laws, as well as changing conditions or compensation philosophies within the organization. Second, by consolidating the various vehicles in one plan, a company can avoid having to seek shareholder approval several times for the modification or adoption of numerous plans.

EXECUTIVE BENEFIT ARRANGEMENTS

Though executive benefits typically do not provide as much value on an annualized basis as long-term incentives (or base salary and bonus), they are an important piece of an executive's total compensation package. In fact, the types and amounts of executive benefits offered by an employer can be a critical factor when it comes to executive recruitment and retention. Generally speaking, executive benefit arrangements are typically an extension of broad-based (all-employee) benefit plans and are designed to meet one or more of the following objectives:

- Restore retirement benefits that would otherwise have been provided under the broad-based qualified plans were it not for tax law limitations;
- Provide welfare benefits that would otherwise have been provided under the broad-based plans were it not for vendor limits (e.g., disability insurance coverage maximums) or tax rules (e.g., treatment of discriminatory group term life plans);
- Enhance the overall level of retirement or welfare benefits beyond that of the broad-based plan; and
- Introduce new retirement or welfare benefits not available under the organization's broad-based arrangements.

These objectives can be met by using one or more of the following executive/nonqualified benefit plan arrangements: nonqualified defined benefit and defined contribution restoration programs, nonqualified supplemental executive retirement plans (SERPs), nonqualified voluntary pay deferral plans, executive vacation benefit plans, executive death and disability plans, and executive medical plans. The balance of this chapter focuses on nonqualified executive benefit programs that fall under the areas of retirement and capital accumulation.

What is a Nonqualified Plan?

In this context, when we refer to a "nonqualified plan" we are speaking about an unfunded retirement program for a select group of management or highly compensated employees that does not qualify for preferential tax treatment under the IRC. This type of plan is also called a "top hat" plan because of the limited number of employees eligible to participate. There is another type of nonqualified plan that usually encompasses a larger group of employees called an "ERISA Excess Plan." An ERISA Excess Plan is also an unfunded arrangement, and its sole purpose is to restore benefits lost on account of the operation of IRC Section 415. (This code section restricts the annual benefit payable from a pension plan and the annual contribution by an employer to a defined contribution plan.)

What is an Unfunded Plan?

From an ERISA and income tax perspective, an unfunded plan is one where assets have not been set aside in a fully secure manner to pay benefits. An employer may informally earmark corporate assets to pay future benefits. An employer can even arrange for a third-party trustee to hold assets for plan benefit obligations, provided the assets are subject to the claims of creditors in the event of corporate bankruptcy. (This arrangement is commonly called a "rabbi trust" arrangement.) However, if assets are irrevocably set aside for the exclusive benefit of plan participants (i.e., in a fully secured manner) then the plan is no longer considered unfunded.

What is the Importance of an Unfunded Nonqualified Arrangement? When a nonqualified plan is unfunded, a company is not required to comply with various Employee Retirement Income Security Act (ERISA) requirements, and is free to design the nonqualified plan in any manner it chooses. For example, it can restrict eligibility, it can use any vesting schedule desired, and it can establish discriminatory levels of benefits within the plan. Furthermore, if a plan is unfunded, then plan participants will be taxed on benefits when they are paid. (If a nonqualified plan is funded, participants are generally taxed when they have a vested right to the assets that have been set aside.)

What Are the Main Types of Nonqualified Plans?

Today, there are three main types of nonqualified plans:

- **Restoration Plans.** These are plans that only make up for IRS tax limits. In a typical restoration plan, retirement benefits are calculated with and without regard to particular IRS limits. The nonqualified plan pays the difference.

■ **Supplemental Executive Retirement Plans (SERPs).** These plans go beyond pure restoration. For example, the plan formula may include a form of pay not covered under the broad-based qualified plan (such as bonus pay). Or, the plan may simply increase the level of benefit (say from a broad-based benefit of 40 percent of final average pay to an executive-only benefit of 50 percent of final average pay). Sometimes the plan pays a supplement to the qualified plan based on adding years of service to the years counted under the qualified plan. (For example, the SERP pays the additional amount the participant would have received from the qualified plan if the number of years of service were increased by ten.)

■ **Voluntary Salary/Bonus Deferral Plans.** These plans allow participants to defer some or all of their compensation, usually salary and/or bonus, to a future date with interest (or other method of earnings).

The balance of this chapter describes these plans in more detail and discusses approaches to secure (or informally fund) them.

Defined Benefit and Defined Contribution Restoration Plans

The IRC contains a number of restrictions that limit the amount of retirement benefits that can be delivered through a tax-qualified retirement or savings plan. For example, IRC Section 401(a)(17) restricts the amount of annual wages that can be used in benefit formulas to determine benefits under a tax-qualified plan. (For plan years beginning on or after January 1, 2001, the recognizable pay limit is $170,000.) To illustrate how this limit operates, consider a participant in a tax-qualified profit-sharing plan whose annual compensation is $200,000. Under the profit-sharing plan, the employer contributes 6 percent of annual compensation to each participant's account. Because of IRC Section 401(a)(17), the employer may contribute only 6 percent of $170,000 rather than 6 percent of $200,000.

Other tax law limits commonly affecting retirement benefit levels include:

IRC Section 415(b) Limits the annual benefit payable from a defined benefit plan ($140,000 for 2001);

IRC Section 415(c) Limits the annual addition to an employee's defined contribution account (lesser of $35,000 or 25 percent of compensation);

IRC Section 402(g) Limits the amount of annual elective deferrals under 401(k) plans ($10,500 for 2001); and

IRC Section 401(m) Limits the percentage of pay that high-paid employees may defer under a 401(k) plan.

In response to these restrictions, companies commonly provide non-qualified plan benefits that make up for one or more of these limitations. These plans are called "restoration" plans because they restore the amount of benefit lost due to IRC limits. Restoration plans that solely make up for IRC Section 415 limits are called ERISA Excess Plans, and these plans may cover all employees who have had retirement benefits reduced on account of IRC Section 415. Restoration plans that make up for any other tax law limit must be unfunded and must restrict eligibility to a select group of management or highly compensated employees (to avoid having to comply with all of ERISA's rules).

Considerations in Designing Restoration Plans

Because restoration plans are nonqualified, the employer is free to design the plan in virtually any manner it desires. The most common practice is to mirror the operation of the qualified plan as closely as possible except, of course, without regard to the IRC tax limitation. There are, however, six design areas that frequently require attention:

- **Picking which tax limits will be restored.** Because of administrative, tax, and/or ERISA considerations, some tax law limits (such as the 402(g) dollar contribution limit to 401(k) plans) are not restored.
- **Determining the level of restoration.** For cost reasons, some employers choose to limit the amount of benefit restored. Though the qualified plan calls for a profit-sharing contribution on all cash compensation up to the recognizable pay limit, the restoration plan may still limit the total pay to a specific dollar amount (e.g., all cash compensation up to $1 million).
- **Deciding who is eligible to participate in the plan.** In some cases, qualified plan participants affected by a particular tax law limit may not be considered a "top hat" individual. In other cases, an employer may simply want to limit participation to reinforce the notion that the plan has been established for an exclusive group.
- **Choosing the vesting schedule.** An employer is free to make vesting shorter or longer under the nonqualified plan. For exam-

ple, vesting might be lengthened to support retention objectives. Or, vesting might be automatic to make an employment offer more attractive. (Note: Vesting schedules can vary by participant if desired.)

■ **Establishing payout options.** Though the qualified plan may contain several payout options, an employer may decide to use a smaller number or options (or even just one option) for the non-qualified plan. Often this is done to simplify administration. In some cases a payout option chosen by the employer for the non-qualified plan may not even be offered under the qualified plan. For example, the nonqualified plan may only pay benefits in the form of a lump sum whereas the qualified plan may not even permit a lump-sum form of payment.

Defined contribution restoration plans pose a particular issue with regard to investment choices. The qualified plan may allow plan participants discretion on how account balances will be invested. The restoration plan need not offer investment discretion, may offer the same (or a more limited) number of investment options, or may simply offer a different array of investment options.

Prevalence of Restoration Plans

Private survey data suggests that restoration plans are very common, especially among larger companies. Smaller employers are less likely to have a restoration plan for a number of reasons including cost, low number of employees affected by the tax law limits, and lack of internal resources to administer the plan.

Supplemental Executive Retirement Plans (SERPs)

A SERP is another type of nonqualified retirement plan that can be used to address a variety of compensation objectives. From a technical perspective it is no different from a restoration plan in that a SERP is an unfunded top hat plan, and the employer is not restricted with regard to plan design. What makes the SERP different from a restoration plan is its purpose. A restoration plan's primary purpose is to replace benefits lost due to one or more IRS limits. A SERP's primary purpose may include one (or more) of the following:

■ **Deliver an overall higher level of retirement benefit.** Typically this is reflected as a higher accrual rate than provided under the broad-based plan. The SERP also may use a different method of calculating final average pay to increase the level of benefit (e.g., highest three years out of last five rather than highest consecutive five years out of ten).

■ **Include a form of compensation not covered under the qualified plan.** For example, the qualified plan may only use base salary under the plan formula, whereas the SERP may use base salary and annual bonus (to reflect the variable nature of executive compensation).

■ **Provide full-career pension benefits to short-term (or "midcareer") new hires.** To facilitate recruiting, an employer may need to supplement the broad-based pension plan benefit to reflect a shorter period of employment expected from the new hire. This can be done by granting additional years of service, waiving vesting requirements, or setting minimum levels of benefit to be paid.

■ **Encourage early retirement.** To facilitate an orderly transition of leadership (and to help make way for executives coming up within the organization), many organizations allow executives the opportunity to receive unreduced pension benefits at an earlier age than allowed under the qualified retirement plans.

SERPs are different from restoration plans in other respects. For example, vesting requirements under restoration plans typically parallel the requirements under the related qualified plan. (Sometimes, vesting under a restoration plan is shorter for ease of administration or to make the plan more attractive.) SERPs on the other hand often have lengthy vesting requirements. This is particularly evident where the SERP benefit is somewhat rich and the company wants to do everything possible to reinforce retention of executive talent.

SERPs also may include "offsets" to reflect the employer's contributions to other (unrelated) retirement benefit programs. For example, if a company has both a broad-based (qualified) profit-sharing plan and a "target" SERP for executives (e.g., a fixed percentage of final average pay commencing at age 60 with 20 years service), then the SERP benefit formula may include an offset to reduce the final amount payable from the SERP. (The offset would be the "actuarial equivalent annuity value" of the profit-sharing plan contributions.) In other words, the actual SERP benefit will be less than the percentage of final average pay targeted. Also, it is common for SERPs to reflect an employer's contributions to Social Security.

Finally, SERPs can include special features to reflect concerns the executives may have. For example, if the SERP only pays benefits in the form of a lump sum, the benefit formula may use a more generous (lower) interest rate to calculate the lump-sum amount. This would be one way to address executive concerns about paying income taxes upfront rather than over time. A SERP may also provide a more generous (subsidized) form of benefit payable to an executive's spouse if the executive dies first. (Or the SERP could provide for a minimum number of payments regardless of when death occurs.)

Voluntary Salary/Bonus Deferral Plans

The third common form of nonqualified retirement plan is one that allows an executive the opportunity to defer receipt of some of the compensation otherwise payable. In a typical voluntary nonqualified deferred compensation (VNDC) plan, the employer maintains a bookkeeping account to keep track of the amount of compensation deferred by each participant. The participant's account balance is then adjusted upwards or downwards to reflect the manner in which the deferrals are deemed invested by the employer. The method of crediting earnings to the account is completely at the employer's discretion; however, if the method is not attractive, the plan will have little value to the executive participants.

If the employer considers the deferrals as business loans from the participant, the employer may use a fixed or floating interest rate to adjust the participant accounts. These interest adjustments may be based on any rate the employer chooses (e.g., prime rate, long-term borrowing rate, T-Bill investment rate, etc.). Alternatively, the employer could treat the deferrals as investments in the company's common stock and will increase or decrease participant accounts to reflect changes in the market value of the common stock (as well as to reflect dividend payments made to real shareholders). In some cases the employer may use a higher-than-market rate of interest to make the plan more compensatory in nature. This might be done in situations where other forms of compensation (e.g., stock options) are not available.

Recently, there has been a trend towards treating the voluntary deferral accounts like 401(k) plans and allowing nonqualified plan participants the opportunity to "hypothetically" invest the deferrals among a variety of mutual funds. When the plan is designed in this manner, participant accounts move up or down along with the direction of the particular funds specified by the executive.

Economic Implications of VNDC Plans

Because the employer cannot take a current tax deduction when the executive defers pay, the net amount of cash retained from the deferral is less than the deferral itself. For example, a $50,000 pay deferral might result only in a $30,000 current cash savings for the employer (because a $20,000 tax benefit has been delayed). Consequently, there are two economic "rules" that should be reviewed whenever a VNDC plan is considered:

Rule No. 1 If the crediting rate used to determine earnings on participant deferral accounts is higher than the after-tax investment return the employer can make on the funds retained from the deferral, then the VNDC plan will have a real economic cost to the employer. For example, if the plan credits 10 percent interest on the deferral accounts, but the employer only earns 6 percent (after-tax) on the cash retained as a result of the deferrals, the employer will incur a cost.

Rule No. 2 If the VNDC plan is fully "funded" with segregated assets (but not actually funded from an ERISA perspective), and if the after-tax return on the segregated assets is less than the employer's after-tax cost of funds, then the full funding of the VNDC plan will cause a real economic cost to the employer.

VNDC Plan Design Considerations

Because VNDC plans are nonqualified, the employer is free to design the plan in any manner desired. The major design parameters to be considered include:

- **Eligibility requirements.** Often times eligibility is broader for VNDC plans than for restoration plans and SERPs (however, top hat rules must still be observed).
- **Types of pay to be deferred.** Salary and bonus deferrals are the most common, but long-term incentives can also be deferred.
- **Amount of pay to be deferred.** Typically, up to 100 percent of bonus may be deferred; salary deferrals are generally more restricted (though they need not be).
- **Length of time pay can be deferred.** Termination of employment usually triggers payment, but deferral for a fixed number of years and other design alternatives are available.
- **Manner of determining earnings credits on deferrals.** Not only can an employer use a variety of indices or rates, but the employer can modify the rate according to corporate performance, length of service, or other factors.

■ **Form of payment.** Lump-sums and annual installments usually are offered.

Nonqualified Plan Accounting Considerations

Accounting for *nonqualified* restoration plan, SERP plan, and deferral plan benefits is the same as accounting for the related qualified plans with one important exception. With a qualified plan, assets placed in a trust for the benefit of participants are counted as "plan assets" and reduce the amount of obligation reflected on the employer's balance sheet. With a nonqualified plan, assets segregated and expected to be used for the benefit of participants are in most cases still treated as general assets of the employer, and may not be counted as plan assets. In other words, the gross nonqualified benefit obligation is reported in the financial accounts. For example, if an employer establishes a rabbi trust and puts assets in the trust to pay benefits for plan participants, the assets in the trust are recorded as general corporate assets for accounting purposes (and do not offset the nonqualified benefit plan obligation).

Nonqualified Plan Tax Considerations

Nonqualified plan benefits generally are not taxable income to the executive participant until paid. Accordingly, the employer does not receive a tax deduction until benefits are paid. (The informal segregating of assets for future payment of benefits will not necessarily trigger taxation for the executive and tax deduction for the employer.)

Securing Nonqualified Plan Benefits

By design, nonqualified retirement and deferral arrangements are unfunded promises of the employer and generally lack security for the specific purpose of avoiding early taxation. Furthermore, while the U.S. Department of Labor regulates the operation of tax-qualified programs through the provisions of ERISA, virtually all nonqualified arrangements are structured purposely to be exempt from most ERISA protections.

Without the protections of ERISA or a secured funding vehicle, nonqualified arrangements remain (unsecured) general asset promises of the employer. Although the nonqualified benefit plan creates an enforceable contractual obligation, most plan participants would prefer greater security than a breach-of-contract lawsuit. Events that could lead to a loss of benefits (or a substantial delay in receiving them due to litigation) include:

- A change of heart (by existing management or the board of directors regarding the payment of benefits when they otherwise would be due).
- Change in company ownership or control.
- Regulatory intervention.
- Poor company cash flow.
- Bankruptcy or insolvency.

Comparing Approaches

Practitioners have devised a number of different approaches to decrease the level of risk inherent in nonqualified arrangements, but there still is no perfect approach. The list of approaches for securing nonqualified benefits include:

- Rabbi trusts.
- Employee-grantor trusts.
- IRC Section 402(b) trusts.
- Employee-owned annuities (or life insurance).
- Split dollar life insurance offsets.
- Qualified supplemental retirement benefit offsets.
- Executive benefit payment insurance.
- Elective lump-sum payment options.
- Haircut withdrawal rights.
- Event trigger payouts.
- Repudiation penalty clauses.
- Earmarking corporate investments (e.g., corporate-owned life insurance).

A detailed comparison of these approaches is outside the scope of this chapter; however, each one has unique advantages and drawbacks that should be weighed carefully before making a decision on which (if any) to use to back nonqualified retirement and deferral plan benefit promises. Regardless of the approach being considered, the following points should be kept in mind when making comparisons:

- "Funded" can mean several things. When the word "funded" is used with respect to nonqualified plans, it may have at least three distinct meanings:
  - For tax purposes, "funded" can mean that amounts are set aside without a risk of forfeiture, resulting in immediate taxation of benefits to participants.
  - For ERISA purposes, "funded" generally means that dollars irrevocably are contributed to a trust or insurance company contract for the benefit of a plan participant, possibly resulting in the full applicability of Title I tax-qualified retirement plan ERISA requirements.
  - To a company chief financial officer, "funded" generally may mean simply that general assets have been earmarked to pay a particular obligation in the future, regardless of whether the assets have been contributed to a trust or irrevocably set aside without a risk of forfeiture.

When discussing the various mechanisms used to back nonqualified arrangements, it always is useful to clarify whether the vehicle will be considered "funded" for purposes of tax and/or ERISA rules, or whether funded means simply earmarking a general company asset where no additional security actually is provided.

Note that certain vehicles, such as 402(b) trusts or employee-owned annuities, by definition, are constructed to be "funded" for tax and/or ERISA purposes

- Direct comparisons of approaches is difficult. A direct, "apples-to-apples" comparison of the various approaches to securing nonqualified arrangements is difficult at best for a variety of reasons:
  - Actual level of security differs by vehicle.
  - Cost and administrative concerns can vary in their significance with respect to cash-flow requirements, commissions and trust fees, record-keeping, accounting treatment, and ERISA applicability.
  - Tax consequences vary by vehicle and significantly impact the economic analysis from the employer and executive points of view.

- As shown in Figure 32–1, the degree of security and taxation are linked. As the level of security increases, there is a greater chance that participants will be subject to immediate taxation of

F I G U R E   32–1

Trade Off Between Security and Taxation

Security to Executive

A	C	E
B	D	F

Low   High

Taxation to Executive

A				
B				
C	D	E	F	

Deferred   Immediate

Legend

A—General asset promises

B—Corporate-owned life insurance

C—Rabbi trusts

D—Split dollar life insurance

E—Employee-owned annuities

F—Employee-grantor trusts

---

benefits under the tax doctrines of constructive receipt and/or economic benefit. (Unlike tax-qualified arrangements, nonqualified plans are not exempt from these tax doctrines.)

Reasons for Securing/Funding Nonqualified Plan Benefits

The reasons companies choose to secure nonqualified benefit plan obligations varies from situation to situation. Often there is no one clear reason for securing or funding; rather, a combination of circumstances makes securing or funding a reasonable course of action to take. The most common reasons (circumstances) that rationalize securing or funding are discussed below.

Need For Executive Security

In some situations, executives may depend heavily on retirement income or retirement savings. Recent poor stock performance or a history of poor incentive payouts may leave the executive with little in the way of capital accumulation, and the nonqualified retirement or savings vehicles may become critical to sustain an executive's post-retirement standard of living.

Also, some boards of directors believe that nonqualified restoration plan benefits, or SERP benefits that simply expand the definition of pay to take into account the unique manner in which executives are compensated, deserve as much protection as qualified plan benefits.

Finally, where there has been a change in ownership (takeover), corporate reorganization, or change in management, or prior insolvency, executives may become preoccupied with benefit security. Adding security measures could eliminate these management distractions, and increase the likelihood that management energy will be devoted to the future performance of the company.

Liability Management

The 1993 decrease in the IRS pay limits for qualified plans (to $150,000) caused a significant increase in nonqualified benefit obligations, and some employers have become concerned with the large projected unfunded liabilities associated with their nonqualified plans. In some situations, companies have adopted a "fund your own obligation" attitude so that current management rather than future management has to deal with the liability problem. This could mean simply investing in earmarked corporate assets (e.g., corporate-owned life insurance) or something more secure such as a funded rabbi trust. In either case, today's management is setting aside assets currently, to match the liability accrual, and to "fund" the benefits they will ultimately receive.

Cash Flow Management

In some companies, those responsible for managing corporate cash flows may prefer to avoid large fluctuations in their cash accounts or available lines of credit. When the potential for significant lump-sum payouts exist under the nonqualified plan, there may be a desire to budget for these cash flows ahead of time.

Competitive Practice

Often the most compelling reason for securing or funding is simply to maintain a competitive posture within a particular industry or group of "comparator" companies. Securing nonqualified benefits, particularly through the use of a rabbi trust, has become quite popular. Thus, to maintain a competitive posture, some action may be required.

Provide a Message to Executives

There are a number of positive messages to executives that are explicitly or implicitly linked to benefit security and funding:

- Management places a high value on benefits.
- Management wants to alleviate fears related to the risk of non-payment of benefits.
- Management's desire to retain executives is strong enough to be backed by assets.
- Management wants to align executive interests with shareholder interests (as is the case when corporate stock is the asset used for funding).

Alleviating fears and distractions and retaining key management are probably the most common messages employers expressly want to communicate by funding. Typically, this is found in two types of situations: one is where there are strong financial concerns because of large consumer lawsuits pending or large net operating losses; the other is where there is merger/reorganization activity pending. In both cases, executives are seeking reassurance related to their retirement benefits, and employers are seeking to retain the executive talent through difficult times.

Provide a Message to Outsiders

Though not reason enough to justify funding, setting assets aside can send a message to outsiders such as hostile acquirers and/or stock analysts. For example, funding a rabbi trust to back "worst-case" benefit payouts related to a change in control might warn an acquirer not to act too swiftly to make management changes. Or, setting aside large blocks of company stock in a rabbi trust to back nonqualified benefits may signal to stock analysts a company's strong conviction regarding the value of its stock.

Materiality

In many instances, the size of the nonqualified benefit obligation is immaterial to the overall financial position of the company. Where that is the case, management may feel that a strong reason against funding is missing and because of immateriality, will go forward with a funding transaction.

Reasons for Not Funding
Nonqualified Plan Benefits

Just as there are a variety of reasons why companies choose to fund their nonqualified plans, there are a variety of reasons why companies choose not to fund.

Costs Associated with Funding

Perhaps the most often cited argument against funding is it results in a cost to the company. Though nearly all financial analysts agree there is a cost to segregating corporate assets, there is disagreement among them on how to measure that cost.

For example, "Company A" always has excess cash invested in overnight deposits. It takes a portion of that excess cash for funding non-qualified benefits and still has excess cash remaining in overnight deposits. Therefore, the cost of funding (if any) should be the lost investment income on the overnight deposit offset by any investment gain resulting from reinvesting the cash in the segregated environment.

"Company B," on the other hand, strives to put every available dollar into operations where the risk-adjusted return on investment is 20 percent (after tax). Since money set aside for benefit funding cannot be used in the business, the cost of funding should be the lost opportunity (20 percent) offset by the after-tax return on the funding.

There are other perspectives on how to measure funding costs. For example, if a company has a relatively small obligation to fund and believes funding will not constrain its ability to borrow, then the cost of funding will be measured with reference to the company's after-tax borrowing costs.

On the other hand, a company may feel that regardless of where the cash comes from and how the cash is used, it ultimately affects the company's ability to raise capital. Therefore, the cost of funding should be measured with reference to the company's after-tax weighted cost of capital.

Shareholder Perception

An adverse reaction by shareholders is another frequently cited reason for not funding. If there is already shareholder tension related to executive compensation, the tension may increase if the funding becomes public. Even where there is not already tension, funding may result in an unfavorable shareholder reaction. For example, establishing a rabbi trust and funding it with assets may create the impression that management is going to shop the company for a takeover or management is contemplating a reorganization. Similarly, creating a so-called secular trust may create the impression that management is worried about the financial soundness of the company.

Note: In most cases, public disclosure of funding is not required. However, informal disclosure may occur when news of the underlying transactions is inadvertently communicated to third parties. Sometimes disclosure is used intentionally to explain other transactions that must be disclosed. (For example, disclosing the funding might help explain related tax reimbursements which must be disclosed in the proxy.) Finally, disclosure may occur simply out of confusion as to what is really required in the proxy (such as details of the CEO's employment contract).

Lack of Security Concerns

Some companies dismiss the idea of funding simply because there is no perceived risk of nonpayment. After all, a properly drafted nonqualified plan document provides executives with a means to legally enforce payment of benefit. Furthermore, where a company has always enjoyed favorable employee/employer relations and there has never been a hint of financial trouble for the company, there may be no apparent risk of nonpayment. If there is no perceived risk of nonpayment, then why fund?

Lack of Tax-Effective Bankruptcy Protections

In situations where the only possible concern is bankruptcy, companies may be unwilling to fund because there are no proven funding vehicles that provide protection from creditors and avoid early taxation of benefits. There are some funding vehicles that can mitigate the bankruptcy risk (e.g., split dollar life insurance and Section 83 option trusts). However, there are questions on how these vehicles are taxed.

Note: There is one proven approach to bankruptcy that is not really a funding approach. So-called "executive benefit insurance" policies can be purchased that protect the executive from nonpayment of benefits. The period of coverage can be as long as five years, and with some policies, the period can be extended to maintain a constant five-year period of protection as long as certain financial and business underwriting requirements are met. These policies are generally unpopular because of the perceived high cost relative to the protection provided (i.e., the cost is highest for those who are most at risk for loss of benefit due to bankruptcy).

CHAPTER 33

Section 403(b) Plans for Nonprofit Organizations

Michele F. Davis

INTRODUCTION

A Section 403(b) plan, also referred to as a tax-sheltered annuity (TSA) Plan or a tax-deferred annuity (TDA) Plan, is a type of defined contribution plan available only to employees of tax-exempt organizations such as colleges, universities, research organizations, hospitals, churches, charitable organizations, independent schools, and public teaching institutions (e.g., state universities, community colleges, and K-12 public school systems). A 403(b) plan offers employees of tax-exempt organizations the same tax advantages as other types of defined contribution plans. Specifically, employer contributions and earnings on those contributions as well as employee elective pretax deferrals or contributions (known as salary reduction contributions) and earnings on those deferrals or contributions are generally excluded from taxable income until the employee receives a distribution from the plan.

This chapter provides an overview of 403(b) plans that accept only employee elective deferrals (which are always 100 percent vested) and in which the employer has limited involvement (as provided for in applicable Department of Labor Regulations). As a result, these plans are not considered employee benefit plans subject to the Employee Retirement Income Security Act (ERISA) of 1974.

LEGISLATIVE HISTORY OF 403(b) PLANS

Prior to 1959, tax-exempt organizations under Section 501(c)(3) of the Internal Revenue Code (IRC or Code) were permitted to purchase tax deferred annuities or TDAs for their employees. (See the section *Eligible Employees* for the definition of a Section 501(c)(3) organization.) Unlike the Section 403(b) contracts of today, it was not clear whether employee salary reduction contributions were permitted. In 1958, in response to Treasury's concerns over what limits should apply to amounts deferred under TDAs, Congress passed the Technical Amendments Act of 1958 that added Section 403(b) to the Internal Revenue Code. The newly enacted Section 403(b) made it clear that an employee was entitled to enter into a salary reduction agreement and make contributions to his or her Section 403(b) contract on a tax-deferred basis. This Act also placed a limit on the amount that could be tax-deferred (the "maximum exclusion allowance"). In 1961, legislation extended eligibility to faculty and staff of public schools, colleges, and universities.

Many of the provisions of ERISA were extended to 403(b) plans upon its passage in 1974. In particular, Section 415(c)(1), which imposed a limit on the annual additions to an employee's account, was also imposed on Section 403(b) plans. To compensate for this limitation, the statute included three special elections for 403(b) contracts that are purchased by tax-exempt educational institutions, hospitals, home health service agencies, certain churches, and health and welfare organizations or their employees. These came to be known as the "catch-up elections." The Tax Reform Act of 1986 (TRA '86) further restricted the annual elective deferral limit. It mandated that the limitation on annual elective deferrals under Section 402(g) applies to elective deferrals to Section 403(b) plans as well as to other defined contribution plans. To compensate for this limitation, the statute included another special "catch-up election" for 403(b) contracts purchased by tax-exempt educational institutions, hospitals, home health service agencies, certain churches, and health and welfare organizations or their employees.

Originally, there were no rules requiring 403(b) plan distributions. Other regulatory and legislative action was taken to address this issue. In 1973, the Internal Revenue Service (IRS) said that more than 50 percent of the money should be taken out during a participant's lifetime, but the IRS did not specify a mandatory starting point for the distributions. In the late 1970s, the IRS informally indicated that distributions should start by age 75. TRA '86 mandated that post-1986 accumulations (deferrals or contributions and all earnings) must comply with the minimum distributions requirements. Subsequently, an IRS agency spokesperson indicated accumulations in 403(b) plans before January 1, 1987, need not be distributed before the annuity holder attains age 75.[1]

In addition, TRA '86 provided that withdrawals of salary reduction amounts from 403(b) annuity contracts could only be made upon attainment of 59½, separation from service, death, disability, or financial hardship. These restrictions always applied to all amounts contributed to 403(b) plans funded with mutual funds, from the time mutual funds were allowed to be funding vehicles for 403(b) plans (as first permitted under ERISA).

The Small Business Job Protection Act (SBJPA) of 1996 eliminated the requirement that an employee could only complete one salary reduction agreement each calendar year.[2] (An employee may now complete more than one salary reduction agreement in a calendar year, but the employer's plan may limit the number of agreements that can be entered into in a given calendar year.) The SBJPA also offered tax-exempt organizations the option of offering a 401(k) plan to its employees.

ELIGIBLE EMPLOYERS

Two types of employers may offer a 403(b) plan:

- An organization exempt under Section 501(c)(3) of the IRC.
- A public educational organization under Section 170(b)(1)(A)(ii) of the IRC.

In addition, a duly ordained, commissioned or licensed minister of a church who is either self-employed or part of an organization that, although not exempt under Section 501(c)(3) shares a common religious bond with such a minister whom it employs, also may be covered under a 403(b) plan.

A Section 501(c)(3) organization is defined as a nonprofit organization organized and operated exclusively for religious, charitable, scientific, public safety testing, literary, or educational purposes. It also includes tax-exempt organizations that are organized and operated exclusively to encourage national or international amateur sports competition (but only if

---

1 Internal Revenue Service's Employee Plans Examination Guidelines Handbook 7.7.1, Chapter 13, 403(b) Plans, Section 13.7.3.

2 An agreement between the employee and the employer whereby the employee elects to have compensation contributed on a pretax basis to the 403(b) plan that would otherwise be paid to him or her as cash.

no part of its activities involve the provision of athletic facilities or equipment), or for the prevention of cruelty to children or animals. The organization can be a corporation, community chest, fund, or foundation. A public educational organization is one that normally maintains a regular faculty and curriculum and normally has a regularly enrolled body of students in attendance at the place where it regularly carries on educational activities, such as public primary and secondary schools, state colleges and universities, and public junior colleges.

ELIGIBLE EMPLOYEES

Individuals at eligible employers may participate in a 403(b) plan if they are present, former, or retired common-law employees. These individuals must meet criteria similar to those applied for determining employee status for the Federal Insurance Contributions Act or FICA (Social Security and Medicare), for the Federal Unemployment Tax (FUTA) purposes, and for federal income tax withholding. Individuals considered independent contractors are not eligible to participate in a 403(b) plan.

PLAN DESIGN OPTIONS

Voluntary Plan

Tax-exempt organizations may offer a 403(b) plan that is funded purely by salary reduction (employee elective deferrals or contributions). This type of plan can be the sole retirement plan offered by the organization or serve as a supplemental plan. These types of plans are relatively easy to administer because they require very little employer involvement and can avoid being subject to ERISA. See section on Application of ERISA.

Employer Contributory or Noncontributory Plan

Many tax-exempt organizations, especially colleges and universities, offer a 403(b) plan as their core retirement plan for their faculty and some or all of their staff. This type of plan can be funded either as a contributory or noncontributory plan, or as a combination of both. In a contributory plan, the employer's nonelective contribution (matching contribution) is contingent upon an employee contribution. Both are usually a percentage of compensation and also may be based on the employee's age or length of service with the employer. In a noncontributory plan, the plan is entirely funded by the organization; in other words, the plan does not require the employee to contribute in order to receive the employer non-elective contribution. The nonelective amount contributed by the employer is usually a percentage of the employee's compensation. In some plans, the percentage of the compensation that is contributed by the employer is also based on the employee's age or length of service, or is integrated with Social Security. As noted previously, this chapter will not address employer contributory or noncontributory 403(b) plans.

Assuming the 403(b) rules are followed, employer contributions and salary reduction contributions (employee elective deferrals or contributions) and all earnings on both of these types of contributions are not subject to federal income tax until the employee begins to receive distributions from the plan. However, salary reduction contributions are treated as wages and are therefore subject to FICA and FUTA, and some states impose a state income tax on salary reduction amounts. Earnings on employee after-tax contributions, if any, are not subject to federal income tax until the employee begins to receive distributions from the plan.

ANNUAL INDIVIDUAL LIMITS ON CONTRIBUTIONS

Over the past 42 years, Congress has placed three limits on the amount that may be contributed to a 403(b) plan. As noted previously, the first limit was imposed in the 1958 statute (the "maximum exclusion allowance" or MEA) under Section 403(b)(2). The second limit was imposed in 1974 when ERISA mandated that the limit on annual additions[3] to a defined contribution plan [Section 415 (c)(1)] applies to 403(b) plans as well. The third limit, which applies to elective deferrals or contributions only, was imposed by TRA '86 under Section 402(g). The MEA and 402(g) calculations must be completed on a tax-year (calendar year) basis for each individual for whom the employer is making contributions to a 403(b) plan. The 415 limit can be applied on a plan year basis, though as a practical matter, most employers choose to apply it on a calendar year basis, as well.

All amounts contributed to a 403(b) plan are considered to be made by the employer on behalf of the employee. There are two major types of contributions to a 403(b) plan: (1) elective, and (2) employer or nonelective contributions. Elective deferrals or contributions are those made as a result of a salary reduction agreement whereby the employee elects to

---

3 The term annual additions means: (1) employer contributions (including salary reduction amounts); (2) employee after-tax contributions; and (3) forfeitures

have compensation deferred or contributed on a pretax basis to the 403(b) plan that would otherwise have been paid to the employee as cash. Salary deduction contributions are employee voluntary contributions made on an after-tax basis, and some plans permit employees to make such contributions to their 403(b) plans as well.

In performing the calculations, it is important to determine if the contributions to the 403(b) plan are elective, after-tax, or nonelective.

SECTION 403(b)(2) CONTRIBUTION LIMIT—THE MAXIMUM EXCLUSION ALLOWANCE (MEA)

When completing the calculation for this limit, one must take into account the employee's *includible compensation*, *years of service*, and *excludable contributions*. These terms are defined as follows:

- *Includible Compensation.* Generally, this is the compensation earned, though not necessarily received, from the employer for the most recent period that is counted as one year of service. For purposes of the exclusion allowance calculation, the most recent one-year period of service is the year of service that ends not later than the close of the tax year for which the exclusion allowance is determined.[4]

  Under the Taxpayer Relief Act of 1997 (TRA '97), certain salary reduction contributions are included in the definition of includible compensation beginning January 1, 1998. They are: (1) elective deferrals to a 403(b) plan under a salary reduction agreement; (2) elective deferrals to a 401(k) plan; (3) elective deferrals or contributions to a Section 125 plan (cafeteria plan); and (4) deferrals made under a Section 457 plan. Nonsalary contributions (e.g., nonelective basic or matching contributions to a 403(b) or 401(k) plan) are not included in the definition of includible compensation. Elective deferrals to a Section 132(f) Transportation Spending Account are also included in the definition of includible compensation pursuant to a technical correction enacted into law in December of 2000.

- *Years of Service.* Generally, this is the number of years the employee has worked for the employer who remits the premium. A part-time employee receives pro rata credit based on the employer's full-time standard, as does a full-time employee who

---

4 Treas. Regs. Section 1.403(b)-1(f)(7).

works part of the year. However, in no event will the number of years of service be less than one.

- *Prior Excludable Amounts.* Generally, this consists of contributions to certain plans that were excluded from the employee's gross income in years prior to the year for which the maximum exclusion allowance is being calculated. Only contributions made in prior years by the employer sponsoring the 403(b) plan are included in the prior excludable amount. Applicable contributions are those made in prior years to: (1) any qualified pension or profit-sharing plan under Section 401(a) or Section 403(a), including a defined benefit plan, whether vested or nonvested; (2) a qualified bond purchase plan; (3) a 403(b) plan (including payments derived from a reduction in employee's salary if 100 percent nonforfeitable or vested when made); (4) contributions to a 403(b) plan made in prior years that were in excess of the 415 limits, even though these amounts were not excludable; and (5) employer contributions to a qualified state teacher's retirement plan.

Under Section 403(b)(2), the maximum exclusion allowance is determined using the following formula:

Step 1:   Multiply the employee's *includible compensation* for taxable year by 20 percent.

Step 2:   Multiply the result of Step 1 by the employee's number of *years of service* with the employer as of the last day of the taxable year.

Step 3:   Subtract the total *prior excludable amounts* from the result of Step 2.

SECTION 415(c)(1) CONTRIBUTION LIMIT—LIMIT ON ANNUAL ADDITIONS

The term *annual additions* means: (1) employer contributions (including salary reduction amounts); (2) employee after-tax contributions; and (3) forfeitures. When completing this calculation, one must take into account the employee's compensation. *Compensation* is defined as taxable compensation. However, under the TRA '97, beginning January 1, 1998, certain salary reduction contributions are included in the definition of compensation. They are: (1) elective deferrals to a 403(b) plan under a salary reduction agreement; (2) elective deferrals to a 401(k) plan; (3) elective deferrals or contributions to a Section 125 plan; and (4) deferrals made under a Section 457 plan. Elective deferrals to a Section 132(f) Transportation Spending Account are included in the definition of compensation pursuant to a technical correction enacted into law in December of 2000.

In the year 2001, the limit on *annual additions* to a 403(b) plan by an employer on behalf of an employee cannot exceed the *lesser of:*

- $35,000 (this amount will be indexed for changes in the consumer price index (CPI) rounded down to the lower multiple of $5,000 in future years); or
- 25 percent of the employee's *compensation.*

This limit applies to all contributions to all 403(b) plans, regardless of whether the contributions are fully vested (nonforfeitable).

When comparing the results of this calculation to the results of the maximum exclusion allowance calculation, the maximum excludable amount of contributions to a 403(b) plan is the lesser of the maximum exclusion allowance under Section 403(b)(2) or the limit under Section 415(c)(1).

Section 415(c)(4) provides special alternative limits that are available to employees of tax-exempt educational institutions, hospitals, home health service agencies, certain churches, and health and welfare organizations. See the section on Alternative Limits.

SECTION 402(g) CONTRIBUTION LIMIT–LIMIT ON SALARY REDUCTION CONTRIBUTIONS

This section of the Code imposes a limit on the amount that an employee can contribute on an elective (salary reduction) basis to the plans (e.g., 403(b) and 401(k)) offered by all of his or her employers in a calendar year. For calendar year 2001, the limit is $10,500. (The $10,500 is indexed to the cost of living in $500 increments with any changes effective January 1 of each calendar year.)

Section 402(g)(8) provides special alternative limits that are available to employees of tax-exempt educational institutions, hospitals, home health service agencies, certain churches, and health and welfare organizations who have completed at least 15 years of service with the current eligible employer purchasing the Section 403(b) annuity contract. (The years of service do not have to be consecutive, but they must all have been with the current employer.)

The maximum amount that an employee may tax-defer or contribute, is the lesser of the amount calculated under the three contribution limits—"maximum exclusion allowance" [Section 403(b)(2)], limit on annual additions [Section 415(c)(1)], and the limit on salary reduction contributions [Section 402(g)].

ALTERNATIVE LIMITS

As noted previously in this chapter, Section 415(c)(4) provides some contribution flexibility in the form of alternative limits. These limits are available to employees of:

- Educational institutions.
- Hospitals.
- Home health service agencies.
- Certain churches.
- Health and welfare organizations.

The alternative limits are not available to employees of associations, research foundations, museums, and libraries.

Each alternative limit is calculated differently and produces a distinct maximum deferral allowance amount. Once an employee elects a particular alternative limit, he or she can only elect that same limit or the general limit in subsequent years with the same employer. However, when an employee changes jobs, he or she can elect a different alternative limit with his or her new employer.

It is important to note that because the calculation results depend on changing variables, such as salary and years of service, there is no guarantee that an alternative limit that provides the maximum deferral this year, will continue to do so in future years.

ALTERNATIVE A–SECTION 415(c)(4)(A)–THE "YEAR FROM SEPARATION OF SERVICE LIMIT"

This limit is only available to an employee in the calendar year in which he or she terminates employment and can be used only once by an employee under that employer's plan. In other words, if the employee is rehired, the maximum amount that may be tax deferred is the amount allowable under the general limit. No other alternative limit may be elected while the employee remains with that particular employer.

This alternative limit may help an employee who is terminating employment or retiring who has made minimal prior deferrals during the course of his or her tenure with the employer. The purpose of this limit is to permit an employee to disregard the Section 415(c)(1) 25 percent limitation and contribute the "maximum exclusion allowance" under the Section 403(b)(2) limit. However, the $35,000 limit under Section 415 (c)(1) still applies. It is important to note that when completing this calculation, no more than 10 years of service may be taken into account.

ALTERNATIVE B–SECTION 415(c)(4)(B)–THE "ANY YEAR LIMIT"

This limit tends to be best for an employee with many years of service who has not taken full advantage of past deferral opportunities. For any taxable year (calendar year), an employee can elect to substitute the 25 percent of compensation limit under Section 415(c)(1) with the smallest of the following three limits:

1. The "maximum exclusion allowance" for the taxable year,
2. 25 percent of includible compensation (as defined earlier) for the taxable year plus $4,000, or
3. $15,000.

ALTERNATIVE C–SECTION 415(c)(4)(C)–THE "OVERALL LIMIT"

This limit tends to be best for a new employee who plans to take full advantage of deferral opportunities each year. It permits an employee to ignore the "maximum exclusion allowance" calculation under Section 403(b)(2) and contribute up to the Section 415(c) limit. That limit is the lesser of 25 percent of compensation (as defined earlier) or $35,000 (indexed). This limit applies to the employer's contributions to a defined contribution plan and/or defined benefit plan and the employee's contributions to the 403(b) plan.

SECTION 402(g)(8) CONTRIBUTION LIMIT–THE "15-YEAR RULE"

This contribution limit, which was made available under TRA '86, permits an employee who has completed at least 15 years of service with the current eligible employer to exceed the limit on contributions made under a salary reduction agreement. Eligible employers are:

- Educational institutions.
- Hospitals.
- Home health service agencies.
- Certain churches.
- Health and welfare organizations.

The alternative limits are not available to employees of associations, research foundations, museums, and libraries.

There is a $15,000 lifetime limit on the amount of additional contributions above the 403(b)(2) limit that may be contributed under the Section 402(g)(8) contribution limit. This one limit applies to service with all employers.

Section 402(g)(8) permits an employee to contribute the lesser of:

1. an additional $3,000 per taxable year above the 403(b) limit ($10,500 in calendar year 2001);
2. $15,000 reduced by prior contributions excluded under the 403(g)(8) election; or
3. $5,000 times the number of years of service with the present employer minus total elective deferrals made by the employer on the employee's behalf in previous years.

FUNDING VEHICLES

Generally, contributions to a 403(b) plan must be invested in individual or group annuity contracts issued by an insurance company. When ERISA was passed in 1974, it permitted contributions to a 403(b) plan to be invested in mutual funds held in a custodial account. These are known as 403(b)(7) accounts. Most 403(b) plans permit the employees to direct the investment of the amounts allocated to their accounts among the investment options offered by the plan.

Most 403(b) contracts, like the tax-sheltered annuity or tax-deferred annuity contracts used before 1958, are owned by the participant and fully portable. This type of flexibility is particularly important for faculty members who may work for several different institutions during their careers. The contracts are also fairly easy for the plan sponsor to administer, as the insurer is responsible for administering the contracts.

NONDISCRIMINATION

An employee elective deferral 403(b) plan satisfies the nondiscrimination rules if each employee is eligible to make salary reduction (pretax defer) contributions annually that are greater than $200. However, the plan is permitted to exclude certain employees, including: (a) students providing services as described in Section 3121(b)(10); (b) part-time employees who normally work less than 20 hours per week; c) nonresident aliens with no U.S. source income; (c) employees who are participants in a Section 457(b) deferred compensation plan; and (d) employees eligible to make salary reduction contributions to other employer plans maintained under Section 401(k) or 403(b).

It is important to note, however, that employees who work less than 20 hours per week and students who provide services described in Section 3121(b)(10) can be excluded for testing purposes only if the plan excludes all employees in that category.

The Average Deferral Percentage (ADP) test that applies to salary reduction (pretax deferrals) contributions under a Section 401(k) plan does not apply to elective deferral contributions under a 403(b) plan.[5]

APPLICATION OF ERISA

Any 403(b) plan, other than those maintained by a church or government entity, including public schools and colleges and universities, in which the employer's involvement goes beyond the narrow limitations found in the Department of Labor (DOL) regulations would be subject to ERISA. In that case, the plan would be subject to ERISA's participation, vesting, joint and survivor annuity, disclosure and reporting, and fiduciary requirements. In addition, many of the same rules applicable to qualified plans, such as maintaining a written plan document, issuing a Summary Plan Description (SPD), submitting a Form 5500 to the DOL–Pension Welfare Benefits Administration (PWBA), and issuing a Summary Annual Report (SAR) to plan participants, would apply.

403(b) plans are, under the applicable DOL regulation, exempt from ERISA where participation by the employees is completely voluntary; all rights under the annuity contract or custodial account are enforceable solely by the employee or beneficiary; and the employer has minimal involvement with the plan, such as making information available as to funding

---

5 However, if there are employer contributions, the actual contribution percentage (ACP) test is applicable to the employer contributions.

vehicles, withholding employee pretax elective (salary reduction) contributions, and forwarding those contributions to the 403(b) providers.

COMPARING 401(k) PLANS WITH 403(b) PLANS

Many individuals are more familiar with 401(k) plans than they are with 403(b) plans. The 403(b) plans are the counterpart of 401(k) plans for tax-exempt organizations, such as educational institutions. The two plans are alike in many ways as illustrated by Table 33–1.

T A B L E   33–1

Comparison of 401(k) and 403(b) Plans

Feature	401(k) Plan	403(b) Plan
1. Employer Contributions	Yes.	Yes.
2. Employee Salary Reduction	Yes.	Yes.
3. Employee Salary Deduction	Yes.	Yes.
4. Determination Letter	Not required, but strongly recommended.	Not applicable.
5. IRS Form 5500 Filing (private institutions only)	Yes; more complicated than 403(b).	Yes, easy to complete.
6. Employee Salary Reduction Contribution Limit	$10,500[1] or less. Governed by Sections 402(g) and 415.	Generally, $10,500[1] or less. Governed by Sections 402(g), 403(b), and 415. Some employees may be able to contribute more than $10,500 through the "15-Year Rule."
7. Total Contribution Limit (employer + employee)	Cannot exceed lesser of $35,000[1] or 25 percent of compensation. Governed by Section 415.	Cannot exceed lesser of $35,000[1] or 25 percent of compensation, or the "maximum exclusion allowance." Governed by Section 415 and 403(b)(2).
8. Minimum Distribution Requirements	Applicable to entire accumulation at age 70½ or retirement, if later.	Applicable to post-1986 accumulations at age 70½ or retirement, if later: on pre-1987 accumulation at age 75 or retirement, if later.
9. Salary Reduction Agreements	No limit on number of agreements each year.	No limit on number of agreements each year.
10. Average Deferral Percentage Test (nondiscrimination test applicable to employee elective deferrals)	Yes.	Not applicable.

1 Under the Internal Revenue Code, these amounts are indexed and are periodically increased to keep pace with cost-of-living adjustments.

Source: TIAA-CREF, 730 Third Avenue, New York, NY, 10017-3206.

Section 457 Deferred Compensation Plans

Daniel J. Ryterband

BACKGROUND

Deferred compensation plans allow employees to postpone receiving income for future service until some later date—most commonly at retirement. Deferred amounts and income earned generally are not taxed until either paid or "made available" to plan participants. Deferred amounts generally are considered made available when participants acquire an immediate, nonforfeitable right to them.

Deferred compensation plans can be structured as pure deferred compensation plans, supplemental benefit arrangements, or a combination of both. In pure deferred compensation plans, employees enter into an agreement with their employer to reduce present compensation or to forgo a raise or bonus in return for the employer's promise to pay benefits at a future date. In supplemental benefit plans, the employer pays an additional, supplemental benefit (sometimes based on a qualified retirement plan benefit formula), without reducing the employee's present compensation, raise, or bonus.

When properly structured, deferred compensation plans shield participants' deferred income from what are termed the tax "doctrines" of economic benefit and constructive receipt. The *doctrine of economic benefit* generally states that an economic benefit results when an economic or financial benefit, even though not in cash form, is provided to an employee as compensation, such as when an employee receives beneficial ownership of amounts placed with a third party, or when assets are unconditionally and irrevocably paid into a fund to be used for the employee's sole benefit. The *doctrine of constructive* receipt generally states that income, although not necessarily received in hand by an individual, is considered received and, therefore, currently taxable when it is credited to an account or set aside so it may be drawn upon at any time and amounts receivable are not subject to substantial limitations or restrictions.[1] Generally, events triggering economic benefit or constructive receipt result in deferred amounts becoming made available to plan participants, and thus, subject to current taxation. A mere unsecured promise to pay, however, does not constitute receipt of income.[2]

INTRODUCTION TO SECTION 457 PLANS

Section 457 plans are nonqualified deferred compensation plans available only to state and local government employers (including rural electrical cooperatives) and nongovernment organizations exempt from tax under Internal Revenue Code (IRC) Section 501. Examples of tax-exempt organizations under Section 501 include nongovernmental schools, private hospitals, labor unions, farmers' cooperatives, and certain trade associations, business leagues, private clubs, and fraternal orders. For the most part, they are nonprofit organizations serving their members or a public or charitable cause.

The Revenue Act of 1978 created IRC Section 457, allowing employees of state and local governments to defer up to $7,500 of compensation annually in plans meeting specified requirements. The Tax Reform Act of 1986 (TRA '86) extended Section 457's provisions to nonqualified deferred compensation plans of nongovernment tax-exempt employers. Section 457 limits deferral opportunities for employees of eligible employers.

Eligible employers generally use Section 457 plans in two ways:

1. As pure deferred compensation plans that allow participants to reduce their taxable salary in a manner similar to that of private-sector 401(k) plans. [401(k) plans generally are not available to state and local government organizations.]

2. As supplemental benefit plans that provide executives with supplemental retirement income.

---

1 Reg. Sec. 1.451-2(a).
2 Rev. Rul. 60-31, 1960-1 CB 174; Rev. Rul. 69-650, 1969-2 CB 106.

Plans meeting the complex requirements of Section 457 as well as related laws and regulations receive favorable tax treatment (deferral of income tax), but deferred income is subject to Social Security and federal unemployment withholding at the time of deferral.[3] Section 457 classifies plans as either "eligible" or "ineligible," each subject to the following specific requirements.

ELIGIBLE PLAN REQUIREMENTS

In eligible plans, deferred income and its earnings are tax free until paid or made available to participants or beneficiaries.[4]

Eligibility for Plan Participation

Plan participation must be limited to employees and independent contractors performing service for the employer.[5] Before deferring compensation in any given month, participants must have previously entered into an agreement authorizing the deferrals.[6] Therefore, an active worker must wait until the beginning of the month after entering into an agreement before deferring any income. New employees can make deferrals in their first month of employment if they enter into an agreement on or before their first day of employment.[7] It is not necessary to execute a new agreement for each month.

Maximum Annual Deferral

The plan ceiling, or maximum annual deferral, is $7,500 or 33⅓ percent of includible compensation (generally the equivalent of 25 percent of gross compensation), whichever is less.[8] The $7,500 limit is adjusted annually, in amounts rounded down to the nearest $500, with an annual limit for 2001 of $8,500. Includible compensation is payment for service performed for the employer includible in current gross income and excludes amounts deferred.[9] Gross compensation generally equals gross income plus amounts deferred. For example, a participant with total compensation of

---

3 IRC Sec. 3121(a)(5)(E), 3121(v)(3), 3306(b)(5)(E).
4 IRC Sec. 457(a).
5 IRC Sec. 457(b)(1), Reg. Sec. 1.457-2(d).
6 IRC Sec. 457(b)(4).
7 Reg. Sec. 1.457-2(g).
8 IRC Sec. 457(b)(2).
9 IRC Sec. 457(e)(5).

$20,000 generally can defer a maximum of $5,000, which is the equivalent of 33⅓ percent of includible compensation or 25 percent of gross compensation. Deferred amounts exceeding this limit generally are treated as made available and subject to normal taxation in the taxable year deferred.

For purposes of the plan ceiling, deferred income must be taken into account at its current value (in the plan year deferred, rather than the year received).[10]

Catch-Up Provision

During any or all of the three taxable years ending before the year the participant reaches normal retirement age, participants may defer more than $7,500 or 33⅓ percent of includible compensation. This "catch-up" provision increases the annual deferral ceiling to $15,000 or, if less, the participant's normal ceiling plus aggregate unused annual ceiling amounts for deferrals in prior years.[11] For example, a 62-year-old participant, with gross compensation of $20,000 in an eligible plan with a normal retirement age of 65, who has underutilized deferrals in prior years by $10,000 could elect to defer a maximum of $15,000 in the present year. This amount is computed by adding the available catch-up limit of $10,000 to the normal limit of $5,000 (computed as 25 percent of $20,000).

Participants may not use the catch-up provision after the expiration of the three-year period even if it was not fully used in the three years preceding normal retirement age and whether or not the participant or former participant rejoins the plan or participates in another eligible plan after retirement.[12] Normal retirement age may be specified in the plan and defined as a single age or range of ages ending no later than 70½. In plans that do not specify normal retirement age, it is generally age 65 or the latest normal retirement age specified in the employer's pension plan, if later.[13]

Coordination with Other Plans

Maximum deferrals in 457 plans must be coordinated with amounts excluded from income under 401(k) plans, simplified employee pensions (SEPs), 403(b) plans, and amounts deductible under IRC Section 501(c)(18).[14] Amounts contributed to such plans reduce the amount par-

---

10 IRC Sec. 457(e)(6), Reg. Sec. 1.457-2(e)(3).
11 IRC Sec. 457(b)(3).
12 Reg. Sec. 1.457-2(f)(3).
13 Reg. Sec. 1.457-2(f)(4).
14 IRC Sec. 457(c)(2).

ticipants can defer in an eligible 457 plan on a dollar-for-dollar basis. For example, if someone participates in both a 403(b) plan and a 457 plan and defers $4,000 to the 403(b), the 457 plan limit would be reduced to $4,500 in 2001. Aggregate amounts in excess of eligible 457 plan limits generally are considered made available and taxable to the participant in the year deferred.[15]

Funding Requirements

In plans maintained by tax-exempt organizations, deferred amounts and earnings must remain the sole property of the employer until made available to participants, subject only to the claims of the employer's general creditors.[16] However, plans maintained by government organizations are required to hold all plan assets in a trust, custodial account, or annuity contract for the exclusive benefit of participants and their beneficiaries.[17] The terms of the trust must make it impossible for plan assets or income to be diverted to any purpose other than participant benefits until all liabilities of the plan have been satisfied. The trust requirement is designed to prevent loss of participant retirement benefits to the claims of the government's general creditors. Before the trust requirement was instituted as part of the Small Business Job Protection Act of 1996, participant benefits were held as employer assets and subject to the general claims of the plan sponsor's creditors.

Investment Options Available to Participants

In government plans, which are required to irrevocably set aside assets to pay participant benefits through a formal trust, custodial contract, or annuity contract, participants are generally permitted to choose among various investment alternatives offered under the plan. In plans maintained by tax-exempt organizations, in which deferred amounts and earnings must remain the property of the employer until distributed to the participant, only "informal" funding is permitted. In these plans, employers can earmark assets and allow the participants to direct investment, but they cannot be given a secured interest in the purchased assets. As a result, participants in plans sponsored by tax-exempt organizations can exercise some ownership rights, but remain at risk that the employer may be unable to pay promised benefits.

---

15 Reg. Sec. 1.457-1(b)(2), Example 6.
16 IRC Sec. 457(b)(6).
17 IRC Sec. 457(g).

Most employers that offer 457 plans offer participants a variety of investment choices, including equity, bond, and money market funds; guaranteed interest contracts; bank deposit accounts; and fixed- and variable-annuity contracts.

Insurance companies are the predominant investment manager. Other managers include mutual funds, brokerage firms, banks, and investment advisers. In-house investment management is uncommon. Investment managers frequently are responsible for plan implementation, administration and record keeping, and participant enrollment as well, but these functions can be contracted to service providers or performed in-house.

Availability of Loan Provisions

Participant loans are not permitted in 457 plans maintained by tax-exempt employers. This is because participants have no secured, nonforfeitable benefit from which to secure the loan and because assets must remain subject to the employer's general creditors until made available. However, in plans maintained by government employers, participant loans may be permitted under the general terms that apply to qualified retirement plans (e.g., 401(k) plans).

Availability of Benefits

Plan benefits generally cannot be made available (other than through a loan feature in a plan maintained by a government employer) until the participant separates from service or is faced with an "unforeseeable emergency," or until the calendar year when the participant attains age 70½, if later.[18] Separation from service generally occurs at the employee's termination, disability, death, or retirement.[19] Independent contractors are considered separated from service when their contracts expire, assuming the expiration constitutes a good-faith and complete termination of the contractual relationship. If the employer expects to renew the contract or hire the independent contractor as an employee, separation from service generally has not occurred.[20] An unforeseeable emergency is a severe financial hardship resulting from a sudden and unexpected illness, loss of property because of casualty, or other similar extraordinary and unforeseeable circumstance outside participant control. Sending a child to

18 IRC Sec. 457(d)(1).
19 Reg. Sec. 1.457-2(h)(2).
20 Reg. Sec. 1.457-2(h)(3).

college or purchasing a new home are not considered unforeseeable emergencies.[21] In addition, participants may not withdraw money if insurance, liquidation of the participant's assets, or discontinuing plan deferrals will relieve the hardship. Emergency withdrawals are permitted only in amounts necessary to satisfy the emergency need.[22]

An exception to the above rules is available for participants with amount balances up to $5,000 (indexed annually for inflation) if no amount has been distributed to the participant during the two-year period that precedes the distribution and there has been no prior plan distribution to the participant.[23]

Plan Distributions

Distributions from eligible plans must begin within 60 days after the later of the close of the plan year in which a participant attains or would have attained the plan's normal retirement age; or the day the participant separates from service.[24] Eligible 457 plans are subject to distribution beginning date requirements similar to those of qualified plans. As such, plan distributions must begin no later than April 1 of the calendar year following the calendar year in which an employee either retires or attains age 70½, whichever is later.[25]

Distributions beginning before a participant's death generally must satisfy the qualified plan incidental death benefit rules. The plan must pay beneficiaries amounts not distributed during the participant's lifetime using a method at least as rapid as the method used before death.[26] When distributions begin after a participant's death, the beneficiary must receive the entire amount within 15 years or, in the case of a spouse, within the beneficiary's life expectancy.[27]

Distributions paid over a period of one year or more must be made in substantially nonincreasing amounts.[28] Eligible 457 plan distributions (and amounts considered made available) are subject to regular income tax withholding as wages, and payments are reported on Form W-2.[29]

---

21 Reg. Sec. 1.457-2(h)(4).
22 Reg. Sec. 1.457-2(h)(5).
23 IRC Sec. 457(e)(9).
24 Reg. Sec. 1.457-2(i)(1).
25 IRC Sec. 457(d)(2) and 401(a)(9)
26 IRC Sec. 457(d)(2)(B)(i).
27 IRC Sec. 457(d)(2)(B)(ii).
28 IRC Sec. 457(d)(2)(C).
29 Rev. Rul. 82-46, 1982-1 CB 158.

However, amounts made available are not taxed if the participant or beneficiary irrevocably elects before distribution to defer payment until a later date.[30] For example, if someone separates from service at age 60 and elects to defer payment until age 65, the amount is not treated as made available (even though the person had the right to receive it) and remains tax deferred until received.

Former participants may have any amount made payable to them transferred to another eligible plan without having amounts treated as made available.[31] However, a 457 plan distribution cannot be rolled over into an individual retirement account.[32] Distributions from 457 plans are exempt from the 10 percent penalty tax on withdrawals made before age 59½.[33]

IRS Approval

Unlike qualified plans, eligible 457 plans need not apply to the IRS for approval but can and often apply for private letter rulings indicating the plan meets the requirements of Section 457. Plans not administered according to the law can lose the tax benefit of deferral. State and local government plans that do not comply with the statutory requirements of eligible 457 plans must be amended as of the first plan year beginning more than 180 days after IRS notification of any inconsistencies. A plan not amended within this grace period will be treated as an ineligible plan and becomes subject to the rules of Section 457(f). There is no grace period for plans of nongovernmental tax-exempt employers that must maintain compliance at all times to maintain favorable tax treatment.[34]

INELIGIBLE PLAN REQUIREMENTS

Ineligible 457 plans are governed by separate rules under Section 457(f). To receive tax-preferred treatment in an ineligible plan, amounts deferred must be subject to a substantial risk of forfeiture. Unlike eligible plans, ineligible plans place no limits on the amount of deferrals made. Employers, therefore, can use ineligible plans to allow employees a contribution level above the eligible plan limit or to provide supplemental retirement benefits to selected executives. However, ineligible plans are

30 Reg. Sec. 1.457-1(b).
31 IRC Sec. 457(e)(10).
32 Rev. Rul. 86-103, 1986-2 CB 62.
33 IRC Sec. 72(t).
34 IRC Sec. 457(b) last paragraph, Reg. Sec. 1.457-2(1).

better suited for employer contributions than for salary reduction due to the substantial risk of forfeiture provision. If an employer maintains both an eligible and an ineligible plan, it is preferable that they be maintained and administered separately for cost and compliance reasons.

Ineligible 457 plan deferred amounts are included in participant or beneficiary gross income in the first taxable year where there is no substantial risk of forfeiture, even if amounts are not received.[35] For a substantial risk of forfeiture to exist, a person's right to receive deferred amounts must be conditioned on future performance of substantial services.[36] Whether the risk of forfeiture is substantial depends on the facts and circumstances of each situation. For example, a substantial risk of forfeiture likely exists when rights to deferred payment are lost at termination of employment for any reason, but a requirement that rights are lost only at termination for cause or committing a crime generally would not create a substantial risk.

Taxation of distributions or amounts made available in ineligible plans is determined under IRC Section 72 annuity rules.[37]

NONDISCRIMINATION ISSUES

Unlike qualified retirement plans (e.g., 401(k) plans), Section 457 plans are not subject to complex IRS rules that require benefits to be nondiscriminatory. As a result, 457 plans can be offered on a discriminatory basis with participation limited to only a few employees or even to a single employee.

The requirement that 457 plans maintained by tax-exempt employers be unfunded, however, limits availability to certain employee groups in such plans. This is because Title I of the Employee Retirement Income Security Act (ERISA) requires plans be funded, which conflicts with the Section 457 requirement that plans be unfunded. Tax-exempt employers' plans generally are subject to Title I requirements and, therefore, must fall within one of the special Title I exceptions to meet both ERISA and IRC requirements. This conflict generally requires nongovernment tax-exempt employer 457 plans to restrict participation to a select group of management or highly compensated employees ("top-hat" plans) to avoid ERISA's funding requirements.[38] Prior to the Small Business Job Protection Act of

---

35 IRC Sec. 457(f)(1)(A).
36 IRC Sec. 457(f)(3)(B).
37 IRC Sec. 72 and 457(f)(1)(B), Reg. Sec. 1.457-3(a)(3).
38 IRS Notice 87-13, 1987-1 CB 432.

1996, tax exempt employers were prohibited from offering 401(k) plans to their employees, which left these organizations with no effective salary deferral arrangement for the bulk of their workforces. Fortunately, these employers can now use 401(k) plans as their primary plan for all employees, and rely on ineligible 457 plans to provide "restoration" plan benefits (i.e., contributions above IRS limits in qualified 401(k) plans) for their highly paid employees.

457 PLAN REPORTING AND DISCLOSURE

State and local government employer 457 plans are exempt from ERISA's reporting and disclosure requirements.[39] These employers do not have to comply with requirements for summary plan descriptions; summary annual reports and summary descriptions of material plan modifications; annual registration statements; and plan descriptions, annual reports, and other materials frequently requested by participants. Certain returns and reports (such as Form W-2 and 1099-MISC), however, must be filed with the IRS, and participants and beneficiaries must receive information about their benefits when they terminate employment or receive benefit distributions.

Nongovernmental tax-exempt employer plans must meet ERISA's requirements for reporting and disclosure.[40] However, tax-exempt employer plans maintained for a select group of management or highly compensated employees can satisfy ERISA's reporting and disclosure requirements through an alternative compliance method under Department of Labor regulations. Under this method, a statement must be filed with the Secretary of Labor declaring the plan is maintained primarily to provide deferred compensation for a select group of management or highly compensated employees. Plan documents must be provided upon request by the Department of Labor.[41]

DEFERRED ARRANGEMENTS NOT CONSIDERED DEFERRED COMPENSATION PLANS

A 1987 IRS Notice interpreted Section 457 requirements as applying to all deferred arrangements. This was interpreted as meaning benefits such

---

39   ERISA Sec. 4(b)(1).
40   ERISA Sec. 4(a), 201, 301, and 401.
41   Labor Reg. Sec. 2520.104-23.

as accrued sick time and vacation not used in the present year (as well as elective deferrals of compensation) would be subject to Section 457 restrictions.[42] The dollar value of these benefits that employees received then would directly reduce their allowable compensation deferral amount in eligible plans. Under this interpretation, state and local government and tax-exempt employers were severely restricted in providing deferred compensation and supplemental retirement benefits. Section 457 was later amended so that the following plans generally are excluded from Section 457 restrictions and are not considered as providing compensation deferral:[43]

1. Vacation and sick leave.
2. Compensatory time.
3. Severance pay.
4. Disability pay and death benefits.

To be exempt from Section 457, an arrangement must be legitimate and not an indirect method of deferring cash amounts.

DEFERRED COMPENSATION PLANS NOT SUBJECT TO SECTION 457

Certain deferred compensation plans of state and local government and tax-exempt employers generally are not subject to Section 457 restrictions if certain conditions are met.

Nonelective Deferred Compensation of Nonemployees

Plans providing nonelective deferred compensation for services not performed as an employee (e.g., independent contractors) are exempt from Section 457 restrictions for tax years beginning after December 31, 1987. To be considered nonelective, a plan must be uniform for all participants, offer no variations or options, and cover all persons with the same relationship to the employer.[44] For example, if a hospital gives a nonemployee doctor deferred compensation, the deferred compensation is considered nonelective only if all other nonemployee doctors are covered by the same plan.

---

42 IRS Notice 87-13, 1987-1 CB 432.
43 IRC Sec. 457(e)(11).
44 IRC Sec. 457(e)(12).

Church and Judicial Deferred Compensation Plans

Deferred compensation plans of churches and church-controlled organizations for their employees generally are exempt from Section 457 requirements for tax years beginning after December 31, 1987.[45]

State judges' government deferred compensation plans use the tax rules for funded and unfunded nonqualified deferred compensation plans, rather than Section 457 rules, if certain requirements are met. In addition, participants are not subject to the substantial risk of forfeiture rule for ineligible plans.[46] Qualified state judicial plans must have existed continuously since December 31, 1978, and must require:

1. All eligible judges to participate and contribute the same fixed percentage of compensation.
2. The plan to provide no judge with an option that would affect the amount of includable compensation.
3. Retirement benefits to be a percentage of the compensation of judges holding similar positions in the state.
4. Benefits paid in any year not to exceed either 100 percent of a participant's average compensation for the highest three years, or if less, $90,000 adjusted for inflation ($120,000 in 1996).[47]

Nonqualified state judicial plans that do not meet these requirements are taxed as ordinary Section 457 deferred compensation plans.

Nongovernment Tax-Exempt Employer Deferred Compensation Plans

Grandfather provisions may apply to nongovernment tax-exempt employer plans in certain cases. Amounts deferred in tax-exempt employers' plans in taxable years beginning before January 1, 1987, generally are exempt from Section 457 restrictions. Amounts deferred after December 31, 1986, are exempt from Section 457 restrictions if deferrals are based on an agreement that on August 16, 1986, was in writing and stipulated deferrals of a fixed amount (or a fixed percentage of a fixed base amount) or an amount determined by a fixed formula. For example, participants who were deferring 5 percent of compensation according to a written plan

---

45 IRC Sec. 457(e)(13), 3121(w)(3)(A), 3121(w)(3)(B).
46 Sec. 1107(c)(4) of P.L. 99-514 (TRA '86).
47 Sec. 252 of P.L. 97-248 (TEFRA).

on August 16, 1986, must make all subsequent deferrals at 5 percent for the amount to be considered fixed. An example of a fixed formula is a deferred compensation plan designed as a defined benefit plan in which deferrals to be paid in the future are in the form of an annual benefit equal to 1 percent per year of service times final average salary. Changes in the fixed amount or fixed formula result in loss of grandfathered status.[48]

Nonelective Government Employer Deferred Compensation Plans

A grandfather provision also is available to amounts deferred before July 14, 1988 in nonelective government plans by participants covered by a written agreement. To avoid Section 457 restrictions, the agreement must stipulate determining annual deferrals as a fixed amount or by a fixed formula. Amounts deferred on or after July 14, 1988 are exempt from Section 457 restrictions until the tax year ending after the effective date of an agreement modifying the fixed amount or fixed formula.[49]

Collectively Bargained Deferred Compensation Plans

Collectively bargained plans of both state and local government and nongovernment tax-exempt employers allowing nonelective income deferral may be excluded from Section 457 restrictions if certain conditions are met. To be grandfathered, a plan must cover a broad group of employees; have a definite, fixed, and uniform benefit structure; and have been in existence on December 31, 1987. A plan loses grandfathered status upon the first material plan modification after December 31, 1987. Modifications to nonelective plans are considered material only if they change the benefit formula or expand the class of participants. This grandfather rule generally applies only to union employees participating in a nonqualified, nonelective plan under a collective bargaining agreement. The rule also is available to nonunion employees if, as of December 31, 1987, participation was extended to a broad group of nonunion employees on the same terms as the union employees and union employees account for at least 25 percent of total participation.[50]

---

48 IRS Notice 87-13, 1987-1 CB 432.
49 Sec. 6064(d)(3) of P.L. 100-647 (TAMRA).
50 IRS Notice 88-98, 1988-2 CB 421.

TAXATION OF NONELECTIVE DEFERRED COMPENSATION SUBJECT TO SECTION 457

The above discussion on deferred compensation plans not subject to Section 457 indicates that, under certain circumstances, nonelective deferred compensation is exempt from Section 457 rules and current taxation. However, many employees of state and local government and nongovernment tax-exempt employers are taxed on nonelective deferred compensation before they are entitled to receive it. For example:

> A nonprofit organization hires an employee under a five-year employment agreement to pay $50,000 annually. Assuming the employee works the entire five-year period, an additional $10,000 will be paid annually in years six through 10. Under Section 457 rules, the employee would be taxed in year six on the entire present value of all five $10,000 payments. If we assume the discounted present value of the $10,000 payments equals approximately $41,000[51] and the entire amount is subject to 28 percent tax, $11,480 would be paid in tax in year six even though only $10,000 is actually received.

This results in current taxation on amounts the taxpayer:

1. Has not yet received.
2. Has no current right to receive.
3. May not actually ever receive.

Because similar rules do not apply to private-sector employers, this practice places state and local government and nongovernmental tax-exempt employers at a disadvantage in recruiting employees. Current Congressional efforts aim to correct this inequity by uniformly providing that nonelective deferred compensation is not taxable until actually received.

CONCLUSION

Most 457 plans are maintained by state and local government employers for the purpose of salary reduction. Without these plans, governmental employers would be precluded from offering salary deferral opportunities that are common among for-profit employers. Section 457 plans used for purposes other than salary reduction are less common but are rapidly gaining in importance. Nongovernmental tax-exempt employers can use in-

---

51 Calculated using a 7 percent discount rate, the present value of $10,000 received annually over five years equals $41,001.97.

eligible 457 plans to provide supplemental retirement benefits and salary continuation to certain high-paid executives. These plans function to:

1. Provide benefits over IRC Section 415 limits on contributions to, or benefits from, qualified plans.
2. Offset the effect of the $170,000 maximum compensation cap of IRC Section 401(a)(17) when determining benefits or contributions to qualified plans.
3. Give valued employees additional death and disability benefits.
4. Impose "golden handcuffs" on valued employees or enhance early retirement benefits.
5. Increase benefits for executives recruited in mid-career who are unable to accrue maximum pension benefits in a qualified plan by normal retirement age.
6. Reward key employees for their contributions to the organization.

Keen competition for talented employees forces employers to design plans attractive to an increasingly mobile workforce. For state and local government and nongovernmental tax-exempt employers, 457 plans play an important part in meeting overall employee benefit plan objectives. A successful program, however, requires compliance with the complex requirements governing design, operation, and administration of Section 457 plans.

Investment of Defined Contribution Plan Assets*

Jack VanDerhei

Sarah Holden

Carol Quick

OVERVIEW

In a traditional defined benefit plan, retirement income is typically a function of the participant's compensation level and/or years of participation with the plan sponsor. The employer agrees to provide the employee with a defined nominal benefit at retirement and the responsibility to fund that benefit falls on the employer. In a defined contribution plan, the benefit received at retirement depends on the participation experience of the employee in the plan and, in addition, on the investment experience of the participant's account. Because a defined contribution plan shifts the investment risks (and rewards) to the participants, plan sponsors often allow the participants to choose the asset allocation of at least a portion of their account balances. This is particularly true of 401(k) plans that typically will be funded in part by salary deferrals. This chapter focuses on the types of investment decisions made with respect to 401(k) plans.

It is important to note that there are several types of defined contribution plans (VanDerhei and McDonnell, 2000):

---

* This chapter was adapted from Jack VanDerhei, Sarah Holden and Carol Quick, "401(k) Plan Asset Allocation, Account Balances, and Loan Activity in 1998," published in *ICI Perspective,* Vol. 6, No. 1, January 2000, and *EBRI Issue Brief,* No. 218, February 2000. Copyright by the Employee Benefit Research Institute and the Investment Company Institute, all rights reserved.

- Savings and thrift plans. Under these retirement plans, employees may contribute a predetermined portion of earnings to an individual account, all or part of which the employer matches. Employers may match a fixed percentage of employee contributions or a percentage that varies by length of service, the amount of employee contribution, or other factors. Contributions are invested as directed by the employee or employer. Although usually designed as a long-term savings vehicle, savings and thrift plans may allow preretirement withdrawals and loans.
- Deferred profit-sharing plans. This is a retirement plan under which a company credits a portion of company profits to employees' accounts. Plans may set a fixed formula for sharing profits, but this is not a requirement. Most plans hold money in employee accounts until retirement, disability, or death.
- Money purchase pension plans. Under these retirement plans, fixed employer contributions (usually calculated as a percentage of employee earnings) are allocated to individual employee accounts. Some of these plans may allow employee contributions, but employees are usually not required to make any contributions.
- Employee stock ownership plan (ESOP). Under ESOP retirement plans, the employer pays a designated amount, often borrowed, into a fund which then invests primarily in company stock. Any debt incurred in the purchase of the stock is repaid by the company. The stocks are then distributed to employees according to an allocation formula.

Over the past two decades, there has been a shift in the composition of pension coverage in the United States toward defined contribution pension plans. Within defined contribution plans, plans with a 401(k) feature have risen in importance and at year-end 1999 assets in 401(k) retirement plans stood at an estimated $1.7 trillion (see Figure 35–1), or close to two-thirds of total defined contribution plan assets.

As 401(k) retirement plans have grown to be a significant part of the private pension landscape in the United States, interest in examining the behavior of 401(k) plan participants also has grown. To enhance the understanding of 401(k) plan participants' investment decisions, account balances, and loan activity, the Employee Benefit Research Institute (EBRI)[1]

---

1 The Employee Benefit Research Institute (EBRI) is a nonprofit, nonpartisan, public policy research organization that does not lobby or take positions on legislative proposals.

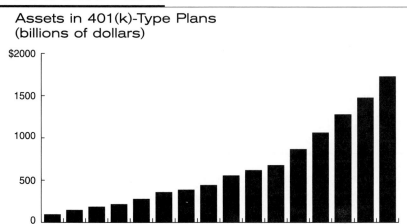

F I G U R E   35–1

Assets in 401(k)-Type Plans
(billions of dollars)

Sources: Investment Company Institute and U.S. Department of Labor.

and the Investment Company Institute (ICI)[2] have collaborated during the past three years in the collection of data on participants in 401(k) plans. In this collaborative effort, known as the EBRI/ICI Participant Directed Retirement Plan Data Collection Project, EBRI and ICI have collected data from some of their members who serve as plan record keepers and administrators. The data include demographic information, annual contributions, plan balances, asset allocation, and loan balances.

The January 1999 issues of the *EBRI Issue Brief* and *ICI Perspective* reported findings on 401(k) plan asset allocation, account balances, and loan activity for year-end 1996, using data from the EBRI/ICI Participant-Directed Retirement Plan Data Collection Project.[3] The project has now collected data for year-end 1997 and year-end 1998. The purpose of this chapter is to report findings from the year-end 1998 data.[4]

---

2 The Investment Company Institute (ICI) is the national association of the American investment company industry. Its membership includes 7,932 open-end investment companies ("mutual funds"), 495 closed-end investment companies, and eight sponsors of unit investment trusts. Its mutual fund members have assets of about $6.2 trillion, accounting for approximately 95 percent of total industry assets, and have more than 78.7 million individual shareholders.

3 Jack VanDerhei, Russell Galer, Carol Quick, and John Rea, "401(k) Plan Asset Allocation, Account Balances, and Loan Activity," *EBRI Issue Brief,* No. 205 and *ICI Perspective*, Vol. 5, No. 1 January 1999. The article is available through EBRI's Web site at www.ebri.org and ICI's Web site at www.ici.org/economy/perspective.html.

4 Summary figures for year-end 1997 are available at ICI's Web site at www.ici.org/pdf/per06-01_appendix.pdf. A hard copy may be requested by calling ICI's research department at 202-326-5913. The 1997 EBRI/ICI database contains 29,899 401(k) plans with $290 billion of assets and 7,056,418 active participants.

At year-end 1998, the EBRI/ICI Participant Directed Retirement Plan Data Collection Project database contained 7.9 million active 401(k) plan participants in 30,102 plans with $372 billion of assets. The 1998 EBRI/ICI database accounts for 11 percent of all 401(k) plans, 22 percent of all 401(k) participants, and about 27 percent of the assets held in 401(k) plans.

THE EBRI/ICI DATABASE

Source and Type of Data

Plan administrators that are either EBRI or ICI members provided records on active participants in 401(k) plans administered by these organizations in 1996, 1997, and 1998. These administrators include mutual fund companies, insurance companies, consulting firms, and investment management companies. The universe of plan administrators varies from year to year, and thus these aggregate figures should not be used to estimate time trends. However, future research will focus in more detail on participants and plans common to all three years to study their evolution over time. Records were encrypted to conceal the identity of employers and employees but were coded so that both could be tracked over multiple years.

Data provided for each participant include participant date of birth, from which an age cohort is assigned; participant date of hire, from which a tenure range is assigned; outstanding loan balance; funds in participants' investment portfolios; and asset values attributed to those funds. An account balance for each participant is the sum of the participant's assets in all funds.[5] Plan balances are constructed as the sum of participant balances. Plan size is estimated as the sum of active participants in the plan, and, as such, does not necessarily represent the total number of employees at the sponsoring firm.

Investment options are grouped into nine categories. *Equity funds* consist of pooled investments primarily investing in stocks. These funds include equity mutual funds, bank collective trusts, life insurance separate accounts, and other pooled investments. Similarly, *bond funds* are any pooled accounts primarily invested in bonds, and *balanced funds* are pooled accounts invested in both stocks and bonds. *Company stock* is

---

5 Account balances are net of unpaid loan balances. Thus, unpaid loan balances are not included in any of the nine asset categories.

equity in the plan's sponsor (the employer). *Money funds* consist of those funds designed to maintain a stable share price. *Guaranteed investment contracts* (GICs) are insurance company products that guarantee a specific rate of return on the invested capital over the life of the contract. *Other stable value funds* include synthetic GICs[6] or similar instruments. The *"other fund"* category is the residual for other investments such as real estate funds. The final category, *"unknown,"* consists of funds that could not be identified.

Distribution of Plans, Participants, and Assets by Plan Size

The 1998 database contains 30,102 401(k) plans with $372 billion of assets and 7,910,030 participants (see Figure 35–2).[7] The average account balance (net of plan loans) for all participants in the EBRI/ICI database was $47,004 at year-end 1998. Most of the plans in the database are small, whether measured by the number of plan participants or by total plan assets. Indeed, almost 50 percent of the plans have 25 or fewer participants, and another 30 percent fall within the range of 26 to 100 participants (see Figure 35–2). In contrast, only 4 percent of the plans have more than 1,000 participants. Similarly, about 40 percent of the plans have assets of $250,000 or less, and another 30 percent have plan assets between $250,001 and $1,250,000 (see Figure 35–3). However, participants and assets are concentrated in large plans. For example, 73 percent of participants are in plans with more than 1,000 participants, and these same plans account for 82 percent of all plan assets (see Figure 35–2).

Relationship of Database Plans to the Universe of Plans

The 1998 EBRI/ICI database appears to be a representative sample of the estimated universe of 401(k) plans. Cerulli Associates (1999) estimates that there were 273,485 401(k) plans at the end of 1998, with about 37

---

6 A synthetic GIC consists of a portfolio of fixed-income securities "wrapped" with a guarantee (typically by an insurance company or a bank) to provide benefit payments according to the plan at book value.

7 Some administrators supplying data were unable to provide complete asset allocation detail on certain pooled asset classes for one or more of their clients. Only plans in which at least 90 percent of all plan assets could be identified were included in the final EBRI/ICI database.

FIGURE   35–2

EBRI/ICI Database: 401(k) Plan Characteristics by
Number of Plan Participants, 1998

Number of Plan Participants	Total Plans	Total Participants	Total Assets	Average Account Balance
1 – 10	6,344	42,670	$ 990,267,821	$23,208
11 – 25	8,260	139,233	2,847,264,244	20,450
26 – 50	5,243	188,250	4,406,105,858	23,406
51 – 100	3,772	268,474	7,282,494,601	27,126
101 – 250	3,074	481,007	13,856,068,577	28,806
251 – 500	1,356	474,999	15,121,584,036	31,835
501 – 1,000	821	580,458	20,726,730,416	35,708
1,001 – 2,500	682	1,062,235	43,261,242,177	40,727
2,501 – 5,000	276	970,332	42,518,558,692	43,819
5,001 – 10,000	155	1,069,482	47,945,432,588	44,831
> 10,000	119	2,632,890	172,844,680,237	65,648
All	30,102	7,910,030	371,800,429,248	47,004

Source: Tabulations from EBRI/ICI Participant Directed Retirement Plan Data Collection Project.

FIGURE   35–3

EBRI/ICI Database: 401(k) Plan Characteristics by
Plan Assets, 1998

Total Plan Assets	Total Plans	Total Participants	Total Assets	Average Account Balance
$0 - $250,000	12,016	191,603	$1,232,688,023	$ 6,434
>$250,000 – $625,000	5,409	182,412	2,190,383,704	12,008
>$625,000 – $1,250,000	3,682	198,828	3,260,917,926	16,401
>$1,250,000 – $2,500,000	2,790	254,042	4,883,644,111	19,224
>$2,500,000 – $6,250,000	2,560	442,385	10,042,189,520	22,700
>$6,250,000 – $12,500,000	1,274	435,739	11,207,589,519	25,721
>$12,500,000 – $25,000,000	847	529,531	14,705,824,867	27,771
>$25,000,000 – $62,500,000	735	905,758	29,236,893,865	32,279
>$62,500,000 – $125,000,000	339	804,765	30,433,154,974	37,816
>$125,000,000 – $250,000,000	216	869,237	36,847,790,558	42,391
> $250,000,000	234	3,095,730	227,759,352,181	73,572
All	30,102	7,910,030	371,800,429,248	47,004

Source: Tabulations from EBRI/ICI Participant Directed Retirement Plan Data Collection Project.

million participants and $1.397 trillion in assets.[8] The 1998 EBRI/ICI database accounts for 11 percent of all 401(k) plans, 22 percent of all 401(k) participants, and about 27 percent of the assets held in 401(k) plans. The distribution of assets, participants, and plans in the EBRI/ICI database for 1998 is similar to that reported for the universe of plans estimated by Cerulli Associates. The shares of the assets and participants in the EBRI/ICI database falling within each of the five plan size classifications are close to those found in the 401(k) universe (see Figure 35–4). In addition, the distribution in the number of plans is virtually identical between the EBRI/ICI database and the universe estimate.[9]

F I G U R E   35–4

401(k) Plan Characteristics by Number of Participants: EBRI/ICI Database vs. Cerulli Estimates for All 401(k) Plans, 1998 (percent)

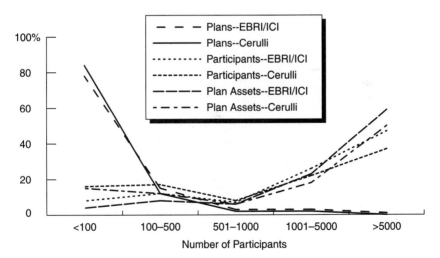

Sources: Tabulations from EBRI/ICI Participant Directed Retirement Plan Data Collection Project. Cerulli Associates estimates for all 401(k) plans.

8 The latest U.S. Department of Labor (1999/2000) estimates of the universe of 401(k)-type plans for plan-year 1996 tallied 230,808 plans covering 31 million active participants, with $1.062 trillion in assets.

9 Please refer to the *EBRI Issue Brief*, January 1999 or *ICI Perspective* for a comparison of the EBRI/ICI database with other participant-level databases.

Asset Allocation

On average, participants in the 1998 EBRI/ICI database have 49.8 percent of their account balances invested in equity funds, 17.7 percent invested in company stock, 11.4 percent in GICs, 8.4 percent in balanced funds, 6.1 percent in bond funds, 4.7 percent in money funds, and 0.3 percent in other stable value funds (see Figures 35–5 and 35–6).[10] Only 0.8 percent of account balances is invested in other investments, and the final 0.8 percent is in unidentified investments. Summing the asset shares of equity funds, company stock, and the equity portion of balanced funds[11] shows that nearly three-quarters of plan balances are invested in some form of equity securities.

F I G U R E   35–5

Average Asset Allocation for All Plan Balances, 1998 (percent)

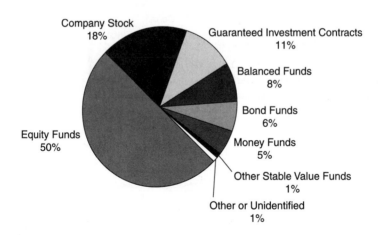

Source: Tabulations from EBRI/ICI Participant Directed Retirement Plan Data Collection Project.

---

10 Unless otherwise indicated, all asset allocation averages are expressed as dollar-weighted averages.

11 At the end of 1998, approximately 60 percent of balanced mutual fund assets were invested in equities. See Investment Company Institute, Quarterly Supplemental Data.

F I G U R E   35-6

Average Asset Allocation by Age, 1998
(percent of account balances)

Age Cohort	Equity Funds	Balanced Funds	Bond Funds	Money Funds	Guaranteed Investment Contracts	Company Stock	Other Stable Value Funds	Other	Unknown	Total
20s	62.1%	8.2%	4.7%	4.5%	4.7%	13.6%	0.1%	1.3%	0.8%	100%
30s	58.1	8.2	4.8	4.0	5.7	17.4	0.1	1.0	0.8	100
40s	52.6	8.4	5.3	4.5	8.5	18.9	0.1	0.9	0.8	100
50s	48.0	8.5	6.4	4.7	12.3	18.1	0.3	0.7	1.0	100
60s	39.8	8.2	9.0	5.7	20.6	14.7	0.7	0.7	0.7	100
All	49.8	8.4	6.1	4.7	11.4	17.7	0.3	0.8	0.8	100

Source: Tabulations from EBRI/ICI Participant Directed Retirement Plan Data Collection Project.

Asset Allocation by Age and Investment Options

Participant asset allocation varies considerably with age (see Figure 35–6). Younger participants tend to favor equity funds, while older participants are more disposed to invest in GICs and bond funds. On average, participants in their 20s have 62.1 percent of their account balances invested in equity funds, in contrast to 39.8 percent for those in their 60s. Participants in their 20s invest 4.7 percent of their assets in GICs, while those in their 60s invest 20.6 percent. Bond funds, which represent 4.7 percent of the assets of participants in their 20s, amount to 9.0 percent of the assets of participants in their 60s. Company stock accounts for 13.6 percent of the plan balances of participants in their 20s, rises to 18.9 percent for participants in their 40s, and tapers off to 14.7 percent for those in their 60s.

The mix of investment options offered by a plan sponsor significantly affects asset allocation. Figure 35–7 presents four combinations of investment offerings, starting with a base group consisting of plans that generally offer equity, balanced, bond, and money funds as investment options but do not offer company stock or GICs.[12] Participants in plans having these basic investment options have 66.4 percent of their assets

---

12 Plans falling into this category cover 26 percent of the participants in the database and 18 percent of the assets.

F I G U R E   35–7

Average Asset Allocation by Age and Investment Options, 1998 (percent of account balances)

	Equity Funds	Balanced Funds	Bond Funds	Money Funds	Guaranteed Investment Contracts	Company Stock
ALL AGES COMBINED						
Investment Options						
Equity, Bond, Money & Balanced Funds	66.4%	13.0%	9.8%	8.4%		
Equity, Bond, Money & Balanced Funds & GICs	58.2	10.0	4.7	4.0	20.9%	
Equity, Bond, Money & Balanced Funds & Company Stock	40.7	5.8	11.5	6.7		32.7%
Equity, Bond, Money & Balanced Funds, and GICs & Company Stock	44.4	7.1	2.1	2.3	18.7	24.3
PLANS WITH NO COMPANY STOCK OR GUARANTEED INVESTMENT CONTRACTS						
Age						
20s	74.3	10.0	7.6	6.0		
30s	73.3	11.5	7.6	5.9		
40s	69.0	12.7	8.9	7.2		
50s	63.4	14.0	10.5	9.0		
60s	52.7	15.1	15.4	13.8		
PLANS WITH GUARANTEED INVESTMENT CONTRACTS						
20s	70.7	8.4	3.6	3.5	11.3	
30s	68.7	8.8	3.9	3.1	13.2	
40s	62.5	9.7	4.4	3.8	17.4	
50s	55.6	10.5	5.1	4.0	22.7	
60s	41.9	10.0	5.8	4.9	35.8	
PLANS WITH COMPANY STOCK						
20s	47.4	6.0	5.9	6.4		32.5
30s	47.4	6.1	6.8	6.0		32.2
40s	44.0	6.2	8.7	6.8		32.6
50s	38.4	5.7	12.5	6.8		33.7
60s	31.0	5.1	20.7	7.1		31.7
PLANS WITH COMPANY STOCK AND GUARANTEED INVESTMENT CONTRACTS						
20s	53.1	7.7	1.7	2.1	7.9	25.2
30s	49.5	7.2	1.7	1.8	9.7	28.5
40s	45.4	7.2	2.0	2.1	13.7	28.2
50s	44.9	7.3	2.3	2.3	19.3	22.9
60s	39.5	6.9	2.3	2.9	31.6	16.0

Source: Tabulations from EBRI/ICI Participant Directed Retirement Plan Data Collection Project.

Note: Minor investment options are not shown; therefore, percentages by row will not add to 100 percent.

invested in equity funds, 13.0 percent in balanced funds, 9.8 percent in bond funds, and 8.4 percent in money funds.[13] Adding GICs to the base group lowers the allocation in all four investment options, with the greatest reduction in relative percentage of account balance occurring in bond and money funds.[14] Alternatively, adding company stock as an investment option to the base group results in substitution away from equity funds and balanced funds.[15] Finally, in those plans that offer GICs and company stock in addition to the base options, a combination of the two effects occurs: Company stock appears to displace equity and balanced fund holdings, while GICs appear to displace other fixed-income investments.[16] These effects tend to occur across all ages of participants.

Asset Allocation by Plan Size and Investment Options

Examining whether participants' behavior varies with plan size (measured by the number of plan participants) reveals whether small plans provide access to a variety of investment options similar to that provided by larger plans. In aggregate, the asset allocation of account balances varies with plan size (see VanDerhei, Holden and Quick, 2000 for details). For example, the percentage of plan assets invested in equity funds falls as plan size rises, decreasing from 66.4 percent for plans with 100 or fewer participants to 45.4 percent for plans with more than 5,000 participants. Because few small plans offer company stock as an investment option, in aggregate, company stock represents a negligible percentage of small plans' assets and a much higher percentage in larger plans. However, these aggregate figures do not consider the influence of the differing investment options offered by plan sponsors.

Asset allocations by plan size also are affected by the number of investment options. For those plans generally offering equity, balanced, bond, and money funds, asset allocation does not appear to be related to the number of participants in the plan (see VanDerhei, Holden and Quick, 2000 for details). When GICs are added to the basic investment choices,

---

13 For convenience, minor investment options are not shown.

14 Plans falling into this category cover 26 percent of the participants in the database and 17 percent of the assets.

15 Plans falling into this category cover 20 percent of the participants in the database and 24 percent of the assets.

16 Plans falling into this category cover 28 percent of the participants in the database and 41 percent of the assets.

differentiation in participant behavior by plan size is more discernible. Participants in smaller plans tend to invest a bit more heavily in equity and bond funds, compared with those in larger plans, while participants in larger plans invest a bit more heavily in GICs and balanced funds than those in smaller plans. When company stock is an investment option, but GICs are not offered, participants in the smallest and largest plans have a higher percentage of assets invested in company stock than those in plans with between 101 and 5,000 participants. When both company stock and GICs are added to the four basic investment options, asset allocation to equity funds does not vary significantly across plan size. However, among such plans, allocations to all other investments do vary, particularly GICs and company stock. For example, participants in plans with 100 or fewer participants have 19.7 percent of their assets invested in company stock, compared with 25.2 percent for those in plans with more than 5,000 participants.

Asset Allocation of Employee and Employer Contributions

In a typical 401(k) plan, an employee contributes a portion of his or her salary to a plan account and determines how the assets in the account are invested, choosing among investment options made available by the plan sponsor (employer). In many plans, the employer also makes a contribution to the participant's account, generally matching a portion of the employee's contribution. Some employers require that the employer contribution be invested in company stock, rather than as directed by the participant.[17] In these plans, it is instructive to examine the participant-directed balances separately from the employer-directed balances.

Participants in plans with mandatory investment in employer stock tend to invest a higher percentage of their self-directed balances in company stock than participants in plans without an employer-directed contribution. Company stock represents 31.5 percent of the participant-directed account balances in plans with such employer-directed contributions (see Figure 35–8, middle panel), compared with 23.4 percent in plans offering company stock as an investment option but not requiring

---

17 Source of contribution (employer versus employee) can be matched to fund information for a subset of the data providers in our sample. Of those plans in the 1998 EBRI/ICI database for which the appropriate data are available, less than 0.5 percent require employer contributions to be invested in company stock. However, most of the plans with this feature are large, covering 9 percent of participants and 14 percent of plan assets (in the subset).

F I G U R E   35-8

Impact of Company Stock on Asset Allocation by Age, 1998 (percent of account balances)

	Equity Funds	Balanced Funds	Bond Funds	Money Funds	Guaranteed Investment Contracts	Company Stock
PLANS WITH EMPLOYER-DIRECTED AND PARTICIPANT-DIRECTED BALANCES						
Total Balances (Employer-Directed and Participant-Directed)						
20s	36.1%	5.5%	0.7%	1.9%	6.8%	48.9%
30s	32.0	5.0	0.7	1.7	7.3	53.1
40s	26.8	5.4	1.2	3.3	7.8	55.2
50s	25.2	6.1	1.7	4.2	10.4	52.1
60s	23.6	6.7	3.1	7.5	17.4	41.6
All	26.7	5.7	1.6	3.9	10.0	51.9
Participant-Directed Balances Only						
20s	49.4%	7.5%	0.9%	2.5%	9.3%	30.3%
30s	46.9	7.3	1.0	2.4	10.7	31.5
40s	40.1	7.9	1.8	4.8	11.8	33.2
50s	36.0	8.5	2.5	6.1	14.2	32.3
60s	30.1	8.4	4.0	9.7	21.4	26.1
All	38.3	8.1	2.3	5.5	14.0	31.5
PLANS WITH COMPANY STOCK INVESTMENT OPTION BUT NO EMPLOYER-DIRECTED CONTRIBUTIONS						
Total Balances						
20s	51.5%	10.5%	2.2%	6.5%	5.3%	19.1%
30s	49.4	10.1	2.5	5.3	6.4	23.2
40s	44.7	10.4	3.1	5.6	8.9	24.4
50s	40.0	11.4	3.9	6.5	12.5	23.3
60s	30.8	11.5	4.6	9.1	20.1	21.6
All	42.2	10.8	3.4	6.4	11.1	23.4

Note: Minor investment in other stable value funds and "other" are not shown; therefore, percentages by row will not add to 100 percent. Employer-directed balances are invested in the plan sponsor's company stock.

Source: Tabulations from EBRI/ICI Participant Directed Retirement Plan Data Collection Project.

that employer contributions be invested in company stock (see Figure 35–8, lower panel). Offsetting the higher allocations to company stock are lower shares of assets in most other plan investments, particularly in equity funds and balanced funds. As a result, participants in plans with employer-directed contributions have 74.7 percent of their participant-directed balances invested in equity securities (defined as company stock, equity funds, and the equity portion of balanced funds). Similarly, participants in plans without employer-directed contributions have 72.1 percent of their assets invested in equity securities. However, it is important to note that the composition of these equity security investments varies.

When total account balances are considered, the overall exposure to equity securities through company stock and pooled investments is considerably higher for participants in plans with employer-directed contributions. For example, company stock, equity funds, and the equity portion of balanced funds represent 82.0 percent of the total account balances for those participants in plans with employer-directed contributions, compared with the 72.1 percent exposure in plans without employer-directed contributions (see Figure 35–8). This higher allocation to equity securities holds across all age groups.

Distribution of Equity Fund Allocations and Participant Exposure to Equities

Among individual participants, the allocation of account balance to equity funds varies widely around the average of 49.8 percent for all participants in the 1998 EBRI/ICI database. Indeed, 28.5 percent of participants have more than 80 percent of their account balances invested in equity funds, while about the same percentage hold no equity funds at all (see Figure 35–9). The percentage of participants holding no equity funds increases with age and tenure. For example, 26.8 percent of participants in their 20s have no equity investments, compared with 43.1 percent of those in their 60s. Similarly, 22.6 percent of participants with two or fewer years of tenure have no equity fund investments, compared with 42.8 percent for those with more than 30 years of tenure.

Participants with no equity fund balances may still have exposure to the stock market through company stock or balanced funds. Indeed, 58.6 percent of participants with no equity funds have investments in either company stock or balanced funds (see Figure 35–10). As a result, participants with no equity funds still have close to half[18] of their account balances in equity-related investments (see VanDerhei, Holden and Quick, 2000, for details).

Asset Allocation by Salary

Salary information is available for a subset of participants in the 1998 EBRI/ICI database. For these participants, asset allocation differs some-

---

18   Estimated as the sum of account balances that are in company stock and 60 percent of the account balances that are in balanced funds.

Asset Allocation Distribution of Participant Account
Balances to Equity Funds by Age and Tenure, 1998
(percent of participants)

	Zero	< 20%	20%–80%	> 80%	Total
TOTAL	28.3%	5.7%	37.4%	28.5%	100%
AGE COHORT					
20s	26.8%	3.3%	35.9%	34.0%	100%
30s	24.3	5.0	38.6	32.1	100
40s	27.2	6.2	39.0	27.6	100
50s	30.8	7.2	37.3	24.8	100
60s	43.1	7.5	30.9	18.6	100
TENURE (years)					
0 to 2	22.6%	2.7%	39.1%	35.6%	100%
>2 to 5	26.0	3.7	38.1	32.2	100
>5 to 10	27.5	6.0	38.9	27.6	100
>10 to 20	31.1	7.6	38.5	22.8	100
>20 to 30	35.2	8.4	35.6	20.8	100
> 30	42.8	8.4	30.7	18.1	100

Source: Tabulations from EBRI/ICI Participant Directed Retirement Plan Data Collection Project.

what with salary.[19] For example, the percentage of account balances
invested in equity funds rises from 49.8 percent for participants earning
between $20,000 and $40,000 per year to 59.6 percent for those earning
more than $100,000 per year (see VanDerhei, Holden and Quick, 2000 for
details). In contrast, the percentage of account balances invested in GICs
declines as salary increases. In addition, the percentage of account balances invested in company stock is similar across each of the income
groups earning $100,000 or less, but drops to 7.8 percent for those earn-
ing more than $100,000.

Changes in Participants' Accounts from 1996–1998

Approximately 3.3 million (or 50.3 percent) of the participants present in
the 1996 EBRI/ICI database also are in the 1997 and 1998 EBRI/ICI data-

---

19 For the most part, asset allocation of participants missing salary information is similar to the
    asset allocation for those with such information, in aggregate. The only notable exception is
    with respect to the percentage of account balances invested in company stock, which is
    higher for participants missing salary information than for those with such information.

F I G U R E   35–10

Percentage of Participants Without Equity Fund
Balances Who Have Equity Exposure by Age and
Tenure, 1998

	Percentage with Company Stock and/or Balanced Funds
AGE COHORT	
20s	49.1%
30s	59.3
40s	62.5
50s	63.9
60s	52.2
All	58.6
TENURE (years)	
0 to 2	48.6
>2 to 5	47.9
>5 to 10	56.3
>10 to 20	65.2
>20 to 30	67.2
> 30	62.8
All	58.6

Source: Tabulations from EBRI/ICI Participant Directed Retirement Plan Data Collection Project.

bases.[20] This consistent group of participants held $224 billion in assets at the end of 1998, up 62.3 percent from $138 billion at the end of 1996.[21] These participants appear to be representative of the aggregate EBRI/ICI database in terms of their distribution across age, tenure, account balance, and plan size, and thus they provide an opportunity to examine the developments in their 401(k) accounts over the two-year time period.

---

20 Employees included in this analysis are active participants with positive account balances in their 401(k) plans in 1996, 1997, and 1998. Participants who enter or exit the database in 1997 or 1998 are not included in this analysis.

21 These participants' aggregate assets rose 30 percent in 1997 and 25 percent in 1998. Because the subsample requires that participants be present in all three years, while in 401(k) plans more generally, participants enter and leave, the growth in assets experienced by our constant group of participants exceeds growth estimates for the universe of 401(k) plans. Indeed, the U.S. Department of Labor reports an average growth rate in 401(k)-type plan assets of 18 percent per year over 1991 to 1996. Cerulli Associates (1999) estimates that 401(k) plan assets grew 20 percent in 1997 and 15 percent in 1998.

FIGURE 35-11

Changes in Participants' Investment in Equity Securities, 1996–1998 (percent of participants)

PERCENTAGE OF ACCOUNT BALANCE INVESTED IN EQUITY FUNDS

Percentage in 1998

		None	1 to 33%	34 to 66%	67 to 99%	100%
Percentage in 1996	None	17.7%	2.4%	1.3%	0.8%	0.5%
	1 to 33%	0.5	10.2	4.1	1.1	0.6
	34 to 66%	0.5	1.6	18.9	5.1	1.3
	67 to 99%	0.4	0.5	1.7	15.7	1.4
	100%	0.2	0.3	0.3	1.0	12.1

Sum of Diagonal: 74.6%

PERCENTAGE OF ACCOUNT BALANCE INVESTED IN EQUITY FUNDS, BALANCED FUNDS,* AND COMPANY STOCK

Percentage in 1998

		None	1 to 33%	34 to 66%	67 to 99%	100%
Percentage in 1996	None	11.1%	1.5%	0.7%	0.6%	0.4%
	1 to 33%	0.2	6.5	3.0	0.9	0.3
	34 to 66%	0.3	0.8	15.0	5.6	0.7
	67 to 99%	0.5	0.7	2.0	30.5	2.7
	100%	0.2	0.3	0.4	1.8	13.3

Sum of Diagonal: 76.4%

*Because approximately 60 percent of aggregate balanced fund assets are invested in equities, 60 percent of participants' balanced fund assets are counted here as equity investments.

Source: Tabulations from EBRI/ICI Participant Directed Retirement Plan Data Collection Project.

Changes in Asset Allocation from 1996 to 1998

Despite the sharp rise in equity prices between 1996 and 1998, the percentage of assets allocated to equity funds did not change significantly for the vast majority of participants. To examine changes in asset allocation, participants are placed into five groups based on the percentage of their account balance invested in equity funds in 1996. The five groups corresponding to the percentages invested in equity funds are: 0 percent, 1 percent to 33 percent, 34 percent to 66 percent, 67 percent to 99 percent, and 100 percent. The participants within each of these groups are then grouped according to the percentage of account balance allocated to equity funds in 1998, using the same five ranges.

The results of this cross-classification are shown in Figure 35–11. A percentage along the diagonal shows the share of all the participants who remain within the same group in 1996 and 1998.[22] The figures above the diagonal represent participants who moved to a higher allocation in equity funds in 1998, whereas figures below the diagonal represent participants with a lower allocation to equity funds in 1998. For example, 18.9 percent of all participants in 1996 remained within the 34 percent to 66 percent range in 1998. In addition, 5.1 percent of the participants moved from the 34 percent to 66 percent range in 1996 to the 67 percent to 99 percent range in 1998, while 1.6 percent moved from the 34 percent to 66 percent range in 1996 to the 1 percent to 33 percent range in 1998.

The vast majority of participants remained within their 1996 equity asset allocation group in 1998. This is indicated by the sum of the diagonal elements in Figure 35–11, which shows that 74.6 percent are in the same cell in both 1996 and 1998. That is, 74.6 percent of participants maintained the 1996 share of their account balances in equity funds in 1998. The other 25.4 percent of the participants experienced a change in groups between 1996 and 1998. More than twice as many participants experiencing a change in equity allocation ended up with a higher equity allocation than ended up with a lower equity allocation. Indeed, the sum of the elements above the diagonal indicates that 18.6 percent ended up with a higher allocation in 1998, whereas the sum of the elements below the diagonal shows that 7.0 percent ended up with a lower allocation. The conclusions of this section are broadly similar when the allocation of account balance to equity securities is defined more generally to include equity funds, the equity portion of balanced funds, and company stock (see Figure 35–11, lower panel).

CONCLUSION

For all 401(k) participants in the 1998 EBRI/ICI database, almost three-quarters of plan balances are invested directly or indirectly in equity securities. Specifically, 49.8 percent of total plan balances are invested in equity funds, 17.7 percent in company stock, 11.4 percent in guaranteed investment contracts (GICs), 8.4 percent in balanced funds, 6.1 percent in bond funds, 4.7 percent in money funds, and 0.3 percent in other stable value funds.

---

22 We should note that maintaining a given asset allocation may have required some adjustment in the composition of account balances or contributions to rebalance the portfolio. In addition, this analysis compares changes in year-end asset allocation over a two-year time period and does not capture trading activity of participants.

Participant asset allocation varies considerably with age. Younger participants tend to favor equity funds, while older participants are more disposed to invest in GICs and bond funds. On average, participants in their 20s have 62.1 percent of their account balances invested in equity funds, in contrast to 39.8 percent for those in their 60s. Participants in their 20s invest 4.7 percent of their assets in GICs, while those in their 60s invest 20.6 percent. Bond funds, which represent 4.7 percent of the assets of participants in their 20s, amount to 9.0 percent of the assets of participants in their 60s.

Investment options offered by 401(k) plans appear to influence asset allocation. For example, the addition of company stock substantially reduces the allocation to equity funds and the addition of GICs tends to lower allocations to bond and money funds. Employer contributions in the form of company stock also affect participants' asset allocation behavior.

BIBLIOGRAPHY

Cerulli Associates, Inc. "Market Update: The 401(k) Industry," *The Cerulli Report*, Boston: Cerulli Associates, September 1999.

Investment Company Institute. Quarterly Supplemental Data.

U.S. Department of Labor, Pension and Welfare Benefit Administration, *Private Pension Plan Bulletin, Abstract of 1996, Form 5500 Annual Reports.* Washington DC: U.S. Government Printing Office, Winter 1999–2000.

VanDerhei, Jack, Russell Galer, Carol Quick, and John Rea, "401(k) Plan Asset Allocation, Account Balances, and Loan Activity," *EBRI Issue Brief*, No. 205 and *ICI Perspective*, Vol. 5, No. 1, Washington DC: Employee Benefit Research Institute and Investment Company Institute, January 1999.

VanDerhei, Jack, Sarah Holden and Carol Quick, "401(k) Plan Asset Allocation, Account Balances, and Loan Activity in 1998," published as January 2000, *ICI Perspective* Vol. 6, No. 1 and *EBRI Issue Brief,* No. 218, February 2000.

VanDerhei, Jack and Ken McDonnell, "Current Provisions and Recent Trends in Qualified Single-Employer Defined Contribution Plans in the Private Sector," in *The Future of Private Retirement Plans*, Dallas Salisbury, ed., Washington, DC: Employee Benefit Research Institute, 2000, pp. 39–60.

PART SEVEN

Employee Benefit Plan Administration

Employee benefit administration has changed substantially in the last twenty-five years, and has evolved into a multifaceted discipline requiring a combination of both general managerial skills and technical proficiencies. An overview of the principles of administration of employee benefit plans is presented in the first chapter of this part, Chapter 36.

The presence of flexible benefit plans or so-called cafeteria plans in employee benefits programs adds another level of complexity to employee benefit plan administration. Chapter 37 provides an historical overview of the development of flexible benefit plans, and it also discusses the advantages and limitations associated with flexible benefit plans and the regulatory structure in which they operate.

Chapter 38 discusses in detail how flexible benefit plans operate in practice. The design and administrative considerations in such plans are presented. Also discussed are flexible spending accounts, which are frequently used as a valuable employee benefit planning tool along with a cafeteria plan.

The fiduciary liability that ERISA imposes on benefits professionals in the administration of employee benefits plans is examined in Chapter 39.

The last chapter of this part, Chapter 40, discusses the critical role of employee benefit communications in plan administration.

CHAPTER 36

Managing Employee Benefit Plans

Dennis F. Mahoney

INTRODUCTION

Administering employee benefit plans has changed substantially in the last 25 years and has evolved into a multifaceted discipline. It requires a combination of both general managerial skills and deep technical proficiencies in select areas. It entails coordinating a team of internal and external specialists from the following diverse disciplines: human resources, law, tax, finance, medical care, risk management, and information systems. And it is best accomplished by an individual skilled in leadership, project management, and general management.

The level of complexity in administering an employee benefits program is contingent on a number of factors. Among these are the complexity and comprehensiveness of the benefits design and coverages, the size of the employee group covered, the uniformity of the program for different categories of employees, the geographical dispersion of employees, and the existence of self-funded or self-administered arrangements. Multiple service providers can add to the complexity of plan administration.

An employee benefits program is of strategic importance to an organization from a human resource (HR) perspective and from a risk-management perspective. From an HR perspective, the program itself is instrumental in attracting and retaining a skilled workforce, which allows the firm to be competitive within its industry. Design of a retirement plan can affect retirement patterns and have a direct impact on the replenishment of the workforce. Equally important are risk management issues.

Because of the significant costs involved and the potential to manage risks in various ways, a firm that effectively manages its employee benefits program risks can have a competitive advantage in terms of product and service pricing. Control over potential risks should be fully considered when evaluating the scope and nature of administrative activities.

The nature and scope of benefits administration activities will be based on the organization's philosophy about a benefits program, risk management activities, the availability of various service providers with expertise in relationship to the organization's benefits offerings, and the ability of these service providers to administer the benefits program in the way that meets the organization's needs. In addition, today's employee benefits management function is profoundly affected by the extent to which the administration is retained in-house or outsourced.

FOCUS OF BENEFITS MANAGEMENT ACTIVITY

Recognizing that scope and function of employee benefits administration differs within organizations, there are a number of core activities. The benefits manager must be able to wear different hats in dealing with a range of issues:

1. Benefits plan design.
2. Benefits plan delivery.
3. Benefits policy formulation.
4. Communications.
5. Applying technology.
6. Cost management and resource controls.
6. Management reporting.
7. Legal/regulatory compliance.
8. Monitoring the external environment.

Benefits Plan Design

A critical function within the purview of employee benefits administration is the initial design and ongoing modification of the employee benefits program to meet changing market conditions, new regulatory requirements, or changing organizational and/or human resource objectives. Often, the benefits manager is not operating completely free of constraints in the design of employee benefit plans. Cost considerations, the culture of the organization, employee needs, and the historical development of benefit programs affect benefits design. Industry trends and competition as well as local market conditions concerning service providers also have a bearing on the design process. Collective bargaining agreements and benefit plan design changes that are negotiated between union and management are another determinant. Even when collective bargaining agreements do not exist, many employers will try to build employee consensus around benefit plan changes, especially if a plan change may be perceived as a "take-away." This was clearly the case when many organizations changed their medical programs from traditional indemnity plans to managed care alternatives.

Benefits design entails making structural decisions at a macro level as well as at a more micro level. Whether an organization uses a noncontributory defined benefit plan or a contributory 401(k) defined contribution plan as its primary retirement program can result in very different outcomes from a financial, human resources, and risk-management perspective. Use of a defined benefit plan means the organization commits to a final pension formula and retains the risk for investing plan assets. In a defined contribution plan, the organization's responsibility to plan participants is largely fulfilled when assets are transferred to the investment custodian and investment risk is shifted to plan participants. These alternate pension forms may affect recruitment and retention as they present different opportunities for capital accumulation that ultimately affect retirement income. The choice of retirement plan forms also can have major impact on the administrative and communication activities. Inclusion of a loan feature with a 401(k) program can lead to more costly administrative and systems support but may result in greater plan participation, which could be necessary to pass plan nondiscrimination tests.

Successful plan design occurs when a benefits program properly addresses the needs of the organization and can be effectively administered and communicated to employees. Any design effort therefore starts with an understanding of the organization's underlying compensation and benefits program and philosophy and the specific objectives that the benefits plan is intended to address.

The plan also should be considered within the wider tax and marketplace contexts to determine whether it is achieving optimal efficiencies. Plans should be considered from a risk-management perspective to determine whether they are subjecting the organization to any special liabilities or creating a situation where the organization is exceeding the level of risk exposure that it is willing to bear. All of these considerations should help in refining the ultimate benefits program approach.

Benefits design is an ongoing and continual process. It is not generally performed once. Organizations often review their plans and make changes after significant company changes, market changes, and technology changes. A good plan design will take into consideration short-term, intermediate, and long-term objectives and conditions, such as the maturing of a workforce. However, the benefits environment changes so rapidly, these long-term (and even intermediate) objectives can easily become obsolete. Examples include the adoption of *Financial Accounting Standard 106 (FAS 106)* and its impact on the reporting of the financial conditions of various organizations. Changes in Medicare policy or other social insurance programs could alter long-term (and short-term) objectives of organizations' retiree medical plans.

Though all future events impacting on plan design will not be known with certainty, management should be aware of possible longer-term impacts to the firm and balance these possible contingencies against the rationale for plan creation. Many times, a benefit plan can be justified on economic grounds when one examines some of the hidden costs in the absence of a plan, such as the continued service of employees who are not operating at a high level of productivity in the absence of a retirement plan or disability plan.[1]

Benefits Plan Delivery

Employee benefits administration is a customer service business with employees/management as the "clients." Serving plan participants can encompass a variety of activities, which again will dramatically vary depending on the scope of the benefits program, the nature of the organization, and the characteristics of the employee workforce. There are certain critical activities that will nevertheless be required, though the scope of activity and emphasis will vary:

- New employee benefits orientation.
- Policy clarification on benefits eligibility, coverage, and applicability of plan provisions.
- Dealing with exceptional circumstances and unusual cases.
- Collection and processing of enrollment information, claims information, and requests for plan distributions either via the Internet or through submission of paper forms.

---

1 Everett T. Allen, Jr., Joseph J. Melone, Jerry S. Rosenbloom, and Jack L. VanDerhai, *Pension Planning*, 8th ed. (New York: Irwin/McGraw-Hill, 1997), p. 10.

■ Benefits counseling and response to employee inquiries for active employees.

■ Benefits counseling for terminating and retiring employees and employees with disabilities.

The scope of these activities will be affected by the characteristics of the organization. For instance, an employer that experiences high employee turnover will have to devote more resources to the new employee benefits orientation and to activities resolving benefits issues for terminating employees. Employers in mature industries are more likely to have a retiree population that exceeds the number of currently employed active workers. In such a situation, the benefits department may find itself routinely handling a greater number of inquiries from retirees on issues such as how the corporate health plan benefits are integrated with Medicare or how outside earnings will impact benefits provided from Social Security. In this instance, the mode of communication selected for disseminating plan information might be different than in other organizations. For example, use of certain technologies such as the Internet may be ineffective because some retirees may not have access to this medium in their homes. If many retirees have relocated to sunbelt states, the network of managed care providers would need concentrations of providers in these areas.

As is true in any customer service endeavor, the organization will attempt to achieve excellent customer service results meeting the valid requirements of the customer base with the given resources allocated for this purpose. Management must make determinations on the appropriate amount of resources to allocate to this endeavor given resource constraints. Management must ultimately seek the strategic deployment of all organizational resources.

There are two quality standards that might be used to evaluate customer service satisfaction. One would be the desired outcome in terms of quality as determined by management, given resource allocations to the benefits administrative function. This targeted level of quality would be the maximum level targeted by management. The other standard would involve the minimum customer service standards that must be met to ensure a benefits program is in compliance with federal and state legal requirements. The special tax preferences that have historically been afforded to benefit programs also come with certain required obligations that plan sponsors have to plan participants. Management should be aware that some of these legal obligations take the form of certain levels of customer service quality, which are legally mandated and that might result in severe penalties if not met. Though certainly not exhaustive, the following are some of the customer service requirements that must be met in sponsoring an employee benefits plan:

1. Requirement to provide a personnel benefits statement at least annually if requested by an employee.

2. Employee Retirement Income Security Act (ERISA) mandated standards for responding to requests for benefits and stipulated time periods to deny claims and respond to appeals.

3. Requirements to make plan financial information available to participants and disclosure requirements of certain plan information.

4. Standards imposed by the Consolidated Omnibus Budget Reconciliation Act of 1985 (COBRA) regarding notification requirements to terminating employees on rights to coverage continuation under the plan sponsor's group plan.

5. Certificates of creditable coverage must be provided to those losing coverage under a group health plan or those requesting a certificate of creditable coverage as mandated by the Health Insurance Portability and Accountability Act (HIPAA).

Benefits Policy Formulation

As part of the benefits management function, there are continuously arising human resource questions and issues that must be resolved. These include issues such as denial of claims by a carrier, confusion over waiting periods, service areas of a managed care network, and whether or not a new medical procedure will be covered by a benefit plan. Many of these must be codified in the form of policy to avoid future problems. Management may take either a proactive or reactive role in formulating policies related to the benefit plans.

Although this component of benefit plan administration has always existed, it assumes a more significant role when benefit programs change or there is substantial change in the contextual environment. Changes in technology, plan design, compliance requirements, outsourcing, and the restructuring of the medical delivery system have forced a new emphasis on the policy formulation aspect of benefits management.

Because many benefit functions are contracted out to insurance carriers, mutual fund companies, and third-party administrators, policy issues surface as these entities provide administrative services. For these issues, policy formulation takes the form of a vendor liaison role. The benefits manager must be continually apprised of issues that surface, give direction for resolution, seek consistency among multiple providers, and at times exert pressure and negotiate to ensure these third parties are administering the benefit programs as the plan sponsor intends. Because these third parties are performing functions such as claims payment, deciding on adequate claims documentation, and monitoring appeal processes for claims denial, there are many areas requiring sound judgment and policy development.

Communications

A principal activity in benefits plan management is to effectively communicate benefit plan programs, their plan provisions, and proper procedures to access these programs. A number of characteristics make the communication of benefit programs challenging. First, within many organizations, the workforce is diverse in composition, with various levels of education, financial sophistication, and interest in understanding plan provisions. Second, some benefits are of little interest to a majority of employees until point of use or access. For instance, there may be little interest in knowing much about a disability income plan until an individual contracts an illness that could result in a disabling condition; then there will be an intense desire to learn about and understand the plan. Similarly, many of the fine points associated with medical plan coverages are not completely understood until the onset of a particular medical condition. Third, multiple regulatory requirements often affect plan features and lead to confusion. Sometimes it is difficult for employees to distinguish between plan stipulations imposed by the Internal Revenue Service, a plan custodian, and the employer sponsoring a given plan. An employee may believe he or she has certain flexibilities permitted by law, while the plan sponsor may be more restrictive, not permitting these plan features. Or, federal law may impose limits on highly compensated employees that are more restrictive than those of the employer. This is often particularly true in the realm of retirement and capital accumulation plans. For instance, the includable cap of compensation for computing pension contributions under Internal Revenue Code (IRC) Section 401(a)(17) may cause an employer to curtail the employer matching contributions an employee is expecting based upon the plan's standard contribution formula. Another example may be the ability to access loans from a 401(k) plan. Although there are restrictions on these loans, governmental rules allow for such plan provisions. A particular investment custodian may not offer that feature on a particular product, or the plan sponsor may choose not to offer such a plan feature, finding it contrary to its plan objectives. The potential for confusion is exacerbated when an employer offers multiple mutual funds or insurance companies as investment custodians with differing features.

Plan complexity also makes communicating benefits a challenge. Increased investment choices with participant-directed accounts; increased program choices in flexible benefits programs; corporate mergers; and continuing market, technology, and legal changes contribute to the complexity.

New technologies, in particular, are dramatically altering employers' communications choices. In addition to written materials, employers have multiple alternatives: audio, video, interactive voice response (IVR) and the Internet. These mediums allow employees to procure information on their personal benefits situation and direct changes in such areas as investment allocations and withholding amounts. Voice response technology is also used to allow employees to procure automated recorded messages on plan provisions and enroll in benefits plans. Increasingly, benefit plan information is displayed in multiple mediums to provide increased awareness of benefit programs.

As with customer service quality standards, there are dual standards to meet in benefits communications—the maximum standards being those the company sets for creating a proper understanding and use of the plans, and a minimum standard specified by ERISA for meeting the legal compliance requirements for disclosure to plan participants. Use of electronic communications is increasing along with traditional standard print materials. Though not exhaustive, the following list delineates some of the most common communication requirements that a plan must meet to be in compliance with federal law:

1. *Summary plan descriptions (SPDs).* These are written materials that provide a summary of the benefit plan's provisions in language that is supposed to be understandable to the average plan participant. In order to be considered a bona fide SPD, certain information must be included:

   a. The requirement to describe how a participant covered by the plan can make a claim for benefits.

   b. The procedure for appeal if a participant's claim for benefits is denied.

    c. The name and address of the person or persons to be served with legal process should a legal action be instituted against the plan.

It is important to note that there are precise time frames for making SPDs available to employees initially when a plan becomes subject to Title I of ERISA, and on an ongoing basis. New participants must receive an SPD 90 days after beginning plan participation. Subsequently, the SPDs must be revised every five years if the plan or information requirements have changed; otherwise, an SPD must be reissued every 10 years.

2. *Summary of Material Modification (SMM).* This is a written document that describes any "material" change that has occurred in the plan and must be issued if the plan sponsor has not issued an updated SPD describing the plan change. Like the SPD, there is a prescribed time frame for the issuance of this document. It must be issued within 210 days after the plan year in which the material modification was adopted. HIPAA reduced this 210-day period to 60 days for group health plans that make changes of "material reductions in covered services or benefits."

3. *Summary Annual Report (SAR).* This is a summary of the latest annual report for a benefit plan, in other words, a summary of the data reported to the Internal Revenue Service (IRS) on Form 5500. Although the IRS has statutory oversight for 5500s, the Department of Labor (DOL) serves as a contractor to the IRS for processing Form 5500s under the ERISA Filing Acceptance System (EFAST). Unless an extension was granted for the filing of the Form 5500, the SAR must be distributed by the last day of the ninth month after the end of the plan year.

In addition to the required reporting and disclosure about general plan provisions, a number of targeted communication messages must be provided by the benefits administrator when specific events occur or certain conditions are met:

1. *Benefit statement to terminated vested participants.* Any terminated employee who is entitled to a benefit under a pension benefit plan must be advised of this entitlement by the time this information is reported to the IRS as part of the Form 5500 reporting.

2. *COBRA rights.* The Consolidated Omnibus Budget Reconciliation Act of 1985 requires employers with 20 or more employees to offer continued health care coverage to employees and their dependents who are losing their health coverage under the employer plan. There is an initial notification requirement at the time that an employee first becomes covered by the health plan and a requirement to notify eligible participants of a 60-day election period when they experience a qualifying event such as termination of employment.

3. *Explanation of tax withholding for rollover distributions.* The Unemployment Compensation Amendments of 1992 imposed a 20 percent mandatory withholding tax on pension plan distributions that are not directly transferred to another eligible plan. Generally, employers are to notify employees no earlier than 30 days and no later than 90 days before the eligible rollover distribution.

4. *Joint and survivor information.* Most pension plans must correspond with their participants between the plan year in which the participant first reaches age 32 and the plan year preceding the plan year in which the participant attains age 35, to advise the pension participant of the rules concerning death benefits for a spouse and the rules regarding survivor annuities and waiver of survivorship rights.

5. *Certificates of creditable coverage.* These must be provided automatically by the sponsor of a group health plan when an individual loses coverage under the plan, exhausts COBRA continuation coverage, or is requested by an individual before losing coverage or within 24 months of losing coverage. The requirement to provide certificates of creditable coverage was instituted by the Health Insurance Portability and Accountability Act of 1996.

Both the general and targeted communications are prescribed by law and must occur within noted time periods for the benefit plan to be in compliance. Failure to provide such communications within the mandated time requirements can subject the plan to financial penalties or result in other legal remedies against a plan. These financial penalties are by no means insignificant. For instance, failure to provide information on COBRA rights can result in a penalty equal to $100 per day, while willful violations of ERISA reporting and disclosure provisions can result in criminal prosecution carrying prison terms and fines up to $100,000 for a corporation.

Applying Technology[2]

New technological applications are constantly emerging and have direct impact on the means to handle information, interface with customers, and enhance service. In recent years, benefits administrators have been dramatically affected by technological innovations and will continue to be dramatically impacted as other innovations emerge, especially continuing dramatic advances in communications and record-keeping functions. Many innovations that did not exist in widespread commercial use a decade ago have become commonplace in administering benefit plans. Among these would be voicemail, electronic mail, fax, automated voice response, and interactive Internet applications. Implementing state-of-the-art administrative technology in benefits management has transformed the service delivery benefits function and revolutionized the way benefits managers monitor the effectiveness of their programs.

The growth of flexible benefits programs in the 1980s and early 1990s spurred advanced record-keeping systems and communication technology. These more complex plans required the functionality of modern technology, which required an employee benefits information system that integrated participant demographic characteristics, cost data, and plan information into one source. The goal was to consolidate information that may need to be cross-referenced into one integrated source with easy access for multiple users. Such an approach made employee self-service the next progressive step as access to the Internet became commonplace.

The power of information technology is rooted in the way data is retained and stored (informational architecture), the expanded ability to retrieve relevant information (data-accessing capabilities), the development of features allowing nontechnical persons to easily extract the information they need (end-user tools), and a realization that this repository of data can be used by both plan administrators for plan management functions and by plan participants for customer service needs.

Informational Architecture

A *common relational database* is at the heart of the informational architecture and becomes the centralized repository of information for census, demographic characteristics, eligibility, and plan information for multiple

---

2 The author gratefully acknowledges the extensive and comprehensive use of internal memos and
   explanations provided by Gary Truhlar, Director of Human Resources: Information
   Management at the University of Pennsylvania, in categorizing and describing information
   management principles and tools. Any errors in description are entirely the responsibility of
   the author.

benefit plans. The goal is to avoid the fragmentation of information that prevents an integrated and complete analysis when viewing benefits coverages by organizational unit, by individual employee, or by various employee types or certain demographic stratas such as geographic location or age. When effectively designed, a common relational database eliminates information "silos" where information is housed in one location and is inaccessible to decision-makers because of organizational, database, or benefit plan boundaries. A common relational database creates a universal repository of information that can be accessed directly by the plan participant on an as-needed basis to engage in financial planning, check balances in capital accumulation accounts, or monitor the status of coverages or pending claims made against a benefit plan. Such an approach also helps the plan administrator in the numerical analysis for nondiscrimination requirements and actuarial valuations.

Data-Accessing Capabilities

The way individuals work and the way customers receive service has changed. Information technology allows self-service, and customers want the freedom of easy access. *Customer-driven processes* enable applications that can be initiated by plan participants. Plan participants are empowered to access individualized benefits information from a common relational database without requiring the intervention of a human benefits specialist. Creating a customer-driven process results in a paradigm shift for servicing employees and becomes the primary, as opposed to secondary, means by which employees access information. The human benefits specialist adds specialized value, counseling, and training but should not be supplying answers related to eligibility, account balances, or standard available information such as claims procedures. Such generic, objective inquiries are more efficiently obtained through automated access.

The newly hired employee without specialized computer training should be able to obtain benefit plan information from the benefits information system. This occurs when user presentation has a reasonably consistent "look and feel." Data to the system is entered once, from the source, and appropriate edits and verification are performed throughout the initiation, review, approval, and submission processes. Access to the data is always available, and the data is always current and consistent when accessed by multiple users.

Security

Security is important because the same database is used for administrative processing as well as communications to plan participants.

Information security is important to protect against fraudulent plan disbursements; unauthorized access to proprietary plan participant information; and entry into other proprietary and protected information, such as medical records or defined contribution investment selections.

The issue of privacy regarding medical records took on greater prominence following passage of HIPAA in 1996. As part of this Act, Congress was to pass further legislation on the privacy of medical records by August 1999. If Congress did not meet this self-imposed deadline, HIPAA called for the Department of Health and Human Services to issue proposed rules. The Department of Health and Human Services issued these proposed rules in November 1999. At the time this chapter was being written, there were various bills on medical privacy issues pending in both the House and Senate.

Unleashing Information Technology Potential

Today's benefits manager can apply a variety of information tools on this landscape of an on-line, relational database supporting customer-driven processes:

- *Executive information systems (EIS)* are powerful end-user tools that provide management information in summary format. The user can immediately access "portraits" that summarize, analyze, and present in graphical display the information from the database that the benefits manager routinely needs to understand and manage the firm's benefit plans. EIS can be designed to profile utilization patterns, risk exposures, and factors driving benefit plan costs.

- *Imaging and optical storage* eliminates paper records and creates "virtual records" (sharing of documents over a network). Use of this technology can improve customer access; eliminate misfiles attendant with manual record sorting; provide more efficient and timely data storage; and, through efficient electronic duplicative backup, reduce the potential for data loss in the event of a disaster, such as a fire or flood.

- *Interactive voice response (IVR)* are technologies that link telephone systems to the employee benefits information system. Employees can access recorded messages explaining plan features and eligibility criteria. These systems allow benefits plan enrollment over the phone and provide a cost-effective means for offering 24-hour-a-day, seven-day-a-week customer service. Coupled with the proper edits for data input, the systems disallow input of obviously contradictory data, improving accuracy and reducing administrative rework. IVR is particularly well-suited for handling large volumes of transactions, such as for open enrollments or new hire sign-ups.

■ *Electronically sent information* allows direct file transfer from the plan sponsor to insurance carriers, investment custodians, and third-party administrators without the physical exchange of paper files or computer tapes. This greatly reduces the amount of time required to forward data, which improves efficiency. Given the decision by many organizations to outsource some component of benefits administration and the necessity to share plan data with specialized experts, such as consultants and actuaries, to monitor compliance and construct asset and liability valuations, such methods greatly enhance the ability of plan sponsors to expeditiously share information.

■ *Client-server technology* integrates networked applications with desktop tools that are familiar to the user (windows, mouse, drag and drop, etc.). Networked workstations allow connection to a virtually unlimited array of resources, including mainframe computers, electronic mail, the Internet, intranets, commercial databases, and vendor systems. Such technology opens tremendous opportunities to support decentralized management of various programs, distill information throughout the organization, and provide plan information through customer-driven processes supporting a more empowered and self-sufficient plan participant.

■ *Employee self-service* allows customer-driven updating of personal data, benefits modeling, retirement planning, and so on. Ideally, applications are delivered directly to each employee's personal technology devices. In organizations where many employees do not have access to personal technology devices, an alternative is to place kiosks at strategic areas of an employer's work site, thus allowing for universal access.

Cost Management and Resource Controls

Increasingly, cost management has become a critical issue for benefit plan administration as the costs of benefit programs have risen. What sometimes was viewed as a purely financial function handled by an organization's finance department is now more often viewed as a partnership with a finance department and an area where benefit plan management can significantly add value to decisions. There are various reasons for an expanding benefits management role in fiscal accountability. Beyond the obvious recognition that plan costs represent a significant operating expenditure as a component cost of total compensation, there are other environmental factors that have expanded the role of benefits management in this area. Many of these trends had their inception in the 1980s and 1990s. Among them were some of the compliance issues that arose during the late 1980s and early 1990s. Issuance of *FAS 106* by the Financial Accounting Standards Board on December 21, 1990, meant that companies had to show on their balance sheets the liabilities associated with their retiree health plan programs. For most organizations, compliance was required in 1993. Because most organizations had not previously shown these liabilities and were accounting for their retiree health care costs on a pay-as-you-go basis, recognition of these liabilities was a major disclosure event for most organizations. Although some organizations chose to terminate their retiree health programs, many other organizations tried to balance the financial (and shareholder) impact of the accounting recognition with their human resource considerations. Those involved in benefits management were able to add value to the decision process because of detailed knowledge on compliance with *FAS 106* requirements and because some of the means to decrease plan liabilities could occur through plan design modification.

Similarly, failure to comply with the nondiscrimination tests of the Tax Reform Act of 1986 could have severe financial impacts. Again, many of the remedies available involved balancing plan design modifications with cost issues. Hence, the benefits management knowledge and expertise in plan design was required to find the optimal financial solutions for the firm. What is significant about both *FAS 106* and many of the nondiscrimination requirements of the Tax Reform Act of 1986 is that there are very real and very substantial financial impacts to an organization related to the firm's knowledge of demographics, health trends, and utilization within benefit programs. Those responsible for the benefits management and plan administration are often best positioned to have knowledge of these nuances and impact the firm in a significant financial way.

Benefits managers have special expertise and knowledge, not only of the cost experience of the firm's employee group, but of insurance arrangements and the pricing of these risk-shifting devices in the marketplace. This knowledge of insurance pricing is useful in evaluating proposals from insurers and in developing the firm's risk-management approach.

On insured products, a benefits manager should carefully evaluate the underlying actuarial assumptions and reserve requirements, and compare these underlying costing determinants with plan experience. Actuarial assumptions that vary substantially from plan experience should be questioned. Even if a plan is being administered on a cost-plus basis, actuarial assumptions can be important. Reserve requirements or a stop-loss fee can be computed based upon expected claims experience. Retention, interest, and penalty charges should be thoroughly understood and negotiated. Some carriers include interest and penalty charges in retention. Because these computation methods may not be clearly elaborated in a contract, analysis of complete computation methodology is required.

As companies have attempted to compete more effectively in a technologically changing world, labor shortages, especially among information technology (IT) workers, have been a threat to many organizations in the new millennium. Design of compensation programs capable of recruiting and retaining the best IT workers have been viewed as a strategic imperative. Use of stock options in the total compensation package has been a widely used device to attract these workers. See Chapter 30 for a detailed description of stock options.

Management Reporting

With the accentuation of the benefits program as a consumer of firm resources and a pivotal ingredient in strategic success, management reporting responsibilities have expanded for benefits staff. It is important for those responsible for benefits management to have the management information systems in place that will allow them to monitor financial results, track program utilization, assess risk exposures, note deviations from compliance targets, and measure progress toward overall human resource objectives. Such metrics go beyond traditional financial measures of plan costs. The management information component of benefits administration has expanded and requires ongoing refinement as the environment changes.

Program Costs

Measuring direct program costs is necessary, but a wide array of other metrics are also necessary to fully understand the forces that are driving benefits costs. To understand hospitalization expenses, for instance, it is necessary to know the various medical procedures that are frequently used and the utilization patterns for hospitalizations and lengths of stay. As health costs have risen, health insurers, managed care companies, and health care coalitions have built community databases to better measure costs and quality. They look at physician practice patterns, and treatment regimens and outcomes. Although cost and quality measures are in their infancy and no single set of standards is universally accepted, benefit managers would be wise to develop at least a cursory understanding of the measures. The measures will provide one way for managers to benchmark their own plan performance with norms and will ultimately help in purchasing better value health care.

To effectively manage health plan costs, the benefits manager must understand the demographic characteristics of the company's covered population and establish a context for comparison. Even relative pricing between multiple plan offerings can be deceptive if pricing of options is viewed in isolation without adjusting for age and geographic selection patterns since these factors are highly correlated with the cost of health care. If a plan attracts a certain population cohort, its higher cost may reflect this dominant demographic feature and may not be indicative of truly higher cost relative to other plans if adjustments are made for population characteristics. For example, health maintenance organizations (HMOs) have often attracted younger employees for various reasons. Even though a health maintenance organization's premium is sometimes lower than a traditional indemnity plan, the HMO may not look as attractive if the employer makes an adjustment for this demographic characteristic and recompares relative pricing with expected pricing given uniform demographic assumptions.

Demographic and utilization patterns are necessary components for computing program liabilities and testing plan compliance. Though the requirement to book defined benefit pension obligations had been in use for some time, *FAS 106* established similar financial reporting requirements for retiree health plans. The Tax Reform Act of 1986 ushered in specific numerical testing to determine whether highly compensated employees were being advantaged under pension programs. Because of the adverse consequences resulting from failing the nondiscrimination tests, testing must be conducted regularly and be included in a management reporting system. The reports will identify any divergence from expected results and give lead time for remedial action such as additional contributions to the accounts of nonhighly compensated employees or redesign of benefit plan structures.

Comparison to the Competition

In order to judge the competitive position of a total compensation program, employers often seek to compare their benefits programs to similar employers. This endeavor is often difficult because the many plan provisions of benefit programs do not make for a homogeneous commodity that is directly comparable. Also, because an employer may have a geographically dispersed workforce and attract some employees from a local labor market and other employees from either a national or international labor pool, the relevant survey group can vary with type of employee. Often, employers find it necessary to segment their employee populations and compare both for their local marketplace and within their particular industry for professional and management personnel.

Survey data often are used, and some benefits consulting firms have attempted to develop comparative databases that give overall comparability ratings for benefit programs. Various approaches can be used to make benefit plan comparisons more relevant, depending on the particular objective for undertaking the analysis. Some experts have identified various comparative methodologies, which include the following:

1. Compare the benefits actually payable to representative employees under different circumstances.
2. Compare actual costs to the employer for different benefit plans.
3. Measure plans on a basis that uses uniform actuarial methods and assumptions and focuses on the relative value of the different benefits provided.[3]
4. Compare benefit plans feature by feature to isolate specific plan provisions that may be appealing to certain employee groups and offer a competitive advantage. Such a comparison may result in amending plan provisions or highlighting specific plan provisions in communication materials in order to attract and retain employees.

Measuring Achievement of Human Resource Objectives

Management often will be interested in knowing whether benefit plans are successfully achieving their objectives. As with conducting benefit

3 Everett T. Allen, Jr., Joseph J. Melone, Jerry S. Rosenbloom, and Jack L. VanDerhai, *Pension Planning*, 8th ed. (New York: Irwin/McGraw-Hill, 1997), pp. 33-34.

plan comparisons, various approaches can be used, depending on the particular evaluative objective. Surveys of the industry can be a starting point to assess overall competitive standing. Employee surveys may be conducted to determine satisfaction levels with the current program and what particular modifications could be implemented to enhance existing programs. Focus groups can be conducted to receive more detailed explanations on how programs meet employee needs. Other approaches use actuarial calculations. For instance, an employer attempting to assess the adequacy of a retirement program can compute income-replacement ratios for representative groups of employees at varied income levels and with various lengths of service. These determinations can then be balanced against target replacement ratios. Alternatively, retirement patterns could be examined to determine whether the employer is achieving desired results in replenishing its workforce.

At times, a purely quantitative measure of HR objectives may not be available. Nevertheless, the benefits manager must be cognizant of the human resource rationale for plan sponsorship and monitor on an ongoing basis the effectiveness of the plans in meeting strategic organizational objectives.

Assessing and Managing Program Risks

Benefit managers should have a clear understanding of the risks the organization is assuming, the costs involved, and a means for managing them. This assessment can only be completed by understanding the characteristics of the benefits program, its historical experience, the demographic characteristics of the employee group and the alternative risk-management techniques that are available in the marketplace. Risk-management techniques must be understood in terms of how they operate and how they are priced. Only with this information can the benefits manager prudently assess whether the selected strategy is attuned to the organization's needs.

A benefits manager must evaluate program risk by comparing past plan outcomes or modeling possible future outcomes under various risk-management techniques. For instance, a benefits manager could model life insurance claims experience over various time intervals, comparing insured approaches to a cost-plus approach. The benefits manager may alter the cost-plus approach by adding either an individual or aggregate stop-loss reinsurance feature. See Chapter 43 for a description of these two stop-loss approaches. Even putting an existing insured benefit plan out for bid can result in compelling plan savings. Many plan sponsors will develop a cycle for rebidding their benefit plans, although this cycle will be modified if marketplace conditions are known to be changing, creating favorable pricing opportunities.

Legal/Regulatory Compliance

Benefit programs must comply with a number of requirements. These include reporting and disclosure requirements (as discussed earlier in the Communications section); certain performance requirements in connection with claims for benefits (as discussed in the Benefit Plan Delivery section above); and fiduciary, funding, and other requirements as prescribed by various pieces of legislation that have been passed over the years. Many compliance standards, particularly for retirement plans, were codified with the passage of the Employee Retirement Income Security Act of 1974. ERISA set the framework for employer responsibilities in sponsoring a benefit plan; establishing broad and pervasive funding; and actuarial, fiduciary, and reporting and disclosure requirements. Since its initial passage, ERISA has been amended on an ongoing basis incorporating new public policy initiatives into this important legislative framework.

A number of benefits compliance issues stem from the fact that benefit plans enjoy preferential treatment under the tax code. Such preferential tax treatment seems constantly to be reevaluated as the legislatures change. An examination of benefits legislation will indicate that almost every budget act for a number of prior years has had a number of benefits-related provisions. This was especially true during the 1980s and early 1990s in light of the large federal deficits. Benefit plans were seen as a potential source of federal revenue generation and the preferential tax treatment was especially in jeopardy if the benefit plans were not seen to be benefiting a substantial segment of an employer's workforce. Hence, a fair amount of regulatory activity and compliance testing revolves around the issue of ascertaining who "benefits" under a benefit plan and whether highly compensated employees are unduly benefited.

The Tax Reform Act of 1986 was especially significant in that it instituted rigorous mathematical testing to ascertain whether a benefit plan is nondiscriminatory. Although the Section 89 testing requirements for health and welfare plans were subsequently repealed, as discussed later, rigorous mathematical testing to ensure nondiscrimination is required for tax-qualified pension and profit-sharing plans. This testing has become a major ongoing benefits administration function since passage of this legislation. Subsequently the Small Business Job Protection

Act of 1996 saw an initiative to simplify some of these testing procedures in the hope of encouraging small employers to extend pension coverage.

As the millennium began and at the time this chapter was being written, the stage was set for major benefits legislation in a number of potential areas. The disappearance of federal budget deficits and the appearance of a budget surplus could mean governmental policy regarding employee benefits will be less revenue-driven. Much more in the realm of pension reform may be possible. Favorable tax treatment may be extended for retirement savings, and bipartisan support seems possible. In the health arena, a patients' bill of rights, Medicare reform, adding prescription drug coverage to Medicare, and more universal access to health coverage are all on the federal health policy agenda.

Adhering to legal requirements involves not only compliance with federal legislation but attention to state and local statutes and requirements. Legal compliance also involves ongoing monitoring of pronouncements from regulatory agencies and the judicial review of the courts, which rule on many of the intricacies that federal and state statutes fail to address. Benefits managers must continually review benefits trade periodicals and specialized compliance publications to remain current on benefit plan legal requirements.

Monitoring the External Environment

As with any type of business activity, employee benefits management is affected by the larger business context in which these programs operate. Recently, the environmental context in which benefits programs operate has experienced major change and has been a major determinant in setting the agenda for benefits plan design and other aspects of the benefits management activity. A review of some of these environmental factors helps illustrate the myriad factors a benefits manager must monitor and gives a sense of some emerging trends that are likely to impact the benefits management activity in future years:

- General business and competitive conditions.
- Governmental policy.
- Workforce demographic shifts.
- New product development.
- New organizational structures.
- Technological enhancement and innovation.

General Business and Competitive Conditions

In the new millennium, the emergence of a more integrated world economy exerted influence on benefit programs in a number of different ways. First and foremost, benefit costs were a major component of labor cost and accordingly had a direct impact on the competitiveness of industries in the global marketplace. After a reprieve of a few years, the health care industry began to experience significant cost escalation once again. Accordingly, the price rise in this single benefit program brought a need for action to control costs as these programs not only outpaced the general price level but were increasing more quickly than many companies' direct compensation costs. This extreme cost pressure resulted in a number of changes in the medical and health benefits offerings of companies. Companies redesigned their medical benefit programs, introducing new ways of delivering care and changed pricing strategies for these benefits; yet they balanced the need for these pricing strategies with tight labor markets that made it difficult to pass cost increases on to employees.

An integrated global marketplace also means that companies must attract and retain employees to remain competitive. Employee benefits are playing an increasingly important role in this. To remain competitive, firms must offer benefits plans that are competitive in design and in ease of access, utilizing state-of-the-art technology.

The growth of benefits consulting firms has been instrumental in bringing technological enhancements to the marketplace. The existence of these firms and their state-of-the-art capabilities have accelerated the trend towards benefits outsourcing. Interesting business combinations are emerging as some larger benefits consulting firms are merging with investment custodians, creating expanded record-keeping and financial services capabilities to plan sponsors. There are also other new entrants in the marketplace with new services being offered by e-health providers.

Governmental Policy

During the 1980s and 1990s, benefit programs were the subject of intense scrutiny as policymakers concentrated on reducing the federal budget deficit. Because many benefit programs are designed to coordinate with social insurance programs such as Social Security, Medicare, and Workers Compensation, benefit plans are affected not only by direct statutory and regulatory pronouncements but also by any alteration in governmental social insurance.

Policymakers also have become involved in benefit "protection" issues, such as employment nondiscrimination for persons with disabilities, required leave time for employees when they or family members are ill, legislation protecting employment rights for military personnel called into active service, further protections for employees covered by pensions, and nondiscrimination issues related to age. Many of these protections have been codified into law.[4]

Because all legislative initiatives that become law require clarifying the statute into regulations, the complete impact of the law unfolds over a period of years. Hence, those responsible for monitoring the external environment for benefit plans must be attuned to continuing regulatory pronouncements and judicial case determinations. At times, the necessity for clarification of the law is so pervasive that a second major law is required merely to fully implement the first measure. Such was the case with the Technical and Miscellaneous Revenue Act of 1988, which clarified many of the changes instituted by the Tax Reform Act of 1986 (TRA '86). So pervasive were the changes applicable to tax qualified retirement plans originally instituted by TRA '86, that it was not until five years later, on September 12, 1991, that the Treasury Department and the Internal Revenue Service issued the long-awaited, final regulations for qualified pension and profit-sharing plans. These final regulations amounted to a 600-page document.

At times, some of the policy initiatives of major regulatory bodies will directly conflict with each other. An example includes the requirement to make contributions into retirement accounts of the working aged to avoid age discrimination in employment and the Treasury Department's requirements to make mandatory distributions from these same retirement accounts in pursuit of tax revenues.

Beyond the need to conform to benefits laws, benefits managers must constantly monitor proposed benefits legislation. Numerous benefits measures were passed in the 1980s and 1990s that were either significantly modified, retroactively amended, or repealed outright before full compliance was required. The scuttled initiatives are still important because the deadline for original compliance often necessitates that organizations make an investment in systems modifications and data collection in order to comply. Many of these initiatives have been far-reaching

---

4 For a more comprehensive explanation of benefit protection issues consult the following laws: Consolidated Omnibus Budget Reconciliation Act of 1985, American with Disabilities Act of 1990, Older Workers Benefit Protection Act of 1990, Family Medical Leave Act of 1993, Uniformed Services Employment and Reemployment Rights Act of 1993, General Agreement on Tariffs and Trade of 1994, Mental Health Parity Act of 1996, and Health Insurance Portability and Accountability Act of 1996.

in their intents and effects. These initiatives have included proposals for expansive benefit plan compliance testing,[5] modifications in social insurance programs and their coordination with employer plans,[6] very substantial additions to federal annual reporting requirements on plan participant dependents,[7] and a fundamental reorganization of the U.S. health care delivery system.[8]

Passage and repeal of benefits legislation before implementation because of public outcry, inability to cost-effectively administer, or an immediate policy reversal creates an onerous responsibility for the man-

---

5 The Tax Reform Act of 1986 instituted comprehensive nondiscrimination testing for health and welfare plans, commonly referred to as Section 89. Originally, compliance was to occur for plan years beginning after the earlier of December 31, 1988, or three months after regulations were issued unless regulations were issued in 1987. Subsequently, President Bush signed a law on November 8, 1989 that abolished Section 89.

6 The Medicare Catastrophic Coverage Act of 1988 provided catastrophic benefits coverage through the Medicare program. Benefits under Part A of Medicare went into effect in 1989 while benefits under Part B were scheduled to commence in 1990. Congress approved the Medicare Catastrophic Repeal Act in November of 1989. Accordingly, Medicare participants were not required to pay an income surtax for 1989, and a supplemental Part B premium was repealed prospectively. Employers had to maintain Maintenance of Effort (MOE) provisions for 1989, whereby either additional benefits were provided to Medicare eligible retirees and their spouses or cash payments of up to $65 were provided to these same retirees. Compliance with the original legislation meant actuarial calculations for MOE and affected the calculation of *FAS 106* liabilities. It was not until the repeal legislation was passed that Congress clarified the FICA and FUTA exclusion of MOE payments.

7 The Omnibus Budget Reconciliation Act of 1993 (OBRA '93) required employers to annually report individuals covered by an employer's health plan (both employees and dependents) starting with the 1994 calendar year by February 28, 1995 to the Medicare/Medicaid Coverage Data Bank. This was particularly onerous to many employers who did not keep detailed electronic records of employee dependents within their human resource databases. On May 10, 1994, the Health Care Financing Administration (HCFA) published preliminary guidance on the employer reporting requirements. Near the time of issuance, HCFA and President Clinton's administration recommended that Congress pass legislation giving an 18-month delay on implementation of the requirement. The Labor/Health and Human Services/Education appropriations bill for fiscal year 1995 spending approved by Congress in the last week of September 1994 prohibited the Department of Health and Human Services from using federal funds in fiscal 1995 to implement the databank. Then HCFA announced in the first week of October 1994 that it was formally putting the requirements on hold.

8 President Clinton's health care plan was formally proposed in 1993. This legislative initiative would have resulted in a dramatic overhaul of the employer-sponsored health insurance system. Provisions included: (1) creating a series of regional cooperatives, (2) assessing 1 percent of continued payroll assessment in 1996 unless the employer irrevocably waived its right to sponsor a corporate alliance, (3) prohibiting the purchase of health coverage on a pretax basis through cafeteria plans or flexible spending accounts beginning January 1, 1997. Employers spent much of 1994 analyzing potential impacts to their plans and developing strategic responses while alternate bills were proposed by Congressional leaders. It was not until late 1994 that it was evident that this legislative initiative had stalled and that passage of health care legislation seemed unlikely in either 1994 or 1995.

ager of benefits programs because compliance activities and their attendant resource commitments must be approached as uncertain eventualities addressed in a prudent and discerning way, balancing the risks of immediate noncompliance with the costs of compliance. Some practitioners have noted the dangerous situation that the flurry of legislative reversals has caused, in that some practitioners will now refrain from immediate compliance and take a "wait and see" approach to see if the law will simply "go away."

Workforce Demographic Shifts

Demographic changes in the composition of the workforce have a profound impact on employee benefits plans. Transition from a homogeneous workforce primarily dominated by men with nonworking spouses to a workforce with a greater concentration of working mothers and nontraditional families has changed the nature of benefit plan offerings. A homogeneous workforce generally translated to "one size fits all" in benefits programs. These plans included less choice and were designed around needs of the traditional family model. Changing workforce demographics, coupled with advances in record-keeping technology and new product offerings, have spurred flexible benefit plan offerings that allow workers to customize their benefits program. Dependent care benefits also have become more important with more dual working couples, more single parents, and more aging parents.

Flexible benefits and family/life benefits often result in employee self-selection that affects the actuarial assumptions of programs and their cost underpinnings. Allowing employees to trade various benefit options results in the necessity to impute costs on an individual basis, and the pricing of plan offerings becomes an important exercise for the benefits manager. Benefits pricing will affect selection patterns by employees and hence will impact the risks attracted to a particular plan and, in the longer term, will impact ultimate costs. Pricing policies of other employers now have become important, too, as employees sometimes choose medical coverage on the basis of whether one employer provides cash payments for opting out of coverage.

The aging of the workforce has created greater interest in retiree health, capital accumulation, and pension programs. Because the aging of the workforce has important implications for social insurance programs such as Medicare and Social Security, the benefits manager must consider the impact to private employer-sponsored programs as the government modifies these social insurance programs. Many employer programs were designed to coordinate with Medicare and Social Security. Thus, any reduction in social insurance programs affects the adequacy of employer programs and is likely to erode targeted benefit levels or increase the costs of employer plans if the employer programs absorb the impacts of government retrenchment.

New Product Development

Innovation in a global systems economy means a more rapid introduction of new products and services in the marketplace. This creates opportunities for the benefits manager to better serve plan participant customers and more effectively administer benefit programs. An important aspect of a benefit manager's job involves developing a means to evaluate these new product/service offerings and to determine capabilities to integrate these products/services into existing plan offerings or administrative structures. This often is difficult to accomplish in practice. For instance, a benefits manager may identify substantial benefits to incorporating a disease-management program into an existing medical plan. A prescription management firm may have the expertise and systems to provide monitoring of drug utilization, increase greater utilization of generic drugs, and ensure greater quality control of the drug dispensing system through computer linkage to network pharmacies. While achieving these advantages, the benefits manager may need to integrate systems to ensure deductibles and co-insurance are merged and tracked for the dual systems; compare definitional differences between the old and new programs to ensure that discrepancies do not emerge when the program is introduced; and communicate changes in the way benefits will be accessed for plan participants. Dislocations that may occur may not be readily apparent and often surface as the new plan is introduced. For instance, certain drug therapies with inpatient hospitalizations or supplied with home health care visits could be potential areas where dislocations can surface.

The timing of new product/service introductions can be critical. Because plan changes necessitate a strategy for communicating changes to participants, they are typically introduced on plan year anniversary dates and communicated to plan participants in advance of open enrollment periods. This timing allows plan participants to make informed benefit selections coordinating elections under the medical plan, flexible spending accounts (FSAs), and so on. Plan anniversary dates often make the most sense because deductibles and copayment schedules often run on plan anniversary dates. However, sometimes when a plan year is not the calendar year, there can be arguments for transitioning on the calendar year. This becomes compelling when the plan change will impact a tax limitation that is measured on the calendar year. This would be the case for an amount that can be contributed to a dependent care expense account.

Benefits managers often must schedule reviews of programs and rebid plan offerings on a cyclical schedule and synchronize the benefits program planning function with the overall business planning cycle of the organization.

New Organizational Structures

Major transformations of organizational structures have occurred in the workplace, often with significant downsizings of the workforce. The elimination of various managerial levels within organizations, the flattening of hierarchical structures, the move toward decentralized organizations, the outsourcing of noncore activities, and greater use of specialized consulting services are among the trends shaping organizations. These changes, many of which are facilitated by changing technology and the more integrated global economy, have important implications for the benefits management function. Many plan designs were crafted with a very different workforce in mind. Therefore, benefits managers are called upon to redesign plans that are appropriate to the "new economy" organization. Benefits programs are now called upon to represent the strategic direction of the organization, to contribute to the firm's bottom line, and to achieve certain goals, such as retention, team performance, and so on. For instance, a retirement plan where the benefit is significantly affected by years of service can be a retention incentive. Profit-sharing plans can be designed to reward accomplishment of team-based goals.

As a firm is redesigned, benefits managers need to be involved in a variety of ways. Benefit managers can craft early retirement options such as window plans when downsizing occurs, and assess the cost shifts that occur in other benefit plans with organizational transition. For example, offering an early retirement window plan could have multiple effects on other benefit plans. More retirees could mean greater expense for a retiree health plan and shifts in the *FAS 106* liability, which must be shown on the balance sheet. If a pension plan is on the margin with passing nondiscrimination tests, a shift in the workforce may cause noncompliance, necessitating a redesign of the existing core pension benefit for the active remaining workforce.

Technological Enhancement and Innovation

As noted earlier, technological enhancement and innovation in plan administration play an important role in benefits management. Clearly, these are environmental factors that need to be monitored by the benefits manager. Ideally, the benefits manager is keeping abreast of this technological change and proactively planning its introduction in administrative and communication activities. At times, the pace of environmental technological change may surpass existing modes of doing business within the organization. Because many benefits programs require exchange of data with insurance carriers, third-party administrators, and consultants, the necessity to interface has major implications for the pace at which advanced technology must be introduced into the host company if it is to remain compatible with marketplace products. The use of compatible technology has profound effects on the efficiency with which programs can be run, the amount of rework that must be done in monitoring and processing transactions, and the level of timely and useful management information that can be made available to plan administrators and top executives. In short, the ability to keep pace with technological change and rapidly integrate advanced technology into an organization's administration and culture can significantly impact its efficiency and effectiveness in meeting customer satisfaction and valid needs.

THE OUTSOURCING ALTERNATIVE

In recent times, many organizations, both large and small, have explored the issue of whether to outsource benefits administration or retain this function as an internal human resource activity. Depending on the scope and complexity of the organization's benefits program, the outsourcing decision can be a complex one. Outsourcing can involve whole programs or certain functions within benefits programs. The manager of employee benefits is faced with some critical tradeoffs when it comes to an outsourcing decision, particularly if only portions of the benefits administration are outsourced. Outsourcing certain functions to third parties can result in fragmentation and lack of integration in the benefits information database. The procedures to access benefits and the manner in which benefits are communicated also can vary, causing confusion for plan participants. If outsourcing is chosen, the organization retains an oversight and supervisory role as well as the coordinating role to ensure benefits programs serve larger human resource and organizational objectives.

Outsourcing has become a very attractive alternative as organizations have downsized their workforces and jettisoned noncore business activities. Benefits administration has been a prime candidate for outsourcing because of the complexity of the function; the efficiencies attendant with specialized service providers; the ability of these specialized service providers to achieve beneficial pricing because of their business volume; and the ability of the service providers to more readily implement technological applications and to monitor the regulatory and market trends that occur within the employee benefits field. Some observers have noted that outsourcing has been especially attractive to organizations that have been faced with the necessity to upgrade their systems capabilities and make significant investments in advanced recordkeeping and communications technology.[9] Because many of these technological innovations have occurred within the last 15 years, most organizations have been confronted with the decision to retain or outsource benefits administration.

Introduction of new technology has affected the organizational design for employee benefits service delivery whether retained in-house or outsourced. Many organizations have created employee benefits service centers where benefits specialists equipped with the latest technology facilitate access to customer-driven processes and handle nonroutine queries accessing computer menus that summarize plan policies and provisions. This automated environment can electronically monitor telephone volume so that managers can reallocate service center human resources at high-volume times. This customer service delivery approach is the model used by consulting firms to administer a variety of plans that have been outsourced from multiple firms.

Despite the level of administrative delegation, the employer providing the benefits program is still considered the plan sponsor and will continue to retain the legal responsibilities related to plan sponsorship under federal law. Application of state insurance laws can vary, depending on whether a program is being provided as an insured arrangement by an insurance company, is self-funded, or is a contracted administrative-services type of contract. Therefore, the decision on which type of service provider and whether the organization will retain or outsource administration can have a different regulatory impact, which should be considered in choosing the appropriate administrative alternative. These issues are more complex within the multinational and truly global organization because of varied national insurance regulations, the ability to leverage financial and underwriting approaches across national boundaries, and the human resource issues of staff transfers between operating companies within different countries and the extent to which similar benefit structures will encourage or impede workforce mobility. In short, larger organizations

---

9 Rod Zolkos, "System Update Costs Overwhelm Benefit Departments," *Business Insurance*, Vol. 29, No. 10 (March 6, 1995), pp. 3, 6.

have more alternatives, and often these alternatives have implications that are interwoven with other strategic considerations for the firm

Decisions on whether to outsource the employee benefits administrative function can be quite different across different benefit programs as well. For instance, a national organization with a geographically dispersed workforce may find it advantageous to contract with a large managed care provider who in turn contracts with local and regional medical care providers. However, the same employer may find that it is more efficient to retain as an internal function the administration of a defined benefit pension plan because it is not subject to the same degree of regional difference and local market specialization.

SUMMARY AND CONCLUSIONS

Administering employee benefit plans is a multifaceted discipline that integrates broad managerial skills and thinking with a high level of technical expertise in a variety of specialty areas. Whether the majority of benefits management activities are retained within the organization or outsourced, benefits management almost always includes coordinating with other departments and groups, necessitating leadership, team building, and project management skills. The scope and nature of the internal organizational benefits plan function is contingent on both the organization's internal capabilities and the availability of external services. There are certain core activities and compliance requirements inherent in plan sponsorship. Management should clearly understand how these activities are affected by the rapidly changing and dynamic environmental context in which benefits plan management operates.

BIBLIOGRAPHY

Allen, Jr., Everett T., Joseph J. Melone, Jerry S. Rosenbloom, and Jack L. VanDerhei. *Pension Planning*, 8th ed. New York: Irwin/McGraw-Hill, Inc., 1997.

APPWP, *Health Notes*, September 15, 2000.

APPWP, *Pension Notes*, September 15, 2000.

Frost, Karen, Dale Gifford, Christine Seltz, and Ken Sperling. *Fundamentals of Flexible Compensation*, New York: John Wiley & Sons, Inc., 1993.

Hewitt Associates, *Employers to Face Double Digit Health Care Cost Increases for Third Consecutive Year*, October 23, 2000.

Hewitt Associates, *On Flexible Compensation*, January–February 1993.

Hewitt Associates, *Washington Status Report*, Vol. 10, No. 41 (October 10, 1994).

Pemberton, Carolyn and Deborah Holmes, eds; Celia Silverman, Michael Anzick, Sarah Boyce, Sharyn Campbell, Ken McDonnell, Annmarie Reilly, and Sarah Snider, *EBRI Databook on Employee Benefits*, 3rd ed. Washington, DC: Education and Research Fund, 1995.

Schultz, Ellen E. "State Street Enters the Benefits Business," *The Wall Street Journal*, December 7, 1995.

Shutan, Bruce. "Fidelity Pursuit Changing Face of 'Total' Benefits Outsourcing," *Employee Benefit News,* Vol. 9, No. 5 (May 1995).

Stright, Jay F., Jr., "The Revolution in Benefit Technology," Presentation at Employee Benefits Symposium, San Francisco, October 8–11, 1995.

Towers Perrin, "Congress Home for the Holidays—Wraps Up Budget Bill and Catastrophic Repeal; IRS Extends Qualified Plan Relief," *TPF&C Update*, November 1989.

Towers Perrin, "Employers Seeking People Strategies for Their E-Business," April 2000.

Towers Perrin, "The Nondiscrimination Rules: They're Finally Final," *TPF&C Update*, September 1991.

Truhlar, Gary, "Information Management Principles and Tools," Internal Memos, University of Pennsylvania, 1994–1995.

U.S. Department of Labor, *General Facts on Women & Job-Based Health Benefits*, April 2000.

U.S. Department of Labor, *In Brief: 1999 Form 5500*, February 2000.

Zolkos, Rod, "System Update Costs Overwhelm Benefit Departments," *Business Insurance,* Vol. 29, No. 10 (March 6, 1995).

CHAPTER 37

Cafeteria Approaches to Benefit Planning

Burton T. Beam, Jr.

INTRODUCTION

Employee benefit plans that provide employees with some choice in the types and amounts of benefits they receive have become quite common. Traditionally, the cost of the optional or supplemental benefits made available under these plans was borne by the employee on an after-tax, payroll-deduction basis. A significant number of employers have established benefit programs in which all or a large segment of the employees are permitted to design their own benefit packages by using a prespecified number of employer dollars to purchase benefits from among a number of available options. Almost a third of employers with more than 1,000 employees have full-fledged cafeteria plans (also referred to as flexible benefit plans or cafeteria compensation plans). Many more of these larger employers and numerous small employers make premium-conversion plans and/or flexible spending accounts (FSAs) available. Premium-conversion plans and FSAs are discussed later in this chapter.

While all employee benefit plans offering employee options might be viewed broadly as being flexible approaches to benefit planning, this chapter focuses primarily on those plans giving employees some choice in selecting the types and levels of benefits provided with employer contributions. The chapter first describes the structure of the plans available and continues by analyzing the reasons for employer interest in these plans, the historical barriers to their establishment, and the design decisions that must be made by employers.

A cafeteria plan can be broadly defined as any employee benefit plan that allows an employee some choice in designing his or her own benefit package by selecting different types or levels of benefits funded with employer dollars. At this extreme, a benefit plan that allows an employee to select a health maintenance organization (HMO) instead of an insured medical expense plan can be classified as a cafeteria plan. However, the more common use of the term *cafeteria plan* denotes something much more definite—a plan in which choices can be made among several different types of benefits and cash: that is, taxable and nontaxable benefits.

Prior to the addition of Section 125 to the Internal Revenue Code (IRC) by the Revenue Act of 1978, the use of cafeteria plans had potentially adverse tax consequences for an employee. If an employee had a choice among benefits that normally were nontaxable (such as medical expense insurance or disability income insurance) and benefits that normally were taxable (such as cash or life insurance in excess of $50,000), the doctrine of constructive receipt resulted in the employee being taxed as if he or she had elected the maximum taxable benefits that could have been obtained under the plan. Therefore, if employees could elect cash in lieu of the employer's medical expense plan, an employee who elected the medical expense plan would have taxable income merely because cash *could have* been elected. Obviously, this tax environment was not conducive to the use of cafeteria plans unless the only benefits contained in them were of a nontaxable nature.

Section 125 provides more favorable tax treatment to a cafeteria plan. As defined in that code section, such plans are those under which all participants are employees and under which all participants may choose among two or more benefits consisting of qualified benefits and cash. Qualified benefits include most welfare benefits ordinarily resulting in no taxable income to employees if provided outside a cafeteria plan. There are some exceptions, and the following benefits cannot be provided under a cafeteria plan: scholarships and fellowships, transportation benefits, educational assistance, no-additional-cost services, employee discounts, and long-term care insurance. However, one normally taxable benefit—group term life insurance in excess of $50,000—can be included. In general, a cafeteria plan cannot include retirement benefits other than a 401(k) plan.

Internal Revenue Service (IRS) regulations define the term *cash* as being broader than it would otherwise appear. In addition to the actual receipt of dollars, a benefit in a cafeteria plan is treated as cash if two conditions are met. First, the benefit is not specifically prohibited by Section 125. This means that the benefit cannot defer compensation or be among the list of previously mentioned exceptions. Second, the benefit is provided on a taxable basis. This means that either (1) the cost of the benefit is paid by the employee with after-tax dollars on a payroll-deduction basis, or (2) employer dollars are used to obtain the benefit, but the employer reports the cost of the benefit as taxable income for the employee. The IRS regulations, for example, allow the inclusion of group automobile insurance in a cafeteria plan, with the value of the coverage being reported as taxable income for each employee who selected the benefit. They also allow long-term disability coverage to be provided on an after-tax basis so disability income benefits can be received tax-free.

As long as a cafeteria plan meets the Section 125 requirements, the issue of constructive receipt is of no concern. Employees have taxable income only to the extent they elect normally taxable benefits. An employer can have a benefit plan that offers choice but does not meet the statutory definition of a cafeteria plan. In such a case, the issue of constructive receipt will come into play if the plan contains benefits that normally result in taxable income.

TYPES OF PLANS

Core-Plus Plans

Probably the most common type of full-fledged cafeteria plan is one that offers a basic core of benefits to all employees, plus a second layer of optional benefits from which an employee can choose the benefits he or she will add. These optional benefits can be "purchased" with dollars, or credits, given to the employee as part of the benefit package. If an employee's credits are inadequate to purchase the desired benefits, the employee can make additional purchases with after-tax contributions or with before-tax reductions under an FSA.

The following is an example of the plan of one employer. The basic benefits provided to all employees include term life insurance equal to 1½ times salary, travel accident insurance, medical expense coverage for the employee and dependents, and disability income insurance. Employees also are provided with "flexible credits" equal to from 3 percent to 6 percent of salary, depending on length of service. Each year, an employee is permitted to use his or her flexible credits to purchase benefits from among several options, including additional life insurance equal to one times salary, term life insurance on dependents, dental insurance for the employee and dependents, an annual physical examination for the employee, up to two weeks of additional vacation time, and cash. If an employee's flexible credits are insufficient to purchase the desired benefits, additional amounts can be contributed on a payroll-deduction basis. In addition, a salary reduction may be elected for contributions to an FSA that provides dependent care benefits.

A variation of this approach is to have the core plan be an "average" plan for which the employee makes no contribution. The employee then may receive credits if certain benefits are reduced. These credits can be used either to increase other benefits or, if the plan allows, to increase cash compensation.

Modular Plans

Another type of plan allows an employee a choice among several predesigned benefit packages. Typically, at least one of the packages involves no employee cost, and, if an employee selects a more expensive package, the employee contributes to the cost of the package. Some employers also may include a bare-bones benefit package with cash paid to an employee who selects it.

Under some plans using this modular approach, the predesigned packages may have significant differences, some being superior to others in certain respects, and inferior in others. Other plans using this approach have virtually identical packages, with the major difference being in the options offered for medical expense coverage. For example, the plan of one large bank offers a traditional insured plan, two HMOs, and a preferred provider organization.

Payroll Deductions and Salary Reductions

Under some cafeteria plans, employees are allowed to allocate only a predetermined employer contribution for benefits. Other cafeteria plans are so designed that employees can obtain additional benefits with optional payroll deductions or salary reductions.

Many cafeteria plans that provide a wide array of benefits allow an employee to elect an after-tax payroll deduction to obtain additional benefits. For example, under a cafeteria plan, an employee might be given $200 per month with which to select varying types and levels of benefits. If the benefits the employee chooses cost $240, the employee has two options—either to decrease the benefits selected or to authorize a $40 payroll deduction. Even though the payroll deduction is on an after-tax basis, the employee will gain to the extent that the additional benefits can be selected at a lower cost through a group arrangement than in the individual marketplace.

Section 125 also allows employees to purchase certain benefits on a before-tax basis through the use of a premium-conversion plan or an FSA. Premium-conversion plans or FSAs, which are technically cafeteria plans, can be used by themselves or incorporated into a more comprehensive cafeteria plan. They are most commonly used alone by small employers who are unwilling to establish a broader plan, primarily for cost reasons. The cafeteria plans of most large employers contain one or both of these arrangements as an integral part of the plan.

Before-tax salary reductions reduce taxable income for federal income tax purposes. In most (but not all) states, they also reduce the income subject to state tax.

Premium-Conversion Plans

A premium-conversion plan (also called a premium-only plan) allows an employee to elect a before-tax salary reduction to pay his or her premium contribution to any employer-sponsored health or other welfare benefit plan. For example, an employer might provide medical expense coverage to employees at no cost but make a monthly charge for dependent coverage. Under a premium-conversion plan, the employee can pay for the dependent coverage with a before-tax salary reduction.

As a rule, premium-conversion plans are established for medical and dental expenses only. If such plans are used for group term life insurance, the cost of coverage in excess of $50,000 must be reported as income, which defeats the purpose of the salary reduction. If these plans are used for disability income coverage, benefits will be taxable as noncontributory employer-provided coverage, because the amount of any salary reduction is considered to be the employer's money.

Flexible Spending Accounts

An FSA allows an employee to fund certain benefits on a before-tax basis through a salary reduction, which then is used to fund the cost of any qualified benefits that are included in the plan. However, they most commonly are used for medical expenses not covered by the employer's plan and dependent care expenses.

The amount of any salary reduction is credited to an employee's reimbursement account, and benefits are paid from this account when an employee properly files for such reimbursement. The amount of the salary reduction must be specified on a benefit-by-benefit basis prior to the beginning of the plan year during an enrollment period. Once made, changes are allowed only under certain circumstances, discussed later in this chapter.

When FSAs first appeared, one issue faced by employers was whether to limit benefit payments to the amount of a current account balance or allow an employee at any time during the year to receive benefits equal to the amount of his or her total annual salary reduction. For example, if an employee contributed $50 a month to an FSA to cover the cost of unreimbursed medical expenses, during the first month of the plan there would be only $50 of the $600 annual contribution in the account. If the employee incurred $400 of unreimbursed medical expenses during the month, should he or she be allowed a reimbursement of $50 or the full $400? The objection to allowing a $400 reimbursement is that the employer would lose $350 if the employee terminated employment before making any further contributions. Consequently, most plans limited aggregate benefits to the total contributions made at the time benefits are received. However, IRS regulation changed the rules, and medical and dental expense FSAs now must allow an amount equal to the full annual contribution for these benefits to be taken as benefits anytime during the year. Therefore, the employee in the previous example would be entitled to a benefit payment of $400 after the first month. However, this regulation does not apply to other types of benefits such as dependent care under an FSA, and employers still have a choice of reimbursement policies for these.

If the monies in the FSA are not used during the plan year, they are forfeited. Since forfeited funds are considered plan assets, they can be used only for the payment of benefits and reasonable administrative expenses. Under ERISA rules, forfeitures may be used to do the following:

- Defray the administrative costs of the plan.
- Protect the underwriting integrity of the plan. This includes the use of these funds to reimburse the plan for benefits paid that exceed a terminated employee's contributions.
- Reallocate contribution to the following plan year. Such reallocations must be on a per capita basis for all participants and cannot be based on amounts each employee originally contributed.

An election to participate in an FSA not only reduces salary for federal income tax purposes, it also lowers the wages on which Social Security taxes are levied. Therefore, those employees who are below the wage-base limit after the reduction will pay less in Social Security taxes, and their future income benefits under Social Security also will be smaller. However, the reduction in benefits will be very small in most cases unless the salary reduction is very large. It should be noted that the employer's share of Social Security tax payments also will decrease, and in some cases the employer's savings actually may be large enough to fully offset the cost of administering the FSA program.

REASONS FOR EMPLOYER INTEREST

Employer interest in cafeteria plans can be attributed to a number of factors. Many employers are concerned that employees may not fully appreciate the value of the benefits provided under conventional plans and hope that, by giving an employee a specified total number of dollars for purchasing benefits and a list of available benefits and their costs, the employee will better perceive the total value of the benefits and the nature and relative costs of the individual benefits themselves.

The inflexible benefit structure of conventional employee benefit plans does not adequately meet the varying benefit needs of different employees and often leads to employee dissatisfaction. For example, single employees or older employees whose children are grown may see little value in substantial life insurance benefits. Also, the combined benefits of working couples may provide excessive coverage, the cost of which could be used for other purposes. Employers view the cafeteria approach to benefit planning as not only a means of more effectively meeting the benefit needs of different employees at a particular time but also as a way of enabling an individual employee to better meet his or her needs as they change over time. Closely related is the feeling among employers that cafeteria plans are viewed as being less paternalistic than conventional employee benefit programs.

Employers also see the cafeteria approach to benefit planning as providing opportunities to control escalating benefit levels and costs associated with inflation and with the need to comply with federal and state legislation. (In fact this is the sole reason many employers establish cafeteria plans.) Because a cafeteria plan essentially is a defined-contribution plan, rather than a defined-benefit plan, it provides a number of opportunities for controlling increases in benefit levels and costs. For example, it may encourage employees to choose medical expense options with larger deductibles to more efficiently use the fixed number of dollars allotted to them under the plan. It also may enable the employer to pass on to employees any increased benefit costs arising out of compliance with legislation prohibiting age and sex discrimination or mandating additional benefits. In addition, because increases in employer contributions for benefits are not tied directly to increases in benefit costs, the employer has the opportunity either to maintain its contributions at a fixed level or to grant percentage increases for benefits that are below the actual overall increase in employee benefit costs. However, for self-funded plans, the employer's ability to contribute a targeted dollar or percentage amount is contingent on how well the employer (or its plan administrator) can prospectively calculate plan costs.

POTENTIAL BARRIERS

The potential barriers to employers establishing a cafeteria plan have included, among other things: (1) the legislative environment; (2) the difficulty in satisfying nondiscrimination rules; (3) potential problems associated with unwise benefit selection by employees; (4) negative attitudes on the part of employees, insurers, and unions; (5) adverse selection; and (6) increased implementation and administration costs. However, many of these barriers have been largely overcome or are less of an obstacle than in the past.

The Legislative Environment

Undoubtedly the largest obstacle to cafeteria plans for several years was the unsettled federal income tax picture. This picture was finally clarified in 1984 by the passage of the Tax Reform Act and the IRS issuance of regulations governing cafeteria plans. Since then, the number of cafeteria plans has grown significantly, particularly among large firms. However, almost every year either a federal tax bill alters Section 125 in some way, new IRS regulations are issued, or proposals for change are made by elected officials. The benefits that can be included in a cafeteria plan are changed, the nondiscrimination rules are altered, or the rules for FSAs are "clarified."

Nondiscrimination Rules

Section 125 imposes complex nondiscrimination tests on cafeteria plans, initially causing many employees to view the establishment of a cafeteria plan unfavorably. If these tests—an eligibility test, a concentration test, and a contributions and benefits test—are not met, highly compensated employees or key employees, or both, must include in gross income the value of the taxable benefits that could have been chosen under the plan. However, other employees suffer no adverse tax consequences.

The nondiscrimination tests are usually met by a full-fledged cafeteria plan that applies to all employees. However, particular care must be exercised in designing a plan that either covers only a segment of the employees or has only a small percentage of employees participating. The latter situation often occurs with FSAs.

The Eligibility Test

Cafeteria plans are subject to a two-part eligibility test, both parts of which must be satisfied. The first part of the test stipulates that no employee be required to complete more than three years of employment as a condition for participation and that the employment requirement for each employee be the same. In addition, any employee who satisfies the employment requirement and is otherwise entitled to participate must do so no later than the first day of the plan year following completion of the employment requirement, unless the employee has separated from service in the interim.

The second part of the test requires that eligibility for participation must not be discriminatory in favor of highly compensated employees, who are defined as any of the following: officers; shareholders who own more than 5 percent of the voting power or value of all classes of the firm's stock; employees who are highly compensated based on all facts and circumstances; or spouses or dependents of any of the above.

The eligibility test uses Table 37–1, which is contained in IRS regulations and can best be explained with an example:

An employer has 1,000 employees, 800 nonhighly compensated and 200 highly compensated. The percentage of nonhighly compensated employees is 80 percent (800/1,000), for which the table shows a "safe-harbor" percentage of 35. This means that, if the percentage of nonhighly compensated employees eligible for the plan is equal to at least 35 percent of the percentage of highly compensated employees eligible, the plan satisfies the eligibility test. Assume that 160 people, or 80 percent of the highly compensated employees, are eligible. Then at least 28 percent, or 224, of the nonhighly compensated employees must be eligible (0.80 × 0.35 = 0.28 and 0.28 × 800 = 224). The table also shows an unsafe-harbor percentage of 25 percent. Using this figure instead of 35 percent yields 160 employees. If fewer than this number of nonhighly compensated employees are eligible, the eligibility test is failed.

If the number of eligible nonhighly compensated employees falls between the numbers determined by the two percentages (from 160 to

T a b l e   37–1

IRC Section 125 Eligibility Test Safe- and Unsafe-Harbor Percentages

Nonhighly Compensated Employee Concentration Percentage	Safe-Harbor Percentage	Unsafe-Harbor Percentage
0—60	50	40
61	49.25	39.25
62	48.50	38.50
63	47.75	37.75
64	47	37
65	46.25	36.25
66	45.50	35.50
67	44.75	34.75
68	44	34
69	43.25	33.25
70	42.50	32.50
71	41.75	31.75
72	41	31
73	40.25	30.25
74	39.50	29.50
75	38.75	28.75
76	38	28
77	37.25	27.25
78	36.50	26.50
79	35.75	25.75
80	35	25
81	34.25	24.25
82	33.50	23.50
83	32.75	22.75
84	32	22
85	31.25	21.25
86	30.50	20.50
87	29.75	20
88	29	20
89	28.25	20
90	27.50	20
91	26.75	20
92	26	20
93	25.25	20
94	24.50	20
95	23.75	20
96	23	20
97	22.25	20
98	21.50	20
99	20.75	20

224 employees in this example), IRS regulations impose a facts-and-circumstances test to determine whether the eligibility test is passed or failed. According to the regulations, the following factors will be considered: (1) the underlying business reason for the eligibility classification, (2) the percentage of employees eligible, (3) the percentage of eligible employees in each salary range, and (4) the extent to which the eligibility classification is close to satisfying the safe-harbor rule. However, the regulations also state that none of these factors alone is determinative, and other facts and circumstances may be relevant.

The Concentration Test

Under the concentration test, no more than 25 percent of the tax-favored benefits provided under the plan can be provided to *key employees*. A key employee of a firm is defined as any person who at any time during the current plan year or the preceding four plan years is any of the following:

- An officer of the firm who earns from the firm more than 50 percent of the IRC limit on the amount of benefits payable by a defined-benefit plan. This amount is $70,000 in 2001, subject to indexing. For purposes of this rule, the number of employees treated as officers is the greater of 3 percent or 10 percent of the firm's employees, subject to a maximum of 50. In applying the rule, the following employees can be excluded: persons who are part-time, persons who are under 21, and persons with less than six months of service with the firm.
- One of the 10 employees owning the largest interests in the firm and having an annual compensation from the firm of more than $35,000 in 2001. The amount is subject to indexing.
- A more-than-5-percent owner of the firm.
- A more-than-1-percent owner of the firm who earns more than $150,000 per year.
- A retired employee who was a key employee when he or she retired or terminated service.

This test is a particular problem if an employer has a large percentage of key employees and if they, being higher paid, contribute large amounts to FSAs.

Contributions and Benefits Test

Cafeteria plans cannot discriminate in favor of highly compensated participants with respect to contributions or benefits. Section 125 states that a cafeteria plan is not discriminatory if the plan's nontaxable benefits and total benefits (or the employer contributions allocable to each) do not discriminate in favor of highly compensated employees. In addition, a cafeteria plan providing health benefits is not discriminatory if contributions under the plan for each participant include an amount equal to 100 percent of the health benefit cost for the majority of similarly situated (i.e., family- or single-coverage) highly compensated employees or to at least 75 percent of the health benefit cost for the similarly situated participant with the best health benefit coverage.

Contributions exceeding either of these amounts are nondiscriminatory if they bear a uniform relationship to an employee's compensation.

Unwise Employee Benefit Selection

Often employers are concerned that many employees may not have the expertise to select the proper benefits from among the alternatives offered under a cafeteria plan. Among other things, unwise employee benefit selection may result in inadequate employee protection following a catastrophic loss, in employee dissatisfaction with the plan, and in an increased potential for liability suits against the employer. To avoid, or at least minimize, these problems, employers offering cafeteria plans must maintain effective ongoing communication programs aimed at educating (and perhaps even counseling) employees about the full implications of various benefit choices available to them. However, despite the employer's best efforts, there remains a risk that the communication of incomplete or incorrect information may give rise to increased corporate liability. An employer with a strong conviction that the organization has a moral obligation to protect employees from financial injury through faulty decisions may offer core benefits within a cafeteria plan that the employee may not waive.

Negative Attitudes

Although negative attitudes on the part of employees, insurers, and unions have abated over the years, these reactions have served as obstacles to the institution of a cafeteria plan.

Employees

Negative reactions on the part of employees to an announced proposal to convert from a conventional fixed benefit plan to a cafeteria plan can arise from a variety of sources: suspicion concerning the employer's motivation in making the change, a fear that some important long-standing benefits may be lost, and an apprehension about now having to make choices among benefits of which the individual employee has little knowledge. Because employee support is critical if a cafeteria plan is to be truly successful, the employer must be willing to commit the time and resources necessary to combat these negative attitudes through adequately informing the employees about the reasons for the proposed program, its advantages and disadvantages, and its future implications for them. Moreover, by soliciting the opinions of employees on their perceived benefit needs and incorporating those findings into the decision-making process, the employer will not only help to allay initial employee concerns but also minimize negative employee attitudes once the cafeteria plan has been instituted.

Insurers

The growth of the cafeteria approach to benefit planning also has been inhibited by the reluctance or inability of some insurance companies to underwrite the optional benefits an employer may wish to include in a cafeteria plan, or to provide meaningful assistance in connection with the implementation and administration of such a plan. While few insurers seem unwilling to experiment with almost any new concept, most have been concerned with the problem of adverse selection because of employee choice. Although the potential for adverse selection is a real problem that must be faced in underwriting a cafeteria plan, insurers are finding it is possible to control the problem at an acceptable level by incorporating certain safeguards in plan design. As a result, the number of insurers willing to underwrite cafeteria plans and provide administrative services for them has grown, and this barrier has been overcome to a significant degree.

Unions

Unions generally have had a negative attitude toward employee benefit plans that contain optional benefits. Union management often feels that bargaining over optional benefits is contrary to the practice of bargaining for the best benefit program for all employees. As a result, most cafeteria plans do not apply to union employees.

Adverse Selection

When employees are allowed choice in selecting benefits, the problem of adverse selection arises, because those employees who are likely to have claims will choose the benefits that will minimize their out-of-pocket costs. For example, an employee who previously selected a medical expense option with a high deductible might switch to a plan with a lower deductible if medical expenses are ongoing. An employee who previously rejected dental insurance or legal expense benefits is likely to elect these benefits if dental care or legal advice is anticipated in the near future.

It should be noted that adverse selection is a problem whether a plan is insured or self-funded. It also exists outside of cafeteria plans if choice is allowed. However, the degree of choice within a cafeteria plan tends to make the potential costs more severe unless actions are taken to combat the problem.

Several techniques are used to control adverse selection in cafeteria plans. Benefit limitations and restrictions on coverage can be included if a person wishes to add or change coverage at a date later than initial eligibility. This technique has been common in contributory benefit plans for many years. Another technique is to price the options accordingly. If an option is likely to encourage adverse selection, the cost to the employee for that option should be increased above the level that would have been charged if the option had been the only one available. Such pricing has been difficult in the past but is becoming easier and more accurate as more experience with cafeteria plans develops. The control of adverse selection is also one reason for the use of modular plans. If, for example, the medical expense plan in one option is likely to encourage adverse selection, the option may not include other options for which adverse selection is also a concern (such as dental or legal expense benefits). To further counter increased costs from the medical expense plan, the option also may offer minimal coverage for other types of benefits.

Administrative Costs

Cafeteria plans involve a number of additional developmental, administrative, and benefit costs over and above those associated with conventional employee benefit programs. Because of the greater complexity associated with employee choice, employers establishing cafeteria plans encounter higher initial and continuing administrative costs associated with, among other things, the need for additional employees to administer the program, additional computer time to process employee choices, and a more comprehensive communication program. However, as cafeteria plans have grown in popularity, numerous vendors have developed products that enable employers to carry out these administrative functions in a more cost-effective manner.

There are also other factors associated with cafeteria plans that might lead to increased benefit costs. For example, if an employee elected to divert a portion of the employer's contribution from a deferred compensation benefit (such as a profit-sharing plan) to an option involving current benefit payments (such as health insurance), the employer would lose the opportunity to recapture that contribution if the employee were to leave the company before becoming fully vested. Also, the establishment of a cafeteria plan may involve what one benefit consulting firm terms *buy-in* costs for the employer. While conventional employee benefit plans generally require employees to contribute at a uniform rate for group life insurance, cafeteria plans usually charge employees at rates that vary according to age. Because a shift from a conventional benefit plan to a cafeteria plan would increase substantially the cost of group life insurance for older employees, the employer may be required to subsidize that group.

CONSIDERATIONS IN PLAN DESIGN

Before committing itself to the establishment of a cafeteria program, an employer must be sure a valid reason exists for converting the company's traditional benefit program to a flexible benefit approach. For example, if there is strong employee dissatisfaction with the current benefit program in general, the solution may lie in clearly identifying the sources of dissatisfaction and making appropriate adjustments in the existing benefit program, rather than shifting to a cafeteria plan. However, if employee dissatisfaction arises from widely differing benefit needs on the part of the employees, conversion to a cafeteria plan may be appropriate. Beyond having a clearly defined purpose for converting from a traditional benefit program to a cafeteria program and being willing to bear the additional administrative costs associated with a flexible benefit approach, the employer faces a number of considerations in designing the plan and the system for its administration.

Plan Design

Numerous questions must be answered before a cafeteria plan can be designed properly. What benefits should be included in the plan? How should benefits be distributed between the basic and optional portions of the plan? How should an employee's flexible credits be calculated? To what extent should employees be allowed to change their benefit selections?

Benefits to Be Included

Probably the most fundamental decision in designing a cafeteria plan is determining what benefits to include. If an employer wants the plan to be viewed as meeting the differing needs of employees, it is important to receive employee input concerning the types of benefits perceived as being most desirable. An open dialogue with employees undoubtedly will lead to suggestions that every possible employee benefit be made available. The enthusiasm of many employees for a cafeteria plan will then be dampened when the employer rejects some, and possibly many, of these suggestions for cost, administrative, or philosophical reasons. Consequently, it is important that certain ground rules be established regarding the benefits that are acceptable to the employer.

The employer must decide whether the plan should be limited to the types of benefits provided through traditional group insurance arrangements or be expanded to include other welfare benefits, retirement benefits, and, possibly, cash. At a minimum, it is important to ensure that an overall employee benefit program provide employees with protection against all major areas of personal risks. This suggests that a benefit program make at least some provision for life insurance, disability income protection, medical expense protection, and retirement benefits. However, it is not necessary that all these benefits be included in the cafeteria plan. For example, most employers have retirement plans separate from their cafeteria plans because of Section 125 requirements. Other employers make a 401(k) plan one of the available cafeteria options.

One controversial issue among employers who have adopted cafeteria plans is the extent to which cash should be an available option. Arguments in favor of a cash option often are based on the rationale that employees should not be forced to purchase optional benefits if they have no need or desire for them. In addition, cash may better fulfill the needs of many employees. For example, a young employee's greatest need may be the down payment for a home, and an older worker's greatest need may be the resources to pay college tuition for children. Some employers may believe the primary purpose of a cafeteria plan is to provide employee benefits only and not current income. If more than a modest amount of cash is available, employees will view the plan as a source of increasing their wages or salary, rather than as an employee benefit. Therefore, the amount of cash that may be withdrawn often is limited. Also, experience has shown that the majority of employees will elect nontaxable benefits in lieu of cash.

In some respects, a cafeteria plan may be an ideal vehicle for providing less traditional types of benefits. Two examples are extra vacation time and child-care. Some plans allow an employee to use flexible credits to purchase additional days of vacation. When available, this has proven a popular benefit, particularly among single employees. A problem may arise, however, if the work of vacationing employees must be assumed by nonvacationing employees in addition to their own regularly assigned work. Those not electing extra vacation time may feel resentful of doing the work of someone else who is away longer than the normal vacation period.

In recent years, there has been increasing pressure on employers to provide care for the children of employees. This represents an additional cost if added to a traditional existing benefit program. By including child-care benefits in a cafeteria plan, those employees using them can pay for their cost, possibly with dollars from an FSA. However, lower-paid employees may be better off financially by paying for child-care with out-of-pocket dollars and electing the income tax credit that is available for dependent care expenses. This issue is discussed more fully in Chapter 19 of the *Handbook*.

Another important consideration is the number of benefits to include in the plan. The greater the number of benefits, particularly optional benefits, the greater the administrative costs. A wide array of options also may be confusing to many employees and require the need for extra personnel to counsel employees or answer their questions.

A final concern is the problem of adverse selection. As previously mentioned, this problem can be controlled by proper plan design.

Basic Versus Optional Benefits

As mentioned earlier, many cafeteria plans consist of two portions—a core of basic benefits received by all employees, and a second layer of optional benefits that may be purchased by each employee with flexible credits provided by the employer. Once a list of benefits has been determined, it is necessary to decide which benefits should be basic core benefits and which should be optional. At a minimum, the basic benefits should provide a reasonable level of protection against the major sources of personal risk and probably should include at least some life insurance, disability income, medical expense, and retirement benefits (unless these are included under a separate retirement plan). Some employers have included additional but less-critical benefits, such as travel accident insurance or dependent life insurance in the basic portions of their plans.

The optional layer of the plan may include additional benefits not included in the basic plan and additional amounts of coverage for some of the basic plan's benefits, such as additional amounts of life insurance on the employee. In addition, the employee may have the option of electing alternative benefits to some or all of the benefits provided in the basic plan. For example, for an additional cost an employee may elect a medical expense plan with a smaller deductible. The plan will be more meaningful to employees if all or most employees can purchase at least some of the optional benefits.

Because of the current provisions of Section 125, cafeteria plans that include both taxable and nontaxable benefits should not include deferred compensation arrangements other than those involving 401(k) plans in the optional benefit layer if the issue of constructive receipt is to be avoided.

Level of Employer Contributions

An employer has considerable latitude in determining the number and value of flexible credits made available to employees to purchase benefits under a cafeteria plan. These credits may be a function of one or more of the following factors: salary, age, family status, and length of service.

The major difficulty arises when the installation of a cafeteria plan is not accompanied by an overall increase in the amount of the employer's contributions to the employee benefit plan. It generally is felt that each employee should be provided with enough flexible credits so he or she can purchase some optional benefits, which, together with basic benefits, are at least equivalent to the benefits provided by the old plan. This probably will lead an employer to determine the amount of flexible credits necessary for each employee to receive an amount of flexible credits comparable to the difference in value between the benefits under the old plan for that employee and the basic benefits under the new cafeteria plan.

Including a Premium-Conversion or an FSA Option

A premium-conversion or an FSA option under a cafeteria plan enables employees to lower their taxes and, therefore, increase their spendable income. Ignoring any additional administrative costs, there probably is no reason not to offer this option to employees for such benefits as dependent care. However, salary deductions for medical expenses pose a dilemma. While they save taxes for the employees, they also may result in an employee obtaining nearly 100 percent reimbursement for medical expenses. This may have the effect of negating many of the cost-containment features contained in the employer's medical expense plan.

Employees' Ability to Change Benefits

Because the needs of employees change over time, a provision regarding employees' ability to change their benefit options must be incorporated into a cafeteria plan. This typically occurs on an annual basis, because Section 125 requires that benefit elections under a cafeteria plan be made prior to the beginning of a plan year. These elections cannot be changed during the plan year, except under certain specified circumstances if the plan allows such changes. While there is no requirement that a plan allow these changes, allowances for some or all of them are included in most plans.

IRS regulations regarding election changes had remained unchanged through most of the 1990s. In 1997, however, regulations with proposed changes were issued, and employers were allowed to use either the old or the new regulations. In early 2000, the proposed regulations were made final with some modifications; they must be used for plan years beginning on or after January 1, 2001. At the same time, the IRS issued another set of proposed regulations to address issues not covered by the new regulations. In early 2001, a few changes were made to the 2000 final regulations and the 2000 proposed regulations were made final with some modifications.

The regulations allow new cafeteria plan elections for specified *changes in status*. In addition, the regulations specify that any new cafeteria plan elections are allowed only if an employee, spouse, or dependent gains or loses eligibility for coverage, and the cafeteria plan election change corresponds with that gain or loss in coverage. The acceptable changes in status include the following:

- Legal marital status (including marriage, death of a spouse, divorce, legal separation, or annulment).
- Number of dependents (resulting from birth, adoption, commencement or termination of an adoption proceeding, or death).
- Employment status (the termination or commencement of employment by the employee, spouse, or dependent).
- Work schedule (a reduction or increase in hours of employment by the employee, spouse, or dependent, including a switch between part-time and full-time employment, a strike or lockout, and commencement of or return from an unpaid leave of absence).
- Dependent status under a health plan for unmarried dependents.
- Residence or worksite of the employee, spouse, or dependent.

The final regulations address several specific issues. For example, increases or decreases in group term life insurance coverage and disability income coverage are allowed for all change-in-status events. The regulations also allow employees to make election changes if, during the plan year: (1) the cost of a benefit plan increases or decreases significantly, (2) a new benefit or benefit package is offered or a benefit or benefit package is eliminated or curtailed significantly, or (3) a change is made in the coverage of an employee's spouse or dependent. Note that when there is a significant decrease in the cost of a benefit or benefit package, those employees who previously had not participated in the cafeteria plan may elect to participate for purposes of that benefit or benefit package. In addition, an employee can make a change as a result of an open-enrollment change by a spouse or dependent when their employer's plan has a different period of coverage. Finally, an employee can make a change as a result of a spouse's or dependent's change under his or her own cafeteria plan as long as that change conforms to the regulations.

Even if none of the above rules is met, election changes are permitted in cafeteria plans as a result of changes in coverage or premiums because of the Health Insurance Portability and Accountability Act (HIPAA); Consolidated Omnibus Reconciliation Act (COBRA); eligibility for Medicare; or legal judgment, decree, or order resulting from divorce, legal separation, annulment, or change in legal custody.

Two situations may arise to complicate the issue of benefit changes. First, the charges to employees for optional benefits must be adjusted periodically to reflect experience under the plan. If the charges for benefits rise between dates on which employees may change benefit selections, the employer must either absorb these charges or pass them to the employees, probably through increased after-tax payroll deductions. Consequently, most cafeteria plans have annual dates on which benefit changes may be made that are the same as the dates when charges for benefits are recalculated. This also usually relates to the date on which any insurance contracts providing benefits under the plan are renewed.

The second situation arises when the amount of the employees' flexible credits are based on their compensation. If an employee receives a pay increase between selection periods, can the employee be granted additional flexible credits to purchase additional benefits at that time? (Is this a change in family status that will allow additional benefits to be elected?) Under most cafeteria plans, the flexible credits available to all employees are calculated only once a year, usually at a date prior to the date by which any annual benefit changes must be made. Any changes in the employee's status during the year will have no effect on an employee's flexible credits until the following year on the date a recalculation is made.

Communication

The complexity of a cafeteria plan, compared with a traditional employee benefit plan, requires additional communication between the employer and the employees. Since the concept is new, employees will have many questions. It is doubtful if all these questions can be answered through written information, and group and individual meetings between employees and representatives of the employer probably will be required to explain the operation of the plan. Obviously, the need for these meetings will be greatest when a cafeteria plan is first installed and for newly hired employees.

Many employees unaccustomed to making choices about benefits also will seek advice concerning their benefit selections, and an employer must decide whether to require employees to make their selections with little guidance or to provide counseling services. Either alternative may have legal as well as moral implications. When counseling is provided, it is imperative that it be provided by a qualified and competent staff.

Updating the Plan

Any employee benefit plan will need periodic updating. However, some unique situations exist for cafeteria plans. Because such plans are advertised as better meeting the needs of individual employees, the employer must continually monitor the changing needs and desires of employees. As employee interest increases for benefits not included in the plan, they should be considered for inclusion. If little interest is shown in certain available benefits, a decision must be made regarding their continued availability, and, if certain optional benefits are selected by most employees, perhaps they should be incorporated as basic benefits.

The employer is faced with a dilemma if employee benefit costs rise more rapidly than the increases in flexible credits made available to the employees. For example, if the allocation of flexible credits is a function of an employee's salary, which is usually the case, an increase of 10 percent in salary results in an increase of 10 percent in flexible credits. However, at the same time, the employee may be faced with an increased cost of 20 percent to retain the optional benefits currently selected under the plan. The employee must either reduce benefits or pay for a portion of the increased cost through additional payroll deductions. Obviously, neither situation is appealing to the employee. In deciding whether to increase flexible credits further, so the employee can choose the same benefits as previously selected, the employer is faced with the difficult task of balancing employee satisfaction with benefit cost control.

CONCLUSION

This chapter has discussed the concept of cafeteria approaches to benefit planning, the attractiveness of cafeteria plans to employers and employees, obstacles to their establishment, and basic issues in their design. Chapter 38 continues the discussion of flexible benefits from an operational viewpoint.

CHAPTER 38

Cafeteria Plans in Operation

Melvin W. Borleis

The number of cafeteria plans in the United States has been growing steadily since the mid-1970s. As soon as the preferential tax treatment of these plans was codified by the addition of Section 125 to the Internal Revenue Code (IRC or code) in 1978, a number of employers adopted them, at least to permit employees to make what were previously taxable medical plan contributions on a tax-deductible basis or to establish flexible spending accounts (FSAs), or both. While these basic arrangements were communicated to employees as being flexible benefit plans designed to meet diverse employee needs and help increase spendable income by reducing federal tax, it is most likely that the tax savings were, in many instances, the prime motivation for their existence. Later, as the plans became more commonplace and they began to offer many more choices than before, they were used to achieve additional objectives including: permitting the employee some true discretion over how his or her compensation is received, giving the employer an advantage over competitors in recruiting new employees, and creating a more favorable impression of the employer to promote productivity and help decrease turnover.

Then, as employers became more familiar with such plans, attention turned to using them to help control spiraling employer costs in the health care area. As this purpose has materialized, plans have become more complex, and now typically include a selection among a number of indemnity type plans, health maintenance organizations (HMOs), preferred provider organizations (PPOs), and other managed care arrangements. One object of increased choice is clearly how to encourage the employee, through skillful pricing techniques, to select the most efficient medical and/or dental arrangement. This chapter describes how these plans operate to achieve all these objectives, from the rudimentary objective of the delivery of tax-efficient compensation, to cost-transfer and cost-control techniques, to meeting employee needs. Emphasis is on the "nuts and bolts" issues involved in operating these somewhat complex plans, as opposed to the design and strategic issues discussed in Chapter 37.

HOW CAFETERIA PLANS OPERATE

A cafeteria plan is defined by the IRC, in Section 125(d)(1)(B), as a plan that permits the participant to choose between two or more benefits consisting of cash and qualified benefits. The inclusion of a requirement to have a choice involving cash is important, because it means that a choice between two otherwise nontaxable benefits, such as an HMO or a medical indemnity plan, would not meet the definition of a cafeteria plan for purposes of the law. Therefore, the employer could provide that choice without the existence of a cafeteria plan. However, the concept of salary reduction (reducing one's taxable income by some amount and directing that amount be used to purchase nontaxable benefits) is a choice between taxable cash and a qualified benefit. This choice, assuming that the benefit plan in question is not solely a 401(k) plan, would require the existence of a cafeteria plan. Thus, the choice between cash and an otherwise nontaxable benefit is a necessary, as well as a sufficient, condition to have a cafeteria plan.

A cafeteria plan is an intriguing device, in that by itself it does not have to provide any benefits in a traditional sense. Most traditional benefit plans provide specified benefits to participants in certain events, such as disability or death. The cafeteria plan simply permits the participant to choose between other benefit plans or cash. If such cash would already have been paid to the employee, say in the form of salary, the plan itself may not necessarily be providing a direct benefit other than the benefit of tax avoidance. Certainly, if the employer makes independent contributions to the cafeteria plan, those contributions constitute a benefit. In essence though, what a cafeteria plan does is direct contributions to, and participation in, other benefit plans. As such, the cafeteria plan is relatively simple in concept but more involved in operation.

To some extent, employers offered benefit choices to employees long before there were flexible benefit plans. Many contributory plans permitted employees to elect the level at which they would participate.

An example might be to offer group term life insurance to employees on an after-tax contributory basis and to permit the employee to elect one, two, or three times pay as coverage, with contributions varying based on the election. Such an arrangement does not meet the the definition of a cafeteria plan, nor does it require the existence of one, but nonetheless offers the employee a choice in the level of coverage he or she desires. However, permitting the employee to reduce salary by $100 per month and have $1,200 placed in a medical spending account annually is a choice between *a taxable cash amount* and *a nontaxable medical benefit* and, therefore, requires the existence of a formal cafeteria plan. Both types of choices can be integrated into one program for any given employer, and the employer may communicate all choices to the employee as part of a flexible benefit plan. However, only one of the choices would truly require the existence of a formal "cafeteria plan" as defined in the IRC. From the employee's standpoint, the flexible benefit plan would include all the choices but, from a legal standpoint, only certain choices would be considered under the cafeteria plan. Thus, there is a distinction between the appearance of the plan (the way the plan is presented to participants) and the provisions in the actual cafeteria plan document itself. For purposes of this chapter, the term cafeteria plan is used to mean a legally defined plan that meets all the criteria of Section 125 of the IRC, while *flexible benefit plan* is used to represent the plan communicated to employees, since this latter plan may contain more choices and elements than the former.

It is possible to have a cafeteria plan that includes after-tax contributions from the employee, but there seems to be little or no advantage in this structure, because such contributory benefit plans are permitted without the use of the cafeteria plan. Today, most employers offering flexible benefit plans that include after-tax employee contributions may communicate those benefits as part of the flexible benefit plan but do not include them in the formal cafeteria plan document. Again, there is a distinction between the presentation of the plan and the plan itself.

The Role of a Cafeteria Plan

The role of the cafeteria plan can best be seen by examining the flow of contributions to other plans controlled by the cafeteria plan. In a traditional (noncafeteria) benefit structure, as shown in Figure 38–1, three kinds of benefits are provided. "Benefit A" represents benefits paid for solely by the employee. These might include such optional benefit plans as long-term disability coverage or a contributory group life insurance

F I G U R E   38–1

Traditional Benefit Plan Structure

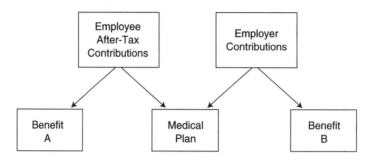

plan. "Benefit B" represents those plans funded or provided solely by employer contributions. Included here may be the pension plan, any employer-provided welfare coverage, and paid time off. Lastly, the structure includes a medical plan to which both the employee and the employer contribute. The arrows in Figure 38–1 represent the contributions to these various benefit plans.

Figure 38–2 illustrates this same set of benefits using a cafeteria plan. In this case, the cafeteria plan serves solely to permit the employee to make what were previously taxable contributions on a now pretax basis. All other benefits and contributions in the program have remained as they were in the traditional structure.

In Figure 38–3, the cafeteria plan has been expanded to include flexible spending accounts (FSAs), the choice of three different medical plans, and an option to receive cash if there are any unused employer contributions. Employer contributions are directed to the cafeteria plan and dispersed from there, based on employee election. This does not mean all employer contributions are funneled through the cafeteria plan—only those over which the employee has some choice. The employer could— and this is the most common case—continue to pay part of the medical plan cost directly. This is simply a function of deciding how much control the employer wishes to give to the employee. For example, if the annual cost of Medical Plans 1, 2, and 3 were $4,000, $3,500, and $3,300, respectively, the employer contribution to the cafeteria plan could be any amount desired. Assume Plan 2 for $3,500 provides coverage under the traditional medical indemnity plan in place prior to creating the cafeteria plan and the employer wants to ensure that employees have enough "flexible dollars" to buy coverage under that plan without making any additional contributions. In this case, the employer can contribute $3,500 to

Basic Cafeteria Plan

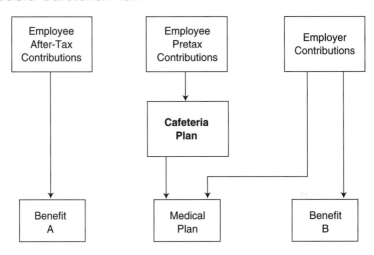

the cafeteria plan, and, if an employee elects medical coverage under Plan 2, the full employer contribution is consumed by that choice. If the employee elects Plan 1, costing $4,000 for a higher level of coverage, he or she must contribute the additional $500 through salary reduction. Also, if this employee wants a medical FSA, the amount placed in the FSA would have to come from salary reduction. There could be no cash election in either of these situations because there are no remaining unused flexible dollars. However, if the employee were to elect Medical Plan 3, an HMO or other managed care arrangement, with a cost of $3,300, there would be $200 remaining that could be taken as taxable cash or placed in the spending account.

   If the employer did not wish the full cost of the coverage to be directed by the employee, it might contribute $3,300 to the medical plan directly and only $200 to the cafeteria plan. In this case, the cost of Plan 2, as far as the cafeteria plan is concerned, would be $200, Plan 1 would be $700, and Plan 3 would be $0. The cost to the employee (paid by salary reduction) for Plan 2 still is $0, and $500 for Plan 1, and Plan 3 yields $200 of available cash. The same result is achieved; only the contribution and the cost of the options as communicated to the participants are different.

   If the employer wished to transfer some of the cost of Plans 1 and 2 to the employee, the employer contribution to the medical plan might still be $3,300 directly, but the contribution to the cafeteria plan would be perhaps only $100 as opposed to the $200 in the example. In this situation,

F I G U R E   38–3

Expanded Cafeteria Plan

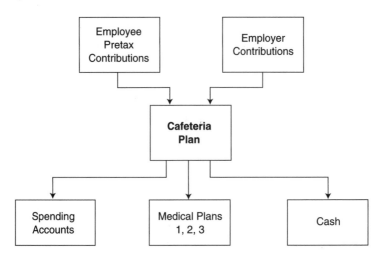

Note: Those benefits provided solely by employee after-tax contributions and those paid for solely by the employer (Benefits A and B, respectively, in Figure 38–2) have been removed from this figure because they are assumed to be outside the cafeteria plan.

it would now cost the employee (through salary reduction) $100 to purchase coverage under Plan 2 and $600 to purchase coverage under Plan 1, and now the election of Plan 3 would produce only $100 of taxable cash. This also can be used as an incentive to attract people to Plan 3, which may be a plan designed to control medical costs more efficiently than the other plans.

Naturally, any combination of contributions and option pricing is possible to achieve plan objectives. However, employers have quickly determined that it pays to provide a sufficient number of flexible dollars as an employer contribution, so employees can purchase the same coverage they had prior to the creation of the cafeteria plan without additional cost. At least this may be the case in the first year of the cafeteria plan, and it is particularly true if no employee contributions were ever taken for medical coverage before implementation of the cafeteria plan. However, some employers may include some cost transfer immediately upon implementation of a flexible benefit plan.

In Figure 38–4, the cafeteria plan has been expanded to include a number of other benefit choices and a new source of flexible dollars has been added, those that result from trading other benefits. The most common benefit traded is paid time off, so an employee might elect to trade a

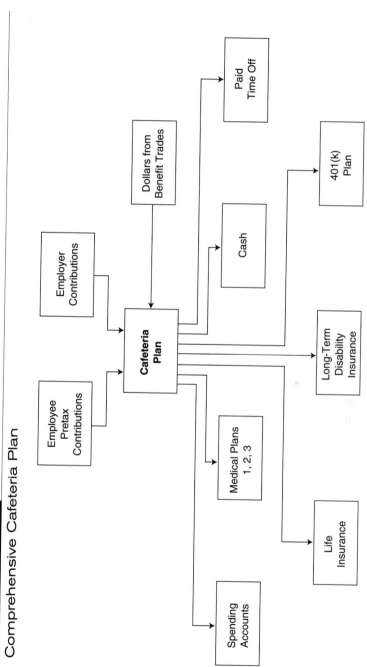

FIGURE 38-4

Comprehensive Cafeteria Plan

few days of vacation time for additional flexible dollars to be spent on other benefits. (The concept of vacation trading is discussed later in this chapter.) The figures show cafeteria plans in varying degrees of complexity. However, the role of the cafeteria plan in all cases is to direct the contributions to and, therefore, the participation in the other plans. Plans maintained outside the cafeteria plan to which employees make contributions on an after-tax basis can continue to be so provided and can even be included on the employee election form and communicated as part of the flexible benefit plan provided by the employer. They do not have to be part of the cafeteria plan.

Salary Reduction Implications

The cornerstone of many cafeteria plans is the concept of salary reduction. Through salary reduction, the employer uses a cafeteria plan to permit employees to make otherwise taxable contributions to existing traditional plans on a pretax basis. The most common example of this is using a cafeteria plan to permit employees to make monthly contributions to a medical plan and to have those contributions be extracted from salary before the application of federal or Social Security tax. This arrangement has come to be known as "salary reduction."

It is important to note that, while the employee views this arrangement as a reduction and redirection of the amount in question to purchase benefits, what really is happening is that the amount has become an employer contribution. For example, consider an employee earning $25,000 annually as taxable income and contributing $83.33 a month after taxes toward the cost of providing family coverage under a medical indemnity plan. The employee sees the $83.33 as a salary deduction and considers it a direct cost to himself or herself. Under a cafeteria arrangement, the $83.33 deduction becomes a salary reduction and is taken from salary before the application of tax. In this case, the employee is still likely to consider the salary *reduction* as his or her own contribution. However, the reason that the $83.33 now escapes taxation is because it is now considered as an employer contribution to a medical plan. Thus, for tax purposes, this employee is assumed to have an annual wage of $24,000 and the employer is making a $1,000 ($83.33 × 12 [rounded]) nontaxable contribution to the medical plan on his or her behalf.

The concept of salary reduction is important to the operation of many cafeteria plans, because it serves as a primary means of creating contributions to the plan. However, while such salary reductions result in nontaxable employer contributions to these plans, the employee will view the contribution as his or her own. This is particularly true in the case of flexible spending accounts being funded wholly from salary reduction amounts.

Salary reduction has implications beyond simply providing a method for making contributions to a cafeteria plan that are free from federal income tax. For example:

■ To the extent the salary reduction reduces an employee's annual compensation below the Social Security wage base ($80,400 in 2001) or, if the salary prior to any reductions does not exceed this amount, the employee will pay less Social Security tax. The payment for Medicare tax (applicable to all salary) is also reduced. Likewise, the tax paid by the employer on behalf of this employee will also be less, representing a cost savings for the employer. It should be noted that if a 401(k) plan is a part of the cafeteria plan, contributions to that plan (even though they pass through the cafeteria plan) do not escape consideration for Social Security and Medicare.

■ Social Security benefits will be computed based on the new, reduced salary. While this has minimal impact (the reduction in ultimate benefit is small compared with the Federal Insurance Contributions Act (FICA) tax saving), it is nonetheless a result of salary reduction.

■ Since most states and other municipal taxing entities base their income tax on the amount taxable for federal purposes (at least as far as wages are concerned), the use of salary reduction also can serve to reduce these taxes. However, each state and local government has its own laws in this regard and they should be reviewed before establishing a cafeteria plan. Also, a number of states include salary reduction amounts in compensation for purposes of determining the tax for unemployment insurance and workers' compensation.

■ Other benefit plans may be affected. Group life insurance, long-term disability, and sick-leave plans may base benefits on actual salary. Pension and profit-sharing plans also may need to be revised to reflect the desired level of compensation on which benefits are based.

■ The new pay could affect those eligible for overtime or similar base-pay-related payments. Bonus policies also should be reexamined.

■ The new salary amount is used for personal financial purposes, such as eligibility for a mortgage and other credit applications.

■ The employer also may need to recognize a difference between a salary reduction and a salary deduction. If an employer were providing medical coverage at no cost to an employee and the employee is on an authorized leave of absence, the employer might continue coverage during such leave. (The employer does not have to do this, but many do.) If the employer, however, required a monthly contribution from the employee for the coverage while the employee was working, chances are the employer would want that contribution to continue during periods of unpaid leave. The argument can be made that the sample employee, who is now earning $24,000 a year (as opposed to the $25,000 before the cafeteria plan), truly has a salary of $24,000 and is now covered by an employer-provided (free from contribution by the employee) medical plan.

It is interesting to note that the above issues appear only because of salary reduction. Had the employee in the example above been hired at a salary of $24,000 and had the employer been providing the medical coverage at no cost to the employee (a structure yielding the same financial result as the salary-reduction approach), none of these issues would be likely to arise. Of course, such other considerations as the competitiveness of starting salaries, the involvement of the employee in the medical plan, and the way employees view their direct compensation and benefits would have to be addressed. All these issues should be evaluated when considering any significant amounts of salary reduction.

Creating and Spending Flexible Dollars

As discussed in Chapter 37, while flexible benefit plans come in different sizes and shapes and may be presented to employees as having significantly differing structures, all such plans have as their core element the creation and spending of flexible credits or dollars. Because these plans serve to direct contributions to other benefit plans as employees choose to participate in them, the flexible benefit plan must have a source of credits or dollars that can be so directed. The remainder of this chapter refers to this medium of exchange as flexible dollars. Regardless of whether a flexible benefit plan is a simple salary-reduction type, a reduction-to-core type, a modular or a prepackaged plan, or a plan offering a broad array of choices and exchanges, it will, at its innermost level, look and operate the same as any other flexible benefit plan. This is true because the primary purpose of the plan is to provide a mechanism for the participant to create flexible dollars and a means for those dollars to be spent. The only differences are the number of sources of flexible dollars and the number of ways they can be expended. This can be seen by further analysis of the possible types of flexible benefit plans.

■ *Salary-Reduction Arrangements.* Employees elect to reduce salary, using the approach discussed earlier in this chapter, and direct that portion of their income to buy other benefits. In the simplest case, this may involve reducing salary to pay for medical plan contributions and possibly to fund a medical spending account or a dependent care account, or both. Even in this rudimentary structure, the flexible plan is facilitating the creation and spending of flexible dollars. In this case, there is only one means by which the employee can create flexible dollars—that of salary reduction. There are three ways these dollars can be spent: to pay premiums to a medical plan, to fund a medical care spending account, to fund a dependent care spending account, or any combination thereof.

■ *Core-Plus Options.* The employer provides the traditional benefit programs as a core program with lower levels of coverage than in the original plans. The employer is saving money (because plans providing lesser coverage are assumed to have less cost associated with them), and the employer passes along some portion of that savings to the employee in the form of an employer contribution to the flexible benefit plan. The employee can then use this contribution to purchase additional benefits to bring his or her coverage back up to the level originally provided under the traditional program, to purchase other offered benefits, or (if the plan permits) to take all or part of the difference in cash. Should the employee desire to purchase more benefits than can be bought with the flexible dollars provided by the employer, additional dollars may be created through salary reduction. This popular flexible benefits plan design still exhibits the same characteristics of creating flexible dollars and spending them. In this case, there are two sources of flexible dollars: employer contributions that result from reducing the level of coverages in the traditional benefit plans, and salary reduction. The employee may have more places to spend those dollars, including a cash election and spending accounts.

■ *Modular or Prepackaged Plans.* The only difference between this type of flexible benefit plan and the plan described above is that the employee may not select individual benefit coverages independently from one another. Rather, the benefit plans are prepackaged in modules or groups that must be selected in their entirety. For example, if the employee wants the better medical coverage, he or she may have to select a higher amount of life insurance, because this latter benefit is packaged with the former. These arrangements had, in the past, been thought to be easier to administer and were designed to further eliminate some elements of adverse selection. However, the plans are not exceptionally popular with employees, because they do not permit the employee the full range of possible choices, and their use to control adverse selection has been shown to be unnecessary. Nonetheless, these structures still involve the creation and spending of flexible dollars.

■ *Full-Choice Plans.* In these arrangements, employees are permitted to choose among a wide variety of benefits and may have a greater number of flexible dollars to spend. Here, the employer provides the employee with a set amount of flexible dollars, may permit salary reduction, and also may permit the employee to trade existing benefits (such as excess vacation time) for yet more flexible dollars. These dollars then could be spent on a wide array of benefits, including cash elections, deposits to 401(k) plans, and FSAs. However, the internal structure of this flexible benefit arrangement still involves the creation of flexible dollars and the spending of these dollars to purchase desired coverages.

Thus, one could conclude that all flexible benefit plans operate in essentially the same manner. They revolve around the creation and spending of flexible dollars or credits. It is possible in any of the structures discussed above to incorporate after-tax contributions. Thus, an employee could pay for a long-term disability plan or group term life insurance in excess of $50,000 with traditional after-tax contributions, while paying for group life insurance up to $50,000 and other benefits with pretax flexible dollars that have been created from any number of sources.

Sources of Flexible Dollars

There are a variety of ways to create flexible dollars. First, existing employer contributions to some or all of the benefits to be provided can be made to the flexible benefits plan and redirected by the employee. Additionally, new employer contributions can be used, but this increases the employer's cost for the plan. Employees can create flexible dollars through the use of salary reduction or by selling off vacation time that would otherwise be taken in the next year. Prior vacation that has already been carried forward might be frozen by the employer and sold off to create flexible dollars as well. Using carry-forward vacation for this purpose can result in a cost saving, because the number of dollars given for an hour or day of vacation can be frozen until all such time is consumed. Further, carry-forward vacation can be eliminated.

Additional sources of flexible dollars can come from reducing the benefit program to a lesser level or by the employee's election of lesser coverage or nonelection of unneeded coverage.

Spending Flexible Dollars

The flexible dollars created in the flexible benefit plan can be used to provide coverage under any of the following:

- Medical indemnity plans, including those with preferred provider organizations (PPOs).

- Health maintenance organizations.
- Dental plans.
- Vision care plans.
- Flexible spending accounts.
- Group term life insurance, including accidental death and dismemberment insurance.
- Short-term disability insurance.
- Long-term disability insurance.
- 401(k) plans.
- Cash.
- Vacation or other time-off plans.
- Adoption assistance plans.

Flexible (tax-free) dollars cannot be used for scholarships or fellowships; transportation benefits (such as van-pooling); educational benefits; long-term care insurance or plans; certain de minimis benefits, such as those described in Section 132 of the IRC (including dependent term life insurance); or meals and lodging. With the number of sources of flexible dollars available and the number of ways they can be spent, a wide variety of combinations is possible in the plan design.

USING CAFETERIA PLANS TO CONTROL COSTS

As the costs of benefit plans have continued to rise, primarily because of increasing medical costs, employers have effectively used cafeteria plans as a framework within which such cost increases could be managed.

Controlling Medical Plan Costs

There are two ways that medical cost control can be achieved through a cafeteria plan. The first is to transfer a portion of the cost to the employee or the government. The second is to use the mechanism to provide an incentive for employees to participate in plans that encourage more efficient delivery of health care. The former results in an immediate savings to the employer, while the latter has a longer-term payoff for both the employer and the employee. To illustrate the use of a cafeteria plan to effect cost transfer, consider an employer who is providing an indemnity-type medical plan with a cost per employee unit of $3,500 per year. Assume also that the employee is making a contribution toward that cost of $60 per month, or $720 a year on an after-tax basis. This represents a traditional benefit structure and is shown in column I of the chart in Figure 38–5.

Under the traditional approach to funding this medical plan, the employee's contribution is $720 a year after tax and the employer's is $2,780 per year. The true cost to the employee on an after-tax basis is $720 per year. As shown in column II, if a cafeteria plan is introduced into the structure and is used to permit the employee contribution on a pretax basis, the employee still contributes $720 per year and the employer $2,780 per year; but the employee's real cost would be reduced to $504 per year, resulting in a savings of $216 for the employee. However, if, as shown in column III, concurrent with the introduction of the cafeteria plan the employer were to raise the employee premium $120 from $720 per year to $840 per year, the employer cost of the plan would decrease by $120 to $2,660 per year, and the new $840 per-year contribution on the part of the employee would have a net cost of $588. Thus, the employer cost is decreased and the real (after-tax) cost to the employee also is decreased. In essence, the employer has transferred part of the cost to the employee by raising the annual employee contribution and part of the cost to the government by consuming some of the tax savings that would otherwise have passed to the employee. Taken to its extreme, the employer could have increased the employee cost to well over $1,000 per year and, at the assumed tax rate of 30 percent, still not altered the after-tax cost to the employee. However, since employees still view the pretax salary reduction amount as their own contribution, such a plan design would not likely have been popular when first implemented. (For purposes of determining the figures above, a 30 percent rate has been used to represent the combination of federal taxes as well as Social Security taxes.) The num-

F I G U R E   38–5

Medical Plan Contributions–Cost Transfer

	I Before Flex	II After Flex A	III After Flex B
Employee	$ 720	$ 720	$ 840
Employer	$2,780	$2,780	$2,660
After-tax cost to employee*	$ 720	$ 504	$ 588

* Assumes a 30% rate for the combination of federal taxes and Federal Insurance Contributions Act (FICA).

bers will, of course, vary depending on the tax rate assumed, but 30 percent seems reasonably conservative.

Another method of transferring cost through a cafeteria plan involves the use of multiple medical plans. Assume that an employer had provided a fairly lucrative medical plan to employees at no cost to them and this plan had a cost of $3,500 per year per employee unit. This plan is called "Medical Plan 1" as shown in Figure 38–6. Assume further that two additional medical plans are created: Plan 2 is not quite as lucrative as Plan 1 and is estimated to cost $3,000 per employee unit per year, and Plan 3 is yet a lesser benefit plan and is estimated to cost $2,800 per employee unit per year.

To encourage employees to participate in Plan 2, the employer might contribute $300 per year to the cafeteria plan for each person who selects Plan 2. This could be directed to a spending account, used for other benefits, or possibly taken in cash. If the employee wanted to participate in Plan 3, the employer would contribute $400 to a spending account or permit the employee to take this amount in cash. The advantage of this arrangement to the employee is that he or she can use the money in the spending account to cover expenses, such as eyeglasses, that would typically not be covered under even the most generous comprehensive medical plan. Of course the money in the spending account also can be used to pay deductibles and coinsurance amounts.

The advantage to the employer is clear, in that, if all employees switched from Plan 1 to Plan 2, the employer would save $200 per employee. This savings comes from the fact that Plan 2 provides lesser benefits and, therefore, has a lesser cost. To the extent that benefits are less and claims remain the same, the cost has been transferred to the employee. It should be noted here that the employer will never realize the full amount of

F I G U R E   38–6

Cost Control Using Multiple Medical Plans

	Real Cost	Spending Account
Medical Plan 1	$3,500	0
Medical Plan 2	$3,000	$300
Medical Plan 3	$2,800	$400

savings because of adverse selection. In the worst possible case of adverse selection, the employer could lose a substantial amount. This results if all employees who do not have medical claims elect to participate in Plan 3, thus receiving $400 each from the employer, and all those who typically had claims remain in Medical Plan 1 and claims are the same as they were in the previous year. In this case, the employer has simply given away $400 to each employee who did not incur any medical claims. In that first year, adverse selection has created a loss for the employer.

The remedy for this situation is to adjust the prices for Plan 1 in the following year. Perhaps in the next year, that plan may require an employee contribution, and the amount given to encourage people to move to Plan 3 might remain the same. Additionally, changes may be made in Plan 1 to increase deductibles or copayment amounts to compensate for the adverse selection. This, in turn, may necessitate changes in Plans 2 and 3.

Thus, the design and pricing of medical plan options in a cafeteria plan is an ongoing process. Each year, prices and incentives can be adjusted to achieve the desired result. Five additional points regarding cost transfer through the use of a cafeteria plan remain to be made.

■ There is an absolute limit to the amount of cost that can be transferred to employees in any situation. This will be a function of the compensation levels of the employees involved. Once that limit is reached, additional cost transfer is counterproductive.

■ The real purpose in using multiple medical plans as shown in Figure 38–6 is not to create employer savings by using an incentive that is less than the real differential between the plans, but to encourage employees into plans that may provide slightly lesser benefits or that may promote more efficient delivery of health care services. To the extent this is achieved, some measure of cost control is possible.

■ The difference between most medical plan options (other than a choice between an indemnity plan and an HMO or PPO) usually is the level of deductible, co-payment, and the maximum out-of-pocket expense that can be borne by the employee. Care must be taken in setting these values, because, in achieving the objective of cost transfer, one may begin to cause the plan to fail to meet its primary objective of providing benefits to those truly in need. Raising the deductible and/or the co-payment amount for an employee who is seriously ill, incurring significant medical expenses, and in dire financial need may not be in the best interest of all concerned.

■ As the differences between these plans become more complex, it becomes more and more difficult for employees to make informed choices about them.

■ Lastly, it is not the cafeteria plan that has saved any cost; it is the fact that cost has been transferred to the employee and that lesser benefits have been provided. The cafeteria plan is simply the mechanism used to facilitate this and the mechanism itself has a cost. The maximum employer savings occurs by simply changing from Plan 1 to Plan 3 as the employer-provided plan with no contribution to a cafeteria plan; however, this is not likely to be as popular with employees.

Controlling Total Benefit Costs

The previous examples deal solely with costs for medical plans. This is appropriate, because the medical plan offers the largest potential savings in any cafeteria plan arrangement. Many of the other plans require only minimal contributions and, therefore, present limited cost-saving opportunities. However, to the extent that any employee contributions to any plan that previously were being made on an after-tax basis are transferred to a pretax basis, the employer will have some cost savings. For all those employees who are earning below the Social Security wage base, the employer's contribution to Social Security on any salary reduction amounts represents reduced cost. This, also, is true, regardless of salary level, for the Medicare tax.

Also, the concept of employer contributions that can be directed to purchase benefits applies equally across all benefit plans. Thus, an employer could limit cost increases in the benefit package as a whole by opting for what is referred to as a *defined contribution approach*. In this case, the employer fixes the amount of contribution it will make to the benefit plan as a whole, contributes that amount to the cafeteria plan, and the employee directs that amount to be spent as he or she wishes. If additional amounts are needed to purchase the same benefits in future years, as will most certainly be the case, those amounts will come from the employee, unless the employer decides to increase its contribution. The employer, though, exercises this control.

Another means of controlling costs involves the use of vacation trades. Permitting employees to purchase time off by using credits created by electing lesser levels of other benefits or through salary reduction does result in less salary expense. Of course, it also means that the employee has more time off; but, if business is slowing down and if this essentially unpaid absence is not disruptive to the workflow, then a true cost saving results. Employers with large amounts of carryover vacation (unused days from prior years) and who are concerned about the associated increasing liability, could use vacation selling as a means to reduce the future buildup of such expenses. Also, a large amount of banked time could be frozen in value (for purposes of the cafeteria plan only) and employees could be required to trade this time for flexible credits in workable increments each year until the entire bank is consumed. This results in more flex credits for individuals (affecting corporate cash flow) but may decrease corporate expenses in the long run. The implementation of such a policy is also an ideal time to eliminate the ability to carry over any additional amounts of vacation time. Vacation trades are further discussed in the "Special Rules" section of this chapter.

ADMINISTRATION OF A CAFETERIA PLAN

Administration of a cafeteria benefit plan is quite different from that of a traditional program where the employee enrolls once and remains until employment terminates. In a traditional plan, all employees have essentially the same coverage, or coverage is determined the same way so the administration generally is the same. In the case of a flexible benefit plan, the employee enrolls and re-enrolls each year and makes choices on how and where to apply his or her flexible dollars. Each employee will spend those dollars differently, and, because of this heavy employee involvement and the differences between individuals, the task of administration becomes doubly important. The plan administrator must be able to quickly answer questions concerning the program and determine the benefits that each participant has.

When flexible benefit plans were first being designed and implemented, the administration was thought to be onerous, and concern over burdensome administrative tasks was the single biggest obstacle to their adoption. In some instances it remains so today. However, while a flexible benefit plan involves more administrative tasks than a traditional approach, it need not result in overly difficult or extremely expensive administration. Today, most payroll systems easily accommodate salary reduction amounts for cafeteria and 401(k) plans or a combination of the two. Also, human-resource systems, including microcomputer-based systems for smaller employers, have sufficient capacity to store benefit election data, provide data for enrollment forms, permit inquiries on coverages, and facilitate management and administrative reporting. Software to perform many of these tasks is available commercially and can easily be customized to fit most plan designs.

Five administrative tasks are of critical importance: development of administrative rules, the annual enrollment process, payroll and accounting issues, administering the flexible spending account, and communicating the plan to participants.

Development of Administrative Rules

Once the program has been designed, there is a need for a very specific and detailed set of administrative procedures and practices. Throughout each year, administrative situations will arise that generally are not contemplated in the design of the plan, and, to ensure uniform administration, proper administrative procedures and rules should be developed in advance. Examples of issues to be addressed in the administrative document may include the following:

- How are flexible dollars computed? What happens in the case of different pay periods, such as hourly, weekly, biweekly?
- How are the prices for the various options determined for each payroll type?
- What happens in the case of unpaid leaves of absence? Will contributions to the various plans be continued and, if so, how? Will the employee make after-tax contributions during such periods and, if so, to which plans? What happens if only a portion of such contributions is received?
- How are newly hired employees enrolled in the plan, and which choices are they given? How are credits calculated for such employees?
- What changes are permitted during the course of the year, and exactly how will they be administered?
- All administrative forms used in the operation of the plan should be contained in the administrative manual, along with instructions on how to complete the forms and what to do with them after completion.
- The administrative procedure should set forth how conversions and trades of salary and vacation time into flexible dollars take place and what result is obtained.
- Exactly what types of expenses will be covered by any flexible spending accounts? What degree of claims adjudication is required, and how will it be accomplished?
- What reports will employees receive throughout the year, and who will prepare them? What management reports will be produced, who will prepare them, and to whom will they be sent?

- How will changes in salary during the course of the year affect the various benefits selected?
- What impact will the various choices have on other benefit plans and personnel policies, and what changes are being made in them to accommodate the flexible benefits program?
- If there are default values that result from employees not returning enrollment forms, what are they and how will they be implemented? Are they different in the first year of enrollment than in subsequent years?

The size and complexity of the administrative procedures and rules are, of course, a function of the complexity of the flexible benefit plan involved. The administrative document may be small in the case of a plan offering only a few choices or more sizeable in the case of more comprehensive programs. In any event, the document should be maintained from year to year as situations arise and decisions are made regarding them.

Annual Enrollment Process

The most important administrative task in any flexible benefit program is the annual enrollment process. It is at this time that the employee must have all the information necessary to make the choices he or she desires. Most likely, this also is the single largest administrative effort in operating the plan. The annual enrollment process involves the following tasks: obtaining the basic employee data; performing the calculations for enrollment and preparing the individual enrollment form; distributing the form to employees; obtaining the completed form back from employees, editing and correcting data, recording the information, and issuing a confirmation report; and preparing all administrative reports necessary for the orderly operation of the program.

Obtaining the basic employee data may be as simple as extracting information from the payroll system. However, additional information may be required, depending on the complexity of the plan. For example, if the plan involves the use of previously carried-forward vacation amounts, that information may have to be gathered from a separate source. Typically, the basic employee data required includes such elements as employee name, address, identification number or Social Security number, or both, work location, employment status (exempt, nonexempt), birth date, date service began (for either computing the number of flexible dollars the employee has or for determining vacation eligibility or sick leave eligibility), salary amount, frequency of pay, accrued carryover vacation, current medical coverage (single, family), marital status, and the like. These data allow the plan administrator to calculate the number of flexible dollars the employee will have or be able to create, and the prices of the benefits on which those dollars may be spent. The amount of data required clearly is a function of the complexity of the plan and the amount of computation to be performed. This task usually is more involved in the first year of the enrollment process, and in future years the validity of the data tends to increase.

Creation and distribution of the enrollment form consists of performing the calculations mentioned above and posting them on an individual enrollment form for each employee. For very simple plans involving only a few choices—where prices of the benefits are not dependent on any individual data, and where a number of flexible dollars is easily determined or they come solely from salary reduction—the amount of computation in the preparation of the enrollment form is small. However, in the case of plans involving vacation trades, employer contributions based on service and pay or other factors, or where prices are a function of family status or other demographic information, more elaborate computations are required. Experience with the enrollment process has shown that enrollment errors can be significantly reduced if employees are not required to perform computations. Thus, everything that can be calculated beforehand and placed on the enrollment form serves to reduce future error. Enrollment forms can be mailed to employee homes, sent to office or work locations, or distributed at meetings. A two-part form offers an advantage, in that the employee may keep one part of the completed enrollment form for his or her records.

Obtaining the completed form is the next step. Usually, completed forms are returned to the plan administrator to check and edit for completeness and accuracy. In the case of large employers, the checking and editing may be performed on an automated basis. At a minimum, editing involves seeing that the number of flexible dollars each employee has spent is, in fact, equal to the number of dollars available. In this case, a cash election is assumed to be dollars spent. Invalid elections must be identified. The administrator must keep track of all returned election forms, so employees who have not returned them can be contacted in advance of the final date on which enrollment forms will be accepted. Those employees whose enrollment forms contain invalid elections or are illegible or incomplete, must be contacted directly, so elections can be corrected. Alternatively, default elections can be invoked. Once any employee's enrollment form is complete and correctly recorded, a confirmation report can be produced. This report serves to confirm to the employee that the elections he or she has made have been recorded by the plan administrator.

Management reports and administrative reports can be produced once the enrollment process is concluded. Part of this process also involves computing salary reduction amounts and other deductions that need to be passed to the payroll system. Also, coverage and eligibility reports to the various insurance carriers and claims administrators should be produced.

Using technology to reduce the amount of paper involved in the enrollment process is an approach that appeals to large employers, and some employers have established automated voice response systems to provide information to participants and to permit enrollment over the telephone. Touch-screen interactive computer systems installed in kiosks at various work sites can help increase the efficiency of the enrollment process. The Internet also is revolutionizing the process. Employers of all sizes are bypassing or transitioning from voice-response systems to Web-enrollment. Sophisticated Web sites are enabling employees not only to make their annual elections but to search for in-network primary care providers, compare medical plans, and review under what circumstances mid-year changes are permitted.

Payroll and Accounting Issues

Payroll and accounting issues are mentioned here briefly, because the establishment of a flexible benefit plan impacts the interaction between payroll and accounting. Decisions need to be made on how the various salary-reduction amounts will be shown on the paycheck stub. If amounts are shown individually by benefit choice, these must be computed and a new pay-stub design may be required in order to accommodate them. Alternatively, if only one amount is shown, an insert in the paycheck may be required to explain that amount. If there is automatic reporting between the payroll and general ledger systems, some modification may be required as items (as a result of salary reduction or vacation trade) may now appear on different lines in the general ledger. Also, additional liability accounts will need to be created in the general ledger to reflect the difference between flexible dollars created through salary reduction (or possibly other means) and those actually spent in the same time period. This is particularly true in the case of spending accounts funded by salary reduction. The dollars removed from salary in each pay period must accumulate in a liability account until such time as they are spent. On the other hand, in the case of a medical reimbursement account, the employee may file a claim for more than the number of dollars yet extracted from pay. In this case, appropriate accounting entries must be made.

Flexible dollars created from different sources may accrue at different rates. For example, dollars created as a result of salary reduction normally accrue each pay period, while those created from vacation trade may accrue monthly or over whatever time period vacation is computed. Dollars created from the sale of carryover vacation may accrue at the beginning of the year. Flexible dollars spent for various plans also accrue at different rates. Contributions to medical plans accrue periodically in concert with payroll periods. However, the use of vacation days may occur at any time during the course of the year. Appropriate procedures and methods should be developed in advance to deal with these issues.

Administering a Flexible Spending Account

As indicated earlier in this chapter, most flexible benefit programs involve the establishment of spending accounts for employees. Typically, two accounts are possible, one for medical and the other for dependent care expenses—both funded by flexible dollars. Employees file claims for reimbursement from the accounts—a process that involves the completion, examination, and adjudication of the claim form; the recording of the appropriate accounting entries; and the preparation of a check and explanation of benefit report for the employees and miscellaneous management and accounting reports. Periodic statements may be provided to employees advising them how much they have used to date and how much remains in their spending accounts.

The operation of a spending account is treated in a manner similar to a medical claim, and most insurance companies or third-party administrators who provide medical claim services also provide claims processing for a flexible spending account. There are distinct advantages to this approach, since it can reduce the number of forms the employee has to file and the amount of time between filing and payment. For example, one typical expense claimed against a medical spending account is for medical expenses claimed under the medical plan but not reimbursed therefrom. In this situation, the employee files a claim for the medical expense against the medical plan, receives an explanation of benefits, and then files a claim (for the difference between the original claim and the payment) against the flexible spending account. If the same entity is receiving both claims, the second claims process can be made a part of the first process, so, when the medical claim is filed, the employee simply indicates on that claim form that any unreimbursed amounts should be paid from his or her spending account.

Alternatively, the plan sponsor may choose to administer the spending account directly. In the case of a small number of participants, this can be a manual process. However, with a large number of participants (500 or more), some mechanized process probably is warranted. Again, software is commercially available for this purpose.

Communicating the Plan

The success of a flexible benefit plan hinges in great part on how well employees understand what the program is designed to do and how to utilize it. It is important to recognize that, although a flexible benefit plan can become complex in design and administration, the concept behind it is relatively straightforward. The employees simply need to understand what the plan is intended to do and how they can make it work for them. This involves understanding how many flexible dollars can be created, how they are created, where they can be spent, and the advantages and disadvantages of creating or spending them in a particular way. The ability of employees to understand even very complex programs should not be underestimated. Once the concept is clear, employees will find ways of using the program to their advantage, and this level of involvement is necessary for a successful program.

The communication program associated with a flexible benefit plan is broader in scope than that used with traditional plan design, and represents, at least in the year of implementation, an additional administrative task. However, it is one where commensurate return is possible.

Communication programs for flexible benefit plans typically involve four phases:

1. *Announcement Phase.* During this time the intention to implement a flexible benefit program is communicated to the employees. This is the time to communicate the general concepts and the plan objectives to employees through any of the communication vehicles available, such as letters, pamphlets, and payroll stuffers. The use of group meetings and audiovisual techniques is ideal.

2. *Educational Phase.* Employees must be educated about the plan. Once the objectives and concepts are known, detailed information about how the plan will operate and what the employee needs to do to use the plan for best results must be provided. There is no such thing as too much communication material, and employees should be provided with newsletters, bulletins, brochures, and pamphlets—as much detailed information as possible. Again, group meetings and audiovisual presentations are helpful.

3. *Enrollment Phase.* This is the most important phase in the communication program. Here, the employer's objectives are at least three-fold: reduce the amount of administrative effort and errors in the enrollment process, reduce the amount of time the enrollment process consumes, and ensure that employees have a positive feeling about the plan and their enrollment in it. In more complex plans, employees may have difficulty making choices and develop a negative view of the plan for that reason. Individually prepared enrollment forms and kits are helpful. Group meetings using audiovisual presentations are strongly encouraged at this point. Some employers have prepared videotapes detailing the process for completing the enrollment form that can be made available to employees on an individual basis. The tapes also could be taken home, so employees could view them with their families as they are going through the enrollment process. Technology-based communications techniques, including voice-response systems, interactive video systems, and Internet and intranet programs have been used in this phase not only to communicate but also to facilitate the enrollment process.

It is important that the enrollment process be completed in a reasonably short time. Even though this may involve the physical distribution of a multipart form to the employee and follow-up to receive the form back, the shorter the time frame during which this is accomplished, the better the result will be. As soon as forms are received and the enrollment data entered into the administrative system, a confirmation report should be distributed to the employee.

Because most flexible benefit plans operate on a calendar-year basis, the enrollment phase will be completed during the late fall of the year before the year in which the plan becomes effective. Confirmation reports should be issued to employees before the start of the year. In fact, if a confirmation report was issued in October or November, it may be appropriate to have an additional report effective January 1 to advise employees that the program has commenced and to reaffirm their participation in it.

4. *Continuation Phase.* Throughout the year, miscellaneous reports to employees advising them of such things as amounts remaining in spending accounts are appropriate. Occasional communication, on how the plan is operating and how many tax dollars have been saved, is helpful. A continuing newsletter is ideal. During this phase it is appropriate to communicate how the plan is performing with respect to the objectives set for it. This is so even if the objective is cost control; it simply requires an honest and credible approach.

SPECIAL RULES FOR CAFETERIA PLANS

Section 125 of the IRC is a relatively brief section of the code, and to date there have been only a few regulations with respect to it. Proposed regulation 1.125-1, issued in 1984, deals primarily with elections, constructive receipt, and selected nondiscrimination issues. This regulation was designed, in part, to put an end to certain practices regarding spending accounts. Regulation 1.125-2T appeared in 1986. This temporary regulation deals only with the types of benefits that can be provided by a cafeteria plan and was replaced by regulation 1.125-2, published in 1989, which provided more detailed guidance regarding these same issues, as well as addressing the operation of spending accounts and vacation trades. The Family Medical Leave Act also had an effect on cafeteria plans and regulation 1.125-3, published in 1995 deals with that. Regulation 1.125-4T issued in late 1997, provides more guidance regarding election changes. This regulation was supposedly made final with the revisions published in March 2000. At the same time a set of proposed regulations (again revising regulation 1.125-4T) was issued. Regulation 1.125-4 was refined and made final by revisions issued by the IRS in January 2001.

It is well beyond the scope of this chapter to provide a detailed discussion of the rules set forth by these various regulations; rather, the purpose of mentioning them here is to alert the reader as to their existence and to encourage a more thorough review of them before designing and implementing a cafeteria plan. However, the following is a brief summary of several of the more important rules to be followed.

Nondiscrimination Rules

Because the cafeteria plan serves to direct contributions to and participation in other (presumably nontaxable) benefit plans, those plans must each meet their own nondiscrimination tests as prescribed by tax law and regulation. For example, medical plans have their own nondiscrimination rules as set forth in Section 105 of the IRC. Therefore, if an election to participate in a nontaxable medical plan is allowed as part of the cafeteria plan, each medical plan in question must meet the nondiscrimination requirements applicable to it. This also is true for dependent-care plans, 401(k) plans, life insurance plans, and the like.

Beyond the above rules, the cafeteria plan itself will probably provide some nontaxable benefits to employees. No definition of these exists in tax regulation at the time of this writing, but they are assumed to at least include such benefits as salary-reduction amounts and employer contributions. A cafeteria plan must meet three nondiscrimination tests: the eligibility test, the benefits test, and the concentration test. (These tests, which are covered in Chapter 37 as well, are repeated here because of their importance and for further emphasis.)

■ *Eligibility Test.* This test simply requires that the benefits be available to a classification (a group) of employees which itself does not discriminate in favor of highly compensated employees. For this purpose, a highly compensated employee is defined as any officer; a shareholder owning more than 5 percent of the voting power or value of employer stock; or a highly paid person (interpreted as one who has earned $80,000, adjusted for inflation, in the prior year); or the employed spouse or dependent of an employee who meets any of the previously mentioned criteria.

■ *Contribution and Benefits Test.* Under this test, the benefits under the plan and the contributions to the plan cannot favor highly compensated participants. The definition of a highly compensated participant is the same as that for a highly compensated individual, but refers only to those who are participants in the plan.

■ *Concentration Test.* This test requires that no more than 25 percent of the total nontaxable benefits under the plan can be for the benefit of "key" employees. A key employee is defined in Section 416 of the Internal Revenue Code and is, generally: any officer who earned more than $67,500 annually in 2000 (amount is adjusted each year); any of the 10 largest employee shareholders earning in excess of $30,000 annually (2000 amount); any 5 percent owner of the employer; or any 1 percent owner earning more than $150,000.

No regulations about how to specifically apply the three tests above have as yet been issued by the IRS. Employers who sponsor cafeteria plans should make a good-faith effort to comply.

Making and Changing Elections

In a cafeteria plan, employees make elections regarding the various benefits they want to receive. These elections must be made prior to the point where the period of coverage under those benefits begins. In most cases a cafeteria plan will operate on a calendar-year basis; thus, employee elections for one year must be made before the end of the previous year. Once employee elections have been made and the year of coverage begins, those elections are relatively immutable. However, it is clear that situations will arise where it is important that employees be allowed to make changes in their elections. This has been an area of great concern to plan administrators as well as the IRS; the latter having made several attempts to define when and what types of election changes are permissible. In March 2000, the IRS issued a set of final as well as a set of proposed regulations addressing these issues. Then, in January 2001, a new set of final regulations (refining those that had been promulgated earlier) was issued. Shown below is a brief summary of the resulting key requirements.

In general, changes in cafeteria plan elections after commencement of the plan year in which they are effective are permitted only in the following circumstances:

I.   A change in coverage under a group health plan is permitted if it corresponds with the special enrollment rights prescribed by the Health Insurance Portability & Accountability Act (HIPAA). This would include such events as marriage, the loss of other health care coverage, termination of employment, a spouse's death, a dependent who reaches an age at which point he or she loses eligibility for coverage, and changes in cost or coverage under the plan.

II.   Election changes can be made if they are "on account of and correspond to" a change in status that affects those who may benefit from coverage under an employer's plan and are due to:

      a. A change in marital status including death of spouse, divorce, legal separation, and annulment.

      b. A change in the number of dependents including births, deaths, adoptions, and placements for adoption.

      c. A change in the employment status of the employee, the employee's spouse, or the employee's dependent including: strike or lockout, taking an unpaid leave of absence, returning from an unpaid leave of absence, a change in worksite, and changing from salaried to hourly or vice versa.

      d. If a dependent satisfies or ceases to satisfy eligibility requirements.

      e. A change in residence of the employee, spouse, or dependent.

      f. The commencement or termination of an adoption proceeding. This applies only to election changes in adoption assistance plans.

III. An election change can be made to comply with any judgment, decree, or court order that results in a change in coverage.

IV.   If an employee, spouse, or dependent who is enrolled in an accident or health plan becomes entitled to Medicare or Medicaid, appropriate election changes can be made.

V.   If there are significant cost or coverage changes in a plan, the employee may change elections with respect to that plan (this does not apply to health care FSAs). Note that the employer can automatically adjust salary reduction amounts to cover less than significant changes in plan costs, but not health care FSAs.

VI.   An employee who is taking a leave under the Family and Medical Leave Act (FMLA), can change an election under an accident or health plan for the remaining period of coverage as provided by the FMLA.

If a 401(k) plan is part of the cafeteria plan, then elections with respect to participation in and contributions to that plan continue to be governed by the various 401(k) regulations, and are separate from the rules above.

Again, the above is merely a summary of the primary provisions of the applicable regulations, but they appear to provide plan sponsors with sufficient flexibility to operate their plans without undue hardship on employees who incur legitimate need to change elections in mid-year. It should be noted that the regulations define when changes in elections are permitted. They do not, however, require that any cafeteria plan permit such changes in election. In other words, the plan itself could limit the ability of the participants to change elections more severely than the regulations provide. The plan could not be more liberal. Thus, employers could apply more strict limitations on their flexible spending accounts to reduce the risk of loss. Careful consideration should be given to these issues during the plan design stage and during the development of administrative rules.

Spending Accounts

Two types of spending accounts are common in most cafeteria plans— one for health care expenses and one for dependent-care expenses. In the past, spending accounts also were used for certain legal expenses permitted under a group legal services plan under Section 120 of the IRC. However, because of the fact that Section 120 has had a tendency to expire and be revised on a frequent basis, the use of a spending account to pay expenses under this type of a plan is virtually nonexistent. Also, nonhighly compensated employees have a tendency not to participate in such legal expense plans. Even dependent-care plans, while they do form a part of a number of cafeteria plans, tend to have limited participation. Recent surveys have found that, of all the dollars paid out of spending accounts, it is reasonable to assume that more than 90 percent come from health care spending accounts.

A wide variety of expenses can be covered by a health care spending account. Generally, such a plan can reimburse for any expenses covered by Section 213 of the IRC, including expenses for services in a hospital or any care by physicians, dentists, or registered nurses; prescription drugs; dental services; vision care, including eyeglasses, contact lenses, or prescription sunglasses; psychiatric and psychological care; therapy, including special education for the handicapped; travel expenses to receive medical treatment, including ambulance service; and a host of miscellaneous expenses, including hearing aids, prosthetics, and guide dogs. A full description of covered expenses can be found in IRS Publication 502. Certain expenses cannot be reimbursed, including undocumented services (such as automobile mileage on a private car), premiums for health coverage of any type, or expenses for cosmetic surgery or cosmetic procedures intended to improve appearance as opposed to promoting proper functioning of the body for the prevention or treatment of an illness. (Procedures to correct birth defects or to correct disfigurement resulting from an accident or a disease can be reimbursed.) There is no prescribed maximum for reimbursements from a health care spending account, but, to not discriminate in favor of highly compensated employees, a fixed dollar amount is required. Most employers use a $1,000 to $3,000 maximum.

In general, the expenses that can be paid from a dependent-care account are those that would otherwise be payable from a dependent-care assistance plan as provided for in Section 129 of the IRC. The maximum amount of reimbursable expense is $5,000 for a single taxpayer or a married couple filing jointly (the maximum includes the amounts in the spending accounts of both spouses, if applicable); it is $2,500 for a married person filing separately. Dependent care expenses must be for a "qualifying individual" and the expense must be "employment-related." A "qualifying individual" is a dependent of the employee, for federal income tax purposes, who is under age 13. Alternatively, a qualifying individual can be a dependent of the employee (or can be the employee's spouse) who is physically or mentally incapable of self-support if the individual spends at least eight hours each day in the employee's home. To be employment-related, the expenses must have been incurred so as to permit the employee to work. Expenses for services rendered outside the home are covered as well. If the facility providing the care does so for more than six individuals, the facility must be a licensed dependent-care facility and/or comply with all state laws. A number of additional rules and definitions apply to dependent-care expenses, each of which is described in IRS Publication 503.

The basic rules for operating a health care or dependent-care spending account are similar. Key procedures to follow include the following:

■ The coverage period for benefits under a flexible spending account must be one year. This can be violated if there is a short plan year when a plan is established or if the plan year is changed. This requirement is relatively easy to follow, because most cafeteria plans operate on a calendar-year basis anyway.

■ Flexible spending accounts are permitted to reimburse only those claims incurred during the period of coverage. A claim is assumed to be incurred when the service is actually rendered. Thus, if a medical service is provided late in a given year, the expense is incurred at that point. This expense, if claimed, must be paid from that year's flexible spending account, even though the invoice for the expense may not be received until the following year. From an administrative standpoint, this means that the ability to file claims against a flexible spending account applicable for a given year will most likely stand for several months into the following year. A two- to three-month grace period is generally followed by most employers operating such accounts.

■ Money deposited into a flexible spending account during a specific year must be consumed by qualifying expenses incurred against that account during that same year or be forfeited. The forfeiture remains an asset of the employer; it does not revert to the government. The employer may do anything with the forfeiture it likes, including redistributing it to the participants in the plan in the following year. The general rule is that the amount given to any employee cannot in any way be linked to the amount forfeited by that employee.

■ For a health care flexible spending account, the plan must operate under the "uniform coverage" rule. This means that the amount of coverage applicable to the full year must be available throughout each day in the plan year. Thus, expenses are reimbursed as they are submitted, no matter how many flexible dollars have actually accrued (from an accounting standpoint) in the individual's account at that point. For example, if an employee elects to have coverage under a health care flexible spending account of $1,200, the salary reduction for such coverage is $100 per month and the total amount of coverage available at any time during the year is $1,200. So, if the employee submitted a qualified expense of $1,200 in the second month of coverage, this expense would be paid from the flexible spending account even though only $200 of the funding for the account existed at that point.

While this may seem to pose a financial risk to the plan sponsor, when contributions are taken in the aggregate (considering the amount of salary reduction taken from all participants versus the total number of claims settled at any point in time), this does not pose a true risk. There is the risk that, upon receiving payment for an expense in excess of the funded amount, the employee may terminate service and cease making payments into the spending account. This risk is borne by the plan sponsor. Offsetting this, however, is the ability of the plan sponsor to recapture forfeitures and the fact that no interest need be paid on accumulated funds. Therefore, the uniform coverage rule has not been a major obstacle to the use of flexible spending accounts. It should be noted that the uniform coverage rule does not apply to flexible spending accounts established to pay dependent-care expenses.

Lastly, because medical FSAs provide health care benefits, they may be subject to the continuation of coverage rules prescribed by the Consolidated Budget Reconciliation Act of 1985 (COBRA). Note that dependent-care FSAs are not subject to such rules, but how COBRA rules affect medical FSAs (while originally thought to be somewhat academic) has been an area of concern to cafeteria plan administrators for some time.

The application of COBRA to a medical FSA depends in part on whether or not the FSA is an "excepted benefit" as defined by the Health Insurance Portability and Accountability Act of 1996 (HIPAA), but HIPAA specifies that this definition is to be provided by regulations, which at the time of this writing, have not been issued. A reasonably reliable indication from the governing agencies is that a medical FSA would be an "excepted benefit" if the employee involved has coverage under the employer's medical plan (which itself must not be limited to benefits which are excepted) and if the amount of benefit available from the FSA for the year is not more than the greater of (a) twice the amount of the affected employee's salary reduction for that year, or (b) the amount of salary reduction plus $500. If the FSA is an "excepted benefit," then continued coverage in future years need not be offered if the amount of benefit available from the FSA is less that the required premium (including the additional 2 percent permitted by COBRA). Continued coverage need not be offered even for the remainder of the year in which the qualifying COBRA event occurred if all the previous conditions are satisfied and the benefit available from the FSA for the remainder of the year in question is less than the remaining required premium (again including the 2 percent fee).

While seemingly complex, these are relatively reasonable requirements. Most sponsors of cafeteria plans will want to be sure to design the medical FSA so that it is an "excepted benefit," and so that coverage beyond the year in which the qualifying event occurs is not required. Continued coverage during the remainder of that same year is not administratively difficult.

The above discussion is conceptual in nature, and there are many rules and nuances involved in operating spending accounts. Again, the reader is encouraged to review the regulations thoroughly.

Vacation Trades

Only a few regulations exist governing the use of vacation time in a cafeteria plan, but thoughtful administrative procedures are required to deal with them. Basically, all that is involved in trading time off for dollars is to permit the employee to either agree to take less vacation time in a given year than that to which he or she is entitled and to receive flexible dollars in return, or to permit the employee to purchase additional time off with flexible dollars that have been created through other means.

If any of these elections are incorporated into the flexible benefits plan, the days of vacation over which the employee has control are referred to as *elective days* and all other days as *nonelective days*. The regulations prescribe that nonelective days be used first and elective days last in any year. Elective days cannot be carried over into future years, as that would cause the flexible benefits plan to create a mechanism whereby the employee could defer compensation into another year. However, if elective days are not used in the year in question, they can be cashed out (i.e., the employee can receive taxable dollars for them) at the end of that year.

For example, if an employee has 10 days of vacation to be taken in a calendar year, and if he or she elects (assuming the plan so permits) to buy three additional days in that year, by consuming the appropriate number of flexible dollars, then the employee has 13 days of vacation for that year. Those three purchased days are the elective days and are assumed to be used last. Thus, if this employee uses only eight vacation days in the year, he or she would have two nonelective days and three elective days unused. If the normal policy of the employer was to permit unused vacation time to be carried over into the next year, only the two unused nonelective days would qualify. The remaining three elective days would have to be either forfeited or cashed out before the year ends.

Carrying this example one step further, assume the flexible benefits plan permitted the employee to purchase a maximum of three days, but that it also permitted the employee to trade up to five days of time off to create additional flexible dollars. In this case, the employee who does not purchase any additional time off would still have five elective days, because that is the number of days that could have been traded. If this employee (who has 10 days of regular vacation in the year) took only five days of vacation in the year, the remaining five days (because they are elective days) cannot be carried over. They can, of course, be cashed out. The employee who purchases three extra days in this case would have eight elective days and five nonelective days, or 13 days of vacation in total. If this employee uses eight of those days, none of the remaining five days can be carried over, because they were all elective days.

When vacation trades are used, three key administrative issues must be addressed:

■ A decision must be made about how much vacation time will be subject to trade, and at what rate. Because the election to trade or not must be made before the start of the year, the base salary on some fixed date prior to the start of the year may be the appropriate exchange rate. In this case, salary increases in the next year are ignored for this purpose. Adequate communication of this fact is required.

■ It is also important to determine the unit of trade. Trading in days is easier to administer than trading in hours, unless the employer is accustomed to operating the vacation plan on an hourly basis.

■ Because it is likely that those with longer service will have more discretionary vacation time available to trade, and because it is probable that these longer service employees are being paid more than those with much less service, care must be taken to ensure that the plan is not discriminating in favor of highly compensated individuals. This same issue must be examined in the situation where existing carried-over vacation days are being traded for flexible dollars.

The use of vacation trades can serve to permit employees to create more flexible dollars without salary reduction. However, these dollars actually come from the employer and, thus, represent a true additional cost. This may be offset by the fact that the employee will be working during the time that would otherwise be spent on vacation. Also, the business needs of the employer should play a major role in deciding whether to include vacation trading in the flexible benefit plan. For example, if the employer would like to encourage employees to take unpaid leave because of declining business conditions, then a plan where employees can purchase additional time off by using salary reduction can help accomplish this objective. Alternatively, if there is a large backlog of work, a plan that permits employees to sell time off may be beneficial.

IMPACT OF A CAFETERIA PLAN ON OTHER PLANS AND POLICIES

While one of the primary points made in this chapter is that the cafeteria plan serves to direct contributions to and participation in other plans, one cannot conclude that it has absolutely no effect on those plans. Indeed, the existence of choice among many plans will result in design changes within those plans. Also, the cafeteria plan can affect other plans, policies, and administrative procedures even though they may not be a part of it.

For example, if the flexible benefit plan provides a choice between two or more medical indemnity plans, there must be a discernible difference between those plans. This applies to the benefits provided from those plans as well as the price tag placed on them. Thus, small differences ($100, for example) in deductibles are relatively meaningless. This may not be totally true if the employer is moving from a medical plan with a very low deductible, such as $50. In this instance, the next best plan in the set of choices may well have a $100 or $150 deductible. However, if there is a third plan, it should probably have a $300 or $500 deductible. While small differences in plan design may not be significant, the same is not necessarily the case with regard to price. Here, a difference of $100 per year for coverage can cause employees to select a plan providing lesser benefits. Naturally, these amounts will vary depending on the employee group and the price for all options. The pricing of the various options, particularly with respect to the medical plans, should be reviewed each year to ensure that the plan is operating as desired.

The existence of flexible spending accounts also may affect other plans. For example:

■ The existence of a health care flexible spending account can mean there is not much need for a vision care plan, because such expenses can be paid from the flexible spending account. Also, vision care plans tend to have relatively small benefits, compared with the cost of vision care services.

■ There may not be as much need for a very lucrative dental plan, as these expenses also can be paid from the flexible spending account. This is particularly true for such coverage as orthodontia and prosthetic devices. However, this result may only be fully achieved if the employer also makes some type of contribution to the spending account on behalf of employees.

■ The use of a dependent-care flexible spending account can reduce some pressure to have other types of dependent-care benefits. However, if the account is funded solely through salary reduction, it does not have the same intensity; and it competes, specifically in the case of lower-paid employees, with the child-care tax credit. However, if the employer makes a contribution to the cafeteria plan and if those flexible dollars can be directed to the dependent-care account (as well as other benefits), then the flexible spending account will be perceived as providing better coverage for those who need it. This approach also will seem more fair to those employees who do not have a need for dependent care, as they can use the employer contribution for other benefits.

Using vacation trading in the cafeteria plan can have an impact on the vacation policies themselves. First, the issue of carrying forward vacation time should be reevaluated when using the cafeteria approach. The introduction of the cafeteria plan may serve as an ideal time to eliminate this practice if the employer so desires. Also, if the cafeteria plan permits the employee to purchase time off, personnel and business policies must be examined to ensure that the process can work. In these cases, employees may come to the end of the year with some unused time that they will want to take before the year is ended. This can result in more than expected vacation time being used in the last month of the year, a time when vacation and holiday time normally is high anyway. Also, for those who must work during that time, procedures must be established so that unused elective days can be cashed out as needed.

The general administration of the vacation plan also must accommodate the cafeteria plan. For example:

- A policy of requiring six months of full-time employment before vacation can be taken may conflict with the ability to trade days for flexible dollars for newly hired employees.
- If supervisors typically grant time off without involvement of the benefit department, or if such time is not recorded, the cafeteria plan can be defeated.
- Lastly, the vacation tracking system may have to be modified.

One additional plan that is worthy of discussion is the long-term disability (LTD) plan. If an LTD plan exists and if it is wholly paid for by employee after-tax contributions, then the benefits from that plan are (under current tax law) not subject to federal tax when received. In this case, a benefit level of two-thirds of normal earnings would result in the employee having essentially the same level of spendable income in the event of disability as he or she had while actively employed, at least in the first few years. A benefit level of 50 percent of normal earnings may be deemed as acceptable, because work-related expenses disappear in the case of disability. (The actual level of benefit will have been set by the employer and will be commensurate with its philosophy regarding the spendable income needs of a person who is disabled.) However, if this plan is incorporated into the cafeteria plan and is paid for with flexible (pretax) dollars, then the benefits are subject to federal income tax when they are received. In this case, a benefit level of 50 percent will not achieve the same result as it did before.

It is possible to permit the employee to choose whether to let the benefit or the premium be taxable, and it is also possible to have an election between LTD plans with different levels of benefits. This structure probably should be avoided, because it is very difficult for all but the most astute employees (or those who know they are going to be eligible for LTD) to determine what is best for them.

In essence then, one must carefully evaluate the plans to be included in the cafeteria plan, looking for the possible impact the cafeteria plan has on them. General personnel policies and administrative procedures and systems also should be reexamined for possible impact.

SUMMARY

The cafeteria plan is clearly a plan whose time has come. Through the use of such plans, employers can construct programs that permit employees to have more command over their own compensation; employer costs, within some reason, can be controlled; and, compensation can become more tax-efficient. The workings of such programs are, as shown in this chapter, relatively straightforward, but care must be taken in the design phase to be sure of the impact on other plans and policies.

The administration of these types of programs is not to be feared and can be accommodated, given the sophistication of today's payroll and human-resource systems, the availability of software packages to perform such functions as the enrollment process, and the willingness of third-party administrators to perform services in all areas, including the administration of flexible spending accounts. The tax environment currently, and for the foreseeable future, favors these arrangements.

Fiduciary Liability Issues under ERISA

Alan P. Cleveland

An appreciation of the legal duties and responsibilities of a fiduciary to the participants and beneficiaries of a trusteed employee benefit plan is both fundamentally simple and exceptionally difficult. Legal definitions and statements of basic principles that seem straightforward in concept often prove elusive when applied in real situations. A plan fiduciary in the discharge of his or her duties under the Employee Retirement Income Security Act of 1974 (ERISA) is well-advised to err on the side of caution, to resolve doubt in favor of a liberal interpretation of plan benefits, to be well-informed at all times of the duties and responsibilities of all the fiduciaries of the plan, and to act uniformly and in strict accordance with the plan document but with a broad reading given to the fiduciary responsibilities and standards of the Act.

FIDUCIARY DUTIES UNDER THE COMMON LAW OF TRUSTS

In the employee benefits area, fiduciary relationships are fundamental to the administration and investment of employee benefit trusts. When does a fiduciary relationship exist? Under the common law of trusts, it is said that a person is in a fiduciary relationship with another if the person who receives certain powers or property does so on the condition that with such receipt is the corollary duty to utilize that conferred power or property for the benefit of that other. A trust is recognized as a formal fiduciary relationship concerning property and imposing on the person (the trustee) who holds title to that property (trust assets) certain fiduciary duties to deal with that property for the benefit of another (the beneficiary). When a person as trustee accepts ownership of such property "in trust" for a beneficiary, the trustee at the same time accepts the fiduciary responsibility and duty to use the power over trust assets for the benefit of the beneficiary of that trust.

Under the common law of trusts, a trustee has several basic fiduciary duties to the beneficiaries of the trust: a duty to see that the property of the trust is legally designated as trust property; a duty not to delegate to others trustee powers over trust property; a duty of undivided loyalty to the beneficiaries of the trust; and a duty to invest prudently by maximizing return on and ensuring the safety of trust assets. Primary among these trustee responsibilities are the duties of loyalty and prudence.

Duty of Loyalty

A trustee's duty of loyalty is the duty to act in the interest of the trust as if the trustee had no other competing interests to protect, especially his or her own. The trustee must resolve all conflicts between his or her personal or other interests and those of the trust and its beneficiaries in favor of the trust beneficiaries. This duty of loyalty is a component of all fiduciary relationships, but is particularly important in the case of a trust created to provide economic support or benefits for a specific beneficiary. A much-cited court opinion by Justice Benjamin Cardozo articulates this high standard of loyalty, and warrants quoting at length:

> Many forms of conduct permissible in a workaday world for those acting at arm's length are forbidden to those bound by fiduciary ties. A trustee is held to something stricter than the morals of the marketplace. Not honesty alone, but the punctilio of an honor the most sensitive, is then the standard of behavior. As to this there has developed a tradition that is unbending and inveterate. Uncompromising rigidity has been the attitude of courts of equity when petitioned to undermine the rule of undivided loyalty by the "disintegrating erosion" of particular exceptions. Only thus has the level of conduct for fiduciaries been kept at a level higher than that trodden by the crowd.[1]

This extreme expression of singular loyalty under the common law of trusts sets out that strict prohibition against fiduciary conflicts of interest which has been the hallmark of subsequent legislation and judicial law under ERISA in regulating the fiduciary management of employee benefit plans.

1 *Meinhard v. Salmon*, 294 N.Y. 458, 464, 164 N.E. 545, 546 (1928).

Duty of Prudence: The Prudent Man Rule

In addition to the duty of undivided loyalty to the beneficiaries of a trust, a trustee under the common law of trusts has the duty of prudence in managing trust assets. This duty of prudence established a standard of performance in managing trust assets measured as equivalent to that care exercised by a person of ordinary prudence in dealing with the fiduciary's own personal property. The standard of skill and care established under traditional American trust law—that of a person of ordinary prudence, or the prudent man rule—is largely derived from a decision of the Supreme Judicial Court of Massachusetts in 1830, the case of *Harvard College* v. *Amory*, 26 Mass. (9 Pick.) 446, 461, which held:

> All that can be required of a trustee to invest is that he shall conduct himself faithfully and exercise a sound discretion. He is to observe how men of prudence, discretion, and intelligence manage their own affairs, not in regard to speculation, but in regard to the permanent disposition of their funds, considering the probable income, as well as the probable safety of the capital to be invested.

This flexible standard under the common law later proved so vague that trustees, including the fiduciaries of employee pension plans, found little comfort in making individual investment choices on behalf of the trust. Likewise, beneficiaries who were disappointed in the investment of a trust often found it difficult to maintain a legal action in proving a fiduciary's lack of prudence and breach of trust. The prudent man rule also was applied on an investment-by-investment basis rather than looking to the overall performance of the trust's portfolio of assets as a whole. All in all, the common law of trusts ultimately proved a poorly stocked tool box in meeting the special requirements of employee pension plans.

EXCLUSIVE BENEFIT RULE UNDER THE INTERNAL REVENUE CODE

As a precondition for the substantial tax advantages afforded contributing employer sponsors and the participants and beneficiaries of qualified pension plans as tax-exempt organizations, Congress had long included in the Internal Revenue Code (IRC or Code) certain limitations and safeguards analogous to those provided under the common law of trusts. The code provisions were intended to ensure that a pension plan in fact was operated for the exclusive benefit of its members. This intent is codified as the *exclusive benefit rule.* A key provision under Section 401(a) of the Internal Revenue Code, which enumerates the general qualification requirements for a pension plan's tax-exempt status, mandates that a trust created by an employer as part of a pension or profit-sharing plan must be "for the exclusive benefit" of the plan's covered employees and their beneficiaries, and that it must be "impossible . . . for any part of the corpus or income . . . to be . . . used for or diverted to, purposes other than for the exclusive benefit" of the employees or their beneficiaries. The duty of loyalty of the trustee of a pension plan qualified under code Section 401(a) is, therefore, threefold:

- To be qualified as tax-exempt, a plan must be established for the "exclusive benefit" of the covered employees and their beneficiaries.
- All contributions received by the plan must be "for the purpose of distributing to such employees or their beneficiaries the corpus and income of the fund accumulated by the trust."
- And, under the express terms of the trust, it must be impossible for trust assets to be diverted to purposes "other than for the exclusive benefit of [the] employees or their beneficiaries" prior to the satisfaction of benefits due under the plan.

Failure of an employee benefit pension plan to operate in accordance with the exclusive benefit rule would cause it to lose its tax-exempt status under the Code, further resulting in a loss of deductibility of employer contributions to the plan as well as loss of the tax-preferred treatment enjoyed by the plan's participants and beneficiaries.

FIDUCIARY STANDARDS UNDER ERISA

Immediately prior to the passage of ERISA, it was estimated that more than 35 million employees were dependent for their retirement benefits on a private pension system whose noninsured trust assets then exceeded $130 billion. Congress determined that the rapid and substantial growth in size and scope of hundreds of thousands of pension plans had such economic impact on the continued well-being and security of their millions of covered employees that it was in the national public interest to establish under ERISA adequate safeguards to ensure the adequacy of funds to pay the retirement benefits promised under those pension plans. Toward these ends, ERISA mandated national standards of conduct, responsibility, and obligation for the fiduciaries of employee benefit plans, and further provided appropriate remedies, sanctions, and access to the federal courts for the enforcement of such fiduciary standards.

Before ERISA, pension plan fiduciaries were largely subject to the common law of trusts, the principles of which were developed and refined primarily during the 19th century to order personal trust relationships between private parties. Unfortunately, traditional trust law proved inapposite to the special purposes of pension plans, which had evolved to such a massive scale in the postindustrial period. Before ERISA, the only real sanction under federal law for fiduciary breaches involving an employee pension plan was revocation of the plan's tax-exempt status for violation of the exclusive benefit rule under the IRC. However, it was realized early that the adverse consequences of withdrawal of a plan's tax preferences would bear most heavily on innocent employees as the plan's beneficiaries, and the sanction was rarely applied in practice.

Under ERISA, Congress intended to establish a comprehensive federal regulatory scheme for the operation of pension and other employee benefit plans based on new and unwavering principles of fiduciary duty to be enforced with uncompromised rigidity. This new federal law of employee benefit trusts had four main objectives:

■ A uniform legal culture of fiduciary duties would be developed incrementally by the federal courts to define further the statutory standards of ERISA on a case-by-case basis that would supersede the traditional common law of trusts unevenly applied and interpreted under the individual laws of each state.

■ Those fiduciary standards developed under ERISA would be clarified and modified purposely to accommodate the special needs and purposes of pension funds.

■ Employee pension plan beneficiaries would have liberal access to the federal courts in enforcing the fiduciary standards of ERISA, and those plan fiduciaries found to have breached their duties could be held personally liable for resulting plan losses.

■ Fiduciaries of employee benefit plans not utilizing the trust form as a funding vehicle would still be subject to the fiduciary standards of the Act.

ERISA in a number of important respects went beyond the common law of trusts in establishing or extending new legal standards of conduct for plan fiduciaries.

■ By combining the exclusive benefit rule under the IRC with the "sole benefit standard" as stated under the Labor Management Relations Act, ERISA now required plan fiduciaries to *act solely in the interest* of the plan's participants and beneficiaries for the *exclusive purpose* of providing plan benefits or defraying the reasonable administrative expenses of the plan. This established the *sole benefit standard* of fiduciary conduct under ERISA.

■ For the future, a plan fiduciary could take little comfort in acting for a plan with only the ordinary prudence required under the traditional prudent man rule. Instead, a fiduciary needed to act under ERISA with the care, skill, prudence, and diligence under the circumstances then prevailing that a prudent man *acting in a like capacity and familiar with such matters* would use in the conduct of an *enterprise of a like character and with like aims*. This established the *prudent expert rule* of ERISA.

■ A fiduciary was still required to diversify the investments of a plan portfolio so as to minimize the risk of large losses unless under the circumstances it was clearly prudent not to do so. This closely resembled the fiduciary principle well known under the common law of trusts as the *diversification rule*.

■ A fiduciary needed to follow strictly the terms of the written plan document (unless otherwise in violation of ERISA) and to administer the plan in a fair, uniform, and nondiscriminatory manner. This principle has come to be called the *plan document rule*.

■ Unless otherwise exempted, a fiduciary could not allow the plan to engage directly or indirectly in transactions prohibited under ERISA, a caveat known as the *prohibited transactions rule*.

The Sole Benefit Standard

The sole benefit standard of ERISA borrows from the previously discussed exclusive benefit rule of Section 401(a) of the IRC and also in large part from Section 302(c)(5) of the Labor Management Relations Act (LMRA). The LMRA had long required that a collectively bargained employee benefit trust fund be maintained "for the sole and exclusive benefit of the employees . . . and their families and dependents."

The United States Supreme Court in *NLRB* v. *Amax Coal Company*, 453 U.S. 322, 335 (1981), stressed the legislative intent of ERISA as designed to prevent a fiduciary "from being put into a position where he has dual loyalties, and, therefore, he cannot act exclusively for the benefit of a plan's participants and beneficiaries." The federal courts have continued to strengthen this fiduciary duty of unwavering loyalty under ERISA to require a fiduciary to act with an "eye single to the interests of the participants and beneficiaries" and to impose liability against plan fiduciaries "at the slightest suggestion that any action taken was with other than the beneficiaries in mind." At this point in the evolution of the national fiduciary law of pension trusts under ERISA, the sole benefit standard should be understood as imposing on the fiduciary a rigid, complete, and undivided loyalty to act for the beneficiaries of the employee benefit trust devoid of any other motivating considerations by the fiduciary.

The Prudent Expert Rule

In an effort to draw attention to the distinction between the standard of ordinary prudence under the common law of trusts and the prudent expert standard contemplated under ERISA as particular to pension plans, the U.S. Department of Labor promulgated prudency regulations in 1979 that introduced the new ERISA standard as one "built upon, but that should and does depart from, traditional trust law in certain respects." For example, unlike traditional trust law, the degree of riskiness of a specific investment would not render that investment per se prudent or imprudent. Rather, the prudence of the investment decision would be judged under ERISA in the context of the plan's overall portfolio.

The prudent expert standard of ERISA differs from the traditional prudent man standard under the common law of trusts in three important respects. First, the plan fiduciary under ERISA must invest plan assets not in the same way as he or she would handle his or her personal estate but must look to how similar pension plans under similar circumstances are being invested. Second, it is not enough for an ERISA fiduciary to be merely "prudent," but he or she additionally must exercise the skill of a prudent person especially knowledgeable and experienced—that is, an expert—in the management of pension plans. Third, the focus is not to be on the performance of the individual plan investment but on how the investment contributes to the net performance of the pension portfolio as a whole, which assumes the conceptual framework of modern portfolio theory in its broadest terms. In investing a pension plan portfolio under the prudent expert rule, the fiduciary should weigh the risk of loss against the opportunity for gain, taking into consideration the following elements: (1) the liquidity and current return of the portfolio relative to the liquidity requirements of the plan; (2) the projected return of the portfolio relative to the funding objectives of the plan; and (3) the composition of the portfolio with regard to diversification.

The Diversification Rule

Consistent with the traditional common law of trusts, an ERISA fiduciary is required to diversify plan investments "so as to minimize the risk of large losses, unless under the circumstances it is clearly prudent not to do so." The legislative history of ERISA suggests the elements a fiduciary should consider in diversifying a plan's portfolio include: the purposes of the plan, the amount of plan assets, the overall financial and industrial conditions of the economy, the special characteristics of the particular type of investment (such as mortgages, bonds, and shares of stock), distribution as to geographical location, distribution as to industries, and dates of maturity. There are, unfortunately, no clear-cut tests under the statute on what would constitute a plan's lack of diversity or undue concentration in any particular investment.

During the legislative hearings leading to the enactment of ERISA, Congress heard testimony that under the common law of trusts, fiduciaries had rarely been held liable for investment losses unless trust holdings in a single investment exceeded 50 percent. Also under the pre-ERISA common law of trusts, a plan's concentration of investments of 25 percent or less of portfolio assets in an individual security or geographic locale did not ordinarily result in sanctions by the courts. However, since passage of ERISA, fiduciary liability has been imposed by the courts in a case where 23 percent of a plan's assets were invested in a single real estate loan. In a separate case, the investment of 85 percent of a profit-sharing plan's assets in long-term government bonds without the fiduciary having first adequately investigated the plan's liquidity needs was found to be a breach of the fiduciary duty to diversify plan assets.

The Plan Document Rule

Plan fiduciaries are required to act in strict accordance with the documents and instruments governing the plan insofar as such documentation is consistent with the provisions of ERISA. As a corollary to this statutory mandate, and in part a derivative of the sole benefit standard, the federal courts are now developing a growing body of fiduciary law under ERISA relating specifically to fiduciary conduct in the administration of plans, especially concerning the role of the plan administrator in the disposition of benefit claims. Plan fiduciaries are required in all cases to uniformly follow the express, written terms of the plan's documents. A plan administrator's decisions on benefits claims are normally accorded deference by the courts unless there is a substantive issue raised on whether (1) the relevant terms of the plan are overly vague or ambiguous, (2) the plan document fails to expressly include a provision that the courts should defer to the administrative decisions of the plan's fiduciaries, or (3) there is an apparent conflict of interest and the fiduciary would be personally or institutionally affected by the benefit decision. The holding of the United States Supreme Court in *Firestone* v. *Bruch*, 109 S. Ct. 948 (1989) is significant for its apparent rejection of the judicial deference normally accorded administrative benefit decisions under case law decided under the Labor Management Relations Act and, instead, has substituted those governing principles developed under the law of trusts in cases involving abusive discretion by plan fiduciaries in deciding benefit claims.

Prohibited Transactions Rule

Arising from yet going well beyond the common trust law duty of loyalty, ERISA prohibits a fiduciary from causing a plan to directly or indirectly enter into transactions with certain persons defined as "parties-in-interest." This group is similar to but more narrowly defined than the class of "disqualified persons" identified under companion provisions of the IRC. A fiduciary may not cause the plan to directly or indirectly engage in a transaction with a party-in-interest, as either buyer or seller, that would constitute a (1) sale or exchange, or leasing, of any property between the plan and a party-in-interest; (2) lending of money or other extension of credit between the plan and a party-in-interest; (3) furnishing of goods, services, or facilities between the plan and a party-in-interest; (4) transfer to or use by or for the benefit of a party-in-interest of any assets of the plan; or (5) the acquisition, on behalf of the plan, of any employer security or employer real property not otherwise specifically exempted by law or regulation.

Congress recognized the great potential for abuse in self-dealing with plan assets and so made fiduciaries liable for any losses sustained by a plan resulting from a prohibited transaction. Under ERISA, the fiduciary has a duty to make a thorough investigation of any party's relationship to the plan to determine if that person is a party-in-interest with respect to the plan. The term *party-in-interest* is broadly defined as including nearly everyone who has a direct or indirect association with a plan and specifically includes, but is not limited to, the following persons listed under Section 3(14) of ERISA:

1. A plan fiduciary (such as an administrator, officer, trustee, or custodian of the plan).
2. The legal counsel or employee of the plan.
3. Any other person providing services to the plan.
4. An employer whose employees are covered by the plan.

5. An employee organization (such as a union) any of whose members are covered by the plan.

6. A direct or indirect 50 percent or more owner of an employer sponsor of the plan.

7. Certain relatives of the foregoing persons.

8. The employees, officers, directors, and 10 percent shareholders of certain other parties-in-interest.

9. Certain persons having a statutorily defined direct or indirect relationship with other parties-in-interest.

Even as the prohibited-transaction provisions of ERISA precisely codify what would in many instances be considered only a possible conflict of interest under the common law of trusts, the ERISA rules in this area are less tolerant and more strictly applied than those of the traditional law of trusts. For example, a plan's engaging in a prohibited transaction would still result in a fiduciary breach even if the plan profited by the prohibited transaction.

Upon application to the Secretary of Labor, however, a plan fiduciary may request an exemption to prospectively enter into what otherwise would be deemed a prohibited transaction upon the secretary's finding that granting such an exemption would be administratively feasible, demonstrably in the interests of the plan and of its participants and beneficiaries, and otherwise protective of the rights of the plan's participants and beneficiaries. Administrative exemptions may be granted for specific transactions on an individual plan basis or as a class exemption for certain categories of transactions typical of the industry for a substantial number of unrelated plans. Under a 1978 accord between the two agencies, administrative exemptions from the prohibited transaction rules granted by the Department of Labor are also binding upon the Internal Revenue Service.

The comprehensive definitional scope of what would constitute a "prohibited transaction" as defined under ERISA, the involved attribution rules identifying persons as "parties-in-interest" (many of whom may themselves have no personal knowledge of the plan), the broad regulatory definition about what property constitutes "assets" of the plan for purposes of applying the prohibited transaction rules, and the severe sanctions and excise taxes assessed for such prohibited transactions dictate that a fiduciary should approach this area with great caution, be well-counseled, and seek an administrative exemption in questionable cases before causing the plan to enter into the transaction.

WHO IS A FIDUCIARY?

ERISA defines a plan fiduciary as any person who (1) exercises any discretionary authority or control over the management of a plan, (2) exercises any authority or control concerning the management or disposition of its assets, or (3) has any discretionary authority or responsibility in the administration of the plan. Fiduciary status extends not only to those persons named in the plan documents as having express authority and responsibility in the plan's investment or management but also covers those persons who undertake to exercise any discretion or control over the plan regardless of their formal title. Fiduciary status under ERISA depends on a person's function, authority, and responsibility and does not rest merely on title or label. To illustrate: A person who exercises discretion in the administration of a plan by making the final decision on a participant's appeal of a denial of a benefit claim would be considered a plan fiduciary under ERISA, even if the plan document makes no express provision authorizing such person's discretionary responsibility. However, those persons simply performing ministerial functions for a plan under administrative procedures established by others would not be considered fiduciaries. Professional service providers to a plan, such as attorneys, accountants, actuaries, and consultants, acting strictly within their professional roles and not exercising discretionary authority or control over the plan or providing investment advice for fees or other compensation, are unlikely to be considered fiduciaries of the plan. Plan trustees and administrators, on the other hand, by the very nature of their functions and authority would be considered fiduciaries.

A written plan document is required to provide for "named fiduciaries" having authority to control and manage the plan so that employees may know who is responsible for its operation. A named fiduciary may in fact manage or control the plan, or merely be identified in the document by name or office as the person authorized to appoint those fiduciaries who actually will exercise discretion and control in administering the plan or investing its assets. Only the named fiduciary may appoint a plan's investment manager and allocate investment responsibility to such manager as to make him or her a plan fiduciary. ERISA forbids persons convicted of any of a wide variety of specified felonies from serving as a fiduciary, adviser, consultant, or employee of a plan for a period of the later of five years after conviction or five years after the end of imprisonment for such crime. A fine of up to $10,000 or imprisonment for not more than one year may be imposed against the named fiduciary and others for an intentional violation of this prohibition.

LIABILITY FOR FIDUCIARY BREACHES UNDER ERISA

A plan fiduciary breaching the fiduciary requirements of ERISA is to be held personally liable for any losses sustained by the plan resulting from the breach. The fiduciary is further liable to restore to the plan any profits realized by the fiduciary through the improper use of the plan assets. Additionally, the fiduciary is subject to a broad panoply of other equitable relief, including removal, as may be ordered by the courts. If found to have engaged in a prohibited transaction with a plan, a disqualified person may be subject to an excise tax payable to the U.S. Treasury equal to 15 percent of the amount involved in the transaction occurring after August 5, 1997, for each year the prohibited transaction was outstanding, plus interest and penalties on the excise tax. (Different rates of excise tax apply before that date). This excise tax increases to 100 percent of the amount involved upon failure to remedy the transaction upon notification. A fiduciary acting solely in such capacity with a plan, however, is not liable for the tax.

Co-Fiduciary Liability

A plan fiduciary, moreover, is liable for the fiduciary breaches of other fiduciaries for the same plan if such fiduciary participates knowingly in or knowingly undertakes to conceal an act or omission of a co-fiduciary knowing such action constitutes a breach; imprudently fails to discharge his or her own fiduciary duties under the plan (and thereby enables the co-fiduciary to commit the breach); or has knowledge of the co-fiduciary's breach and makes no reasonable effort under the circumstances to remedy the breach.

Enforcement

Enforcement of the fiduciary provisions of ERISA may be by civil action brought in federal or state court by a plan participant or beneficiary (individually or on behalf of a class of plan participants and beneficiaries), by the Secretary of Labor, or by another plan fiduciary.

Exculpatory Provisions

Exculpatory provisions written into a plan document or other instrument to relieve a fiduciary from liability for fiduciary breaches against the plan are void and to be given no effect under ERISA. A plan may purchase liability insurance for itself and for its fiduciaries to cover losses resulting from their acts or omissions if the insurance policy permits recourse by the insurer against the fiduciaries in case of a breach of fiduciary responsibility.

Bonding and Fiduciary Insurance

Every fiduciary of an employee benefit plan and every other person who handles plan funds or property is required to be bonded, naming the plan as the insured, in an amount fixed at the beginning of each plan year as not less than 10 percent of the amount of funds handled, but in no event less than $1,000. Certain insurance companies, banks, and other financial institutions handling plan assets may be relieved of the bonding requirement if such institutions meet certain capital and other regulatory criteria established by the Secretary of Labor.

Further Sanctions for Breaches of Fiduciary Responsibility

In addition to a fiduciary's personal liability to restore losses sustained by the plan as a result of a breach of the fiduciary's responsibilities, the fiduciary also may be liable for (1) court-ordered attorneys' fees and costs incurred to remedy the breach, (2) punitive damages awarded by a court against the fiduciary, (3) special damages in an amount equal to the profits received by a fiduciary resulting from the wrongful use of plan assets, and (4) mandatory assessment of a civil penalty equal to 20 percent of the amount recovered by the Secretary of Labor on account of a fiduciary breach.

Attorneys' Fees. Under ERISA, a court in its discretion may award attorneys' fees to a prevailing plaintiff against a plan fiduciary by taking into account certain factors, including the degree of the fiduciary's culpability or bad faith, the offending party's ability to satisfy the award of attorneys' fees, whether its award would deter other fiduciaries from acting similarly under like circumstances, the relative merits of the parties' positions in the litigation, and whether the action conferred a common benefit on the plan's participants and beneficiaries.

Punitive Damages. The courts have broad discretion under ERISA to award punitive damages to a plan for fiduciary breaches in cases where it is found a fiduciary acted with malice or wanton indifference. On awarding such damages, a court would take into consideration

(1) the trust and pension laws as developed by the state and federal courts in a particular jurisdiction, (2) whether the allowance of such relief would conflict with other public-policy objectives under ERISA, and (3) whether granting such relief would best effectuate the underlying purposes of ERISA.

Restitution for Wrongful Profits. Where a fiduciary has personally profited by wrongfully using plan assets for the fiduciary's own account, even where the plan itself has sustained no direct loss and may actually have gained by the transaction, the fiduciary likely will be required by the courts to disgorge to the plan the full amount of those personally realized profits. And if there is any commingling of plan assets with the fiduciary's personal property, all issues of apportionment of the wrongful profit will be resolved against the fiduciary and in favor of the plan. The purpose of this disgorgement requirement is to remove any incentive for the fiduciary to misuse plan assets whether or not the plan sustains a loss by the fiduciary breach. As a matter of equity, the fiduciary will not be permitted to gain by his or her wrongful acts.

Twenty Percent Civil Penalty. Added by the Omnibus Budget Reconciliation Act of 1989 (OBRA '89), ERISA was amended to require the Secretary of Labor to assess a civil penalty against fiduciaries who breach their fiduciary responsibilities under ERISA and also to make such assessments against any nonfiduciary who knowingly participates in such breach. The amount of civil penalty is equal to 20 percent of the amount of applicable recovery obtained pursuant to any settlement agreement with the Secretary of Labor or ordered by a court to be paid in a judicial proceeding instituted by the Department of Labor. The 20 percent civil penalty assessment is to be reduced by the amount of any excise tax payable to the U.S. Treasury on account of a prohibited transaction. In the Secretary of Labor's sole discretion, the civil penalty may be waived or reduced if the secretary determines in writing that the fiduciary or other person so assessed acted reasonably and in good faith, or that it is reasonable to expect that as a consequence of the penalty's assessment it would not be possible to restore all losses to the plan without severe financial hardship unless the waiver or reduction were granted.

ALLOCATION OF FIDUCIARY RESPONSIBILITIES

Plan documents may provide that specific duties may be allocated by agreement among the fiduciaries, provided those duties are specifically delineated in writing, the procedures for such allocations are sufficiently detailed, and the fiduciaries act prudently in implementing the established allocation procedure. If fiduciary responsibilities are allocated in accordance with the plan documentation, the fiduciary would not be held liable for any plan loss arising from the acts or omissions of those other fiduciaries to whom such responsibilities had been properly delegated. Regardless, a plan fiduciary will remain fiduciarily responsible if he or she does not act in general accordance with the prudency requirements of ERISA in making the delegation, or if the fiduciary had knowledge of another's fiduciary breach and yet failed to make reasonable efforts to remedy the breach.

Only the named fiduciary of a plan may allocate or delegate duties involving the management and control of plan assets. In duly appointing an investment manager in writing and in accordance with the procedural requirements of ERISA, the fiduciary responsibility of investing or otherwise managing the assets of the plan may be transferred to the manager within the terms of the delegation. Yet, the named fiduciary would still be held liable for imprudently selecting or retaining the manager or for permitting, concealing, or failing to remedy a known breach of that fiduciary's responsibility to the plan.

A fiduciary also must demonstrate procedural prudence in the management of the plan's affairs and must be able to show that the fiduciary's reliance on the plan's advisers and other fiduciaries was reasonable and informed. As fiduciary status is functionally determined; so, too, is prudency measured by conduct no less than result. The court in a lead ERISA case, *Donovan v. Cunningham*, 716 F.2d 1455, 1467 (5th Cir. 1983), aptly summarized the fiduciary obligation of affirmative vigilance in holding that "a pure heart and an empty head are not enough" to avoid liability for a breach of fiduciary responsibility under the Act.

SUMMARY

This brief survey has reviewed the changing course of the fiduciary standards of *employee pension plans* from their traditional meaning under the common law of trusts to the passage of the broad statutory standards set out under ERISA. The national fiduciary law of pension trusts is continuously shifted by the decisions of the federal courts and by administrative rule-making. For example, the Department of Labor by interpretive bulletin and administrative announcement has established a fiduciary duty of plan trustees to cause the proxies of plan-owned stock to be voted solely in the interests of the participants and beneficiaries without regard to the interests of the plan sponsor. Similarly, where appropriate, the Department of Labor is now prompting trustees to recover stock value losses on behalf of their plans by serving as lead plaintiff in securities fraud litigation.

This chapter merely touches the surface of the deep, swift-running, and ever-wandering stream that plan fiduciaries must negotiate. Knowing its ways and understanding their own roles, fiduciaries may guide the plan and its beneficiaries to their intended destination in trust without upset or misadventure.

Chapter 40

Communicating Employee Benefits Programs

Serafina Maniaci

OBJECTIVES OF EMPLOYEE BENEFITS COMMUNICATIONS

The Information Age as characterized by the Internet is spawning a new generation of communication applications in employee self-service. Web-based applications are replacing interactive voice-response (IVR) systems in human-resources (HR) administration. Employees empowered by the Web are educating themselves, modeling plan costs, enrolling in health plans, and opening retirement accounts. To Internet enthusiasts a paperless HR department seems more certain than ever with the passing of the Electronic Signatures in Global and National Commerce Act into law in June 2000. Yet regardless of the accuracy of such a prediction, technological advancements with friendly government policies do not change the fundamental nature of benefits communications. Communicating either in print or nonprint media, the objectives remain the same and can be classified into three areas:

1. Adhering to statutory reporting and disclosure requirements.
2. Supporting employer efforts for cost-effective programs.
3. Supporting recruitment and retention objectives.

MANDATORY DISCLOSURE REQUIREMENTS

In general, an employer[1] in the private sector that voluntarily sponsors an employee benefit plan is required to meet disclosure requirements. The basic requirements were established by Title I of the Employee Retirement Income Security Act of 1974 (ERISA) and since then other legislation has expanded and/or amended the ERISA provisions. Two major Acts that affect disclosure requirements, among other requirements, are the Consolidated Omnibus Budget Reconciliation Act of 1985 (COBRA) and the Health Insurance Portability and Accountability Act of 1996 (HIPAA). The government agency that has principal jurisdiction over the reporting and disclosure requirements of Title I of ERISA is the Department of Labor (DOL). The Internal Revenue Service (IRS) is the other government agency that has regulatory and interpretive responsibility for legislation related to employee benefits plans. This chapter's focus is on employer disclosure requirements and not on DOL or IRS reporting requirements.

An employer that sponsors an employee benefit plan is required to provide to participants and beneficiaries a summary plan description (SPD) which describes in "understandable terms" the participants' and beneficiaries' rights as well as the benefits and responsibilities under the plan. The employer also must provide participants with a summary of any material modifications (SMM) to the plan or changes to the information contained in the summary plan description. In addition, plan administrators must furnish participants and beneficiaries with a summary of the annual report (IRS Form 5500 Series). Shown in Table 40–1 are the documents that must be provided to participants at various times and upon the occurrence of specific events.[2] Table 40–2 illustrates items from IRS Form 5500 that Pension Plans and Welfare Plans must include in their Summary Annual Reports (SARs).

Timing and Methods of Distribution Requirements for Key Documents

In general, the Statement of ERISA rights (often included in the SPD) and the SPD must be provided within 90 days after the person becomes a par-

---

1 An " employer" is any person acting directly as an employer, or indirectly in the interest of an employer, in relation to an employee benefit plan, and includes a group or association of employers acting for an employer in such capacity. Frank J. Bitzer, J.D., CEBS and Nicholas W. Ferrigno, Jr., JD., CLU, ChFC, *ERISA Facts 2000* (The National Underwriter Company), p. 1.

2 Ibid., pp. 78-79.

T a b l e   40–1

Documents Required By ERISA for Plan Participants

1. Statement of ERISA rights
2. Summary Plan Description (SPD)
3. Notice of Material Plan Changes (Summary of Material Modifications ([SMM])
4. Summary Annual Reports (SAR)
5. Written Explanation of Joint Survivor Annuity Option and the Preretirement Survivor Annuity Option
6. Rollover Distribution Notice
7. Statement of Participant's Rights
8. Statement of Participant's Accrued and Vested Benefits
9. Notice to Participants in Underfunded Plans
10. Notice of Failure to Fund
11. Notice to Missing Participants
12. COBRA Notices
13. HIPAA Notices

ticipant (or a beneficiary) in the plan or within 120 days after the plan becomes subject to the reporting and disclosure provisions of ERISA.[3] If a change is made to the plan that affects information contained in the SPD, an SMM must be provided within 210 days after the close of the plan year in which the modification was adopted. HIPAA reduced the 210-day period to 60 days for group health plans that make changes of "material reductions in covered services or benefits." The SAR is required to be provided no later than nine months after the close of the plan year. As for the method of distribution, the general disclosure requirements by the DOL's Pension and Welfare Benefits Administration state that "the plan administrator shall use measures reasonably calculated to ensure the actual receipt of the material by plan participants and beneficiaries."[4] The regulation states that materials such as SPDs and SMMs that are required to be furnished to all plan participants must be sent by a method or methods of delivery likely to result in full distribution. The regulation states that it is not acceptable to merely place copies in locations that are frequented by participants.

---

3 An updated SPD must be issued every five or ten years if no changes are made to the plan during that period.

4 29 CFR 2520.104b-1.

T A B L E   40–2

Pension Plans and Welfare Plans Must Include the Following Items from IRS Form 5500s in their Summary Annual Reports (SARs)

PENSION PLAN

1. Funding arrangement
2. Total plan expenses
3. Administrative expenses
4. Benefits paid
5. Other expenses
6. Total participants
7. Value of plan assets (net):
   a. End of plan year
   b. Beginning of plan year
8. Change in net assets
9. Total income
   a. Employer contributions
   b. Employee contributions
   c. Gains (losses) from sale of assets
   d. Earnings from investments
10. Total insurance premiums
11. Funding deficiency:
    a. Defined benefit plans
    b. Defined contribution plans

WELFARE PLAN

1. Name of insurance carrier
2. Total (experience-rated and nonexperienced-rated) insurance premiums
3. Experience-rated premiums
4. Experience-rated claims
5. Value of plan assets (net):
   a. End of plan year
   b. Beginning of plan year
6. Change in net assets
7. Total income
   a. Employer contributions
   b. Employee contributions
   c. Gains (losses) from sale assets
   d. Earnings from investments
8. Total plan expenses
9. Administrative expenses
10. Benefits paid
11. Other expenses

Source: www.dol.gov/dol/pwba/public/regs/fedreg/final/2000009611.htm; PWBA Final Rule; Annual Reporting and Disclosure Requirements; Final Rule (April 19, 2000).

On January 28, 1999[5], the DOL issued proposed regulations on the use of electronic communication (and record-keeping) technologies by employee pension and welfare benefit plans. The proposed regulations establish a safe harbor pursuant to which all pension and welfare benefit plans covered under Title I of ERISA may satisfy their obligation to furnish SPDs, SMMs, updated SPDs, and SARs using electronic media. As of this writing the final regulations have not been issued. The proposed regulations specify that electronic media could be used if the following conditions are satisfied:[6]

- The plan administrator must take appropriate and necessary measures to ensure that the system for furnishing documents results in actual receipt by participants, such as the use of a return-receipt electronic mail feature or periodic reviews or surveys by the plan administrator to confirm the integrity of the delivery system.
- Electronically delivered documents must be prepared and furnished in a manner consistent with the style, format, and content requirements applicable to the disclosure. For example, for an electronic document to be considered an SPD it must qualify as an SPD.
- The plan administrator must notify each participant, through electronic means or in writing, of the disclosure documents that are furnished electronically and the significance of the documents. For example, the electronic document being furnished is a summary of material modifications made to your health plan which describes changes in your level of coverage effective on July 1. Also, the plan administrator must notify participants of their right to request and receive, free of charge, a paper copy of each such document.

The safe harbor applies only to participants who meet certain requirements:

- They can effectively access electronic documents at their "work sites." A work site is any location where an employee is reason-

---

5 Under a separate directive of HIPAA, in April 1997 the DOL had issued proposed disclosure rules just for group health plan participants. The January 1999 proposed regulations broaden the rules for using electronic media to pension and welfare plans.

6 Federal Register Online via GPO Access (wais.access.gpo.gov), Part III, U.S. Department of Labor, Pension and Welfare Benefits Administration, 29CFR 2520, *Use of Electronic Communication and Recordkeeping Technologies by Employee Pension and Welfare Benefit Plans.*

ably expected to perform his or her duties, and where access to the employer's electronic information system is an integral part of those duties. The actual location of the work site (e.g., an employee's home, a client's office, or an employee's hotel room) is less important than the reasonable expectation that the employee will have access to the employer's information system on the job, thus being more likely to receive timely communication of plan information.

- At their work sites, they can readily convert furnished documents from electronic to paper form free of charge. Employers may satisfy this requirement by ensuring that participants have access to a printer at their principal work sites.

- Their "principal work site" would be determined by facts and circumstances. For example, if an employee works at home four days a week and at his or her employer's office one day a week, the employee's home would be considered the principal work-site location. On the other hand, if an employee travels to various clients' offices four days a week and is in the employer's office once a week, the employer's office would be considered the employee's principal work site.

The proposed rules do not apply to other plan disclosures[7] such as individual benefit statements, COBRA notices upon a "qualifying event," or notices concerning qualified domestic relations orders.

Information Mandated for SPDs

The original regulations governing the required content for Summary Plan Descriptions were issued in 1977. On September 9, 1998, the DOL proposed new regulations affecting mostly health plan SPDs and on November 21, 2000 it published amended final regulations that take effect on the first day of the second plan year beginning on or after January 22, 2001. The final regulations eliminate the exemption of federally qualified health maintenance organizations (HMOs) from SPD requirements. An SPD must contain information on:

---

7 The IRS did issue final rules on using electronic media for certain qualified plan distribution transactions including notifying participants of distribution options, obtaining a participant's signature, and notifying payees of their right not to have income tax withheld from their distributions. The final regulations are effective for plan years beginning on January 1, 2001. The IRS rules generally approve the use of any electronic media that is "reasonably accessible" to the participant including automated telephone systems and Internet and Intranet Web sites.

1. Plan administration.
2. Plan eligibility requirements.
3. Summary of benefits, rights, and obligations.
4. The Pension Benefit Guaranty Corporation (PBGC) for pension plans.
5. Claims and appeals processes.
6. ERISA rights.

Selected detailed items that fall into these categories are:[8,9]

1. The plan sponsor's name, address, and the employer identification number (EIN).
2. A statement clearly identifying circumstances that may result in disqualification, ineligibility, denial, loss, forfeiture, or suspension of any benefits that a participant or beneficiary might otherwise reasonably expect the plan to provide on the basis of other information provided in the SPD.
3. For an employee pension benefit plan, information about whether the plan is insured with the Pension Benefit Guaranty Corporation and, if not, the reason for the lack of insurance.
4. For an employee welfare benefit plan that is a group health plan, any cost-sharing provisions, including premiums, deductibles, coinsurance, and co-payment amounts for which the participant or beneficiary will be responsible.
5. For an employee welfare plan that is a group health plan, provisions governing the use of network providers, the composition of the provider network, and whether, and under what circumstances, coverage is provided for out-of-network services.
6. The identity of any funding medium used for the accumulation of assets through which benefits are provided.
7. The procedures to be followed in presenting claims for benefits under the plan and the remedies available under the plan for the redress of claims that are denied in whole or in part.

To draft an SPD, there are various sources of expertise available. There are employee benefits consultant firms that specialize in writing

---

8 For a complete list, see www.dol.gov/dol/allcfr/PWBA/Title_29/Part_2520/29CFR2520.102-3.htm.
9 For the final regulations regarding employee pension welfare benefit plans, refer to www.dol.gov/dol/pwba/public/regs/fedreg/final/2000029765.htm.

SPDs; some of these firms also offer software programs that require the plan sponsor to simply insert plan specific information to generate customized SPDs. Also, some insurance carriers and other third-party administrators are willing to assist employers in drafting these documents. However, before these documents are distributed to plan participants, an attorney who specializes in employee benefits should review the documents to ensure compliance and limit litigation risk. It is important to remember that courts generally follow the legal principle of interpreting unclear or confusing SPD language in favor of the "nondrafting party," that is, employees and their beneficiaries.

EDUCATING EMPLOYEES

Plan sponsors offering the most basic employee benefits program have to concern themselves with ERISA, COBRA rights, HIPAA provisions, and other legislation while striving to merge business needs with employee needs. The programs offered must be communicated to new hires, workers experiencing life changes, terminating individuals, and retirees. Not only does the content differ for each of the groups but so does the delivery.

New-Hire Communication Objectives

Newly hired employees are an important audience because their initial exposure to communications materials can affect overall employee morale. In most companies the benefits communications materials and media used for this group usually are the best of whatever the companies can provide. For the new-hire process, human-resources departments have developed communication tools that incorporate notification and disclosure requirements and present their benefits program with its most advantageous aspects. In most cases, the new-hire processes in place are capable of delivering the benefits package, providing counseling services, and enrolling a new hire with remarkable efficiency. Whether the processes are through a one-on-one contact, an IVR system, or a Web application, they communicate the benefits program; provide the means for the new hire to perform the required actions (select plans, authorize payroll deductions, designate beneficiaries); and confirm participant choices in the program.

Common problems that can arise are misunderstandings about actual benefits offered, missing applications, vendor enrollment delays, and challenges to mandatory benefits. A good communication process can alleviate some of these problems. For instance, communication materials can be used to educate hiring officers on the pitfalls of miscommunicating benefits to prospective employees. System-generated notifications to new employees on the types of vendor confirmations to expect can reduce interfacing vendor problems.

Annual Open Enrollment Communication Process

Once the new-hire process is established, it requires periodic attention for maintenance and potential alteration when plan changes occur. These changes often are easier to communicate if they are adopted during the open enrollment period. Often, the open enrollment communication process requires a major commitment of HR resources. Four to six months prior to the effective date of a new plan year, HR professionals begin to work on the open enrollment process. Much effort is expended on updating and revising personal data reports, printed materials, IVR menus, and Web-application programs. All available communications media are employed to communicate plan design changes, changes related to new legislation, and vendor administration changes. Other changes that must be communicated each year are plan cost increases, changes in family members' eligibility statuses, and flexible spending accounts notifications.

However, with the exception of communicating benefits cutbacks when applicable, the most challenging task of open enrollment communications is securing employee participation. The best practices call for a communication campaign that motivates employees to take the time to understand the plan changes and their impact, get their questions answered, and make informed decisions on next year's choices. A high employee participation rate should be pursued to ensure employees are well-informed on their benefits. Employees who take the time to study and make informed decisions during the open enrollment period are less likely to need assistance or misinterpret plan provisions. Thus, designing the best open enrollment Web application or the most comprehensive open enrollment brochure is not enough, the communication campaign must attract employees' attention and then convince them that access to the information is easy and the information is relevant to them. Benefits fairs, newsletters, e-mails, and memos from senior management and employee representatives are examples of actions used to encourage employee participation.

Communications Throughout the Year

Today, many HR offices, benefits call centers, IVR systems, and Web applications are using the "life-events approach" to communicate with employees who experience life changes mid-year. Using this approach, the plan sponsor extracts from each of its benefits plans applicable information for a specific event (e.g., marriage, adoption, or divorce) and then in one place the sponsor communicates step-by-step the options available and actions required to make benefits changes as a result of the particular life-event. For example, acquiring a new dependent has an impact on medical, dental, and life plans; flexible spending accounts; and even pension contributions. Selecting/clicking on the "Adding A New Dependent" button would show all benefits affected by the event, the options available to the employee, and the actions required to make any change. The communication medium also can provide educational materials on child safety precautions, child-care facilities, and tax-advantaged savings plans for college tuition. Although the life-events approach in communications materials is not new, IVR systems, Intranet and Internet technology are enabling plan sponsors to standardize and integrate the approach into their communication function with modest investment. Without this technology, the life-events based approach could not be as effectively employed.

An employee who has access to a fully interactive HR Web site that uses a life-events approach is an empowered individual. The employee can now maximize his or her benefits with minimal transactional cost to the plan sponsor. And with the linking capability of the Web, an employee's opportunities expand beyond what the employer has to offer. An employer can link to various external informational resources. The employer's overall employee benefits' cost may actually increase from such enhancements in benefits communication. Still, plan savings can be derived from effective benefits communications as discussed later in the Employer Objectives section.

Communications to Retirees

In the days of free, lifetime retiree medical benefits, once an employee retired, periodic mass communications were unnecessary. The records of those who retired before age 65 and their dependents were monitored and retirees were notified when they or their dependents became Medicare eligible. The other contact occurred, if applicable, when a life insurance policy claim was filed. Defined benefit pension payments were routinely processed each month. Retiree communications dealt with operational matters such as maintaining current addresses. That is no longer possible. The adoption of *Financial Accounting Standard 106* which achieved its objective of having employers recognize their retiree medical expenses on an accrual basis; the Medicare+Choice program, the catalyst for the growth of managed care in the retiree population; and the escalating increases in health care costs are factors for today's frequent design and pricing changes in retiree medical plans. Consequently, employers are expending more resources on retiree communications and it is not unusual today for employers to hold open enrollment periods for retirees.

The mode of communication for the retiree group remains predominantly printed materials. Limited use of IVR systems and Web-based programs does exist but a broad application of these technological innovations requires the arrival of a new generation of retirees with greater access to computers and more familiarity with the e-world. More so than for materials to active participants, communication to retirees should state clearly *what* has not changed, be very specific of *how* a change will affect the recipient, if possible include personalized materials, and give step-by-step instructions on the actions that the retiree must take and by when. Again, as with any other employee communications, the literature should use short sentences, avoid jargon (include a glossary of terms if necessary), avoid using the passive voice, whenever possible give examples, and, of course, avoid small font sizes. If feasible, materials should be tested first with a subset of the group. A phone number should be prominently displayed on all communications to facilitate inquiries. Retirees' inquiries should be handled by dedicated HR or call center representatives who have the required training. Also, employers with retirees living nearby may find that some retirees still prefer face-to-face communications. The cost of offering this type of service should be measured against the value placed on maintaining good relations with retirees and its effect on employee morale.

Retiree communication needs also have changed because of changes in pension benefits. As more individuals retire with defined contribution plan accumulations, more educational programs are needed to assist retirees not only upon retirement but also throughout their retirement years. HR offices and their third-party administrators are learning that retirees who continue to keep balances in their 401(k) and other similar accounts expect their former employer to provide investment and financial planning advice. Web-based education applications are being utilized for this younger retiree group. However, investment education poses unique communication challenges to employers as discussed in the following section.

Investment Education

Section 404(c) of ERISA states that sponsors of participant-directed plans can avoid responsibility for investment decisions made by a participant with respect to his or her own account if the participant "exercises control."[10] Participant-directed accounts include those from 401(k), money purchase, profit-sharing, or 403(b) plans. A plan is deemed to allow exercise of control by participants or beneficiaries if participants are provided with the opportunity to:[11]

1. Choose from a broad range of investment alternatives, which consist of at least three diversified investment alternatives, each of which has materially different risk and return characteristics.

2. Give investment instructions with a frequency that is appropriate in light of the market volatility of the investment alternatives, but no less frequently than once within any three-month period. (The plan must allow transfers among investment options at least quarterly.)

3. Diversify investments within and among investment alternatives.

4. Obtain sufficient information to make informed investment decisions with respect to investment alternatives available under the plan.

To avail themselves of Section 404(c) protection, plan sponsors must provide certain information automatically to participants. One required disclosure is an explanation that the plan intends to comply with Section 404(c), which limits the liability of plan fiduciaries. Other items of disclosure include the following:[12]

1. A description of the investment alternatives under the plan and a general description of the investment objectives and risk/return characteristics of each alternative, including information relating to the type and diversification of assets comprising that portfolio.

2. Identification of any designated investment managers the plan might provide for the participants.

3. An explanation of how to give investment instructions, any limits/restrictions on giving instructions (including information of withdrawal penalties and valuation adjustments) as well as any restrictions on the exercise of voting, tender, or similar rights.

4. A description of transaction fees or expenses that are charged to the participant's account (e.g., commissions).

---

10 29 CFR 2550.404 (c).

11 Frank J. Bitzer, J.D., CEBS and Nicholas W. Ferrigno, Jr., JD., CLU, ChFC, *ERISA Facts 2000* (The National Underwriter Company), p. 215.

12 Bitzer and Ferrigno, pp. 222-223.

5. If the plan provides for investment in employer securities, a description of those procedures established to provide for confidentiality to participants regarding their transactions in those securities. This requirement includes the name, address, and telephone number of any fiduciary in charge of maintaining such confidentiality and information on independent fiduciaries that are required in transactions that involve employer securities where there is a high potential for a conflict of interest.

6. Shareholder information, subsequent to a specific investment, including any material the plan receives regarding the exercise of voting and ownership rights to the extent such rights are passed through to the participant, along with any references to any plan provisions regarding the exercise of these rights.

7. A copy of the most recent prospectus must be provided to participants immediately after they have made an initial purchase of an investment which is subject to the Securities Act of 1933. (This also may be satisfied by providing the prospectus prior to the initial purchase.)

8. A description of those materials available only upon request and the identification of the person responsible for providing that information.

Yet, despite the issuance of these final 404(c) regulations in 1992, a number of employers still refrained from offering investment education because of fears of widening their fiduciary liability. In 1996, hoping to encourage more employer-sponsored financial education, the DOL issued *Interpretive Bulletin (IB) 96-1* which established guidelines on what constitutes investment education versus advice. Although perfectly legal and offered by some plan sponsors, investment advice has fiduciary implications that can weaken Section 404(c) protection.[13] The DOL's *IB 96-1* stated that benefits communications comprising general plan information, general financial and investment information, asset allocation models that follow generally accepted investment theories, and interactive investment material are providing investment education not advice. Many plan sponsors today do offer investment education, and the Internet is the ideal vehicle for the delivery of this service.

With a few clicks, participants can learn about general investment principles, read about the investment objectives of particular funds,

---

13 At the writing of this chapter, a bipartisan group is proposing legislation to ease ERISA liability regulations and make it easier to offer investment advice. Opponents to the legislation include the DOL.

request prospectuses, and obtain current benchmark performance data as well as compare fund fees and expenses and their ultimate impact on earnings. Not many years ago HR professionals were demonstrating the power of compounding by using brochures with cardboard slides that allowed for several different assumptions on retirement age, inflation, and interest rates. Today the number of permutations that Internet investment models can accommodate is limitless.

However, offering employees financial and retirement planning services via the most innovative medium is not enough. Similar to open enrollment communication, a communication campaign is needed for financial education. The services that are offered only on the Internet must be publicized through other media and supplemented with other activities. General financial planning seminars should be offered throughout the year as well as other sessions targeting specific groups. Those sessions targeting groups near retirement age should include topics such as Social Security benefits, retiree medical insurance, and long-term care. One-on-one counseling sessions could be offered by contracting with independent financial planners when employers are willing to augment investment education with investment advice.

EMPLOYER OBJECTIVES

The common employer objectives of benefits communications are to meet statutory requirements, educate plan participants on the provisions of programs, and demonstrate the value of benefits to the employee's total compensation package. But another critical objective is to support employers' efforts in managing employee benefits program costs. As discussed, effective employee communication can do much to assist employers in averting plan administration problems and lowering administrative costs. Well-developed benefits communications also can assist in managing direct benefits costs. Employers have successfully utilized benefits communications tools to increase employee participation in defined contribution plans such as 401(k) plans in order to pass nondiscrimination test requirements. Another area where employers have used effective benefits communication tools in controlling costs has been in workers' compensation programs. The capacity of occupational safety training programs to reduce job injuries increases when their messages are reinforced through employee/supervisor communication campaigns.

Similarly, dynamic benefits communication programs are supporting health care cost-containment efforts of employers that attack the problem via managed care products. These employers' plans require more than a description of the medical plan benefits. As employers continue to shift cost increases to employees and larger portions to those whom they consider unwise consumers of health care, the role of the communication programs expands. It must compare and contrast medical plans, detail the advantages of in-network providers, promote the benefits of preventive care, and emphasize healthy lifestyles; its objective is to influence the behavior of plan participants. Ultimately, effective benefits communication tools can contribute toward increasing the number of visits to primary care physicians and decreasing those to specialists, increasing mammogram screenings, and increasing smoking-cessation enrollment. All are outcomes proven to have a positive impact on health care costs.

SUMMARY

As companies continue to reduce paper-based processes and empower employees with Web-based self-service applications, HR departments are diverting resources from transactional activities to value-added strategic activities. HR professionals have begun to devote their energies to: (1) designing plans that reduce the risk of moral hazard in group plans; (2) improving the quality of health care by interpreting data on providers, utilization, and outcomes; and (3) developing financial planning education that assists plan participants in balancing current needs with future ones.

The challenge for HR professionals in the Information Age is to sift through mounds of data and design applications with information technology (IT) specialists that convert this mass of information into a knowledge base. Using this knowledge base, HR professionals can then continue to enrich employee benefit programs both for employees and employers.

Employee Benefit Plan Financial Management

Part Eight covers the crucial areas of accounting, reporting, and funding of employee benefit plans. Chapters 41 and 42 review employer's accounting and reporting for employee benefits programs.

Chapter 43 discusses the alternative methods available through insurance companies to fund health and welfare plans, from full insurance to administrative services-only type arrangements, and also discusses self-funding techniques.

Chapter 44 focuses on employer's accounting for pension costs, while the topic of utilizing the appropriate actuarial cost methods to determine the cost of retirement plans is covered in the first part of Chapter 45. The balance of the chapter reviews the different funding vehicles that can be used to set aside assets to meet retirement plan obligations.

Chapter 46 continues the discussion of the investment process for retirement plans by concentrating on investment objectives that must be the starting point in appropriately designing the correct investment strategy.

CHAPTER 41

Employee Benefit Plan Accounting and Reporting

Donald A. Doran

JulieAnn Verrekia

Since the enactment of the Employee Retirement Income Security Act of 1974 (ERISA), there has been a continued emphasis and focus on the financial management of assets held in trust for the benefit of plan participants. Significant other changes since that time have been mandated by the Tax Reform Act of 1986 (TRA '86), the Retirement Protection Act of 1994 (RPA '94), and most recently, the Tax Reform Act of 1997 (TRA '97). As a result, the role of benefit plan financial statements has increased in importance causing the Financial Accounting Standards Board (FASB) and other accounting regulatory bodies, including the American Institute of Certified Public Accountants (AICPA), to address the needs of the users of the plan financial statements and the objectives of those statements.

The most important objective of the plan financial statements is to assist the user in assessing the ability of the plan to pay benefits when due. Who is the user? Obviously, the plan is for the benefit of the participants, and the ability of the plan to pay benefits when due is of critical importance to the participant. However, "the *typical* plan participant would be uninterested in or unable to properly assimilate the information presented in plan financial statements and, thus, would be confused and possibly misled."[1] The FASB concluded that, even if some participants might need to be educated regarding the plan financial statements, those financial statements should nonetheless focus on their needs. Thus, the

---

1 *Statement of Financial Accounting Standards No. 35*, Paragraph 48.

primary users or those who advise or represent them are deemed to be the participants.

This chapter presents an overview of the general financial reporting and accounting requirements of employee benefit plans. Employers' accounting for pension plans is discussed in Chapter 44.

FINANCIAL REPORTING REQUIREMENTS

ERISA requires that many different reports be prepared and filed with the Department of Labor (DOL) and furnished to participants, beneficiaries, and others. ERISA requires that most plans file an annual report with the DOL.

While it is ERISA that requires the plans to file an annual report, it is DOL regulations that specify the filing requirements for plan financial statements. Principally, the requirements are that each plan must file an annual report containing Form 5500 plus certain attachments. The attachments include, among other things, financial statements, notes thereto, supporting schedules, and an accountant's report. Pursuant to DOL regulations, the following plans are not required to file financial statements:

- Small plans (fewer than 100 participants at the beginning of the plan year or plans with more than 100 participants but fewer than 120 that file Form 5500 C/R under the 80–120 rule of DOL Reg. 2520.103-1(d)).
- Insured plans funded exclusively through allocated insurance contracts and whose benefits are fully guaranteed by the insurance carrier.
- Unfunded plans.

ACCOUNTING LITERATURE

Prior to 1980, there were no published guidelines on the application of generally accepted accounting principles (GAAP) to employee benefit plans. Consequently, there was great diversity in the accounting principles adopted and the types of disclosure used in plan financial statements. For example, where one plan may have reported its assets at its cost basis, another plan may have adjusted the cost basis of the assets to reflect market appreciation or depreciation.

In March 1980, the FASB issued *Statement of Financial Accounting Standards (SFAS) No. 35, Accounting and Reporting by Defined Benefit Pension Plans.* Since *SFAS No. 35* addressed only defined benefit plans, the

AICPA incorporated accounting and reporting guidelines for defined contribution and health and welfare plans when it issued its *Audit and Accounting Guide: Audits of Employee Benefit Plans* (the *Guide*) in 1983. Since that time, the *Guide* has been updated numerous times, including a new edition in 1991, and, most recently, reprinted with conforming changes as of May 1, 2000. In August 1992, the FASB issued *Statement of Financial Accounting Standards No. 110, Reporting by Defined Benefit Pension Plans of Investment Contracts*, which expanded fair value accounting to certain contracts with insurance companies.

The Employee Benefit Plans Committee (Committee) of the AICPA also has issued Statements of Position (SOP), periodically amending the *Guide*. SOPs issued by the committee include:

- *SOP 99-2, Accounting for and Reporting of Postretirement Medical Benefit (401(h)) Features of Defined Benefit Pension Plans.*

- *SOP 99-3, Accounting for and Reporting of Certain Employee Benefit Plan Investments and Other Disclosure Matters.*

- *SOP 94-4, Reporting of Investment Contracts Held by Health and Welfare Benefit Plans and Defined Contribution Pension Plans.*

- *SOP 92-6, Accounting and Reporting by Health and Welfare Benefit Plans.*

ACCOUNTING RECORDS

As with any entity, certain records are needed to produce information necessary for effective management of the entity and for preparing its financial statements. Such records for employee benefit plans are usually maintained by a number of individuals at different locations, such as the employer, the trustee, and the actuary or administrator, or both. Depending on the plan, typical records include (but are not limited to):

- *Investment Asset Records.* Such records should include a portfolio listing of all investments and investment transactions. A plan trustee must be able to provide sufficient detail of investment transactions and balances to satisfy both GAAP and ERISA financial reporting and disclosure requirements.

- *Participant Records.* Demographic records are needed to determine eligibility for participation, contributions, benefit calculations, benefit payments, and actuarial valuations.

- *Contribution Records.* Records of contributions received and due are particularly important for plans having more than one contributor.
- *Claim Records.* Records of claims for health and welfare plans are not only important for establishing claims history but also for determining when benefit limits have been reached.
- *Distribution Records.* These records, including entitlement, commencement data, forfeitures, terminations, and the like, are necessary to support all distributions from the plan.
- *Separate Participants' Accounts.* Defined contribution plans require separate accounts to be maintained for each participant reflecting his or her share of the net assets of the plan.

EMPLOYEE BENEFIT PLAN FINANCIAL STATEMENTS

The general requirements for financial statements prescribed by the FASB and AICPA are applicable for defined benefit, defined contribution, and health and welfare plans and are similar in many aspects. This section of the chapter is organized into a discussion of the general requirements equally applicable to all types of plans, followed by some of the particular requirements applicable to the specific types of plans. Sample financial statements of a defined benefit pension plan are included in the appendix at the end of this chapter. Financial accounting and reporting standards for defined contribution plans are similar to those of defined benefit plans to the extent appropriate. For example, under a defined contribution plan, information regarding the actuarial present value of accumulated plan benefits would not be applicable, because the amount of benefits a participant receives is based on contributions made to the plan, as opposed to a calculation of benefits made by applying a formula to participant census data. In other respects, the financial statements of defined contribution plans are substantially the same as those of defined benefit plans.

Overview of General Requirements

SFAS No. 35 requires that every plan issuing financial statements present a statement of net assets available for plan benefits as of the end of the plan year, a statement of changes in net assets for the year then ended, and the related notes to the financial statements.

All plans filing under ERISA must present the financial statements in comparative form—that is, statements for the current year must be presented alongside statements for the previous year.

Under GAAP, the financial statements must be presented using the accrual basis of accounting, whereby financial recognition is given to an event when it occurs, regardless of whether cash was paid or received. The accrual basis also contemplates that, generally, purchases and sales of securities must be recognized on a "trade-date" basis, as opposed to a "settlement-date" basis. The DOL does accept financial statements prepared using a modified cash accounting basis; however, these statements would not qualify as being in conformity with GAAP.

Statement of Net Assets Available for Plan Benefits

The statement of net assets available for plan benefits shall present information regarding net assets in such reasonable detail as is necessary to identify the plan's resources available to pay plan benefits. Plan resources typically include investments, contributions receivable, cash, and operating assets, if any, less any liabilities of the plan.

Investments

Because investments are usually a pension plan's largest asset, their valuation is particularly important. Most plan investments are required to be stated at fair value as of the date of the financial statements.

Determining Fair Value. The fair value of an investment is the amount a pension plan could realistically expect to receive in a transaction between a willing buyer and a willing seller. Fair value is often difficult to determine, because of the nature of the investment. For securities traded on an active market, the determination is relatively easy—fair value is the quoted market price. For securities for which there is no quoted market price, the determination of fair value becomes more difficult. Securities of closely held companies or investments in real estate generally will not have an active market. In these cases, market price must be determined by using alternative means, such as discounted cash flow or valuations performed by independent experts.

Contracts with Insurance Companies. Contracts with insurance companies are valued differently, depending on the type of plan. Valuation of investment contracts with insurance companies held by health and welfare benefit plans and defined contribution plans is governed by *SOP 94-4, Reporting of Investment Contracts Held by Health and Welfare Benefit Plans and Defined Contribution Pension Plans*, issued by the Employee Benefit Plans Committee of the AICPA. The *SOP* requires that most contracts be valued at fair value, except contracts that incorporate mortality or morbidity risk, or that allow for current withdrawals for benefits at contract value. In such cases, the contract can be reported at contract value. Additionally, the presentation will generally depend on whether the payment to the insurance company is allocated to purchase insurance or annuities for the individual participants, or whether the payments are accumulated in an unallocated fund to be used to pay retirement benefits. These are referred to as *allocated* and *unallocated* arrangements, respectively.

Allocated funding arrangements include contracts in which the insurer has a legally enforceable obligation to make the benefit payments to the participant. The obligations of the plan have been transferred to the insurer, through the payment of premium, and the investment in the allocated insurance contract should be excluded from plan assets. Conversely, unallocated funding instruments apply to any arrangement under which contributions are held in an undivided fund until they are used by the plan to pay retirement benefits.

Unallocated funds, therefore, are included in plan assets. Examples of allocated contracts include individual insurance, annuity contracts, and group permanent insurance contracts. Unallocated arrangements include guaranteed investment contracts, group deposit administration contracts, and immediate participation guarantee contracts.

Commingled and Master Trust Funds.

Common or commingled trust funds, pooled separate accounts of insurance companies, and master trust funds generally contain the assets of two or more plans that are pooled for investment purposes. Common or commingled funds and insurance company pooled separate accounts generally contain plans sponsored by two or more employers. Master trusts hold the assets of plans sponsored by a single employer or by members of a controlled group. In a common or commingled fund or pooled separate account, the plan generally has units of participation in the fund. The value of these investments is based on the unit value of the fund or separate account, and must be stated at fair value.

The accounting and reporting requirements for master trusts present certain additional considerations. Plans are required to present their interest in the master trust as one line—that is, as "Investment in master trust."

Summarized financial information (the investments of the master trust, the net change in fair value of each significant type of investment of the master trust, and total investment income of the master trust by type) of the master trust should be presented in a footnote along with the information mentioned above regarding the method of determining fair value and general types of investments. The notes to the financial statements also should include a description of the basis used to allocate net assets, net investment income, gains and losses to participating plans, and the plan's percentage interest in the master trust.

Participant Loans. Many defined contribution plans allow for participants to borrow funds from the plan. Participant loans are reported as investments in the benefit plan financial statements at their unpaid balances. Participant loans are typically restricted in amount and sometimes as to the use of the funds. Examples of restrictions might be that loans are only made up to a percentage of the vested portion of the participant's account or that the proceeds from loans may only be used to purchase a home. Interest charges on loans provide investment revenue to the plan.

Disclosure. Disclosure must be provided, usually in the footnotes, of whether fair value was measured using quoted market prices in an active market or was otherwise determined. The method of valuation of insurance contracts also must be disclosed. Detail of the investments must be provided either on the face of the statement of net assets available for plan benefits or in a footnote. Investments must be segregated, where material, by general types, such as corporate stocks, bonds, and the like. In addition, individual investments representing 5 percent or more of net assets available for plan benefits must be separately disclosed.

Receivables

Receivables must be stated separately, if material, for the following:

- Employer contributions.
- Participant contributions.
- Amounts due from brokers for securities sold.
- Accrued interest and dividends.
- Other.

Contributions receivable may only include amounts due as of the reporting date. Participant contributions receivable, generally, are those amounts withheld from participants' pay and not yet remitted to the plan. Employer contributions can be evidenced by the following:

- A legal or contractual obligation.
- A formal commitment evidenced by:

— A resolution by the employer's governing body.

— A consistent pattern of making payments after the plan's year-end, pursuant to an established funding policy.

— A deduction for federal income taxes by the employer.

— The employer's recognition of a liability (although recognition of a liability by the employer in and of itself may not be sufficient to justify recording a receivable).

All of the foregoing should be tempered by the need to establish an appropriate allowance for estimated uncollectible receivables and, if material, disclose such allowance. For example, assume an employer has a contractual obligation to make a contribution to the plan. If the employer is a financially troubled company, there may be some uncertainty that the full amount of the contribution will be received. In this situation, the amount of the contribution receivable should be reduced by the amount estimated to be uncollectible, and this fact should be disclosed in the footnotes. Additionally, if a deficiency in the plan's funding standard account exists at year-end, consideration should be given to establishing a receivable from the employer.

Other Assets

Typically, most plans do not have significant assets, other than investments and contributions receivable. However, other types of assets that may exist are residual cash that has not yet been invested and operating assets, such as buildings and equipment.

Cash and cash equivalents are recorded at face value but should be segregated between interest-bearing and noninterest-bearing deposits.

GAAP requires that operating assets be recorded at cost less depreciation and amortization. ERISA requires these assets be recorded at fair value. This should rarely present a significant difference.

Liabilities

Liabilities, such as those for the purchase of investments and other administrative expenses, should be stated at the amount owed by the plan.

Statement of Changes in Net Assets Available for Plan Benefits

Information regarding changes in net assets available for plan benefits is intended to present the effects of significant changes in net assets during the reporting period. At a minimum, this disclosure should include:

■ The net appreciation or depreciation includes realized gains or losses from sales of investments and unrealized gains or losses from market appreciation or depreciation. Separate disclosure of realized gains or losses is not required by GAAP but is required for Form 5500. The DOL instructions to Form 5500 require that realized and unrealized gains and losses be determined using the value of the asset as of the beginning of the plan year ("current value method"), rather than the historical cost basis. The current value method often requires additional record-keeping to track changes in investment values from year to year.

■ Investment income exclusive of amount included in net appreciation of investments.

■ Contributions from employer(s) and participants.

■ Benefits paid to participants.

■ Payments to insurance companies to purchase contracts that are excluded from plan assets.

■ Administrative expenses.

■ Other changes such as the transfer of assets to or from other plans.

Statement of Cash Flows

FASB Statement No. 102, Statement of Cash Flows—Exemption of Certain Enterprises and Classification of Cash Flows from Certain Securities Acquired for Resale, exempts employee benefit plans that present financial information required by *SFAS No. 35* from the requirement to present a statement of cash flows. However, benefit plans are encouraged to include a statement of cash flows with their annual financial statements when that statement would provide relevant information about the ability of the plan to meet future obligations.

Additional Financial Statement Disclosures

Requirements for financial statement disclosures come from a variety of sources, including *SFAS No. 35*, the *Guide*, and various SOP and ERISA regulations. Many of the significant disclosure requirements are as follows:

General

■ A description of the plan, including vesting and benefit provisions, significant plan amendments during the year, and the policy regarding the disposition of forfeitures.

- A description of coverage provided by the Pension Benefit Guaranty Corporation (PBGC) if applicable, as well as benefit payment priorities in the event of plan termination.
- The plan's funding policy, including any changes during the year.
- The policy regarding the purchase of allocated insurance contracts that are excluded from plan assets.
- Methods and significant assumptions used to value investments.
- Significant actuarial assumptions and changes during the current year.
- The federal income tax status of the plan, including whether a favorable IRS tax determination letter has been received. Additionally, disclosure should be made if the plan has been amended subsequent to the receipt of the latest determination letter.
- Individual investments that represent more than 5 percent of total net assets. For defined contribution plans that provide for both participant-directed and nonparticipant-directed investment programs, specific identification of nonparticipant-directed investments that represent 5 percent or more of total net assets is required.
- Significant transactions with related parties that include, but are not limited to, the sponsor, plan administrator, employees, and employee organizations.
- Significant events or transactions occurring subsequent to the financial statement date.
- Accounting policies that represent variances from GAAP.
- Certain significant risks and uncertainties including significant estimates used.
- Commitments and contingencies.
- Information regarding financial instruments with off-balance-sheet risk of accounting loss and significant concentrations of credit risk.
- Disclosure regarding derivative financial instruments.
- Differences between the financial statements and amounts required to be reported on Form 5500. For example, Form 5500 requires the accrual of a liability representing amounts payable to participants at year-end, while GAAP assumes that liability is included in the actuarial present value of accumulated plan benefits.

Defined Contribution Plans

- Investment allocation provisions, including any unallocated assets.
- The policy regarding the disposition of forfeitures.
- Basis for determining contributions.
- Net assets and significant components of the changes in net assets relating to nonparticipant-directed investment programs for defined contribution plans that provide for both participant-directed and nonparticipant-directed investment programs.
- Amounts allocated to persons who have elected to withdraw from the plan but remain unpaid at the financial statement date.

Health and Welfare Plans

- Policy regarding participant contributions to the plan.
- A description of the methods and significant actuarial assumptions used to determine the plan's benefit obligations, as well as any changes in the current year.
- If the benefit obligation exceeds plan assets, the method of funding the deficit must be disclosed.
- The types and extent of insurance coverage that transfers risk from the plan.
- Assumed health care cost-trend rates used to measure the cost of benefits covered by the plan.
- For plans providing post-retirement benefits, the effect of a one-percentage-point increase in the assumed health care cost-trend rates.

Supplemental Schedules

In addition to the requirements of *SFAS No. 35* and the *Guide*, ERISA and DOL regulations specify separate schedules of:

- Investment assets (one schedule of assets held at the plan year-end and another showing plan assets acquired and disposed of during the plan year) showing both cost and current (fair) value or sales proceeds.
- Nonexempt transactions.
- Loans or fixed-income obligations in default or classified as uncollectible.

■ Leases in default or classified as uncollectible.

■ Reportable transactions, which includes any single transaction that involves more than 5 percent of the current value of plan assets, or a series of transactions with the same person in excess of 5 percent of the current value of plan assets.

DEFINED BENEFIT PLANS

A defined benefit plan is one that promises to pay participants' benefits that are determinable based on such factors as age, years of service, and compensation.

In addition to the general financial statement requirements, defined benefit plans also must disclose information regarding the actuarial present value of accumulated plan benefits (PVAB) as of either the beginning or end of the plan year and changes in the PVAB from year to year.

It is important to understand that the PVAB will generally not be the same amount as the actuarially determined liability pursuant to the cost method in the plan. This actuarial liability represents the present value of the estimated benefits that will be payable to participants on retirement. The PVAB represents only those benefits that have accumulated as of a specific date, as opposed to estimated benefits at retirement. There is no requirement that the assumptions used to calculate the PVAB (e.g., discount rates, investment rates, and the like) be the same as for the actuarial liability. Consequently, significant differences could exist.

Statement of Accumulated Plan Benefits

Information regarding the PVAB may be presented in the financial statements (on the same page as the statement of net assets available for plan benefits or as a separate statement) or in the footnotes and must be segmented into the following categories:

■ Vested benefits of participants currently receiving benefits (including benefits due and payable as of the benefit information date).

■ Other vested benefits.

■ Nonvested benefits.

A description of the method and significant assumptions (e.g., assumed rate of return, mortality rates, and retirement ages) used to determine the PVAB must be disclosed in the footnotes. The benefit information should exclude benefits to be paid by insurance companies pursuant to contracts that are excluded from plan assets.

Note that *SFAS No. 35* requires a statement of net assets available for plan benefits only as of the end of the plan year. However, when the accumulated benefit information is presented as of the beginning of the plan year, a statement of net assets available for plan benefits must be included as of the preceding plan year-end. The reason is to give the reader the ability to make a comparison between plan assets available to pay benefits with the related PVAB as of the same date. If the plan assets are as of the end of the year and the benefit information is as of the beginning of the year, such comparability does not exist. By including plan assets as of the preceding year-end, there is comparability with the beginning-of-the-year benefit information. For plans complying with ERISA, this will not pose any problems because, as mentioned, ERISA requires comparative financial statements.

Statement of Changes in Accumulated Plan Benefits

Information regarding changes in the PVAB from the preceding to the current benefit information dates can be presented as a separate financial statement or in the footnotes, and in either a narrative or reconciliation format. The effects of any changes in accumulated plan benefits should be accounted for in the year of the change, not by restating amounts previously reported.

If significant, either individually or in the aggregate, the effects of certain factors affecting the change in the PVAB from the preceding to the current benefit-information dates shall be identified. Minimum disclosure shall include the following:

- Plan amendments.
- Changes in the nature of the plan (e.g., a plan spinoff or merger).
- Changes in actuarial assumptions.

The significant effects of other factors also may be identified, including, for example, benefits accumulated (including actuarial gains or losses), the increase (for interest) as a result of the decrease in the discount period, and benefits paid.

If the minimum required information is presented in a manner other than a reconciliation format, the PVAB as of the preceding benefit-information date also shall be presented.

DEFINED CONTRIBUTION PLANS

A defined contribution plan is one that provides individual accounts for each participant's benefits based on amounts contributed to the participants' accounts, investment experience, and, if applicable, forfeitures allocated to the account.

The additional key financial statement issue to address is the allocation of the plan assets to the participants' accounts. Required financial statement disclosures include:

- Amount of unallocated assets.
- The basis used to allocate asset values to participants' accounts when that basis differs from the one used to record assets in the financial statements.
- Net assets and significant components of the changes in net assets relating to nonparticipant-directed investment programs for defined contribution plans that provide for both participant-directed and nonparticipant-directed investment programs.
- Amounts allocated to participants who have withdrawn from the plan.
- Specific identification of nonparticipant-directed investments that represent 5 percent or more of total net assets.

Some plans allow for the participant to make investment decisions between a number of investment options. Typical plans of this type would include a range of investment options that would provide various levels of risk and return. Examples would include money market funds, government bond funds, balanced funds, equity funds, and growth funds.

Some defined contribution plans, such as employee stock purchase plans, are required to register with and report to the Securities and Exchange Commission (SEC). The form and content of the financial statements that must be filed with the SEC are prescribed in Regulation S-X.

The general requirements are included in Articles 1, 2, 3, and 4 of Regulation S-X. Article 6A of Regulation S-X includes the specific requirements applicable to employee stock purchase, savings, and similar plans.

Article 6A requires that plans present their net assets available for plan benefits in statements of financial condition for the two most recent years. Plan assets to be disclosed in this statement include:

- Investments in securities of participating employer(s), stated separately for each employer.
- Investments in securities of unaffiliated issuers, segregated between U.S. government obligations and other.

- Investments other than securities.
- Dividends and interest receivable.
- Cash.
- Other assets, stating separately amounts due from participating employers, directors, officers or principal shareholders, trustees or managers of the plan, and other.

Liabilities and equity that must be disclosed include:

- Liabilities, stating separately any payables to employers, employees, and other.
- Reserves and other credits.
- Debt.
- Plan equity, which is equivalent to the net assets available for plan benefits.

In addition, statements of income and changes in plan equity are required for the three most recent years. These statements must include:

- Net investment income, stating separately:
    — Income, stating separately cash dividends, interest, and other. Income from investments in or indebtedness of participating employers shall be segregated.
    — Expenses.
    — Net investment income.
- Realized gain or loss on investments, stating separately gains or losses from investments in securities of participating employer(s), other investments in securities, and other investments.
- Unrealized appreciation or depreciation of investments. In addition, in a footnote, the unrealized appreciation or depreciation as of the beginning and end of the period must be disclosed.
- Contributions and deposits, separated between employer(s) and employees.
- Withdrawals, lapses, and forfeitures, stating separately the balances of the employees' accounts, the amounts disbursed in settlement of the accounts, and the disposition of the remaining balance.
- Plan equity at the beginning of the period and at the end of the period.

In addition, Article 6A requires certain schedules to be filed if the information is not readily apparent from the financial statements. These are:

- Schedule I—Investments.
- Schedule II—Allocation of plan assets and liabilities to investment programs.
- Schedule III—Allocation of plan income and changes in plan equity to investment programs.

The form and content of these schedules are specified in Rule 6A–05.

In lieu of the aforementioned requirements, plans subject to ERISA may file plan financial statements and schedules prepared in accordance with the financial reporting requirements of ERISA.

HEALTH AND WELFARE PLANS

Employee health and welfare plans are those plans providing benefits, such as medical, dental, scholarship, and the like, to employees of a single employer or group of employers. Such benefits may be provided by the plan or transferred to an insurance company. Whether a premium paid to an insurance company represents a deposit (i.e., an investment) or a transfer of risk depends on the exact nature of the contract.

Payment of a premium where the risk is transferred to the insurance company represents a reduction in the net assets of the plan. Premiums paid that represent deposits should be reflected as plan assets until such time as the deposit is refunded or applied against claims.

In an insured plan, claims reported and claims incurred but not reported will be paid by the insurance company. Such claims should not appear in the plan's financial statements. Self-insured plans should report those amounts. The footnotes should describe the significant assumptions and changes in assumptions used to determine such liabilities.

Certain group insurance contracts provide for experience-rating adjustments that could result in a refund (premiums exceed claims) or deficit (claims exceed premiums). If the amount of a refund can be reasonably estimated, then a receivable should be recorded. If the amount of a deficit can be reasonably estimated and if it will be applied against future premiums, then a payable should be recorded. If a payable for a deficit is not recorded, because one of the two conditions has not been met, disclosure should be made.

Some plans provide for payment of insurance benefits for a time period subsequent to the financial statement date for participants who have accumulated a certain number of eligibility credits. Such credits will permit payment of benefits during times of unemployment and represent a liability of the plan as they have arisen from prior employee service. The liability should be calculated as follows:

- Insured plans—current insurance premium rates should be applied to the accumulated credits.
- Self-insured plans—the average cost per person of the benefits should be applied to the accumulated credits.

As previously noted, *SOP 92-6, Accounting and Reporting by Health and Welfare Benefit Plans*, was issued by the Employee Benefit Plans Committee of the AICPA. This SOP requires, among other things, that the benefit obligations for health and welfare plans include the actuarial present value of post-retirement benefits and claims incurred but not reported.

More detailed coverage of accounting and reporting for health and welfare benefit plans is presented in Chapter 42.

AUDITOR'S REPORT

The purpose of an audit is to attest to management's representations in financial statements. An auditor's report on employee benefit plan financial statements is generally included as part of the annual report required by ERISA standards. The *Guide* contains illustrative auditor's reports that have been prepared in accordance with *SFAS No. 58, Reports on Audited Financial Statements*. The audit report is typically addressed to the plan, plan administrator, board of trustees, or participants. Illustrative examples of standard reports and certain departures therefrom are provided in the appendix at the end of this chapter. The general form of the illustrative examples are in accordance with the *Guide*.

Standard Report

A standard auditor's report provides users with a reasonable assurance that the plan's financial statements have been presented fairly, in all material respects, in conformity with generally accepted accounting principles. The chapter appendix contains illustrative examples of standard audit reports for a defined benefit, a defined contribution, and a health and welfare benefit plan. The exact wording of each report in practice will depend on the relevant circumstances involved. For example, although the illustrative reports included here are for financial statements covering one year, the two-year comparative statements are frequently presented.

Supplemental Schedules

As indicated earlier in this chapter, in addition to the requirements of *SFAS No. 35* and the *Guide*, ERISA and DOL regulations require certain supplemental schedules. These schedules must be covered by the auditor's report, which requires a modification to the standard report. The modification includes the addition of a fourth paragraph to the standard. The additional paragraph is illustrated as follows:

> Our audit was made for the purpose of forming an opinion on the basic financial statements taken as a whole. The supplemental schedules of (identify) are presented for purposes of complying with the Department of Labor's Rules and Regulations for Reporting and Disclosure under the Employee Retirement Income Security Act of 1974 and are not a required part of the basic financial statements. The supplemental schedules have been subjected to the auditing procedures applied in the audit of the basic financial statements and, in our opinion, are fairly stated in all material respects in relation to the basic financial statements taken as a whole.

Nonstandard Reports

The standard auditor's report will not always be appropriate. Some of the more common circumstances in which the auditor might use nonstandard wording include the preparation of financial statements on a non-GAAP basis (e.g., on a cash or modified cash basis), scope limitations imposed by the plan administrator pursuant to DOL regulations, and inadequacies related to investment valuation.

Plan administrators commonly limit the scope of the auditor's examination to exclude information provided by a bank or insurance company, subject to certain stipulations. This limitation restricts the scope of the auditor. Due to the significance that this information generally carries, the restriction prevents the auditor from reaching an opinion on the financial statements taken as a whole. An illustrative example of a report that might be issued in this situation also is provided in the appendix.

At times, benefit plans may hold material investments that do not have a readily determinable market value. This may cause a standard report to be inappropriate. An illustrative report, of when the plan's procedures to determine the fair value of investments are not adequate, appears in the appendix.

When the auditor concludes that departures from generally accepted accounting principles are so material that the financial statements of the plan do not fairly present the plan's financial position and results, the auditor issues an adverse opinion.

SUMMARY

This chapter serves as a general description of the accounting and financial reporting requirements of employee benefit plans. It does not replace authoritative accounting and auditing literature, ERISA, or other official instructions or published regulations of the DOL or IRS. Readers of this chapter should refer to those specific sources for more detailed information.

Participation in employee benefit plans, and the invested assets of employee benefit plans, has continued to grow over the past several years. It has been estimated that there are approximately 90 million participants and beneficiaries of employee benefit plans in the United States alone. The assets of the associated plans are estimated to exceed $1.5 trillion dollars, which makes employee benefit plans a significant factor in the overall economy.

Accompanying this growth, the various regulatory authorities governing these plans have increased their focus on compliance with the various laws and regulations governing employee benefit plans. Form 5500 filings are being subjected to more detailed and comprehensive review by the DOL. Along with the laws and regulations come stiff penalties for noncompliance. In many instances, noncompliance could cost the plan's sponsor or administrator up to $1,000 per day. There is no doubt that this increased focus will continue in the future and add to the complexity of accounting and reporting by employee benefit plans.

A P P E N D I X   41–1

Sample Pension Plan Financial Statements

SAMPLE COMPANY PENSION PLAN

Statements of Net Assets Available for Plan Benefits and Accumulated Plan Benefits

As of December 31, 20X2 and 20X1

Net Assets Available for Plan Benefits	20X2	20X1
Investment contract with insurance company	$2,278,000	$1,934,000
U.S. government securities	250,000	150,000
Employer contributions receivable	41,000	41,000
Net assets available for plan benefits	$2,569,000	$2,225,000
Accumulated Plan Benefits as of January 1, 20X2		
Actuarial present value of accumulated plan benefits:		
Vested benefits:		
Participants currently receiving payments	$2,330,000	$1,980,000
Other participants	195,000	177,000
Total	2,525,000	2,157,000
Nonvested benefits	286,000	264,000
Total actuarial present value of accumulated plan benefits	$2,811,000	$2,421,000
Excess of actuarial present value of accumulated plan benefits over net assets available for plan benefits	$ 242,000	$ 196,000

The accompanying notes are an integral part of the financial statements.

Statement of Changes in Net Assets Available for Plan Benefits and Accumulated Plan Benefits

For the Years Ended December 31, 20X2 and 20X1

Net Increase in Net Assets Available for Benefits	20X2	20X1
Additions:		
Contributions from employer	$ 183,000	$ 141,000
Net appreciation of U.S. government securities	20,000	10,000
Interest income	250,000	201,000
Total additions	453,000	352,000

Deductions:		
Benefits paid	101,000	80,000
Administrative expenses	8,000	8,000
Total deductions	109,000	88,000
Net additions	344,000	264,000
Net assets available for plan benefits, beginning of year	2,225,000	1,961,000
Net assets available for plan benefits, end of year	$2,569,000	$2,225,000

Net increase in Actuarial Present Value of Accumulated Plan Benefits

Increase (decrease) during the year attributable to:	
Benefits accumulated	$208,000
Increase for interest due to the decrease in the discount period	153,000
Benefits paid	(71,000)
Net increase	290,000

The accompanying notes are an integral part of the financial statements.

Notes to Financial Statements

A. General Description of the Plan

The Sample Company Pension Plan (Plan) is a noncontributory defined benefit plan covering all employees of Sample Company who have at least one year of service. It is subject to the provisions of the Employee Retirement Income Security Act of 1974 (ERISA). Participants should refer to the Plan agreement for more complete information regarding benefit, vesting, and termination provisions.

B. Summary of Significant Accounting Policies

The following are the significant accounting policies followed by the Plan:

1. *Basis of accounting.* The accompanying financial statements are prepared on the accrual basis of accounting.

2. *Investment valuation.* U.S. government securities are valued at quoted market prices. The investment contract is valued at fair value by discounting the related cash flows based on current yields of similar instruments with comparable durations. Funds under the investment contract that have been allocated and applied to purchase annuities guaranteed by the insurance company are excluded from plan assets. Purchases and sales of securities are recorded on a trade-date basis.

3. *Income recognition.* Interest income is recorded on the accrual basis.

4. *Payment of benefits.* Benefit payments to participants are recorded upon distribution.

5. Administrative expenses of the Plan are paid by the Plan.

C. Funding Policy

The Company's funding policy is to make annual contributions, at a minimum, to meet the ERISA minimum funding standards and at a maximum, amounts deductible by the Company for federal income tax purposes. The Company's contributions for 20X1 and 20X2 exceeded the minimum funding requirements of ERISA.

D. Plan Termination

Although it has not expressed any intention to do so, the Company has the right under the Plan subject to the provisions set forth in ERISA. In the event the Plan terminates, the net assets of the Plan will be allocated as prescribed by ERISA and its related regulations. Certain benefits under the Plan are insured by the Pension Benefit Guaranty Corporation (PBGC), a U.S. government agency, if the plan terminates. Generally, the PBGC guarantees most vested normal age retirement benefits, early retirement benefits. However, the PBGC does not guarantee all types of benefits under the Plan and coverage is subject to certain limitations.

E. Contract with Insurance Company

The Company entered into a contract with the Emerald Insurance Company. The underlying assets of the contract are invested in the unallocated general assets of the insurance company. The contract provides, among other matters, that the investment account is to be credited with the contributions received during the contract period plus its share of the insurance company's actual investment income. Annuities purchased to provide and guarantee benefits are excluded from Plan assets.

F. Significant Actuarial Information

Accumulated plan benefits are those future periodic payments, including lump-sum distributions, that are attributable under the Plan's provisions to the service employees have rendered. Accumulated plan benefits include benefits expected to be paid to (a) retired or terminated employees or their beneficiaries, (b) beneficiaries of employees who have died, and (c) present employees or their beneficiaries. Benefits under the Plan are based on employees' compensation during their last full 60 months of service. The accumulated plan benefits as of January 1, 20X2, for active employees are based on their service rendered and history of compensation as of December 31, 20X1. Benefits payable under all circumstances (retirement, death, disability, and termination of employment) are included to the extent they are deemed attributable to employee service rendered to the valuation date.

The actuarial present value of accumulated plan benefits is that amount that results from applying actuarial assumptions to adjust the accumulated plan benefits to reflect the time value of money (through discounts for interest) and the probability of payment (by means of such decrements as for death, disability, withdrawal, or retirement) between the valuation date and the expected date of payment. The significant assumptions used in the actuarial valuation and/or the computation of the present value of accumulated plan benefits as of January 1, 20X2, are as follows:

Actuarial Factor	Assumption
Actuarial method	Projected unit credit
Rate of return on investments	7.5 percent per annum compounded annually
Mortality basis	1971 Group Annuity Table
Expenses	4.0 percent of estimated plan costs
Retirement age	Normal, attained age 65; Early, attained age 55
Withdrawal rates	Table 6 of *The Actuary's Pension Handbook*

G. Tax Status

The Internal Revenue Service has determined and informed the Company by a letter dated September 30, 20XX, that the Plan and related trust are designed in accordance with Section 401(a) of the Internal Revenue Code (IRC) and is, therefore, exempt from federal income taxes under provisions of Section 501(a). The Plan has been amended since receiving the determination letter. However, the Plan administrator and the Plan's tax counsel believe the plan is designed and is currently being operated in compliance with applicable requirements of the IRC.

ILLUSTRATIONS OF AUDITOR'S REPORTS ON FINANCIAL STATEMENTS

Standard Auditor's Reports

A Defined Benefit Plan

Independent Auditor's Report

Addressee:

We have audited the accompanying statements of net assets available for benefits and of accumulated plan benefits of XYZ Pension Plan as of December 31, 20X2, and the related statements of changes in net assets available for benefits and of changes in accumulated plan benefits for the year then ended. These financial statements are the responsibility of the Plan's management. Our responsibility is to express an opinion on these financial statements based on our audit.

We conducted our audit in accordance with auditing standards generally accepted in the United States. Those standards require that we plan and perform the audit to obtain reasonable assurance about whether the financial statements are free of material misstatement. An audit includes examining, on a test basis, evidence supporting the amounts and disclosures in the financial statements. An audit also includes assessing the accounting principles used and significant estimates made by management, as well as evaluating the overall financial statement presentation. We believe that our audit provides a reasonable basis for our opinion.

In our opinion, the financial statements referred to above present fairly, in all material respects, the financial status of the Plan as of December 31, 20X2, and the changes in its financial status for the year then ended in conformity with accounting principles generally accepted in the United States.

[Signature of Firm]

[City and State]

[Date]

A Defined Contribution Plan

Independent Auditor's Report

Addressee:

We have audited the accompanying statement of net assets available for plan benefits of XYZ Company Savings Plan as of December 31, 20X1, and the related statement of changes in net assets available for plan benefits for the year then ended. These financial statements are the responsibility of the Plan's management. Our responsibility is to express an opinion on these financial statements based on our audit.

We conducted our audit in accordance with auditing standards generally accepted in the United States. Those standards require that we plan and perform the audit to obtain reasonable assurance about whether the financial statements are free of material misstatement. An audit includes examining, on a test basis, evidence supporting the amounts and disclosures in the financial statements. An audit also includes assessing the accounting principles used and significant estimates made by management, as well as evaluating the overall financial statement presentation. We believe that our audit provides a reasonable basis for our opinion.

In our opinion, the financial statements referred to above present fairly, in all material respects, the net assets available for plan benefits of the Plan as of December 31, 20X1, and the changes in net assets available for plan benefits for the year then ended in conformity with accounting principles generally accepted in the United States.

The Fund Information in the statement of net assets available for benefits and the statement of changes in net assets available for benefits is presented for purposes of additional analysis, rather than to present the net assets available for plan benefits and changes in net assets available for plan benefits of each fund. The Fund Information has been subjected to the auditing procedures applied in the audits of the basic financial statements and, in our opinion, are fairly stated in all material respects in relation to the basic financial statements taken as a whole.

[Signature of Firm]
[City and State]
[Date]

A Health and Welfare Benefit Plan

Independent Auditor's Report

Addressee:

We have audited the accompanying statement of net assets of XYZ Corporation Employee Health and Welfare Benefit Plan as of December 31, 20X1, and the related statement of changes in net assets for the year then ended. These financial statements are the responsibility of the Plan's management. Our responsibility is to express an opinion on these financial statements based on our audit.

We conducted our audit in accordance with auditing standards generally accepted in the United States. Those standards require that we plan and perform the audit to obtain reasonable assurance about whether the financial statements are free of material misstatement. An audit includes examining, on a test basis, evidence supporting the amounts and disclosures in the financial statements. An audit also includes assessing the accounting principles used and significant estimates made by management, as well as evaluating the overall financial statement presentation. We believe that our audit provides a reasonable basis for our opinion.

In our opinion, the financial statements referred to above present fairly, in all material respects, the net assets of the Plan as of December 31, 20X1, and the changes in net assets for the year then ended in conformity with accounting principles generally accepted in the United States.

[Signature of Firm]
[City and State]
[Date]

Nonstandard Auditor's Reports

A Non-GAAP-Basis Financial Statement

Independent Auditor's Report

Addressee:

We have audited the accompanying statements of net assets available for plan benefits (modified cash basis) of XYZ Pension Plan as of December 31, 20X2 and 20X1, and the related statement of changes in the net assets available for plan benefits (modified cash basis) for the year ended December 31, 20X2. These financial statements are the responsibility of the Plan's management. Our responsibility is to express an opinion on these financial statements based on our audits.

We conducted our audits in accordance with auditing standards generally accepted in the United States. Those standards require that we plan and perform the audit to obtain reasonable assurance about whether the financial statements are free of material misstatement. An audit includes examining, on a test basis, evidence supporting the amounts and disclosures in the financial statements. An audit also includes assessing the accounting principles used and significant estimates made by management, as well as evaluating the overall financial statement presentation. We believe that our audits provide a reasonable basis for our opinion.

As described in Note X, the Plan's policy is to prepare its financial statements and supplemental schedules on a modified cash basis of accounting, which differs from accounting principles generally accepted in the United States. Accordingly, the accompanying financial statements and schedules are not intended to be presented in conformity with accounting principles generally accepted in the United States.

In our opinion, the financial statements referred to above present fairly, in all material respects, the financial status of XYZ Pension Plan as of December 31, 20X2 and 20X1, and the changes in its financial status for the year ended December 20X2, on the basis of accounting described in Note X.

Our audits were made for the purpose of forming an opinion on the financial statements taken as a whole. The supplemental schedules (modified cash basis) of (1) assets held for investment, (2) reportable transactions, and (3) investments in loans and fixed-income obligations in default or classified as uncollectible as of or for the year ended December 31, 20X2, are presented for purposes of complying with the Department of Labor's Rules and Regulations for Reporting and Disclosure under the Employee Retirement Income Security Act of 1974 and are not a required part of the basic financial statements. The supplemental schedules have been subjected to the auditing procedures applied in the audits of the basic financial statements and, in our opinion, are fairly stated in all material respects in relation to the basic financial statements taken as a whole.

[Signature of Firm]

[City and State]

[Date]

A Limited-Scope Audit under DOL Regulations

Independent Auditor's Report

Addressee:

We were engaged to audit the financial statements and schedules of XYZ Pension Plan as of December 31, 20X1, and for the year then ended, as listed in the accompanying index. These financial statements and schedules are the responsibility of the Plan's management.

As permitted by Section 2520.103-8 of the Department of Labor's Rules and Regulations for Reporting and Disclosure under the Employee Retirement Income Security Act of 1974, the Plan administrator instructed us not to perform, and we did not perform, any auditing procedures with respect to the information summarized in Note X, which was certified by ABC Bank, the trustee of the Plan, except for comparing the information with the related information included in the 20X1 financial statements and supplemental schedules. We have been informed by the Plan administrator that the trustee holds the Plan's investment assets and executes investment transactions. The Plan administrator has obtained a certification from the trustee as of and for the year ended December 31, 20X1, that the information provided to the plan administrator by the trustee is complete and accurate.

Because of the significance of the information that we did not audit, we are unable to, and do not, express an opinion on the accompanying financial statements and schedules taken as a whole. The form and content of the information included in the financial statements and schedules, other than that derived from the information certified by the trustee, have been audited by us in accordance with auditing standards generally accepted in the United States and, in our opinion, are presented in compliance with the Department of Labor's Rules and Regulations for Reporting and Disclosure under the Employee Retirement Income Security Act of 1974.

[Signature of Firm]
[City and State]
[Date]

A Defined Benefit Plan Audit Assuming Inadequate Procedures to Value Investments

Independent Auditor's Report

Addressee:

We have audited the accompanying statements of net assets available for benefits and of accumulated plan benefits of XYZ Pension Plan as of December 31, 20X2, and the related statements of changes in net assets available for benefits and of changes in accumulated Plan benefits for the year then ended. These financial statements are the responsibility of the Plan's management. Our responsibility is to express an opinion on these financial statements based on our audit.

We conducted our audit in accordance with auditing standards generally accepted in the United States. Those standards require that we plan and perform the audit to obtain reasonable assurance about whether the financial statements are free of material misstatement. An audit includes examining, on a test basis, evidence supporting the amounts and disclosures in the financial statements. An audit also includes assessing the accounting principles used and significant estimates made by management, as well as evaluating the overall financial statement presentation. We believe that our audit provides a reasonable basis for our opinion.

As discussed in Note X, investments amounting to $ (percent of net assets available for benefits) as of December 31, 20X2, have been valued at estimated fair value as determined by the Board of Trustees. We have reviewed the procedures applied by the trustees in valuing the securities and have inspected the underlying documentation. In our opinion, those procedures are not adequate to determine the fair value of the investments in conformity with generally accepted accounting principles. The effect on the financial statements and supplemental schedules of not applying adequate procedures to determine the fair value of the securities is not determinable.

In our opinion, except for the effects of the procedures used by the Board of Trustees to determine the valuation of investments as described in the preceding paragraph, the financial statements referred to above present fairly, in all material respects, the financial status of XYZ Pension Plan as of December 31, 20X2, and the changes in its financial status for the year then ended, in conformity with accounting principles generally accepted in the United States.

Our audit was made for the purpose of forming an opinion on the financial statements taken as a whole. The additional information presented in supplemental schedules of (1) assets held for investment, (2) reportable transactions, and (3) investments in loans and fixed-income obligations in default or classified as uncollectible as of or for the year ended December 31, 20X2, are presented for purposes of complying with the Department of Labor's Rules and Regulations for Reporting and Disclosure under the Employee Retirement Income Security Act of 1974 and is not a required part of the basic financial statements. That additional information has been subjected to the auditing procedures applied in the audit of the basic financial statements for the year ended December 31, 20X2; and in our opinion, except for the effects of the valuation of investments, as described above, the additional information is fairly stated in all material respects in relation to the basic financial statements taken as a whole.

[Signature of Firm]
[City and State]
[Date]

CHAPTER 42

Accounting and Financial Reporting for Health and Welfare Benefit Plans

Paula J. Conroy

NATURE OF THE PLANS

Health and welfare benefit plans can be either defined benefit or defined contribution plans, and they share a number of characteristics with pension plans. Whereas pension plans primarily provide for income benefits during retirement,[1] health and welfare benefit plans provide a wide variety of benefits primarily to active employees, although certain types of benefits commonly are provided to retirees as well. The range of benefits offered by these plans includes:

- Medical, dental, vision, hearing, prescription drug, dependent-care, psychiatric, and long-term care benefits.
- Life insurance benefits.
- Accidental death or dismemberment benefits.
- Unemployment, severance, or disability pay.
- Vacation or holiday pay.
- Other miscellaneous benefits, such as legal services, daycare, tuition assistance, apprenticeships, and housing allowances.

Like pension plans, health and welfare benefit plans can be single-employer or multiemployer plans, often require actuarial valuations, and, in most cases, are subject to the Employee Retirement Income Security Act of 1974 (ERISA). The form of most plans is governed by tax law.

---

1 Some pension plans provide ancillary benefits of the same nature as the benefits provided by health and welfare plans.

Contributions may be voluntary or through a collective-bargaining agreement and may be paid by the plan sponsor, plan participants, or both. Some plans may be funded through a trust arrangement, such as a voluntary employees' beneficiary association (VEBA) trust under Internal Revenue Code Section 501(c)(9).

In recent years, companies have focused increasing attention on the health and welfare benefit plans they sponsor for two reasons. First, many plan sponsors are modifying their plans in an effort to better manage escalating costs and are monitoring changing trends in the health care industry for other cost-effective plan design changes. Second, plan sponsors are operating in a more competitive labor market and combining various types of welfare benefits with compensation to attract and retain qualified employees.

PLAN ACCOUNTING AND REPORTING

The requirements for accounting and reporting by health and welfare benefit plans are prescribed in the American Institute of Certified Public Accountant's (AICPA) *Statement of Position 92-6* (*SOP 92-6*), *Accounting and Reporting by Health and Welfare Benefit Plans* (that amended Chapter 4 of the AICPA audit and accounting guide, *Audits of Employee Benefit Plans* (the *Guide*)), and *Statement of Position 99-2* (*SOP 99-2*), *Accounting for and Reporting of Postretirement Medical Benefit (401(h)) Features of Defined Benefit Pension Plans.* While the rules in *SOP 92-6* are similar in many respects to those prescribed by *SFAS No. 35* for defined benefit pension plans, some important differences are discussed below. Although the 401(h) feature is not widely utilized, *SOP 99-2* addresses accounting and reporting for Section 401(h) of the Internal Revenue Code (IRC), which allows some defined benefit pension plans to provide a post-retirement medical benefit component. This is accomplished by funding a portion of a health care plan's retiree medical cost through a transfer of excess pension assets (as defined by the IRC) or through additional contributions to the 401(h) account. Contributions may be made by the employer, employee, or both.

Health and welfare benefit plans reporting under generally accepted accounting principles (GAAP) are required to use the accrual basis of accounting, although modified cash basis financial statements are sometimes prepared (in accordance with rules governing reporting under a basis of accounting other than GAAP. Note also that, as to reporting of retiree benefits, *SOP 92-6* borrows significantly from the related measurement principles of *Statement of Financial Accounting Standards No. 106* (*SFAS No. 106*), *Employers' Accounting for Postretirement Benefits Other Than Pensions*.

For health and welfare plans, it is especially important to understand the nature of the plan benefits and any related insurance arrangements before determining the appropriate accounting. Specifically, it must be determined who is at risk for the benefit obligations. An insurance company may assume all or a portion of the financial risk, or it may provide only administrative, benefit payment, or investment management services. In a situation that is considered to be "fully insured," the plan generally has no obligation for the covered benefits (other than for payment of premiums to the insurance company) and, accordingly, the benefit obligation is not reported in the plan's financial statements.

The financial statements of a defined benefit health and welfare benefit plan consist of:

- A statement of net assets available for benefits as of the end of the plan year.
- A statement of changes in net assets available for benefits for the year then ended.
- Information regarding the plan's benefit obligations as of the end of the plan year.
- Information regarding the effects, if significant, of certain factors affecting the year-to-year change in the plan's benefit obligations.

The information regarding a plan's benefit obligations and the changes in those obligations may be separately reported in individual statements or may be combined with the statements of net assets available for benefits and the statement of changes in net assets available for benefits. In either case, this is a significant change from prior practice where such amounts were reported as liabilities in the statement of net assets. This new basic financial statement presentation also differs significantly from the common presentation by defined benefit pension plans, for which *SFAS No. 35* permits footnote presentation of the benefit obligation. (Also, if a defined benefit health and welfare plan were to present its financial statements on a basis of accounting other than generally accepted accounting principles, for example a modified cash basis, it still should disclose information regarding benefit obligations.)

Plan benefit obligations (at actuarial present value as applicable) of a defined benefit health and welfare plan include the following:[2]

---

2 Note that in a change from prior practice, benefit obligations no longer include death benefits actuarially expected to be paid during the active service period of participants.

- Insurance premiums payable.
- Claims payable and currently due for active and retired participants. For plans that are at least partly self-insured, claims that are reported but unpaid generally are determined by the records of the plan.
- Estimated claims incurred but not reported (IBNR) for active participants.[3] For plans that are at least partly self-insured, these obligations generally are determined by a specialist, such as the plan's actuary. The obligations are the present value of the estimated ultimate cost of settling the claims, including estimated costs to be incurred after the financial statement date.
- Estimated future benefits for accumulated eligibility credits for active participants. Some plans provide insurance payments or direct benefit amounts for a period of time after year-end for participants who have accumulated sufficient "eligibility credits." Such credits permit eligible participants to receive benefits during periods of subsequent unemployment. This obligation generally is estimated by applying current insurance premium rates or the average benefit cost (for self-insured plans) to the accumulated eligibility credits, considering assumptions for mortality and expected employee turnover.
- Estimated post-retirement benefits. Some plans continue to provide benefits to participants after the participants retire. This obligation normally is determined by a specialist, such as the plan's actuary, and, as mentioned above, generally is based on the employer's related calculations under *SFAS No. 106.* Disclosure should segregate benefits for retired participants (including their beneficiaries), active or terminated participants who are fully eligible to receive benefits, and active participants not yet fully eligible to receive benefits. (Note that a proposed AICPA Statement of Position is presently under consideration. The SOP will clarify certain *SOP 92-6* matters, primarily the presentation of post-retirement benefit obligations.)

The computation of the preceding benefit obligation amounts, especially those requiring an actuary, can be time-consuming and complex

---

3 IBNR may be combined for active and retired participants or the IBNR for retired participants may be included in the postretirement benefit obligation.

due to the amount of data that must be collected, annual enrollment of participants, and selection of actuarial methods and assumptions.

The financial statements of a defined contribution health and welfare benefit plan consist of:

- A statement of net assets available for benefits of the plan as of the end of the plan year.
- A statement of changes in net assets available for benefits of the plan for the year then ended.

Because a defined contribution plan's obligation to provide benefits is limited to the amounts accumulated in an individual's account, further information regarding benefit obligations is not applicable.

After considering the above-mentioned reporting of the benefit obligation amounts in the basic financial statements, footnote disclosures for health and welfare benefit plans generally are similar to those of pension plans, but differ somewhat in their requirements for descriptions of:

- The nature of the benefits provided and the accounting policy regarding purchase of insurance contracts excluded from plan assets.
- Significant actuarial assumptions used in estimating certain plan benefit obligations and the effects of significant changes therein.
- The plan's funding policy, including, if applicable, the method of funding the amount by which benefit obligations exceed the net assets of the plan.
- For plans that provide post-retirement health care benefits, the assumed health care cost trend rate(s) used to measure the expected cost of plan benefits and a general description of the direction and pattern of change in the rate(s) used, the ultimate trend rate and when that rate is expected to be achieved, and the effect of a one-percentage-point increase in the assumed health care cost trend rate(s).

SUMMARY

While health and welfare benefit plans share a number of characteristics with pension plans, they also have unique distinguishing features and, thus, have their own important place in the overall structure of an employer's benefits program.

As pointed out in this chapter, these plans, their increasing costs, and their complex accounting and financial reporting are receiving more attention. This additional focus is likely to continue for some time, especially as the costs for health care continue to escalate and the labor market remains highly competitive.

The sample financial statements in the appendix that follows illustrate the financial reporting for a typical defined benefit health care plan.

A P P E N D I X   42–1

Health Care Plan
Financial Statements

SAMPLE COMPANY HEALTH CARE PLAN

Statement of Net Assets Available for Benefits

December 31, 20X2 and 20X1

	20X2	20X1
Assets		
Investments at fair value:		
U.S. government securities	$217,000	$142,000
Corporate bonds	200,000	103,000
Common stock	289,000	394,000
	706,000	639,000
Receivables:		
Contributions of Sample Company	111,000	101,000
Contributions of participants	64,000	54,000
Accrued interest and dividends	13,000	9,000
	188,000	164,000
Cash	70,000	90,000
Total assets	964,000	893,000
Liabilities		
Due to broker for securities purchased	25,000	26,000
Accounts payable for administrative expenses	12,000	18,000
Total Liabilities	37,000	44,000
Net assets available for benefits	$927,000	$849,000

See notes to financial statements.

SAMPLE COMPANY HEALTH CARE PLAN

Statement of Changes in Net Assets Available for Benefits

For the Years Ended December 31, 20X2 and 20X1

	20X2	20X1
Additions		
Contributions:		
Sample Company	$ 709,000	$ 704,000
Participants	214,000	213,000
	923,000	917,000
Investment income:		
Net realized and unrealized appreciation (depreciation) in fair value of investments	73,000	(4,000)
Interest	39,000	20,000
Dividends	11,000	16,000
	123,000	32,000
Less investment expenses	(8,000)	(6,000)
	115,000	26,000
Total additions	1,038,000	943,000
Deductions		
Payments for health claims	884,000	801,000
Disability and death benefits	43,000	42,000
	927,000	843,000
Administrative expenses	33,000	29,000
Total deductions	960,000	872,000
Net increase	78,000	71,000
Net assets available for benefits at beginning of year	849,000	778,000
Net assets available for benefits at end of year	$ 927,000	$ 849,000

See notes to financial statements.

SAMPLE COMPANY HEALTH CARE PLAN

Statement of Plan Benefit Obligations

For the Years Ended December 31, 20X2 and 20X1

	20X2	20X1
Amounts currently due:		
Health claims payable	$ 670,000	$ 625,000
Death and disability benefits payable	30,000	25,000
	700,000	650,000
Other obligations for current benefit coverage—claims incurred but not reported	225,000	200,000
Total obligations for current benefit coverage	925,000	850,000
Post-retirement obligations:		
Current retirees	100,000	75,000
Other participants:		
Fully eligible for benefits	500,000	475,000
Not yet eligible for benefits	475,000	350,000
	1,075,000	900,000
Total benefit obligations	$ 2,000,000	$ 1,750,000

See notes to financial statements.

SAMPLE COMPANY HEALTH CARE PLAN

Statement of Changes in Plan Benefit Obligations

For the Years Ended December 31, 20X2 and 20X1

	20X2	20X1
Amounts currently due:		
Balance at beginning of year	$ 650,000	$ 600,000
Claims reported approved for payment	977,000	893,000
Claims paid (including disability)	(927,000)	(843,000)
Balance at end of year	700,000	650,000
Other obligations for current benefit coverage:		
Balance at beginning of year	200,000	150,000
Net change during year	25,000	50,000
Balance at end of year	225,000	200,000
Total obligations for current benefit coverage	925,000	850,000
Post-retirement obligation:		
Balance at beginning of year	900,000	800,000
Increase (decrease) during the year attributable to benefits earned and other changes	175,000	100,000
Balance at end of year	1,075,000	900,000
Total benefit obligations at end of year	$ 2,000,000	$ 1,750,000

See notes to financial statements.

SAMPLE COMPANY HEALTH CARE PLAN

Notes to Financial Statements

For the Years Ended December 31, 20X2 and 20X1

General Description of the Plan

The Sample Company Health Care Plan (Plan) provides health care benefits covering substantially all employees of the Company. The following description provides only general information; participants should refer to the Plan agreement for more complete information regarding operation of the Plan.

The Plan provides health benefits (hospital, surgical, and major medical) and death benefits to full-time Company employees with at least 1,000 service hours annually. The Plan also provides similar benefits to retired employees provided that they have attained at least age 62 and have 10 years of service with the Company. Benefits presently are self-insured, although claim processing is handled by an insurance company.

The Company's policy is to contribute the maximum amounts allowed as a tax deduction by the Internal Revenue Code. Employee and retiree contributions are required, relative to the coverage received, as determined annually by the Plan Committee. Certain dependent coverage may be elected at extra cost to the employee.

Administrative expenses are paid by the Plan, except that certain professional fees and administrative overhead costs are borne by the Company.

The Plan is subject to the provisions of the Employee Retirement Income Security Act of 1974 (ERISA). Although it has not expressed any intent to do so, the Company has the right to modify the benefits provided to active employees, to discontinue its contributions at any time, and to terminate the Plan subject to the provisions of ERISA.

Summary of Significant Accounting Policies

Investments of the Plan are reported at fair value. Quoted market prices were available to value virtually all investments during 20X2 and 20X1.

Benefit obligations for claims incurred but not reported are estimated by the Plan's actuary in accordance with accepted actuarial principles.

The post-retirement obligation represents the actuarial present value of those estimated future benefits that are attributed to employee service rendered to December 31. The post-retirement obligation includes future benefits expected to be paid to or for (1) currently retired employees and (2) active employees after retirement from service with the Company. Prior to an active employee's full eligibility date, the post-retirement obligation is the portion of the expected post-retirement obligation that is attributed to that employee's service rendered to the valuation date.

The actuarial present value of the expected post-retirement obligation is determined by an actuary and is the amount that results from applying actuarial assumptions to historical claims-cost data to estimate future annual incurred claims costs per participant and to adjust such estimates for the time value of money (through discounts for interest) and the probability of payment (by means of decrements such as those for death, disability, withdrawal, or retirement) between the valuation date and the expected date of payment, and to reflect the portion of those costs expected to be borne by Medicare, the retired participants, and other providers.

For measurement purposes at December 31, 20X2, a 9.5 percent annual rate of increase in the per capita cost of covered health care benefits was assumed for 20X3; the rate was assumed to decrease gradually to 6.0 percent for 20X9 and to remain at that level thereafter. These assumptions are consistent with those used to measure the post-retirement obligation at December 31, 20X1.

The following were other significant assumptions used in the valuations as of December 31, 20X2 and 20X1.

Weighted-average discount rate	7.5%
Average retirement age	60
Mortality	1971 Group Annuity Mortality Table

The foregoing assumptions are based on the presumption that the Plan will continue. Were the Plan to terminate, different actuarial assumptions and other factors might be applicable in determining the actuarial present value of the postretirement obligation.

The health care cost-trend rate assumption has a significant effect on the postretirement obligation that is reported. If the assumed rates increased by one percentage point in each year, that would increase the obligation as of December 31, 20X2 and 20X1, by $125,000 and $105,000, respectively.

The Plan's deficiency of net assets over benefit obligations at December 31, 20X2 and 20X1, relates primarily to the post-retirement obligation, which will be funded by subsequent Company contributions to the Plan.

Investments

Investments of the Plan are held in a bank trust fund. No individual investments represent 5 percent or more of total plan assets. Net appreciation (depreciation) in the fair value of Plan investments during 20X2 and 20X1 (as determined by quoted market prices) was as follows:

	20X2	20X1
U.S. government securities	$ (2,000)	$ 6,000
Corporate bonds	(3,000)	4,000
Common stocks	78,000	(14,000)
	$73,000	$ (4,000)

Income Tax Status

A September 27, 20X1, Internal Revenue Service letter states that the Plan and its trust qualify under Section 501(c)(9) of the Internal Revenue Code and, thus, are not subject to tax under the present income tax law. The Company believes that the Plan continues to qualify and operate as designed.[4]

---

4 None of the schedules that may be required under ERISA nor certain other ERISA disclosures are provided in this appendix.

CHAPTER 43

Alternative Insured and Self-Funded Arrangements

Richard L. Tewksbury, Jr.

The cost of health and welfare benefit plans has become a substantial budget item for employers, causing them to take steps that control plan cost and liabilities. Employers—particularly large ones—are demanding that conventional insurance products become funding arrangements that are used as corporate financing tools. In response, insurance companies and third-party administrators have designed a number of alternative funding arrangements for group insurance programs. This chapter first explains a conventional insurance arrangement, then highlights the development of alternative funding arrangements and describes each in detail.

CONVENTIONAL INSURANCE ARRANGEMENT

Definition

In a conventional insurance arrangement, an employer purchases a group insurance contract and agrees to pay premiums to an insurance company. In return, the insurance company agrees to pay specific benefit amounts for such events as death, medical care expenses, or disability. The employer's annual premium is based on historic claims cost experience of employers of similar size and characteristics and the underwriting factors and administrative expenses of the insurance company.

The insurance company uses the premiums paid by all employers to pay the claims incurred under the group insurance plans. Employers whose actual claims costs are less than their premium payments subsidize employers whose claims costs exceed their premium payments. In a conventional insurance arrangement, there is no reconciliation of an employer's premium payments to its actual plan expenses. Instead, any adjustment of premium charges reflects the loss experience of all employers.

Premium Cost Factors

The insurance company considers a number of factors in determining the total cost of insuring a risk.

Paid Claims

This is the total benefits paid to insured employees or their dependents during the policy period.

Reserves

This cost reflects the insurance company's liability to pay benefits in the future for a loss incurred during the policy year. The most common reserve is the incurred but unreported claim reserve established to pay losses incurred during the policy year but not reported for payment until after the policy year has ended. Reserves also are established for deferred benefit payment liabilities such as reserves for the life insurance waiver of premium, retiree life insurance, and future disability benefit payments.

Other Claim Charges

Several additional costs are assumed by the insurance company for providing special benefit coverages such as extended liability coverage and conversion to an individual insurance policy when a participant terminates employment.

Administrative Charges

Although the terminology and allocation of administrative expenses vary by insurance company, there are six main cost categories:

1. *Commissions.* This is the payment to a licensed insurance agent or broker for helping the employer obtain the insurance coverage and administer the plan. The commission amount normally is determined as a percentage of the premium paid with the percentage either remaining level or declining as the premium increases.

2. *Premium Taxes.* A state tax is levied on the premiums received by insurance companies in the resident states of insured employees. This tax expense is passed directly to the employer, normally as a percentage of premium paid. The current tax rate averages about 2 percent of premium but varies from state to state.

3. *Risk Charge.* Each insured employer contributes to the insurance company's contingency reserve for unexpected, catastrophic claims. The risk charge normally is determined by a formula based on the premium amount.

4. *Claims Administration Expenses.* These are the expenses incurred by the insurance company to investigate claims and calculate and pay the appropriate benefits. These expenses normally are fixed per claim, with the per-claim cost varying by the type of benefits paid. For example, life insurance benefits are relatively simple and quick to administer and have a low administrative cost per claim compared to disability and medical claims, which often require medical review and more difficult benefit calculations.

5. *Other Administrative Expenses.* Charges for actuarial, legal, accounting, and other such services plus overhead expenses are shared by all contract holders. These expenses are determined either as a percentage of the premium amount, a fixed charge, or a variable charge based on the insurance company's actual services provided to the employer.

6. *Insurance Company Profit (stock company) or Contribution to Surplus (mutual company).*

ALTERNATIVE FUNDING ARRANGEMENTS

Definition

An alternative funding arrangement *defers, reduces,* or *eliminates* the premium paid by the employer to transfer risk and receive plan administration services. Essentially, this saving is accomplished in various ways that affect the standard reserves, claim charges, and administrative costs of a conventional insurance arrangement.

The deferral, reduction, or elimination of the premium provides an employer *direct* and *indirect* savings. Direct savings result from the reduction or elimination of specific insurance and administration charges.

Indirect savings are gained through the more profitable employer use of monies that otherwise are held and invested by the insurance company.

The tradeoff for these savings is the employer's assumption of insurance company functions and/or risk. For example, the employer might assume all or part of the financial liability—that is, benefit payments to employees—and therefore reduce the necessary premium paid to the insurance company to pay benefit claims. Similarly, an employer might agree to administer all or part of the plan to reduce the insurance company's administrative charges, or to purchase administration services at a lesser cost from an independent service firm, typically referred to as a third-party administrator.

Reasons for Alternative Arrangements

Premium Charges

An employer's main reason for purchasing group insurance is to transfer a personnel risk that has unpredictable occurrence and costs potentially greater than the insurance company's premium charge. If a substantial loss occurs, the insurance is a valuable investment. But if losses over a period of time are less than the premium charges, employers begin to analyze the insured risk and the conventional insurance arrangement for ways to reduce or eliminate the fixed cost of premium charges.

Employers with large insured employee groups have more predictable loss experience. They can reasonably project the expected claims costs of their employee groups over time and determine the expected annual cost to provide health and welfare benefits. The value of the conventional insurance arrangement then becomes protecting against unexpected catastrophic losses.

Because large employers can reasonably project their future benefit costs, they can determine the financial advantages and tradeoffs of participating in the financing and assumption of the risk. This participation reduces the premium paid to the insurer and potentially reduces the overall cost to the employer through reduced claims charges, premium tax, risk charge, and other administrative charges. These financial advantages have been the impetus to such alternative insured arrangements as *participating* and *experience-rated contracts*.

In some cases, employers are willing to assume total financial responsibility for providing health and welfare benefits to employees. This arrangement, called *self-funding*, eliminates premium payments to an insurance company and potentially reduces overall plan costs through reduced reserves, premium tax, risk charge, and other administrative expenses. In addition, a self-funding arrangement may enable the multi-state employer to lower plan costs by avoiding different state-mandated benefits and administrative regulations through the preemption clause of the Employee Retirement Income Security Act of 1974 (ERISA).[1]

Corporate Value of Money

The significance of corporate value of money increases when premium costs and interest rates are rising. Under a conventional insurance arrangement, the insurance company invests the excess premiums when the paid premium exceeds plan costs. The insurance company also invests the various claim reserves it maintains for each group insurance plan.

Some of this investment income is credited to the employer. However, if the employer can earn more than this interest credit, it is advantageous to minimize the transfer of funds to the insurer. This factor has encouraged the development of deferred premium arrangements, reduction or waiver of accumulated reserves, and various self-funding arrangements.

Competition

There is intense competition among insurance companies for insuring "good" risks. As already mentioned, under the conventional insurance arrangement, employers have similar premium charges, which means that employers with favorable loss experience (premiums exceed plan costs) subsidize employers with unfavorable loss experience (plan costs exceed premiums). Employers with favorable loss experience—the "good" risks—will look for funding alternatives that better reflect their actual costs. The availability of alternative funding and administration arrangements is often the key factor in an employer selecting and continuing with an insurance company. This shift to alternative funding arrangements is especially true for medical expense plans. One survey reports that on average 77 percent of employers currently self-fund one or more of their plans, ranging from 25 percent for small employers (less than 500 employees) to 97 percent for the largest employers (20,000 or more employees).[2]

INSURED ALTERNATIVE FUNDING ARRANGEMENTS

There are a number of ways an employer potentially may reduce total plan costs and still remain in an insured arrangement that transfers the

---

1 ERISA Sec. 514.

2 Mercer/Foster Higgins, *National Survey of Employer-Sponsored Health Plans*, 1999.

underlying benefit plan risk and plan administration to the insurance company. These alternatives can be classified in three ways, based on the employer objective(s) for the arrangement:

Sharing Year-End Plan Financial Results

Participating arrangement.

Experience-rating arrangement.

Minimizing Plan Assets Held by the Insurer

Deferred premium arrangement.

Annual retrospective premium arrangement.

Terminal retrospective premium arrangement.

Extended plan-year accounting.

Exclusion of the waiver of premium provision (life insurance).

Minimizing Premium Payments during the Plan Year

Claims-plus premium arrangement (life insurance).

Partial self-funding arrangement (long-term disability).

Large deductible arrangement (medical).

Minimum premium arrangement (health care, short-term disability).

The prevalence and importance of managed care plans in today's health care benefits programs have caused employers to expect similar alternative funding arrangements for these plans. The insurers, including health maintenance organizations (HMOs), have adopted some of the arrangements that share year-end results or minimize annual premium payments. However, the details often differ because managed care plans also must satisfy provider reimbursement contracts and unique state regulations.

Each insured alternative funding arrangement is described in the following sections.

Participating Arrangement

In a *participating insurance arrangement*, the employer shares in its favorable or unfavorable financial experience during the policy period. If the financial experience is favorable—that is, the claims and administrative costs are less than the premium paid during the policy period—the employer receives the surplus premium from the insurance company at the end of the policy year. If the financial experience is unfavorable—that is, the claims and administrative costs are greater than the premium paid during the policy period—the plan is considered to be in a deficit balance equal to the difference between total plan costs and paid premium. In most instances, this deficit balance is carried forward by the insurance company to be recovered from the employer in future years of favorable experience.

Therefore, in a participating insurance arrangement, the true cost, or *net cost*, of a group insurance plan is the premium paid during the policy year, adjusted for the balance remaining at year-end.

Underwriting Factors

Because the insurance company shares with each employer in the net cost of its group insurance plans, several underwriting factors are included in a participating insurance arrangement that are unnecessary in a conventional insurance arrangement.

Employer Participation.   An insurance company will vary the *percentage of employer* participation in the actual financial experience depending on two key factors: the "spread" of risk and the predictability of losses.

Spread of risk refers to the ability of the employer's benefit plan to absorb a major, catastrophic loss relative to its paid premium base. The larger the employee group, the easier it becomes to incur a major loss from one or a few plan participants without substantially affecting the year-end actual financial experience. The reason is that the total paid premium is large enough to pay the infrequent major losses as well as the expected plan benefit and administration costs. The risk is effectively "spread" across the premium base of the insured employee group. For health care plans, employee groups of more than 50 employees typically are considered large enough for a participating insurance arrangement. For life insurance and disability plans, the insured employee groups typically must be much larger—at least 250 employees—for a participating contract.

Predictability of losses is the most important factor in determining the percentage of participation. Essentially, the more predictable the total losses for each year, the greater the percentage of employer participation. Plans such as medical care, dental care, and short-term disability cover risks in which losses normally occur frequently and at relatively low benefit costs per occurrence. The predictability of loss experience for these plans is much better than for life insurance and long-term disability plans that cover risks with less frequent losses and normally much higher total benefit costs per loss. For this reason, participating insurance arrangements are more common in indemnity and preferred provider organization (PPO) medical care, dental, and short-term disability plans. Point of service (POS) and HMO managed medical care plans tend not to offer participating arrangements due to the prefunding and incentive provisions of their provider reimbursement contracts.

To control the employer's percentage of participation in the plan's actual financial experience, the insurance company sets *individual pooling points for each plan*. A pooling point is the annual dollar limit of individual benefit costs that will be included in the actual financial experience of the participating insurance arrangement. Any individual benefit costs in excess of the pooling point will not be included in the plan's financial experience. Instead, this excess amount is included in the insurance company's "pool" of conventional insurance arrangements for the same risk. For example, a medical insurance plan could insure employees with unlimited lifetime medical care benefits but have an annual pooling point of $50,000. This means an individual's benefits claims costs up to $50,000 are included in the plan's actual financial experience, and any benefit amounts in excess of $50,000 are assumed by the insurance company.

The employer pays an additional premium charge, called a *pooling charge*, for the exclusion of benefits amounts in excess of the individual pooling point. This charge is based on the loss experience of the conventional insurance "pool" and reflects the type of risk and expected average benefit costs that each employer will have in excess of the pooling point. For instance, a life insurance plan pooling charge normally equals the volume of life insurance in excess of the pooling point, multiplied by the insurance company's conventional premium rate. The medical care plan pooling charge normally is determined as a percentage of annual premium or paid claims.

Table 43–1 illustrates a typical schedule of pooling point levels for medical care and life insurance plans, which are the most common participating insurance arrangements requiring pooling points.

Underwriting Margin. The premium paid under a participating insurance arrangement includes a charge for the possible fluctuation of actual costs in excess of the expected total plan costs during the policy year. This charge commonly is called the insurance company's *underwriting margin*.

Underwriting margin reflects the normal range of deviation of the plan's actual loss experience in any year from the expected loss experience. The underwriting margin is determined from actuarial studies on the fluctuation of actual claims experience relative to insurance company norms for similar employee groups and types of insurance coverage. In

T A B L E   43-1

Pooling Points

Life Insurance Plan Volume of Insurance	Pooling Point
$ 1 million	$ 20,000
2.5 million	25,000
5 million	35,000
10 million	60,000
25 million	85,000
50 million	135,000
Medical Care Insurance Plan Annual Claims (000s)	Annual Benefit Pooling Point
$ 200–600	$ 30,000
600–1,000	40,000
1,000–2,000	50,000
2,000–4,000	75,000
4,000–8,000	100,000
Over 8,000	150,000 or more

general, the underwriting margin decreases as the predictability of the plan's expected claims experience increases.

The underwriting margin for a basic group life insurance plan varies between 10 percent and 20 percent of premium, depending on the size of the employee group and volume of life insurance. As the number of employees and volume of insurance increases, the underwriting margin decreases. Table 43–2 illustrates the typical level of underwriting margins for medical care plans.

Determining the Year-End Balance

The underlying principle in a participating insurance arrangement is that the employer's final or net cost equals paid premiums adjusted for the year-end balance (surplus or deficit). The year-end balance is determined by the actual plan costs in relation to the paid premium.

Basic Formula. The determination of a surplus or deficit year-end balance for group insurance plans is straightforward.

Paid premium – Claims costs – Administrative costs = Balance

T A B L E   43–2

Underwriting Margin for Medical Care Plans

Number of Covered Employees	Percent of Premium
Fewer than 500	10%–15%
500 to 1,000	7%–12%
Over 1,000	5%–10%

Paid premium refers to the employer's total payments to the insurance company during the plan year, plus any fund transfers from a premium stabilization reserve or surplus carry-forward account.

The *claims costs* factor is made up of various charges:

1. *Paid Claims.* The actual benefit payments during the policy year.
2. *Reserve Charge.* The establishment of or adjustment to claims reserves held for incurred but unreported claims and any other specific pending liabilities, such as waiver of premium life insurance claims and unsettled claims payments at year-end.
3. *Pooling Charge.* The additional cost for having large individual claims "pooled" in excess of a specific pooling point.
4. *Other Claim Charges.* The most common charge is a penalty charge levied against the employer when a terminated employee converts from a group to an individual insurance policy.

The *administrative costs* essentially are the same six expense categories mentioned previously for a conventional insurance arrangement.

Surplus Balance. If the year-end balance is positive, there will be surplus premiums available to be returned to the employer. The following example illustrates how a surplus year-end balance is determined.

During the policy year, the employer pays $500,000 of group insurance premiums to the insurance company. Claims paid during the year are $375,000, reserve charges are $10,000, pooling charges are $20,000, and other claim charges are $5,000, for a total of $410,000 in claims costs. Total administrative costs equal $60,000. These total costs subtracted from the paid premium result in a year-end balance of $30,000 surplus premium.

Surplus premium that accumulates with the insurance company during the plan year normally is credited with interest earnings that are used to reduce the insurance company's administrative costs. The credited interest rate is based on the investment performance of the insurance company's general assets.

The insurance company can return the surplus balance by issuing a *dividend* check equal to the surplus amount. This dividend reduces the year-end employer-paid premium total that is tax deductible as an ordinary business expense under Section 162 of the Internal Revenue Code.

Alternatively, the insurance company deposits the surplus balance in a special reserve, normally called a premium stabilization reserve. The major advantages of a *premium stabilization reserve* are as follows:

- Avoids a reduction in the tax-deductible paid premium amount at year-end.
- Helps stabilize the future budget and cash-flow requirements of the plan by supplementing future premium rate increases with funds from the special reserve.
- Receives tax-free investment earnings on the reserve balances held for active employees' benefit plans.

A disadvantage of a premium stabilization reserve is the low interest rate typically credited by the insurance company on the reserve amount. Also, an insurance company may be able to retain and use these funds after contract termination to pay unexpected plan costs.

Another disadvantage of premium stabilization reserves is the potential tax implications if the reserve amount does not meet specific definitions of a "welfare benefit fund." The "fund" definitions were established in the 1984 Deficit Reduction Act (DEFRA) under Section 419 of the Internal Revenue Code. The principal purpose of this law is to prevent employers from taking premature deductions for expenses that have not yet been incurred. In essence, a premium stabilization reserve is considered reasonable, and deposits to the reserve tax-deductible, if there is no guarantee of renewal of the insurance contract and the reserve amount is subject to "significant current risk of economic loss," as defined under Section 419.

Deficit Balance.   A negative year-end balance, or deficit balance, occurs when the employer's premium paid during the policy year is insufficient to pay the plan's total costs during the year. Such a situation is illustrated in the following example.

The premium and plan costs are the same as in the previous example, except paid claims during the year are $425,000, and the total administrative costs are $70,000. The total plan expenses now result in a year-end deficit balance of $30,000 premium.

The deficit balance is offset during the policy year from the insurance company's corporate surplus to pay all claims and other immediate costs of the plan. In a sense, these insurance company funds act as a "loan" to the employer. While a plan deficit exists, the outstanding balance is charged with an interest expense similar to the interest credited on surplus premiums of other policyholders.

An employer's deficit balance will be carried forward and will be repaid by the employer through surplus premium balances that may result in future policy years. However, the employer normally is not contractually required to repay this insurance company "loan" and can switch insurance companies while a plan deficit is outstanding. This is a risk assumed by the insurance company and is reflected in the risk charge and the underwriting margins of the insurer.

Instead of repaying the deficit balance through future surplus premium, the employer can negotiate with the insurance company to repay the "loan" in a lump sum or in installments over a specified period. However, the insurance company interest charge on the outstanding deficit balance often is less than the interest charge if the employer were to borrow monies from another financial institution. In these instances, it is more cost-effective to repay the outstanding deficit balance through future surplus premiums.

In some participating insurance arrangements, the insurance company contractually cannot recover deficit balances from future employer surplus balances but still shares annual surplus balances with the employer. This type of arrangement reduces the insurance company's risk of an employer switching insurance companies before repaying a deficit balance. Also, this type of participating insurance arrangement may be more favorable for the employer because it participates only in years of positive financial results. The tradeoff will be a higher annual risk charge or underwriting margin compared to an arrangement that participates in both year-end surplus and deficit-balance situations.

Employer Advantages

The advantage of a participating insurance arrangement is that the employer pays its "net" insurance cost and is rewarded for favorable financial experience by the return of year-end surplus premium. During a policy year of favorable experience, cost savings can be gained in two additional ways:

1. *Premium tax* is reduced because it is based on the net premium received by an insurance company; that is, the employer's premium paid during the policy year less the surplus balance returned at year-end.

2. *Administrative costs* are reduced by lower general overhead charges based on net premium paid and by interest income earned on the surplus premium during the policy year.

The financial tradeoff to the employer of a participating insurance arrangement is a higher risk charge and underwriting margin in comparison with a conventional insurance arrangement. Also, the carryover of deficit balances will increase the future years' plan costs due to interest charges on the outstanding deficit balance and possibly additional underwriting margins required by the insurance company.

Experience-Rating Arrangement

Whereas a participating insurance arrangement lets the employer share in year-end surplus or deficit balances, an *experience-rating insurance arrangement* enables the actual financial experience of previous policy years to affect the employer's future premium charges. If the employer's actual financial experience has been favorable in the past, the future premium rates will be less than the conventional premium rate of other similar employers. If the historic financial experience has been unfavorable, future premium rates will be increased more than the conventional insurance rates for similar employers.

An experience-rating arrangement can be included with either a participating or a conventional insurance arrangement. In either case, the actual historic financial experience of the employer's plan is the basis for determining the future plan year's premium rates.

Underwriting Factors

If an employer's actual loss experience has fluctuated significantly in the past, substantial changes can occur in the experience-rated premium charges from year to year. For example, a plan year with favorable loss experience will reduce the next year's premium charges. If unfavorable experience actually occurred during that next year, subsequent premium charges will increase to reflect this unfavorable year. Such yearly swings in premium costs usually disturb employers and hinder their ability to budget future costs and control cash-flow needs. Similarly, the insurance company usually finds it more difficult to satisfy the employer when the required premium charges vary significantly from year to year.

To minimize this problem, the insurance company controls the significance of an employer's historic loss experience in determining premium charges. This is done through underwriting factors based on the statistical credibility of the actual paid claims experience and the type of risk.

Statistical Credibility. *Statistical credibility* refers to the validity of an employee group's actual paid claims experience representing the expected loss experience for such a group. The greater the statistical credibility, the greater the significance given to the group's historic financial results in determining future premium rates.

Statistical credibility is based on the applicability of the *law of large numbers,* which states that: *The larger the number of separate risks of a like nature combined into one group, the less uncertainty there will be as to the relative amount of loss that will be incurred within a given period.*[3]

Statistical credibility is determined by the size of the employee group and number of years of actual paid claims experience that can be analyzed. The statistical credibility of cumulative years of actual experience for a smaller employee group will be similar to the one-year historic results of a much larger employee group. For example, the cumulative five-year life insurance experience of a 350- to 400-employee group has similar statistical credibility to the one-year experience of a 1,750- to 2,000-employee group.

The importance of the *type of risk* is similar to the underwriting of a participating insurance arrangement. Statistical credibility of actual loss experience is greater for risks that occur more frequently and have a lesser average cost per occurrence, such as medical care and short-term disability. Therefore, greater significance can be given to the actual paid claims experience for these types of risks. For instance, only one to three years of loss experience normally are necessary to determine the experience-rated premium charges of medical care, dental, or short-term disability coverages.

On the other hand, the insurance company applies statistical credibility to the employer's life insurance and long-term disability loss experience only if three to five years of paid claims experience are available for review. This caution is due to the greater volatility of loss experience

---

3 For a good explanation of the law of large numbers, see S.S. Huebner and K. Black, *Life Insurance,* 10th ed. (Englewood Cliffs, NJ: Prentice-Hall, 1982), p. 3.

(lesser frequency, greater cost per occurrence) from year to year for these types of risk. By analyzing three to five years' loss experience, individual years of unusually favorable or unfavorable loss experience are blended into a more typical historic trend of claims costs.

Credibility Factors. There are several ways an insurance company values the statistical credibility of historic loss experience in an experience-rating arrangement. The most common method is to use a weighted average of the employer's actual claims experience and the insurance company's standard loss factors for a similar conventional insurance arrangement. The percentage weighting given to the employer's actual paid claims experience is called the credibility factor. The greater the statistical credibility of the risk, the closer the *credibility factor* is to 100 percent—which would imply that the employer's prior loss experience is wholly representative of future loss experience.

Table 43–3 shows typical credibility factors applied to life insurance and medical care plans. The life insurance factors are determined by the number of covered employees and the number of available years of actual claims experience. The factors for a medical plan typically are based on the number of employees covered by the plan.

T A B L E   43–3

Credibility Factors

Life Insurance Plan	*Number of Years of Experience*		
Number of Covered Employees	**1**	**3**	**5**
250–500	10%	25%	35%
500–1,000	20	55	75
1,000–2,500	40	65	85
2,500–5,000	65	85	100
5,000–10,000	80	100	100
Over 10,000	100	100	100

Medical Care Insurance Plan	
Number of Covered Employees	**Credibility Factors**
50–100	25%–30%
100–250	30–60
250–500	60–100
Over 500	100

For example, if an employer's medical plan covers 200 employees and incurred $800,000 of paid claims last year, a 50 percent credibility factor may be applied to this loss experience. If the insurance company's expected losses for a similar size and type of employee group are $700,000, the expected paid claims for this employee group would be $750,000.

Employer's past year's actual claims ($800,000)
× Credibility factor (.50) = $400,000

Plus

Insurer's expected losses ($700,000)
× Noncredible factor (.50) = $350,000

Equals

Expected claims cost = $750,000

Pooling Points. A second method of controlling loss experience volatility is to establish *pooling points*, as described previously in the section on participating insurance arrangements. By placing dollar maximums on the individual and total plan claim costs that will be included in each plan year's actual financial experience, the volatility of losses in any year is substantially limited. For providing this limitation on the employer's "experience-rated" losses, the insurance company levies a fixed annual charge, or pooling charge.

With a life insurance plan, the pooling charge is added to the average of the prior years' experience-rated paid claims to determine the expected claims costs for the next policy year. For example, if the average experience-rated claims cost over the last five plan years is $100,000, the life insurance volume in excess of the pooling point is $2,500,000, and the monthly pooling charge is $.60 per $1,000 of life insurance, the expected claims costs for the next policy year are $118,000, as calculated here:

Average annual experience-related claims = $100,000

Plus

Monthly pooling charge ($.60)
× Excess insurance volume ($2,500)
× 12 months = $18,000

Equals

Expected claims cost = $118,000

The medical insurance pooling charge normally is stated as a percentage of annual premium or paid claims. For instance, if the paid premium is $1,000,000, the pooling point is $75,000 per individual, and the pooling charge is 6 percent of premium, a charge of $60,000 would be included in determining the necessary premium charges for the next year.

Determining the Experience-Rated Premium

The exact method for determining the experience-rated premium charges varies by the type of insurance coverage and the insurance company. The explanation here describes the common principles for life insurance and medical care coverages.

Life Insurance. The life insurance premium charge is based on the expected paid claims, underwriting margin, reserve adjustment, pooling charge, and administrative costs.

Expected Paid Claims. Determining the next year's expected paid claims depends on the credibility factor given to the employer's historic actual loss experience. The credibility factor is applied to the average actual paid claims total for a three- to five-year period. This average actual annual paid claims total also should reflect annual changes in the volume of life insurance to provide a meaningful comparison of year-to-year claims experience.

Reserve Adjustment. The incurred but unreported reserve initially is established as a percentage of premium or paid claims and is adjusted each year thereafter to reflect changes in these factors. An estimate of the next year's adjustment is included in the premium-charge calculation based on expected paid claims or premium.

Underwriting Margin. This charge normally is stated as a percentage of expected paid claims and reserve adjustments or of total premium. If a participating insurance arrangement is included with the experience-rated arrangement, additional underwriting margin is added.

Pooling Charge. An annual charge is included based on the volume of "pooled" life insurance and premium rate for the employee group.

Administrative Costs. These costs normally are determined as a percentage of the experience-rated premium charges.

The sum of these factors determines the experience-rated life-insurance-premium charge for the next policy year. An example of calculating a required premium rate is illustrated in Figure 43–1.

Medical Care Insurance. The medical care insurance premium charge for traditional indemnity plans and for preferred provider organizations and for point of service managed care plans is based on expected paid claims, inflation/utilization trend, underwriting margin,

F I G U R E   43–1

Life Insurance Experience-Rating Calculation

Assumptions: Five-year average actual paid claims	$100,000
Expected annual losses*	80,000
Credibility factor	.60
Underwriting margin	10% of incurred claims
Reserve adjustment	2,000
Pooling charges	6,600
Administrative costs	10,000
Example:	
1. Expected paid claims: ($100,000 × .6) + ($80,000 × .4)	$ 92,000
2. Reserve adjustment	2,000
3. Incurred claims	94,000
4. Margin: 10% of incurred claims	9,400
5. Pooling charges	6,600
6. Administrative costs	10,000
Required premium	$120,000

*Based on insurance company's actuarial statistics.

reserve adjustments, pooling charge, and administrative costs. These factors are applied similar to the life insurance premium charges with the following exceptions.

Expected Paid Claims. Much greater credibility is given to the historic loss experience of the most recent plan year, so evaluating average loss history over more than three years normally is unnecessary. For PPO and POS plans, total claims charges may include fixed costs for delivery of specific services, such as a capitated or a percentage-of-premium fee arrangement, plus variable costs for all other services based on a negotiated discounted fee per transaction.

Inflation/Utilization Trend. Rising medical care prices (inflation) and utilization of services are distinct economic factors that will increase the next year's paid claims; therefore, the expected paid claims are increased by a trend factor projected for the next policy year. This factor will vary by the type of medical care plan and the included cost-management features, such as pre-authorization of hospital admissions and concurrent review of high-cost individual medical care cases. For example, the typical rates of cost increase (trend) applied to health care plans in 2000 are illustrated in the table below:

Plan Type	Trend Factor
Indemnity	10%–15%
PPO	9%–12%
POS	7%–10%
HMO	7%–10%

Pooling Charge. This charge normally is a percentage of paid claims or premium.

Administrative Costs. For PPO and POS plans, these costs include an *access fee* expense to pay for the initial development and ongoing management of the provider network. This cost normally is set as a cost per participant or a cost per employee per month.

The sum of these factors determines the experience-rated medical premium charge, as illustrated in Figure 43–2.

The experience-rated premium calculation for a health maintenance organization is based on these same factors but typically has less impact on future premium rates than the other types of health care plans, for several reasons:

1. The HMO rate-setting process is more closely regulated by the licensing states. The states often limit the weighting given to an employer's actual loss experience in determining future rates.

2. Compared to the other plans, HMO claims costs are influenced more by the service fees and fixed-cost reimbursement arrangements negotiated with hospitals, physicians, and other health care providers. These arrangements tend to be one- to three-year contracts that become "fixed" claims costs in calculating the next year's premium. The "variable" claims costs—which drive the experience-rated premium calculation—become a smaller part of total plan costs.

A variety of experience-rating methods are used by HMOs. For example, some HMOs apply the same methodology as previously described but place a limit—such as 5 percent of current premium—on the annual change in rates. In other words, if the current experience-rated monthly premium rate for a single employee is $200, the maximum rate reduction or increase for the next year can be 5 percent, that is, $190 or $210, respectively. Another common technique is to use several years—

F I G U R E   43–2

Medical Care Experience-Rating Calculation
(Traditional Indemnity)

Assumptions:	Prior year's paid claims	$500,000
	Expected annual losses*	700,000
	Credibility factor	.50
	Pooling charge	6% of paid claims
	Inflation/utilization trend	12% of expected claims costs
	Underwriting margin	10% of trended losses
	Reserve adjustment	20,000
	Administrative costs	75,000

Calculation:

1. Expected paid claims			$600,000
Actual experience factor	($500,000 × .50)	$250,000	
Insurance company factor	($700,000 × .50)	350,000	
2. Pooling charge: (1) × .06			36,000
3. Inflation/utilization trend: [(1) + (2)] × .12			76,320
4. Trended losses: (1) + (2) + (3)			712,320
5. Underwriting margin: (4) × .10			71,232
6. Reserve adjustment			20,000
7. Administrative costs			75,000
Required premium: (4) + (5) + (6) + (7)			$878,552

*Based on insurance company's actuarial statistics.

typically three years—of claims cost experience in calculating the next year's rates.

Employer Advantage

An experience-rated insurance arrangement is much more a financing method for the employer's actual plan costs than a true insurance arrangement in which employers collectively share in the loss experience and have a common premium rate. With the experience-rating arrangement, the primary insurance protection is against the unexpected catastrophic losses in one plan year that might severely affect the ongoing financial condition of the plan. To the employer with favorable and predictable claims experience, this arrangement is a very cost-effective way to share the plan's financial gains without assuming substantial financial risks.

Deferred Premium Arrangement

In a deferred premium arrangement, one to three months' premium payments to the insurance company can be deferred and used more advantageously by the employer. If and when the insurance contract terminates, the deferred premium must be paid to the insurance company.

In essence, this arrangement allows the employer to retain an amount similar to the plan's incurred but unreported reserves until it is actually needed by the insurance company at contract termination. The necessary amount of reserve varies by the type of coverage, with life insurance plan reserves equaling one to two months' premium, and disability and medical plan reserves equaling two to four months' premium. These reserves are part of the insurance company's total corporate assets and typically earn investment income that either reduces the employer's administrative charges or reduces the reserve amount held by the insurer. The interest credit is related to the insurance company's after-tax investment return on its general assets, which often is significantly less than an employer's after-tax rate of return earned on assets.

If this is the case, the deferred premium arrangement allows an employer to invest more effectively the reserve amount otherwise held by the insurer, and thus enhance its cash flow and year-end earnings level.

To illustrate this advantage, assume an employer normally pays monthly premiums of $50,000 and has an after-tax corporate value of money of 14 percent. The insurance company currently credits 7 percent interest on incurred but unreported reserves. If the employer and insurer agree to a three-month deferred premium arrangement, the financial advantage is the annual *additional* investment earnings the employer earns on the three-month deferred premium amount. In this case, the employer would earn an additional 7 percent return on each of the $50,000 monthly premium deferrals for the remainder of the policy year, which provides an annual cash flow advantage of $9,625. This is shown in Table 43–4.

The loss of the interest credits from the insurance company is reflected in higher annual administrative or reserve charges. However, these increases should be more than offset by the additional employer investment earnings.

Deferred premium arrangements are most common in health care plans that have substantial reserve requirements. Managed medical care plans typically offer only a one-month premium deferral if they have capitated or prefunded financing arrangements in their provider contracts.

T A B L E   43–4

Example of Savings to Employer Under a Three-Month Deferred Premium Arrangement

Month	Deferred Premium	Additional Interest Credit		Duration of Policy Year		Savings
1	$50,000	× 7%	×	1 year	=	$3,500
2	50,000	× 7%	×	11/12 year	=	3,208
3	50,000	× 7%	×	10/12 year	=	2,917
				Total	=	$9,625

Annual Retrospective Premium Arrangement

An annual retrospective premium arrangement reduces the employer's monthly premium payments by a specified percentage with the understanding that this percentage of premium will be paid to the insurance company at year-end if the plan's actual claims and administrative costs exceed the paid premium. The specific percentage reduction of premium normally relates to the insurance company's underwriting margin. The employer gains a cash-flow advantage through the corporate use of this premium amount during the plan year if the corporate value of money exceeds the insurance company's interest credit on surplus premium.

Underwriting margin provides the insurer with premium in excess of the funds necessary to pay expected claims and administrative charges, as illustrated below. During the plan year, any surplus premiums held by the insurance company are credited with interest based on the investment return of the insurance company's general corporate assets. In a participating insurance arrangement, this surplus premium is returned to the employer at the end of the plan year.

Annual Retrospective Premium

	Underwriting margin	Retrospective premium
Total premium payable to insurance company	Administrative charges	Premium paid during plan year
	Expected claim charges	

If the insurance company's interest credit is less than the corporate value of money, an annual retrospective premium arrangement is advantageous. By investing during the plan year the premium amount otherwise held by the insurer as underwriting margin, the employer can improve its current cash flow and its year-end earnings level through the additional investment income earned.

For example, assume an employer's annual premium cost is $3 million, or $250,000 per month, and the plan's underwriting margin is 10 percent of premium. A 10 percent annual retrospective premium arrangement would reduce the premium payments to $2.7 million per year and provide $300,000 premium to be invested by the employer during the plan year. The financial advantage is the *additional* investment earnings the employer can earn on the $300,000 reduced premium amount. If the corporate after-tax value of money is 14 percent and the insurance company interest credit is 7 percent, the additional investment income to the employer is approximately $10,500. (This value assumes premiums are paid monthly and that the additional investment earnings equal the monthly interest rate multiplied by the remaining months of the plan year.)

As part of the annual retrospective premium arrangement, the employer agrees to pay a part or all of the reduced premium amount to the insurance company at the end of the policy year if the actual claims and administrative charges exceed the actual premium paid during the plan year. The insurance company pays charges in excess of paid premium during the year from its capital or surplus accounts. An interest charge is applied to these excess charges that represents the insurance company's lost investment earnings.

Terminal Retrospective Premium Arrangement

With a terminal retrospective premium arrangement, the employer agrees to pay the outstanding deficit that may exist at the time the insurance contract is terminated with the insurance company. The agreement usually specifies a maximum percentage of premium or dollar amount up to which the employer will indemnify the insurance company at contract termination.

In this arrangement, the insurance company substantially reduces the annual risk charge and the underwriting margin. The terminal retrospective premium arrangement transfers some or all of the unexpected claims costs to the employer; therefore, these charges can be reduced. This reduction is reflected in lower monthly premium costs and gives the employer use of this reduced premium amount for potentially more profitable corporate investment.

Also, this arrangement offers more underwriting flexibility for insuring high benefit limits and special plan design features that pose a potentially greater financial risk to the insurance company. Because some of the risk of underestimating the losses from these special benefit arrangements is transferred to the employer, the insurance company is more apt to underwrite the coverage to satisfy the employer's needs.

Both annual and terminal retrospective premium arrangements can be included to maximize the reduction of the risk charge and underwriting margin and the potential cash flow savings. However, the terminal retrospective premium arrangement is less common than the annual arrangement. Insurance companies are less apt to offer a terminal retrospective premium arrangement because its long-term nature makes it difficult to determine a reasonable value to the insurer. Secondly, its attractiveness is limited to the very large employer that is willing to assume a potential long-term liability and that is considered a good, long-term credit risk by the insurance company. Therefore, the applicability and current use of this alternative insurance arrangement is limited.

Extended Plan-Year Accounting

Some insurance companies extend the plan year's accounting of claims paid as a means of reducing or eliminating the necessary incurred but unreported claims reserves. These insurers record the claims *incurred before* the end of the plan year but *paid after* the plan year as actual paid claims during that plan year. This extended accounting period, which normally is an additional one- to three-month period, allows the actual incurred but unreported claims to be more accurately accounted to the appropriate plan year and substantially reduces or even eliminates the incurred but unreported claims reserves maintained by the insurance company.

For example, if the accounting period for a life insurance plan is extended an additional month, the incurred but unreported reserve, which normally is about 10 percent of premium, often is reduced to 2 percent to 3 percent of premium. Similarly, extending by two months the plan year accounting for a traditional indemnity or PPO medical care plan may reduce the incurred but unreported reserve by 50 percent or more.

This financial alternative normally is available only to large employers with predictable monthly claims experience. For such employers, this arrangement provides an accurate accounting of incurred but unreported claims. To the extent these actual claims are less than the insurance company's normal reserve factors, the employer gains a direct savings and cash-flow advantage. In addition, the insurance company substantially reduces the required reserve levels held during the contract period. The employer gains a cash-flow advantage on the reserve difference equal to the additional investment income earned by the employer using these funds in its business compared to receiving an interest credit from the insurance company.

Exclusion of the Waiver of Premium Provision (Life Insurance)

The waiver-of-premium provision is common in a group life insurance program. It continues coverage for a totally and permanently disabled employee without continued premium payments by the employer for the employee's coverage. Although such a provision sounds attractive, the additional cost to include it in the life insurance plan often is greater than its actual value, especially for large employers.

Monthly premium costs typically increase 10 percent to 15 percent due to the increase in incurred but unreported claims reserves and the additional risk of the waiver of premium provision. The additional monthly cost of this provision can be avoided in large part by the employer eliminating the waiver of premium provision and continuing to pay monthly premiums for the disabled employees. In most cases, the total cost of these continued premium payments after the disability date will be substantially less than the additional 10 percent to 15 percent monthly premium charge for *all* employees.

A potential disadvantage to excluding the waiver of premium provision occurs if the employer changes insurance companies. There can be a problem continuing life insurance coverage for previously disabled employees with the new insurer because most contracts only insure employees actively at work as of the effective date of the new life insurance coverage. Insurance companies often waive this provision for large employers, but they may hesitate to do so for smaller employers if the inclusion of disabled employees' coverage could adversely distort the expected loss experience. Therefore, excluding the waiver of premium provision often is suggested only for larger employers.

Claims-Plus Premium Arrangement (Life Insurance)

A claims-plus premium arrangement bases the employer's monthly life insurance premium on the *actual* loss experience of previous months *plus* fixed monthly administrative and reserve charges. To the extent actual monthly loss experience is *less* than the level monthly premium payments normally paid during the plan year, this difference can remain with the employer as additional cash flow. If the employer's corporate value of money is greater than the insurer's interest credit on surplus premium, the employer gains additional investment income on this difference during the plan year.

To limit the risk of the employer having a cash-flow loss by incurring benefit claim payments in one or more months in excess of the level monthly premium amount, insurance companies set the maximum monthly employer cost at the level monthly premium amount plus any "surplus" accumulated from prior months. Also, the maximum annual employer cost is the same as the annual premium cost based on the level monthly premium amounts. In this way, the employer still is fully insured against unexpected or catastrophic loss experience that may occur during any policy year.

To illustrate how this claims-plus premium arrangement works, assume the employer's normal annual life insurance premium cost is $360,000, or a level monthly premium payment of $30,000. This $30,000 monthly premium payment is based on $27,000 of expected losses per month and a standard monthly administrative and reserve charge of $3,000. Table 43–5 shows the actual monthly premium costs under a claims-plus arrangement given the above assumptions and assumed actual loss experience during the plan year.

The normal administration of the claims-plus arrangement is for the first month's premium payment to equal the level monthly premium pay-

T A B L E   43–5

Life Insurance Claims-Plus Arrangement ($ thousands)

	Months												
	1	2	3	4	5	6	7	8	9	10	11	12	Total
Normal premium	$30	$30	$30	$30	$30	$30	$30	$30	$30	$30	$30	$30	$360
Actual losses	20	0	20	50	10	0	0	70	20	50	30	20	290
Administrative/ reserve	3	3	3	3	3	3	3	3	3	3	3	3	36
Actual monthly payment	30	23	3	23	53	13	3	3	73	23	53	26	326
Cumulative balance	—	7	34	41	18	35	62	89	46	53	30	34	34

ment amount and thereafter to equal the actual loss experience of the previous month plus the standard administrative and reserve charge. In the example illustrated in Table 43–5, the employer pays the normal monthly premium payment of $30,000 in month 1 and from then on pays the actual losses of the previous month plus the standard monthly administrative and reserve charge of $3,000. For instance, the premium payment for month 2 is $23,000; that is, $20,000 of actual losses in month 1 plus the $3,000 administrative charge. The cumulative balance for month 2 and thereafter equals the cumulative difference between actual monthly payments and the normal monthly premium payments. In months 5, 9, and 11, the employer pays substantially more than the normal premium payment, reflecting the previous months' high actual losses. This can occur under this arrangement as long as any monthly premium amount does not exceed the normal premium payment plus the cumulative balance as of that date. At the end of the plan year a reconciliation occurs between the actual annual plan expenses and the year-to-date (11 months) actual monthly payments. In month 12 the employer pays the reconciling balance required to cover actual annual plan expenses, subject to the maximum annual plan premium of $360,000. In the example, the employer pays a reconciling balance of $26,000:

Actual Annual Plan Expenses:		$326,000
▪ Actual losses:	$290,000	
▪ Administrative/reserve:	$36,000	
Actual Monthly Payments (11 months)		$300,000
Monthy 12 Reconciling Balance		$26,000

Insurance companies have various trade names for this arrangement, the most common being *flexible funding* or *minimum premium* arrangement. Normally, such an arrangement is offered only to large employers that have substantial monthly life insurance premiums. Normally, for employers with less than a $15,000 monthly life insurance premium, this arrangement is not advantageous because of the increased internal administration and administrative costs, the volatile fluctuation in monthly claims, and limited potential financial gain.

Partial Self-Funding Arrangement (Long-Term Disability)

Long-term disability (LTD) insurance promises to pay a significant percentage of an employee's income for the duration of his or her total and permanent disability. Typically, the number of claims incurred by an employer is few, but the total cost per claim is quite large because of the duration of benefit payments. In the plan year that a LTD claim is incurred, a reserve is charged to that year's financial experience equal to the discounted expected cost of all future benefit payments. Often, the reserve charge is greater than the annual paid premium. However, the limited number of claims over a three- to five-year period allows the insurance company to set the premium rate at the expected average annual cost over this time period, thereby keeping it relatively stable and affordable for the employer.

The employer can partially self-fund its group LTD plan by assuming the financial liability of any claim for a specific duration and transferring the remaining liability to the insurance company. This arrangement reduces the monthly premium payments to the insurance company, provides potential cash-flow savings through increased investment earnings on the premium difference, and still provides the employer substantial insurance protection against a catastrophic claim situation. Two other financial advantages to a partial self-funding arrangement are (1) the incurred but unreported reserve requirement normally is reduced, and (2) the premium tax liability is reduced.

There are two ways this arrangement can be designed. The more common method is for the insurer to assume the benefit payment liability for the first two to five years and the employer to continue benefit payments beyond this specific time period. There are several advantages of this plan design:

1. The average duration for an LTD claim is less than two years, so the long-term financial liability and administration assumed by the employer is limited.

2. The insurance company establishes minimal reserves for future benefit payments in comparison to a fully insured arrangement, which reduces the required premium payment and offers cash-flow savings to the employer.

3. Because an extended period exists before the employer assumes financial liability and begins periodic benefit payments, the employer typically prefunds its liability only when the disability actually occurs.

The second plan design option is for the employer to pay the LTD benefits for the initial two to five years and the insurance company to assume the risk thereafter. The main employer advantage is that premiums are substantially reduced because the employer is assuming the full liability of most LTD claims.

As a general rule, this alternative insurance arrangement is offered only to employers with at least 1,500 to 2,000 insured employees. For smaller plans, typically the claim occurrence is too volatile and the potential long-term financial liability normally too large for the employer to effectively self-insure the risk.

Large Deductible Arrangement (Medical)

Like the partial self-funding arrangement for LTD plans, the large deductible arrangement for medical care plans has been designed for employers to assume the financial liability for a substantial part of each medical plan participant's initial annual covered medical expenses and transfer only the excess claims costs to the insurance company. This arrangement substantially reduces the monthly premium payments to the insurance company, provides potential cash-flow savings through additional investment earnings on the unused premium difference, and still provides the employer substantial insurance protection against a catastrophic individual claim situation.

Other potential advantages of this arrangement are (1) the incurred but unreported reserve requirement normally is reduced, (2) the premium tax liability is reduced, and (3) it facilitates the employee sharing some of the assumed claims costs. A large deductible arrangement typically is used with traditional indemnity or PPO plans.

The typical design of this arrangement is illustrated below and shows the three parties—the employee, employer, and insurance company—assuming some of the annual benefits cost.

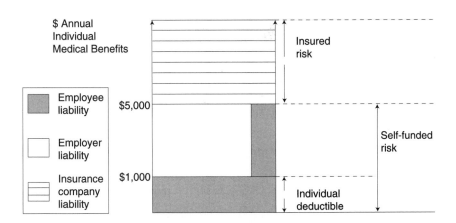

The employer typically assumes the financial liability for the initial $1,000 to $5,000 of annual medical plan benefit payments per participant, which is called the *self-funded risk*. In turn, the employer typically requires the employee (and dependents) to assume the financial liability for a budgetable amount of the self-funded risk—normally the initial $200 to $1,000 of covered expenses per year per family member (referred to as the *individual deductible*) and 10 percent or 20 percent of the remaining self-funded risk. Usually there is a family maximum annual expense, defined either as a dollar limit or when two or three family members have each reached the individual deductible limit.

The financial liability in excess of the self-funded risk level is transferred to the insurance company, which also serves as plan and claims administrator for the total program.

This arrangement is of greatest interest to employers that want to manage utilization, assume total financial liability for the high-frequency, relatively low-cost health care services, and be protected from the infrequent and unbudgetable high-cost individual medical episodes. Large deductible arrangements also have been an outgrowth of the popularity of flexible spending accounts, medical savings accounts, and similar employee-funded medical reimbursement accounts.

Recent legislation has encouraged the use of medical savings accounts (MSAs) for eligible individuals participating in a "high deductible health plan"[4] sponsored by a small employer (defined as an employer with 50 or fewer employees on average) or a self-employed individual. An MSA is a trust created exclusively for paying qualified medical expenses of a participating individual. Contributions to the MSA by the individual and/or the small employer and qualified distributions from the MSA are treated with the typical favorable tax advantages of an employer-sponsored plan. The intent of this legislation is to help self-employed individuals and small employers have greater access to affordable health care coverage for themselves and their employees.

Minimum Premium Arrangement (Health Care, Short-Term Disability)

In a minimum premium arrangement, the employer pays the health care and/or short-term disability benefits directly from a corporate cash

---

4 IRC Section 220 defines a "high deductible health plan" as having, for tax years beginning in 2000, an individual-coverage annual deductible in the range of $1,550 to $2,350 and a family-coverage annual deductible in the range of $3,100 to $4,650.

account instead of transferring funds in the form of premium payments to the insurance company. The employer essentially self-funds the payment of benefits up to the expected loss level for the plan year, with the insurance company assuming the financial liability for any claims costs in excess of the expected loss level. The only premium paid to the insurer is for the normal administrative, risk, and reserve charges.

This arrangement typically is used for traditional indemnity or PPO medical plans, dental, and short-term disability plans.

The primary advantages of this arrangement are reduced premium tax liability and potential cash-flow savings. The payment of benefits from a corporate cash account is not considered an insurance arrangement in most states;[5] therefore, no premium tax liability is incurred. This offers a direct annual savings on the average equal to 2 percent of the normal premium amount used to pay benefits. Normally, a minimum premium arrangement is suggested only for employers with at least $500,000 in premiums. At this minimum level of premium, approximately 85 percent of premium, or $425,000, is used to pay benefits. This implies the annual savings from reduced-premium tax liability is approximately $8,500 (2 percent of $425,000). As the premium size increases, the percentage of premium used to pay benefits similarly increases and the premium tax savings becomes more substantial. For instance, an employer paying $5 million in annual medical premium may use 93 percent of the normal premium to pay benefits, or $4.65 million. At this level, the annual premium tax savings would be $93,000.

The second advantage is potential cash-flow savings gained by the employer having the corporate use of "surplus" funds during the plan year. Minimum premium arrangements are generally designed so the employer pays benefit claims during the plan year up to the annual expected loss level determined by the insurance company. This limit often is called the *employer maximum liability*. The employer pays benefits periodically from a separate cash account[6] to meet the plan's claims liability. If the actual claims paid during the initial months of the plan year are less than the expected monthly claims costs, a "surplus" develops in the cash account. To the extent the investment return earned by the corporation on this "surplus" is greater than the insurance company's interest credit on surplus premium, the employer gains additional investment earnings and a cash-flow advantage.

---

5 Connecticut and California assess a premium tax on all benefits paid through a minimum premium arrangement.

6 This corporate cash account typically is either a direct-deposit account of a bank or savings institution or a 501(c)(9) trust.

By paying benefit claims as they are reported during the plan year, the employer also can have a cash flow *loss* if claims in the initial months are greater than the expected monthly claims costs. To avoid this possibility, a minimum premium arrangement can be designed to limit the maximum monthly payment of claims from the employer cash account equal to the monthly level of expected claims costs *plus* any "surplus" funds accumulated during the plan year. If the actual claims costs in a month exceed this limit, the insurance company pays all excess benefit claims from its funds. If "surplus" funds develop in future months, the insurer immediately uses these funds to recoup its payment amount of prior months. The insurance company normally increases its administrative and risk charges to reflect the potential additional monthly liability it assumes in this specific case.

In a minimum premium arrangement, the insurance company administers all claims payments and assumes the risk of claims costs in excess of the annual expected loss level, just as in conventional or other alternative insurance arrangements. Figure 43–3 illustrates the flow of a benefit claim from its initial receipt, review, and benefit determination by the insurance company to the issuing and clearing of a corporate check through the corporate account.

The insurance company typically has similar administrative, risk, and reserve charges as in a conventional or other alternative insurance arrangement. The employer pays a monthly premium to the insurer equal to the expected annual cost of these charges. Premium taxes must be paid by the

FIGURE 43–3

Claim Flow of Minimum Premium Arrangement

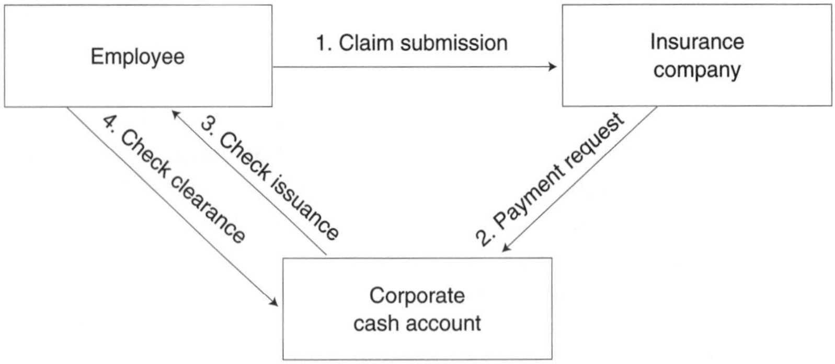

employer on these monthly premium amounts. In the previous examples, where 85 percent and 93 percent of normal premium are deposited into the corporate cash account to pay expected claims costs, the remaining 15 percent and 7 percent of normal premium, respectively, reflect the monthly premium charge for administrative, risk, and reserve costs.

Minimum Premium— No Reserve Arrangement

A significant difference between a minimum premium arrangement and self-funding (see next section) is that the insurance company still maintains a substantial reserve for incurred but unreported claims in the minimum premium arrangement. As in other alternative insurance arrangements, the employer potentially can gain a cash-flow savings by gaining the corporate use of the reserves. To meet this employer demand, the insurance companies offer a minimum premium-no reserve arrangement.

The employer gains the use of these reserves by the insurance company returning the incurred but unreported reserves it has been holding and reducing the future premium charges paid to the insurance company. This arrangement allows the corporation to use the reserve funds until they are required to pay incurred but unreported claims at the time of plan or contract termination. Because of state insurance regulations, it is generally agreed by insurance companies that they cannot fully release to the employer the financial liability for incurred but unreported claims at termination of its insurance contract with the employer. Therefore, the employer must either repay the reserve amount to the insurer at time of termination, or specifically pay the incurred but unreported claims up to the insurer's normal reserve amount for a similar medical and/or short-term disability plan.

The minimum premium-no reserve arrangement offers most of the financial advantages of self-funding, plus limits the employer's liability for benefit payments in excess of the expected annual loss level. The liability for these possible unexpected costs is still assumed by the insurance company. A disadvantage to the minimum premium-no reserve arrangement is administrative costs will be higher than the minimum premium arrangement because the interest credited by the insurance company on reserves, which is applied to reduce the administrative charges, no longer exists. However, the additional investment income gained through the corporate use of these funds significantly offsets this disadvantage.

Multi-Option Arrangements

HMO, PPO, and/or POS plans are included now in most employers' health care programs. These managed care plans are designed to control costs by steering patients to hospitals and physicians that have agreed to a reduced or fixed payment, and by managing utilization of services. Employees often choose between an existing indemnity medical benefits plan and these managed care options. Employers often establish separate benefit, funding, administrative, and insurance arrangements to manage each plan.

While a multi-option benefit program helps control total claim costs, the additional plan administration and separate funding arrangements can cause problems. Plan administration is more complex due to the additional reporting, employee communication, and tracking of eligibility, payments, and expenses. This complexity increases internal and third-party administration costs. When employee participation is spread among several plans, the previously discussed alternative insured arrangements may have less impact or even be inappropriate. For instance, the employer's credibility factor may be substantially less in an experience-rating arrangement if the number of participants in the indemnity plan significantly decreases. And if this insured group becomes too small, cash-flow arrangements such as minimum premium may not be feasible.

In addition, the separate financial arrangements can limit the employer's ability to share in the overall claims cost savings. HMO coverage typically is provided through a fully insured arrangement, with premium rates based on the average community costs of all HMO participants and the employer unable to participate in the year-end financial settlement. If the actual claims costs of the employer's HMO participants are less than the overall community costs, the employer is subsidizing the plan and not gaining the total savings of the HMO option.

In response, insurance and managed care companies are offering employers the indemnity and managed care options as one funding, administrative, and insurance arrangement. After the employees make their plan choices, a multi-option arrangement essentially works as if it is one plan. The enrollment, reporting, and communications activities are consolidated, typically reducing both internal and third-party administrative expenses. The financial results of each plan option are combined to determine the year-end balance, which enables the employer to fully share in any plan savings. And the insurance or managed care company may offer the alternative funding arrangements previously discussed in this chapter.

Table 43–6 illustrates the potential financial advantages of a multi-option arrangement. Assume there are three plans—indemnity, PPO, and HMO—with 1,000 employees covered in each plan. The indemnity and PPO plans are separate, participating insurance arrangements, whereas the HMO is conventionally insured, which means the employer doesn't participate in a year-end surplus balance. The premiums and total expenses for each plan are different, resulting in a $200,000 deficit balance for the indemnity plan, a $50,000 surplus balance for the PPO, and a $350,000 surplus balance for the HMO. The balance in the Separate Plan Totals column is a $150,000 deficit balance because the employer doesn't collect the $350,000 surplus balance from the conventionally insured HMO plan. However, with a multi-option funding arrangement, the employer has a $300,000 surplus balance total at year-end. This favorable result is due to the HMO surplus balance being included in the total balance and a $100,000 reduction in administration expenses under the multi-option arrangement.

The multi-option arrangement is relatively new and still being developed by many companies. The arrangement is available primarily to large employers—typically those with at least 500 employees—whose employee locations match the locations of the insurer's managed care networks. Also, some states limit the scope of this arrangement by restricting the consolidation of actual HMO financial results with the other employer-sponsored plans.

T A B L E   43–6

Multi-Option Arrangement Financial Advantages ($000)

	Indemnity	PPO	HMO	Separate Plan Total	Multi-Option Total
Employees	1,000	1,000	1,000	3,000	3,000
Premiums	$3,100	$2,700	$2,500	$8,300	$8,300
Expenses					
Claims	$3,000	$2,250	$1,700	$6,950	$6,950
Administration	300	400	450	1,150	1,050
Total	$3,300	$2,650	$2,150	$8,100	$8,000
Balance	($ 200)	$ 50	$ 350	($ 150)	$ 300

NONINSURED (SELF-FUNDING) ARRANGEMENTS

The final step in potentially reducing total plan costs is for the employer to assume essentially the total financial risk of the benefit plan, which is called *self-funding*. In this arrangement, the only plan costs are the actual paid claims, claims administration and other administrative expenses, and in some cases, excess loss premium expense. By eliminating the other insurance-related expenses, the employer is in a position to pay only the basic administration expenses and fully capture favorable loss experience. Of course, the employer also is responsible for all unfavorable loss experience because there is little or no transfer of risk to an insurance company.

The most common benefits plans being self-funded are medical, dental, and other health care plans and short-term disability benefits. Self-funding arrangements for managed care plans are relatively new because of restrictive state insurance laws and only recent employer interest in such arrangements. However, the same self-funding principles apply to managed care plans as to the traditional indemnity health care plans, except where noted in this section. Life insurance benefits plans generally are not self-funded because noninsured death benefits are taxable to the beneficiary. And, the number of employers self-funding long-term disability benefits recently has been decreasing because of a competitive insurance market and 1993 federal tax law changes that limit self-funded coverage for compensated employees using a tax-exempt trust.

Corporate employers have been self-funding benefits plans for 20 years or more, especially after the courts clarified in 1974 that self-funding should not be construed as *doing an insurance business*, which otherwise would subject these plans to state insurance laws. Governmental and not-for-profit employers and Taft–Hartley welfare plans have lagged behind corporate employers in implementing self-funding arrangements, due in part to unique legislation authorizing this alternative funding arrangement and in part to their greater hesitancy to assume total financial risk. However, at this point, self-funding is applicable and common for all types of employers and benefit plan sponsors (see Table 43–7).

Definitions

Self-funding refers to a funding arrangement in which the ultimate financial and legal responsibility for providing the plan benefits is assumed by the employer. These arrangements typically must comply with federal disclosure, documentation, and fiduciary requirements under ERISA.

T A B L E   43-7

Percentage and Type of Employees with Self-Funded Indemnity and PPO Medical Plans

		Indemnity	PPO
Manufacturing		87%	82%
Wholesale/retail trade		57%	75%
Finance		77%	56%
Services		61%	60%
Government		83%	86%
Total	Large Employers	72%	70%
	Small Employers	25%	20%

Source: Mercer/Foster Higgins, *National Survey of Employer-Sponsored Health Plans,* 1999.

Although the "payor of last resort" in this type of funding arrangement is the employer, the risk of losses exceeding an affordable threshold often is transferred to an insurance company through the purchase of excess loss insurance. This insurance coverage also is referred to as stop-loss insurance or reinsurance.

There are two types of excess loss insurance: individual and aggregate. *Individual excess loss* insurance covers the claims costs incurred by and/or paid for an individual during a specified time period (typically a 12-month plan year) that exceed a specific threshold. For example, an employer may purchase medical plan individual excess loss insurance that applies to any plan participant's medical service costs exceeding $100,000 (the typical threshold ranges from $50,000 to $200,000) that are incurred and paid during a calendar year. *Aggregate excess loss* insurance protects an employer from total plan claims costs exceeding a specified threshold during a specific time period. For example, if medical plan paid claims exceed 125 percent (the typical range is 110 percent to 125 percent) of an agreed-upon, expected cost threshold (e.g., $5 million) during the calendar year, all costs in excess of $6.25 million are reimbursed by the aggregate insurance coverage.

The claims and other plan administration services for a self-funded arrangement can be performed by the employer or, more often, by a third-party administrator (TPA) or an insurance company as part of an *administrative services only* (ASO) *contract*. No risk is assumed by the TPA or insurance company, so the contract charges are related only to claims payment transactions and other plan administration processes. Typical administrative charges of an insured funding arrangement, such as premium tax, risk charge, commissions, and general administrative and underwriting expenses, are not included in an administrative services contract.

Advantages of Self-Funding

Self-funding arrangements can provide employers both financial and plan-management advantages. The primary advantages include capturing favorable claims experience, reducing administrative and other claims expenses, avoiding state-mandated benefits, and having greater flexibility in managing the benefit plans.

Capturing Favorable Claims Experience

Self-funding is most effective for group insurance plans with a substantial number of claims transactions and a relatively low cost per transaction, such as medical, dental, and short-term disability benefit plans. The expected financial result for these types of plans is more predictable. This predictability helps an employer project its expected annual claims costs and assess whether these costs are less than similar costs in an insured arrangement. If the employer is confident its actual plan costs will be less than the insurance company's premium charges and the potential savings are worth taking the risk, the employer should consider self-funding.

For example, insurance companies often use factors in addition to historical claims experience to calculate future premium charges, such as demographics of the insured group, industry-specific actuarial factors, and the average claims experience of other similar employers. Let's say that, looking at these factors, the insurance company determines an employer's short-term disability claims costs for next year will be $500,000. The employer knows that actual claims costs for the last two years have been 15 percent to 20 percent less than the insurance company's projections. If the employer is confident this historical experience should repeat itself, this situation is appropriate for self-funding.

Reducing Administrative and Other Claims Expenses

While capturing favorable claims experience offers the greatest potential savings, the more certain savings of self-funding come from lower "fixed" plan costs—that is, administration, reserves, and other claims charges.

Because the employer assumes the financial risk, the types of administrative services and charges of an insurance company or TPA differ in several ways from an insured arrangement:

1. No premium tax liability is incurred by the insurance company or TPA, so no premium tax charges are transferred to the employer.
2. There is no risk charge because the insurance company or TPA assumes no financial liability for benefit payments.
3. Normally, no commission payments are included in a self-funding arrangement.
4. General administrative and underwriting services performed by the insurance company or TPA normally are much less than in an insured arrangement, so the charges for these activities are comparatively much less.

The insurance company or TPA administers the plan and determines the benefit payments under a self-funded arrangement in the same way as a conventional insured arrangement. The typical services provided under this arrangement include the following:

- Claims processing.
- Financial and administrative reports.
- Plan descriptions for employees.
- Banking arrangements.
- Government reporting and compliance.
- Basic underwriting and actuarial services.
- Individual conversion policies.
- COBRA administration.
- Legal, clinical, and other professional services.

By performing these services, the insurance company or TPA accepts the fiduciary responsibilities and powers necessary to administer the plan. However, they do not assume financial responsibility for the plan. The benefit payment checks are drawn against the employer's general assets or assets deposited into an employer-sponsored trust (see Funding and Accounting Considerations later in this chapter). Often, the insurance company or TPA isn't even identified on these checks.

Many employers also consider internally administering the plan to further reduce their administrative costs. However, there are a number of reasons why purchasing administrative services from a third-party may be more cost-effective:

1. The initial investment expense and ongoing operating costs of computer hardware and storage can be spread over a larger customer base.

2. Typically, it's more economical to purchase rather than internally develop the computer software for a health care claims payment system because the details of the system are complex and unfamiliar to the employer's computer programmers.

3. The ongoing employee training to stay current with legal, clinical, and operating changes can be costly and time-consuming to the employer.

4. The insurance company or TPA can achieve greater economies of scale for standard operating procedures.

5. It's more economical for the insurance company or TPA to be staffed with legal, clinical, and other technical expertise necessary to administer health care and disability plans.

6. The employer maintains a third-party "buffer" in disputing or denying benefit payments.

Avoiding State-Mandated Benefits

ERISA preempts self-funded employee benefits programs from state laws that mandate minimum benefits coverage, regulate financial management of the plans, or assess taxes on "insured" arrangements. This preemption gives the employer greater authority and flexibility in designing and funding the benefits programs. This advantage of self-funding is especially important to multistate employers, that can establish a similar benefits program for all employees and avoid the expense and complexity of meeting the unique benefits and financial requirements of each state.

Almost every state currently has some state-mandated benefits, typically involving minimum benefit levels of specific health care services, such as physical therapy or mental health/substance abuse, or minimum coverage requirements, such as preexisting condition or surviving-spouse coverage provisions. The ability of self-funded benefit plans to avoid these mandates has been continually tested by state and federal legal actions. However, the courts have been relatively consistent in upholding the ERISA preemption. The preemption issue also has gained significant political interest as Congress and the executive branch look to the states for creative solutions to national health care cost, access, and quality problems.

Greater Flexibility and Control

In addition to the legal requirements avoided or at least simplified by self-funding, employers have greater authority on plan design, financing, and administration than in an insured arrangement. Because the financial risk is assumed by the employer, the insurance company or TPA isn't as restricted by state or federal insurance laws and is less concerned with the underlying benefit levels and cost of the health care plan. Therefore, their underwriting, funding, contractual, and operational requirements are relatively minor in a self-funded arrangement.

The employer has greater flexibility to design and finance a benefits plan that fits its business, human-resources, and benefits strategies and meets the needs of its workforce. With the dynamic changes in managed care and cost-containment options, self-funding can help employers change their health care plans quickly and creatively in response to savings and quality of care opportunities. These advantages don't lessen the need to follow prudent underwriting, plan design, and administrative principles—they give the employer greater control in implementing them.

Potential Disadvantages of Self-Funding

As noted earlier, a recent survey found that more than 70 percent of large employers currently self-fund their traditional indemnity or PPO medical plans, compared to around 20 percent of small employers (fewer than 500 employees).[7] One of the primary reasons small employers use an insured arrangement is a concern over the predictability of annual plan costs and the ultimate financial responsibility that comes with self-funding. Most of these employers weigh the availability, security, cost, and financial protection of an insured arrangement with a self-funded plan and excess loss insurance—and decide on the insured arrangement.

The following are other reasons an employer may decide not to self-fund health care benefits:

- To gain the additional underwriting, legal, and administrative services available through an insured arrangement.
- To avoid potential employee concerns about the financial security of their health care benefits.
- To respond to specific collective-bargaining negotiations and stipulations.

---

7 Mercer/Foster Higgins, *National Survey of Employer-Sponsored Health Plans*, 1999.

- To have a financial and administrative third-party buffer with employees.
- To avoid the additional financial risk of numerous COBRA participants.
- To gain the cost advantages of HMOs and other managed care plans that are limited or prohibited from self-funding by state insurance laws.
- To capture the lower costs of a community-rated, insured arrangement compared to the expected actual costs of an employee group based on its demographics, health status, and/or previous claims experience.

An emerging concern about self-funding medical plans is the possibility of increased employer liability for medical malpractice and third-party denial of employees' medical care claims. Several legislative measures currently are being considered in Congress that would impose responsibility on the health care plan sponsor for medical benefit and coverage decisions. If this increased liability is placed on the employer, it is expected that many employers will move away from sponsorship and management of medical care benefit plans for their employees.

Funding and Accounting Considerations

Because the employer assumes ultimate financial and fiduciary responsibility, specific attention should be given to how a self-funded plan is structured to hold and invest assets (funding) and how the plan accounts for plan expenses and liabilities.

The expenses of a self-funded plan typically are paid from one of three employer funding sources: the general assets of the organization, a tax-favored trust, or a captive insurance company. The differences between these funding vehicles center on security and use of assets, tax treatment of fund deposits and investment income, and employer access to surplus assets.

General Assets of the Organization

Plan expenses are paid directly from the general assets of the organization, similar to the payment of any general organization expenses. Assets to pay plan costs are commingled with all other assets. Employee contributions withheld through payroll deduction can be reported as specific plan assets but also are commingled with the general assets of the organization. The plan liabilities and expenses are recognized as a general operating expense, and the claimant is a general creditor of the organization.

Self-funded short-term disability and wage continuation plans typically are funded on this basis. If there is no insurance involved, the benefit payments are considered and administered much like a payroll expense. Payments are drawn from general assets but reported as a separate benefit plan expense. The employer recognizes the benefit payments as a general operating expense for tax purposes, and any additional funding of plan liabilities is tax-deductible only when the liability has been incurred and can be determined. The benefit payments for these wage continuation and disability plans are typically ordinary taxable income to the employee, excluding any portion of the benefit attributable to employee contributions.

The advantages of this funding arrangement are primarily administrative. Initial qualification filings are avoided, and annual government reporting is simplified. General plan administration typically is included with the daily payroll and treasury functions.

The primary disadvantages involve the tax treatment of plan assets and the security of future benefit payments. As mentioned before, the accumulation of plan assets in a general asset-funding arrangement are tax-deductible only if the liability has been incurred and can be determined. This tax treatment limits the applicability of general asset funding to pay-as-you-go benefit plans, such as self-funded paid time-off plans. In addition, the promise to pay benefits in the future is only as good as the financial condition of the organization. For this reason, most organizations are encouraged by their employees and financial advisers to use another funding source for a benefit plan with any extended liabilities.

Tax-Exempt Trust

If any plan assets are accumulated to pay extended plan benefit liabilities, a special trust typically is used that exempts from federal tax the investment income earned on these assets. This special tax-exempt entity technically is called a voluntary employees' beneficiary association (VEBA) but is better known as a 501(c)(9) trust.

A VEBA can be created to fund "for the payment of life, sick, accident or other benefits" to the members, and their designated dependents/beneficiaries, participating in the trust. Medical and other health care, and disability benefits for active employees are the most common plans funded through a VEBA. Benefits payments for retiree plans, such as postretirement life insurance and medical and other benefit plans can be funded through a VEBA in a limited manner if specific regulations are followed.

To qualify for this special tax status, the VEBA must satisfy several requirements:

1. Membership eligibility essentially is limited to employees with an employment-related common bond, such as common employer or employers in the same line of business in the "same geographic locale."

2. The eligibility or benefits provided through the trust cannot discriminate in favor of officers, shareholders, or highly compensated employees.

3. The VEBA must be controlled by the participating members or trustees designated by the members.

4. The assets or earnings of the VEBA can be used only to pay permissible benefits (including specified insurance premiums). At plan termination, the contributing employers can receive any remaining assets only after all plan liabilities have been satisfied.

5. The VEBA must apply to the IRS and receive approval of its tax-exempt status.

In addition, there are detailed regulations limiting the tax-deductible annual contributions and the accumulated assets in a VEBA, referred to as the trust's "qualified cost." Basically, this "qualified cost" is the actual annual cash payments for benefits, administration, and other reasonable direct plan costs and the annual additions to actuarially reasonable accumulated assets held in the trust to pay incurred but unpaid claims liabilities.

A VEBA operates as an independent entity with financial reporting and auditing requirements. The participating employers and/or employees make periodic contributions into the trust to fund current and accrued liabilities. A VEBA is common when employee contributions are required, especially after-tax contributions or substantial contribution amounts that need to be segregated from the general assets of the organization. Assets are distributed from the trust as required to meet the plan's financial obligations. The federal income tax treatment of employer contributions into the trust and of benefit payments from the trust follows the applicable tax rules of any qualified employee benefit program.

The primary advantages of the VEBA are the tax-exempt treatment of investment income (except for retiree health care reserves) and the increased security of benefit payment for employees. Standard accounting rules and reporting requirements serve as a monitor of the financial integrity of the plan. The trustees have fiduciary responsibilities for the appropriate management of the VEBA. And plan assets can only be used for the payment of plan benefits and expenses.

The primary disadvantages are the compliance requirements and related expenses to operate the trust. The regulations are complex and often require professional advice and technical support. And, the IRS is stepping up its auditing activity of VEBAs to ensure excess assets are not accumulating on a tax-favored basis. This interest has increased the scope and expense of actuarial and auditing services required to manage plan funding.

Captive Insurance Company

A captive insurance company is formed by an organization to transfer some or all of its own business or personnel risks and to potentially capture a proportionate profit from the captive insurance arrangement. The captive essentially underwrites and operates as a regular insurance company, accepting risk-related premiums and paying contractual claims liabilities. Captives typically can accept two to five times their capital, depending on the type of risk. Certain U.S. states, especially Vermont and Colorado, and offshore countries are the primary captive domiciles due to their favorable tax treatment, financing, and regulation of captives.

ERISA defines use of a captive insurer as a self-funding arrangement and governs the arrangement from this perspective unless less than 50 percent of the captive's premiums are for its own risks. The Department of Labor and IRS continue to scrutinize the validity of this funding vehicle. For these reasons, a captive insurer is not often used today as an employee benefit funding source.

CONCLUSION

This chapter has described a number of creative solutions for reducing or, at least, controlling the employer costs of health and welfare benefit plans. However, as these costs continue to increase, employers and the insurers and other third-party service firms supporting their plans will be designing additional alternative funding arrangements to meet employers' needs. This trend will be most prevalent in funding HMOs and other managed care plans.

At the same time, federal and state regulatory and legislative branches are increasingly interested in how employers finance and administer their benefit plans. This oversight will add another dimension to designing and administering alternative funding arrangements in the future.

These dynamic market forces ensure continued activity and creativity in the funding of employee benefit programs.

Employers' Accounting for Pension Costs

William E. Decker

Kenneth E. Dakdduk

This chapter explains the pension accounting standards contained in *Statement of Financial Accounting Standards (SFAS) No. 87, Employers' Accounting for Pensions,* as amended by *SFAS No. 132, Employers' Disclosures about Pensions and Other Postretirement Benefits,* and *SFAS No. 88, Employers' Accounting for Settlements* and *Curtailments of Defined Benefit Pension Plans and for Termination Benefits,* and addresses certain interpretations of those standards published by the staff of the Financial Accounting Standards Board (FASB) and by the FASB's Emerging Issues Task Force (EITF).

FASB Statement No. 87

SFAS No. 87, Employers' Accounting for Pensions, prescribes financial accounting and reporting standards for employers that offer pension benefits to their retired employees. Such benefits are ordinarily periodic pension payments, but also may include lump-sum payments and other types of benefits (such as death and disability benefits) provided through a pension plan.

While the provisions of *SFAS No. 87* apply to any arrangement that is similar in substance to a pension plan, regardless of its form or the means of financing,[1] they have the most significant impact on defined benefit pension plans.

---

1 *SFAS No. 87* does not apply to a plan that provides retirees with life and/or health insurance benefits or other post-retirement health care benefits. *SFAS No. 106, Employers' Accounting for Postretirement Benefits Other Than Pensions,* prescribes the accounting for plans of this nature.

SFAS No. 87:

- Requires that a single attribution (or actuarial cost) method be used to calculate pension cost and obligations.[2]
- Provides specific guidance on how to select (actuarial) assumptions.
- Requires amortization of (actuarial) gains and losses in excess of a prescribed amount.
- Limits the acceptable methods and time periods for amortizing prior service cost.
- Requires that the transition amount computed when *SFAS No. 87* was adopted be amortized to expense on a straight-line basis over future periods.
- Specifies that an employer's balance sheet should reflect a liability for any unfunded accumulated pension benefits (without considering salary progression), generally offset by an intangible asset.

For purposes of *SFAS No. 87*, a defined benefit pension plan is any pension plan that is not a defined contribution pension plan. Generally, a defined benefit pension plan defines an amount of pension benefit to be provided, usually as a function of one or more factors such as age, years of service, or compensation. A defined contribution pension plan, on the other hand, provides an individual account for each plan participant and specifies how contributions to the individual's account are to be determined, instead of specifying the amount of benefits the individual is to receive. The benefits a participant will receive depend solely on the amount contributed to his or her account, the returns earned from investing those contributions, and forfeitures of other participants' benefits that may be allocated to the participant's account.

SFAS No. 87 does not provide guidance on determining whether an arrangement to provide pension or other retirement income benefits constitutes a pension plan. That determination depends on the particular facts and circumstances of each case. The authors believe a key characteristic of a pension plan is that benefits would be available to all employees or to a group of employees that meet stipulated eligibility criteria that define who may participate in the plan and when they may join.

In *SFAS No. 87*, the FASB expresses the view that it would be conceptually appropriate and preferable to recognize a net pension liability or asset measured as the difference between the projected benefit obligation

---

2 *SFAS No. 87* generally avoids using the term "actuarial." In certain instances, the term actuarial is included parenthetically herein as an aid in understanding the language in *SFAS No. 87*.

and plan assets, either with no delay in the recognition of gains and losses, or perhaps with gains and losses reported currently in comprehensive income but not in earnings. Under this approach, if there were no delay in the recognition of gains and losses, pension cost would be the difference between what the FASB considers to be the conceptually appropriate balance-sheet amounts at the beginning and end of any period. However, the FASB decided that this approach represented too great a change from past practice to be viable at the time. Therefore, the statement allows for gains and losses, the cost of plan amendments that give credit for past service, and the effects of adopting *SFAS No. 87* to be recognized in pension cost over future periods. Many of the complex aspects of *SFAS No. 87* result from the provisions developed to accomplish the delayed recognition of these off-balance sheet amounts.

FASB Statement No. 88

SFAS No. 88 defines an event (a settlement) that requires, among other things, immediate recognition of previously unrecognized gains and losses and another event (a curtailment) that requires immediate recognition of previously unrecognized prior service cost.

FASB Statement No. 132

SFAS No. 132 revises employers' financial statement disclosures about pension plans that were previously contained in *SFAS No. 87, No. 88,* and *No. 106.*

Figure 44–1 highlights some of the key terms used in *SFAS No. 87, No. 88*, and *No. 132.*

FASB Staff Special Reports

The FASB does not attempt to anticipate all of the implementation questions that may arise in connection with a particular accounting pronouncement, nor to provide answers to those questions when a pronouncement is issued. Accordingly, many implementation issues are addressed by the FASB staff. Because of the unusually high number of questions raised and the inherent complexities of pension accounting, the FASB staff published two special reports, one entitled *A Guide to Implementation of Statement 87 on Employers' Accounting for Pensions,* and the other entitled *A Guide to Implementation of Statement 88 on Employers' Accounting for Settlements and Curtailments of Defined Benefit Pension Plans and for Termination*

FIGURE 44–1

Glossary of Terms

accumulated benefit obligation (ABO).
Actuarial present value of benefits as of
a specified date, determined according
to the terms of a pension plan and
based on employees' compensation
and service to that date. (Salary progression is not considered in making
this computation.)

actuarial gains or losses. Same as gains
or losses.

adjusted plan assets. Fair value of plan
assets *plus* previously recognized
unfunded accrued pension cost or *less*
previously recognized prepaid pension
cost on the employer's balance sheet.

benefit approaches. A group of basic
approaches for allocating benefits or
the cost of benefits to service periods
(sometimes referred to as *actuarial*
methods). These approaches determine
the amount of pension benefits earned
during a period based on the terms of
the plan, and they calculate the service
cost component for the period as the
actuarial present value of those benefits. The projected unit credit method
and the unit credit method are benefit
approaches.

career average pay plan. A pension plan
with a benefit formula that bases benefits on the amount of compensation
earned over an employee's entire service life.

corridor approach. Method of accounting
for gains and losses whereby an
employer amortizes only the portion of
the accumulated net gain or loss that
exceeds a prescribed limit—10 percent
of the greater of the market-related
value of plan assets or the projected
benefit obligation.

cost approaches. A group of basic
approaches for allocating benefits or
the cost of benefits to service periods
(sometimes referred to as *actuarial*
methods). These approaches assign
pension cost to periods so the same

amount of cost or the same percentage
of compensation is allocated to each
period. The entry age normal, attained
age normal, individual level premium,
and aggregate methods are cost
approaches.

curtailment. An event that significantly
reduces the expected years of future
service of present employees or eliminates for a significant number of
employees the accrual of defined benefits for some or all of their future services.

defined benefit pension plan. A plan that
specifies a determinable pension benefit, usually based on such factors as
age, years of service, and compensation. Under *SFAS No. 87*, any plan that is
not a defined contribution pension plan
is considered a defined benefit pension
plan.

defined contribution pension plan. A
plan that provides an individual account
for each participant and specifies how
contributions to the individual's account
are to be determined, instead of specifying the amount of benefits the individual
is to receive. Under a defined contribution pension plan, the benefits a participant will receive depend solely on the
amount contributed to the participant's
account, plus any income, expenses,
gains or losses, and forfeitures of other
participants' benefits that may be allocated to such participant's account.

discount rate. The assumed interest rate
at which the pension obligation could
be effectively settled—used to adjust for
the time value of money between a
specified date and the expected dates
of payment. Also referred to as the *settlement rate.*

earnings rate. Average long-term rate of
return expected to be earned on pension fund assets.

final pay plan. A pension plan with a benefit formula that bases benefits on the

amount of employee compensation earned over a specified period near the end of the employee's service life.

flat benefit plan. A pension plan that provides retirement benefits based on a fixed amount for each year of employee service.

gains or losses. Changes in the value of either the projected benefit obligation or plan assets resulting from experience different from that assumed and from changes in assumptions.

market-related asset value. Either the fair-market value of a plan asset or a calculated value derived by systematic and rational adjustments to fair-market value over a period of not more than five years.

multiemployer plan. A pension plan to which two or more unrelated employers contribute, usually pursuant to one or more collective-bargaining agreements.

participating annuity contract. An annuity contract that provides for the purchaser to participate in the investment performance and possibly other experience, both favorable and unfavorable (e.g., mortality), of the insurance company.

prior service cost. The cost of retroactive benefits granted in a plan amendment (or a new plan).

projected benefit obligation (PBO). The actuarial present value of all benefits attributed to employee service up to a specific date, based on the terms of the plan. A salary progression factor is included for final pay and career average pay plans.

projected unit credit method. A benefit/years-of-service actuarial approach generally required to be used for final pay and career average pay plans. Under this method, an equal portion of the total estimated benefit (including a salary progression factor) is attributed to each year of service. The cost of that benefit is then computed,

with appropriate consideration to reflect the time value of money (discounting) and the probability of payment (e.g., mortality and turnover). Accordingly, this method results in progressively higher benefit costs each successive year for each participant, because the probability of survival to normal retirement increases and the discount period decreases.

salary progression. Projection of the assumed rate of salaries to be earned in future years, based on all components of future compensation levels (i.e., merit, productivity, and inflation).

service cost. Portion of benefits attributed to employee service for the period.

settlement. An irrevocable action that relieves the employer (or the plan) of primary responsibility for a pension benefit obligation, and eliminates significant risks related to the obligation and the assets used to effect the settlement.

settlement rate. See discount rate.

transition amount. The difference between the projected benefit obligation and the fair value of adjusted plan assets at the date *SFAS No. 87* was adopted. If the projected benefit obligation exceeded adjusted plan assets, there was an unrecognized net obligation and loss (transition debit) at the date of transition to *SFAS No. 87*. Conversely, if adjusted plan assets exceeded the projected benefit obligation, there was an unrecognized net asset and gain (transition credit) at the date of transition to *SFAS No. 87*.

unit credit method. Accumulated benefits approach generally required to be used for flat benefit plans. Under this method, benefits earned to date are based on the plan formula and employees' history of pay, service, and other factors.

volatility. Changes in pension cost from period to period.

Benefits. The special reports contain the FASB staff members' views on a wide range of issues relating to the implementation of SFAS *Nos. 87* and *88.* In addition, certain questions and answers in the FASB staff's special report on *SFAS No. 106, Employers' Accounting for Postretirement Benefits Other Than Pensions,* entitled *A Guide to Implementation of Statement 106 on Employers' Accounting for Postretirement Benefits Other Than Pensions,* deal directly with pension-related issues. Several other questions and answers contained in that report may be useful in accounting for pensions because of the similarities between accounting for pensions and accounting for other post-retirement benefits.

These publications clearly state that the opinions expressed are those of its authors and should not be considered the official positions of the FASB. However, the Securities and Exchange Commissions (SEC) staff has taken the position that companies subject to SEC reporting requirements should be prepared to justify any significant deviations from the guidance set forth in the special reports.

DEFINED BENEFIT PENSION PLANS: ANNUAL PROVISION FOR PENSION COST

Components of Pension Cost

Under *SFAS No. 87,* an employer is required to select a consistent date on which to measure plan assets and obligations (and thus determine pension cost) from year to year. This "measurement date" is defined as either the employer's fiscal year-end or a date not more than three months before that date. The FASB staff's special report on *SFAS No. 87* indicates that:

- Although the pension obligation (and thus pension cost) must be based on census data and actuarial assumptions as of the measurement date, a full actuarial valuation is not required if a company is satisfied that the amount of the pension obligation determined by rolling forward data based on a valuation prior to the measurement date is substantially the same as the amount that would be determined by an actuarial valuation as of that date.

- If an employer remeasures plan assets and obligations or performs a full actuarial valuation as of an interim date other than the established measurement date, pension cost for the period prior to the remeasurement should not be restated. However, pension cost for the remainder of the year should be based on the revised measurements.

SFAS No. 87 specifies that an employer's pension cost should consist of several components, computed as follows:

- **Service Cost.** The increase in the projected benefit obligation attributable to employee service for the period calculated using the beginning-of-the-year discount rate and the required cost method.

- **Interest Cost.**[3] The increase in the projected benefit obligation attributable to the accrual of interest on the beginning-of-the-year balance of the obligation, calculated using the beginning-of-the-year discount rate. Anticipated changes in the projected benefit obligation for employee services rendered and benefit payments made during the year need to be considered in determining interest cost. Interest cost is often the biggest component of pension cost.

- **Return on Plan Assets.** The expected earnings on plan assets calculated using the beginning-of-the-year assumed long-term earnings rate and the market-related value of plan assets taking into consideration anticipated contributions and benefit payments expected to be made during the year. Although paragraph 20 of *SFAS No. 87* specifies that the "actual" return on plan assets is a component of pension cost, paragraph 34(a) states that the difference between the actual and expected return on plan assets should be deferred and accounted for as part of the gain or loss component of pension cost. The net result of these paragraphs is that the expected return on plan assets is used to calculate pension cost for the period.

  The market-related value of plan assets is defined as fair value or a calculated value that recognizes changes in fair value in a systematic or rational manner over not more than five years. Employers may use different methods of calculating the market-related value for different classes of assets (e.g., an employer might use fair value for bonds and a five-year moving average value for equities), provided that the methodologies are applied consistently from year to year. Some employers find that the use of a calculated value rather than fair value reduces pension cost volatility somewhat, because the expected return component is based on a smoothed asset value.

---

3 The interest cost component of pension cost is not considered to be interest for purposes of applying *SFAS No. 34, Capitalization of Interest Cost.*

- **Prior Service Cost.** The amortization of the cost of retroactive benefits granted in a plan amendment. Amendments that increase pension benefits are expected to result in future economic benefits to the employee. Thus, the cost of the retroactive benefit is amortized generally over future employee service periods.
- **Gains and Losses.** The amortization of the change in the amount of either the projected benefit obligation or plan assets (or both) resulting from experience different from that assumed and from changes in assumptions.
- **Transition Amount.** The amortization of the transition asset or obligation.

An illustrative example of the manner in which pension cost is calculated under *SFAS No. 87* is included in Figure 44–2.

Attribution Method

Companies are required to use a single attribution method based on the plan's terms to determine pension cost (a benefits approach). For final pay and career average pay plans, this is equivalent to the projected unit credit method. For flat benefit plans, the unit credit method is required. Companies may not use cost approaches (e.g., entry age normal or aggregate method) for accounting purposes, although they may do so for funding purposes.

Substantive Commitments

Paragraph 41 of *SFAS No. 87* indicates that a company may have a present commitment to make future amendments and that the substance of the plan is to provide benefits greater than the benefits defined by its written terms. In these situations, the "substantive commitment" is required to be taken into consideration in determining pension cost and obligations.

Question 52 of the FASB staff's special report on *SFAS No. 87* provides guidance in determining whether a substantive commitment exists and points out that the company's past actions, including communications to employees, may embody a commitment to have a benefit formula that provides benefits beyond those specified by the written terms of the plan. The special report also indicates, however, that it is not the intent of paragraph 41 to permit the anticipation of an individual plan amendment (i.e., one that is not part of a series).

In the authors' experience, most companies have concluded that they do not have a substantive commitment to make future plan amendments. Consequently, they do not include the cost of anticipated amendments in the calculation of pension cost and obligations until they have been contractually agreed to. However, some companies have concluded that they have such a commitment and make their pension calculations accordingly; in these cases, paragraph 41 requires footnote disclosure of the existence and nature of the commitment.

Selecting Assumptions

Explicit Assumptions

Each significant assumption required under *SFAS No. 87* should reflect the best estimate solely with respect to that individual assumption (referred to as an explicit approach). This means employers may not apply an approach that looks to the aggregate effect of two or more assumptions that individually do not represent the best estimate of the plan's future experience with respect to those assumptions, even though their aggregate effect may be approximately the same as that of an explicit approach.

Three Different Rates

Companies are required to select three different rates in calculating pension obligations: (1) an assumed discount (or settlement) rate based on the rate at which the pension obligation could be effectively settled, (2) an expected long-term rate of return on plan assets (earnings rate), and (3) a salary progression rate.

Discount Rate

The discount rate is used to measure the projected, accumulated, and vested benefit obligations and the service and interest cost components of pension cost. A certain degree of latitude is permissible in selecting this rate. In this connection, paragraph 44 of *SFAS No. 87* states:

> Assumed discount rates shall reflect the rates at which the pension benefits could be effectively settled. It is appropriate in estimating those rates to look to available information about rates implicit in current prices of annuity contracts that could be used to effect settlement of the obligation (including information about available annuity rates currently published by the Pension Benefit Guaranty Corporation). In making those estimates, employers also may look to rates of return on high-quality fixed-income investments currently available and expected to be available during the period to maturity of the pension benefits.

This rather broad guidance has given rise to a number of questions with respect to the appropriate methodology for determining the discount rate. The FASB staff's special report on *SFAS No. 87* indicates that select-

F I G U R E 44-2

Illustrative Example of the Pension Cost Calculation

XYZ Company has a defined benefit pension plan covering substantially all of its employees. The company adopted *SFAS No. 87* as of January 1, 1989.

Plan Data and Key (Actuarial) Assumptions

Benefit formula	Career average
Accounting policies:	
Amortization of gains and losses	Corridor approach
Amortization of transition amount	Average future service period of employees
Market-related value of plan assets	Equal to fair value

	January 1, 2000	January 1, 2001
Assumed discount rate	8%	7.5%
Assumed salary progression rate	5%	5%
Assumed earnings rate	7%	6%
Plan assets and obligations (as of beginning of year):		
Vested benefit obligation (VBO)	$ 8,500,000	$11,700,000
Accumulated benefit obligation (ABO)	10,000,000	13,800,000
Projected benefit obligation (PBO)	11,500,000	14,653,000
Fair value of plan assets	$12,000,000	$15,000,000
Prepaid pension cost as of January 1, 2000	$ 1,000,000	
For the year ended December 31, 2000:		
Service cost	$ 300,000	
Benefit payments made	360,000*	
Contributions made	500,000†	
Actual return on plan assets	$ 2,860,000	

XYZ Company's pension cost for the year ended December 31, 2000 was $435,555, computed as follows:

Service cost		$300,000
Interest cost‡		
PBO at 1/1/2000	$11,500,000	
Discount rate at 1/1/2000	× 8%	920,000

Expected return on plan assets:

Market-related value at 1/1/2000	12,000,000	
Earnings rate at 1/1/2000	× 7%	(840,000)

Amortization of prior service cost	—§
Amortization of gains and losses	—‖
Amortization of transition amount	55,555@
Pension cost for the year ended	
December 31, 2000	$435,555

The company's additional liability at December 31, 2000 was $0, computed as follows:

Fair value of plan assets at 12/31/2000		$15,000,000
Less prepaid pension cost at 12/31/2000:		
Prepaid pension cost at 1/1/2000	$1,000,000	
Contribution on 12/31/2000	500,000	
Pension cost for the year ended 12/31/2000	(435,555)	(1,064,445)
Less ABO at 12/31/2000		(13,800,000)
		$135,555
Amount of additional liability	$0#	

* Benefits payments are made ratably during the year.

† Contributions are made on December 31.

‡ The calculation of the interest cost component should take into consideration anticipated benefit payments; however, they were not considered for purposes of this illustrative example.

§ There have been no plan amendments.

‖ The corridor approach requires amortization of the beginning-of-the-year unrecognized net gain or loss. At January 1, 2000, this amount was $0.

@ The transition obligation is computed at adoption of *SFAS No. 87* as the difference between the projected benefit obligation and adjusted plan assets and is amortized on a straight-line basis over the average remaining service period of active employees at adoption.

Since adjusted plan assets exceed the ABO at December 31, 2000, no additional liability is required to be recorded. Note that *SFAS No. 87* does not permit companies to record a pension asset in this situation.

ing the discount rate is not a mechanical process based on a standard formula. It states that the primary objective of selecting the discount rate is to select the best estimate of the interest rates inherent in the price at which the pension obligation could be effectively settled currently, given the pension plan's particular facts and circumstances and current market conditions, and that the methodology used in the selection process is subordinate to that primary objective.

The following guidance on selecting the discount rate is provided in the special report:

■ A methodology for determining the discount rate, once selected, should be followed consistently. If the facts and circumstances surrounding the pension plan do not change from year to year, it would be inappropriate to change the methodology, particularly if the intent in changing it is to avoid a change in the discount rate.

- A change in facts and circumstances may, however, warrant the use of a different approach for determining the discount rate. This change in methodology—which, in the authors' view, would occur infrequently—would be a change in accounting estimate, not a change in accounting method.

- The discount rate should be reevaluated each year to ensure that it reflects current market conditions. The discount rate generally is expected to change as interest rates decline or rise.

- It would be inappropriate to use a range of rates (e.g., from Pension Benefit Guaranty Corporation (PBGC) rates at one end to high-quality bond rates at the other), and to arbitrarily select any rate within the range or use the same rate each year provided it falls within the range.

- If the pension plan has a "dedicated" bond portfolio, that yield should not be used as the discount rate, because it is the current rates of return on those investments (not historical rates of return as of the dedication date) that are relevant.

Earnings Rate

The earnings rate is used in connection with the market-related value of plan assets to compute the return-on-assets component of pension cost. In estimating that rate, consideration needs to be given to current returns being earned and returns expected to be available for reinvestment.

As a general rule, the expected long-term rate of return on plan assets is less volatile than the actual rate of return on assets because the expected rate contemplates not only current rates of return but also expected reinvestment rates. The expected long-term rate of return is not the equivalent of the discount rate used to measure interest cost related to the projected benefit obligation, because the discount rate is intended to be the current rate at which the obligation could be effectively settled immediately. *SFAS No. 87* does not preclude the selection of different rates of return for different classes of plan assets (e.g., one rate for bonds and another for equity securities).

Salary Progression Rate

In determining the salary progression rate, employers are required to consider all salary-increase components (e.g., merit, productivity, promotion, and inflation) as well as changes under existing law in Social Security benefits or benefit limitations that would affect benefits provided by the plan.

All assumptions are required to be consistent to the extent that each reflects expectations of the same future economic conditions, such as rates of inflation. However, the FASB staff's special report on *SFAS No. 87* points out that it is not required that all assumptions contain the same future inflation component unless that would be appropriate under the circumstances to reflect the best estimate of the pension plan's future experience. For example, if an employer uses a 5 percent inflation factor for purposes of determining the earnings rate, that same factor is required to be used to determine the inflation component of the salary progression rate when the employer's labor costs over time have been highly correlated with that inflation factor and the employer expects that correlation to continue.

Amortization of Prior Service Cost

Amortization Period

SFAS No. 87 requires that pension cost include amortization of prior service cost, generally over the future service period of employees active as of the date of a plan amendment, who are expected to receive benefits under the plan. If all or almost all of a plan's participants are inactive, prior service cost should be amortized based upon the remaining life expectancy of the inactive participants. Amortization begins at the date of adoption of the plan amendment, not the effective date of the amendment, and prior service cost arising from each plan amendment should be amortized separately. The FASB staff's special report on *SFAS No. 87* indicates that once an amortization period has been established, it may be revised only if a curtailment (as defined in *SFAS No. 88*) occurs or if events indicate that (1) the period benefited is shorter than originally estimated, or (2) the future economic benefits of the plan amendment have been impaired. The special report also indicates that the amortization period would not necessarily be revised for ordinary variances in the expected future service period of employees.

Amortization Method

Prior service cost and the related interest on the unrecognized amount are required to be accounted for separately. The interest component of pension cost includes the interest on the unamortized prior service cost, while the principal is amortized to expense using an accelerated method that results in a declining amortization pattern. This method assigns an equal amount of prior service cost to each future period of service of each employee active at the date of the plan amendment, who is expected to receive benefits under the plan. In other words, the method (similar to sum-of-the-years' digits) is based on the relationship between the total expected employee years of service and the service years expected to expire in a period.

SFAS No. 87, however, also indicates that methods that result in amortization that is more rapid than the method described above can be used—including straight-line amortization over the average remaining service period of employees expected to receive benefits.

Using the amortization method set forth in *SFAS No. 87* results in accelerated principal amortization of prior service cost. If an alternative method (such as straight-line) is selected, the amortization period must be reduced to no more than the average remaining service period to achieve the more rapid amortization called for by the standard.

Some employers have expressed the view that immediate recognition of prior service cost resulting from all plan amendments (present and future) is an acceptable alternative amortization method. The special report indicates that immediate recognition is appropriate only if, after assessing the facts and circumstances surrounding the retroactive plan amendment, the employer does not expect to realize any future economic benefits from that plan amendment. Accordingly, an employer may not adopt an accounting policy to immediately recognize prior service cost, because such a policy would preclude the employer from making this assessment for future plan amendments as they occur.

Plans with a History of Regular Amendments

SFAS No. 87 indicates that a shorter amortization period for prior service cost may be warranted for certain plans. Paragraph 27 states that if a company has a history of regular plan amendments (e.g., when flat benefit plans are amended with each renegotiation of a union contract), that practice, along with other evidence, may indicate a shortening of the period during which the company expects economic benefits from each amendment. When a situation of this nature is deemed to exist, amortization is required over the period benefited. In its deliberations, the board considered, and rejected, recommendations that the final statement specify that the "period benefited" (and, thus, the prior service cost amortization period) is the period between contract renegotiations.

The determination of what constitutes a history of regular plan amendments and what amortization period should be used if such a situation exists can be difficult. While it addresses these issues, the special report on *SFAS No. 87* provides little additional guidance, essentially indicating that the assessment of whether such a situation exists and, if so, what amortization period should be used, is fact specific. It therefore appears that the appropriate amortization period in a situation of this nature is not necessarily the contract period of a collectively bargained agreement. The authors are aware of a number of companies that, based on an assessment of the particular facts and circumstances involved, have been able to support an amortization period, in such a situation, that is longer than the contract period but not longer than the future service period of active employees expected to receive benefits under the plan.

Paragraph 27 is not limited to pension plans that are subject to collective-bargaining agreements. An employer with a non-union shop that regularly grants cost-of-living increases also must consider the provisions of paragraph 27.

If a plan amendment eliminates the accrual of defined benefits for future services, it is considered a curtailment under *SFAS No. 88*, and all prior service cost related to years of service no longer expected to be rendered is eliminated in computing the gain or loss on curtailment.

If a plan amendment reduces (but does not eliminate) benefits, it is a negative plan amendment. An example of a negative plan amendment is the reduction in benefits that occurs when a union agrees to give back a portion of benefits that have been earned based on past service. In such instances, the reduced benefits are offset against existing unrecognized prior service cost. When a company has unrecognized prior service cost relating to several plan amendments that have differing amortization periods, the issue arises as to which plan amendment should first be offset by the effects of a subsequent plan amendment that reduces the projected benefit obligation. The FASB staff's special report on *SFAS No. 87* indicates that unless the retroactive plan amendment that reduces benefits can be specifically related to a prior amendment, any systematic and rational method (e.g., last-in, first-out [LIFO]; first-in, first-out [FIFO]; or pro rata), applied on a consistent basis, is acceptable. If an employer terminates a defined benefit pension plan and establishes a successor plan that provides reduced benefits for employees' future service, that transaction is also required to be accounted for as a negative plan amendment.

Gains and Losses

Gains and losses are defined as changes in either the projected benefit obligation or plan assets (or both) resulting from experience different from that assumed and from changes in assumptions. All gains and losses, including those arising from changes in the discount rate, are accounted for on a combined basis. Companies are permitted to consistently apply any systematic and rational amortization method, as long as it results in the amortization of the net gain or loss in an amount at least equal to the minimum based on the so-called corridor approach. The FASB staff's special report on *SFAS No. 87* indicates that companies may immediately recognize gains and losses (instead of delaying their recognition) provided that (1) this approach is applied consistently; (2) the method is applied to both gains and losses (on plan assets and obligations); and (3) the method used is disclosed.

Under the corridor approach, only the portion of the net gain or loss that exceeds a prescribed amount (10 percent of the greater of the market-related value of plan assets or the projected benefit obligation, both as of the beginning of the year) must be amortized. The excess is required to be amortized on a straight-line basis over the average remaining service period of active employees expected to receive benefits. If all or almost all of a plan's participants are inactive, amortization should be based upon the average remaining life expectancy of the inactive participants. Asset gains and losses not yet reflected in the market-related value of plan assets (the difference between the fair value and the market-related value of plan assets) are not, however, required to be included in the computation.

Controlling Volatility

Pension cost under *SFAS No. 87* can be volatile. However, any attempt to manage the assumptions or acceptable accounting methods under *SFAS No. 87* to avoid volatility or manage reported earnings (even through immaterial misstatements) is inappropriate. While there is some latitude regarding the methodology that may be selected to determine the discount rate, the approach selected should be followed consistently (unless circumstances change).

The FASB developed the corridor approach and the market-related value of plan assets concept in an attempt to reduce the volatility of pension cost as follows:

- First, only the asset gains or losses reflected in the market-related value of plan assets must be considered for amortization (as little as 20 percent per year).

- Second, all gains and losses may be offset; amortization is required only if the net gain or loss is in excess of the corridor amount.

- Third, the excess may be spread over the average remaining service period of active employees expected to receive benefits.

Balance Sheet Recognition

Under *SFAS No. 87*, a pension liability is recorded if, on a cumulative basis, the employer's contributions to the plan are less than net periodic pension cost. Conversely, a pension asset is recorded only if, on a cumulative basis, the contributions are more than the recorded cost. *SFAS No. 87* also requires that an additional liability be recognized when the unfunded accumulated benefit obligation (the excess of the accumulated benefit obligation over the fair value of plan assets) exceeds the balance-sheet liability for accrued pension cost. Under this approach, when an additional liability is recorded, an intangible asset is also recognized to the extent that unamortized prior service cost and/or an unamortized transition obligation exists. If the additional liability exceeds the total of these two items, the excess (on a net of tax basis) is recorded as a separate component (i.e., a reduction) of accumulated other comprehensive income in stockholders' equity. Recording of the additional liability does not affect net income; however, the change in the stockholders' equity adjustment is included as a component of other comprehensive income under *SFAS No. 130, Reporting Comprehensive Income*. The FASB staff's special report on *SFAS No. 87* points out that because prior service cost and the transition obligation are amortized as part of pension expense, the intangible asset is not subject to separate amortization, because that would result in double-counting of expense.

For companies with more than one plan, liability recognition is determined on a plan-by-plan basis. Unless an employer clearly has a right to use the assets of one plan to pay the benefits of another, the excess assets of an overfunded plan cannot offset the additional liability for unfunded accumulated benefits of another plan sponsored by the same company. Thus, as a general rule, companies are required to recognize a liability under *SFAS No. 87* if they sponsor any underfunded plans.

SFAS No. 87 does not allow companies with overfunded plans to reflect surplus plan assets as an asset on their balance sheets.

Debt or equity securities of the employer, or an affiliate of the employer, that are held by the pension plan may be included in plan assets if those securities are transferable. The answer to question 88 of the FASB staff's special report on *SFAS No. 106* explains what is required for an employer's securities to be transferable and clarifies that it is not enough that nontransferable securities held by the plan can be converted into transferable securities. The securities held by the plan must be transferable in their present state.

With respect to the appropriate balance-sheet classification of the additional liability and intangible asset required to be recognized, the

FASB staff's special report on *SFAS No. 87* indicates that the criteria for current and noncurrent classification of the additional liability are the same as for any other liability. Thus, the classification of any additional liability should be based on the company's intent to fund the amount involved. However, the special report states that the intangible asset should be classified as noncurrent, since it represents either unrecognized prior service cost or the remaining unamortized portion of the transition obligation.

Transition

SFAS No. 87 required a "transition amount" to be computed as of the measurement date for the beginning of the fiscal year in which the statement was first applied. This transition amount is the difference between:

- The projected benefit obligation, including a salary progression factor and computed using the attribution method and the assumption guidance set forth in *SFAS No. 87*, and
- Adjusted plan assets, an amount representing the fair value of plan assets plus the pension liability or less the pension asset on the employer's balance sheet at the measurement date.

To the extent the projected benefit obligation exceeded adjusted plan assets, a transition obligation resulted; if adjusted plan assets exceeded the projected benefit obligation, a transition asset resulted. In either case, the transition amount (which is not immediately recorded in the financial statements) is required to be amortized on a straight-line basis over the average remaining service period of active employees expected to receive benefits under the plan, except that the employer may elect to use a 15-year period if the average remaining service period is less than 15 years. If all or almost all of a plan's participants are inactive, however, the employer must use the average remaining life expectancy of the inactive participants.

Figure 44–2 provides an illustrative example of the pension cost calculation for a company with a single defined benefit pension plan.

Consistency

There are three methodologies under *SFAS No. 87* where acceptable alternatives are available: the calculation of the market-related value of plan assets, the approach used to recognize gains and losses, and the measurement date. If the methodology for calculating any of these three items has changed, it is considered to be a change in accounting principle subject to the requirements of *Accounting Principles Board (APB) Opinion No. 20, Accounting Changes.* The term "accounting principle" includes not only accounting principles and practices but also the method of applying them (*APB Opinion No. 20*). For example, if the method of computing the market-related value of plan assets is changed from a five-year average to a three-year average, it would be considered to be a change in application of an accounting principle. In addition, a change in discount rate from a single discount rate to multiple discount rates to reflect differences in the maturity and duration of pension benefit programs is also considered a change in application of an accounting principle. On the other hand, if market conditions indicate that the expected rate of return on plan assets is 9 percent rather than 10 percent as had been used previously, the change is considered to be a change in accounting estimate.

It is necessary to justify as preferable a change in accounting principle not mandated by the issuance of an authoritative accounting pronouncement. The authors believe it may be difficult for an employer to justify certain changes on the basis of preferability. For example:

- An employer that measures plan assets and obligations as of the date of the financial statements may have difficulty justifying the preferability of performing those measurements as of a date other than the financial statement date.

- Regular interim measurements that are performed by an employer because interest rates have changed since the last measurement date would be indicative of a policy of performing interim measurements whenever interest rates subsequently fall or rise by the same or a greater margin. In this situation, it may be difficult to justify the preferability of deviating from such an established practice.

- It may be difficult for an employer that uses fair value in determining the market-related value of plan assets to justify switching to a calculated value that defers the recognition of changes in fair value.

- Justifying a gain/loss recognition approach that introduces more delayed recognition is generally difficult (e.g., switching from amortization of all gains and losses to a 10 percent corridor approach).

To determine the cumulative effect of the change, an employer should apply the new method retroactively to all prior periods that would have been affected. Generally this requires that the new method be applied retroactively to the year *SFAS No. 87* was initially applied and to each year thereafter. For example, for a company that adopted *SFAS No. 87* in 1986, a change in determining the market-related value of plan assets would be applied retroactively starting in 1986 and pension cost for each year thereafter would be recomputed under the new method up to the beginning of the year that the new method is adopted.

DEFINED CONTRIBUTION PENSION PLANS

The periodic cost of a defined contribution pension plan is measured by the required contribution amount determined using the plan formula, because, in a defined contribution plan, the pension benefits that participants will receive depend only on the amount contributed to the participants' accounts, the returns earned on investments of these contributions, and forfeitures of other participants' benefits that may be reallocated. If a plan requires contributions to continue after participants retire or terminate, the cost of these benefits also should be accrued during the participants' service periods.

When a plan has both a formula for plan contributions and a scale for plan benefits, a careful analysis is required to determine whether the substance of the plan is to provide a defined contribution or a defined benefit. If the plan history indicates that the scale of benefits is adjusted to reflect the amount actually contributed, as a general rule the plan should be treated as a defined contribution plan. If, however, a company's liability for pension benefits is not limited by the amount of the pension fund or if the plan history indicates (and/or the current employer policy contemplates) the maintenance of benefit levels regardless of the amount of defined contribution or legal limitation of the employer's liability for such benefits, as a general rule the plan is required to be treated as a defined benefit plan. The accounting and disclosure requirements are determined by the applicable provisions of *SFAS No. 87*.

CASH BALANCE AND OTHER HYBRID PLANS

Arrangements referred to as "cash balance plans," "hybrid plans," "guaranteed individual account plans," or "lump-sum pension plans" typically have the following characteristics:

- Benefits are intended to be paid primarily in lump-sum form.
- Employer contributions to "separate accounts" and account balances are communicated periodically to employees. However, separate investment accounts are not actually maintained. Instead,

the "separate accounts" are maintained on paper only and are "credited" with a guaranteed rate of investment earnings.

■ Actual plan earnings below the guaranteed rate are required to be made up by the employer; earnings in excess of the guaranteed rate serve to reduce the employer's cost.

Legally, and in substance, these types of arrangements are defined benefit plans and should be accounted for as such. While the account-balance-reporting feature may be somewhat similar to a defined contribution plan, like any defined benefit plan, a cash balance plan must be funded on an actuarial basis in accordance with ERISA. The employer, not the employees, bears the investment risks and rewards. As with any defined benefit plan, *SFAS No. 87* requires the accounting to be based on the attribution of benefits earned in each service period under the terms of the plan.

MULTIEMPLOYER PENSION PLANS

A multiemployer pension plan is a plan to which two or more unrelated employers contribute, usually pursuant to one or more collective-bargaining agreements. A characteristic of multiemployer plans is that assets contributed by one participating employer may be used to provide benefits to employees of other participating employers, because assets contributed by an employer are not segregated in a separate account or restricted to provide benefits only to employees of that employer.

An employer participating in a multiemployer plan is required to recognize as pension cost the required contribution for the period and recognize as a liability any contributions due and unpaid. In other words, even though a multiemployer plan may be a defined benefit plan, the employer is able to account for its participation as though it were a defined contribution plan. This would be the case even if the employer, as part of entering a multiemployer pension plan or amending the benefits under the plan, unconditionally promises to pay certain future contributions to the plan (calculated based on the plan's prior service cost associated with the participants entering the plan or the improved benefits), and executes an agreement that specifies the amounts of those future contributions.

DISCLOSURE

SFAS No. 132 revised the disclosure requirements contained in *SFAS Nos. 87* and *88*. Under *SFAS No. 132*, a significant amount of information must be disclosed by all sponsors of defined benefit plans. The primary disclosures that are required for public companies include changes in the projected benefit obligation and plan assets; the components of pension cost; the assumed discount rate, salary progression rate and expected long-term rate of return on plan assets; and a reconciliation of the funded status of the plan to the asset or liability recorded on the company's balance sheet. Non-public companies may elect reduced disclosure requirements. Disclosures regarding defined contribution and multiemployer plans are also required. Figure 44–3 summarizes these disclosure requirements.

The reconciliation of the funded status of the plan to the balance-sheet amounts recorded by sponsors of defined benefit plans provides users of financial statements with information that is consistent with the FASB's theoretical preference that the asset or liability should be the difference between the projected benefit obligation and the fair value of plan assets. The remaining items in the reconciliation reflect the delayed recognition of prior service cost, gains and losses, and the transition amount.

Under *SFAS No. 132*, disclosures may now be aggregated for all of an employer's defined benefit pension plans. Thus, if an employer elects, disclosures about plans with assets in excess of the accumulated benefit obligation may be aggregated with disclosures about plans with accumulated benefit obligations in excess of assets. If those disclosures are combined, the employer is required to disclose the aggregate projected benefit obligation and aggregate fair value of plan assets for plans with projected benefit obligations in excess of plan assets, and the aggregate accumulated benefit obligation and aggregate fair value of plan assets for pension plans with accumulated benefit obligations in excess of plan assets. However, the balance sheet should continue to present prepaid benefit costs and accrued benefit liabilities separately.

Additionally, disclosures about plans outside the United States may now be combined with those for U.S. plans unless the projected benefit obligations of the plans outside the United States are significant relative to the total projected benefit obligation and those plans use significantly different assumptions.

Figure 44–4 provides an illustrative example of the financial statement disclosures of the XYZ Company (based on the same hypothetical facts used in the illustrative example in Figure 44–2). The footnote format presented is consistent with Illustration 1 in *SFAS No. 132*.

FUNDING AND PLAN ADMINISTRATION

In many cases, pension cost determined pursuant to *SFAS No. 87* is greater than the maximum deductible amount permitted under the Internal

F I G U R E   44–3

Required Pension Disclosures under *SFAS No. 132*

Defined Benefit Plans—Public Company

A reconciliation of beginning and ending balances of the projected benefit obligation showing separately, if applicable, the effects during the period attributable to each of the following: service cost, interest cost, contributions by plan participants, actuarial gains and losses, foreign-currency exchange-rate changes, benefits paid, plan amendments, business combinations, divestitures, curtailments, settlements, and special termination benefits.

A reconciliation of beginning and ending balances of the fair value of plan assets showing separately, if applicable, the effects during the period attributable to each of the following: actual return on plan assets, foreign-currency exchange-rate changes, contributions by the employer and by plan participants, benefits paid, business combinations, divestitures, and settlements.

The funded status of the plans, the amounts not recognized in the statement of financial position, and the amounts recognized in the statement of financial position, including:

1. The amount of any unamortized prior service cost.
2. The amount of any unrecognized net gain or loss (including asset gains and losses not yet reflected in market-related value).
3. The amount of any remaining unamortized, unrecognized net obligation or net asset.
4. The net pension prepaid assets or accrued liabilities.
5. Any intangible asset and the amount of accumulated other comprehensive income recognized.

The amount of net periodic benefit cost recognized, showing separately the service cost component, the interest cost component, the expected return on plan assets for the period, the amortization of the unrecognized transition obligation or transition asset, the amount of recognized gains and losses, the amount of prior service cost recognized, and the amount of gain or loss recognized due to a settlement or curtailment.

The amount included within other comprehensive income for the period arising from a change in the additional minimum pension liability

On a weighted-average basis, the following assumptions used in the accounting for the plans: assumed discount rate, rate of compensation increase (for pay-related plans), and expected long-term rate of return on plan assets.

The amounts and types of securities of the employer and related parties included in plan assets, the approximate amount of future annual benefits of plan participants covered by insurance contracts issued by the employer or related parties, and any significant transactions between the employer or related parties and the plan during the period.

A description of any alternative amortization methods used to amortize prior service amounts or unrecognized net gains and losses.

Any substantive commitment, such as past practice or a history of regular benefit increases, used as the basis for accounting for the projected benefit obligation.

The cost of providing special or contractual termination benefits recognized during the period and a description of the nature of the event.

An explanation of any significant change in the projected benefit obligation or plan assets not otherwise apparent in the other disclosures required by *SFAS No. 132*.

Amounts related to the employer's results of operations shall be disclosed for each period for which an income statement is presented. Amounts related to the employer's statement of financial position shall be disclosed for each balance sheet presented.

F I G U R E   44–3 (continued)

Reduced Disclosure Requirements for Nonpublic Entities

A nonpublic entity may elect to disclose the following for its defined benefit pension plans in lieu of the disclosures required for public companies:

1. The projected benefit obligation, fair value of plan assets, and funded status of the plan.
2. Employer contributions, participant contributions, and benefits paid.
3. The amounts recognized in the statement of financial position, including the net pension prepaid assets or accrued liabilities and any intangible asset and the amount of accumulated other comprehensive income recognized.
4. The amount of net periodic benefit cost recognized and the amount included within other comprehensive income arising from a change in the minimum pension liability.
5. On a weighted-average basis, the following assumptions used in the accounting for the plans: assumed discount rate, rate of compensation increase (for pay-related plans), and expected long-term rate of return on plan assets.
6. The amounts and types of securities of the employer and related parties included in plan assets, the approximate amount of future annual benefits of plan participants covered by insurance contracts issued by the employer or related parties, and any significant transactions between the employer or related parties and the plan during the period.
7. The nature and effect of significant nonroutine events, such as amendments, combinations, divestitures, curtailments, and settlements.

Defined Contribution Plans

A description of the nature and effect of any significant changes during the period affecting comparability, such as a change in the rate of employer contributions, a business combination, or a divestiture.

The amount of cost recognized during the period.

Multiemployer Plans

The amount of contributions during the period. Total contributions may be disclosed without disaggregating the amounts attributable to pensions and other post-retirement benefits.

A description of the nature and effect of any changes affecting comparability, such as a change in the rate of employer contributions, a business combination, or a divestiture.

If withdrawal from a multiemployer plan is probable or reasonably possible, the amount (if reasonably estimable) of obligation the employer would have on withdrawal from the plan. If the amount is not reasonably estimable, the best reasonably available general information about the extent of the obligation the employer would have on withdrawal from the plan.

Revenue Code or less than the minimum required contribution under ERISA. Some companies have modified their funding policies in an attempt to attain some level of consistency with the methodology under *SFAS No. 87*. This consistency, however, may be difficult to achieve. Certainly, companies that historically have used a different actuarial cost method from the one required by *SFAS No. 87* may switch to the *SFAS No.*

F I G U R E   44–4

Illustrative Example of Financial Statement Disclosures

NOTE P: PENSION PLAN

The following table sets forth information related to the Company's defined benefit pension plan as of and for the year ended December 31, 2000 (in thousands):

Change in projected benefit obligation (PBO)

Projected benefit obligation at beginning of year	$11,500
Service cost	300
Interest cost	920
Actuarial loss	2,293
Benefits paid	(360)
Projected benefit obligation at end of year	14,653

Change in plan assets

Fair value of plan assets at beginning of year	12,000
Actual return on plan assets	2,860
Employer contribution	500
Benefits paid	(360)
Fair value of plan assets at end of year	15,000
Funded status	347
Unrecognized net actuarial loss*	273
Unrecognized transition obligation	444
Prepaid benefit cost	$ 1,064

Weighted-average assumptions

Discount rate	7.5%
Expected return on plan assets	6.0%
Rate of compensation increase	5.0%

Components of net periodic pension cost

Service cost	$ 300
Interest cost	920
Expected return on plan assets	(840)
Amortization of transition obligation	56
Net periodic benefit cost	$ 436

* The sum of (1) a loss ($2,293) equal to the difference between the expected PBO at December 31, 2000 ($11,500 + 300 + 920 – 360) and the actual PBO at December 31, 2000 ($14,653), and (2) a gain ($2,020) equal to the difference between the actual return on plan assets ($2,860) and the expected return on plan assets ($840).

87 method for funding purposes as well. However, the methods and periods for amortizing prior service cost and gains and losses, and certain other requirements of *SFAS No. 87*, are not permissible for purposes of computing the maximum allowable income tax deduction. Furthermore, actuarial assumptions are likely to differ because the discount rate assumption required by *SFAS No. 87* may be too high to use for funding purposes. Accordingly, many companies may find it necessary to perform separate actuarial calculations for funding and accounting purposes.

Moreover, companies are confronted with another problem:

- If funding levels are reduced to reflect lower pension cost, appropriate explanations and communications are needed to explain the reduced funding levels to plan participants and other interested parties.

- If funding levels are not reduced even though pension cost is lower, management needs to explain to stockholders, the board of directors, plan participants, and other interested parties the difference between these levels and the reduced pension cost, as well as the potentially large assets included on the company's balance sheet based on the excess of amounts funded over amounts expensed.

ACCOUNTING FOR SETTLEMENTS AND CURTAILMENTS OF DEFINED BENEFIT PLANS AND TERMINATION BENEFITS

SFAS No. 88 defines an event—a settlement—that requires, among other things, immediate recognition of previously unrecognized gains and losses but no accelerated recognition of prior service cost, and another event—a curtailment—that requires immediate recognition of previously unrecognized prior service cost, but no accelerated recognition of previously unrecognized gains and losses.

SFAS No. 88 also requires all companies to accelerate the recognition of prior service cost when it is probable a curtailment will occur, thus providing more consistent accounting among companies for the same types of transactions.

Accounting for Settlements

SFAS No. 88 defines a settlement as a transaction that:

- Is an irrevocable action.
- Relieves the employer (or the plan) of primary responsibility for a pension benefit obligation.
- Eliminates significant risks related to the obligation and the assets used to effect the settlement.

The statement indicates that purchasing annuity contracts or making lump-sum cash payments to plan participants in exchange for their rights to receive specified pension benefits constitutes a settlement, because all three criteria are met. However, a decision to invest in a portfolio of high-quality, fixed-income securities with principal and interest payment dates similar to the estimated payment dates of benefits does not constitute a settlement, because such a decision (1) may be reversed, (2) does not relieve the employer of primary responsibility for the obligation, and (3) does not eliminate mortality risk.

The FASB staff's special report on *SFAS No. 88* confirms that a settlement generally does not occur until an exchange has been accomplished (i.e., cash has been disbursed to participants or annuities have been purchased). Other actions, including the intent to complete the exchange, the probability of completing the irrevocable action, the completion of negotiations, or committing to purchase annuities, are not sufficient to effect a settlement.

SFAS No. 88 requires that companies accelerate the recognition of previously unrecognized gains and losses when a settlement occurs, because the possibility of these gains and losses being offset by future losses or gains related to the obligation and to the assets used to effect the transaction is eliminated. Specifically, *SFAS No. 88* requires companies to immediately recognize a pro rata portion of (1) the unrecognized net gain or loss, (2) the gain or loss arising from the settlement (i.e., the difference between the expected value of the pension obligation and plan assets and their actual [remeasured] value at the time of the settlement), and (3) the unamortized transition asset based on the percentage of the projected benefit obligation eliminated by the settlement. The amortization of prior service cost and/or transition obligation (if any) is not, however, accelerated because unless a curtailment also takes place, the benefits derived from the future services of employees (which is one of the bases for delayed recognition of prior service cost) are not affected by the settlement. Figure 44–5 illustrates how a settlement gain would be calculated.

Whenever a defined benefit plan is terminated (and a settlement occurs) and a replacement defined benefit plan is established, the gain (or loss) recognized is to be determined not by the amount of assets that revert to the company, but by the settlement computation discussed in the preceding paragraph. The difference between the recognized gain (or loss) and the reverted assets is accounted for as an asset or liability on the company's balance sheet. In theory this asset or liability will be eliminated by differences between funding and expense over future years.

F I G U R E   44–5

Illustrative Example of a Settlement Gain Calculation

ABC Company sponsors a final pay, defined benefit pension plan. On July 15, 2000, the plan settled its accumulated benefit obligation through the purchase of nonpartici-pating annuity contracts for $18 million. To determine the settlement gain of $5,148,000, the company remeasured its plan assets and obligations as of the settle-ment date, July 15, 2000.

	Revaluation (in thousands)		
	Expected Values at 7/15/2000	Revaluation*	Actual Values at 7/15/2000
Accumulated benefit obligation (ABO)	($16,000)	($ 2,000)	($18,000)
Projected benefit obligation (PBO)	($23,700)	($ 3,600)	($27,300)
Fair value of plan assets	31,300	2,700	34,000
Funded status	7,600	(900)	6,700
Unamortized transition asset	(8,700)		(8,700)
Unrecognized net loss	-0-	900	900
(Accrued) pension cost	($ 1,100)	$0	($ 1,100)

Settlement Gain Calculation (in thousands)

Maximum gain:		
Unrecognized net gain/loss before the revaluation	$ 0	
Loss arising from the settlement	900	
Unamortized transition asset	(8,700)	$ 7,800
Percentage of the PBO settled:		
ABO after the revaluation	$18,000	
PBO after the revaluation	÷ 27,300	× 66%
Settlement gain		$ 5,148*

* The revaluation is necessary in this situation because the discount rate (9 percent) at July 15, 2000 is lower than the assumed discount rate (10 percent) at January 1, 2000, and the actual return on plan assets is greater than the expect-ed return.

SFAS No. 88 indicates that routine annuity purchases (for retiring employees, for example) result in a settlement. However, employers may elect to adopt a consistent policy of not recognizing a gain or loss if the cost of all settlements in a year is less than or equal to the sum of the ser-vice cost and the interest cost components of pension cost for the year.

Figure 44–6 discusses how settlement accounting is applied in some common situations.

F I G U R E   44-6

Settlement Accounting in Common Situations

Annuities are purchased and the defined benefit plan is terminated (i.e., the obligation is settled and the plan ceases to exist) and replaced with a defined contribution plan.

This type of transaction is both a curtailment (because pension benefits cease to accumulate) and a settlement. As a result, the unrecognized prior service cost, the unrecognized net gain or loss, and the remaining transition amount are recognized immediately, with the amount of any gain generally being equal to the excess assets that revert to the company. The FASB staff's special report confirms that the gain should not be recorded as an extraordinary item.

A defined benefit plan is terminated and replaced with another defined benefit plan.

Because employees continue to earn benefits under the successor plan, this transaction is not considered a curtailment, and unrecognized prior service cost continues to be amortized as before the termination. It is considered to be a settlement, however, because annuities must be purchased under IRS/Department of Labor/PBGC (Pension Benefit Guaranty Corporation) guidelines. The gain is to be computed as follows:

- **Flat benefit plans:** Because 100 percent of the projected benefit obligation (PBO) (before termination) is settled by purchasing annuities—salary progression is not considered in actuarial calculations for flat benefit plans—the entire unrecognized gain (including any gain or loss arising directly from the annuity purchase and any remaining unamortized transition asset) is recognized immediately.

- **Final pay or career average plans:** Because to the best of our knowledge insurance companies do not sell annuities for the salary progression component of the PBO, it is impossible to settle 100 percent of the PBO for such plans. Pro rata recognition is required when less than 100 percent of the PBO is settled. The immediate gain or loss recognized is computed:

   Recognized amount = Percentage reduction of the PBO × Maximum gain or loss

   The maximum gain or loss equals the unrecognized net gain or loss (including asset gains and losses not yet reflected in the market-related value of plan assets as discussed in paragraphs 30 and 31 of *SFAS No. 87*) plus or minus the gain or loss first measured at the time of the annuity purchase plus any remaining unamortized transition asset (see paragraph 77 of *SFAS No. 87*).

- The FASB staff's special report on *SFAS No. 88* indicates that both plan assets and obligations are required to be remeasured as of the date of settlement in order to compute the maximum gain or loss and the percentage reduction in the PBO.

Annuities are purchased without plan termination or asset reversion.

If a company purchases annuities to settle all or part of the vested benefits portion of the PBO, a pro rata portion of the maximum gain or loss is recognized immediately. It is, therefore, not necessary to terminate the plan and recover the assets in order to recognize a gain. Thus, companies in an overfunded situation can trigger gain recognition by purchasing annuities at any point in time.

- **Negative contributions:** An employer in the United States is generally precluded from withdrawing excess plan assets from a pension plan without settling the obligation by making lump-sum payments or by purchasing annuities. Excess assets may be transferred to an employee stock ownership plan (ESOP) or to 401(h) accounts in the pension plan to be used to pay post-retirement medical benefits. The FASB staff's special report on *SFAS No. 88* indicates that an ESOP transfer not involving the purchase of annuities does not constitute a settlement. The withdrawal of assets in both situations should be recorded as a "negative contribution" by increasing cash and reducing prepaid pension cost or increasing accrued pension liability.

F I G U R E   44-6 (continued)

- **Annuities purchased from an affiliate:** Annuities purchased from an insurance company controlled by the employer do not constitute a settlement, because the risk has not been eliminated but merely transferred within the group. The FASB staff's special report on *SFAS No. 88* indicates that when a subsidiary purchases annuities from an insurance company that is a subsidiary of the same parent company, settlement accounting should be reflected in the separate company financial statements of the subsidiary purchasing the annuities; however, for consolidated financial statement purposes, no settlement is deemed to have occurred.

If the insurance company is less than majority owned and not controlled by the employer, the special report states that the entire settlement gain may be recognized by the employer. (For example, if the insurer is a 40-percent-owned investee, 100 percent of the settlement gain should be reflected in the employer's financial statements.) The special report acknowledges that this conclusion is a departure from traditional accounting under the equity method and is not intended to be a precedent for nonpension intercompany transactions.

The critical factor in determining whether settlement has occurred in situations of this nature is whether risk has been transferred. As discussed in footnote 1 of *SFAS No. 88* and in the FASB staff's special report on *SFAS No. 88,* transfer of risk within a controlled group does not constitute settlement; risk transferred outside the group does. Risk also has not been transferred if there is reasonable doubt that the insurer will meet its obligations under an annuity contract, and, therefore, the purchase of the contract from such an insurer does not constitute settlement.

The pension obligation is settled using participating annuity contracts.

SFAS No. 88 describes some contracts with insurance companies (participating annuities) that allow a company or the plan to receive dividends if the insurance company has favorable experience. *SFAS No. 88* indicates that if the substance of a participating annuity contract is such that the employer remains subject to all or most of the risks and rewards associated with the benefit obligation covered or the assets transferred to the insurance company, the purchase of the contract does not constitute a settlement. In interpreting this provision, however, the prevailing view appears to be that if an employer transfers the risks associated with the benefit obligation and plan assets but retains some potential rewards, the transaction should be considered a settlement.

If the purchase of a participating annuity contract constitutes a settlement, *SFAS No. 88* stipulates that the cost of the settlement is the cost of the contract less the amount attributed to the participation right. For example, the cost of settling a $100 obligation by purchasing a contract for $80 that includes a $10 participation right is $70. The $30 difference ($100 − $70) would be the gain first measured at the time of settlement. That amount would be treated as an unrecognized gain under *SFAS No. 87,* which is a component of the maximum gain subject to recognition under *SFAS No. 88.* However, *SFAS No. 88* requires that the maximum gain (but not the maximum loss) be reduced by the cost of the participation right. This requirement recognizes the continuing risk related to the participation right (i.e., the possibility of a subsequent loss is not completely eliminated with a participating contract), because realization of the participation right is not assured. Thus, for the transaction described, the maximum gain subject to recognition would be $20. The cost of the participation right is recognized as an asset and amortized systematically over the expected dividend period under the contract. Its carrying value should be assessed for recoverability on an ongoing basis. Dividends actually received by the plan are considered to be a return on plan assets and are accounted for like any other fund earnings.

Accounting for Curtailments

SFAS No. 88 defines a curtailment as an event that significantly reduces the expected years of future service of present employees or eliminates, for a significant number of employees, the accrual of defined benefits for some or all of their future services. Curtailments include:

- Termination of employees' service earlier than had been expected, which may or may not involve closing a facility or discontinuing a segment of a business.
- Termination or suspension of a plan so employees do not earn additional defined benefits for future services.

When it is probable a curtailment will occur and its impact (dollar effect) can be reasonably estimated, an employer is required to compute a net gain or loss from the curtailment that includes accelerated recognition of previously unrecognized prior service cost. Unless an employer also settles the pension obligation, accelerated recognition of previously unrecognized gains or losses is not permitted, because the employer has not been relieved of the primary responsibility for the pension obligation and remains subject to the risks associated with it as well as the related plan assets. If the result of this computation is a net loss, an employer must recognize the amount immediately. (Curtailment losses associated with a business combination are discussed later in the chapter.) However, if the result is a net gain, an employer should recognize this amount when realized (i.e., when the related employees terminate, or the plan suspension or amendment is adopted). *SFAS No. 88* sets forth the computations to be made to determine the net curtailment gain or loss. The net gain or loss represents the sum of two items:

- A loss computed as the portion of unrecognized prior service cost that relates to years of service no longer expected to be rendered, and
- A gain or loss computed as the net change in the projected benefit obligation resulting from the event. If the net change is a gain, it must first be offset against any existing unrecognized net loss. If the net change is a loss, it must first be offset against any existing unrecognized net gain.

For purposes of these computations, any remaining unamortized transition asset is treated as an unrecognized net gain; any remaining transition obligation is treated as unrecognized prior service cost. The percentage recognition of the unrecognized transition obligation and of prior service cost from each plan amendment are calculated separately based on the expected years of future service being eliminated for participants who are being curtailed and were active at transition and at the date of each amendment, respectively, compared with expected years of future service of all participants who were active at each date.

Termination Benefits

The accounting provisions of *SFAS No. 88* also deal with "special termination benefits offered 'only for a short period of time' to employees in connection with their termination of employment." An employer is required to recognize a liability and a loss when its employees accept an offer of special termination benefits and the amount can be reasonably estimated. The FASB staff's special report on *SFAS No. 88* indicates that an employer may not recognize a loss at the date the offer is made based on the estimated acceptance rate.

SFAS No. 88 also addresses "contractual termination benefits" provided by the existing terms of a plan but payable only if a specified event (such as a plant closing) occurs. An employer should recognize a liability and a loss for contractual termination benefits when it is probable that employees will be entitled to such benefits and the amount can be reasonably estimated. (Termination benefits associated with a business combination are discussed later in the chapter.) The FASB staff's special report on *SFAS No. 88* indicates that supplemental early retirement benefits should not be considered contractual termination benefits because they are not based on the occurrence of a specific event that causes employees' services to be involuntarily terminated. However, termination indemnities paid only in the case of involuntary termination of employment due to a specific event qualify as contractual termination benefits.

A situation involving termination benefits also would generally involve a curtailment if the terminated employees represent a significant portion of the workforce.

EITF Issue 94–3, Liability Recognition for Certain Employee Termination Benefits and Other Costs to Exit an Activity (Including Certain Costs Incurred in a Restructuring), provides guidance on accounting for involuntary termination benefits that are not associated with a disposal of a segment and that an employer decides to pay to involuntarily terminated employees absent a benefit plan or deferred compensation contract that requires such payments. The guidance in that issue does not change the way *SFAS No. 88* should be applied in practice. Under *SFAS No. 88*, as with all authoritative literature covering employers' accounting for employee benefits, the benefit plan is the unit of accounting. *EITF Issue 94–3* provides guidance for situations in which benefits to be paid are not pursuant to the terms of a plan (i.e., prior to management's decision to pay benefits to employees to be involuntarily terminated, they would not have been entitled to receive those benefits upon the occurrence of such an event). The main consensus reached by the EITF requires that an employer recognize a liability for the cost of involuntary termination benefits when it meets several conditions that include (a) making a decision prior to the financial statement date to terminate employees and pay them a termination benefit; (b) communicating to employees about benefit entitlements; (c) specifically identifying the number of employees to be terminated, their job classifications, and their locations; and (d) being able to complete the plan of termination in a period that indicates that significant changes to it are unlikely.

Recognition, Classification, and Disclosure

SFAS No. 88 contains the following provisions regarding financial statement recognition, classification, and disclosure for settlements and curtailments of defined benefit pension plans and for termination benefits.

■ Requires disclosure of the effects during the period of a curtailment, settlement, or special termination benefit on the benefit obligation and plan assets; the amount of gain or loss resulting from settlement, curtailment, or termination benefits; the cost of providing special or contractual termination benefits during the period; and a description of the nature of the event.

■ Extraordinary item treatment is not permitted unless the requirements of *APB Opinion No. 30, Reporting the Results of Operations—Reporting the Effects of Disposal of a Segment of a Business, and Extraordinary, Unusual, and Infrequently Occurring Events and Transactions,* are met (i.e., the event must be both unusual and infrequent). Appendix A (paragraph 48) of *SFAS No. 88* and the FASB staff's special report on *SFAS No. 88* indicate that gains or losses resulting from settlements, curtailments, or termination benefits generally do not result from the type of unusual and infrequent event that under *APB Opinion No. 30* would be reported as an extraordinary item. The authors agree with this interpretation.

■ The effect of a settlement and/or curtailment and/or termination benefits directly related to a disposal of a segment of a business should be recognized as part of the gain or loss associated with the disposal, not as part of pension cost. The gain or loss on disposal of a segment of a business is computed and recognized in accordance with *APB Opinion No. 30.*

■ Unless the settlement or curtailment or termination benefits are directly related to a disposal of a segment (see the preceding paragraph), *SFAS No. 88* calls for the recognition criteria of each event to be followed, even if a single management decision results in recognizing gains or losses in different reporting periods. For example, a settlement gain or loss is recognized when the transaction is completed; a curtailment loss is recognized when it is probable a curtailment will occur and the amount can be estimated; a curtailment gain is recognized when realized; a special termination benefits loss is recognized when the employees accept the offer; and a contractual termination benefits loss is recognized when it is probable that employees will be entitled to benefits and the amount can be estimated. Therefore, a situation could arise in which a plan is terminated and a curtailment loss and the loss relating to contractual termination benefits are recognized in one period (when it is probable that the events will occur and the amounts can be estimated), the loss relating to special termination benefits offered in the same period is recognized in a later period (when the offer is accepted), and the gain on settlement is recognized in still another later period (when the annuities are purchased).

■ A gain or loss from settlement or curtailment may occur after the pension plan's measurement date but prior to the employer's fiscal year-end. The FASB staff's special report on *SFAS No. 88* indicates that the employer should generally not include that gain or loss in determining that fiscal year's results of operations. The gain or loss should be recognized in the financial statements for the subsequent fiscal year. However, if the gain or loss results from the employer terminating the pension plan and not establishing a successor pension plan, the effect of the settlement and curtailment should be recognized in the current fiscal year. If the gain or loss is directly related to another event of the current fiscal year (e.g., a disposal of a segment of a business or the sale of a division requiring that a portion of the pension obligation be settled), the gain or loss should be recognized in the current fiscal year.

The special report also notes that if the gain or loss is not recognized in the current fiscal year, and the employer's financial position or results of operations would have been materially affected had it been recognized, disclosure of the event, its consequences, and when recognition will occur should be made in the financial statements for the current fiscal year. Although it is more stringent than the guidance in the special report, the authors believe the necessity of disclosing the effect of a post-measurement date event should be evaluated in relation to the respective reportable components of the plan, not solely the employer's financial position and results of operations.

OTHER ISSUES

Business Combinations

In a business combination accounted for under the purchase method prescribed in *APB Opinion No. 16, Business Combinations*, the acquiring company is required to recognize a liability (or asset) if the acquired company has a defined benefit pension plan with a projected benefit obligation in excess of (or less than) the fair value of plan assets. For purposes of this calculation, the projected benefit obligation and the fair value of plan assets at the date of the acquisition should reflect current interest rates and assumptions, and the effects of the acquiror's intention regarding the plan and the acquired operations (e.g., plan restructuring, termination, or plant closings). It is also generally appropriate to restart the calculation of the market-related value of plan assets at acquisition. The pension asset or liability thus recorded eliminates any previously unrecognized gain or loss, unrecognized prior service cost, and transition asset or obligation related to the acquired plan. Although the eliminated unrecognized items will not affect the acquiror's net pension cost subsequent to the combination, they may still need to be considered for funding purposes. To the extent that those items are considered in determining funding requirements, differences between the acquiror's net pension cost and amounts contributed will occur. Those differences will reduce or increase the asset or liability recognized at the date of the combination.

Interest on the acquired pension liability or asset is included in the interest cost or return-on-assets component of net periodic pension cost as it arises subsequent to the acquisition. Because interest is included in accounting for the pension plan (i.e., through the pension cost computation), it is inappropriate to accrue additional interest on the acquired pension obligation or asset.

Some pension plans or contractual relationships provide employees with termination benefits if the employee is terminated as a result of a business combination. In *EITF Issue 96–5, Recognition of Liabilities for*

Contractual Termination Benefits or Changing Benefit Plan Assumptions in Anticipation of a Business Combination, the EITF reached a consensus that the liability for the contractual termination benefits and the curtailment losses under employee benefit plans that will be triggered by the consummation of the business combination should be recognized when the business combination is consummated, even if consummation is probable at an earlier date.

Some companies have questioned the appropriate accounting when the acquiring company includes in its pension plan employees of an acquired company that did not have a pension plan of its own and grants them credit for prior service. The FASB staff's special report on *SFAS No. 87* indicates that careful consideration of the facts and circumstances surrounding the acquisition is required to determine the appropriate accounting. If the granting of credit by the acquiring company for prior service is required by the terms of the acquisition agreement, such amount should be considered as part of the cost of the acquisition to be accounted for as a purchase. Otherwise, the credit for prior service should be accounted for as a plan amendment.

For a multiemployer plan, the estimated withdrawal liability should be recorded only when it is probable that the acquiring company will withdraw from the plan.

Income Tax Considerations

For income tax purposes, the tax deduction for pension expense is generally equal to the amount contributed to the plan for the year. Thus, the *SFAS No. 87* pension cost usually results in an amount different from that allowable as a deduction for income tax purposes. In addition, to be deductible in a particular year, amounts must be paid on or before the extended due date of the income tax return. Differences between the cumulative pension cost recorded under *SFAS No. 87* and the cumulative pension contributions deductible for income tax purposes (i.e., often the unfunded accrued/prepaid pension cost) should be accounted for as a temporary difference in accordance with *SFAS No. 109, Accounting for Income Taxes*. The reversal of a pension asset or liability should be based on estimates of how and when the recorded asset or liability will actually be reduced. If increases in the recorded asset or liability are expected before reductions will occur, those increases should be ignored. The first reductions anticipated should be deemed to apply to the asset or liability existing at the balance-sheet date. This approach is similar to that for depreciable assets where increases in the temporary difference are ignored and reversals are applied on a FIFO basis.

Other book/tax differences may result from different computational methods. For example, pension costs capitalized as part of the cost of inventory for financial reporting purposes may differ from the pension costs required to be capitalized for income tax purposes. For employers using the LIFO method for costing inventory, the use of different pension cost methods for financial reporting and income tax purposes does not raise a LIFO conformity issue; rather, it is a LIFO computational difference. Separate actuarial reports may be required if there are substantial differences between the financial reporting and income tax methods. A change in the method of determining pension cost for income tax purposes, in an effort to eliminate the need for separate actuarial reports, may be a change in funding method for income tax purposes requiring advance approval from the Internal Revenue Service.

Rate-Regulated Enterprises

SFAS Nos. 87 and *88* do not contain special provisions relating to employers subject to certain types of regulation. In this connection, paragraph 210 of *SFAS No. 87* states:

> For rate-regulated enterprises, *FASB Statement No. 71, Accounting for the Effects of Certain Types of Regulation,* may require that the difference between net periodic pension cost as defined in this *Statement* and amounts of pension cost considered for rate-making purposes be recognized as an asset [if the criteria in paragraph 9 of *SFAS No. 71* are met] or a liability [if the situation is as described in paragraph 11(b) of *SFAS No. 71*] created by the actions of the regulator. Those actions of the regulator change the timing of recognition of net pension cost as an expense; they do not otherwise affect the requirements of this *Statement*.

Paragraph 9 of *SFAS No. 71* states:

> Rate actions of a regulator can provide reasonable assurance of the existence of an asset. An enterprise shall capitalize all or part of an incurred cost that would otherwise be charged to expense if both of the following criteria are met:
>
> a. It is probable that future revenue in an amount at least equal to the capitalized cost will result from inclusion of that cost in allowable costs for rate-making purposes.
>
> b. Based on available evidence, the future revenue will be provided to permit recovery of the previously incurred cost rather than to provide for

expected levels of similar future costs. If the revenue will be provided through an automatic rate-adjustment clause, this criterion requires that the regulator's intent clearly be to permit recovery of the previously incurred cost.

Paragraph 11(b) of *SFAS No. 71* states:

Rate actions of a regulator can impose a liability on a regulated enterprise. Such iiabilities are usually obligations to the enterprise's customers. The following are the usual ways in which liabilities can be imposed and the resulting accounting:

b. A regulator can provide current rates intended to recover costs that are expected to be incurred in the future with the understanding that if those costs are not incurred future rates will be reduced by corresponding amounts. If current rates are intended to recover such costs and the regulator requires the enterprise to remain accountable for any amounts charged pursuant to such rates and not yet expended for the intended purpose, the enterprise shall not recognize as revenues amounts charged pursuant to such rates. Those amounts shall be recognized as liabilities and taken to income only when the associated costs are incurred.

The FASB staff's special report on *SFAS No. 87* indicates that continued use of different methods of determining pension cost for rate-making purposes and financial accounting purposes would result in the criteria in paragraph 9 of *SFAS No. 71* being met, in which case an asset would be recorded due to the actions of the regulators. However, the special report also indicates that the criteria in paragraph 9 of *SFAS No. 71* would not be met, and thus an asset could not be recorded, if:

(a) it is probable that the regulator soon will accept a change for rate-making purposes so that pension cost is determined in accordance with *Statement 87* and (b) it is not probable that the regulator will provide revenue to recover the excess cost that results from the use of *Statement 87* for financial reporting purposes during the period between the date that the employer adopts *Statement 87* and the rate case implementing the change.

Similarly, the special report indicates that the situation would not be as described in paragraph 11(b) of *SFAS No. 71*, and a liability due to the actions of the regulator would not be required to be recorded, if it is probable that:

(a) the regulator soon will accept a change for rate-making purposes so that pension cost is determined in accordance with *Statement 87*, (b) the regulator will not hold the employer responsible for the costs that were intended to be recovered by the current rates and that have been deferred by the change in method, and (c) the regulator will provide revenue to recover those same costs when they are eventually recognized under the method required by *Statement 87.*

The special report indicates that rate-regulated enterprises may record an asset only if it is probable that the "excess" costs will be recovered from the ratepayers in the future.

Plan Compliance with ERISA

SFAS No. 87 requires companies to compute pension cost in accordance with the plan's requirements. If the plan is not in compliance with ERISA, the provision for pension cost may be based on plan provisions that do not comply with ERISA. This may result in a loss contingency that may need to be reflected in the financial statements in accordance with *SFAS No. 5, Accounting for Contingencies.* To illustrate, if a plan instrument does not conform to ERISA's participation requirements, the provision for pension cost would be computed excluding certain legally eligible participants, and the pension accrual will be inadequate. Thus, a determination would need to be made as to the likelihood (as defined by *SFAS No. 5*) that a liability will be incurred for the additional benefits, and for any fines and penalties that may be imposed due to lack of compliance.[4]

---

4 ERISA specifies that certain penalties are levied against the plan or against the plan administrator. However, the employer may ultimately become liable for such penalties even if it is not the plan administrator.

Costing and Funding Retirement Benefits

Vincent Amoroso*

Introduction

Funding retirement benefits includes setting aside contributions, investing them in a funding medium, and making benefit payments from the amounts set aside. It involves administrative and accounting functions and important tax considerations.

This chapter discusses funding retirement programs that are qualified plans under the Internal Revenue Code (IRC). Special considerations, not discussed here, apply to plans covering employees of governmental bodies and churches.

FUNDING MEDIA

The funding medium is the vehicle containing the plan's assets, from which the benefits are paid. All pension plan assets must be held by one or more trusts, custodial accounts, annuity contracts, or insurance contracts.[1]

Trusts

Trusts are the investment medium for about two-thirds of all pension plan assets. Governed by state law, a trust is a legal entity under which a

---

* The author acknowledges the significant contribution of Don Grubbs in the preparation of this chapter.

1 Employee Retirement Income Security Act of 1974 (ERISA) Sec. 403; IRC of 1986 Secs. 401(a),(f), 403(a), 404(a)(2).

trustee holds assets for the benefit of another. Whereas the Internal Revenue Service (IRS) deems a trust to exist even before it has a corpus (assets), most state laws require a corpus for a trust to exist.[2] A trust agreement is entered into between the employer or other plan sponsor and the trustee(s).

The trust instrument states the purpose of the trust and defines the authority and the responsibilities of the trustee. It includes provisions for terminating the trust and for replacing the trustee. A trust must provide that plan assets are to be used for the exclusive benefit of participants and beneficiaries.[3]

Trustees

Generally, trustees may be either individuals or institutions with trust powers, such as banks or trust companies. A bank usually is designated as trustee. Some large plans divide plan assets among two or more banks serving as trustees.

Some plans have a board of trustees consisting of a group of individuals. Collectively bargained multiemployer plans usually follow this approach. In such a case, the board of trustees usually enters a second trust agreement with a bank, delegating responsibility for holding and investing plan assets. Sometimes the trustee is a single individual, but many individuals are reluctant to assume the fiduciary responsibilities of trustees.

The duties of trustees differ from plan to plan. In every case the trustee must hold the plan assets and account for them. Some trustees have complete responsibility for determining investment policy and making investment decisions. Under other trust agreements, the trustee is required to follow investment decisions made by the employer or investment manager. For many plans, the trustee's authority lies between these two extremes; for example, the trustee may make individual investments in accordance with investment policies or limitations established by the employer, an investment manager, or trust agreement.

Trustees usually pay the plan's benefits to participants and often assume other administrative responsibilities as well. Sometimes the trustee is designated plan administrator with full responsibility for administering the plan. The trustee is a fiduciary of the plan and subject to ERISA's fiduciary responsibilities.

---

2 Rev. Rul. 57-419, 1957-2 CB 264.
3 IRC Sec. 401(a)(2).

Trust Investments

Many banks maintain one or more collective trust funds to pool the assets of a number of plans for investment purposes. These commingled trust funds are very similar to mutual funds. They may provide more diversification, better investment management, and reduced investment expense—particularly for small plans—compared to a single trust investing in individual securities. Many banks have several separate commingled funds for particular types of investments; for example, common stocks or bonds. For the same reasons that some trusts invest in commingled funds, others invest in mutual funds as an intermediary. Most larger trusts acquire individual securities, rather than use commingled funds or mutual funds.

Many trusts invest only in securities listed on a major stock exchange to assure marketability, avoid valuation problems, and reduce fiduciary problems. Common stocks and corporate bonds are the most common investments. Trusts also often invest in preferred stocks, certificates of deposit, commercial and government notes, government bonds, mortgages, and real estate. Occasionally, they invest in art, precious metals, and other collectibles, but this is, in effect, prohibited if individuals direct the investment of their own accounts in a defined contribution plan.

A plan may invest in securities of the employer only if they are "qualifying employer securities." A qualifying employer security is either a stock or a marketable security of the employer that meets several criteria of ERISA. A defined benefit plan generally may not invest more than 10 percent of its assets in securities of the employer; but stock bonus plans, profit-sharing plans, and some money purchase pension plans are not so limited.

Insured Plans

A significant portion of pension plan assets are held by insurance companies. Many different kinds of contracts are used. These include group contracts covering a group of participants and individual contracts covering each participant. While the following descriptions of investment media point out what were traditional insurance company approaches to funding pensions, it should be noted that over the years, to meet demands for greater flexibility, insurers have expanded their offerings and can now tailor the funding approach to the specific needs of the employer. This flexibility also has been accelerated by the trend to defined contribution plans.

Annuity contracts and insurance contracts are used, and both generally provide annuity income after retirement. Life insurance contracts generally guarantee to pay death benefits exceeding the reserve for the individual participant, while annuity contracts generally do not. The extent to which the contracts guarantee the payment of benefits or the employer's costs varies greatly among contract types.

Deposit Administration Group Annuity Contract

A deposit administration (DA) contract has a deposit fund into which all contributions to the plan are deposited. For defined benefit plans, the fund is not allocated among participants. The insurance company credits the fund with interest at a guaranteed rate and may assess the fund with a stipulated expense charge. When a participant becomes eligible for a pension, a withdrawal is made from the deposit fund to purchase an annuity. Sometimes lump-sum distributions, disability payments, or other benefits are paid directly from the deposit fund without the purchase of an annuity.

The DA contract specifies the guaranteed rate of interest to be credited to the deposit fund, the expense charge to be subtracted from the deposit fund, and the rates that will be used to purchase annuities when individuals retire. There generally is no expense charge for larger plans. The insurer guarantees payment of the pensions after annuities have been purchased but does not guarantee that the deposit fund will be sufficient to purchase the annuities.

The guaranteed interest rates and annuity purchase rates generally are quite conservative. When actual experience is more favorable than the guaranteed assumptions, the difference may be recognized by adding dividends or experience credits to the deposit fund. Consulting, administrative, and actuarial services for the plan may be provided by the insurance company, independent consultants, or the employer.

If the contract is discontinued, it may allow the employer either to apply the balance of the deposit fund to purchase annuities, or to transfer it to a trust or another insurance company. If the fund is transferred in a lump sum, the insurance company may deduct a surrender charge or a market-value adjustment or, alternatively, the insurer may require that the transfer be made in installments over a period of years.

The assets of the deposit fund represent a contractual obligation of the insurer but do not represent any particular assets of the insurer. The insurer invests the monies received as part of the total assets of the insurance company, usually primarily in bonds and mortgages. The insurer usually reflects the investment earnings of its entire portfolio in determining the amount of interest to credit in dividends or experience credits.

In determining the interest to credit, most insurers use the "investment year" or "new money" method, which determines the rate of investment earnings on investments made by the insurance company in each year deposits were added to the deposit fund.

Many DA contracts provide that part or all of the employer contributions to the plan may be invested in separate accounts, rather than in the deposit fund. Separate accounts operate similarly to mutual funds and are invested in common stocks or other forms of investment. The employer may direct transfers from the deposit account into the separate account. As in a mutual fund, deposits to the fund are converted to units by dividing by the current unit value of the separate account. The unit value equals the total market value of the fund divided by the number of units held by all of the contracts that invest in the separate account. Withdrawals also are based upon the current unit value. Many insurance companies maintain separate accounts for common stocks, bonds, mortgages, and other classes of investment.

Immediate Participation Guarantee Contract

An immediate participation guarantee (IPG) contract, like a DA contract, has a deposit account into which employer contributions are paid. The insurance company generally agrees to credit to the deposit account the actual rate of investment earnings it earns on its general portfolio using the investment-year method and to deduct an allocation of expenses for the particular contract based on accounting records for that contract. Pensions are paid from the deposit account monthly as they become due, rather than from a purchased annuity. Thus, the contract immediately participates in its actual experience for mortality, expenses, and investment income. Annuity purchase rates are guaranteed under the contract, but annuities are not usually purchased unless the contract is discontinued. Some companies use an accounting device that appears to purchase annuities, but ordinarily no annuities are actually purchased. Some insurers call such contracts *pension administration* or *investment only* contracts, rather than IPG contracts. Separate accounts generally are used with IPG contracts, just as they are with DA contracts.

Guaranteed Investment Contract

A guaranteed investment contract (GIC) guarantees the rate of interest to be credited to the deposit account for a limited period, usually from 30 days to 20 years. Most GICs guarantee that the full principal will be paid out with no surrender charge or adjustment at the end of that period. It may provide only for an initial deposit or may provide for continuing deposits during a "window" period. It may allow benefits to be paid from the deposit account during that period. These characteristics can be particularly valuable for a thrift plan or a regular profit-sharing plan where the entire fund balance is allocated to individual participants; many participants want a guarantee of principal and interest.

The GIC may include all the plan's assets, or it may be only one of several investments held by the plan's trust. At the end of the guarantee period, the entire balance of the GIC will be paid out to the trust or other funding medium of the plan, or it may be left on deposit and a new guarantee period established. The GIC may have annuity purchase options, but in practice annuities usually are not purchased.

Group Deferred Annuity Contracts

A deferred annuity contract is one under which the insurance company promises to pay a monthly annuity beginning at a future date. Under a group deferred annuity contract, the employer purchases a deferred annuity for each participant each year to fund the amount of pension earned in that year. The insurance company guarantees payment of the pension purchased to date, beginning at the normal retirement date, or payment of a reduced pension beginning at an early retirement date. For example, assume a pension plan provides a pension at age 65 equal to $10 monthly for each year of participation in the plan. Each year the employer pays a premium for each participant to purchase a deferred annuity of $10 monthly to begin at age 65. Premium rates are based on the participant's age and sex. Because a small deferred annuity is purchased and guaranteed each year, by the time a participant reaches age 65 his or her entire pension will be purchased.

Before DA contracts became popular, group deferred annuities were the most common type of group annuity. In recent years, however, very few new deferred annuity contracts have been issued, except to purchase annuities under terminated plans. Most plans that formerly used deferred annuities have changed to other methods of funding pensions earned after the date of change, but deferred annuities purchased before the change remain in force.

Individual Level Premium Annuities

Under some plans, usually small ones, an individual level premium annuity contract is purchased to fund the projected pension of each participant.

The insurance company deducts an expense charge from each premium and accumulates the balance at a guaranteed rate of interest. At retirement the balance of the account is converted into a monthly annuity, applying guaranteed purchase rates. The insurance company actually may use interest credits and annuity purchase rates more favorable than the conservative rates guaranteed in the contract.

The annual premium is the level annual amount so determined that the accumulation at normal retirement age is sufficient to purchase the promised pension. If the participant receives a salary increase that causes the originally projected pension to increase, a second level premium annuity is purchased to fund the increase. Further salary increases may require purchase of a third level, fourth level, and so on.

Upon termination of employment before retirement, the accumulated balance (cash value) of each policy is available to provide a benefit for the employee if he or she is vested, or a credit for the employer if the employee is not vested. Upon death before retirement, the death benefit usually equals the greater of the cash value or the sum of the premiums paid.

Individual Retirement Income Insurance Contracts

An individual retirement income insurance contract (sometimes called income endowment) is similar to an individual level premium annuity, except the death benefit equals the greater of the cash value or 100 times the projected monthly pension. The retirement income contract also has level annual premiums, but these must be larger than under the level premium annuity to provide the larger death benefit.

Split-Funded Plans—Individual Life Insurance and an Auxiliary Fund

Many plans are funded by a combination of individual life insurance policies plus an auxiliary fund ("side fund"). The type of policy used is most frequently an ordinary life ("whole life") policy or a universal life policy. In many defined benefit plans, the amount of life insurance equals 100 times the projected pension, as in the retirement income contracts. The life insurance contract builds up a cash value sufficient to provide part of the pension. Deposits are made to the auxiliary fund to provide the balance. The auxiliary fund may be held by the insurance company or may be in a trust.

At retirement, two alternatives are available to provide a pension. Some plans surrender the insurance contract at retirement, deposit the cash value in the trust, and pay pensions monthly out of the trust. Other plans make a transfer from the trust to the insurance company at the time of retirement; the amount transferred is the amount required, together with the policy cash value, to purchase an annuity from the insurer to guarantee payment of the pension.

Many plans originally funded with retirement income insurance contracts have been converted to a split-funded basis to reduce the cost of funding the plan and to allow part of the plan's assets to be invested in common stocks. In turn, many split-funded plans have been converted to fund the pensions with a trust or group annuity contract and to provide the death benefits outside the pension plan under group term insurance in order to reduce the employer's cost. Because individual policies generally have a higher cost than group policies, the purchase of individual policies may constitute a breach of fiduciary responsibility.

When death benefits are funded with individual insurance under a qualified plan, the employee has current taxable income equal to the cost of the insurance ("P.S. 58" cost). On the other hand, if death benefits are funded outside the plan with group term life insurance, the cost of providing the first $50,000 of insurance paid by employer contributions is tax-free to the employee, and the cost of insurance on amounts over $50,000 is computed on a less expensive basis than under individual contracts. Thus, employees pay less income tax if death benefits are funded outside the plan with group term insurance.

Group Permanent Contracts

Group permanent insurance contracts are designed to preserve the characteristics of individual insurance contracts while achieving some of the economy of group insurance. Whole life, universal life, and other types of contracts are available. All participants are covered under a single contract that has cash values, death benefits, and other characteristics similar to a collection of individual contracts. Because the group contract pays lower commissions and has lower administrative expense than individual contracts, the premiums are lower. Such contracts are termed *permanent* insurance to distinguish them from group term insurance.

FACTORS AFFECTING FUNDING

Many factors affect the amount an employer contributes to the pension plan. Different considerations affect different plans.

Type of Plan

The type of plan and its provisions often completely or partially determine the amount of the employer contribution. A thrift plan, for example, may require the employer to match employee contributions up to 6 percent of pay. A profit-sharing plan may require the employer to contribute 20 percent of profits but not more than 15 percent of pay. A money purchase pension plan may require contributions of 10 percent of pay. Such plans leave no discretion in the amount of contribution. But most profit-sharing plans provide the employer complete discretion in determining what, if anything, to contribute, and most defined benefit pension plans allow substantial discretion in determining how much to contribute each year. Details on the factors affecting the funding of specific retirement plans are contained in the respective chapters of the *Handbook*.

Laws and Regulations

An employer may want to contribute more in a year when it is in a higher tax bracket and less in a year when it is in a low tax bracket or has no taxable income at all. Minimum funding requirements under ERISA set an absolute minimum on the contributions for most pension plans. These are described later.

If the employer is a taxpayer, it is subject to limits on the amount of pension contribution that may be claimed as a deduction for income tax purposes. Employers are subject to a 10 percent excise tax on any contributions greater than can be deducted currently.[4]

Other governmental requirements affect the amount of contributions of some employers. Federal Procurement Regulations and Defense Acquisition Regulations control pension costs assessed under federal contracts. The Department of Housing and Urban Development has rules applicable to reimbursement of pension costs for local housing authorities. Public utilities commissions regulate the amount of pension contributions that may be recognized for rate-making purposes by utilities.

Collective Bargaining

Collective-bargaining agreements affect the funding of many plans. Some collective-bargaining agreements set the amount of employer contributions specifically in cents per hour, as a percent of pay, or as, for example,

---

4 IRC Sec. 4972.

cents per ton of coal produced. Other collective bargaining agreements, however, specify what benefits the plan provides but do not specify the amount of employer contributions.

Funding Media

Under most plans funded with group annuity contracts or with trusts, the funding medium does not usually limit the amount of contributions. Under a traditional DA group annuity contract, the deposit fund must be sufficient to purchase annuities for individuals currently retiring. Usually, the deposit fund is far more than sufficient for this purpose, so this requirement has no impact. But occasionally the deposit fund is not sufficient, particularly if a number of employees with large pensions retire shortly after the plan is established; this may require additional employer contributions to purchase annuities. To solve this problem, DA contracts often are modified to allow annuities to be purchased in installments after retirement.

Accounting

Generally accepted accounting principles (GAAP) establish the charge for pension expense in the employer's profit and loss statement. This does not directly control the amount actually contributed, but some employers prefer the amount contributed to approximate the charge to expense. For the largest U.S. companies, expense charges have become even more significant in recent years. The effect on accounting charges has become more important than the corresponding effect on required contributions when such companies consider adopting plan improvements or any plan change of substance.

Financial Considerations

An employer often considers its cash position in determining the amount of contribution to the plan. Cash shortages may stem from lack of profits or from a need to reinvest earnings in the business or to reduce indebtedness. Reducing pension contributions helps solve cash shortages. But an employer in a strong cash position may want to increase its pension contributions, since an additional dollar paid this year reduces the required contributions in future years and earns tax-free income in the pension trust. For an employer with lots of cash, larger pension contributions may help in avoiding the accumulated earnings tax on accumulated earnings in excess of the greater of $250,000 or the amount required for the reasonable needs of the business.[5] Larger contributions also reduce the cash available for dividends.

Interest rates often are considered. Increasing the pension contribution may require increased borrowing by the employer or may prevent reducing debts. The rate of interest on debt may be compared with the rate of investment earnings of the pension fund, but taxes also should be considered. Similarly, an employer with no indebtedness may consider how much could be earned by additional investments in the business, using amounts that would otherwise be contributed to the pension fund.

Employers may establish a funding policy based on many other considerations. Most employers want the plan to be soundly funded to ensure that it will be able to pay promised benefits. Some employers want pension costs to be stable as a percent of pay over future years. The employer may decide to fund the unfunded liabilities over a fixed period, such as 20 years. Future trends in pension costs may be projected, based on projected increases or decreases in the number of future participants, changes in work pattern histories, investment earnings, future salary increases, anticipated plan amendments, or possible plan termination or merger.

Statutory Requirement for Funding Policy

ERISA requires every employee benefit plan to "provide a procedure for establishing and carrying out a funding policy and method."[6] Many plan documents merely state the employer will contribute to the trust each year the minimum amount required by ERISA's minimum funding standards and such additional amounts as the employer determines at its discretion. This retains the maximum discretion to change the funding policy without a plan amendment.

ACTUARIAL COSTS

Fundamental concepts of actuarial science are used in the costing of retirement benefits. The following illustrate the factors involved in the actuarial costing of such benefits.

---

5   IRC Sec. 531–537.
6   ERISA Sec. 402(b)(1).

Probability

When rolling an honest die, the probability of getting a 3 is ⅙ (or 0.16667). This statement does not tell us what the outcome of the next roll will be, but it does tell us something about the average experience that might be expected if many dice were rolled.

Mortality tables show the probability of dying at each particular age of life. This probability is determined by examining the experience of many thousands of lives. For example, according to one mortality table the probability of a man's dying at age 30 is 0.000991. This means if there were 1 million men aged 30, it might be expected that 991 of them would die before reaching age 31. It does not tell us which ones might die and which ones might live and, hence, tells us nothing about the expected life-time of any one individual. But it does give us information about the average experiences to be expected in a large group of men aged 30.

Interest Discount

If someone deposits $100 in a savings account at 5 percent interest, one year later it will have grown to $105 (1.05 × $100). If the individual leaves the funds on deposit for a second year they will grow to $110.25 (1.05 × 105). Thus, if an individual wants to obtain $110.25 two years from now (assuming 5 percent interest), $100 must be deposited today. The $100 is the "present value" of $110.25 payable two years from now.

Viewed another way, the present value of an amount payable two years from now is 0.907029 times that amount (determined by dividing $100 by $110.25). At 5 percent interest, 0.907029 is the present value factor, or *interest discount factor*, for two years. To know the present value of any amount due two years from now (assuming 5 percent interest), simply multiply it by 0.907029.

There is a discount factor for any number of years for any interest rate. Sample discount factors for zero years to five years at 5 percent interest and 6 percent interest are shown in Table 45–1.

Present Value of Future Amounts

Suppose a woman agrees that two years from now 600 dice will be rolled and that she will pay $1 for each 3 that results. Further suppose that she wants to know the present value—the amount that she can set aside in a savings account today—that can be expected to be sufficient, together with interest, to pay the amounts when they become due. The total

T A B L E   45–1

Sample Discount Factors

Number of Years	Interest Discount Factor	
	5 Percent	6 Percent
0	1.000000	1.000000
1	0.952381	0.943396
2	0.907029	0.889996
3	0.863838	0.839619
4	0.822702	0.792094
5	0.783526	0.747258

expected payments are $100 (⅙ × 600 × $1). Assuming 5 percent interest, the present value of that is $90.70 (the two-year discount factor or 0.907029 × $100). Thus, if she deposits $90.70 today it will have grown to $100 two years from now, which will be sufficient to make the expected payments if exactly one-sixth of the 600 dice turn up a 3. Thus, $90.70 is the present value of the expected future payments. Of course, it might turn out to be more or less than needed, if the account earns more or less than the 5 percent assumed, or if more or less than exactly one-sixth of the dice turn up a 3. *The present value of any future event is the number of exposures* (600 dice) *times the probability of occurrence* (⅙) *times the amount of payment on each occurrence* ($1.00) *times the interest discount factor* (0.907029).

Suppose, in addition to the obligation related to the 600 dice to be rolled two years from now, the woman has an obligation to pay $3 for each head that results from flipping 1,000 coins five years from now. The present value of the coin flipping could be determined similarly to that for the dice throwing. Then the two present values for dice rolling and coin flipping could be added to get the total present value of both obligations combined. Similarly, total present value can be determined for combinations of many possible future events, each with its own exposure, probability of occurrence, amount of payment, and time of occurrence.

Actuarial Cost Methods

Underlying actuarial concepts of pension funding are the actuarial cost methods that establish the level of pension contributions needed to fund promised pension benefits.

When a pension plan is first established, it may give past service credit to provide benefits related to employment before the effective date. Employees then covered under the plan will work for various amounts of time in the future. When employees terminate employment, some of them will be eligible to receive benefits, either beginning immediately or deferred into the future. After pension benefits begin, they usually continue for the retiree's lifetime, and sometimes payments are made after death to beneficiaries.

Actuarial cost methods are merely methods for assigning the cost of the benefit payments to particular years. Ultimately, the cost of a pension plan equals the sum of all the benefits and expenses paid from the plan, less any employee contributions and less the plan's investment return. If the employer contributes an additional dollar in any year, that dollar together with the interest it earns reduces the amount the employer needs to contribute in future years. Actuarial cost methods do not affect these ultimate costs, although they indirectly may influence the amount of investment income by influencing the size of the fund or the timing of contributions.

To the extent that any insurance or annuity contracts guarantee the costs of the plan, the employer's cost equals the premiums paid to the insurance company reduced by any dividends or credits, rather than the plan's own experience of benefits and expenses paid, and investment return.

Basic Categories of Actuarial Cost Methods

All actuarial cost methods for pensions fall into three categories: current disbursement, terminal funding, and advance funding. All are in current use, although advance funding is most commonly used and is required for plans subject to ERISA's minimum funding requirements.

Under the *current disbursement* method, also called *pay as you go,* each year the employer contributes the current year's benefit payments. This is not really an actuarial cost method at all. However, actuarial techniques can be used to project payments in future years, which may assist those responsible for the plan's operation. If a plan is funded precisely under the current disbursement method, the plan will have no assets whatsoever available to pay future benefits; next month's benefits will depend on next month's contributions.

Under *terminal funding,* as under current disbursement, no cost is recognized for a participant while he or she continues employment. The entire cost of the participant's future benefits is recognized, however, at the moment the participant retires and benefits begin. If a participant terminates and is entitled to a deferred pension beginning at a later date, the cost of the pension may be recognized either at the time of termination of employment or at the time payments begin, under two variations of the terminal funding method. If a plan is funded under the terminal funding method, the assets are expected to be sufficient to pay all the future benefits for those already retired (and terminated vested participants, if they also have been funded); no assets would be available to provide benefits for those not yet retired.

With *advance funding*, the cost of a participant's pension is spread over his or her working lifetime. It recognizes the cost of a worker's pension as a cost of employment. If all the costs attributable to the past have been funded, the plan assets usually are larger than under the terminal funding method and usually are expected to be sufficient to provide all future benefits for those already retired and terminated and to have some additional assets available to provide benefits for those still employed. Advance funding usually results in more rapid funding than terminal funding, but that is not always the case.

Except as otherwise noted herein, all actuarial cost methods are assumed to be advance funding methods.

Present Value of Future Benefits

For any group of individuals, the present value of their future benefits is the amount expected to be sufficient to pay those future benefits. If the present value of the future benefits were invested in a fund today, it would be sufficient, together with the investment income, to pay all such future benefits as they become due; no additional contributions would be needed, but the fund would be exactly exhausted when the last individual dies.

A participant or beneficiary may become eligible to receive future benefits if he or she retires (before or after normal retirement date), becomes disabled, dies, or otherwise terminates employment. The present value of future benefits is determined by the same principles as described earlier.

Consider a new employee just hired at age 25 under a pension plan that provides normal retirement benefits at age 65, assuming all payments are made annually at the beginning of the year. The present value of the single payment he or she may receive at age 65 is determined by multiplying the number of exposures (one person) times the probability of occurrence (the probability he or she will not die or terminate employment before age 65 and will then retire) times the amount of payment (the annual pension) times the interest discount factor (for 40 years from age

25 to 65). The present value of the payments to be received at 66, and each later age, could be similarly calculated. In each case the probability would need to consider not only the employee's chance of receiving the first payment, but of continuing to survive to receive subsequent payments, and the interest discount factor would be smaller as the years become more distant. By adding the present value of each future normal retirement payment, the present value of all normal retirement payments can be determined. By similar techniques the present value of the payments that may be paid for this worker in the event of early retirement, disability, death, or vested termination can be determined. Adding all these together, the present value of all future benefits that may become payable to the individual or his or her beneficiary is ascertained.

For this individual, the present value may be meaningless. He or she may quit before becoming vested and never receive a cent. Or he or she may collect a pension until age 99, with costs greater than anticipated. But if the plan has a large number of participants, the sum of their present values will accurately reflect the amount needed to pay all future benefits, if the assumptions are correct concerning the various probabilities, the interest rate, and the amount of each future payment that might become payable. This concept is key to all actuarial cost methods.

Components of Present Value of Future Benefits

Actuarial cost methods generally divide the present value of future benefits into two portions, the part attributable to the past and the part attributable to the future. The part attributable to the past is called the *accrued liability*. It also has sometimes been called *past service liability*, *prior service liability*, *actuarial liability, supplemental present value*, and the like. The part of the present value of future benefits attributable to the future is called the *present value of future normal costs*. This present value of future normal costs is the portion of the present value expected to be paid in the future for "normal costs," the cost attributable to each of the future years.

If the same assumptions are used, all actuarial cost methods have the same present value of future benefits (although under one of the methods it is not required to calculate the present value of future benefits). The methods differ in how they divide this present value between the accrued liability and the present value of future normal costs. Obviously, a method that produces a larger accrued liability has a smaller present value of future normal costs and vice versa. Under some methods, when a plan is first established no accrued liability exists at all, even though benefits are actually credited for past service. In this case, the present value of future normal costs equals the entire present value of future benefits.

Except when a plan is first established, it usually will have assets equal to part of the accrued liability. Any excess of the total accrued liability over the assets is the "unfunded accrued liability," or the "unfunded past service liability."[7]

If the assets exactly equal the accrued liability, there is no unfunded accrued liability, and the plan is "fully funded" for its accrued liability; this is also a tax concept. Under some actuarial cost methods, the assets always exactly equal the accrued liability and there never is an unfunded liability.

Each actuarial method determines the normal cost for the current year.[8] The normal cost usually is calculated for the year beginning on the valuation date, but under one method it is sometimes calculated for the year ending on the valuation date. The normal cost may be calculated in dollars or in a number of other ways, including as a percent of payroll, cost per employee, per hour, or per shift. If not originally expressed in dollars, it is converted to dollars by multiplying by the actual or expected payroll, number of employees, hours, shifts, and so on. The normal cost for the coming year is, of course, part of the present value of future normal costs.

Gain or Loss

As part of the actuarial valuation, the actuary can calculate what the present unfunded liability would have been expected to be currently if the experience since the date of the last actuarial valuation had exactly followed the actuarial assumptions. This expected unfunded liability can then be compared with the actual unfunded liability calculated in the current valuation. The difference between the expected unfunded liability and the actual unfunded liability is the gain or loss since the last valuation. This gain or loss shows the extent to which the actual experience was better or worse than would have been expected by the actuarial assumptions.

Under some actuarial cost methods ("spread gain" methods) the actual unfunded liability is assumed to equal the expected unfunded liability and, thus, there is no gain or loss. Under these methods, deviations between expected and actual experience are spread over the future working lifetimes of participants as increases or decreases in the normal cost.

---

7 ERISA Sec. 3(30), 302(b)(2)(B), IRC Sec. 412(b)(2)(B).

8 ERISA Sec. 3(28).

Summary of Valuation Results

Under every actuarial cost method, the valuation produces the following results:

1. Normal cost for the current year.
2. Accrued liability.
3. Assets.
4. Unfunded accrued liability (the accrued liability less the assets, assumed $0 under one method).
5. Gain or loss (assumed $0 under spread gain methods).

ACTUARIAL COST METHODS

Statutory Requirements for Actuarial Cost Methods

ERISA states the term *advance funding actuarial cost method* or *actuarial cost method* means a recognized actuarial technique utilized for establishing the amount and incidence of the annual actuarial cost of pension plan benefits and expenses. Acceptable actuarial cost methods shall include the accrued benefit cost method (unit credit method), the entry age normal cost method, the individual level premium cost method, the aggregate cost method, the attained age normal cost method, and the frozen liability cost method. The terminal funding cost method and the current funding (pay-as-you-go) cost method are not acceptable actuarial cost methods. The Secretary of the Treasury shall issue regulations to further define acceptable actuarial cost methods.[9]

Under the statute, the IRS may recognize other methods as "acceptable" for determining ERISA's minimum funding requirements. The IRS has so far recognized one additional method, the shortfall method. The same actuarial cost method and the same assumptions must be used for determining deductible limits as are used for minimum funding purposes.[10] The actuarial cost method and actuarial assumptions must be reasonable in the aggregate and must offer the actuary's best estimate of anticipated experience under the plan; in addition, actuarial assumptions, generally are subject to an individually reasonableness standard under which each assumption must be reasonable.[11]

9　ERISA Sec. 3(31).
10　IRC Sec. 404(a)(1) (A).
11　ERISA Sec. 302(c) (3), IRC Sec. 412(c)(3).

Classification of Actuarial Cost Methods

There are a variety of ways in which actuarial cost methods may be classified. Only advance funding methods are considered in the following classifications.

1. Methods may be divided between (a) those that allocate the *benefits* of the plan to particular plan years and then determine the actuarial present *value* associated with the benefits assigned, and (b) those that allocate the actuarial present value of all future benefits to particular plan years without allocating the benefits themselves. Those methods that allocate the benefits to particular plan years may be further divided between those that allocate the benefits according to the plan's provisions describing the accrued benefit, and those that allocate the projected benefits as a level dollar benefit for each year of service.

2. A second way of classifying actuarial cost methods is between accrued benefit methods and projected benefit methods. An accrued benefit method is based on the amount of benefit earned to date, while a projected benefit method is instead based on the projected amounts of benefits expected to be paid from the plan on retirement or other termination of employment. This is similar to the first classification above, because all *accrued* benefit methods allocate the *benefits* to particular years, while *projected* benefit methods generally allocate the actuarial present *value* to particular years.

3. A third way of classifying divides actuarial cost methods between those that directly determine the actuarial gain or loss, and those that do not. Actuarial cost methods that do not directly determine the actuarial gain or loss have the effect of automatically spreading the gain or loss over the future working lifetimes of all active participants as part of the normal cost; such methods are called *spread gain methods*.

4. A fourth way of classifying divides actuarial cost methods between individual methods and aggregate methods. Under an individual method, the normal cost and the accrued liability may be calculated for each individual participant; the normal cost and the accrued liability for the entire plan are the sums of these respective items for all of the participants. Under an aggregate method, the costs are determined for the group as a whole in such a way that they cannot be determined separately for individuals.

5. A fifth way of classifying is between methods that result in an initial accrued liability when the plan is established or amended (usually related to past service benefits or plan amendments that increase accrued benefits) and those that do not. If a method does not produce an initial accrued liability, the cost of all benefits (including past service benefits) must be funded through normal costs.

6. A sixth way of classifying is between methods that use an entry age basis and those that use an attained age basis. Under an attained age basis, the normal cost is determined on the basis of the participants' current attained ages, without reference to their ages at entry. Under an entry age basis, age at entry is a key element in determining normal cost.

7. A seventh way of classifying is between open group methods and closed group methods. A closed group method considers only the group of present plan participants, while an open group method considers employees expected to be hired in the future as well.[12] Except as otherwise specifically noted, this chapter considers only closed group methods. All six methods listed in ERISA are this type.

The above classifications are each presented as dichotomies. A number of methods exist that combine elements of the dichotomies.

Accrued Benefit Cost Method

The plan document usually defines the "accrued benefit," the annual amount of benefit earned to date that is payable at normal retirement age. If a participant is 100 percent vested, the participant's vested benefit equals his or her accrued benefit.[13]

The accrued benefit cost method, also called the *unit credit cost method*, defines the accrued liability as the present value of the plan's accrued benefits. The normal cost equals the present value of the benefit accrued during the current year.

The traditional accrued benefit cost method is based on the accrued benefit defined in the plan. This does not recognize future salary increases. If a plan's benefits are based on final average pay, salary increases will cause the benefit credited for past years to increase from year to year as salaries increase, causing liabilities to increase and creating actuarial losses. For this reason, the IRS will not allow a final average pay plan to use the traditional accrued benefit cost method.

A modified accrued benefit cost method may be used for final average pay plans and other plans. Under this method, the projected benefit at normal retirement age is first calculated based on projected service to normal retirement age and future salary increases. A modified accrued bene-

---

12 For a discussion of an open group method, see Donald R. Fleischer, "The Forecast Valuation
    Method for Pension Plans," *Transactions 27* (1975), pp. 93–154, Society of Actuaries.
13 ERISA Sec. 3(23), 204, IRC Sec. 411(b).

fit is then calculated; generally equal to the projected benefit multiplied by the ratio of the participant's actual years of service to date to his or her projected years of service at normal retirement age. This modified accrued benefit cost method, sometimes called *the projected unit credit method*, does not have the problems of increasing liabilities and actuarial losses because of salary increases that are part of the traditional method.

Entry Age Normal Cost Method

The entry age normal cost method is a type of projected benefit cost method. This means the cost is based on the projected amount of pension expected to be payable at retirement, rather than the accrued benefit earned to date.

The entry age normal cost equals the level annual amount of contribution (level in dollars or as a percent of pay) from an employee's date of hire (or other entry age) to retirement date, calculated as sufficient to fund the projected benefit. The accrued liability equals the present value of all future benefits for retired and present employees and their beneficiaries, less the portion of that value expected to be funded by future normal costs.

Under the entry age normal cost method, unlike the accrued benefit cost method, the normal cost of each individual is expected to remain level each year. For plans with benefits not related to pay, the normal cost is calculated to remain level in dollars; for a plan with benefits expressed as a percentage of pay, the normal cost is calculated to remain level as a percentage of pay. The average normal cost for the entire group also can usually be expected to remain fairly level per employee or as a percentage of pay, even if the average attained age increases, unless there is a change in the average *entry* age.

Under the entry age normal cost method, when the plan is first established an initial accrued liability exists that equals the accumulation of the normal costs for members for years prior to the effective date. Similarly, if an amendment increases benefits, there is an increase in the accrued liability equal to the accumulation of prior normal costs for the increase in projected benefits.

Individual Level Premium Cost Method

The individual level premium cost method determines the level annual cost to fund each participant's projected pension from the date participation begins to normal retirement date. When participation begins, the plan has no accrued liability, even if the participant has substantial benefits credited for past service. Usually no salary increase assumption is used in projecting the benefit at retirement. If a participant's projected benefit increases during a year, this increase in the projected benefit will be separately funded by an additional level annual cost from the participant's then-attained age to normal retirement age. If a plan amendment increases benefits, the increase in the projected benefit for each individual is funded by a level premium from his or her then-attained age to retirement age, with no immediate increase in the accrued liability.

Under the individual level premium cost method, the accrued liability for each individual equals the present value of future benefits less the present value of future normal costs. The accrued liability for the entire plan, less the plan assets, equals the unfunded accrued liability.

An allowable variation of this method is the "individual aggregate method." Under this variation, the normal cost for the first year is the same as previously described. To determine the normal cost in subsequent years, it is first necessary to allocate the plan's assets. The assets attributable to retired or terminated vested employees are assumed to equal the present value of their benefits; those assets attributable to retired and terminated employees are subtracted from the total actual assets to determine the portion of the actual assets attributable to active employees. Several methods are used to allocate assets among active employees. Each individual's allocated assets are subtracted from the present value of future benefits to obtain the remaining unfunded cost of his or her benefits. This unfunded cost is spread as a level premium (level in dollars or as a percentage of pay) from attained age to the participant's retirement age.

Aggregate Cost Method

The aggregate cost method is another projected benefit cost method. Under this method, there is no unfunded liability. The accrued liability is, in effect, assumed to equal the assets. Thus, all costs are funded through the future normal costs, determined as a level percent of pay (or level in dollars) during the future working lifetimes of all current employees from their current attained ages.

The excess of the present value of future benefits over the value of any plan assets is the portion of that present value that must be funded by normal costs in the future. This excess is the present value of future normal costs. The actuary then determines the present value of all future compensation for all employees. By dividing the present value of future normal costs by the present value of future compensation, the actuary determines the ratio of future normal costs to future compensation. The actuary multiplies this ratio by the current year's compensation to determine the current year's normal cost. A similar procedure is used to determine the normal cost per employee, rather than as a percent of compensation, if benefits are not related to compensation.

Costs are determined in the aggregate and cannot be determined individually. Thus, the normal cost is calculated as a percentage of the total payroll, or a cost per employee for the entire group. The aggregate cost method automatically spreads gains and losses through the future normal costs and has no separately identifiable gains or losses.

Attained Age Normal Cost Method

The attained age normal method combines the unit credit cost method with either the aggregate cost method or the individual level premium cost method. The accrued liability at the plan's effective date is calculated using the accrued benefit cost method. The cost of the excess of the projected benefit over the accrued benefit on the effective date is funded by level costs over the future working lifetimes of participants, using either the individual level premium cost method or the aggregate cost method. Both individual and aggregate variations have long been recognized as the attained age normal cost method, but some use the name only to apply to one or the other variation.

If the individual variation is used, each individual's original past-service benefit is valued every year using the unit credit cost method to determine the accrued liability. The difference between the employee's total projected benefit and this frozen past-service benefit is valued as under the individual level premium cost method, without spreading gains. This method funds any increase in projected benefits, because of salary increases from the then-attained age to retirement age.

If the aggregate variation is chosen after the first year, the frozen initial liability technique, described below, is used. In that event, gains and losses are spread over the future working lifetimes of employees.

Frozen Initial Liability Cost Method

ERISA lists the frozen initial liability method. Many actuaries do not regard this as an actuarial cost method at all but, rather, a method for spreading gains under other methods. This latter group might describe a method as "entry age normal cost method with frozen initial liability" or as "attained age normal cost method with frozen liability." But this difference of viewpoint does not reflect an actual difference in how the method operates.

The frozen initial liability method is not a method for determining the plan's initial accrued liability. The entry age normal cost method usually is used to determine the initial accrued liability and the first year's normal cost, but sometimes the attained age normal cost method is used, instead. In subsequent years the unfunded liability is "frozen" and does not reflect actuarial gains and losses. This method has no gain or loss. What would be a gain or loss is spread over the future working lifetimes of all participants through increases or decreases in future normal costs.

To accomplish this, the unfunded accrued liability on the valuation date is set equal to the expected unfunded liability; that is, what the unfunded liability would be if the actuarial assumptions had been exactly realized during the prior year. This unfunded liability plus the plan assets equals the total accrued liability. The excess of the present value of all future benefits over the accrued liability is the portion of that present value that must be funded by future normal costs and is designated as the present value of future normal costs. From this present value of future normal costs, the current year's normal cost is determined in the same manner as for the aggregate cost method.

Shortfall Method

The shortfall method is not really an actuarial cost method but a way of adapting other actuarial methods to ERISA's funding requirements.[14] It was created to solve a problem created by ERISA's minimum funding requirements and applies only to collectively bargained plans.

Retired and Terminated Participants and Beneficiaries

Under the traditional accrued benefit cost method, the accrued liability equals the value of accrued benefits. This is true for retired participants, terminated participants with vested rights, and beneficiaries of deceased participants, as well as for active employees.

This same approach is used for retired and terminated members and beneficiaries under all actuarial cost methods that determine the accrued liability on an individual basis. Thus, the accrued liability for retired and

14 Treasury Reg. 1.412(c)(1)-2.

terminated members and beneficiaries is the same under the entry age normal cost method as under the accrued benefit cost method.

For aggregate methods, this same value for retired and terminated members and beneficiaries is part of the present value of future benefits.

Table 45–2 summarizes the actuarial cost methods.

Actuarial Assumptions

Purpose of Assumptions

Determining the present value of future benefits is basic to all actuarial cost methods. *The present value of any future benefit is the amount of the future benefit times the probability it will be paid, discounted to present value at interest.* For example, a plan may provide a disability benefit equal to 50 percent of pay to workers who become disabled after 15 years of service. The amount of future benefits depends on the probability each worker will survive in the group to become eligible; that is, that he or she will not die, retire, become disabled, or otherwise terminate employment before becoming eligible for such benefits. The amount of future benefits also depends on the probabilities of becoming disabled, as well as the period of disability before either death or recovery. It also depends on future salary increases. Actuarial assumptions are used to predict these matters.

The present value of future benefits is calculated using an interest discount. It may not be apparent why an assumption concerning the assets is used to determine the present value of future benefits. The present value of a future benefit is the amount of assets that would need to be invested today to ensure that the assets plus the interest they would earn would be sufficient to provide the expected benefits in the future. The interest to be earned is key to determining what amount of present assets are needed. Apart from minimum funding requirements, the interest assumption affects the incidence of contributions, and, therefore, can affect equities among different generations of contributors. This can be an especially important consideration in plans where unrelated employers make contributions, as in multiemployer and multiple employer plans.

The actuarial valuation allocates the present value of benefits to various periods of the past and future. Frequently, that allocation is made in proportion to periods of employment or to compensation. For example, actuarial assumptions are used to estimate those periods of employment or amount of compensation. Thus, the selection of the assumptions affects the allocation of present values between periods of the past and future.

T A B L E   45–2

Summary of Actuarial Cost Methods (excluding shortfall)

	Accrued Benefit or Projected Benefit	Calcu- lates Gain or Loss	Indi- vidual or Aggre- gate	Initial Accrued Liability	Age Used for Compu- tation of Normal Cost
1. Accrued benefit cost	Accrued	Yes	Individual	Yes	Attained
2. Entry age normal cost					
a. Individual ages	Projected	Yes	Individual	Yes	Entry
b. Average entry age	Projected	Yes	Aggregate	Yes	Entry (average)
3. Individual level premium cost					
a. No spread	Projected	Yes	Individual	No	Attained
b. Spread gain	Projected	No	Individual	No	Attained
4. Aggregate cost	Projected	No	Aggregate	No	Attained
5. Attained age normal cost					
a. Individual	Mixed	Yes	Individual	Yes	Attained
b. Aggregate	Mixed	No	Aggregate	Yes	Attained
6. Frozen initial liability cost	Projected	No	Aggregate	Yes	Attained

Note: For a more detailed presentation of actuarial cost methods, see C. L. Trowbridge and C. E. Farr, *The Theory and Practice of Pension Funding* (Burr Ridge, IL: Richard D. Irwin, 1976); and B. N. Berin, *The Fundamentals of Pension Mathematics* (Schaumburg, IL: Society of Actuaries, 1989).

Long-Range Nature of Assumptions

For an employee now aged 25, the actuarial assumptions are used to esti-mate whether he or she will be eligible for a pension 40 years in the future, what the employee's salary will be after 40 years, how long the employee will live to receive a pension, and what the fund will earn over the entire period.

Thus, the actuarial assumptions are extremely long-range in nature. The more distant any event is, the less likely it can be predicted accurate-ly. Mortality rates for next year are fairly predictable (barring a war), but mortality rates 50 years hence may depend on events that cannot possibly be predicted, such as remarkable medical discoveries or a disastrous deterioration of the environment. Other assumptions than mortality are even less predictable for long periods. The experience of last year, or the expected experience of next year, is relevant to the process of establishing assumptions only to the extent that it may indicate long-term trends.

Most experts will not even conjecture for such long periods. When economists talk of long-range projections, they often mean five years. Yet such long-range assumptions are essential to actuarial valuations. The actuary, faced with this difficult task, usually assumes the future will be generally similar to the present.

ERISA Requirements for Assumptions

ERISA requires the actuary to use reasonable actuarial assumptions and methods (taking into account the experience of the plan and reasonable expectations), which, in combination, offer the actuary's best estimate of anticipated experience under the plan.[15] The statutory language provides more questions than answers. What is the meaning of reasonable? How can the assumptions be reasonably related to the plan's experience when the large majority of plans are so small that their experience is not statistically valid? Is the "best estimate" one that has a 50 percent chance of being on the high side and a 50 percent chance of being on the low side? *In an effort that lasted about 10 years, the IRS challenged the deductibility of pension contributions made by thousands of plan sponsors—consisting mostly of professionals who practiced law or medicine. The IRS claimed in these cases that plan sponsors overstated the required contributions by using actuarial assumptions that did not comply with the reasonableness standard. The tax authorities abandoned their efforts in 1995 after a series of judicial defeats.* Detailed discussion of the individual assumptions can be found in the actuarial literature.[16]

In addition to the above requirements, *which apply to actuarial assumptions used for the generally applicable minimum funding standard,*

---

15 ERISA Sec. 302(c)(3), IRC Sec. 412(c)(3).

16 Study notes of the Society of Actuaries and articles and discussions in numerous volumes of the *Transactions and Record* of the Society of Actuaries, and the *Proceedings* of the Conference of Actuaries in Public Practice. See also, "Deductible Limits for Pension Plans: How We Got Here," by Vincent Amoroso, *NYU 48th Institute on Federal Taxation*, 1990, Matthew Bender & Co., Inc.

other standards apply to the interest and mortality assumptions used for those funding requirements that apply to certain underfunded plans.

Asset Valuation Methods

Under some actuarial cost methods, the value of plan assets affects the unfunded liability, which must be funded by amortization payments. Under other actuarial cost methods, the value of plan assets affects the normal cost. Under either approach, the method used to determine the value of plan assets determines the required employer contributions for a particular year and the fluctuation in contributions from year to year.

Some plans use the market value of assets for the actuarial valuation. It is argued this is the real value of the plan's assets and, therefore, makes the valuation more realistic. The disadvantage of this method is that fluctuations in market value may result in substantial fluctuation in the required employer contributions from year to year, which is generally undesirable.

Some plans use cost or book value of assets for the actuarial valuation. Using this method, the plan can avoid the problems of fluctuation in plan costs. However, if the asset value used differs substantially from market value, it may present an unrealistic picture of the true costs and liabilities.

A variety of actuarial methods of asset valuation are used to avoid these problems. Some plans use the cost or book value so long as it lies within a stated corridor around market value; for example, not less than 80 percent or more than 120 percent of market value. Some plans use a formula or method to gradually recognize asset appreciation; for example, five-year average market value. A wide variety of methods are used to gradually recognize appreciation but avoid extreme asset value fluctuation. ERISA requires plans to use "any reasonable actuarial method of valuation which takes into account fair-market value and which is permitted under regulations." Regulations generally require that the asset value used be between 80 percent and 120 percent of market value.

MINIMUM FUNDING REQUIREMENTS

General Requirements

ERISA established minimum funding requirements to provide greater assurance that pension plans will be able to pay the promised benefits.

Applicability

The minimum funding requirements appear twice in ERISA in duplicate language, in Title I and Title II.[17] The IRS issues regulations that apply to both Title I and Title II.

Under Title II, the minimum funding requirements apply to almost all qualified pension plans (excluding profit-sharing and stock bonus plans) except government plans, church plans, and "insurance contract plans."

Under Title I, the minimum funding requirements apply to nonqualified plans as well as qualified plans. The exemptions described above for Title II also apply under Title I, along with a few other ones. Plans exempt from the funding requirements include "a plan which is unfunded and is maintained by an employer primarily for the purpose of providing deferred compensation for a select group of management or highly compensated employees" and "excess benefit plans."[18]

The broad definition of pension plan under ERISA makes the funding requirements apply to many deferred compensation arrangements, previously unfunded plans, and other arrangements not previously thought of as pension plans.

Basic Requirements

Employers are required to contribute at least the normal cost plus amounts calculated to amortize any unfunded liabilities over a period of years. The required amortization period ranges from five to 40 years, depending on when it arose and its source. Additional requirements apply to certain plans with a low level of funding. If contributions in any year exceed the minimum required, the excess reduces the minimum required in subsequent years.

Penalties and Enforcement

If contributions are less than required, the shortfall is an "accumulated funding deficiency." If an accumulated funding deficiency exists at the end of the plan year, a 10 percent excise tax is assessed on the deficiency. If the funding deficiency is not corrected within a prescribed timeframe, an additional tax is imposed equal to 100 percent of any uncorrected deficiency. In addition to paying these nondeductible taxes, the

---

17 ERISA Sec. 301–306, IRC Sec. 412.

18 See also, "SERP Sponsors Beware," by Vincent Amoroso, *BNA Pension & Benefits Reporter*,
    Vol. 24, April 21, 1997.

employer also must correct the accumulated funding deficiency itself. These taxes apply only to qualified plans. Whether or not the plan is qualified, the Secretary of Labor, participants, beneficiaries, and fiduciaries may bring civil actions to enforce the minimum funding requirements.

Funding Standard Account

A "funding standard account" is an accounting device used to keep track of the funding requirements. Amounts that increase the funding obligation for the year are charges to the funding standard account. These include the normal cost and annual payments needed to amortize any unfunded liabilities. Amounts that decrease the employer's obligation are credits to the funding standard account. These include employer contributions and annual amounts that may be used to amortize any decrease in the unfunded liability.

If the credits exceed the charges for a year, the excess is carried over as a credit balance to decrease the contributions required for the following year. Similarly, if the credits are less than the charges, the resulting accumulated funding deficiency is carried forward to increase the contributions required in the following year.

Reporting

For defined benefit pension plans, the plan administrator must engage an enrolled actuary "on behalf of all plan participants." Satisfaction of the minimum funding requirements is demonstrated on Schedule B "Actuarial Information," which must be certified by an enrolled actuary and attached to IRS Form 5500. For defined contribution pension plans, satisfaction of the requirements is shown on Form 5500 itself.

Timing of Contributions

The entire contribution required for a plan year must be paid no later than eight and one-half months after the end of the year. In addition, a portion of the required contribution must be paid no later than each of four quarterly contribution dates.

Minimum Contribution Requirement

Additional funding requirements generally apply to any plan with more than 100 participants if its assets are less than 90 percent of its "current liability" (the liability for accrued benefits on a plan-termination basis). If the "deficit reduction contribution," which includes the amount needed to amortize the unfunded current liability exceeds the otherwise applicable minimum contribution amount under the regular minimum funding standards, the excess must be added to the regular funding requirement.

Full Funding Limitation

No employer is required or allowed to contribute more than the amount needed to fully fund the accrued liability or the amount needed to fund a percentage that is scheduled to increase to 170 percent of the current liability by the year 2005. This full funding limitation may reduce or eliminate the minimum contribution otherwise required. Special rules govern the determination of the amounts of assets and liabilities for this purpose.

Alternative Minimum Funding Standard

Some plans are allowed to use the alternative minimum funding standard to determine their minimum funding requirement. If a plan uses the alternative minimum funding standard, it must nonetheless also maintain records for the regular funding standard account. A plan may not use the alternative minimum funding standard unless it uses the entry age normal cost method under its regular funding standard account. If an alternative minimum funding standard account is maintained, it is charged with (1) the lesser of the normal cost under the actuarial cost method used under the plan or the normal cost determined under the unit credit cost method; (2) the excess, if any, of the present value of accrued benefits over the fair-market value of assets; and (3) any credit balance in the account as of the beginning of the year. The alternative minimum funding standard account is credited with employer contributions for the year.

The alternative minimum funding standard is based on a plan-discontinuance concept, and very few plans use it.

Waiver

The IRS may grant a waiver of part or all of the minimum funding requirement. A waiver will be approved only if the employer faces "substantial business hardship" and if failure to approve the waiver would be "adverse to the interests of plan participants in the aggregate." IRS standards in considering waiver requests are similar to a banker acting on a request for a loan: Is the employer's financial hardship sufficient to warrant granting the waiver *and* is such hardship likely to be temporary?

Extension of Amortization Period

Another form of relief from the minimum funding requirement is an extension of the amortization periods. The IRS may extend the time required to amortize any unfunded liability by up to 10 years. Extending an amortization period reduces slightly the required employer contribution. Employer's generally apply for outright waivers instead of amortization extensions.

Multiemployer Plan Requirements

ERISA contained slightly different funding requirements for collectively bargained multiemployer plans than for other plans. The Multiemployer Pension Plans Amendment Act of 1980 (MEPPA) and other statutory changes made further changes for multiemployer plans. The most significant difference is that an employer that withdraws from a multiemployer plan may be assessed "withdrawal liability," requiring significant contributions after the withdrawal.

TAX DEDUCTION OF EMPLOYER CONTRIBUTIONS

Purposes

Like most other business expenses, contributions to qualified pension plans must be deducted as ordinary and necessary business expenses. In addition, Section 404 of the IRC sets maximum limits on the amount that may be deducted in each year. Section 404 reflects two concerns of Congress.

First, Congress wanted to encourage employers to establish qualified plans for their employees. Congress also wanted to encourage employers to soundly fund the plans to ensure that promised benefits would be paid. Thus, Congress wanted to allow tax deductions for the amounts needed to soundly fund the plans.

Second, Congress wanted to limit the deduction for a particular year to expense attributable to that year. This would serve to minimize an employer's ability to manipulate its taxable income. However, it is not clear how much of the payments for past service costs and actuarial gains and losses should be considered attributable to a particular year.[19]

---

19 See "Deductible Limits for Qualified Pension Plans: Yesterday, Today and Tomorrow," by Vincent Amoroso with others, "*NYU 57th Institute on Federal Taxation, 1999*," published by Matthew Bender and Co., Inc.

Timing of Deductible Contributions

To be deductible, contributions to pension and profit-sharing plans for a year must be paid no later than the tax filing date for the year, including extensions. No deduction may be claimed for the contribution of a promissory note of the employer, even if secured.

If the employer contributes more than the deductible limit for a year, the excess is carried over to be deducted in future years, subject to the deductible limit in future years. However, a 10 percent excise tax is generally assessed on any contributions that exceed the maximum deductible amount for the year.[20]

Maximum Deductible Limit for Pension Plans

In addition to a special rule that applies for certain plans with unfunded current liability, Section 404 has three alternative ways to determine the maximum limit on deductible employer contributions for a pension plan. Usually, the maximum deductible limit equals the normal cost plus the amount needed to amortize any past service liability over 10 years. If a plan has no unfunded liability, its deductible limit does not include a past service amount.

The amount of past service cost to be amortized is called a *10-year amortization base*. For a new plan, the 10-year amortization base equals the initial unfunded accrued liability base. If the unfunded accrued liability is changed by a plan amendment, change in the actuarial method or assumptions, or actuarial gains or losses, the amount of change in the unfunded accrued liability becomes an additional 10-year amortization base. The old base continues until it is fully amortized. Any event that increases the unfunded liability creates a new positive base. Any event that decreases the unfunded liability creates a new negative base. A plan may have many bases.

The amount required to amortize each 10-year amortization base over 10 years is the "limit adjustment." Each 10-year amortization base has its own limit adjustment. The limit adjustment is positive if its base is positive and negative if its base is negative. All of a plan's limit adjustments are added to determine the plan's maximum deductible limit for past service contributions. Detailed regulations provide rules for determining the amount of bases and limit adjustments.[21]

---

20 IRC Sec. 4972.
21 Treasury Reg. Sec. 1.404(a).

The second method of determining the maximum deductible limit is the individual aggregate method. The maximum deductible limit for each participant is the amount necessary to provide the remaining unfunded cost of the projected benefit distributed as a level amount, or a level percentage of compensation, over the participant's remaining future service. But if the remaining unfunded cost for any three individuals exceeds 50 percent of the unfunded cost for the entire plan, then the unfunded cost for each such individual must be distributed over at least five years.

The third alternative for determining the deductible limit equals the amount required to satisfy the plan's minimum funding requirement. The full-funding limitation determined under the minimum funding requirements is an overriding maximum limit on the amount that may be deducted for a year.

Maximum Deductible Limits for Profit-Sharing and Stock Bonus Plans

The maximum deductible limit for a profit-sharing plan or stock bonus plan is 15 percent of the compensation paid or accrued for all participants during the tax year. The limitation is on the aggregate contributions for all participants, not the contribution for each. Thus, more than 15 percent may be contributed and deducted for a particular participant if the aggregate limit is not exceeded.

Maximum Deductible for Combined Plans

If an employer maintains more than one profit-sharing or stock bonus plan, they are treated as a single plan for purposes of determining the deductible limit. If an employer maintains both a defined benefit plan and a defined contribution plan that have one or more participants in common, there is an additional limitation on deductible contributions. Deductible contributions to the combined plans are limited to 25 percent of compensation of all of the participants in either plan or, if greater, the pension plan contribution required by the minimum funding requirements. This is so even though an employer that has no defined contribution plan may deduct more than 25 percent of pay under a defined benefit plan. If contributions to combined defined benefit and defined contribution plans exceed the combined 25 percent limit, they may be carried over for deduction in a later year, but the 10 percent excise tax on nondeductible contributions applies.

DEDUCTION OF EMPLOYEE CONTRIBUTIONS

Some plans require employees to contribute to the plan as a condition for participation or for receiving certain employer-provided benefits. Some plans allow employees to make voluntary contributions to increase the benefits otherwise provided under the plan. Neither mandatory nor voluntary employee contributions are deductible by employees.

Under a 401(k) plan, an employee may elect to defer receipt of part of his or her compensation and have the employer contribute it to the plan. Subject to limits, the amount deferred is excluded from the employee's taxable income and is treated as an employer contribution.

ACCOUNTING FOR PENSION PLAN LIABILITIES AND COSTS

There are two parts to pension plan accounting: accounting for the plan itself and accounting for the employer. A brief description of each follows. For a more detailed discussion of plan accounting, see Chapter 41. Employer accounting for pension plans is covered in Chapter 44.

Accounting for the Plan

Form 5500 or a related form must be filed each year through the Department of Labor with the Internal Revenue Service. Form 5500 includes a statement of plan assets and liabilities, a statement of income and expenses, and certain other financial information. For plans with 100 or more participants, the plan administrator is required to engage an independent qualified public accountant. A statement from the accountant, prepared in accordance with generally accepted accounting principles, must be attached to Form 5500. *Statement of Financial Accounting Standards, No. 35* of the Financial Accounting Standards Board (FASB) established generally accepted accounting principles for pension plans.

Both Form 5500 and *Statement No. 35* also require a statement of assets and liabilities (other than actuarial liabilities), a statement of changes in fund balances, and additional information.

Accounting for the Employer

An employer's accounting for a defined contribution plan usually is simple. Contributions paid for the employer's fiscal year are treated as an expense. An employer's accounting for a defined benefit plan is more complex. It requires certain disclosures in addition to determining the charge to expense and possible balance-sheet entries.

For a defined benefit plan an employer's charge to expense for pension cost is the subject of *Statements No. 87* and *No. 88* of the Financial Accounting Standards Board. *Statement No. 87* requires the profit and loss statement to include a charge for pension expense that represents the pension cost properly attributable to the current year, regardless of the amount contributed for the year.

The employer's pension expense is the "net periodic pension cost." It must be determined using the projected unit credit cost method.

The net periodic pension cost consists of six components:

1. Service cost.
2. Interest cost.
3. Actual return on plan assets.
4. Amortization of any prior service cost.
5. Gain or loss (including the effect of changes in actuarial assumptions).
6. Amortization of unrecognized obligation at the date of initial application of *Statement No. 87.*

The service cost is the plan's normal cost. The interest cost equals one year's interest at the valuation interest rate ("discount rate") on the plan's accrued liability ("projected benefit obligation"). The "actual return on plan assets," which reduces the net periodic pension cost (but as noted below is modified by expected returns on plan assets), equals the investment income earned plus realized and unrealized appreciation and depreciation of the fair value of plan assets. The initial projected benefit obligation for a new plan, or the increase in the projected benefit obligation resulting from a plan amendment, generally must be amortized over the expected future period of service of participants expected to receive benefits; this forms the annual amortization of any prior service cost. To smooth fluctuations in pension cost from year to year, *Statement No. 87* includes rules for delaying and spreading the recognition of actuarial gains and losses, so only a portion of the gain or loss is included in the net periodic pension cost for any year. However, any difference between the actual return on plan assets and the expected return on plan assets in the year is recognized currently, immediately offsetting any investment return greater or smaller than expected. The difference between the projected benefit obligation and the fair value of plan assets on the effective date of *Statement No. 87*, adjusted for any accrued or prepaid pension cost at that date, is the plan's unrecognized net obligation or asset at that date. This amount is to be amortized over the expected future period of service of participants expected to receive benefits, although the employer may elect to use a 15-year amortization period if that is longer.

Negative components of the net periodic pension cost may exceed positive components, resulting in a negative net periodic pension cost.

Differences between the net periodic pension cost and the amount of contribution to the plan result in a balance sheet asset or liability for prepaid or accrued pension cost. In addition, any excess of the value of accrued benefits ("accumulated benefit obligation") over the fair value of plan assets will require recognition on the balance sheet as a liability. In this case, an offsetting intangible asset is usually allowed on the balance sheet.

Statement No. 87 also requires certain disclosures in the employer's financial statements. It contains accounting rules related to termination or curtailment of plans, purchase of annuities, and payment of lump-sum distributions under plans.

Relationship of Accounting and Funding

Accounting for the pension plan itself and accounting for the employer do not directly control the plan's funding. However, there may be an important indirect effect, since the manner in which accountants report funding influences some employers' decisions concerning funding.

CHAPTER 46

Funding Retirement Plans—Investment Objectives

Eugene B. Burroughs

The successful funding of the future pension benefit payment promise through investment operations is made possible through the exercise of prudence, the application of time-proven principles, the dedication of people conducting themselves in a professional manner, and the resultant efficacy of the adopted policy and practices. The growth in real asset value over time through successful investment funding activities will require fewer contributions and will allow greater potential for enhancing retirement benefit payments.

Representatives of sponsors of employee benefit plans play a significant role in the benefit payments funding process, for if they collectively address the asset management part of their responsibilities in an objective and professional manner, their stewardship may produce the major portion of the benefit payments stream from the pension plan. The power of compounded interest, reinvested earnings, redeployed rents, and realized capital appreciation are powerful elements in the wealth-enhancement process. To the degree the supervising fiduciaries are successful in systematically adding value over time from investment operations, less of a need exists to increase employer, or employee, contributions to the plan.

Therefore, it behooves the supervising group to endeavor through knowledge and insight into the workings of the financial markets to propitiously allocate plan assets. Unfortunately, plan sponsors may miss their opportunities to add value to the plan by:

- The frequent hiring of "winning" managers and firing of "losing" managers.
- Excessive turnover in the portfolio.
- Inordinate emphasis on stock-picking activities as opposed to the more productive asset-allocation decisions.
- Assuming unrealizable return expectations based on the most recent market experience and ignoring the long-term risk/return relationships in the securities markets.

Since asset stewardship activities so significantly impact the net bottom line, choosing among funding vehicles is extremely important. This chapter's discussion of funding pensions through asset management activities provides the elements basic to the process. The discussion is necessarily limited to investing alternatives. The important point of this discussion is to grasp the principles and process to achieve a plan's funding goals through investment operations.

The discussion includes:

1. Four elements fundamental to successful investing of employee benefit plan monies.
2. Attributes of the prudent fiduciary.
3. Characteristics of the three favored classes of investments.
4. Identification of appropriate investment objectives.
5. Evaluation and selection of the investment facility.
6. Development and documentation of investment policy.
7. Exercising the option to engage in strategic asset deployment activities.
8. Monitoring, reevaluation, and modification of policy and strategy.

FOUR FUNDAMENTAL ELEMENTS OF SUCCESSFUL INVESTING

Before proceeding with the discussion of investment planning as it relates to achieving funding objectives, it is necessary to review four principles fundamental to the investment process:

1. The level of risk assumed by a fund determines the level of return achieved (Figure 46–1).
2. Returns normally attributed to variable assets (common stock, long-duration bonds, and real estate) are assured only as the holding period is extended (Figure 46–2).

F I G U R E   46–1

Risk Versus Return

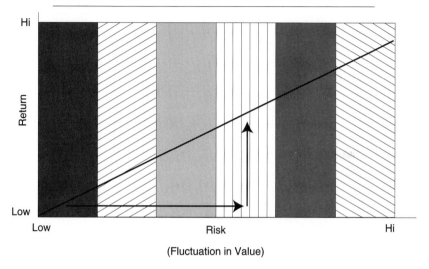

Level of Risk Assumed Determines Level of Return Achieved

(Fluctuation in Value)

3. The time permitted to lapse before converting an investment
   position to cash determines the level of return.
4. Market studies have confirmed the orderliness that exists
   between risk and reward in the financial markets (Figure 46–3).

ATTRIBUTES OF THE PRUDENT FIDUCIARY

Because successful investment programs are a product of human judgment, it is also important to consider briefly the attributes of a prudent
fiduciary. ERISA, Sec. 404(a)(1)(B), stipulates that a fiduciary shall discharge his or her duties with respect to a plan solely in the interest of the
participants and beneficiaries, and "with the care, skill, prudence, and
diligence under the circumstances then prevailing that a prudent man acting in a like capacity and familiar with such matters would use in the conduct of an enterprise of a like character and with like aims."

To qualify as prudent, in retrospect, fiduciaries of plans must have
conducted themselves as *prudent experts*, having set up an administrative
approach to facilitate the decision-making process, considered internal
factors of the fund, hired and listened to investment experts and qualified
legal counsel, obtained independent studies when advisable, considered

F I G U R E   46–2

Return Expectations Versus Realized Variable Assets
Stocks, Long Bonds, Real Estate

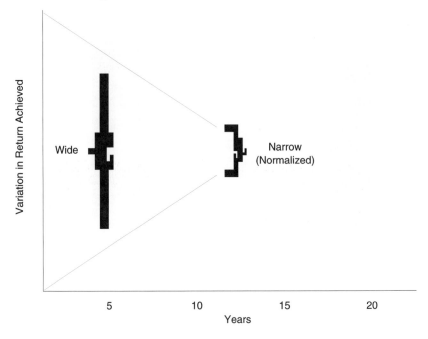

the financial variables of the prospective course of action, and set up an arm's-length mechanism to negotiate with any parties-in-interest. Such a documented sequence of activities probably should be sufficient to stand the test of prudence required by the law.

In any technically demanding investment course of action, there should be an effective blending of the judgment of those charged to be the overseers of a trust fund with the opinions of the experts who provide counsel and research in support of a defensible conclusion. If done properly, this team approach will most likely be judged sufficient to support a sound decision. There also should be a careful preservation of the lines of demarcation among cofiduciaries. Plans go afoul with the counsel of too few. Sufficient counsel increases the likelihood of success. This is not a carte blanche vote in favor of multimanagement investment systems, but recognition that, just as the diversification requirement calls for balance in assembling the components of the portfolio, prudence calls for balance and effectiveness in the selection of people and how they perform their varied assignments.

F I G U R E   46–3

Orderliness in Financial Markets
Types of Mutual Funds

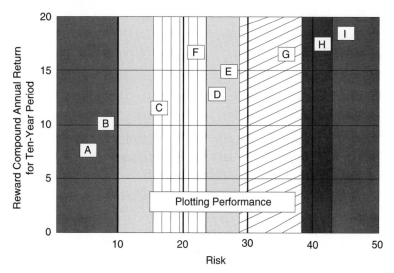

Maximum Fluctuation, in Percentage Points,
Between Best and Worst Quarters Over a Ten-Year Period

Categories of Funds

A. 91-Day U.S. Treasury Bills (Short-Term Instruments)
B. Money Market Funds (Short-Term Fixed-Income Pool)
C. Fixed-Income Funds (More than 75% in Fixed Income Assets)
D. Balanced Funds (Conserves Principal; Mix of Stocks and Bonds)
E. Growth and Income Funds (Stock Mix Aimed for Short and Long Term)
F. Equity Income Funds (Mostly Stocks with High Current Value)
G. Growth Funds (Stocks with Higher Growth than Market Average)
H. Capital Appreciation Funds (Diverse Means to Build Capital)
 I. Small Company Growth Funds

Source: Lipper Advisory Services, Inc., Milwaukee.

There is no substitute for the fiduciary's exercise of informed and reasoned judgment. The fiduciary must pursue each alternative until he or she gets to the heart of the matter, examining all the facts available prior to making the decision. In addition to exercising resourceful due diligence, there appears to be unanimous agreement among legal counselors on the necessity for the preparation of resourceful documentation on the part of all fiduciaries party to the process.

Put succinctly, the "prudent" fiduciary possesses the following characteristics:

1. Determination.
2. Knowledge that leads to insightful decisions.
3. Organization.
4. Open-mindedness.
5. Objectivity.
6. Realistic expectations.
7. Patience.

There are myriad investment vehicles available as funding vehicles—insured, noninsured; pooled separate accounts; aggregated pools of individual securities; privately placed and publicly traded. The characteristics of the investment medium chosen should be conducive to the attainment of the investment objectives sought. To recognize which vehicles are most appropriate, a fiduciary needs to understand the differing characteristics of the various classes of investments.

CHARACTERISTICS OF THE THREE FAVORED CLASSES OF INVESTMENTS

To understand why fiduciaries choose to blend equity and fixed-income securities in portfolios, the characteristics of common stock, fixed-income securities, and real estate are reviewed. Common stock is the preferred investment medium, with bonds, cash equivalents, and real estate vehicles following.

Common Stock

The characteristic that most attracts the employee benefit plan investor to common stock is its ability to add real value to a portfolio. According to the Vanguard Group, the Standard & Poor's 500 achieved +16.81 percent per year in return over the 10 years ending September 30, 1999. If, during this time, a plan manager was able to constructively exploit this class of investment, the fund was able to compete effectively with, and substantially outdistance, inflation's impact on portfolio values. Because one of the long-range goals for many employee benefit plans is to pay benefits in inflation-adjusted dollars, the choice of common stock as the preferred asset class has proven to be a productive funding facility.

The driving forces behind stock prices are *earnings*, *return on equity*, and the issuing firm's *dividend policy*. Increased earnings influence the company's board of directors to increase dividend payouts, which in turn influences stock analysts to pay a higher price for the shares. As demand for the shares increases, at some point the stock becomes fully valued, or overvalued, which should lead the investment manager to take the plan's profits and reinvest the proceeds in a stock that is still passing through the undervalued part of its pricing cycle. Such portfolio management should produce the historical 6 percent real return expected from common stock ownership. The astute manager picks up additional return from his or her superior information-processing ability.

The rewards of stock ownership, resulting from a combination of an increasing dividend stream and appreciation in the value of the shares, can be unlimited. These rewards accrue from investors' willingness to pay a higher multiple for the increased earnings and the ability of the firm to "manage its store" successfully. The increases in the price/earnings (p/e) multiple and dividend-payout stream flow in part from the firm's ability to capitalize on its research and development activity. This in turn fosters consumer acceptance of its products or services and eventually leads to increased sales. If costs are efficiently controlled, increasing sales should lead to growing earning power, profitable reinvestment opportunities for the earnings, and ultimately increased confidence shown by the investment community in the firm's ability to manage its affairs successfully in the future. Investors, reflecting their increased confidence in the future fortunes of the firm, will increase their activity in accumulating the stock, which in turn will bid up the price/earnings multiple. Thus, the p/e multiple becomes a measure of the attractiveness of a particular security versus all other available securities as determined by the investing public.

Even though common stock as a class has proven to be an attractive funding facility, plan sponsors need to identify stock managers who have developed and can apply superior selection techniques. Unless the manager can consistently buy stock with a present price at or below its intrinsic value, the sponsor may have to forsake active management and opt for dollar-cost averaging into a passively managed index fund. The sponsor in turn must exercise patience permitting the long-term investment trends to overcome the shorter-term cyclical influences in the determination of share value. Actively managing a portfolio of common stock can achieve superior results, but the results do not come automatically. It takes superior stock selection, or insightful market timing, or a combination of both, to outperform the passive "market" portfolio.

Charles Ellis of Greenwich Research Associates sums this up well when he says that the "keys to successful common-stock management are: (1) adopt a policy (style) and apply it consistently; (2) strive for excellence in a few areas; (3) concentrate on when to sell; and (4) maintain modest expectations."

Many plan sponsors have adopted passive stock management (a style of management that seeks to obtain average, risk-adjusted performance), because the net returns achieved from active management have not compared favorably to the net returns achieved by index funds. To justify its use, the return from active management must exceed the return from a comparable market index plus a recoupment return for the higher relative transaction costs. Plan sponsors are also adopting passive strategies to implement asset redeployment moves, to complement their existing active managers, and as a temporary parking place for equity-destined monies while undertaking a management search.

Common stock has evolved over time to become the favored investment medium of the funds because it offers the possibility of providing the most attractive real rate of return. However, before that possibility becomes a reality, a plan sponsor has two options. The sponsor can find a manager who can recognize change early, select those stocks whose emerging positive attributes will be discovered by other analysts, and pay attention to the price paid for stocks as a class, and for his or her stocks in particular. Or, in the absence of finding such a manager, the sponsor can participate in a passively supervised stock portfolio for that portion of the total portfolio dedicated to long-term common stock ownership.

Fixed-Income Securities

Fixed-income securities have traditionally been the bellwether asset in employee benefit plan portfolios. However, the turbulence created in interest rates several years ago by unanticipated and volatile inflation rates has shaken confidence in the traditionally passive approach to bond management. Because of the resultant concern for volatility, bond managers have developed a number of strategies and products to more effectively compete with the challenging environment.

There are many alternatives to choose from in the fixed-income area. Within the money market area alone, one can choose from a broad spectrum of securities. The advent of money market deposit accounts and short-term investment fund (STIF) accounts offered by banks in the deregulation environment has increased both the options and relative yields for monies limited to short-term maturities. For a plan willing to embrace a higher degree of credit risk, Eurodollar CDs, corporate master notes, and repurchase agreements are available. Consumer Auto Receivables (CARS), Certificates of Accrual on Treasury Securities (CATS), and Treasury Investment Growth Receipts (TIGRS) are examples of the many fixed-income products available in the bond markets.

With the proliferation of products has come an increase in the number of ways of increasing wealth in a portfolio through the use of fixed-income securities. Whether a plan's supervising fiduciaries accomplish their goals through a high- or low-turnover approach, there is no substitute for the adoption of and adherence to a reasoned, disciplined strategy. To the degree possible, a plan should exploit its longer-term planning horizon and forsake the extreme comfort of money market instruments by extending the duration of its fixed-income portfolio. Here again there are a number of alternatives and strategies—active/active, passive/active, passive/passive. You can make active bets on interest-rate movements while also engaging in sector swaps, etc.; you can forgo (or limit) your interest-rate anticipation moves while still actively trading the portfolio with arbitrage moves; or you can immunize or dedicate the portfolio and forgo shorter-term upside potential (or limit downside risk) through a wholly passive approach. These strategies can be implemented using governments, corporates, and utilities or the more recent market entrants—mortgage-backed securities and derivative instruments. Another recent entrant is the "accounts receivable-backed bond," which securitizes credit card and automobile purchases.

Why would a fiduciary include bonds as a part of a plan's funding mechanism? First, the plan (the lender) has a preferred claim on the income and assets of the issuer (the borrower). The lender has a contractual right to the return of stated principal and a contractual right to receive the periodic stated interest payments. From this right springs a plan's expectation of receiving and cultivating an income stream. It is the periodic reinvestment of this income stream that permits a plan to exploit the principle of the "power of compounding interest." In just 20 years, $100 growing at 7 percent (i.e., 4 percent inflation + 3 percent "rent" for loaning money) results in an accumulation of $386. The tax-exempt status of the plan increases all the more the efficacy of compounding interest.

The success of a bond investment depends on whether the financial accumulation from ownership compares favorably with the original expectations at purchase. If a plan's objective is to produce a real rate of return, the income stream from the bond should exceed the loss caused by inflation in the purchasing power of the principal. Unfortunately, this is only one of the risks faced in bond investment. Others are credit (default) risk (if the issuer goes bankrupt), interest-rate risk (if bonds must be sold below the price paid), call risk (if the issuer calls in the bond in a lower interest-rate environment), and reinvestment risk (if comparable, credit-worthy bonds are paying a lower rate of interest when principal or coupons are being reinvested).

Bond risk can be controlled. In addition to the use of interest-rate futures (not in the scope of this discussion), there are many portfolio management techniques that can provide comfort to the plan sponsor. Inflation risk can be reduced by buying bonds only when the real spread (interest rates minus probable inflation) is at a historical premium. Correctly assessing when a premium spread is available takes a combination of astute historical perspective, forecasting ability, and luck! The phenomenon of lagging return premiums probably exists because bond buyers, having previously erred in their forecasting of inflation's rise, demand high rates long after inflation has subsided in intensity. Credit risk can be controlled through the exercise of superior credit analysis and adequate quality-threshold guidelines. Interest-rate risk can be reduced by keeping maturities short, dollar-cost-averaging purchases, and adopting the various immunization and dedication strategies.

Partitioning out the retired lives and purchasing bonds dedicated to meet these benefit payments as they fall due has become a popular planning technique. This strategy can be attractive when interest rates are relatively high and as benefit payments begin to exceed contributions in a mature fund. In some cases, the potential this technique offers for with-drawal-liabilities reduction (or elimination) to the multiemployer plans has been sufficient to justify the trustees' implementing such a risk-reduction strategy. Single-sponsor plans also have chosen such techniques to control the fluctuation in plan surplus, or the rate at which contributions are required. To manage call risk, one must simply "read the fine print." Reinvestment risk can be eliminated by purchasing zero-coupon bonds or laddering the bond maturities.

Real Estate

A third and less popular funding facility is the fee ownership of real properties. The class of equity real estate is added to a portfolio within the context of a pension plan's objectives (a) to exploit its long-term time horizon, (b) to defend against the possibility that higher inflationary periods may reappear (repeat of the 1976–81 environment), (c) to add a third asset class that offers the potential to produce real rates of return in all price environments, and (d) because of its noncovariance characteristics when combined with stocks and bonds in a portfolio.

Like common stock, equity real estate has the potential to add significant real value over time. Its hybrid nature as both financial (leases) and tangible (bricks and mortar) enables its owner to hedge effectively against either low or high inflation. Overage rents, net net leases, expense-escalation clauses, equity-equivalent loans, and so on, all result in the investor being assured that his or her principal will stay competitive with inflation. The hybrid nature of convertible participating mortgages enables the pension fund sponsor to hedge against an unknown future.

Successful real estate investing requires attention to *location, product*, and *management*. Therefore, a fund must retain a real estate manager with a resourceful research staff. Because real estate is a relatively inefficient market, a real estate management organization should, by processing information in an effective manner, ultimately acquire those properties whose configurations of attributes will ensure relatively high demand. Building on a firm base of research capability, the manager(s) must have developed a strategic approach compatible with the plan and have demonstrated the ability to acquire properties astutely through analytical talent and negotiating skills. An underrated resource of a manager is his or her property (asset) management capability, whether developed in-house or successfully retained and monitored. It also is important to determine that the principals of the firm have formed a team that enjoys industry peer-group respect. It takes time and effort to develop marketing packages for complex properties. Those management teams who (a) have attracted a sufficient client base to provide continuing cash-flow availability, (b) have available the diverse disciplines to evaluate a deal effectively, and (c) can quickly respond to the offer to capitalize on a market opportunity will be afforded priority in being shown the more desirable properties.

Other caveats that must be considered are that: (1) the properties acquired must be well-conceived, well-located, and well-managed; (2) the sponsor must be willing to undergo "income only" years in anticipation of the slower-emerging capital-appreciation years; (3) the manager must purchase the properties using the current effective rents as the basis for determining value; (4) a plan just beginning to invest in real estate may be well-advised to dollar-cost-average into the market over several years; and (5) if a plan is going into open-ended funds that use net-asset valuations supported by yearly appraisals of the portfolio properties, due diligence should be performed by the plan sponsor to ensure that the net-asset valuation used reflects the realities of the current marketplace. One would not want to place new dollars indirectly into real estate assets at inflated valuations resulting from a lagging recognition of deteriorating portfolio values.

Asset Allocation

Although collectively the classes of domestic common stock, bonds, and equity real estate represent the preponderance of allocations in employee benefit plan portfolios, other vehicles used in the funding process include foreign securities, guaranteed investment contracts, mortgages, venture capital, timber, and oil and gas investments. To protect a fund's future valuations from being overly vulnerable to the fortunes of any one class, supervising fiduciaries construct diversified portfolios. An employee benefit plan portfolio's value is the sum of its component parts. If the plan is to reach its ultimate performance objectives, these component parts must, each in its own way, make a contribution to the whole fund. No class of assets exists in isolation. Such an orderly blending of related units is not happenstance but must be carefully orchestrated to produce a harmonious conclusion. Thus, a cardinal rule in plan investing is "diversify, diversify, diversify."

Someone, or some group, usually serves in the role of "investment coordinator" for a plan. The following list describes the coordinator's duties and responsibilities:

1. Lead the plan's professional team in the identification of the investment and noninvestment constraints of the plan and the subsequent development of the appropriate portfolio performance objectives, policies, and strategies.

2. Continually examine and evaluate all acceptable investment alternatives, and recognize and value the strengths that each team member can bring to the task.

3. Watch for early warning signs of weaknesses evidenced by people, policies, or practices of the program, and foster the reasonable expectations of investment performance, recognizing the inherent limitations in the investment management process.

4. Recognize the importance of establishing an appropriate risk posture for the fund predicated on a thorough examination of the risk/reward tradeoffs.

5. Set targets in ranges, rather than in absolutes.

6. Recognize and be responsive to change, and be knowledgeable about techniques on the cutting edge of contemporary investment management.

7. Respect the opinions of gray-haired peers, realizing that to ignore the past may cause the fund to repeat it.

8. Foster a spirit of meaningful review, evaluation, and modification of previous policy decisions.

Because numerous studies have confirmed that the single most significant decision in terms of its potential to add value to the portfolio is the asset allocation decision, it is important that the plan's portfolio be effectively supervised in the aggregate. Because one is always dealing with an uncertain future, portfolios must be broadly diversified and, thus, hedged against the possibilities of higher inflation, continuing stable inflation, or the onset of deflation. Having diversified the bulk of the portfolio's assets, strategic moves with a smaller portion of the assets can be made from cycle to cycle in the quest to achieve rates of return above the rates of return the longer-term policy portfolio produces. Any strategic moves made will be the result of an assessment of changes in the general prices within the economy, the profits of the companies in which assets are invested, and, ultimately, the valuation of the asset classes themselves, both now and projected into the future. All this activity is for the purpose of tilting the portfolio toward investment success. Producing real gains in value is the ultimate goal of asset management, since such gains will be used to replace the lost wages of the deserving retirees and to pay benefits to the beneficiaries of the plans.

The extent of permitted flexibility in asset allocation and asset shifting depends on the volatility constraint that logically evolves from the investment objectives and goals adopted by the benefit plan's representatives. Before a discussion can proceed to conclusion on what would appear to be the "best" allocation of the assets, a constraints analysis must be performed from time to time. Such analysis coordinates the portfolio-building activities of the investment manager with the objectives and goals as perceived and articulated by the plan sponsor.

The place to begin in the asset allocation process is with the plan sponsor representative(s). As previously mentioned, this could be the investment coordinator. An ideal plan sponsor representative:

1. Has researched and properly analyzed the demographics of the plan.

2. Can speak for the intentions of the principals of the contributing source as to their attitudes toward funding and risk-taking policies.

3. Understands the risk/reward dimensions of the investment markets.

4. Has thorough knowledge, insight, and experience, and is emotionally capable of handling investment fluctuations without abandoning the adopted long-term policy.

Asset allocation decisions are policy and strategy decisions that are separate and distinct from objective setting. Objective setting has to do with the sponsor targeting a desired result or range of results. The characteristics of the plan are the driving force in objective setting. Policy and strategy are implementation phases, which evolve logically in the quest to attain the objectives. Thus, the ideal fiduciary sets out initially to articulate, as succinctly as possible, the appropriate objectives for the investment program and then adopts the appropriate policy and strategy methodology.

IDENTIFICATION OF APPROPRIATE INVESTMENT OBJECTIVES

Setting portfolio guidelines should not be confused with *setting investment objectives*. Guidelines are adopted to facilitate the attainment of the objectives and, thus, form the building blocks of policy and strategy. Not only do some fiduciaries confuse objectives with guidelines, but they adopt guidelines that impede the attainment of their stated objectives!

Investment objective setting by employee benefit plan representatives is a delicate balancing act. The supervising fiduciaries find their loyalties pulled in different directions because of the natural tendencies that exist among the economic players in the process. These understandable tendencies create tensions among fiduciaries when adopting policy. The contributing sponsor wants to pay the highest level of benefits for the least cost. The participant wants the assurance that the pension promise will be fulfilled at an acceptable cost-of-living standard. The regulators want "prudent management," resulting in principal protection and growth in assets to ensure that private plans in the aggregate will fulfill the socially redeeming goal of providing financial security during retirement. The plans' fiduciaries themselves often have their own agendas; in addition to embracing worthy and constructive goals, they often desire personal fulfillment and respect from their peer group, reelection to office, promotion in a job, and so on. Because it is impossible to satisfy all these conflicting aspirations and influences simultaneously, investment objective setting in many instances becomes a process of negotiation and compromise. The goals of the various constituencies are weighted according to importance and, in the process, policy and strategy evolve. To the extent that the process can remain professionally objective, the probability increases that the objectives ultimately adopted will be the most appropriate given the long-term needs of the plan. Investment objectives should be set in tandem with the overall funding policy of the plan. Conservative funding—that is, accelerated reduction in the unfunded liabilities—can be accompanied by an aggressive investment posture. Conversely, a sponsor who chooses to fund the liabilities as minimally as possible out of current resources may be obligated to the participants to manage those fewer accumulated assets in a conservative manner. However, sponsors' attitudes toward risk may very well reverse these relationships. In any event, an important principle to apply in objective setting is funding coordination.

What are some of the specific elements in objective setting? Foremost, the objectives adopted should be in conformance with the plan's documents and with the fiduciary standards of ERISA and related regulations. Also, an objective fundamental to all plans is that cash be available to make benefit payments in a timely manner. No investment course of action is complete until cash has been returned to the fund. To facilitate the setting of this objective, the consulting actuary should develop a financial profile of the fund that projects the immediate, short-term, and long-term cash-flow requirements. In such an analysis, the present value of assets, investment return expectations, anticipated contributions, and liabilities are considered, and the fiscal integrity of the sponsoring entity is projected.

After the cash-flow needs are identified and targeted, the planning process turns to risk/reward considerations. To what degree can the fund sustain volatility in values in the quest for higher returns? How important is it to the sponsors that the future flow of contributions be stabilized and controlled? Is there a limit on the level of contributions that can be expected? Must principal value be preserved or enhanced? Does it seem wise, in the case of a plan with a relatively young workforce, to place added importance on seeking growth in value in real terms? Conversely, in the case of a mature plan, should the manager seek cash flow from income-producing investments to augment dwindling contributions? How willing is the control group to exercise patience and accept short-term disappointment as a "contrarian investor" in the search for long-term positive results? The answers to these questions become the portfolio constraints. The aggregation of constraints influences policy and strategy decisions, including asset allocation. Portfolio guidelines, beta, quality, diversification, and so on, also emanate from the constraints analysis.

Part and parcel with establishing the investment-return objectives is the selection of the performance measurement period and the comparative benchmarks to be used in the monitoring process. The performance objectives can be set in nominal terms, or real terms, and several performance objectives can be adopted for the same fund. For instance, it may be deemed appropriate to compare the *aggregate* portfolio on a *real* basis—that is, compare the total return to a cost-of-living index—while comparing *segments* of the fund to referenced benchmarks on a nominal basis—that is, comparing the growth-stock component to an index of growth-stock portfolios, and the bond component to the Lehman Brothers Government/Corporate Bond Index. A set of performance objectives, both nominal and real, spanning differing time frames, may be more insightful to the stewards of the fund than relying on a single measurement statistic.

Very few sponsors still express their performance objectives using a single absolute number. Since most fiduciaries are aware that the investment-earnings assumption used by the actuary for planning purposes is an inappropriate performance target (it should follow, not lead, the investment experience), any other single absolute number chosen is even more of an arbitrary target. An 8 percent absolute target return would seem reasonable and attainable in a disinflationary environment; it may be less meaningful and attainable in higher-inflation periods. More funds seem to be favoring the adoption of relative return objectives—returns relative to the consumer price index (CPI), returns relative to chosen referenced benchmarks, and the like. The acceptance of relative return objectives recognizes the inherent economic, financial, and market limitations that exist in the management of institutional portfolios.

Producing a real rate of return can be a formidable, and rewarding, task for an employee benefit plan. There is obviously no single way to accomplish this quest, but careful attention to detail and skillful consideration of many alternatives just may add sufficient basis points to a fund's bottom line to enable it to compete effectively with the problem of purchasing-power erosion. Certainly, with a modicum of success from the management process, real value may very well be added to the plan's portfolio if the responsible fiduciaries:

- Assume responsibility for allocating the portfolio's assets in the aggregate.
- Develop a resourceful information system resulting in group conviction on which direction the general prices in the nation are heading.
- Understand historically the attractiveness of various investment media in different price environments.
- Consistently diversify a majority of the portfolio to hedge

against the occurrence of general price-level extremes in either direction.

■ Preserve flexibility in the management of a minority of the portfolio to exploit the evolving price-environment scenario.

The following objectives, excerpted from a plan's statement of investment policy, exemplify the use of relative *and* real rate-of-return objectives:

> The long-term investment objective of the Trust is to produce a total rate of return of three percent (3 percent) in excess of the rate of inflation as measured by the Department of Labor, Bureau of Labor Statistics Consumer Price Index, All Cities Average, 1992 = 100. Since the duration, direction, and intensity of inflation cycles vary from cycle to cycle, it is recognized that the return experienced by the Trust over any one cycle may vary from this objective; but it is deemed reasonable to expect a three percent (3 percent) real rate of return over succeeding cycles. A complementary investment objective of the Trust is that the total rate of return achieved by the Trust competes favorably, when compared over comparable periods, to other trust funds having similar objectives and constraints and using similar investment media.

Other examples of portfolio performance objectives, stated or implied, include the following:

1. To achieve the rate of return of a published index, including income, plus x percent.
2. To achieve the rate of return of a special benchmark index reflecting a chosen risk/reward preference.
3. To achieve performance comparability to other accounts having similar objectives.
4. To achieve a minimum of x percent.
5. To preserve portfolio value sufficient to eliminate the potential for withdrawal liability (Taft-Hartley funds).
6. To achieve total return sufficient to stabilize contributions at x percent of payroll.
7. To maintain a specified level of plan surplus.

Performance objectives expressed in risk-adjusted returns are preferred. Returns expressed in risk-adjusted terms are the most precise in objective setting, because they take into account volatility as well as return. Unfortunately, risk-adjusted return analysis has not been broadly practiced, and, thus, statistics are not readily available for comparative purposes.

It has been said that the application of portfolio management operations is both an art and a science. Engineering the portfolio to attain the stated objectives would seem to be more scientific in nature, particularly since the advent of computer technology to assist in modeling and portfolio-control activities. The fact-finding and related analysis so vital to the objective-setting process also requires resourceful analytical activities. The "artful" part of the process would seem, in the present environment, to be at the plan sponsor level. The supervising fiduciaries must examine the facts, balance what appear to be opposing agendas of the various constituencies, fend off any potentially inhibiting subjective influences, objectively adopt the most appropriate set of investment objectives, and carefully articulate them to the managers of the assets. Choosing appropriate objectives points the manager of the assets in the proper direction in the quest to assist in fulfilling the benefit payment promise.

EVALUATION AND SELECTION OF THE INVESTMENT FACILITY

Having identified appropriate investment objectives, the supervising group can next turn to evaluating and selecting the investment facility. If the sponsor decides to invest passively, then an organization is sought that can administratively replicate the return of the chosen benchmark portfolios. If, however, the sponsor chooses value-added management, the structure of the organization is not nearly as important as is its demonstrated ability to add value to the portfolio. Success in investment decision-making is indifferent to the structure of the organization as well as to its size and location. Whether the firm is organized as a bank, insurance company, mutual fund organization, or independent counsel firm, the keys to success are its people and program. To the degree any one of these four organizational classes becomes more successful in attracting, compensating, and motivating the best and brightest professionals, this group as a class should eventually produce superior performance.

To be successful, an investment management firm should possess certain characteristics. It should have an approach to investing that has proven successful in the past. It should consistently apply that approach and articulate it clearly. The firm should have highly intelligent, insightful, well-trained, experienced people and motivate them with performance incentives. It should cultivate an environment conducive to creativity and innovation. It should target investment management activities that will attain the client's objectives and goals. It should have resourceful, quantitative support systems. It should maintain high internal quality-control systems in the delivery of investment services and communicate effectively with the client's representatives.

Funding the benefit payment promise through asset-enhancement activities requires systematic planning and execution. Having identified the objectives and with the manager in place, the supervising fiduciaries, together with a consultant, can address themselves collectively to finalizing an investment policy statement.

DEVELOPMENT AND DOCUMENTATION OF INVESTMENT POLICY

To produce a cohesive, well-organized, investment policy statement, fiduciaries of an employee benefit plan, assisted by the plan's legal counsel, actuary, administrator, investment manager, and other consultants (as deemed appropriate) must identify, debate, and define the relevant issues and identify the investment objectives that will complement and augment the overall funding process.

The policy development process includes the identification and analysis of various internal compelling forces:

- Characteristics of the plan's sponsors that produce a certain attitude toward risk taking.
- Trends within the sponsors' industries.
- The current funding level of the plan's obligations.
- The cash-flow projection from a financial profile analysis.

Thus, the sponsors' attitude toward risk, the industry and company trends, the plan's status (underfunding, full funding, or overfunding), and the prospective cash-flow needs all impact investment policy choices because they impact funding requirements. Funding policies necessarily influence investment policies, because the return from investments over the life of the plan plays such an important part in the benefit payment delivery process.

After examining the internal plan factors and other noninvestment criteria embraced by the group, one can move next to the external factors, an examination of the capital markets themselves. Risk and reward trade-offs are considered. Will the fiduciaries be satisfied with achieving the markets' rates of return, or do they want to attempt to achieve returns, with the accompanying volatility, above the markets' returns? This decision has an impact on the investment management structure that is adopted. The range of choices includes:

1. Using only accounts that replicate the markets' returns (*passive* approach).
2. Using accounts that replicate the return of a chosen referenced (benchmark) portfolio (*passive-plus* approach).
3. Using accounts that are supervised within the discretion of the investment management organization (*active* approach).
4. Using a weighted combination of the above (*passive-active* approach).

As mentioned previously, a supervising group's *attitude* toward risk will affect the degree of flexibility in policy. Is the group willing to achieve slower growth in value in exchange for less volatile returns, or does it seek faster growth in value accompanied by higher volatility? The former would constrain the system to include, at the riskiest level, balanced growth and income stocks and real estate vehicles; the latter would permit moving out further on the risk spectrum and include the use of growth and capital-appreciation stocks and small-company growth stocks.

How much management risk is the group willing to embrace? The answer to this question indicates how much of the portfolio can be deployed to value-adding active managers. Fiduciaries desiring to eliminate investment management risk completely must content themselves with the markets' rates of return and suffer the accompanying short-term volatility. The group in reality trades off investment-manager vulnerability for market vulnerability; it accepts prices set by the masses in lieu of a value assessment by a professional.

Part and parcel of finalizing the investment policy statement is an articulation of the investment performance objectives, as previously reviewed. Choices of objectives are influenced by the somewhat conflicting goals of preserving principal value, producing current income, enhancing principal value, preserving purchasing power, producing capital gains, and enhancing purchasing power. To the degree one emphasizes the performance objective of value enhancement over value preservation, one must be willing to move out on the risk/reward spectrum. The wider the range of alternatives granted the investment managers, the less control the supervising group maintains over portfolio values. Objectives to preserve and enhance principal value, produce current income, and preserve purchasing power would most probably encourage the use of money market accounts, fixed-income accounts, equity-income accounts, and real estate accounts. Performance objectives to enhance purchasing power and produce capital gains would most probably encourage the use of real estate accounts, balanced (stocks and bonds) accounts, growth and income accounts, growth-stock accounts, capital-appreciation accounts, small-company growth-stock accounts, and even venture capital.

Once the objectives are articulated, a decision must be made whether to adopt a *fixed* asset mix, a *flexible* posture, or some *combination* of both. A fixed posture is constrained to accept the long-term risk/reward tradeoffs in the markets. A flexible posture assumes that a management system can periodically exploit the occasional undervaluations that exist and do it consistently enough to add value over and above what a passive fixed policy would have achieved. Because of the difficulty in correctly and consistently timing the markets, many funds prefer a combination of the two approaches. An example would be the decision to allocate 80 percent of the assets to be fully invested at all times, weighted among the classes in accordance with long-term historical returns and attendant volatility, and then to grant discretion to an investment manager to strategically redeploy the remaining 20 percent of the fund based on an assessment of the short-term cyclical pricing outlook.

If the supervising group has the confidence in its manager to grant the use of either a flexible policy or a fixed/flexible posture, it needs to adopt procedures that can be accomplished in a timely enough fashion to opportunistically exploit market turns. In most cases, boards and committees function poorly with such time constraints. This is the reason that the majority of funds embracing such a market approach use an in-house coordinator, an investment consultant, and/or an investment manager(s), or some combination of these professionals. Timely market awareness to capitalize on market turns is generally only available through a full-time information-gathering and analysis process. Thus, supervising fiduciaries who attempt cyclical redeployment activities must realize they are competing with highly trained professionals who work full-time in their search for value. And, for all their effort and expertise, the record reveals that a majority of the professionals attempting to fortuitously time the markets fail to add value to the portfolios. Part-time fiduciaries, to be successful in this highly competitive game, must either be unusually prescient or lucky, or both.

Prior to implementing any strategic portfolio moves permitted within the plan's overall policy constraints, a methodology must be adopted to assess the levels of investment risk. Financial (business) risk, market (interest rate) risk, inflation (purchasing power) risk, political (confiscation) risk, and social-change risk should be evaluated. Within the context of such an analysis, an assessment is next made about whether a class or subclass of investments is undervalued, fully valued, or overvalued. If sufficient belief in the evaluation system exists, the supervising group may comfortably grant full discretion to the professional(s) to implement such periodic asset shifts. The degree to which discretion is granted is influenced by the willingness of the group to embrace timing risk, the group's confidence in the manager to whom full discretion is delegated, and the previous experience of the fiduciaries in asset-shift activities.

Needless to say, those boards or committees who have seen portfolio values squandered due to poor timing decisions generally are inclined to constrain such activities in the future. Also, it is better to learn from observation or through published studies than from disappointing first-hand experience.

Even when an employee benefit fund permits strategic asset-mix shifts, it generally permits only a small shift at any one time. Portfolio repositioning phased in over time profits from the *principle of time diversification*. Significant asset shifts implemented all at once place at risk the long-term value enhancement objective of most funds. Contrariness is wonderful when it's right, but the opportunity costs (or real losses) can be very expensive if proven wrong.

Both the approach to policy adoption and the approach to strategy implementation should be systematic. A step-by-step "seek and search" mission should coalesce into both policy decisions, which enable the fund to attain its long-term investment objective, and strategic decisions that add value over time, above what the policy alone would have achieved. Resourceful documentation accumulated during the dialogue when policy and strategy constraints were considered can be very helpful when finalizing the investment policy statement.

In investing, the way one approaches the process is just as important as the choice of the particular vehicles. Thus, the policy statement becomes the necessary road map to successful funding. The absence of a cohesive written statement results in an investment context composed of a loose aggregation of ideas, which usually results in a fuzzy understanding of the objectives. The investment manager may be seeking objectives incompatible with the needs of the plan, or the investment vehicles selected for the plan may be inappropriate, given its needs. If a policy is not in writing, it cannot be mutually understood, and the absence of understanding between the supervising groups and professionals is the most significant cause of poor investment results.

The investment policy statement becomes the overall "game plan" from which all substrategies and implementation of those strategies evolve. Investment decisions will then be in concert with the needs of the plan, and the group's stewardship role will have been fulfilled as the "management of risk" directives have been effectively articulated. Cohesive investment policy fosters good understanding among all participants in the process. Lines of demarcation are carefully drawn, permitting appropriate accountability and adjustments in the review, reevaluation, and modification process. Diverse areas—the requirements of ERISA, fiduciary liability, acceptable performance, diversification, the discretion delegated to managers, and any attitudes toward social investing—need to be addressed. Without the development of policy and its subsequent reduction to a written statement, the plan, like a ship without a rudder, may flounder in a dynamic economic environment.

Such an empirical process is an ongoing effort. The policy and evolving strategies of the plan must respond to its dynamic political, social, and economic environment. The policy statement for the plan in the aggregate then becomes the stepping stone for the individual policy statements for the particular investment manager.

Reducing a plan's investment policy to a written statement provides legal protection, improves communication, and supplies instructions to investment managers. The statement prepared for the fund in the aggregate generally includes at least the following elements:

1. Background information on the fund.
2. Identification of fiduciaries.
3. Organizational structure.
4. Cash-flow requirements.
5. Lines of authority and delegation.
6. Diversification of the portfolio.
7. Active/passive strategies.
8. Definition of assets.
9. Performance objectives.
10. Guidelines.
11. Brokerage.
12. Voting of proxies.
13. Trusteeship/custodianship.

The statement related to each investment manager would include background information; future fund and cash-flow projection; investment objectives; policies related to the voting of proxies; portfolio guidelines; reporting requirements; and review, evaluation, and modification methods.

Monitoring, reevaluation, and modification of the investment funding process is an unending task because of the dynamic spheres of influence affecting policy selection. Characteristics of the plan sponsor change, plan demographics change, markets change, and investing facilities change. Thus an ongoing ability to effectively monitor and modify, if necessary, is important to long-term success. Independent performance measurement services assist in objective evaluation. Plan liability studies assist in achieving objective-setting precision. Analysis of expected rates of return helps in portfolio-tilting activities. The exercise of patience on the part of the plan fiduciaries is important to ensure that counterproductive changes do not unnecessarily squander portfolio values.

Quality control in management procedures is important to attain maximum productiveness from the accumulated assets. In summary, the ultimate result of this procedural quest for successful funding techniques through successful stewardship of accumulated assets is to adopt an appropriate long-term investment policy, and, if one is so inclined, to periodically implement successful investment strategy moves permitted within the overall policy constraints.

The investment funding process begins with those fiduciaries charged with the stewardship responsibility. Determined to ask the right questions and resourcefully armed with knowledge of basic investment principles, the fiduciaries can add significant value to a plan's portfolio. With such determination, knowledge, and insight, the supervising fiduciaries need to examine the internal factors to adopt investment objectives appropriate to the plan's requirements. They must next examine the long-term historical risk/reward characteristics of the various investment classes. Then, with the objectives in mind, and with an awareness of which classes and subclasses of securities can best facilitate the attainment of those objectives, they can next turn to the selection of the funding vehicles. The most appropriate investment-management structure is identified, evaluated, and selected. Part and parcel with the adoption of these policy decisions is the asset-mix policy decision—whether it will over time be fixed, flexible, or a combination of both.

If an element of flexibility is permitted in the asset-mix policy, then an additional set of procedures must be adopted that provides the context within which strategy moves are implemented. It is in the strategy area that most groups supervising employee benefit plans choose to retain either an in-house coordinator or an independent investment consultant, and/or to engage investment manager(s). And finally, the process of monitoring, reevaluation, and modification must be accomplished with thoroughness and insight.

PART NINE

Employee Benefit Plan Issues

The final part of the *Handbook* is devoted to issues of special interest in employee benefit planning and begins with Chapter 47 on the topic of employee plans compliance resolution systems (EPCRSs). Chapter 48 discusses welfare benefits for retirees, a topic that will continue to have major implications for employers as long as health care cost increases continue to escalate and there is no relief from government programs such as Medicare.

Chapter 49 compares the major components and issues relating to multiemployer plans as contrasted with single employer plans. Chapter 50 examines the characteristics, magnitude, and differences involved in pension plans for public employees.

In an increasingly global economy, international employee benefit planning assumes a much greater role in corporate planning. This topic is explored in Chapter 51.

The final chapter in the *Handbook*, Chapter 52, takes a visionary look at the future of employee benefits.

The Employee Plans Compliance Resolution System for Qualified Plans

C. Frederick Reish

Bruce L. Ashton

Nicholas J. White

INTRODUCTION

In establishing broad-based retirement programs for employees, employers design and operate these programs as qualified plans in order to obtain favorable tax treatment under the Internal Revenue Code (the "Code"). This favorable treatment includes: current deductibility of the contributions to the plan by the employer[1]; deferral of the income tax on the earnings on the plan assets[2]; and no current taxation to the employees of the contributions to the plan made on their behalf, as well as the ability to further defer taxation by rolling over the benefits to another qualified plan or an individual retirement account.[3] In order to obtain these benefits, the plan must meet *each* of the requirements of Code Section 401(a).[4]

If a qualified plan violates any of the qualification rules in Code Section 401(a), it becomes subject to disqualification by the Internal Revenue Service (IRS). Plan disqualification results in the immediate loss of the tax advantages noted above. More specifically, plan disqualification results in the following:

---

1 Code Section 404.

2 Code Section 501(a).

3 Code Sections 401(a), 402(b) and 402(d).

4 Qualified plans include defined benefit plans, money purchase pension plans, profit-sharing plans, Section 401(k) plans and stock bonus plans, including employee stock ownership plans. A discussion of the dozens of specific qualification rules is beyond the scope of this chapter.

The employer loses its deduction for contributions to the plan during the open tax years under the statute of limitations to the extent the contribution is not vested for the plan participants.[5] In the case of a defined benefit plan, plan disqualification results in a total loss of the deduction (other than for a one-person plan).[6]

- For tax years still open under the applicable statute of limitations,[7] the employee recognizes as income the *vested* portion of his or her account.[8]
- For tax years still open under the applicable statute of limitations, the plan's related trust recognizes any earnings as income for income tax purposes.[9]
- Distributions become ineligible for special tax treatment and cannot be rolled over on a tax-deferred basis (e.g., any amounts rolled over to an IRA or another qualified plan would not be excluded from income by reason of the rollover).[10]

Thus, maintaining the qualified status of a plan has substantial benefits for the plan sponsor and the participants in the plan. This requires diligent efforts in properly administering the plan and in making certain that the plan document meets current legal requirements. Inevitably, however, mistakes happen, in part because of the complexity of the qualification rules. This chapter discusses how to bring a plan back into compliance with the qualification requirements once a disqualifying defect has occurred.

In an effort to mitigate the harsh effects of plan disqualification, in 1990 the IRS introduced the first of a series of administrative programs that allowed sponsors of qualified plans with disqualifying defects to *retroactively* fix those defects and, thus, to maintain the plan's qualified status. Each of these remedial correction programs had different eligibility requirements, addressed different types of violations, and required various methods of correction. This chapter describes the programs in detail and explains when and how they can (or should) be used.

In 1998, the IRS issued Revenue Procedure (Rev. Proc.) 98-22, 1998-12 IRB 11, which modified, restated, and consolidated its remedial correc-

---

5 Code Section 404(a)(5).
6 Treas. Reg. 1.404(a)-12(b).
7 Code Section 6501.
8 Code Section 402(b).
9 Code Section 501(a).
10 Code Section 402(d).

tion programs for plan qualification defects into a single, comprehensive system called the Employee Plans Compliance Resolution System (EPCRS). The programs included in EPCRS are the Administrative Policy regarding Self-Correction (APRSC), the Voluntary Compliance Resolution (VCR) program (including the Standardized VCR Procedure [SVP]), the Walk-in Closing Agreement Program (Walk-in CAP), the Audit Closing Agreement Program (Audit CAP), and the Tax Sheltered Annuity Voluntary Correction (TVC) program.[11] The Rev. Proc. established the specific eligibility requirements for each program, set forth general correction principles, and described the operation of each program in detail, including the application procedures for these programs which can only be used with IRS supervision.

In 1999, Rev. Proc. 99-31, 1999-34 IRB 280 supplemented EPCRS with additional guidance on corrections that the IRS will accept for specified types of defects, in effect creating "safe-harbor" corrections for those types of violations. In January of 2000, the IRS issued Rev. Proc. 2000-16, 2000-6 IRB 10, which updated EPCRS to include the correction guidance from Rev. Proc. 99-31, and provide certain clarifications and minor modifications to the various remedial programs.

In the remainder of this chapter, we will describe what constitutes a qualification defect and how to correct those defects under each of the remedial programs for a qualified plan.

TYPES OF DISQUALIFYING PLAN DEFECTS

EPCRS uses specific terminology to describe various types of violations of the qualified plan rules. These are generically referred to as "Qualification Failures."[12] There are five categories of such failures, as follows:

1. **Plan Document Failures.** A "Plan Document Failure" exists if a plan provision violates the requirements of Section 401(a) *or* if a Qualification Failure does not fall within one of the other categories.[13] Plan Document Failures may be corrected retroactively only under one of the CAP programs, either Audit CAP if the IRS discovers the failure on audit or Walk-in CAP if the plan sponsor seeks to self-correct the defect.

---

11 Because this chapter focuses on qualified retirement plans, we have not addressed tax sheltered annuities under Code Section 403(b) or the Tax Sheltered Annuity Voluntary Correction program, the remedial program for such arrangements.

12 Rev. Proc. 2000-16, Section 5.01(2).

13 Rev. Proc. 2000-16, Section 5.01(2)(a).

2. **Operational Failure.** An "Operational Failure" is a failure to follow the terms of the plan document. This is true even if the plan operation would have been permitted under the qualified plan rules had the document been written in conformance of such operation.[14]

3. **Demographic Failure.** A "Demographic Failure" is a failure to satisfy the nondiscrimination testing requirements of Code Section 401(a)(4), the coverage requirements under Code Section 410(b), or the minimum participation requirements of Code Section 401(a)(26), that requires a substantive amendment to the plan document to correct.[15] Like Plan Document Failures, Demographic Failures may only be corrected under one of the CAP programs.

4. **Egregious Operational Failures.** The IRS has not specifically defined what it considers to be an "egregious operational failure;" however, it does offer guidance by way of the following two examples: "If an employer has consistently and improperly covered only highly compensated employees, or if a contribution to a defined contribution plan for a highly compensated individual is several times greater than the dollar limit set forth in Code Section 415, the failure would be considered egregious." Egregious operational failures are *not* eligible for correction under APRSC or VCR. They are, however, eligible for correction under Walk-in CAP.[16]

5. **Diversion or Misuse of Plan Assets.** A diversion or misuse of plan assets is a violation of the rule in Code Section 401(a) that plan assets must be held for the exclusive benefit of plan participants and their beneficiaries. The IRS will determine that there has been a violation of the "exclusive benefit rule" only in cases where there has been a *substantial* diversion or misuse of plan assets (the general rule of thumb is that 70 percent or more of the plan's assets must be involved). None of the EPCRS programs may be used to correct failures relating to the diversion or misuse of plan assets.[17]

---

14 Rev. Proc. 2000-16, Section 5.01(2)(b).
15 Rev. Proc. 2000-16, Section 5.01(2)(c).
16 Rev. Proc. 2000-16, Section 4.07.
17 Rev. Proc. 2000-16, Section 4.08.

EVENTS NOT ELIGIBLE FOR CORRECTION UNDER EPCRS

EPCRS is only available for correction of *Qualification Failures*. It is not available to correct violations for which the Code provides tax consequences other than those associated with plan disqualification (such as excise or penalty taxes). For example, funding deficiencies, prohibited transactions, and failures to timely file IRS Form 5500 cannot be corrected under EPCRS.

In some situations it may be difficult to determine whether the defect is a Qualification Failure or another type of violation, for which there is only a tax or penalty ramification. For example, a failure to meet the minimum funding requirements in a defined benefit or money purchase plan could be viewed as an Operational Failure, based on failing to follow the plan's terms regarding contributions to the plan (pension plans routinely require, by their terms, that contributions be made to the plan). However, in published interviews, IRS officials have indicated that, in general, such violations are not viewed as Qualification Failures, but rather non-disqualifying events for which a tax or penalty is imposed.[18]

If a violation is a Qualification Failure and it *also* produces a tax or penalty consequence, then EPCRS can be used to correct the failure; however, the tax or penalty must still be paid. For example, if a plan violated its terms limiting the outstanding balance on participant loans to $50,000, the Operational Failure (e.g., the failure to follow the plan's terms) could be corrected under EPCRS; however, the income tax resulting from exceeding the limit under Code Section 72(p) must be paid.

There is an exception to this rule. The IRS takes the position that the failure of a plan to make a required minimum distribution under Code Section 401(a)(9) is an Operational Failure. In addition, the participant is subject to a 50 percent excise tax on the amount of the missed distribution under Code Section 4974. In Rev. Proc. 2000-16, the IRS indicates that it will waive the Section 4974 excise tax in "appropriate cases."[19] The situations where the excise tax will be waived are not described, but generally the tax will be waived if the distribution is to a nonhighly compensated employee[20]; if a distribution is to a highly compensated employee, the tax will generally be waived if the employee did not cause the failure.

Finally, EPCRS is not binding on the Department of Labor or plan participants or their beneficiaries, whose benefits are protected under

---

18 See interview with senior IRS EP Division officials, CCH *Pension Plan Guide* (July 1993).

19 Rev. Proc. 20000-16, Section 6.04(3).

20 For a definition of "highly compensated employee," see Code Section 414(q).

Title I of the Employee Retirement Income Security Act of 1974 (ERISA). Therefore, although a Qualification Failure may be resolved under EPCRS, it will not necessarily protect the plan sponsor or the plan fiduciaries from related liability under Title I of ERISA.[21]

THE REMEDIAL CORRECTION PROGRAMS

The Administrative Policy Regarding Self-Correction (APRSC)

APRSC is a voluntary correction program for resolving "significant" and "insignificant" Operational Failures that are *not* "egregious." It does not require any disclosure or payment of fees to the IRS. In this respect, it is a true "self-correction" program. Because of the lack of IRS oversight of the correction, as a condition of eligibility for the program APRSC requires that, at the time the Operational Failure occurred, the plan had in place practices and procedures reasonably designed to prevent the failure. Such practices and procedures must have been routinely followed, but through oversight, a mistake in application, or perhaps an inadequacy in the procedures themselves, the Operational Failure occurred.[22]

What is an Insignificant Operational Failure?
Whether a violation is "insignificant" is determined based on all the facts and circumstances of the particular case. In Section 8.02 of Rev. Proc. 2000-16, the IRS lists seven *non*-exclusive factors to be considered in making this determination. They are: (1) whether other failures occurred, (2) the percentage of assets/contributions involved, (3) the number of years the violation occurred, (4) the number of participants affected relative to the total number of participants in the plan, (5) the number of participants affected by the failure relative to the number that could have been affected, (6) whether correction was made within a reasonable time of discovery, and (7) the reason for the failure.

Why does it matter whether an Operational Failure is significant or insignificant? The relevance of
this question is that (1) a significant failure must be corrected by the end of the second plan year following the plan year in which it occurred;

---

21 Rev. Proc. 2000-16, Section 6.06. Note, however, that if correction is made under one of the IRS remedial programs, there may be little incentive on the part of the DOL or participants to pursue any claim against the plan sponsor or other plan fiduciaries.

22 Rev. Proc. 2000-16, Sections 4.04.

(2) the plan cannot be under audit by the IRS at the time correction is made; and (3) the plan must have a current favorable determination letter ruling or its equivalent.[23] In contrast, insignificant Operational Failures can be corrected anytime, even if the plan is under audit, and there is no requirement that the plan have a favorable letter ruling.[24]

What happens if a significant Operational Failure is not corrected in a timely manner? If a significant Operational Failure is not corrected within the two-year correction period, then the failure is not eligible for self-correction under APRSC. The failure could be voluntarily submitted for resolution under either VCR or Walk-in CAP, by making a formal application and paying a fee. Alternatively, if the IRS audited the plan before the failure was voluntarily submitted under VCR or Walk-in CAP, the failure could be resolved under Audit CAP, at a significantly higher cost, as discussed later in this chapter. This highlights the importance of conducting internal audits and self-correcting any identified Operational Failures as quickly as possible.

The Voluntary Compliance Resolution (VCR) Program and Standardized VCR Procedure (SVP)

VCR is a voluntary program similar to APRSC for resolving Operational Failures. The primary differences between VCR and APRSC are that VCR involves (1) disclosure of the failure to the IRS through the filing of a formal application with the IRS in Washington, D.C., (2) the payment of a fixed "Compliance Fee" based on the size of the plan,[25] and (3) formal IRS approval of the method of correction through the issuance of a Compliance Statement that describes the terms of correction. VCR does not distinguish between significant and insignificant Operational Failures, and there is no limit on the time in which the plan sponsor has to correct the failure.[26] As previously noted, Plan Document and Demographic Failures cannot be resolved through VCR or SVP.

---

23 Rev. Proc. 2000-16, Sections 4.03, 4.05, and 9.01.
24 Rev. Proc. 2000-16, Section 8.
25 The Compliance Fee is $500 for a plan with less than $500,000 in plan assets and no more than 1,000 participants; $1,250 for plans with more than $500,000 in assets but no more than 1,000 participants; $5,000 for a plan with between 1,000 and 10,000 participants; and $10,000 for a plan with 10,000 participants or more.
26 Rev. Proc. 2000-16, Section 10.

In order to be eligible for VCR, the plan cannot be under audit and it must have a current favorable determination letter or its equivalent.[27] Although the IRS may evaluate and discuss with the plan sponsor the appropriateness of the plan's existing administrative procedures, there is no requirement under VCR, as there is under APRSC, that the plan have "practices and procedures" reasonably designed to avoid the Operational Failure that occurred.[28]

SVP is a subset of VCR that provides for expedited processing (120 days) and a limited filing fee (currently $350). The Operational Failures eligible for SVP are the 11 identified in Appendices A and B of Rev. Proc. 2000-16 (see discussion of these failures below, under "Correction of Plan Qualification Failures"). The plan sponsor may not submit more than two SVP failures in a single application.[29]

What factors should the plan sponsor consider in choosing between VCR and APRSC? Because VCR and APRSC are both programs for resolving Operational Failures, plan sponsors and their advisers need to be aware of the key factors to consider in choosing the appropriate program. These key factors include, but are not necessarily limited to, the following:

1. **Reliance.** This is arguably the most important factor. Under VCR, the plan sponsor will receive a "compliance statement." The compliance statement provides the plan sponsor with a "guarantee" that if the Operational Failure is corrected as described in the VCR application, the IRS will not disqualify the plan based on that failure. This is to be contrasted with APRSC, where there is no disclosure to the IRS and, thus, no document ensuring that the method of correction will be acceptable to the IRS. This means the IRS could subsequently audit the plan and, if it disagrees with how the Operational Failure was corrected, propose to disqualify the plan. (As a practical matter, prior to proposing plan disqualification, the IRS would almost certainly offer to resolve the failure under Audit CAP. In addition, if the defect is one of those listed in Appendix A or B of Rev. Proc. 2000-16 and is corrected as specified in the Appendices, the IRS will not seek disqualification.)

---

27 Rev. Proc. 2000-16, Sections 4.03 and 4.04.
28 Rev. Proc. 2000-16, Section 10.06.
29 Rev. Proc. 2000-16, Section 10.11 and Appendices A and B.

Accordingly, the prudent approach is to generally limit APRSC correction to routine Operational Failures that can be corrected using one of the "safe-harbor" methods described in Appendices A or B of Rev. Proc. 2000-16. (These "safe-harbor" methods are discussed later in this chapter in the Correction of Plan Qualification Failures section). If the violation is unique or the plan sponsor uses a "creative" method of correction, then the safest approach would be to submit the failure for resolution under VCR.

2. **Cost.** There is no IRS fee under APRSC. Under VCR, there is a fixed fee; however, it is generally not significant when compared to the cost of plan disqualification. The actual cost of correcting the Operational Failure under VCR or APRSC should be the same. Of course, because of the application process, plan sponsors are likely to use professional advisers more extensively when resolving a failure under VCR, thus making VCR somewhat more expensive overall. And, if a "creative" method of correction is being used, the prudent approach is for the plan sponsor to consult with retirement plan professionals and correct the failure under VCR (see discussion under No. 1, above).

3. **Expiration of the Two-Year Self-Correction Period.** If the two-year self-correction period under APRSC for a significant Operational Failure has expired, the plan sponsor must correct under VCR, unless the Operational Failure is insignificant under all the facts and circumstances of the case. Because it is often difficult to know with any great degree of certainty what the IRS will consider *insignificant*, if the plan sponsor has any doubt in this regard, the prudent approach is to submit the failure under VCR.

The Walk-in Closing Agreement Program (Walk-in CAP)

Walk-in CAP is a voluntary program operated in much the same way as VCR, except the fee is usually significantly higher and the application is filed with a Closing Agreement Coordinator in the local IRS area office. Under Walk-in CAP, a plan sponsor can correct Plan Document Failures (in fact, this is the only program under which such failures can be resolved), Operational Failures, Demographic Failures, and egregious failures. If, however, a Qualification Failure is eligible for correction under APRSC or VCR, it cannot be corrected under Walk-in CAP, unless the plan also has a Plan Document Failure or Demographic Failure.[30] The only eligibility requirement for Walk-in CAP is that the plan must not be under audit at the time the application is filed.[31] The plan is not required to have a current favorable determination letter.

As part of resolving the failure under Walk-in CAP, the IRS and the plan sponsor will have to agree on the appropriate method(s) of correction and a "compliance correction fee" to be paid to the IRS. The compliance correction fee can be negotiated within a range based on the number of participants in the plan. The fee range indicates a "minimum fee" (which corresponds to the fee that would be paid under VCR), a "presumptive amount" (which is the fee the IRS expects to impose and, therefore, constitutes the starting point for negotiation), and a "maximum fee."[32] In cases involving "egregious" failures, the fee is substantially increased.[33]

Once an agreement is reached, the plan sponsor and the IRS will sign a closing agreement, concurrently with payment of the compliance correction fee. The closing agreement describes the failure(s) and approved method(s) of correction, and states that the IRS will not disqualify the plan based on those failures. If an agreement cannot be reached, the IRS may refer the case to examination, where the failure can be resolved under Audit CAP, where the correction fees (called "sanctions") are greater.

"John Doe" Submissions. Some IRS area offices permit the submission of "John Doe" or anonymous Walk-in CAP applications. A plan sponsor may want to take this approach if it is concerned about the acceptability of a contemplated method of correction and/or the compliance correction fee, and wants to "test the waters" in this regard on an anonymous basis.

The "John Doe" application is filed based on "sanitized" documentation. That is, all of the relevant information and documentation are provided; however, the identity of the plan sponsor and the participants is withheld. On this basis, the IRS will discuss with the plan sponsor's representative the appropriateness of the proposed method(s) of correction and give some indication of what might be expected in terms of a compli-

---

30 Rev. Proc. 2000-16, Sections 4.01 and 11.
31 Rev. Proc. 2000-16, Section 4.03.
32 Rev. Proc. 2000-16, Section 13.05. The maximum fee ranges from $4,000 for plans with 10 or fewer participants to $70,000 with plans of more than 1,000 participants. The "presumptive amount" in each case is one-half of the maximum.
33 Rev. Proc. 2000-16, Section 13.05(3).

ance correction fee. If the plan sponsor finds the tentative terms of the agreement unacceptable, it may withdraw the application without disclosing its identity. Otherwise, a complete, or "unsanitized," application package is filed and the Walk-in CAP process goes forward on the usual basis.

"Reformation" Walk-in CAP. In appropriate circumstances, a plan sponsor may be able to use Walk-in CAP to correct an apparent operational failure by adopting a plan amendment that modifies the plan's terms to conform to its prior operation. This type of correction is permitted by the IRS only if the amendment does not cause the plan to violate one of the qualified plan rules—particularly those having to do with discrimination, coverage, and the prohibition against reducing an accrued benefit.[34] This method of correction is sometimes referred to as "reformation CAP," because the plan document is being "reformed" after the fact to comply with the way the plan was operated.

A plan sponsor is most likely to be successful in securing this method of correction if it can establish to the satisfaction of the IRS that its intent was to have the plan operate in one manner, but the document was erroneously prepared to indicate a different operation. For example, assume a profit-sharing plan allocated employer contributions to participant accounts in proportion to compensation (e.g., on a "comp-to-comp" basis), which is what the plan sponsor intended in establishing the plan. However, the retirement plan professional who prepared the plan document provided that employer contributions were to be allocated on an integrated basis. In this case, the plan sponsor would likely be successful if it proposed correcting the Operational Failure (e.g., failure to operate the plan in accordance with its allocation formula) by adopting a retroactive amendment to the plan, conforming its terms to its operation. The fact that the "comp-to-comp" formula is more generous to rank-and-file employees than the integrated formula would make the IRS even more likely to accept the corrective amendment.

Audit Closing Agreement Program (Audit CAP)

Audit CAP becomes available when a *significant* Qualification Failure is discovered during the course of an IRS examination of the plan. (If the Qualification Failure were *insignificant*, Audit CAP would be unnecessary, because the failure could be corrected under APRSC.) To resolve the failure under Audit CAP, the plan sponsor must agree to (1) correct the

---

34 Rev. Proc. 2000-16, Section 4.06(2).

failure for all years in which it occurred, (2) enter into a written closing agreement with the IRS, and (3) pay a monetary "sanction."[35]

The amount of the sanction under Audit CAP is negotiated based on the total tax liability that could be imposed if the plan were disqualified. Thus, the Audit CAP sanction is potentially much more expensive than the "compliance correction fee" under Walk-in CAP, which is negotiated based on a limited range of fees designed to "reward" the plan sponsor for having *voluntarily* disclosed the failure to the IRS. In negotiating the sanction, the IRS will take into account the nature, extent, and severity of the Qualification Failure to ensure that the sanction is not excessive based on all the facts and circumstances of the case.[36]

With the exception of the sanction, Audit CAP operates in the same manner as Walk-in CAP.

CORRECTION OF PLAN QUALIFICATION FAILURES

For purposes of EPCRS, correction is the process of retroactively bringing a plan back into compliance with the qualification requirements of the Code. Once correction is complete, the plan is no longer subject to disqualification for the years in which the qualification failure existed.

Rev. Proc. 2000-16 describes "general principles and rules of general applicability" for correcting qualification failures under EPCRS.[37] The Rev. Proc. also describes specific "safe-harbor" methods for correcting certain types of Operational Failures. These safe-harbors consist of the SVP-mandated forms of correction, and appear in Appendix A and Appendix B of Rev. Proc. 2000-16.

In distilling the correction guidance under EPCRS, three *fundamental* principles emerge. The first is that plan documents must comply with the requirements of the law as to form. Accordingly, the correction for a Plan Document Failure is to amend the plan document to comply with the applicable legal requirements. The second principle is that correction of an Operational Failure should put the plan and its participants back in the position they would have been in had the failure not occurred; however, certain exceptions to this principle are found in the SVP-mandated forms of correction. A third fundamental principle is that correction must be made for all relevant plan years and affected participants; this is true even

---

35 Rev. Proc. 2000-16, Section 14.01.
36 Rev. Proc. 2000-16, Section 15.01.
37 Rev. Proc. 2000-16, Section 6.01.

if the correction is inconvenient or burdensome, or the year of the failure is otherwise closed by the statute of limitations.[38]

The following section discusses the general principles of correction under EPCRS, the SVP-mandated forms of correction and the use of plan amendments to correct Plan Document and Demographic Failures.

General Correction Principles

In Section 6 of Rev. Proc. 2000-16, the IRS lists 15 "general" correction principles to be followed under EPCRS. They are as follows:

1. The correction method should restore the plan to the position it would have been in had the qualification failure not occurred, including restoration of current and former participants and beneficiaries to the benefits they would have had if the Qualification Failure had not occurred.[39] Essentially, this means to put the plan back to where it would have been if it had been administered correctly.

2. The correction should be reasonable and appropriate for the qualification failure. Taken alone, this is not very helpful guidance. However, the IRS then goes on to explain that "there may be more than one reasonable and appropriate correction for the failure." This statement is very helpful, particularly when contemplating a correction method which does not fall within one of the safe harbors specified in the Appendices to Rev. Proc. 2000-16.[40]

3. Any correction method permitted under Appendix A or Appendix B of Rev. Proc. 2000-16 (e.g., one of the "safe-harbor" correction methods, which are discussed in the next section) will be *deemed* to be a reasonable and appropriate method of correcting the related Qualification Failure under any of the other correction programs.[41] Although this principle applies to VCR, Walk-in CAP, and Audit CAP, it is most helpful in the case of APRSC, which is an unsupervised remedial correction program. This is because it allows plan sponsors to self-correct with the confidence that, in the event of a plan

---

38 FN: Rev. Proc. 2000-16, Sections 6.02 (opening paragraph) and 6.02(6).
39 Rev. Proc. 2000-16, Section 6.02(1).
40 Rev. Proc. 2000-16, Section 6.02(2).
41 Rev. Proc. 2000-16, Section 6.02(2).

audit, the IRS will accept the correction as reasonable, appropriate, and complete. Therefore, the IRS will not seek to disqualify the plan as a result of the failure.

4. The correction method should, to the extent possible, resemble
one already provided for in the Code, Regulations, or other
guidance of general applicability, relevant to the Qualification
Failure being corrected.[42]

5. The correction for failures of the nondiscrimination rules
should provide additional benefits to nonhighly compensated
employees (NHCEs), as opposed to reducing benefits for highly compensated employees (HCEs).[43]

The IRS provides two examples to explain this principle.
The first describes a situation where, under the qualified plan
rules, the discrimination failure can be corrected by either (1)
amending the plan to cover more employees, or (2) taking
advantage of certain aggregation and/or restructuring rules to
pass very technical numerical tests. (This is commonly referred to as "cross-testing," and it is used to determine whether
a plan is discriminatory in favor of HCEs). In this example,
the IRS indicates that the plan amendment form of correction
should be used, because it is the "typical" means of correcting
discrimination-type failures.

The second example describes a Section 401(k) plan that
fails the actual deferral percentage (ADP) or actual contribution
percentage (ACP) tests. (These are discrimination tests that
measure the disparity in amounts deferred or contributed on
behalf of the HCEs, as compared to the NHCEs.) Under the
Code, correction could be made by distributing excess amounts
made by the HCEs. However, the IRS states in this example
that correcting "solely by distributing excess amounts to highly
compensated employees would not be the typical means of correcting such a failure." Therefore, under EPCRS, the plan sponsor would generally be required to correct this failure by using
the alternative form of correction, which is to make qualified
nonelective contributions (QNECs) or qualified matching contributions (QMACs) to the NHCEs.

6. The correction method should keep plan assets in the plan,
except to the extent the Code, Regulations, or other guidance

---

42 Rev. Proc. 2000-16, Section 6.02(2)(a).
43 Rev. Proc. 2000-16, Section 6.02(2)(b).

of general applicability provides for correction by distribution to participants or beneficiaries, or the return of assets to the plan sponsor.[44] The IRS notes that, for example, if an excess allocation (not in excess of the benefit limitations under Code Section 415) was made for a participant under a profit-sharing plan, the excess should be reallocated to other participants or used to reduce future employer contributions, rather than being returned to the employer.

7. The correction method should not violate another qualification rule, such as the nondiscrimination rules under Code Section 401(a)(4) or the anti-cutback rules under Code Section 411(d)(6).[45] For example, if a plan sponsor were to attempt to correct an operational failure by retroactively amending the plan to conform its terms to its prior operation, such correction would not generally be acceptable to the IRS if the amendment resulted in a reduction of benefits, and particularly if the affected participants consisted of rank-and-file employees.

8. Where more than one correction method and/or earnings calculation is available to correct a particular type of Operational Failure, the correction method and/or earnings calculation should be applied consistently in correcting all Operational Failures of that type. This is referred to in Rev. Proc. 2000-16 as the "Consistency Requirement."[46]

9. In distributing "excess amounts," the plan sponsor is required to notify the affected participant that the amount was not eligible for the favorable tax treatment accorded to distributions from qualified plans, such as eligibility for a tax-free rollover under Code Section 402(c).[47] An "excess amount" is an amount in excess of the plan's and/or Code limits. Such contributions include, for example, contributions in excess of the Code Section 415 limit, or deferral contributions that exceed the Code Section 402(g) limits (e.g., $10,500 for 2000), or deferral and matching contributions that exceed the ADP and ACP tests, respectively.

10. Corrective allocations under a defined contribution plan should be based upon the terms of the plan and other applica-

---

44 Rev. Proc. 2000-16, Section 6.02(2)(c).
45 Rev. Proc. 2000-16, Section 6.02(2)(d).
46 Rev. Proc. 2000-16, Section 6.02(3).
47 Rev. Proc. 2000-16, Section 6.02(4).

ble information at the time the Qualification Failure occurred (including the compensation that would have been used under the plan for the period for which a corrective allocation is being made).[48] This relates to general principle No. 1, and it means that the correction should be made as if the plan had been properly administered for the year in which the failure occurred.

11. Corrective allocations, as well as corrective distributions, should be adjusted for earnings and forfeitures that would have been allocated to the participant's account if the failure had not occurred. For administrative convenience and in lieu of determining the exact rate of return on each investment in a participant's account, the IRS permits a plan that allows participants to self-direct the investments in their accounts to use the highest rate earned by any one of the available investment options to calculate the earnings adjustment; however, this "rule" of administrative convenience is only available if most of the employees receiving the corrective allocations are nonhighly compensated, as determined under Code Section 414(q).[49]

12. Corrective allocations may be adjusted for losses. This principle is derived by implication from Section 6.02(5)(a) of Rev. Proc. 2000-16, where it states that "corrective allocation(s) need not be adjusted for losses."

13. A corrective allocation made for a prior year will not be considered an annual addition for the year in which the correction is made; rather, the corrective allocation will be considered an annual addition for the year to which the corrective allocation relates. This means that, for purposes of the annual maximum limit under Code Section 415(c) on allocations to a participant's account, the limit applies the year in which the allocation should have been made, as opposed to the year in which the corrective allocation was actually made. However, the deductibility of the contribution under Code Section 404 is determined based on the plan sponsor's tax year in which the contribution is actually made, not the tax year in which the failure occurred. The IRS has not provided any guidance on whether the deductibility of corrective earnings is to be deter-

---

48 Rev. Proc. 2000-16, Section 6.02(5)(a).
49 Rev. Proc. 2000-16, Section 6.02(5)(a).

mined under Code Section 162 (as an ordinary business expense) or Code Section 404.[50]

14. Corrective allocations under a defined contribution plan should come only from employer contributions, including forfeitures, if the plan permits their use to reduce employer contributions.[51] However, there are certain exceptions to this principle, which allow for correction through "re-administration" of the plan.

15. For a defined benefit plan, a corrective distribution for an individual should be increased to take into account the delayed payment, consistent with the plan's actuarial adjustments.[52]

Exceptions to Full Correction

As indicated in the discussion of the *fundamental* principles of correction in the previous section, the IRS requires that correction be made for all relevant plan years and for all affected participants. This is commonly referred to as the "full correction" requirement. Section 6.02(6) of Rev. Proc. 2000-16 lists three exceptions to this requirement.

1. Reasonable Estimates. The first exception relates to the use of reasonable estimates in calculating the appropriate correction. In Section 6.02(6)(a) of Rev. Proc. 2000-16, the IRS describes this exception as follows: "If it is not possible to make a precise calculation, or the probable difference between the approximate and the precise restoration of a participant's benefits is insignificant and the administrative cost of determining the precise restoration would significantly exceed the probable difference, reasonable estimates may be used in calculating appropriate correction."

The IRS applies the "reasonable estimates" exception literally; therefore, it is difficult to meet the standard. For this reason, it is generally inadvisable to use reasonable estimates for purposes of self-correction under APRSC. Rather, if the plan sponsor is unable to make precise calculations or the cost and administrative burden of performing such calculations would be excessive, the plan sponsor should correct under one of the

---

50 Rev. Proc. 2000-16, Section 6.02(5)(b).

51 Rev. Procurther claim. 2000-16, Section 6.02(5)(c).

52 Rev. Proc. 2000-16, Section 6.02(5)(d).

IRS-supervised programs, such as VCR, SVP, or Walk-in CAP, as appropriate.

2. **Small Benefits.** The second exception to the "full correction" requirement has to do with the "delivery of very small benefits." Under Section 6.02(6)(b) of Rev. Proc. 2000-16, if the total corrective distribution due a participant or beneficiary is $20 or less, and the cost of delivering the distribution would exceed the amount of the distribution, the plan has the option of not making the distribution.

3. **Locating Lost Participants.** The final exception deals with locating "lost" participants. The general rule is that "reasonable" action must be taken to locate all current and former participants and beneficiaries to whom additional benefits are due. However, even if lost participants are not found, the plan will be considered to have met the "full correction" requirement if it uses the IRS Letter Forwarding Program (under Rev. Proc. 94-22, 1994-1 CB 608) or the Social Security Administration Reporting Service to locate them. The only caveat is that additional benefits must be provided to these participants if they are later located.[53]

Safe-Harbor Corrections

Appendices A and B of Rev. Proc. 2000-16 identify 10 common Operational Failures and list mandated forms of correction for each. All of the identified failures are eligible for correction under SVP. In addition, with the exception of two correction methods that require a plan amendment and, thus, the use of Walk-in CAP, all of the mandated forms of correction are acceptable under SVP. Furthermore, in the opening paragraph of Section 6.02(2) of Rev. Proc. 2000-16, the IRS states that "(a)ny correction method permitted in Appendix A or Appendix B is deemed to be a reasonable and appropriate method of correcting the related Qualification Failure."

Thus, the guidance in Appendices A and B of Rev. Proc. 2000-16 creates "safe-harbor" correction methods under *all* of the remedial correction programs. The greatest impact of the guidance, other than for SVP, has been on unsupervised correction under APRSC. This is because the safe harbors allow a plan sponsor to self-correct using the prescribed methods

---

53 Rev. Proc. 2000-16, Section 6.02(6)(c).

and rest assured that, in the event of a plan audit, the IRS will accept the correction as reasonable, appropriate, and complete under EPCRS.[54]

The following is a list of the Operational Failures identified in Appendices A and B of Rev. Proc. 2000-16, along with a brief discussion of the prescribed (e.g., "safe-harbor") methods of correction. In the case of a defined contribution plan, any corrective allocations or distributions must be adjusted for earnings. Corrective distributions for a defined benefit plan must be adjusted consistent with the plan's actuarial assumptions regarding delayed payments. (See previous discussion of the general correction principles.)

1. **Failure to provide top-heavy minimum benefits under Code Section 416.** The correction method differs depending on the type of plan. In a defined contribution plan, the plan sponsor must contribute and allocate the required top-heavy minimums to the plan's non-key employees in the manner provided for in the plan. In a defined benefit plan, the minimum required benefit must be accrued in the manner provided in the plan.[55]

2. **Failure of a Section 401(k) or 401(m) plan to pass the ADP or ACP tests.** Under Appendix A, Section .03, and Appendix B, Section 2.01, of Rev. Proc. 2000-16, there are two methods of correction for this failure. The first is for the plan sponsor to make qualified non-elective contributions (QNECs) or qualified matching contributions (QMACs) to the accounts of the NHCEs in an amount sufficient to enable the plan to satisfy the tests. (QNECs and QMACs are employer contributions that are fully vested when made and subject to the same distribution restrictions as elective deferrals.) The contributions must be either the same flat dollar amount or the same percentage of compensation for all eligible NHCEs.

   The second method of correction is for the plan sponsor to use the "one-to-one" alternative. The one-to-one method has two steps. First, an excess contribution amount (adjusted for earnings through the date of correction) is determined for each

---

54 As previously discussed, IRS approval of the correction (either formally through one of the supervised programs or informally through a safe harbor) is not "binding" on plan participants or the DOL. However, as also discussed, from a practical standpoint, once correction is made in accordance with IRS guidelines, there may be little incentive to pursue a further claim.

55 Rev. Proc. 2000-16, Appendix A, Section .02.

HCE, and then either distributed to the highly compensated employees or forfeited from their accounts (depending on the source of the funds). And, second, an amount equal to the excess contribution amount is then contributed to the plan and allocated to the accounts of the NHCEs.

To properly evaluate how to correct ADP or ACP failure, plan sponsors and their advisers should be aware that there are alternatives to the "safe-harbor" use of QNECs or the one-to-one correction method. The first is to distribute the excess contributions to the HCEs only. It is likely this will be available, if at all, only where it can be clearly established that making the QNECs would impose a severe financial hardship on the plan sponsor (e.g., subject it to a risk of bankruptcy). In the authors' experience, the IRS is likely to require compelling evidence about the plan sponsor's financial hardship, such as tax returns and other documentation establishing its impaired financial status for the past several years. While the authors have had some success in this regard under Walk-in CAP for a plan incurring both ADP and plan document failures, the authors are not aware of any cases where the IRS has accepted distributions as the sole method of correction.

The second alternative under VCR to the safe-harbor correction methods is to use "bottom up" (or targeted) QNECs, as opposed to QNECs for all NHCEs. The "bottom up" QNEC is allocated to the lowest paid eligible employee up to his or her maximum Code Section 415 limit (currently, 25 percent of pay) in order to raise the overall ADP or ACP of the NHCEs. This process is repeated until the ADP or ACP test is passed. Although the QNECs paid may be relatively high as a percentage of compensation, the plan sponsor may actually have to pay less into the plan overall because the QNECs are made to the lowest paid employees. Under VCR, "bottom up" QNECs have been permitted even if the plan document does *not* provide for them.

Although the IRS has indicated that it is considering the appropriateness of using "bottom up" QNECs to self-correct under APRSC, it has *not* yet announced anything official in this regard. Therefore, it would *not* be prudent at this time for plan sponsors to use "bottom up" QNECs outside an IRS-supervised correction program (e.g., VCR, Walk-in CAP, or Audit CAP).

In deciding which of the two safe-harbor correction methods to use, the primary issue is whether the cost of the QNEC will be greater than the amount the plan sponsor will have to contribute under the one-to-one correction method. In analyzing those costs, plan sponsors also will have to factor in a less precise cost in terms of the ill will that may result if HCEs are required either to forfeit their benefits or receive taxable distributions that cannot be rolled over into an IRA or another qualified plan.

The costs of the safe-harbor corrections will then have to be compared to the alternatives available under VCR, where no contribution (based on financial hardship) or only a small contribution (based on "bottom up" QNECs) may be required. Unlike APRSC, the VCR program does require the payment of a compliance fee, and it may be considerably greater than the $350 fee required under SVP. In addition, there may be significant costs in preparing and processing the VCR application (as opposed to APRSC where there is no application, and SVP which may allow for a more simple application). However, depending on the facts of the particular case, these costs may be preferable to the monetary cost of across-the-board QNECs or the "cost" of impairing the employer-employee relationship, which could result if the correction required HCEs to either forfeit their benefits or receive taxable distributions.

3. **Failure to distribute elective deferrals in excess of the annual limit.** Code Section 402(g) imposes a limit on the maximum elective deferrals that an employee may make each year to a plan. (For 1999, the limit was $10,000; for 2000, the limit was $10,500). The Code also provides that any excess over that amount (plus earnings) may be returned to the employee by April 15th of the next year and is treated as taxable income in the deferral year, as opposed to the distribution year.

If an employee defers more than the maximum in a year and the excess deferral is not returned in a timely manner, the correction is to distribute the excess amount and report the excess as taxable in both the year of deferral (e.g., the calendar year in which the deferral was contributed to the plan) and the year of the corrective distribution. This means the employee receiving the corrective distribution is taxed twice on the corrective distribution amount. This safe-harbor correction also requires that the excess amount deferred by a highly compensated employee be included in the plan's ADP test for the deferral year; however, the excess amount for any nonhighly compensated employee is not.[56]

4. **Improper exclusion of eligible employees from all contributions or accruals.** The safe-harbor correction for this failure depends on the type of plan involved:

   a. **Defined Benefit Plan.** In the case of a defined benefit plan, the correction is to make the affected participant whole through an adjustment to his or her accrued benefit.[57]

   b. **Defined Contribution Plan.** In the case of a defined contribution plan, the basic correction is to provide a make-up allocation (adjusted for earnings) on behalf of each affected employee, equal to what the employee would have received if the employee had properly shared in the employer contribution.[58] Specific rules for Section 401(k), profit-sharing, and stock bonus plans are discussed below.

   c. **Section 401(k) Plan.** The correction here depends on whether a participant has been denied an opportunity to make elective deferrals to the plan for an entire plan year or for only part of the year.

      (i) **Full Plan-Year Exclusion.** In Appendix A of Rev. Proc. 2000-16, Section .05, the IRS describes the correction for exclusion of an eligible employee from contributions under a 401(k) plan for one or more full plan years. The correction is for the plan sponsor to make QNECs to the plan on behalf of the employee equal to the ADP of the employee's group (i.e., either highly or nonhighly compensated). If an eligible employee was excluded from sharing in matching contributions or from making employee after-tax contributions, the correction is for the plan sponsor to make a QNEC to the plan on behalf of the employee equal to the ACP for the employee's group. In either case, the corrective contribution must be adjusted for earnings. Because the corrective contribution is equal to the ADP and/or ACP of the eligible

---

56 Rev. Proc. 2000-16, Appendix A, Section .04.
57 Appendix A of Rev. Proc. 2000-16, Section .05.
58 Appendix A of Rev. Proc. 2000-16, Section .05.

employee's group, the contribution does not alter the ADP or ACP test results; therefore, using the safe-harbor correction for a full plan-year exclusion eliminates the need to rerun the tests.

(ii) **Partial Plan-Year Exclusion.** In Appendix B of Rev. Proc. 2000-16, Section 2.02(1), the IRS discusses how to correct *partial*-year exclusions of eligible employees from contributions under a 401(k) plan. In the authors' experience, it is more common for a 401(k) plan to improperly exclude eligible employees for a portion of the plan year than for the entire plan year. Therefore, this correction method is very useful, because it helps the plan sponsor address the more typical case.

The approved correction is for the plan sponsor to contribute an amount equal to the ADP and/or ACP for the employee's group (either highly or nonhighly compensated), multiplied by the employee's plan compensation for the portion of the year the employee was improperly excluded. The corrective contribution must be reduced to the extent it would cause a violation of the maximum deferral limitation under Code Section 402(g). Similarly, the corrective contributions must be reduced to the extent necessary to prevent the plan from exceeding any of its specified limits. Any corrective contribution must be adjusted for earnings.

(iii) **Brief Exclusion Exception.** The general rule under EPCRS is that a Qualification Failure is not corrected unless *full* correction is made with respect to all participants and beneficiaries, and for all taxable years, regardless of whether the tax year is closed under the statute of limitations. (See previous discussion of general correction principles.) Furthermore, the correction should restore the plan to the position it would have been in had the qualification failure not occurred. This includes restoring current and former participants, and their beneficiaries, to the benefits they would have had absent the failure.[59]

---

59 Appendix B of Rev. Proc. 2000-16, Section 2.02(1)(E).

However, under Rev. Proc. 2000-16, there is a special exemption to the general correction principles where there has been a "brief exclusion" of an eligible employee from making elective deferrals. The exception applies to any eligible employee who had the opportunity to make elective deferrals at the maximum level under the plan, not in excess of the Code Section 402(g) limit, for at least the last nine months of the plan year.

Plan sponsors will find the "brief exclusion" rule helpful, because it provides relief from having to make a contribution equal to the amount the excluded employee *could* have deferred absent the exclusion. Arguably, this takes into account the realities of plan operations. Thus, in Appendix B of Rev. Proc 2000-16, the IRS appears to be striking a balance between the interests of an excluded employee who is not substantially impaired by the exclusion, and a plan sponsor at a substantial risk of having to provide what might be viewed as a "windfall" to the excluded employee. The "brief exclusion" rule also indicates that the IRS is willing, at least to some extent, to recognize that the ability to make "catch-up" deferrals can be part of a safe-harbor correction.

d. **Profit-Sharing or Stock Bonus Plan.** Under Appendix A, Section .05, and Appendix B, Section 2.02(2)(a), of Rev. Proc. 2000-16, there are two safe-harbor corrections for the improper exclusion of an eligible employee from a profit-sharing or stock bonus plan. The first is the "contribution correction method" and the other is the "reallocation correction method." These alternatives are discussed separately below.

(i) **The Contribution Correction Method.** Under this correction method, the amount of the corrective contribution must be determined using the "same basis" of allocation as was used for all participants who received an allocation for that year, plus earnings. That is, the allocations to the excluded employees must equal what was given to the other employees as a percentage of their individual compensation under the plan's allocation formula. To the extent an amount was improperly allocated to the account of an eligible employee who

shared in the original allocation (because not all eligible employees were included), no reduction is made to the account of that employee. This means that once an allocation is made to a participant's account, even if it is improper, no correction is required if it would reduce the participant's account.

The correction principles under EPCRS generally require that any correction place the plan in the same position it would have been in had the failure not occurred. The contribution correction method is an exception to this principle, because it does not require correction of improper allocations if correcting them would have the effect of reducing a participant's account.

Although the contribution correction method may be costly because it requires an additional contribution to the plan, plan sponsors may find it helpful in cases where correction by "re-administration" (discussed in the next section) would create ill will among the plan participants or where the re-administration would be complex and/or expensive (e.g., there is high turnover, multiple investment options, etc.) Correction by re-administration requires a reallocation of the employer contribution in accordance with the plan's allocation formula, taking into account the previously excluded eligible employees. The "funding" of the excluded employee accounts necessarily requires a reduction in the accounts of the employees who shared in the original contribution. To the extent the participants become aware of the reduction, they may object to it and focus their dissatisfaction on the plan sponsor.

(ii) **The Reallocation Correction Method.** Under this correction alternative, the plan is "re-administered" to adjust the account balances of all participants, taking into account the excluded employees. In substance, this means that the employer contribution (plus earnings) is reallocated in accordance with the plan's allocation formula to all participants, including the excluded employees who were improperly excluded. As a result, the accounts of the excluded employees are increased (with earnings) by the amount they would have received had

they shared in the original allocation. At the same time, the accounts of the employees who shared in the original allocation are reduced by the "excess" amount they received due to the improper exclusion of eligible employees, adjusted for earnings. To the extent the aggregate of the reductions is less than the aggregate of the increases, the plan sponsor must contribute the difference. This could happen, for example, if distributions occurred prior to the date of correction or reductions were calculated using a lower earnings rate than the rate used to calculate the increases.[60] (The possibility of using a lower earnings rate for the reductions is specifically provided for in Appendix B, Section 2.02(2)(a)(iii)(C)(2), of Rev. Proc. 2000-16, if most of the employees for whom account balances are being reduced are NHCEs.)

Generally, under the "reallocation correction method," there is only the administrative cost of reallocating the employer contribution among the accounts of the plan participants. Therefore, this correction method provides plan sponsors with a low-cost option for complying with the general correction principle under EPCRS that the corrective contributions should restore the plan and its participants to the position they would have been in absent the improper exclusion. At the same time, it treats all employees fairly and consistently, which satisfies another general correction principle.

5. **Failure to pay timely minimum distributions required under Code Section 401(a)(9).** In a defined contribution plan, the correction is to recalculate the amount that should have been distributed for each year and distribute those amounts to the affected participant. In a defined benefit plan, the correction is the same; however, the distribution amount should be grossed up for earnings attributable to "the loss of use of such amounts."[61]

6. **Failure to obtain participant and/or spousal consent to a distribution subject to the joint and survivor annuity rules.**

---

60 Rev. Proc. 2000-16, Appendix B, Section 2.02(a)(iii).
61 Rev. Proc. 2000-16, Appendix A, Section .06.

The correction is to give each affected participant a choice between receiving a qualified joint and survivor annuity (QJSA) and providing an informed consent for the distribution previously received. To correct this failure under SVP, the plan sponsor must have contacted and received responses from each affected participant and relevant spouse *before* filing the SVP application; otherwise the failure would have to be corrected on a "non-safe-harbor" basis under APRSC, VCR, or Walk-in CAP.

If the participant's consent cannot be obtained, he or she must receive a QJSA, offset by any amounts previously received. This means if the participant already received a single-sum distribution equal to the actuarial equivalent of the QJSA, no further benefit should be paid to the participant. If the spouse's consent cannot be obtained, the correction is to provide the spouse with a survivor annuity which is unreduced by any amounts distributed to the participant.[62]

7. **Failure of defined benefit plan to satisfy the Code Section 415 (b) limit.** There are two alternatives for correcting a defined benefit plan that has paid benefits in excess of the Code Section 415(b) limit: the "Return of Overpayment Correction Method" and the "Adjustment of Future Payments Correction Method."

   a. **Return of Overpayment Correction Method.** Under this alternative, the plan sponsor (1) notifies the affected participant of the "overpayment," (2) requests that it be paid back with earnings (in effect, the participant receives a "bill" from the plan in the amount of the overpayment, plus earnings), and (3) takes "reasonable steps" to have the money returned to the plan. (According to conversations the authors have had with IRS officials, the requirement to take "reasonable steps" to have the money returned does not obligate the plan sponsor to engage in litigation.) To the extent the money is not returned, the plan sponsor or another responsible fiduciary contributes the difference. In addition, the plan sponsor must notify the affected participant that any overpayment amount not returned to the plan is ineligible for favorable tax treatment applicable to distribu-

---

62 Rev. Proc. 2000-16, Appendix A, Section .07.

tions from qualified plans and, specifically, is ineligible for tax-free rollover.[63]

b. **Adjustment of Future Payments Correction Method.** Under this alternative, if distributions are being made on the basis of periodic payments, then future payments are reduced not only to comply with the Code Section 415(b) limit, but as necessary to recoup the overpayment amount (adjusted for earnings) over the remaining payments. If the participant is receiving his or her benefit in the form of a QJSA, the reduction to recoup the overpayment applies *only* to the benefits paid during the joint lives; there can be no reduction to the spouse's death benefit.[64]

8. **Failure of defined contribution plan to satisfy Code Section 415.** There are potentially three alternatives for correcting a defined contribution plan that has allocated contributions in excess of the annual addition limitation under Code Section 415(c): the "SVP Correction Method," the "Forfeiture Correction Method," and the "Return of Overpayment Correction Method."

a. **The SVP Correction Method.** Under the SVP Correction Method, excess amounts attributable to elective deferrals and/or employee after-tax contributions must be distributed to plan participants, along with related earnings in accordance with Treasury Regulations Section 1.415-6(b)(6)(iv). Matched elective deferrals and employee after-tax contributions can be returned, provided that the matching contributions relating to those elective deferrals and employee contributions are forfeited. The forfeited matching contributions must be placed in an unallocated account to be used by the plan sponsor to make future contributions.[65]

To the extent the excess is not corrected by distributing elective deferrals and/or employee after-tax contributions, the excess amounts should be placed in an unallocated account, similar to the suspense account described in Treasury Regulations Section 1.415-6(b)(6)(iii). The unallocated account is then used to make employer contributions

---

63 Rev. Proc. 2000-16, Appendix B, Section 2.04(1)(a)(i).
64 Rev. Proc. 2000-16, Appendix B, Section 2.04(1)(a)(ii).
65 Rev. Proc. 2000-16, Appendix A, Section .08, and Appendix B, Section 2.04(2)(a)(i).

in succeeding years. The plan sponsor may not make any additional contributions to the plan until the amount in the suspense account is fully allocated.[66]

b. **Forfeiture Correction Method.** This correction method provides more favorable tax treatment for elective deferrals than the SVP Correction Method. It is available for NHCEs who, in the year of the failure, meet the following conditions:

(i) their annual additions consist of both (1) elective deferrals and/or employee after-tax contributions, *and* (2) matching and/or nonelective contributions;

(ii) their matching and/or nonelective contributions equal or exceed the Code Section 415 excess amount; and

(iii) they have terminated with no vested interest in the matching and/or nonelective contributions (and have not been reemployed at the time of correction).

If each of these conditions is met, the NHCEs Code Section 415(c) excess amount is "deemed to consist solely of the matching and/or nonelective contributions." If the NHCE's Code Section 415(c) excess (adjusted for earnings) has been previously forfeited, the failure is deemed corrected. If it has not, then it is placed in a unallocated account, similar to the suspense account described in Treasury Regulations Section 1.415-6(b)(6)(iii), to be used to reduce the employer contribution in succeeding years (or, if the amount would have been reallocated to other employees for the year of the failure, then the amount is reallocated to such employees in accordance with the plan's allocation formula).[67]

c. **Return of Overpayment Correction Method.** This correction method is conceptually the same as the method described in 7a, above, for correcting Code Section 415 failures in a defined benefit plan.[68]

9. **Vesting failures.** There are two methods of correction for a defined contribution plan that fails to properly apply its vesting schedule, resulting in excess forfeitures. One is the

---

66 Rev. Proc. 2000-16, Appendix A, Section .08, and Appendix B, Section 2.04(2)(a)(i).
67 Rev. Proc. 2000-16, Appendix B, Section 2.04(2)(a)(ii).
68 Rev. Proc. 2000-16, Appendix B, Section 2.04(2)(a)(iii).

Contribution Correction Method and the other is the Reallocation Correction Method. Under the Contribution Correction Method, the corrective contribution to the affected employee equals the amount of the improper forfeiture, adjusted for earnings. If the forfeiture resulted in an improper allocation to the accounts of other employees, no reduction is made to their accounts.[69]

In a defined contribution plan under which forfeitures are reallocated to the accounts of other participants, the plan sponsor may use the Reallocation Correction Method to "re-administer" the plan. The process of adjusting participant account balances is similar to what is described in 4d(ii), above, concerning correction of improperly excluded employees in a profit-sharing or stock bonus plan.[70] (See also the discussion in 4d(i) and (ii), above, indicating the pros and cons of the "Contribution" and "Reallocation" Correction Methods, and why the Contribution Correction Method is an exception to the general correction principles.)

10. **Section 417 failures in a defined contribution plan.** The IRS provides two safe harbors for correcting allocations of contributions or forfeitures in a defined contribution plan that are based on compensation in excess of the Code Section 401(a)(17) limit: (1) the Reduction of Account Balance Method, and (2) the Contribution Correction Method. Under the Reduction of Account Balance Method, the plan reduces the participant's account by the amount of the improperly allocated contribution or forfeiture (adjusted for earnings). If the improperly allocated amount would have been allocated to other participants in the year of the failure, the improperly allocated amount (adjusted for earnings) must be reallocated to those participants in accordance with the plan's allocation formula in effect at the time of the failure. If the plan provides that forfeitures reduce employer contributions, the improperly allocated amount (adjusted for earnings) must be placed in a suspense account to be used to reduce future employer contributions.[71]

Under the Contribution Correction Method, the plan sponsor makes an additional contribution to the plan. The contribu-

---

69 Rev. Proc. 2000-16, Appendix B, Section 2.03(1)(a).
70 Rev. Proc. 2000-16, Appendix B, Section 2.03(1)(b)
71 Rev. Proc. 2000-16, Appendix B, Section 2.06(1).

tion is allocated to the accounts of all the participants, other than the participant for whom there was a Code Section 401(a)(17) violation. As part of this correction, the plan sponsor must file a Walk-in CAP application to obtain retroactive approval of a plan amendment permitting the additional contribution.[72]

In all likelihood, use of the Contribution Correction Method will be limited. It may be helpful in a closely held business where the plan covers the business owners and only a few NHCEs. In this case, the owners may feel that the cost of the additional contribution to the NHCEs is worth preserving their "improper" allocations for the HCEs. The Contribution Correction Method also may be helpful where the Reduction of Account Balance Method could cause an employee morale problem. That is, the cost of the additional contribution may be small when compared to the potential ill will that may result if employees are informed that their account balances are going to be reduced because of an administrative error.

11. **Hardship distribution failures.** The Operational Failure of making hardship distributions in a plan that does not, by its terms, provide for them may be corrected under the Plan Amendment Correction Method. Under this correction method, the plan is amended retroactively to provide for the hardship distributions that were made. The only caveat is that the plan sponsor must be able to establish (1) that the retroactive amendment satisfies Code Section 401(a) (i.e., the "current and effective availability" requirements in Code Section 401(a)(4) and Treasury Regulations Section 1.401(a)(4)-4), and (2) that the plan, as amended, would have satisfied the requirements applicable to hardship distributions under Code Section 401(k) at the time such distributions were first made.[73]

CONCLUSION

Given the importance of plan qualification and the complexity of the qualification requirements for plans, the availability of EPCRS is important for plan sponsors and plan participants. Use of the EPCRS programs

---

72 Rev. Proc. 2000-16, Appendix B, Section 2.07(1)(a).
73 Rev. Proc. 2000-16, Appendix B, Section 2.07(2)(a).

helps preserve the favorable tax treatment for the plan and enables the plan to deliver the promised benefits to the participants.

Equally important is knowing how to use the programs and which program to use. Table 47–1 is designed to help you understand what each of the programs covers and when to use them.

T A B L E   47-1

Summary of EPCRS Programs

	Monetary Penalty	Form Disqualifying Defect	Operational Disqualifying Defect	Available if Audited	IRS Approval of Correction
Two-Year APRSC (Significant Failures)	No	No	Yes, except for*	No	No
Regular APRSC	No	No	Yes, if insignificant and except for*	Yes	No
SVP	No, but a filing fee is required	No	Yes	No	Yes
VCR	No, but a filing fee is required	No	Yes	No	Yes
Walk-in CAP	Yes, in the form of a Compliance Correction fee	Yes	No, except for**	No	Yes
Audit CAP	Yes, in the form of a sanction	Yes	Yes	Yes	Yes

*(1) Demographic Failures requiring an amendment to correct and (2) exclusive benefit violations involving a misuse of plan assets where the Department of Labor has jurisdiction.

**Demographics Defects Failures requiring a plan amendment to correct and cases rejected by the IRS in Washington D.C. under the VCR program.

CHAPTER 48

Welfare Benefits for Retirees

Richard Ostuw

$\mathbf{M}$ost large companies provide life insurance and health care benefits for their retired employees. Because most of the U.S. workforce is employed by small- to medium-sized companies, however, only a minority of workers are currently eligible for post-retirement welfare benefits. Nonetheless, these benefits are an important component of retiree income and a significant cost to employers providing them.

Many employers began providing post-retirement benefits when their retiree populations were small and the costs of the benefits were low. Costs have grown tremendously since then because of growing numbers of retirees, increases in health care costs, and changes in the accounting for the benefit. As a result, companies are paying close attention to their retiree benefit programs and are attempting to ensure that they meet specific objectives, including the following:

- Protecting retirees against the cost of unbudgetable medical expenses and providing a modest life insurance benefit to cover burial expenses.
- Promoting cost-effective use of medical care and discouraging the use of unnecessary care.
- Ensuring that employer contributions make the program competitive with those of other companies and that the employee contributions are affordable.
- Attracting and retaining experienced workers.
- Containing employer costs.

The following pages review current practices with respect to retiree benefits, starting with an overview of trends and issues affecting these benefits. After a brief discussion of life insurance, the remainder of the chapter focuses primarily on medical benefits.

CURRENT TRENDS AND ISSUES

Employers have made major changes to their retiree welfare benefit programs over the years. Continued fine-tuning and occasional major changes are necessary to maintain a suitable balance between cost control and employee relations in a dynamic environment. The study by the Financial Accounting Standards Board (FASB) of possible changes in accounting rules prompted many companies to make significant changes in the late 1980s and early 1990s. The new rules were published in December 1990 as *Financial Accounting Standard, No. 106 (FAS 106)*.

Under *FAS 106*, the company's actuary determines the Expected Post-retirement Benefit Obligation (EPBO), which represents the current value of employer payments for current and future retirees and their dependents. The calculation of the EPBO reflects the following facts and assumptions:

- The provisions of the "substantive plan," including the benefit payable and the retirees' share of the contribution toward the premium.
- The percentage of eligible retirees and dependents who enroll in each plan.
- The mortality rate of the plan participants.
- The age at retirement for future retirees.
- The rate of termination of employment.

The Accumulated Post-retirement Benefit Obligation (APBO) represents the portion of the EPBO attributable to past service. This represents the full value of benefits for current retirees and a prorated portion for future retirees. The APBO is the key measure of the employer's obligation earned to date.

The annual expense for post-retirement benefits is as follows:

- The *service cost*, or the value of future benefits attributable to the current year of employee service.
- The *interest cost*, or the growth in the APBO due to the change in the interest discount for future payments.

- Amortization of the *initial transition obligation* (unless the employer recognized the entire APBO as a one-time charge when adopting *FAS 106*).
- Adjustments to amortize the effect of (a) actuarial gains and losses, and (b) plan changes.

The *FAS 106* rules are similar to the *FAS 87* and *FAS 88* rules applicable to pensions.

Companies will continue to modify their retiree benefits to reflect changes in the environment, such as general pressure on the cost of business operations, changes in health benefits for active employees, and increases in plan costs for retirees. Most employers have focused on health benefits rather than life insurance benefits. The specific steps vary from employer to employer but often include the following:

- Revisions in the definition of covered expenses, and/or their reimbursement.
- Increases in employee contribution, especially for short-service retirees and for dependent coverage.
- Limits on the dollar amount of employer contribution.
- Greater use of managed care techniques.

In their ongoing efforts to balance cost concerns with the specific program objectives cited earlier, employers have to address the following issues in their decision to retain or modify their current plans:

- Should we continue to offer a plan to retirees?
- Where and how should we offer health maintenance organizations (HMOs) or other managed care options?
- What benefits provisions should the plans include? Should the medical plan, for example, have a low deductible and high coinsurance or vice versa? Should the life insurance formula represent a percentage of final salary or a uniform dollar amount?
- How should the premium cost be shared between the company and employees for each optional plan?
- How should retiree welfare benefits be integrated with other components of the retirement program?
- What special grandfather or transition rules, if any, should apply?
- What are the appropriate elements of the expensing policy?
- How should the plan cost be funded?

LIFE INSURANCE

In general, retirees' death benefit needs are less than those of active employees and are met to some extent by survivor-income benefits under the pension plan and Social Security, or by significant savings or profit-sharing balances at retirement. Many employers also provide some form of retiree life insurance, and some provide a modest death benefit through the pension plan.

Benefit Design

Life insurance for active employees typically takes the form of a basic employer-paid benefit amount that can be supplemented with optional employee-paid insurance. For retirees, the life insurance benefit is usually a flat dollar amount—generally in the range of $3,000 to $20,000—that the employer may update from time to time for new retirees. Ad hoc increases for current retirees are unusual. Another common approach, particularly for salaried employees, is to express the post-retirement life insurance schedule as a percentage of the employee's final preretirement life insurance amount or final preretirement salary. Some employers reduce the benefit amount during retirement. They might, for example, reduce life insurance of two times salary for active employees by 20 percent per year during retirement to an ultimate level of 20 percent of the preretirement benefit; that is, 40 percent of final pay. Such a benefit also may have a modest post-retirement coverage maximum of perhaps $20,000.

Group universal life programs (GULP) are common for salaried employees. They provide a flexible vehicle for employees to tailor the amount of insurance to their needs, reflect changes in their needs over time, and prefund post-retirement costs as desired. For a detailed discussion of group universal life programs, see Chapter 16.

Cost

Growth in the size of the retiree population—exacerbated in many companies by downsizing—has increased the cost of post-retirement benefits substantially. *FAS 106* requires that employers recognize the cost of these benefits on a pension-style expensing basis.

On such an advance-expensing basis, the cost of post-retirement life insurance is typically about 0.5 percent or less of the active employee payroll. In those companies that provide significant post-retirement life insurance (such as two times pay without reduction), however, the advance-expensing cost can approach 2 percent of payroll.

HEALTH BENEFITS

Few employers provided medical coverage to retirees before 1965 because the cost of doing so was prohibitive. When Medicare became effective in 1966, however, companies realized they could supplement Medicare coverage for their retirees at a modest cost. Over the years, the share of medical expenses covered by Medicare has diminished—although Medicare is still the primary payer for retirees—and the benefits provided by employers have become more and more liberal. Thus, what was once low-cost post-retirement medical coverage has become enormously expensive.

Medical Plan Design Elements

Medical plan design elements are the same for retirees and active employees. There are key differences between the two groups, however. For example:

- Age differences make retiree medical costs substantially higher than those of active employees. The average annual cost per person for retirees under age 65 commonly is about two times the average cost for active employees. Both the frequency and intensity of health care (including hospitalization, physician visits, and use of prescription drugs) increase with age.
- Certain health conditions, such as hearing impairments and the need for various prostheses, are more common among the elderly.
- Elderly individuals require more time to recover from serious medical conditions and therefore are likely to require longer hospital stays and more care after a hospital discharge.

Medicare assumes the bulk of the cost of hospital and physician services after age 65. The relative share of employer plan costs by type of expense for retirees over 65 thus differs from the cost share for active employees. For example, prescription drugs might represent 10 percent of the plan cost for active employees and 50 percent for Medicare-eligible retirees.

Covered Services

As with active-employee plans, retiree medical plans generally cover a wide rage of care and treatment, including hospital care, surgery, doctors' visits, therapy, and prescription drugs. Typically excluded from coverage are hearing and vision care, cosmetic surgery, and experimental procedures. Routine physical examinations are typically covered only in managed care plans.

New developments in technology will have a substantial impact on medical costs for retirees. How the plan defines experimental procedures and how the administrator updates the rules will have significant consequences.

Coordination with Medicare

Retirees usually receive the same medical benefits as active employees and often have the same or similar array of optional plans, including HMOs. When they reach age 65 and become eligible for Medicare, however, their employer-provided benefits are coordinated with Medicare in one of two ways:

- *Offset.* The employer plan continues to provide the same benefits structure, but those benefits are offset by Medicare payments. This can preserve cost sharing.
- *Medigap.* Plan coverage is limited to expenses that are not paid by Medicare. This Medicare fill-in approach often is called Medigap coverage.

There are three general forms of the offset approach. Under "Medicare carve-out," the net benefit is the regular plan benefit less the amount paid by Medicare. Under "government exclusion," the Medicare benefits are subtracted from covered expenses before calculating the plan benefits. Under traditional "coordination of benefits" (COB), the net benefit is the amount of covered expenses less the amount paid by Medicare but not more than the regular plan benefit.

Under the Medigap approach, the employer plan might pay all or part of the following hospital expenses for its retirees:

- The first level of expenses for each hospital admission; that is, the Medicare Part A deductible ($792 in 2001).
- The Medicare co-payment amounts beginning on the 61st day of hospitalization ($198 in 2001).
- Co-payment amounts during the lifetime reserve days ($396 in 2001).
- The cost of hospital care extending beyond the period covered by Medicare.

Similarly, the employer plan may pay all or part of the expenses for physician and other nonhospital services not reimbursed by Medicare Part B. It also may cover all or part of the expenses commonly excluded by both parts of Medicare, such as prescription drugs and private nursing. Few employer-sponsored plans cover long-term custodial care in a nursing home. Some employers offer long-term care insurance, usually on an employee-pay-all basis, to address the cost of such care. See Chapter 13 for a discussion of long-term care insurance.

We can use the Medicare Part A deductible to illustrate two methods of updating retiree medical coverage. Under one approach, the employer plan defines covered expense as the Medicare Part A deductible. When the Part A deductible amount increases, the employer plan automatically fills the gap. Under the other approach, the employer specifies a coverage amount (such as $700) and increases that amount only by plan amendment. The latter approach gives the employer the ability to control the impact of inflation and Medicare changes on its plan and its costs.

Liberal Medigap plans virtually eliminate out-of-pocket medical expenses for retirees; more restrictive plans may provide only modest benefits. For example, some plans do not cover hospital stays beyond the Medicare limit, physicians' fees not fully covered by Medicare, prescription drugs, and nursing care.

The Medicare program theoretically reimburses 80 percent of physicians' fees after a modest deductible. In actual practice, however, the reimbursement level has been much lower—as low as 50 percent—because of Medicare's low level of allowed charges. This was a problem until 1989, when Medicare fees changed to the Resource Based Relative Value Scale (RBRVS) and placed restrictions on "balance billing" by physicians. By limiting the physicians' fees, these rules significantly reduce the retiree's share of the cost and therefore the cost under the employer's medical plan.

Eligibility

In the typical retiree benefit program, eligibility rules for post-retirement health care and life insurance benefits follow the employer's pension plan definition of retirement. The most common definition specifies termination of employment after attainment of age 55 and 10 years of active service. An employee hired at age 40, for example, first becomes eligible for retirement at age 55; a person hired at age 50 becomes eligible at age 60. Some plans impose no minimum service requirement for employees who terminate employment at or after age 65.

Employees also may be eligible for retirement after 30 years of service regardless of age, or upon attaining a specified number of years of age plus service. The "Rule of 80," for example, would be satisfied by any combination of age and service that equals or exceeds 80. This approach is common for both unionized and salaried employees in industries with a strong union presence.

Nearly all retiree medical plans extend coverage to the spouses and children of retirees, as those relationships are defined in the active employee plan. Some plans are more restrictive, however, and may, for example, exclude the spouses of marriages that occur after employees retire.

Employee Contributions

The level and nature of retiree contributions varies significantly among large employers. For many current retirees, the plans are noncontributory because of grandfathering provisions. But nearly all employers require contributions for new retirees.

In general, it is more common for employers to require contributions from retirees than from active employees. Post-age-65 retiree contributions typically represent a greater percentage of total plan cost than do contributions by pre-age-65 retirees or active employees. Employee-pay-all coverage is rare for active employees, for example, but not for retirees over 65. Retirees' contributions may represent a percentage of plan cost, a flat dollar amount, or the excess of the plan premium over the fixed employer contribution.

Under a percentage-of-cost approach, retirees are required to contribute a specified percentage of the expected plan cost for the coming year—usually 20 percent to 33 percent but sometimes as much as 100 percent. If a plan requires a 25 percent employee contribution and plan costs are expected to be $120 per month per covered person, for example, retirees would have to contribute $30 per month. As the plan cost increases due to inflation and utilization changes, the retirees' contribution increases proportionately.

It is also common for employers to require specified dollar contributions. Although such an approach may reflect a cost-sharing policy, the underlying percentage of plan cost is not necessarily disclosed to employees or retirees. Employers using this approach usually update dollar amounts every few years. Nonetheless, updates generally have failed to keep pace with increases in plan costs. Employers often procrastinate in making changes that employees and retirees will view as benefit reductions. Further, planning for and implementing such updates is time-consuming.

The percentage approach has become more popular because it allows employers to update contribution amounts without creating the perception of a benefit take-away. This is especially important in view of recent court decisions limiting employers' ability to reduce retiree benefits and the ability to recognize changes in employee contributions under *FAS 106*. By indicating that retiree contributions will increase as plan premiums increase, retirees accept the year-to-year changes, the courts accept the employer's right to change the amount, and *FAS 106* allows the employer to anticipate future increases in retiree contributions.

Retiree contributions generally are payable by deduction from the retiree's pension check, although in some companies retirees send a monthly check to the employer. Coverage is terminated if payment is not made on a timely basis.

Plan Types and Benefit Levels

Plan types include indemnity plans and network/managed care plans. Under indemnity plans, the benefit represents reimbursement of eligible expenses for use of any health care provider. Under network or managed care plans, the program administrator contracts with selected providers and benefits are more liberal when the participant uses a network or preferred provider.

During the 1980s, many employers changed from "basic plus major medical" programs to comprehensive plans for both active employees and retirees. Consequently, basic plus major medical programs now typically apply only to a closed group of retirees. Future retirees are generally covered under comprehensive plans or network/managed care plans.

In addition to or in lieu of the change to comprehensive coverage, many employers have established utilization review programs or incentive arrangements to minimize the use of unneeded medical care. Such provisions can be summarized as follows:

- *Reimbursement differences.* The plan pays a higher level of reimbursement (such as 100 percent instead of 80 percent) for types or locations of services presumed to be more cost-efficient, including preadmission testing and outpatient surgery. The benefit differential may apply only in certain circumstances—for specific surgical procedures identified by the employer, for example.

- *Review requirements.* The plan pays a higher reimbursement when there is a pretreatment review such as a second surgical opinion or hospital preadmission review.

The goal of these incentives is to reduce the use—and cost—of unnecessary care or to substitute less costly forms of care for expensive procedures. To achieve these savings, a plan will incur some added cost in the form of administration expenses and more liberal benefits for selected services. For active employees and retirees who are not eligible for Medicare, the employer will experience a net cost reduction. There may, however, be a net cost increase to the employer for retirees covered by Medicare. This is because the employer pays administration expenses and the cost of benefit increases while Medicare enjoys most of the savings from reduced in-hospital care or surgery costs.

The types of plans—indemnity as well as the various approaches to managed care—are summarized below.

Basic Plus Major Medical

Basic benefits provide 100 percent reimbursement of covered expenses for certain types of services. Examples might include the following:

- Hospital inpatient services for up to 180 days.
- Surgery.
- Diagnostic X-ray and laboratory procedures.
- Emergency treatment for an accident.

The major medical component supplements basic benefits but reimburses less than the full expense—usually 80 percent of the expense in excess of an annual deductible of between $100 and $200 per person.

Comprehensive

The typical plan pays 80 percent of expenses for all services, with an annual deductible of perhaps $300 per person, until the individual incurs out-of-pocket covered expenses of a specified amount—perhaps $2,000 in a year (taking into account the 20 percent coinsurance and the deductible). The plan pays 100 percent of eligible expenses thereafter.

Employers shifted to comprehensive programs for a number of reasons, including the following:

- Medical costs almost doubled between 1982 and 1984 for many employers. Many companies that were unable or unwilling to absorb the full increase changed to a comprehensive program to reduce plan costs.

- Basic/major medical programs provide no financial incentives for patients to avoid costly in-hospital treatment and, in fact, often provide an incentive to use inpatient care rather than less expensive outpatient care. The change to a comprehensive plan redefines the reimbursement basis to establish financial incentives for using medical care more efficiently.

- Relatively low-cost services such as laboratory work and treatment for accidents add up to a significant portion of basic/major medical plan costs. Comprehensive plans shift this budgetable cost to the employee through application of the annual deductible.

Health Maintenance Organizations (HMOs)

U.S. employers generally offer HMOs to active employees as an alternative to their traditional medical plan. Most employers also offer the same HMOs to their retirees. Because retirees are more geographically dispersed than actives, some employers offer additional HMOs to retirees in retirement destinations such as Florida and Arizona.

The HMO offering for retirees under age 65 is generally the same as for active employees. The nature of the arrangement differs, however, for Medicare-eligible retirees. Medicare pays a fixed monthly premium, and the HMO takes the risk for the cost of providing the care. Because of HMO efficiencies in many parts of the country, the amount paid by Medicare is more than enough to cover the HMO's cost of providing the Medicare level of benefits, allowing the HMO to offer supplemental benefits and charge a small premium for these benefits.

Preferred Provider Organizations (PPOs)

A preferred provider organization is much like an HMO, in that it contracts with a network of physicians and health care facilities to provide services to members at a reduced cost. There are, however, some important differences. Unlike HMOs, most PPOs do not require members to name a primary care physician, and members are free to select a specialist from the network without first obtaining a referral. Because PPO networks are not subject to the same regulations as HMOs, employers generally have greater flexibility with PPOs than with HMOs in plan design and financing.

Point of Service (POS) Managed Care

During the late 1980s and the 1990s, many companies implemented point-of-service (POS) managed care programs for employees and retirees. Each time the employee or retiree needs health care, he or she chooses between hospitals and physicians who participate in the managed care network or choose non-network providers. When they use in-network services, the benefits are more liberal than those applicable to non-network services. Because of negotiated fee discounts and managed care techniques, the networks substantially reduce the cost of care for employees and retirees not yet eligible for Medicare.

Medicare+Choice

The Balanced Budget Act of 1997 (BBA '97) ushered in a major change in Medicare—perhaps the most important revisions since Medicare's inception some 32 years earlier. By authorizing the development of new Medicare plans (known as Medicare+Choice), the bill is intended to expand competition in the delivery of medical services and, consequently, the choices for all Medicare enrollees.

The name Medicare+Choice indicates that this is traditional Medicare plus the opportunity for enrollees to choose from an array of new, coordinated care plans (including HMOs with or without point of service options, PPOs, and provider-sponsored organizations). Thus, Medicare+Choice encompasses traditional fee-for-service Medicare as well as new managed care services as they become available.

The Balanced Budget Act also made provisions for medical savings accounts (MSAs), offered on a limited basis as a pilot project. The MSA approach allows the enrollee to purchase a high-deductible plan, with the premium covered by the Health Care Financing Administration (HCFA). The difference between the capitation payment to the provider and the premium is deposited in a medical savings account. For retirees who are in good health and can absorb the high deductible, this may be an attractive option.

To expand network/managed care options, BBA '97 prepared the way for HMOs and other service providers to contract with HCFA for delivery of services. The payment arrangements are similar to those for the Medicare risk contracts in use prior to BBA '97. That is, the plans assume full risk for providing benefits to enrollees in return for a fixed premium from HCFA. In addition to adjusting payment rates by blending county-specific and U.S. data, HCFA set a minimum payment rate ($367 per month per enrollee in 1998).

While these changes to Medicare are significant, the underlying structure remains intact. Many plan sponsors, for example, had been using Medicare HMOs for their retirees prior to BBA '97 and were already familiar with the arrangement. Also, the methods used by managed care providers to evaluate costs and set premiums remains very much the same. Still, there are important implications:

- The increases in Medicare payments to network providers will likely fall short of actual increases in the cost of providing care. For several years, the payment by HCFA was sufficient to fund the full HMO benefit level. With the limitation on future increases, zero premium plans will disappear as costs increase. Plan sponsors as well as retirees should recognize, however, that managed care options will be less costly than traditional Medicare supplement plans in many locations.

- HCFA will introduce a risk adjustment based on the health risk of the covered group. Managed care organizations whose enrollees are healthier than average will receive reduced payments; those with less healthy participants will receive increased payments. This risk adjustment may prompt managed care plans to deliberately seek out less healthy Medicare beneficiaries.

- Although BBA '97 allows an array of products, there will be relatively few organizations willing to accept the risk, except under HMO programs.

The Changing Nature of the Promise

Defined Dollar Benefit Approach

Under a traditional retiree medical plan, the employer "promises" to provide a stated level of benefits (with the possibility of changes in the benefit provisions). The key element is the benefits level. Under a newer approach, the key element is the dollar amount the employer will pay toward the cost of the benefits. The employer contribution is the defined dollar benefit (DDB). Many large companies have implemented this approach since the late 1980s or early 1990s. Here is an illustration of how the DDB approach works:

- The employer offers a medical plan with benefit features comparable to those offered to active employees.

- The employer contributes up to $200 per month per person for coverage until age 65 and $100 per month thereafter. The retiree must pay the balance of the plan cost. The employer contribution is available only as a subsidy toward the cost of the medical plan.

- The employer updates benefit features from time to time and will consider ad hoc increases in the defined dollar benefit.

The defined dollar benefit approach has these advantages:

- The employer has full control over future increases in its benefit costs because it determines the amount and timing of any increases in its contributions. (However, employee concern about benefit adequacy and competition may create pressure for ad hoc increases.)
- Benefit features can be updated more easily than in traditional programs. This is because the employer's promise involves its contribution—not the benefits themselves—and any reduction in the benefit level will directly reduce retiree contributions.
- Because benefit costs are communicated, employees will better understand the substantial value of the benefits they receive.
- The approach facilitates service-related benefit coverage, which is discussed below. In the above illustration, for example, the $200 and $100 employer contribution amounts could be prorated for service of less than 25 years.
- Retirees can be offered choices in how to apply their defined dollar benefit.

Tying Contributions and Benefit Levels to Service

The cost of retiree medical benefits has prompted many employers to tie retiree contributions to service.

As an example, the employer contribution may be 3 percent of the plan cost for each year of employee service. Alternatively, service brackets, such as the following, may be used.

Years of Service	Retiree Contribution As Percentage of Plan Cost
10–14	70%
15–19	55
20–24	40
25–29	25
30+	10

It is theoretically possible to vary the benefit level by length of service. Because this approach is more difficult to administer than one that uses variable contributions, few employers use this approach.

Retiree Health Accounts

One of the problems with retiree health programs is that employees do not understand the value of the employer's contributions. To raise the level of understanding, some companies have introduced retiree health accounts, a nontraditional approach similar to cash balance and pension equity pension plans. Under a retiree health account program, the employer makes an annual "contribution" to an account for each employee. The account may grow with interest, depending on provisions established by the employer. During the individual's retirement, the account can be used to pay for medical premiums. If the account runs out, the retiree becomes fully responsible for medical plan premiums. The appeal of this approach is that the employee is aware of the value of the employer contributions. Moreover, the program is more equitable with reference to employees who retire at different ages as well as to those who enroll their dependents and those who do not. By contrast, under traditional programs, the employer typically contributes much more for employees who retire early and for those who enroll dependents.

FINANCING

The three key considerations in financing retiree benefits are expense recognition, level of cost, and the funding vehicle.

Expense Recognition

Nearly all employers initially recognized the cost of retiree welfare benefits on a pay-as-you-go basis. In a sense, this is a historical accident. When employers began providing these benefits, they believed they were making a year-by-year commitment rather than a lifetime promise. They did not consider post-retirement benefits to be a form of deferred compensation earned during an employee's working career. This was in sharp contrast to prevailing views applicable to post-retirement income benefits, that is, pension plans. Court decisions (discussed below) have prompted many employers to change their views on the nature of their commitment, and accounting rules now require most employers to recognize these costs during the working years of employees.

The Financial Accounting Standards Board (FASB) considered the issue of how retiree welfare benefits should be expensed during the 1980s. The key question is this: Should companies be required to recognize the expense of post-retirement welfare benefits during the working careers of employees and charge such amounts against current earnings? As a first step, *FASB Statement 81* required the disclosure of the amount expensed for these benefits and the basis for expensing. Pay-as-you-go cost recognition still was permitted.

The FASB subsequently published new accounting rules (*FAS 106*), effective December 15, 1992, that require a pension-type expensing approach for life insurance and medical benefits on the grounds that such benefits represent a form of deferred compensation whose cost should be charged against earnings during the period when employees are productive. Under *FAS 106*, companies must recognize the accruing cost of post-retirement coverage during the working years of employees and must disclose specific information about the plan, the aggregate value of accrued benefits, and the actuarial assumptions used to calculate the results.

Cost

On a pay-as-you-go basis, retiree medical plan costs typically are about $4,000 per year per person until age 65 and $2,000 per year thereafter. (The cost for individual employers may be significantly higher or lower.) The present value of these costs depends on employee age at retirement and, of course, on the assumptions for the interest discount rate, mortality rates, and increases in health care costs. Representative amounts are as follows.

Age at Retirement	Present Value of Medical Benefits (per retiree)	
	Single Coverage	Family Coverage
55	$75,000	$150,000
60	45,000	90,000
65	30,000	60,000

Roughly 60 percent of the cost is attributable to retired employees and 40 percent to their dependents. By comparison, the cost commonly is split 50-50 between active employees and their dependents, reflecting the larger average family size of these employees. Relatively few retirees have children who are still eligible under the medical plan.

Pay-as-you-go costs will rise in the future as a result of the following:

- Price increases measured by the consumer price index (CPI).
- The introduction of new medical technology and new procedures.
- Changes in the frequency or utilization of health care or in the mix of services.

The health care share of the gross domestic product (GDP) is now more than 14 percent, compared with 9.1 percent in 1980 and 7.3 percent in 1970. While the growth of national medical care costs in the last 20 years has been significant, the rates of change have been quite variable. There is not a consensus on the rate of future growth.

Expensing annual retiree benefit costs on a pension-type basis during the working years of employees under *FAS 106* has the following results for representative groups of employees:

Cost as Percent of Payroll

Normal cost	2–3%
Amortization of unrecognized past service liability	2–3
Interest on past service liability	3–5
Total expense	7–11

Funding

Several funding alternatives are available to employers. These include the following:

Book reserve. The employer accrues the cost on its financial statement and retains the assets within the organization. *FAS 106* requires pension-type expensing, but there are no requirements that assets be maintained in a separate trust.

Voluntary Employees' Beneficiary Association (VEBA). Under Section 501(c)(9) of the Internal Revenue Code, the employer contributes funds to an independent trust from which benefits subsequently are paid. Section 419 of the Internal Revenue Code severely restricts the use of VEBAs for retiree health plans by limiting the amount of tax-deductible contributions to such trusts and subjecting the investment income to the unrelated business income tax. Neither of these problems applies to prefunding of retiree life insurance, the welfare plans of a not-for-profit organization, or health benefits provided through collective-bargaining agreements.

Pension plans. A special account for medical benefits may be maintained as part of a pension plan under Section 401(h) of the Internal Revenue Code. Within limits, contributions to the account are deductible when made and investment income is exempt from tax. Because benefits represent health care cost reimbursement, payments from the 401(h) account are tax free.

Insurance contracts. Insurance contracts can be used in either of two ways to prefund retiree welfare benefits. Assets can be accumulated in an insurance continuation fund for subsequent payment of pay-as-you-go costs. Paid-up insurance also may be used. Under the latter approach, a one-time premium is paid to fund benefits for the lifetime of the retirees. These insurance approaches may be used for either life or medical insurance but are much more common for the former. The life insurance contracts are issued to the employer, and the arrangement is often labeled corporate-owned life insurance (COLI). If issued to the trust, the arrangement may be labeled trust-owned life insurance (TOLI). The use of offshore captive insurance companies is sometimes helpful.

Union funds. Under many multiple-employer union-negotiated plans, contributions are made to a Taft-Hartley fund. The fund is responsible for the benefits to retirees.

LEGAL ISSUES

Unlike pension benefits, ERISA does not provide for the statutory vesting of retiree medical benefits. As such, employee communication materials usually describe the employer's right to modify or terminate the overall benefit plan. Without such effective disclaimers, employers may be accused of having voluntarily offered lifetime medical benefits.

Employer attempts to reduce or eliminate medical benefits for current retirees have resulted in significant litigation. (It is interesting to note that no case has involved the issue of whether such actions improperly infringed on the rights of active employees.) Following is a summary of several representative cases.

In *U.A.W.* v. *Yardman*, the employer attempted to terminate medical coverage for retirees. A federal appeals court held that the employer was obligated to continue the benefits because it had promised coverage to retirees. Once an individual achieved the status of retiree, the benefits could be discontinued only if the individual no longer held that status. Thus, the employer was obligated to continue lifetime coverage for retirees.

In *Eardman* v. *Bethlehem Steel*, the employer attempted to reduce the level of benefits and increase the level of required contributions by retirees. A federal district court ruled that, in effect, the employer had given up its right to make such changes by omitting the required language in written communications and by making oral promises to retirees at exit interviews. The company and its retirees subsequently reached a compromise whereby benefit reductions and increased contributions were implemented, but the company promised not to attempt such changes again.

In the case of *In Re White Farm Equipment*, a federal district court went further than the above cases. It concluded that benefits were vested and could not be reduced or eliminated, regardless of any statements by the employer. On appeal, however, this reasoning was not accepted, and the case was returned to the lower court for review on its merits. More representative, perhaps, is *Moore* v. *Metropolitan*, where a federal court of appeals confirmed that, absent fraud, an unambiguous plan document reserving the employer's right to alter or amend the plan makes allegations of conflicting oral and written communications irrelevant.

These cases have been widely reported and have received a great deal of attention. Many other employers have made changes in their medical benefits for current retirees, usually concurrent with and similar to changes in their active-employee plans, but these actions have not been reported by the press because there has been no litigation.

At this time, neither the employer's ability to modify retiree benefits nor the employee's rights under the plans are fully defined. Further litigation—and perhaps legislation—probably will help clarify the situation.

In 1995, the U.S. Supreme Court confirmed in *Curtiss-Wright* v. *Schoonejongen*, for example, that plan language to the effect that "a company reserves the right at any time to amend a plan" establishes an amendment procedure that satisfied ERISA Section 402(b)(3).

Multiemployer Plans

Cynthia J. Drinkwater

Multiemployer plans provide benefits to employees in unionized industries such as the apparel trades, professional and consumer services, the entertainment industry, transportation, and construction. Often these employees are highly mobile, working for several employers a year. If it were not for multiemployer plans, which are arranged by industry (or related industries) on a local, regional, or national level, such employees would be forced to switch plans as often as they do employment. Benefit coverage would be haphazard and incomplete.

Within the structure of a multiemployer plan, employers contribute to one trust fund from which benefits are paid to all eligible employees. Staff of a separate, centralized office perform administrative functions, such as determination of eligibility, maintenance of participant records, claim processing, and payment of benefits. Contributing employers, thus, avoid the details of administering and delivering benefits. To some extent, contributing employers also enjoy economies of scale inherent in the maintenance of a common plan versus numerous separate ones. This accounts for multiemployer plans maintained even by employers with relatively more permanent workforces, such as those in the retail trade industry.

As with collectively bargained single-employer plans, employer contributions to (or, less frequently, benefits of) multiemployer plans are negotiated between the respective employees and employers and formalized contractually in collective-bargaining agreements. Unlike single-employer collectively bargained plans, which are likely to be administered unilaterally by the employer, multiemployer plan responsibility falls upon a board of trustees equally representative of labor and management. The board of trustees is charged with making plan decisions in the interests of plan participants and beneficiaries without regard to the labor or management constituency that designates the board.

It is not always logical or feasible to apply benefit knowledge appropriate for a benefit plan designed, funded, and administered by one employer to a multiemployer plan. In some areas, such as withdrawal liability, plan termination, and plan insolvency, special multiemployer plan rules have been established. In other areas, such as plan qualification, most requirements apply to multiemployer plans as well as single-employer plans, but sometimes multiemployer plan practice is more liberal than what is specified in the requirements, or the requirements are at odds with the multiemployer plan structure. And at times, employee benefits law has been modified to fit the multiemployer plan framework as well as that of the single employer plan, as evidenced by amendments to the Consolidated Omnibus Budget Reconciliation Act of 1985 (COBRA).

The unique features of a multiemployer plan—mobile employees, numerous contributing employers, a common trust fund with centralized administration, collectively bargained benefits, and a joint board of trustees—have the potential to complicate the responsibilities of trustees, plan administrators, and professionals who carry out the day-to-day tasks of running a plan. Yet, advantages of multiemployer plans to both employees and employers is evidenced by their continued presence in the United States for nearly 45 years. Multiemployer plans in 1992 numbered approximately 7,000 plans, with about 8.5 million total participants in welfare plans and about 10.5 million total participants in pension plans.[1] Multiemployer plans have been and will remain an important part of the employee benefits environment.

MULTIEMPLOYER PLAN DEFINED

Two characteristics of an employee benefit plan make it multiemployer in nature: the number of contributing employers and a collective-bargaining origin. As indicated by its name, more than one employer contributes to a multiemployer plan. Employers contribute to the plan pursuant to a collective-bargaining agreement (or agreements) with one or more employee organizations. Typically, these employee organizations are unions.

---

1 Terence Davidson, "Characteristics of Multiemployer Plans," *Employee Benefit Basics*, Second Quarter (Brookfield, WI: International Foundation of Employee Benefit Plans, 1996).

Employer contributions to multiemployer plans are negotiated through the collective-bargaining process and fixed in the collective-bargaining agreement—usually on a dollars-per-hour, unit-of-production, or percentage-of-compensation basis. A distinguishing feature of a multiemployer defined benefit plan is that it actually resembles both a defined benefit and a defined contribution plan—although employer contributions are fixed, participants' benefits are based on a formula. Because contributions to multiemployer plans are calculated on some basis of work performed, a multiemployer plan's income is dependent on the level of economic activity in participants' industries. Contributions and benefits, therefore, are adjusted periodically to reflect the actual experience of the plan.

The description "multiple employer" plan is sometimes incorrectly interchanged with "multiemployer" plan. A multiple employer plan has only the first feature of a multiemployer plan—more than one employer contributes. There are no collective-bargaining agreements requiring contributions in a multiple-employer plan.

THE TAFT-HARTLEY CONNECTION

"Taft-Hartley" plan, too, often is used synonymously with "multiemployer" plan. It is not the number of contributing employers, however, that distinguishes a Taft-Hartley plan but its joint, labor-management administration. Under Section 302(c) of the Taft-Hartley Act of 1947 (also referred to as the Labor-Management Relations Act), it is a criminal act for an employer to give money or anything else of value to employee representatives or a union, including contributions to an employee benefit plan administered solely by the union. An employer is permitted, though, to contribute to a jointly administered employee benefit trust fund for the "sole and exclusive benefit" of employees, their families, and dependents.[2]

Joint labor-management employee benefit plan administration required by the Taft-Hartley Act can be found in either a multiemployer or single-employer plan. Single-employer Taft-Hartley plans, in which an individual employer enters into a collective-bargaining agreement with union employees and administers a benefit plan jointly with the union, are not common. Multiemployer plans always are jointly administered.

Contributions to a jointly administered trust fund are legal under the Taft-Hartley Act only if (1) payments are in accordance with a written agreement with the employer, (2) the agreement provides for employers

---

2 LMRA Sec. 302(c)(5). Trust funds established before January 1, 1946 that are unilaterally administered by a union are valid.

and employees to agree upon an impartial umpire for disputes (if no neutral persons are authorized to break deadlocks), (3) the trust fund is audited annually, and (4) the employer and employees are represented equally in fund administration. Furthermore, Taft-Hartley plans may be established only to fund certain types of employee benefits. The types of benefits have expanded over the years, generally from just medical/hospital care; pensions; occupational illnesses/injuries; unemployment; and life, disability/sickness, or accident insurance to include vacation, holiday, or severance benefits; apprenticeship and training programs; educational scholarships; child-care centers; and legal services. In 1990, Congress added financial assistance for employee housing to the list of valid purposes for establishment of a Taft-Hartley trust fund.

Purposes of Taft-Hartley Funds

Medical/hospital care	Pooled vacation/holiday/severance benefits
Pensions	Apprenticeship/training programs
Occupational illness/injury	Educational scholarships
Unemployment benefits	Child-care centers
Life insurance	Legal services
Disability/sickness insurance	Financial assistance for housing
Accident insurance	

"BUILT-IN" PORTABILITY OF BENEFITS

One of a multiemployer plan's greatest advantages for a mobile workforce is its built-in portability. Portability refers to the ability to transfer benefits from one employer's plan to another. Although they might work for numerous employers over the course of their work lives, employees covered under collective bargaining agreements that require employer contributions to multiemployer plans usually do not have to be concerned with losing benefits from or transferring benefits among employers' plans. In multiemployer pension plans, for example, employees will be credited years of service for vesting and participation purposes as long as they work for a contributing employer in covered service or in contiguous noncovered service with the same employer. Contiguous noncovered service is nonbargaining unit service, such as supervisory work, preceding or following covered service.[3]

In addition to built-in portability, some multiemployer plans enter into reciprocal agreements with other multiemployer plans—both pen-

---

3 29 CFR Sec. 2530.210(c). For benefit accrual purposes, covered service with any employer maintaining the plan will be taken into account.

sion, and health and welfare. Not only, then, are benefits portable from one employer to another through the multiemployer plan, but benefits of employers contributing to different multiemployer plans also are portable among multiemployer plans.

In multiemployer pension plans, reciprocity agreements are arranged in two ways. Among some funds, pension contributions "follow the man." Contributions on behalf of a "traveler" to a local fund are paid to the traveler's home fund, which distributes the entire benefit to the participant based on its own formula. In other reciprocity agreements, no contributions are transferred. Instead, years of service among funds are combined for purposes of plan participation and vesting. Each fund pays benefits based only on its own years of service, or a pro rata share. In health and welfare plans, reciprocity agreements are arranged similarly and used to avoid a period of noncoverage while an employee waits to satisfy another multiemployer plan's eligibility requirements.

First developed in the mid-1960s, reciprocal agreements are most common among the building and construction trades. In 1987, almost one-half of all multiemployer funds were party to reciprocity agreements.[4] In some instances, these agreements extend portability among multiemployer plans to a national level.

JOINT BOARD OF TRUSTEES

A unique feature of multiemployer plans is equal representation of employers and employees in plan administration. Unlike a unilaterally administered single-employer plan, where the employer directly administers the plan without employee participation, a multiemployer plan is administered by a joint board of trustees. The board of trustees is the "plan sponsor" of a multiemployer plan (the equivalent of an employer in a single-employer plan) as well as the plan's "named fiduciary" and has exclusive authority and discretion to manage the assets of the plan.

Multiemployer plan trustees are designated by labor and management and do not necessarily have a background in employee benefits or any specific aspects of plan administration, although professional trustees do exist. How, then, can a politically and economically divided board of trustees administer a plan solely in the interests of plan participants and beneficiaries? Moreover, how can multiemployer plan trustees prudently administer a plan without appropriate skills and experience? The answer lies in the

---

4 "Reciprocity and Multiemployer Funds: A Model of Portability," *Employee Benefit Notes*, February 1987, p. 5, contributed by the Martin E. Segal Company.

trustees' awareness of and dedication to fulfilling fiduciary duties to plan participants and the trustees' ability to delegate, within limitations, plan responsibilities to experts.

Multiemployer plan trustees, unlike trustees of unilaterally administered single-employer plans who have been selected by management, inevitably face conflicts of interest given their labor or management backgrounds. Often, multiemployer trustees also are officers or agents of either a contributing employer or a union, and therefore have loyalties both to employee benefit plan participants and to the bargaining party they represent.

Working under what is described by many as the "two-hat dilemma," multiemployer plan trustees are inevitably faced with making decisions that promote the interests of plan participants and beneficiaries but conflict with positions they would take if they were not plan trustees. Advising legal action for the collection of delinquent employer contributions, for example, is an area of potential conflict of interest, particularly for management trustees. Despite union or employer selection, the multiemployer plan trustee's labor or management "hat" comes off when administering the plan. "[A]n employee benefit fund trustee is a fiduciary whose duty to the trust beneficiaries must overcome any loyalty to the interest of the party that appointed him," the Supreme Court has declared in an oft-repeated statement.[5]

As with all employee benefit plan fiduciaries, multiemployer plan trustees are charged with administering a plan with the care, skill, prudence, and diligence that a prudent person acting in a similar capacity and familiar with such matters would use. Most labor and management trustees have full-time jobs outside of their plan responsibilities, are not paid for their efforts (except for reasonable expenses), and are not necessarily skilled or experienced in employee benefit plan operation. Fiduciary, trustee, and other responsibilities of multiemployer plan trustees, therefore, frequently are delegated to other individuals. This delegation of responsibility is proper as long as it is authorized and prudent.

Under the overview of the joint board of trustees, plan administrators and such professionals as attorneys, accountants, actuaries, consultants, and investment managers handle the daily functions of multiemployer plans. Some multiemployer plan administrators are salaried, working solely for the fund in an employee status. Other plan administrators work under contract for several benefit plans (sometimes both single and

---

5 *NLRB* v. *Amax Coal Co.*, 453 U.S. 322, 323 (1981).

multiemployer) at one time. The administrators of most Taft-Hartley funds are salaried.[6]

Through education of multiemployer plan trustees about the two-hat dilemma and prudent delegation of plan responsibilities, potential weaknesses of multiemployer plans can turn into strong points. As a well-known employee benefits attorney has said about the contribution of lay labor and management trustees to multiemployer plan operation: "The greatest strength that the trustee brings to the Taft-Hartley trustee table is his or her knowledge and feeling for the industry and the people in it."[7] The interests of plan participants, when trustees separate labor and management duties from plan duties and prudently delegate responsibilities to other persons better equipped to perform them, are well-served by the multiemployer plan.

WITHDRAWAL LIABILITY

In addition to joint labor-management administration and the unique characteristic of built-in portability, the multiemployer plan is notable for a somewhat perpetual existence independent of individual contributing employers. Because other employers participate in a multiemployer plan, an individual employer's withdrawal does not cause the plan to terminate.

This structural aspect of multiemployer plans, specifically of multiemployer pension plans funded for benefits payable far in the future and not on a pay-as-you-go basis, is potentially hazardous to participants. Without some sort of safeguard, employers remaining in a multiemployer defined benefit plan could owe vested benefits earned by employees of employers opting out of the plan. Given this disincentive to remain in a multiemployer plan, particularly one covering employees in a declining industry, many employers would want to withdraw and the plan would be unable to pay participants the retirement benefits they had been promised.

The Employee Retirement Income Security Act of 1974 (ERISA) originally addressed this problem, but did not go far enough in discouraging employers from withdrawing from a financially weak multiemployer defined benefit plan. Employers faced liability for unfunded vested benefits only if they contributed to a multiemployer plan within five

---

6 Bernard Handel, "Forms and Functions of Administration," chapter in *Trustees Handbook*, 5th ed., ed. Marc Gertner (Brookfield, WI: International Foundation of Employee Benefit Plans, 1998), p. 323.

7 Marc Gertner, "Basic Concepts of Trusteeship," chapter in *Trustees Handbook*, p. 19.

years of the plan's termination. Moreover, liability was limited to 30 percent of the employer's net worth.

In 1980, Congress recognized the precarious financial condition the multiemployer defined benefit plan structure placed on both employers and the Pension Benefit Guaranty Corporation (PBGC) and passed the Multiemployer Pension Plan Amendments Act (MPPAA). The MPPAA amended ERISA's withdrawal liability rules, making withdrawal liability harsher for withdrawing employers but fairer for those remaining in the plan. Under the MPPAA, any employer withdrawing from a multiemployer defined benefit plan that has unfunded, vested benefits is liable for its proportionate share of the benefits—whether the plan terminates or not. Hence, remaining employers no longer shoulder the full burden of the plan's unfunded vested benefits.

PLAN TERMINATION AND INSOLVENCY

Although an employer's withdrawal from a multiemployer plan does not terminate the plan, a mass withdrawal (all employers withdrawing) will. Also, a multiemployer plan terminates if a plan amendment is adopted to either freeze service credits or change a defined benefit plan to a defined contribution plan. When a multiemployer plan does terminate, no reversion of residual assets to a contributing employer is allowed. In contrast, a single-employer sponsor may recover surplus plan assets upon plan termination (but also will encounter an excise tax of up to 50 percent of the reversion).

Unlike the guarantee of nonforfeitable benefits under a single-employer plan upon plan termination, the PBGC guarantees the nonforfeitable benefits of participants of a multiemployer defined benefit plan only upon plan insolvency—not plan termination. When the available resources of a multiemployer plan are not sufficient to pay benefits for a plan year, the PBGC provides the insolvent plan with a loan.

The PBGC's insolvency insurance program for multiemployer plans is funded and maintained separately from its termination insurance program for single-employer plans. The multiemployer program covers about 8.7 million participants in about 2,000 plans; the single-employer program covers about 33 million participants in about 42,000 plans.[8] The PBGC insolvency insurance premium for multiemployer plans, unlike the termination insurance premium for single-employer plans, is not risk-related. The annual premium for each participant of a multiemployer plan

---

8 Pension Benefit Guaranty Corporation, *1998 Annual Report to the Congress*, (Washington, D.C.), pp. 17,19.

is $2.60. In comparison, the annual PBGC premium for single-employer plans is $19 per participant, plus $9 per participant for every $1,000 of unfunded vested benefits.[9]

With the more stringent withdrawal liability provisions MPPAA introduced in 1980, the majority of multiemployer plans are now fully funded and chances of plan insolvency have decreased. In 1994, about 3 percent of multiemployer plans were underfunded by a total of $27.4 billion. In comparison, 55 percent of single-employer plans were underfunded by a total of $64 billion in 1996.[10]

PLAN QUALIFICATION

Unlike withdrawal liability and PBGC insolvency insurance, which are areas distinct to multiemployer plans, Internal Revenue Code (IRC) plan qualification provisions generally apply to single-employer and multiemployer plans alike. These qualification provisions, such as the minimum participation, minimum coverage, and minimum and full-funding rules, permit tax advantages to pension plans that meet them. As with single-employer plans, if a multiemployer plan is "qualified," contributions are tax-deductible for contributing employers, and benefits (including investment income) are tax-deferred for employees until distribution.

In some instances, bargaining-unit employees in multiemployer plans are excluded from or easily meet plan qualification rules. For example, a plan of which a qualified trust is a part must benefit the lesser of 50 employees or 40 percent of the employees of an employer. This minimum participation standard does not apply to employees in a multiemployer plan who are covered by collective-bargaining agreements.[11]

Plan qualification provisions designed to prevent discrimination in favor of highly compensated employees similarly call for a disaggregation of a multiemployer plan into a plan covering the bargaining-unit employees and plans covering nonbargaining-unit employees. In the case of the minimum coverage requirements, bargaining-unit employees are excluded from the testing of that portion of the plan covering nonbargaining-unit employees if retirement benefits were the subject of good-faith bargaining. Tested separately and as employees of one employer, the collectively

---

9 ERISA Sec. 4006(a)(3).

10 *Pension Benefit Guaranty Corporation: Financial Condition Improving but Long-Term Risks Remain*, (Washington, D.C: General Accounting Office, 1999), pp. 8, 12, 13.

11 IRC Sec. 401(a)(26)(E). A special testing rule for nonbargaining-unit employees allows the plan to meet the minimum participation standard if 50 employees, including those covered by a collectively bargained agreement, benefit from the plan.

bargained portion of a multiemployer plan should automatically pass the minimum coverage test because all other employees are excluded (i.e., 100 percent of the nonhighly compensated and 100 percent of the highly compensated employees in the bargaining unit will be covered).[12]

In nondiscrimination tests that compare the benefits actually provided to highly and nonhighly compensated employees, rather than the coverage, such as the 401(k) actual deferral percentage and actual contribution percentage tests, plan qualification requirements become more difficult for multiemployer plans. Bargaining-unit employees, again, are similarly treated as employees of one employer and tested as a separate plan. However, multiemployer plan administrators have to rely on contributing employers for identification of highly compensated employees, and it is unclear whether an employer's failure to do so will disqualify the plan. As with other nondiscrimination testing, each employer's nonbargaining-unit employees are treated as a separate plan.[13]

As mentioned earlier, sometimes multiemployer plan practice is more liberal than the plan qualification rules under the IRC, and sometimes plan qualification rules are more liberal for multiemployer plans than for single-employer plans. To constitute a qualified trust, for example, the plan of which it is a part generally cannot require an employee to be over 21 years of age or to complete a period of service longer than one year (if over age 21) to participate. Because most collective-bargaining agreements require contributions for individuals within a bargaining unit or classification—regardless of age—multiemployer plans seldom have an age prerequisite for participation.[14]

Compliance with qualification requirements either intended for single-employer plans or incognizant of multiemployer plans, is, at times, difficult for multiemployer plan trustees and administrators. Compliance with the full funding limitation changes of the Omnibus Budget Reconciliation Act of 1987 (OBRA '87) was particularly problematical. OBRA '87 placed a cap of 150 percent of current liabilities over plan assets on the deductible contributions an employer may make to a pension plan. This full-funding limitation modification, which in 1999 began a phased-in increase to 170 percent by 2005, was intended to prevent the loss of tax revenue through the overfunding of pension plans for liabilities not yet

---

12 Treas. Reg. Sec. 1.410(b)–6(d)(1).
13 See Gerald E. Cole, Jr., and Gregory A. Delamarter, "401(k) for Negotiated Plans," *Employee Benefits Digest*, March 1990, pp. 6, 7.
14 Daniel F. McGinn, "Minimum Participation and Vesting, Postretirement Age Benefit Adjustments and General Benefit Distribution Rules," chapter in *Trustees Handbook*, p. 233.

incurred—particularly the overfunding of single-employer plans targeted for recovery of surplus assets upon termination.

Because most multiemployer plans are fully funded, and employer contributions are negotiated over a fixed number of years, contributing employers were concerned about their possible inability to deduct obligatory, negotiated contributions that exceeded the full funding limitation (as well as the related 10 percent excise tax on nondeductible contributions). Options to counter OBRA '87's effects, such as increasing benefits or reopening bargaining, were either impractical or potentially harmful to multiemployer plans. Even more frustrating was the fact that neither unions nor employers had much incentive to overfund a multiemployer plan.[15]

The sometimes arduous application of plan qualification rules and other benefit laws and regulations to multiemployer plans is one contributing factor to a comparatively slow appearance of employee benefit trends, such as flexible benefit plans and 401(k) plans, among multiemployer plans. It is understandable that employers contributing to multiemployer plans for employees who often change jobs with seasons, business cycles, or construction projects are somewhat reluctant to handle administrative matters that must be taken care of at the employer level. Salary deferrals to a multiemployer 401(k) plan, for example, have to be withheld from payroll by each employer and forwarded to the plan administrator. Inherent multiemployer plan differences also somewhat impede experimentation with health and welfare benefit plan designs. The extent of employee assistance and wellness programs among multiemployer plans, although increasing, lingers well behind that found among single-employer plans.

COBRA

Multiemployer employee benefit plan regulation by ERISA, the Internal Revenue Code, and other benefits-related law, outside of the plan qualification rules, also sometimes is incongruous with the structure and operation of multiemployer plans. COBRA is an excellent example of a federal statute that, while originally enacted with little acknowledgment of multiemployer plans, has since been interpreted through regulations and amended to clarify and ease the compliance process for multiemployer plans and contributing employers.

---

15 "Relentless Pursuit of Fair Funding Treatment: Making Sense of Pension Funding Limitations," *NCCMP Update*, Spring 1989, p. 7.

One of the first questions COBRA posed for those connected with the administration of multiemployer health plans was its application to contributing employers with fewer than 20 employees. Treasury regulations confirmed the worst: Each of the employers maintaining a multiemployer health plan must have fewer than 20 employees during the preceding calendar year for the plan to be excluded from COBRA. Employers maintaining multiple-employer welfare plans, conversely, are treated as maintaining separate plans, and, therefore, are excluded from COBRA if they have fewer than 20 employees.[16]

Even the intent of COBRA—to allow qualified beneficiaries who lose employer-sponsored group health plan coverage to elect continued coverage at their own expense—was not as relevant in the multiemployer plan context because most multiemployer plans already had continued health coverage options in place. Historically, multiemployer health plans provide an extended period of eligibility to participants during times of temporary unemployment, often based on an hours bank or through a series of self-payments.

Because many multiemployer health plan participants do continue their eligibility for health benefits for a time period despite a reduction in hours or termination (many times without even accessing their hours bank), there often is no loss of coverage upon these events as there is for participants in single-employer plans. Accordingly, employers contributing to multiemployer plans, who are required under COBRA to notify a plan administrator of certain qualifying events, are not always aware whether an employee's reduction in hours or termination has resulted in a loss of coverage, i.e., whether a qualifying event has taken place. Advised to err on the side of caution, employers were likely to notify the plan administrator of every reduction in hours and every termination. The plan administrator, in turn, was obliged to notify qualified beneficiaries if continued coverage could not be verified within COBRA's 14-day notification period.

COBRA has since been amended to introduce alternative means of notification for reductions in hours and terminations of employees covered

---

16 Treas. Reg. Sec. 54.4980B-2 Q&A 5(a) (1999). The confusion over the characteristics of a "small employer plan" persists in applying other group health plan statutes to multiemployer plans. For example, the Medicare secondary-payer provisions for group health plans that cover the working aged also, like COBRA, apply to employers with 20 or more employees. But, in the case of the Medicare secondary-payer provisions, employers contributing to multiemployer or multiple-employer plans that have less than 20 employees can elect out if the plan so provides, leaving Medicare as primary payer for employees (and spouses) 65 and older.

by multiemployer plans, and also longer notification periods for employers contributing to and administrators of multiemployer plans. If a multiemployer plan so provides, the determination of a reduction in hours or termination as a qualifying event may be made by the plan administrator instead of the contributing employer. Also, if the plan so provides, contributing employers may take longer than 30 days to notify the plan administrator of qualifying events, and the plan administrator may take longer than 14 days to notify qualified beneficiaries of their rights. Finally, for any group health plan, notice by the employer to the plan administrator and extension of coverage may begin with the loss of coverage instead of the qualifying event.[17]

COBRA also has been amended since its passage in 1985 to change the entity directly liable for the noncompliance tax burden as well as the form of the sanction. Somewhat atypically placed, the tax penalty for COBRA violations (generally, a $100 excise tax for each day of noncompliance per qualified beneficiary up to a maximum of the lesser of 10 percent paid for medical care or $500,000) now falls on the multiemployer plan, not contributing employers.[18] Prior to amendment by the Technical and Miscellaneous Revenue Act of 1988 (TAMRA), the failure of one contributing employer to comply with COBRA caused all contributing employers to lose their respective tax deductions for contributions to any multiemployer group health plans they maintained, and highly compensated employees of all employers to be denied an income exclusion for employer group health coverage.

CONCLUSION

A multiemployer plan has five basic features: (1) numerous employers contribute to the plan; (2) employees frequently change jobs without loss of benefits (or benefit eligibility); (3) a joint labor-management board of trustees, not contributing employers, manages the plan and its assets, which (4) are placed in a trust fund; and (5) the plan is maintained under a collective-bargaining agreement or agreements. These features have led to separate legislation for multiemployer plans in some instances, such as withdrawal liability and plan insolvency insurance. In other employee

---

17 ERISA Sec. 606; IRC Sec. 4980B(f)(6), as amended by the Omnibus Budget Reconciliation
    Act of 1989, Sec. 7891(d), effective for plan years beginning on or after January 1, 1990.
18 IRC Sec. 4980B(e). Other persons who are responsible for administering or providing benefits
    under the plan, such as contributing employers, also can be liable for the excise tax if they
    cause a COBRA failure.

benefit areas, such as certain plan qualification rules and the continued health care coverage requirements of COBRA, multiemployer plans either have had to adapt to a framework set up for single-employer plans or modify the framework.

In a number of aspects of employee benefit plan design, funding, and administration too numerous to mention in this chapter, application to multiemployer plans differs. In areas even as basic as investment policy, where multiemployer plans historically are more conservative than single-employer plans, multiemployer plans are something of a wrinkle in an otherwise smooth spread of employee benefits. Yet, significantly, multiemployer plans are the only way to provide meaningful benefits to skilled, frequently mobile employees at a cost and level of responsibility acceptable to the industry employers who employ them.

State and Local Pension Plan Developments

Olivia S. Mitchell*

David McCarthy

Pension plans of state and local government employees in the United States command substantial attention in financial and labor market circles. One reason is that they are so large, controlling more than $2.4 trillion in assets, on a par with private pension plan systems in the U.S. Another is that they cover so many people: Currently these systems pay benefits to more than 5 million retirees, and they cover more than 13 million active participants.[1] In this chapter we outline three key aspects of public sector pension plans in the U.S. having to do with their overall structure, their benefit and financing arrangements, and their governance structure. In addition, we outline key challenges facing these plans in the next decade.[2]

---

*Mitchell is the International Foundation of Employee Benefit Plans Professor of Insurance and Risk Management and executive director of the Pension Research Council at The Wharton School, as well as research associate at the National Bureau of Economic Research. McCarthy is a Ph.D. candidate in Insurance and Risk Management at the Wharton School. The authors acknowledge research support from The Wharton School and the Pension Research Council. Conclusions and opinions are those of the authors and do not reflect the views of any of the institutions with which they are affiliated.

1 These statistics, along with much of the information in this chapter, are derived from our analysis of public sector pensions in North America by Mitchell and Hustead (Reference 21); see in particular Mitchell, McCarthy, Wisniewski, and Zorn, (Reference 22; henceforth MMWZ).
2 For early discussion of public pension plans see Bleakney (Reference 2), Inman (Reference 13), and Phillips (Reference 26); more recent analyses include Mitchell and Carr (Reference 18), Hsin and Mitchell (Reference 8, 9, and 10), and Mitchell and Smith (Reference 23).

PUBLIC PENSION PLAN STRUCTURE

Public employee pension plans in the United States cover a diverse set of participants, with membership and composition varying from state to state.[3] In some states separate plans cover uniformed officers (police officers and firefighters), teachers, the judiciary, and members of the legislature, while in other states a few large plans encompass the range of state and local workers.[4] These pension plans have evolved over time differently, one from the other, as a result of having emerged from distinct constituencies and histories. One interesting aspect of public plans in the U.S. is that they are not regulated at the Federal government level. This is because individual states have developed and constructed their pension systems independently from the Federal government, and in turn the benefits promised ultimately rely on each state's individual taxing capability and authority, rather than having a Federal government guarantee. In practice, however, many state and local governments require their pension systems to conform to generally accepted accounting principles, and as a result many (though not all) tend to follow pension measurement and reporting requirements specified by the Governmental Accounting Standards Board (GASB).

Other common elements are also characteristic of state and local pension systems. One is that public sector pensions have tended to be of the defined benefit (DB) variety, meaning that workers were promised a pension benefit specified in terms of the individual's age, years of service, and salary at the time of retirement. Contributions needed to keep the plan solvent would be determined on the basis of actuarial valuations, and plan investments would be managed by a pension board, perhaps with investment management outsourced to financial experts. DB plans could be underfunded if assets on hand are insufficient to meet promised benefits; in that event, DB participants might bear the risk of benefits being reduced, and/or taxpayers could be asked to pay additional taxes to meet promised benefits. Recently some public sector jurisdictions have either adopted or expressed an interest in adopting a defined contribution (DC) plan, wherein plan contributions are specified instead of retiree benefit formulas or specific retirement payments. DC participants tend to have

---

3 In this effort, a primary source of comparative information we use for state and local government pension systems is the public pension survey conducted periodically by the Public Pension Coordinating Council (hereafter PENDAT; see Zorn, Reference 35), along with Bureau of Labor Statistics (BLS) surveys on state and local pension plans, and Census of Government reports.

4 We do not discuss federal civilian or military retirement systems in this chapter; for more on these systems, see Hustead and Hustead (Reference 12).

some say over where their pension investments are directed, given a menu of options determined by the employer. At retirement, DC benefits depend on the accumulations in participants' accounts; larger accruals can generate larger benefits, but the brunt of poor investment performance must be borne by retirees.[5] At present however, the large majority of public pension plans in the U.S. are of the defined benefit variety.

To outline the overall structure of state and local pension plans in the U.S., Table 50–1 presents information on system membership, receipts, and total investments for 1987 and 1997.[6] These data show that system financial flows have grown markedly over time: State and local pension plan revenues rose from $99 billion to $225 billion from 1987 to 1997, mostly due to robust investment earnings over the period. These earnings, combined with employer and employee contributions, quadrupled total system assets and resulted in an aggregate state and local government pension pool of more than $2 trillion at the end of the 1990s.

To better understand who is covered by these state and local pensions, it is worth examining system membership by plan type.[7] It is interesting to note some consolidation over time, with the number of plans declining slightly (from 2,414 to 2,264 between 1987 and 1997). However, active membership grew almost 20 percent (from 10.7 million to 12.8 million) and the number of retirees grew even faster (from 3.7 million to 5.3 million). On the whole, the net result was that the ratio of active to retired members dropped (from 2.9 million to 2.4 million) for the combined systems. Had these plans not had substantial investment reserves, the decline in active members might have required more employer contributions, because retiree benefits were rising relative to active member payrolls. Most of the active members population—some 57 percent—is covered by state-administered retirement systems, approximately 29 percent is in systems specifically for teachers or school employees, one-tenth is in locally administered systems primarily serving general employees, and the remaining 3 percent is in systems specifically for public safety employees (i.e., police officers and firefighters). Similar breakdowns apply for the retiree/beneficiary breakdowns. Of the 4 million retirees and beneficiaries covered by plans surveyed, 56 percent were in state-administered systems, 27 percent were in systems for teachers and school employees, 11 percent

---

5 For early discussion of public pension plans see Bleakney (Reference 26), Inman (Reference 13), and Phillips (Reference 26); more recent analyses include Mitchell and Carr (Reference 18), Hsin and Mitchell (References 8, 9, and 10), and Mitchell and Smith (Reference 23).

6 The 1997 PENDAT data were the most recent available as of this writing.

7 The PENDAT survey (Zorn, Reference 35) covered plans employing more than 80 percent of active state and local system members.

T A B L E   50–1

State and Local Pension Plan Features

	1986–87			1996–97		
	State	Local	Total	State	Local	Total
I. Number of Plans	201	2,213	2,414	212	2,052	2,264
II. Membership (M)						
Active members	9.2	1.5	10.7	11.2	1.6	12.8
Inactive members	1.0	0.1	1.1	2.3	0.1	2.4
Retirees and beneficiaries	3.0	0.7	3.7	4.3	1.0	5.3
Total Members	*13.2*	*2.3*	*15.5*	*17.8*	*2.7*	*20.5*
Active/Retired ratio	3.1	2.1	2.9	2.6	1.6	2.4
III. Receipts ($B)						
Employee contributions	$ 9.4	$ 1.8	$ 11.2	$ 17.4	$ 3.4	$ 20.8
Government contributions	23.3	7.1	30.4	37.1	7.8	44.9
Earnings on investment	45.0	12.7	57.7	133.9	25.1	159.0
Total Receipts ($B)	*$77.7*	*$21.6*	*$99.3*	*$188.4*	*$36.3*	*$224.7*
Employee contributions	12.1%	8.3%	11.3%	9.2%	9.4%	9.3%
Government contributions	30.0	32.9	30.6	19.7	21.5	20.0
Investment earnings	57.9	58.8	58.1	71.1	69.1	70.8
IV. Total Invested Assets ($B)			$530.1			$2,094.1

Source: Adapted from MMWZ (Reference 22), from U.S. Bureau of the Census (various years) and Board of Governors of the Federal Reserve System (Reference 3).

Note: Total investment values not completely comparable with contributions and earnings on investment due to discrepancies in different data sources.

were in general local systems, and the remaining 4 percent in public safety systems. Systems that cover only local employees have a higher ratio of active to retired members (2.4 active/retired), than for state-wide systems (2.7 active/retired). Furthermore, the active/retired ratio for teacher and school employees is somewhat higher than the average (3.0), and for public safety employees it is lower than average (1.9).[8]

DESIGNING BENEFITS FOR PUBLIC PENSION SYSTEMS

As a rule, a retirement system seeks to provide retirees with old-age benefits, which combined with other sources of retirement income such as

8 This section draws on Zorn (Reference 34).

Social Security can meet retirement needs. To this end, employers offering a pension typically specify rules regarding who can be included in the plan after completing a certain period of service on the job, what legal vesting rights are, and what benefit formulas entail. Public and private sector practice varies along these dimensions, with state and local employees often being required to work longer before they gain a legal right to an eventual benefit—that is, to vest—than their private sector counterparts. For example, in 1994 (the last time the U.S. Bureau of Labor Statistics tallied these figures), 43 percent of the public sector workforce had to remain on the job at least 10 years before becoming legally entitled to a benefit. In the private sector, double that number, or 85 percent, can vest in the pension after five years (in 1997; Reference 17). Some public sector plans also permit "purchase of service" credits, where a public employee who moves from one job to another within a state can purchase credit for past service under the plan on the new job. This is virtually unknown in private sector defined benefit plans.

Turning to benefit formulas, state and local pension plans tend to emphasize final average earnings, a practice now also common among private-sector plans.[9] But benefit formulas differ substantially across sector: Almost two-thirds of public-sector pensions use the last three years of an employee's pay to determine the benefit amount (61 percent), while private plans more commonly use five years to determine the fraction of pay used in the benefit formula (78 percent). It is also evident that state and local pension formulas tend to use a higher benefit multiplier per year of service worked, as compared to private-sector pension plans. That is, 43 percent of the public plans provide a benefit accumulation of 2+ percent of pay per year of service, while only 7 percent do so in the private sector.

A reader knowledgeable about public-sector pensions will recognize that these public/private comparisons must be qualified in at least three ways. First, many governmental employees in state/local jurisdictions are required to contribute to their DB pension plans—on the order of one-third of total contributions are made by employees—while employee contributions are uncommon in the private sector. As a result, it is often argued that benefits can be higher in the public sector, as a result of the higher employee payments to the plans. Second, the DB tabulations do not include payments to and from defined contribution plans, though many private-sector employers offer both DB and DC plans (Zorn, Reference 33). Hence a

---

9 These public-private comparisons are based on MMWZ (Reference 22) for the public plan data, and Mitchell (Reference 17) for the private plan information (the latter include employees in medium and large private establishments).

focus on DB benefits alone may overstate the relative advantage of public-sector pensions, compared to private plan offerings. Finally, many public employees are not covered by Social Security (as many as one-quarter are not currently included; U.S. House Ways and Means, Reference 30), and hence their employer-provided DB plans must provide higher retirement benefits to partially offset this lack of Social Security benefits. We also note that those without Social Security benefit coverage would seek automatic (though not necessarily full) indexation to inflation after retirement; such escalators are prevalent in state and local pension plans, but rare among private plans.

Public pension plans also appear to be more likely to offer different kinds of retirement benefits—disability benefits—as compared to corporate plans.[10] For instance, 91 percent of state and local pensions contained disability retirement provisions in 1994, as compared with only 75 percent of private plans in 1997. Almost half (42 percent) of public plans allowed workers to retire with unreduced normal benefits compared with fewer (30 percent) of private plans. Qualifying age and service conditions for disability retirement also tend to be less restrictive in the public sector, perhaps because disability may be covered through disability insurance plans in the corporate sector, rather than through the pension plan. In addition, some occupations in the public sector (e.g., police officers and firefighters) are more inherently risky than those found in the private sector; hence one would anticipate that these riskier jobs would provide more generous disability provisions.

A few public plan benefit changes over time are worth mentioning. One is that public pension DB programs do not tend to integrate benefits with Social Security, for those three-quarters of state and local employees with Social Security coverage, and the fraction is decreasing over time. The fraction of public plans with a benefit formula integrated with Social Security fell from 10 percent to 4 percent between 1992 and 1994. Among private plans, the fraction has risen from around 45 percent in 1980 to 63 percent in 1989, and fallen again to 49 percent in 1997 (MMWZ, Reference 22; Mitchell, Reference 17). Another trend is that over time, requirements for early retirement appear to have been lowered, with fewer public plans now requiring the "age 55/service 10" combination for early retirement, and more moving to combinations requiring less service. A similar pattern is observed among private DB plans.

---

10 The data in this comparative exercise are derived from MMWZ (Reference 22) for public plans, and Mitchell (Reference 17) for medium and large private plan establishments.

FINANCING PUBLIC PENSION SYSTEMS

In public DB pensions, the sponsoring employer—be it a state or municipal or some other jurisdiction—takes on the responsibility of ensuring that the promised benefits will be paid. One way of securing these promises is to prefund the pension system, by having the employer and/or employee contribute to the plan. In addition, investment returns on plan assets can help reduce contributory obligations. To this end, a public pension plan's board of trustees in concert with staff (and frequently outside consultants) must carry out the task of determining plan liabilities, deciding how much contributions should be, and directing asset investments. Actuaries will be required to measure DB plan obligations, by assessing how projected benefits will change with current and projected employee age, service, and compensation, as well as mortality, disability, retirement rates, and economic assumptions regarding wage increases and long-term rates of return on plan investments (Hustead, Reference 11). In addition, actuaries make an informed guess about projected asset returns, to judge likely investment performance in the long term.

Clearly, the choice of actuarial assumptions is highly influential in determining a plan's financial status, yet there is a fair degree of leeway for cross-plan differences in the selection of these. The average assumed rate of return in public plans was 7.8 percent in 1997 (Zorn, Reference 34), with marginally higher rates assumed by systems serving state employees and teachers (8.0 percent for both groups) and the same or slightly lower rates for systems serving public safety and general local employees (7.8 and 7.7 percent, respectively). Assumptions related to wage increases (including inflation and step/merit increases) varied more across groups: On average the figure was 5.9 percent, but 6.4 percent for systems covering teachers, and 5.7 percent for plans covering general public employees. By contrast, assumptions regarding anticipated inflation were similar across surveyed plans, averaging 4.4 percent overall, with little variance.

In addition to differences in assumptions, pension plans differ according to the actuarial method used to calculate plan liabilities. Around two-thirds of state and local plans use an entry age actuarial cost method, so as to smooth employer contributions (targeting a level percent of payroll over time; see McGill et al., Reference 15). This approach is appealing in the political context inasmuch as it tends to stabilize pension contributions for long-term budgeting purposes. Actuaries also must forecast how plan assets will evolve over time, to determine whether these are sufficient to pay promised benefits. The gap between the actuarial value of assets and the actuarial accrued liability is referred to as the "unfunded actuarial accrued liability," and this gap tends to be amortized through a smooth contribution stream over a 20- to 30-year period.[11]

Because actuarial methods and assumptions differ across plans, so too will the resulting asset/liability measures. This means that funding comparisons across plans are not strictly comparable (because all plans do not apply the same actuarial method and set of assumptions), but each plan's reported asset/liability measures reflect the methods and assumptions actually used to fund that plan.[12] Bearing this in mind, Table 50–2 shows that the actuarial accrued liability amounted to almost $1.3 trillion across the subset of all public plans responding to the PENDAT 1997 survey, with approximately $1.1 trillion in assets available to fund the liability (Zorn, Reference 34). It is instructive to focus on the "funding ratio," which may be calculated by dividing the actuarial value of assets by actuarial accrued liabilities. Though it is an imperfect measure of year-to-year efforts to fund past obligations, it is often used as a summary measure of funded status. Table 50–2 shows that the average public plan funding ratio was estimated at 87 percent for survey respondents in 1996, with the median at 91 percent; the average period for amortizing the unfunded actuarial accrued liability was approximately 23 years. The typical public pension plan reported actuarially based assets of $4.32 billion and an average reported liability of $4.95 billion, for an average actuarial unfunded liability of about $630 million per plan. On an active participant basis, the median dollar-weighted value of assets per participant in 1996 was $116,000 with $148,000 in accrued liabilities. Table 50–2 also indicates a "flow" funding measure, showing whether employer contributions

---

11 The actuarial value of assets is often determined in a manner that smooths year-to-year market fluctuations over a three- or five-year averaging period. This dampens the impact of short-term investment volatility on the measure of plan assets and tends to stabilize contributions.

12 Prior to June 15, 1996, the Governmental Accounting Standards Board (GASB) required public plans to disclose the Pension Benefit Obligation (PBO), a measure of the actuarial accrued liability based on the projected unit credit actuarial method, in the notes to their financial statements. This was reported in addition to the actuarial accrued liability determined under the actuarial method actually used to calculate the plan's liabilities and required contributions. The purpose of disclosing the PBO was to provide a more consistent measure with which to compare funding progress across public plans. In 1996, GASB (1996) eliminated the PBO disclosure requirement after substantial debate, on the grounds that it did not substantially clarify funded status and was possibly responsible for a reduction in employer contributions for some plans. Currently GASB provides for the use of any one of the following actuarial cost methods: entry age, frozen entry age, attained age, frozen attained age, projected unit credit, and aggregate actuarial cost. With the spread of GASB reporting among retirement systems, the PBO statistic has been de-emphasized or dropped entirely from public employee pension system annual financial reports.

T a b l e   50–2

Financial Status of State and Local Pension Plans

	Average	Median
I. Assets and Liabilities ($000)		
Pension plan assets[1]	$4,318,185	$562,873
Pension plan liabilities[2]	4,954,381	679,507
Total underfunding	636,196	39,533
Stock funding ratio (%):		
Assets/Liabilities ($-weighted)	87%	91%
II. Contributions ($000)		
Req. employer contributions	105,168	14,580
Actual contributions	162,846	20,930
Employer	102,662	14,580
Employee	60,184	5,316
Flow funding ratio (%):		
Required/actual contributions	98%	100%
III. Benefit Payments ($000)		
Total benefit payments	$204,289	$18,048
Retirement	177,823	12,623
Disability	16,047	1,333
Survivors	8,086	971
Lump Sum	2,333	0
IV. Per Active Participant ($000)		**$-weighted**
Actuarial value of assets		$165
Actuarial accrued liability		211
Contributions		5.5

Source: Adapted from MMWZ, Reference 22; data from 1997 PENDAT sample of reporting plans.
Notes:
1 Measured as the actuarial value of plan assets.
2 Measured as the actuarial accrued liability.

in a given year cover the amounts necessary to systematically fund the plan. It should be noted that the average flow funding rate stood at 98 percent and the median at 100 percent in 1996, indicating that public employers typically met their new pension obligations as they arose.

One source of pension financing is employer contributions, which in the public-sector PENDAT plans averaged 9.5 percent of payroll. As noted above, public employee retirement systems are also usually contributory, that is, they require contributions by their members, averaging

5 percent in the PENDAT sample.[13] An additional and quite important source of state and local pension system revenue is investment returns, which in turn highlights the role of asset allocation in pension investment portfolios. Thirty years ago, state and local retirement systems rarely held anything but fixed-income assets which earned them relatively low rates of return. This practice was in part attributable to legally-set portfolio limits prescribed by state legislatures that frequently ruled out equity investments. The so-called portfolio caps were eased over time and replaced with a "prudent person" requirement, which typically allow pension boards a freer choice of investments, as long as standards of prudence and diversification are met.[14] Flowing from this regulatory change, equities have been introduced into most public plan portfolios, and now more than 40 percent of these assets are held in domestic equities (Table 50–3). Among the top 1,000 pension systems, half or more of total assets are held in equities, more than one-third in bonds, and the rest in real estate, cash, and other forms of investments (Anand, Reference 1). Public pensions today still do hold slightly less equity (59 percent) than do private funds (64 percent), and slightly more bonds (35 percent versus 29 percent). The international equity exposure of public funds (11 percent) is also slightly lower than that of private funds (14 percent). Other holdings (real estate, cash) are similar across plan types.

Even today, however, some state and local pension systems are still required to seek out, or avoid, specific investment categories. For example, 19 percent of the PENDAT plans have constitutional restrictions on investments, while 12 percent are now or have been prohibited from making certain investments (e.g., countries such as South Africa and Northern Ireland, that do not follow McBride principles). Other times, public plans must meet mandates favoring certain investments: For example, 4 percent of the PENDAT plans are required to direct a percentage of their plan investments to in-state holdings. In addition, many other funds have internal policy limitations on asset allocations, or other statutory limits on asset allocations. The extent to which such asset restrictions influence investment policy and investment returns as well as investment risk is an extremely important and complex issue particularly because rates of return

---

13 Often these contributions are "picked-up" under section 414(h)(2) of the Internal Revenue Code, effectively making them pretax contributions by the employees. In this instance, they are different from private-sector defined benefit plans, under which employee contributions are made after tax. This may be one of the reasons why private-sector defined benefit plans are typically non-contributory.

14 The prudent person concept was codified for private sector plans in the Employee Retirement Income Security Act of 1974 (ERISA).

T a b l e   50–3

State and Local Government Pension System Investments

	All Systems
I. Total Investments ($B)	**1,092.2**
II. Asset Allocation	
Short-term	4.4%
Domestic Stocks	42.7
Domestic Bonds	38.8
Real Estate Mortgages	0.7
Real Estate Equities	1.8
International Equities	6.9
International Fixed-Income	1.7
Other	3.0
III. Investment Returns	
Rate of Return 1996	13.8%
Exp. 1-year Return Given Allocation	11.8
5-year Annualized Return (% 1991–1996)	11.3

Source: Adapted from MMWZ, Reference 22; data from 1997 PENDAT sample of reporting plans.

earned by these plans are generally higher, for more equity-based pools.[15] On average, the investments earned a 13.66 percent return in 1996, higher than the 11.77 percent expected return calculated using the systems' asset allocations and benchmark returns earned on the major security classes.[16] Additional research is required on this topic; in any event, it is not clear whether state taxpayers should be more or less risk-averse than corporate stockholders. We should add that even good investment performance can be substantially eroded by high expenses, suggesting the importance of learning more about administrative costs of public plans. Unfortunately fewer than half of all PENDAT plans currently report their administrative costs; for those reporting, dollar-weighted investment expenses averaged 27 basis points in 1996, with larger funds having lower

15 For more discussion on this topic see Mitchell and Hsin (Reference 19 and 20); Munnell and Sunden (Reference 24); Useem and Hess (Reference 31), and Clark, Craig, and Wilson (Reference 5).

16 On the other hand Nofsinger (Reference 25) compares public pension plan returns to a composite market index and argues that public plan investment performance tends to underperform the market, after correcting for risk.

expense ratios than smaller funds (Mitchell, Reference 16). Further research is required to establish whether public pension plans are, in fact, becoming more efficient over time (Mitchell and Hsin, Reference 20).

GOVERNANCE STRUCTURE

How state and local pensions are governed is not centrally prescribed, in contrast to the private sector where ERISA plays a strong role in standardizing management structures. Typically, however, there is much in common between plans. Most state and local systems are managed by an appointed retirement board with authority for investment decisions, actuarial matters, day-to-day operations, and sometimes, benefit design as well as benefit payment. Table 50–4 indicates that the typical size of public pension boards is usually eight people, with most of the board members appointed by politicians or serving ex-officio.[17] The average number of board members is higher for systems serving state employees and teachers (9.2 and 10, respectively) than for systems serving public safety and general local employees (7.5 and 7.6, respectively; MMWZ, Reference 22); also, systems serving teachers and public safety employees have a somewhat higher percent of elected members and lower percent of appointed members than do systems serving state or local general employees.

The management tasks of a public pension plan tend to be carried out by a paid staff under the supervision of the system's executive director or plan administrator, the latter of which usually reports directly to the pension board. (Some smaller systems established by a single governmental employer are administered by the employer's finance or human-resources department.) Staffing levels stand at around 50, averaged across all PENDAT plans, but state employee and teacher plans have larger staffs (110 to 120) due to the larger size of the pension systems, versus smaller ones for public safety and general local employees (7 to 11 staff members). The typical public pension system has around 2.6 staff members per 1,000 active members, with systems covering state employees and teachers averaging 1.5 each, compared with 5.0 for systems covering public safety and 2.8 for systems covering local government employees. Since state and teacher systems have substantially more members than systems covering public safety and local employees, it is likely that their lower staffing ratios reflect economies of scale.

---

17 Some systems, such as the Florida Retirement System and the Iowa Public Employee
Retirement System operate without a board of trustees, relying instead on authority vested
in a senior official of the sponsoring agency (Wisniewski, Reference 32).

T a b l e   50–4

Public Pension Plan Governance and Structure

	Mean	Median	Number of Sample Points
I. Board Size and Composition			
Number of board members	8.3	8	244
% appointed and ex-officio	62%	60%	231
% elected by members	35	40	224
II. Board Responsibilities (% responsible for)			
Investment	88%		244
Benefits	71		244
Assumptions	89		244
Asset allocation	84		228
III. Constraints on Board Behavior (% subject to)			
Prudent person limitation	88%		236
Ethics standards written	66		233
State legal list	29		238
Constitutional restrictions on investment	19		225
Own investment prohibitions	12		235
In-state investment requirements	4		233
State insurance law	3		235
IV. Public Pension Board Oversight (% requiring)			
Actuarial valuation annually	100%		364
Annual audit	99		252
Independent investment performance audits	86		231

Source: Adapted from MMWZ, Reference 22; data from 1997 PENDAT for sample of plans reporting.

The vast majority of public retirement boards are responsible for overseeing pension investments. As noted above, this is currently an area of substantial debate, because public plans are exempt from the Employee Retirement Income Security Act (ERISA) fiduciary requirements. Nevertheless, identical or very similar "prudent person" language has been adopted in 88 percent of the PENDAT plans, and two-thirds have written ethical standards for public board members. The latter approach seeks to limit potential conflicts of interest with regard to public pension boards, and it has recently been championed by the California Public Employee Retirement System (CalPERS), among others. In addition, most public plans are required to undertake an annual actuarial valuation, and furthermore they are subject to annual actuarial and independent investment audits. These requirements are useful in enhancing information for policymakers, plan participants, and taxpayers.

DISCUSSION

State and local government pension plans in the United States are substantial financial institutions. They also powerfully affect the retirement benefits of millions of public sector employees. Today, defined benefit plans still dominate the public pension marketplace, paying annuity benefits that depend on pay and service and are often indexed to inflation, and they are relatively well-funded, with substantial assets backing the benefit promise. These assets are also relatively diversified, though political factors and governance structures continue to exert an influence over investment allocations.

These signs of pension system maturity are, in the main, strongly positive predictors for the future. Yet public retirement systems also must expect challenges over the next 20 years. Legal developments are pending: For instance, the National Conference of Commissioners on Uniform State Laws recently proposed that all states adopt a uniform set of laws related to public pension plan investments. Called the Management of Public Employee Retirement Systems Act (MPERSA), it is intended to modernize investment decision-making in public pensions (Wisniewski, Reference 32). Whether it will eventually be adopted by state legislatures remains to be seen.

Anticipated demographic and workforce changes also will have an impact. The public sector workforce is aging, and state employers will soon face a spate of retirements; both developments will increase benefit payouts and reduce revenue inflows, in turn putting pressure on underfunded plans. In addition, an economic downturn also might undermine efforts to prefund accumulating benefit promises (Mitchell and Smith, Reference 23). A related issue is that some employee groups want either to move to a defined contribution plan, or to introduce a second-tier DC plan. Examples of public-sector DC plans include the State Employees Retirement System of Nebraska, the Teachers' Defined Contribution Plan of West Virginia, and Michigan's State Employee plan for workers newly hired in 1997 and thereafter (Fore, Reference 6). In addition, some public employers find they need to keep experienced, long-term employees by providing additional benefits for those who remain on the job beyond their "normal" retirement date. Known as DROPs (Deferred Retirement Option Plans), these reward an employee who postpones his or her retirement by providing a partial lump-sum distribution when he or she eventually leaves the job (Eitelberg, Reference 5). This trend has been paired with employee interest in pension portability, particularly among the younger, more mobile workforce.

Whether these complex pressures will increase public employer and employee interest in DC and hybrid plans—pensions that combine defined benefit and defined contribution plan features—is not yet known. If these plans can be shown to curtail administrative and transition costs, they certainly will become more prevalent. Working in the other direction is skepticism on the part of employee groups, especially labor unions, which may see the risks associated with these new plan types as offsetting their benefits. Equity market performance will undoubtedly also play a role.

R e f e r e n c e s

1. Anand, Vineeta, "Defined Benefit Assets Surge 20.3 Percent," *Pensions and Investments*, March 22: p. 1, 1999.
2. Bleakney, Thomas P., *Retirement Systems for Public Employees*, Philadelphia: Pension Research Council, 1972.
3. Board of Governors of the Federal Reserve System, *Flow of Funds Accounts of the United States, Annual Flows and Outstandings, 1982-1990*, Washington, D.C.: Board of Governors, 1999.
4. Clark, Robert L., Lee A. Craig, and Jack W. Wilson, "The Life and Times of a Public-Sector Pension Plan Before Social Security: The U.S. Navy Pension Plan in the Nineteenth Century," In O.S. Mitchell and E. Hustead, eds. *Pensions in the Public Sector*, Pension Research Council, Philadelphia: University of Pennsylvania Press, 2001.
5. Eitelberg, Cathie. "Evolution in Public Pensions," In O.S. Mitchell and E. Hustead, eds., *Pensions in the Public Sector*, Pension Research Council, Philadelphia: University of Pennsylvania Press, 2001.
6. Fore, Douglas. "Going Private in the Public Sector: The Transition from Defined Benefit to Defined Contribution," In O.S. Mitchell and E. Hustead, eds. *Pensions in the Public Sector*, Pension Research Council, Philadelphia: University of Pennsylvania Press, 2001.
7. Government Accounting Standards Board (GASB). *Statement No. 25: Financial Reporting for Defined Benefit Plans and Note Disclosures for Defined Contribution Plans*, Hartford, CT: GASB, 1996.
8. Hsin, Ping-Lung and Olivia S. Mitchell, "Managing Public Sector Pensions," In S. Schieber and J. Shoven, eds., *Pensions for the Twenty-First Century*, New York: Twentieth Century Fund, 1996.
9. Hsin, Ping Lung and Olivia S. Mitchell, "The Political Economy of Public Sector Pensions: Pension Funding Patterns, Governance Structures, and Fiscal Stress," *Revista de Analysis Economico*, July, 1994.
10. Hsin, Ping Lung and Olivia S. Mitchell, "Public Pension Plan Efficiency," In M. Gordon, O.S. Mitchell, and M. Twinney, eds. *Positioning Pensions for the 21st Century, 187–208*, Pension Research Council, Philadelphia: University of Pennsylvania Press, 1997.
11. Hustead, Edwin. "Determining the Cost of Public Pension Plans," In O.S. Mitchell and E. Hustead, eds. *Pensions in the Public Sector*, Pension Research Council, Philadelphia: University of Pennsylvania Press, 2001.
12. Hustead, Edwin and Toni Hustead, "Federal Civilian and Military Retirement Systems," In O.S. Mitchell and E. Hustead, eds., *Pensions in the Public Sector*, Pension Research Council. Philadelphia: University of Pennsylvania Press, 2001.

13. Inman, Robert P., "Public Employee Pensions and the Local Labor Budget," *Journal of Public Economics,* 19: 49-71, 1982.

14. Internal Revenue Service, U.S. Department of the Treasury, *Federal-State Reference Guide: Social Security Coverage and FICA Reporting by State and Local Government Employers*, Washington, D.C.: Internal Revenue Service, 1997.

15. McGill, Dan M., Kyle N. Brown, John J. Haley and Sylvester J. Schieber, *Fundamentals of Private Pensions*, Pension Research Council, Philadelphia: University of Pennsylvania Press, 1997.

16. Mitchell, Olivia S. "Administrative Costs in Public and Private Pension Systems," In M. Feldstein, ed., *Privatizing Social Security*, National Bureau of Economic Research, Chicago: University of Chicago Press, 1998.

17. Mitchell, Olivia S., "New Trends in Pension Benefit and Retirement Provisions," *Pension Research Council Working Paper*, rev. February 2000, (http://prc.wharton.upenn.edu/prc/prc.html).

18. Mitchell, Olivia S. and Rod Carr, "State and Local Pension Plans," In J. Rosenbloom, ed., *Handbook of Employee Benefits,* 1207–1222. Chicago: Irwin, 1996.

19. Mitchell, Olivia S. and Ping-Lung Hsin, "Managing Public Sector Pensions," In J. Shoven and S. Schieber, eds., *Public Policy Toward Pensions,* Twentieth Century Fund, 247–266, Cambridge, MA: MIT Press, 1997.

20. Mitchell, Olivia S. and Ping-Lung Hsin. "Public Sector Pension Governance and Performance," In S. Valdes-Prieto, ed., *The Economics of Pensions: Principles, Policies, and International Experience,* 92–126, Cambridge, MA: Cambridge University Press.

21. Mitchell, Olivia S. and Edwin Hustead, eds., *Pensions in the Public Sector*, Pension Research Council, Philadelphia: University of Pennsylvania Press, 2001.

22. Mitchell, Olivia S., David McCarthy, Stanley C. Wisniewski, and Paul Zorn (MMWZ), "Developments in State and Local Pension Plans," In O.S. Mitchell and E. Hustead, eds. *Pensions in the Public Sector*, Pension Research Council, Philadelphia: University of Pennsylvania Press, forthcoming.

23. Mitchell, Olivia S. and Robert S. Smith, "Pension Funding in the Public Sector," *Review of Economics and Statistics,* 278–290, May 1994.

24. Munnell, Alicia and Annika Sunden, "Economically Targeted Investments in Public Pensions," In O.S. Mitchell and E. Hustead, eds., *Pensions in the Public Sector*, Pension Research Council, Philadelphia: University of Pennsylvania Press, 2001.

25. Nofsinger, John R., "Why Targeted Investing Does Not Make Sense." *Financial Management,* 87–96, 27 (3), Autumn 1998.

26. Phillips, Kristen, "State and Local Government Pension Benefits," In J. Turner and L. Dailey, eds., *Trends in Pensions 1992,* 341–492, Washington, D.C.: USGPO, 1992.

27. Social Security Advisory Council, *Final Report,* 1996. (www.ssa.gov).

28. U.S. Bureau of the Census. Census of Governments, *Employee Retirement Systems of State and Local Governments,* Washington, D.C.: U.S. Department of Commerce, various years.

29. U.S. Bureau of Labor Statistics. *Employee Benefits in State and Local Governments,* Washington, D.C.: U.S. Department of Labor, 1994.

30. U.S. House Ways and Means Committee, *Green Book,* Washington, D.C.: U.S. Government Printing Office, 1998.

31. Useem, M. and Hess, D., "Emerging Issues in Public Pension Governance," In O.S. Mitchell and E. Hustead, eds., *Pensions in the Public Sector,* Pension Research Council. Philadelphia: University of Pennsylvania Press, 2001.

32. Wisniewski, Stanley, "Salient Features of Large Public Employee Retirement Systems With A Focus on Education Employees," *Pension Research Council Working Paper,* Philadelphia: Wharton School, 1999.

33. Zorn, Paul, "Comparing Retirement Benefits Provided by Private Firms and State and Local Governments," *Research Bulletin,* Government Finance Officers Association, January 1995.

34. Zorn, Paul, "Local Government Employee Pension Plans," *Pension Research Council Working Paper,* Philadelphia: Wharton School, 1999.

35. Zorn, Paul, *Survey of State and Local Government Employee Retirement Systems,* Public Pension Coordinating Council, Chicago: Government Finance Officers Association, 1997.

The Globalization of Employee Benefits

Mark S. Allen

Tony R. Broomhead

Around the world, the rationale for supplemental employee benefits is pretty much the same in each country regardless of their legislative environment. They generally are provided to protect employees in the event of retirement, death, disability, and illness to the extent these are not covered by the government. But for most countries, this is where the similarities end. The framework in which these benefits are provided varies significantly from country to country, ranging from comprehensive government programs ("cradle-to-grave" coverage provided by the government) to partnership arrangements (combinations of employer, employee, and government benefits with many options from which to choose).

The challenge for multinational organizations is to manage the design, delivery, and financing of these benefits from a global perspective, not from a local perspective. This process entails a balancing act among:

- Local benefits objectives with local and global business objectives and philosophies.
- The cost and benefits available from old age, survivors, and disability programs with supplemental retirement and capital accumulation plans.
- The cost, quality, and availability of national health insurance programs with emerging private medical practices in many countries.

- Changing regulatory environments that impact the design, delivery, and cost of supplemental benefits plans with local and global benefits objectives.

In order to be effective in this process, most managers will need to gain an understanding of the local environment; assist in establishing global benefits objectives and in designing local plans; and to the extent required, help in the administration and cost management of local plans.

This chapter will review each of these issues from a macro or global perspective. The reader should realize that the benefits environment in many countries is very complex, and that each country and situation needs to be evaluated very carefully.

BACKGROUND CONSIDERATIONS

Benefits for individuals in international operations often are affected by where they were hired and the location of their assignment. For clarification, the main situations are described below.

- *Expatriates or International Assignees.* These are employees that are currently on temporary assignment overseas. Often these employees are paid on terms and conditions that are representative of their home country and not their country of assignment. For U.S. companies, for example, expatriates normally are paid a U.S. base salary and generally are entitled to U.S. benefits.

- *Local Nationals.* This group comprises individuals employed, working, and residing on a long-term basis in a particular country, regardless of the country of which they are citizens. Compensation and benefits programs usually are based on local practices, although there are some exceptions to this as companies attempt to globalize their compensation and benefits. These exceptions are usually found at the executive level

- *Third-Country Nationals* (TCNs). TCNs normally are individuals working for a foreign company on assignment outside of their home country. "True" TCNs will serve in at least two, but usually more, countries during their career. They can be employees of the corporate office, the subsidiary at which they were hired, or the subsidiary where they are working. Consequently, pay and benefits might be provided on a home-country, a host-country, or some special basis designed to suit operational needs. Usually, the duration and number of foreign assignments are key considerations when establishing benefit packages for TCNs. Sometimes these employees are referred to as "career expatriates" or "internationalists."

UNDERSTANDING THE LOCAL ENVIRONMENT

The local issues that need to be understood are:

1. Statutory and government-provided benefits.
2. Regulatory environment and taxation of employee benefits.
3. Economic and labor environment.

Statutory and Government-Provided Benefits

These benefits generally include retirement, death, disability, severance, and medical plans, and the amount and type of coverage will vary significantly from country to country. Some countries, such as Italy and France, have fairly comprehensive government systems that mitigate to some extent the need for supplemental plans. Other countries, such as Australia and Hong Kong, have minimal benefits, while others—usually impoverished or developing countries—have none. The way in which these benefits are financed also will differ. Most are financed by employer and employee taxes on pay, while some countries fund the benefits from general revenues. Most countries fund the benefits on a "pay-as-you-go" basis, although there has been a trend among newly established programs to be funded (as in Chile and Argentina).

Retirement and Old Age Benefits

With respect to retirement, most social security systems provide an income benefit for the life of the individual with reduced benefits to survivors. Benefit formulas range from final pay plans (Russia, Ukraine, Pakistan) to career average plans (Germany, Belgium, U.S.—although Germany and Belgium adjust career-average pay for inflation). Some countries, such as Australia and Hong Kong, provide flat-rate benefits. The most common plan is a final average pay plan with the averaging period ranging from one to 10 years. Table 51–1 provides an example of the approximate level of final pay replaced by some countries in Europe, Latin America, and the Pacific region for an employee earning the equivalent of $25,000, $50,000, and $100,000 after 30 years of coverage. As the table indicates, the level of pay replacement by social security is very high in some countries, while in others social security provides only a limited benefit leaving sufficient scope for supplemental or private retirement plans.

Social security benefit levels correlate closely to the level of contribution. Table 51–2 shows a comparison of the employee and employer contribution rates and applicable contribution ceilings for the retirement portion of social security for each of these countries. Total contributions

T A B L E   51–1

Social Security Pay Replacement

Country	Approximate Percentage of Final Pay Replaced for Employees Earning the Equivalent of		
	$25,000	**$50,000**	**$100,000**
Belgium (married)	56%	40%	20%
Canada (including Canada Pension Plan)	52	26	13
Germany	45	40	21
Italy	76	72	57
Japan	61	46	29
Mexico (new system)	26	13	7
Netherlands (married)	66	30	15
Spain	90	56	28
Taiwan	24	12	6
United Kingdom (contracted in)	61	41	20

Note: Exchange rates effective as of December 13, 1999.

range from a high of 32.7 percent in Italy (which provides a generous benefit) to 5.85 percent in Taiwan (where benefit levels are not as competitive).

Some social security systems provide a two-tier benefit, where the first part is a flat benefit for all eligible employees and the second piece is an earnings-related benefit, which is provided in addition to the flat benefit. The United Kingdom and Japan have this type of system. In both, companies may be able to "contract out" of the earnings-related portion of social security if a private plan that produces equal or greater benefits is provided to all employees. "Contracting out" simply means that companies can divert the contributions earmarked for that part of the social security system to a private plan if certain conditions are met.

In some countries social security retirement benefits are provided in the form of a defined contribution plan. This is most common in Asian, South American, and African countries. Singapore, Malaysia, India, Indonesia, Chile, Egypt, and Nigeria all have a defined contribution arrangement, usually called a "provident fund," from which benefits generally are paid out in a lump sum. One exception to this is France, which has a complicated system of social security and mandatory complementary plans funded on a quasi-defined contribution basis—similar to cash

T A B L E   51-2

Social Security Contribution Levels

	Maximum Employee and Employer Contribution Rates for Old Age and Survivor Benefits				
Country	**Employee**	**Employer**	**Local Currency**	**Earnings Ceiling Local Currency**	**Earnings Ceiling U.S. Dollars**
Belgium (married)	7.50%	8.86%	BF	None	None
Canada (including Canada pension plan)	3.90	3.90	CS	37,600	$25,449
Germany	9.65	9.65	DM	103,200	53,441
Italy	8.89	23.81	Lit	144,000,000	75,322
Japan (contracted in)	8.68	8.68	Yen	6,900,000	67,199
Mexico	1.75	6.90	Peso	245,592	26,080
Netherlands (married)	17.90	0.00	Dfl	48,994	22,517
Spain	4.70	23.60	Pta	4,893,480	29,787
Taiwan	1.30	4.55	NTS	504,000	15,922
United Kingdom (contracted in)	10.00	12.20	£	27,820	45,168

Note: Exchange rates effective as of December 13, 1999.

balance plans in the United States. However, in France, benefits are paid out in the form of an annuity.

Eligibility conditions for qualifying for and receiving benefits also will vary from country to country. In some countries residency is the only requirement, whereas in others, 10 years or more of coverage is needed to qualify for benefit payments. The age at which these benefits commence generally has been different for men and women, but there is a gradual worldwide trend to equalize the retirement age. This trend is perhaps more apparent in Europe where legislation now requires equalization of retirement ages, than it is in other parts of the world. Table 51–3 shows the age at which normal retirement benefits can commence for men and women in several countries, with a brief description of the plan type.

Death and Disability Benefits

Salary continuation, workers' compensation, survivor benefits, and long-term disability benefits commonly are mandated by most countries although the amount of benefit and the length of payment vary considerably.

T A B L E   51–3

Social Security Normal Retirement Age, Required Service or Years of Contributions, and Plan Type

Country	Normal Retirement Ages for		Service or Contribution Requirement for a Benefit	Plan Type
	Men	Women		
Argentina	65	60	30 years	Final 10-year average plus flat amount plus defined contribution
Australia	65	61	Means tested	Fixed amount
Belgium	65	62	30 years	Adjusted career average
Canada	65	65	10 years	Adjusted career average plus flat amount
Colombia	60	55	20 years	Final 10-year average or defined contribution
Egypt	60	60	10 years	Final 2-year average
France	60	60	3 months	Adjusted 17-year average
Germany	65	65	5 years	Adjusted career average
Greece	65	65	15 years	Final 5-year average
Hong Kong	70	70	5 years of residency	Fixed amount
Ireland	65	65	3 years	Fixed amount
Italy	65	60	19 years	Adjusted career average
Japan	65	65	25 years	Adjusted career average plus flat amount
Korea	60	60	20 years	Career average plus flat amount
Mexico	65	65	None	Defined contribution
Netherlands	65	65	None	Fixed amount
New Zealand	64	64	None	Fixed amount
Norway	67	67	3 years	20-year average plus flat amount
Pakistan	60	55	15 years	Final pay
Portugal	65	65	15 years	Highest 10 of last 15 years
Saudi Arabia	60	60	10 years	Final 2-year average
United Kingdom	65	60	1 year	Adjusted career average plus flat amount

Note: Data effective January 2000.

Long-term disability benefits and survivor benefits often are related to the retirement benefits provided through social security.

Medical

Some form of national health insurance for all ages is provided by most countries. Argentina, Brazil, Canada, Mexico, Australia, Japan, Italy, and the United Kingdom are some examples of countries providing comprehensive coverage. Although this would appear to eliminate the need for supplemental medical plans, these plans are common practice in many countries with national health insurance programs. The reasons range from necessity (the poor quality of service from national health providers) to executive compensation (perquisites given to executives but not other employees).

Severance Benefits

In some countries, statutory severance benefits were originally designed to force employers to provide some form of retirement benefit. In these countries, the amounts can be significant and are an important factor in supplemental plan design. As an example, in some Latin American countries, the statutory severance benefit can be as high as two months' pay times years of service where the definition of pay includes all components of compensation, including benefits-in-kind such as company cars, ancillary benefits, nonaccountable cash payments and expense accounts (representation allowances), and the like. For some positions, particularly in those countries where there is a confiscatory tax environment, the value of the benefits-in-kind can exceed 50 percent of base salary.

Bilateral Social Security Treaties for Expatriates and TCNs

Many countries have bilateral social security agreements that enable expatriates, including TCNs, to avoid making simultaneous contributions to both their native and host countries' social security systems. The agreements also permit employees to combine periods of coverage under foreign systems for the purpose of determining eligibility in their home-country programs (totalization). Currently, the United States has agreements with the following 17 countries:

Austria	Germany	Luxembourg	Spain
Belgium	Greece	Netherlands	Sweden
Canada	Ireland	Norway	Switzerland
Finland	Italy	Portugal	United Kingdom
France			

The specific provisions regarding coverage and totalization of benefits will vary among the individual agreements. For U.S. expatriates, most agreements provide that work performed abroad on a permanent basis be covered under the system in the country in which the employee is working. For temporary assignments, generally less than five years, it usually is possible to remain in the U.S. system and not make duplicate contributions.

The European Community (EC) has a special totalization agreement created by the Treaty of Rome. It has three main features:

1. It allows nationals of EC countries to combine their years of participation under the social security systems of all EC countries to establish eligibility for benefits. Each country then pays proportionate benefits for the years of coverage under its own system.

2. It allows employees on temporary assignment to another EC country to remain in their home-country system for pension benefits and to participate in the host-country system for other benefits. "Temporary" is defined as 12 months with the possibility of one 12-month extension.

3. It provides for equal, nondiscriminatory treatment of all EC nationals under the systems of member countries.

Regulatory Environment

Taxation of Benefit Plans

In most countries, employer and employee contributions and pension plan assets receive some form of tax relief. Benefits commonly are taxed as ordinary income, although some countries tax either lump-sum or income benefits on a more advantageous basis. The requirements for this tax relief will differ from country to country, but generally they include provisions similar to those in the United States. However, the requirements usually are not as comprehensive, and they typically permit discrimination in one form or another.

Not all countries offer complete tax relief on pension plans. In Australia, employer contributions (and certain employee contributions) to approved plans are partially taxed, as are the plan assets. In New Zealand pension plans are tax-neutral. Here, employer and employee contributions to pension plans, and the assets are fully taxed, but benefit payments generally are tax-free.

In many countries, discrimination is not as significant a concern as it is in the United States. In those countries where it is not, benefit programs often can discriminate by using different:

- Retirement ages for males and females.
- Required levels of employee contributions.
- Eligibility requirements.
- Benefit formulas for classes of employees.

There are many other ways in which employers may discriminate. What is permitted will depend on the country, and for some countries the ability to discriminate is beginning to disappear. In 1990, in the case of *Barber* v. *the Guardian Royal Exchange*, the European Court of Justice ruled that occupational pension schemes are considered as pay, and, therefore, must be equal between the sexes. It cited the nondiscrimination clause of the Treaty of Rome as the basis for its decision. This case has implications for all companies with operations in the European Community.

Financing and Funding Restrictions

Often the requirements for an approved plan will include restrictions on the funding of the plan or on where the plan assets may be invested. In Japan for example, plans with fewer than 100 employees cannot utilize trust banks—they must insure the benefits with an insurance company or a portion (40 percent) may be book-reserved.

In Germany, employers have several choices for the funding of retirement plans that include a form of trust fund (support fund), book reserves, and direct insurance, but only plans that are book-reserved are free from restriction. Tax-free contributions to direct insurance and support funds are limited.

Many other countries have restrictions. Currently, companies subject to the Labor Standards Law in Taiwan are required to fund retirement benefits with the Central Trust of China, while trustee-managed provident funds in India must be invested 15 percent in specified government securities and government-approved securities, 20 percent in a special deposit bank account with the government, and 40 percent in bonds of public sector companies and financial institutions. In Canada and Switzerland, the restrictions are less onerous, but still are there and include limitations on the amounts that can be invested outside the country and in certain asset classes like real estate and equities.

Other Issues

There are numerous other regulatory issues particular to each country that need to be understood. The principal ones include mandatory indexation of benefits, Works Councils and employee representation, and accounting and reporting requirements.

Mandatory Indexation of Benefits. Typically, most countries do not require that pension payments be indexed to inflation (although it may be customary practice to provide such protection), but this may be changing. Inflation is a worldwide concern, and its effect on the erosion of pension benefits is being addressed by some countries. Recently the United Kingdom enacted the Pensions Act of 1995, which mandates limited indexation of pensions in payment. Similar legislation exists in Germany.

Works Councils and Employee Representation. Many countries, particularly those in Europe, require that employees have a say in the management of a company's activities, and this generally includes issues relating to pay systems (which include employee benefits), dismissals, recruitment, and working hours. The form that this role takes varies, but most common are Works Councils. The degree of authority and control will be different for each country, but these councils almost always cover employee benefit plans. The table below indicates the minimum number of employees in a company before a Works Council is required in five European countries.

	Number of Employees in Company
Belgium	100
Denmark	35
France	50
Germany	5
Netherlands	35

Employee representation may take other forms, such as direct representation on pension committees or boards. As an example, in Spain there has been legislation permitting pension funds on a tax-advantaged basis. However, one of the requirements for achieving the tax-qualified status is that each company must establish a committee to oversee the plan and fund management, and employees must represent a majority of that committee.

Accounting and Reporting Requirements. U.S. multinationals must be concerned with both local and U.S. reporting requirements. Local accounting and reporting requirements usually are not as onerous as the requirements in the United States for domestic plans, but they still exist. In the United States, most of the requirements for foreign plans relate to *Financial Accounting Standards Board (FASB) Statements No. 87 (FAS 87), No. 106 (FAS 106),* and *No. 112 (FAS 112). FAS 87* requires U.S. companies to calculate and report pension costs using explicit assumptions and also requires expanded disclosure in financial statements; *FAS 106* has similar requirements for other post-retirement costs, such as life insurance and medical coverage; *FAS 112* covers other postemployment costs, including severance payments and continued medical coverage while disabled. Most non-U.S. plans must be included on a basis similar to U.S. plans. Similar rules exist in the United Kingdom in the form of *Statement of Standard Accounting Practice 24 (SSAP24)* and its replacement, *Financial Reporting Standard 17 (FRS 17)* which detail how pension costs should be represented in financial statements. Canada, Mexico, Taiwan, Indonesia, Germany, Austria, Japan, Brazil, Portugal, Spain, Sweden, Switzerland, and Norway now have rules that deal with accounting and reporting requirements. *International Accounting Standard 19 (IAS 19)* also provides guidelines and reporting requirements.

Economic and Labor Environment

Prevailing economic conditions can be an influencing factor in the design of international benefit plans and can have a significant impact on plan costs. However, rarely will they dictate the final plan design. The more important factors are inflation and interest rates, but exchange-rate manipulation or currency controls also can have an impact—particularly in countries with high inflation. Normally, currencies appreciate or depreciate in line with inflation, but some countries (Mexico and Brazil, for example) have previously manipulated exchange rates to further other economic goals. In these instances, costs in U.S. dollar terms can be affected. Table 51–4 shows inflation and interest rates in selected countries.

With respect to labor, it is important to have an understanding of the following:

1. The prevalence and types of labor unions—whether they are local or national in scope.
2. The depth of the labor movement—does it encompass management as well as hourly employees?
3. The local supply of and demand for labor.

The makeup of the labor movement will vary significantly in each country. In some, most of the workforce may not be unionized, and those workers that are generally are concentrated in small, loosely organized local unions. In others, most of the country may belong to one union or another, as in Belgium, where more than 80 percent of the workforce is unionized—

T A B L E   51—4

Inflation and Interest Rates

Country	Percent Official Annual Inflation	Percent 10-Year Govt. Bond Yields
Argentina	−1.1%	—%
Australia	1.8	6.2
Belgium	2.3	5.1*
Canada	2.7	5.9
Chile	3.4	—
China	0.7	—
Colombia	9.7	—
Denmark	3.0	5.5
Egypt	2.9	—
France	1.4	5.1*
Germany	1.9	5.1*
Greece	3.1	6.2
Hong Kong	−5.3	—
India	3.6	—
Italy	2.5	5.1*
Japan	−0.6	1.8
Korea	1.6	—
Mexico	10.1	—
Netherlands	1.9	5.1*
New Zealand	2.3	6.8
Sweden	1.3	5.3
Turkey	67.9	—
United Kingdom	2.3	5.2
Venezuela	17.5	—

* Part of European Monetary Union.

Note: Data effective March 2000.

including white-collar or management employees. Unions may operate at the local or national level. In Italy, management employees, or *dirigenti*, generally belong to one of two trade unions, which negotiate on their behalf on a national basis.

Obviously, the supply of and demand for labor also can affect the design and costs of benefit plans. As an example, countries with younger populations generally might find defined contribution plans more acceptable than defined benefit plans. Similarly, older populations probably would prefer the security of a defined benefit plan. Around the industrialized world there is a trend, as there is in the United States, for governments to shift a greater burden of their benefit costs to the private sector. As in the United States, the population in these countries is growing older, and there are fewer workers to contribute to programs such as social security. Table 51–5 shows the population of people under age 15 and over age 64 as a percentage of the population between ages 15 and 64 in eight countries. It shows that the number of older people is steadily increasing (rapidly in Italy and Japan), while the number of young people entering the workforce is stable or declining.

But, this is not the case in every country. Many Latin American countries, as well as some of the developing countries, are currently enjoying a "baby boom" period, and the number of eligible workers far outnumbers older workers and retired employees. For example, in Mexico more than 35 percent of the population is under age 15, which contrasts with 19 percent in Japan and 14 percent in Italy. However, the problem in some of these countries may not be the quantity of labor, but the quality.

GLOBAL BENEFIT OBJECTIVES AND PLAN DESIGN

Most employers recognize the importance of rewarding their employees for their contributions to growth and profits without regard to whether they are domestic or international employees. One of the ways in which employers balance the need for employee reward and business objectives is to develop a statement of policy and objectives that acts as a guide to the establishment, modification, and administration of benefit plans. Usually this statement is an expression of the employer's preferences as opposed to rigid instructions. While most U.S. employers have something similar for their U.S. employees, they generally do not for their foreign operations. Yet, local plans require equal discipline.

Establishing international benefit programs takes place at two levels— determining global objectives, and designing plans for local nationals, expatriates, and TCNs that meet these objectives.

Global Benefit Objectives

Global policy statements and objectives generally state the company's philosophy and overall attitude for employee benefits. The documents also include broad policy statements on total remuneration; definition of competitive practice; uniformity of treatment and internal equity; mergers and acquisitions; costs; and employee communications.

T A B L E   51-5

Population Projections

	Population under 15 as a Percentage of Population 15–64						
					Projections		
Country	1965	1975	1985	1996	2005	2025	2045
United States	51	39	33	33	31	32	33
Japan	38	36	32	23	22	21	24
Germany	35	34	22	24	22	22	23
France	41	38	32	30	28	26	25
Italy	—	—	—	21	21	17	21
United Kingdom	36	37	29	30	27	25	24
Canada	57	41	32	30	26	25	25
Mexico	—	—	—	59	49	35	31

	Population 65 and over as a Percentage of Population 15–64						
					Projections		
Country	1965	1975	1985	1996	2005	2025	2045
United States	16	16	18	20	19	30	34
Japan	9	12	15	22	29	46	62
Germany	18	23	21	23	28	37	49
France	19	22	20	23	25	36	46
Italy	—	—	—	25	29	40	68
United Kingdom	19	22	23	24	24	34	45
Canada	13	13	15	18	19	33	41
Mexico	—	—	—	7	8	13	25

Source: U.S. Bureau of the Census, International Data Base.

Global objectives rarely get into specifics on the type of benefits for each country, because the variations are likely to be too great. The following is a synopsis of the elements in a global policy.

Total Remuneration

This part of the policy encompasses the overall level of competitiveness for each element of pay, including employee benefits. The total package (base pay, regular bonus, incentive bonus, perquisites, allowances, and employee benefits) as well as each individual component of pay usually is addressed. Such items as tax effectiveness and the state of the business (e.g., startup situations require different rewards than mature, stable operations) also are covered.

Preferences for specific levels and types of benefits are included. For example, a policy for retirement plans might state the following:

- Defined contribution plans are preferred to defined benefit plans.
- For defined benefit plans, career average formulas are preferred to final pay plans.
- Where possible, employees should share in the cost of funding the plans.
- Benefits should be at the 60th percentile of comparable companies for management employees, and the 50th percentile for all other employees.
- Plans should take into account social security benefits wherever possible.
- Trust arrangements are preferred to insurance.
- Insurance contracts should be experience-rated where possible by using a multinational pooling arrangement (discussed in detail later in the chapter).
- Actuarial valuations should be performed for defined benefit plans no less frequently than every three years.
- Similar information should be recorded for each benefit area—retirement, death, disability, and medical.

Definition of Competitive Practice

While actual competitive practice is likely to differ from country to country, it is helpful to have some broad guidelines for each local operation to follow. In some countries, it may be appropriate to limit the definition to only those companies that are direct competitors in a specific industry. In other countries, it may make sense to expand to other industries. Much will depend on the state of the business in a particular country—for example, a manufacturer may not want to limit the definition to only those companies in its industry when the competition operates principally sales and distribution facilities and does no or little manufacturing. Similarly, a startup operation in a mature market environment will want to include relatively stable and long-standing companies in its definition.

The definition does not have to be limited to industry alone, nor does one standard have to apply for all groups of employees. Many companies expand it to include geographic location (city, suburb, or country location), ownership (U.S. multinationals, foreign multinational, or indigenous), type of activity (sales or manufacturing), and size, and also will have different definitions for different groups of employees. Figure 51–1 is a useful guideline for determining appropriate comparator groups and companies for different categories of employee.

Uniformity of Treatment

In many countries, it is permissible to differentiate between groups of employees—senior management and other employees, for example—although this differential treatment may not be considered appropriate by U.S. management whether it is permissible or not. This section of the policy usually deals with these issues, and it generally is expanded to include matters concerning internal equity, particularly those that involve cross-border comparisons. Cross-border evaluations are difficult because many factors, such as exchange-rate fluctuations, local taxes, social security, and living standards are involved.

Mergers and Acquisitions

Typically companies have three choices for dealing with mergers and acquisitions issues: (1) integrating immediately with corporate benefit programs and policies, (2) maintaining current arrangements without change, or (3) a gradual integration into corporate programs. To the extent a company's preference is articulated in a global policy statement, local managers will be better equipped to handle mergers and acquisitions situations. Many companies simply follow established U.S. company policy in these instances.

Costs

A global statement will outline how costs are to be budgeted and reported and also indicate the preferred level of employee cost sharing. There also may be a section outlining the company's preferences for funding levels and types of investments.

Employee Communications

This section might indicate the information that employees are entitled to have on existing programs and the frequency with which it should be provided to the employees. It also may specify how the information might be made available to employees.

FIGURE 51–1

Guidelines to Identification of Comparison Companies

Comparison Factor	Production	Clerical and Administrative	Professional and Technical Staff	Salespersons and Middle Managers	Senior Managers
Geographical location			City and Country		
Industry			Type of Industry(ies)		
Ownership of company			Locally Owned, Multinational Companies, U.S.-Owned Subsidiaries		
Type of activity			Manufacturing, Marketing, Sales, and Distribution		
Company size (sales)			Comparable, Smaller, Larger Than Operations		
Competitive level			Quartile Ranking—1st, Median, 3rd, Other		

Local Benefit Plan Design

Local benefits should be determined for each country within the framework of the global policy, but this is not always possible. The employer must try to balance corporate policy against the local realities, which include the following:

- Legislative restrictions.
- Tax implications.
- Other liabilities, such as termination indemnities that are really retirement plans.
- Different actuarial practices.
- Smaller, more volatile local investment markets.
- Cultural differences or preferences.

The local programs can be designed by a corporate benefits manager, but more often they are developed locally for approval by the head office. Generally, it makes sense to involve local management in the decision-making process wherever possible.

Plan Design—U.S. Expatriates

The objective of the vast majority of U.S. employers with respect to benefit plans for expatriates is to keep the employee in the U.S. programs—but this is not always possible. Much will depend on whether the employee is working for a branch or foreign subsidiary of the U.S. company.

Employees working in a foreign branch of a U.S. corporation are automatically covered by their employer's U.S. qualified plan unless specifically excluded. Internal Revenue Code (IRC) Section 410(b)(3)(C) and Section 4(b) of the Employee Retirement Income Security Act (ERISA) allow a U.S. qualified plan to exclude nonresident aliens from plan coverage in cases where they do not receive any U.S. source income. This permits companies to cover only those employees of a foreign branch who are U.S. citizens or resident aliens.

Any company considering this approach should note the following:

- The exclusion of nonresident aliens must be specifically written into the plan document.
- The law in some foreign jurisdictions may treat the accrual of benefits under a U.S. plan as a taxable event.

- The law in some countries may not allow a deduction, for foreign income tax purposes, to the foreign branch; a U.S. tax deduction is allowed, however.

Individuals working in a foreign subsidiary, unlike employees in a branch, are not employees of the U.S. corporation. As such, these employees are not legally entitled to participate in qualified plans maintained in the United States unless specific steps are taken. IRC Section 406 allows such employees to be deemed employees of the U.S. parent company, but, to qualify, companies must elect, under Section 3121(1), to provide U.S. Social Security coverage for all U.S. citizens and resident alien employees of the foreign subsidiary. This election can be made separately for each subsidiary and is irrevocable. The election is made by filing Form 2032 with the Internal Revenue Service.

Alternatively, if the subsidiary is part of the controlled group of the U.S. parent (requiring at least 80 percent ownership of the subsidiary by the U.S. parent), selected U.S. citizens and resident alien employees can be covered in U.S. qualified plans under IRC Section 414.

Plan Design—Third-Country Nationals

By definition, TCNs are expatriate employees, but for benefit purposes they are often treated differently. Few companies will try to maintain a TCN in his or her home-country benefit plan unless the assignment is temporary. If the transfer abroad is clearly denoted as temporary and if the employees can be classified as "on loan" to the foreign office, then it usually is possible to continue home-country coverage for periods up to two or three years. If this is not possible, then the employee is typically "made whole" on his or her return to the home country.

Other TCNs can be either permanent or mobile ("true TCNs"). Permanent TCNs normally are included in the host-country plan and usually are not a problem. True TCNs, on the other hand, create problems because they rarely are in one country long enough to accrue any meaningful service for retirement benefits. For this reason, many companies design international retirement plans that cover this specific category of employee. These plans may provide a benefit based on home- or host-country programs, U.S. levels, or a special benefit formula designed for the TCNs. These plans generally are either book-reserved or funded offshore in order to minimize the tax implications. Many of these plans are umbrella plans, in which the actual benefit provided by the plan generally is offset by other retirement benefits accrued during the employee's career, including social security, termination indemnities, and any company-provided benefits.

ADMINISTRATION AND FINANCIAL MANAGEMENT OF INTERNATIONAL BENEFIT PLANS

The administration and management of international plans, from the corporate perspective, typically involves two key areas—design and financial considerations. But before these can be examined, there probably will be a need to get information concerning the benefit programs at each foreign location.

Most companies conduct periodic audits of their international benefit plans. Generally, this process involves designing a questionnaire, getting the local operations to complete the questionnaire, and analyzing the results. Figure 51–2 provides a list of the items that typically are included on a questionnaire.

Once the data have been collected, it will be possible to determine the potential cost savings with respect to design considerations by evaluating the following:

1. The relative competitive position.
2. Whether the plans are properly integrated with statutory benefits.
3. Whether the program specifications, such as normal retirement age and employee contribution levels, are consistent with the global objectives.
4. The administration of the plans to see if there are more cost-effective methods.

Financial considerations include funding, investment management, and risk management. With respect to funding and investment management, corporate managers need to focus on the issues in each country that are similar to those for their U.S. plans. These include funding costs at each location with respect to acceptable U.S. expense levels; appropriate funding media; whether the plan should be funded at all—or book-reserved; the actuarial process—reporting, methodology, and assumptions; and investment management.

The investment management process probably has the most scope for controlling or reducing benefit costs. It has been estimated that a 1 percent per year improvement in return on plan assets can reduce costs by 10 percent or more per year. In the United States, this area gets considerable

F I G U R E   51-2

Data Collection Items for International Audit

Retirement Plans	Health Care	Long-Term Disability
Type of plan	Type of plan	Type of plan
Eligibility requirements	Eligibility	Eligibility
Definition of covered earnings	Hospital room & board	Benefit amount
Benefit formula	Hospital miscellaneous	Integration
Normal retirement	Surgical	Duration of benefit
Early retirement	Attending physician	Lump-Sum benefits
Integration	In-Hospital	Employee contributions
Benefit payment form	Outpatient	Company contributions/cost
Vesting	Major medical	Claims history
Employee contributions	Deductible	Financing medium
Company contributions/cost	Coinsurance	
Financing medium	Maximum	
	Employee contributions	
	Company contributions/cost	
	Claims history	
	Financing medium	
	Dental	**Severance**
	Vision/Hearing	
	Maternity	Amount of payment
	Prescription drugs	Conditions of payment
	Psychiatric	Notice period

Salary Continuation	Preretirement Death Benefits	Perquisites
Type of plan	Eligibility	Company cars
Eligibility	Lump-sum amount	Driver
Benefit amount	AD&D	Club memberships
Integration	Business travel	Annual medical checkups
Duration of benefit	Survivor income	Subsidized meals
Lump-Sum benefits	Employee contributions	Mobile telephones
Employee contributions	Company contributions/cost	Long-term incentives
	Claims history	Separate executive contracts
	Financing medium	

attention; but this is not so overseas, where the plans generally are smaller and encumbered with different types of legislation. However, in such countries as Australia, New Zealand, Canada, Japan, and the United Kingdom, where trusts are common, or at least an acceptable alternative for pension investing, the same scope exists for managing the investment process, and generally the same principles used in the United States can be exported overseas, and even considered on a global basis.

The risk management aspect of international benefit plans generally revolves around the concept of multinational pooling.

Multinational Pooling

Insured employee benefits in a multinational company generally are undertaken through separate arrangements in each country. Thus, employees in each country will be covered for such benefits as life insurance, medical/dental coverage, disability, and retirement benefits through a local insurance company or financial organization in accordance with local conditions and practices. In the absence of multinational pooling, local insurance arrangements would not enjoy any economies of scale based on the worldwide size of the group.

Using group life insurance as an example, the insurance contract in each country involves a premium payment to the local insurance company in return for the agreed coverage. Dividends may be paid out of the insurer's overall profits (if any) at the end of the contract year. A variation on this, known as "experience-rating," involves the linking of either the dividend or the premium to the actual claims experience of the local subsidiary.

Experience-rating is an advantage when claims are lower than the "average," because the cost of insurance is based partly on the company's own claims, rather than on the average level of claims. Experience-rating also can reduce insurance costs by reducing the "risk charge" made by the insurer. In return, the company incurs an additional risk of loss when claims are high. This generally is more practical if the company has a large number of employees insured under the contract, because there is likely to be greater stability of total annual claim payments.

Multinational pooling enables the principles of experience-rating to be applied to the worldwide insurance arrangements of a multinational company. If the subsidiary companies use insurers associated with an insurance "network," then a "multinational dividend" can be paid based on the actual combined experience of those subsidiaries. Thus, the group will benefit from favorable experience and also bear some of the risk of bad experience.

The multinational pooling arrangement consists of a contract between the parent company and the coordinating insurer of the network. It is thus independent of local practice governing payment of dividends on local contracts. In fact, the existence of the multinational contract has no effect on the premiums, dividends, and claim payments under the local contracts.

A multinational pooling arrangement operates on two levels. First, an employer contracts with an insurance network to share the profits and losses of the network's business with the subsidiaries of the parent company. Second, individual contracts are negotiated between the subsidiary and the local network insurer. These contracts conform with local laws, competitive practice, dividend payments, and the like. A multinational dividend is paid based on the sum total of experience under each of the individual contracts. In essence, this is the meaning of multinational pooling.

Advantages of Multinational Pooling

The primary objective of multinational pooling is a reduction in overall insurance costs, resulting from the receipt of multinational dividends. These dividends arise in years when experience is favorable. If experience is unfavorable, however, the worst that can happen is the cancellation of the dividend, perhaps for several years.

In a sense, an insurance network can afford to give "something for nothing." Multinational dividends arise from the following factors:

- If a company has low claims, the experience-rating approach enables that company to share in the savings.
- In a few countries, local regulations or gentlemen's agreements exist that limit the freedom of the insurers to compete on premiums and dividends. Pooling arrangements may provide a legal means of returning some of the profits resulting from these restrictions.
- Pooling reduces the risk faced by the local insurers, because heavy claims in one country can be met out of the multinational dividend earned from favorable experience in other countries. This can result in reduced "risk charges" by the local insurers.
- Membership in a multinational network offers competitive advantages to a local insurer. Therefore, an insurer may be willing to offer favorable terms to users of a network to become the network's associate insurer in the local country.

Reduced insurance costs are the main advantage of multinational pooling. However, there are a number of other benefits to be gained:

■ *Annual Accounting on a Centralized Basis.* More information is available on a company's group insurance costs around the globe and on how those costs are determined.

■ *Centralized Communication.* In dealing with one "group" office, rather than individual local insurance companies or branches in each country, a company can reduce administrative time and expense.

■ *Relaxed Underwriting Limits.* Because insurance companies wish to protect themselves against high risks, group life and disability coverage for executives typically is subject to satisfactory medical examinations. By pooling lives in a number of locations, the risk of adverse experience is reduced substantially, and the insurance company is more willing to raise or eliminate the limits at which medical evidence is required.

The Multinational Pooling Account

The multinational pooling account sometimes is known as a "second stage account" because it is drawn up after all payments under the local contracts (e.g., premiums, claims, and dividends) have been made. Its principal advantage is that it provides financial information, normally not available from the local insurers, on the foreign benefit programs for each operation in the pooling program.

Although the actual format of a multinational pooling account (or experience statement) will vary from one carrier to the next, it normally will contain the following items:

■ Credits
   Premiums paid by the company.
   Investment earnings on company-paid premiums.

■ Debits
   Claims.
   Risk charges.
   Insurer expenses.
   Commissions.
   Local dividend payments.

■ Funds Retained
   Additions to reserves (most often for pensions but also occasionally for some risk benefits).

■ Balance
   Multinational dividend.

The multinational dividend is the balance of the account, and the anticipated result of a pooling program. Positive balances arising in countries where experience has been favorable are used to offset negative balances in countries where experience has been poor. Any remaining balance is paid by the network as a dividend to the multinational parent company. In some companies, this dividend is then distributed to the subsidiary companies, who have had positive balances.

Where Multinational Pooling May Not Work

Over recent years, many companies have established multinational pooling contracts for their overseas employee benefit coverage, and more can be expected to do so. However, pooling is not necessarily appropriate for every multinational organization or every situation. Examples of situations in which multinational pooling may not work include the following:

- Not enough employees are located overseas. Typically, an employer should have at least 500 employees in at least two countries outside the United States or Canada who are covered by group insurance, although some networks are now offering small groups pools where less than 500 employees are involved.
- In some countries, the network's local insurer may not be competitive or the network may not have a local representative insurer.
- In countries with blocked currencies, some networks may experience difficulty in pooling or in paying dividends outside the country.
- Local management may refuse to change carriers. This could occur for a number of reasons, including excellent service from the existing carrier, long-standing personal relationships, or national pride.
- In some countries, such as the United Kingdom or Australia, premium rates are extremely low. This means that the insurer's profit margin is low and the risk of adverse claims experience might outweigh the expected additional multinational dividend.
- The employer's business is in an industry with above-average claims experience.

SUMMARY

A number of recent events are spurring on the globalization of many U.S. companies. These include the formation of the single market in Europe, the North American Free Trade Agreement (NAFTA), the rapid development of the Pacific Rim economies, and the democratization of many countries in Central and Eastern Europe. Companies are trying to position themselves competitively, either in anticipation of or in reaction to these events, to take advantage of the opportunities that will arise.

The challenge for employee benefit managers is to assist their companies in developing and maintaining their competitive edge while at the same time keeping an eye on issues such as internal equity and cost. In order to accomplish these tasks on a global basis, managers must have a thorough understanding of the employee benefits and related environments in the countries in which they operate.

The Future of Employee Benefit Plans

Dallas L. Salisbury

Predicting the future is a game of chance in which the normal laws of probability do not hold. The passage of time allows numerous unexpected events to intervene, and this has been the rule rather than the exception with employee benefits.

One can predict that the field of employee benefits will be increasingly dynamic and challenging in the years ahead as the world becomes smaller, technology innovations continue, and the population ages. The greatest rewards will go to those who carefully anticipate and plan. This chapter attempts to lay a base for that purpose.

PRE-ERISA PREDICTIONS ABOUT EMPLOYEE BENEFIT PLANS (1970)

In 1970, experts made predictions concerning the future of employee benefits. The predictions were based upon specific beliefs regarding (a) the economy of the 1970s, and (b) expected population changes.

The economy of the 1970s was expected to be strong. Median incomes were expected to rise substantially; they did. Inflation was expected to drop from the abnormally high rate of 4 percent; it didn't. The makeup of the workforce (male–female) was expected to remain fairly constant; it didn't. The population over age 65 was expected to approach 23 million; it did. The average work week was expected to move to 35 hours per week or less; it didn't.

Based on these economic and population predictions, the seers of 1970 specified future benefit trends. They predicted the following:

- Dramatic increases in income replacement, reaching an average of 75 percent of final earnings. For many it did, but it's moving the other way.

- A movement toward encouraging early retirement, with the average moving to age 55. It moved down to the 61–62 range for all individuals; to 58 for large employers. Now it is moving back up, and the early retirement incentives in plans are being eliminated.

- Shorter vesting periods and earlier participation. It happened and continues to grow shorter.

- Dramatic growth of, and pressure for, survivor benefits. It happened.

- Liberalization of eligibility rules for disability benefits. It happened.

- Active and competitive portfolio management. It happened.

The seers were surprisingly accurate. Inflation reached its highest historical point for the United States and then came back down. Median income rose dramatically but then slowed. The over-65 population continued to grow, and the proportion of women in the workforce grew dramatically.

These economic and population trends of the 1970s, 1980s and 1990s are still with us. They will help to shape what occurs in the decades ahead. They are relevant to a number of factors that will determine the future of benefit programs:

- *Families are changing.* Just over one-third of first marriages now remain intact for life. Fewer than one in eight families now consists of a married couple with children in which the mother does not work outside the home. Today, more than half of all women with a child under age 6 are in the paid labor force. More than 7.5 million households with young children are headed by a single parent, and this number continues to increase. Time constraints, competing pressures, and marital dissolution are undercutting the family's ability to perform its role as the mainstay of assistance to dependent family members.

- *Life expectancy has increased, and more people are surviving to older ages.* In 1935, when the Social Security Act was passed, life expectancy in the United States was just below 62 years. Now, it hovers around 75 years and shows continued improvement. By 2030, one in five

Americans will be age 65 or older, compared with just one in eight today. And the number of people aged 85 or older is expected to triple by 2030, accounting for more than 8.6 million people. Nearly half of today's 20-year-olds can expect to reach 80, compared with less than one in four in the 1930s. The increasing number of older Americans will put a significant strain on the nation's health care services and retirement-income programs in the years ahead.

■ *Racial and ethnic diversity is increasing.* Birth rates of the non-Hispanic white population have been at or below replacement level for the past 25 years. Meanwhile, immigration from abroad and higher fertility rates among blacks and some Asian and Hispanic groups are creating greater racial and ethnic diversity in the population. While people of color currently account for 20 percent of the U.S. population, this proportion is expected to grow to more than 30 percent by 2030. As minorities become a larger share of the population and the labor force, their special needs and problems impact directly on the support systems and economic structures of U.S. society. Minorities today are more likely to have lower levels of education, to have fewer job skills, and to be poor. This creates special challenges in terms of delivery of health benefits, achieving participation in defined contribution plans, and more.

■ *The income gap between the rich and the poor is widening.* In 1969, families in the top 20 percent of the nation's income distribution accounted for 41 percent of all income; by 1999, they held 48 percent. Meanwhile, the families at the bottom 20 percent of the income scale lost ground, their share declining from 5.6 percent to 3.6 percent. Middle-income families also held a smaller share of national income by 1999 (15 percent). Twenty-three percent of the nation's children currently live below the U.S. poverty line, and 10.7 million young adults (ages 18 to 34) are in poverty. Economic polarization is affecting the number and composition of people who are poor and raising questions about the vitality of America's middle class as well as social and economic prospects for our youth. And the ability of those people to afford employee benefits with heavy cost sharing could undermine the fabric of economic security.

■ *State and regional differences affect our ability to design employee benefit programs.* During the 1960s, 1970s, 1980s, and 1990s, the U.S. population shifted from the Northeast and Midwest to the South and West. Growth in the Sunbelt states was also spurred by the influx of immigrants. More than 40 percent of new immigrants during the 1990s settled in just three states: California, Texas, and Florida. While most central cities in the Northeast and Midwest lost population during the 1990s, the surrounding outer suburbs grew exponentially. New and growing residential areas often are selective of young adults who are well-educated and have high earnings potential. Left behind are some of the neediest and most vulnerable population groups. Such patterns only widen the breach between those who need supportive services and the community's capacity to pay for and staff them, and limit the ability to meet needs through employment-based programs.

Taken together, these economic and population trends will challenge the employee benefit system in the future, threatening continued erosion of health and retirement security on a total population basis, even as the employed full-time population continues to build stronger economic security prospects. Employers and unions will face a retired population with less to spend and higher health costs due to more uncompensated care for a growing nonemployed uninsured population.

SOCIAL SECURITY/MEDICARE

In 1980, on the 45th anniversary of Social Security, William Driver, then commissioner of the Social Security Administration, made bold predictions about its future. "Social Security will not go bankrupt," he said. "Its benefits will continue to be the basic source of retirement income upon which people rely." By 1982 the program was on the verge of benefit checks not going out, when the Social Security Act Amendments of 1983 brought renewed stability to the retirement portion of the program.

Predicting the future of Social Security or the stability of the entire employee benefit system has never been an easy task, but Social Security was in severe financial trouble in the early 1980s. The strong economy of the late 1990s has extended the trust fund of the program, such that benefits can be paid until almost 2040 before added funds will be needed. The Medicare portion faced the potential of bankruptcy by the year 2001, as recently as 1998, but the strong economy has served to extend the life of the program until about 2015. Both programs are in need of tax increases or benefit reductions in the decades ahead.

For the plan sponsor, participant, and taxpayer, the stability of Social Security has far-reaching implications. The prospects for stability are affected by numerous factors, but the level of inflation, the size and makeup of the workforce, and the selected age for retirement are particularly important.

There is no easy political solution to Social Security's long-term financial problems. The importance of Social Security to all elements of benefit programs and current employee compensation cannot be overstated. Should

Social Security continue to absorb an ever-growing share of our nation's resources, it will limit the expansion of other benefit programs and take-home pay. Incremental change is likely to remain the rule, unless and until one political party controls all the levers of power in Washington. This will cause the cost of the program to go steadily upward and the resources available for other programs to shrink. The government focus on "saving" the Social Security tax surplus will be tested in a weak economy.

The alternatives include significant increases in the retirement age for benefit payment, further benefit formula reductions, turning the program into a means-tested welfare program, proposals for "privatization" to obtain higher returns on the trust fund, or contribution of some funds to individual accounts funded through savings achieved by benefit reductions. These individual account approaches are not a panacea, however, as there will be both winners and losers, with the losers looking to the government to provide a reasonable floor of income as the price of political calm.

THE EMPLOYEE'S DECISION TO RETIRE

The retirement decision is crucial for retirement income programs: It determines the amount of money required by the programs. The difference between paying benefits for 30 years and 20 years and 10 years is much greater than a doubling and tripling. Future trends, therefore, are extremely important.

What motivates a person to leave a job? What are the factors considered by an individual who has worked for 30 or 40 years and has the opportunity to decide whether to continue working or to retire? The worker must examine all sources of income, from Social Security, personal savings, and pensions. To the extent that the income from these sources promises to be inadequate, the worker is likely to delay retirement.

Actions are being taken that will encourage later retirement. Such changes for Social Security have included relaxing the earnings test, raising the age of eligibility for initial benefits to 67, and adjusting the level of indexing by changing the Consumer Price Index (CPI) definition.

Private-plan changes are also taking place. The move to individual account approaches and lump-sum distributions is both a defined benefit and a defined contribution plan movement. Changes in the tax status of benefit program contributions and benefits could alter the future pattern of benefit receipt. Government could require private plans to raise the normal retirement age (with mandatory retirement eliminated, workers may want to work longer) to match Social Security.

But what are the effects of a mandatory retirement age change? Studies indicate that few older workers previously subject to mandatory retirement chose to remain on the job when the mandatory age was lifted to 70. Thus far, work-life extension has been modest. And, while surveys such as the Employee Benefit Research Institute (EBRI) Retirement Confidence Survey have shown for a decade that workers say they will want to work at least part-time after they "retire," only small numbers have yet begun to do so. There continues to be a prediction that this will change in the future, but will it?

High general inflation and health care inflation did cause persons to delay retirement at times in the past, and could again should they return in the future. The worker may anticipate that wages will rise with prices, especially if the older worker expects several years of inflation. The worker also can anticipate that higher wages will result in higher pension benefits, in which case a delay in retirement will pay off. A return of high inflation would affect retirement patterns. In addition, with the provision of employer- and union-provided retiree health insurance being less and less a promise to future retirees, the prospect of individuals working at least until Medicare coverage is available at 65 is more and more likely.

Other factors affecting retirement trends are health, education, personnel policies, and changes in negotiating employee benefit plans. On the whole, health has improved, and further improvements could increase the proportion of older workers in the labor force. Were the result to increase the length of retirement rather than work, the implications for plan financing would be extremely adverse.

Older workers may desire to reduce their hours of work gradually or shift to less arduous tasks while remaining employed. Whether or not unions continue to press for subsidized early retirement features will have an effect on future retirement patterns. Phased retirement and holding "bridge-jobs" prior to full retirement are both expanding at a slow pace, which fits with demographics and the fact the Social Security normal retirement age is increasing. Continued movement towards a phase down from full-time work will continue in the future based upon baby boomer demands, if unemployment is low.

The consequences of retirement age are great for all benefit programs in terms of the period of coverage, the cost of coverage, and the mix of programs. Benefit professionals should watch developing trends carefully and consider strategic initiatives to allow those who wish to continue working beyond "normal" ages to do so as the workforce ages.

DEMOGRAPHIC CHANGE

The makeup of both the retired and working populations affects all public and private benefit programs. In the 1970s, the World War II baby boomers entered the workforce for the first time. By the 1990s, this group was moving into their 50s and focusing for the first time on long-term security issues.

While the Social Security program is sound today, we must consider the prospects for the years beyond 2038, when the last baby boomers will be in retirement. Payroll tax rates could rise to between 18 percent and 64 percent to finance the present program, dependent upon economic performance and population trends. Should rates go this high, numerous other benefit programs could find themselves crowded out.

In the next 10 years, the nation must seriously focus on the implications of the aging baby boomers. The implications of these demographic trends, however, go well beyond the age mix of the population:

- Due to longer life expectancies, the cost of providing health care and retirement income support to current retirees is higher than expected and rising. This will continue to be the case for future retiree groups. The need for long-term care financing will gain increasing recognition.

- Changing family relationships will continue to have a major effect on the stability and future development of benefit programs. The number of families headed by women is increasing, as is their participation in the workforce. Child-care and elder-care will both command increased attention, as will coordination of benefits for two-earner households.

The productive workforce will continue to shrink as a proportion of the total population, increasing the proportion of each worker's income that will be needed to support the young, the old, and the infirm.

These changes will lead to greater flexibility in benefit design. The traditional household model—working husband, housewife, children—around which benefit programs were designed in the past now applies to fewer than 15 percent of households. Employers are already changing benefit plans to accommodate this. The continuing challenge will be in designing programs that match worker desires while still providing economic security in the event of unforeseen problems (health) or poor economic planning (retirement security).

Employers and the government will both need to reevaluate benefit promises, increase the financial involvement of participants and beneficiaries, and focus on catastrophic protection.

ECONOMIC CHANGE

The strength of the economy in the future will also be a principal determinant of the future of employee benefits. A low-growth, high-unemployment, high-inflation economy like that of the 1970s would carry with it very negative consequences. A brief review of those years provides some clues to the future should the 1970s economy carry forward in the new century.

Inflation was a persistent problem during the 1970s, averaging 7.4 percent per year and topping 14 percent in 1979. Because Social Security and many other public benefit programs are indexed to inflation, program costs soared. The 14.3 percent July 1980 adjustment, attributable to 1979 inflation, increased Social Security costs by more than $16 billion per year. The July 1981 increase added approximately $17 billion to annual program costs. The nation would have had difficulty affording such a trend if it had continued, or if it returned.

For private pension plans, a fixed pension or annuity would lose 66 percent of its value over 10 years, and 90 percent over 20 years, at 12 percent inflation—a rate that was exceeded in the 1979–80 period. The recent history of 2 percent per year has erased these memories, and reduced the accompanying consideration of inflation in calculating what one might need as savings in the future.

The only real solution for retirees is the end of inflation, the use of available inflation-indexed bonds as a core investment, or inflation-adjusted benefits. The same is true for active workers. Renewed inflation would jeopardize Social Security, Medicare, and both private pensions and private medical insurance. The fact that one system is indexed and the other is not does not represent a statement of success and failure. Over the long term, society cannot maintain full indexing of social programs without substantial tax increases if initial benefit levels are maintained.

During the 2000s, we are likely to see an acceleration of government and employer emphasis on maintaining retirement income programs with minimum cutbacks, while seeking new ways of paying for increasingly expensive health programs.

GOVERNMENT REGULATION

There was a marked increase in the scope of government regulation of employee benefits—both pension and welfare programs—in the 1970s, 1980s, and 1990s. The movement in this area was part of a broad general expansion of the government's role in numerous areas of the economy. Many of the changes adopted were not preceded by detailed analysis of costs, benefits, or secondary consequences. Experience with the changes indicates that many carried undesired and unexpected results.

Regulatory thrusts that never succeeded were also prominent. Such was the case of government-run national health insurance and comprehensive health care cost containment. During the years ahead, it is unlikely that these initiatives will be enacted into law. In addition, it is likely that regulation imposed by ERISA will be adjusted and in some cases removed, as described below:

- Reporting and disclosure requirements are likely to be reduced in cases where no apparent gain resulted from the requirement.

- Adjustments to the Pension Benefit Guaranty Corporation program are likely to continue as more experience with it is gathered. Past reforms have now led to substantial reserves for the agency, making it likely that future issues will relate to premium reductions or expanded guarantees.

- Emphasis is likely to be given to making all benefit components work better together—including emphasis on integration of savings programs, retirement benefit programs, disability benefit programs, and health benefit programs. For active workers and retirees, this will be essential. Employers will work to individualize benefits and to reduce the employee view of entitlement to employer provision and payment.

- Greater equity is likely to be sought for various benefit programs in terms of tax treatment, particularly savings and retirement programs. This is likely to include maximizing flexibility of program design so that the maximum number of people are accommodated while introducing more cash portability and discouraging consumption of preretirement distributions. At the same time, however, account balances will increasingly be viewed as providing transition funds upon job change or retraining.

- Continued attention will be given to improving the quality and cost effectiveness of health care, with special emphasis on provision for the needy and ensuring that retirement, health, and income promises are kept, once made.

■ States have become the primary agents of health care reform, focused on expansion of health insurance coverage, and this activity will increase in the future.

■ The Internet makes all of these movements very easy. It makes information delivery immediate and cheap, and delivers all of the information to the kitchen table for family decision-making. The Internet allows employees to make decisions and post changes, without the need to visit the personnel office. It allows governments, employers, and unions to deliver services on a 24/7 basis. Technology will make the pace of change and the extent of flexibility to expand on a continuous basis.

While the overall role of government as direct provider is not likely to *expand* significantly beyond children with low-income parents, in the future, government will continue to be very active and will continue to impose new requirements. Knowledge of the regulatory environment will become no less necessary; the years ahead will provide an excellent opportunity for study, review, and refinement, with the public and private sectors increasingly working together as partners rather than adversaries.

EMPLOYEE BENEFIT TRENDS

The period ahead will be one of challenge and change for employee benefits. Their major role in the total compensation package will be recognized, even if the characterization of "fringe benefits" persists. The combined effects of economic, political, and population changes cannot and will not be ignored. The dynamics of change are already in progress, with much of the decade ahead likely to be reinforcing even greater change. The focus on "total rewards," which adds considerations of the work environment to "compensation", underlines the degree to which employee benefits, compensation, and human resources continue to change.

The exact future of employment-based benefits will rest, however, on whether employers continue to focus on why they originally provided retirement and health protection: to enhance economic security. Since the early 1980s, we have increasingly redesigned benefits to provide employees satisfaction and gratification, potentially at the expense of long-term economic security. The growing movement toward individual empowerment and responsibility will continue to increase individual risk and opportunity for reward. These trends may result in less risk protection, economic security, worker wellness, and the ability for people to retire with dignity if not accompanied by increased information and education. When President Clinton proposed the creation of *universal savings accounts* in 1999, it marked movement by the Democratic party towards giving more power and responsibility to the individual.

During the 1970s, 1980s and 1990s, a number of study groups including the National Commission on Social Security (NCSS), the President's Commission on Pension Policy (PCPP), the National Commission for an Agenda for the '80s, the Minimum Wage Study Commission (MWSC), the White House Conference on the Aging, the Entitlements Commission, the Medicare Commission, and the National Commission on Retirement Policy were appointed to look at the future of components of the employee benefits world. These groups produced well over 1,000 recommendations on how to "improve" employee benefit programs.

The private sector also exhibited increasing concern in the late 1970s with the creation of organizations such as the Employee Benefit Research Institute (EBRI) in Washington, D.C., and the development of educational programs such as the Certified Employee Benefit Specialist (CEBS) Program. During the 1980s and 1990s, World at Work expanded its training and certification programs for benefits and compensation, and the International Foundation of Employee Benefit Plans added certificate programs. The Society for Human Resources Management added benefits surveys, and the National Academy of Human Resources was formed to recognize professionals in all areas of specialization. Training and research will continue to expand.

Employee benefit programs are already moving to accommodate changes noted throughout this chapter. The following are some of those changes:

- The design of employee benefits is increasingly recognized as an important and vital business function that should be integrated with business strategy. As such, the function will be given increasing prominence within organizations' planning regime, with increasing responsibility given to benefit managers for strategy and planning. Technology and outsourcing will bring third-party administration to the forefront like never before, with permanent benefits staff focused on planning and monitoring delivery.
- Efficiency in the financing of benefit programs will be increasingly emphasized. Cost management and value are already, and

will continue to be, the watchwords. Some of these changes may be the result of legislative activity. Cutbacks in federal government expenditures will lead to cost shifting to other levels of government and employers, and to greater consumer choice and the development of classes of medical care. (In addition, emphasis on better health and wellness is likely to increase.)

■ Efficiency in benefit design will be increasingly emphasized in an effort to eliminate and prevent overlap and to provide participants with the particular benefits they need. Flexible compensation and benefits will expand as the makeup of the workforce continues to change and as technology makes it easy to deliver choice to the desktop and the kitchen table. Whether flexibility provides economic security will increasingly be determined by employee action.

■ Long-term care insurance, offered on an employee-pay-all basis, preretirement counseling, and financial counseling will expand as employee benefits. Financial and health education will be delivered more aggressively because of technological ease and concerns about liability, and the Internet will facilitate the delivery of investment advice for those who want that next step.

■ The trend toward providing primary and supplemental defined contribution plans will continue among employers. Defined benefit plans will continue to provide the base level of retirement income above Social Security for large employers' long-service employees who become retirees, but for many others the primary benefit will come from defined contribution programs, even where dual coverage is present. It will become increasingly important, as lump sums become the rule, that those who receive lump-sum distributions preserve them, and education programs can be expected to expand.

■ The Internet, backed up by voice-response systems, will revolutionize benefit programs. Beneficiaries will have more information easily available and be able to make decisions at any time. This also will lead to more understanding of programs by participants, will enhance communications, and will make flexible compensation an option for the smallest employers. These same advances, combined with employer reengineering, will continue to lead to more extensive outsourcing of all administration and communication functions.

■ Part-time or contract employment of annuitants will be more and more common. These changes will be a natural addition to a growing emphasis on preretirement counseling, the effects of the Age Discrimination in Employment Act, the dramatic growth of the retired population, and low unemployment levels.
■ Few future retirees will receive medical protection, beyond Medicare, paid for by a former employer.

Beyond these developments, we are likely to see increasing recognition of the advantages of individual and employer benefit provision. The most striking advantage of providing benefits through the employer or union is the natural group and the ease of communication. In addition, flexibility is a major factor: the ability to adjust quickly to changing workforce needs. Flexible benefit programs, whether formally structured or not, are likely to become more common in the future to accommodate changes in tax policy, nontax regulation, the workforce, and government and employee desires to make decisions. The Internet makes this possible on a 24/7 real-time basis, using third parties. And, the employer or union have the choice of whether to allow the third parties to "brand" the programs, or to keep them identified with the employer.

The public and private sectors will see increasing advantages in cooperation, coordination, and nonduplication. Regulatory and legislative initiatives are likely to be consistent with such recognition.

CONCLUSION

Social Security now promises a floor of income protection to most workers, while nonworkers have access to supplemental security income, in-kind benefits, unemployment compensation, workers' compensation, disability income, and other programs. They could all be reduced in the future in response to demographic and economic necessity, placing a growing need on the individual to plan and save.

Supplementing these programs is an array of private income security programs. Private pensions, for example, are now participated in by more than 70 percent of all steady full-time workers over age 21. Over 85 percent of those working for large employers have pensions. One quarter of present retirees now receive private pension income, and the percentage continues to grow. Public pensions provide coverage and benefits to many more workers. Individuals are saving through qualified plans with more frequency as well. But, benefit levels are small for most who get them because of short job tenures and a propensity to spend distributions upon job change. The number of future retirees with adequate income will only grow if planning and saving behavior increases and more individuals roll over distributions upon job change.

The vast majority of public- and private-sector workers now enjoy protection for health care. Through government programs, such protection is available to nonworkers as well. And means will develop to allow access to protection for all individuals. The public/private mix is likely to change in the future, however, with more and more responsibility being placed on the individual. As employer health insurance coverage has grown, the proportion of the population without insurance has continued to grow.

Employers are also providing employees access to a wide array of additional programs discussed in the *Handbook*. Some paid for by employers and many by employees, these programs help to meet the needs of tens of millions of persons. They help to maintain morale, ensure family security, and maintain employee health. Employer sponsorship of programs will become increasingly important in the future as the workforce continues to tighten and the ability to recruit and retain continues to become more difficult. Not offering benefits has come to repel possible candidates, more than offering them attracts them. And, as the total work environment counts for more and more in employee satisfaction, benefits have come to be recognized as a needed element.

Taken together, employee benefit programs provide a blanket of security against numerous risks. For the most part, the programs deliver with reliability, effectiveness, and efficiency to the participants. They are an integral part of our social structure, and with prudent employer and union action in the future, along with public policy that allows employers and unions to act, employee benefit programs will continue to be.